Autodesk Inventor 2027 Black Book Part I

By
Gaurav Verma
Matt Weber
(CADCAMCAE Works)

Edited by
Kristen

ISBN # 978-1-77459-214-4

DEDICATION

To teachers, who make it possible to disseminate knowledge
to enlighten the young and curious minds
of our future generations

To students, who are the future of the world

THANKS

To my friends and colleagues

To my family for their love and support

Training and Consultant Services

At CADCAMCAE Works, we provide effective and affordable one to one online training on various software packages in Computer Aided Design(CAD), Computer Aided Manufacturing(CAM), Computer Aided Engineering (CAE), Computer programming languages (C/C++, Java, .NET, Android, Javascript, HTML, and so on). The training is delivered through remote access to your system and voice chat via Internet at any time, any place, and at any pace to individuals, groups, students of colleges/universities, and CAD/CAM/CAE training centers. The main features of this program are:

Training as per your need

Highly experienced Engineers and Technician conduct the classes on the software applications used in the industries. The methodology adopted to teach the software is totally practical based, so that the learner can adapt to the design and development industries in almost no time. The efforts are to make the training process cost effective and time saving while you have the comfort of your time and place, thereby relieving you from the hassles of traveling to training centers or rearranging your time table.

Software Packages on which we provide basic and advanced training are:

CAD/CAM/CAE: CATIA, Creo Parametric, Creo Direct, SolidWorks, Autodesk Inventor, Solid Edge, UG NX, AutoCAD, AutoCAD LT, EdgeCAM, MasterCAM, SolidCAM, DelCAM, BOBCAM, UG NX Manufacturing, UG Mold Wizard, UG Progressive Die, UG Die Design, SolidWorks Mold, Creo Manufacturing, Creo Expert Machinist, NX Nastran, Hypermesh, SolidWorks Simulation, Autodesk Simulation Mechanical, Creo Simulate, Gambit, ANSYS, and many others.

Computer Programming Languages: C++, VB.NET, HTML, Android, Javascript and so on.

Game Designing: Unity.

Civil Engineering: AutoCAD MEP, Revit Structure, Revit Architecture, AutoCAD Map 3D and so on.

We also provide consultant services for design and development on the above mentioned software packages

For more information you can mail us at:
cadcamcaeworks@gmail.com

Table of Contents

Chapter 3 : Dimensioning and Constraining

Chapter 4 : Creating Solid Models

Chapter 5 : Advanced Solid Modeling Tools

Chapter 6 : Advanced Modeling Tools and Practical

Chapter 7 : Assembly Design and Presentation

Chapter 9 : Application Management

Preface

Autodesk Inventor is a product of Autodesk Inc. Autodesk Inventor 2027 is a parametric, feature-based solid modeling tool that not only unites the three-dimensional (3D) parametric features with two-dimensional (2D) tools, but also addresses every design-through-manufacturing process. The continuous enhancements in the software has made it a complete PLM software. The software is capable of performing analysis with an ease. Its compatibility with CAM software is remarkable. Its seamless integration with Autodesk Assistant AI agent delivers on-the-go support. Based mainly on the user feedback, this solid modeling tool is remarkably user-friendly and it allows you to be productive from day one.

The **Autodesk Inventor 2027 Black Book** is the 7th edition of our series on Autodesk Inventor. The book is divided into two parts **Autodesk Inventor 2027 Black Book Part I** and **Autodesk Inventor 2027 Black Book Part II**. With lots of features and thorough review, we present a book to help professionals as well as beginners in creating some of the most complex solid models. The book follows a step by step methodology. In this book, we have tried to give real-world examples with real challenges in designing. We have tried to reduce the gap between university use of Autodesk Inventor and industrial use of Autodesk Inventor. The Part I of the book covers Sketching, 3D modeling, Advanced 3D Modeling, Assembly Design, Drawing, and Inspection tools. Some of the salient features of this book are :

In-Depth explanation of concepts

Every new topic of this book starts with the explanation of the basic concepts. In this way, the user becomes capable of relating the things with real world.

Topics Covered

Every chapter starts with a list of topics being covered in that chapter. In this way, the user can easy find the topic of his/her interest easily.

Instruction through illustration

The instructions to perform any action are provided by maximum number of illustrations so that the user can perform the actions discussed in the book easily and effectively. There are about 1180 small and large illustrations that make the learning process effective.

Tutorial point of view

At the end of concept's explanation, the tutorial make the understanding of users firm and long lasting. Almost each chapter of the book has tutorials that are real world projects. Moreover most of the tools in this book are discussed in the form of tutorials.

Project

Projects and exercises are provided to students for practicing.

For Faculty

If you are a faculty member, then you can ask for video tutorials on any of the topic, exercise, tutorial, or concept. As faculty, you can register on our website to get electronic desk copies of our latest books, self-assessment, and solution of practical. Faculty resources are available in the **Faculty Member** page of our website (**cadcamcaeworks**) once you login. Note that faculty registration approval is manual and it may take two days for approval before you can access the faculty website.

Formatting Conventions Used in the Text

All the key terms like name of button, tool, drop-down, etc. are kept bold.

Free Resources

Link to the resources used in this book are provided to the users via email. To get the resources, mail us at ***cadcamcaeworks@gmail.com*** with your contact information. With your contact record with us, you will be provided latest updates and informations regarding various technologies. The format to write us mail for resources is as follows:

Subject of E-mail as ***Application for resources of ________ book***.
Also, given your information like
Name:
Course pursuing/Profession:
E-mail ID:

Note: We respect your privacy and value it. If you do not want to give your personal informations then you can ask for resources without giving your information.

About Authors

Gaurav Verma is a Mechanical Design Engineer with deep knowledge of CAD, CAM and CAE field. He has an experience of more than 15 years in CAD/CAM/CAE field. He has delivered presentations in Autodesk University Events on AutoCAD Electrical and Autodesk Inventor. He is an active member of Autodesk Knowledge Share Network. He has provided content for Autodesk Design Academy. He is also working as technical consultant for many Indian Government organizations for Skill Development sector. He has authored books on SolidWorks, Mastercam, Creo Parametric, Autodesk Inventor, Autodesk Fusion, and many other CAD-CAM-CAE packages. He has developed content for many modular skill courses like Automotive Service Technician, Welding Technician, Lathe Operator, CNC Operator, Telecom Tower Technician, TV Repair Technician, Casting Operator, Maintenance Technician and about 50 more courses. He has his books published in English, Russian and Hindi worldwide.

He has trained many students on mechanical, electrical, and civil streams of CAD-CAM-CAE. He has trained students online as well as offline. He also owns a small workshop of 20 CNC and VMC machines where he tests his CAM skills on different Automotive components. He is providing consultant services to more than 15 companies worldwide. You can contact the author directly at cadcamcaeworks@gmail.com

For Any query or suggestion

If you have any query or suggestion, please let us know by mailing us on ***cadcamcaeworks@gmail.com***. Your valuable constructive suggestions will be incorporated in our books and your name will be addressed in special thanks area of our books on your confirmation.

Page left blank intentionally

Chapter 1

Starting with Autodesk Inventor

Topics Covered

The major topics covered in this chapter are:

- ***Starting Autodesk Inventor 2027.***
- ***Starting a new document.***
- ***Autodesk Inventor Interface.***
- ***Opening a document.***
- ***Closing documents.***
- ***Basic Settings for Autodesk Inventor Professional***

DOWNLOADING AND INSTALLING AUTODESK INVENTOR STUDENT EDITION

Autodesk gives a free license of 1 Year for students to practice on Autodesk Inventor and many other software. You cannot use a student edition in manufacturing products but you can use this edition to learn software. The procedure to download and install latest Autodesk Inventor educational version is given next.

- Open the link **https://www.autodesk.com/education/edu-software/overview** in your Web Browser. The web page for Autodesk software will be displayed; refer to Figure-1.

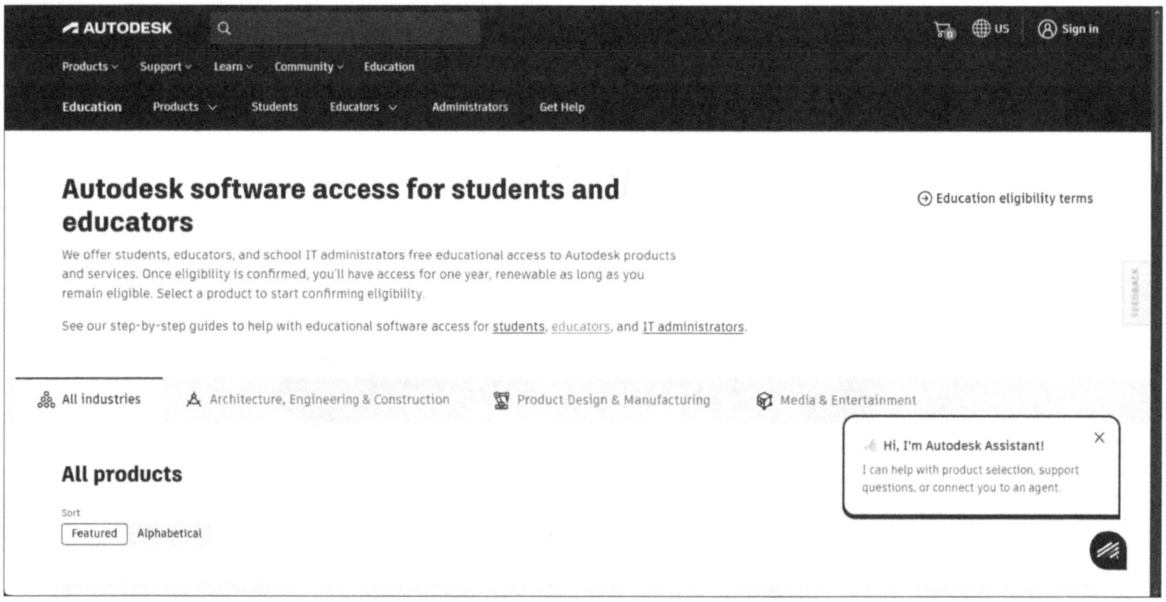

Figure-1. Autodesk page of education software

- Click on **Sign In** link button on this page and sign in with your student account details. If you do not have an Autodesk Student account then click on the **Create account** link button on the Sign In web page and create your account.
- After signing in, the web page of Autodesk educational software will be displayed. Scroll-down the page and click on **Select** button for **Inventor** section; refer to Figure-2. The subscription plan page will be displayed. Select the **Access products** button to start your education access of software. The Products and Services page will be displayed, asking to select the Operating system, Version, and Language of the software.

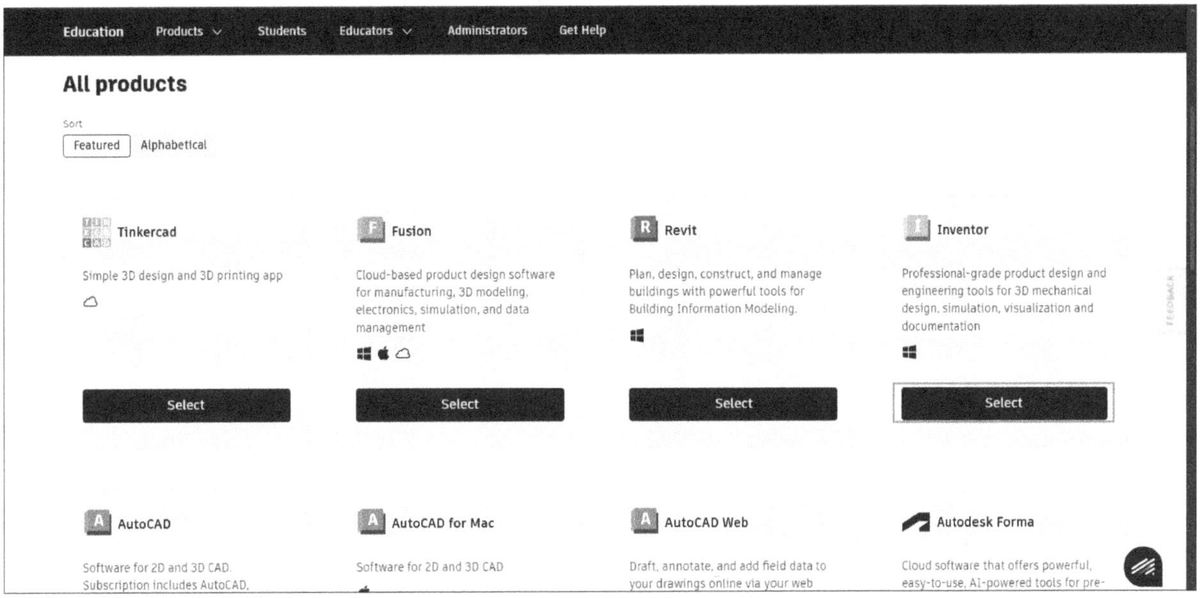

Figure-2. Select button for Inventor

- Set the parameters as required and click on **INSTALL** drop-down button, the two options will be displayed; refer to Figure-3. Click on the **DOWNLOAD** option and the software will begin to download. After downloading the software, install the software by accepting the license terms and following the instructions as displayed.

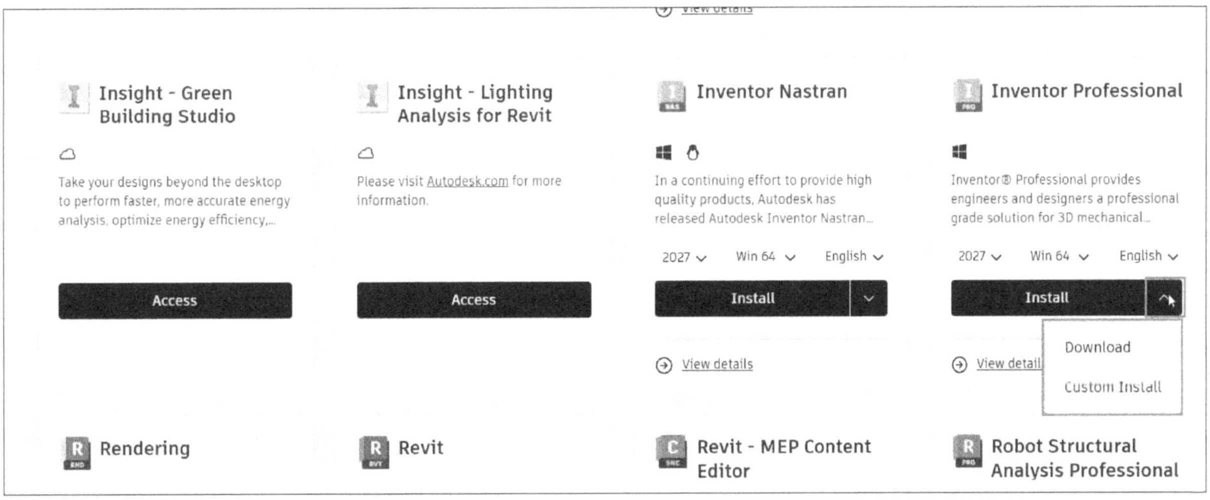

Figure-3. INSTALL drop down options

STARTING AUTODESK INVENTOR

There are various ways to start Autodesk Inventor but we will use the fastest general method to start Autodesk Inventor in Microsoft Windows.

- Click on the **Start** button at the **Taskbar**. The menu of application shortcuts will be displayed.
- Type **Autodesk Inventor** (in Microsoft Windows 11). The applications with the name Autodesk Inventor will be displayed which is only one in our case; refer to Figure-4.

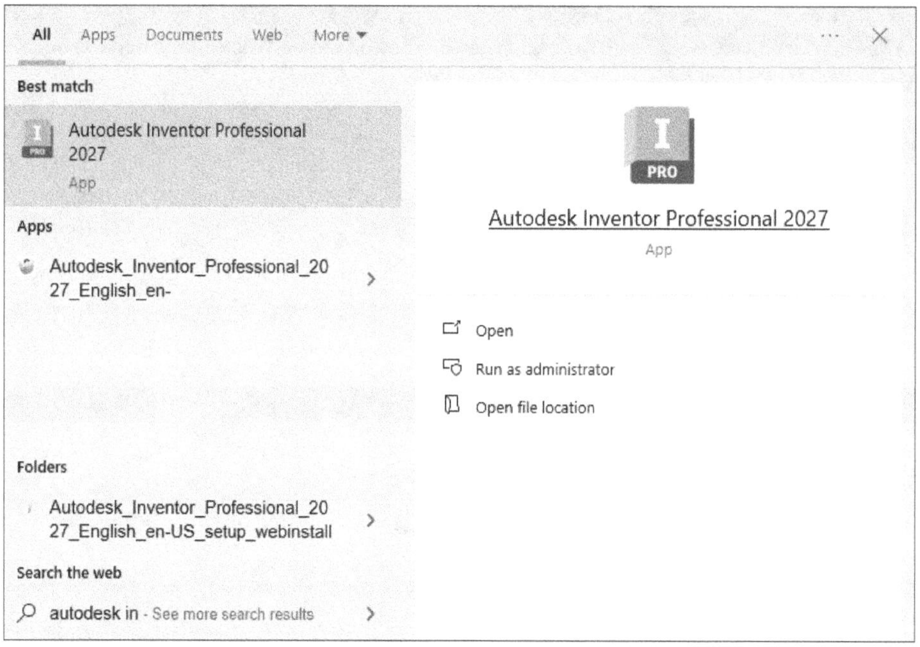

Figure-4. Start menu

- Click on the **Autodesk Inventor Professional 2027** link button. Note that if you have created a desktop icon of Autodesk Inventor then you can double-click on that icon to start application. The application will start along with **Migrate Custom Settings** dialog box; refer to Figure-5.

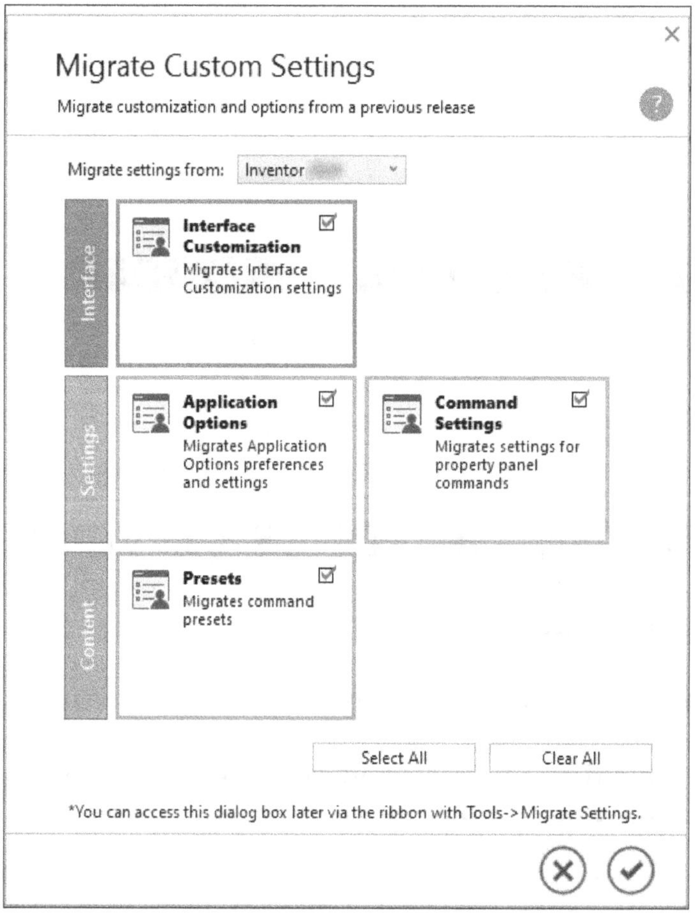

Figure-5. Migrate Custom Settings dialog box

- If you want to migrate the customization and options from the previous version of software into this version of software then select the check boxes of parameters which you want to migrate and click on **OK** button from the dialog box.
- If you do not want to migrate the customization then select **Clear All** button and click on **OK** button from the dialog box. The application interface will be displayed as shown in Figure-6.

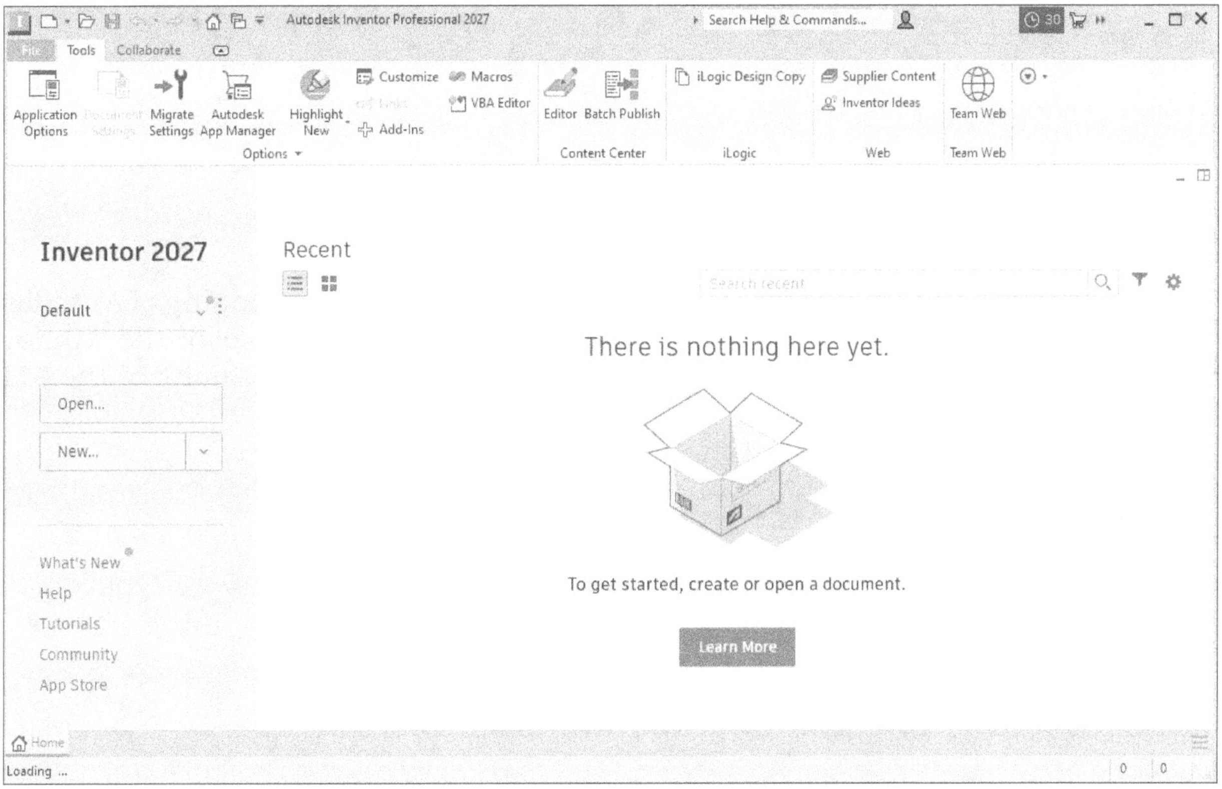

Figure-6. Autodesk Inventor interface

Autodesk Inventor INTERFACE

Autodesk always keeps on improving the interface of Inventor for better usability. The interface of Autodesk Inventor 2027 is displayed as shown in Figure-6. Various components of interface are shown in Figure-7.

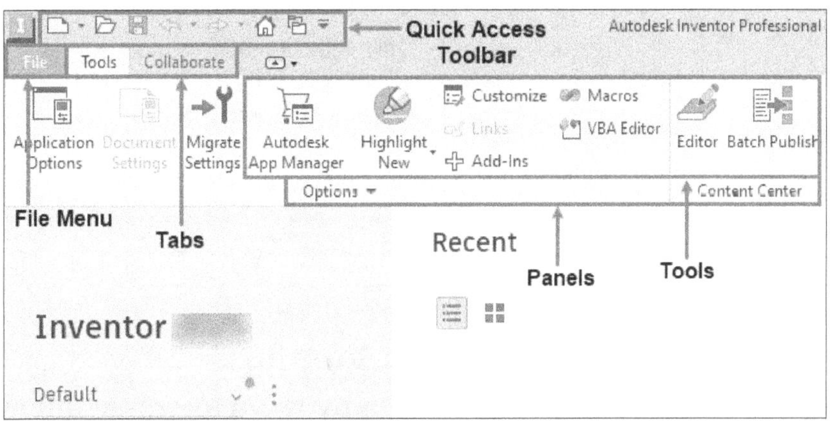

Figure-7. Components of Autodesk Inventor interface

Ribbon

Ribbon is the area of the application window that holds all the tools for designing and editing; refer to Figure-8. **Ribbon** is divided into **Tabs** which are further divided into **Panels**. Each panel is collection of tools dedicated to similar operations. The tools in these panels will be discussed in this chapter and subsequent chapters.

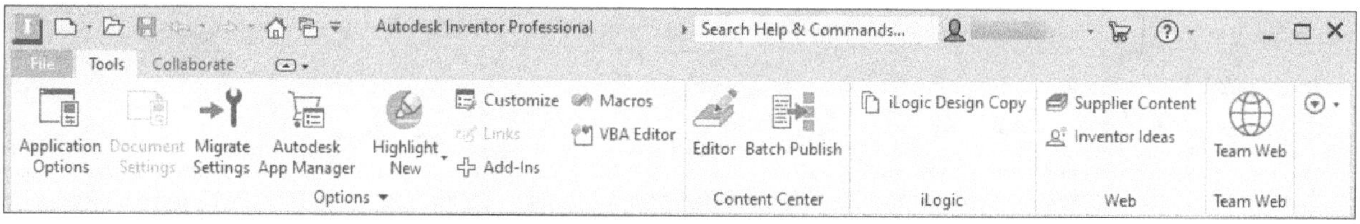

Figure-8. Ribbon

FILE MENU

The options in the **File** menu are used to manage the overall functioning of Autodesk Inventor. Once, you click on the **File** button at the top-left corner of the window, the **File** menu will be displayed as shown in Figure-9. Various options of the **File** menu are discussed next.

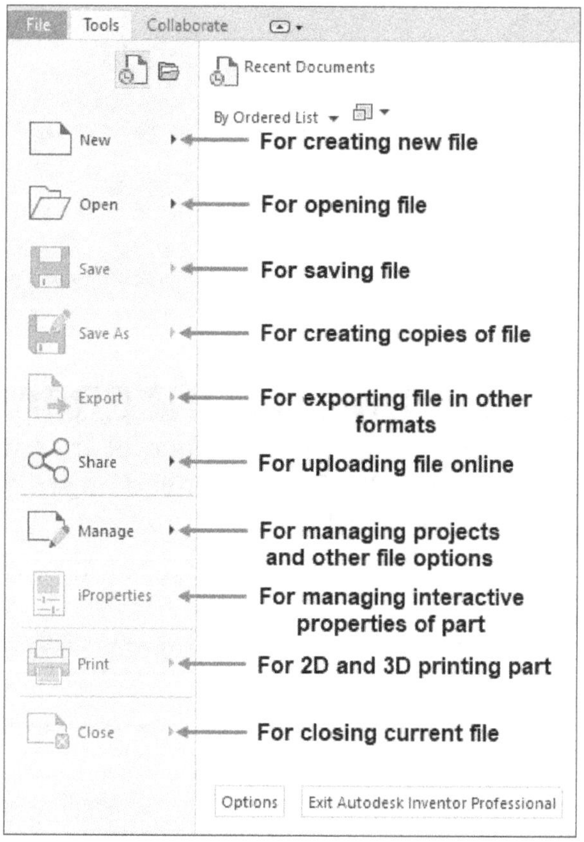

Figure-9. File menu

Creating New File

Like other products of Autodesk, there are many ways to create a new file. To create a new file, use the **New** option from the **File** menu or click on the **New** button from **Home** tab; refer to Figure-10. You can also use the **New** button from the **Quick Access Toolbar** at the top-left of the application window; refer to Figure-11 or press **CTRL+N** from the keyboard.

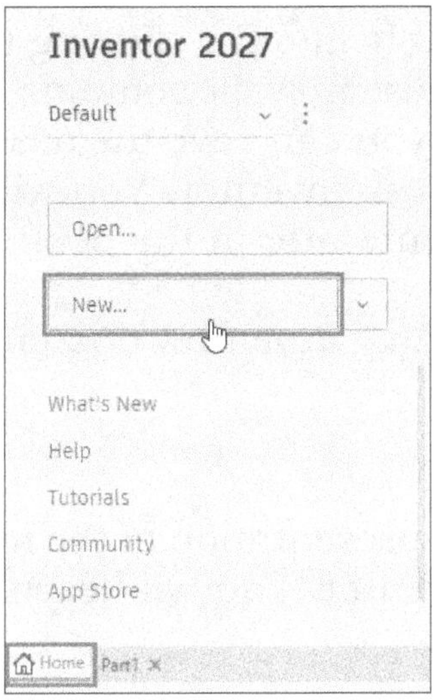

Figure-10. New button in Home tab

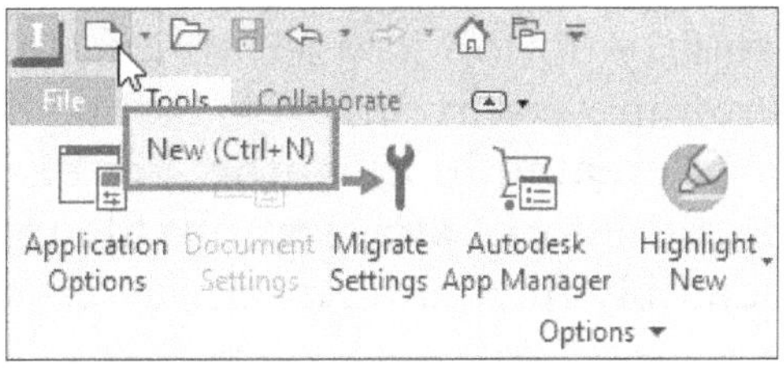

Figure-11. New button in Quick Access Toolbar

We will discuss the method of starting new file using **File** menu here. You will learn about the other methods later in the book.

Starting a New File using File menu

- Click on the **File** button at the top in the **Ribbon**. The **File** menu will be displayed.
- Hover the cursor on the **New** option in the menu. The options for creating new file will be displayed in the **New** cascading menu; refer to Figure-12.

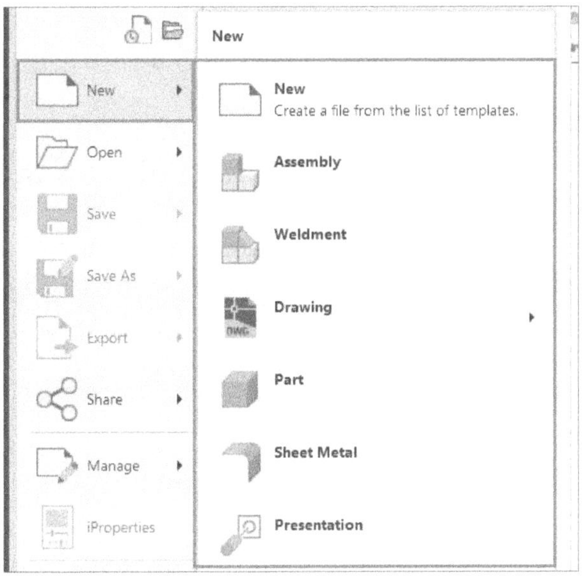

Figure-12. New cascading menu

There are five options in the **New** cascading menu viz. **New**, **Assembly**, **Drawing**, **Part**, and **Presentation**. The functions of these options are discussed next.

 The **New** option is used to create new file by using the templates saved in the Autodesk directory.

The **Assembly** option is used to create assembly file. On clicking the **Assembly** option, the Assembly environment is displayed. An assembly file contains the assembly of various parts created in Inventor. For example, you can save the assembly model of motorbike in the form of assembly file in Autodesk Inventor. You will learn more about the assembly files and Assembly environment, later in the book.

The **Weldment** option is used to start a new welding assembly document. You will learn about weldments in Part 2 of this book.

The **Drawing** option is used to create the 2D representation of the model created in **Part** or **Assembly** environment of Autodesk Inventor. You will learn more in the later chapters.

The **Part** option is used to create the part file for any real-world model. A real-world model means a model that can be manufactured. Although, you can create unreal objects in Autodesk Inventor but that is not the purpose of this software, for creating those objects you should use animation software.

The **Sheet Metal** option is used to create thin metal parts that are produced by sheetmetal bending and other forming processes in manufacturing.

The **Presentation** option is used to create 3D representations of the model for presentation to the client.

We will start with the **Part** environment and then discuss the predefined templates.

- Click on the **New** option from the **New** cascading menu in the **File** menu. The **Create New File** dialog box will be displayed; refer to Figure-13.

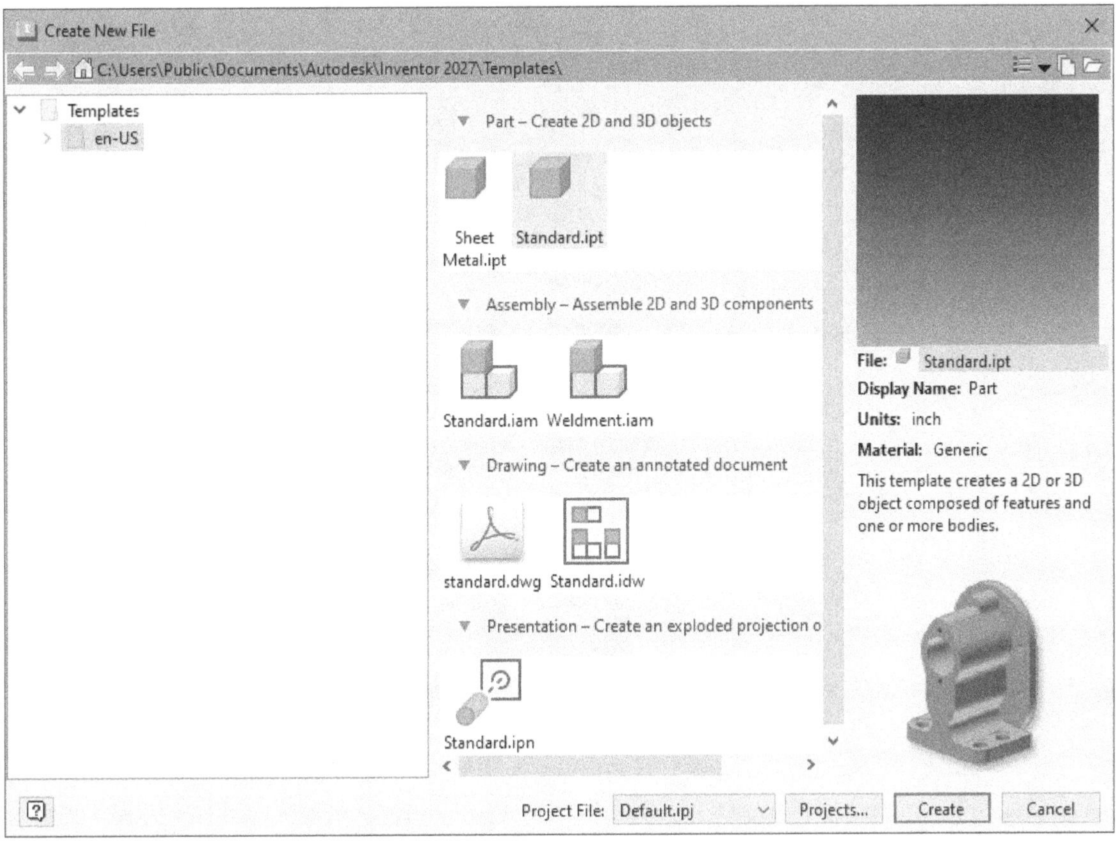

Figure-13. Create New File dialog box

- Expand the **en-US** node from the **Templates** category and select desired folder from **English** or **Metric** in the **Templates** area at the left of dialog box. If you select the **English** folder then the templates with **English** units (Feet and Inches) will be displayed in the right of the dialog box. If you select the **Metric** folder from the left of the dialog box then the templates with **Metric** units (Meters, Millimeters) will be displayed in the right of the dialog box.
- To start a new file with unit as mm, click on the **Metric** folder and then click on the **Standard (mm).ipt** icon from the right of the dialog box; refer to Figure-14.
- Click on the **Create** button from the dialog box. The new file will open and part environment will be displayed; refer to Figure-15.

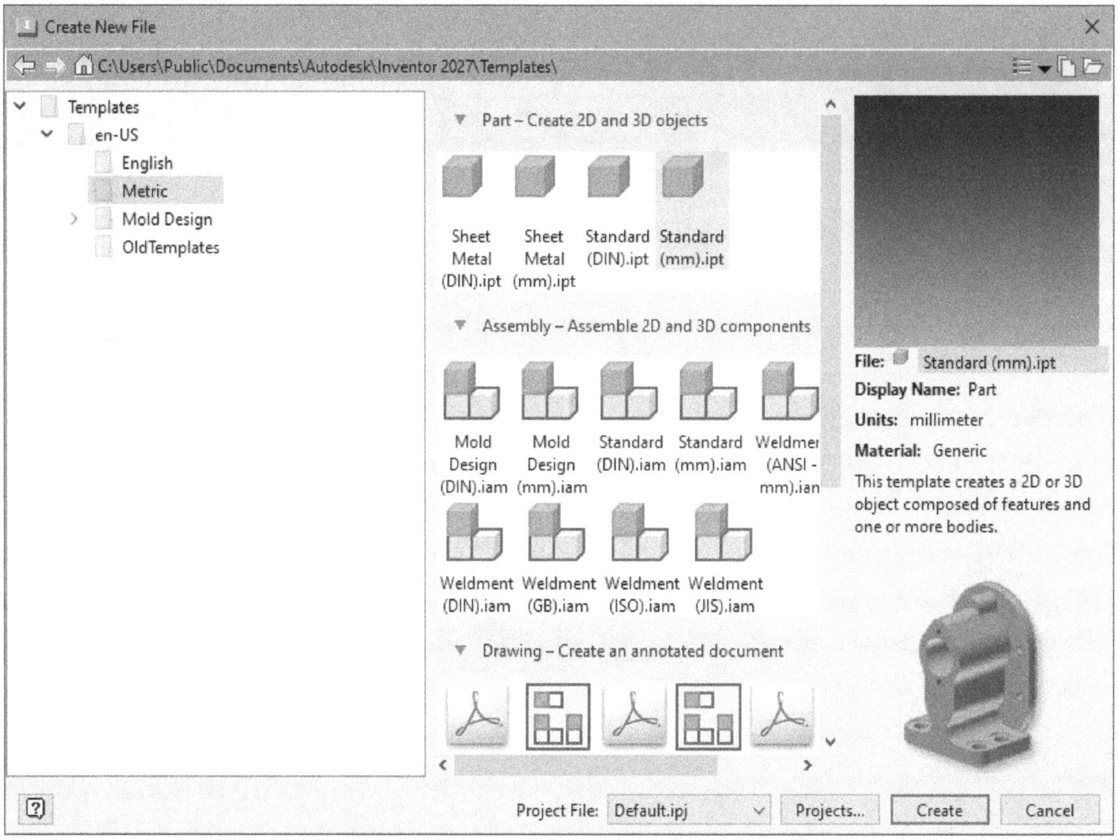

Figure-14. Creating part file in metric

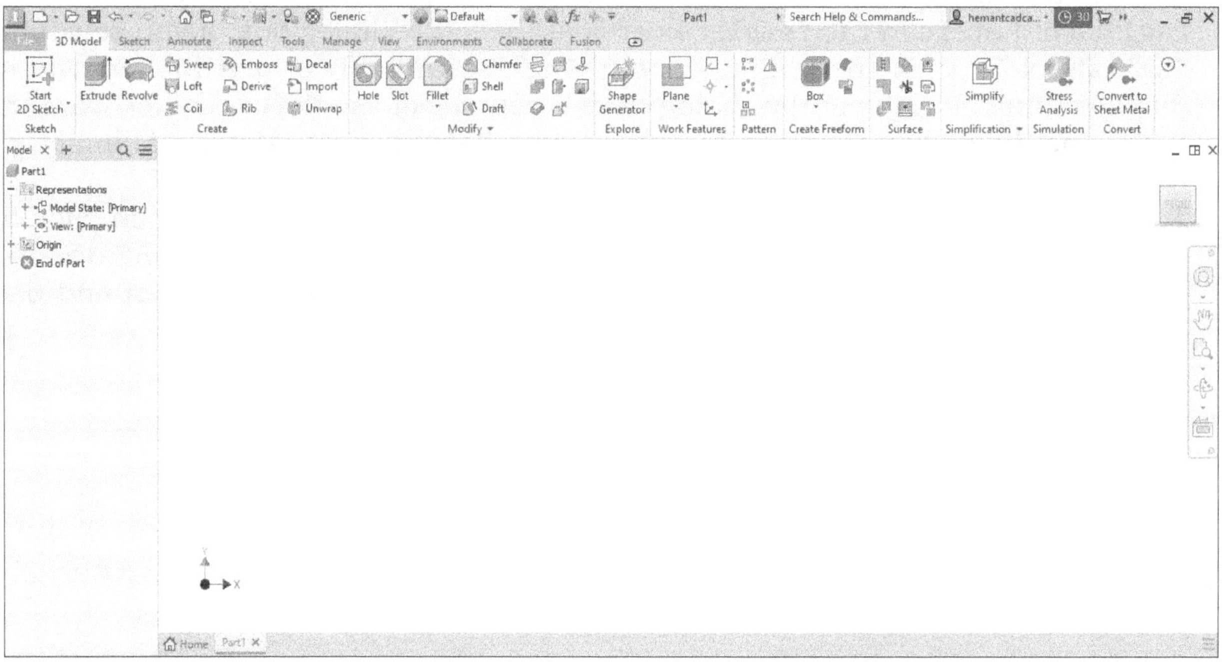

Figure-15. Part environment

Opening a file

Similar to creating new file, there are many ways to open files in Autodesk Inventor like, using the **Open** option from the **File** menu, using the **Open** button from the **Quick Access Toolbar**, or pressing the **CTRL+O** key from the keyboard. Here, we will discuss the procedure to open a file by using the **Open** option from the **File** menu.

Opening a File using File Menu Options

- Click on the **File** menu button at the top-left corner of the application window. The **File** menu will be displayed.
- Hover the cursor on the **Open** option in the **File** menu. The **Open** cascading menu will be displayed; refer to Figure-16.

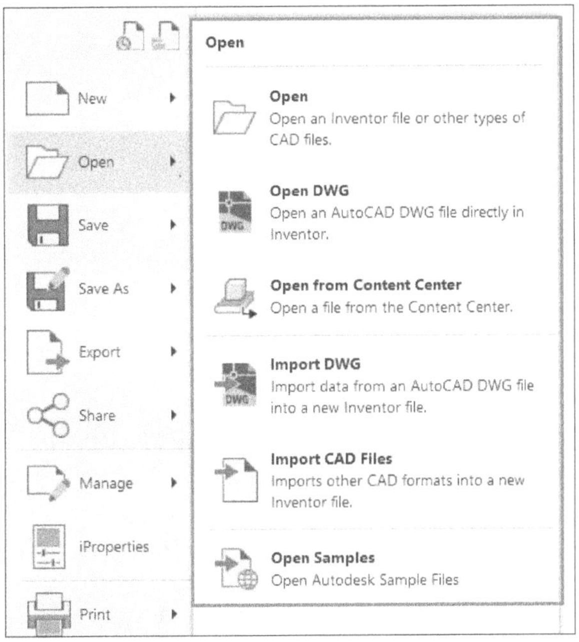

Figure-16. Open cascading menu

There are various options in **Open** cascading menu to open a file. The procedures of opening files by using each of these options are given next.

Opening Inventor file and other CAD files

- Click on the **Open** option from the **Open** cascading menu in the **File** menu. The **Open** dialog box will be displayed as shown in Figure-17.

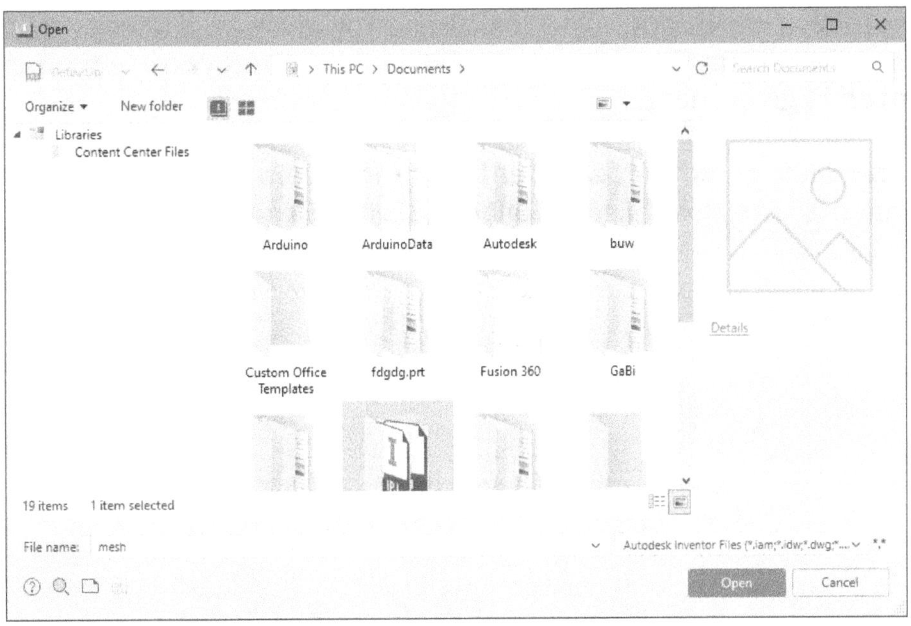

Figure-17. Open dialog box

- Click on the **Files of type** drop-down and select the format of file you want to open; refer to Figure-18.

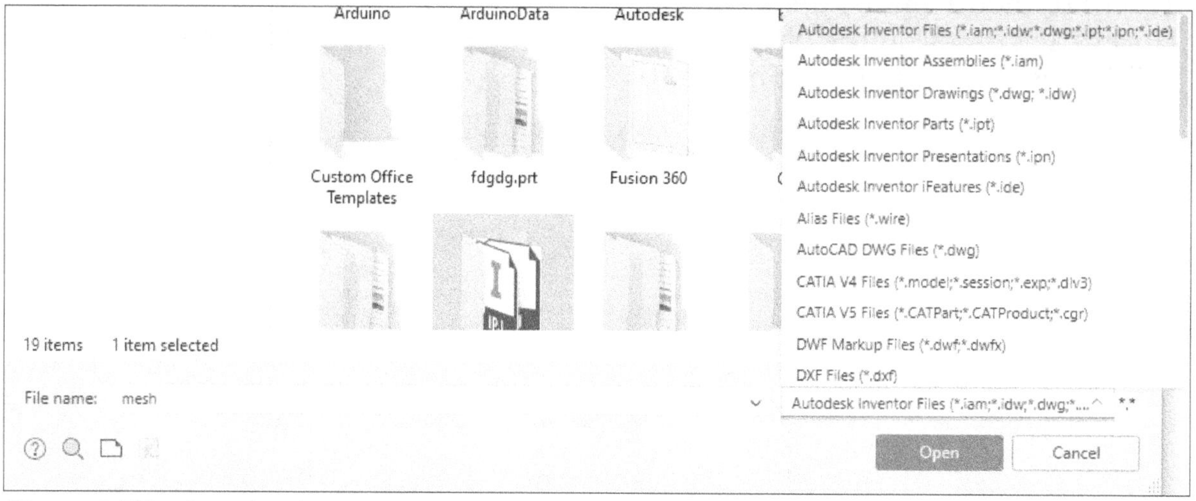

Figure-18. Files of type drop down

- Browse to the location of file by using general Microsoft Windows functions and double-click on the file to open it.

Note that you will learn more options of **Open** dialog box later in the book.

Opening AutoCAD Drawing file in Autodesk Inventor

- Click on the **Open DWG** option from the **Open** cascading menu in the **File** menu. The **Open** dialog box will be displayed similar to the one displayed in previous topic.
- Note that the file type is locked to AutoCAD DWG files only. So, browse to desired AutoCAD file and click on it.
- Click on the **Open** button from the dialog box. The file will open in the layout mode which we will discuss later in the book.

Opening file from Content Center

Like other Autodesk products, Autodesk Inventor gives you access to the library of standard parts like, Gear, bearing, connector, etc. The procedure to open parts from **Content Center** is given next.

- Click on the **Open from Content Center** option from the **Open** cascading menu in the **File** menu. The **Open from Content Center** window will be displayed; refer to Figure-19.

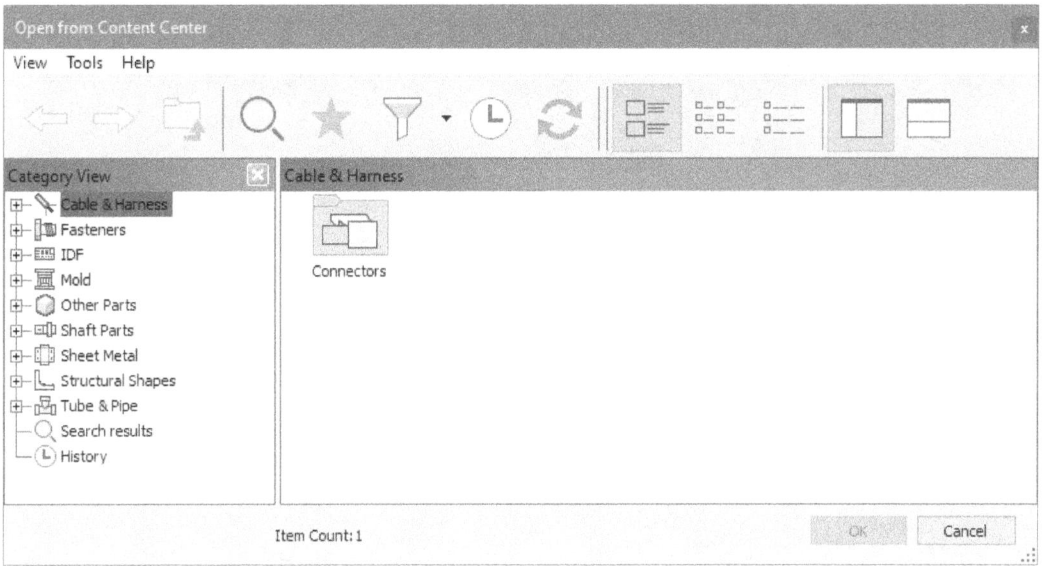

Figure-19. Open from Content Center window

- Click on the plus sign (+) of a category from the left pane of window to check subcategories.
- To open any part, double-click on it from the **Content Center** window. In some of the cases, you will be asked to select the size of component like in Figure-20.

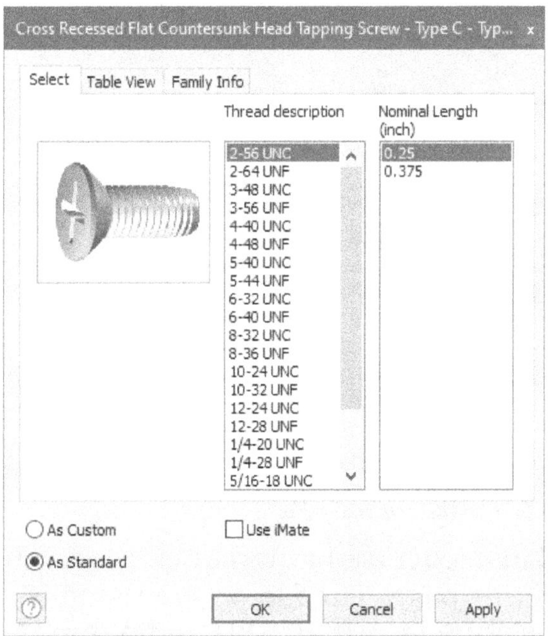

Figure-20. Specifying size for tapping screw

- After selecting the size, click on the **OK** button. The part will open.

Importing AutoCAD DWG files

Importing models of other software can reduces lots of extra work of rebuilding the base sketch for Inventor models. In Autodesk Inventor, we can directly use the AutoCAD drawing files for creating or manipulating the model. The procedure to import the AutoCAD Drawing files is given next.

- Click on the **Import DWG** option from the **Open** cascading menu in the **File** menu. The **Import** dialog box will be displayed as shown in Figure-21.

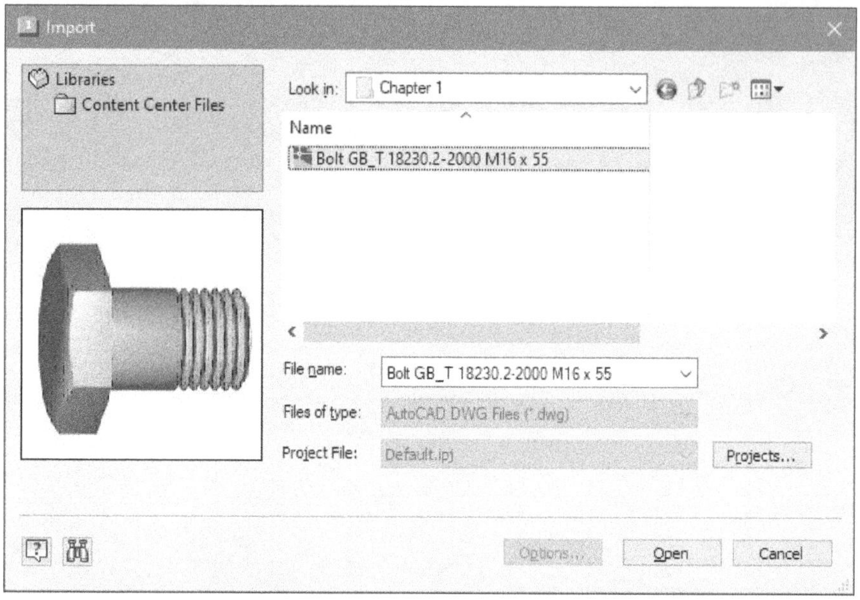

Figure-21. Import dialog box

- Double-click on desired file from the dialog box. The **DWG/DXF File Wizard** dialog box will be displayed; refer to Figure-22.

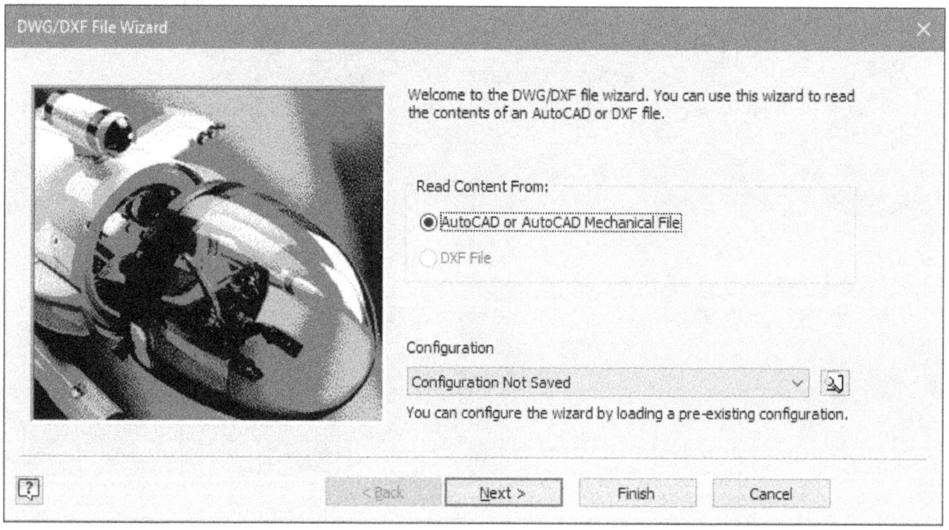

Figure-22. DWG DXF File Wizard dialog box

- The format of file will be recognized automatically and the relevant radio buttons will become active on this page. The file we are using is a dwg file, so it will show only **AutoCAD or AutoCAD Mechanical File** radio button as active. If there is any configuration saved with the file then it will appear in the **Configuration** drop-down. Select desired options and click on the **Next** button. The **Layers and Objects Import Options** dialog box will be displayed; refer to Figure-23.
- Select desired layers/objects from the **Selective import** list box and check the preview in the right of the dialog box. Once the preview is as per your requirement, click on the **Next** button from the dialog box. The **Import Destination Options** dialog box will be displayed; refer to Figure-24.

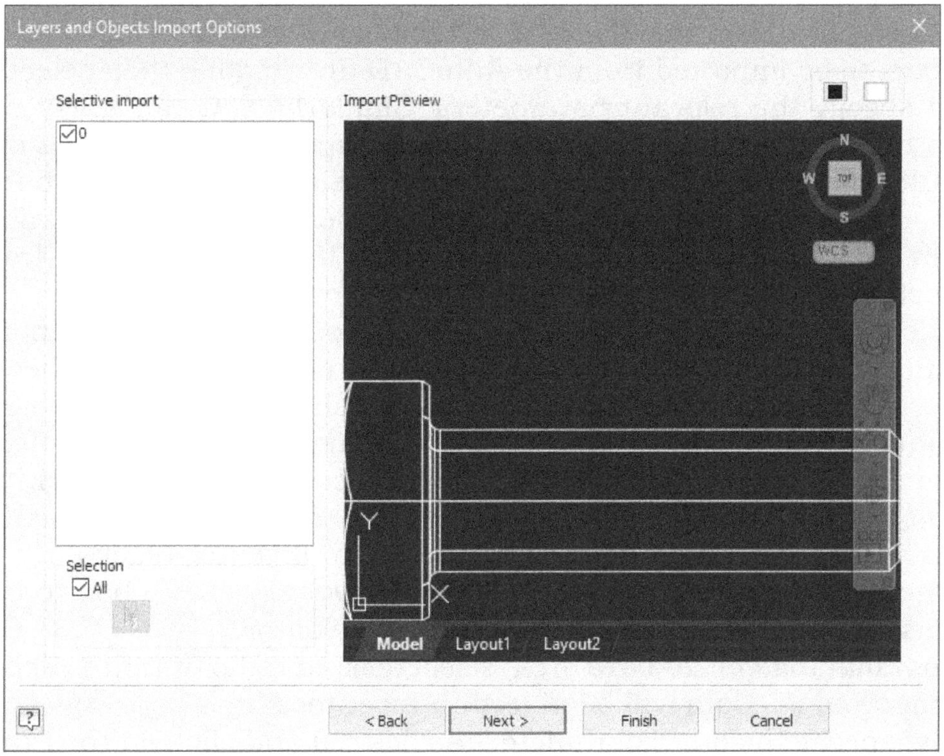

Figure-23. Layers and Objects Import Options dialog box

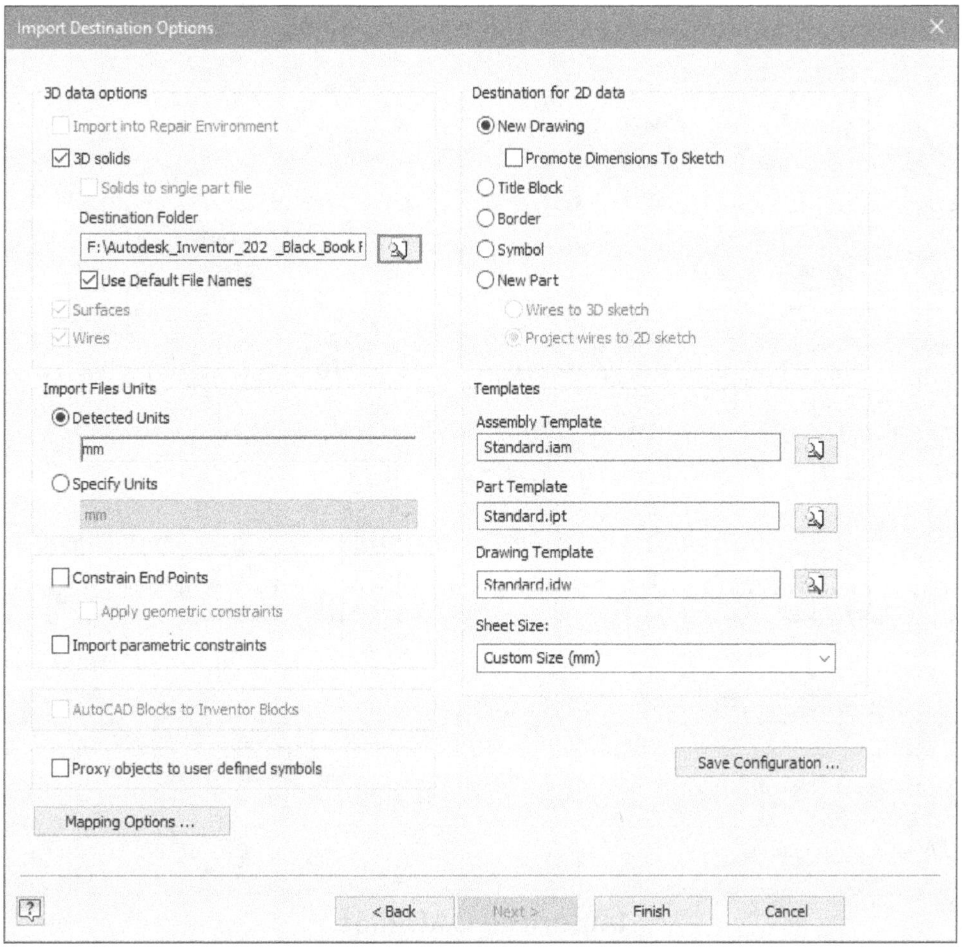

Figure-24. Import Destination Options dialog box

- Since, we do not have a 3D model in our drawing, so we are not selecting the **3D Solids** check box from the **3D data options** area of the dialog box. If you need a 3D model to be imported from the AutoCAD drawing file then select this check box and specify the relevant parameters. Similarly, you can select other check boxes in the 3D data options area to import respective components of file.
- By default, the **Detected Units** radio button is selected in the **Import Files Units** area of the dialog box, so the units of imported files are used. If you want to import the file in different unit then select the **Specify Units** radio button from the area and select desired unit from the drop-down below the radio button.
- Select the **Constrain End Points** check box if you want to constrain all the open end points of the imported drawing model. After selecting this check box, you can select the **Apply geometric constraints** check box for applying geometric constraints of Autodesk Inventor. Select the **Import parametric constraints** check box if you want to import the geometric constraints applied in AutoCAD.
- Select the **AutoCAD Blocks to Inventor Blocks** check box if you want to import blocks from the AutoCAD and convert them into Inventor blocks.
- Select the **Proxy objects to user defined symbols** check box to copy all the objects as user defined symbols in Autodesk Inventor.
- In the **Destination for 2D Data** area, select desired radio button to define location where imported 2D data will be placed in Inventor file.
- Similarly, specify the other parameters as desired and click on the **Finish** button from the dialog box. The view will be placed at the center of the drawing sheet; refer to Figure-25. Also, the tools related to drawing view will be displayed in the **Ribbon**. We will discuss these tools later in the book.

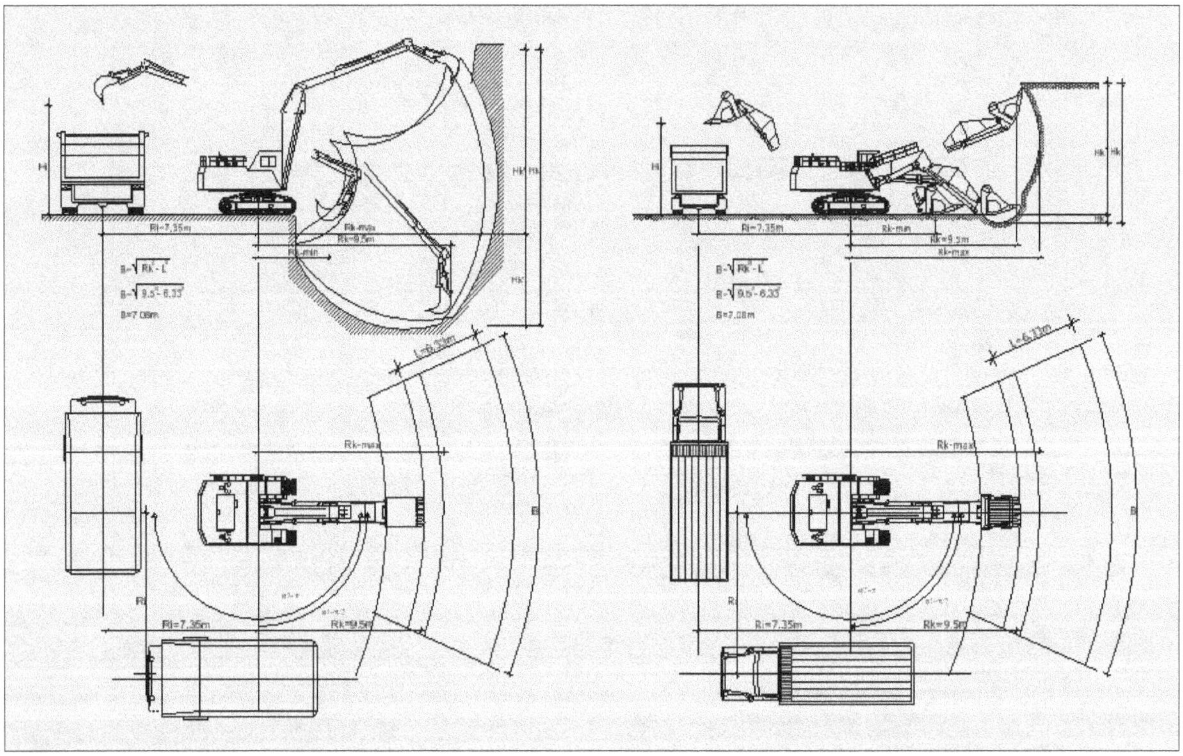

Figure-25. Drawing view placed

Importing CAD files

- Click on the **Import CAD Files** tool from the **Open** cascading menu in the **File** menu. The **Open Document** dialog box will be displayed as shown in Figure-26.

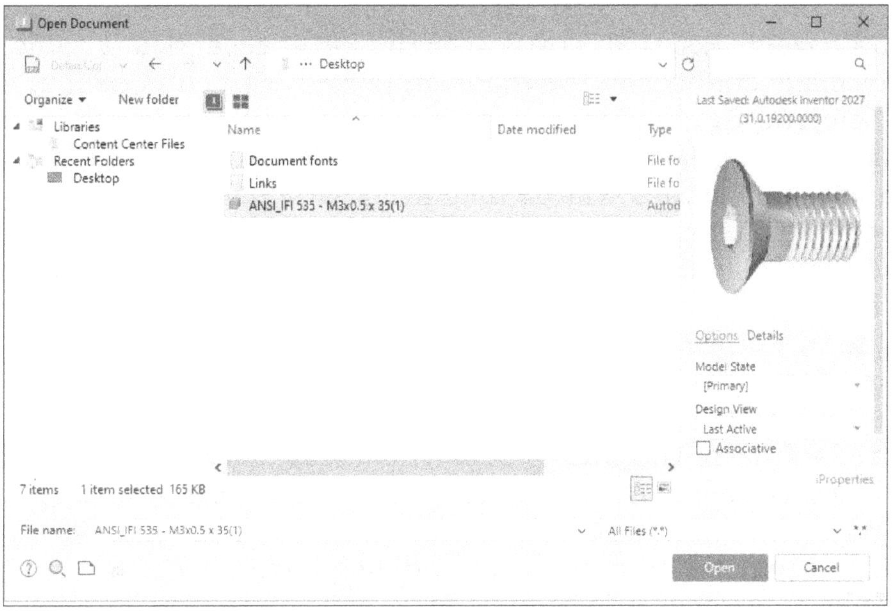

Figure-26. Open Document dialog box

- Double-click on desired CAD file from the dialog box. The **Import** dialog box will be displayed; refer to Figure-27. Note that depending on the type of document, you might get different dialog box for specifying parameters. We get this dialog box when you are opening part file created by Creo Parametric.

Figure-27. Import dialog box

- There are two radio buttons in **Import Type** area of the dialog box; **Reference Model** and **Convert Model**. If you select the **Reference Model** radio button then you cannot make changes in the model imported. You can use it in your inventor model as referenced, make more features on it, and can use it in assembly and drawing as well. On selecting the **Reference Model** radio button, the options related to **Object Filters** will be displayed with **Inventor Length Units** drop-down. Select the check boxes for objects to be imported from the **Object Filters** area and select desired unit from the **Inventor Length Units** drop-down.
- If you select the **Convert Model** radio button then the imported model will be converted to inventor format. After selecting this radio button, specify the name of converted file in the **Name** edit box and set the location of the new file.
- Select the **Individual** or **Composite** option from the **Surfaces** drop-down in the **Part Options** area of the dialog box. The **Individual** option is used to create individual surfaces of the model whereas selecting the **Composite** option will create a combined surface feature.
- Click on the **Select** tab from the **Import** dialog box. The options in the dialog box will be displayed as shown in Figure-28.

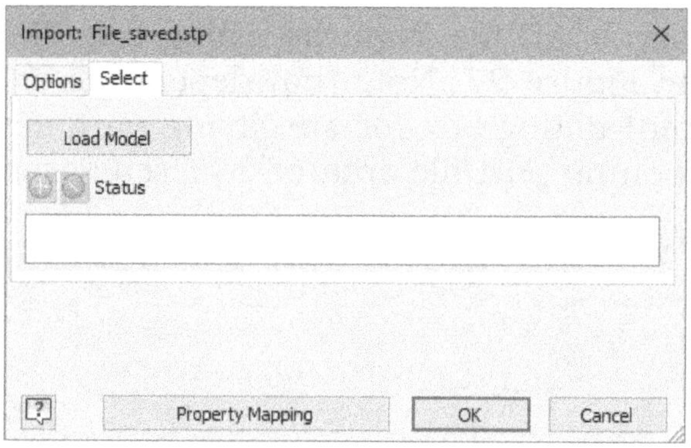

Figure-28. Select tab of Import dialog box

- Click on the **Load Model** button from the dialog box. The objects of the selected model will be displayed; refer to Figure-29.

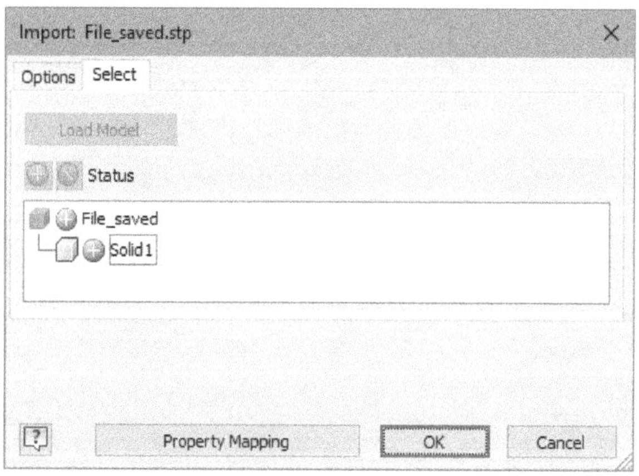

Figure-29. Objects in the Select tab

- Objects with plus sign will be imported and the other objects will be skipped.
- Click on the plus sign against the part to skip it from importing and click on the **OK** button from the dialog box. The object will be displayed in the modeling area.

Opening Sample Files

The **Open Samples** tool in **Open** cascading menu of the **File** menu is used to download and open the sample files provided by Autodesk for Inventor. On clicking this tool, a web page will be displayed in your default Web Browser. Download and open the file as desired.

Saving File

Saving file is as important as planting trees in backyard!! Jokes apart, its very important to save the model created, so that you can reuse it later. There are many options in Autodesk Inventor to save files. These options are discussed next.

Save option

The **Save** option is used to save the active file. This option is available in the **Save** cascading menu of the **File** menu. The procedure to use this option is given next.

- After creating the model, click on the **Save** option from the **Save** cascading menu in the **File** menu; refer to Figure-30 or press **CTRL+S** from keyboard.

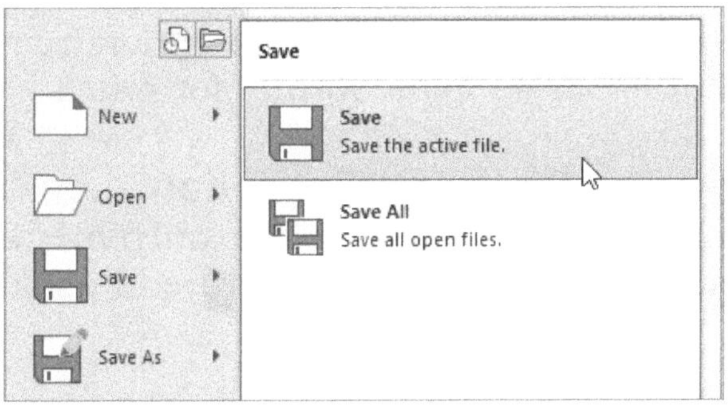

Figure-30. Save option

- If you are saving the file for the first time then the **Save As** dialog box will be displayed; refer to Figure-31.

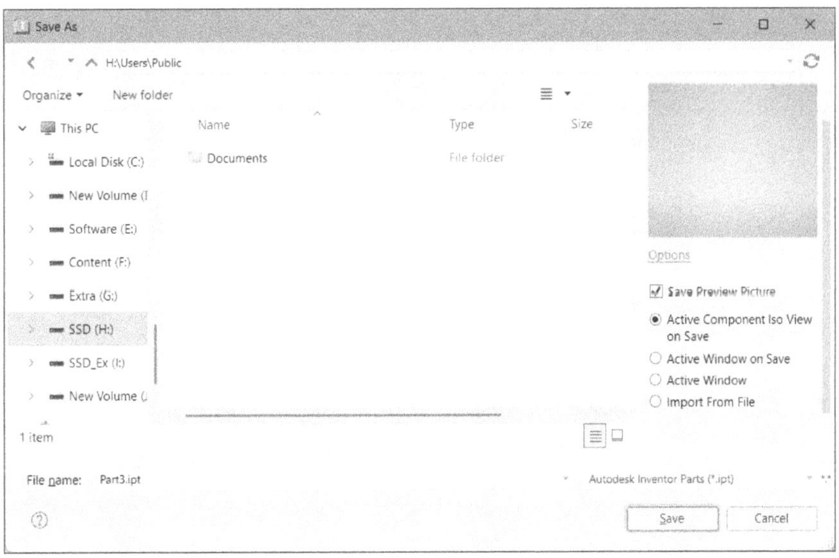

Figure-31. Save As dialog box

- Click on the **Save in** drop-down at the top in the dialog box and select desired location for saving file.

- Specify desired name in the **File name** edit box and click on the **Save** button. The file will be saved by specified name in the selected location.
- If you click again on the **Save** option second time later then the file will be over-written on the previous session of file.

Save All option

The **Save All** option does the same as the **Save** option do but it saves all the open files.

Save As option

The **Save As** option available in the **Save As** cascading menu is used to save the file with new name and at different location. The operation of this tool is same as the operation of **Save** option for the first time.

Save Copy As option

The **Save Copy As** option is used to save another copy of the current file. Note that if you select the **Save Copy As** option then the file will be saved with another name but it will not open in Inventor automatically.

Similarly, you can use the **Save Copy As Template** option from the **Save As** cascading menu to save the current file in template format for reuse.

Pack and Go option

The **Pack and Go** option is used to package the currently active file and all of its referenced files into a single location. The procedure to use this option is discussed next.

- After creating and saving the model, click on the **Pack and Go** option from **Save As** cascading menu in the **File** menu; refer to Figure-32. The **Pack and Go** dialog box will be displayed; refer to Figure-33.

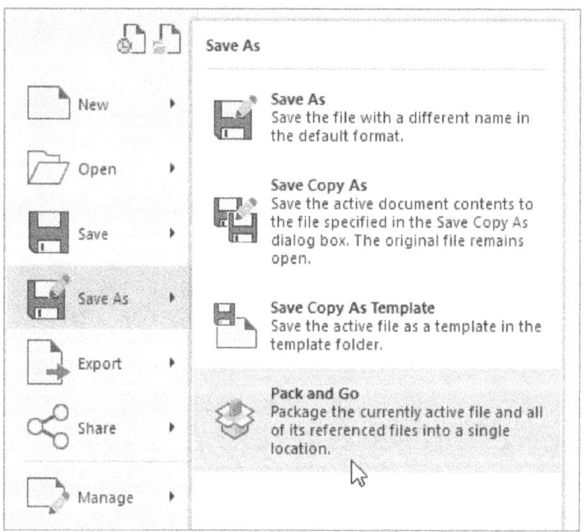

Figure-32. Pack and Go option

- The **Source File** box displays the path and the file name of the file to package.
- Click on **Browse** button from **Destination Folder** box to find the appropriate destination for the packaged files or specify the path and folder name. If the folder does not exist, a prompt to create the folder will be displayed.

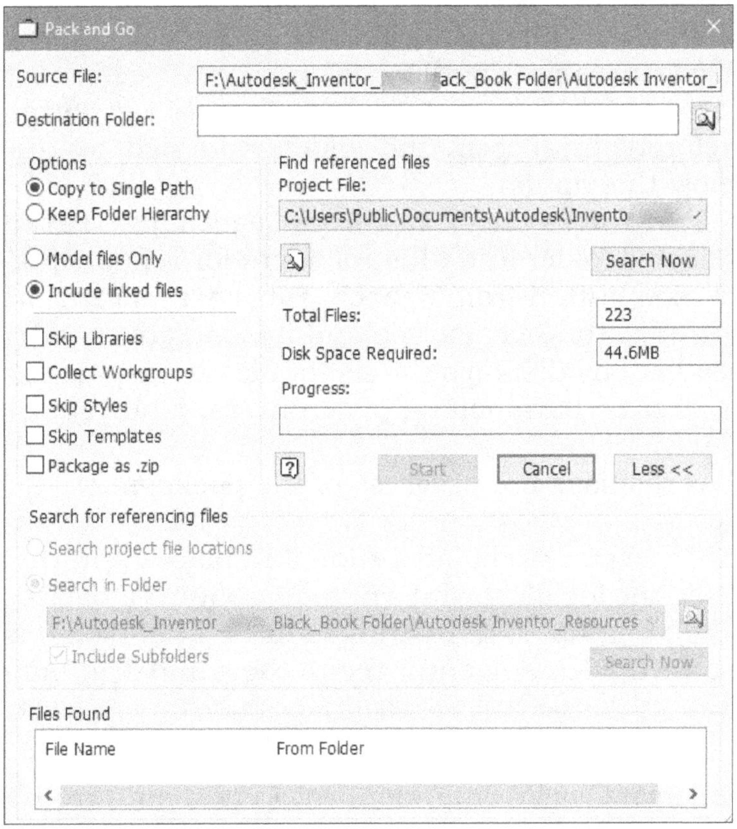

Figure-33. Pack and Go dialog box

- Select **Copy to Single Path** radio button from **Options** area to copy the referenced files to a single folder with the packaged file.
- Select **Keep Folder Hierarchy** radio button from **Options** area to build a folder hierarchy under the destination folder that preserves the folder hierarchy under the original project locations and copies the selected file and its referenced and referencing files to the appropriate subfolders.
- Select **Model files Only** radio button from **Options** area to copy only Autodesk Inventor model files (.ipt, .idw, .ide, .dwg) to the destination folder.
- Select **Include linked files** radio button from **Options** area to copy all referenced files to the destination folder including spreadsheets, text files, and other files.
- Select **Skip Libraries** check box from **Options** area to not copy the library files with the packaged file.
- Select **Collect Workgroups** check box from **Options** area to collect workgroups and the workspace into a single root folder.
- Select **Skip Styles** check box from **Options** area to not copy the styles with the packaged file.
- Select **Skip Templates** check box from **Options** area to not copy the templates with the packaged file.
- Select **Package as .zip** check box from **Options** area to package the files in .zip format.
- The **Project Files** box in the **Find referenced files** area displays the default active project file. Click on the **Browse** button to search for a different project file.
- Click on the **Search Now** button from **Find referenced files** area to search for files that are referenced from the selected file.
- The **Total Files** box displays the total number of files to package.
- The **Disk Space Required** box displays the disk space needed on destination media.

- Select **Search project file locations** radio button from **Search for referencing files** area to search for referencing files in the workspaces, workgroups, and library locations specified in the project file.
- Select **Search in Folder** radio button from **Search for referencing files** area to search for referencing files in the folder identified by the path in the field immediately below this option.
- Select **Include Subfolders** check box from **Search for referencing files** area to search the selected folder and all subfolders for referencing files.
- Click on **Search Now** button from **Search for referencing files** area to search for files that reference the selected file and its transitively referenced files.
- The **Files Found** list box displays the list of files to be packaged.
- After specifying desired parameters, click on **Start** button to begin the process of packaging.
- The **Progress** box displays the progress of the packaging.

Pack and Go creates a log file of the operation and places it in the same directory as the packaged file. See the log file for information about the packaging operation and the names with source paths of all referenced files. The log file is overwritten each time you package an Autodesk Inventor file to the same destination.

Exporting Files

The options in the **Export** cascading menu of **File** menu are used to create alien matter. (No!! I mean it.) Okay, getting back to software terms, the options in the **Export** cascading menu are used to save the inventor files in native format of the other software like, you can save the file for Pro-E, CATIA, AutoCAD, and so on; refer to Figure-34.

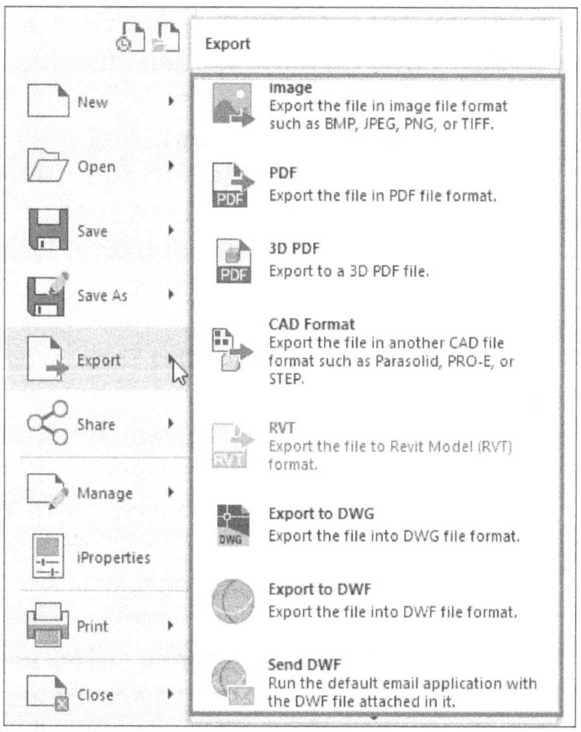

Figure-34. Export cascading menu

The options of **Export** cascading menu are discussed next.

Image option

The **Image** option in the **Export** cascading menu is used to save images of the model. After making the model and export it to image format by using this option, you can get beautiful print of the model (which can be your company product) and paste it to the wall. The procedure to use the **Image** option is given next.

- Click on the **Image** option from the **Export** cascading menu in the **File** menu. A very familiar **Save As** dialog box will be displayed; refer to Figure-35.

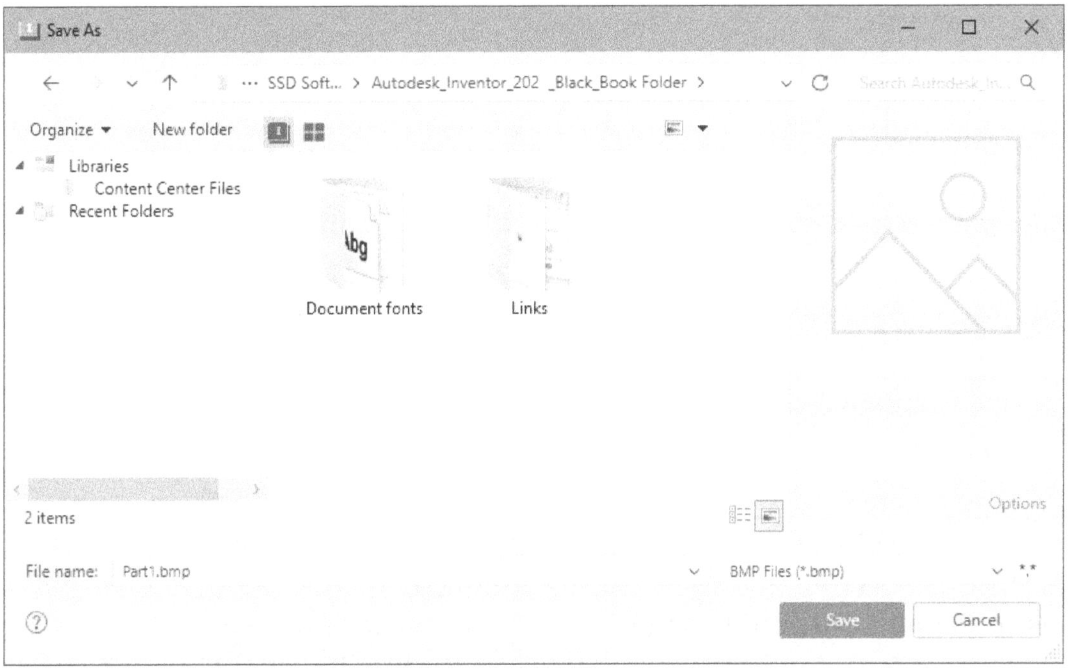

Figure-35. Save As dialog box

- Select desired image format from the **Save as type** drop-down and click on the **Save** button from the dialog box. The current model in the modeling area will be saved in the image with background.

PDF option

PDF is one of the most popular document format. Due to its compact size and easy handling, this format can also be used in presentations of models. Using the **PDF** option in the **Export** cascading menu, you can create the pdf file of Inventor model. Note that the pdf created will be just like image that we created in previous topic.

3D PDF option

Although, iges and other CAD portability formats are useful data for engineers and designers but they are not useful data for marketing. For market executives, there is requirement of a format by which they can display important features of model with some dimensions. 3D PDF is one of the important format for this purpose. The procedure to create 3D PDF is given next.

- Click on the **3D PDF** tool from the **Export** cascading menu in the **File** menu after creating the model. The **Publish 3D PDF** dialog box will be displayed; refer to Figure-36.

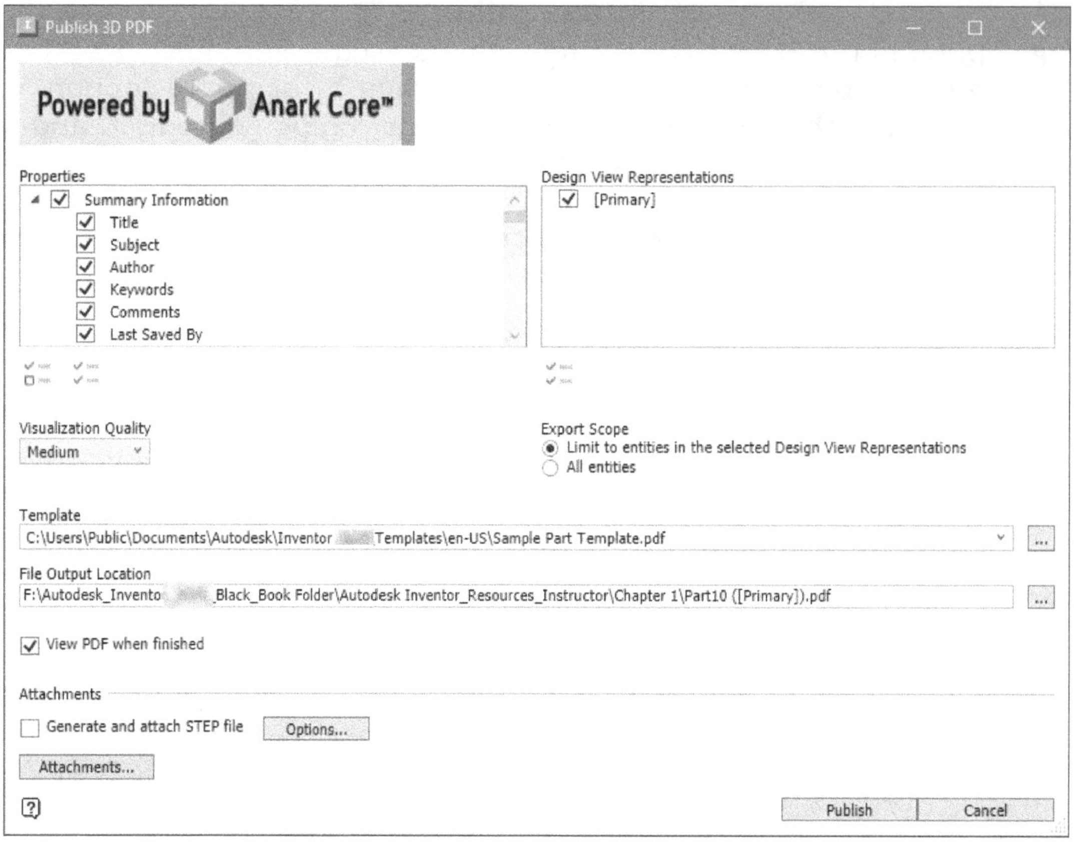

Figure-36. Publish 3D PDF dialog box

- Select the properties and views to be included in the 3D PDF using the check boxes in **Properties** and **Design View Representations** areas of the dialog box.
- Set desired model quality in the **Visualization Quality** drop-down. Note that increasing the quality will increase the PDF size.
- Set desired template and location using the respective fields in the dialog box.
- Select the **Generate and attach STEP file** check box to attach a STEP in PDF. To modify options related to STEP file, click on the **Options** button next to the check box.
- You can add more attachments to the PDF by using the **Attachments** button.
- Click on the **Publish** button after specify desired parameters. The 3D PDF will be generated and displayed in your default PDF Reader Application; refer to Figure-37.

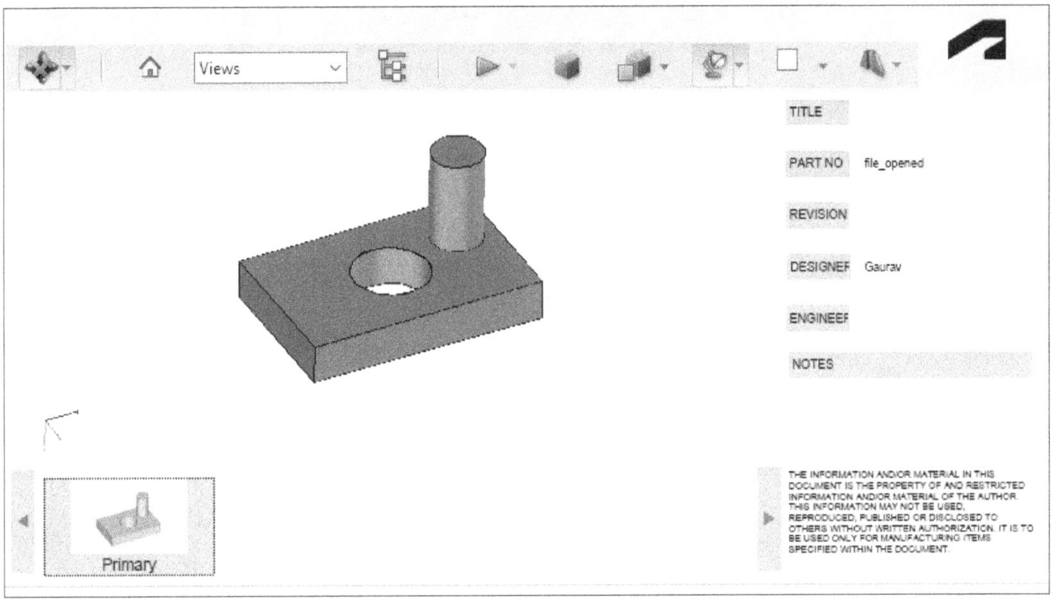

Figure-37. 3D PDF generated

CAD Format option

The **CAD Format** option in the **Export** cascading menu is used to export the Inventor model in other CAD formats like iges, stp, jt, stl, etc. Out of all the export formats, IGES and STP are the most popular formats. So, we will discuss the procedure to export file in these formats.

- Click on the **CAD Format** option from the **Export** cascading menu in the **File** menu. The well known **Save As** dialog box will be displayed. You know what to do now.

Exporting File to IGES Format

- Select the **IGES Files** option from the **Save as type** drop-down; refer to Figure-38.

Figure-38. Save as type drop down

- Click on the **Options** button from the dialog box. The **IGES File Save As Options** dialog box will be displayed as shown in Figure-39.

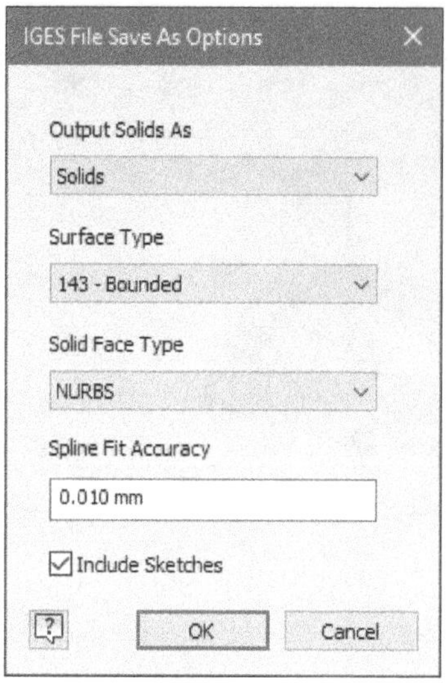

Figure-39. IGES File Save As Options dialog box

- Here, we are exporting a solid part so the options related to solid part are displayed. If you are exporting a surface part or assembly file then the options in the dialog box will change accordingly.
- In the current scenario, select desired option from the **Output Solids As** drop-down. You can export the part as surfaces, solids, or wireframe. On selecting the **Surfaces** option, the **Solid Face Type** drop-down will become inactive and on selecting the **Wireframe** option, the **Surface Type** drop-down will also become inactive.
- Select desired surface type from the **Surface Face Type** drop-down and desired solid face type from the **Solid Face Type** drop-down.
- Using the **Spline Fit Accuracy** edit box, you can specify the accuracy for conversion.
- Select the **Include Sketches** check box to export the sketches along with the solids/surfaces/wireframe.
- Click on the **OK** button from the dialog box to apply the selected parameters.

STEP Format

- Select the **STEP Files** option from the **Save as type** drop-down.
- Click on the **Options** button from the **Save As** dialog box. The **STEP File Save As Options** dialog box will be displayed as shown in Figure-40.

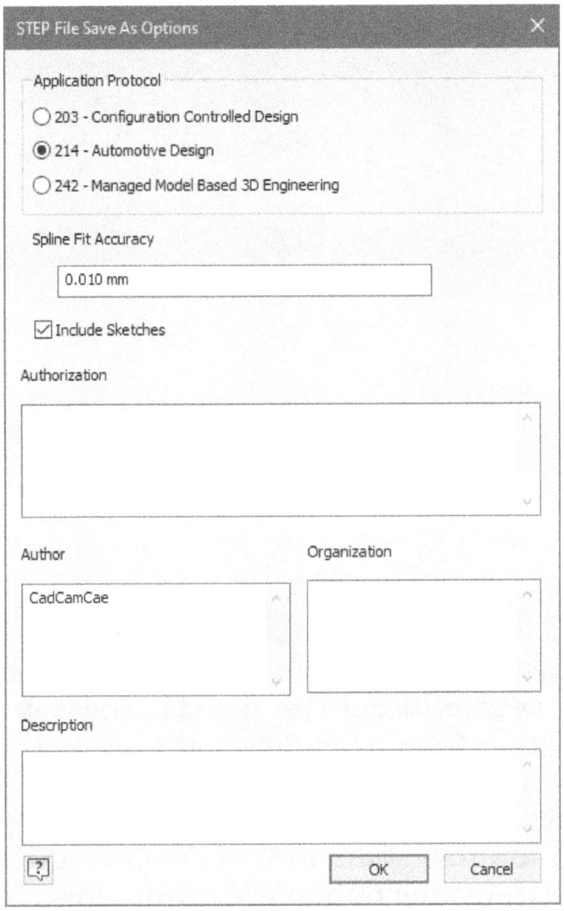

Figure-40. STEP File Save As Options dialog box

- Select desired radio button from the **Application Protocol** area to define the applications of current file.
- As discussed earlier, you can set the accuracy of model by using the **Spline Fit Accuracy** edit box and you can include the sketches in exported file by using the **Include Sketches** check box.
- Specify the other user parameters by using the edit boxes in the dialog box and click on the **OK** button to apply the parameters.
- Click on the **Save** button from the **Save As** dialog box to export the file in selected format.

Similarly, you can export the current model to **DWG** or **DWF** format by using the respective option from the **Export** cascading menu.

RVT option

The **RVT** option in the **Export** cascading menu is used to export a version of an assembly model as RVT file. Revit model do not require manufacturing level detail in models to use for designs. The procedure to use this tool is given next.

- Click on the **RVT** option from **Export** cascading menu in the **File** menu after creating the assembly model. The **Simplify Property** panel will be displayed; refer to Figure-41.

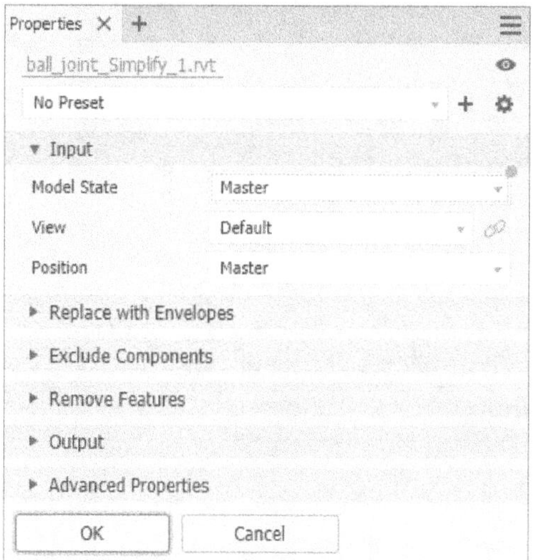

Figure-41. Simplify Property panel

- Select desired built-in preset from **Preset** drop-down. On selecting **Remove the least detail (small parts and features)** option from drop-down, the settings are designed to remove small parts and features resulting in the most detailed model. On selecting **Remove moderate detail (medium sized parts and all listed features)** option from drop-down, the settings are designed to remove a moderate amount of detail. On selecting **Remove the most detail (replace top-level components with envelopes)** option from drop-down, the settings are designed to remove the greatest amount of detail resulting in very basic shapes. On selecting **No Simplification** option from drop-down, the simplified version is full fidelity with respect to the assembly model. All details are visible in the model.
- Click on **Create new preset** button to create your own preset.
- Click on the **Preset Settings** button to create desired settings for the preset.
- The options in the **Model State** drop-down of **Input** rollout define the envelope size. Changes in a model state affect the envelope size; refer to Figure-41.
- Select desired option from **View** drop-down of **Input** rollout to display active design view. Changes in design views do not affect envelope size. Click on the **Associative** button to link the design view with the simplified model.
- The options in the **Position** drop-down of **Input** rollout define the envelope size. Changes in position view can affect the envelope size.
- Select **None** option from **Replace** area of **Replace with Envelopes** rollout if you are not using envelopes for the simplication. Components and Features groups are available for use; refer to Figure-42.

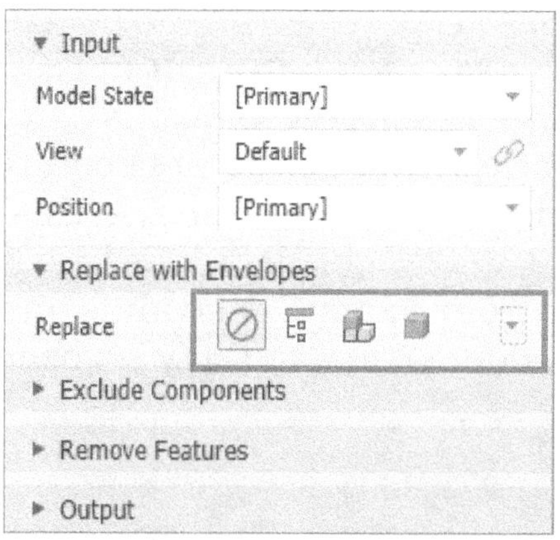

Figure-42. Replace drop down of Replace with Envelopes rollout

- Select **All in One Envelope** option from **Replace** drop-down of **Replace with Envelopes** rollout to create an envelope around the top-level assembly. The result is imprecise and useful for developing a "keep out" area for the design. Components and Features groups are hidden.
- Select **Each Top Level Component** option from **Replace** drop-down of **Replace with Envelopes** rollout to create an envelope around assembly first-level components. Component selection tools display. Feature selection tools are hidden.
- Select **Each Part** option from **Replace** drop-down of **Replace with Envelopes** rollout to create envelopes for all parts in the assembly. Feature selection tools are hidden.
- Select **Exclude parts by size** check box from **Exclude Components** rollout and specify the maximum diagonal value for a bounding box in the **Max. Diagonal** edit box; refer to Figure-43. Click on the arrow button at the end of edit box to select a recently used value. Click on the **Pick a part to get its bounding box diagonal length** button and select a part/component to supply the diagonal value.

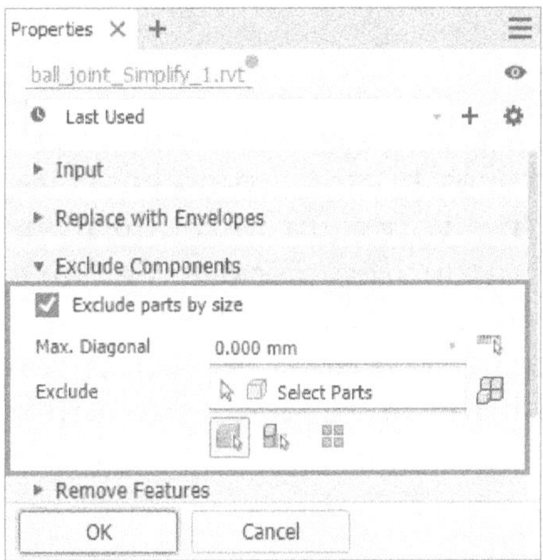

Figure-43. Exclude Components rollout options

- Click on desired selection priority you want to use from **Exclude Components** rollout. Select **Parts** button to select only parts of selected item. Select **Components** button to select only components of selected item. Select **All Occurrences** button to select all occurrences of the selected item.
- Click on the **Show excluded parts** button from **Exclude Components** rollout to display the components being removed in the **Exclude** box. Click on the **Show included parts** button to display the components that are included in the simplified model in the **Include** box.
- The **Remove Features** rollout provides options for selecting features by type or size to include in or exclude from the simplified part. The list of features include holes, fillets, chamfers, pockets (subtractive), embosses (additive), and tunnels (single and multiple entry); refer to Figure-44. On selecting **None** option from drop-down, no features of this type are removed. On selecting **All** option from drop-down, all features of this type are removed. On selecting **Range** option from drop-down, all features equal to or smaller than the specified parameter are removed. Specify the value that defines the maximum size to remove.

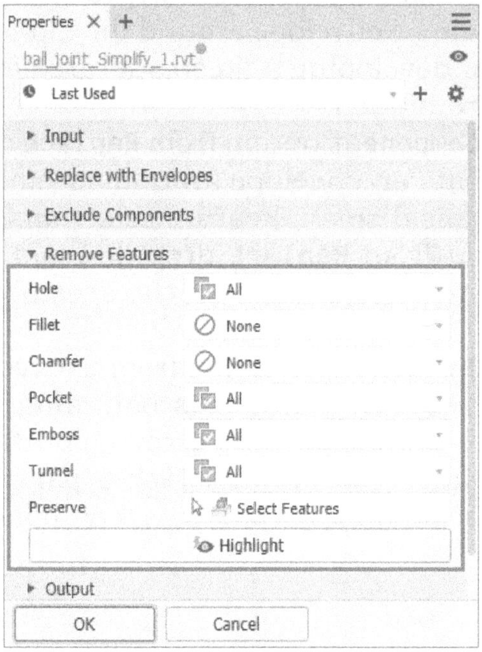

Figure-44. Remove Features rollout options

- Click on the **Select Features** button from **Preserve** section of **Remove Features** rollout to select the features you want to retain from those being removed.
- Click on the **Highlight** button from **Remove Features** rollout to apply a color to the features to be removed.
- The **Type** section of **Output** rollout outputs your inventor design as a Revit model, so you can provide it to building designers or other downstream uses; refer to Figure-45.

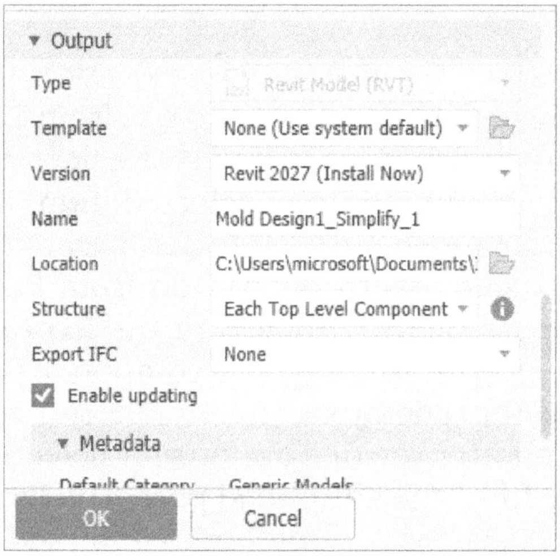

Figure-45. Output rollout options

- Specify desired file name in the **Name** edit box of **Output** rollout or use the default assembly name.
- Select desired option from the **Version** drop-down to specify the Revit version for compatibility during export.
- Specify desired location of the new file in the **Location** edit box of **Output** rollout.

- Select **All in One Element** option from **Structure** drop-down of **Output** rollout to specify a Revit model with one element representing the simplified assembly is output. Select **Each Top Level Component** option from drop-down to specify a Revit model with multiple elements representing the first level components of the simplified model.
- Select **Enable updating** check box from **Output** rollout to create a browser node that enables you to edit the simplification and update the exported RVT.
- Select **Fill internal voids** check box from **Advanced Properties** rollout to automatically filled all internal voids; refer to Figure-46.

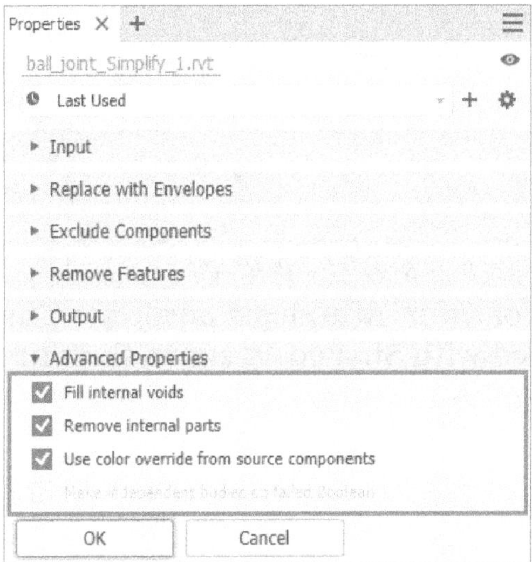

Figure-46. Advanced Properties rollout options

- On selecting **Remove internal parts** check box from **Advanced Properties** rollout, Inventor looks at the model from 14 standard directions (six orthographic and eight isometric) to determine a parts visibility state. Parts deemed not visible are removed.
- Select **Make independent bodies on failed Boolean** check box from **Advanced Properties** rollout to create a multi-body part when a boolean operation fails on one of the single solid body style options. This check box is available only when Style is Single body with no visible edges between planar faces or Single body with visible edges between planar faces.
- After specifying desired parameters, click on **OK** button from the panel or press **ENTER**. The **Exporting New Revit Model (RVT)** window will be displayed exporting the model; refer to Figure-47.

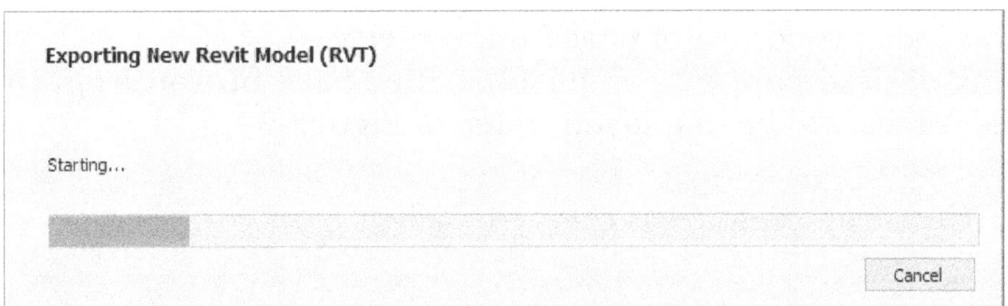

Figure-47. Exporting New Revit Model RVT window

Sharing View

The **Share View** tool in **Share** cascading menu of the **File** menu is used to share views of current model with other. The procedure to use this tool is given next.

- Click on the **Share View** tool from the **Share** cascading menu of the **File** menu. The **Sign in** page will be displayed to sign into your Autodesk account if not logged in; refer to Figure-48.

Figure-48. Sign in page of Autodesk account

- Enter the credentials of your Autodesk account. The **Create a Shared View** window will be displayed with **Shared Views** task pane at the right in application window; refer to Figure-49.

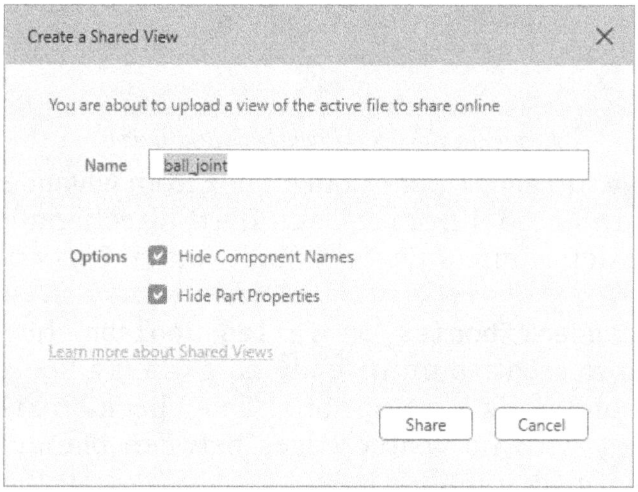

Figure-49. Create a Shared View dialog box

- Specify desired name of view in the **Name** edit box. Select the **Hide Component Names** check box from **Options** area of the dialog box if you want to hide component name from shared view. Similarly, select the **Hide Part Properties** check box if you want to hide properties of part from the view.
- After setting desired parameters, click on the **Share** button from the dialog box. The **Shared Views** will be displayed; refer to Figure-50.

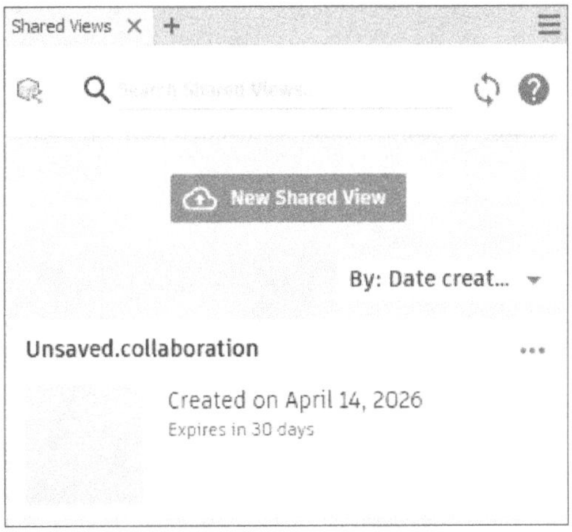

Figure-50. Displaying the shared view

- Click on the button, the flyout will be displayed; refer to Figure-51.

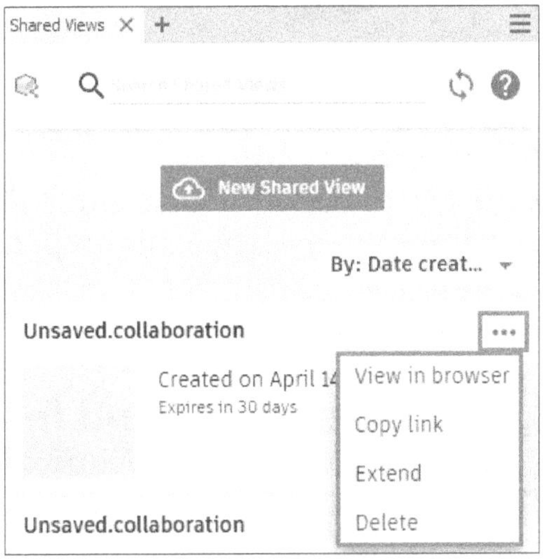

Figure-51. Displaying the flyout of shared view

- Click on the **View in browser** button from the flyout to open the shared view in a web browser; refer to Figure-52.

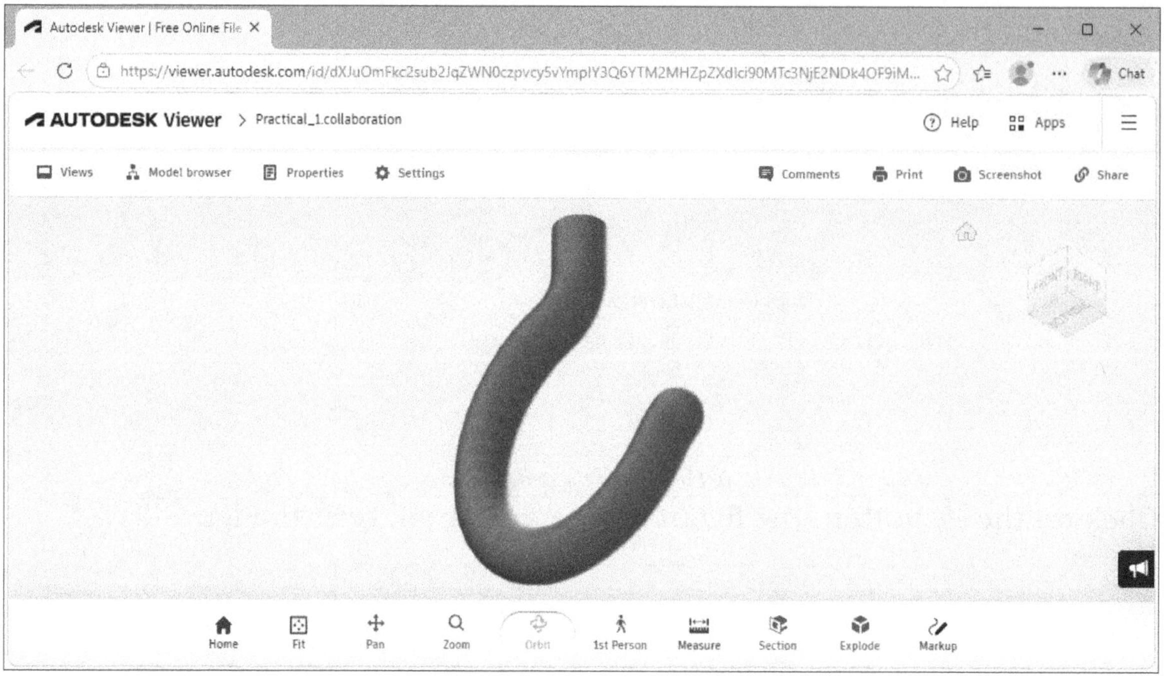

Figure-52. Autodesk viewer displayed

- Click on the **Copy link** button to copy the shareable link of the shared view.
- Click on the **Extend** button to increase the validity period of the shared view.
- Click on the **Delete** button to remove the shared view.
- Once the processing is complete. The view will be available for sharing.

Managing Project files and features

The options to manage project file and other related features are available in the **Manage** cascading menu; refer to Figure-53. Various options of this menu are discussed next.

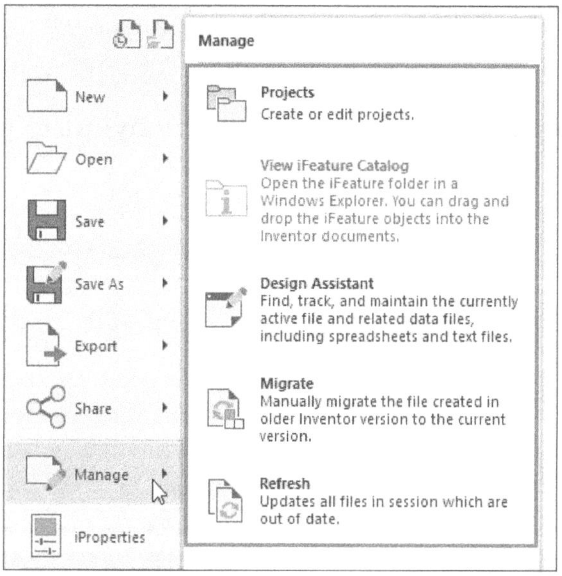

Figure-53. Manage cascading menu

Projects

The **Projects** option is used to create and manage the project files. A project alloys you easily manage drawings and other assets related to current design project. For example, if you are working on a drone project then all files related to the project will be stored in drone project folder in your local drive with all related assets like material, content library components, and so on. The procedure to use this tool is given next.

- Click on the **Projects** option from **Manage** cascading menu in the **File** menu. The **Projects** dialog box will be displayed as shown in Figure-54.

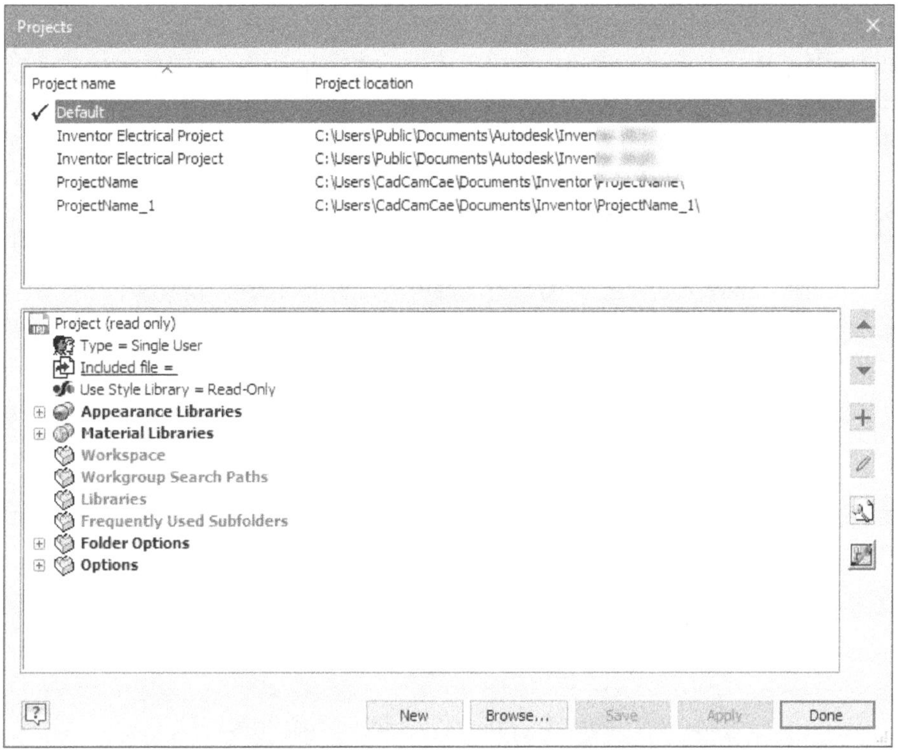

Figure-54. Projects dialog box

- Select the project file that you want to edit from the upper area of the dialog box. The related options will be displayed in the lower area of the dialog box.
- To change any parameter in the dialog box, right-click on it and select the **Edit** option from the shortcut menu.

Adding New Project

- To add new project, click on the **New** button from the **Projects** dialog box. The **Inventor project wizard** dialog box will be displayed; refer to Figure-55.

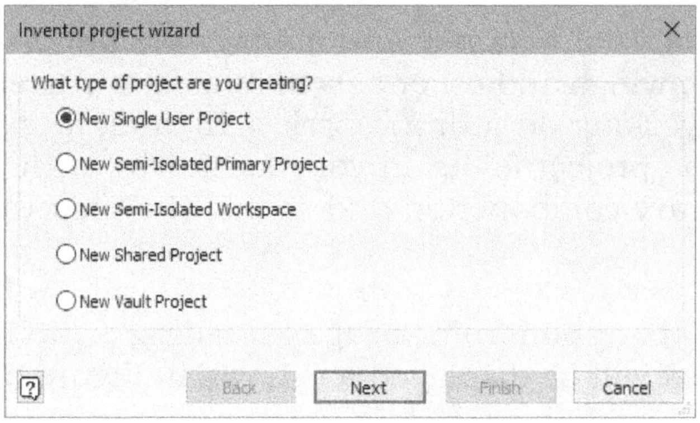

Figure-55. Inventor project wizard dialog box

- If you are using Vault server and want to create a vault project then select the **New Vault Project** radio button. Otherwise, select the **New Single User Project** radio button and click on the **Next** button. The updated **Inventor project wizard** dialog box will be displayed as shown in Figure-56. (Note that we have selected the **New Single User Project** radio button in this case.)

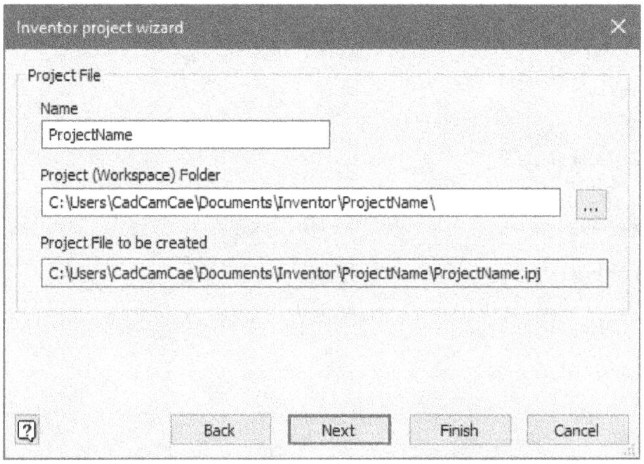

Figure-56. Updated Inventor project wizard dialog box

- Specify desired name of project file in the **Name** edit box. Similarly, you can set the project folder in the **Project (Workspace) Folder** edit box.
- Click on the **Next** button after specifying desired values. The **Select Libraries** page of **Inventor project wizard** dialog box will be displayed; refer to Figure-57.

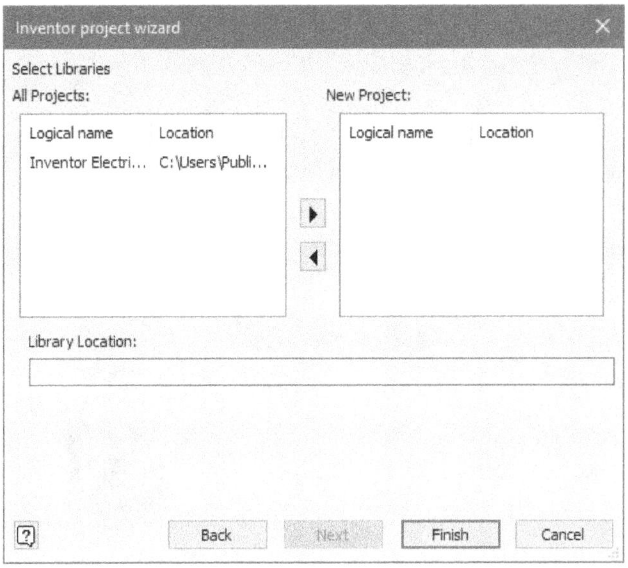

Figure-57. Select libraries page

- Click on the arrow button in the middle of the dialog box to add or remove the library from the new project.
- Click on the **Finish** button from the dialog box to create the project file.
- Click on the **Done** button from the **Projects** dialog box to exit. Now, you can use the newly created file as project while starting new file.
- To make the newly created project as active project, click on the **Projects** button from the **Quick Access Toolbar**; refer to Figure-58. The **Projects** dialog box will be displayed as discussed earlier.

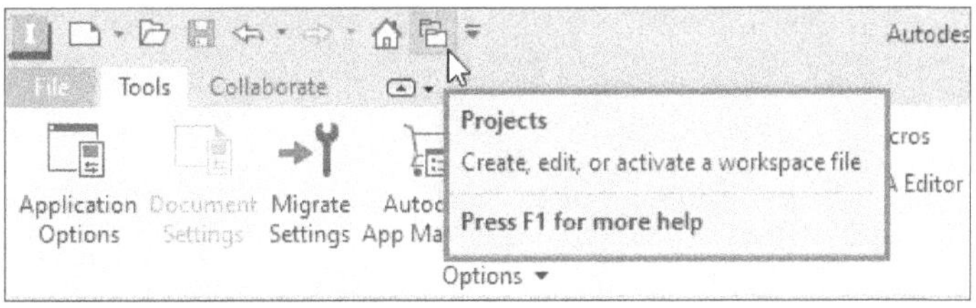

Figure-58. Projects button

- Double-click on the newly created project file that you want to make active project from the upper area of the dialog box. A tick mark will be displayed with the selected project file which means it is the default project.

View iFeature Catalog

In terms of Autodesk Inventor, iFeature means intelligent features. iFeatures are pre-designed features that take a few parameters as input and create real-world designs. For example, there are shapes of punches, cones, rectangular tubes, and so on that can be directly used while creating the model. The procedure to use this tool is given next.

- Make sure a new file is open in the software. Click on the **View iFeature Catalog** tool from the **Manage** cascading menu in the **File** menu. The **Catalog** folder will be displayed in the Windows Explorer; refer to Figure-59.
- Open desired category from the **Windows Explorer** and drag desired feature to modeling area of Autodesk Inventor; refer to Figure-60.

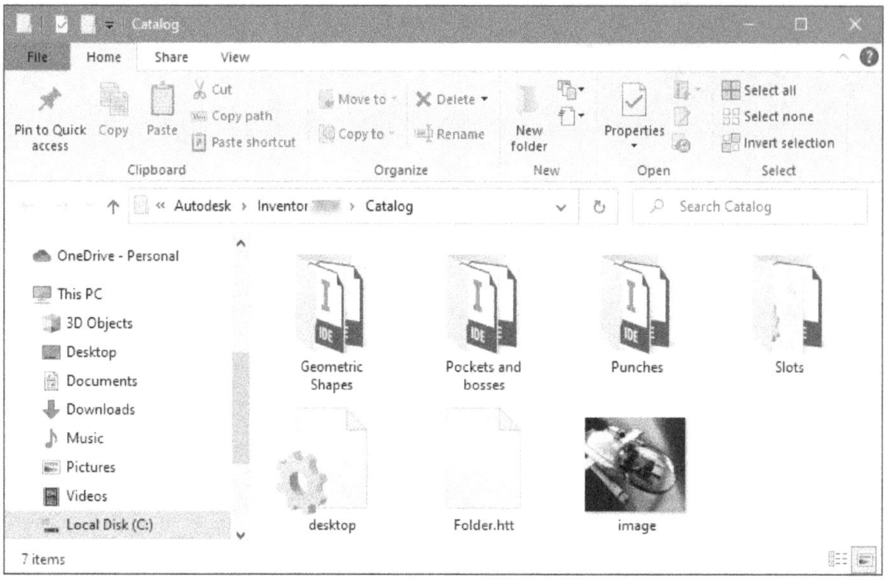

Figure-59. Catalog folder

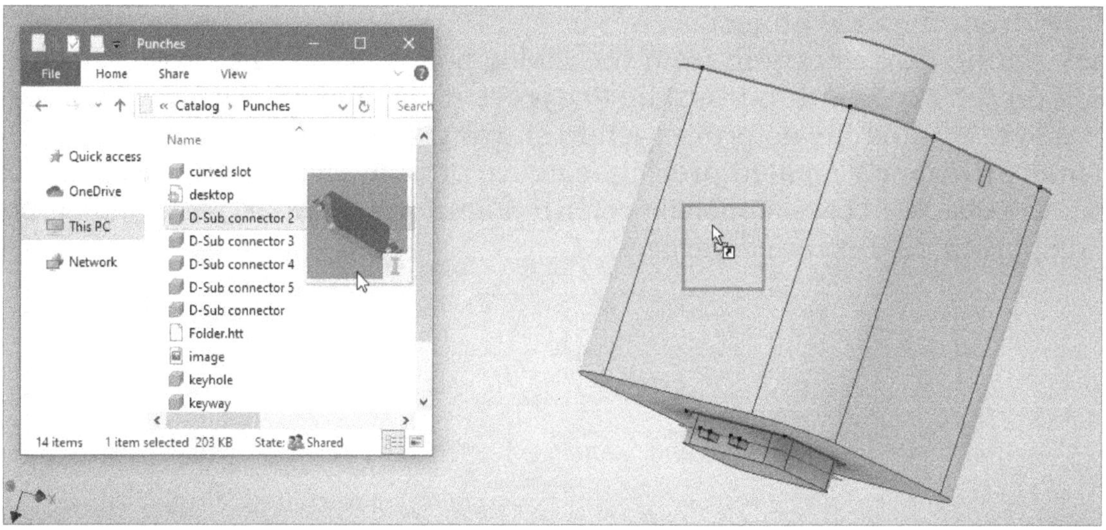

Figure-60. Dragging iFeatures in Inventor

- Once you release the mouse button after dragging the feature on model, the preview of iFeature will be displayed with **Insert iFeature** dialog box; refer to Figure-61.

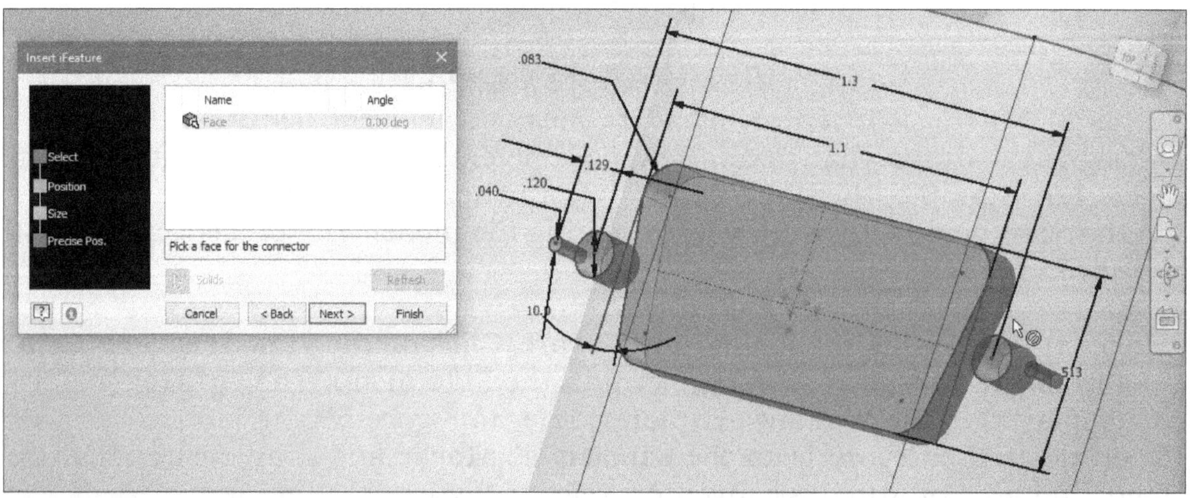

Figure-61. Insert iFeature dialog box

- Click on desired face of the model to place the feature.
- If you want to rotate the feature then click in the field under **Angle** column and specify the value of rotation angle; refer to Figure-62.

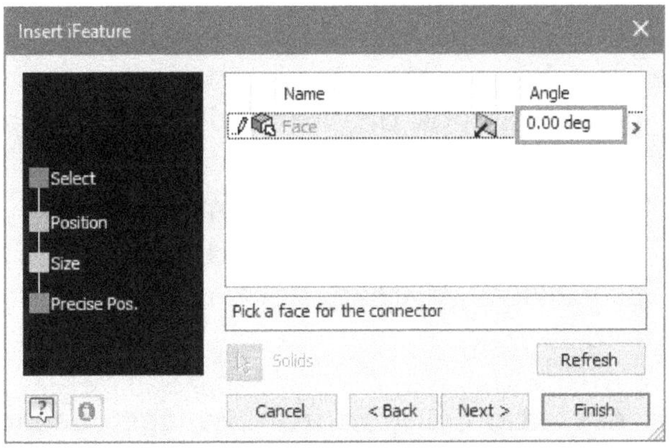

Figure-62. Angle edit box

- Click on the **Next** button from the dialog box. The **Size** page of **Insert iFeature** dialog box will be displayed; refer to Figure-63.

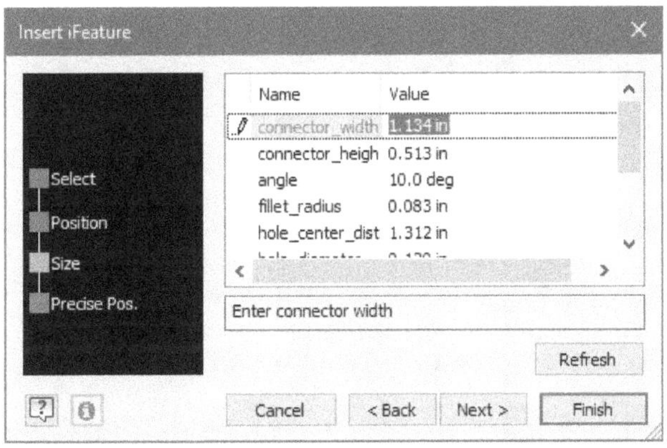

Figure-63. Size page of Insert iFeature dialog box

- Specify desired values for the size parameters of the feature and click on the **Next** button from the dialog box. The **Precise Position** page of **Insert iFeature** dialog box will be displayed; refer to Figure-64.

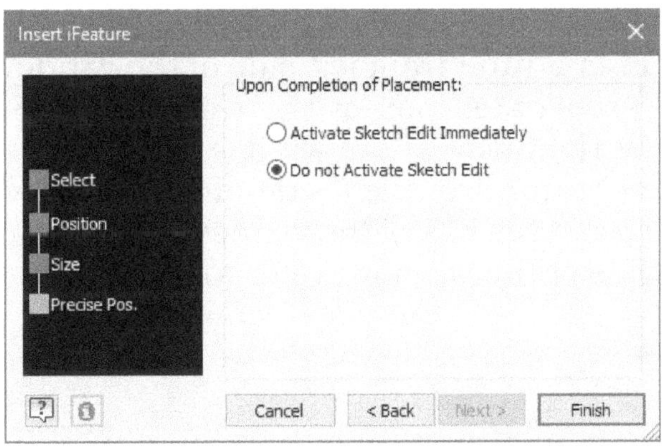

Figure-64. Precise Position page of Insert iFeature dialog box

- Select the **Do not Activate Sketch Edit** radio button from the dialog box if you are satisfied with the current position of the iFeature. If you want to edit the position of the iFeature precisely then select the **Activate Sketch Edit Immediately** radio button and click on the **Finish** button. The sketching environment will be displayed and using the **Dimension** tool, you can place the feature precisely. We will learn about the sketching tools later in the book.
- After specifying the position, click on the **Finish Sketch** button.

Design Assistant

The **Design Assistant** option is used to find, track, and maintain Autodesk Inventor files and related word processing, spreadsheet, or text files. The procedure to use this tool is discussed next.

- Click on the **Design Assistant** option from **Manage** cascading menu in the **File** menu. The **Design Assistant** window will be displayed with the properties and preview of current opened model; refer to Figure-65.

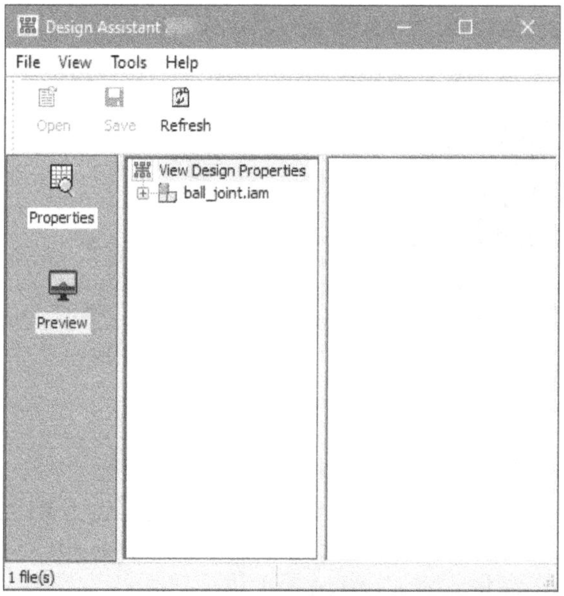

Figure-65. Design Assistant window

- Click on the **Properties** button from left side of the window and select the model from **View Design Properties** box of the window to display the properties of selected model on the right side of the window.
- Click on the **Preview** button from left side of the window and select the model from **View Design Properties** box of the window to display the preview of selected model on the right side of the window; refer to Figure-66.

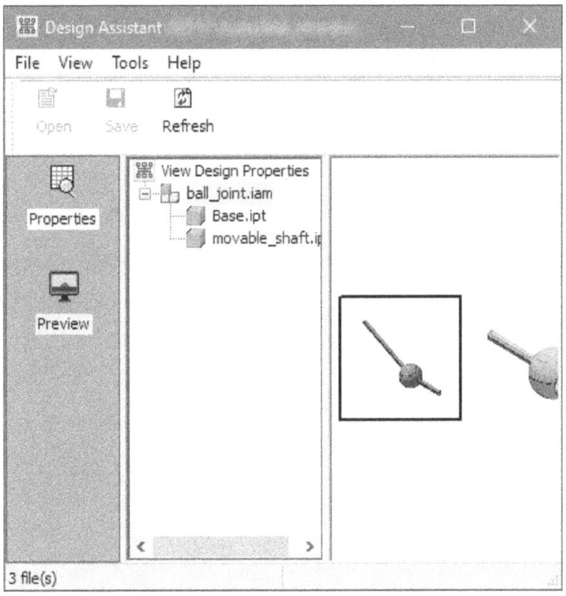

Figure-66. Preview of model

iProperties

The **iProperties** option is used to change general properties of the model. The procedure to use this option is given next.

- Click on the **iProperties** option from the **File** menu. The **iProperties** dialog box will be displayed as shown in Figure-67.
- The options in **General** tab display the general information of the part. Note that you cannot modify any of the values in this tab.
- Click on the **Summary** tab to specify the user details for the part. Similarly, you can specify the project details, status, and other custom details by using the respective tabs.
- The **Physical** tab in this dialog box is generally a major attraction for engineers. Using the options in the **Physical** tab, you can specify and check the mass properties of the model; refer to Figure-68.

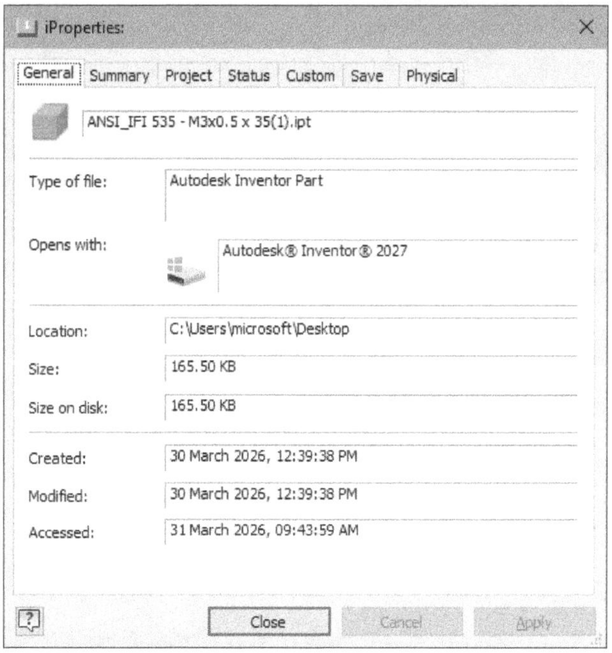

Figure-67. iProperties dialog box

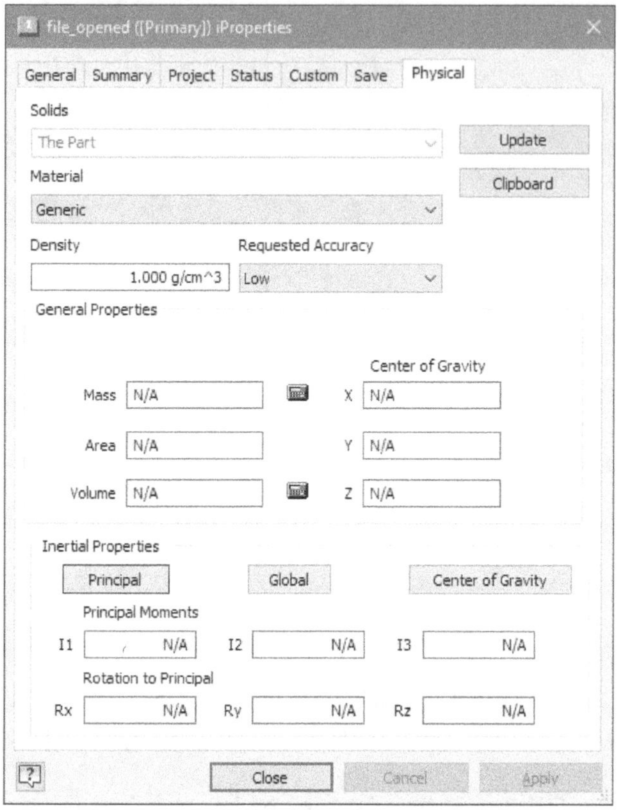

Figure-68. Physical tab of iProperties dialog box

- Select desired material from the **Material** drop-down. The value of density will change accordingly and hence the other property parameters like mass, center of gravity, and so on will change.

Printing Document

Printout is an important requirement in manufacturing area. You can not reach to a boiler/furnace with a tablet/laptop/e-gadgets in your hand as temperature near boiler/furnace is very high. In those cases, we need a copy of engineering drawing as printout that can be used by manufacturers for reference. Also, it is not feasible to hang 100 e-gadgets to display 100 of your products in a presentation room but you can take printouts of your products and display them alongside the products in the presentation room. There are various tools related to printing available in the **Print** cascading menu; refer to Figure-69. Various options in the menu are discussed next.

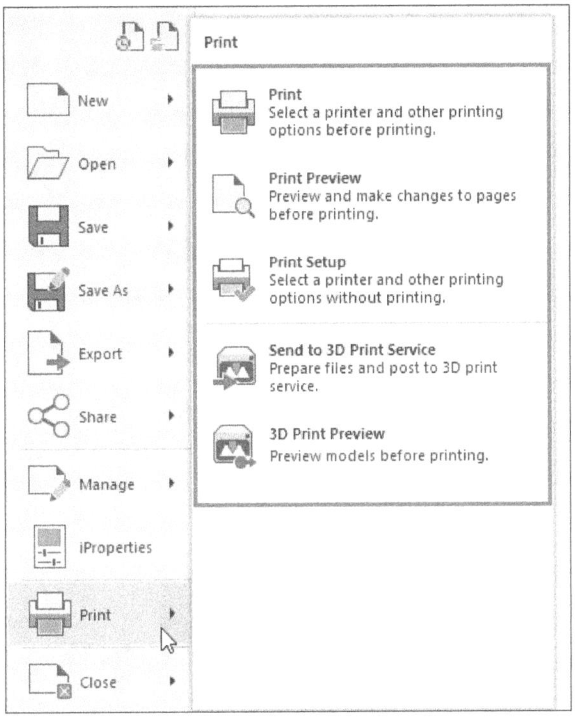

Figure-69. Print cascading menu

Print Tool

As the name suggests, the **Print** tool is used to get print out of the model/drawing on paper. The procedure to use this tool is given next.

- Click on the **Print** tool from the **Print** cascading menu in the **File** menu. The **Print** dialog box will be displayed as shown in Figure-70.

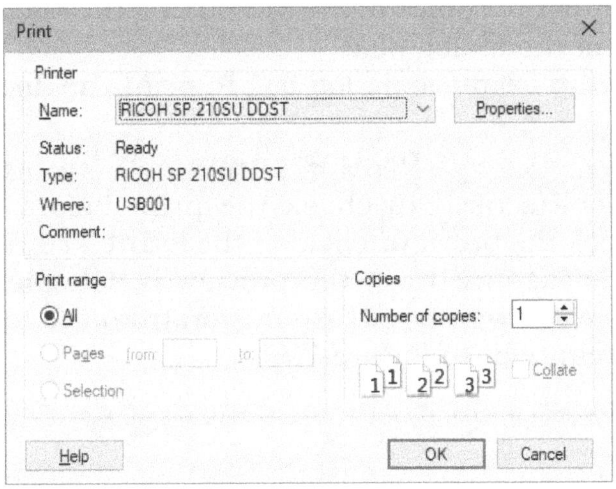

Figure-70. Print dialog box

- Select desired printer from the **Name** drop-down in the **Printer** area of the dialog box.
- Click on the **Properties** button next to **Name** drop-down. The **Printer Properties** dialog box will be displayed as shown in Figure-71.

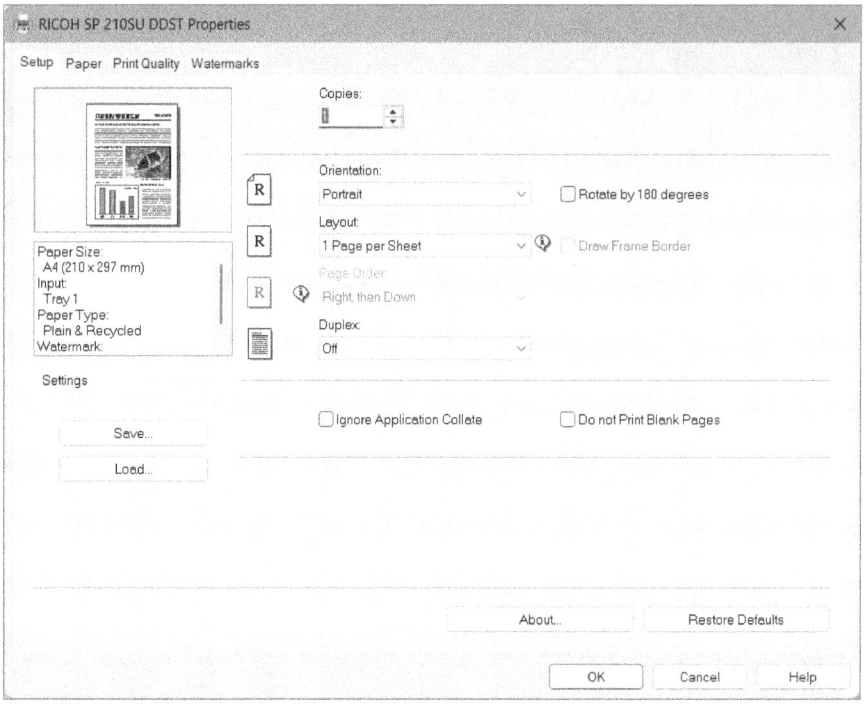

Figure-71. Printer Properties dialog box

- Set desired orientation for the page in **Orientation** drop-down of this page.
- Select desired paper size from the **Document Size** drop-down in the **Paper** tab of the dialog box.
- To apply watermark on the printout, click on the **Watermark** tab and select desired option from the **Watermark** drop-down in the dialog box.
- Click on the **OK** button from the **Printer Properties** dialog box to apply the changes.
- Specify desired number of copies of drawing using the **Number of copies** spinner in the **Copies** area of the dialog box.
- Click on the **OK** button from the dialog box to print the document.

Print Preview

The **Print Preview** tool is used to check the print before sending command to printer/plotter. To check the preview, click on the **Print Preview** tool from the **Print** cascading menu in the **File** menu. If the preview is satisfactory then click on the **Print** button, otherwise click on the **Close** button from the toolbar displayed at the top of the modeling area; refer to Figure-72.

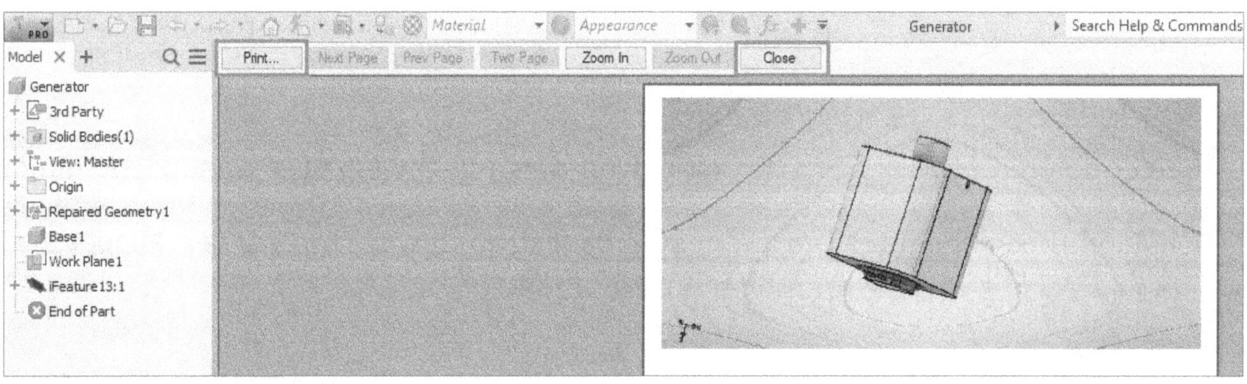

Figure-72. Print preview of the model

Print Setup

The **Print Setup** tool is used to specify settings for the printing. The procedure to use this tool is given next.

- Click on the **Print Setup** tool from the **Print** cascading menu in the **File** menu. The **Print Setup** dialog box will be displayed as shown in Figure-73.

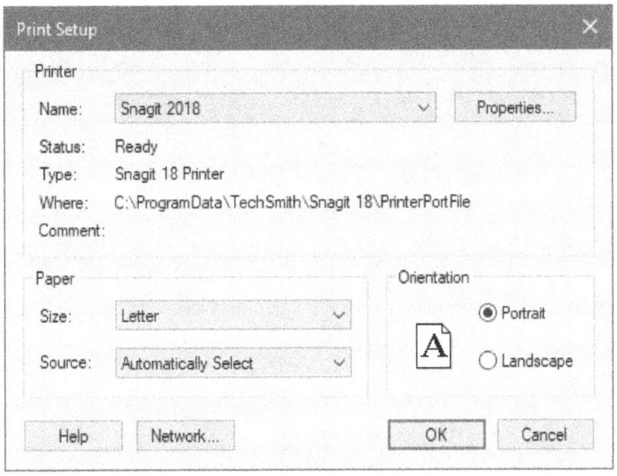

Figure-73. Print Setup dialog box

- The options in this dialog box are same as discussed earlier for the **Printer Properties** dialog box. Specify the size and orientation for the print and click on the **OK** button.

Send to 3D Print service

One of the great invention of this century, 3D Printing facilitate prototype creation at blazing speed. 3D Printing is finding scope in almost every area of engineering whether it is biotechnology or it is Construction engineering. Now, every good CAD package has the option to send file for 3D print service. The procedure to send file for 3D Print service from Autodesk Inventor is given next.

- After creating a solid model, click on the **Send to 3D Print Service** tool from the **Print** cascading menu in the **File** menu. The **Send to 3D Print Service** dialog box will be displayed as shown in Figure-74.

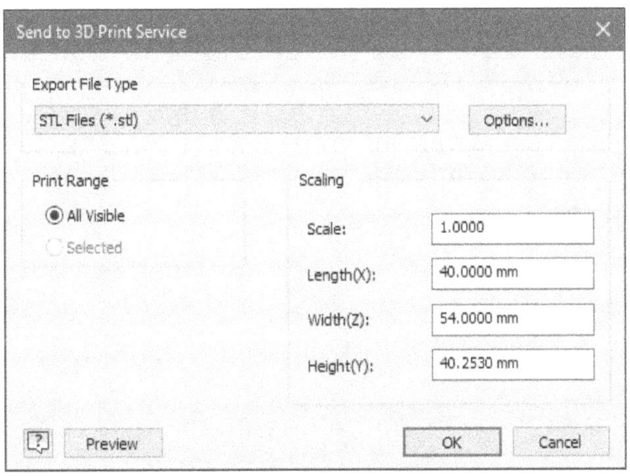

Figure-74. Send to 3D Print Service dialog box

- Experienced CAD users can easily find that the export format in this dialog box, **STL Files** is a very old CAD format and is in use for many years. So, we can understand that the dialog box actually apply some scaling changes and then convert the model to STL file which can be directly used by 3D Printer.
- From the **Scaling** area, specify desired parameters to enlarge or diminish the model.
- Click on the **Options** button next to **Export File Type** drop-down. The **STL File Save As Options** dialog box will be displayed; refer to Figure-75.

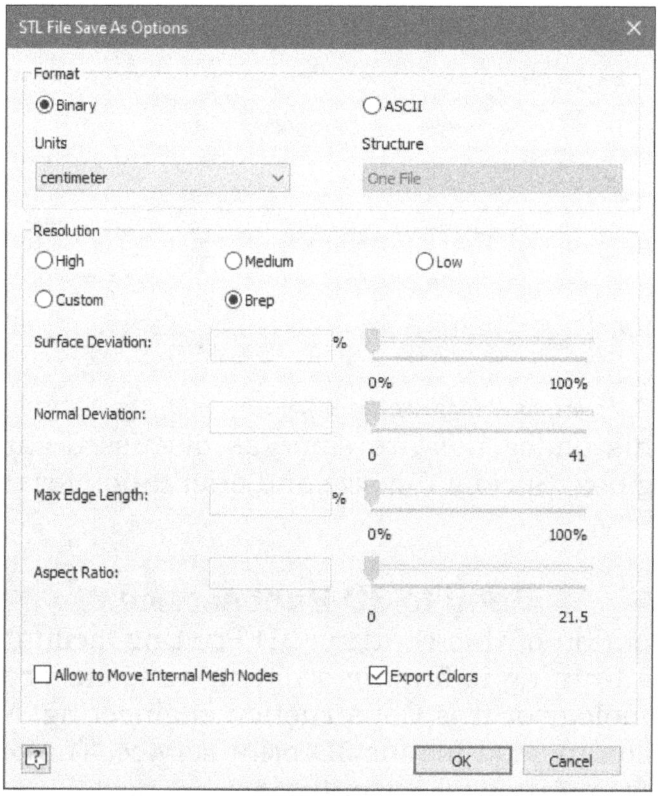

Figure-75. STL File Save As Options dialog box

- Set the quality of export file by using the options in this dialog box and click on the **OK** button.
- Click on the **OK** button from the **Send to 3D Print Service** dialog box to export the file. The **Save Copy As** dialog box will be displayed; refer to Figure-76.

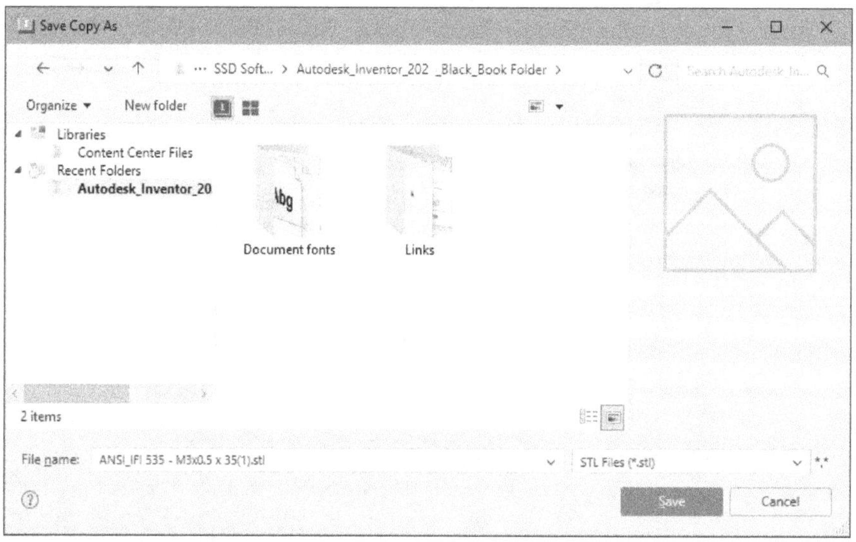

Figure-76. Save Copy As dialog box

- Click on the **Save** button from the dialog box to save the file.

3D Print Preview

The **3D Print Preview** tool works in the same way as the **Print Preview** tool works. Click on this tool and check the quality of 3D print to be created.

Till this point, we have learned about various settings and basic file operations of Autodesk Inventor. This chapter is a reference material and will be utilized in one or another way in all the upcoming chapters. To learn about modifying Application Options, please refer to Chapter 9 of this book. In the next chapter, we will learn about sketching tools and their applications.

Autodesk Assistant

The **Autodesk Assistant** tool is used to allow user to ask questions and receive guidance, suggestions, and step by step solutions directly within the software via AI. The procedure to use this tool is discussed next.

- Click on the **Autodesk Assistant** tool from the **Title bar**. The **Autodesk Assistant** dialog box will be displayed; refer to Figure-77.

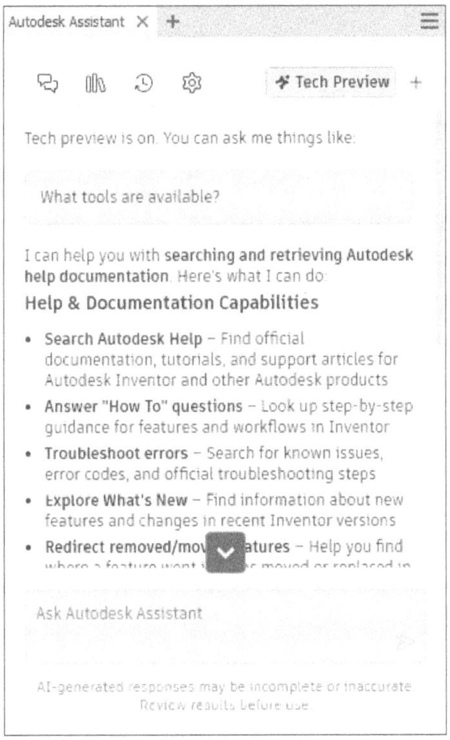

Figure-77. Autodesk assistant dialog box

- Click on the **Prompt Library** button to provide a collection of sample prompts that user can use to interact with the assistant effectively.
- Click on the **Chat History** button to view and return to your previous conversation with the Autodesk Assistant.
- Click on the **Settings** button to manage the assistant's preferences and options within the software.
- Click on the **New chat** button to start a new conversation with the Autodesk Assistant.
- Type and enter the prompt in input field similar to ChatGPT and other AI tools to get response for your queries.

SELF ASSESSMENT

Q1. Which of the following options manages the overall document management of Autodesk Inventor?

a) Tools
b) File menu
c) Get Started
d) Collaborate

Q2. By which of the following options, you cannot create a new file?

a) File menu
b) Get Started
c) Collaborate
d) Quick Access Toolbar

Q3. Which of the following options is used to create the 2D representation of the model?

a) Presentation
b) Drawing
c) Part
d) Assembly

Q4. While importing CAD files in Autodesk Inventor, which option in the dialog box cannot make changes in the imported model?

a) Individual
b) Reference Model
c) Convert Model
d) Composite

Q5. Which of the following options is used to save the file with new name and location?

a) Save As
b) Save Copy As
c) Save All
d) Save

Q6. Which tool in Autodesk Inventor allows you to save the file for other software like Pro-E, Catia, and so on?

a) Save
b) Save Copy As Template
c) Pack and Go
d) Export

Q7. Which of the following options is used to export drawing file in Inventor?

a) Image
b) CAD Format

c) Export to DWG
d) Export to DWF

Q8. By which option the intelligent features like shapes of punches, cones, and rectangular tubes can be directly used in the model?

a) iProperties
b) View iFeature Catalog
c) Design Assistant
d) Projects

Q9. If you are using Vault server and want to create a vault project then select **New Single User Project** in the **Inventor project wizard** dialog box. (True/False)

Q10. The options in the **Manage** cascading menu are used to create and manage the project files. (True/False)

Q11. The .... option is used to package the currently active file and all related files into a single location.

Q12. The .... option is used to find, track, and maintain Autodesk Inventor files and related word processing, spreadsheet, or text files.

REVIEW QUESTIONS

Q1. What is the fastest general method to start Autodesk Inventor in Microsoft Windows?
A. Use the File menu
B. Use the desktop icon only
C. Search Autodesk Inventor from the Start menu
D. Use the Quick Access Toolbar

Q2. What appears when Autodesk Inventor starts and allows you to transfer previous custom settings?
A. Startup Help Guide
B. Migrate Custom Settings dialog box
C. Interface Settings Panel
D. Application Launcher

Q3. In Autodesk Inventor, what is the 'Ribbon'?
A. A place to store files
B. A toolbar for saving and opening documents
C. An area with design and editing tools
D. A panel for managing file paths

Q4. Which menu is used to create a new file in Autodesk Inventor?
A. View Menu
B. Ribbon Tab
C. File Menu
D. Tools Menu

Q5. What shortcut key is used to create a new file in Autodesk Inventor?
A. CTRL+O
B. CTRL+S
C. CTRL+P
D. CTRL+N

Q6. Which file type is used to create a part file in Autodesk Inventor?
A. .iam
B. .dwg
C. .ipt
D. .ipn

Q7. What is the purpose of the 'Presentation' option in the New cascading menu?
A. Create weldment document
B. Create a 3D representation of a model for clients
C. Create electrical circuits
D. Manage content center parts

Q8. To create a new file using metric units, which template should you choose?
A. Standard (in).ipt
B. Standard (mm).ipt
C. Default.ipt
D. MetricDrawing.ipt

Q9. How do you open an AutoCAD drawing file specifically in Autodesk Inventor?
A. Import DXF
B. Click on Open DWG from File menu
C. Use Open from Content Center
D. Click on Insert DWG button

Q10. What feature allows importing AutoCAD blocks directly into Inventor blocks?
A. DWG Merge Tool
B. Object Mapper
C. AutoCAD Blocks to Inventor Blocks
D. 3D Solids Import Tool

Q11. Which of the following is not an option in the New cascading menu of the File menu?
A. Part
B. Sheet Metal
C. Surface Model
D. Assembly

Q12. What is the purpose of the Weldment option in Autodesk Inventor?
A. Create 3D models
B. Create exploded views
C. Create welding assembly documents
D. Import steel material data

Q13. In the process of opening files, which keyboard shortcut is used?
A. CTRL+N
B. CTRL+S
C. CTRL+O
D. CTRL+D

Q14. What is the main purpose of the Content Center in Autodesk Inventor?
A. To manage custom settings
B. To create presentation slides
C. To access standard parts library
D. To import AutoCAD files

Q15. When opening a file from Content Center, what action allows you to explore sub-categories?
A. Right-click the Content Center icon
B. Click on the minus sign (-)
C. Click on the plus sign (+)
D. Double-click the folder

Q16. What is displayed after clicking the Import DWG option?
A. Open dialog box
B. DWG File Wizard dialog box
C. New File window
D. Export dialog box

Q17. In the DWG/DXF File Wizard dialog box, what does selecting "Detected Units" do?
A. Converts the file to imperial units
B. Allows manual unit selection
C. Uses the units already in the DWG file
D. Disables all unit options

Q18. What does selecting the "Constrain End Points" option do during DWG import?
A. Freezes all sketch constraints
B. Applies fillets automatically
C. Connects all open endpoints in the model
D. Imports only 3D elements

Q19. What happens when you check "Apply geometric constraints" during DWG import?
A. All dimensions are removed
B. All geometric relationships from AutoCAD are ignored
C. Geometric constraints of Inventor are applied
D. Only annotations are preserved

Q20. Which of the following options converts AutoCAD symbols into Inventor symbols?
A. DWG Merge
B. Symbol Extractor
C. Proxy objects to user defined symbols
D. Inventor Shape Converter

Q21. What dialog box appears after clicking the Import CAD Files tool?
A. Save As dialog box
B. Open Document dialog box
C. Import Wizard dialog box
D. File Settings dialog box

Q22. Which import type allows editing of the imported model in Inventor?
A. Reference Model
B. Convert Model
C. Dynamic Model
D. Fixed Model

Q23. What happens when you select Reference Model during import?
A. The model is editable
B. The model is converted to .stp format
C. The model cannot be edited
D. The model is saved as an image

Q24. What option creates a combined surface during CAD import?
A. Individual
B. Grouped
C. Composite
D. Unified

Q25. What is the function of the Open Samples tool?
A. Imports 3D PDFs
B. Opens saved custom templates
C. Downloads and opens sample files from Autodesk
D. Opens recently used files

Q26. What keyboard shortcut is used for the Save option?
A. CTRL+A
B. CTRL+S
C. CTRL+Z
D. CTRL+O

Q27. What is the primary difference between Save and Save Copy As?
A. Save Copy As replaces the original
B. Save Copy As does not open the new file
C. Save always asks for a new name
D. Save Copy As deletes the original

Q28. Which feature in Pack and Go keeps the folder structure of the project?
A. Copy to Single Path
B. Keep Folder Hierarchy
C. Include Subfolders
D. Skip Libraries

Q29. What does selecting Package as .zip in Pack and Go do?
A. Compresses files in the source folder
B. Emails the file directly

C. Converts files to .zip format
D. Saves the model in RVT format

Q30. What format is best used for marketing presentations from Inventor?
A. STEP
B. IGES
C. 3D PDF
D. DWG

Q31. Which export option is used to generate CAD-neutral formats like IGES or STL?
A. CAD Format
B. PDF
C. RVT
D. Save As

Q32. What option is used to include sketches in IGES or STEP export?
A. Include Surfaces
B. Output as Wireframe
C. Include Sketches
D. Export Profiles

Q33. In the RVT export, which preset option results in the most simplified model?
A. No Simplification
B. Remove the most detail
C. Remove the least detail
D. Custom Preset

Q34. What is the effect of enabling Fill internal voids in RVT export?
A. Removes all cavities
B. Fills hollow spaces within the model
C. Highlights selected features
D. Converts all solids to surfaces

Q35. What happens if Remove internal parts is selected during RVT export?
A. All parts are merged
B. External surfaces are thickened
C. Non-visible parts from standard views are removed
D. The entire model is deleted

Q36. What does Make independent bodies on failed Boolean do?
A. Joins all parts into one
B. Creates a backup file
C. Saves the failed parts as separate bodies
D. Aborts the export process

Q37. Where is the RVT export log file stored?
A. User's temp folder
B. Autodesk Inventor install directory
C. Same directory as the packaged file
D. Desktop

Q38. What is the result of selecting Each Top Level Component in RVT export structure?
A. Combines all into a single element
B. Outputs each first-level assembly component as a separate Revit element
C. Creates only bounding boxes
D. Excludes all child parts

Q39. What does the Search Now button do in the Pack and Go dialog?
A. Scans the model for fillets
B. Searches for referencing files
C. Compresses the file
D. Checks license status

Q40. Which export feature allows attaching a STEP file within a PDF?
A. PDF Export
B. STEP Export
C. 3D PDF Export
D. Image Export

Q41. What is the primary function of the Share View tool in Autodesk Inventor?
A. To print the current model
B. To manage project files
C. To share views of the current model with others
D. To edit part properties

Q42. What must a user do if they are not signed into their Autodesk account while using the Share View tool?
A. Reboot the software
B. Enter their Autodesk credentials
C. Create a new model
D. Contact technical support

Q43. Which option should be selected to hide component names in a shared view?
A. Hide View Details
B. Hide Component Names
C. Hide File Names
D. Hide Metadata

Q44. What is the purpose of the Projects option under the Manage menu?
A. To share files online
B. To create and manage project files
C. To modify component sketches
D. To view print previews

Q45. What type of project should be selected if not using Vault server?
A. Vault-Enabled Project
B. Cloud-Based Project
C. New Single User Project
D. Shared Network Project

Q46. How is a library added to a new project in the Inventor Project Wizard?
A. Through the File tab
B. Using the Add Component tool
C. Clicking the arrow button in the middle of the dialog box
D. Double-clicking the library file

Q47. What indicates that a project has been made the default active project?
A. It is highlighted in red
B. A tick mark appears next to its name
C. It is listed at the top
D. The name turns bold

Q48. What are iFeatures in Autodesk Inventor?
A. Interactive file sharing tools
B. Intelligent pre-designed features for modeling
C. Export options for 3D printers
D. Print layout templates

Q49. What happens when an iFeature is dragged into the modeling area?
A. It is automatically saved
B. A new window for file sharing opens
C. The Insert iFeature dialog box appears
D. A project folder is created

Q50. What option allows precise positioning of an iFeature?
A. Do not Activate Sketch Edit
B. Manual Adjustment Tool
C. Activate Sketch Edit Immediately
D. Edit Position Mode

Q51. What is the main purpose of the Design Assistant tool?
A. To create new designs
B. To track and manage Autodesk Inventor files
C. To manage users
D. To preview 3D prints

Q52. Which tab in the iProperties dialog allows you to view general part information (but not edit it)?
A. Summary
B. Physical
C. General
D. Custom

Q53. What feature of the Physical tab in iProperties attracts engineers the most?
A. Print settings
B. Export features
C. Mass properties calculation
D. Rendering options

Q54. Why is printout important in manufacturing areas according to the text?
A. Easier to export than digital files
B. Digital devices are not reliable
C. High temperatures make electronic gadgets impractical
D. Printing is faster than modeling

Q55. What allows adding watermark to the printout?
A. Orientation tab
B. Watermark tab in Printer Properties
C. Preview Settings
D. Printer Name drop-down

Q56. What is the use of the Print Preview tool?
A. To edit the drawing
B. To export the model
C. To check the print before printing
D. To save as STL

Q57. How do you specify settings for a print job in Autodesk Inventor?
A. Using the Save As dialog
B. Using the Edit tab
C. Using the Print Setup tool
D. Through the Status tab

Q58. What is the main function of the Send to 3D Print Service tool?
A. To preview the print
B. To create 2D sketches
C. To export the model as an STL file for 3D printing
D. To upload the file to the cloud

Q59. What can be set from the STL File Save As Options dialog?
A. Model dimensions
B. Print orientation
C. Export file quality
D. Printer name

Q60. What does the 3D Print Preview tool allow you to do?
A. Save STL directly
B. Check the quality of 3D print before exporting
C. Add material properties
D. Measure dimensions

Chapter 2

Creating Sketches

Topics Covered

The major topics covered in this chapter are:

- ***Introduction to Sketching***
- ***Sketch creation tools***
- ***Modification tools***

INTRODUCTION TO SKETCHING

Sketch is the back bone (should I say spine!!) of 3D models. If you are creating a wrong sketch then you cannot expect desired results from the 3D model. So, it is very important to understand the tools of sketching as well as method of sketching. The tools related to sketching are available in the **Sketch** tab of the **Ribbon**; refer to Figure-1. In this chapter, we will discuss these tools one by one. But before that let's understand the concept of sketching planes.

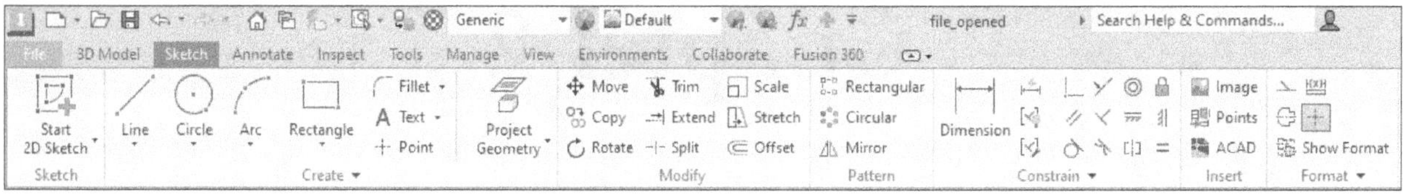

Figure-1. Sketch tab

SKETCHING PLANE

In a CAD software, everything is referenced to other entity like a line created must be referenced to any other existing geometry, so that you can clearly define the position of line with respect to the other geometry. But, what if there is no geometry in the sketch to reference from. In these cases, we have tools to create reference geometries like reference planes, axes, points, curves, and so on. Out of these reference geometries, the sketching plane acts as foundation for other geometries. By default, there are three planes perpendicular to each other in Autodesk Inventor; refer to Figure-2.

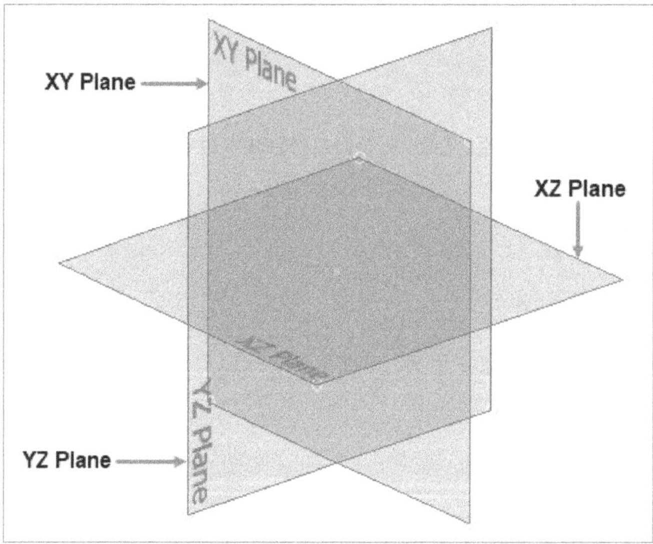

Figure-2. Sketching planes in Inventor

Relation between sketch, plane, and 3D model

Sketch has a direct relationship with planes and the outcome which is generally a 3D model. Refer to Figure-3. In this figure, rectangle is created on the **XY** Plane which is also called **Front** plane. A circle is created on the **YZ** Plane which is also called **Right** plane. A polygon is created on the **XZ** plane which is also called **Top** plane. In a 3D model, the geometry seen from the Front view should be drawn on the **Front** plane. Similarly, geometry seen from the Right view should be drawn at **Right** plane and geometry seen from the Top view should be drawn at the **Top** plane.

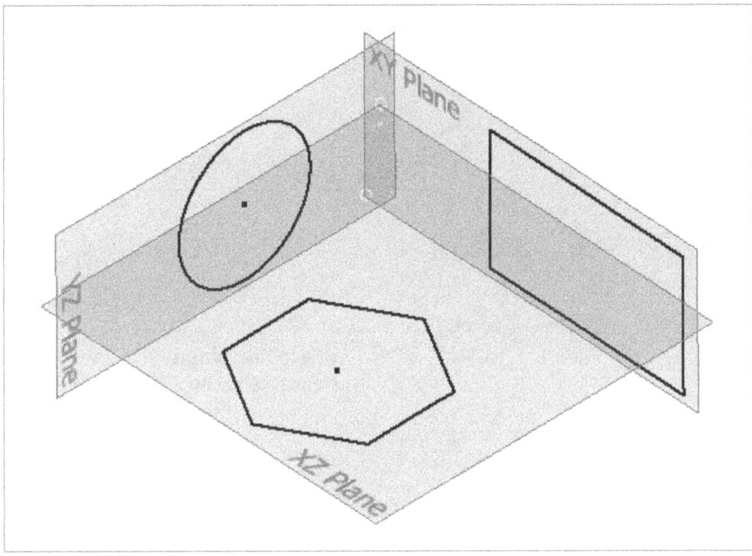

Figure-3. Sketches created on different planes

We will learn more about planes at the beginning of 3D Modeling. We will now start with Sketching tools.

START 2D SKETCH

The **Start 2D Sketch** tool is used to start sketching environment. Once we have started 2D sketch, we will be able to use the sketching tools on the selected plane. The procedure to start 2D sketch is given next.

- Click on the **Start 2D Sketch** tool from the **Start 2D Sketch** drop-down in the **Sketch** tab of the **Ribbon**; refer to Figure-4. You will be asked to select a plane for sketching.

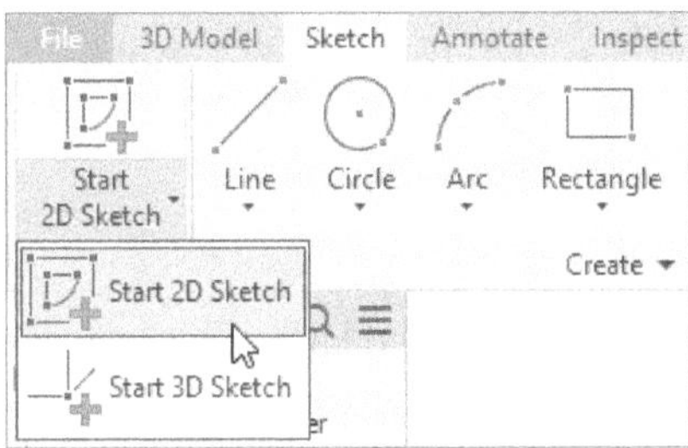

Figure-4. Start 2D Sketch tool

- Click on desired plane from the highlighted planes in modeling area; refer to Figure-5. The sketching environment will be displayed with horizontal and vertical reference lines; refer to Figure-6. Note that these reference lines as actually other two planes.

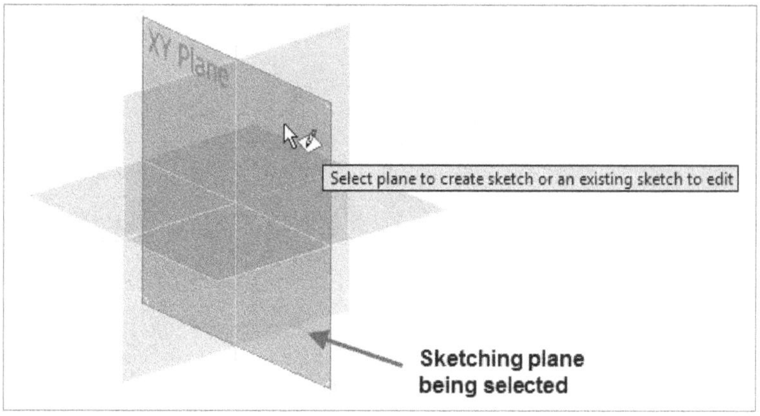

Figure-5. Sketching plane being selected

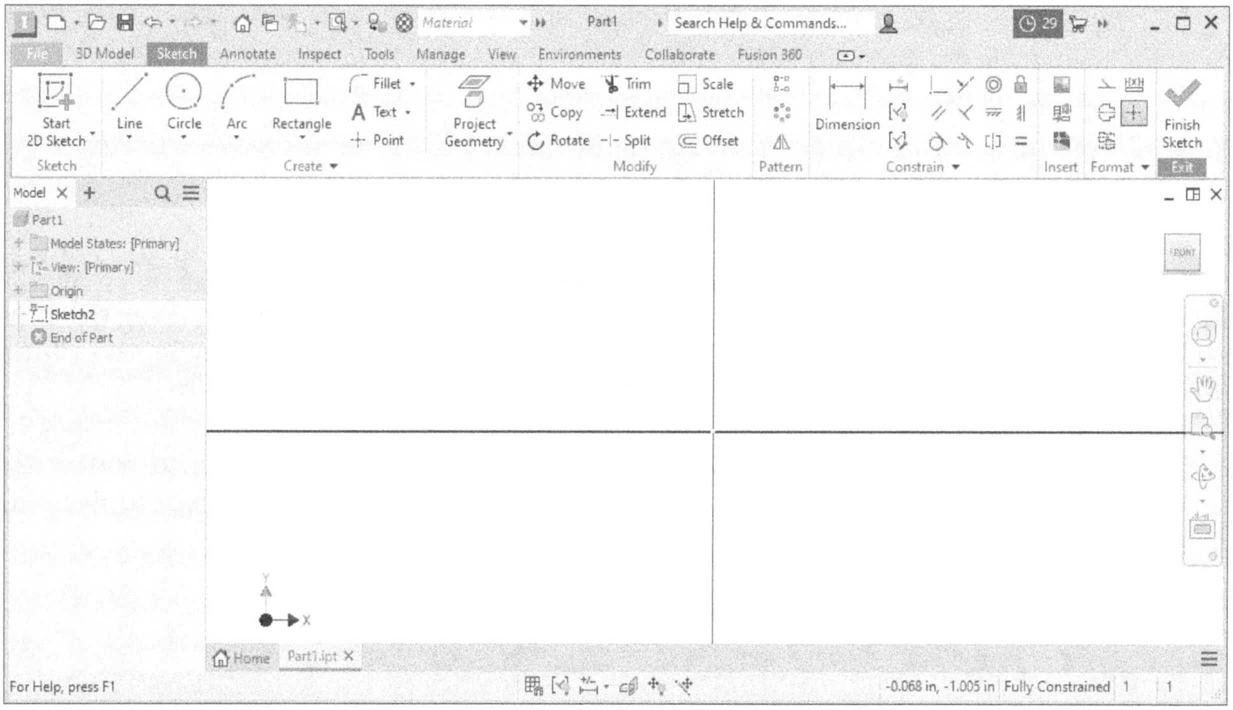

Figure-6. Sketching environment

- After creating sketch, click on the **Finish Sketch** button. Note that we generally use sketching tools after starting sketching environment and before clicking on the **Finish Sketch** button.

SKETCH CREATION TOOLS

The tools that are available in the **Create** panel are named as sketch creation tools. The tools that are most commonly used for sketch creation are given next.

Line tool

As everyone can guess, the **Line** tool is used to create a line in the sketch. The procedure to create a line is given next.

- Click on the **Line** tool from **Create** panel in the **Ribbon**; refer to Figure-7. You will be asked to specify start point of the line. Also, the **Coordinate Input box** will be displayed; refer to Figure-8.

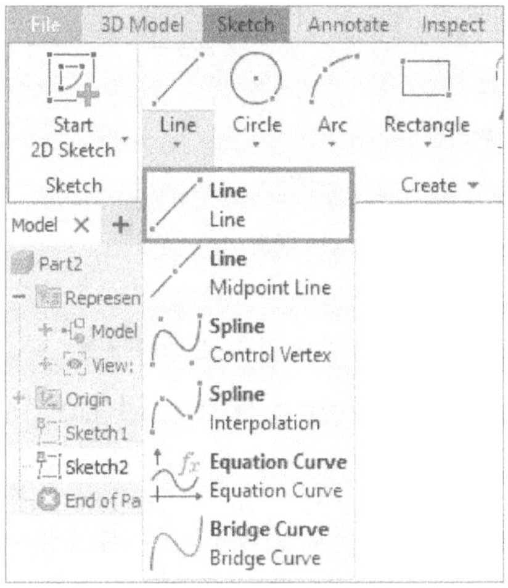

Figure-7. Line tool

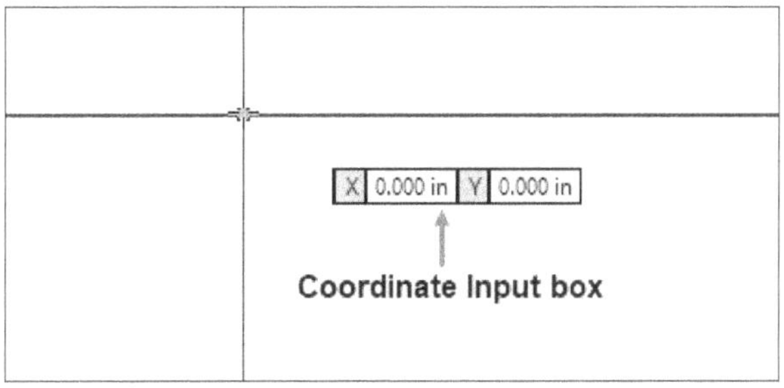

Figure-8. Coordinate Input box

- Specify desired coordinates in the Input box (Note that **X** edit box is used to specify X coordinate and **Y** edit box is used to specify Y coordinate in the Input box) or click in the modeling area to specify the starting point. On doing so, you will be asked to specify the end point of the line; refer to Figure-9.

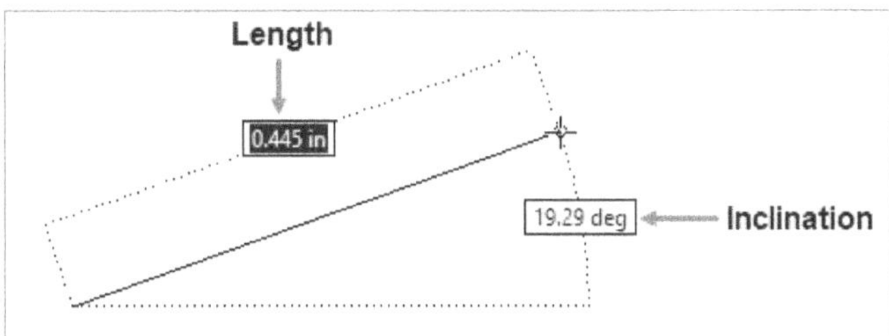

Figure-9. Specifying end point of line

- Specify desired length and angle in the input boxes or click at desired location in the modeling area to specify the end point of the line. Note that if you want to specify the values in the input boxes then press **TAB** to toggle between the two input boxes and press **ENTER** after specifying the values. The specified values will be displayed as dimension along the line; refer to Figure-10.

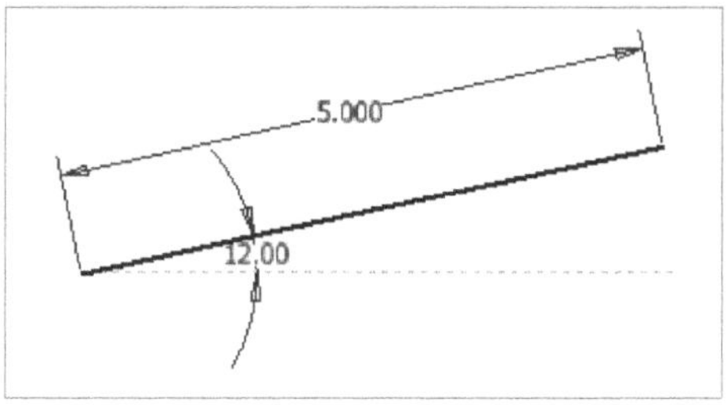

Figure-10. Dimension assigned to line

- Note that you can keep on specifying the end points of the consecutive lines as per your requirement. To stop creation of consecutive lines, press **ESC** button.
- To create an arc using the **Line** tool, click and hold the left mouse button (LMB) after creating a line and drag the cursor to create an arc tangent to previous line; refer to Figure-11.

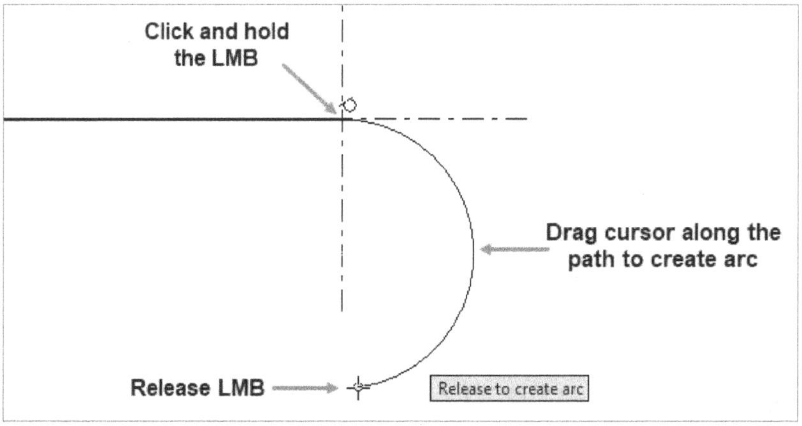

Figure-11. Creating arc with Line tool

Note that if you want to change the unit system for model then click on the **Document Settings** tool from the **Options** panel in the **Tools** tab of **Ribbon**. The **Document Settings** dialog box will be displayed. Click on the **Units** tab and set desired unit system in the dialog box; refer to Figure-12. You will learn more about **Document Settings** dialog box later in the book.

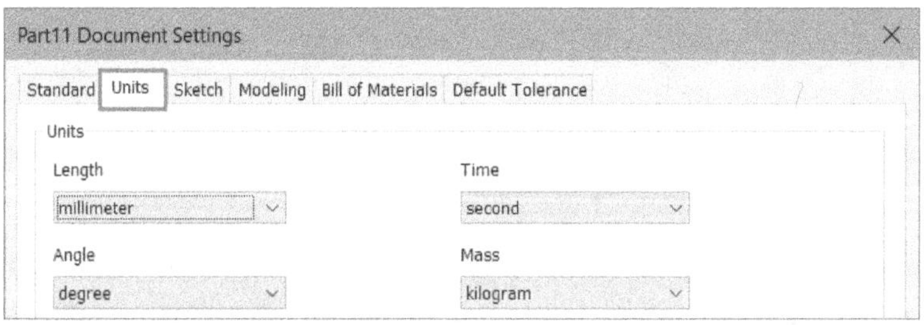

Figure-12. Units tab

Midpoint Line

The **Midpoint Line** tool is used to create a line by defining its midpoint first and then extending it equally in both directions. The procedure to use this tool is discussed next.

- Click on the **Midpoint Line** tool from the **Line** drop-down in the **Create** panel of the **Ribbon**; refer to Figure-13. The edit boxes related to midpoint line will be displayed; refer to Figure-14.

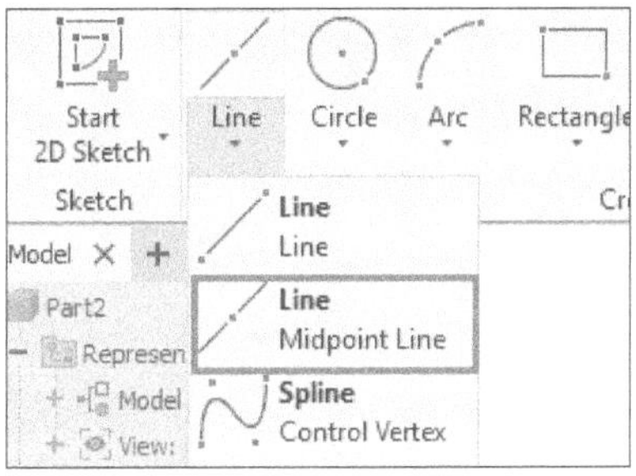

Figure-13. Midpoint line tool

- Click in the graphics window and specify the midpoint of the line; refer to Figure-14.

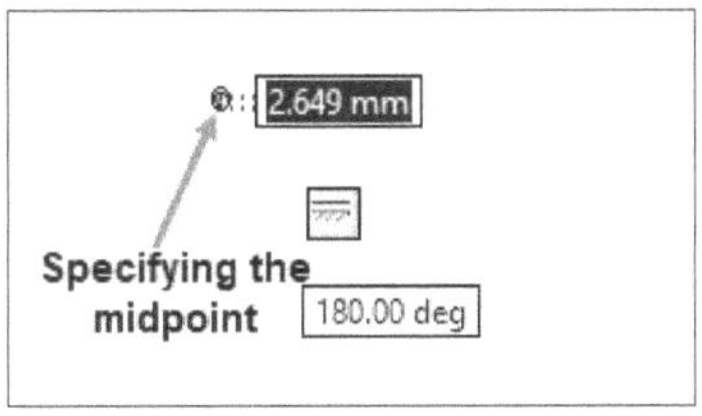

Figure-14. Specifying the midpoint

- Drag the cursor at desired location to define the length and direction. The line is created symmetrically on both side of the midpoint; refer to Figure-15.

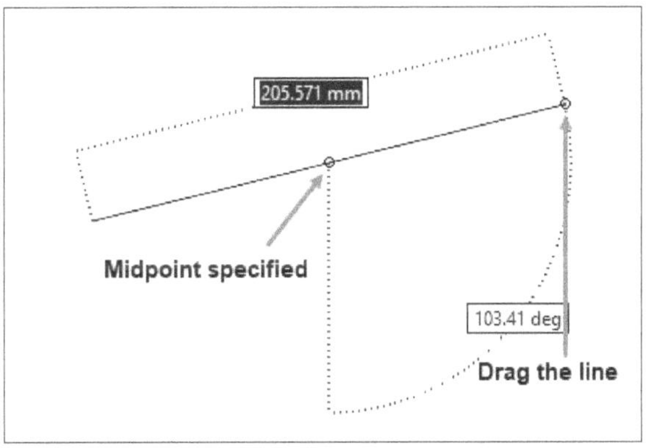

Figure-15. Preview of Midpoint line

- Specify desired values in the edit boxes to create the line and press **ESC** button to exit the tool.

Control Vertex Spline

The **Control Vertex Spline** tool is used to create spline with the help of control verticcs. A spline is a dynamic curve passing through specified points or controlled by specified vertices. Splines are generally used to create models of artistic objects. The procedure to use this tool is given next.

- Click on the **Control Vertex Spline** tool from **Line** drop-down in the **Create** panel of the **Ribbon**; refer to Figure-16. You will be asked to specify the first point of the spline.

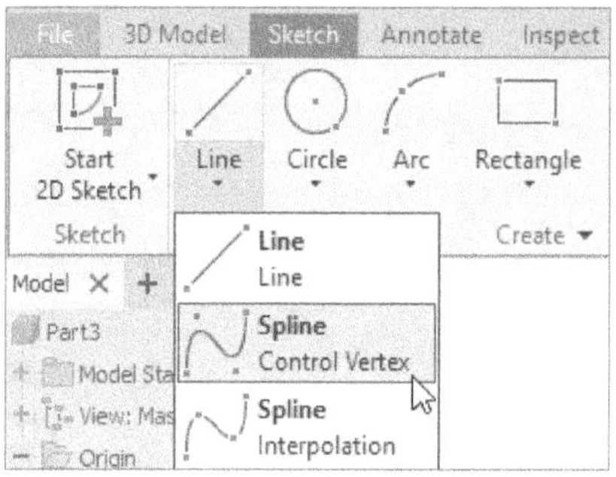

Figure-16. Control Vertex Spline tool

- Click to specify the first point of spline. You are asked to specify the first control vertex of the spline.
- Click to specify the vertex point. You are asked to specify the next control vertices; refer to Figure-17.

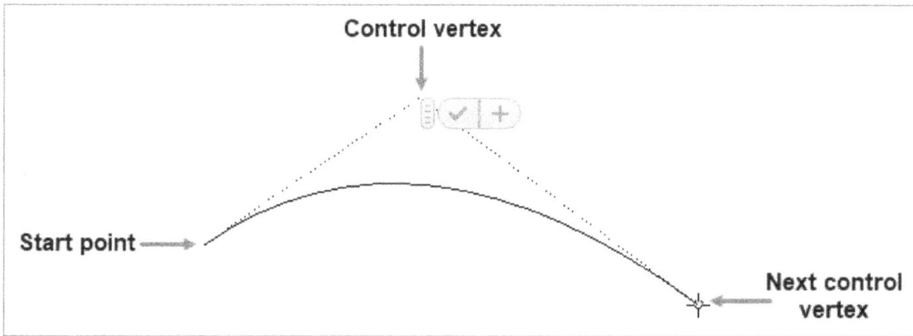

Figure-17. Specifying control vertex

- Keep on specifying the control vertices as per your requirement and press **ENTER** when you have specified control vertices as per your requirement. The spline will be created with the specified control vertices. Press **ESC** to exit the tool.
- Note that to modify the shape of spline, you can drag any of the control vertex to desired position.

Interpolation Spline

The **Interpolation Spline** tool works in the same way as the **Control Vertex Spline** tool works but in case of interpolation spline, we specify the points through which the spline passes. The procedure to use this tool is given next.

- Click on the **Interpolation Spline** tool from **Line** drop-down in the **Create** panel of the **Ribbon**; refer to Figure-18. You will be asked to specify starting point of the spline.

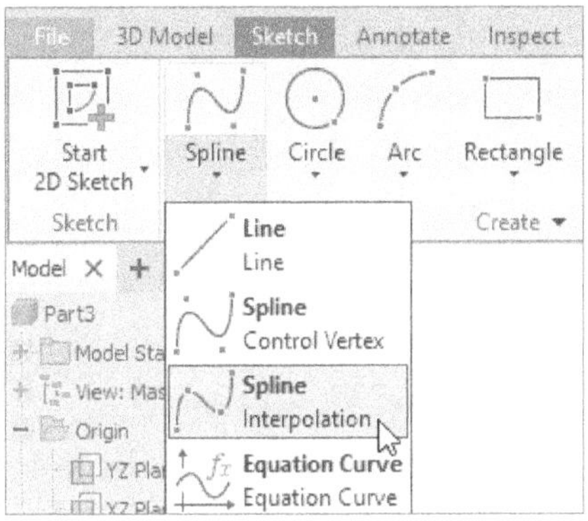

Figure-18. Interpolation Spline tool

- Click to specify the starting point. You are asked to specify the next points of spline.
- Keep on specifying the points through which you want the spline to pass.
- Press **ENTER** to exit the spline creation mode. Press **ESC** to exit the tool.

Equation Curve

The **Equation Curve** tool is used to create curve with the help of an equation. There are three components of equation:

x(t), y(t), and values of t_{min} & t_{max}. Here, x(t) and y(t) are functions of **t** like,

x(t) = t^2
y(t) = t^3+t

t varies from $\mathbf{t}_{min}$ to $\mathbf{t}_{max}$.

To create curve based on equation, follow the steps given next.

- Click on the **Equation Curve** tool from **Line** drop-down in the **Create** panel of the **Ribbon**; refer to Figure-19. The edit boxes related to curve equation will be displayed; refer to Figure-20.

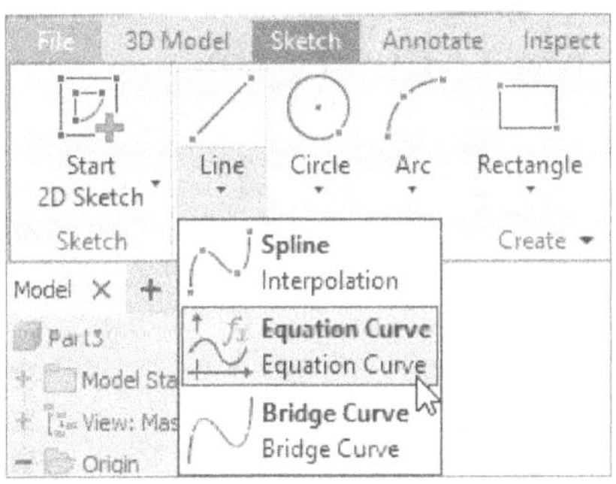

Figure-19. Equation Curve tool

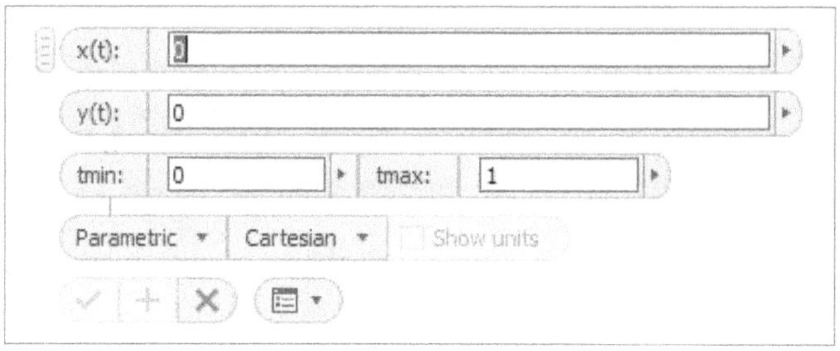

Figure-20. Edit boxes for curve equation

- Specify desired values in the edit boxes and click on the **OK** button to create the curve.

Bridge Curve

As the name suggests, the **Bridge Curve** tool is used to create a curve that connects two curves. The procedure to use this tool is given next.

- Click on the **Bridge Curve** tool from **Line** drop-down in the **Create** panel of the **Ribbon**; refer to Figure-21. You will be asked to select first curve.

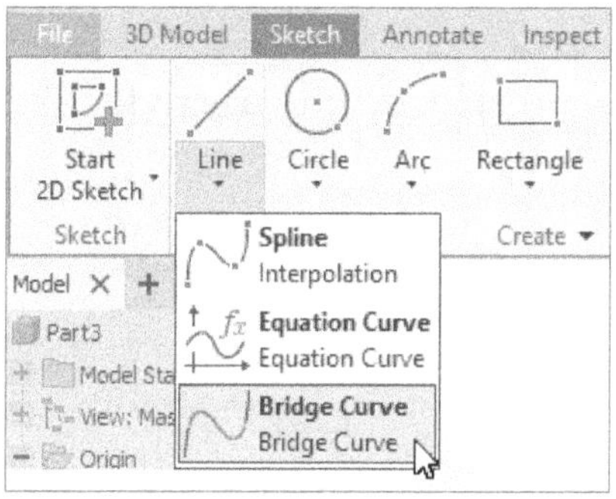

Figure-21. Bridge Curve tool

- Click on the first curve. You will be asked to select the second curve.
- Click on the second curve. A bridge curve will be created connecting both the curves. Note that your selection region of curve will decide the start point/end point of the bridge curve; refer to Figure-22. So, click on the curve near the point which you want to use as start or end point.

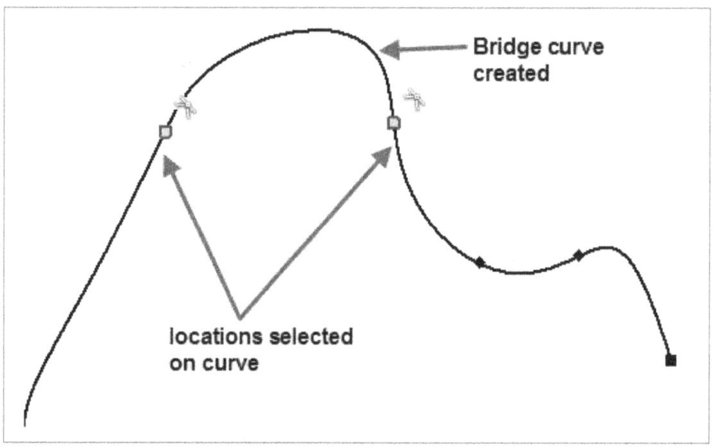

Figure-22. Bridge curve created

Circle

Circle has a great history and it is useful in various designs (No! we will not discuss history here). There are numerous examples where we will be using the circle tool to create designs like wheels, gears, shafts, and so on. The procedure to use this tool is given next.

- Click on the **Center Point Circle** tool from **Create** panel in the **Ribbon**; refer to Figure-23. You will be asked to specify the center point of the circle.

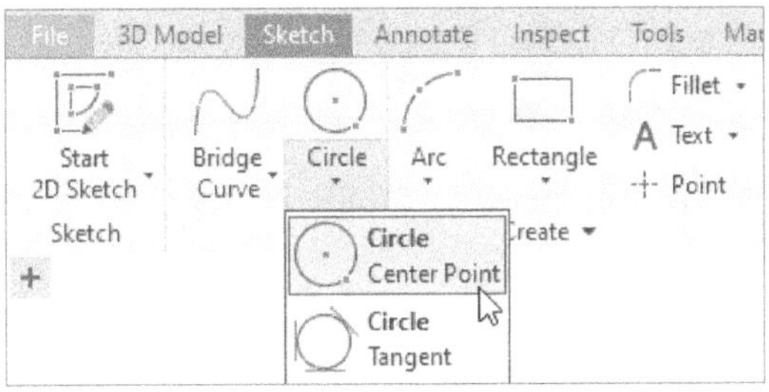

Figure-23. Center Point Circle tool

- Click to specify the center point of the circle. You will be asked to specify diameter of the circle; refer to Figure-24.

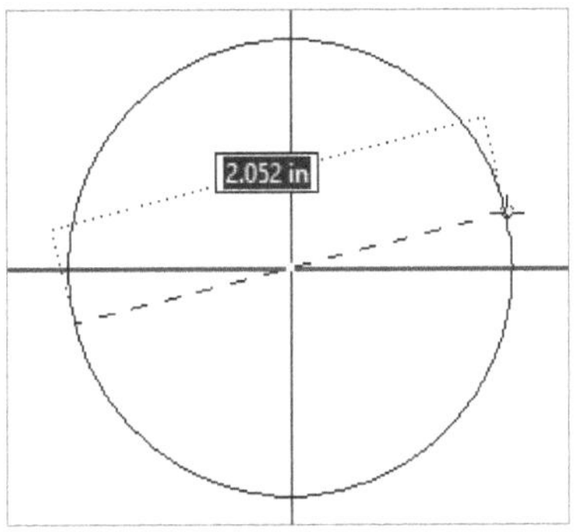

Figure-24. Specifying diameter of circle

- Specify desired diameter value in the edit box. If you want to specify the radius value in place of diameter then right-click in the modeling area before specifying value in edit box. A shortcut menu will be displayed; refer to Figure-25.

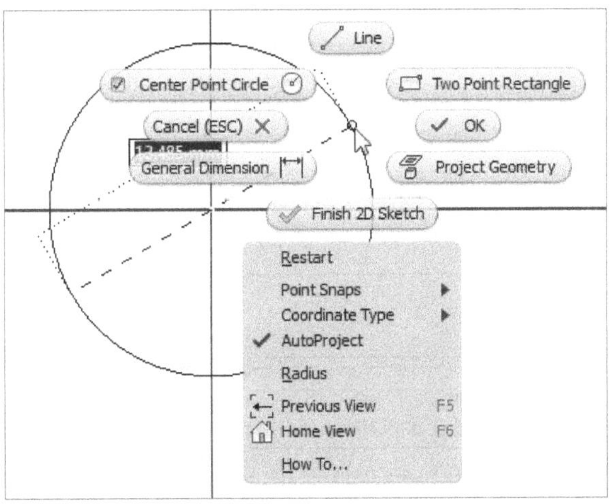

Figure-25. Shortcut menu for circle

- Select the **Radius** option from the shortcut menu. You will be asked to specify radius of the circle; refer to Figure-26.

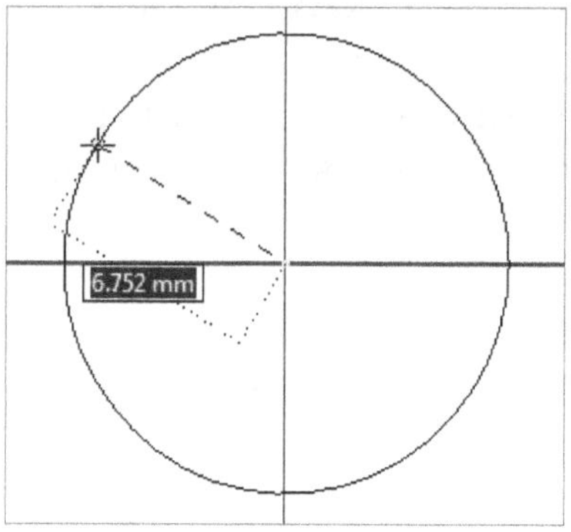

Figure-26. Specifying radius of circle

- After specifying desired value, press **ENTER** from the keyboard to create the circle. Press **ESC** to exit the tool.

Tangent Circle

The **Tangent Circle** tool is used to create circle tangent to three selected lines. The procedure to use this tool is given next.

- Click on the **Tangent Circle** tool from **Circle** drop-down in the **Create** panel of the **Ribbon**; refer to Figure-27. You will be asked to select the first line.

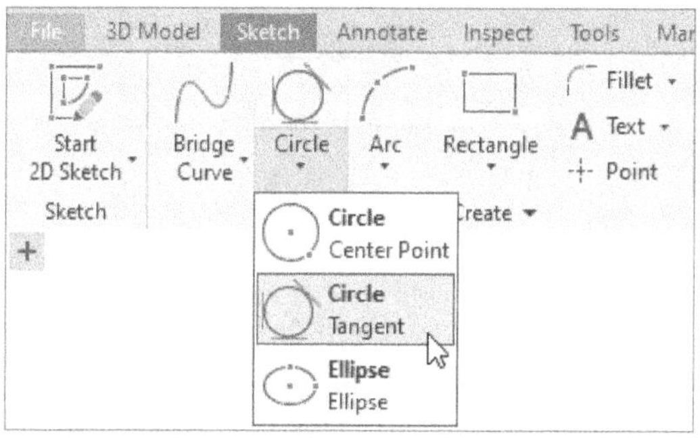

Figure-27. Tangent Circle tool

- Click on the first line in the modeling area; refer to Figure-28. You will be asked to select the second line.

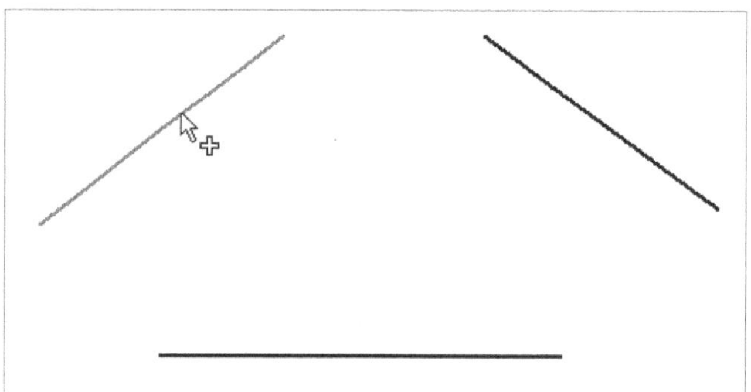

Figure-28. Selecting first line for tangent circle

- Click on the second line and then on the third line. A circle tangent to the three lines will be displayed; refer to Figure-29.

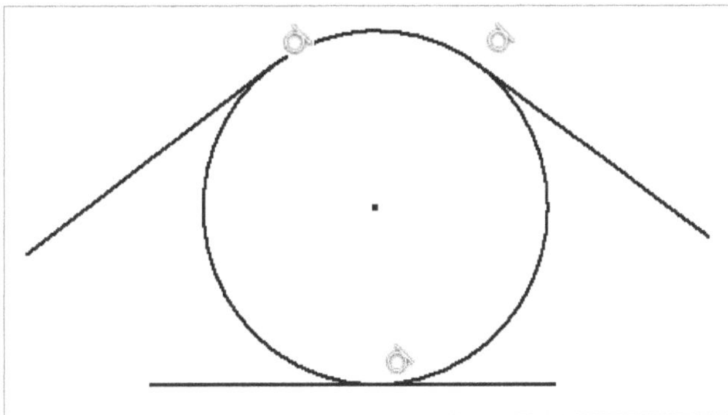

Figure-29. Circle tangent to the lines

Note that it is not compulsory for the circle to touch all the line to be tangent to them.

Ellipse

As the name suggests, the **Ellipse** tool is used to create ellipse in the sketch. The procedure to use this tool is given next.

- Click on the **Ellipse** tool from **Circle** drop-down in the **Create** panel of the **Ribbon**; refer to Figure-30. You will be asked to specify center point of the ellipse.

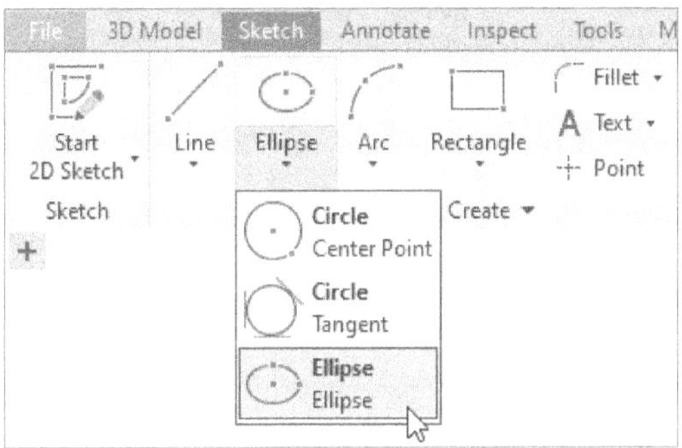

Figure-30. Ellipse tool

- Click to specify the center point of the ellipse. You will be asked to specify the end point of the first axis of ellipse; refer to Figure-31.

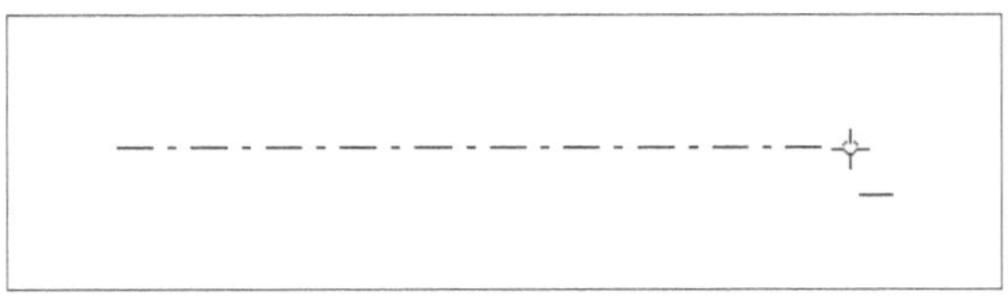

Figure-31. Specifying endpoint of first axis

- Click to specify the end point of axis. You will be asked to specify a circumferential point of the ellipse; refer to Figure-32.

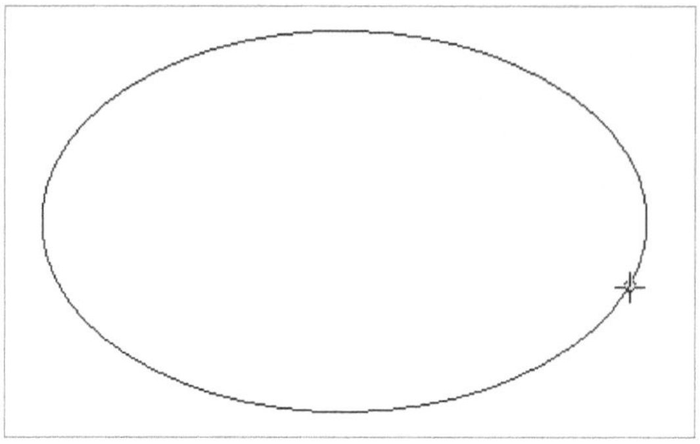

Figure-32. Specifying circumferential point of ellipse

- Click to specify circumferential point of ellipse. The ellipse will be created. Press **ESC** to exit the tool.

Three Point Arc

The **Three Point Arc** tool is used to create an arc passing through specified three points. The procedure to create 3 point arc is given next.

- Click on the **Three Point Arc** tool from **Create** panel in the **Ribbon**; refer to Figure-33. You will be asked to specify the start point of the arc.

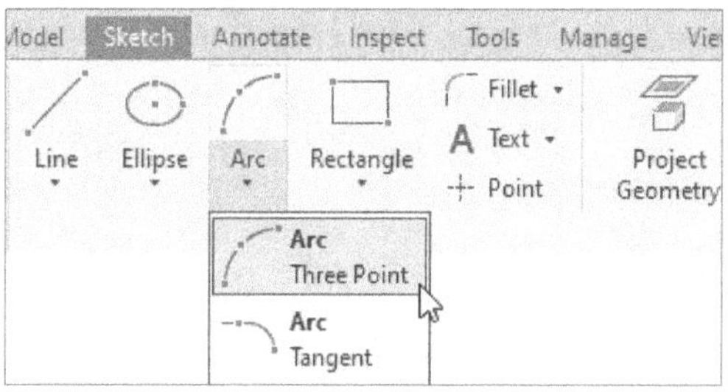

Figure-33. Three Point Arc tool

- Click in the modeling area to specify the start point. You will be asked to specify the end point of the arc; refer to Figure-34.

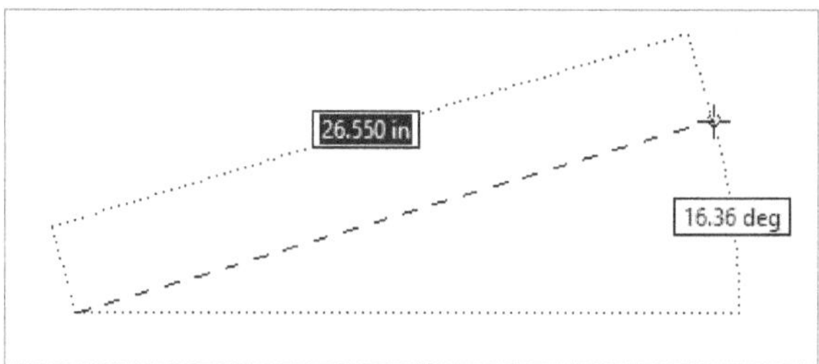

Figure-34. Specifying end point of the arc

- Click to specify the end point of the arc. You will be asked to specify a circumferential point of the arc; refer to Figure-35.

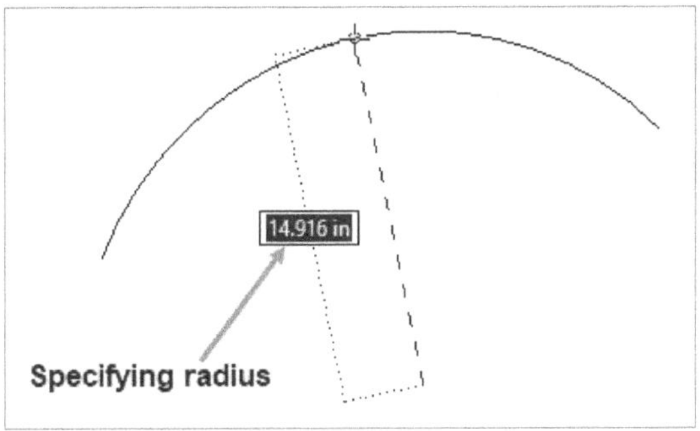

Figure-35. Specifying circumferential point of arc or radius of arc

- Enter desired radius value or click to specify the circumferential point. The arc will be created.

Tangent Arc

As the name suggests, the **Tangent Arc** tool is used to create arc tangent to the selected entity. The procedure to use this tool is given next.

- Click on the **Tangent Arc** tool from **Arc** drop-down in the **Create** panel of the **Ribbon**; refer to Figure-36. You will be asked to select start point of the arc.

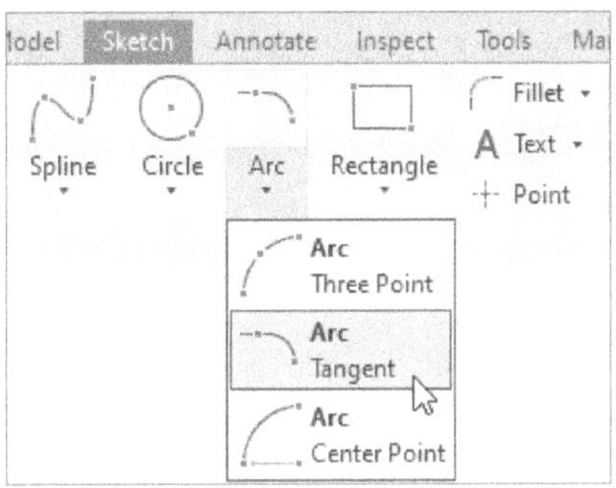

Figure-36. Tangent Arc tool

- Hover the cursor on an entity. The nearest endpoint of the entity will be highlighted in green color.
- Click on the entity when you get desired endpoint. You will be asked to specify the end point of the arc; refer to Figure-37.

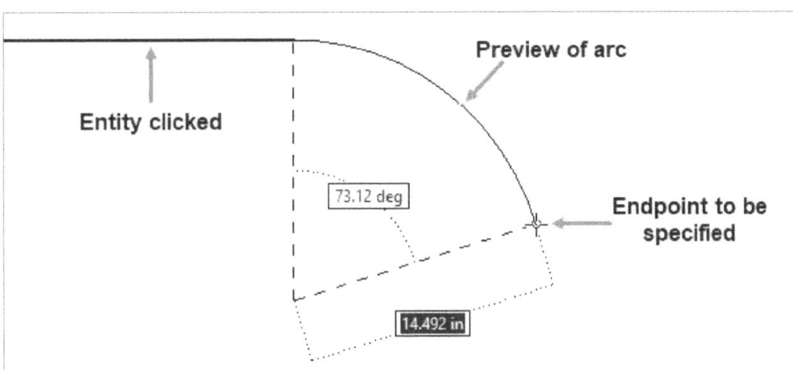

Figure-37. Creating tangent arc

- Click to specify the endpoint of the arc. The arc will be created tangent to the selected entity.

Center Point Arc

The **Center Point Arc** tool is used to create an arc with the help of center point and radius (or circumferential point). If you do not have reference points (for 3 Point Arc) or an entity to make tangent then this is the tool to be used. The procedure to use the **Center Point Arc** tool is given next.

- Click on the **Center Point Arc** tool from **Arc** drop-down in the **Create** panel of the **Ribbon**; refer to Figure-38. You will be asked to specify the center of the arc.

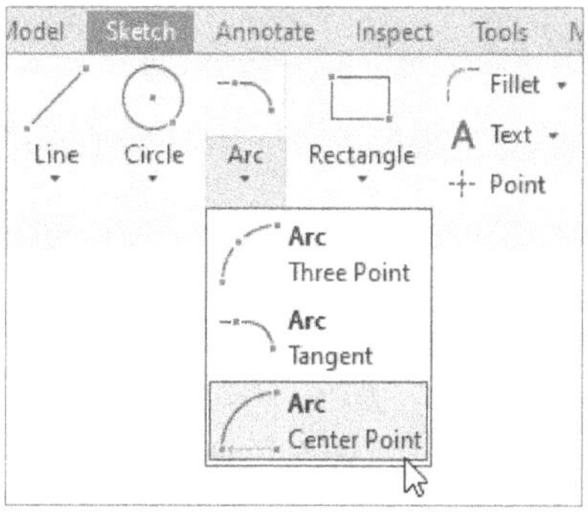

Figure-38. Center Point Arc tool

- Click to specify the center point of the arc. You will be asked to specify the start point of the arc; refer to Figure-39.

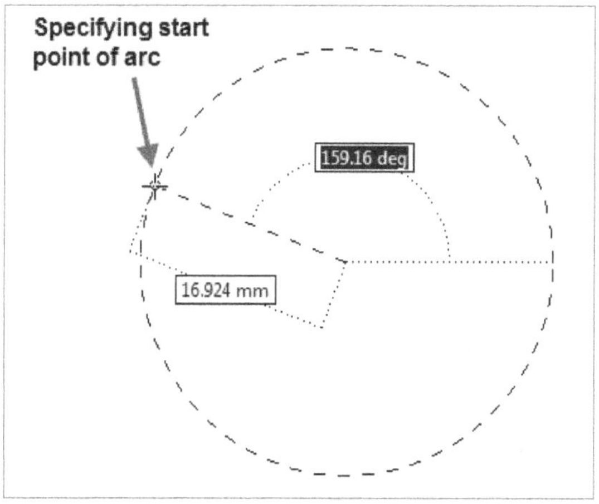

Figure-39. Specifying start point of arc

- Click to specify the start point. You will be asked to specify the span angle of the arc; refer to Figure-40.

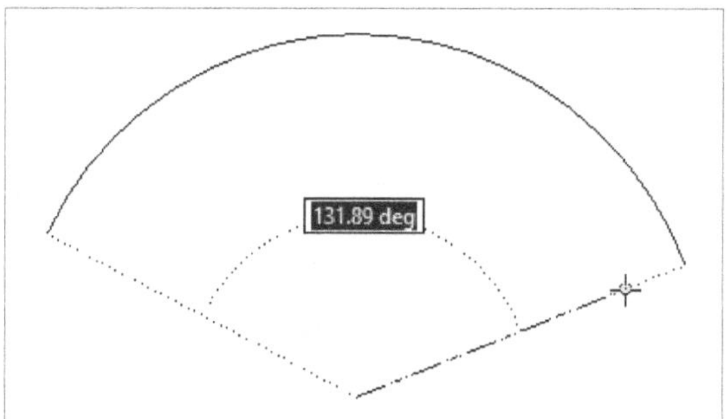

Figure-40. Specifying the angle span value

- Enter the angle span value or click to specify the end point of the arc.

Two Point Rectangle

The **Two Point Rectangle** tool is used to create a rectangle with specified two points. The procedure to use this tool is given next.

- Click on the **Two Point Rectangle** tool from **Create** panel in the **Ribbon**; refer to Figure-41. You will be asked to specify the first corner point of the rectangle.

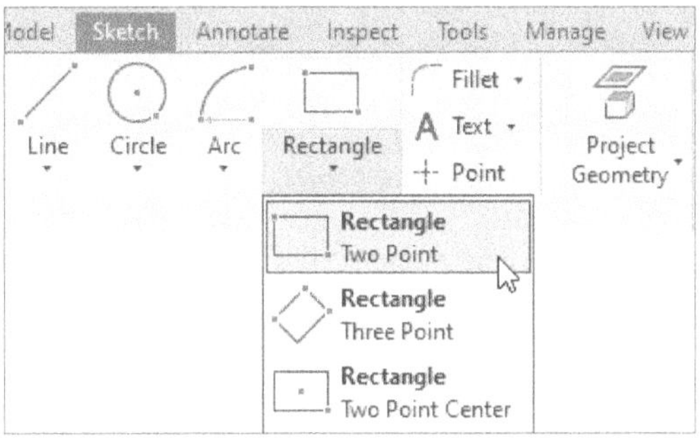

Figure-41. Two Point Rectangle tool

- Click to specify the first corner point. You will be asked to specify the opposite corner point; refer to Figure-42.

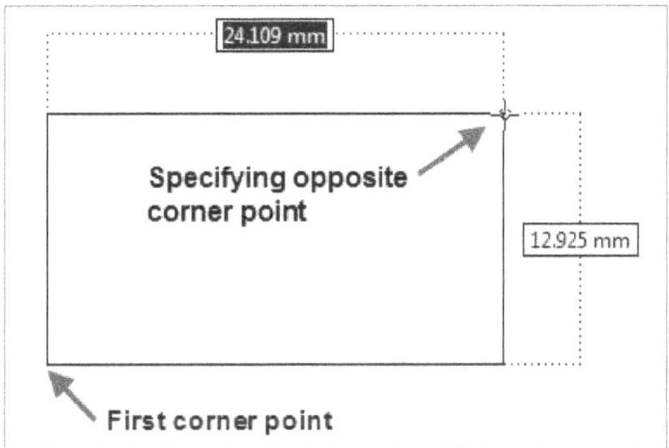

Figure-42. Specifying corner points of rectangle

- Click to specify the other corner point of rectangle. The rectangle will be created. Press **ESC** to exit the tool.

Three Point Rectangle

The **Three Point Rectangle** tool is used to create rectangle by using three points. The procedure to use this tool is given next.

- Click on the **Three Point Rectangle** tool from **Rectangle** drop-down in the **Create** panel of the **Ribbon**; refer to Figure-43. You will be asked to specify a corner point of the rectangle.

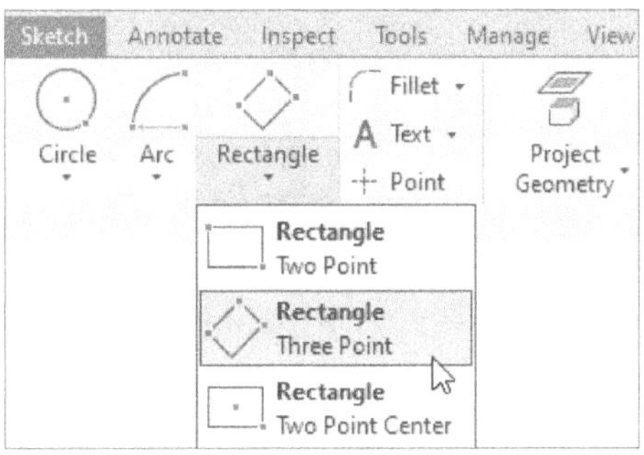

Figure-43. Three Point Rectangle tool

- Click to specify the first corner point. You will be asked to specify second corner point; refer to Figure-44.

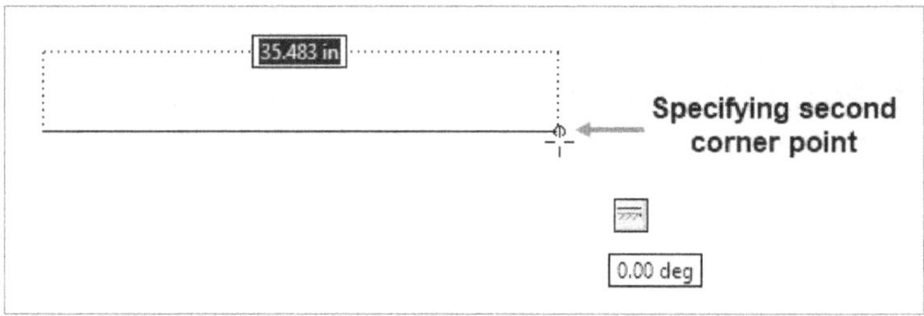

Figure-44. Specifying second corner point

- Click to specify the second corner point. You will be asked to specify the third corner point; refer to Figure-45.

Figure-45. Specifying third corner point

- Click to specify the third corner point or specify the value in the edit box. Press **ESC** to exit the tool.

Two Point Center Rectangle

The **Two Point Center Rectangle** tool is used to create rectangle by specifying center point and corner point of the rectangle. The procedure to use this tool is given next.

- Click on the **Two Point Center Rectangle** tool from **Rectangle** drop-down in the **Create** panel of the **Ribbon**; refer to Figure-46. You will be asked to specify the center point for the rectangle.

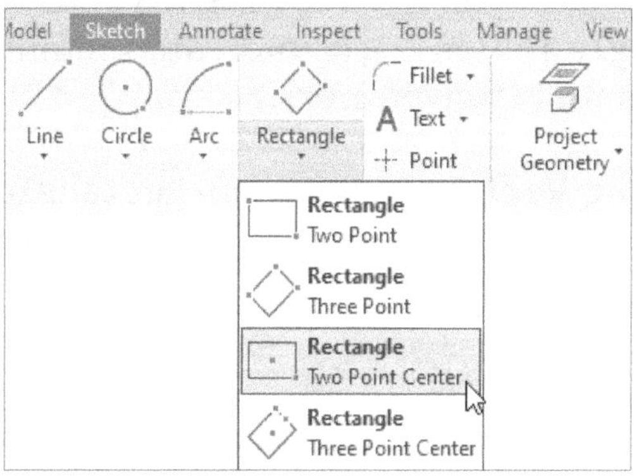

Figure-46. Two Point Center Rectangle tool

- Click to specify the center point for the rectangle. You will be asked to specify one corner point of the rectangle; refer to Figure-47.

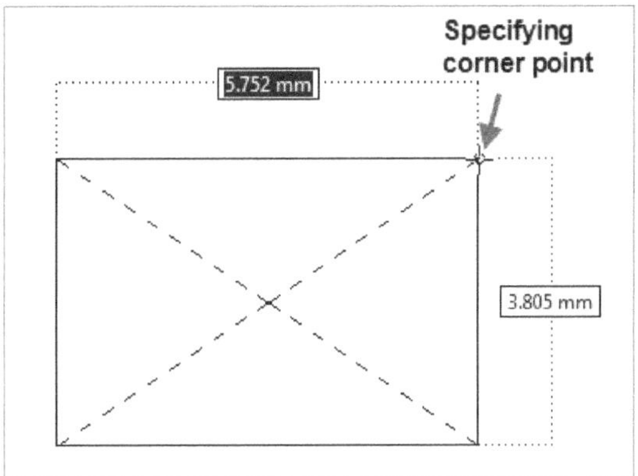

Figure-47. Specifying corner point of center rectangle

- Click to specify the corner point or enter the dimensions of rectangle in the edit boxes. Note that to switch between the edit boxes, you need to press **TAB** from keyboard.

Three Point Center Rectangle

Using the **Three Point Center Rectangle** tool, you can create a rectangle with the help of center point, center line, and corner point. The procedure to use this tool is given next.

- Click on the **Three Point Center Rectangle** tool from **Rectangle** drop-down in the **Create** panel of the **Ribbon**; refer to Figure-48. You will be asked to specify the center point of the rectangle.

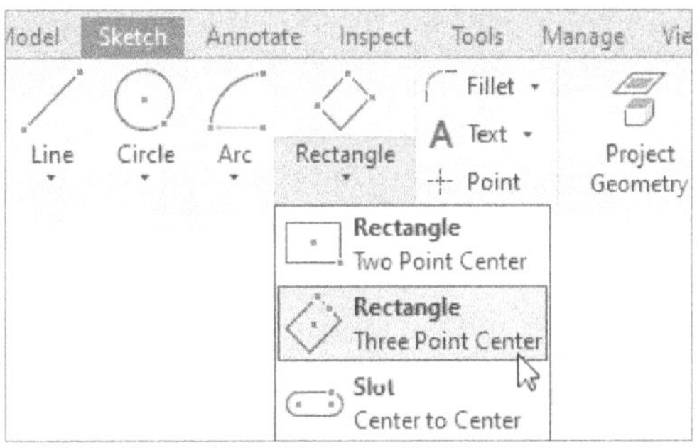

Figure-48. Three Point Center Rectangle tool

- Click to specify the center point of the rectangle. You will be asked to specify second point for the centerline of rectangle; refer to Figure-49.

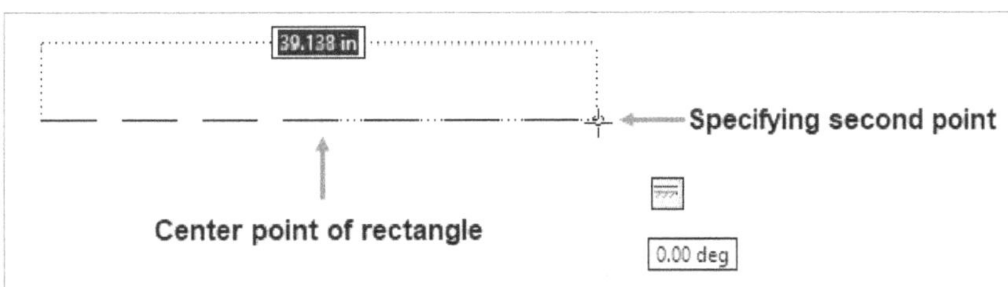

Figure-49. Specifying centerline second point of rectangle

- Click to specify the second point of centerline or enter desired value in the edit box. You will be asked to specify the third point of the rectangle; refer to Figure-50.

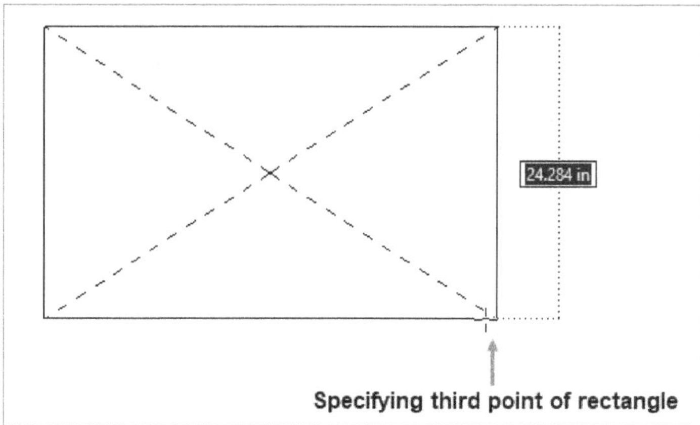

Figure-50. Specifying third point of rectangle

- Click to specify the third point of the rectangle or enter desired dimension in edit box. Press **ESC** to exit the tool.

Center to Center Slot

The **Center to Center Slot** tool is used to create slots in the sketch. In engineering, slots are used to make way for keys, bolts, and other assembly objects. The procedure to use this tool is given next.

- Click on the **Center to Center Slot** tool from **Rectangle** drop-down in the **Create** panel of the **Ribbon**; refer to Figure-51. You will be asked to specify starting center point.

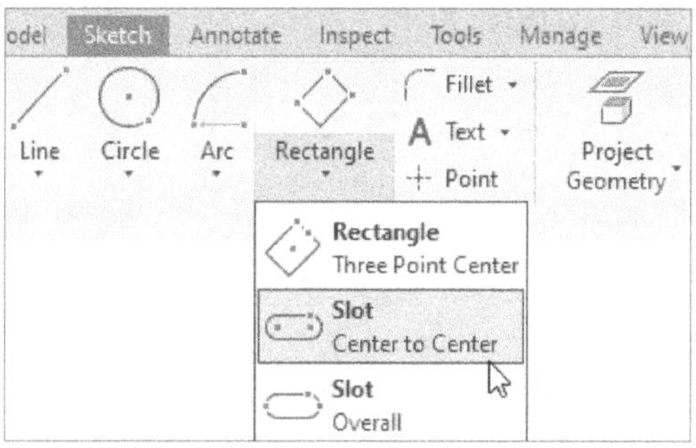

Figure-51. Center to Center Slot tool

- Click to specify the first center point. You will be asked to specify end center point; refer to Figure-52.

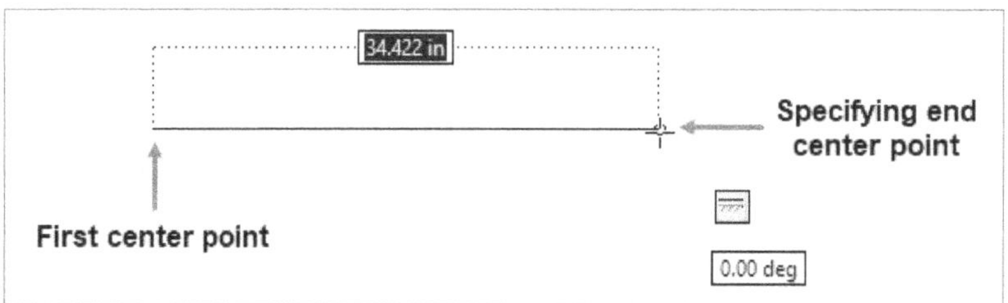

Figure-52. Specifying end center point of slot

- Click to specify the end center point. You will be asked to specify the width of the slot.
- Click at desired location to specify the width of slot or enter desired value in the edit box; refer to Figure-53. The slot will be created.

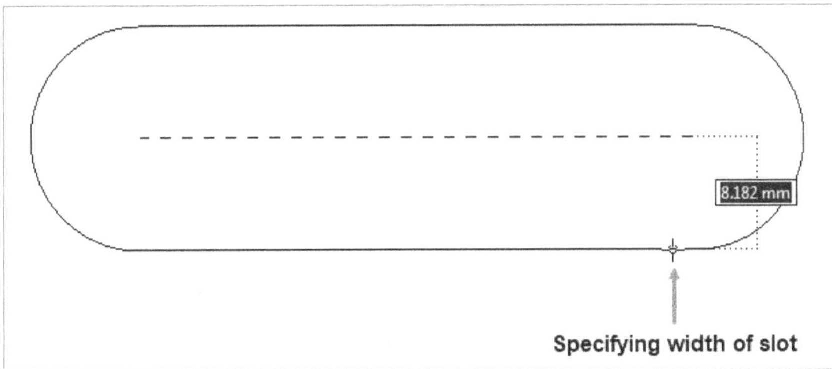

Figure-53. Specifying width of slot

Overall Slot

The **Overall Slot** tool is used to create slot by specifying total length of slot and width of slot. The procedure to use this tool is given next.

- Click on the **Overall Slot** tool from **Rectangle** drop-down in the **Create** panel of the **Ribbon**; refer to Figure-54. You will be asked to specify the start point of the slot.

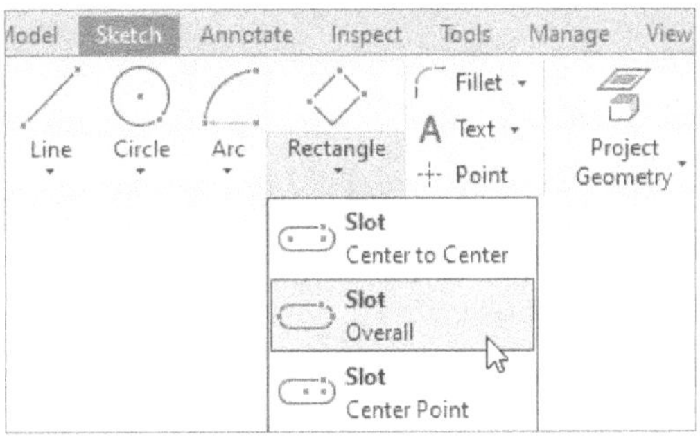

Figure-54. Overall Slot tool

- Click to specify the start point. You will be asked to specify the end point of the slot; refer to Figure-55.

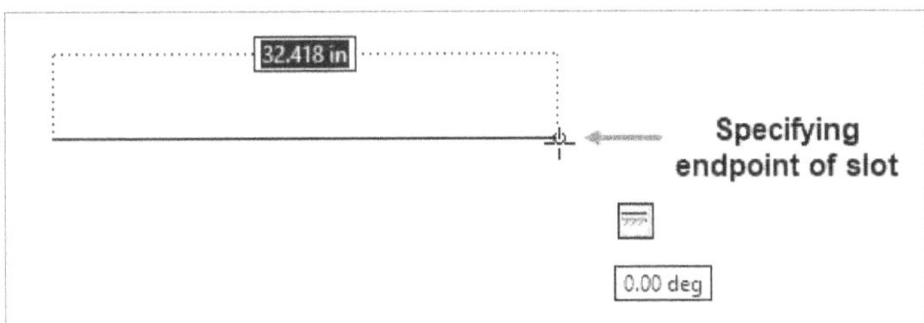

Figure-55. Specifying end point of slot

- Click to specify the end point of the slot. You will be asked to specify the width of the slot.
- Click to specify the width of the slot or enter desired value in the edit box; refer to Figure-56. The slot will be created.

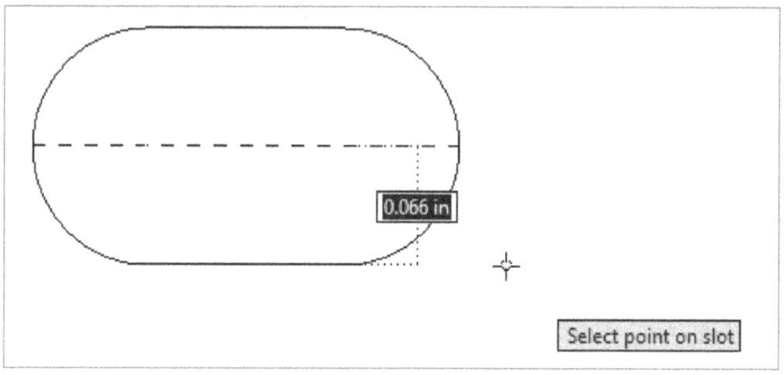

Figure-56. Specifying width of Overall slot

Center Point Slot

The **Center Point Slot** tool is used to create linear slot defined by a center point. The procedure to create slot using this tool is given next.

- Click on the **Center Point Slot** tool from **Rectangle** drop-down in the **Create** panel of the **Ribbon**; refer to Figure-57. You will be asked to specify the center point of the slot.

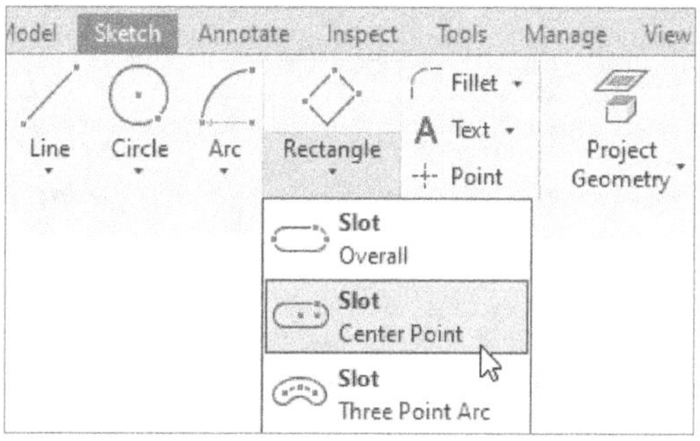

Figure-57. Center Point Slot tool

- Click to specify the center point. You will be asked to specify the second point of the slot; refer to Figure-58.

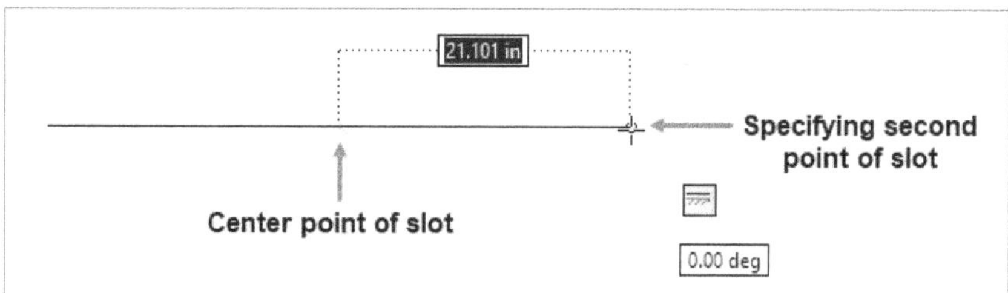

Figure-58. Specifying second point of slot

- Click to specify the second point of the slot. You will be asked to specify the width of the slot.
- Click to specify the width of the slot or enter desired value in the edit box; refer to Figure-59. The slot will be created.

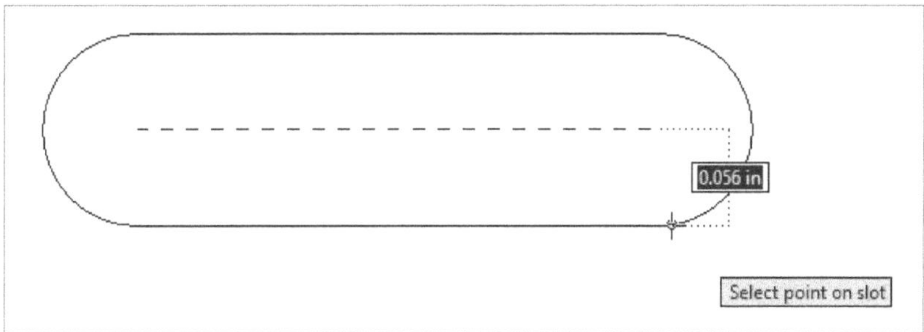

Figure-59. Specifying width of center point slot

Three Point Arc Slot

The **Three Point Arc Slot** tool is used to create slot along the specified arc. The procedure to create slot using this tool is given next.

- Click on the **Three Point Arc Slot** tool from **Rectangle** drop-down in the **Create** panel of the **Ribbon**; refer to Figure-60. You will be asked to specify the start point of the center arc.

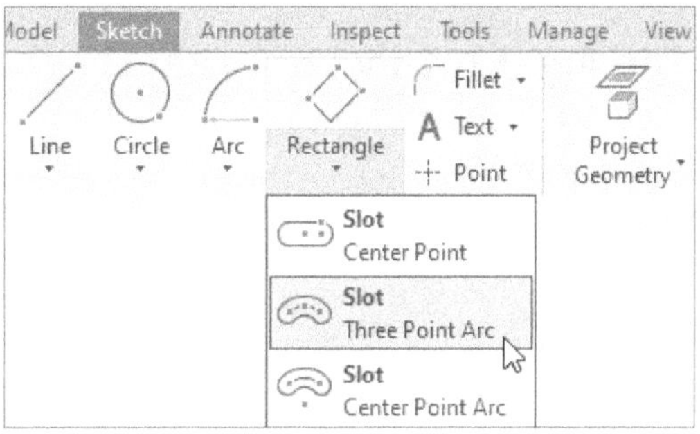

Figure-60. Three Point Arc Slot tool

- Click to specify the start point of the arc. You will be asked to specify the end point of the arc.
- Click to specify the end point of arc or enter desired distance value in the edit box displayed. You will be asked to specify a point on the arc; refer to Figure-61.

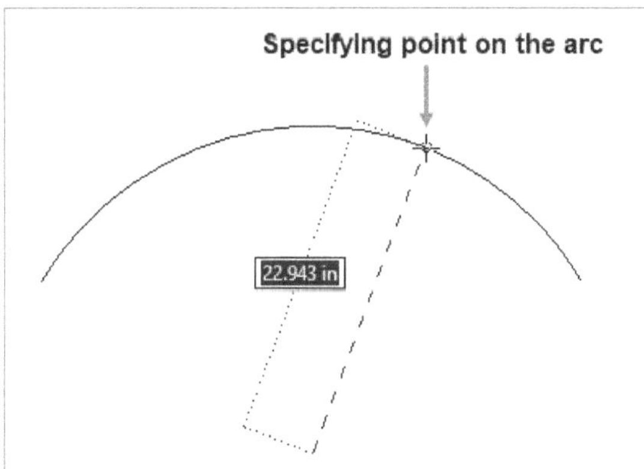

Figure-61. Specifying point on the arc

- Click to specify the arc point or enter desired value in the edit box displayed. You will be asked to specify the width of the slot; refer to Figure-62.

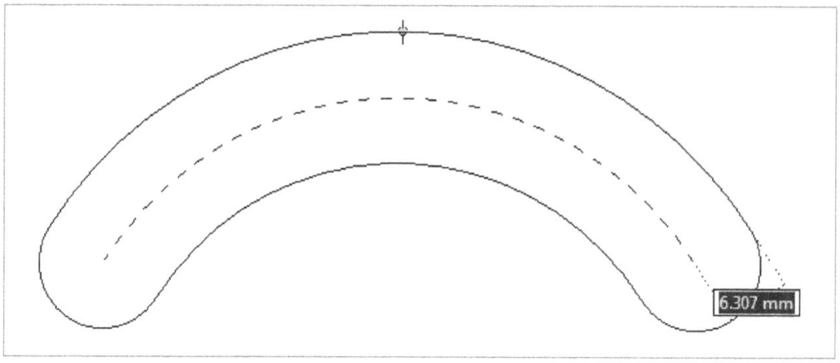

Figure-62. Specifying width of arc slot

- Click at desired location to specify the width or enter desired value of width in the edit box displayed. The slot will be created. Press **ESC** to exit the tool.

Center Point Arc Slot

The **Center Point Arc Slot** tool is used to create slot along the specified arc. The procedure to create slot using this tool is given next.

- Click on the **Center Point Arc Slot** tool from **Rectangle** drop-down in the **Create** panel of the **Ribbon**; refer to Figure-63. You will be asked to specify the center point for the arc.

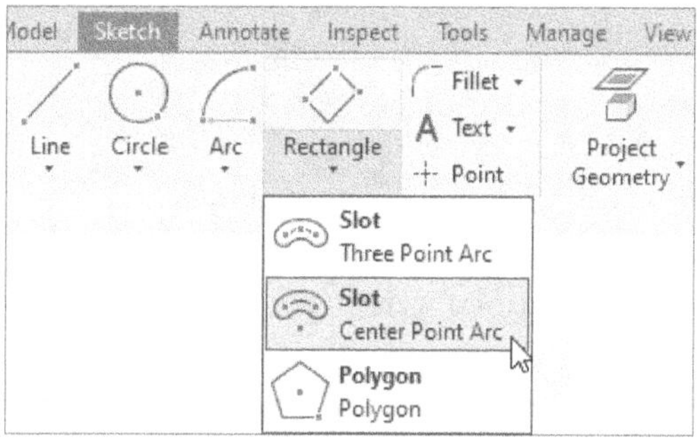

Figure-63. Center Point Arc Slot tool

- Click to specify the center point of the arc. You will be asked to specify the starting point of the arc; refer to Figure-64.

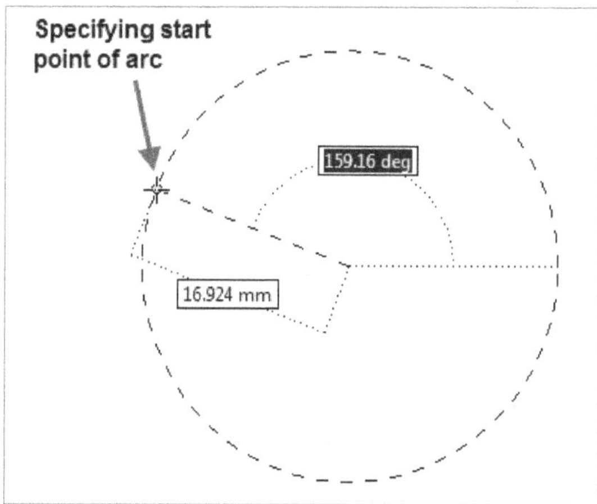

Figure-64. Specifying start point of arc

- Click to specify the starting point. You will be asked to specify end point of the arc; refer to Figure-65.

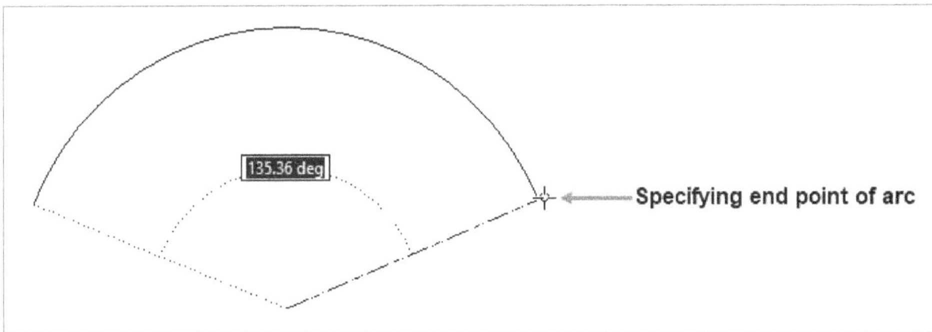

Figure-65. Specifying end point of arc

- Click to specify the end point or enter desired angle value in the edit box displayed. You will be asked to specify the width of slot.
- Enter desired value in the edit box. The slot will be created; refer to Figure-66.

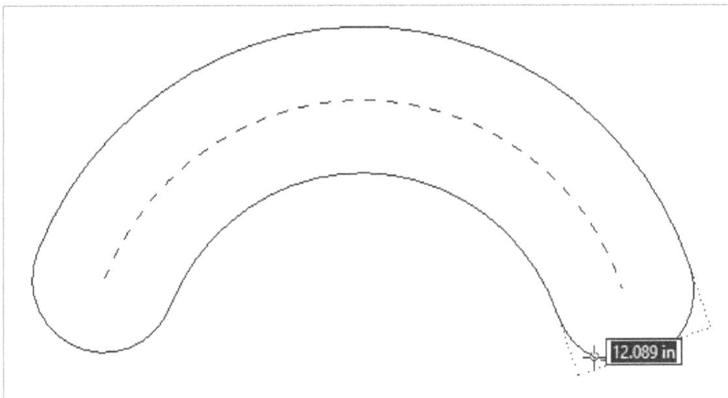

Figure-66. Specifying width of slot

Polygon

As the name suggests, the **Polygon** tool is used to create polygons in the sketch. The procedure to use this tool is given next.

- Click on the **Polygon** tool from **Rectangle** drop-down in the **Create** panel of the **Ribbon**; refer to Figure-67. The **Polygon** dialog box will be displayed; refer to Figure-68.

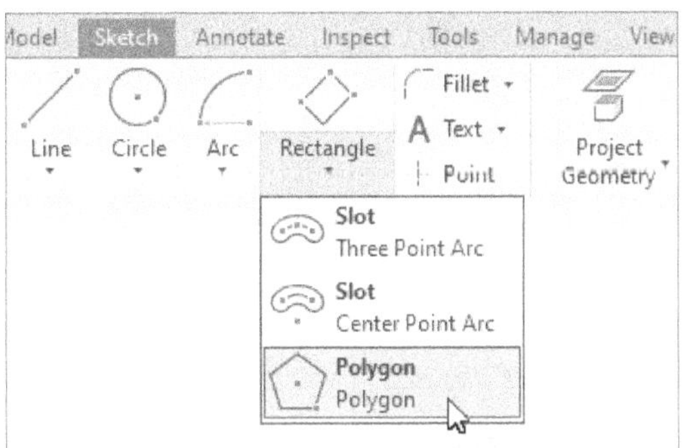

Figure-67. Polygon tool

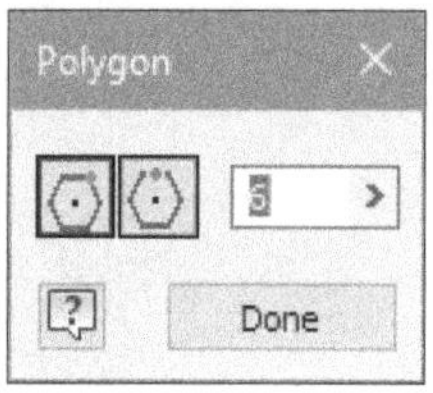

Figure-68. Polygon dialog box

- There are two buttons in the dialog box. **Inscribed** and **Circumscribed**. Click on the **Inscribed** button if you want to create polygon inscribed in the construction circle and click on the **Circumscribed** button if you want to create the polygon circumscribed to the construction circle.
- Click in the edit box and specify the number of sides of polygon.
- Click in the drawing area to specify center of construction circle for polygon. You will be asked to specify a point on the polygon circumference; refer to Figure-69.

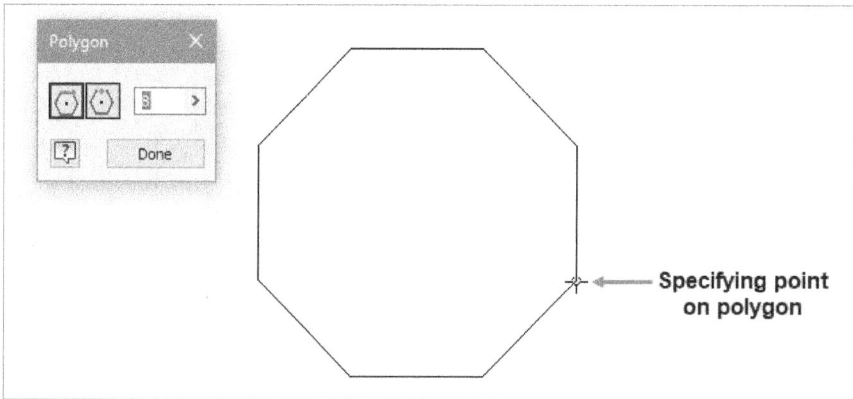

Figure-69. Specifying point on polygon

- Click to specify the point. The polygon will be created. Click on the **Done** button from the dialog box to exit.

Fillet

The **Fillet** tool is used to apply round at the sharp corners. Procedure to use this tool is given next.

- Click on the **Fillet** tool from **Create** panel in the **Ribbon**; refer to Figure-70. The **2D Fillet** dialog box will be displayed as shown in Figure-71.

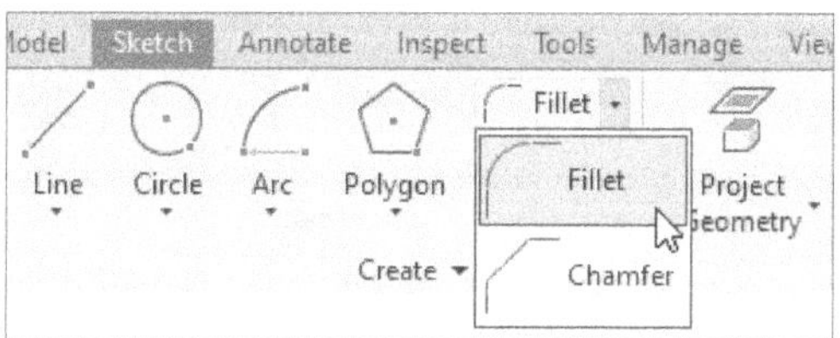

Figure-70. Fillet tool

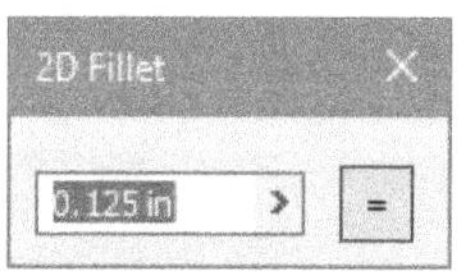

Figure-71. 2D Fillet dialog box

- Specify desired value of radius for fillet in the edit box of dialog box.

- Click on the first edge in sketch and then hover the cursor on other intersecting edge. Preview of the fillet will be displayed; refer to Figure-72.

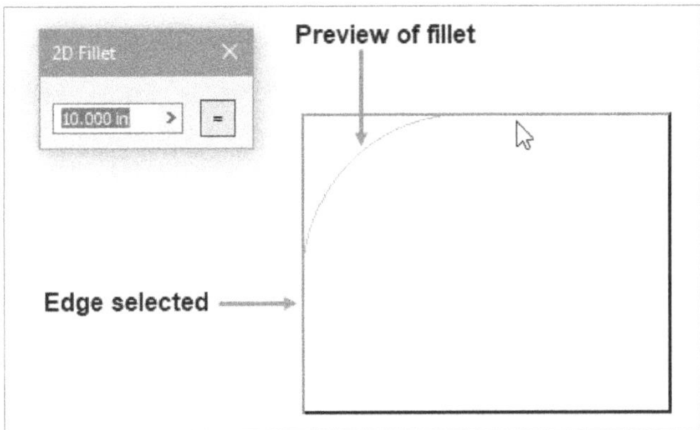

Figure-72. Preview of fillet

- Click on the other edge if preview is as per your requirement. The fillet will be created. Press **ESC** to exit the tool.

Chamfer

The **Chamfer** tool is used to chisel the sharp edges of the model. The procedure to use this tool is given next.

- Click on the **Chamfer** tool from **Fillet** drop-down in the **Create** panel of the **Ribbon**; refer to Figure-73. The **2D Chamfer** dialog box will be displayed; refer to Figure-74.

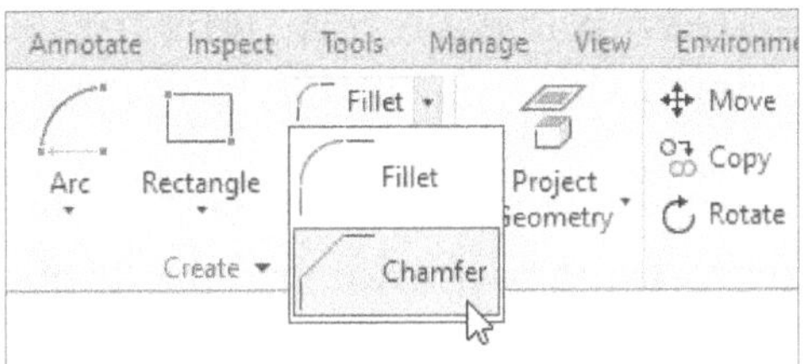

Figure-73. Chamfer tool

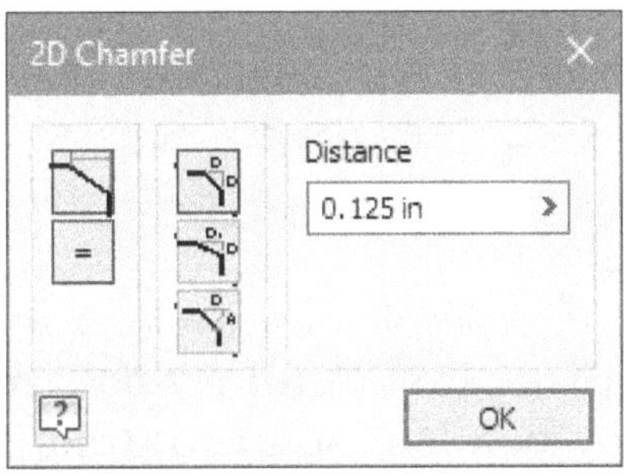

Figure-74. 2D Chamfer dialog box

- There are three buttons for specifying parameters of chamfer, **Distance**, **Distance 1 x Distance 2**, and **Distance x Angle**. If you want to specify equal length of chamfer on both sides to the corner point then select the **Distance** button. If you want to specify different distance on both sides of the corner point then select the **Distance 1 x Distance 2** button. If you want to specify angle and distance for the chamfer then select the **Distance x Angle** button.
- Select desired button from the dialog box and specify the related parameters.

- One by one click on the two intersecting lines. The chamfer will be created; refer to Figure-75. Repeat this step to create more chamfers and press **ESC** to exit the tool.

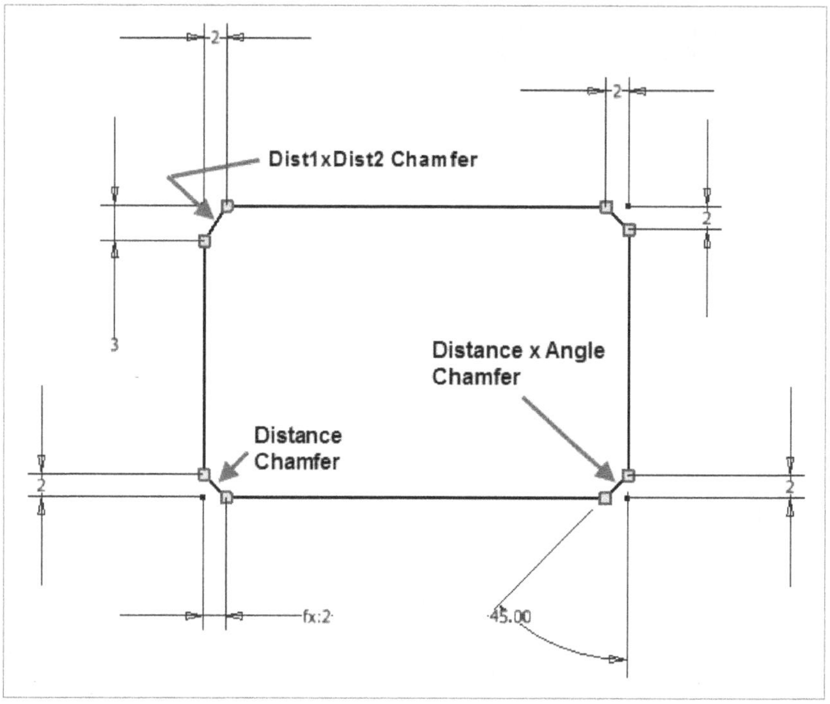

Figure-75. Chamfers in drawing

Text

The **Text** tool is used to write text in the sketch. This text can later be used to engrave marking on the component with the help of CAM software. The procedure to create text is given next.

- Click on the **Text** tool from **Create** panel in the **Ribbon**; refer to Figure-76. You will be asked to create a boundary box by specifying corner points.

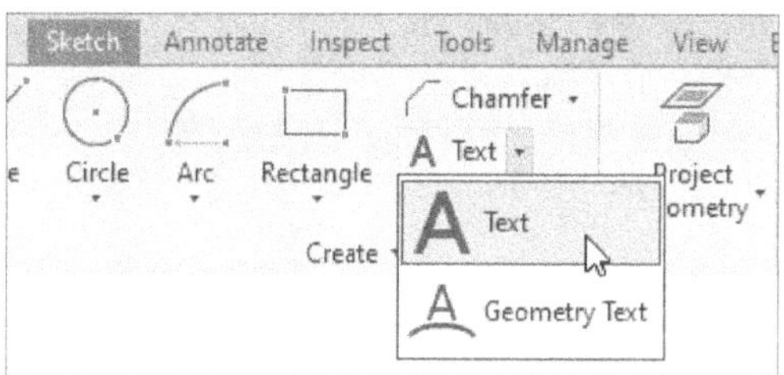

Figure-76. Text tool

- Click and drag the cursor to create boundary box; refer to Figure-77. On creating box, the **Format Text** dialog box is displayed; refer to Figure-78.

Figure-77. Creating boundary box

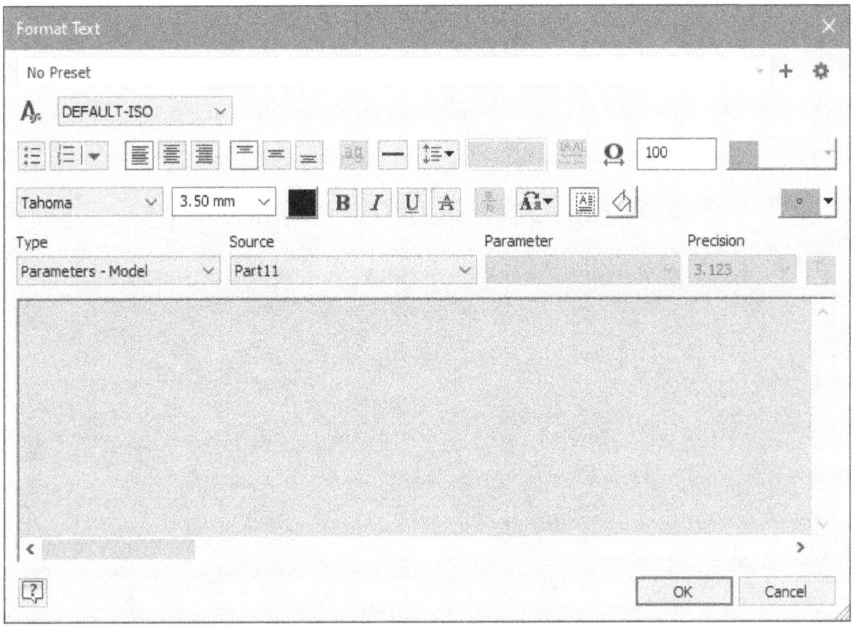

Figure-78. Format Text dialog box

- Type desired text in the input area of the dialog box.
- Set desired format for the text by using buttons in the dialog box like changing color, making text boldface, applying numbering or bullet, and so on.
- Click on the **OK** button from the dialog box. The text will be created; refer to Figure-79.

Figure-79. Text created

Geometry Text

The **Geometry Text** tool is used to create text aligned to the selected geometry. The procedure to create geometry text is given next.

- Click on the **Geometry Text** tool from **Text** drop-down in the **Create** panel of the **Ribbon**; refer to Figure-80. You will be asked to select the geometry to which you want the text to be aligned.

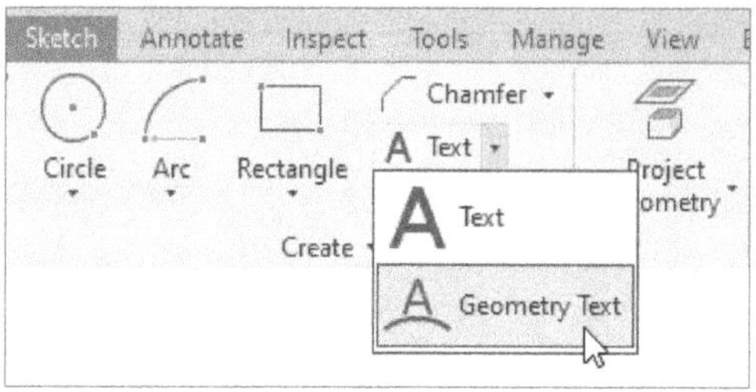

Figure-80. Geometry Text tool

- Click on the geometry; refer to Figure-81. The **Geometry-Text** dialog box will be displayed; refer to Figure-82.

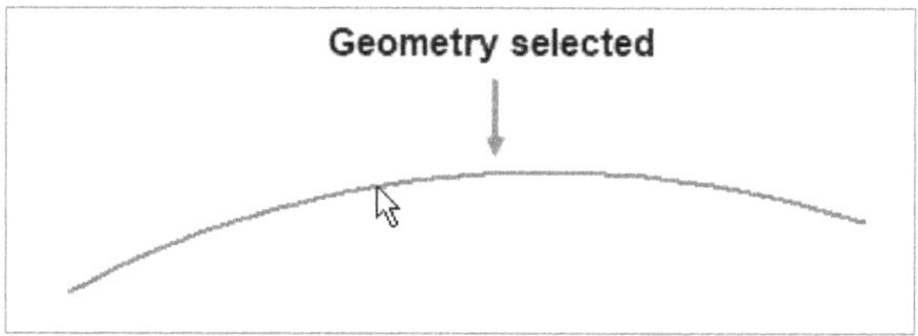

Figure-81. Geometry selected for text

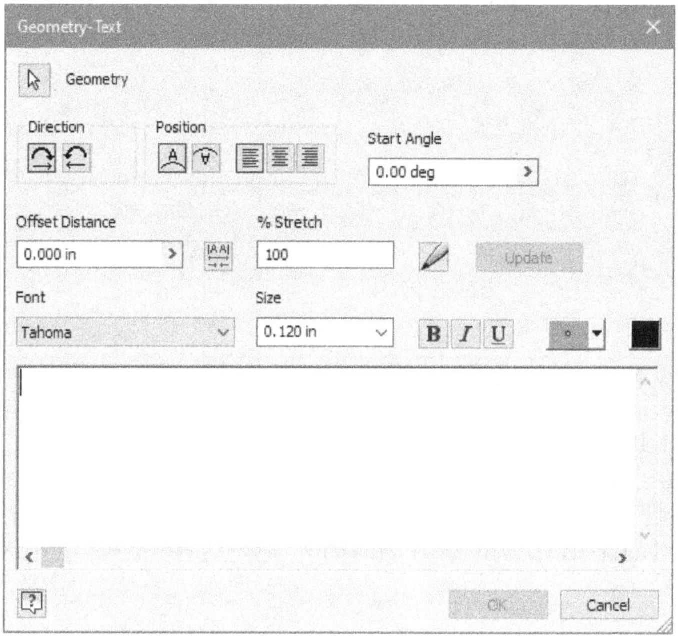

Figure-82. Geometry Text dialog box

- Set the direction and position of the text by using the options in the dialog box.
- Type desired text in the input box and click on the **OK** button from the dialog box. The text will be created; refer to Figure-83.

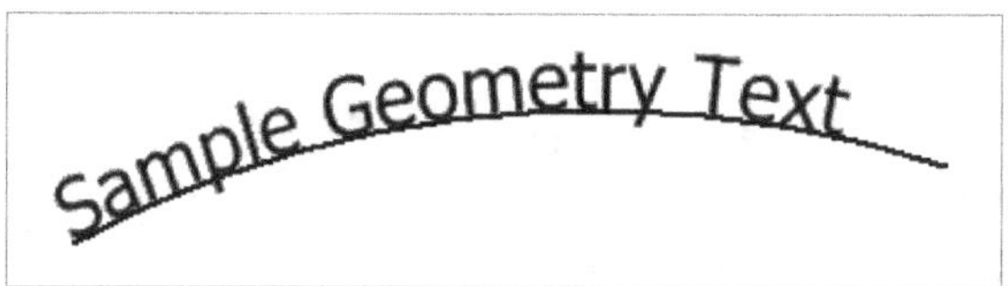

Figure-83. Geometry text created

Point

Point is smallest geometric entity available in any CAD package. Point is mainly used to provide reference for other geometric entities. The procedure to create point is given next.

- Click on the **Point** tool from **Create** panel in the **Ribbon**; refer to Figure-84. You will be asked to specify position of the point; refer to Figure-85.

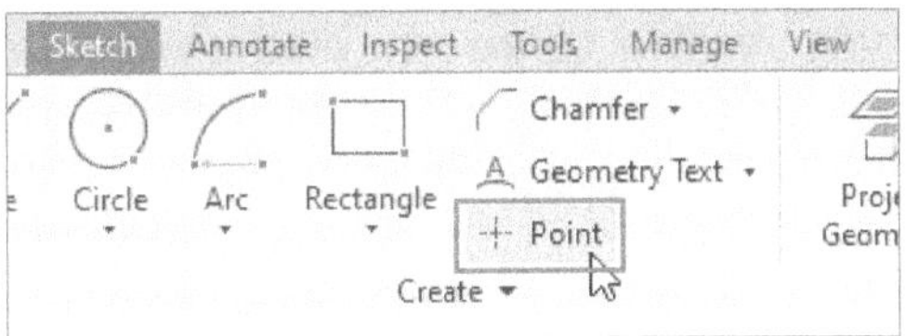

Figure-84. Point tool

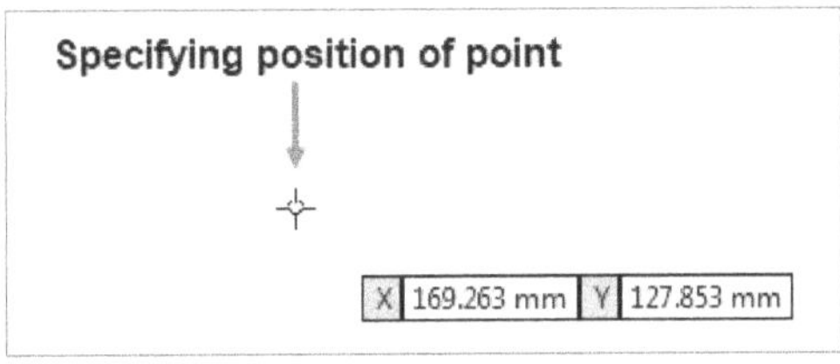

Figure-85. Specifying position of point

- Click to specify the position of point or type desired coordinates for **X** and **Y** directions. Note that you need to press **TAB** to switch between **X** edit box and **Y** edit box.

SKETCH MODIFICATION TOOLS

The sketch modification tools are used to modify the sketch entities. These tools are available in the **Modify** panel of the **Sketch** tab in the **Ribbon**; refer to Figure-86. These tools are discussed next.

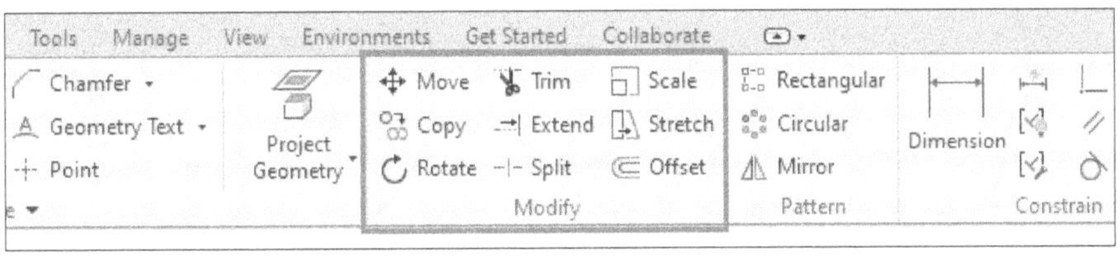

Figure-86. Modify panel

Move tool

The **Move** tool is used to move sketched entities. The procedure to use this tool is given next.

- Click on the **Move** tool from **Modify** panel in the **Ribbon**. The **Move** dialog box will be displayed; refer to Figure-87. Also, you will be asked to select objects.

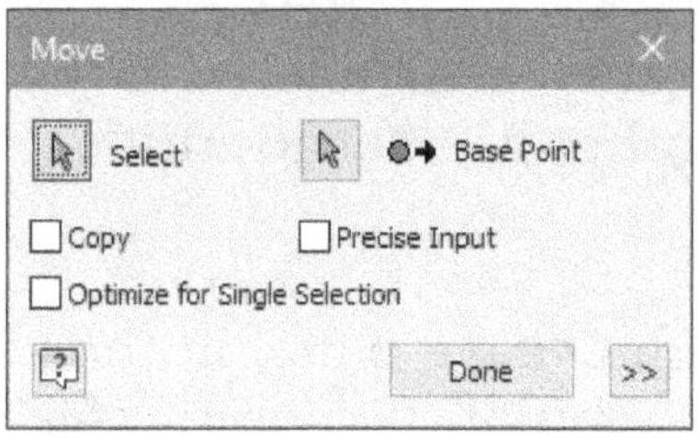

Figure-87. Move dialog box

- Select the object that you want to move; refer to Figure-88. Press **ENTER** from keyboard, you will be asked to select base point for moving the object.

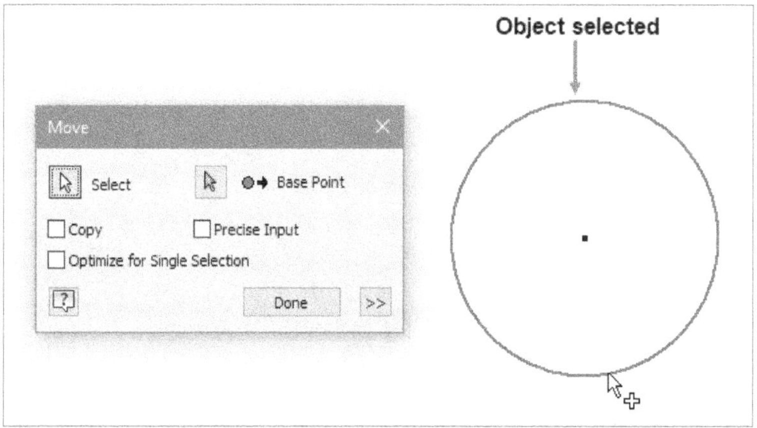

Figure-88. Object selected

- Click on desired location on the object to make it base point. You will be asked to specify the placement position for the object.
- Click to specify the new position. The object will move to the new location as specified; refer to Figure-89.

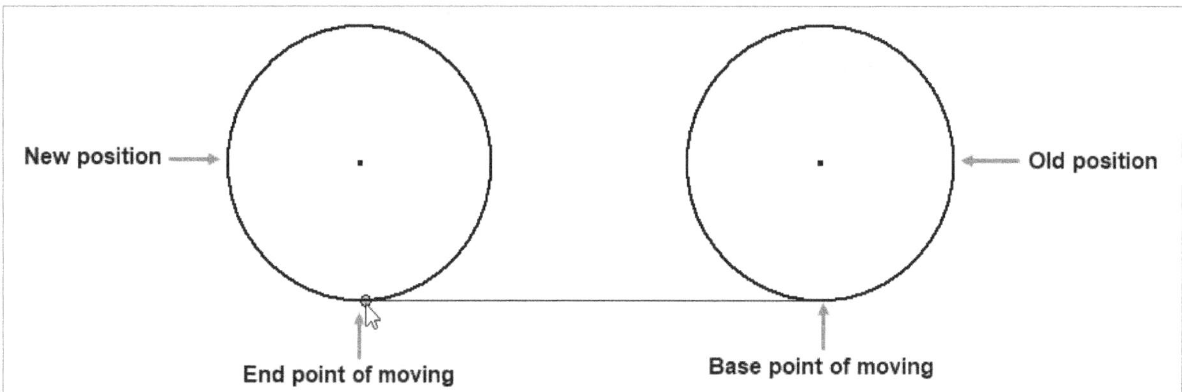

Figure-89. Moving object

- You can create a new copy of the selected object at desired location by selecting the **Copy** check box.
- You can specify the precise positions in the **Inventor Precise Input** box by selecting the **Precise Input** check box.
- Click on the **>>** button from the dialog box to display advanced options of the dialog box; refer to Figure-90.

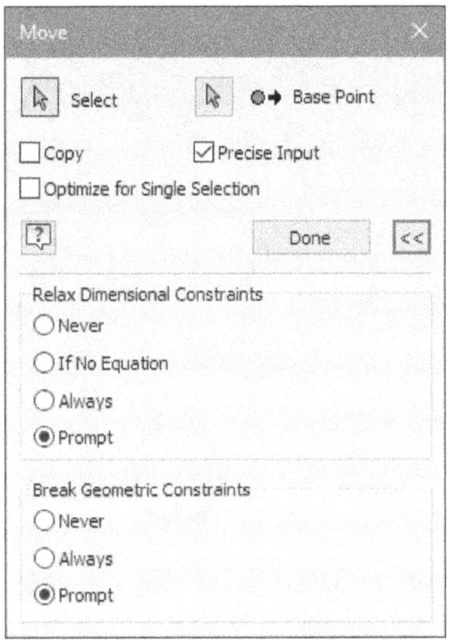

Figure-90. Move dialog box with advanced options

- Select desired radio buttons in the dialog box to relax or apply constraints.
- After moving objects or creating their copies, click on the **Done** button.

Copy tool

The **Copy** tool is used to create copy of the selected entities. The procedure to use this tool is given next.

- Click on the **Copy** tool from **Modify** panel in the **Ribbon**. The **Copy** dialog box will be displayed; refer to Figure-91.

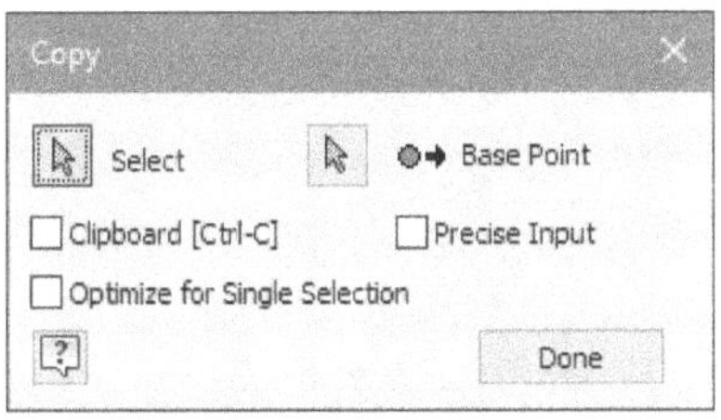

Figure-91. Copy dialog box

- Select the entities that you want to copy. Note that you can select multiple entities to create copy. Press **ENTER** to complete selection of entities. You will be asked to select base point on the entities.
- Click to select the base point. You will be asked to specify the placement location for copied entities.
- Click at desired location. The copies of selected entities will be placed at the specified location. Note that you can create multiple copies by specifying more than one placement points; refer to Figure-92.
- Click on the **Done** button from the dialog box to exit.

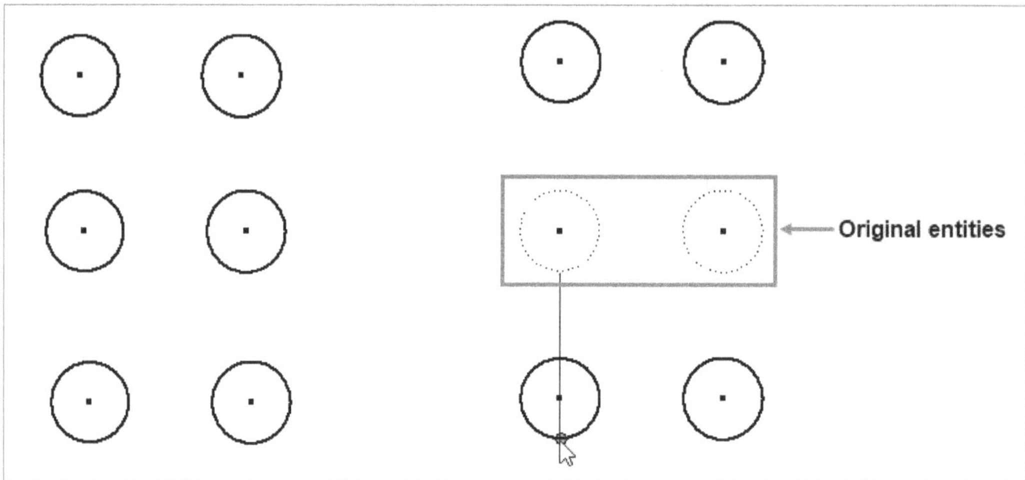

Figure-92. Copies created

Rotate tool

The **Rotate** tool is used to rotate selected entities. Procedure to rotate the entities is given next.

- Click on the **Rotate** tool from **Modify** panel in the **Ribbon**. The **Rotate** dialog box will be displayed; refer to Figure-93.

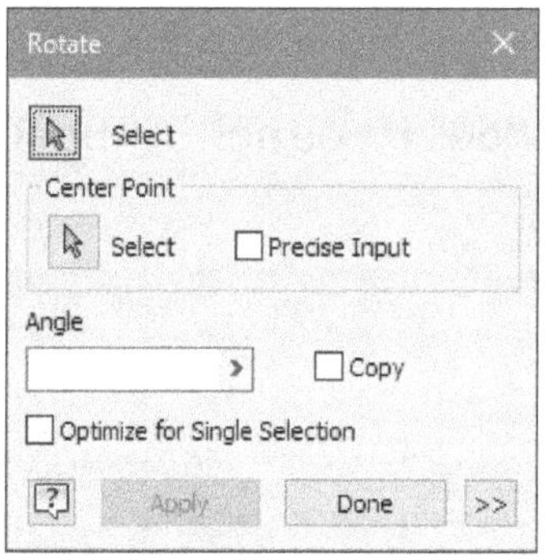

Figure-93. Rotate dialog box

- Select the entities that you want to rotate.

Note that till now we have selected the entities individually. We can also select the entities by windows selection. There are two ways for windows selection; Cross-window selection and Window selection. To select all the entities that intersect with our window is called Cross-window selection. To do so, click in the drawing area and drag the cursor towards left; refer to Figure-94. To make window selection, click in the drawing area and drag the cursor towards right; refer to Figure-95. All the entities that completely come inside the window will be selected.

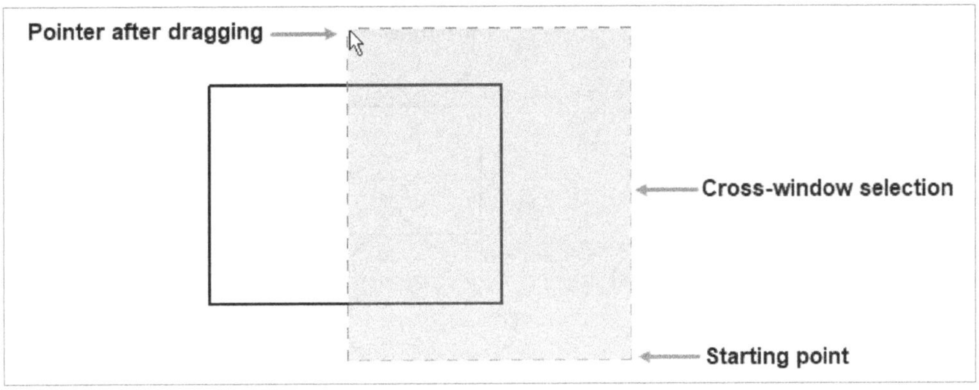

Figure-94. Cross window selection

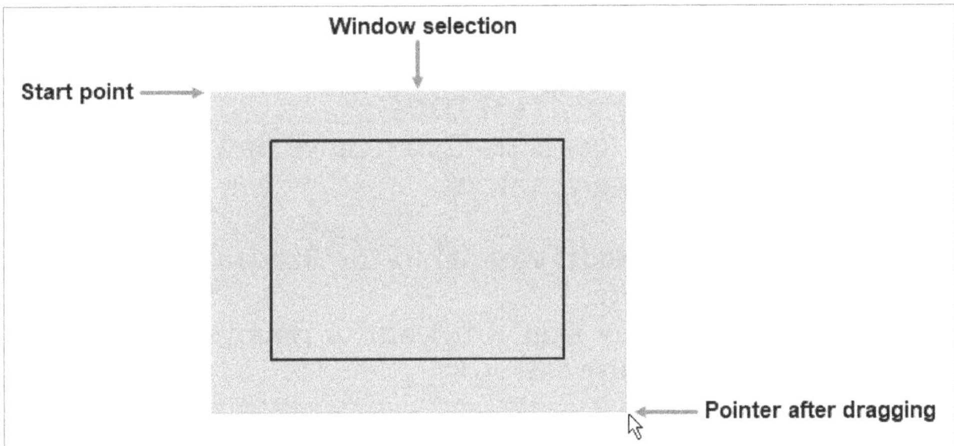

Figure-95. Window selection

- After selecting the entities, press **ENTER** from the keyboard. You will be asked to specify center point for rotation of entities.
- Click at desired location/point to make it pivot point for rotation. If your entities are constrained then a confirmation box will be displayed as shown in Figure-96. Click on **Yes** button to accept the changes.

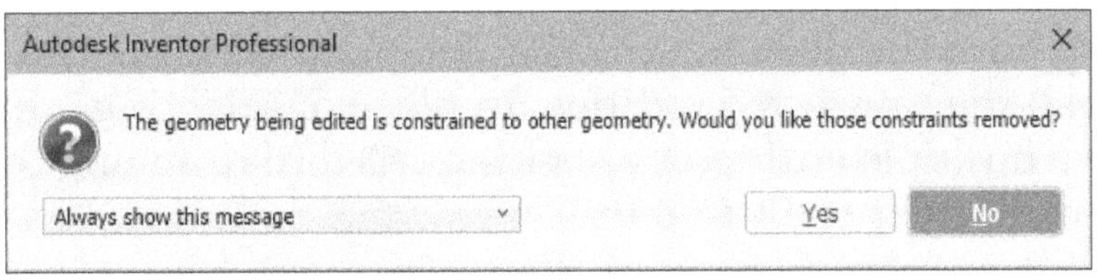

Figure-96. Confirmation box

- You will be prompted to specify the angle value for the rotation; refer to Figure-97. Enter desired angle value in the **Angle** edit box in dialog box and click on the **Apply** button. The entity will be rotated.
- You can create a rotated copy of the selected entity by selecting the **Copy** check box. Click on the **Done** button from the dialog box to exit the tool.

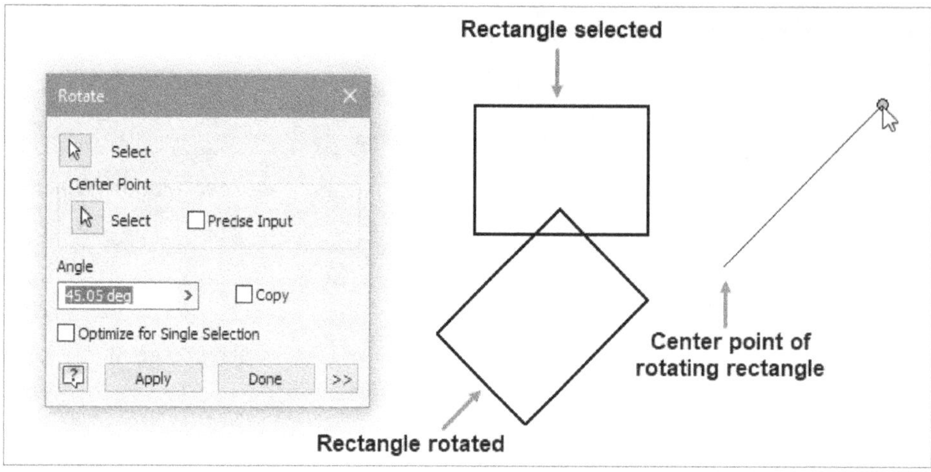

Figure-97. Rotating entities

Trim tool

As the name suggests, the **Trim** tool is used to remove unwanted section of sketch. The procedure to use this tool is given next.

- Click on the **Trim** tool from **Modify** panel in the **Ribbon**. Cursor is ready with a scissor to remove sketch entity.
- Hover the cursor on the entity that you want to remove. It will be displayed in dashed line type; refer to Figure-98.

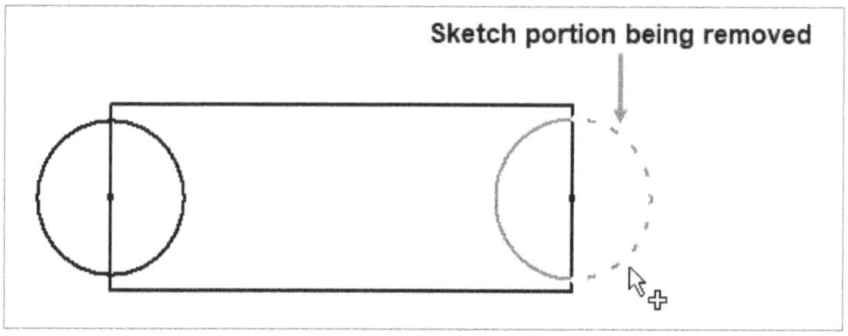

Figure-98. Sketched portion being trimmed

- Click on it to remove the portion. You can keep on selecting the entities until you have removed all the unwanted entities. In place of selecting entities individually, you can remove multiple entities by clicking **LMB** and dragging the cursor over the unwanted entities; refer to Figure-99.

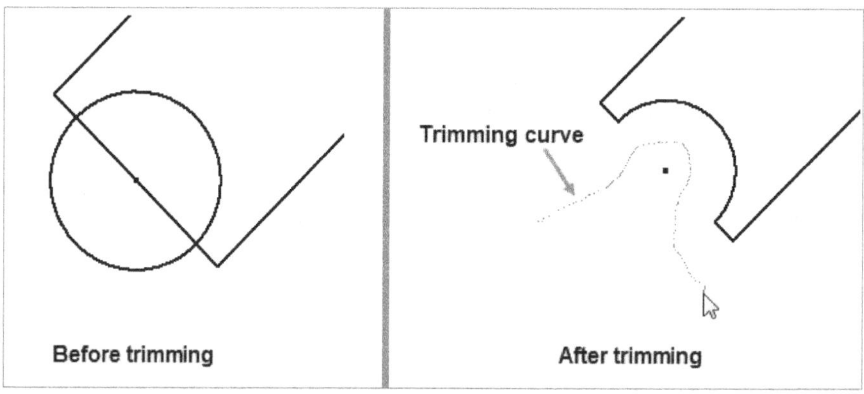

Figure-99. Trimming entities

- Press **ESC** from the keyboard to exit the tool.

Extend tool

The **Extend** tool does reverse of the **Trim** tool. This tool creates link between two entities by extending the selected entity. The procedure to use this tool is given next.

- Click on the **Extend** tool from **Modify** panel in the **Ribbon**. You will be asked to select entities to extend.
- Hover the cursor on the entity. Preview of extension will be displayed; refer to Figure-100.

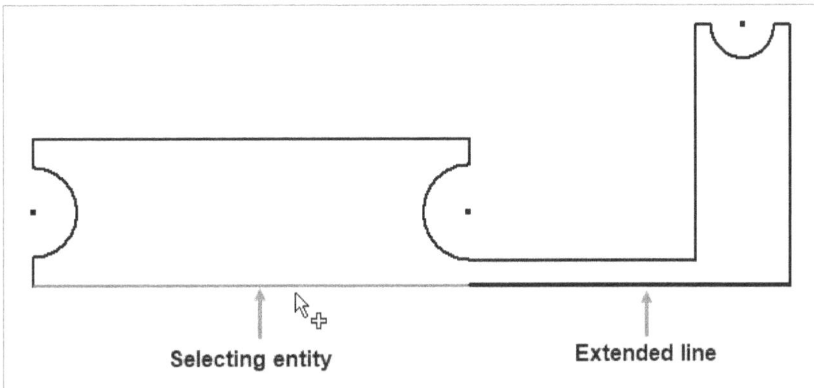

Figure-100. Extending entities

- Click on desired entities to extend them. Press **ESC** to exit the tool.

Split tool

The **Split** tool is used to break the entity into two parts. The procedure to use this tool is given next.

- Click on the **Split** tool from **Modify** panel in the **Ribbon**. You will be asked to select entity to be split.
- Click on the entity near desired snap point from where you want to split the entity; refer to Figure-101. The selected entity will split at the snap point.
- Press **ESC** to exit the tool.

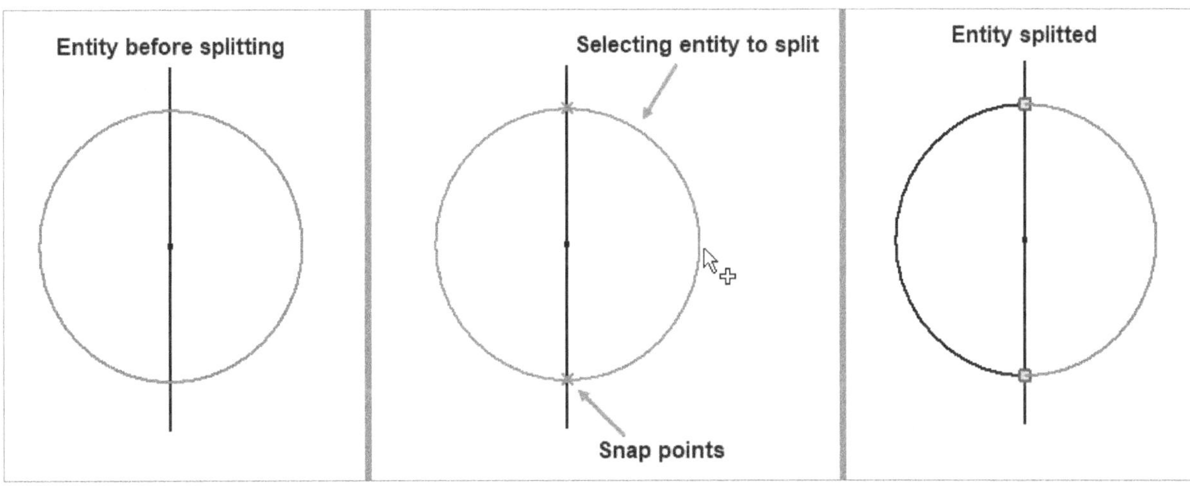

Figure-101. Splitting entity

Scale tool

The **Scale** tool is used to enlarge or diminish the selected entities by same proportion. The procedure to use this tool is given next.

- Click on the **Scale** tool from **Modify** panel in the **Ribbon**. The **Scale** dialog box will be displayed and you will be asked to select the entities; refer to Figure-102.

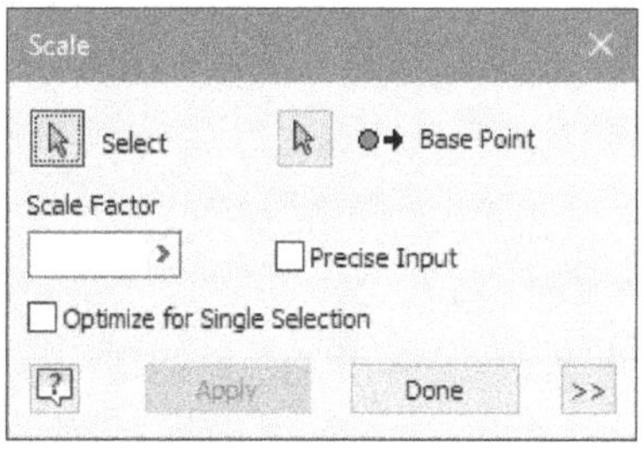

Figure-102. Scale dialog box

- Select the sketch entities that you want to enlarge or diminish and press **ENTER**. You will be asked to specify base point for scaling.
- Click at desired point to make it base point. You will be asked to specify the value of scale factor; refer to Figure-103.

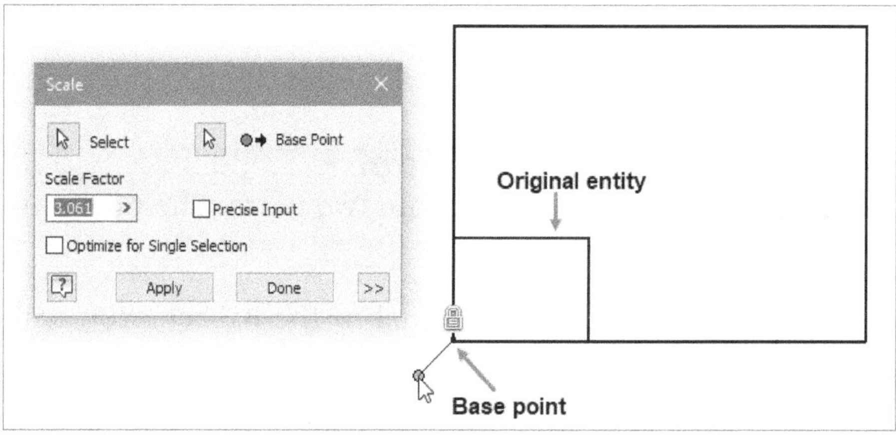

Figure-103. Specifying scale factor

- Specify desired value in the **Scale Factor** edit box in the dialog box. Note that negative values are not applicable for scale factor. Values less than 1 make the selected objects diminish and values greater than 1 enlarge the selected objects.
- Click on the **Apply** button to scale the objects.
- Click on the **Done** button from the dialog box to exit the tool.

Stretch tool

The **Stretch** tool is used to stretch the component by using the selected references. The procedure to use this tool is given next.

- Click on the **Stretch** tool from **Modify** panel in the **Ribbon**. The **Stretch** dialog box will be displayed; refer to Figure-104. Also, you will be asked to select the entities to stretch.

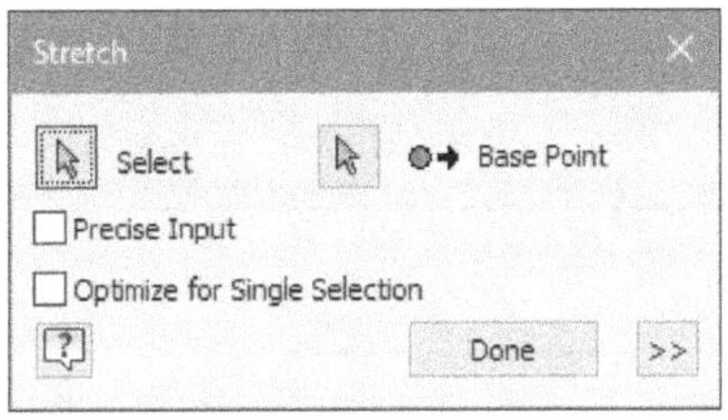

Figure-104. Stretch dialog box

- Select the entities that you want to stretch; refer to Figure-105. Press **ENTER** from the keyboard to complete selection of entities. You will be asked to select the base point.

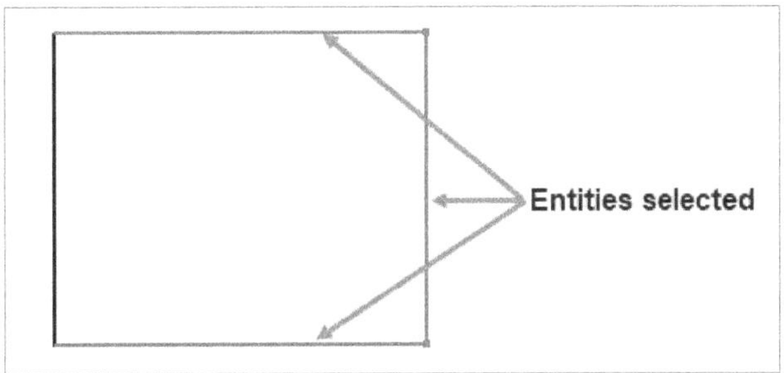

Figure-105. Entities selected for stretching

- Click at desired location to specify base point. If your sketch is constrained then a confirmation box will be displayed. Click on **Yes** button from the confirmation box to allow removal of constraints. You will be asked to specify end point for stretch.
- Click at desired location to specify end point. The object will be stretched by distance between base point and end point; refer to Figure-106.
- Click on the **Done** button from the dialog box to exit the tool.

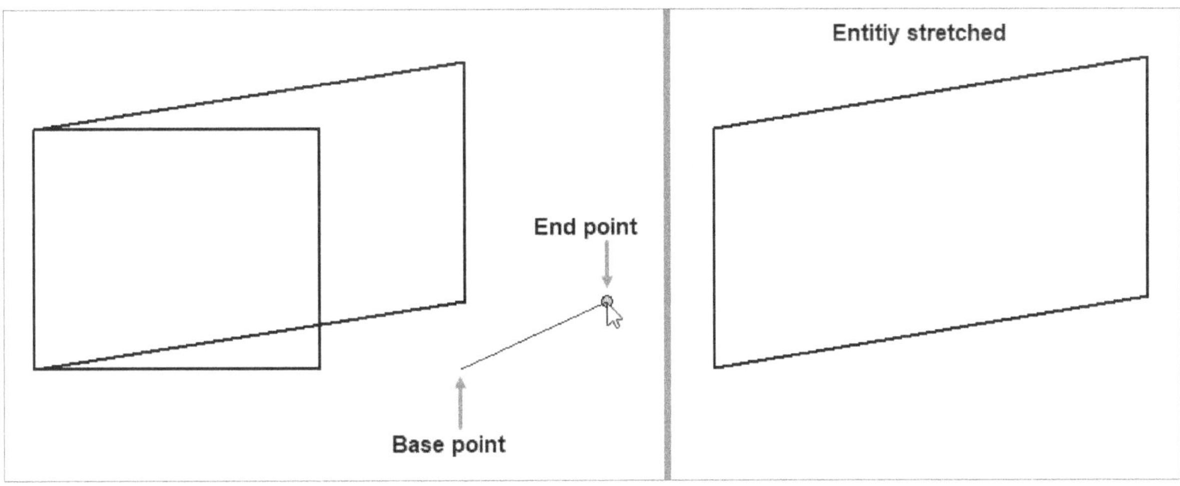

Figure-106. Entitiy stretched

Offset tool

The **Offset** tool is used to create enlarged or diminished copy of the selected entity by specified distance. The procedure to use this tool is given next.

- Click on the **Offset** tool from **Modify** panel in the **Ribbon**. You will be asked to select the curve/entity to offset.
- Select the curve/entity. You will be asked to specify the offset distance; refer to Figure-107.

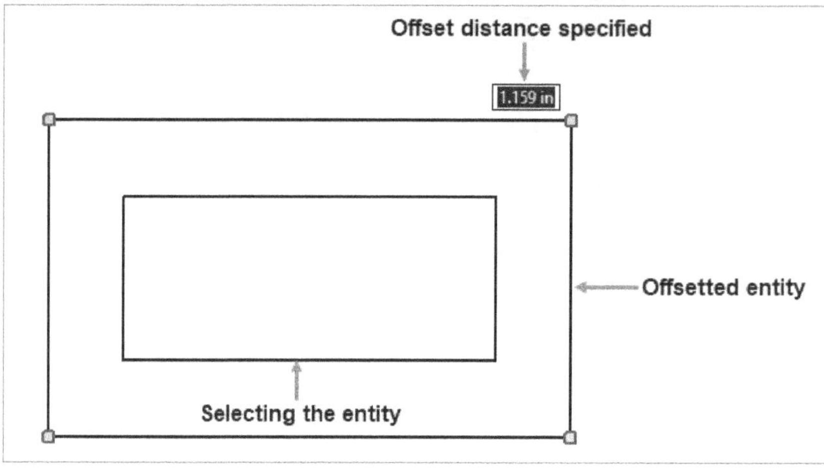

Figure-107. Offset entity created

- Click to specify the offset distance or enter desired value in the edit box. The offset copy of selected curve will be created. Press **ESC** to exit the tool.

CREATING PATTERNS OF SKETCH ENTITIES

Patterns are arrangement of selected entities in symmetric ways. There are three tools in the **Pattern** panel of the **Ribbon**; refer to Figure-108. These tools are discussed next.

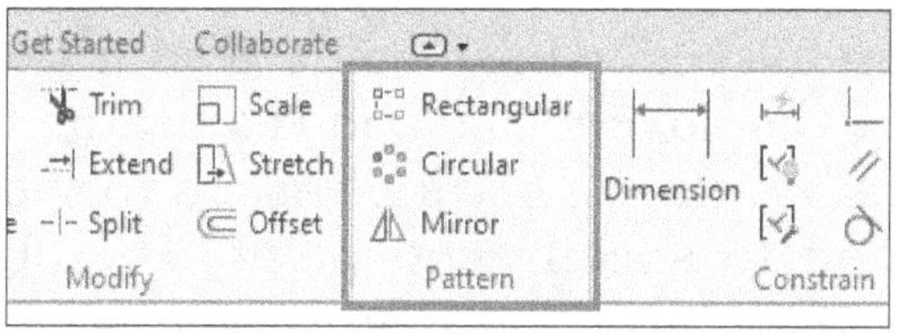

Figure-108. Pattern panel

Rectangular Pattern tool

The **Rectangular Pattern** tool is used to create multiple copies of the selected object in linear symmetry. The procedure to use this tool is given next.

- Click on the **Rectangular Pattern** tool from **Pattern** panel in **3D Model** tab of the **Ribbon**. The **Rectangular Pattern** dialog box will be displayed; refer to Figure-109. Also, you will be asked to select the entity to be patterned.

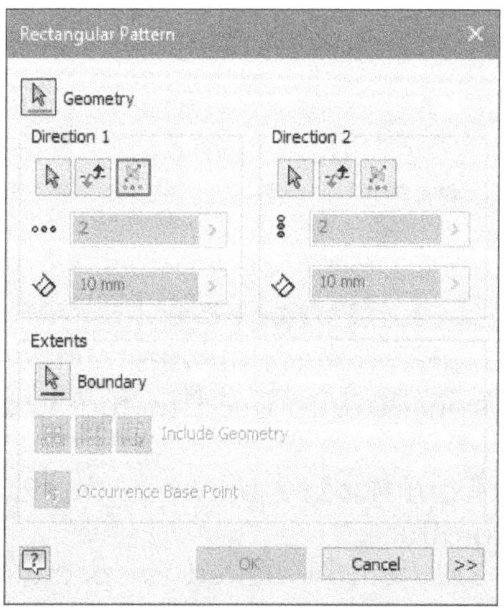

Figure-109. Rectangular Pattern dialog box

- Select the object that you want to pattern and press **ENTER**. You will be asked to select reference for first direction.
- Click on the direction reference like line, edge, and so on. Preview of the pattern will be displayed; refer to Figure-110.

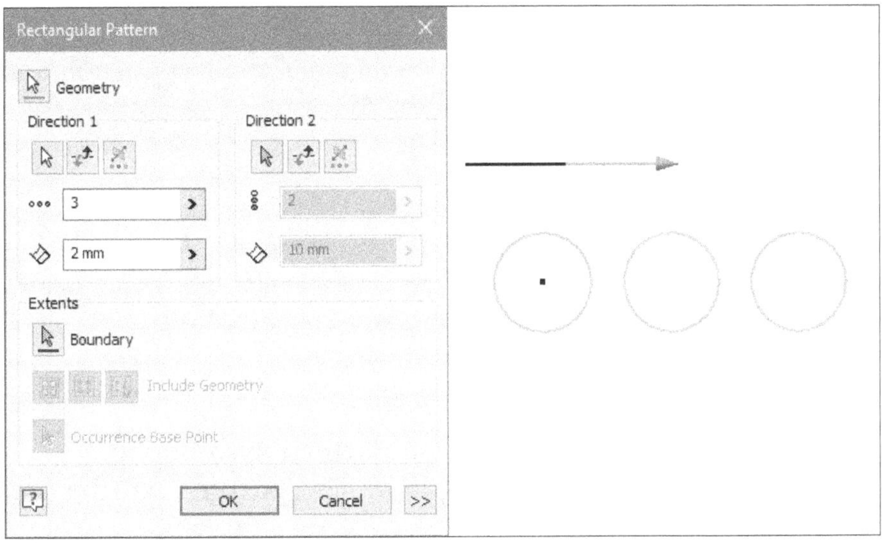

Figure-110. Preview of rectangular pattern

- Click in the **Count** edit box in the dialog box and specify the number of entities.
- Click in the **Spacing** edit box and specify the distance between the two consecutive entities of the pattern.
- To create the pattern in the other direction, click on the **Select** button in the **Direction 2** area of the dialog box; refer to Figure-111. You will be asked to select reference for the other direction.

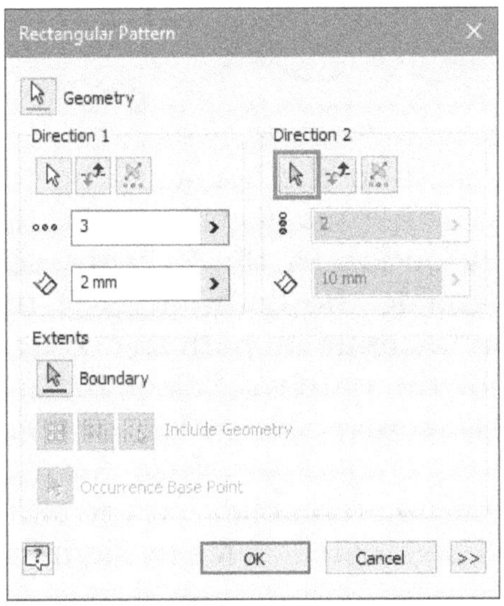

Figure-111. Selection button in Direction 2

- Click on the reference for direction 2, preview of the pattern will be displayed; refer to Figure-112.

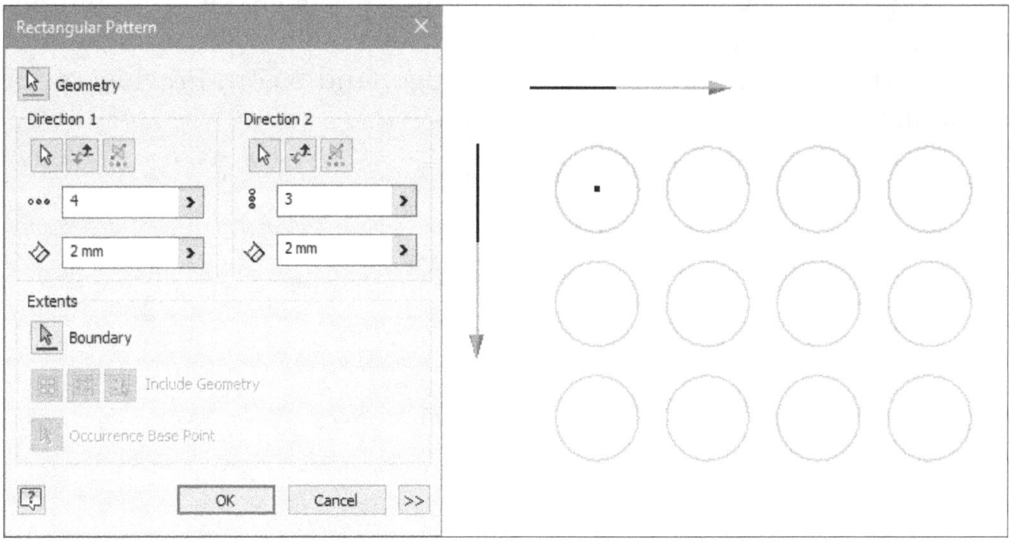

Figure-112. Preview of rectangular pattern in both directions

- Select the **Symmetric** button to create the pattern symmetric.
- Click on the **OK** button from the dialog box. The pattern will be created; refer to Figure-113.

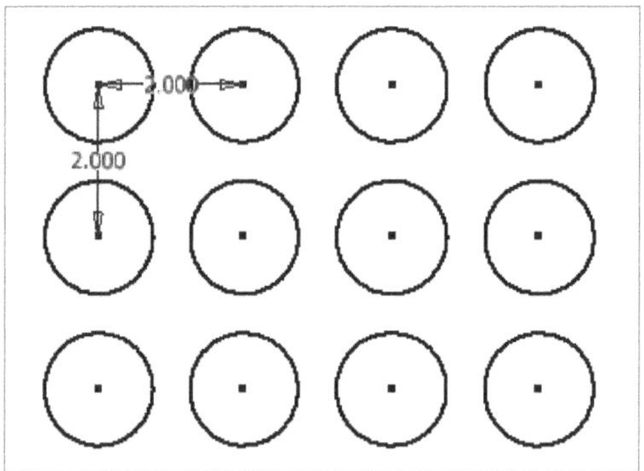

Figure-113. Rectangular pattern created

- In the **Extents** section, click on the **Boundary** button and click inside desired boundary of the sketch. The boundary will be selected.
- Select **Include Geometry** option in the **Extents** section to create all pattern occurrences completely inside the boundary are used for the pattern. Select **Include Centroids** option to create all pattern occurrences with centroids within the boundary are used for the pattern. Select **Include using occurrence base points** option to create all occurrences with base points inside the boundary are used for the pattern.
- After specifying desired parameters, click on the **OK** button from the dialog box. The bounded pattern will be created; refer to Figure-114.

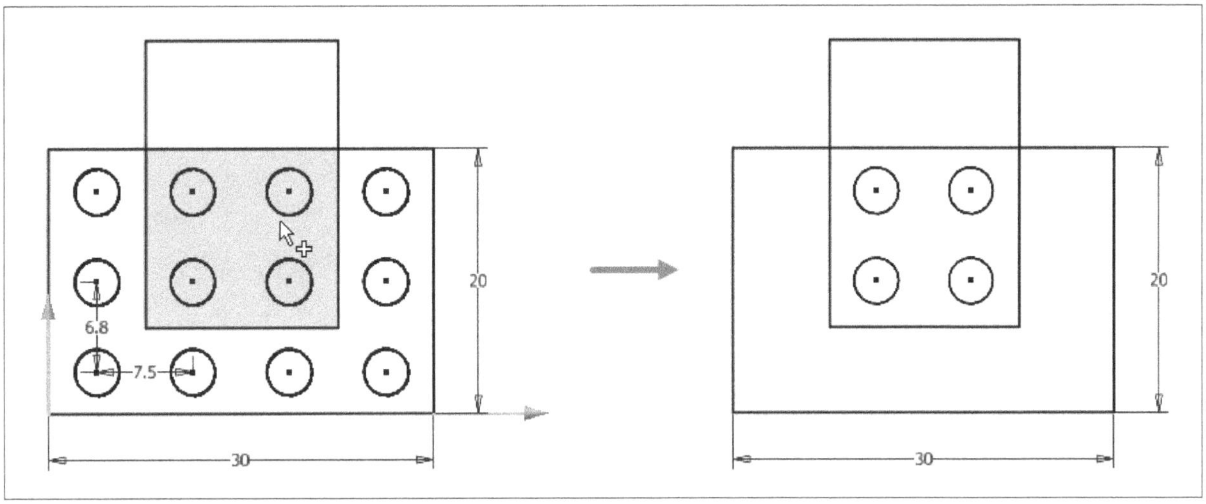

Figure-114. Bounded pattern created

- Click on the **Expand** button, the advanced options will be displayed; refer to Figure-115.

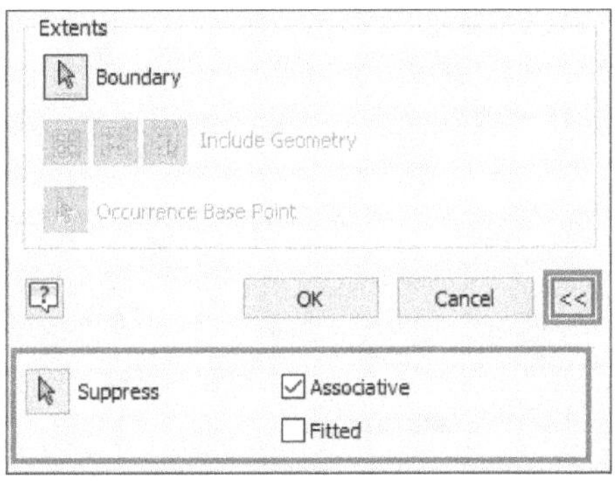

Figure-115. Advanced options of Rectangular Pattern dialog box

- Click on the **Suppress** button and select the elements which you want to suppress. **Suppressed elements** are not included in profiles or drawing sketches.
- On selecting the **Associative** check box, the pattern updates when changes are made to the part.
- Select the **Fitted** check box to specify whether pattern elements are equally fitted within the specified angle.

Circular Pattern

The **Circular Pattern** tool is used to create multiple copies of the selected entity in circular symmetry with respect to the selected axis. The procedure to create circular pattern is given next.

- Click on the **Circular Pattern** tool from **Pattern** panel in the **Ribbon**. The **Circular Pattern** dialog box will be displayed; refer to Figure-116. Also, you will be asked to select the entities for creating pattern.

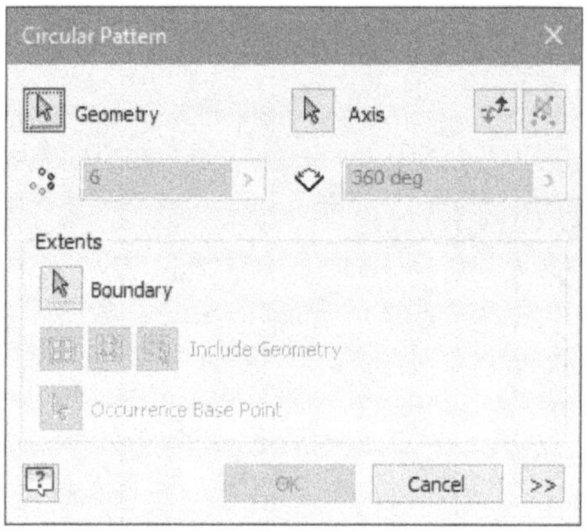

Figure-116. Circular Pattern dialog box

- Select the entity and press **ENTER**. You will be asked to select a reference for axis.
- Click on the reference, preview of the pattern will be displayed; refer to Figure-117.

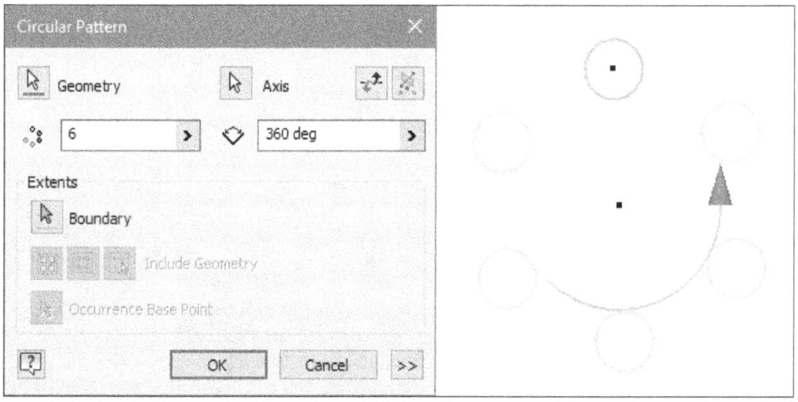

Figure-117. Preview of circular pattern

- Specify the number of entities of pattern in the **Count** edit box and specify the total angle span in the **Angle** edit box. Note that if you clear the **Fitted** check box from the expanded dialog box then you need to specify the angle between two consecutive instances of the object in pattern; refer to Figure-118.

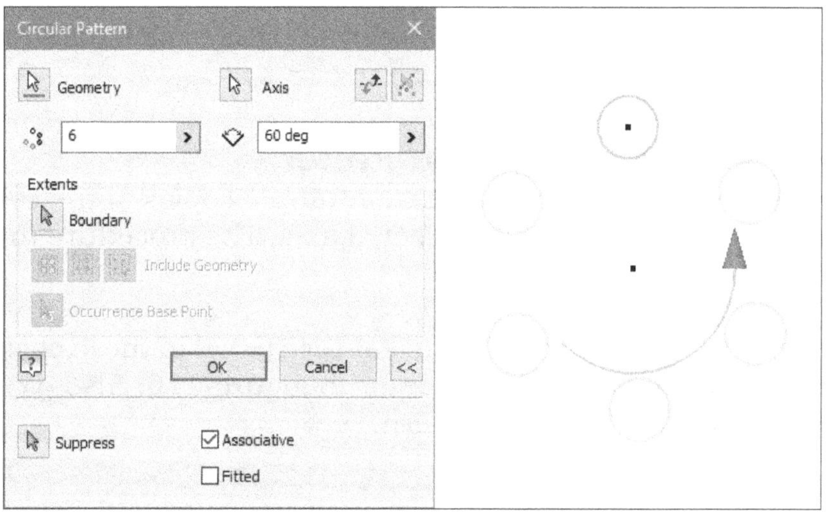

Figure-118. Expanded Circular Pattern dialog box

- You can skip desired instances of pattern by using the **Suppress** button in the expanded dialog box. To do so, click on the **Suppress** button and select the instances from the preview that you do not want to created. The line type of selected entities will be changed to dashed.
- Click on the **OK** button from the dialog box. The circular pattern will be created; refer to Figure-119.

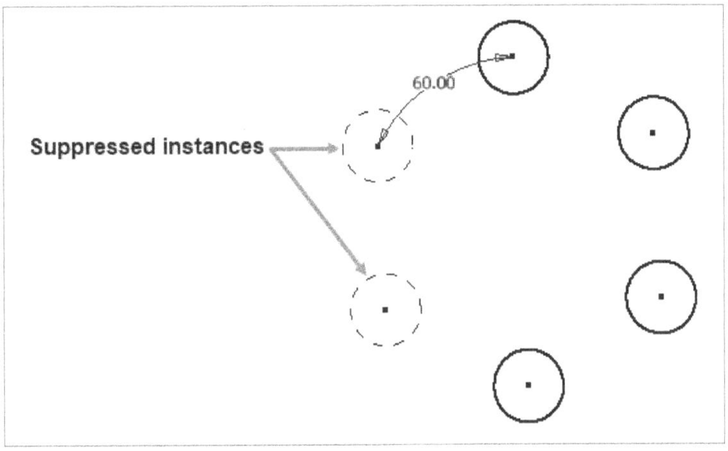

Figure-119. Circular pattern created

- Other parameters in the dialog box are same as discussed in previous tool.

Mirror tool

The **Mirror** tool is used to create a mirror copy of the selected entities. The procedure to use this tool is given next.

- Click on the **Mirror** tool from **Pattern** panel in the **Ribbon**. The **Mirror** dialog box will be displayed; refer to Figure-120. Also, you will be asked to select the entities.

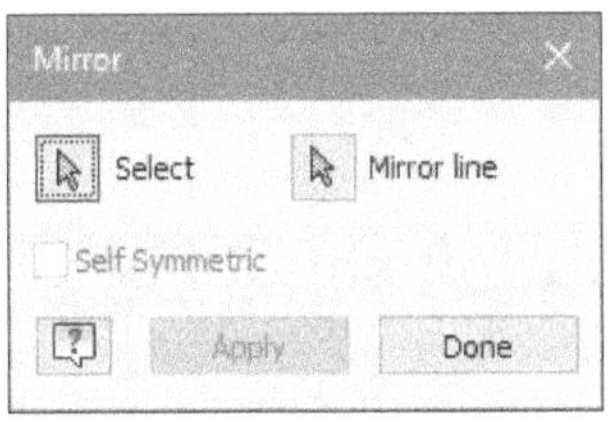

Figure-120. Mirror dialog box

- Select the entity/entities that you want to mirror copy and press **ENTER**. You will be asked to select a mirror line.
- Click on the line that you want to use as mirror line and click on the **Apply** button from the dialog box. The mirror copy will be created; refer to Figure-121.

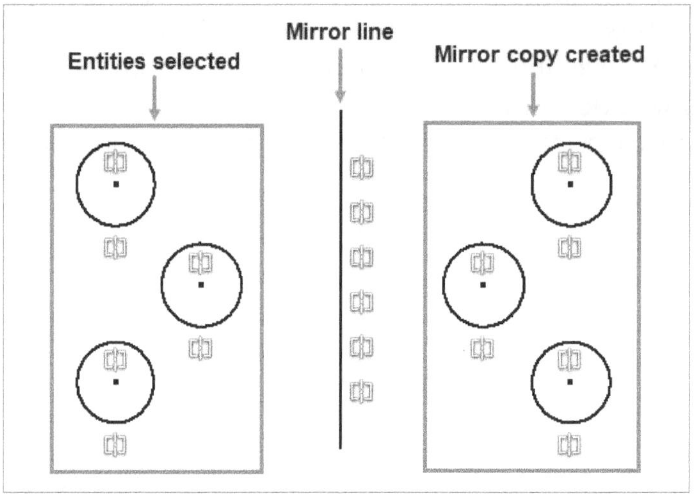

Figure-121. Creating mirror copy

- Click on the **Done** button from the dialog box to exit.

Till this point, we have discussed the tools related to sketching. But, sketches without dimensions and constraints are useless for engineers and designers. In next chapter, we will discuss tools related to dimensions and constraints and then we will work on some practical exercises.

SELF ASSESSMENT

Q1. Which of the following options should be selected first to start sketching environment?

a) Start 2D Sketch
b) Select Plane
c) Finish Sketch
d) Create line

Q2. While creating line, which button should be pressed to toggle between the two input boxes for specifying coordinates?

a) Enter
b) Shift
c) Ctrl
d) Tab

Q3. Which of the following options should be used to create an arc using the **Line** tool?

a) Click and hold the MMB
b) Click and hold the RMB
c) Click and hold the LMB
d) Press the LMB

Q4. By using which of the following options, you can create curve using an equation?

a) Line
b) Interpolation Spline
c) Equation Curve
d) Bridge Curve

Q5. Which of the following tools can be used to create an arc without reference points or an entity?

a) Control Vertex Spline
b) Center Point Arc
c) Tangent Arc
d) Three Point Arc

Q6. Which of the following tools can be used in creating a slot along the specified arc?

a) Overall Slot
b) Center to Center Slot
c) Center Point Slot
d) Center Point Arc Slot

Q7. By the help of which of the following tools, you can apply round at the sharp corners?

a) Chamfer
b) Fillet
c) Polygon
d) Ellipse

Q8. Which of the following is the smallest geometric entity available in any CAD package?

a) Point
b) Text
c) Geometry Text
d) Line

Q9. Which of the following tools is used to enlarge or diminish the entity by same proportion?

a) Extend
b) Stretch
c) Scale
d) Trim

Q10. Which of the following tools can be used to create enlarged or diminished copy of the selected entity?

a) Rectangular Pattern
b) Circular Pattern
c) Offset
d) Mirror

Q11. While creating circular pattern feature, you can skip desired instances of pattern by using the .... button.

Q12. The .... tool is used to create slot by specifying total length of slot and width of slot.

REVIEW QUESTIONS

Q1. What is the purpose of sketching in 3D modeling?
A. To color the model
B. To finalize the design
C. To define the foundation of a 3D model
D. To print the model

Q2. Where are the sketching tools located in Autodesk Inventor?
A. Tools tab
B. File menu
C. Sketch tab of the Ribbon
D. View tab

Q3. What is the main function of a sketching plane in CAD software?
A. To color geometry
B. To provide printing options
C. To act as a foundation for creating other geometries
D. To save the file

Q4. Which of the following is NOT a default plane in Autodesk Inventor?
A. XY Plane
B. YZ Plane
C. XZ Plane
D. ZXZ Plane

Q5. On which plane should geometry seen from the Front view be drawn?
A. XZ Plane
B. YZ Plane
C. XY Plane
D. Any random plane

Q6. What is the first step in starting a 2D sketch?
A. Click Finish Sketch
B. Select dimensions
C. Click the Start 2D Sketch tool
D. Select Line tool

Q7. What appears in the modeling area when you enter the 2D sketch environment?
A. 3D model
B. Axis constraints
C. Horizontal and vertical reference lines
D. Background color options

Q8. Which panel contains sketch creation tools?
A. Tools panel
B. Edit panel
C. Create panel
D. View panel

Q9. What must be done to stop creating consecutive lines using the Line tool?
A. Press TAB
B. Click Finish Sketch
C. Press ESC
D. Click on View tab

Q10. What tool allows you to create an arc tangent to the previous line?
A. Interpolation Spline
B. Tangent Circle
C. Three Point Arc
D. Line tool (click & drag after line creation)

Q11. How do you switch between coordinate input boxes when drawing a line?
A. Click directly
B. Press ESC
C. Press TAB
D. Double-click input box

Q12. How can you change the unit system for the model?
A. Through View tab
B. Using Sketch tab
C. Via Document Settings in Tools tab
D. Using the Print Settings dialog

Q13. Which tool creates a spline controlled by vertices?
A. Interpolation Spline
B. Control Vertex Spline
C. Bridge Curve
D. Equation Curve

Q14. What is used to modify the shape of a spline created by control vertices?
A. Dimension tool
B. Dragging any control vertex
C. Mirror tool
D. Sketch Constraints

Q15. How does the Interpolation Spline differ from the Control Vertex Spline?
A. Uses straight lines
B. Passes through specified points
C. Requires arcs only
D. Can only be created in 3D

Q16. What is required to create a curve using the Equation Curve tool?
A. Center and radius
B. Three points
C. Start and end points
D. Mathematical functions x(t) and y(t), tmin and tmax

Q17. Which tool connects two existing curves?
A. Equation Curve
B. Control Vertex Spline
C. Bridge Curve
D. Tangent Arc

Q18. How is the start or end point of a Bridge Curve determined?
A. Center of the sketch
B. Based on the midpoint of curves
C. Depends on where you click on the curves
D. Always the end of the first selected curve

Q19. What does the Center Point Circle tool require first?
A. Radius
B. Diameter
C. Center point
D. Endpoints

Q20. How can you switch from entering diameter to radius for a circle?
A. Use the View menu
B. Click on the circle twice
C. Right-click in modeling area and select Radius
D. Enter “R” in the input box

Q21. What is the minimum number of lines required to create a Tangent Circle?
A. One
B. Two
C. Three
D. Four

Q22. What does the Ellipse tool require to create an ellipse?
A. A spline
B. Two circles
C. Center point, axis end point, circumferential point
D. Just center and diameter

Q23. What type of arc does the Three Point Arc tool create?
A. Tangent arc
B. Arc with center and radius
C. Arc passing through three specified points
D. Circular arc only

Q24. What tool is used to create an arc tangent to an existing entity?
A. Center Point Arc
B. Interpolation Spline
C. Tangent Arc
D. Three Point Arc

Q25. What is the purpose of the Center Point Arc tool?
A. To connect lines
B. To mirror geometry
C. To create arc using center and span angle
D. To create fillets

Q26. What is the first step in using the Two Point Rectangle tool?
A. Set the length
B. Select the plane
C. Specify the first corner point
D. Draw a circle

Q27. What is the first step when using the Three Point Rectangle tool?
A. Specify the center point
B. Specify the third corner point
C. Specify the first corner point
D. Enter dimensions in the edit box

Q28. Which rectangle tool requires a center point and a corner point to create a rectangle?
A. Three Point Rectangle
B. Two Point Center Rectangle
C. Three Point Center Rectangle
D. Center to Center Slot

Q29. In the Three Point Center Rectangle tool, what is the second input required after selecting the center point?
A. Width of the rectangle
B. Height of the rectangle
C. Second point of centerline
D. Corner point

Q30. Which tool is used to create a slot by defining two center points and a width?
A. Overall Slot
B. Three Point Arc Slot
C. Center to Center Slot
D. Center Point Arc Slot

Q31. What input is required to define an Overall Slot?
A. Radius and angle
B. Center and corner
C. Length and width
D. Centerline and arc

Q32. What is the first step when using the Center Point Slot tool?
A. Specify the end point
B. Enter the angle
C. Specify the center point
D. Specify slot width

Q33. The Three Point Arc Slot tool requires how many main inputs before specifying the width?
A. One
B. Two
C. Three
D. Four

Q34. In the Center Point Arc Slot tool, which point is selected after specifying the arc's center?
A. End point
B. Width
C. Start point
D. Midpoint

Q35. Which button should be selected to create a polygon inscribed in a construction circle?
A. Circumscribed
B. Inside
C. Inscribed
D. Polygon

Q36. What does the Fillet tool apply to sharp corners?
A. A triangle
B. A round
C. A chamfer
D. A fillet box

Q37. When using the Chamfer tool, which option allows you to specify different lengths on both sides?
A. Distance
B. Distance x Angle
C. Distance 1 x Distance 2
D. Equal Distance

Q38. What is the primary use of the Text tool in sketches?
A. To draw dimensions
B. To create labels for CAM engraving
C. To measure distance
D. To apply textures

Q39. What is the first step in using the Geometry Text tool?
A. Type the text
B. Set the font
C. Select geometry
D. Specify center point

Q40. What is a Point used for in sketches?
A. Dimensioning lines
B. Applying text
C. Reference for other entities
D. Creating 3D models

Q41. Which tool allows movement of sketch entities and has an option to create a copy?
A. Fillet
B. Chamfer
C. Move
D. Text

Q42. What is the primary function of the Copy tool?
A. Rotate selected entities
B. Create a copy of selected entities
C. Split entities into parts
D. Enlarge sketch entities

Q43. What must be selected first when using the Copy tool?
A. The base point
B. The placement location
C. The entities to copy
D. The copy option

Q44. How can multiple copies be created using the Copy tool?
A. By pressing ENTER multiple times
B. By selecting multiple base points
C. By clicking Done repeatedly
D. By specifying more than one placement point

Q45. What does the Rotate tool allow you to do with selected entities?
A. Copy in linear pattern
B. Mirror along an axis
C. Rotate around a pivot point
D. Extend to a reference

Q46. What are the two ways of window selection mentioned for the Rotate tool?
A. Cross and Window selection
B. Free and Fixed selection
C. Box and Lasso selection
D. Manual and Auto selection

Q47. What option must be selected to create a rotated copy of an entity?
A. Base Point
B. Rotate Preview
C. Apply
D. Copy check box

Q48. Which tool is used to remove unwanted sections of a sketch?
A. Trim
B. Extend
C. Offset
D. Split

Q49. What appears when hovering over a sketch entity with the Trim tool?
A. A red box
B. A dashed line
C. A pop-up message
D. A green arrow

Q50. What does the Extend tool do?
A. Shortens a curve
B. Cuts part of a curve
C. Joins two entities by extending
D. Creates a duplicate line

Q51. How do you specify where to split an entity using the Split tool?
A. Enter a value
B. Use angle input
C. Select near a snap point
D. Click and drag

Q52. What does the Scale tool do to selected entities?
A. Stretches them at an angle
B. Breaks them into parts
C. Enlarges or diminishes them proportionally
D. Converts them to 3D

Q53. What kind of values are invalid for the Scale Factor?
A. Values over 10
B. Values less than 1
C. Decimal values
D. Negative values

Q54. What is the function of the Stretch tool?
A. Move entities along X-axis
B. Join two sketch lines
C. Create fillet on entities
D. Stretch components between base and end point

Q55. What action allows you to stretch a constrained sketch?
A. Ignore confirmation
B. Click "Yes" in confirmation box
C. Use Copy instead
D. Press ESC

Q56. What is the primary purpose of the Offset tool?
A. Create multiple rotated copies
B. Join two curves
C. Create an enlarged/diminished copy at set distance
D. Delete unwanted entities

Q57. Which value determines the spacing in Rectangular Pattern?
A. Count
B. Radius
C. Spacing
D. Angle

Q58. What option allows patterns to be fitted within a total span in Circular Pattern?
A. Angle span
B. Count
C. Suppress
D. Fitted check box

Q59. What is used as a reference for axis in Circular Pattern?
A. Pattern boundary
B. Reference line or axis
C. Sketch text
D. Origin point

Q60. What does the Suppress button do in pattern tools?
A. Moves the pattern
B. Deletes extra copies
C. Hides selected pattern instances
D. Duplicates pattern

Q61. What does the Mirror tool require to create a mirrored copy?
A. Center point
B. Base point
C. Mirror line
D. Pivot axis

Chapter 3

Dimensioning and Constraining

Topics Covered

The major topics covered in this chapter are:

- ***Introduction to Dimensioning***
- ***Dimensioning Tools***
- ***Introduction to Constraints***
- ***Constrain tools***
- ***Formatting tools***
- ***Inserting objects in sketch***

INTRODUCTION TO DIMENSIONING

Dimensions are used to specify shape and size of entities. Dimensions in sketch environment should not be confused with dimensions in engineering drawing as they can be represented in same way or in a different way. Purpose of dimensions in sketch is to constrain the size and shape of object whereas purpose of dimensions in drawing is to represent engineering intent of the component for manufacturer. You will learn about drawing dimensions later in the book. Here, we will discuss the use of dimensioning tools in sketch.

DIMENSIONING TOOLS

The tools to apply dimensions are given in **Constrain** panel of the **Sketch** tab; refer to Figure-1. The dimensioning tools in this panel are discussed next.

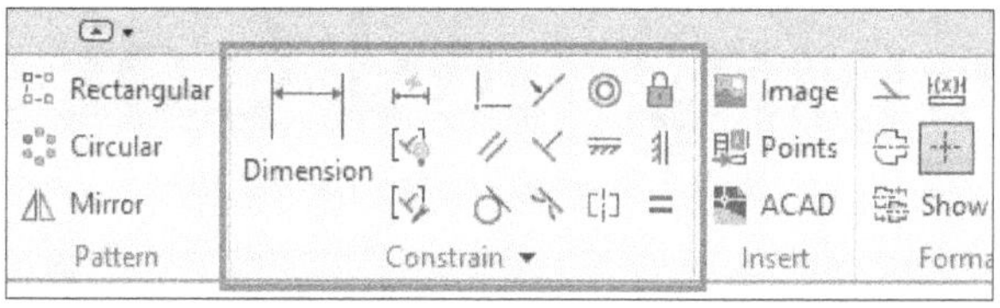

Figure-1. Constrain panel

General Dimension Tool

The **General Dimension** tool is used to apply almost all type of dimensions possible in sketching. Since this single tool is applicable for dimensioning various entities, we will discuss the tool as per its applications.

Dimensioning Line

- Click on the **General Dimension** tool from **Constrain** panel in the **Ribbon**. You will be asked to select entities to be dimensioned.
- Click anywhere in the middle of line, a dimension will get attached to the cursor; refer to Figure-2.

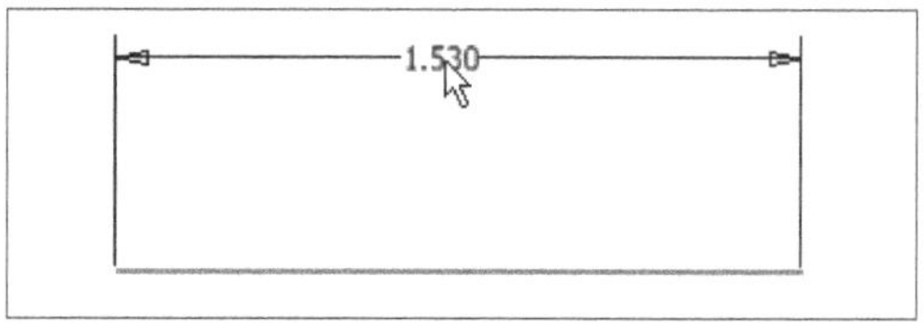

Figure-2. Dimension attached to cursor

- Click at desired location to place the dimension. The **Edit Dimension** dialog box will be displayed; refer to Figure-3.

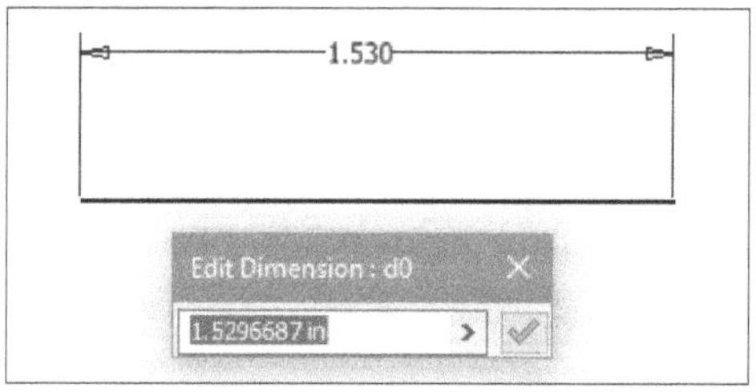

Figure-3. Edit Dimension dialog box

- Specify desired value of dimension and press **ENTER** to apply dimension.

Or

- After clicking on the **General Dimension** tool, one by one click on the end points of the line. Preview of dimension will be displayed; refer to Figure-4.

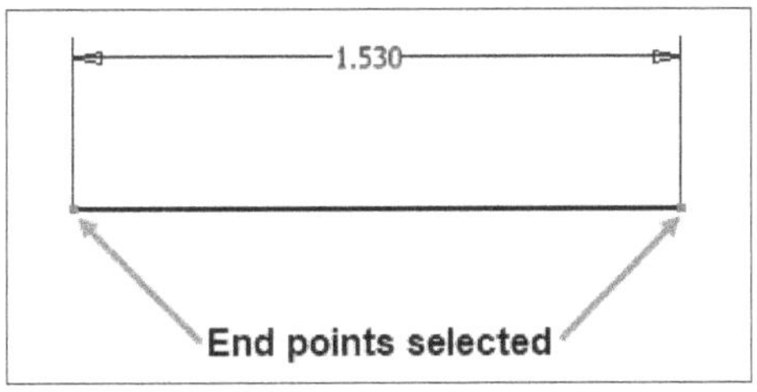

Figure-4. End points of line

- Click to place the dimension and enter desired value in the dialog box displayed.

Aligned Dimension

- After selecting the **General Dimension** tool, click anywhere on the inclined line. Preview of dimension will be displayed as either horizontal dimension or vertical dimension; refer to Figure-5.

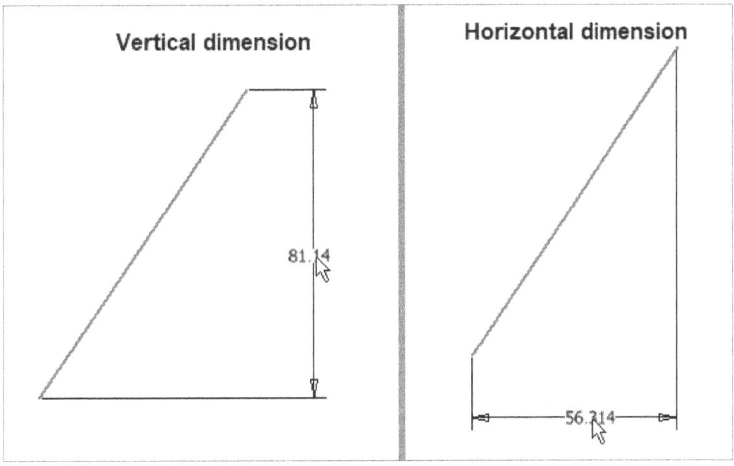

Figure-5. Preview of dimension for inclined line

- Right-click in the drawing area when dimension is attached to the cursor. A shortcut menu will be displayed; refer to Figure-6.

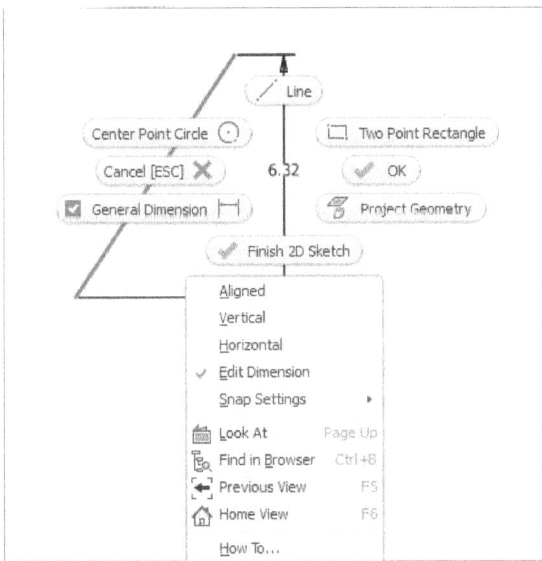

Figure-6. Shortcut menu for dimension

- Click on the **Aligned** option from the shortcut menu. The aligned dimension will get attached to the cursor; refer to Figure-7.

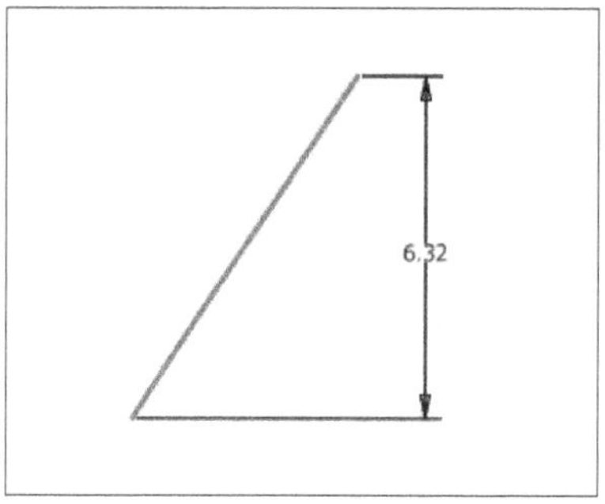

Figure-7. Aligned dimension attached to cursor

- Click at desired location to place the dimension. The **Edit Dimension** dialog box will be displayed. Enter desired dimension value to assign the dimension.

Dimensioning Circle

- Click on the **General Dimension** tool from **Constrain** panel in the **Ribbon**. You will be asked to select entities to be dimensioned.
- Click anywhere on the circle. The diameter dimension will get attached to the cursor; refer to Figure-8.

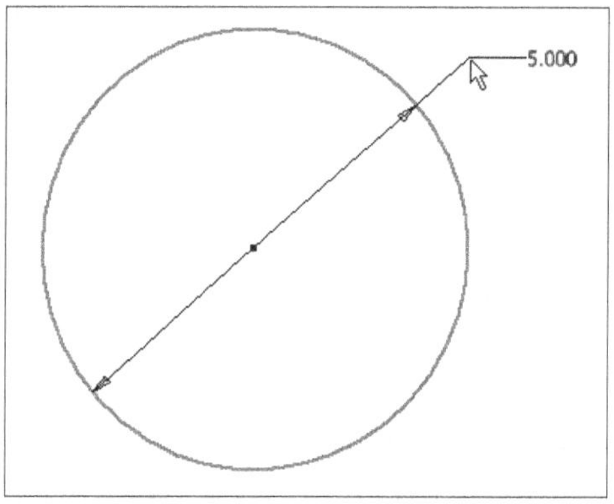

Figure-8. Diameter dimension attached to cursor

- Click at desired location to place the dimension. The **Edit Dimension** dialog box will be displayed; refer to Figure-9.

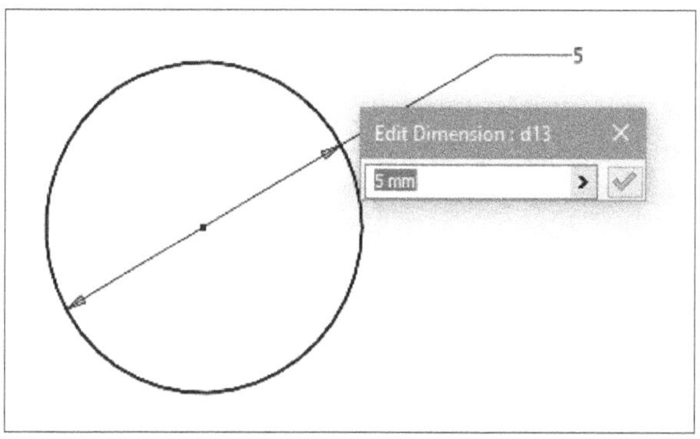

Figure-9. Edit Dimension dialog box for circle

- Enter desired value in the edit box. The dimension will be assigned.

Dimensioning Arc

- Click on the **General Dimension** tool from **Constrain** panel in the **Ribbon**. You will be asked to select entities to be dimensioned.
- Click anywhere on the arc. The radial dimension will get attached to the cursor; refer to Figure-10.

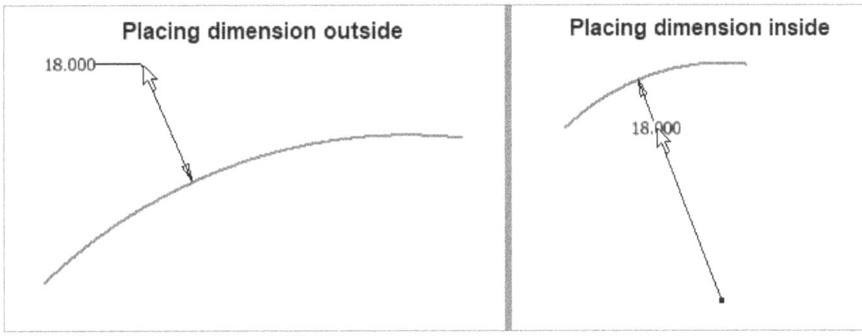

Figure-10. Preview of radial dimension

- Click at desired location to place the dimension. The **Edit Dimension** dialog box will be displayed.
- Enter desired value of dimension. The dimension will be applied to arc.

In the same way, you can assign dimensions to the other sketch entities.

Automatic Dimensions and Constraints

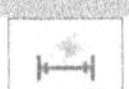 The **Automatic Dimensions and Constraints** tool, as the name suggests, is used to automatically apply dimensions and constraints to all the entities in the sketch. (No! This is not a tool of lazy people, this tool helps to make dimensioning process faster.) The procedure to use this tool is given next.

- Click on the **Automatic Dimensions and Constraints** tool from **Constrain** panel in the **Ribbon**. The **Auto Dimension** dialog box will be displayed; refer to Figure-11. Also, you will be asked to select the entities which are to be dimensioned.

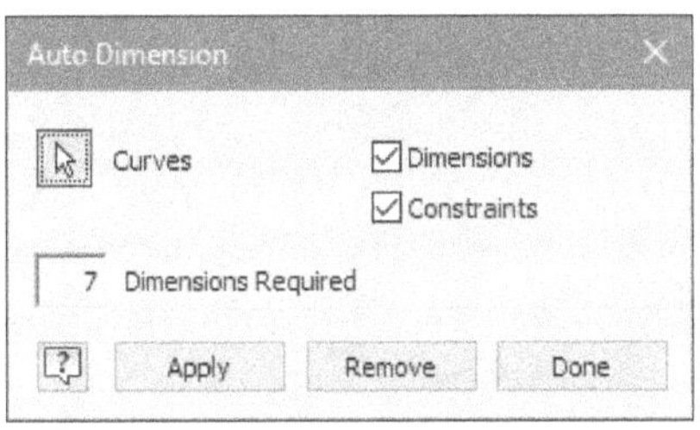

Figure-11. Auto Dimension dialog box

- Select all the entities that you want to dimension and click on the **Apply** button from the dialog box. The dimensions will be applied to the sketch; refer to Figure-12.

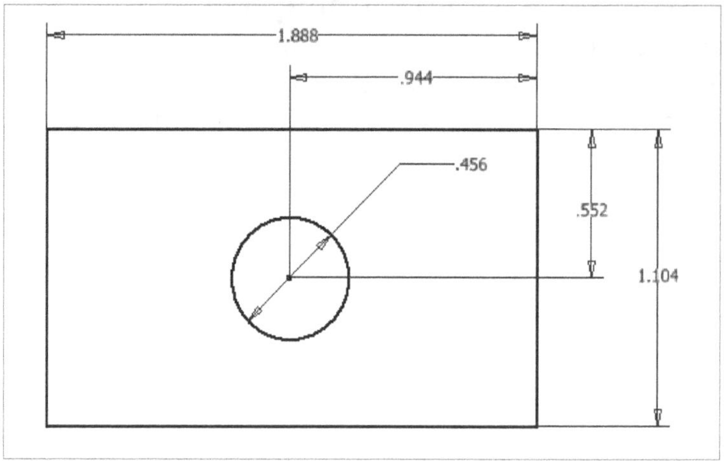

Figure-12. Dimensions applied automatically

- Click on the **Done** button from the dialog box and drag the dimensions to desired locations.

Show Constraints

The **Show Constraints** tool is used to display constraints of the selected sketch entities. The procedure of using this tool is given next.

- Click on the **Show Constraints** tool from **Constrain** panel in the **Ribbon**. You will be asked to select curve/point to display its constraint.
- Click on desired sketch entity. The constraints applied to the selected entity will be displayed; refer to Figure-13.

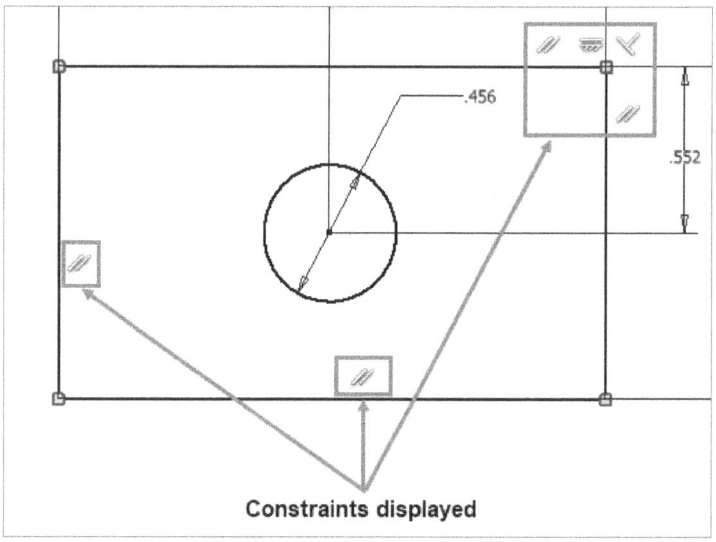

Figure-13. Constraints displayed

Since, we have displayed the constraints and will be using them now onwards, so let's have a brief introduction about them.

CONSTRAINTS

Constraints are used to compel the sketch to retain its shape and position. There are twelve type of constraints available in Autodesk Inventor. These constraints with their respective tools in Inventor are discussed next.

Coincident Constraint

The **Coincident** constraint makes the selected entity coincide with other line, arc, circle, ellipse, point, etc. The procedure to apply this constraint is given next.

- Click on the **Coincident Constraint** button from **Constrain** panel in the **Ribbon**. You will be asked to select first curve/point.
- Select the first curve/point. You will be asked to select second curve/point.
- Select the second curve/point. The two curves/points will become coincident; refer to Figure-14.

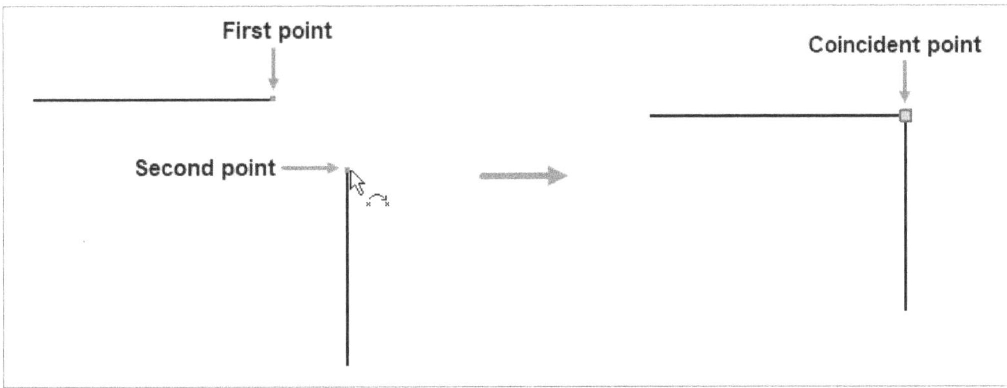

Figure-14. Making points coincident

Collinear Constraint

The **Collinear Constraint** tool is used to make the two or more selected entities collinear. The procedure to use this tool is given next.

- Click on the **Collinear Constraint** tool from **Constrain** panel in the **Ribbon**. You will be asked to select the first line segment or axis.
- Click on the first line segment or axis. You will be asked to select the second line segment or axis.
- Click on the second line segment/axis. The selected entities will become collinear; refer to Figure-15.

Figure-15. Making lines collinear

Concentric Constraint

The **Concentric Constraint** tool is used to make any two of circles, arcs, or ellipses share the same center point. The procedure to use this tool is given next.

- Click on the **Concentric Constraint** tool from **Constrain** panel in the **Ribbon**. You will be asked to select first circle, arc, or ellipse.

- Click on the first circle, arc, or ellipse. You will be asked to select the second circle/arc/ellipse.
- Click on the second circle/arc/ellipse. Both the entities will become concentric; refer to Figure-16.

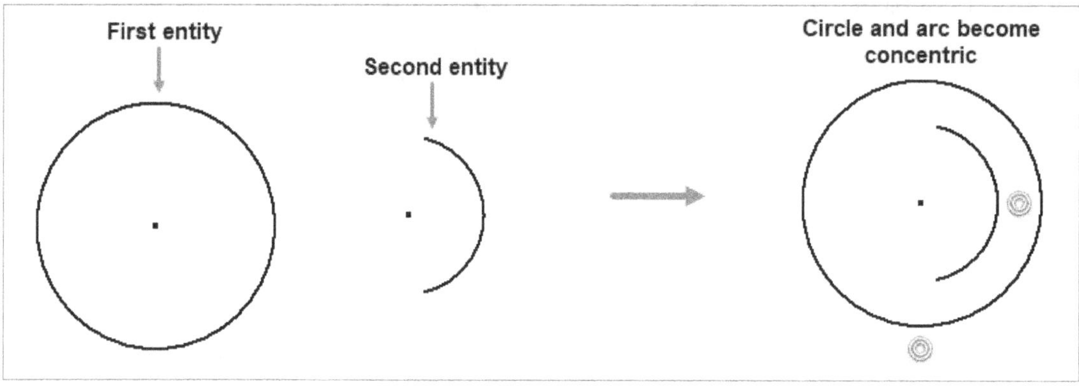

Figure-16. Making entities concentric

Fix Constraint

The **Fix Constraint** tool is used to fix the selected curves/points at their current position with respect to system coordinate system. The procedure to use this constraint is given next.

- Click on the **Fix** tool from **Constrain** panel in the **Ribbon**. You will be asked to select the curve/point which you want to fix.
- Select the curve/point, a lock icon will be attached to the curve/point marking it as fixed; refer to Figure-17.

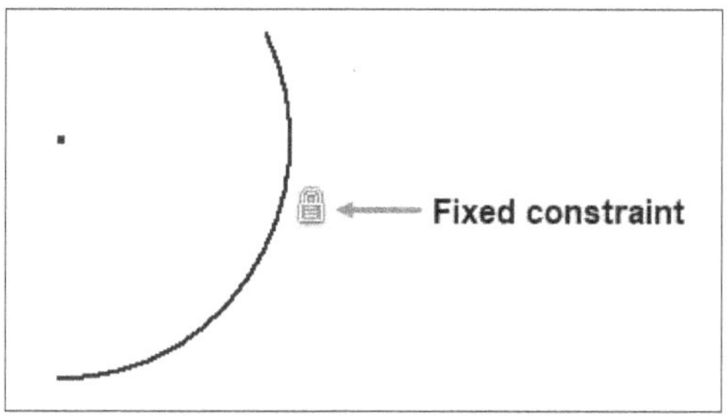

Figure-17. Applying fixed constraint

Parallel Constraint

The **Parallel Constraint** tool is used to make linear geometries parallel to each other. The procedure to make the entities parallel is given next.

- Click on the **Parallel Constraint** tool from **Constrain** panel in the **Ribbon**. You will be asked to select the first line/axis.
- Click on the first line/axis. You will be asked to select the second line/axis.
- Click on the second line/axis. The two lines/axes will become parallel to each other; refer to Figure-18.

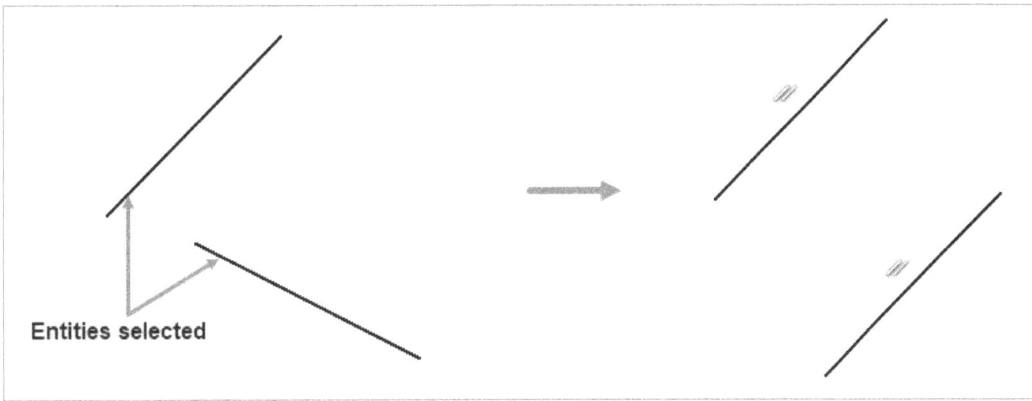

Figure-18. Applying parallel constraint

Perpendicular Constraint

 The **Perpendicular Constraint** tool is used to make geometries perpendicular to each other. The procedure to make the entities perpendicular is given next.

- Click on the **Perpendicular Constraint** tool from **Constrain** panel in the **Ribbon**. You will be asked to select the first sketch entity.
- Click on the first sketch entity. You will be asked to select the second sketch entity.
- Click on the second sketch entity. The two entities will become perpendicular to each other; refer to Figure-19. Note that you can make arc, line, circle, ellipse, and spline handles perpendicular to each other.

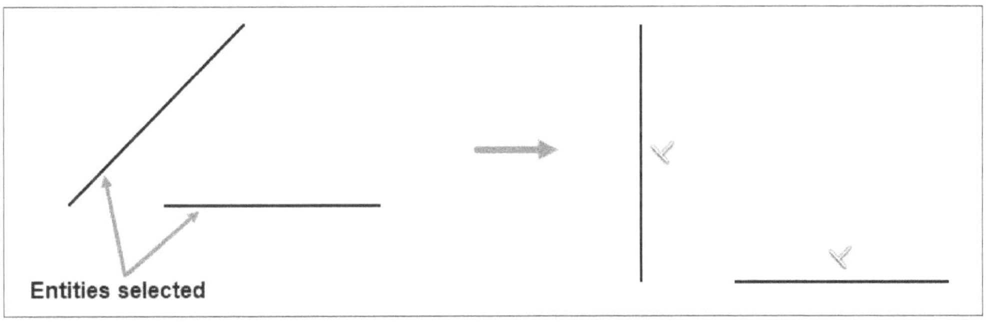

Figure-19. Applying perpendicular constraint

Horizontal Constraint

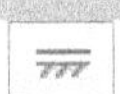 The **Horizontal Constraint** tool is used to make geometries horizontal or two points at the same horizontal level. The procedure to apply Horizontal constraint is given next.

- Click on the **Horizontal Constraint** tool from **Constrain** panel in the **Ribbon**. You will be asked to select the line/axis or point of first entity.
- Click on the line/axis. It will become horizontal.
- To make the two points at same level, click on the first point and then the second point. Both the points will become at same level; refer to Figure-20.

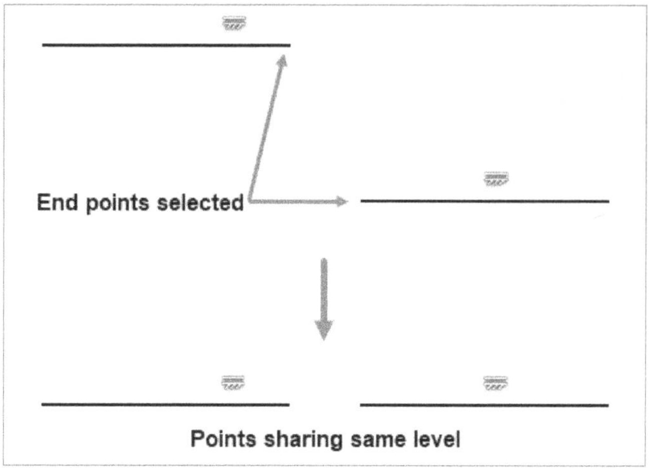

Figure-20. Making points at same level

Vertical Constraint

The **Vertical Constraint** tool is used to make geometries vertical or two points at the same vertical level. The procedure to apply Vertical constraint is given next.

- Click on the **Vertical Constraint** tool from **Constrain** panel in the **Ribbon**. You will be asked to select the line/axis or point of first entity.
- Click on the line/axis. It will become vertical.
- To make the two points at same level, click on the first point and then the second point. Both the points will become at same level; refer to Figure-21.

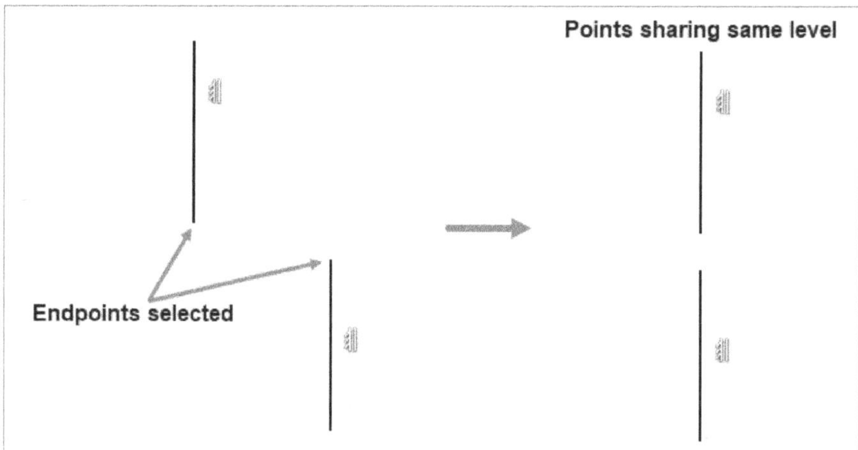

Figure-21. Making points at same level

Tangent Constraint

The **Tangent Constraint** tool is used to make selected curves tangent to the other curve. The procedure to apply this constraint is given next.

- Click on the **Tangent** tool from **Constrain** panel in the **Ribbon**. You will be asked to select the first curve.
- Click on the first curve. You will be asked to select the second curve.
- Click on the second curve. The curves will become tangent to each other; refer to Figure-22.

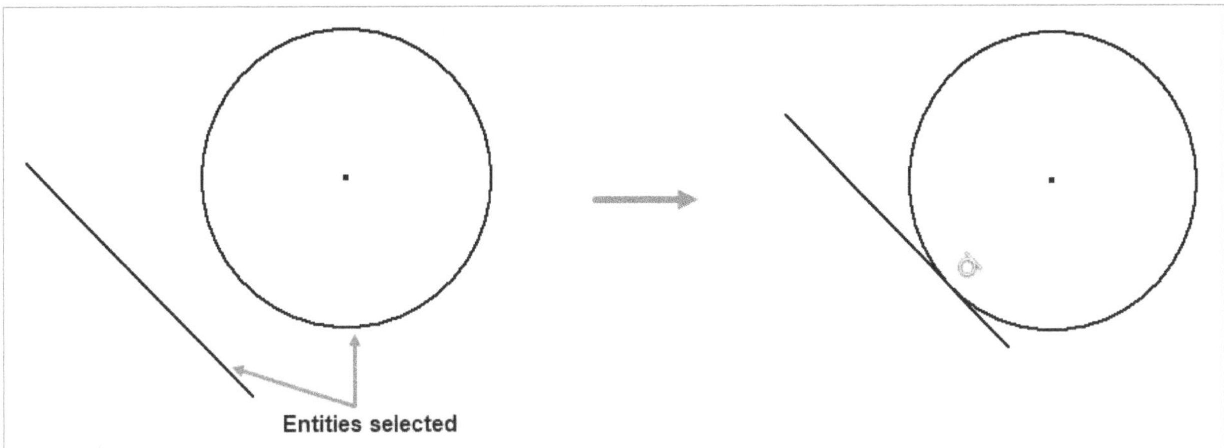

Figure-22. Applying tangent constraint

Smooth (G2) Constraint

The **Smooth (G2) Constraint** tool is used to smoothen the spline by applying curvature continuous condition (G2) on it. The procedure to apply this constraint is given next.

- Click on the **Smooth (G2)** tool from **Constrain** panel in the **Ribbon**. You will be asked to select the first curve.
- Select the first curve. You will be asked to select the second curve.
- Select the spline that you want to smoothen. The Smooth constraint will be applied to the spline; refer to Figure-23.

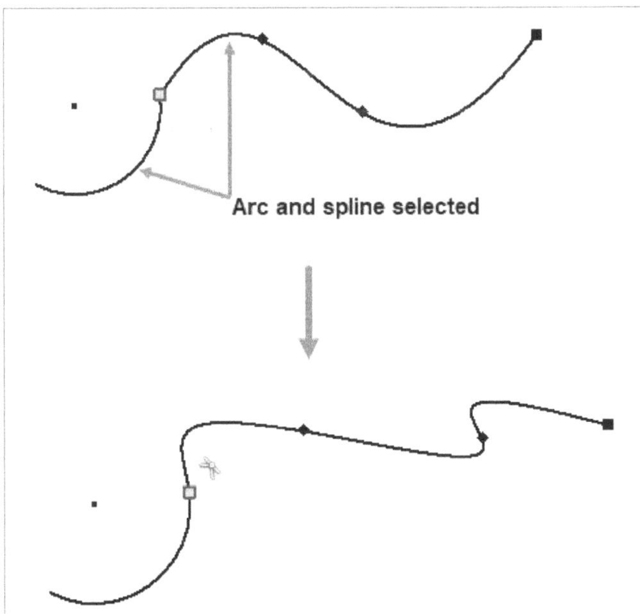

Figure-23. Applying smooth constraint

Symmetric Constraint

The **Symmetric Constraint** is used to make two entities symmetric about a reference line. The procedure to apply this constraint is given next.

- Click on the **Symmetric** tool from **Constrain** panel in the **Ribbon**. You will be asked to select the first curve.

- Select the first curve. You will be asked to select the second curve.
- Select the second curve. You will be asked to select the centerline.
- Click on the centerline. Both the curves will become symmetric with respect to the centerline; refer to Figure-24.

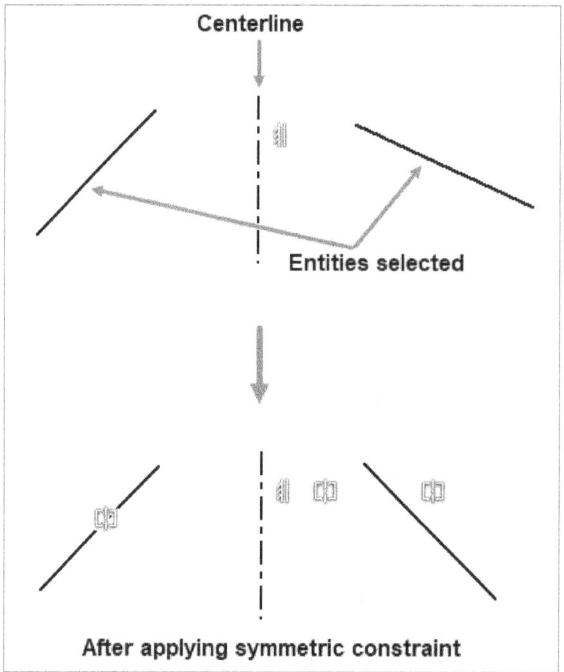

Figure-24. Applying symmetric constraint

Equal Constraint

The **Equal Constraint** is used to make the two selected entities equal in size. The procedure to apply this constraint is given next.

- Click on the **Equal** tool from **Constrain** panel in the **Ribbon**. You will be asked to select the first curve.
- Select the first curve. You will be asked to select the second curve.
- Select the second curve. Both the curves will become equal in size; refer to Figure-25.

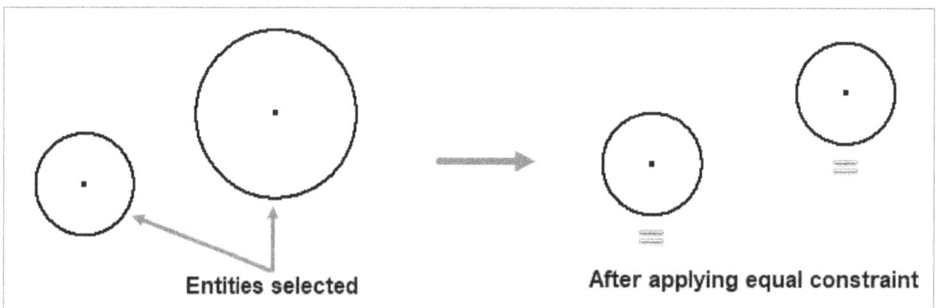

Figure-25. Applying equal constraint

There are a few settings that should be taken care of while applying constraints in sketch. The tool to change these settings is discussed next.

Constraint Settings

The **Constraint Settings** tool is used to change the settings and parameters related to constraint. The procedure to use this tool is given next.

- Click on the **Constraint Settings** tool from **Constrain** panel in the **Ribbon**. The **Constraint Settings** dialog box will be displayed; refer to Figure-26.

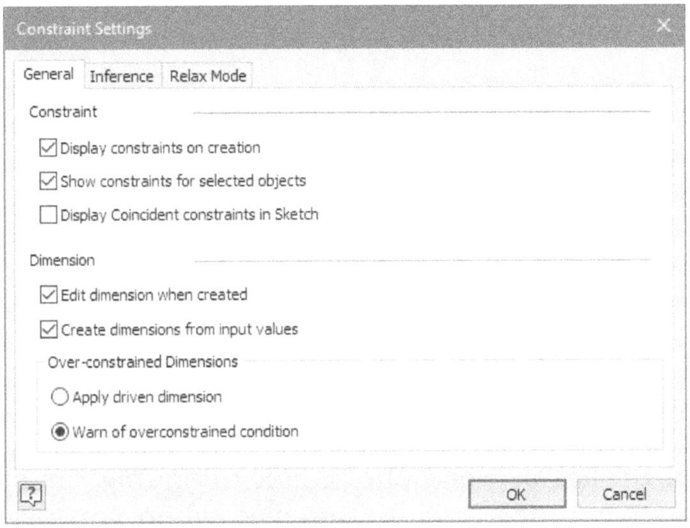

Figure-26. Constraint Settings dialog box

- Select desired check boxes to display respective constraints.
- From the **Dimension** area, select the check boxes to enable editing and assignment of dimension of sketch entity during creation.
- Similarly, select desired radio button from the **Over-constrained Dimensions** area of the dialog box to set solution in case of over-constraining of dimensions.

Inference tab

- Click on the **Inference** tab from the dialog box to display options related to inferencing of constraints (automatic constraining of the entity based on its position and orientation); refer to Figure-27.

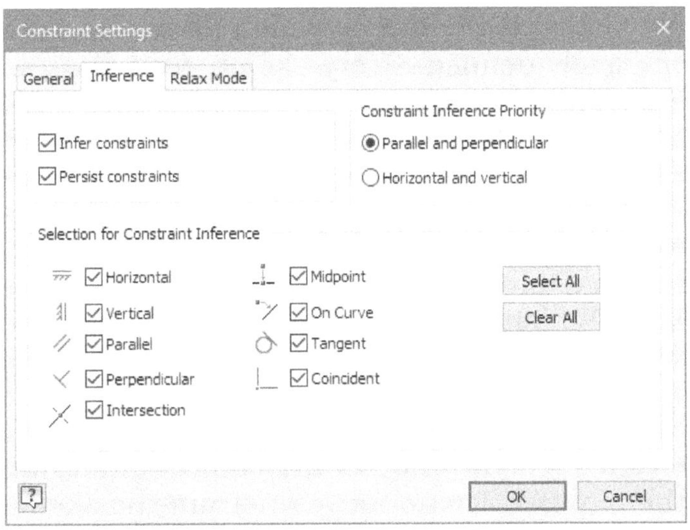

Figure-27. Inference tab in Constraint Settings dialog box

- Select only those check boxes from the dialog box that you want to apply to the sketch entities while creating them.

Relax Mode

- Click on the **Relax Mode** tab from the dialog box to modify settings related to relax mode; refer to Figure-28.

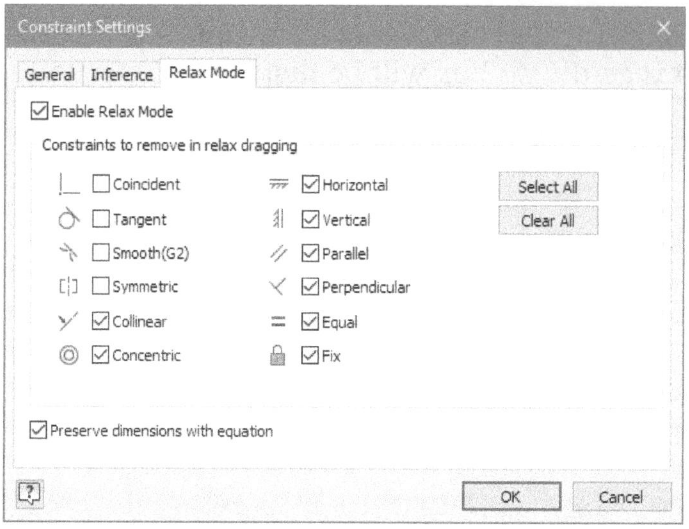

Figure-28. Relax Mode tab in the Constraint Settings dialog box

- Click on the **Enable Relax Mode** check box to enable the relax mode. In relax mode, constraints are automatically removed when you drag the sketch entity by using its key points.
- Select the check boxes against the constraints that you want to be removed in relax mode editing.
- Click on the **OK** button from the dialog box to apply the settings related to constraints.

Concept of Over-constrained, Fully constrained, and Under-constrained

Ah! A new topic, all of a sudden!! Actually, the topic is related to constraining. There are three ways a sketch is constrained; Fully constrained, Over-constrained, and Under-constrained.

Fully Constrained

The Fully constrained sketch is the one in which all the degrees of freedom of each sketch entity are completely defined. Every sketch entity has six degree of freedom denoting rotation and translation in each direction (X direction, Y direction, and Z direction). Once you fix all the degrees of freedom of the entity then it can neither be rotated nor translated in any of the direction.

Under-Constrained

The Under constrained sketch is the one in which some degrees of freedom of the entities are not defined. Which means they are free to move or rotate in directions that are not frozen by constraining their degrees of freedom.

Over-Constrained

The Over constrained sketch is the one in which more constraints are applied on the sketch entity than the required one to fully constrain the sketch.

After understanding the details above, you should always try to fully constrain the sketch, so that it always retains the shape and size which is required as per the drawing or client. Now, question that arises here in some curious minds is, How do I know that my sketch is fully constrained or not? Answer to the question is: check the Bottom Bar of Inventor; refer to Figure-29. In this figure, the sketch is fully dimensioned and constrained, so fully constrained is displayed in the Bottom Bar. If there is any dimension or constrained required then the number of dimensions required to fully define the sketch are displayed in the Bottom Bar; refer to Figure-30.

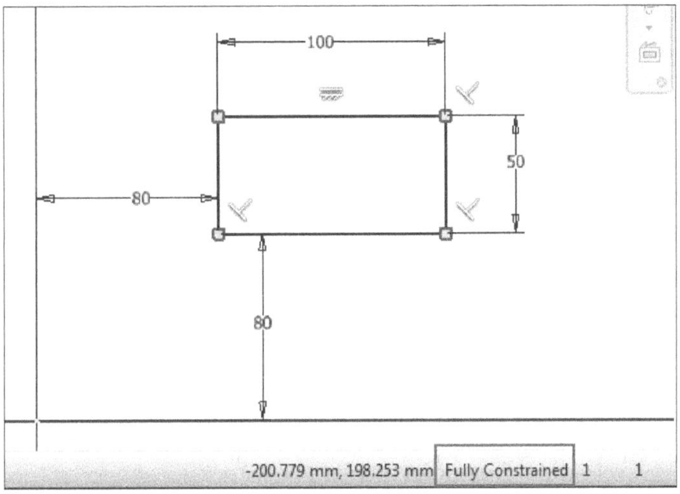

Figure-29. Identifying constrain condition

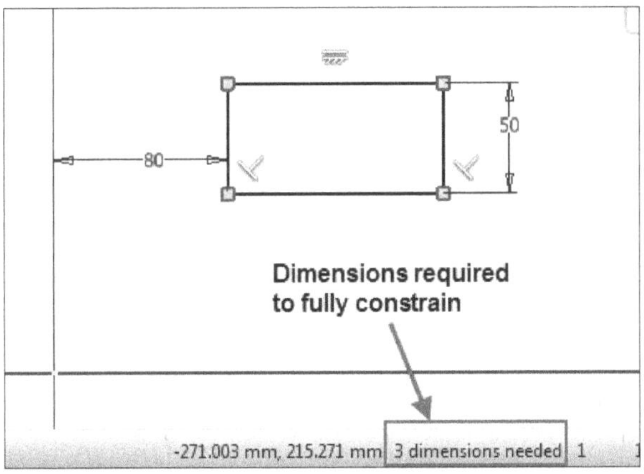

Figure-30. Dimensions required to fully constrain

There are a few miscellaneous tools in the **Insert** panel of **Sketch** tab that are helpful in sketching. These tools are discussed next.

INSERTING OBJECTS IN SKETCH

The tools to insert objects of other software in current sketch are available in the **Insert** panel of **Sketch** tab in the **Ribbon**; refer to Figure-31. There are three tools in this panel which are discussed next.

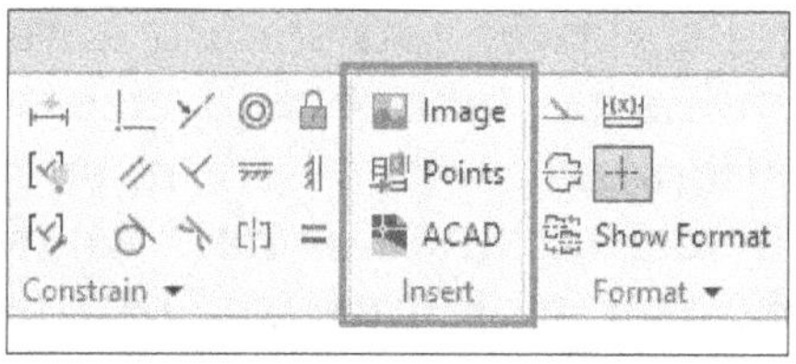

Figure-31. Insert panel

Insert Image Tool

Image The **Insert Image** tool is used to insert image in the current sketch. Using the image, you can create outline of the sketch using the edges of component in the image (photograph). The procedure to use this tool is given next.

- Click on the **Insert Image** tool from **Insert** panel in the **Ribbon**. The **Open** dialog box will be displayed; refer to Figure-32.

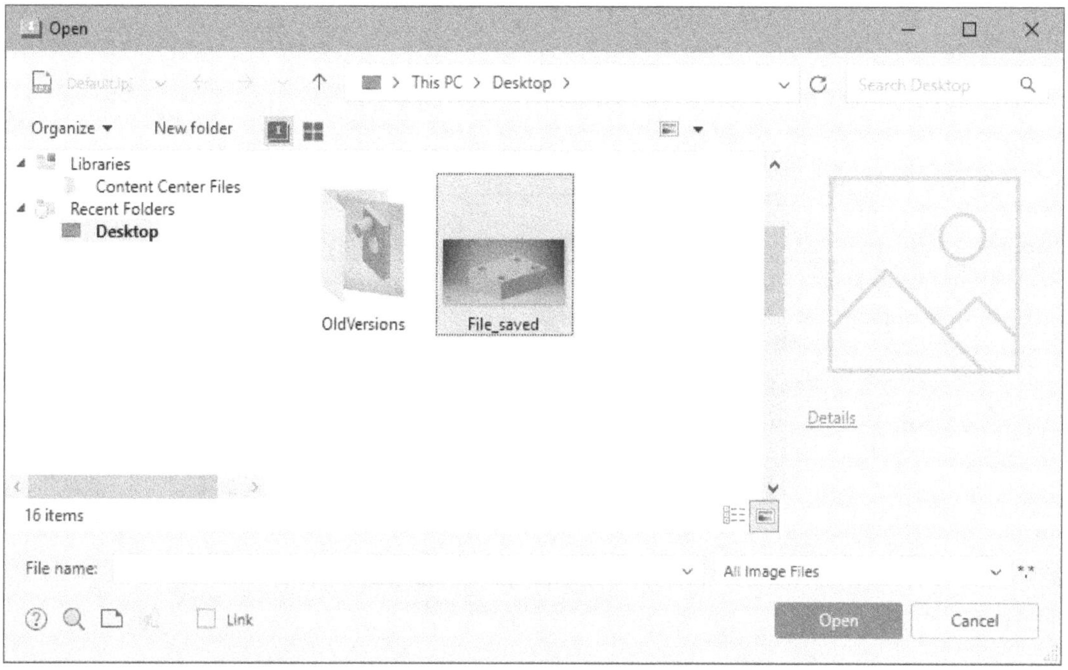

Figure-32. Open dialog box for inserting image

- Double-click on the image file that you want to use in the sketch. The image box will get attached to the cursor; refer to Figure-33.

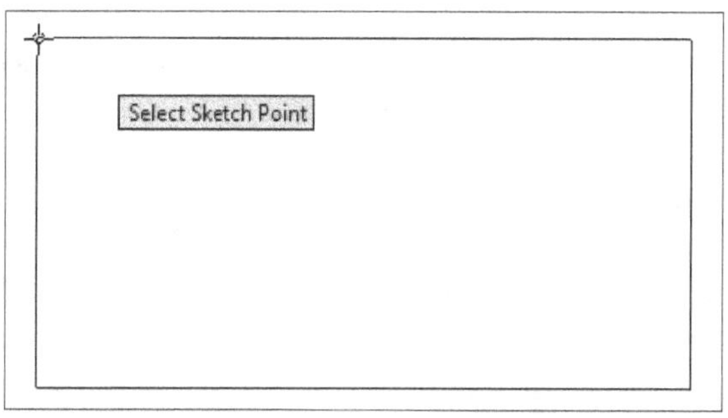

Figure-33. Image box attached to cursor

- Click at desired location to place the image. If the file location is not in folder of active project then a warning box will be displayed asking you to confirm that you want to open the file from its current location.

- Click on the **OK** button from the warning box. The image file will be placed at the specified location. Press **ESC** to exit the tool.

Import Points tool

The **Import Points** tool is used to insert points with the help of excel spreadsheet. The procedure to use this tool is given next.

- Click on the **Import Points** tool from **Insert** panel in the **Ribbon**. The **Open** dialog box will be displayed for selecting the Excel file.
- Select the file which has coordinates of points defined in it in the format as shown in Figure-34. The points will be created in the sketch; refer to Figure-35.

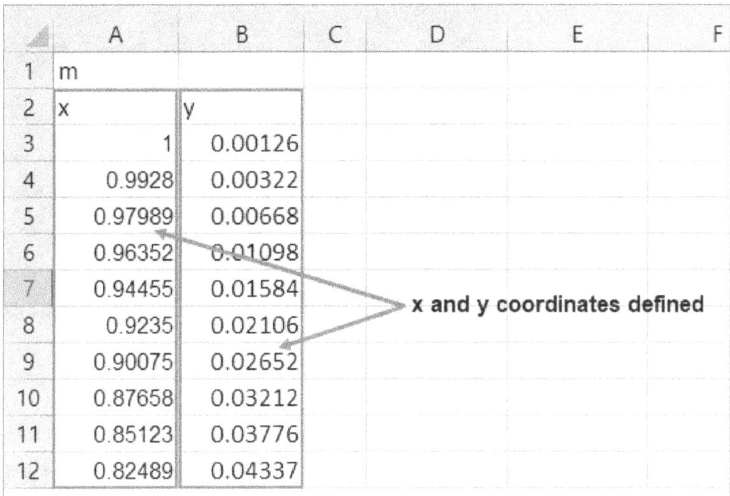

	A	B	C	D	E	F
1	m					
2	x	y				
3	1	0.00126				
4	0.9928	0.00322				
5	0.97989	0.00668				
6	0.96352	0.01098				
7	0.94455	0.01584				
8	0.9235	0.02106				
9	0.90075	0.02652				
10	0.87658	0.03212				
11	0.85123	0.03776				
12	0.82489	0.04337				

Figure-34. Example of spreadsheet

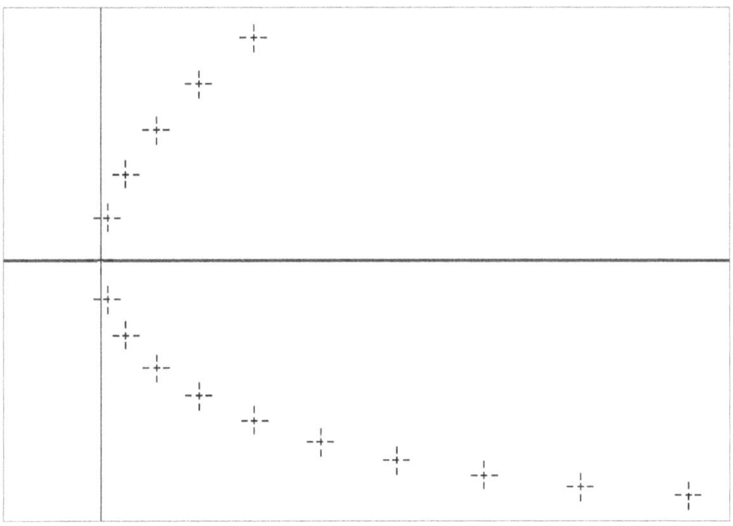

Figure-35. Points created in sketch

Insert AutoCAD File

Using the **Insert AutoCAD File** tool, you can insert a sketch made in AutoCAD into Inventor sketch. The procedure to use this tool is given next.

- Click on the **Insert AutoCAD File** tool from **Insert** panel in the **Ribbon**. The **Open** dialog box will be displayed prompting you to select AutoCAD drawing file.

- Double-click on desired AutoCAD file. The **Layers and Objects Import Options** dialog box will be displayed; refer to Figure-36.

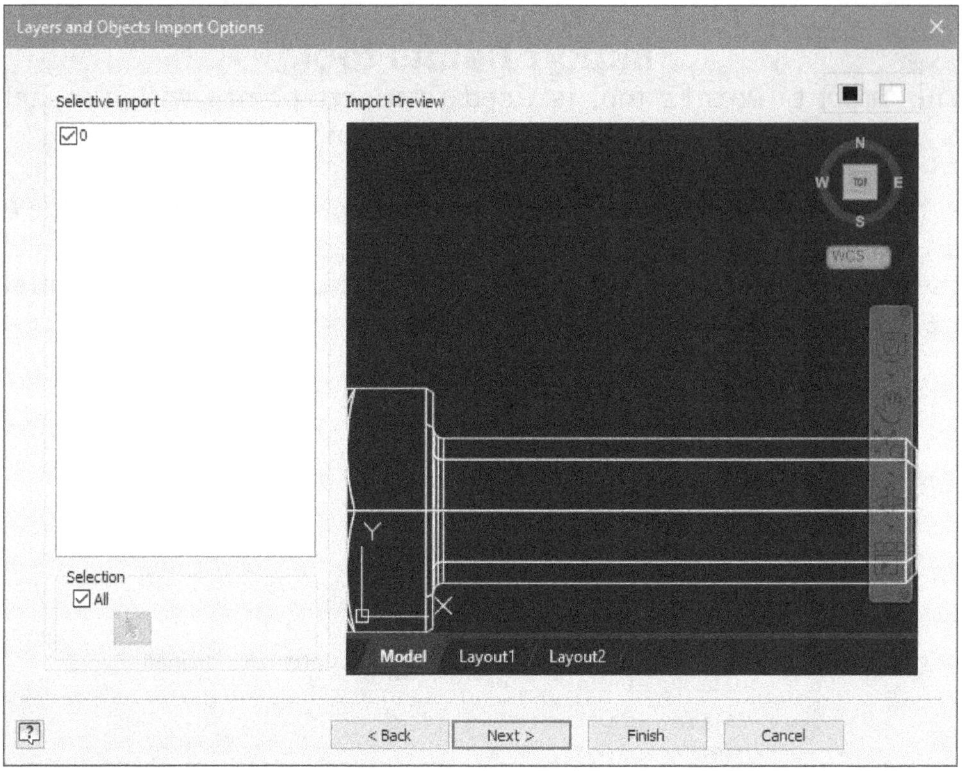

Figure-36. Layers and Objects Import Options dialog box

- Select the layers that you want to import in the sketch and click on the **Finish** button. The objects on selected layers will be inserted in the sketch automatically.

Till this point, we have covered all the important tools required for sketching. I want you to revise all the tools discussed so far with practical implementations. Now, you will work on some practical problems.

PRACTICAL 1

In this practical, we will create a sketch as shown in Figure-37.

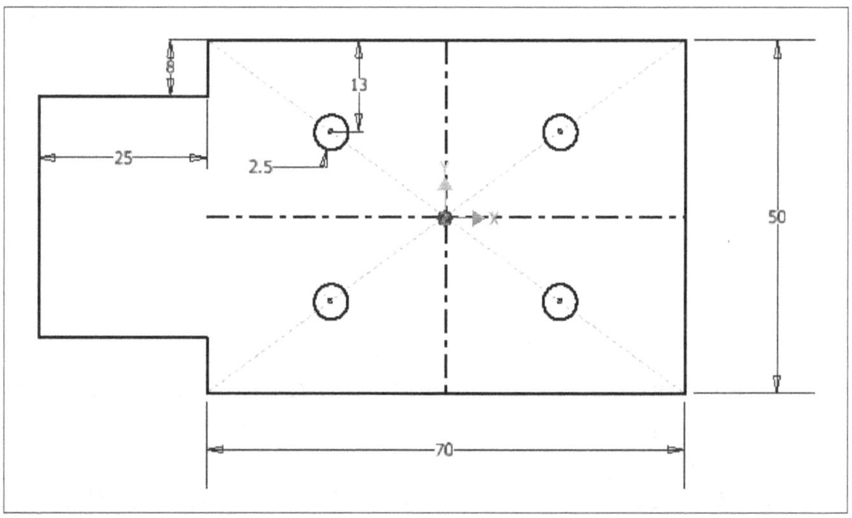

Figure-37. Practical 1

The sketch shown in this figure is not actual drawing that you will get in industry. This sketch is just to help you start in sketching.

Starting Sketch

- Start Autodesk Inventor by double-clicking on the Autodesk Inventor Professional icon from the desktop.
- Click on the **New** button from the **Quick Access Toolbar**. The **Create New File** dialog box will be displayed.
- Double-click on **Standard(mm).ipt** icon from the **Metric** template; refer to Figure-38. The Part environment of Autodesk Inventor will be displayed.

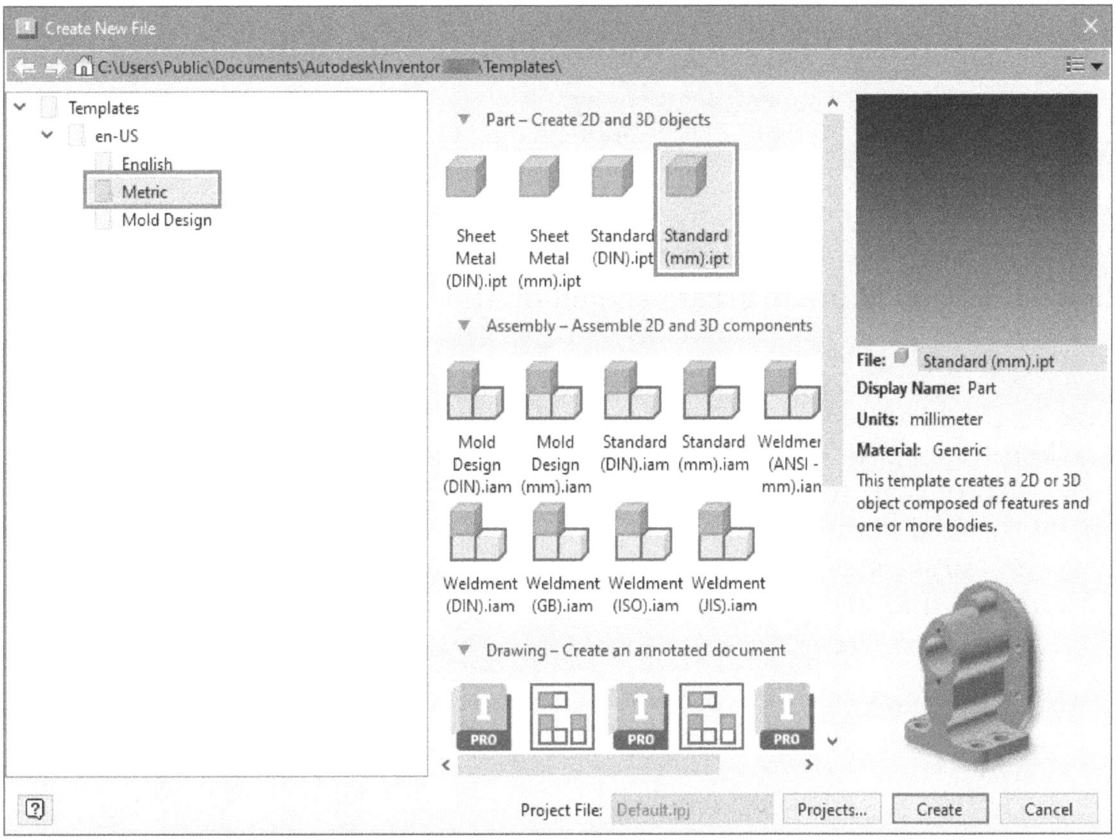

Figure-38. Standard(mm) icon in Create New File dialog box

- Click on the **Start 2D Sketch** button from **Sketch** panel in the **3D Model** tab of the **Ribbon**; refer to Figure-39. You will be asked to select a sketching plane; refer to Figure-40.

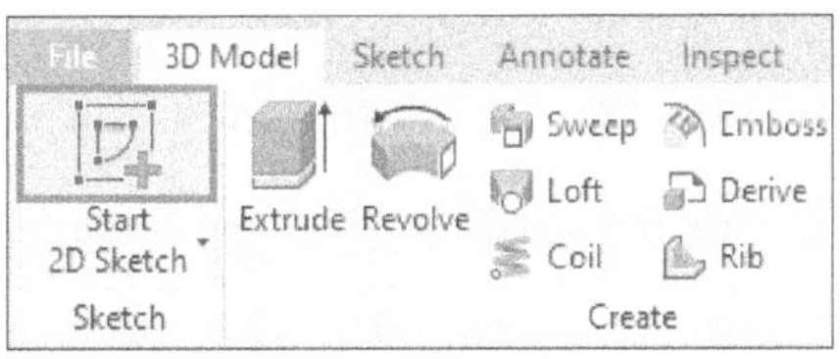

Figure-39. Start 2D Sketch button

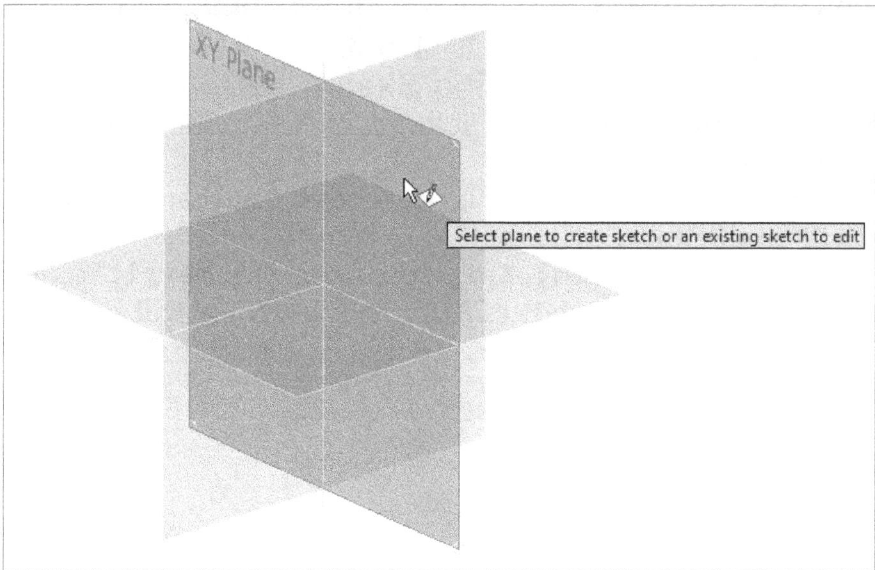

Figure-40. Selecting sketching plane

- Click on desired plane to create sketch on it.

Creating outer loop

- Click on the **Line** tool from **Create** panel in the **Sketch** tab of the **Ribbon**. You will be asked to specify the starting point of the line.
- Click at the origin to specify the starting point of the line. You will be asked to specify the end point of the line.
- Move the cursor straight towards right, type **70** in the input box displayed; refer to Figure-41 and press **ENTER**.

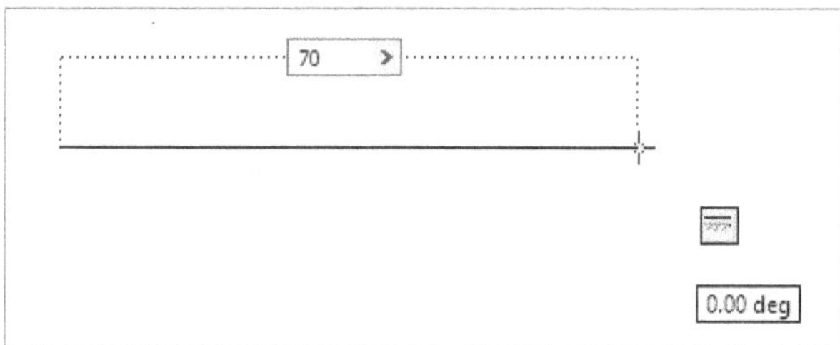

Figure-41. Specifying length of line

- Move the cursor vertically upwards and enter **50** in the input box displayed; refer to Figure-42.

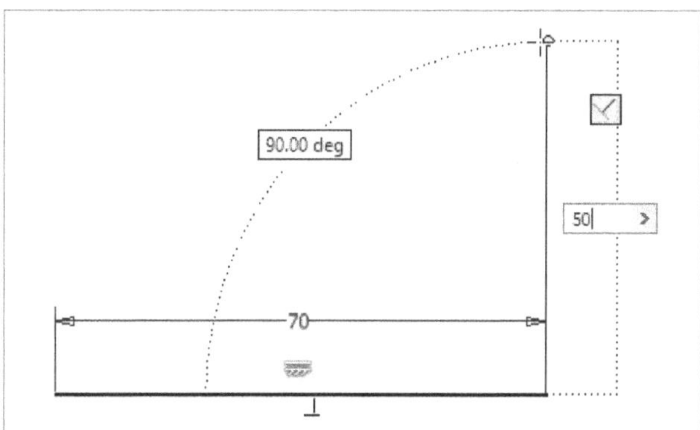

Figure-42. Specifying length of vertical line

- Move the cursor straight towards left and enter the value as **70** in the input box.

- Move the cursor vertically downward and enter the value as **8** in the input box.
- Similarly, create other lines of outer loop; refer to Figure-43.

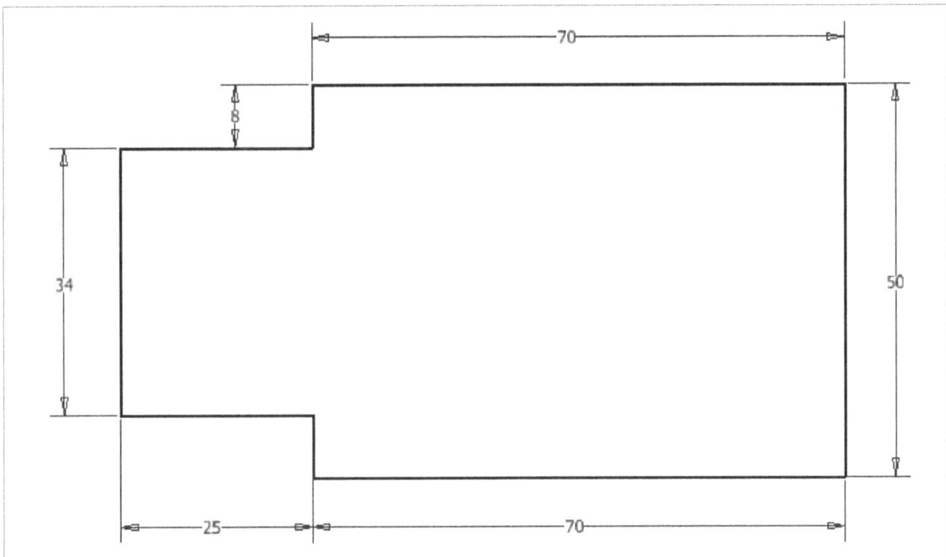

Figure-43. Outer loop

Creating Circles

- Click on the **Construction** button from **Format** panel in the **Sketch** tab of the **Ribbon**; refer to Figure-44. The sketch will be created in construction mode.

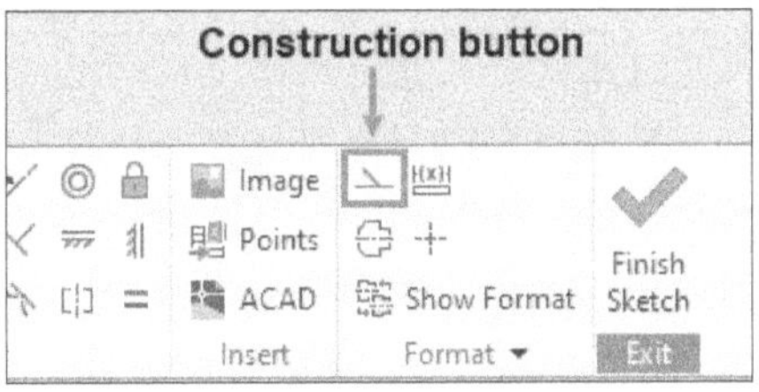

Figure-44. Construction button

- Click on the **Line** tool from **Create** panel in the **Sketch** tab of the **Ribbon**. Create a line as shown in Figure-45, joining the two corners of outer loop diagonally.

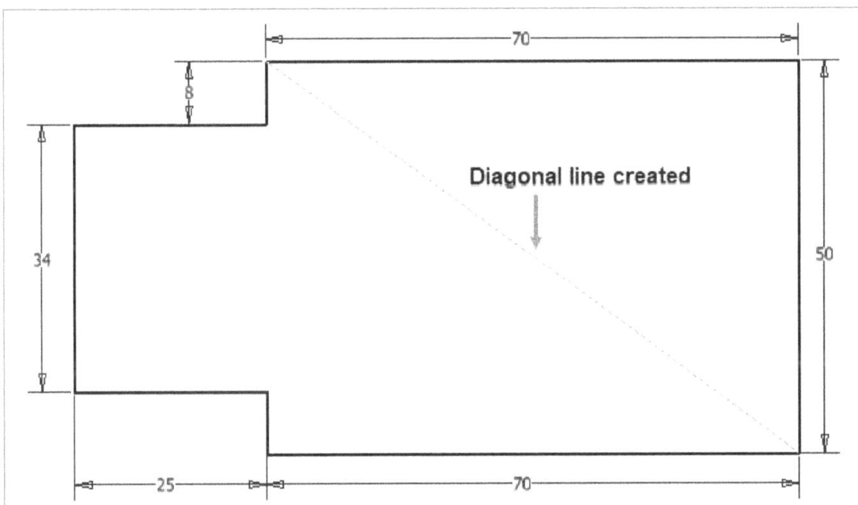

Figure-45. Creating diagonal line

- Similarly, create the other diagonal line; refer to Figure-46.

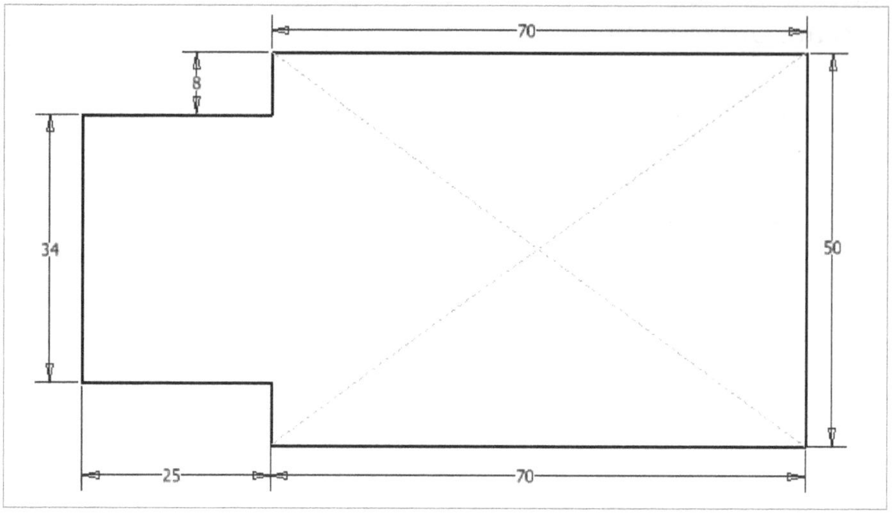

Figure-46. Creating diagonal construction lines

- Click again on the **Construction** button from **Format** panel in the **Sketch** tab to stop creating construction geometries.
- Click on the **Center Point Circle** tool from **Create** panel in the **Sketch** tab of the **Ribbon**. You will be asked to specify the center point of the circle.
- Click on the diagonal line to specify the center point of the circle; refer to Figure-47. You will be asked to specify the radius of circle.

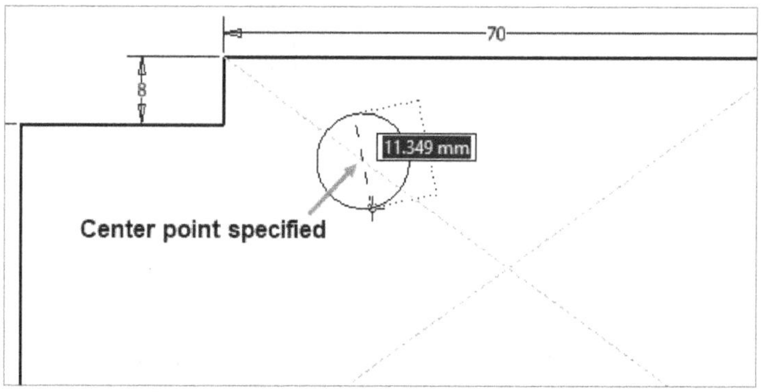

Figure-47. Specifying center point of circle

- Enter the value of radius as **2.5**.
- Click on the **Centerline** button from **Format** panel in the **Sketch** tab of the **Ribbon**; refer to Figure-48. Now, you can create center lines for the sketch.

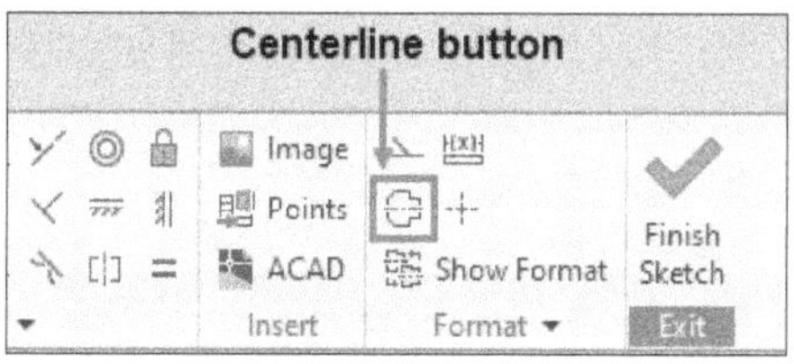

Figure-48. Centerline button

- Click on the **Line** tool from **Create** panel in the **Ribbon** and create the lines as shown in Figure-49. We will use these lines as mirror references.

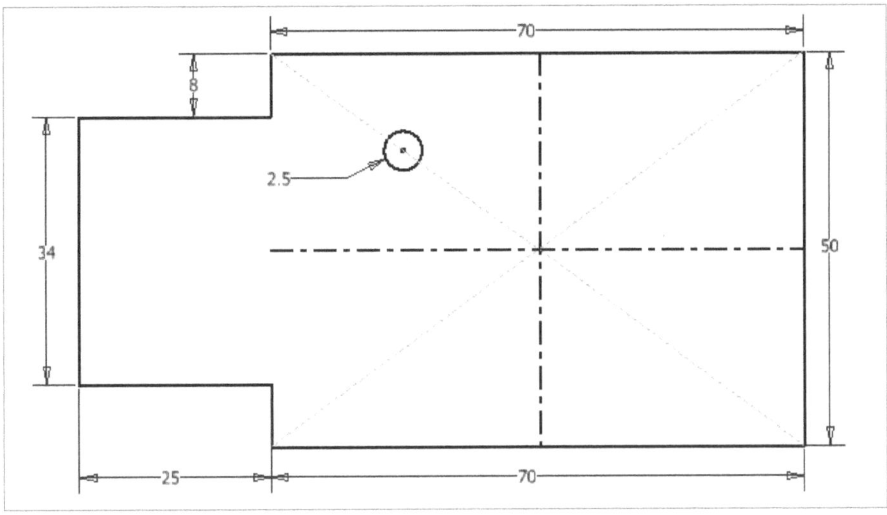

Figure-49. Centerlines created

- Click on the **Mirror** tool from the **Pattern** panel in the **Sketch** tab of **Ribbon**. The **Mirror** dialog box will be displayed and you will be prompted to select entity to mirror.
- Click on the circle created earlier; refer to Figure-50.

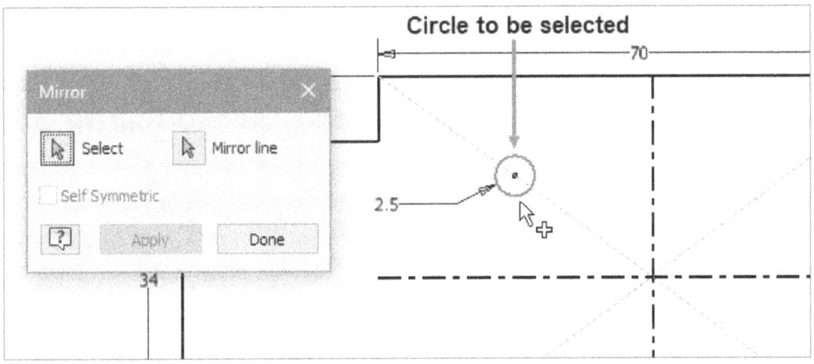

Figure-50. Circle to be selected

- Press **ENTER** and select the vertical centerline. The **Apply** button will become active in the **Mirror** dialog box.
- Click on the **Apply** button to create the mirror copy; refer to Figure-51.

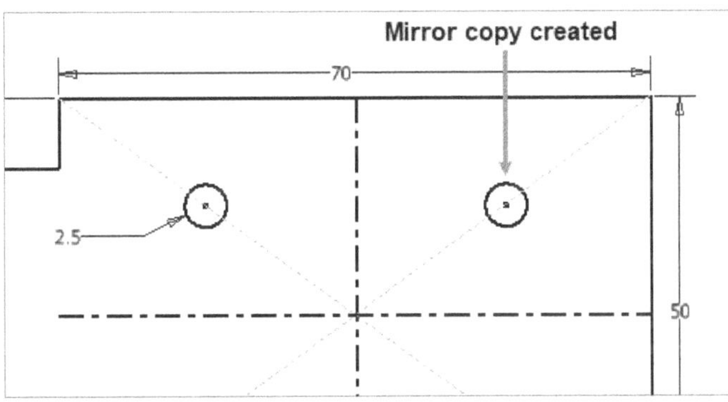

Figure-51. Mirror copy of circle

- Now, select both the circles and press **ENTER**. You will be prompted again to select a mirror line.

- Select the horizontal center line and click on the **Apply** button from the dialog box. The mirror copy of both the circles will be created as shown in Figure-52.

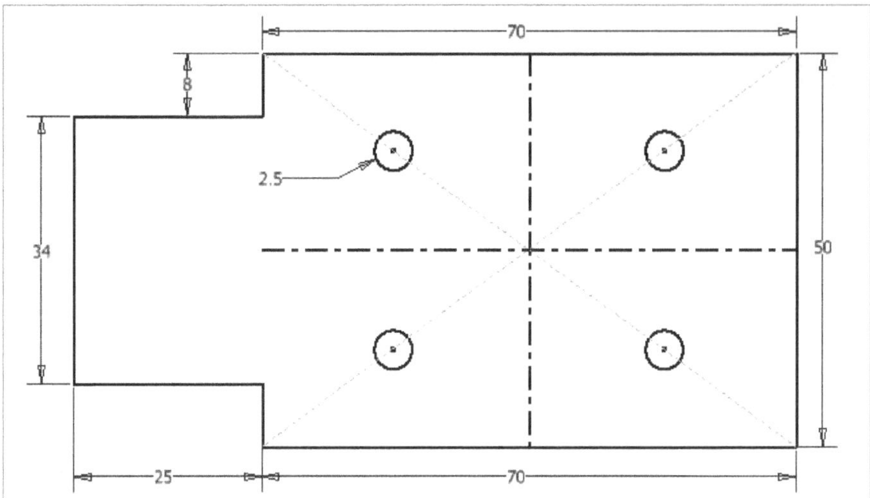

Figure-52. Mirror copies of circle

- Click on the **Done** button from the dialog box to exit the tool.

Applying Dimension to Circle

- Click on the **General Dimension** tool from **Constrain** panel in the **Sketch** tab of the **Ribbon**. You will be asked to select entities to dimension.
- Click on the center point of the circle created at first and then click on the horizontal line above the circle in outer loop; refer to Figure-53. The dimension will get attached to cursor.

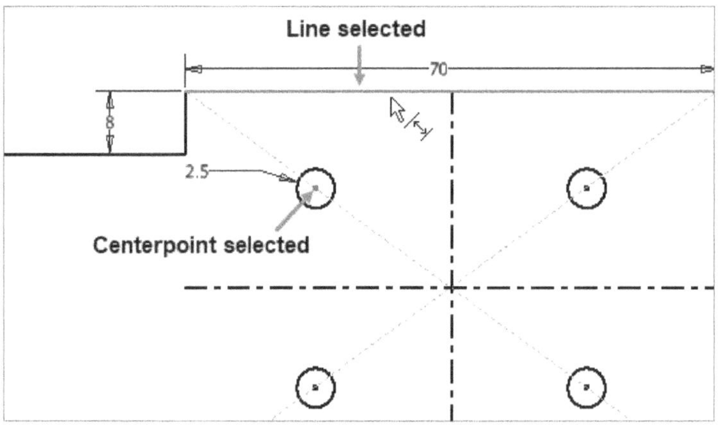

Figure-53. Entities selected for dimensioning

- Click at desired location to place the dimension. The **Edit Dimension** box will be displayed; refer to Figure-54.

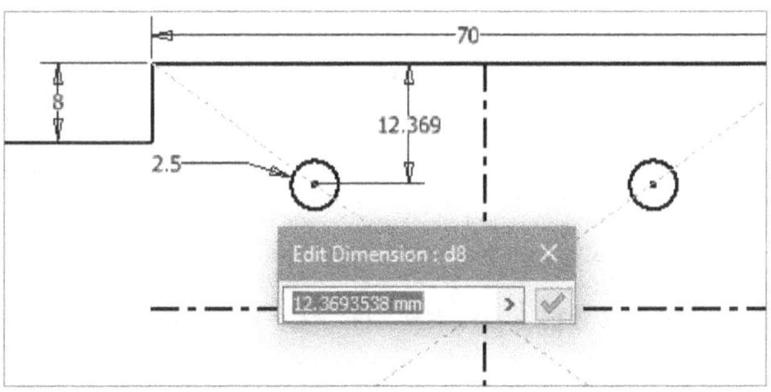

Figure-54. Dimension to edit

- Type the value as **13** and press **ENTER**. The selected circle and all the mirror copies will be dimensioned accordingly; refer to Figure-55.

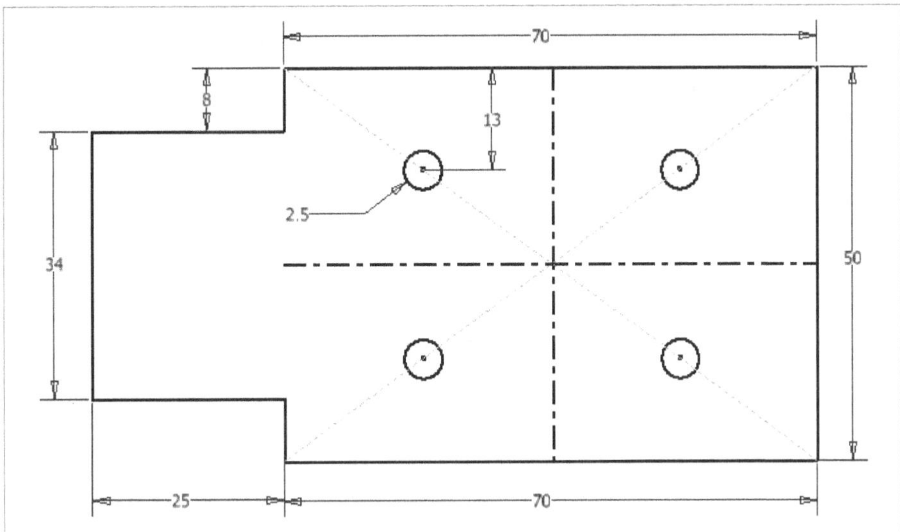

Figure-55. Final sketch of Practical 1

PRACTICAL 2

Create a sketch as shown in Figure-56.

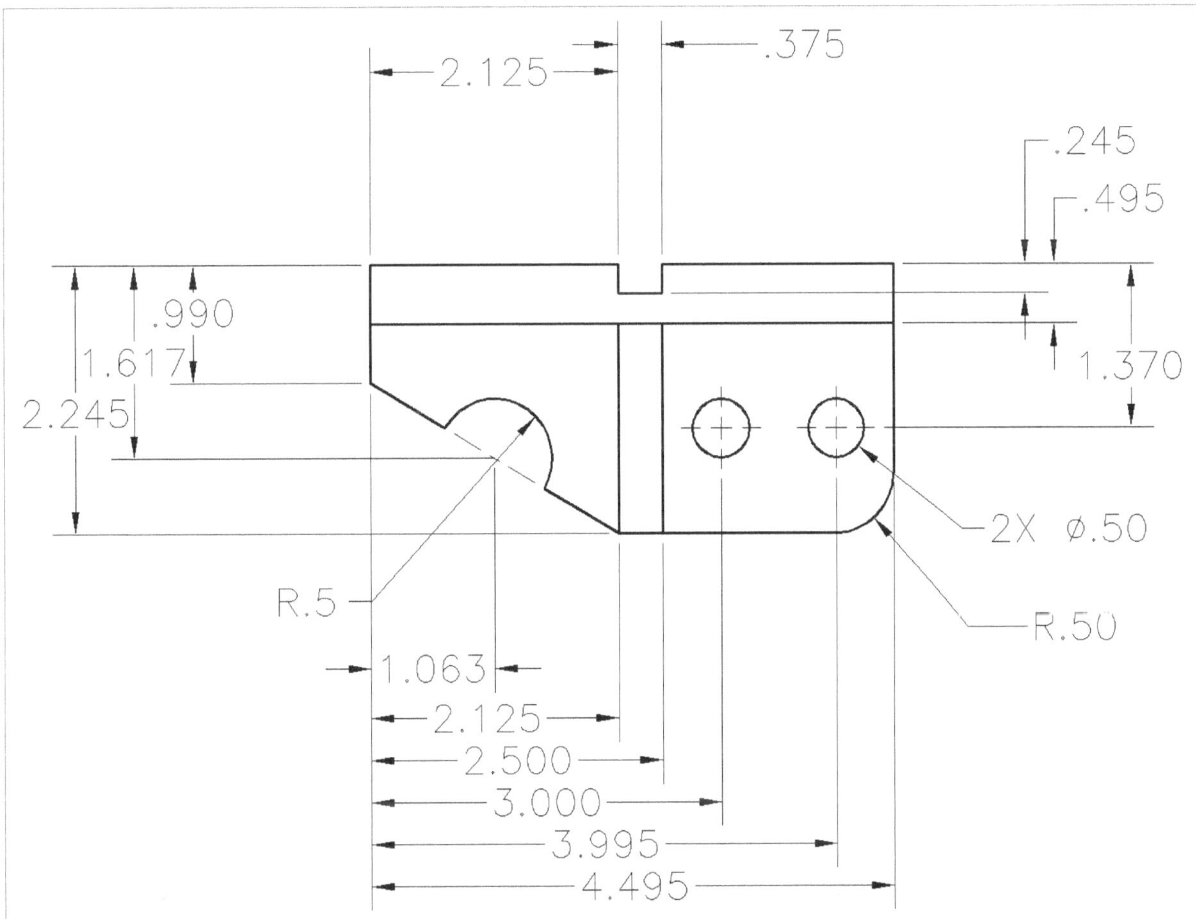

Figure-56. Practical 2

Starting Sketch

- Start Autodesk Inventor by double-clicking on the Autodesk Inventor Professional icon from the desktop. (If not started yet.)
- Click on the **New** button from the **Quick Access Toolbar**. The **Create New File** dialog box will be displayed.
- Double-click on **Standard(in).ipt** icon from the **English** templates. The Part environment of Autodesk Inventor will be displayed.
- Click on the **Start 2D Sketch** button from the **Sketch** panel in the **3D Model** tab of the **Ribbon**. You will be asked to select a sketching plane.
- Click on desired plane to create sketch on it.

Creating Line sketch

- Click on the **Two Point Rectangle** tool from **Create** panel in the **Sketch** tab of the **Ribbon**. You will be asked to specify the starting corner point of the rectangle.
- Click on the origin to specify the starting corner point. You will be asked to specify the end corner point of the rectangle. Type the length and width of rectangle as **4.495** and **2.245**, respectively in the input boxes on screen; refer to Figure-57. Note that you need to press **TAB** from keyboard to switch between the two dimensions.

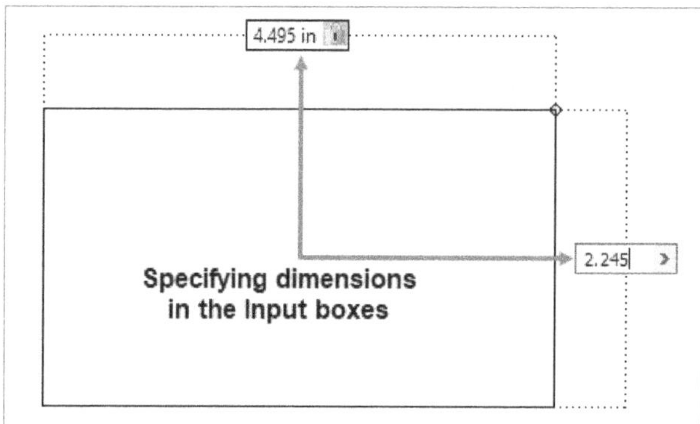

Figure-57. Specifying dimensions of rectangle

- Press **ENTER** to apply the dimensions.
- Click on the **Line** tool from **Create** panel in the **Sketch** tab of the **Ribbon** and create a line intersecting the vertical and horizontal side of rectangle as shown in Figure-58.

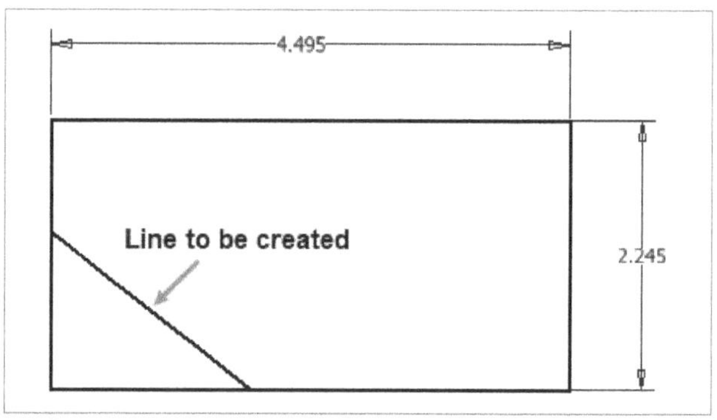

Figure-58. Line to be created

- Click on the **General Dimension** tool from **Constrain** panel in the **Sketch** tab of the **Ribbon** and specify distance of end points of the line as shown in Figure-59.

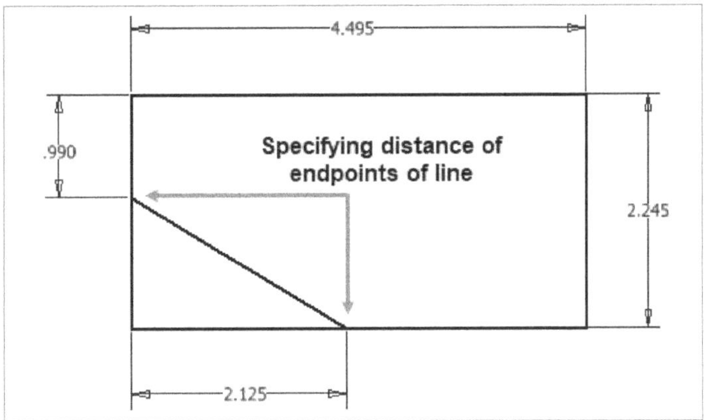

Figure-59. Dimensioning the line

- Similarly, create the other lines of the sketch; refer to Figure-60.

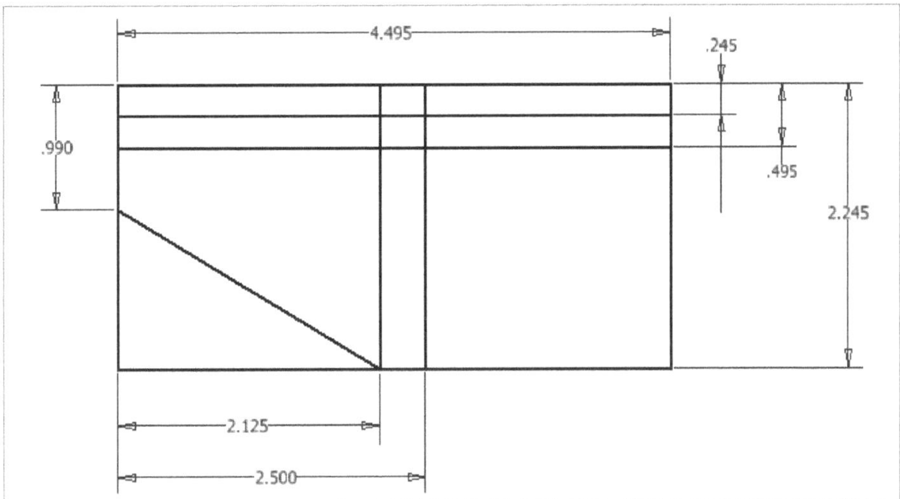

Figure-60. Sketch after creating lines

Creating Circles

- Click on the **Center Point Circle** tool from **Create** panel in the **Sketch** tab of the **Ribbon**. You will be asked to specify the center of the circle.
- Click on the midpoint of the inclined line to specify the center; refer to Figure-61. You will be asked to specify the radius of the circle.

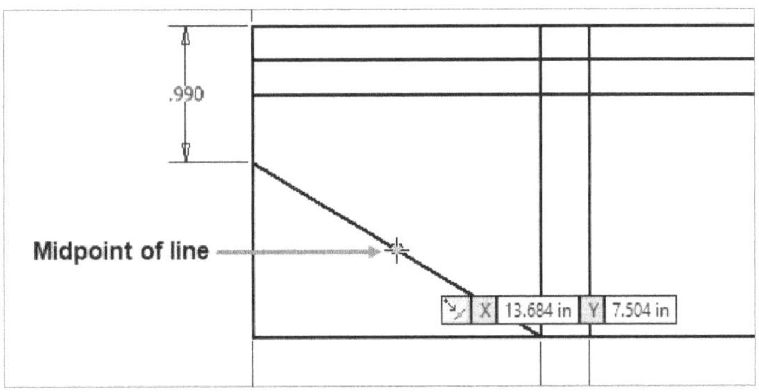

Figure-61. Midpoint of inclined line

- Enter the radius as **0.5** in the input box. The circle will be created.
- Similarly, create the other two circles of diameter **0.5** at random locations as displayed in Figure-62.

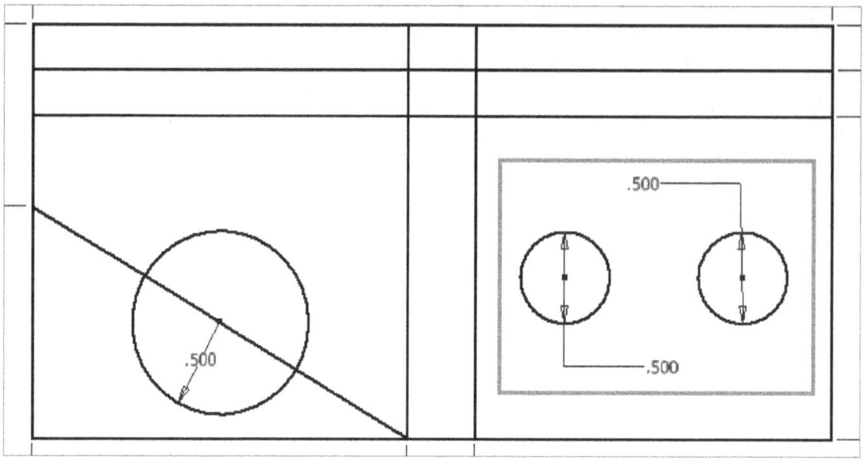

Figure-62. Circles created

- Click on the **General Dimension** tool from **Constrain** panel in the **Sketch** tab of the **Ribbon** and set the dimensions of circles as shown in Figure-63.

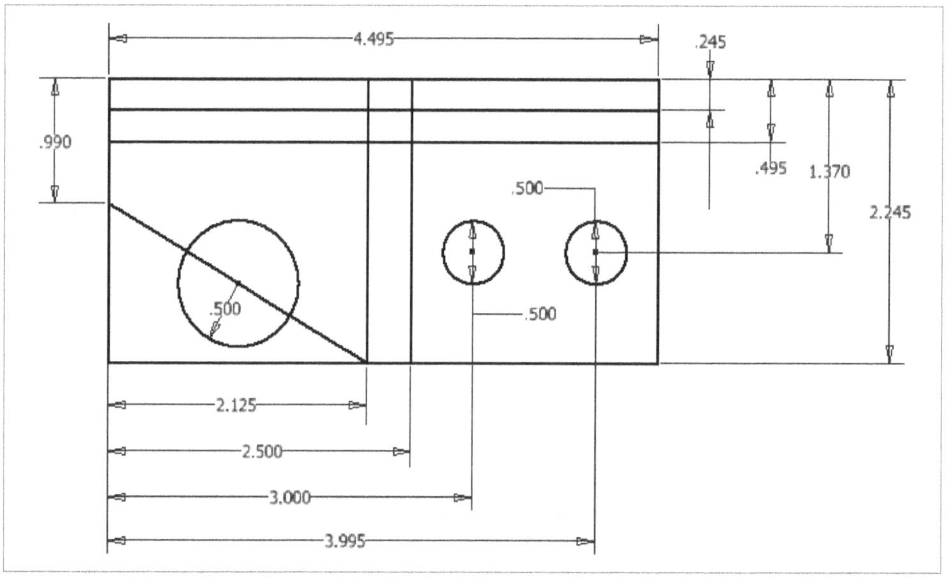

Figure-63. Dimensioning the circles

Now, we are done with creating the entities. There are some extra portions of sketch that need to be trimmed. The procedure is given next.

Trimming

- Click on the **Trim** tool from **Modify** panel in the **Sketch** tab of the **Ribbon** or press **X** from keyboard. You will be asked to select the entities to trim.
- Click on the entities marked in Figure-64 with red dot. The sketch will be displayed as shown in Figure-65.

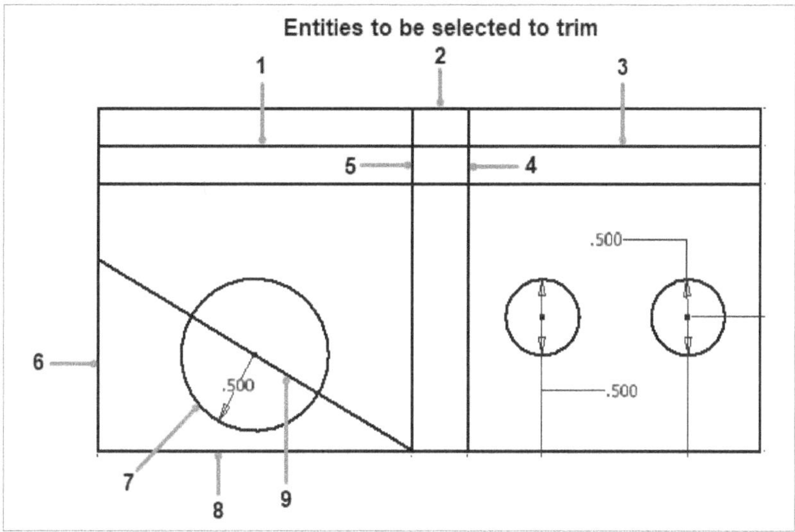

Figure-64. Entities selected for trimming

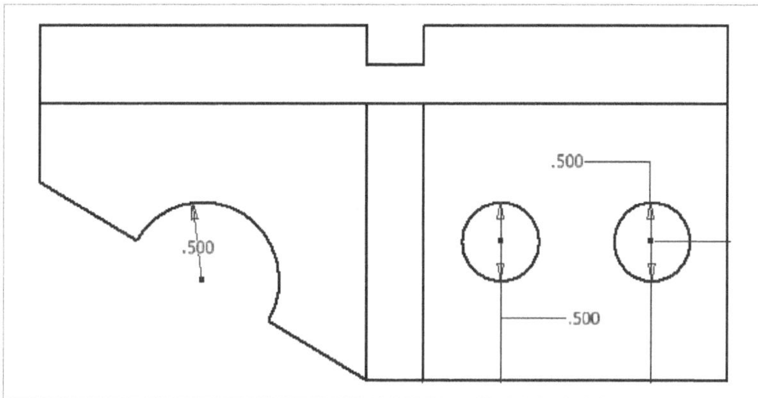

Figure-65. Sketch after trimming

- Create a fillet at the corner by using **Fillet** tool from **Create** panel in the **Sketch** tab of the **Ribbon** and apply rest of the dimensions as given in the drawing; refer to Figure-66.

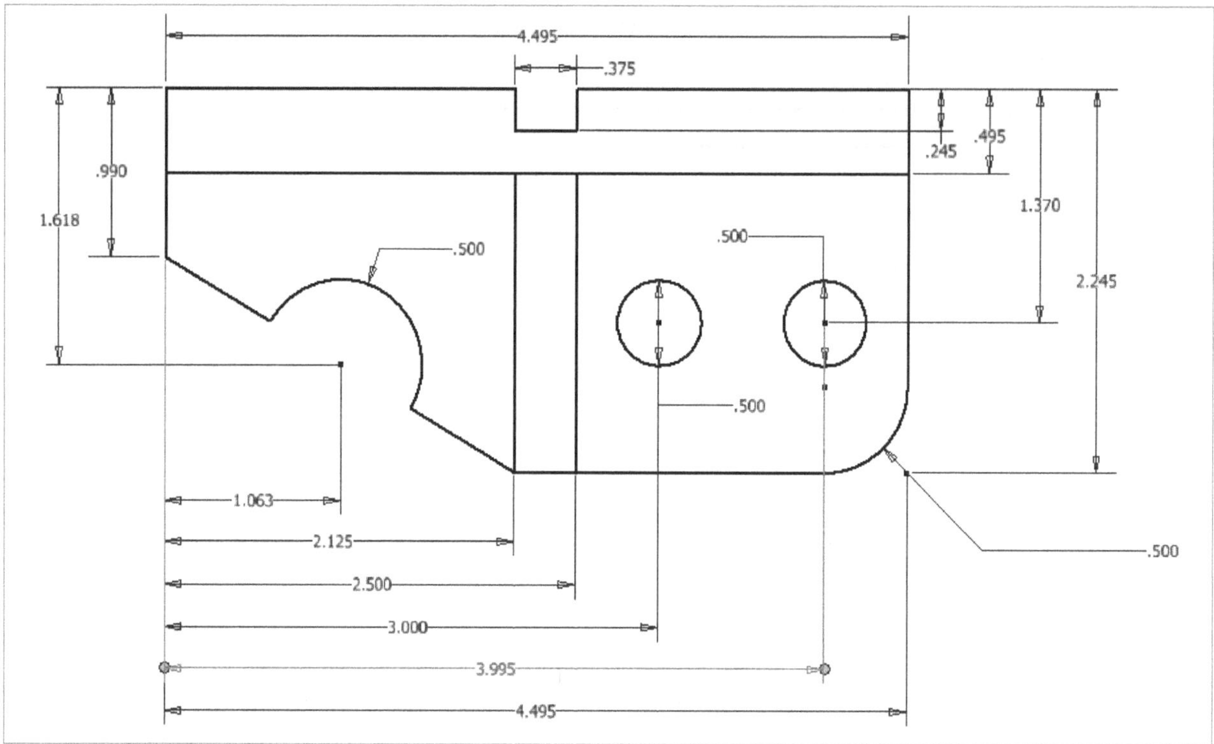

Figure-66. After applying dimensions and creating fillet

PRACTICAL 3

Create the sketch as shown in Figure-67.

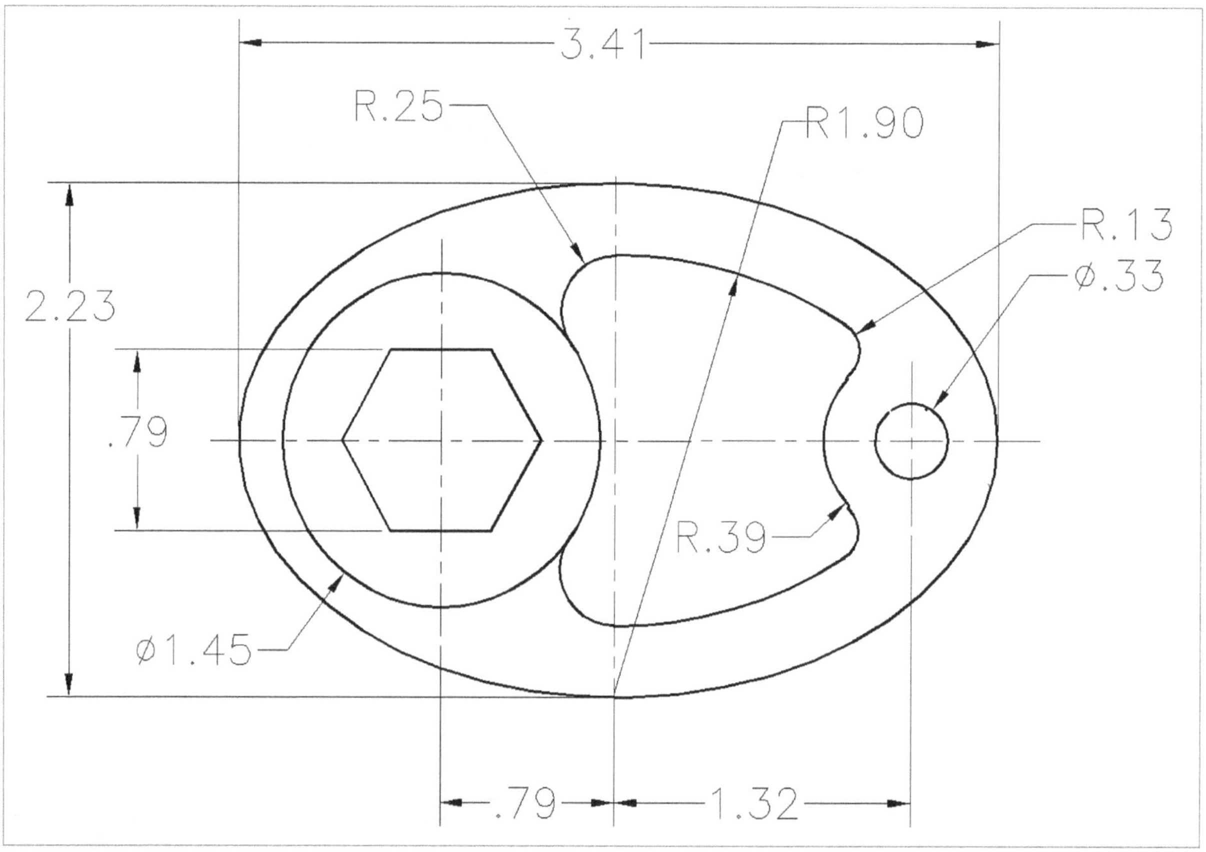

Figure-67. Practical 3

Starting Sketch

- Start Autodesk Inventor by double-clicking on the Autodesk Inventor Professional icon from the desktop. (If not started yet.)
- Click on the **New** button from the **Quick Access Toolbar**. The **Create New File** dialog box will be displayed.
- Double-click on **Standard(in).ipt** icon from the **English** templates. The Part environment of Autodesk Inventor will be displayed.
- Click on the **Start 2D Sketch** button from **Sketch** panel in the **3D Model** tab of the **Ribbon**. You will be asked to select a sketching plane.
- Click on desired plane to create sketch on it.

Creating Ellipse

- Click on the **Ellipse** tool from **Circle** drop-down in the **Create** panel of the **Ribbon**; refer to Figure-68. You will be asked to specify center of the ellipse.

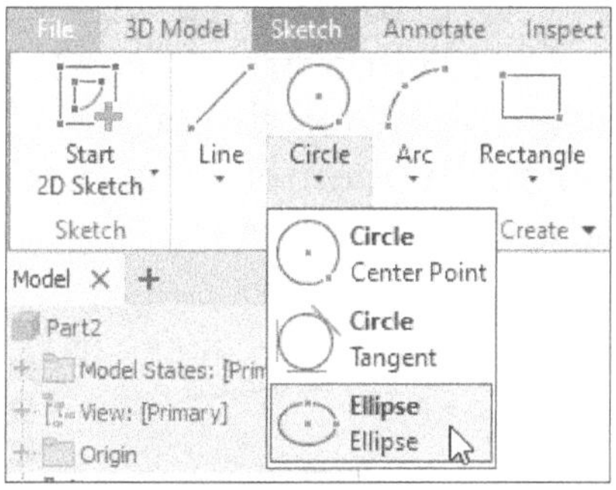

Figure-68. Ellipse tool

- Click on the origin to make it center point of the ellipse. You will be asked to specify the first axis end point.
- Click to specify the first axis end point; refer to Figure-69. You will be asked to specify a point on ellipse; refer to Figure-70.

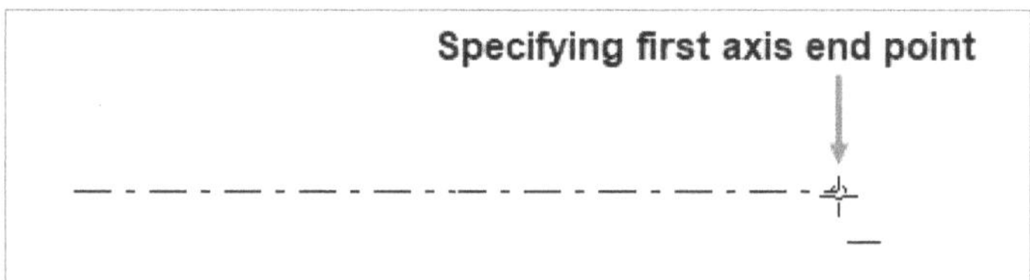

Figure-69. Specifying end point of ellipse axis

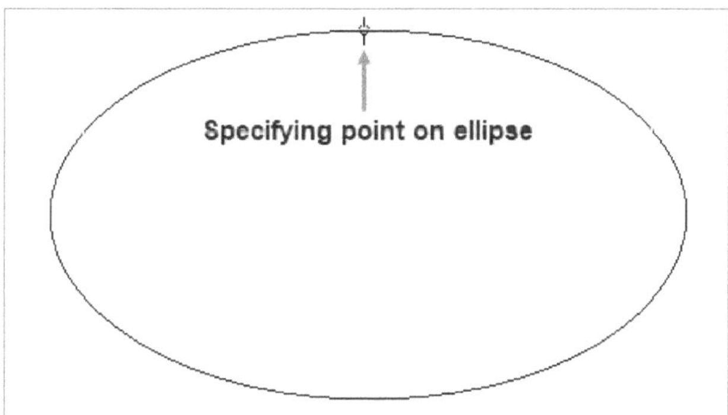

Figure-70. Specifying point on ellipse

- Click at desired location to specify the point on ellipse.
- Click on the **General Dimension** tool and specify the length and width of ellipse as **1.705** and **1.115**, respectively at its axes; refer to Figure-71.

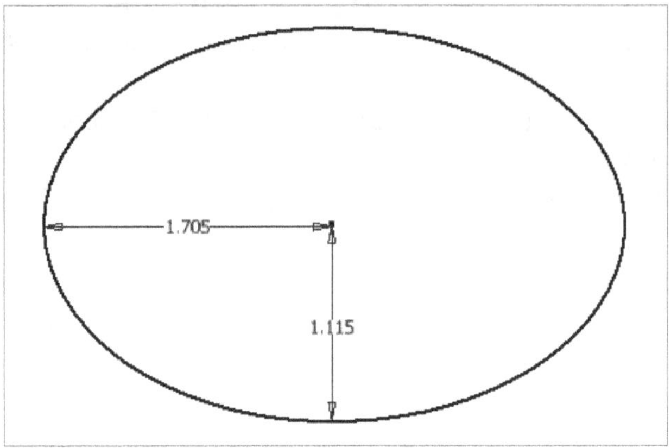

Figure-71. Ellipse after specifying dimensions

Creating Circles

- Click on the **Center Point Circle** tool from **Create** panel in the **Ribbon**. You will be asked to specify the center point for the circle.
- Click at a location collinear to the center of ellipse as shown in Figure-72. You will be asked to specify radius of the circle.

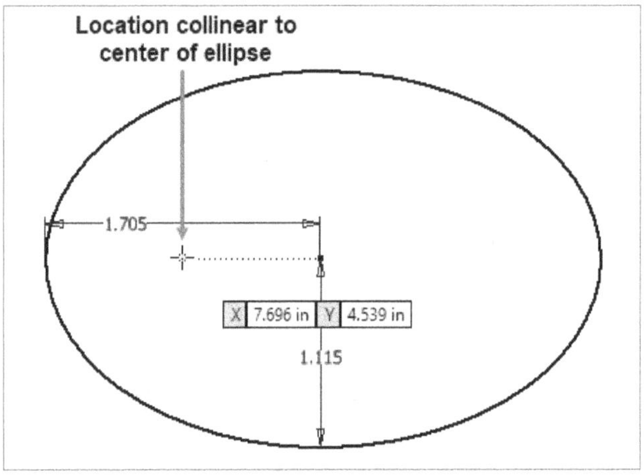

Figure-72. Specifying location for center of circle

- Enter the diameter as **1.45** in the input box. The circle will be created.
- Similarly, create the other circle of diameter **0.33** and specify the distances by using the **General Dimension** tool; refer to Figure-73.

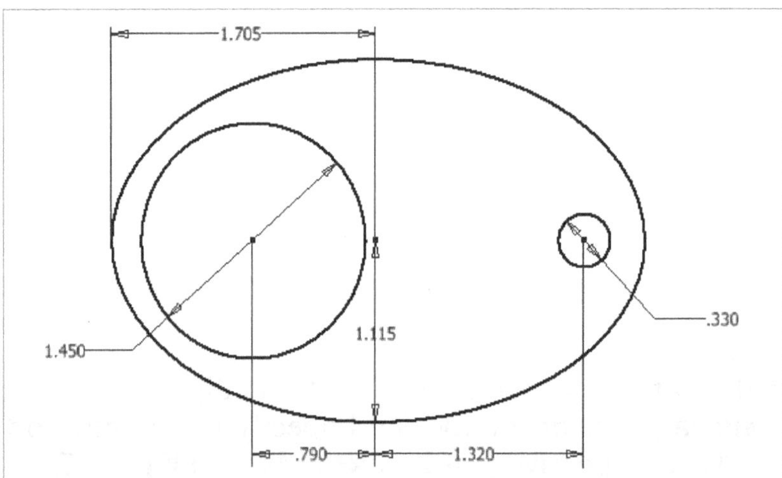

Figure-73. Sketch after creating circles

Creating Arcs and Fillets

- Click on the **Center Point Arc** tool from **Arc** drop-down in the **Create** panel of the **Ribbon**. You will be asked to specify center of the arc.
- Click on the center of the circle with diameter **0.330** to specify center of the arc. You will be asked to specify the starting point of the arc.
- Type the radius of arc as **0.390** in the input box and press **TAB** from keyboard. You will be asked to specify the location of starting point on the construction circle of radius **0.390**.
- Click at the location where angle value is approximately **120** degree; refer to Figure-74. You will be asked to specify end point of the arc.

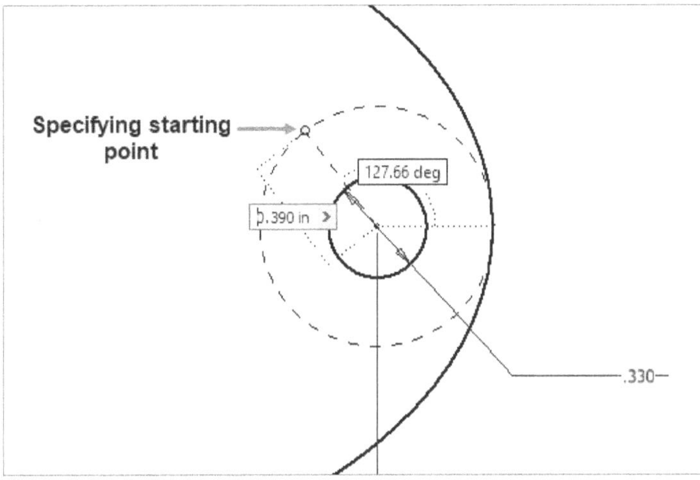

Figure-74. Specifying starting point of arc

- Click at the location where arc angle is approximately **120** degree. The arc will be created.
- Click again on the **Center Point Arc** tool and specify the center point of arc along vertical line of center and at the circle as shown in Figure-75. You will be asked to specify the starting point of the arc.

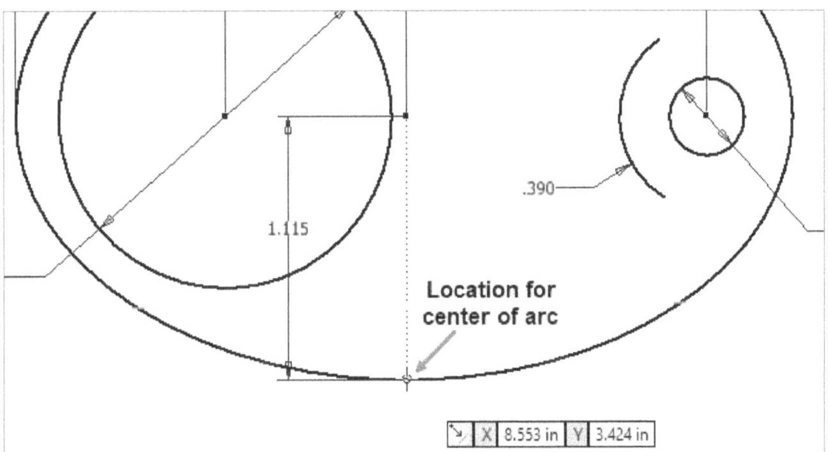

Figure-75. Location for center of arc

- Enter **1.90** in the **Radius** input box and specify the starting point and end point of the arc as shown in Figure-76.

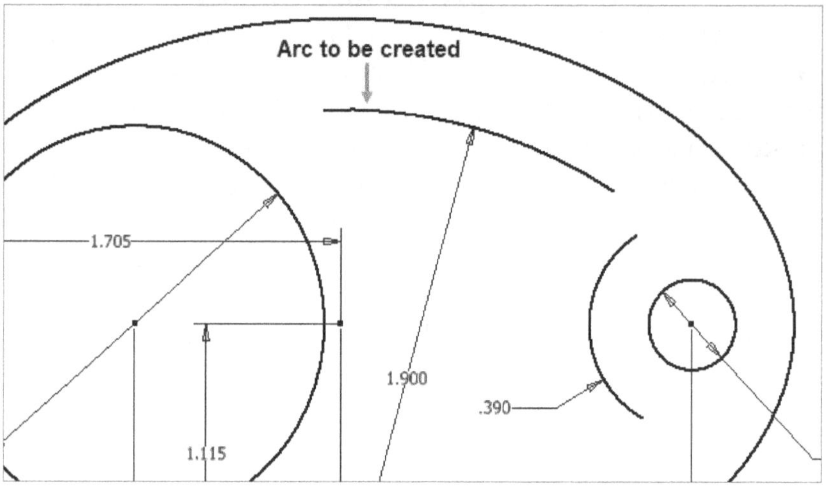

Figure-76. Arc to be created

Applying Constraint

- Click on the **Coincident Constraint** button from **Constrain** panel in the **Ribbon**. You will be asked to select curves or points.
- Select the curves or points to be coincident as shown in Figure-77. The entities will become coincident to each other.

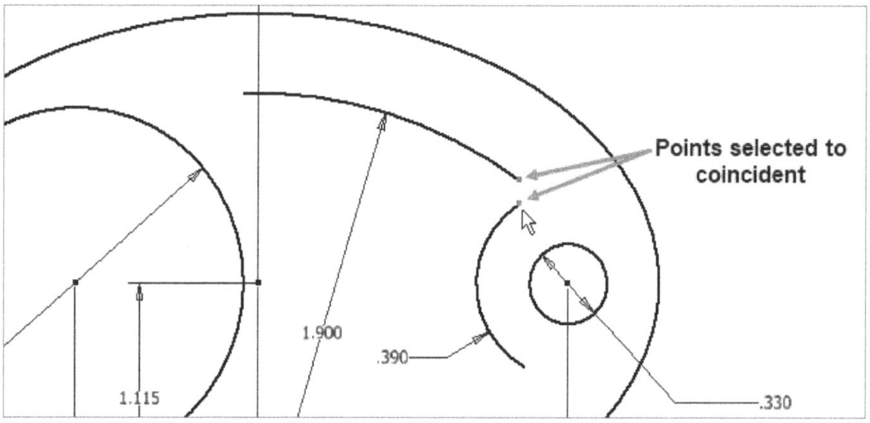

Figure-77. Points selected to coincident

- Press **ESC** from keyboard to exit the tool.

Creating Fillets

- Click on the **Fillet** tool from **Create** panel in the **Ribbon**. You will be asked to select the entities to apply the fillet.
- Type the value of radius for fillet as **0.13** in the edit box displayed in the **2D Fillet** dialog box and click on the arcs as shown in Figure-78. The fillet will be created.

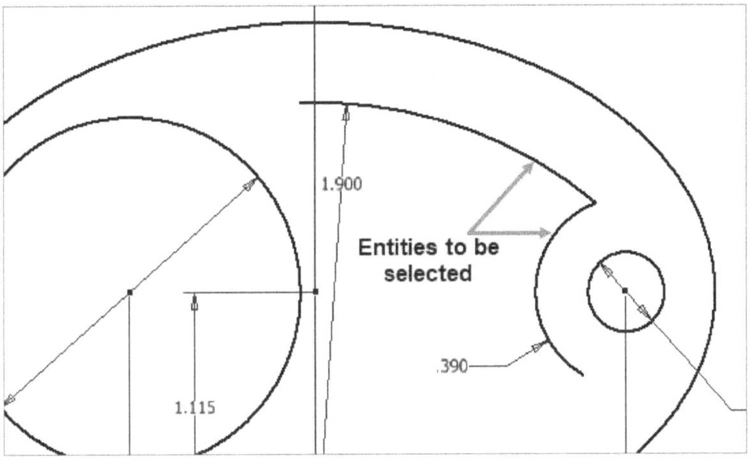

Figure-78. Entities to select for fillet

- If you have earlier tried then you would be knowing that we can not create fillet between arc and circle by using the **Fillet** tool in Inventor. Yes!! We have solution! Click on the **Tangent Arc** tool from **Arc** drop-down in the **Create** panel of the **Ribbon**. You will be asked to specify the starting point of the arc.
- Click on the arc as shown in Figure-79. You will be asked to specify the end point of the arc.

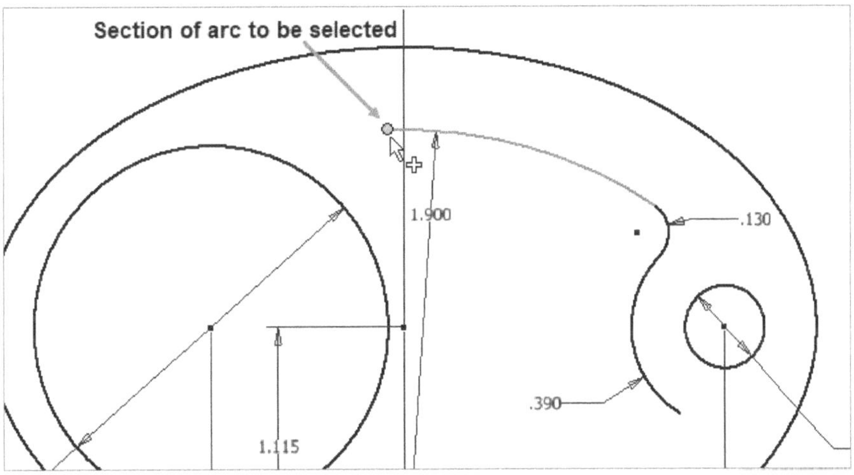

Figure-79. Section of arc to be selected

- Click on the circle at any random location to specify the end point of the arc; refer to Figure-80.

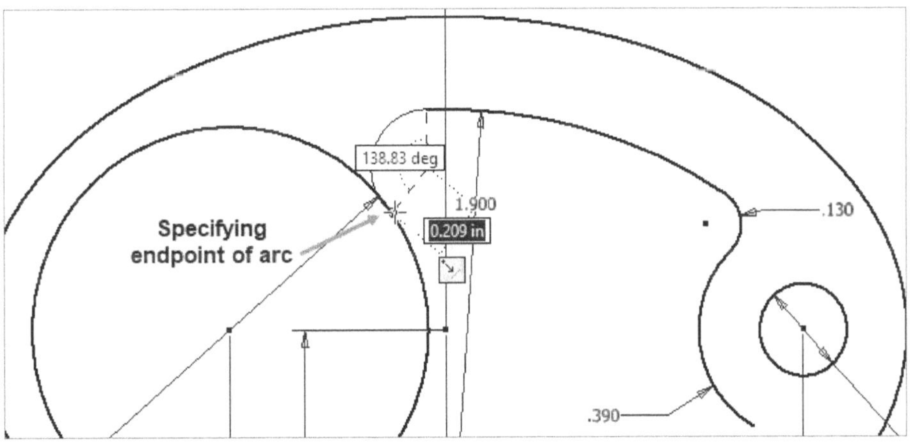

Figure-80. Specifying end point of arc

- Click on the **Tangent** button from **Constrain** panel in the **Ribbon**. You will be asked to select the first curve.
- One by one select the newly created arc and circle as shown in Figure-81. The entities will become tangent to each other. Specify the dimension of the arc as **0.25** using the **General Dimension** tool.

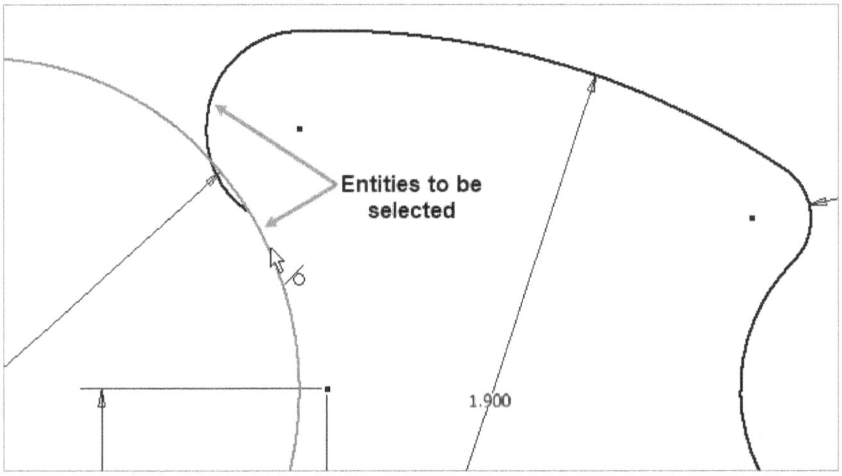

Figure-81. Entities selected for tangency

Creating Mirror copy

- Click on the **Construction** button from **Format** panel in the **Ribbon**. The construction mode will become active.
- Click on the **Line** tool from **Create** panel in the **Ribbon**. You will be asked to specify the starting point of the line.
- Click on the centers of the circles one by one to create the line; refer to Figure-82. Press **ESC** from keyboard to exit the tool.

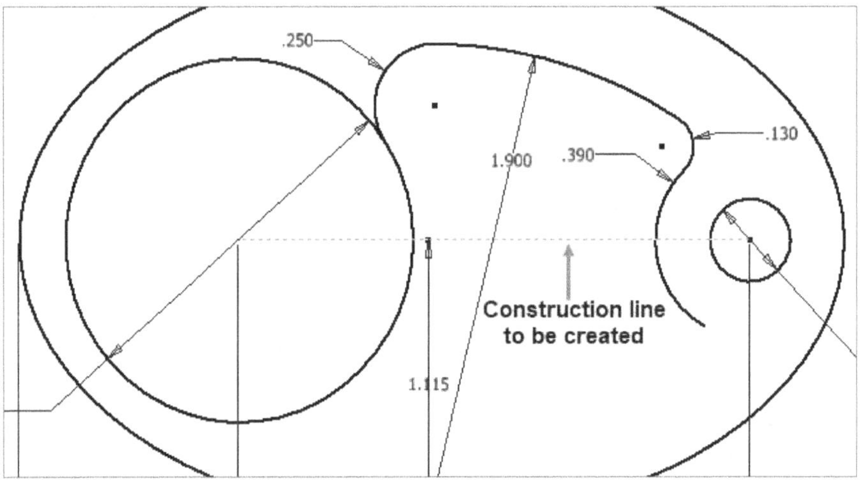

Figure-82. Construction line created

- Click on the **Construction** button again to exit the construction mode.
- Click on the **Mirror** tool from **Pattern** panel in the **Ribbon**. You will be asked to select the entities to be mirrored.
- Select the three arcs as shown in Figure-83 and press **ENTER**. You will be asked to select the mirror line.

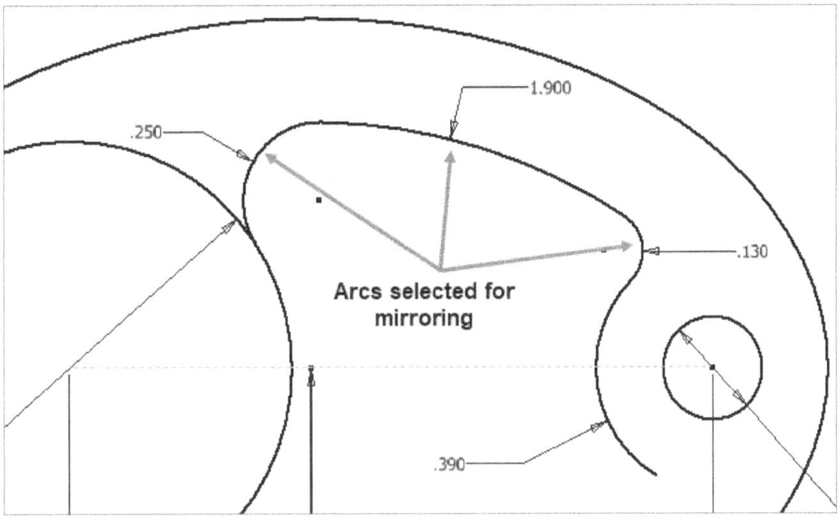

Figure-83. Selecting arcs for mirroring

- Select the construction line recently created. The **Apply** button will become active in the **Mirror** dialog box.
- Click on the **Apply** button. The mirror copy will be created; refer to Figure-84. Click on the **Done** button to exit the dialog box.

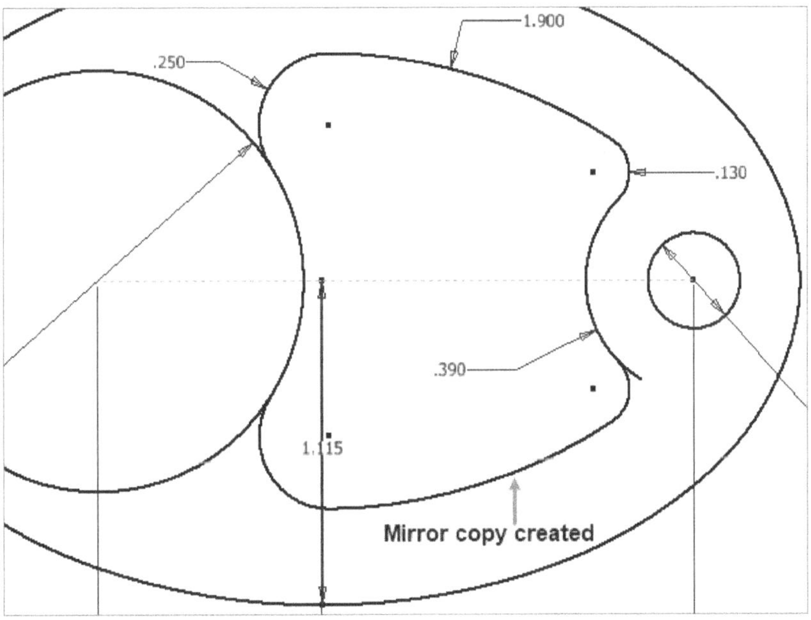

Figure-84. Mirror copy created

Creating Polygon

- Click on the **Polygon** tool from **Rectangle** drop-down in the **Create** panel of the **Ribbon**. You will be asked to specify the number of sides of the polygon in the **Polygon** dialog box; refer to Figure-85.

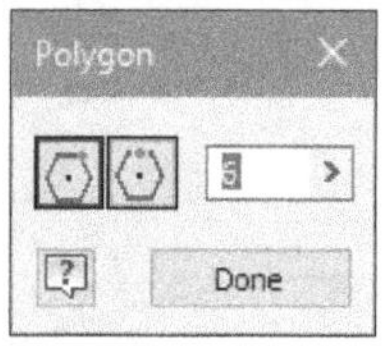

Figure-85. Polygon dialog box

- Specify the value as **6** in the edit box and click at the center of the left circle to specify the center of the polygon. You will be asked to specify a point on the polygon; refer to Figure-86.

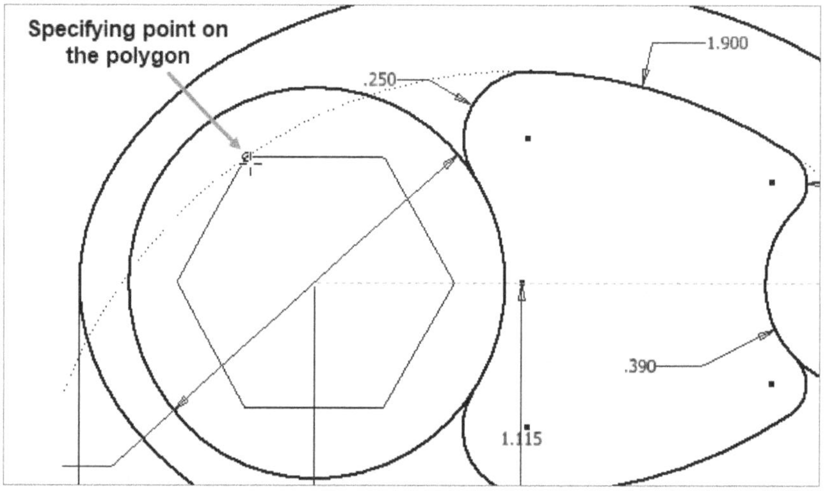

Figure-86. Point to be specified for polygon

- Click randomly at any location inside the circle and press **ESC** from keyboard. The polygon will be created; refer to Figure-87.

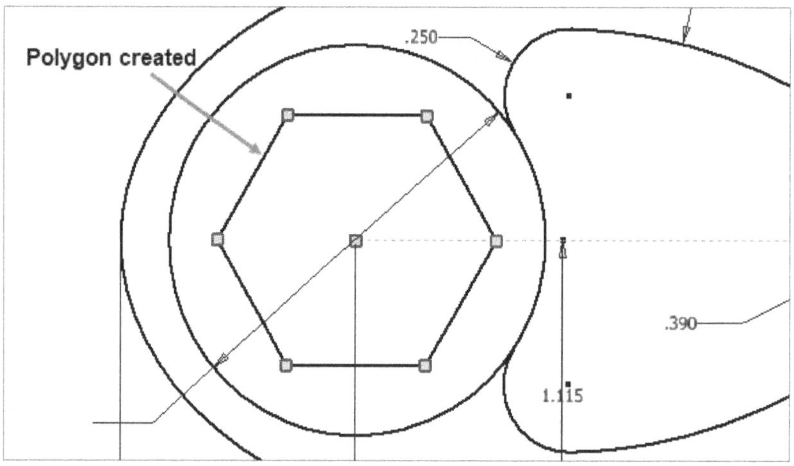

Figure-87. Polygon created

- Click on the **Horizontal Constraint** button from **Constrain** panel in the **Ribbon**. You will be asked to select the entity.
- Click on any line of the polygon to orient it as it is in the drawing.
- Click on the **General Dimension** tool from **Constrain** panel and specify the dimension as given in Figure-88. The final sketch will be created as shown in Figure-89.

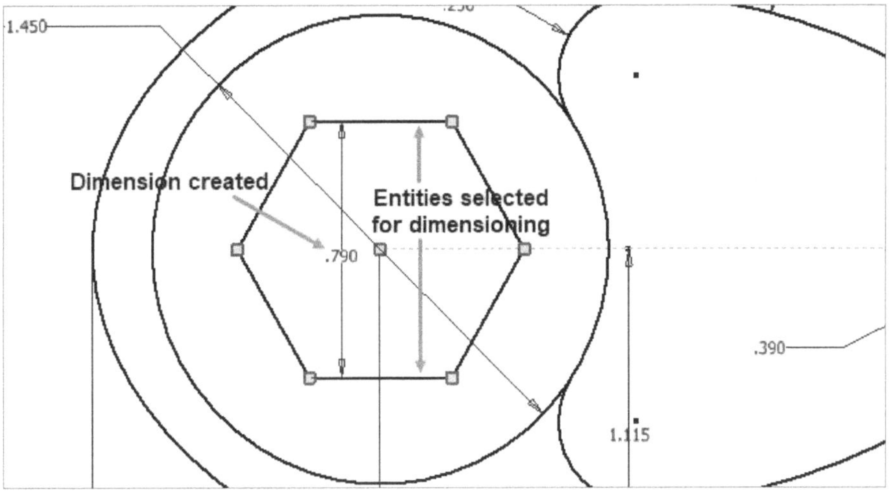

Figure-88. Applying dimension to polygon

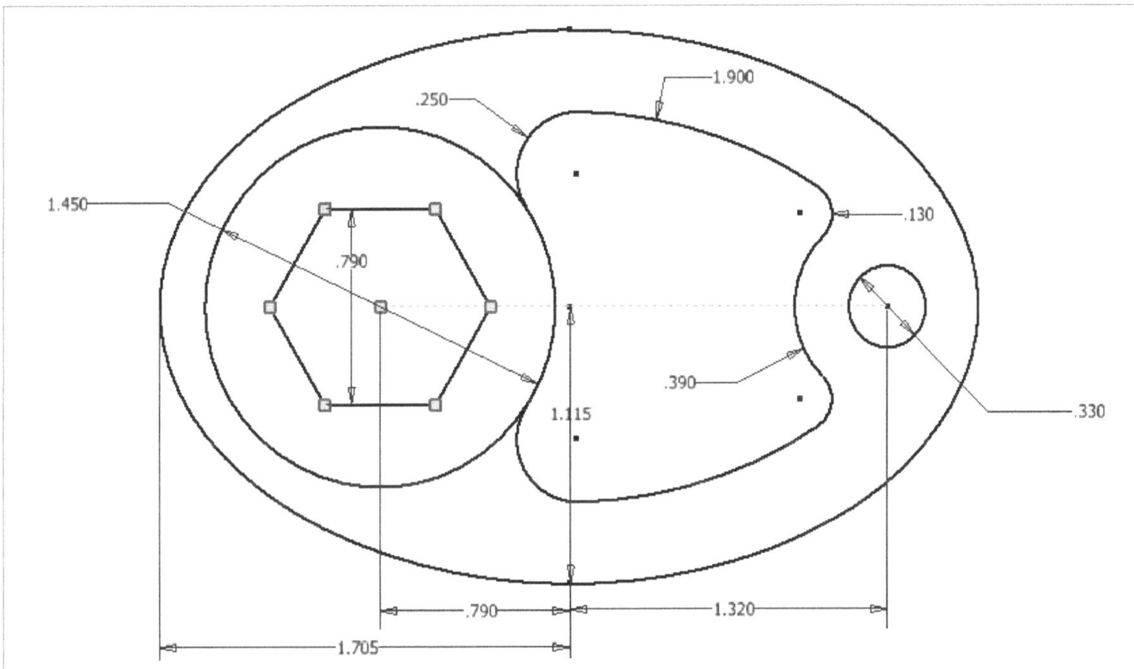

Figure-89. Final sketch for practical 3

PRACTICAL 4

Create the sketch as shown in Figure-90.

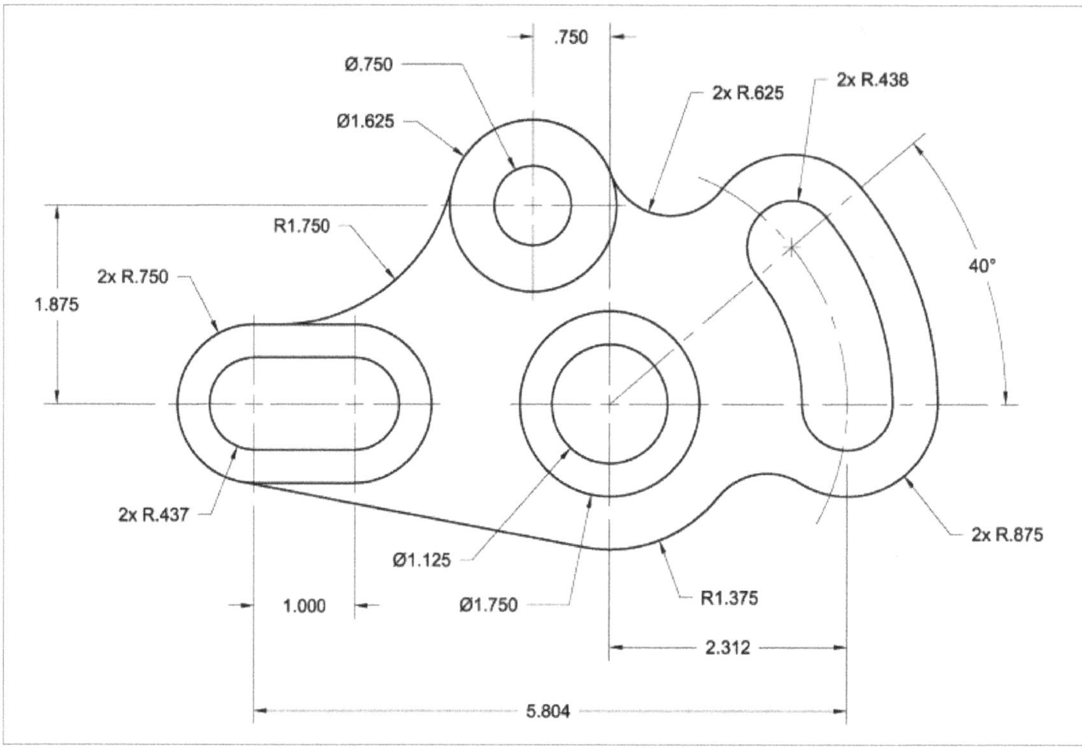

Figure-90. Practical 4

Starting Sketch

- Start Autodesk Inventor by double-clicking on the Autodesk Inventor Professional icon from the desktop. (If not started yet)
- Click on the **New** button from the **Quick Access Toolbar**. The **Create New File** dialog box will be displayed.
- Double-click on **Standard(in).ipt** icon from the **English** templates. The Part environment of Autodesk Inventor will be displayed.
- Click on the **Start 2D Sketch** button from **Sketch** panel in the **3D Model** tab of the **Ribbon**. You will be asked to select a sketching plane.
- Click on desired plane to create sketch on it.

Creating Circles

- Click on the **Center Point Circle** tool from **Create** panel in the **Ribbon** and click on the origin. You will be asked to specify the diameter of the circle.
- Enter the value of diameter as **1.125** in the input box. The circle will be created.
- Similarly, create the circle of diameter **1.75** at the same center; refer to Figure-91.

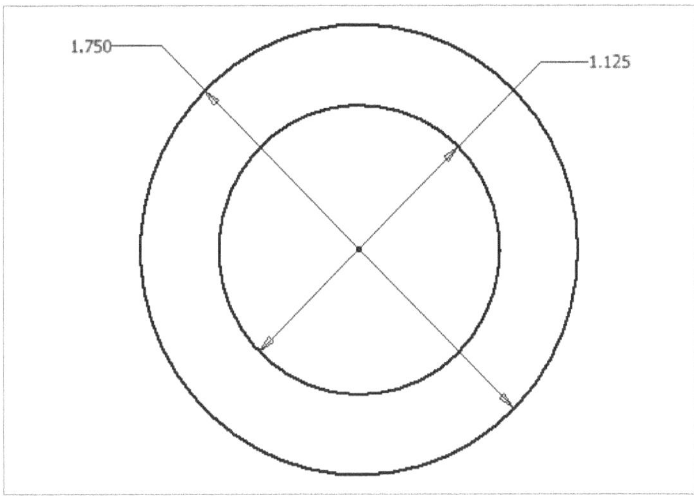

Figure-91. Circles created at origin

- Again, click on the **Center Point Circle** tool from **Create** panel in the **Ribbon** and click at a random location above earlier created circles to specify center; refer to Figure-92.

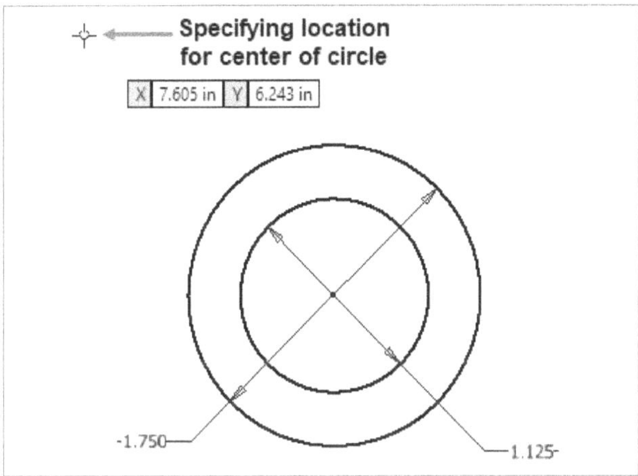

Figure-92. Specifying location for center of circle

- Enter the value of diameter as **0.750** in the Input box. The circle will be created.
- Create a circle of diameter **1.625** at the same center; refer to Figure-93.

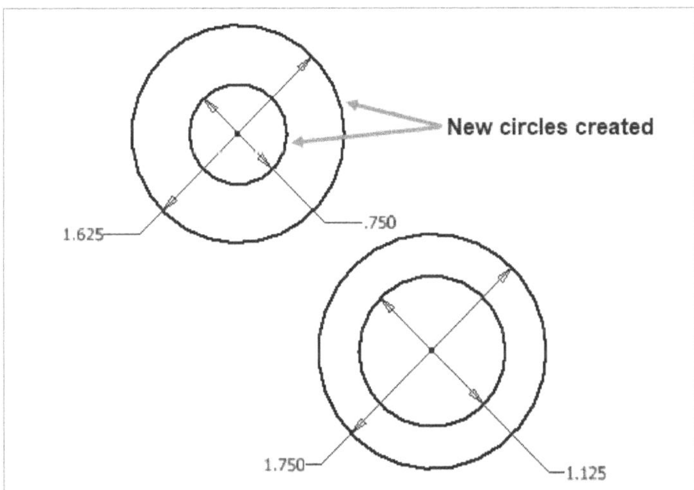

Figure-93. New circles created

- Click on the **General Dimension** tool from **Constrain** panel in the **Ribbon** and specify the position of newly created circles with respect to the origin as shown in Figure-94.

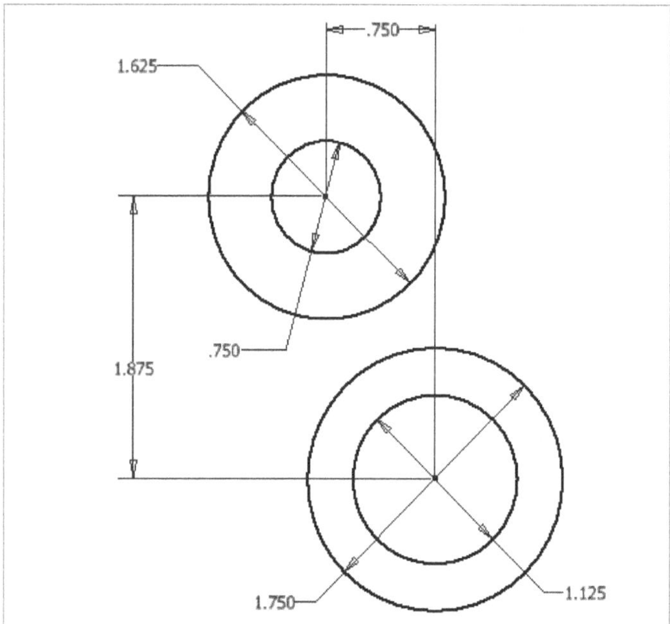

Figure-94. Positioning newly created circle

Creating Slots

- Click on the **Center Point Arc Slot** tool from **Rectangle** drop-down in the **Create** panel of the **Ribbon**. You will be asked to specify center point for center arc.
- Click on the origin to specify center. You will be asked to specify starting point of center arc.
- Type the radius as **2.312** in the Input box and press **TAB**. You will be asked to specify angle for starting point.
- Enter **0** in the Input box. You will be asked to specify end point of the arc.
- Move the cursor above and enter **40** in the Input box. You will be asked to specify diameter of the slot; refer to Figure-95.

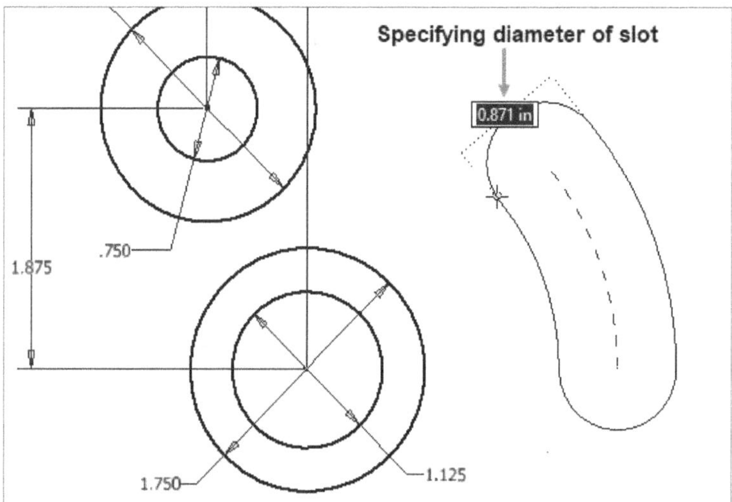

Figure-95. Specifying diameter of slot

- Enter **0.876** (0.438 x 2) in the Input box. The slot will be created; refer to Figure-96.

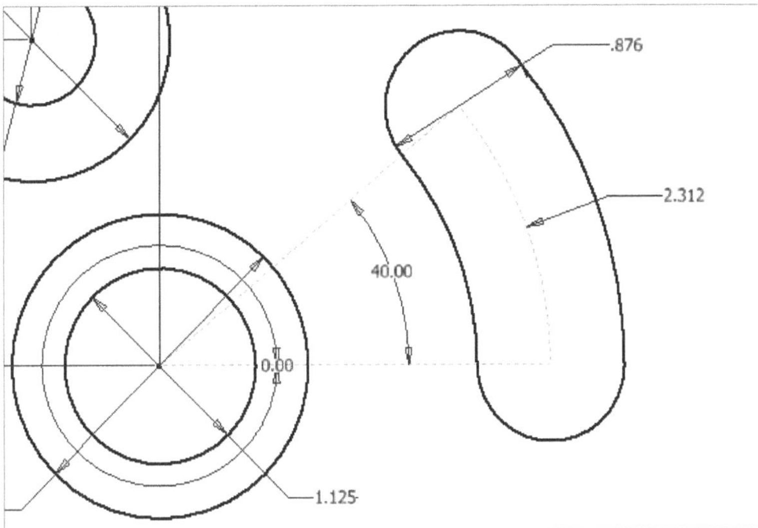

Figure-96. Slot created

- Similarly, create a slot of width **1.75** at the same location; refer to Figure-97.

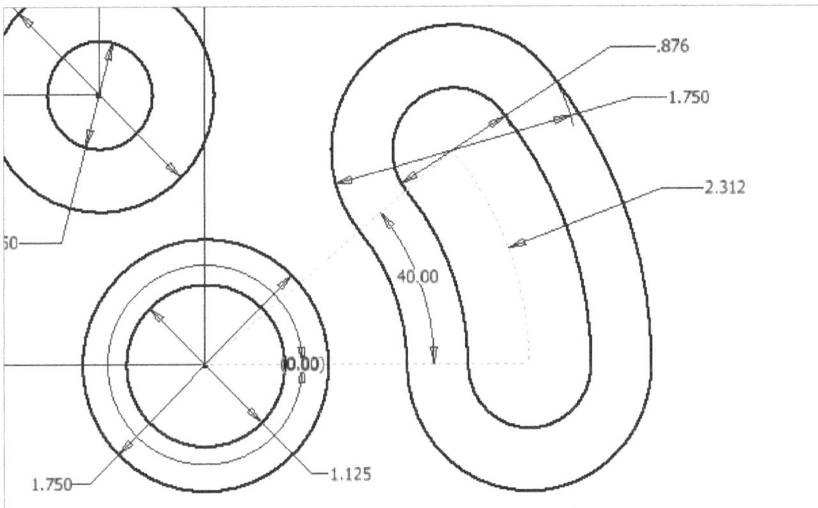

Figure-97. Second slot created

- Click on the **Center to Center Slot** tool from **Rectangle** drop-down in the **Create** panel of the **Ribbon**. You will be asked to specify starting center point of the slot; refer to Figure-98.

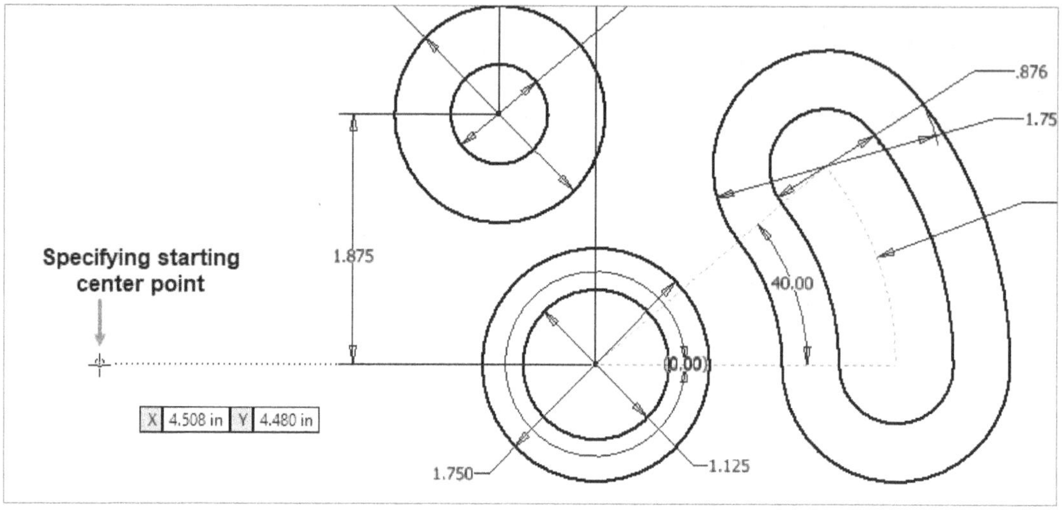

Figure-98. Specifying starting center point of slot

- Click at the location straight left to the origin. You will be asked to specify the end center point for the slot.
- Move cursor towards right and enter **1** in the Input box. You will be asked to specify width of the slot; refer to Figure-99.

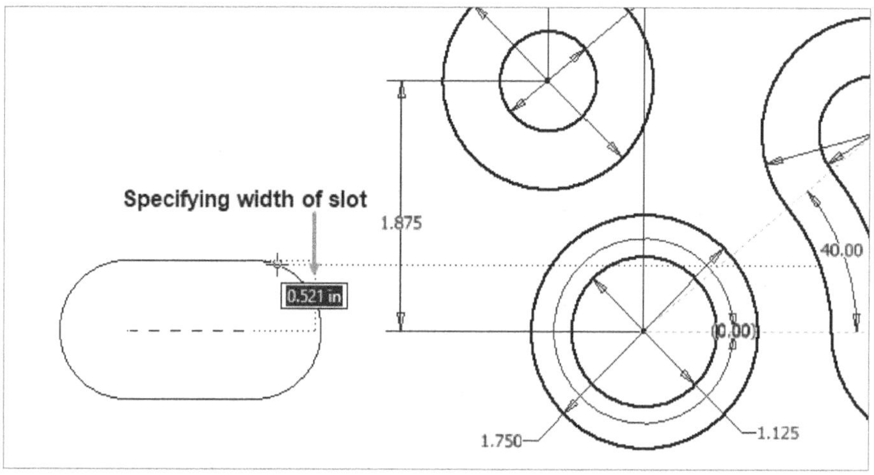

Figure-99. Specifying width of slot

- Right-click and select **Radius** option from the shortcut menu displayed. You will be asked to specify radius for the slot.
- Enter **0.437** in the Input box. The slot will be created.
- Similarly, create a slot of radius **0.75** at the same location; refer to Figure-100.

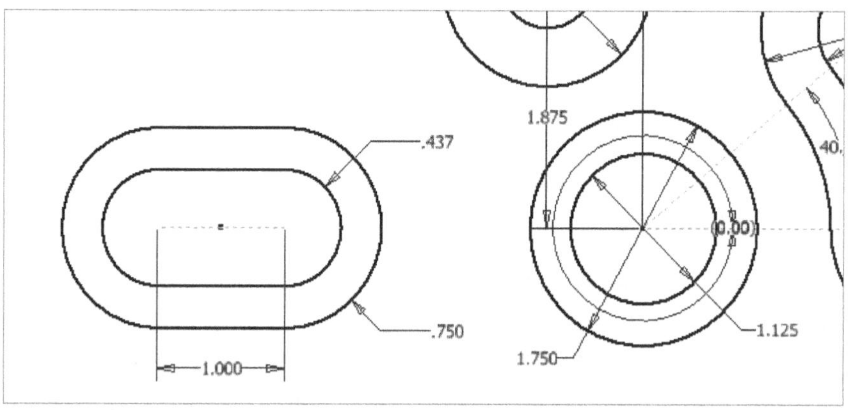

Figure-100. Straight slots created

- Click on the **General Dimension** tool from **Constrain** panel in the **Ribbon** and specify the location of the slot as shown in Figure-101.

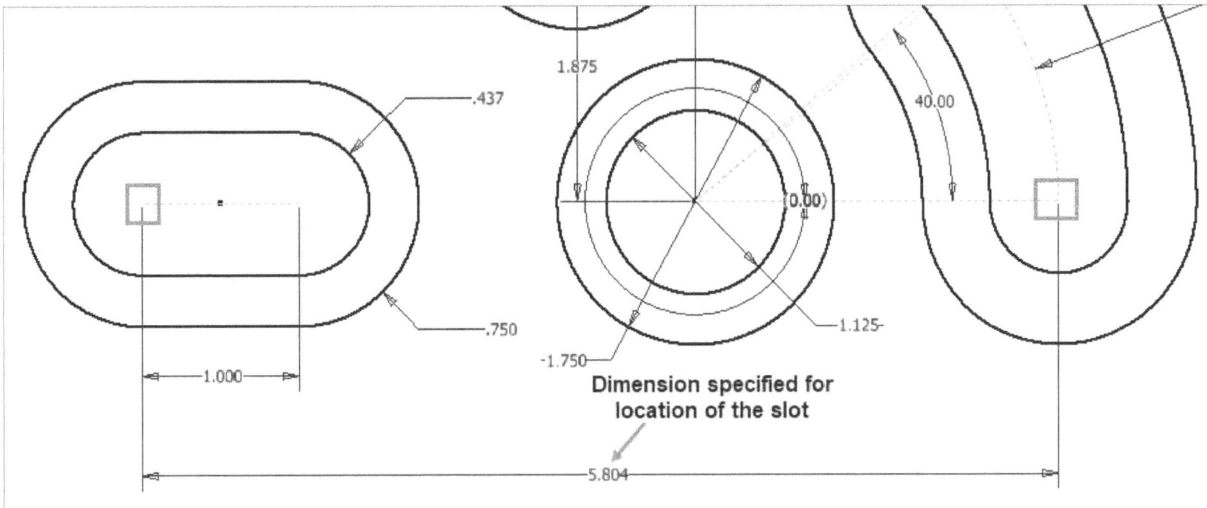

Figure-101. Dimensioning location of the slot

Creating Arcs and Fillets

- Click on the **Center Point Arc** tool from **Arc** drop-down in the **Create** panel of the **Ribbon**. You will be asked to specify the center point of the arc.
- Click on the origin to specify center point. You will be asked to specify start point of the arc.
- Type **1.375** in the Input box and press **TAB** from the keyboard. You will be asked to specify angle of the arc.
- Enter **30** in the Input box. You will be asked to specify angle for end point of the arc; refer to Figure-102.

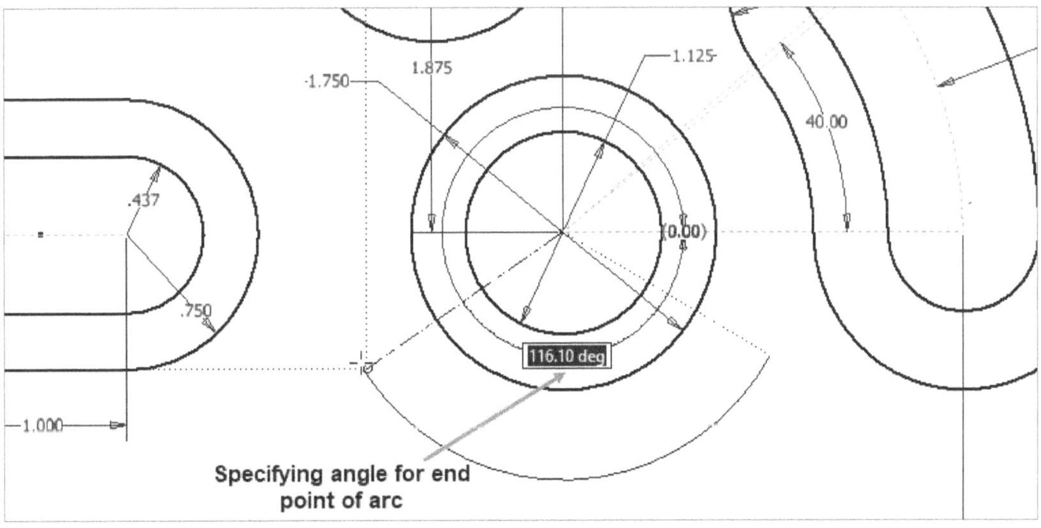

Figure-102. Specifying angle for end point

- Enter **120** in the Input box. The arc will be created.
- Click on the **Three Point Arc** tool from **Create** panel in the **Ribbon**. You will be asked to specify start point of the arc.
- Click on the circle and then on the line to specify start and end points of the arc, respectively; refer to Figure-103. You will be asked to specify radius of the arc.

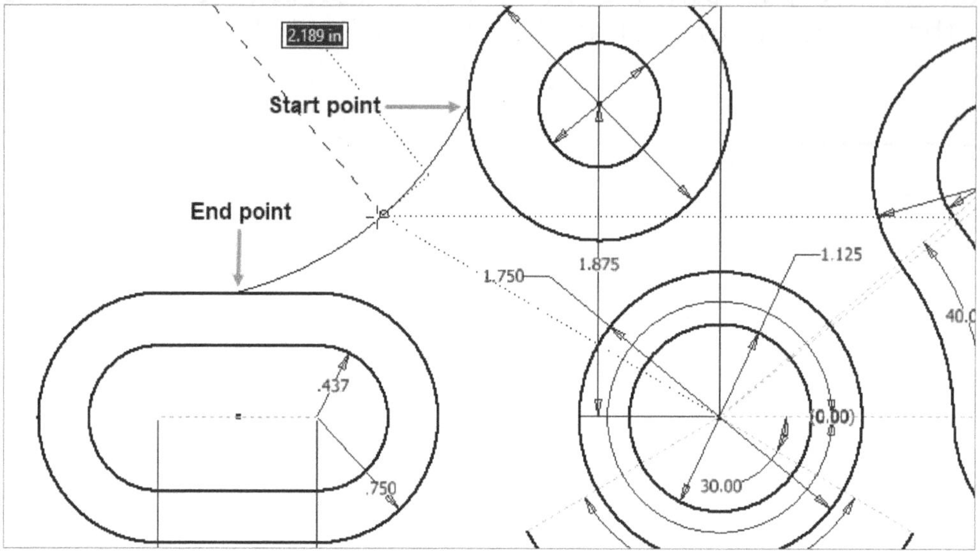

Figure-103. Start and end points of arc

- Enter **1.750** in the Input box. The arc will be created.
- Click on the **Tangent** button from **Constrain** panel in the **Ribbon** and click on newly created arc and then on the connected circle. Similarly, select the newly created arc and then line of slot to make the arc tangent to circle and line of slot.
- Similarly, you can create the other arcs; refer to Figure-104.

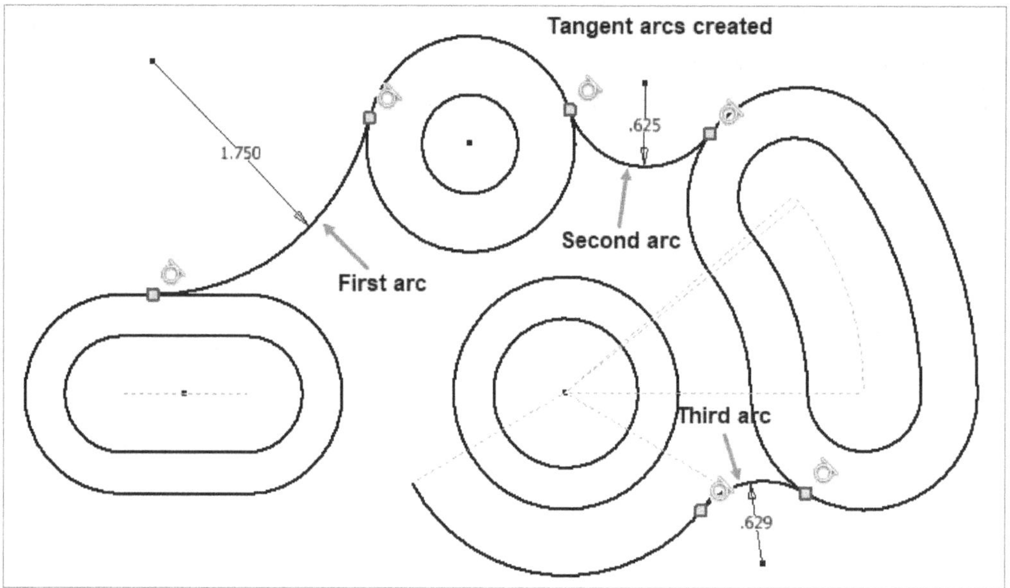

Figure-104. Tangent arcs created

Creating Tangent Line

- Click on the **Line** tool and connect arc of slot to the bottom arc; refer to Figure-105.

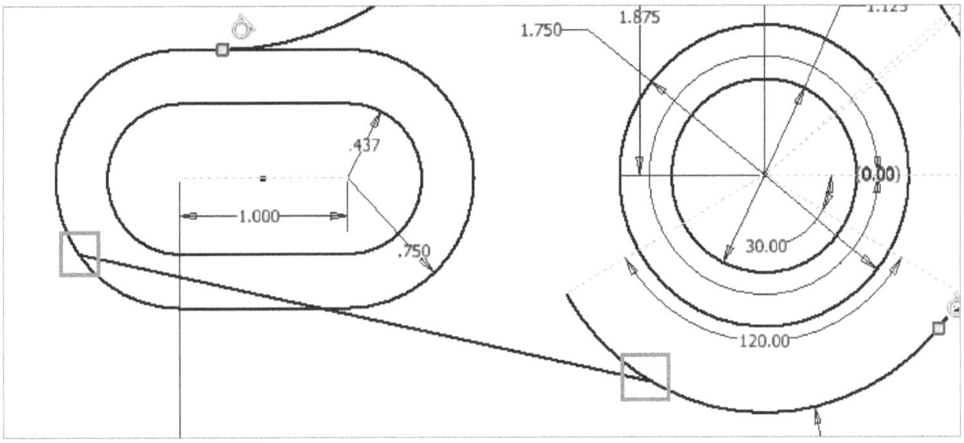

Figure-105. Connecting arc and slot

- Click on the **Tangent** button from the **Constrain** panel and select newly created line and then arc of slot. The entities will become tangent. Similarly, make the line tangent to the bottom arc; refer to Figure-106.

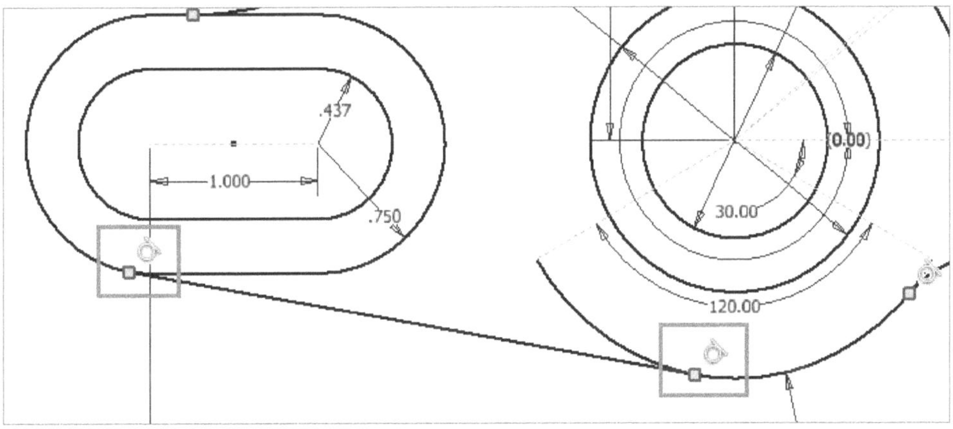

Figure-106. Line tangent to bottom arc and arc of slot

Trimming Extra Sections

- Click on the **Trim** tool from **Modify** panel in the **Ribbon**. You will be asked to select the entities to be removed.
- Click on all the portions of sketch that are not required; refer to Figure-107. The final sketch will be displayed as shown in Figure-108.

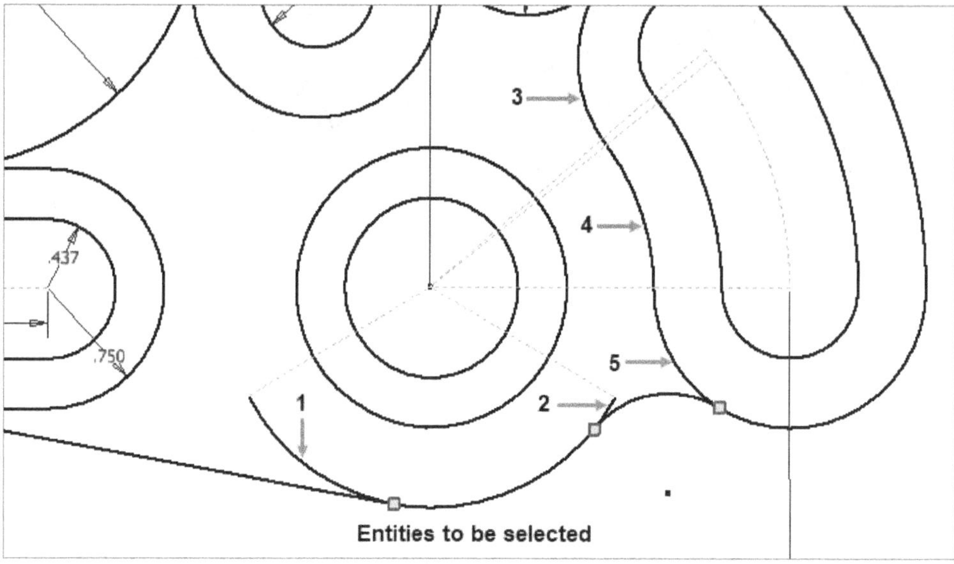

Figure-107. Entities selected for trim

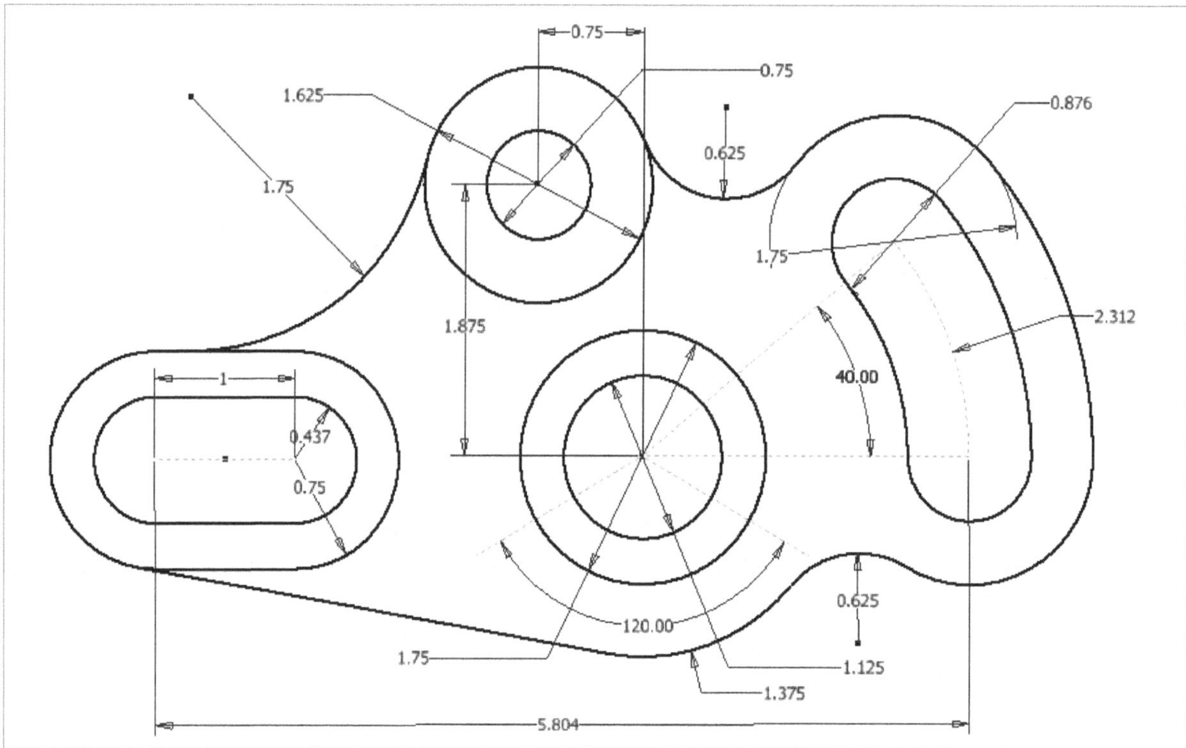

Figure-108. Final sketch for practical 4

PRACTICAL 5

In this practical, we will create a sketch for the drawing given in Figure-109.

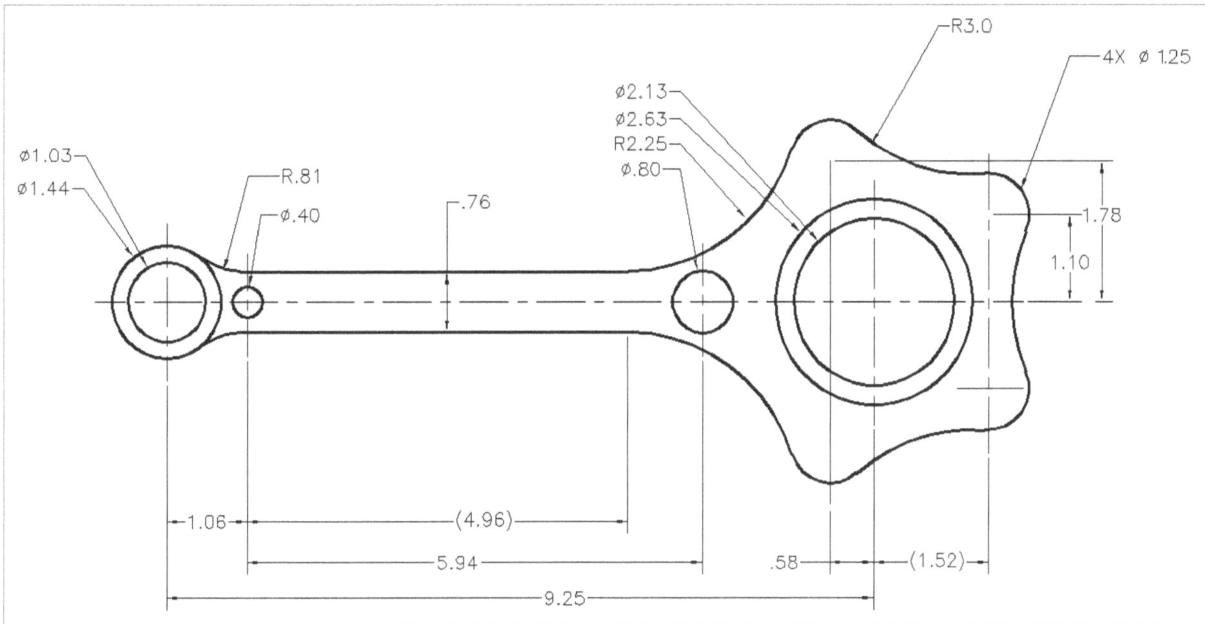

Figure-109. Practical 5

Starting Sketch

- Start Autodesk Inventor by double-clicking on the Autodesk Inventor Professional icon from the desktop. (If not started yet.)
- Click on the **New** button from the **Quick Access Toolbar**. The **Create New File** dialog box will be displayed.
- Double-click on **Standard(in).ipt** icon from the **English** templates. The Part environment of Autodesk Inventor will be displayed.
- Click on the **Start 2D Sketch** button from the **Sketch** panel in the **3D Model** tab of the **Ribbon**. You are asked to select a sketching plane.
- Click on desired plane to create sketch on it.

Creating Circles

- Click on the **Center Point Circle** tool from **Create** panel in the **Ribbon**. You will be asked to specify center for the circle.
- Click at the origin and enter **1.03** in the Input box displayed for diameter. Note that if Input box is displayed for radius then you need to select **Diameter** option from the right-click shortcut menu.
- Similarly, create the circle of diameter **1.44** using the same center point.
- You can create the other circles of the sketch by using the **Center Point Circle** tool and specify their locations using the **General Dimension** tool; refer to Figure-110.

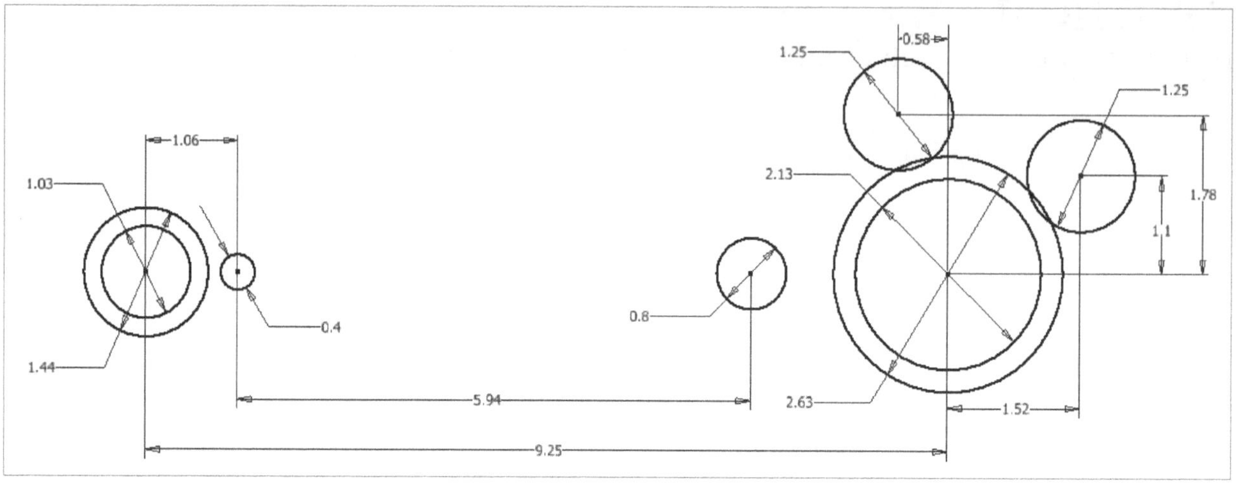

Figure-110. Sketch on creating circles

Creating Mirror Copy

- Click on the **Centerline** button from **Format** panel in the **Ribbon**. The centerline mode will become active.
- Click on the **Line** tool from **Create** panel in the **Ribbon**. You will be asked to specify the starting point of the line.
- Click on the centers of the circles one by one to create the line; refer to Figure-111. Press **ESC** from keyboard to exit the tool.

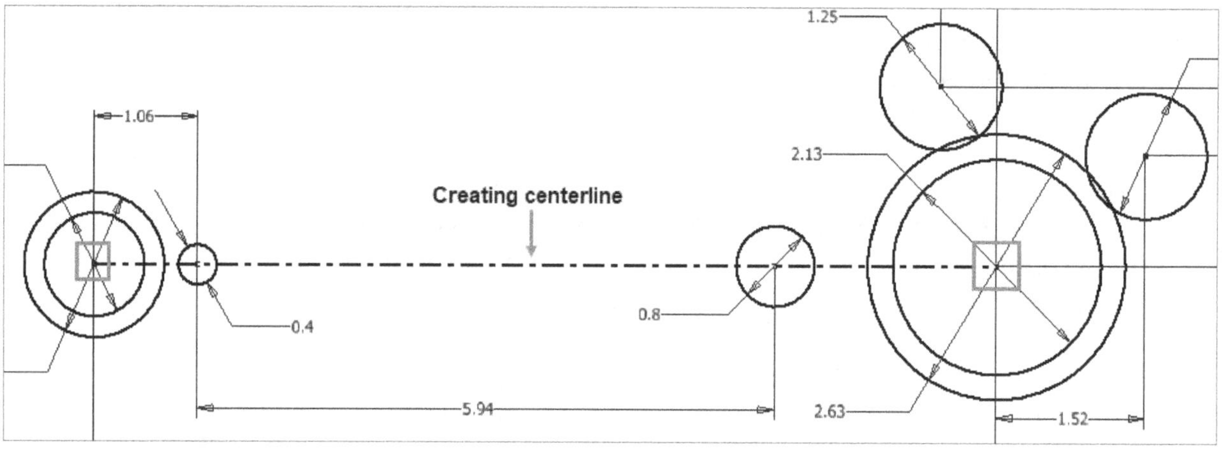

Figure-111. Centerline created

- Click on the **Centerline** button again to exit the centerline mode.
- Click on the **Mirror** tool from **Pattern** panel in the **Ribbon**. You will be asked to select the entities to be mirror copied.
- Select the two circles as shown in Figure-112 and press **ENTER**. You will be asked to select the centerline.

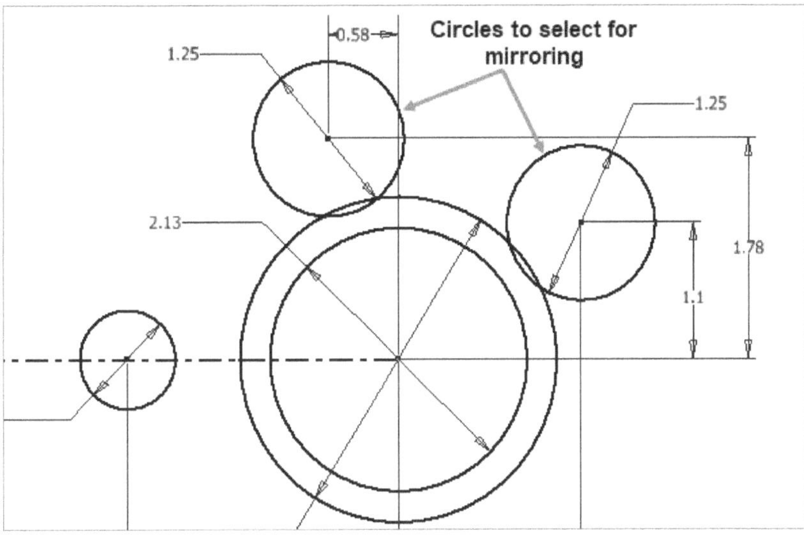

Figure-112. Circles to be selected for mirroring

- Click on the centerline passing through center of circle with diameter **2.130**. The **Apply** button will become active in the **Mirror** dialog box.
- Click on the **Apply** button. The mirror copy of circles will be created. Click on the **Done** button to exit the tool.

Creating Lines

- Click on the **Line** tool from **Create** panel in the **Ribbon**. You will be asked to specify starting point of the line.
- Click on the location which is in vertical line to the center of circle having radius **0.4**; refer to Figure-113.

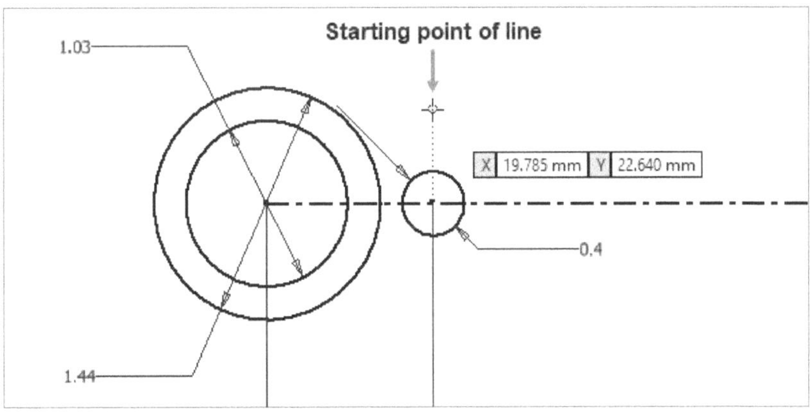

Figure-113. Specifying starting point of line

- Move the cursor straight towards right and enter the distance value as **4.96** in the input box; refer to Figure-114.

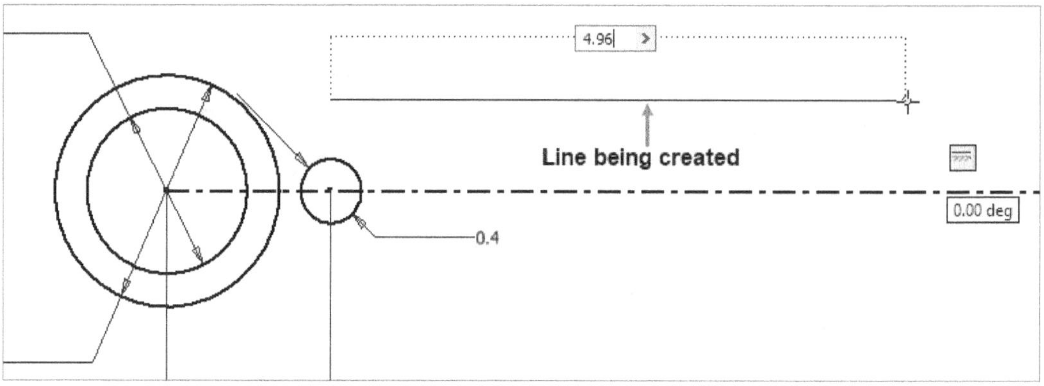

Figure-114. Specifying length of line

- Click on the **General dimension** tool and specify the distance of line from the centerline as **0.38**.
- Create a mirror copy of the line on the other side of centerline; refer to Figure-115.

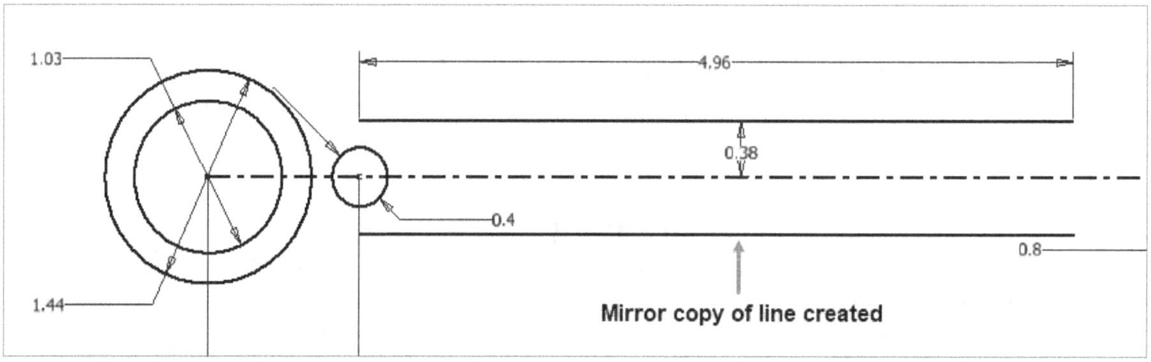

Figure-115. Mirror copy of line created

Creating Arcs

- Click on the **Three Point Arc** tool and click on a point on the circle of diameter **1.44**; refer to Figure-116. You will be asked to specify end point of the arc.

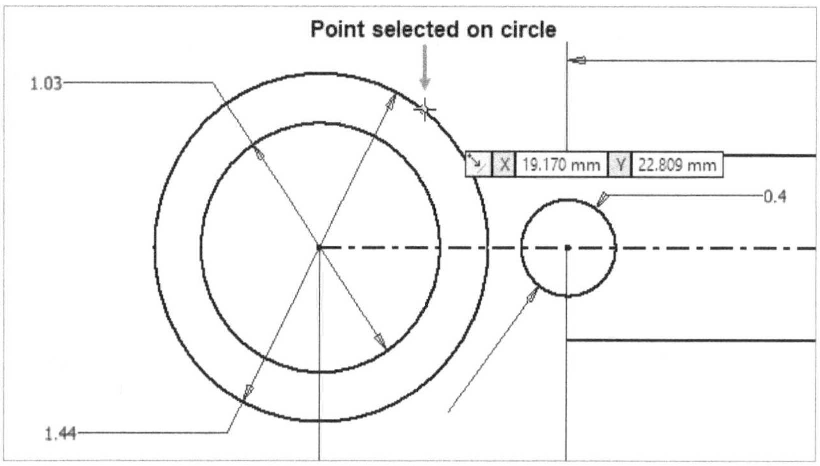

Figure-116. Point selected on circle

- Click at the end point of the line; refer to Figure-117. You will be asked to specify radius of the arc.

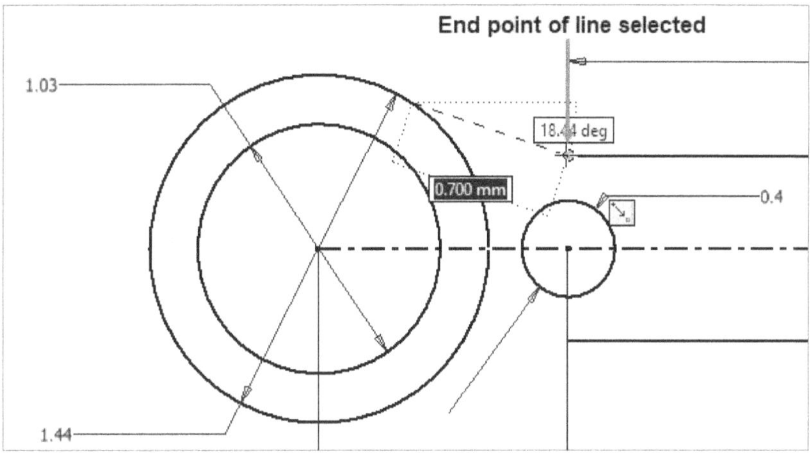

Figure-117. End point of arc specified

- Enter the radius value as **0.81** in the Input box; refer to Figure-118. The arc will be created but it is not tangent to circle and line.

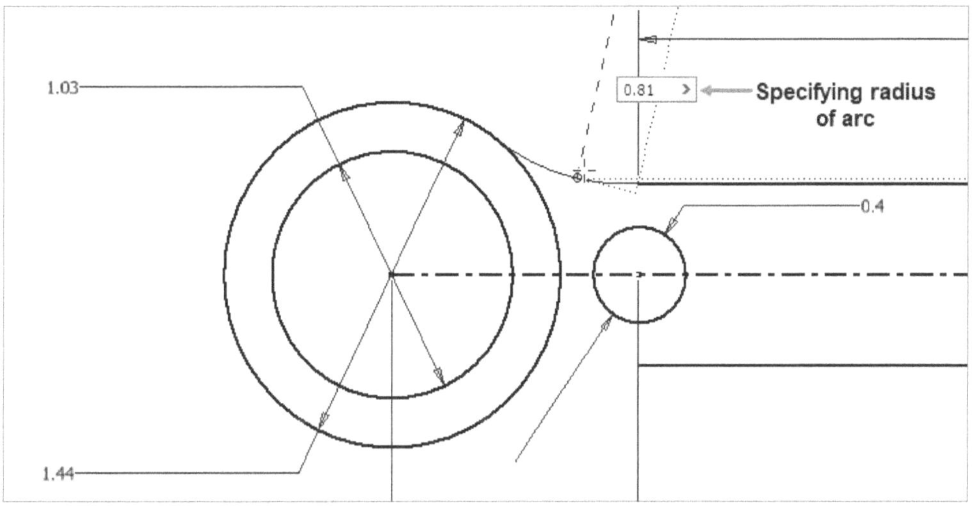

Figure-118. Specifying radius of arc

- Click on the **Tangent** button from **Constrain** panel in the **Ribbon**. You will be asked to select the entities.
- Click on the arc and then on the line near connected end point. Similarly, make the arc tangent to the connected circle; refer to Figure-119.

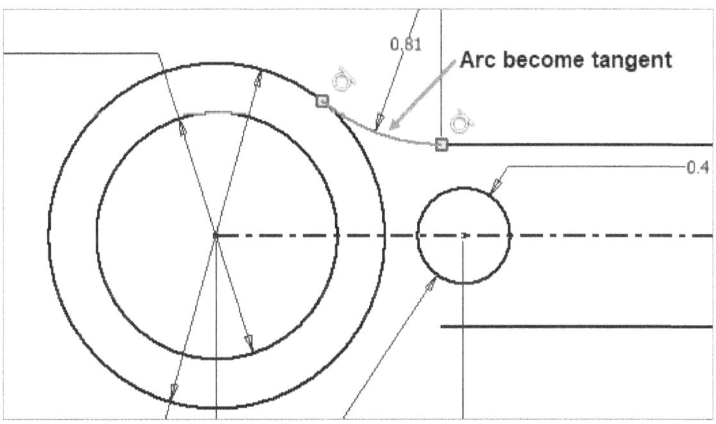

Figure-119. Making arc tangent

- Similarly, create the other arcs and trim the extra sections; refer to Figure-120. The final sketch of Practical 5 will be created; refer to Figure-121.

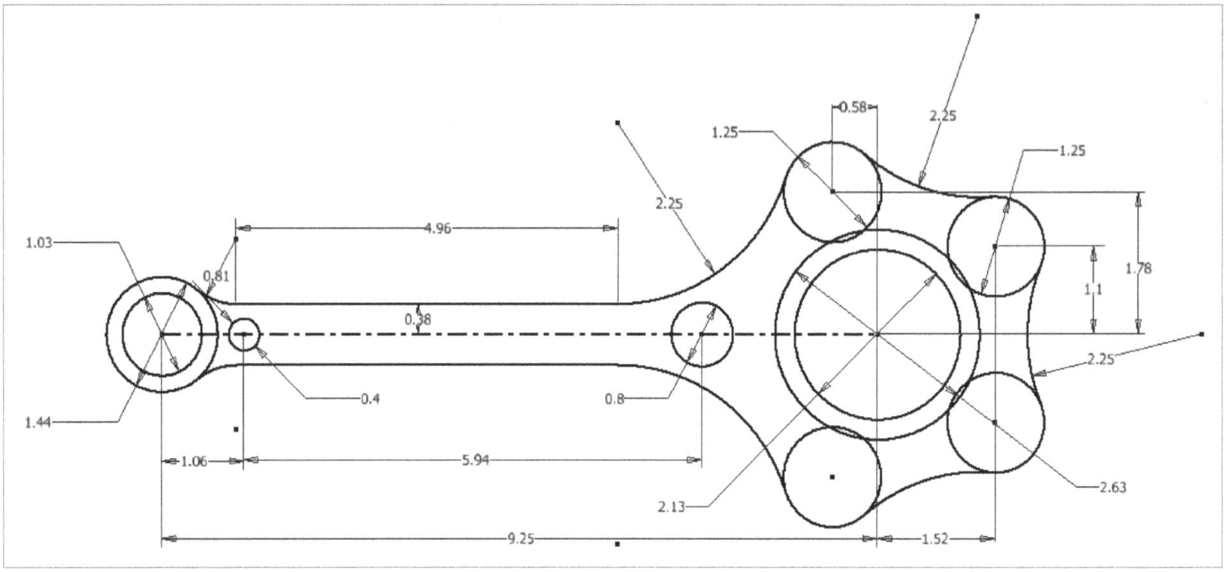

Figure-120. Sketch after creating arcs

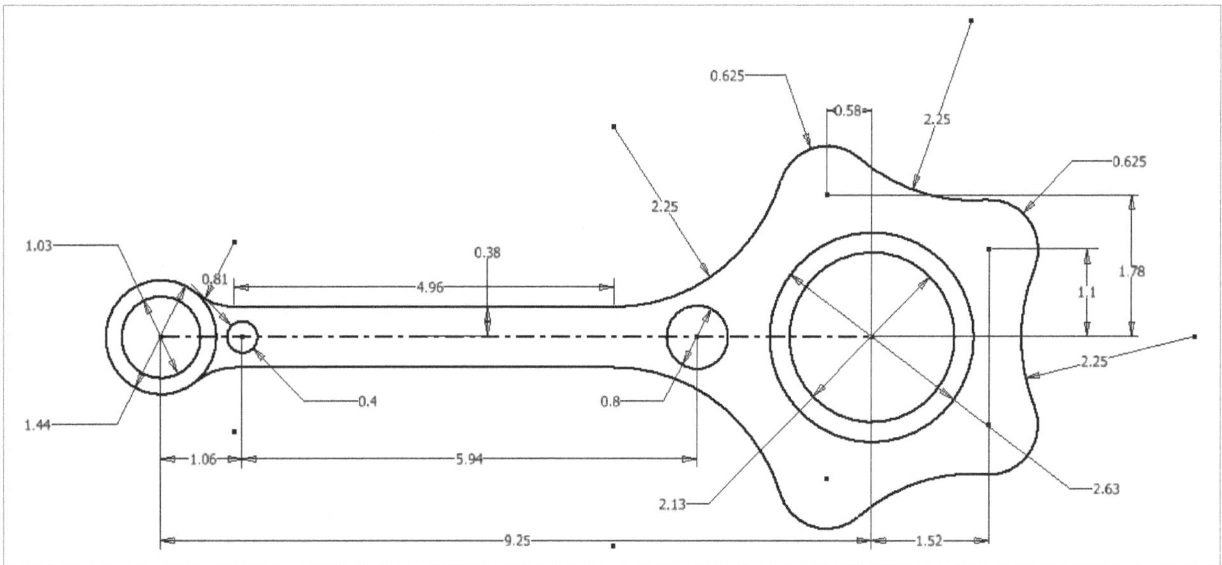

Figure-121. Final sketch for Practical 5

PRACTICE 1

In this practice session, we will create a sketch for the drawing given in Figure-122.

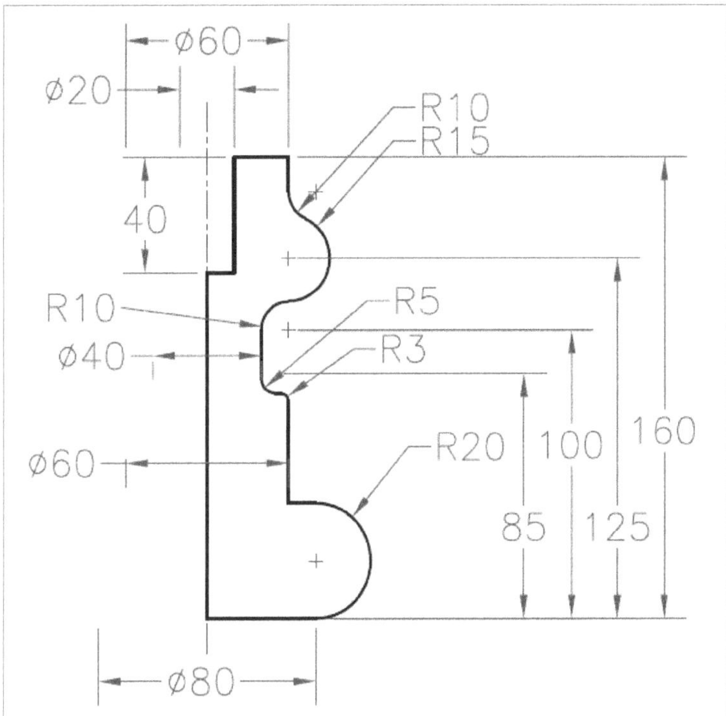

Figure-122. Practice 1

PRACTICE 2

In this practice session, we will create a sketch for the drawing given in Figure-123.

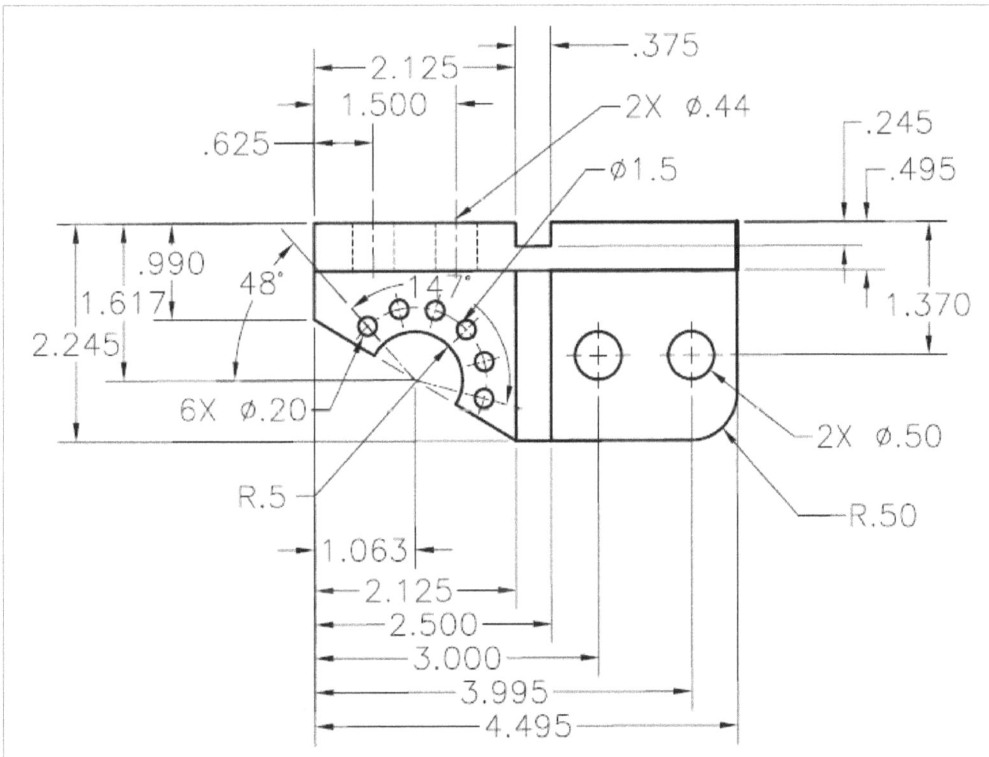

Figure-123. Practice 2

PRACTICE 3

In this practice session, we will create a sketch for the drawing given in Figure-124.

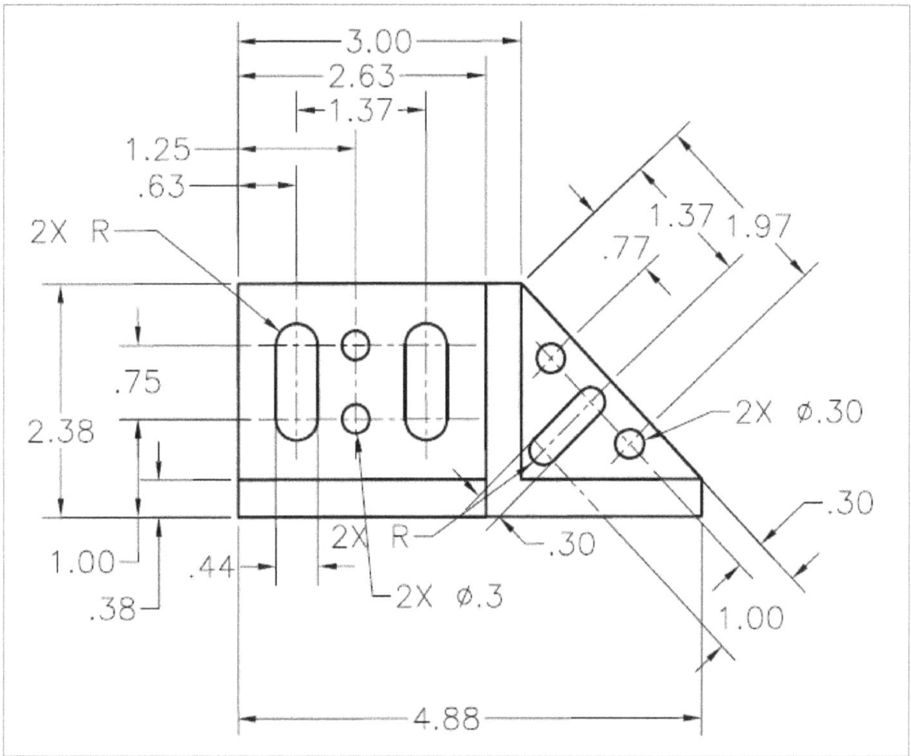

Figure-124. Practice 3

PRACTICE 4

In this practice session, we will create a sketch for the drawing given in Figure-125.

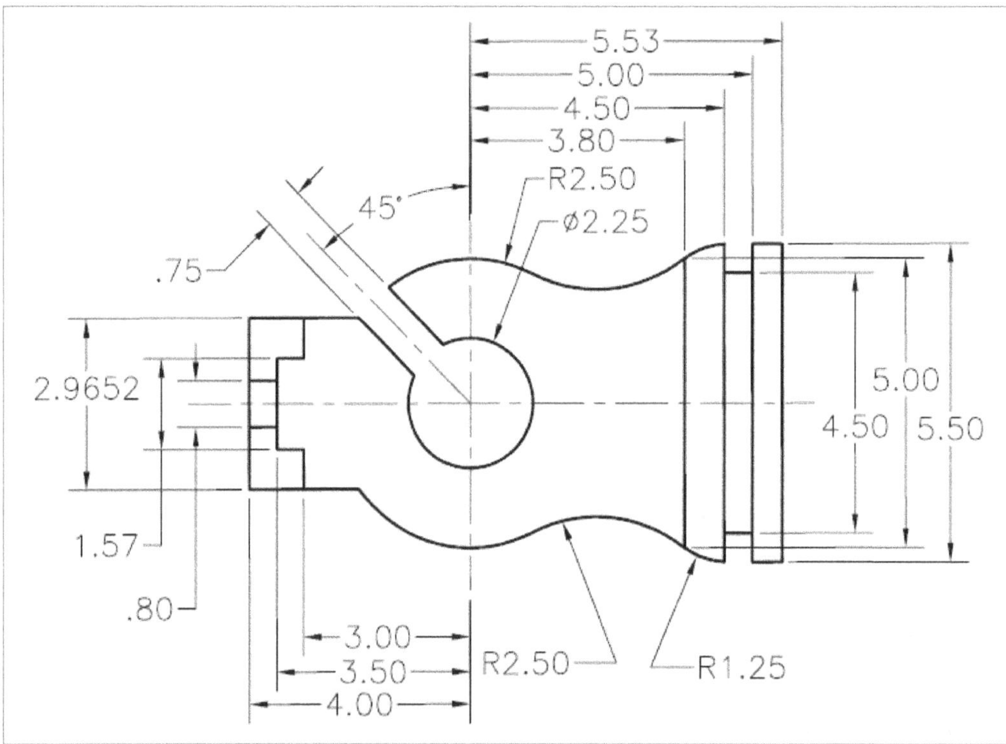

Figure-125. Practice 4

PRACTICE 5

In this practice session, we will create a sketch for the drawing given in Figure-126.

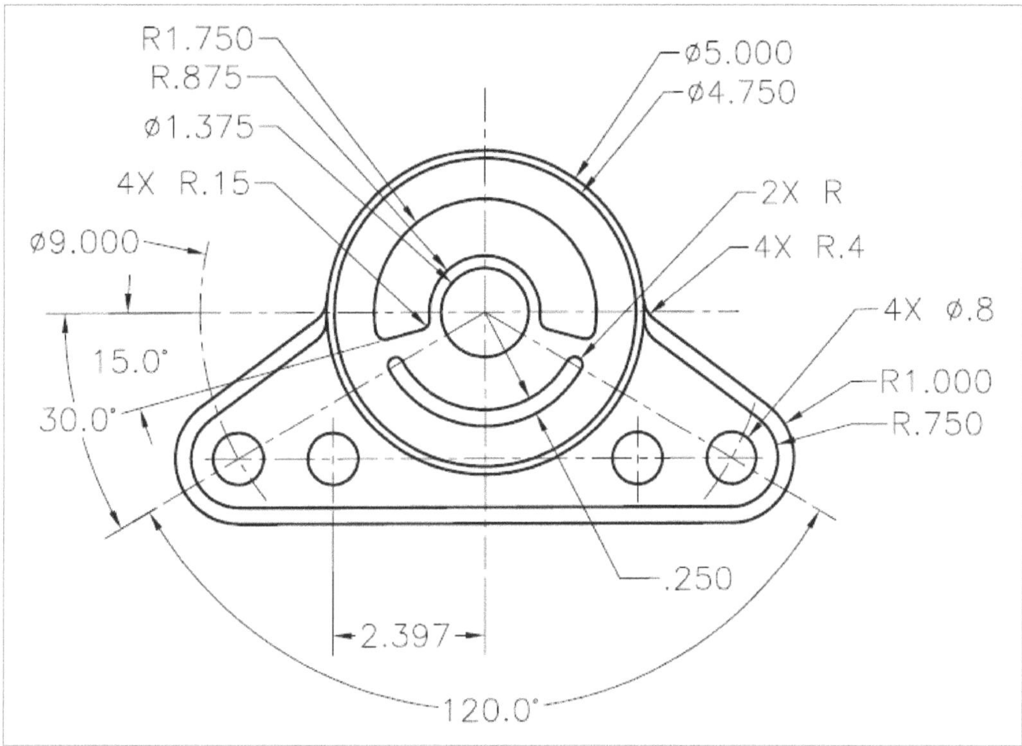

Figure-126. Practice 5

PRACTICE 6

In this practice session, we will create a sketch for the drawing given in Figure-127.

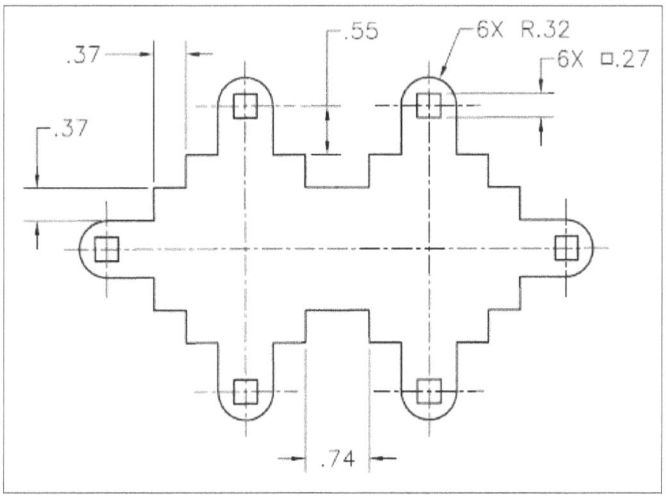

Figure-127. Practice 6

SELF ASSESSMENT

Q1. Which of the following geometries can be dimensioned with **General Dimension** tool?

a) Line
b) Circle
c) Arc
d) All of the above

Q2. Which of the following constraints is used to make two circles, arcs, or ellipses share the same center point?

a) Coincident
b) Collinear
c) Concentric
d) Parallel

Q3. Which of the following constraints is used to make two entities similar about a reference line?

a) Smooth
b) Symmetric
c) Equal
d) Fix

Q4. By enabling which of the following options, the constraints are automatically removed when the sketch entity is selected?

a) Infer constraint
b) Persist constraint
c) Relax mode
d) Fix constraint

Q5. Which of the following objects can be inserted with the help of excel spreadsheet?

a) Text
b) Drawing
c) Image
d) Point

Q6. The **Automatic Dimensions and Constraints** tool is used to automatically apply dimensions and constraints to all the entities in the sketch. (True/False)

Q7. The **Perpendicular** constraint tool is used to make geometries perpendicular to each other. (True/False)

Q8. The **Symmetric** constraint is used to make two selected entities equal in size. (True/False)

Q9. The .... tool is used to display constraints of the selected sketch entities.

Q10. Every sketch entity has .... degree of freedom denoting rotation and translation in each direction.

Q11. .... are used to compel the sketch to retain its shape and position.

Q12. The .... sketch is the one in which more constraints are applied on the sketch entity than the required to fully constrain the sketch.

REVIEW QUESTIONS

Q1. What is the primary use of the General Dimension tool in the Constrain panel?
A. To add color to sketches
B. To draw lines and arcs
C. To apply all types of dimensions in a sketch
D. To import dimensions from another sketch

Q2. What kind of dimension is applied when you select a circle using the General Dimension tool?
A. Radius
B. Circumference
C. Diameter
D. Area

Q3. How can you apply an Aligned Dimension to an inclined line using the General Dimension tool?
A. Select both end points and press ESC
B. Select the line and press ENTER
C. Right-click and choose Aligned from the shortcut menu
D. Double-click the inclined line

Q4. Which tool automatically applies dimensions and constraints to all entities in the sketch?
A. Show Constraints
B. Coincident Constraint
C. Auto Layout
D. Automatic Dimensions and Constraints

Q5. What happens when you use the Show Constraints tool?
A. Constraints are removed
B. The selected entities are deleted
C. Dimensions are converted to constraints
D. Constraints of the selected entities are displayed

Q6. What does the Coincident Constraint do?
A. Makes entities equal in size
B. Fixes entities to the origin
C. Makes entities meet at a point
D. Makes entities tangent

Q7. What is achieved using the Collinear Constraint?
A. Entities are placed on the same line
B. Entities become tangent
C. Entities have the same size
D. Entities share a center point

Q8. What kind of entities can be made concentric using the Concentric Constraint?
A. Circles and lines
B. Arcs, circles, and ellipses
C. Lines and arcs
D. Rectangles and polygons

Q9. Which constraint fixes the position of a curve or point relative to the coordinate system?
A. Coincident
B. Parallel
C. Fix
D. Smooth

Q10. Which constraint ensures two lines are parallel to each other?
A. Tangent
B. Parallel
C. Horizontal
D. Symmetric

Q11. Which entities can be made perpendicular using the Perpendicular Constraint?
A. Only lines
B. Lines and arcs
C. Lines, arcs, and splines
D. Only ellipses

Q12. The Horizontal Constraint can be used to:
A. Rotate the sketch
B. Make lines horizontal or points at the same horizontal level
C. Apply a dimension
D. Make entities symmetric

Q13. What is the function of the Vertical Constraint?
A. Convert entities to vertical lines only
B. Remove all horizontal lines
C. Make entities vertical or points at the same vertical level
D. None of the above

Q14. The Tangent Constraint is used to:
A. Force two entities to be equal
B. Fix the position of a line
C. Make two curves touch at one point
D. Measure distance between curves

Q15. What does the Smooth (G2) Constraint do to a spline?
A. Straightens the spline
B. Deletes the spline
C. Applies a curvature continuous condition
D. Breaks the spline into segments

Q16. What is the Symmetric Constraint used for?
A. Apply equal dimensions
B. Mirror sketch entities
C. Make two entities symmetric about a centerline
D. Convert entities to centerlines

Q17. The Equal Constraint makes:
A. Two entities concentric
B. Two entities of equal size
C. A line equal to a circle
D. Arcs perpendicular

Q18. In the Constraint Settings dialog box, which tab allows you to configure automatic constraint application?
A. Dimension tab
B. Relax Mode tab
C. Inference tab
D. Edit tab

Q19. What happens when Relax Mode is enabled?
A. Constraints are permanently deleted
B. The sketch is locked
C. Constraints are automatically removed when sketch entities are dragged
D. Nothing changes

Q20. What does a Fully Constrained sketch mean?
A. It's constrained to only two degrees of freedom
B. Only horizontal constraints are applied
C. All degrees of freedom of each entity are defined
D. Only dimensions are used

Q21. How can you identify if a sketch is fully constrained in Autodesk Inventor?
A. It says "Under-Constrained" on the top bar
B. The background color changes
C. The Bottom Bar displays "Fully Constrained"
D. Constraints turn red

Q22. Where are the tools for inserting objects from other software into a sketch located in Autodesk Inventor?
A. Constrain panel
B. Annotate tab
C. Insert panel of Sketch tab
D. View tab

Q23. What is the purpose of the Insert Image tool?
A. To convert images into 3D models
B. To create complex parts
C. To insert an image for tracing outlines in a sketch
D. To export images from the sketch

Q24. What happens when you select an image file from outside the active project folder using the Insert Image tool?
A. The file is automatically copied into the project
B. A warning box asks for confirmation
C. The tool closes without inserting
D. The image becomes locked

Q25. What must you do after placing an image with the Insert Image tool?
A. Save the sketch
B. Scale the image
C. Press ESC to exit the tool
D. Convert the image to vector format

Q26. What is the function of the Import Points tool?
A. Import 3D coordinates from CAD files
B. Import data from text documents
C. Insert points using an Excel file with coordinates
D. Create random points in a sketch

Q27. What format must be followed when importing points using an Excel spreadsheet in Autodesk Inventor?
A. Any free-form table layout
B. Columns for X, Y, and Z coordinates in proper order
C. A single row with comma-separated values
D. A list of object IDs and their descriptions

Q28. What is the first step when using the Insert AutoCAD File tool?
A. Click on Import button
B. Select Finish from dialog
C. Click on the Insert AutoCAD File tool
D. Save the file

Q29. What does the Layers and Objects Import Options dialog box allow you to do?
A. Convert 2D sketches to 3D
B. Select specific layers to import from the AutoCAD file
C. Edit AutoCAD drawings
D. Add constraints to the sketch

Q30. What is the final step after selecting layers to import in the Insert AutoCAD File workflow?
A. Press ESC
B. Click Finish
C. Choose a dimension
D. Close the software

Chapter 4

Creating Solid Models

Topics Covered

The major topics covered in this chapter are:

- ***Introduction to 3D Models.***
- ***Work Planes, axes, and geometric point creation.***
- ***Extrude Feature.***
- ***Brief note on Drawings.***
- ***Sketching plane selection.***
- ***Practical and Practice***

INTRODUCTION

We welcome you to the 3D world of Autodesk Inventor. Like any other 3D CAD modeling software, Autodesk Inventor has full set of tools to create 3D models on the basis of specified dimensions. Till this point, we have learned about the 2D sketching tools. Now, we will be using those 2D sketches to create 3D models which can later be used for CAM (Computer Aided Manufacturing) or CAE (Computer Aided Engineering) applications. The tools to create 3D models are available in the **3D Model** tab of the **Ribbon**; refer to Figure-1. We will discuss these tools one by one in this chapter.

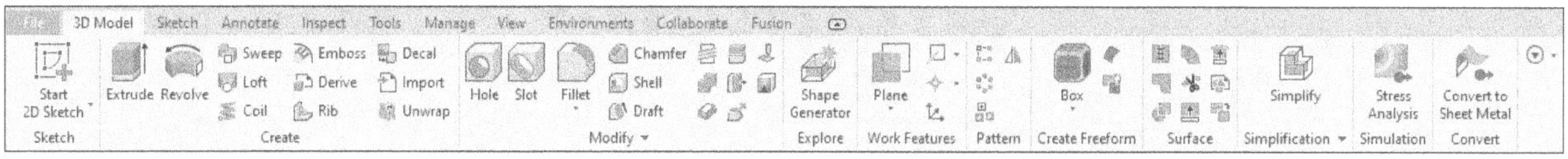

Figure-1. 3D Model tab

Before we starting using the modeling tools, we need to understand the construction geometries like plane, axis, points, and coordinate system. Various construction geometries and their respective tools are discussed next.

WORK PLANE

The Work planes act as floor for 3D model features. By default, three planes are available in Inventor named, XY Plane (Front Plane), YZ Plane (Right Plane), and XZ Plane (Top Plane); refer to Figure-2. To display the default planes, select them from the **Model Browse Bar** in the left of the dialog box while holding the **CTRL** key and right-click on them. A shortcut menu will be displayed; refer to Figure-3. Click on the **Visibility** option from the shortcut menu. The planes will be displayed permanently. We can also create planes whenever required by using the tools available in the **Plane** drop-down of **Work Features** panel in the **Ribbon**; refer to Figure-4. We will learn to use the plane creation tools one by one. Note that there might be some features used for creating plane that you will learn to create later in the book.

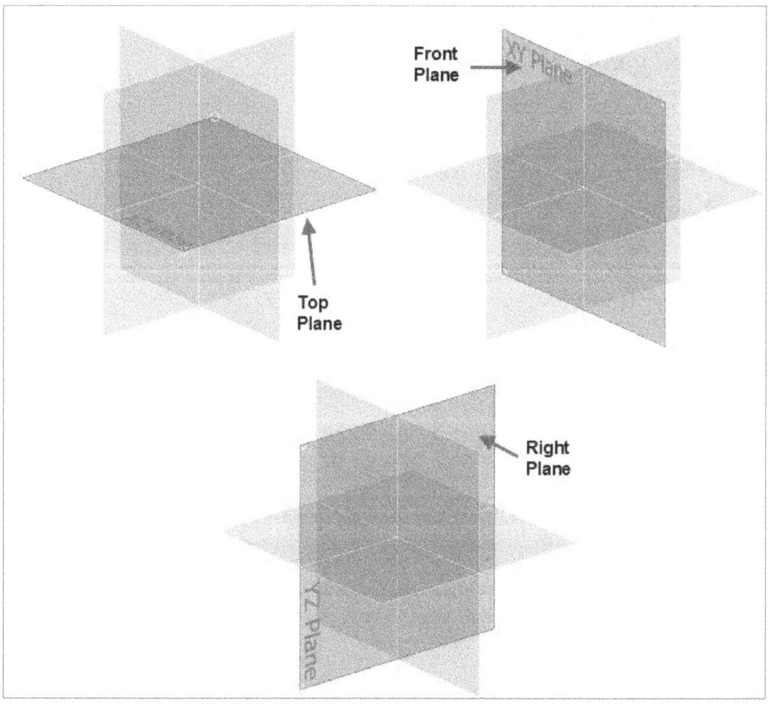

Figure-2. Default Planes

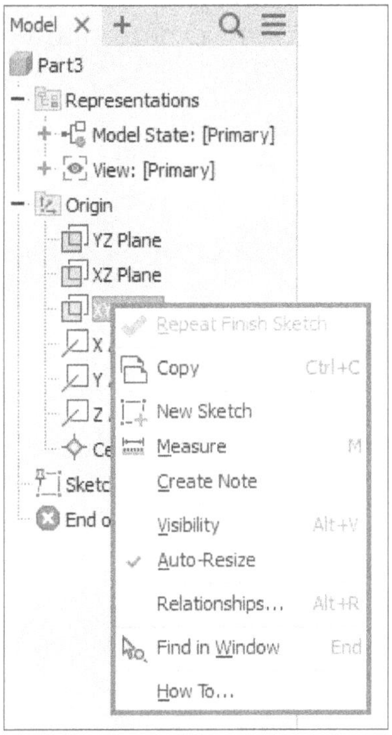

Figure-3. Shortcut menu for planes

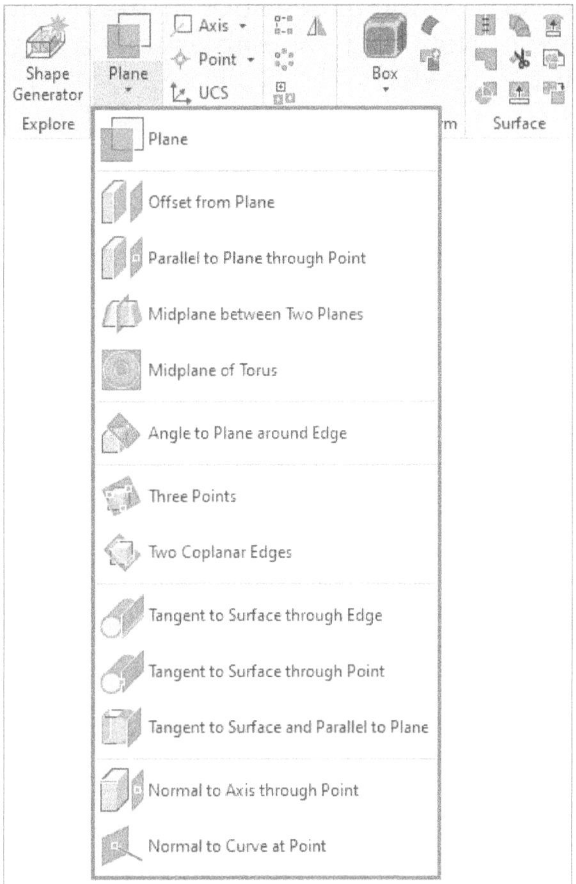

Figure-4. Plane drop-down

Offset from Plane

The **Offset from Plane** tool is used to create a plane at specified offset distance from the selected plane/flat face. The procedure to use this tool is given next.

- Click on the **Offset from Plane** tool from **Plane** drop-down in the **Work Features** panel of the **Ribbon**. You will be asked to select a plane or planar face.
- Select the plane or flat face. You will be asked to specify the offset distance; refer to Figure-5.

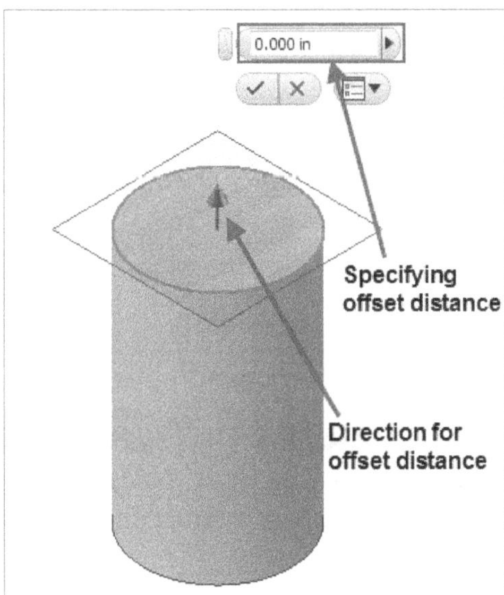

Figure-5. Specifying offset distance for plane

- Enter desired value of distance in the Input box. The plane will be created; refer to Figure-6. Note that you can specify a negative value to create plane in reverse direction.

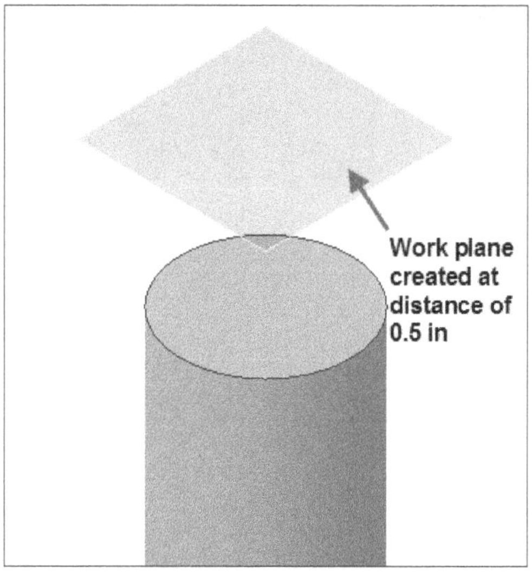

Figure-6. Workplane created

Parallel to Plane through Point

The **Parallel to Plane through Point** tool, as the name suggests, is used to create plane parallel to the selected plane and passing through selected point. The procedure to create plane using this tool is given next.

- Click on the **Parallel to Plane through Point** tool from **Plane** drop-down in the **Work Features** panel of the **Ribbon**. You will be asked to select a point or plane.
- Click on the plane or face to which you want the new plane to be parallel. You will be asked to select a point through which you want the plane to pass.
- Click on the point. The new work plane will be created; refer to Figure-7.

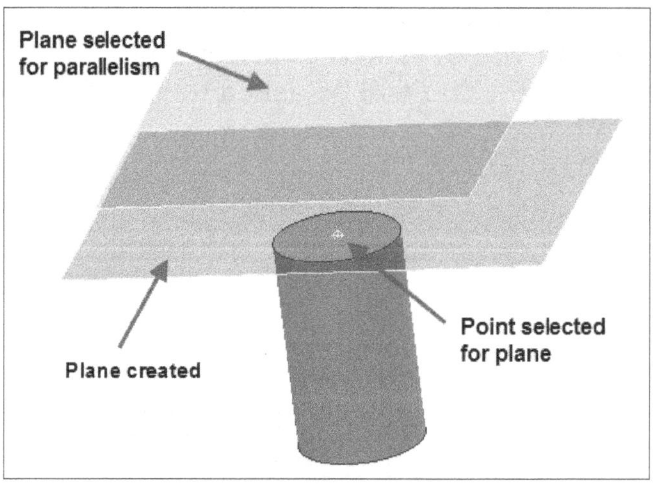

Figure-7. Plane created through point

Midplane between Two Planes

The **Midplane between Two Planes** tool is used to create a plane through the median of selected planes. The procedure to create midplane is given next.

- Click on the **Midplane between Two Planes** tool from **Plane** drop-down in the **Work Features** panel of the **Ribbon**. You will be asked to select the first plane.
- Click on the first plane/face. You will be asked to select the second plane.
- As soon as you hover the cursor on other plane/face, preview of the new plane will be displayed; refer to Figure-8.

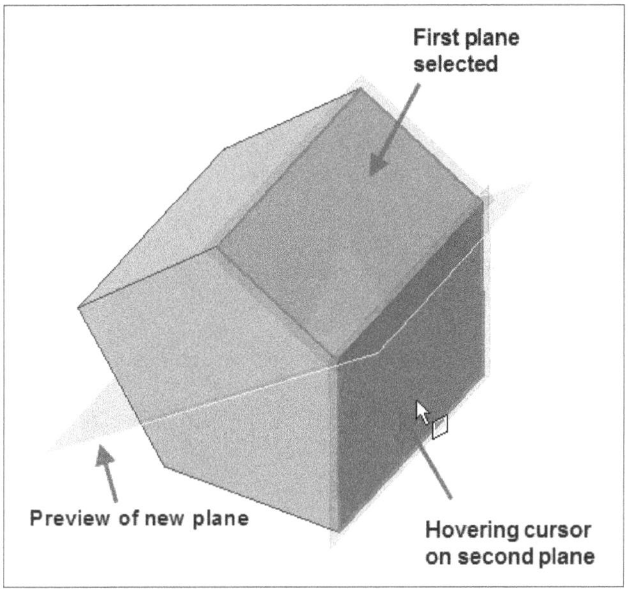

Figure-8. Creating midplane

- Click on the second plane/face to create the mid plane.

Midplane of Torus Tool

The **Midplane of Torus** tool is specific tool to create plane at the middle of torus. The procedure to use this tool is given next.

- Click on the **Midplane of Torus** tool from **Plane** drop-down in the **Work Features** panel of the **Ribbon**. You will be asked to select a torus.
- Click on the torus. A plane will be created dividing the torus at middle; refer to Figure-9.

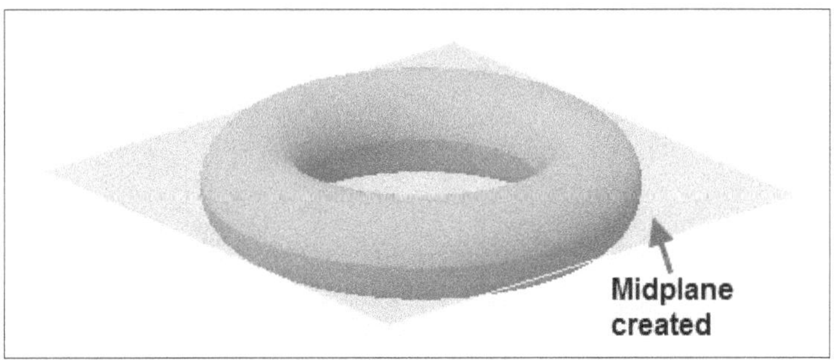

Figure-9. Midplane of torus

Angle to Plane around Edge

The **Angle to Plane around Edge** tool is used to create a plane at an angle to the selected plane around the selected edge. This option is very helpful when you are going to create features at an angle to the other features. The procedure to create plane by using this tool is given next.

- Click on the **Angle to Plane around Edge** tool from **Plane** drop-down in the **Work Features** panel of the **Ribbon**. You will be asked to select a line or a plane.
- Click on the plane which you want to set as reference for angle. In simple words, select the plane to which the new plane will be at angle. You will be asked to select a line or edge.
- Click on the edge or line that you want to use as hinge for rotation of plane. You will be asked to specify the rotation angle; refer to Figure-10.

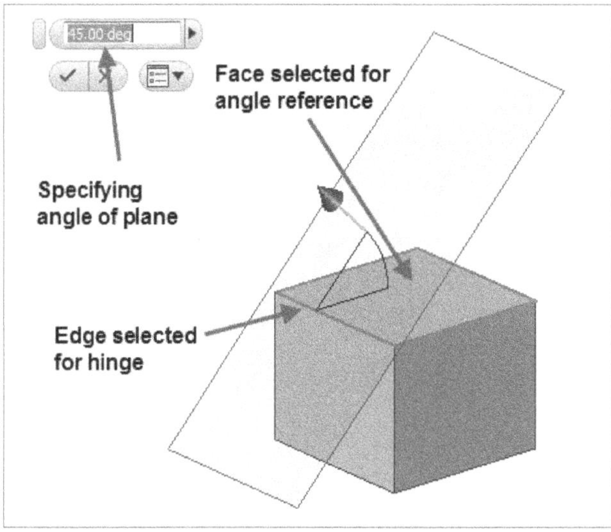

Figure-10. Creating plane at angle

- Enter desired value of angle in the Input box. The plane will be created at specified angle; refer to Figure-11.

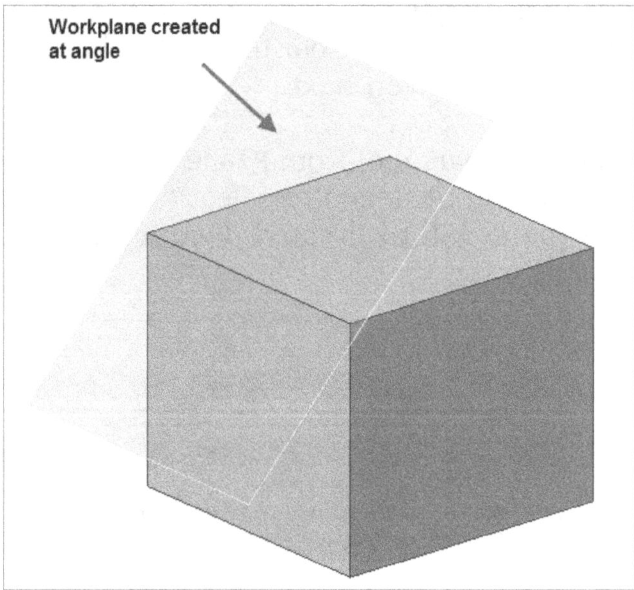

Figure-11. Workplane created at angle

Three Points

The **Three Points** tool is used to create plane passing through the specified three points. The procedure to use this tool is given next.

- Click on the **Three Points** tool from the **Plane** drop-down. You will be asked to select the reference points.

- Click on desired three points one by one. The plane will be created; refer to Figure-12.

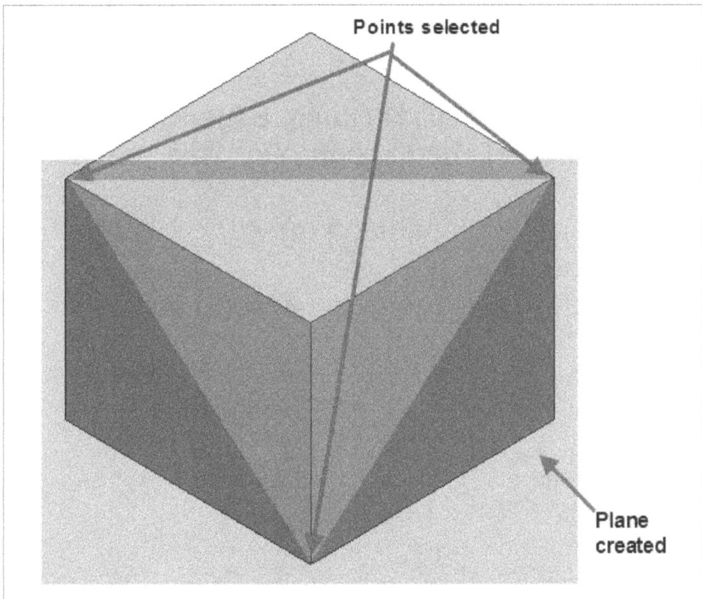

Figure-12. Three point plane created

Two Coplanar Edges

The **Two Coplanar Edges** tool is used to create a plane passing through the two selected coplanar edges. The procedure to create plane by using this tool is given next.

- Click on the **Two Coplanar Edges** tool from **Plane** drop-down in the **Work Features** panel of the **Ribbon**. You will be asked to select an edge, axis, or line.
- Click on desired edge/axis/line. You will be asked to select the second edge/axis/line.
- Hover the cursor on desired edge/axis/line. Preview of the plane will be displayed; refer to Figure-13.
- Click on the edge/line/axis to create the plane.

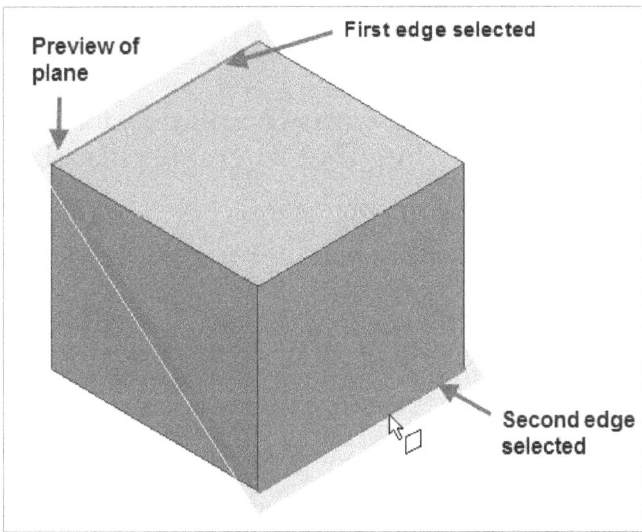

Figure-13. Preview of plane

Tangent to Surface through Edge

The **Tangent to Surface through Edge** tool, as the name suggests, is used to create a plane tangent to the selected surface and passing through the selected edge. The procedure to use this tool is given next.

- Click on the **Tangent to Surface through Edge** tool from the **Plane** drop-down in the **Work Features** panel of the **Ribbon**. You will be asked to select an edge or surface.
- Click on desired round surface to which you want to make the plane tangent. You will be asked to select the edge.
- Click on the edge through which the plane should pass. The plane will be created; refer to Figure-14.

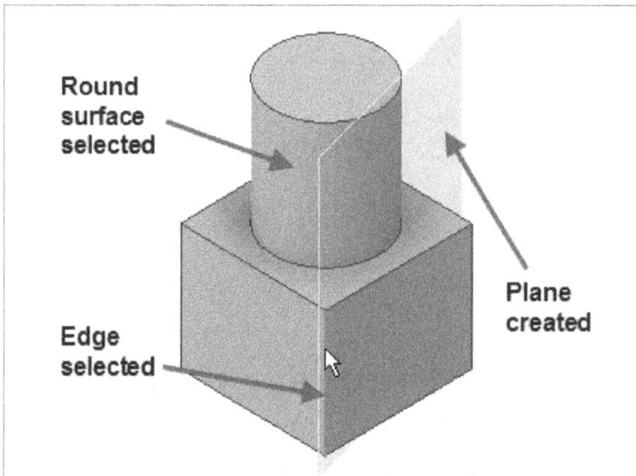

Figure-14. Tangent plane through edge

Tangent to Surface through Point

The **Tangent to Surface through Point** tool is used to create a plane tangent to the selected surface and passing through the selected point. The procedure to create plane by using this tool is given next.

- Click on the **Tangent to Surface through Point** tool from **Plane** drop-down in the **Work Features** panel of the **Ribbon**. You will be asked to select a point or surface.
- Click on the point through which you want the plane to pass. You will be asked to select a round surface.
- Click on the surface to which you want the plane to be tangent. The plane will be created; refer to Figure-15. Note that to create this plane, the point must be on the curved surface.

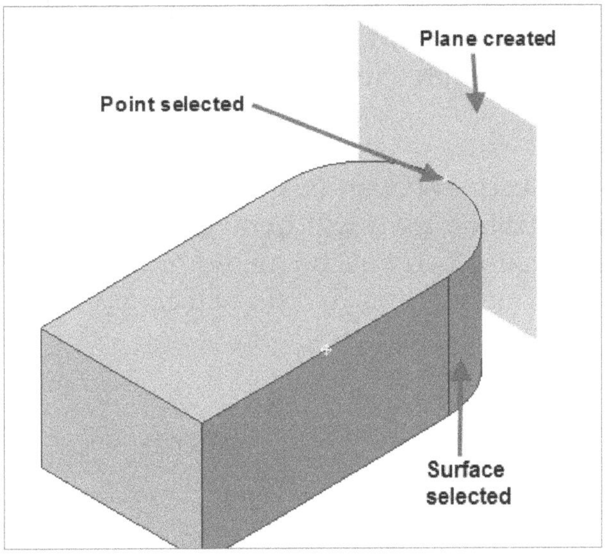

Figure-15. Tangent plane through point

Tangent to Surface and Parallel to Plane

The **Tangent to Surface and Parallel to Plane** tool is used to create a plane tangent to the selected surface and parallel to the selected plane. The procedure to use this tool is given next.

- Click on the **Tangent to Surface and Parallel to Plane** tool from **Plane** drop-down in the **Work Features** panel of the **Ribbon**. You will be asked to select a curved surface or a plane.
- Select the curved surface that you want to be tangent to the plane. You will be asked to select a plane.
- Click on the plane to which you want the new plane to be parallel. The plane will be created; refer to Figure-16.

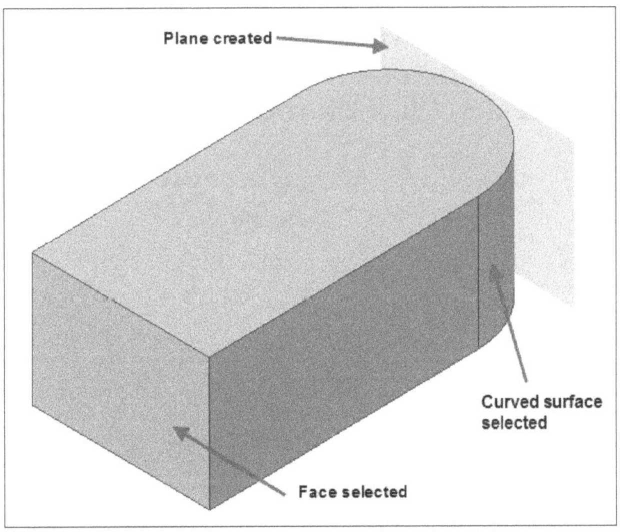

Figure-16. Tangent plane parallel to selected face

Normal to Axis through Point

The **Normal to Axis through Point** tool is used to create a plane normal to the selected axis and passing through the point. The procedure to use this tool is given next.

- Click on the **Normal to Axis through Point** tool from **Plane** drop-down in the **Work Features** panel of the **Ribbon**. You will be asked to select an edge/axis or point.
- Click on desired edge/axis. You will be asked to select a point.
- Click on the point. A plane normal to axis will be created; refer to Figure-17.

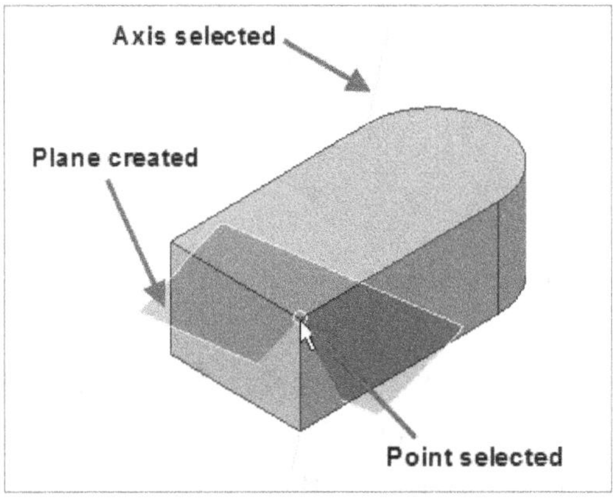

Figure-17. Plane created normal to axis

Normal to Curve at Point

The **Normal to Curve at Point** tool is used to create a plane normal to the selected curve and passing through the selected point. The procedure to use this tool is given next.

- Click on the **Normal to Curve at Point** tool from **Plane** drop-down in the **Work Features** panel of the **Ribbon**. You will be asked to select a curve or point.
- Click on desired point of the curve to which the plane should be perpendicular. You will be asked to select a curve.
- As soon as you hover the cursor on desired curve, a preview of plane will be displayed; refer to Figure-18. Click on the curve to create the plane.

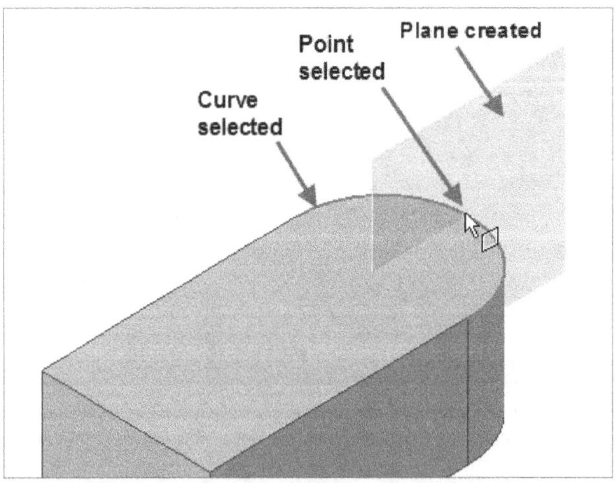

Figure-18. Plane created normal to curve

Plane

Yes!! This was the first tool in the **Plane** drop-down and we are discussing it at the last. This is because the **Plane** tool can create all the type of planes discussed earlier except the offsetted planes. The procedure to use this tool is given next.

- Click on the **Plane** tool from **Plane** drop-down in the **Work Features** panel of the **Ribbon**. You will be asked to select a geometry.
- Select desired geometries one by one. The plane will be created based on the selection.

AXIS

Axis is generally used to support creation of round features and creation of planes. It can also be used as reference for directions. The tools to create axes are available in the **Axis** drop-down in the **Work Features** panel of the **Ribbon**; refer to Figure-19. Tools in this drop-down are discussed next.

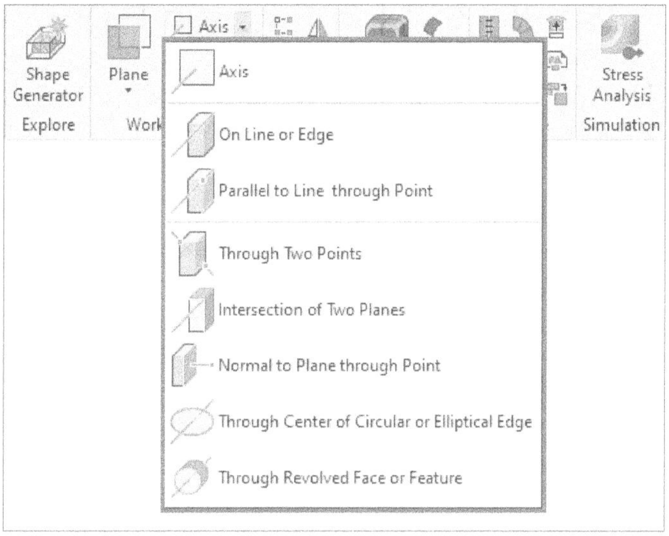

Figure-19. Axis drop-down

On Line or Edge

The **On Line or Edge** tool is used to create an axis on the selected line/edge. The procedure to use this tool is given next.

- Click on the **On Line or Edge** tool from **Axis** drop-down in the **Work Features** panel of the **Ribbon**. You will be asked to select an edge or line.
- Click on the edge or line. An axis will be created along the selected edge/line; refer to Figure-20.

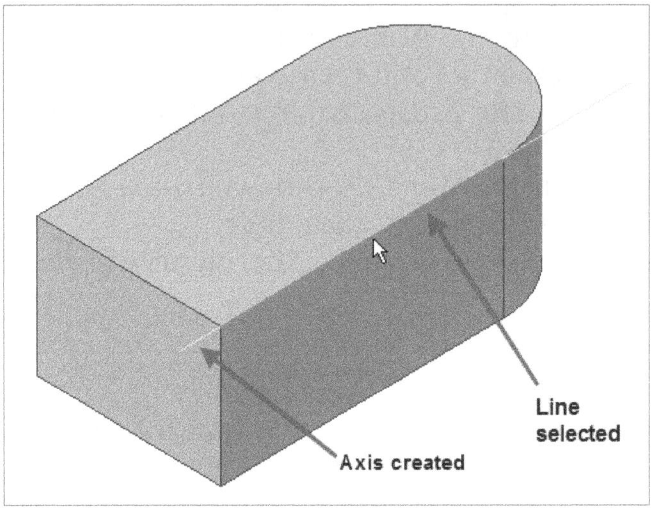

Figure-20. Axis created along selected edge or line

Parallel to Line through Point

The **Parallel to Line through Point** tool, as the name suggests, is used to create an axis parallel to selected edge/line and passing through the selected point. The procedure to create axis by this tool is given next.

- Click on the **Parallel to Line through Point** tool from **Axis** drop-down in the **Work Features** panel of the **Ribbon**. You will be asked to select a line/edge or point.
- Click on desired line/edge. You will be asked to select a point.
- Click on desired point. The axis will be created passing through the selected point; refer to Figure-21.

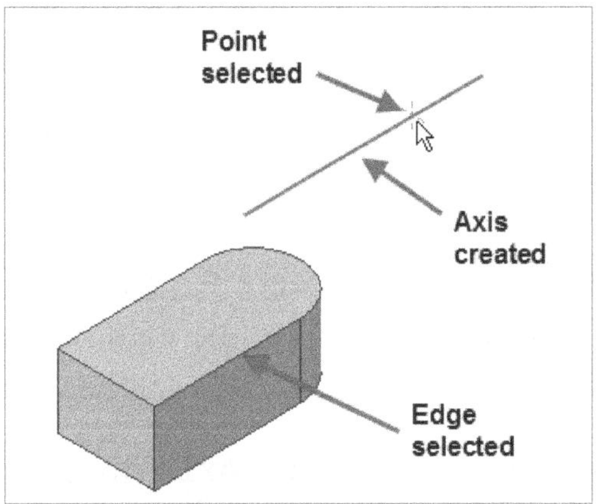

Figure-21. Axis created passing through point

Through Two Points

The **Through Two Points** tool is used to create an axis passing through selected two points. The procedure to use this tool is given next.

- Click on the **Through Two Points** tool from **Axis** drop-down in the **Work Features** panel of the **Ribbon**. You will be asked to select a point.
- Click on desired two points one by one. The axis will be created; refer to Figure-22.

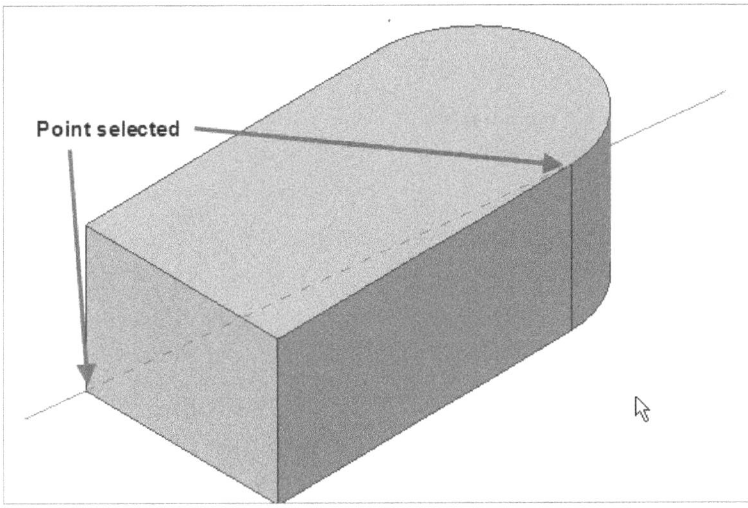

Figure-22. Axis created through points

Intersection of Two Planes

The **Intersection of Two Planes** tool is used to create an axis at the intersection of two planes. The procedure to use this tool is given next.

- Click on the **Intersection of Two Planes** tool from **Axis** drop-down in the **Work Features** panel of the **Ribbon**. You will be asked to select a plane.
- Click on the two intersecting planes/faces. The axis at the intersection of planes/faces will be created; refer to Figure-23.

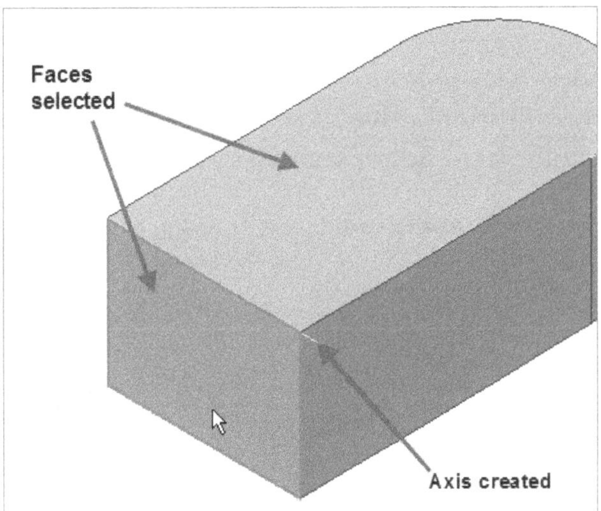

Figure-23. Axis created at intersection

Normal to Plane through Point

The **Normal to Plane through Point** tool is used to create an axis perpendicular to selected plane and passing through the selected point. The procedure to use this tool is given next.

- Click on the **Normal to Plane through Point** tool from **Axis** drop-down in the **Work Features** panel of the **Ribbon**. You will be asked to select a plane or point.
- Select the plane to which the axis should be normal. You will be asked to select a point.

- Click on the point through which the axis should pass. The axis will be created; refer to Figure-24.

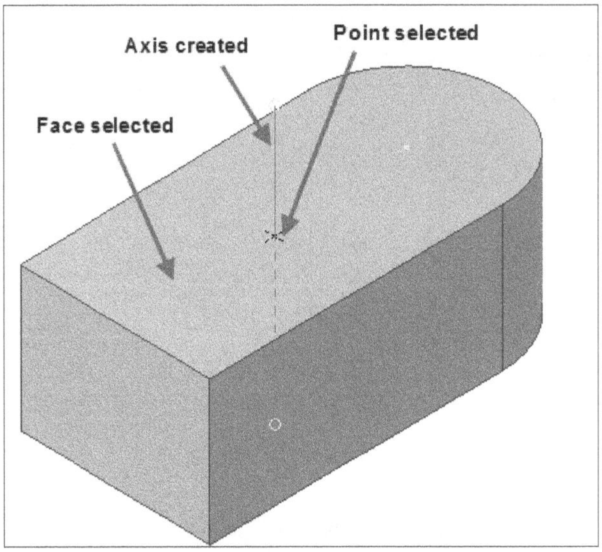

Figure-24. Axis passing through point

Through Center of Circular or Elliptical Edge

The **Through Center of Circular or Elliptical Edge** tool is used to create an axis passing through the center of circular or elliptical edge selected. The procedure to use this tool is given next.

- Click on the **Through Center of Circular or Elliptical Edge** tool from **Axis** drop-down in the **Work Features** panel of the **Ribbon**. You will be asked to select circular/elliptical edge or a sketched curve.
- Click on the circular/elliptical edge. An axis will be created passing through the center of circular or elliptical edge; refer to Figure-25.

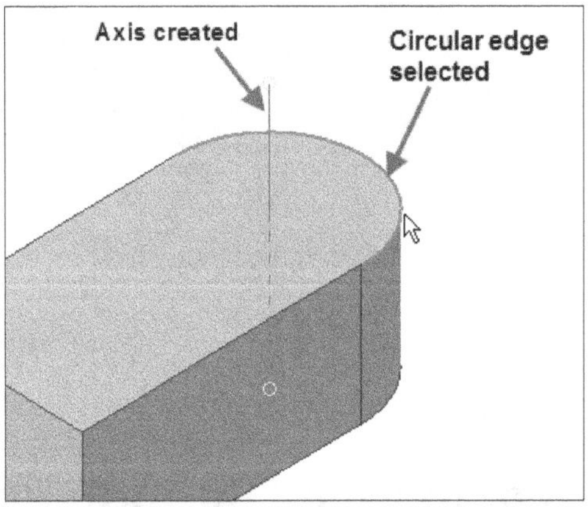

Figure-25. Axis created at center of circular edge

Through Revolved Face or Feature

The **Through Revolved Face or Feature** tool is used to create an axis passing through the centerline of revolved face/feature. The procedure to use this tool is given next.

- Click on the **Through Revolved Face or Feature** tool from **Axis** drop-down in the **Work Features** panel of the **Ribbon**. You will be asked to select a cylindrical or revolved surface.
- Select the cylindrical/revolved surface. An axis will be created; refer to Figure-26.

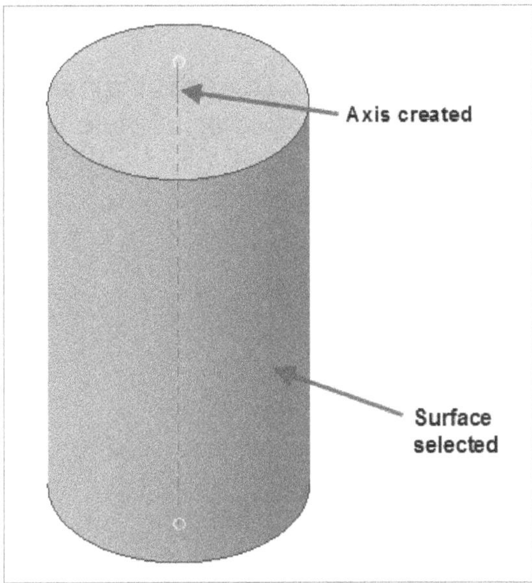

Figure-26. Axis through cylindrical surface

Axis

The **Axis** tool can be used to create any type of axis we have discussed before. After selecting this tool, make the selections based on axis requirement.

POINT

Point is an imaginary smallest geometric entity. Theoretically, point has zero size. Points are used to provide reference for other geometric features. The tools to create point are available in **Point** drop-down in the **Work Features** panel of the **Ribbon**; refer to Figure-27.

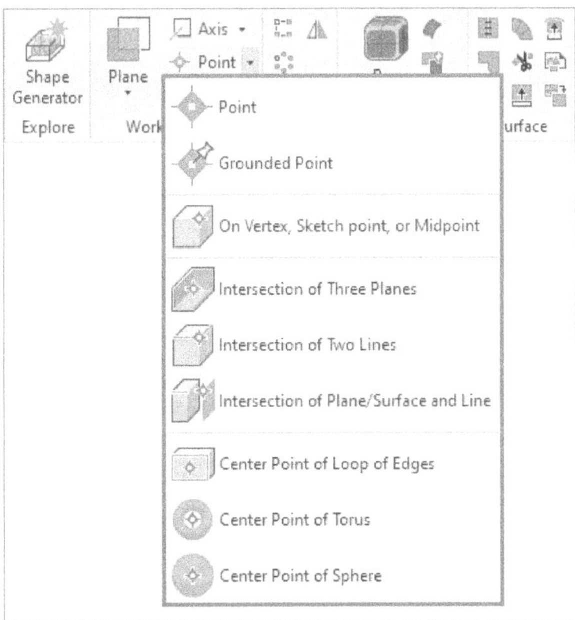

Figure-27. Point drop-down

The tools in this drop-down are discussed next.

Grounded Point

The **Grounded Point** tool is used to create points in reference to selected key point (like end point, mid point, etc.). The procedure to use this tool is given next.

- Click on the **Grounded Point** tool from the **Point** drop-down in the **Work Features** panel of the **Ribbon**. You will be asked to select the vertex or work point.
- Click on desired vertex or work point. A triad will be displayed at the selected vertex; refer to Figure-28.

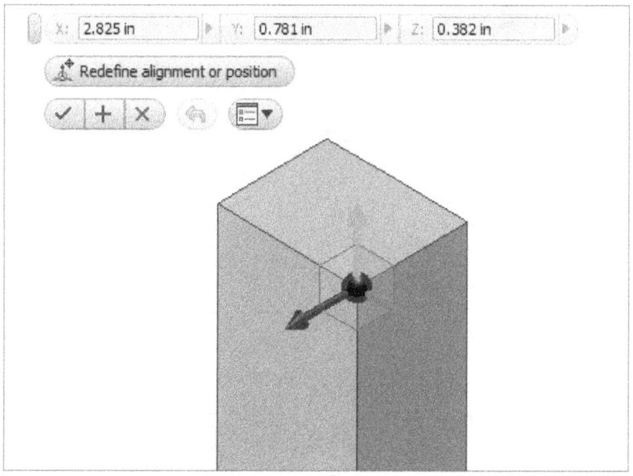

Figure-28. Triad displayed on point

- Click on the arrow to move the point in respective direction. The edit box for selected direction will be active in the Input boxes; refer to Figure-29.

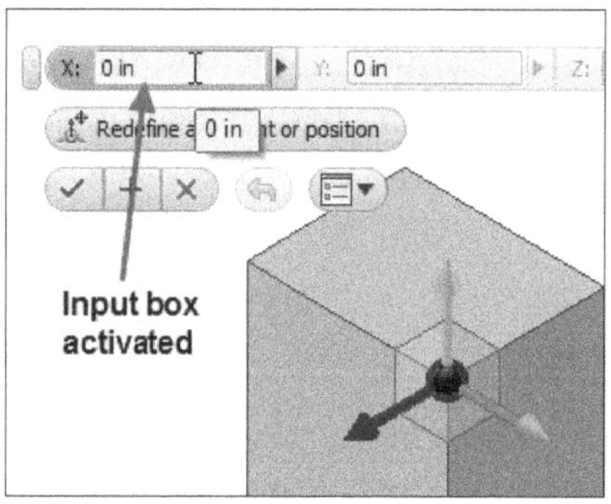

Figure-29. Input box active

- Enter desired distance value in the Input box to specify location of the point in respective direction. Similarly, you can set the location of point in other directions.
- If you want to add more points then click on the **Apply** button + from the Input boxes. You will be asked to specify location of the next point. Repeat the procedure until you get desired number of points.
- Click on the **OK** ✓ button from the Input boxes to create the point.

Similarly, you can use the other tools in the **Point** drop-down to create points at desired locations.

Since, you have basic understanding of planes, axes, and points; it is now time to create some basic solid features. The tools to create solid features are available in the **Create** panel of the **3D Model** tab in the **Ribbon**; refer to Figure-30. These tools are discussed next.

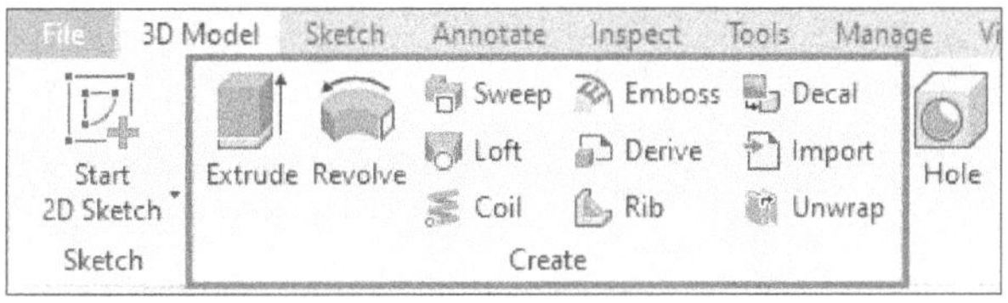

Figure-30. Create panel of 3D Model tab

EXTRUDE TOOL

The **Extrude** tool is used to create a solid volume by adding height to the selected sketch. In other words, this tool adds material by using the boundaries of sketch in the direction perpendicular to the plane of sketch. The procedure to use this tool is given next.

- Click on the **Extrude** tool from **Create** panel in the **3D Model** tab of the **Ribbon**. You will be asked to select a sketching plane.
- Select a plane and create a desired sketch for extrusion.
- Click on the **Finish Sketch** tool to exit the sketching environment. The **Extrude** dialog box will be displayed along with the preview of extrusion; refer to Figure-31.

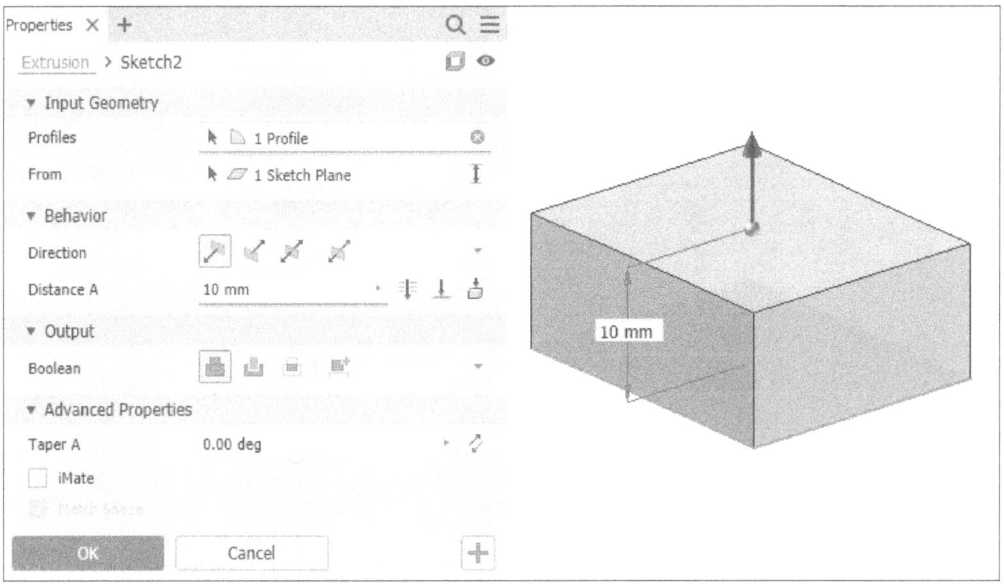

Figure-31. Extrude dialog box with preview of extrusion

Specifying Distance for Extrusion

- To specify the depth of extrusion, enter the desired value in the **Distance A** edit box in the dialog box; refer to Figure-32.

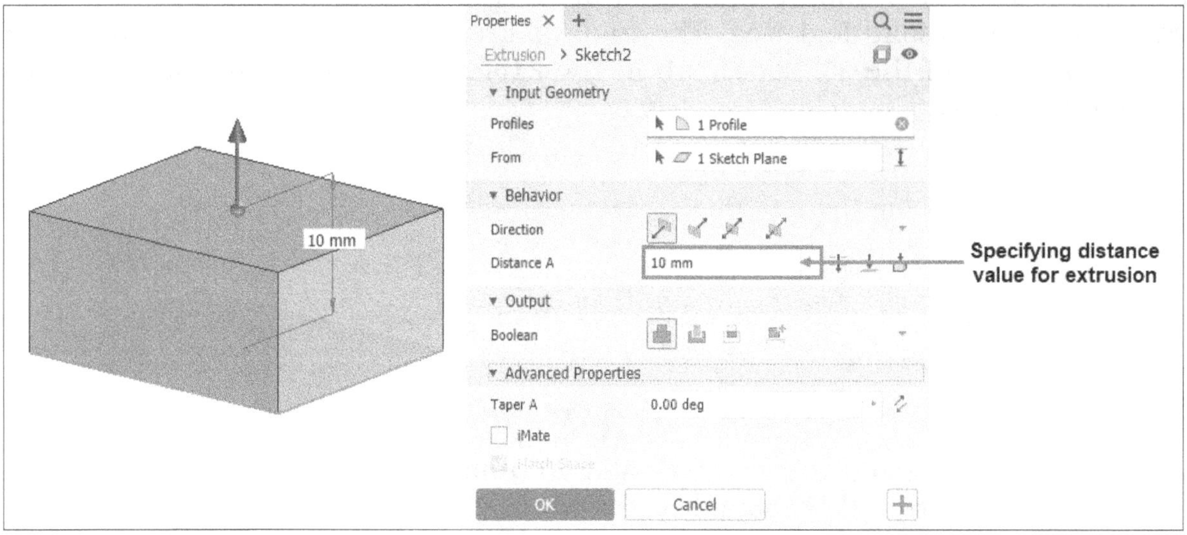

Figure-32. Specifying depth of extrusion

- There are four options to manage direction of extrusion viz. **Default**, **Flipped**, **Symmetric**, and **Asymmetric**; refer to Figure-33.

You can switch between **Icons** and **Dropdown** to display **Direction** options by selecting respective option from the **Selector Style** flyout; refer to Figure-34.

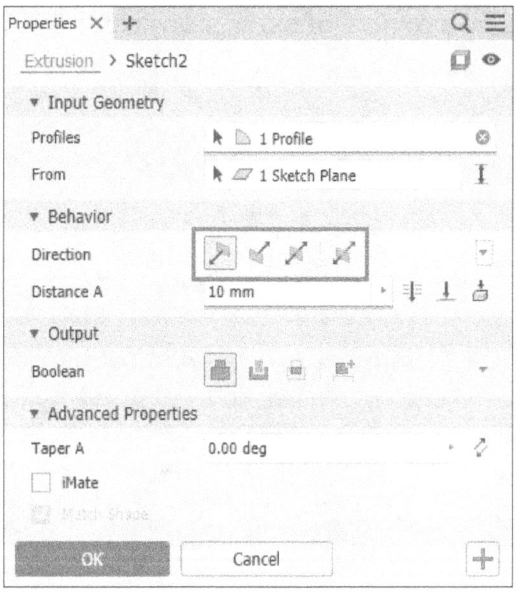

Figure-33. Direction of extrusion

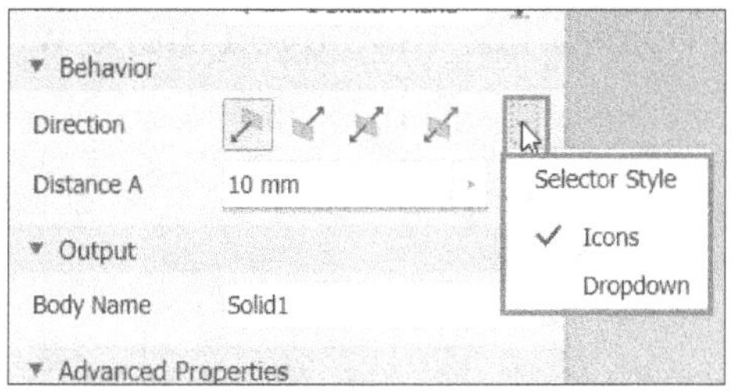

Figure-34. Selector Style flyout

When we were creating planes, you might have noticed two colors of plane, light orange and light blue. If no! Try to rotate the model by holding the **SHIFT** key and dragging the cursor using middle mouse button. The light orange side of plane is positive side and in case of extrusion, Default Direction. The light blue side of plane is negative side and in case of extrusion, Flipped Direction.

- Select the **Default** or **Flipped** button to create the extrusion in respective direction. If you want to create extrusion to both sides of sketching plane with same depth value then select the **Symmetric** button. If you want to create extrusion to both sides of sketching plane but with different depth value in each direction then click on the **Asymmetric** option. On selecting the **Asymmetric** option, two distance edit boxes will be displayed in the dialog box; refer to Figure-35. Specify desired distance for each direction.

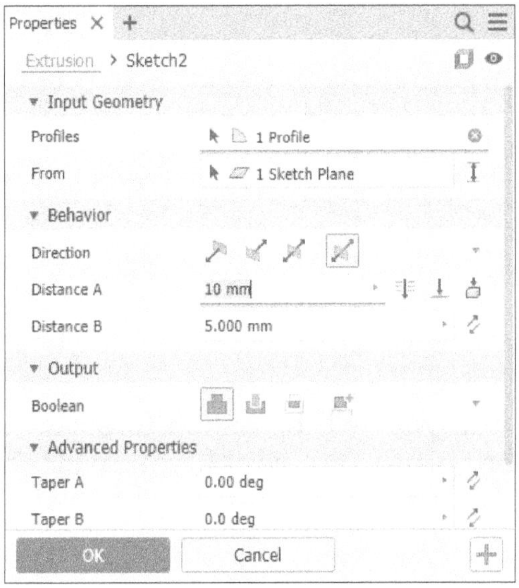

Figure-35. Specifying distances for asymmetric extrusion

Setting Extent of Extrusion

While designing, we might get some reference geometries up to which the extrusion is to be done and we do not have the distance values. To fulfil such conditions, the options are available next to the **Distance A** edit box; refer to Figure-36. These options are discussed next.

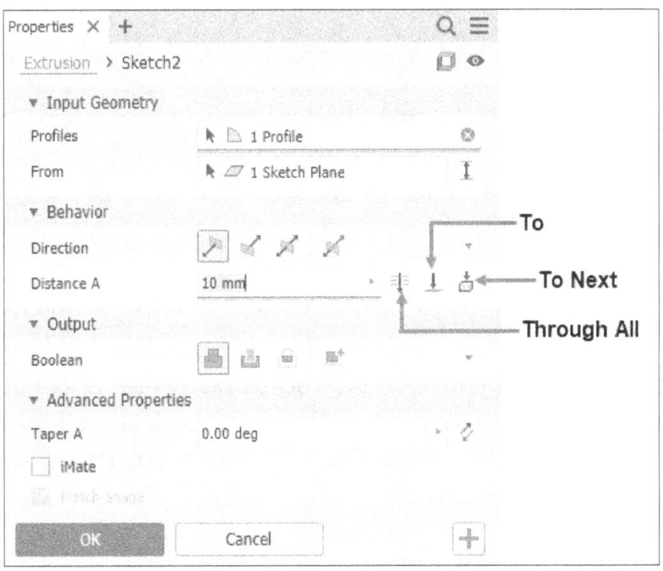

Figure-36. Extent options

- Click on the **Through All** option to create extrusion intersecting with all the solids/ faces coming in the direction of extrusion; refer to Figure-37.

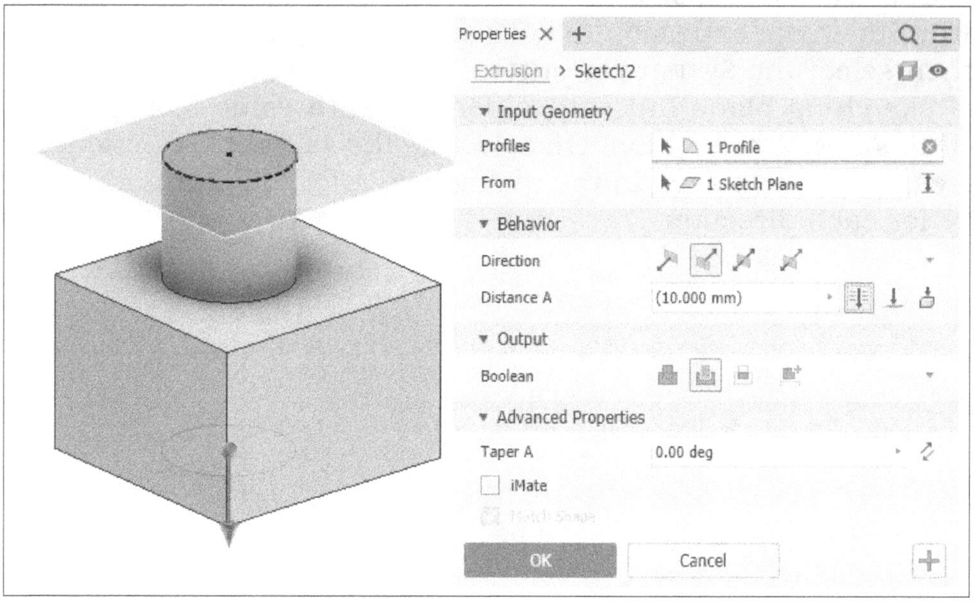

Figure-37. Through All extrusion

- Click on the **To** option and you will be asked to select the terminating geometry. Select the plane, face, or point up to which you want to create extrusion; refer to Figure-38.

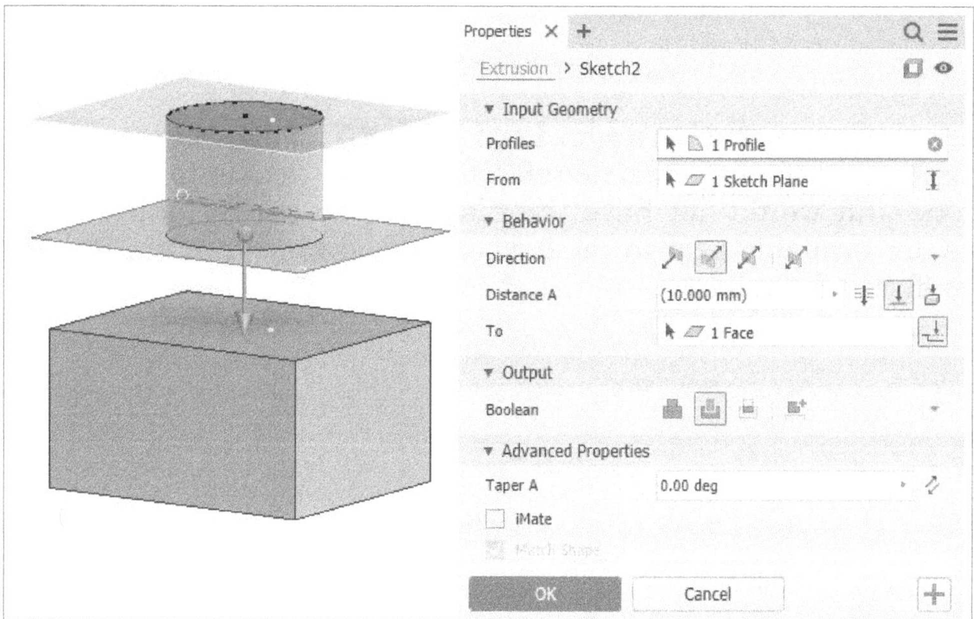

Figure-38. Creating extrusion to plane

- Click on the **To Next** option if there is any solid body/face in the extrusion direction. The extrusion distance will automatically be specified up to the next intersecting body/face; refer to Figure-39. Note that the terminating solid/face must cover the extrusion sketch, completely.

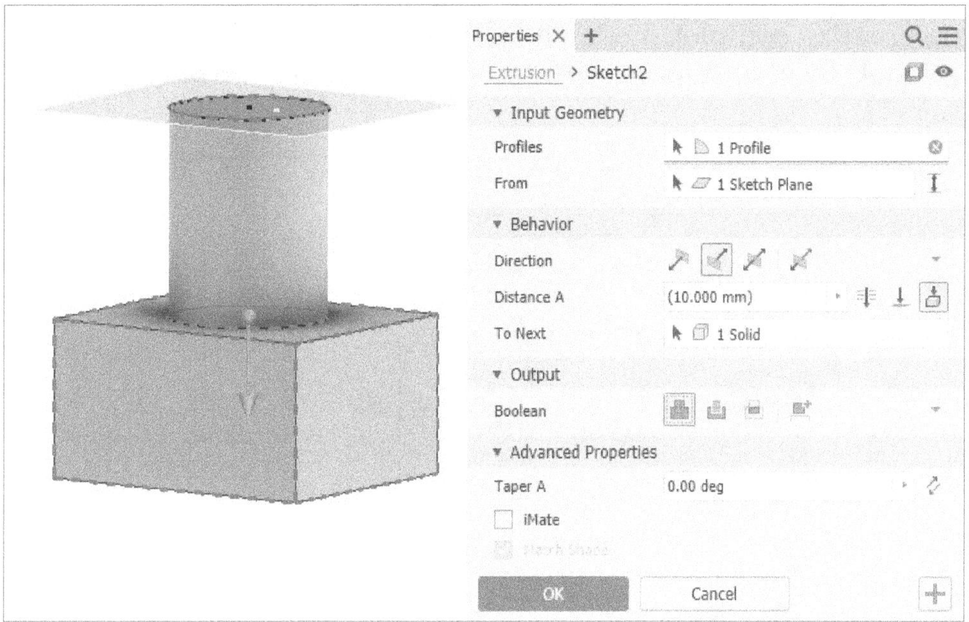

Figure-39. Creating extrusion up to next

Boolean Operations

There are some basic boolean operations that can be performed with solid features like Join (addition), Cut (subtraction), and Intersection. There is one more option by which you can make the newly created solid feature as solid having no relation with other solids in modeling space with the name **New Solid**.

The buttons to apply these options are available from **Boolean** area in **Extrude** dialog box; refer to Figure-40. Note that these buttons will be available only when you have a solid base feature and you are creating another feature on it.

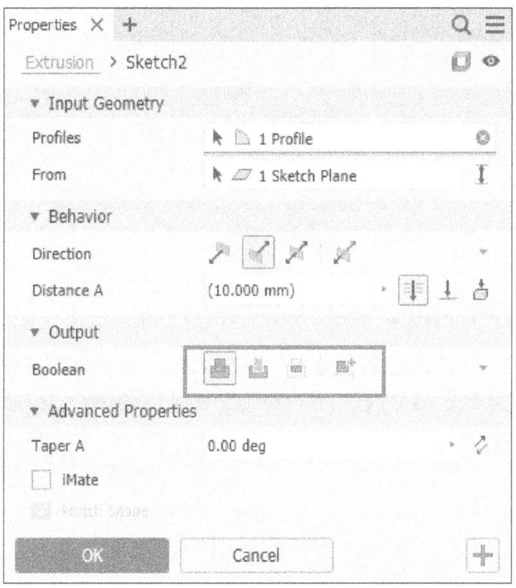

Figure-40. Options to apply Boolean operations

Joining Features

When we are creating complex model, it is not possible to create model by using single operation of tool. In such cases, we may need multiple extrusions joined together like in Figure-41.

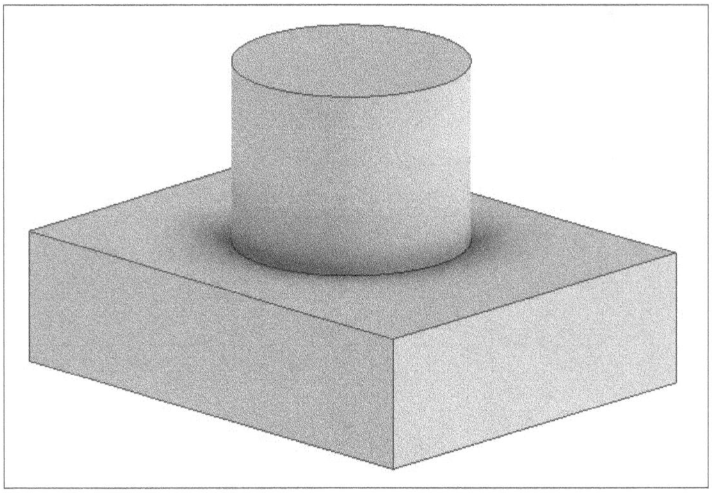

Figure-41. Model created by joining two extrude features

The method to do so is given next.

- Click on the **Extrude** tool from **Create** panel in the **Ribbon** after creating the base extrude feature. You will be asked to select a sketching plane or an existing sketch.
- Select the top face of the base feature as sketching plane; refer to Figure-42. The sketching environment will be activated.

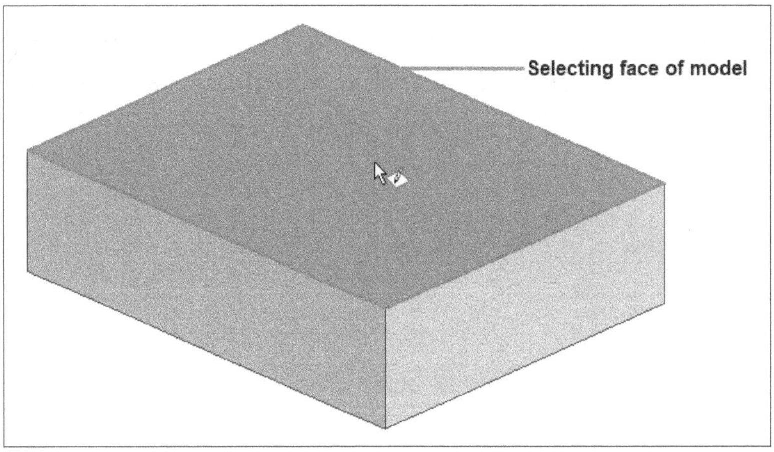

Figure-42. Selecting face of model as sketching plane

- Create the closed sketch and then click on the **Finish Sketch** button from the **Finish** drop-down in the **Exit** panel of the **Ribbon**; refer to Figure-43. Preview of the extrusion will be displayed.

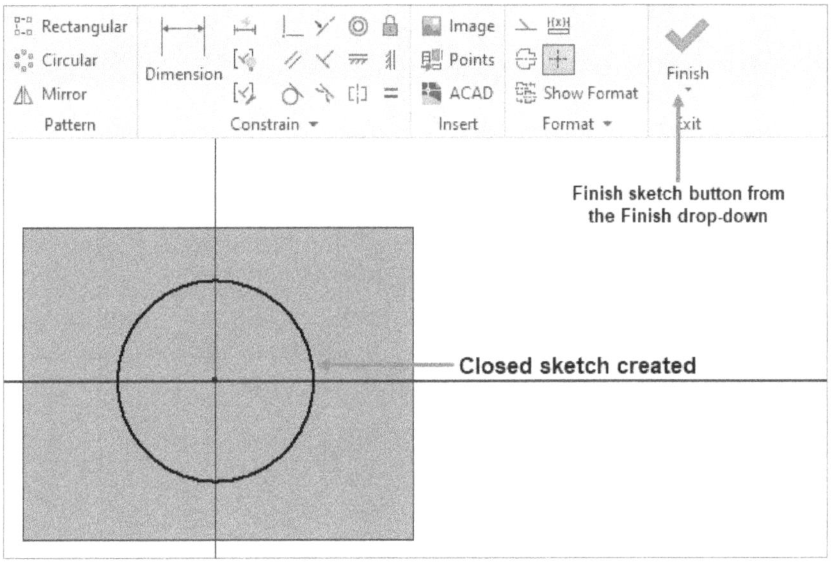

Figure-43. Creating sketch on face of solid feature

- Click on the **Join** button from the **Extrude** dialog box to join the extrusion to base feature; refer to Figure-44.

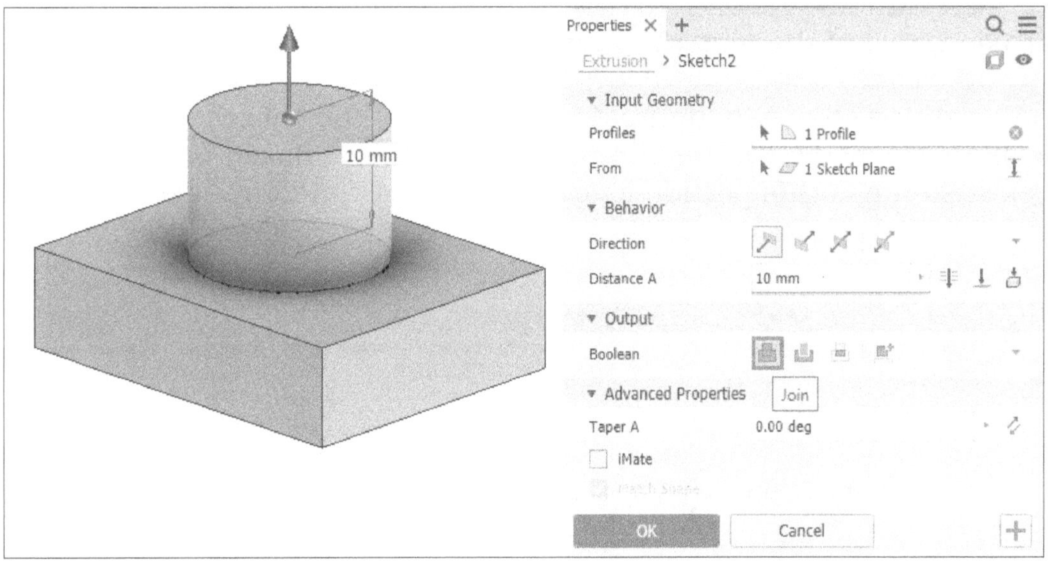

Figure-44. Preview of extrusion joined to base feature

Cutting extrusion from base feature (Cut button)

The **Cut** button is used to remove material from the base feature.

- In the same example, if you reverse the direction of extrusion by clicking on the **Flipped** button and select the **Cut** button then preview of cut feature will be displayed; refer to Figure-45.

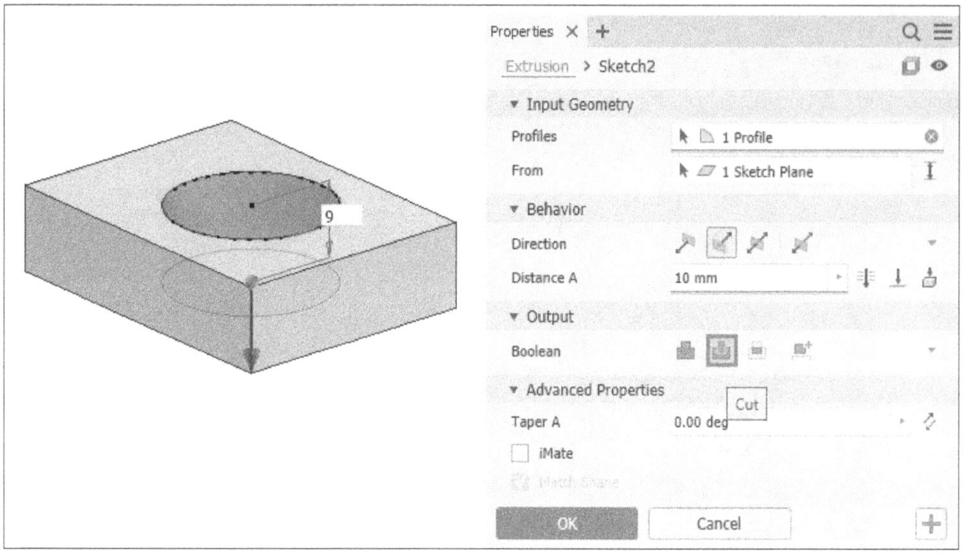

Figure-45. Preview of cut feature

Intersection

The **Intersect** button is used to extract the common portion between base feature and extrusion, rest of the material in model is automatically removed.

- In the condition shown in Figure-45, if you select the **Intersect** button then only the cylindrical model will remain and rest will be removed because base feature and extrusion has this portion as common; refer to Figure-46.

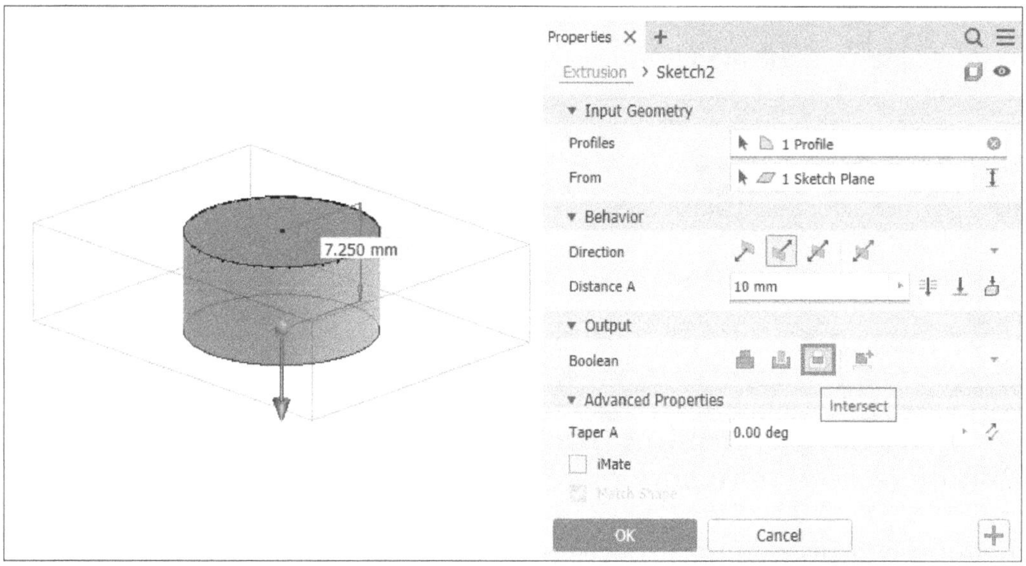

Figure-46. Preview of extrusion with intersect button

New Solid

You can create the extrusion as new solid by using the **New Solid** button from **Boolean** area in the **Extrude** dialog box.

Adding Taper to Extrusion

- To add taper to the extrusion, click on the **Advanced Properties** rollout from the dialog box and specify desired angle value in the **Taper A** edit box; refer to Figure-47. The taper angle will be applied to the extrusion keeping the base of extrusion fixed; refer to Figure-48.

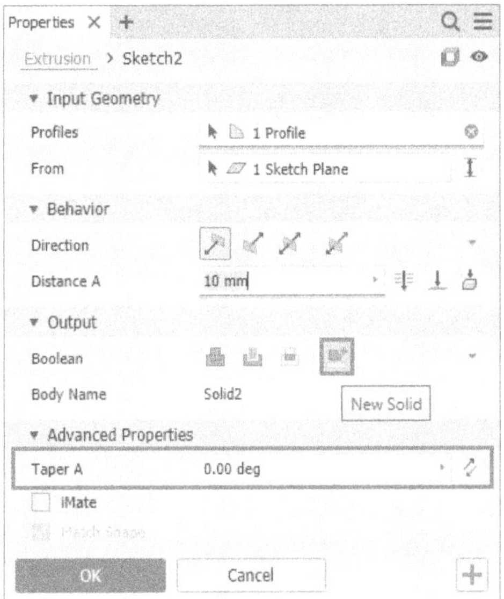

Figure-47. Taper edit box

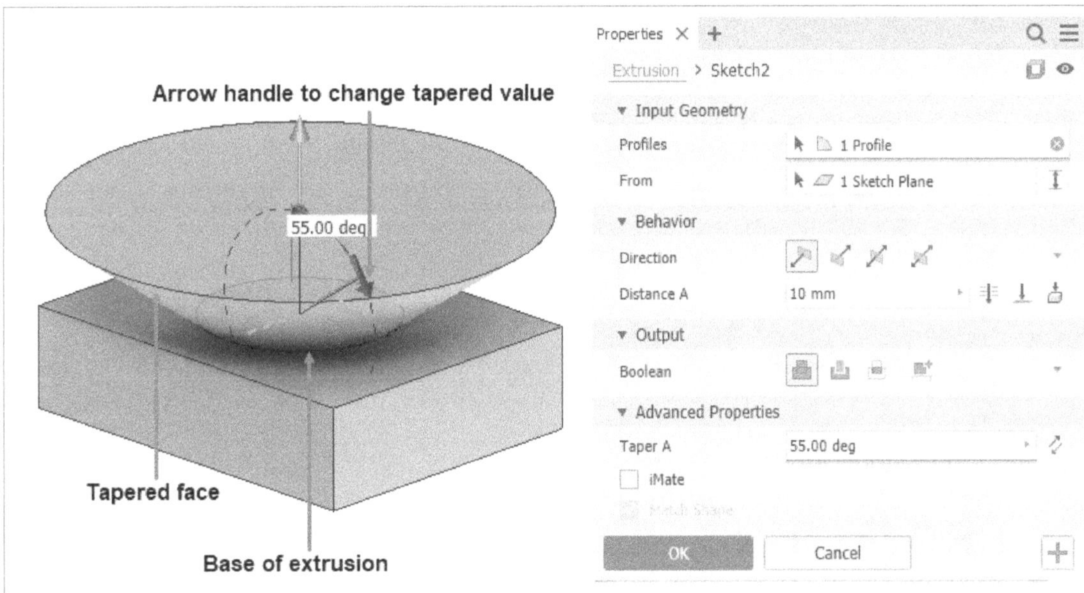

Figure-48. Extrusion with taper angle

And finally, click on the **OK** button from the dialog box to create the extrude feature.

Surface Mode of Extrusion

- Click on the **Surface mode** button from **Extrude** dialog box to create the surface extrusion of feature. The updated **Extrude** dialog box will be displayed with preview of surface extrusion; refer to Figure-49.

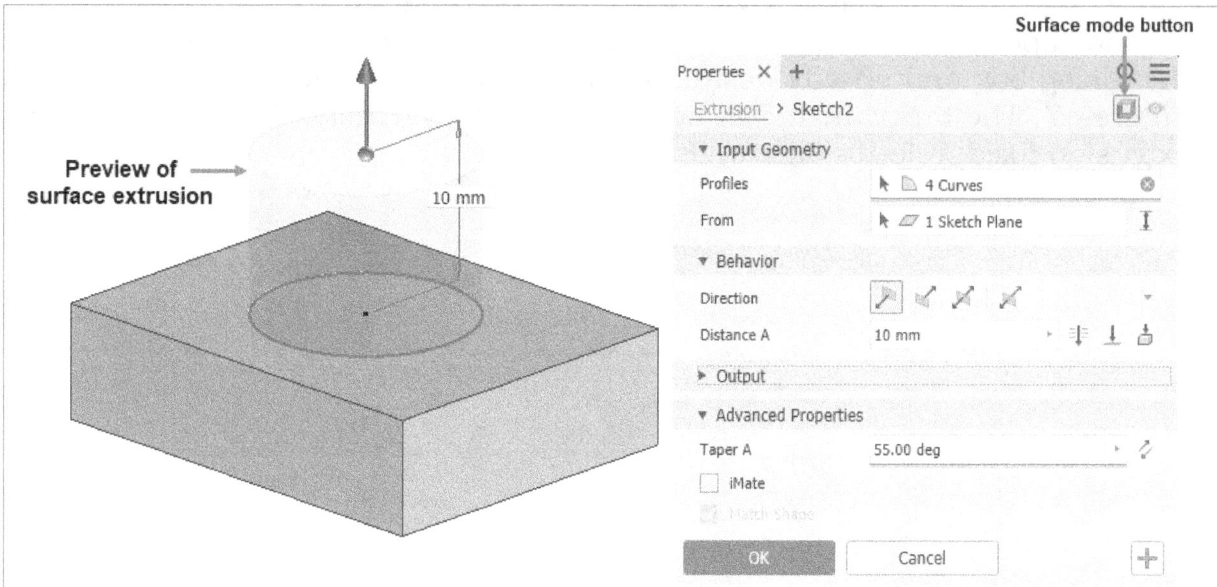

Figure-49. Updated Extrude dialog box with preview of surface extrusion

- Specify desired parameters as discussed earlier and click on the **OK** button from the dialog box to create surface extrusion; refer to Figure-50.

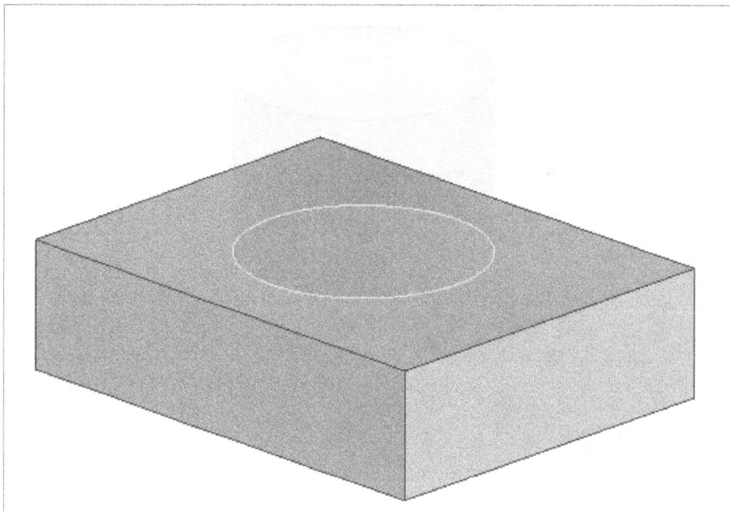

Figure-50. Surface extrusion created

PROJECTING GEOMETRIES IN SKETCH

When you are working with 3D modeling features like extrude, revolve, sweep, and so on; you will find the need to reuse edges and boundaries of various already created features for generating new solid/surface feature. Assume that you want to create a shaft that passes through the hole of model shown in Figure-51 and same diameter as diameter of hole. In such cases, you can use Project tools to generate sketch curves using selected solid features. Various tools for projecting geometries are available in the **Project Geometry** drop-down of **Create** panel in the **Sketch** tab of the **Ribbon** when Sketching environment is active; refer to Figure-52. Various tools of this drop-down are discussed next.

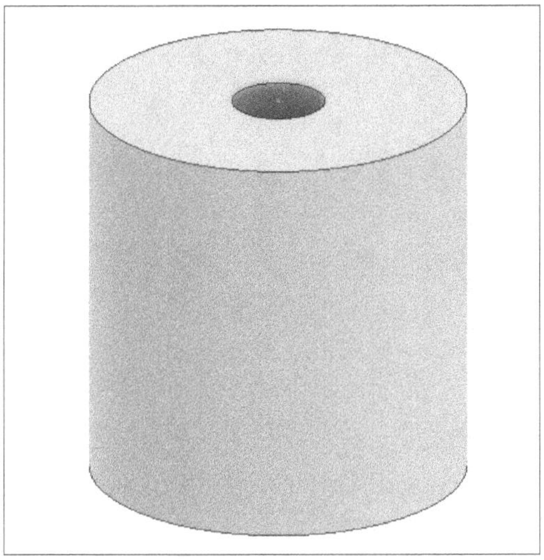

Figure-51. Model for projection

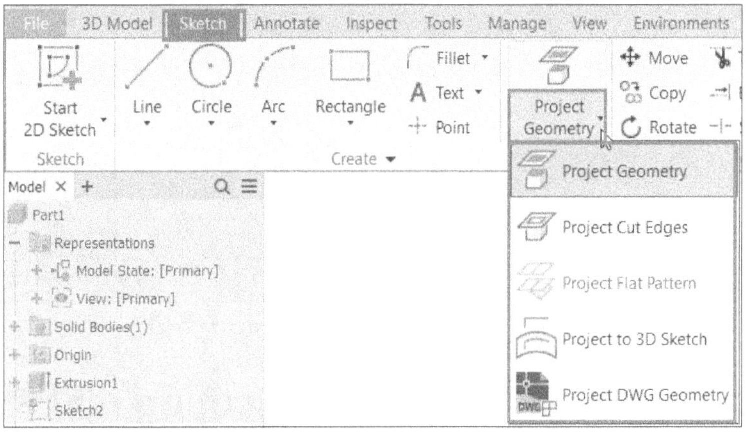

Figure-52. Project Geometry drop-down

Projecting Geometries

The **Project Geometry** tool is used to project vertices, edges, faces, and loops of selected feature on the current sketching plane. The procedure to use this tool is given next.

- Click on the **Project Geometry** tool from the **Project Geometry** drop-down in the **Create** panel of **Sketch** tab in the **Ribbon**. You will be asked to select object/feature to be projected.
- Select desired face/edge/curve/vertex to be projected. The projected geometry will be generated; refer to Figure-53. You can use this geometry as sketch curve or you can use it as reference for creating other sketch entities. Press **ESC** to exit the tool.

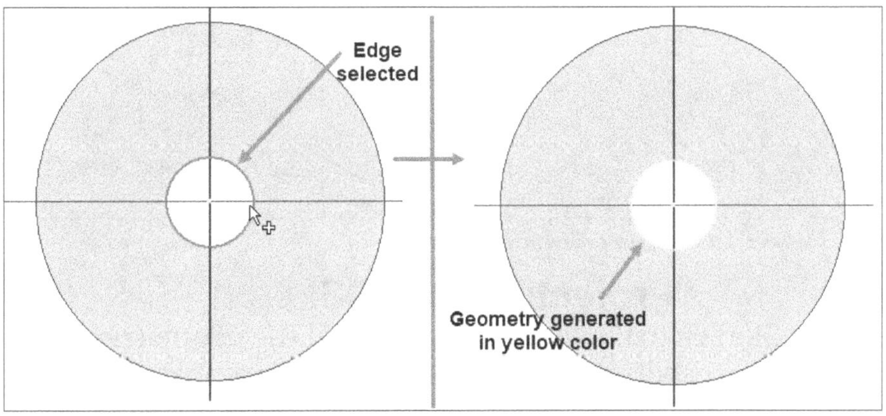

Figure-53. Geometry projected using edge

Projecting Cut Edges

The **Project Cut Edges** tool is used to generate all the edges of model that intersect with the sketching plane. The procedure to use this tool is given next.

- Click on the **Project Cut Edges** tool from the **Project Geometry** drop-down in the **Create** panel of **Sketch** tab in the **Ribbon**. All the edges of model will be generated as projected curves; refer to Figure-54. Press **ESC** to exit the tool.

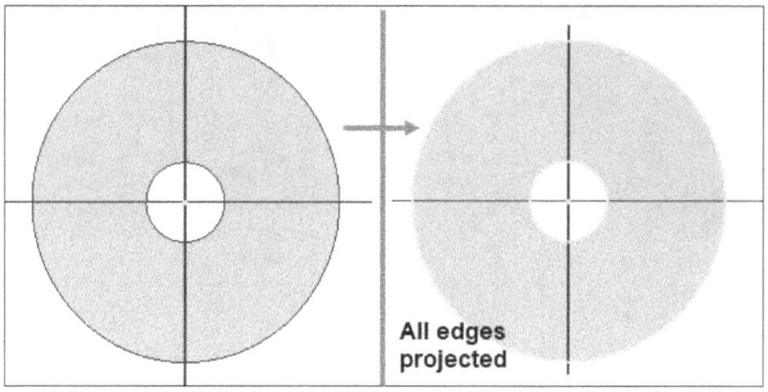

Figure-54. Projected cut edges

Projecting Flat Pattern

The **Project Flat Pattern** tool is used to project boundaries of flat pattern of selected sheet metal objects. The procedure to use this tool is given next.

- Click on the **Project Flat Pattern** tool from the **Project Geometry** drop-down in the **Create** panel of the **Sketch** tab in the **Ribbon** when flat face of sheetmetal part is selected. You will be asked to select faces to be projected.
- Select desired faces of the sheetmetal part; refer to Figure-55. The projected sketch will be generated.

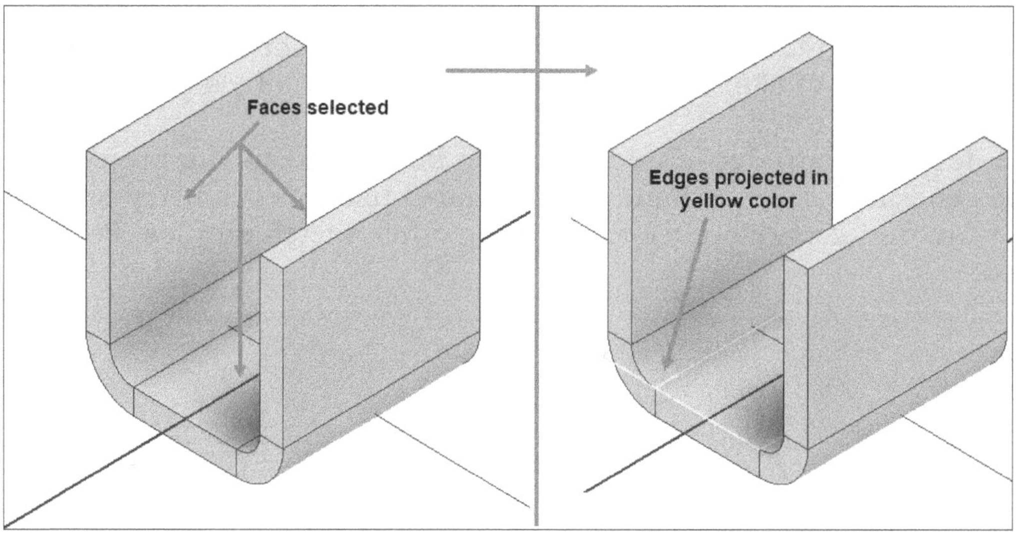

Figure-55. Sheetmetal flat pattern projected

Projecting to 3D Sketch

The **Project to 3D Sketch** tool is used to project all the geometries in current sketch on selected face. The procedure to use this tool is given next.

- After starting a 2D sketch and creating desired sketch geometry, click on the **Project to 3D Sketch** tool from the **Create** panel in the **Sketch** tab of the **Ribbon**. The **Project to 3D Sketch** dialog box will be displayed; refer to Figure-56.

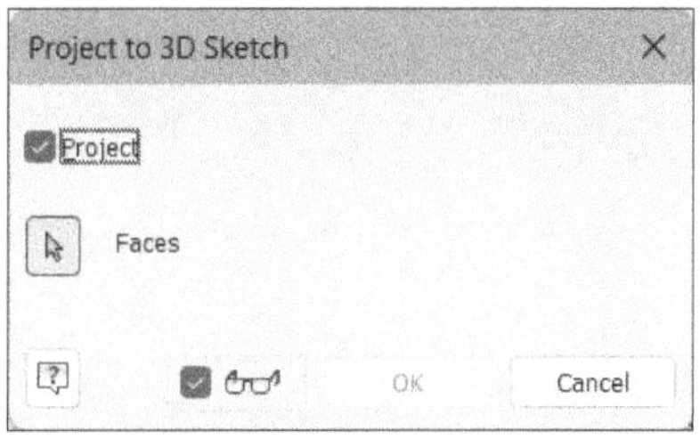

Figure-56. Project to 3D Sketch dialog box

- Make sure the **Project** check box is selected in the dialog box and select the face of 3D model. Preview of projected sketch will be displayed; refer to Figure-57.

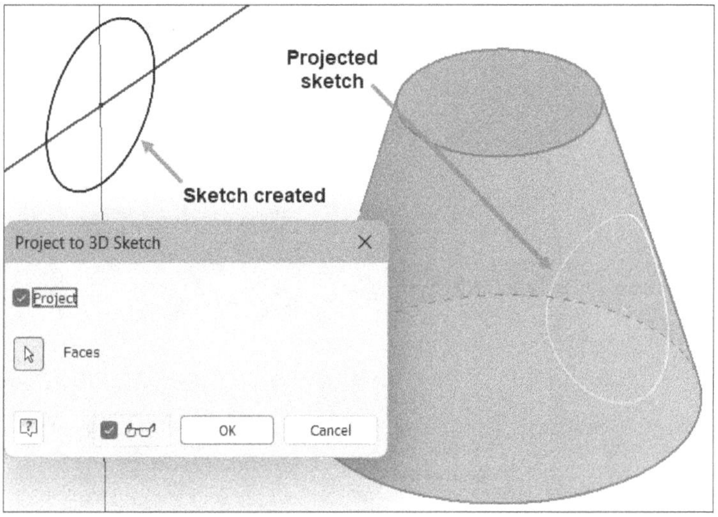

Figure-57. Preview of projected sketch

- Click on the **OK** button from the dialog box to create the projected curves.

Projecting DWG Geometry

The **Project DWG Geometry** tool is used to project curves of imported DWG drawing file onto sketching plane. The procedure to use this tool is given next.

- Click on the **Project DWG Geometry** tool from the **Project Geometry** drop-down in the **Sketch** tab of **Ribbon**. You will be asked to select entities of imported DWG file (using **Import** tool in **Manage** tab of **Ribbon**).
- Select desired geometries of imported dwg file using single entity selection or window selection; refer to Figure-58. After selection press **ENTER**; selected entities will be projected; refer to Figure-59.

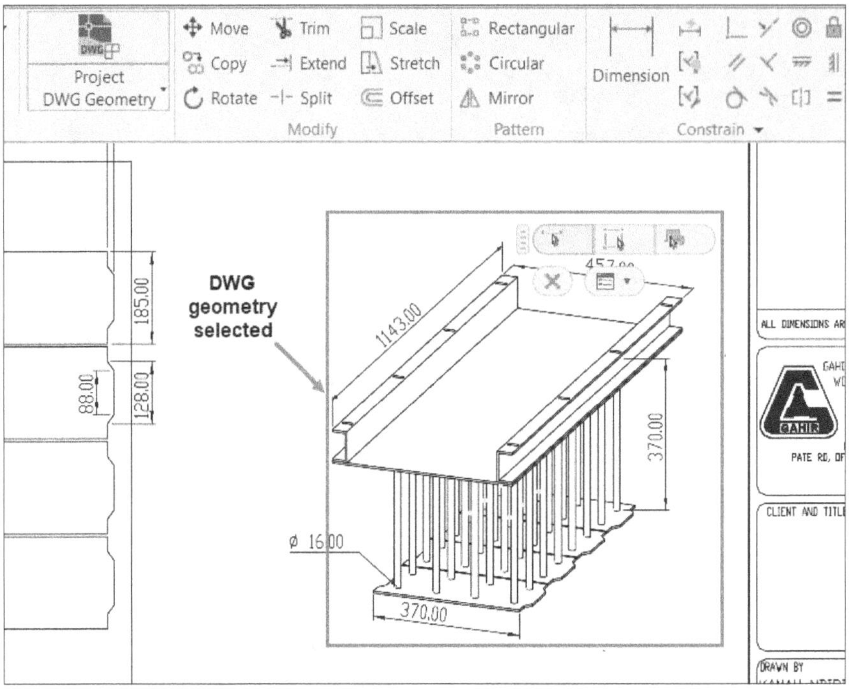

Figure-58. Geometry selected from DWG

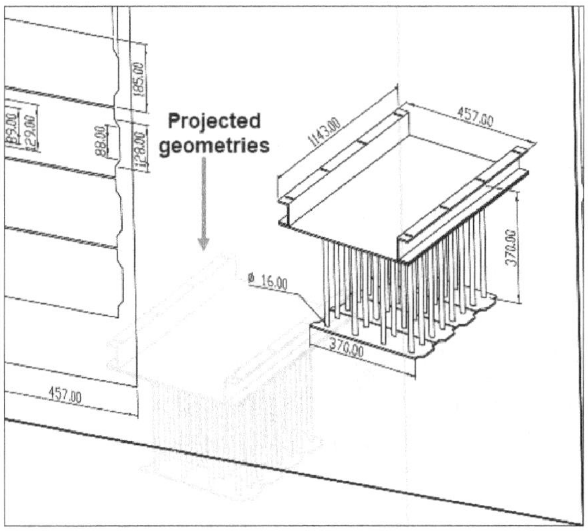

Figure-59. Projected DWG geometry

Now, there is a surprise topic on drawing again before we move to create solid models by using extrusion.

BRIEF NOTE ON DRAWINGS

Till this point, we have created sketches and then we have learned to create extrusion with the help of those sketches. But, in real-world conditions, we are not going to have sketches. We will be finding our sketches from the engineering drawings. Being a mechanical engineer, you should be knowing about the engineering drawings but still its good idea to refresh the topic.

Engineering Drawing is the exact representation of an engineering component on the paper. There are a few qualities in Engineering Drawing given as:

- It is a clear and unmistakable representation of engineering component.
- It shows all the shapes and sizes of the engineering component.
- After reading the drawing, we get only one interpretation and there is no scope of confusion.

The Engineering Drawings are broadly classified into four categories:

Machine Drawing

It is pertaining to machine parts or components. It is presented through a number of orthographic views, so that the size and shape of the component is fully understood. Part drawings and assembly drawings belong to this classification. An example of a machine drawing is given in Figure-60.

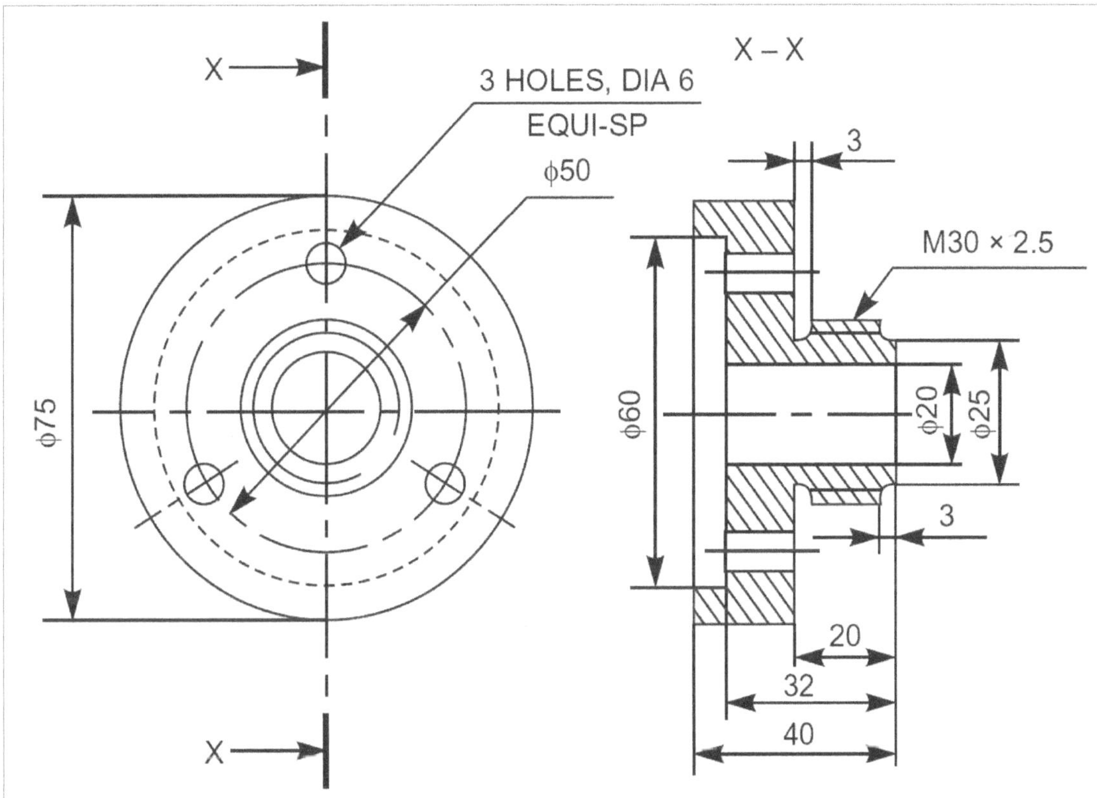

Figure-60. Machine drawing

Production Drawing

A production drawing, also referred to as working drawing, should furnish all the dimensions, limits, and special finishing processes such as heat treatment, honing, lapping, and surface finish to guide the craftsman on the shop floor in producing the component. The title should also mention the material used for the product, number of parts required for the assembled unit, and so on. Figure-61 shows an example of production drawing.

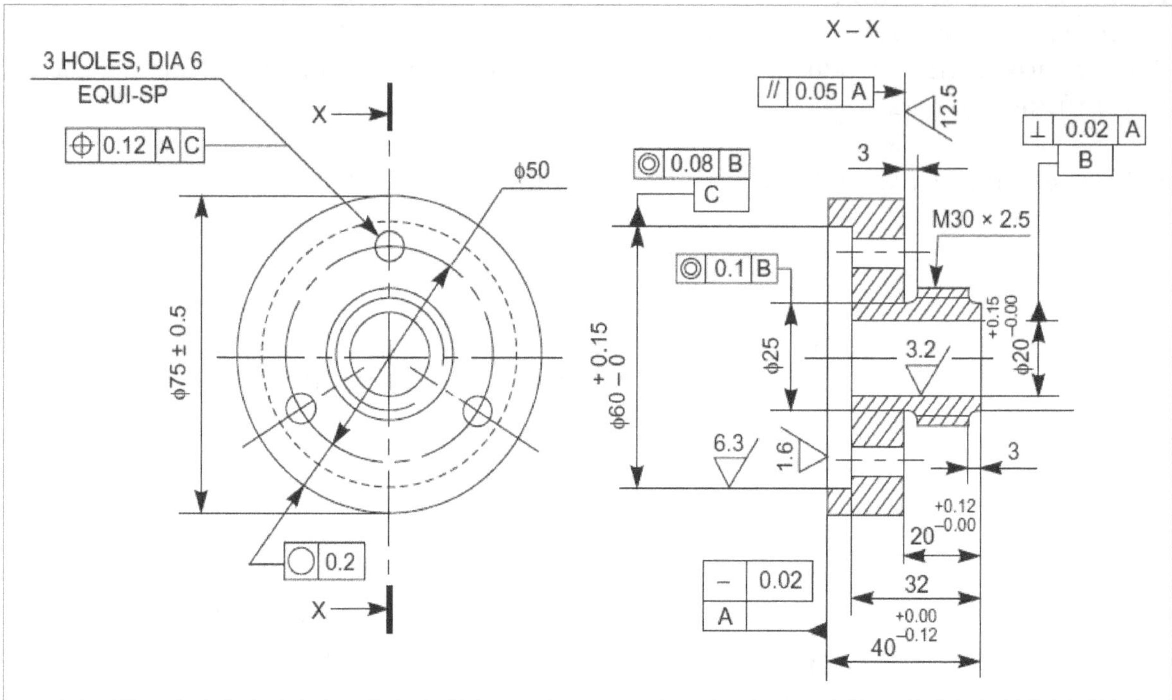

Figure-61. Production drawing

Part Drawing

Component or part drawing is a detailed drawing of a component to facilitate its manufacture. All the principles of orthographic projection and the technique of graphic representation must be followed to communicate the details in a part drawing. A part drawing with production details is rightly called as a production drawing or working drawing.

Assembly Drawing

A drawing that shows various parts of a machine in their correct working locations is an assembly drawing; refer to Figure-62.

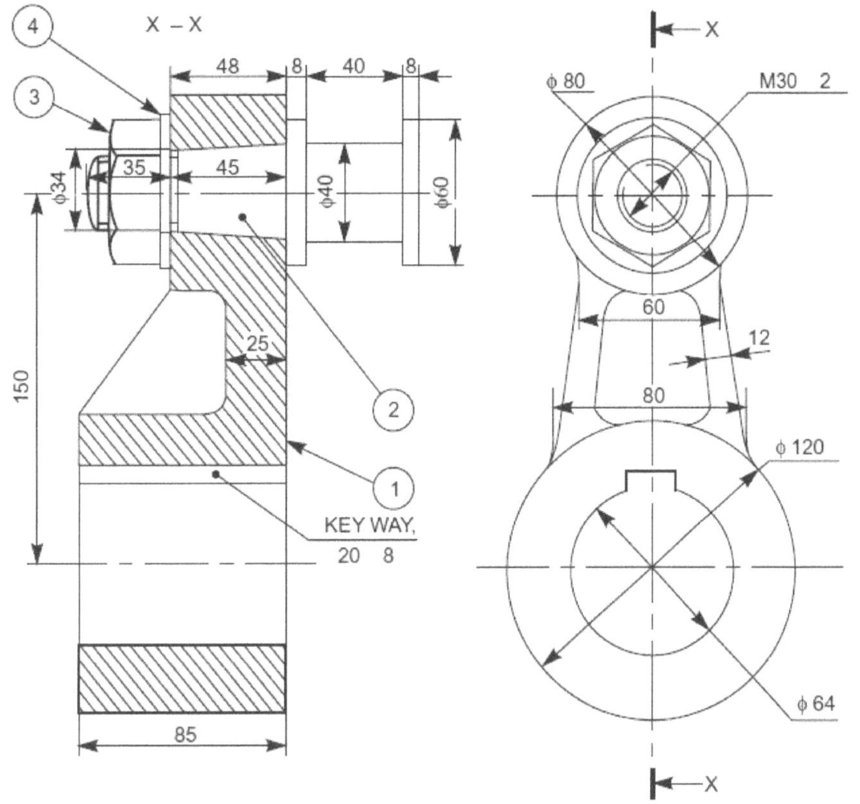

Parts List

Part No.	Name	Material	Qty
1	Crank	Forged Steel	1
2	Crank Pin	45C	1
3	Nut	MS	1
4	Washer	MS	1

Figure-62. Assembly drawing

COMPONENT REPRESENTATION METHODS

Broadly, there are two ways to present a component in engineering drawing; **Orthographic representation** and **Isometric representation**.

The orthographic representation is the method in which component is placed in the form of various views to completely define its shape and size. These orthographic views can be Front view, Right view, Top view, and so on. Refer to Figure-63.

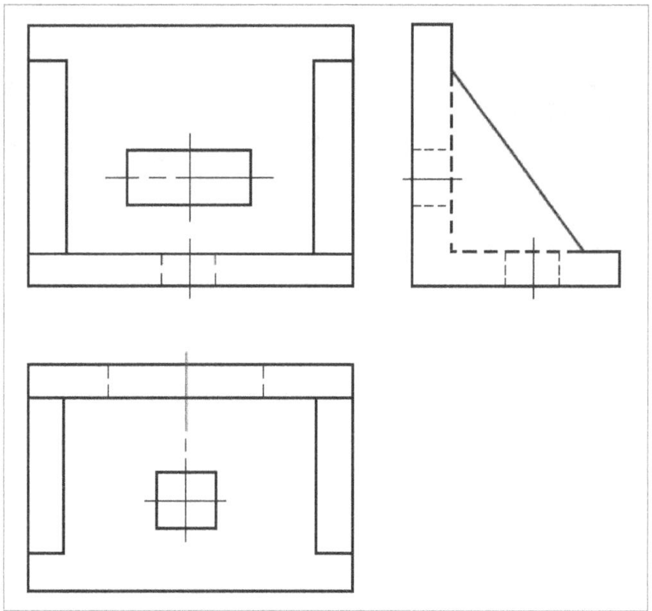

Figure-63. Orthographic views

The isometric representation is the method to display wireframe model of the object with its dimensions at standard angles from base planes. Note that all the objects can not be completely defined by this representation. So, it is useful when we need to represent the shape of the object with some highly needed dimensions; refer to Figure-64.

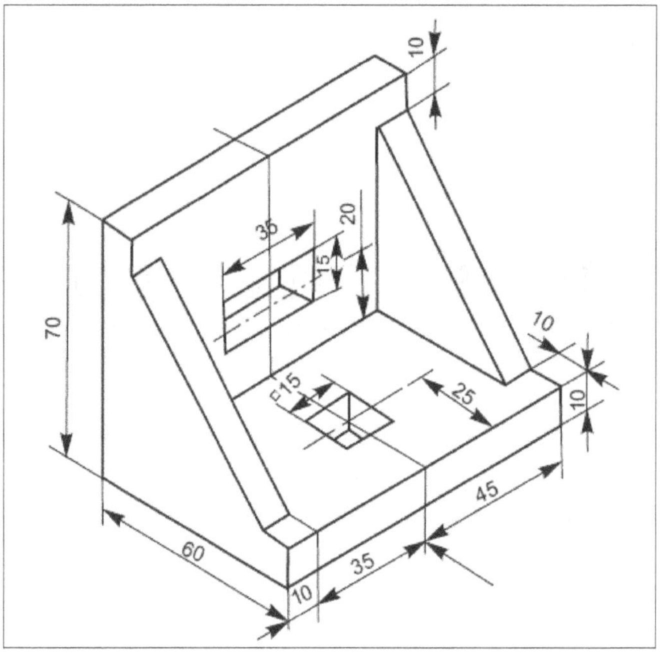

Figure-64. Isometric view

We will be using both the representations to create our models for practice.

SKETCHING PLANE SELECTION

Plane selection is a very important task while creating 3D models because the orientation of the model depends totally on the selection of plane. Since, most of the time we will get orthographic views of the model, so let's check the method of sketching plane selection for orthographic views.

Selecting planes according to orthographic views

Yes!! We know that there are top plane, front plane, right plane, and so on in orthographic views of component. But, how to identify which view is top and which view is front. Answer to this question is projection type. There are two type of projections mainly used for orthographic views; **First Angle Projection** and **Third Angle Projection**. In each engineering drawing, they are shown by their symbols in the Title Block; refer to Figure-65. Let A, B, C, D, and E are the three positions to see a car from front, left, right, top, and bottom. Then car views are placed as shown in Figure-66 for first angle projection and as shown in Figure-67 for third angle projection.

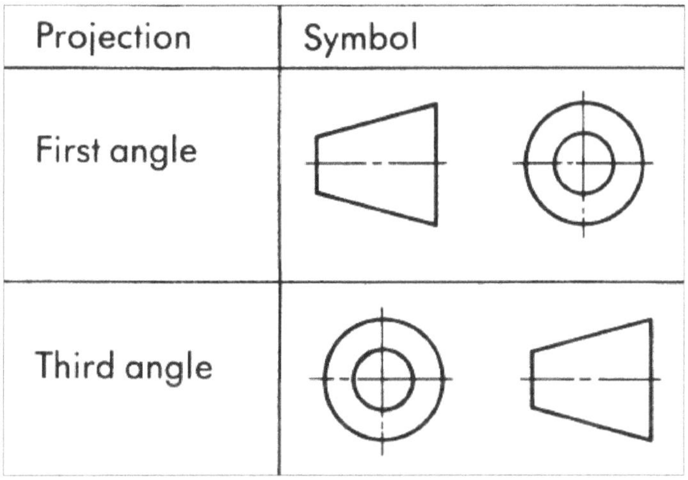

Figure-65. Symbols for projection

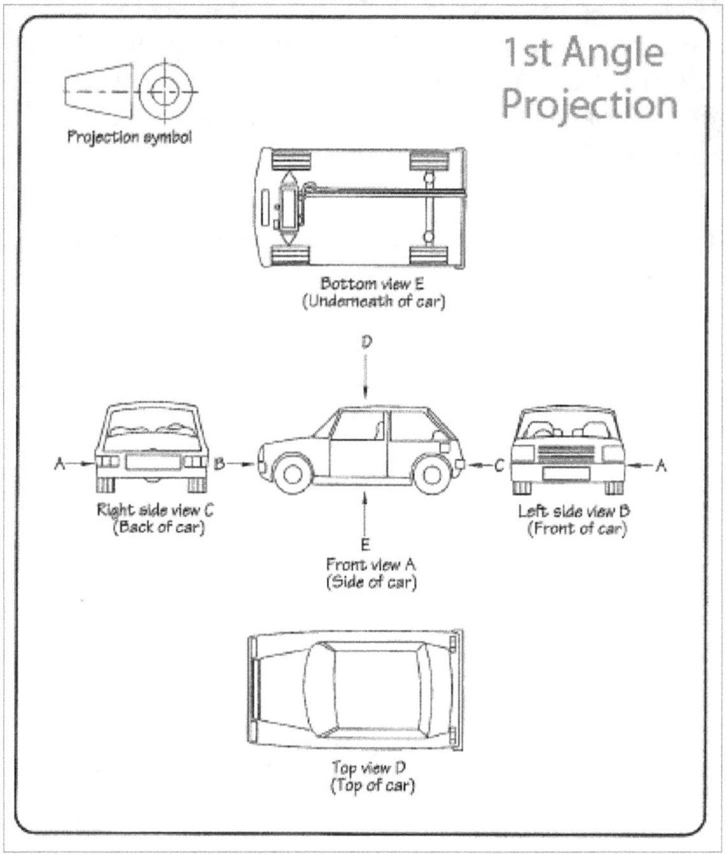

Figure-66. Views in 1st Angle Projection

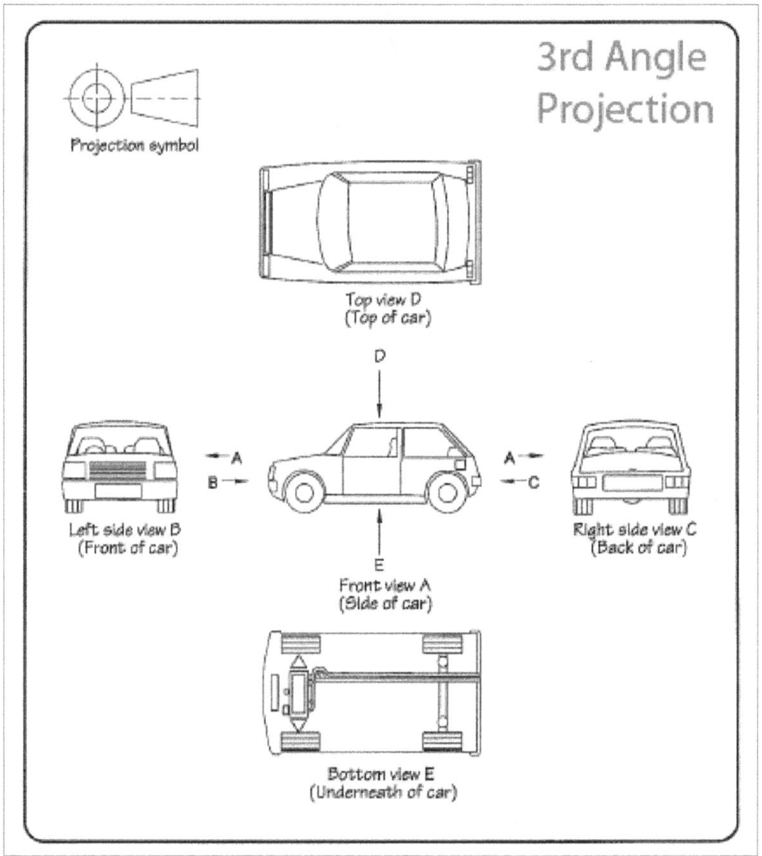

Figure-67. Views in 3rd Angle Projection

PRACTICAL 1

In this practical, we will create a 3D model from the drawing given in Figure-68. The drawing has both isometric as well as orthographic views. You can use any of the two to create the model.

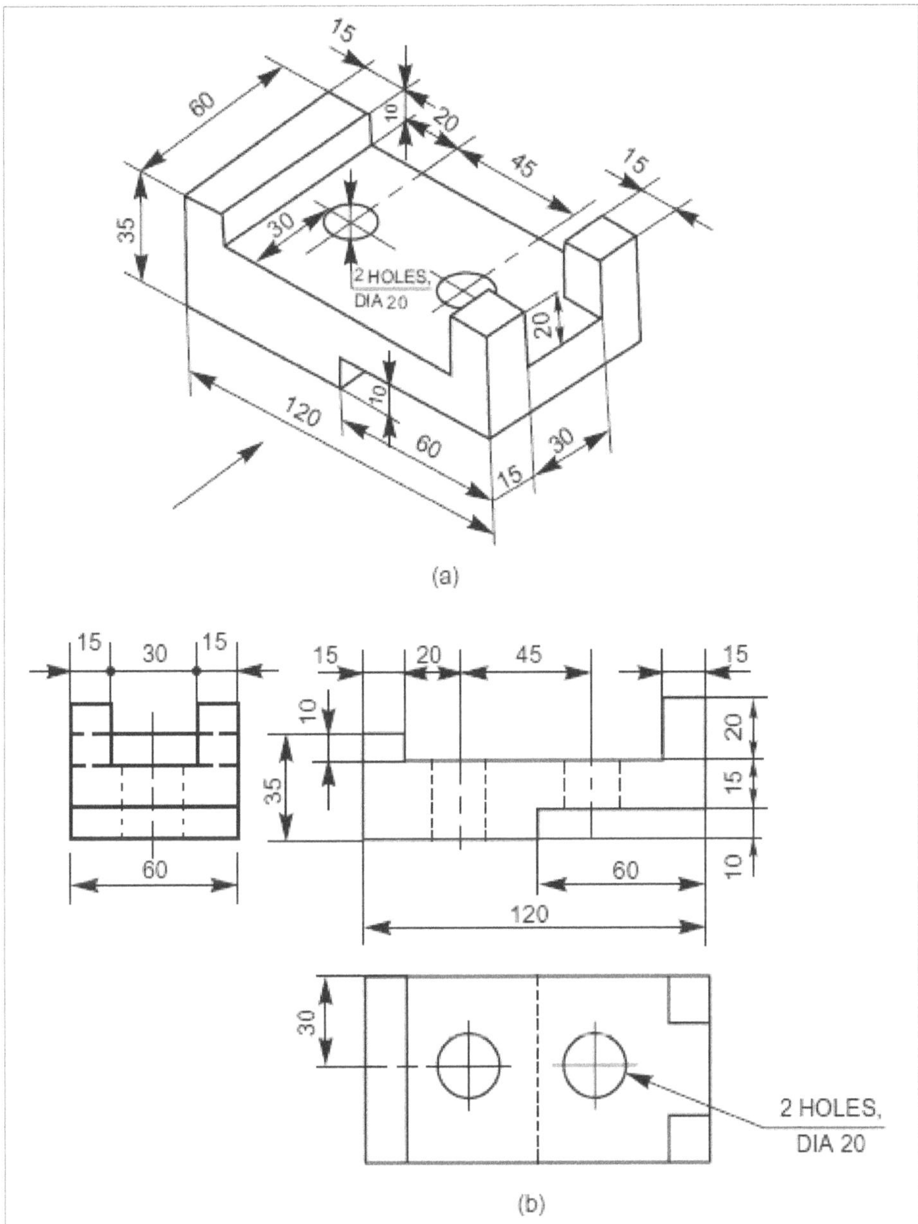

Figure-68. Practical 1

Strategy for Creating model

1. Looking at the isometric view and orthographic views, we can find that the drawing is in **`First Angle Projection`**. Because keeping the arrow direction in isometric view as Front view, the Right view of model is placed at the left of the Front view in Orthographic view. We are going to use Front view from orthographic views for creating sketch for base feature. Because in this way, we will use the extrusion tool at minimum. (Although, we can create this model using any other view and using same tool multiple times but in the end, we are more time which means more cost to the company.)

2. We will create two circles in a sketch and then create an extrude cut from the base feature by using the sketch to create holes.
3. We will use one more extrude cut to remove extra material from the model.

Starting Part File

- Start Autodesk Inventor by double-clicking on the Autodesk Inventor Professional icon from the desktop. (If not started yet.)
- Click on the **New** button from the **Quick Access Toolbar**. The **Create New File** dialog box will be displayed.
- Double-click on **Standard(mm).ipt** icon from the **Metric** templates. The Part environment of Autodesk Inventor will be displayed.

Creating sketch

- Click on the **Start 2D Sketch** button from **Sketch** panel in the **3D Model** tab of the **Ribbon**. You will be asked to select a sketching plane.
- Click on the **XY** Plane (Front Plane) to create sketch on it.
- Click on the **Line** tool from **Create** panel in the **Sketch** tab of the **Ribbon**. You will be asked to specify the starting corner point of the line.
- Click on the origin to specify the starting point of line. You will be asked to specify end point of line.
- Move the cursor straight right and enter **60** in the Input box displayed. You will be asked to specify next end point of line.
- Move the cursor straight upward and enter **10** in the Input box; refer to Figure-69.

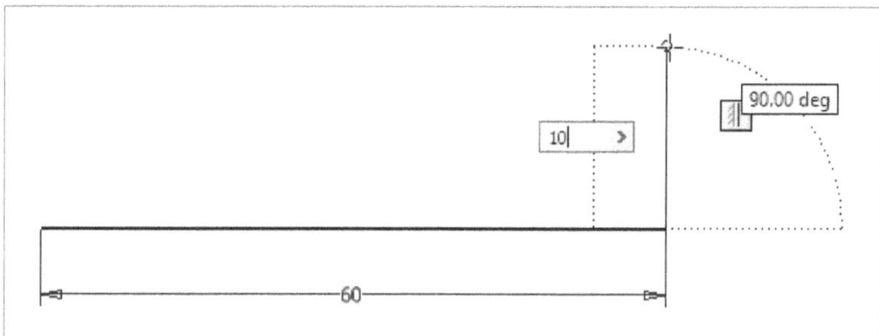

Figure-69. Creating lines

- Similarly, create rest of the sketch; refer to Figure-70.

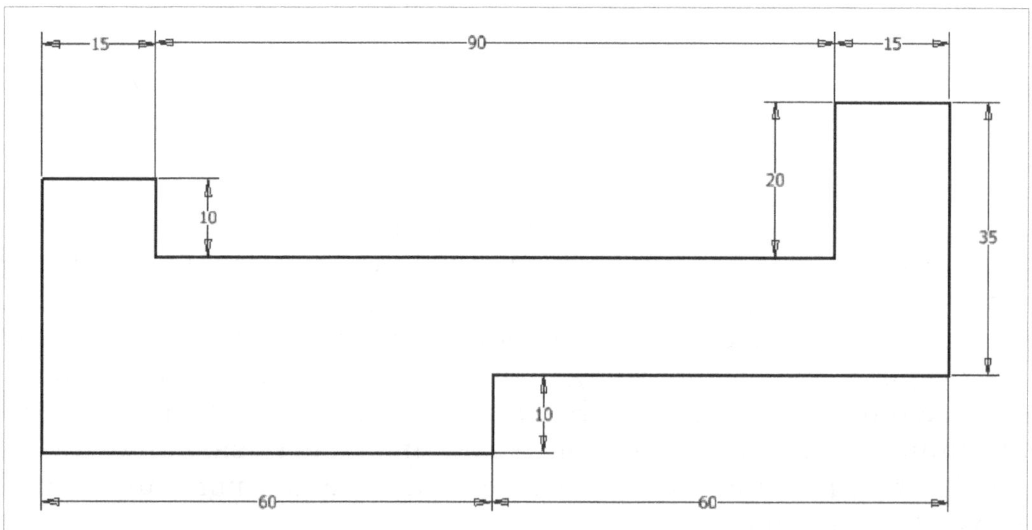

Figure-70. Sketch to be created

- Click on the **Finish Sketch** button from the **Finish** drop-down in the **Exit** panel to exit sketching environment.

Creating base extrude feature

- Click on the **Extrude** tool from **Create** panel in the **3D Model** tab of the **Ribbon**. The **Extrude** dialog box will be displayed with the preview of extrusion; refer to Figure-71.

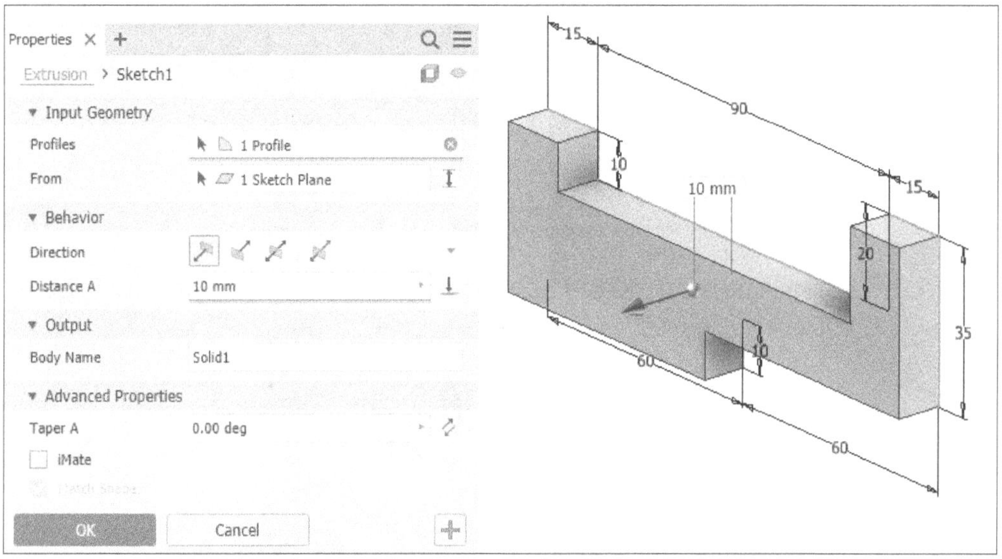

Figure-71. Extrude dialog box with preview of extrusion

- Enter the distance value as **60** in the **Distance A** edit box in the **Extrude** dialog box. The extrusion feature will be created; refer to Figure-72.

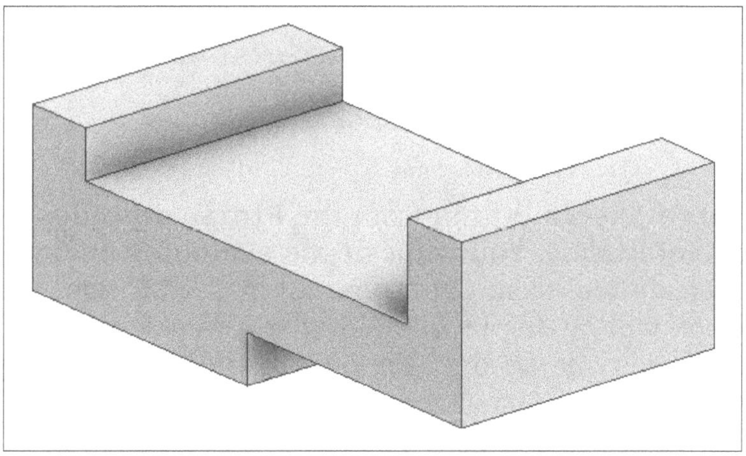

Figure-72. Extrusion created

Creating Holes

- Click on the **Start 2D Sketch** tool from **Sketch** panel in the **3D Model** tab of the **Ribbon**. You will be asked to select a plane/face for sketching.
- Click on the face as shown in Figure-73. The sketching environment will be displayed.

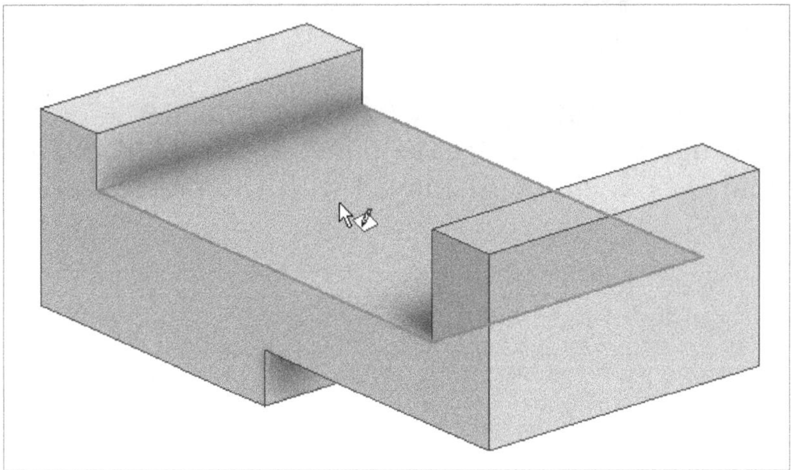

Figure-73. Face to be selected for creating hole

- Create two circles of diameter **20** at the dimensions as shown in Figure-74.

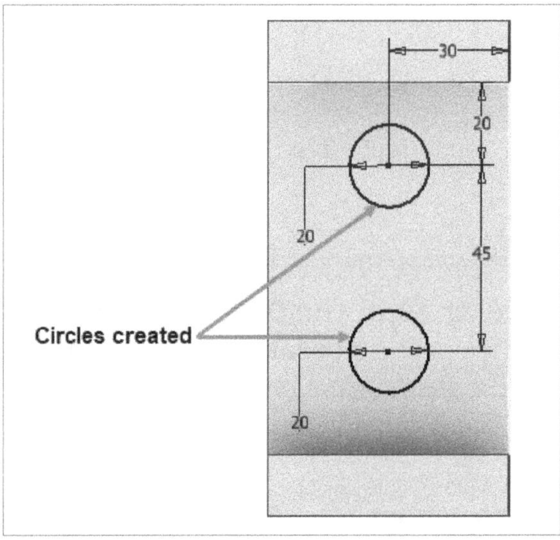

Figure-74. Creating circles

- Click on the **Finish Sketch** button from the **Finish** drop-down of the **Exit** panel in the **Sketch** tab of **Ribbon**. You will exit the sketching environment.
- Click on the **Extrude** tool from **Create** panel in the **3D Model** tab of **Ribbon**. The **Extrude** dialog box will be displayed asking you to select the profiles.
- Select both the circles one by one. Preview of the cut feature will be displayed; refer to Figure-75.

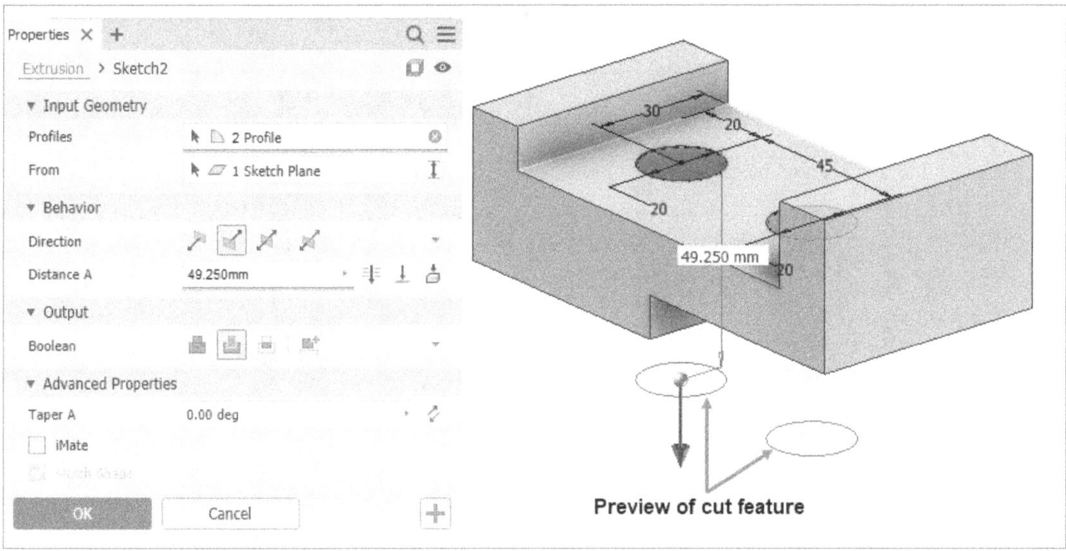

Figure-75. Preview of cut feature

- Make sure the buttons in the dialog box are selected as shown in Figure-75 and enter the distance value as **25** in the **Distance A** edit box. The holes will be created in the base feature; refer to Figure-76.

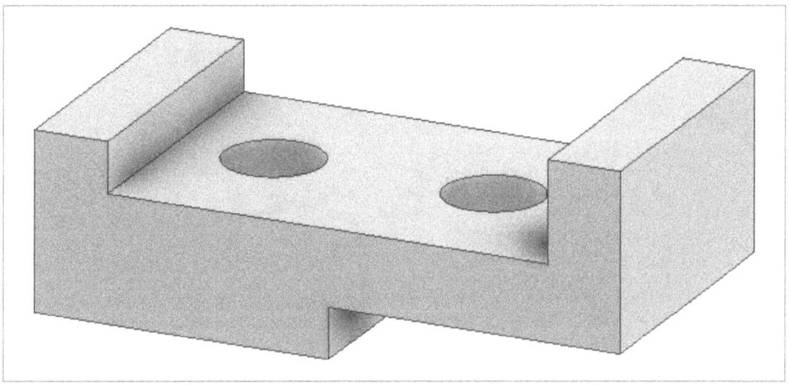

Figure-76. Holes created in the base feature

Creating cut feature

- Click on the **Extrude** tool from **Create** panel in the **3D Model** tab of the **Ribbon**. You will be asked to select a plane/face for sketching.
- Click on the face as shown in Figure-77. The sketching environment will be displayed.

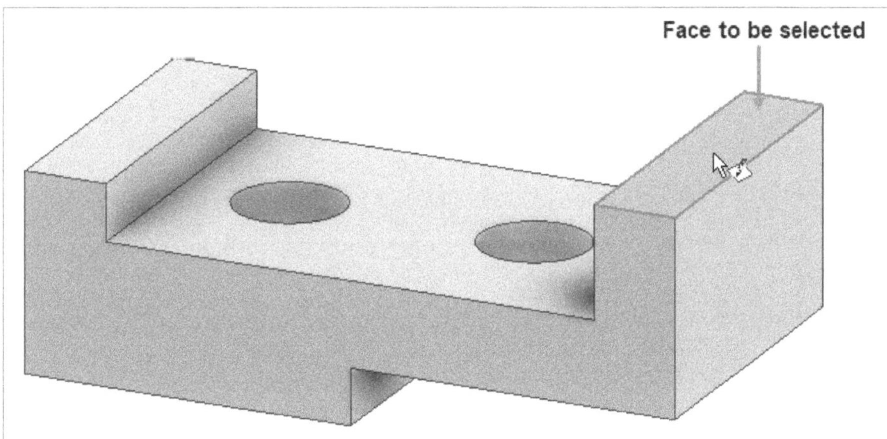

Figure-77. Face to be selected for creating cut feature

- Create the sketch as shown in Figure-78.

Figure-78. Sketch for cut feature

- Click on the **Finish Sketch** button from the **Finish** drop-down in the **Exit** panel of the **Sketch** tab in the **Ribbon** to exit the sketching environment.
- The **Extrude** dialog box will be displayed along with the preview of extrusion; refer to Figure-79.

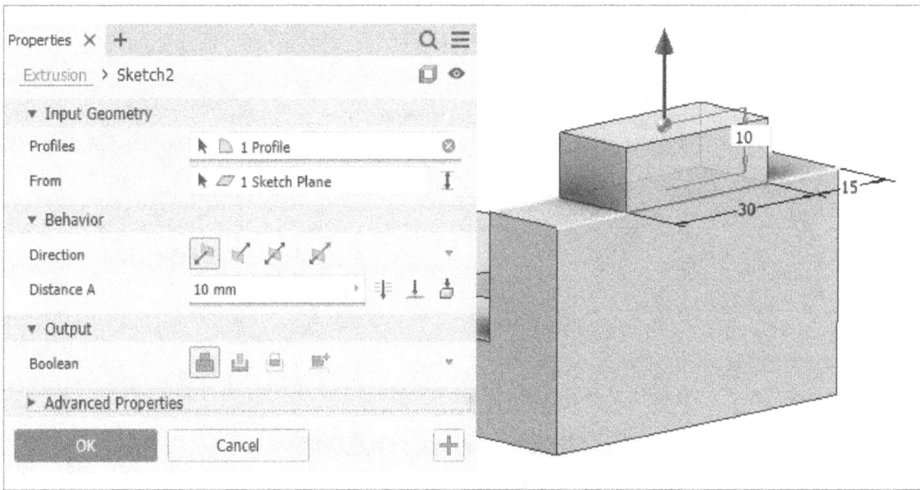

Figure-79. Extrude dialog box with preview of extrusion

- Select the **Flipped** option from **Direction** area and **Cut** option from **Boolean** drop-down from the dialog box and specify the cut depth value as **20** in the **Distance A** edit box; refer to Figure-80.

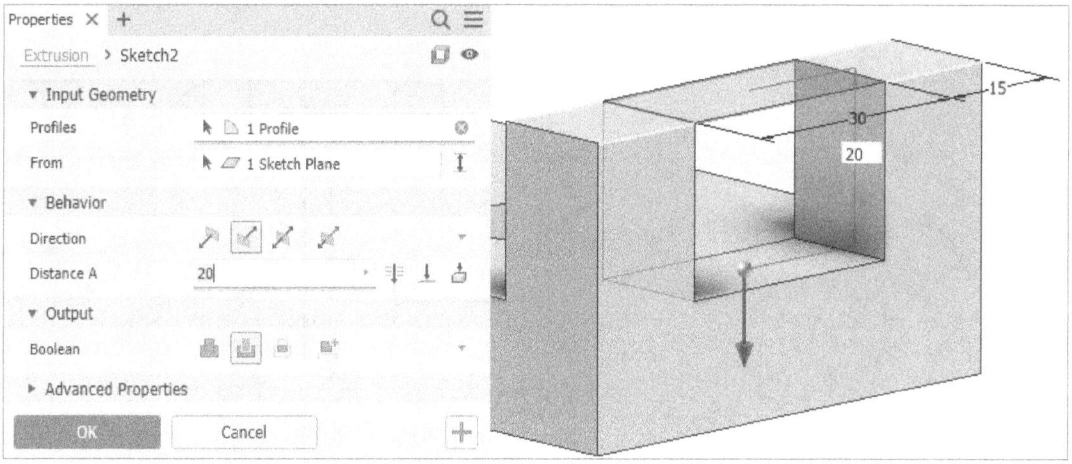

Figure-80. Creating cut feature

- Click on the **OK** button from the dialog box. The final model will be displayed as shown in Figure-81.

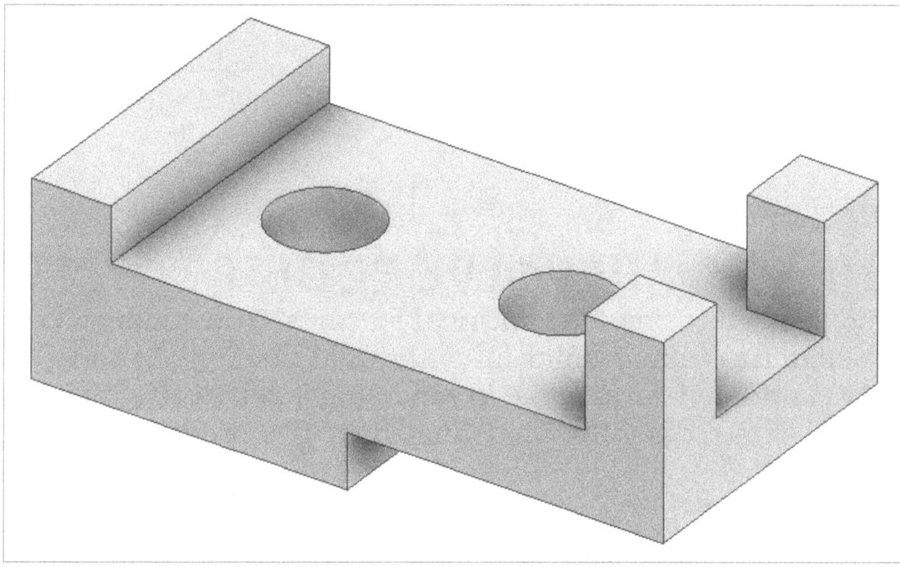

Figure-81. Final Model for Practical 1

PRACTICE 1

Create the model as shown in Figure-82 with the help of extrusion. The orthographic views are as per the Third Angle Projection. Note that you need to first create the basc extrusion by using the outlines of Top view.

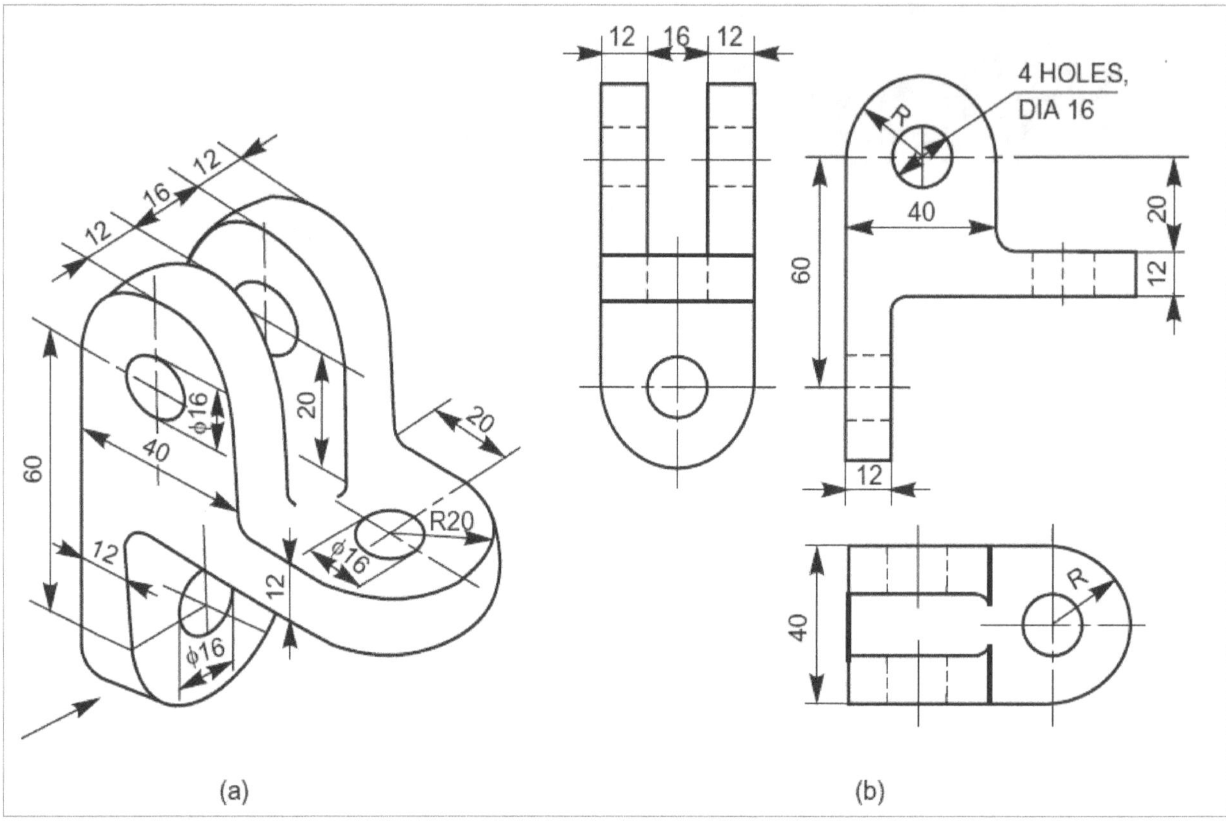

Figure-82. Drawing for Practice 1

REVOLVE TOOL

The **Revolve** tool is used to create cylindrical features. You can also use the **Revolve** tool to remove material from a solid in cylindrical fashion. At most of the places, where we need cylindrical features like in modeling a pen, a shaft, and so on; we can use the **Revolve** tool to reduce the modeling time. The procedure to use this tool is given next.

- Click on the **Revolve** tool from **Create** panel in the **Ribbon**. You will be asked to select a sketching plane.
- Click on the **XY** Plane (Front Plane) to create sketch on it. The sketching environment will be displayed.
- Create closed sketch with a centerline on its either side; refer to Figure-83.

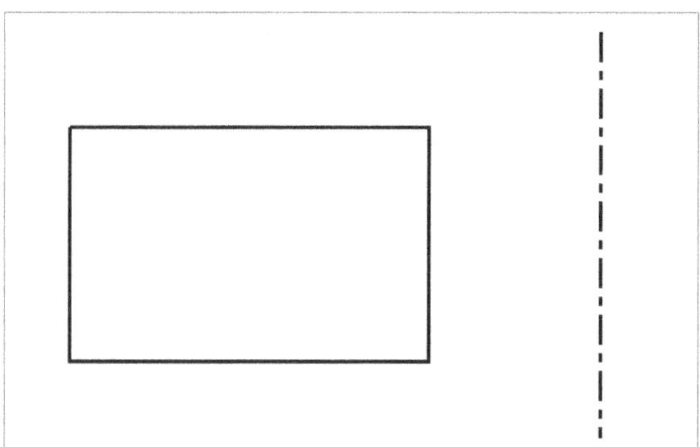

Figure-83. Sketch with centerline

- Click on the **Finish Sketch** button from the **Finish** drop-down in the **Exit** panel of the **Sketch** tab in the **Ribbon**. The **Revolve** dialog box will be displayed along with the preview of revolve feature; refer to Figure-84.

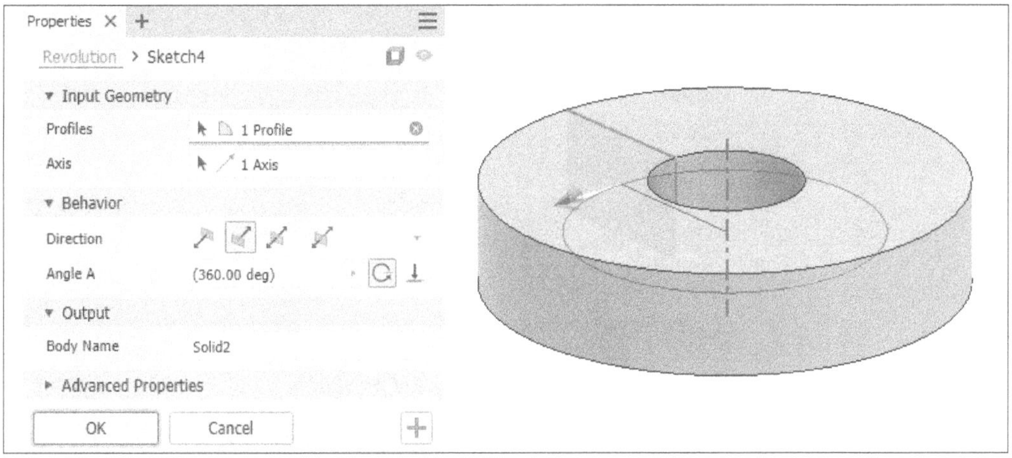

Figure-84. Revolve dialog box with preview of revolve feature

Specifying Angle of Revolution

- Most of the options in this dialog box are same as discussed for **Extrude** tool with the only difference that in place of distance, we will be specifying revolution angle for the revolve feature to define its extents. The options to define angle extent are available next to the **Angle A** edit box; refer to Figure-85.

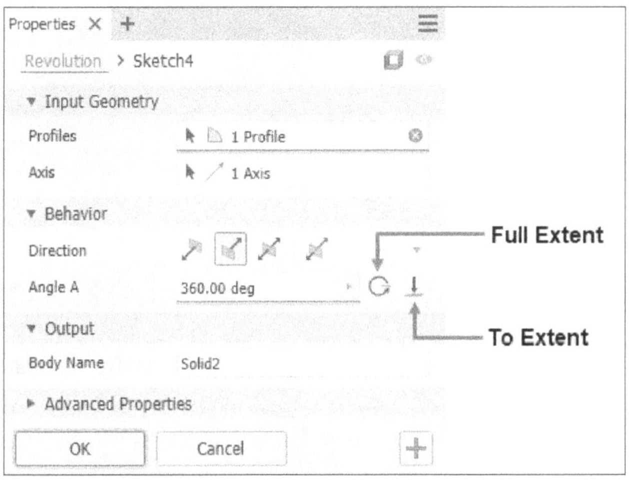

Figure-85. Extent options for revolve feature

- Click on the **Full** option from the **Extent** options. The sketch will be revolved by 360 degree of full revolution.
- Click on the **Angle A** edit box to specify the angle of revolution. Select desired option from **Direction** area to specify the direction of revolve feature. The options will be displayed as shown in Figure-86.

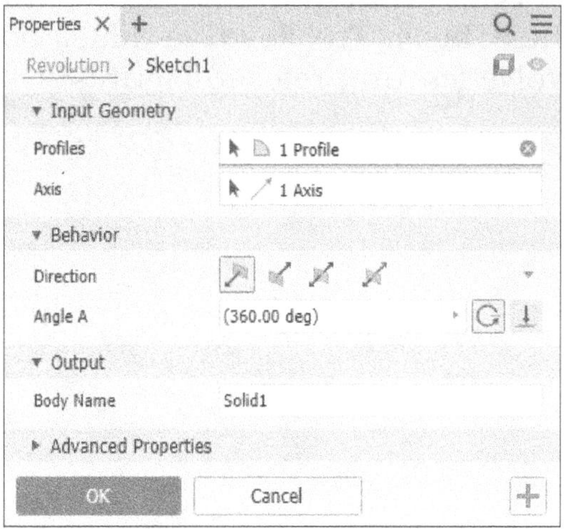

Figure-86. Options to specify angle of revolution

- Specify desired value of angle in the edit box and confirm the revolve feature with preview displayed; refer to Figure-87.

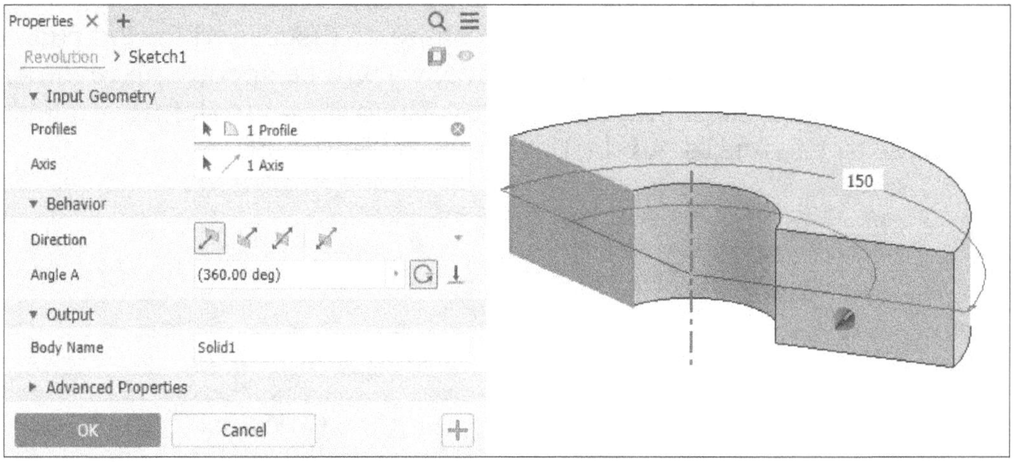

Figure-87. Preview of revolve feature

- You can also use the **To** option for specifying extent in the same way as discussed for **Extrude** tool.
- Click on the **OK** button from the dialog box to create the feature.

PRACTICAL 2

Create the model with dimensions as shown in Figure-88.

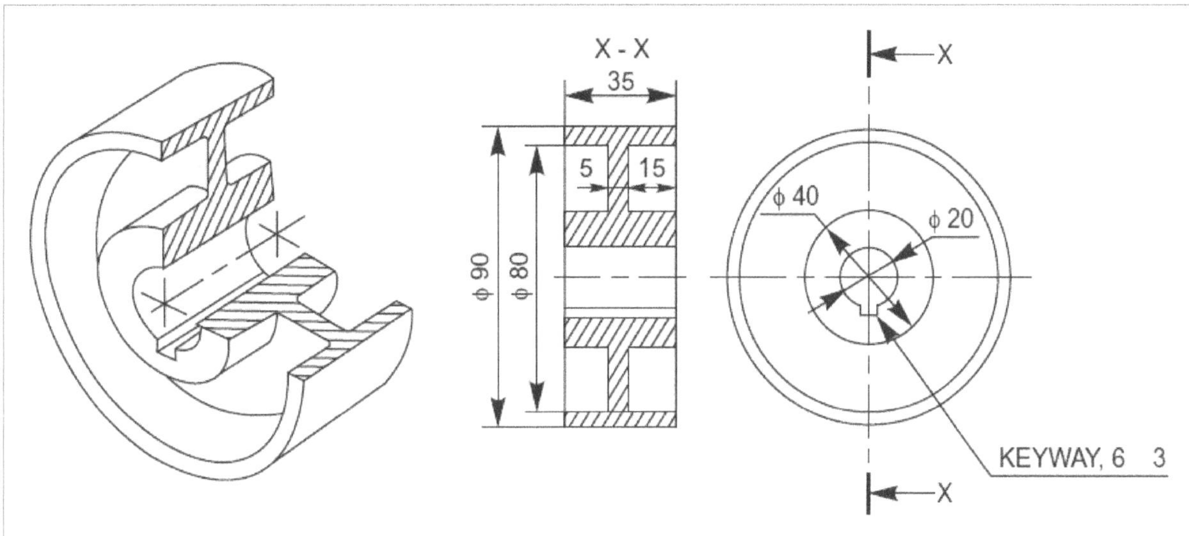

Figure-88. Drawing for Practical 2

Strategy for Creating model

1. Looking at the isometric view and orthographic views, we can find the sketch for revolve feature should be created on the Right plane (YZ Plane).
2. Using the **Revolve** tool, we will create the solid base of the model.
3. Using the **Extrude** tool, we will create the keyway from the base feature.

Starting Part File

- Start Autodesk Inventor by double-clicking on the Autodesk Inventor Professional icon from the desktop. (If not started yet.)
- Click on the **New** button from the **Quick Access Toolbar**. The **Create New File** dialog box will be displayed.
- Double-click on **Standard(mm).ipt** icon from the **Metric** templates. The Part environment of Autodesk Inventor will be displayed.

Creating sketch

- Click on the **Revolve** tool from **Create** panel in the **3D Model** tab of the **Ribbon**. You will be asked to select a sketching plane.
- Click on the **YZ** Plane (Right Plane) to create sketch on it.
- Click on the **Line** tool from the **Create** panel in the **Sketch** tab of the **Ribbon**. You will be asked to specify the starting point of the line.
- Click on the **Centerline** button from **Format** panel in the **Sketch** contextual tab of **Ribbon** and create a centerline as shown in Figure-89.

Figure-89. Centerline created

- Click again on the **Centerline** button to toggle centerline creation.
- Create the sketch as shown in Figure-90.

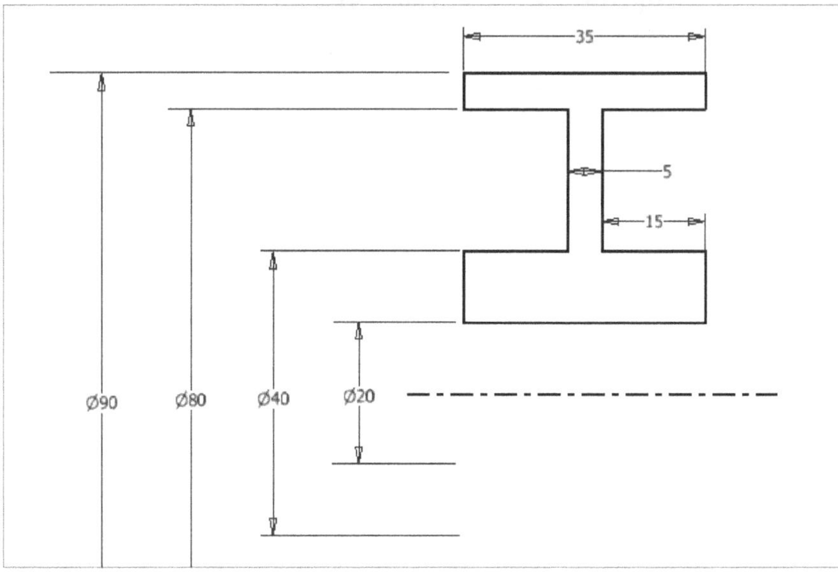

Figure-90. Sketch created for revolve

Creating Revolve Feature

- Click on the **Finish Sketch** button from the **Finish** drop-down of the **Exit** panel in the **Sketch** tab of the **Ribbon**. The **Revolve** dialog box will be displayed along with the preview of revolve feature; refer to Figure-91.

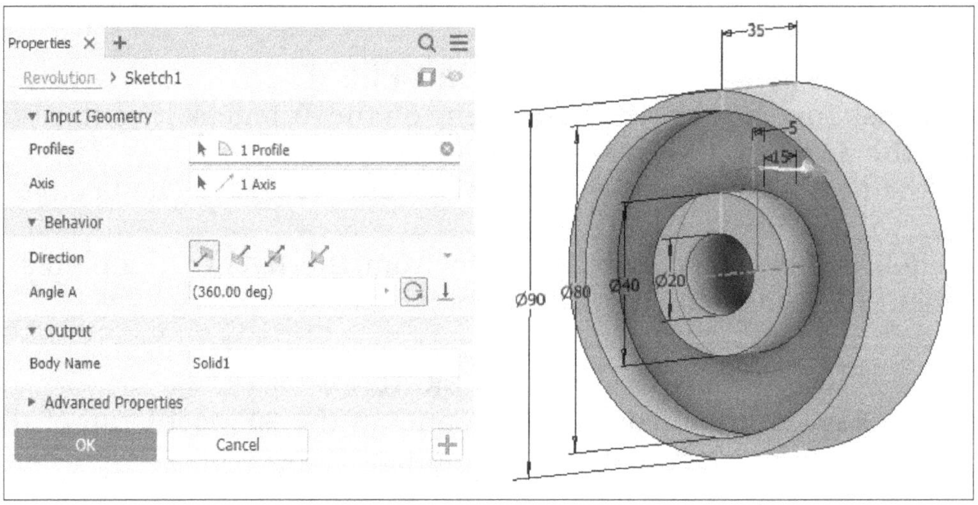

Figure-91. Preview of revolve feature

- Click on the **OK** button from the dialog box to create the feature.

Creating the Cut Feature

- Click on the **Extrude** tool from **Create** panel in the **3D Model** tab of the **Ribbon**. You will be asked to select a plane/face to create the sketch.
- Select the face as shown in Figure-92 and create the sketch as shown in Figure-93.

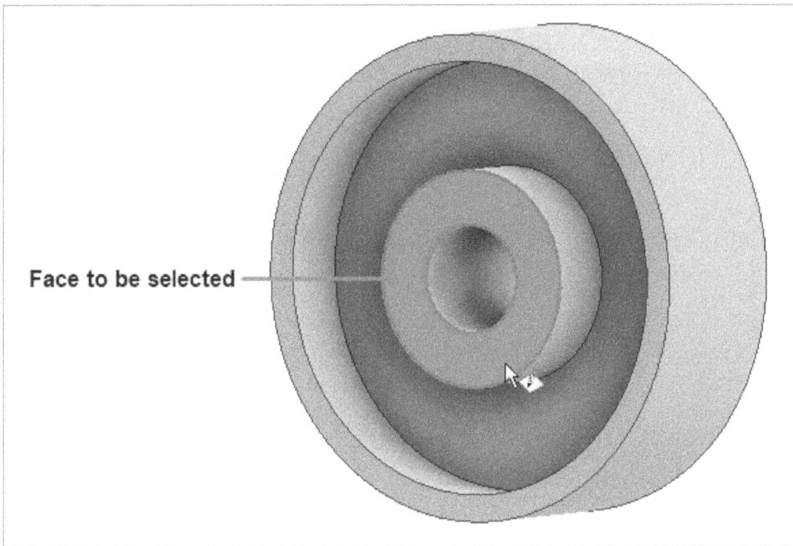

Figure-92. Face selected for extrusion

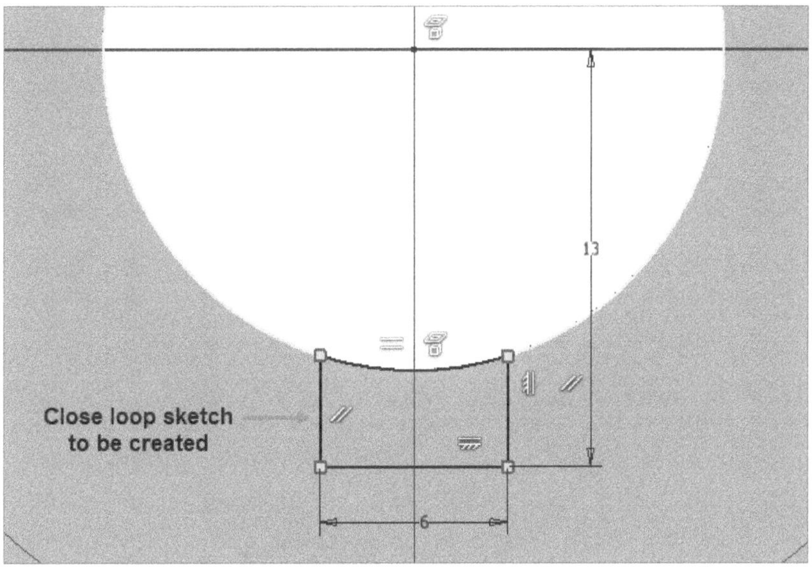

Figure-93. Sketch for extrude cut

- Click on the **Finish Sketch** button from the **Finish** drop-down of the **Exit** panel in the **Sketch** tab of the **Ribbon**. The **Extrude** dialog box will be displayed asking you to select the profiles.
- Select the newly created sketch from the model. The preview of extrusion will be displayed.
- Click on the **To Next** option from the **Extent** options next to the **Distance A** edit box in the dialog box. Preview of the cut feature will be displayed; refer to Figure-94.

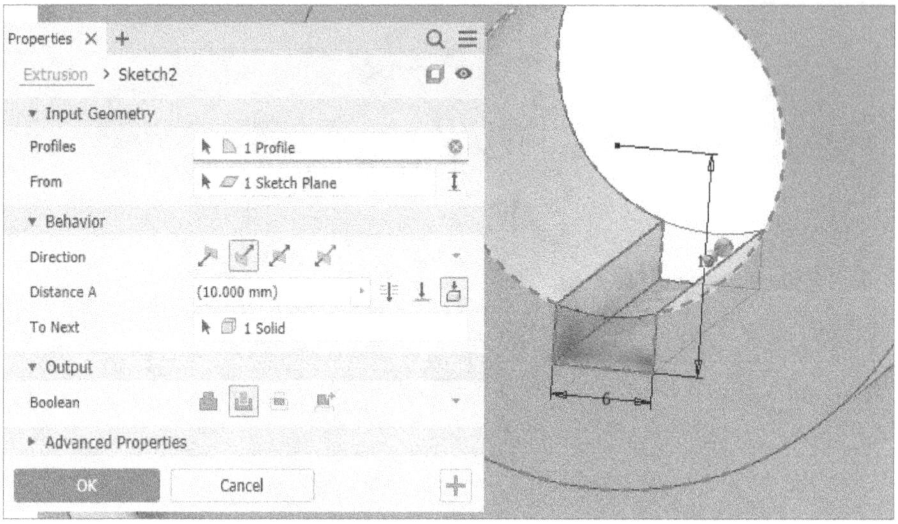

Figure-94. Preview of the cut feature

- Click on the **OK** button from the dialog box to create the cut feature. The final model will be created; refer to Figure-95.

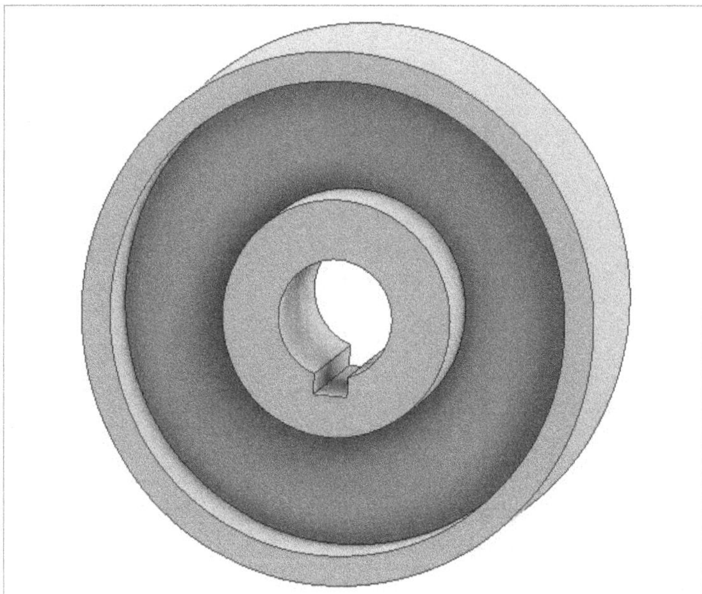

Figure-95. Final model of Practical 2

PRACTICAL 3

Create the model as shown in Figure-96.

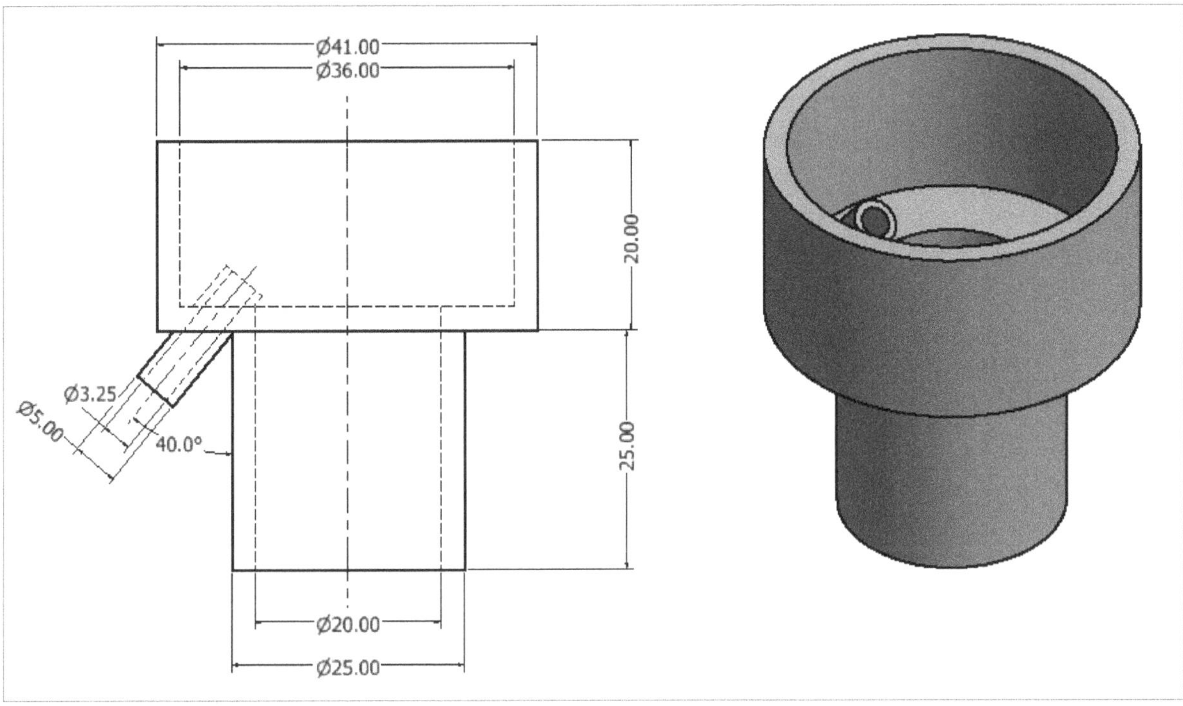

Figure-96. Drawing for Practical 3

Strategy for Creating model

1. Looking at the isometric view and orthographic views, we can find the sketch for revolve feature should be created on the Front plane (YZ Plane).
2. Using the **Revolve** tool, we will create the solid base of the model.
3. Using the Plane tools, we will create a plane at an angle of 40 degree to the vertical wall of base feature.
4. Using the **Extrude** tool, we will create the pipe joined to the base feature.

Starting Part File

- Start Autodesk Inventor by double-clicking on the Autodesk Inventor Professional icon from the desktop. (If not started yet.)
- Click on the **New** button from the **Quick Access Toolbar**. The **Create New File** dialog box will be displayed.
- Double-click on **Standard(mm).ipt** icon from the **Metric** templates. The Part environment of Autodesk Inventor will be displayed.

Creating sketch

- Click on the **Revolve** button from **Create** panel in the **3D Model** tab of the **Ribbon**. You will be asked to select a sketching plane.
- Select the **XY** Plane (Front Plane) as sketching plane. The sketching environment will be displayed.
- Create the sketch as shown in Figure-97.

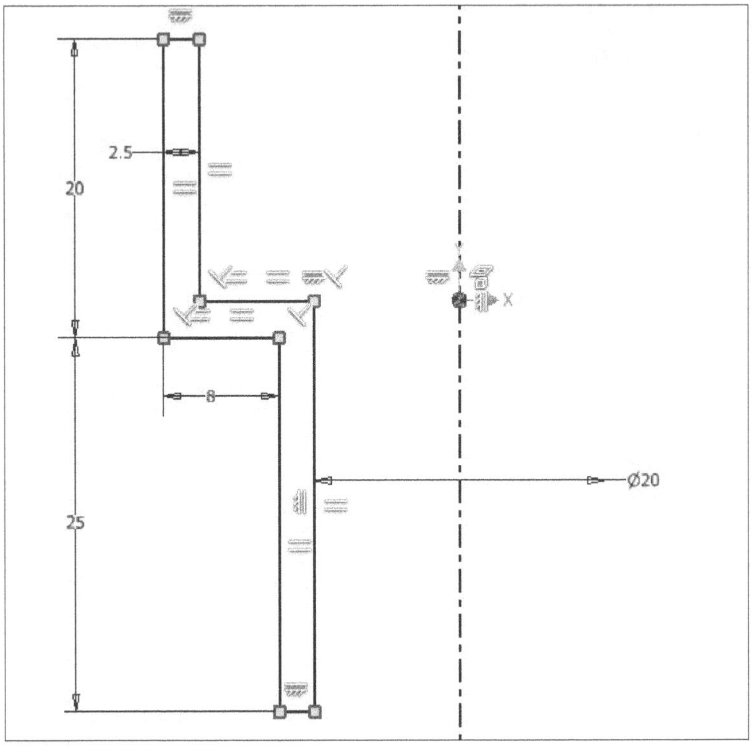

Figure-97. Sketch with constrains

Creating Revolve Feature

- Click on the **Finish Sketch** button from **Exit** panel in the **Sketch** tab of the **Ribbon.** The **Revolve** dialog box will be displayed along with the preview of revolve feature; refer to Figure-98.

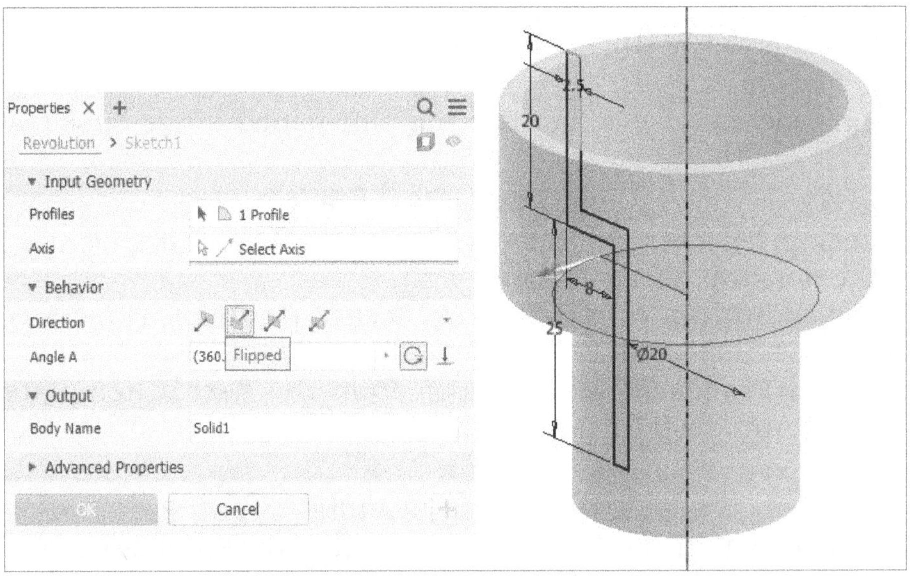

Figure-98. Preview of revolve feature

- Click on the **OK** button from the dialog box to create the revolve feature; refer to Figure-99.

Figure-99. Revolve feature created

Creating Plane at angle

- Click on the **Start 2D Sketch** tool from **Sketch** panel in the **3D Model** tab of the **Ribbon**. You will be asked to select a sketching plane.
- Click on the bottom face of the model as shown in Figure-100 and create a line tangent to the edge of base model as shown in Figure-101.

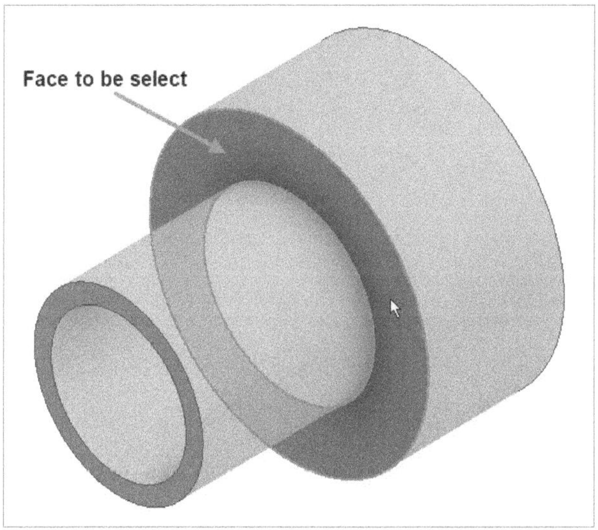

Figure-100. Face to select

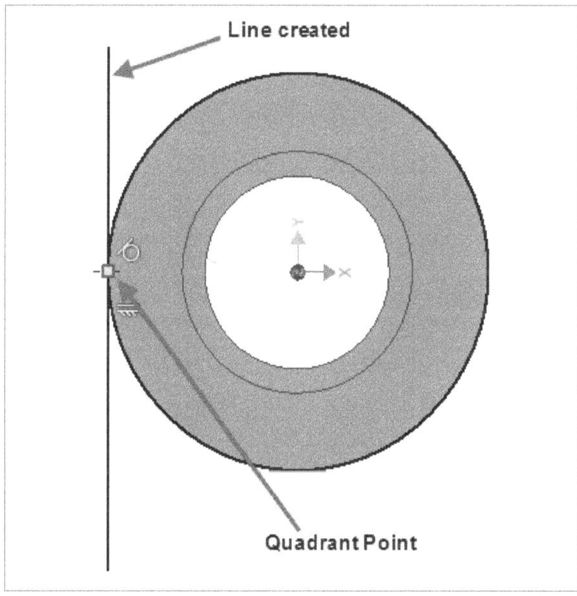

Figure-101. Line to create in sketch

- Click on the **Finish Sketch** button from the **Finish** drop-down in the **Exit** panel of the **Sketch** tab in the **Ribbon**. In isometric view, the sketch should be displayed as shown in Figure-102.

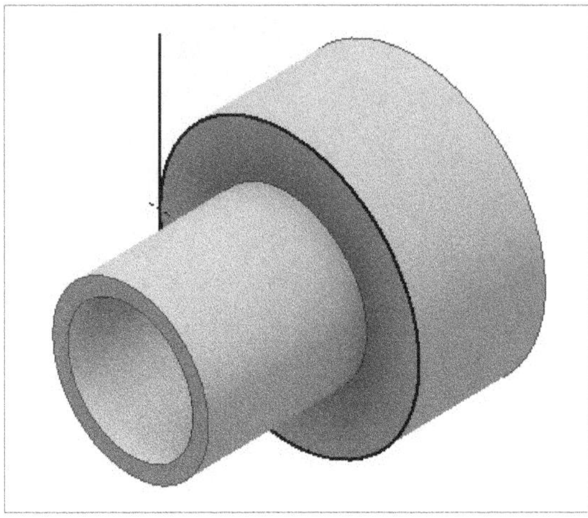

Figure-102. Sketch in isometric view

- Click on the **Angle to Plane around Edge** tool from **Plane** drop-down in the **Work Features** panel of the **3D Model** tab in the **Ribbon**. You will be asked to select a line or plane.
- Click on the line newly created and select the bottom face of the base feature. You will be asked to specify the angle between face and plane; refer to Figure-103.

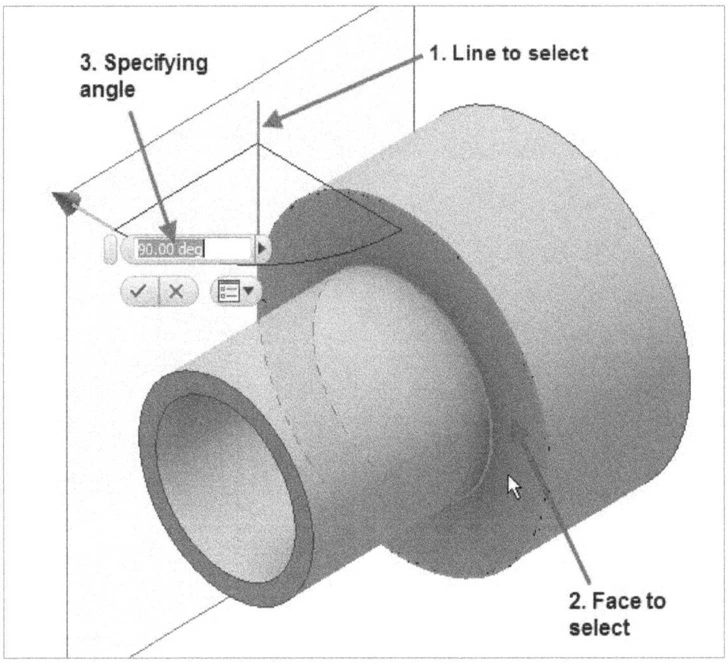

Figure-103. Selecting line and plane

- Specify the angle value as **40** in the edit box and click on the **OK** button to create the plane. The plane will be displayed as shown in Figure-104.

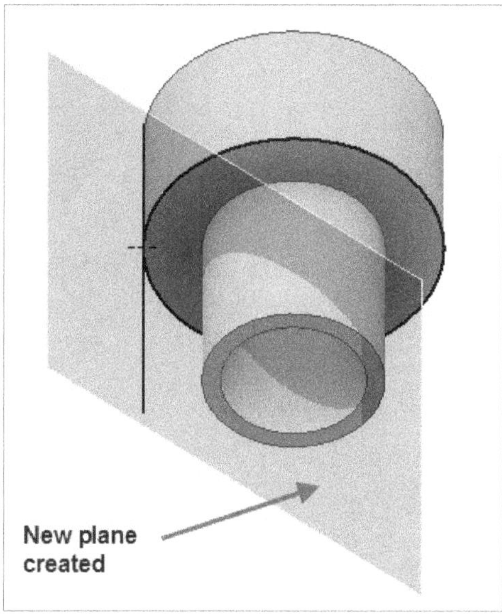

Figure-104. New plane created

Creating Tube

- Click on the **Start 2D Sketch** button from **Sketch** panel in the **3D Model** tab of the **Ribbon**. You will be asked to select the sketching plane.
- Select the newly created plane. The sketching environment will be displayed.
- Create a sketch as shown in Figure-105. Make sure you have applied proper constraint as given in the figure.

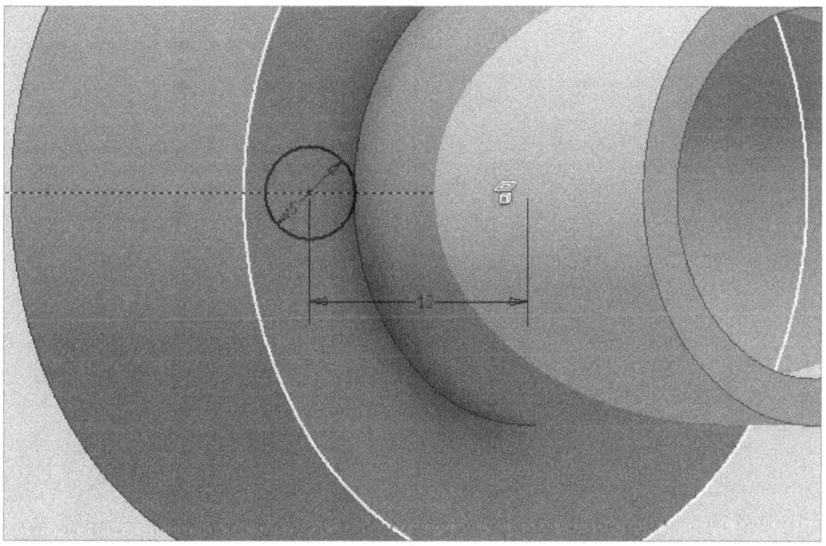

Figure-105. Circle to be created

- Click on the **Finish Sketch** button from the **Finish** drop-down in the **Exit** panel of the **Sketch** tab in the **Ribbon** to exit the sketching environment.
- Click on the **Extrude** tool from **Create** panel in the **3D Model** tab of the **Ribbon**. The **Extrude** dialog box will be displayed along with the preview of extrusion. Specify the distances as 10 inside the base feature and 5 outside the base feature; refer to Figure-106.

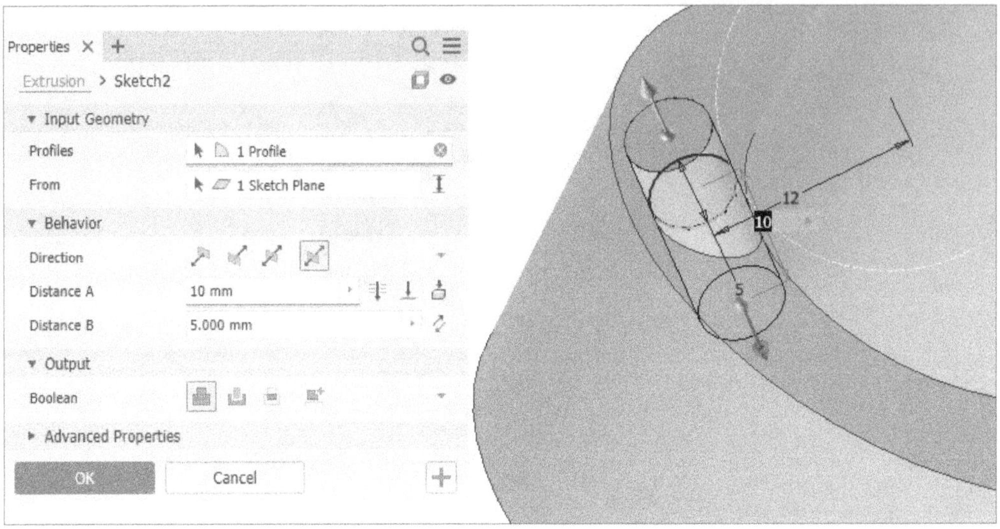

Figure-106. Preview of extrusion

- Click on the **OK** button from the dialog box. The extrusion will be displayed as shown in Figure-107.

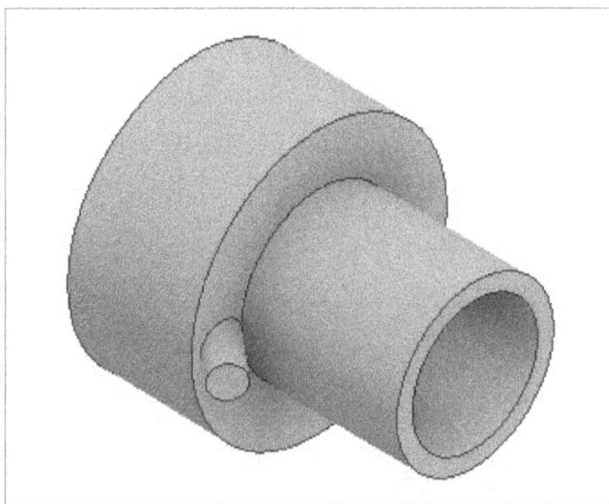

Figure-107. Model after creating extrusion

- Click on the **Extrude** tool again and using the face of newly created extrusion, create a extrude cut for making hole of diameter **3.25**; refer to Figure-108.

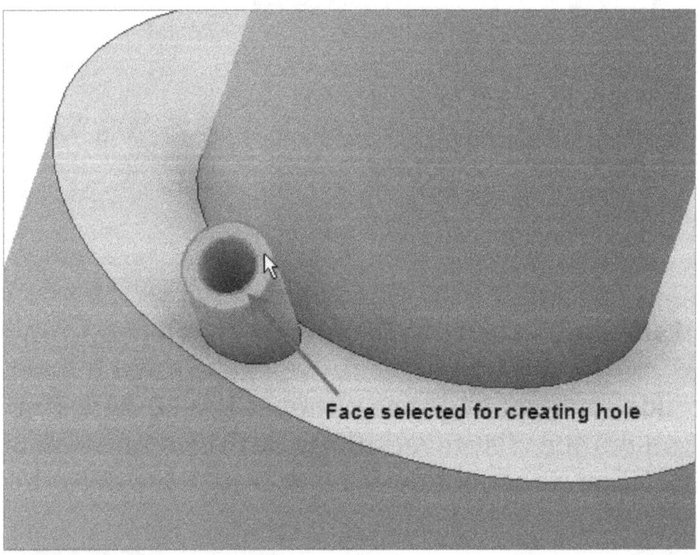

Figure-108. Creating hole

PRACTICE 1

Create the model of pulley by using dimensions given in the Figure-109.

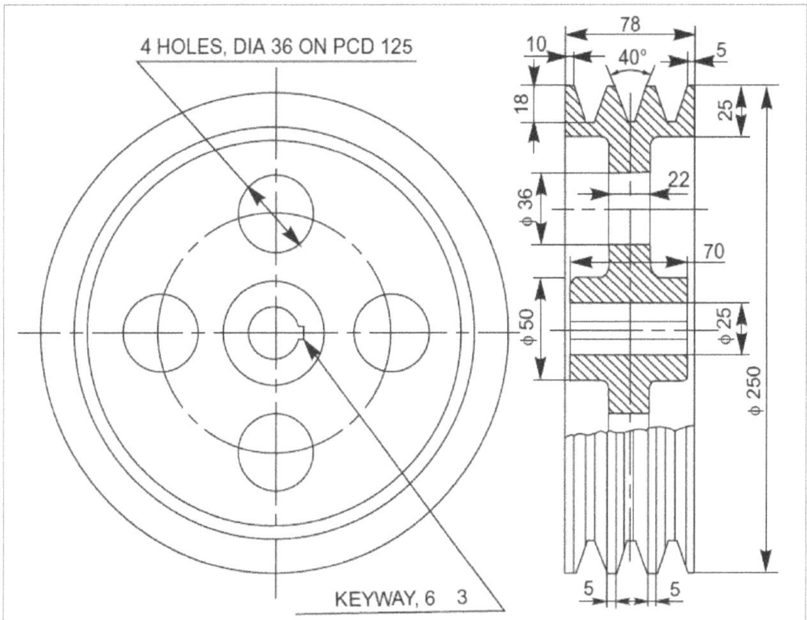

Figure-109. Drawing for Practice 1

PRACTICE 2

Create the model as shown in Figure-110.

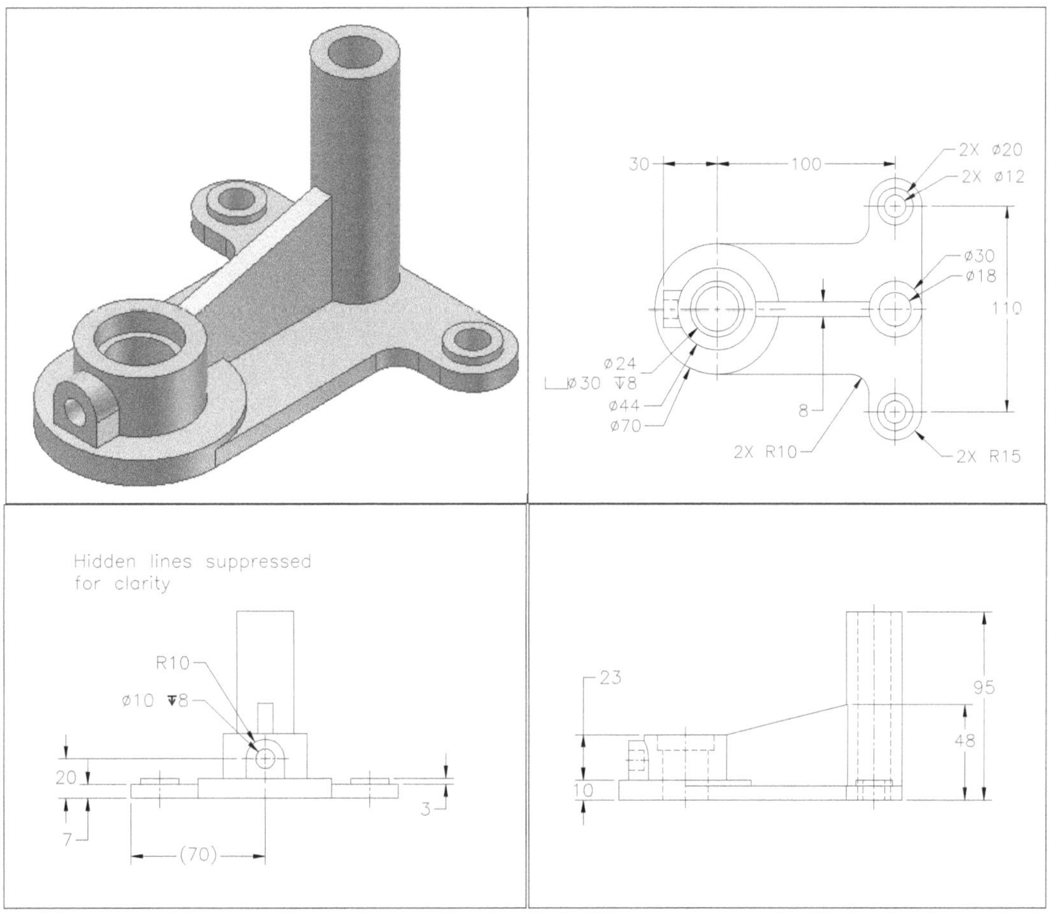

Figure-110. Views and dimensions of the model

PRACTICE 3

Create the model as shown in Figure-111.

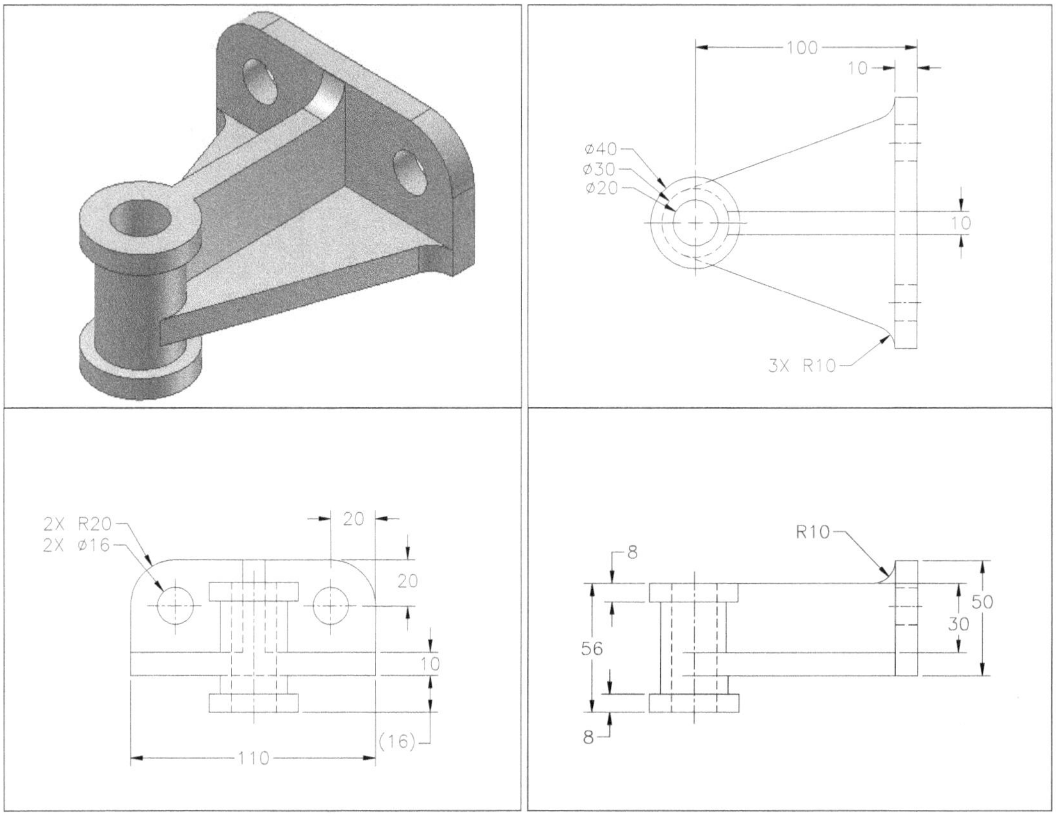

Figure-111. Views and dimensions of the model

PRACTICE 4

Create the model shown in Figure-112.

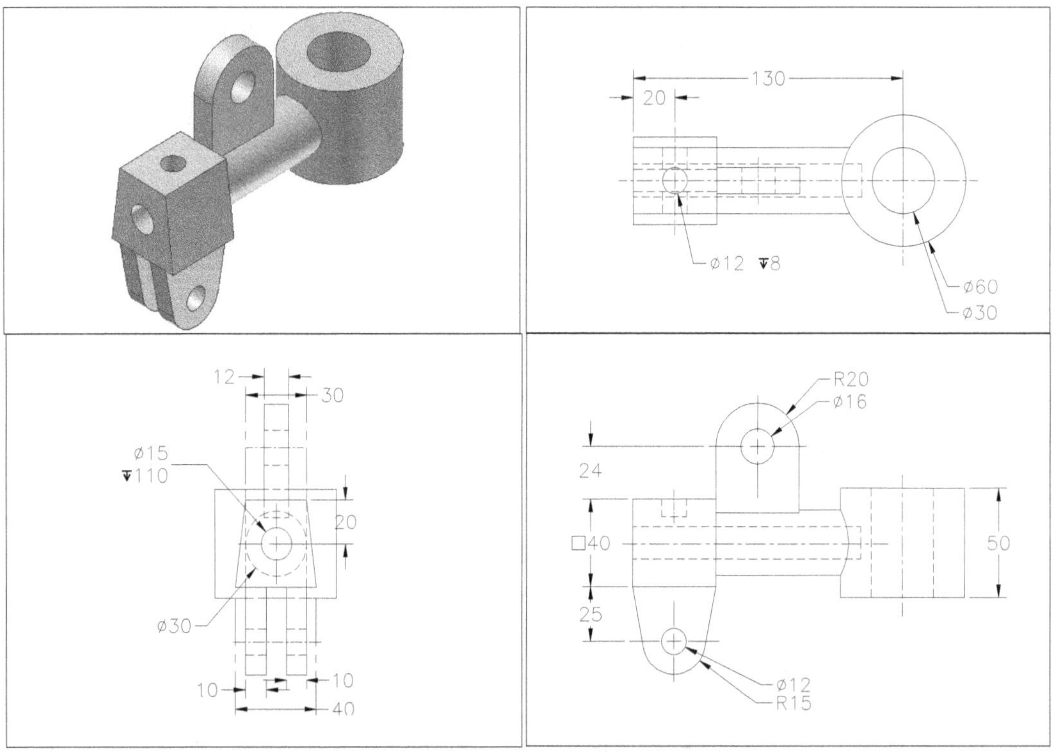

Figure-112. Views and dimensions of the model

PRACTICE 5

Create the model by using the dimensions given in Figure-113.

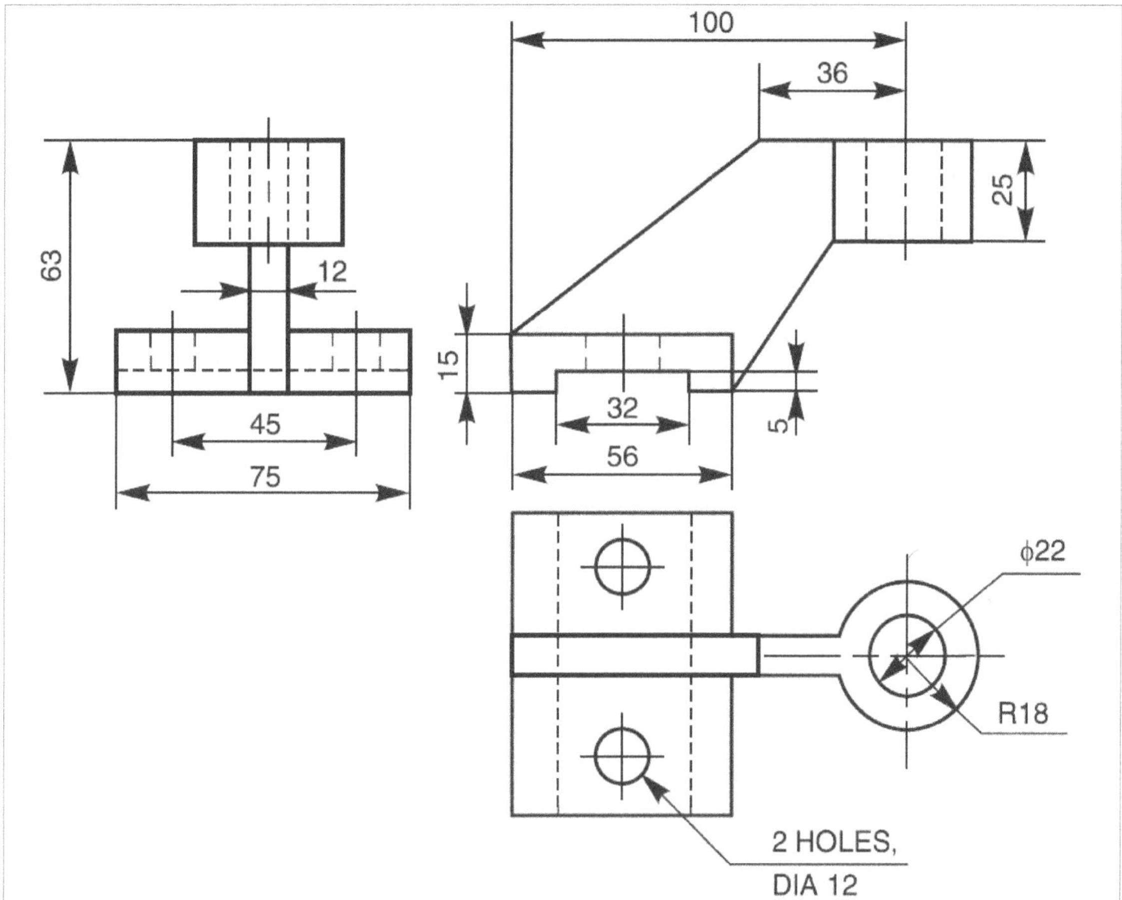

Figure-113. Practice 5

SELF ASSESSMENT

Q1. Which of the following work planes do not exist by default in the software?

a) XY Plane
b) YZ Plane
c) YX Plane
d) XZ Plane

Q2. By which of the following tools can you create a plane through the median of selected planes?

a) Midplane between two Planes
b) Parallel to Plane through Point
c) Midplane of Torus
d) Offset from Plane

Q3. A **Plane** tool can create all the types of plane except one. Which type of plane is it?

a) Normal to Curve at Point
b) Normal to Axis through Point
c) Offset from Plane
d) Two Coplanar Edges

Q4. Which of the following tools can create an axis perpendicular to selected plane and passing through the selected point?

a) On Line or Edge
b) Normal to Plane through Point
c) Through Two Points
d) Axis

Q5. What is the size of Point theoretically?

a) 3
b) 2
c) 1
d) 0

Q6. Which type of Boolean operations should be used to extract the common portion between base feature and extrusion, so that rest of the material in model is automatically removed?

a) Intersect
b) Join
c) Cut
d) New Solid

Q7. Which type of projections are mainly used for orthographic views?

a) First Angle Projection and Second Angle Projection
b) First Angle Projection and Third Angle Projection
c) First Angle Projection and Fourth Angle Projection
d) Third Angle Projection and Fourth Angle Projection

Q8. The **Revolve** tool can be used to remove material from a solid in cylindrical fashion. (True/False)

Q9. If you want to create extrusion to both sides of sketching plane with same depth then select the **Asymmetric** option. (True/False)

Q10. Broadly, there are two ways to present a component in engineering drawing: .... representation and .... representation.

Q11. The .... tool is used to create points in reference to selected key point (like end point, mid point, etc.).

Q12. The .... is the method to display wireframe model of the object with its dimensions at standard angles from base planes.

REVIEW QUESTIONS

1. What is the main function of a Work Plane in Inventor?
A. To apply materials
B. To edit constraints
C. To act as the base for 3D features
D. To create 2D views

Q2. Which default plane is also called the Top Plane?
A. XY Plane
B. YZ Plane
C. XZ Plane
D. ZX Plane

Q3. What must you do to make the default planes visible permanently?
A. Select and drag them to workspace
B. Click on “Show All”
C. Right-click while holding CTRL and choose “Visibility”
D. Enable from Preferences

Q4. Which tool creates a plane at a specific distance from an existing plane or face?
A. Midplane between Two Planes
B. Offset from Plane
C. Tangent to Surface
D. Parallel through Point

Q5. How do you create a plane parallel to another and passing through a point?
A. Use Offset from Plane
B. Use Parallel to Plane through Point
C. Use Plane
D. Use Tangent to Surface through Point

Q6. Which tool is used to create a plane at the midpoint between two selected planes?
A. Angle to Plane
B. Midplane between Two Planes
C. Through Two Points
D. Midplane of Torus

Q7. The Midplane of Torus tool specifically creates a plane at the:
A. Outer edge of torus
B. Center axis of torus
C. Middle of torus
D. Tangent of torus

Q8. Which tool allows creation of a plane at an angle to a selected plane, rotating around an edge?
A. Angle to Plane around Edge
B. Offset from Plane
C. Normal to Curve
D. Plane

Q9. What is required to create a plane using the Three Points tool?
A. Three planes
B. Two edges and one point
C. Three reference points
D. One point and one surface

Q10. The Two Coplanar Edges tool requires:
A. Two parallel planes
B. Two coplanar edges
C. Two intersecting lines
D. One point and one axis

Q11. Which tool creates a plane tangent to a curved surface and passing through an edge?
A. Tangent through Point
B. Tangent to Surface through Edge
C. Midplane between Curves
D. Parallel through Edge

Q12. The Tangent to Surface through Point tool requires the point to be:
A. On the axis
B. On a straight edge
C. On the curved surface
D. At the origin

Q13. What does the Tangent to Surface and Parallel to Plane tool accomplish?
A. Tangent to two curved surfaces
B. Plane parallel to a face and perpendicular to another
C. Plane tangent to a surface and parallel to a plane
D. Midplane between two surfaces

Q14. The Normal to Axis through Point tool creates a plane that is:
A. Tangent to axis
B. Parallel to axis
C. Perpendicular to axis and passes through a point
D. Offset from axis

Q15. The Normal to Curve at Point tool creates a plane that is:
A. Parallel to the curve
B. Perpendicular to the curve at selected point
C. Offset from curve
D. Through curve and surface

Q16. Which tool can create most plane types except Offset from Plane?
A. Parallel to Plane
B. Plane
C. Tangent through Point
D. Midplane

Q17. The On Line or Edge tool creates an axis:
A. At the intersection of planes
B. On a selected line or edge
C. Between three points
D. Offset from edge

Q18. To create an axis parallel to a line and through a point, which tool is used?
A. Through Two Points
B. On Edge
C. Parallel to Line through Point
D. Tangent Axis

Q19. The Through Two Points tool is used to create an axis:
A. Perpendicular to a plane
B. Between two intersecting planes
C. Passing through two selected points
D. Tangent to a curve

Q20. What does the Intersection of Two Planes tool do?
A. Creates a curve
B. Creates a midpoint plane
C. Creates an axis where two planes intersect
D. Rotates a face

Q21. The Normal to Plane through Point tool results in:
A. A plane perpendicular to axis
B. An axis normal to plane through a point
C. Tangent plane creation
D. Curve normal axis

Q22. What is required for the Through Center of Circular or Elliptical Edge tool?
A. Two edges
B. Center point
C. Circular or elliptical edge
D. Revolved face

Q23. The Through Revolved Face or Feature tool creates an axis:
A. At the bottom of the model
B. Along the centerline of revolved face
C. On any flat face
D. Tangent to outermost edge

Q24. What does the general "Axis" tool allow you to do?
A. Create only one type of axis
B. Select multiple axis presets
C. Create any previously discussed type of axis
D. Sketch on plane only

Q25. What is the theoretical size of a point in Inventor?
A. One unit
B. Zero size
C. One pixel
D. Infinite small

Q26. Where can you find the tools to create points in Inventor?
A. Sketch panel
B. Work Features panel of the Ribbon
C. 3D Model tab
D. Extrude dialog box

Q27. What does the Grounded Point tool require for placing a point?
A. A circular edge
B. A plane
C. A selected key point like vertex or mid point
D. A sketch

Q28. How do you create multiple points using the Grounded Point tool?
A. Use the Array tool
B. Use the Pattern tool
C. Click the Apply button in the Input boxes
D. Select multiple vertices simultaneously

Q29. What is the purpose of the Extrude tool?
A. Create a sketch
B. Add materials by projecting sketch into 3D
C. Create planes
D. Create surfaces only

Q30. What must you do before accessing the Extrude dialog box?
A. Create a surface
B. Define a Boolean operation
C. Finish the sketch
D. Change the view mode

Q31. Which option in Extrude dialog specifies the height of extrusion?
A. Taper A
B. Distance A
C. Depth B
D. Height Z

Q32. What color indicates the Default extrusion direction?
A. Light green
B. Light blue
C. Dark gray
D. Light orange

Q33. Which extrusion option allows you to specify different depths in opposite directions?
A. Default
B. Symmetric
C. Asymmetric
D. Through All

Q34. What happens when you select the “To” option during extrusion?
A. Model is mirrored
B. Depth becomes infinite
C. You must select a terminating geometry
D. Tool exits automatically

Q35. What does the “To Next” option in extrusion do?
A. Goes to the next sketch
B. Creates a mirrored feature
C. Extrudes up to the next intersecting solid face
D. Adds a fillet

Q36. What is the function of the “Join” operation in Boolean drop-down?
A. Creates a sketch
B. Joins extrusion to the sketch
C. Combines new extrusion with base feature
D. Splits the model

Q37. Which Boolean operation removes material from the base feature?
A. Cut
B. Join
C. New Solid
D. Intersect

Q38. What does the Intersect button retain in the model?
A. Only thc ncw cxtrusion
B. Entire base body
C. Common portion between base feature and extrusion
D. The cutting section

Q39. What is the result of using the New Solid option in the Extrude dialog?
A. Replaces base model
B. Creates a non-editable model
C. Creates a separate solid
D. Deletes existing model

Q40. How do you add a taper to the extrusion?
A. Use Mirror tool
B. Change Direction settings
C. Enter value in Taper A field
D. Set Distance B

Q41. What does the Surface Mode button in Extrude dialog do?
A. Creates wireframe
B. Creates surface extrusion
C. Converts solid to sheet
D. Removes material

Q42. What does an engineering drawing represent?
A. Blueprint for electrical circuits
B. Exact representation of an engineering component
C. Simple sketch with labels
D. Code for CNC machines

Q43. Which type of drawing shows all dimensions, limits, and processes like heat treatment?
A. Machine Drawing
B. Part Drawing
C. Assembly Drawing
D. Production Drawing

Q44. A drawing showing various parts in their working positions is called:
A. Part Drawing
B. Isometric Drawing
C. Assembly Drawing
D. Orthographic View

Q45. What kind of drawing is typically used to manufacture a component?
A. Part Drawing
B. Assembly Drawing
C. Wireframe Drawing
D. Concept Sketch

Q46. Which drawing method represents a component through multiple standard views?
A. Isometric
B. Orthographic
C. 3D Render
D. CAD View

Q47. Which method is used to show shape of object with some critical dimensions at angles?
A. Wireframe
B. Orthographic
C. Isometric
D. Blueprint

Q48. What does the orientation of the model depend on while creating 3D models?
A. Material type
B. Sketch dimensions
C. Plane selection
D. Axis selection

Q49. How can one identify the top and front views in orthographic drawings?
A. By measuring the dimensions
B. By looking at the component directly
C. By the use of projection type symbols
D. By selecting default planes

Q50. Which projection types are commonly used for orthographic views?
A. Isometric and Dimetric
B. First Angle and Third Angle
C. Top-down and Bottom-up
D. Front-back and Left-right

Q51. What is shown in the Title Block of engineering drawings to indicate the projection type?
A. A legend of symbols
B. A sketch of the part
C. Projection symbols
D. View numbers

Q52. Which tool is used to create cylindrical features or remove cylindrical material?
A. Extrude
B. Fillet
C. Revolve
D. Shell

Q53. What must be created in the sketch to use the Revolve tool effectively?
A. An open sketch without centerline
B. A closed sketch with a centerline
C. A sketch with only construction lines
D. A sketch on the Top Plane

Q54. What does the Revolve tool use instead of a distance to define extent?
A. Radius
B. Volume
C. Angle
D. Height

Q55. What happens when the 'Full' option is selected in the Revolve tool?
A. The sketch revolves halfway
B. The feature is cut by half
C. The sketch revolves by 360 degrees
D. Only one side of the sketch is revolved

Q56. Which option can be used in the Revolve tool to specify a terminating geometry for the revolution?
A. Symmetric
B. To
C. Distance A
D. Through All

Q57. How is the direction of the revolve feature specified?
A. By clicking and dragging the sketch
B. By selecting the correct plane
C. By using the Direction drop-down
D. By editing the angle manually in the sketch

Q58. What is the final step to create the revolve feature after setting all parameters?
A. Click Apply
B. Press Enter
C. Click OK
D. Select the sketch again

Chapter 5

Advanced Solid Modeling Tools

Topics Covered

The major topics covered in this chapter are:

- ***Sweep tool***
- ***Loft tool***
- ***Coil tool***
- ***Emboss tool***
- ***Rib tool***
- ***Derive tool***
- ***Decal tool***
- ***Import tool***

INTRODUCTION

In the previous chapter, we learnt about extrude and revolve features. We also learnt the use of planes, axes, and points. In this chapter, we will learn to use some advanced tools for creating solid models. These tools are also available in the **Create** panel of the **3D Model** tab in the **Ribbon**.

SWEEP TOOL

Sweep The **Sweep** tool is used to create solid/surface feature by sweeping closed loop sketch along the selected trajectory. This tool is generally used when we need to create tubes/bars along a curve. The procedure to use this tool is given next.

- Create a closed loop sketch section and a path in the modeling area; refer to Figure-1.

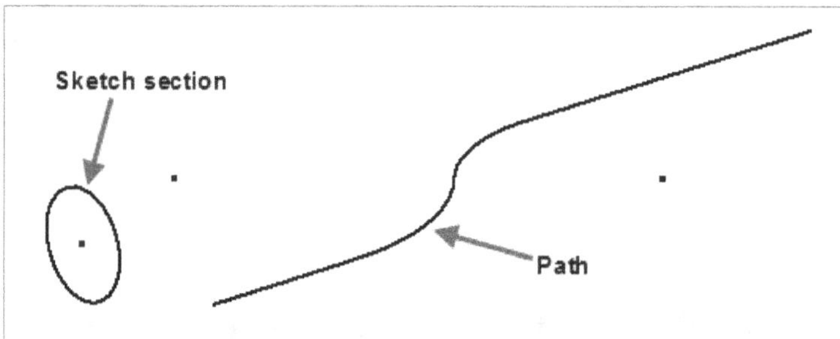

Figure-1. Sketch section and path

- Click on the **Sweep** tool from **Create** panel in the **3D Model** tab of the **Ribbon**. The **Sweep** dialog box will be displayed along with the preview of sweep feature; refer to Figure-2. If there are more than one sections in the modeling space then you will be asked to select a section (Profile).

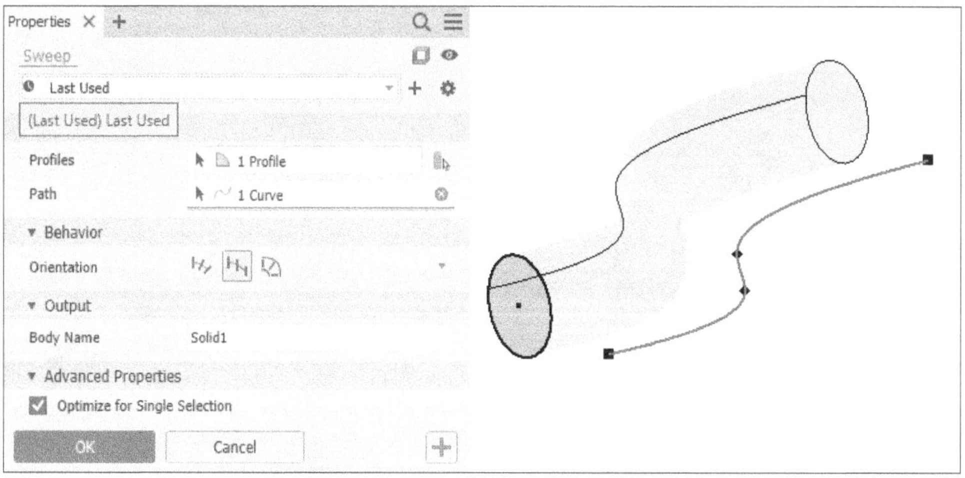

Figure-2. Preview of sweep feature

- There are three types of orientations available for creating sweep feature: **Follow Path**, **Fixed**, and **Guide**; refer to Figure-3.

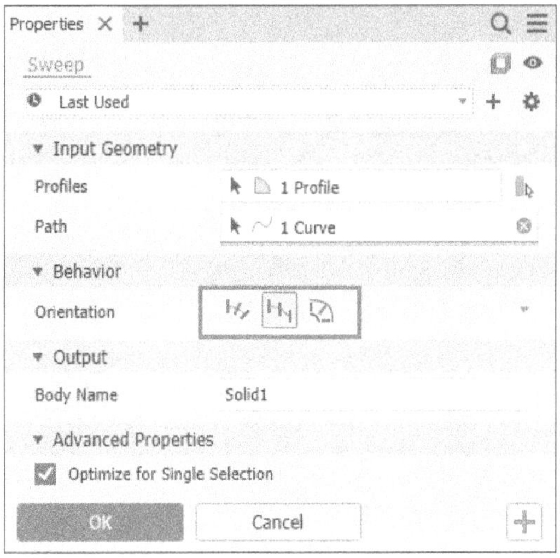

Figure-3. Orientation for sweep

Creating Sweep feature with Follow Path

- If you select the **Follow Path** option from **Orientation** area in the dialog box then profile will be of same shape and size throughout the path followed for sweep; refer to Figure-4.

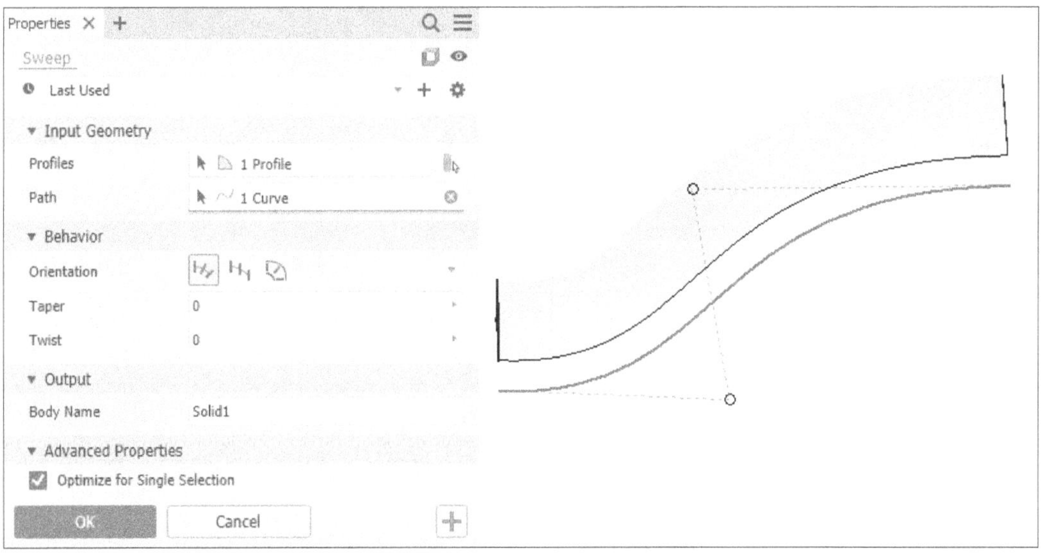

Figure-4. Sweep with Follow Path option

- On selecting the **Follow Path** option, you can specify the taper angle and twist angle in the **Taper** and **Twist** edit boxes of the **Sweep** dialog box, respectively; refer to Figure-5.

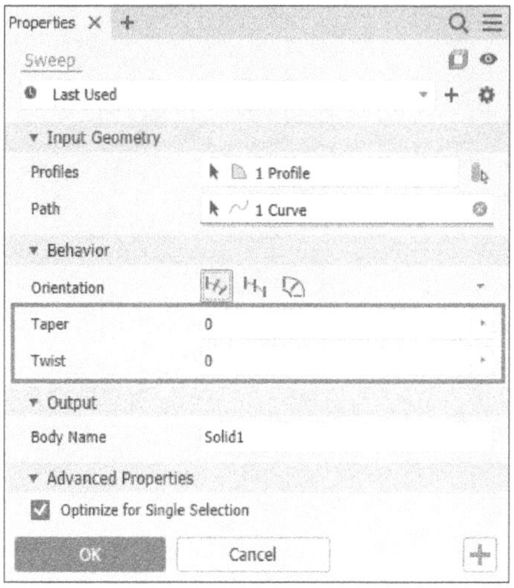

Figure-5. Taper and Twist edit boxes

- Specify the taper angle value in **Taper** edit box, the preview of sweep feature will be displayed; refer to Figure-6.

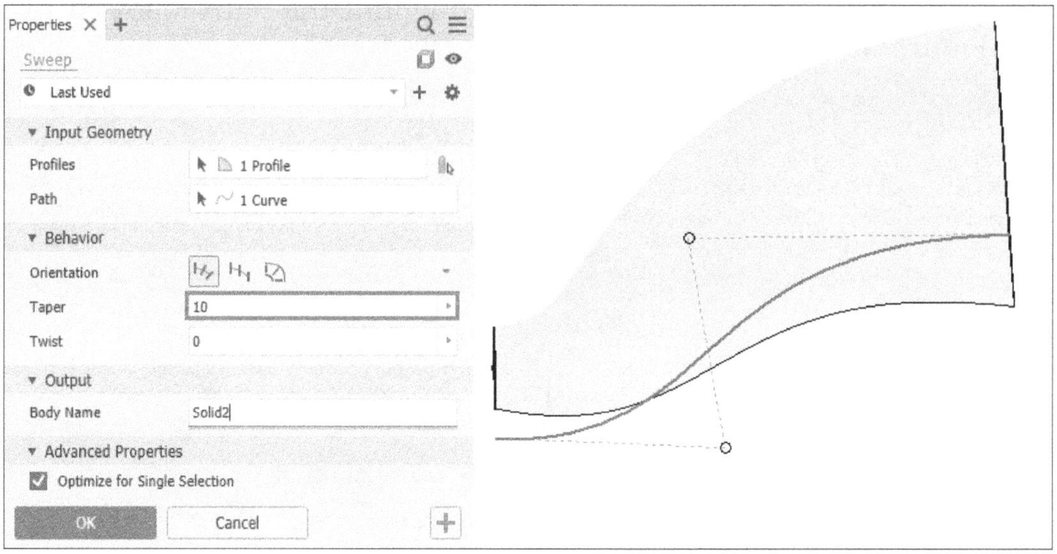

Figure-6. Tapered sweep

- Specify the twist angle value in **Twist** edit box, the preview of sweep feature will be displayed; refer to Figure-7.

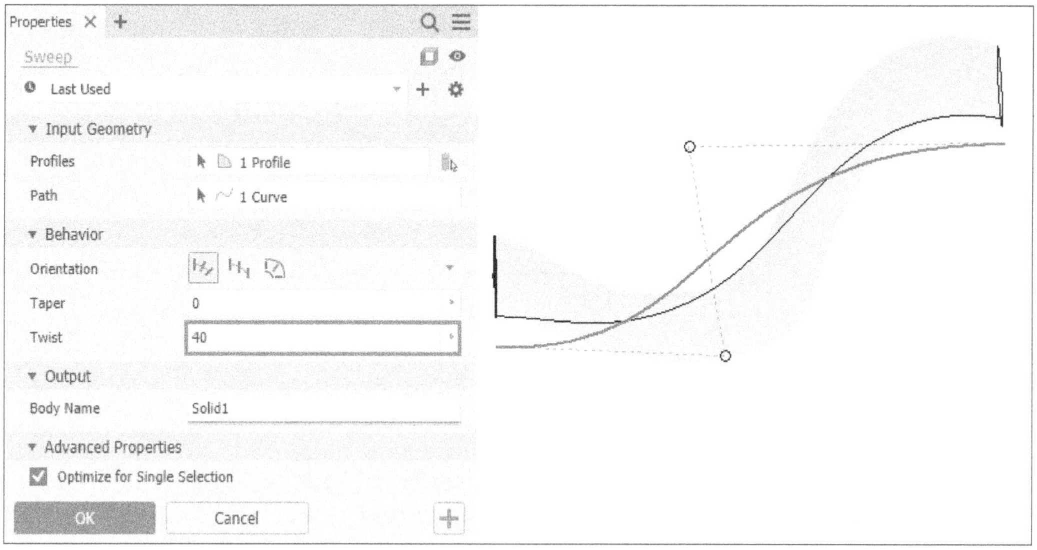

Figure-7. Twisted sweep

Creating Sweep feature with Fixed

- If you select the **Fixed** option from **Orientation** area in the dialog box then shape/ size of the profile can be changed to make it follow the exact shape of path; refer to Figure-8.

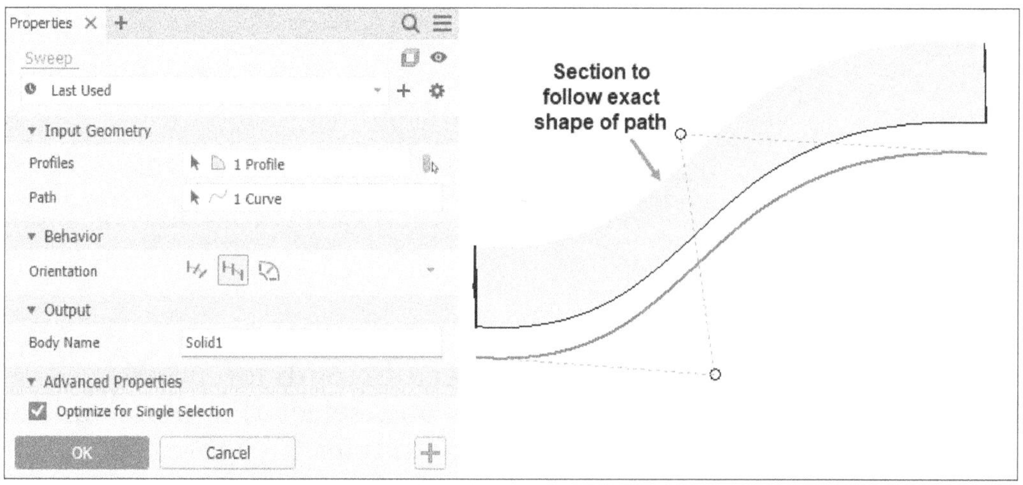

Figure-8. Sweep with Fixed option

Creating Sweep feature with Guide

- Sometimes, it becomes necessary to control the outer shape of the sweep feature. You can create this feature with **Guide** options which is available in **Orientation** area in the dialog box. To use this option, you must have a guide rail curve along with section and path; refer to Figure-9.

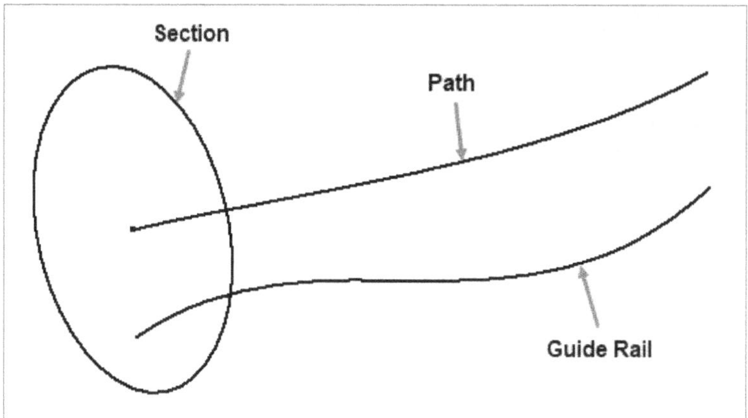

Figure-9. Section with path and guide rail

- Once you have the three sketch entities (section, path, and guide rail), click on the **Sweep** tool from **Create** panel in the **3D Model** tab of the **Ribbon**. The **Sweep** dialog box will be displayed with profile selection and you will be asked to select the path and guide rail; refer to Figure-10.

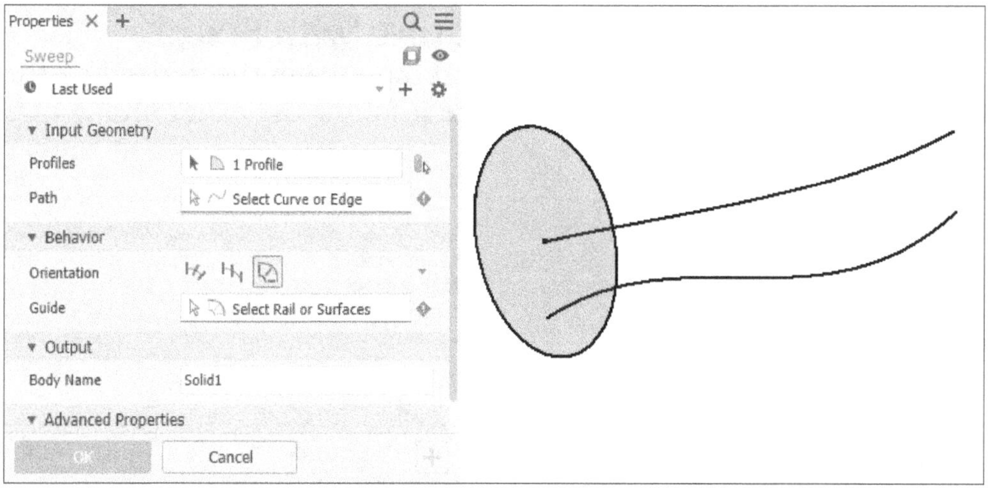

Figure-10. Sweep dialog box with profile selection

- Click on the **Path** selection button and select the path for sweep.
- Next, click on the **Guide** selection button and select the guide rail for sweep. Preview of the sweep feature will be displayed; refer to Figure-11.

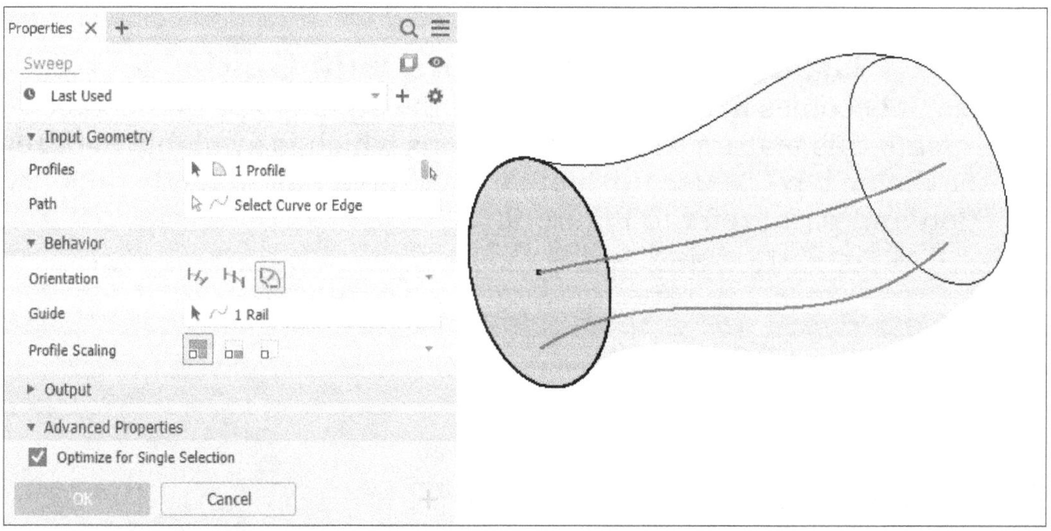

Figure-11. Preview of sweep feature with guide rail

- Options in the **Profile Scaling** area below the **Guide** selection button are used to manage the profile of sweep feature while following the guide rail. There are three options in this area, **X&Y Scaling**, **X Scaling**, and **No Scaling**; refer to Figure-12.

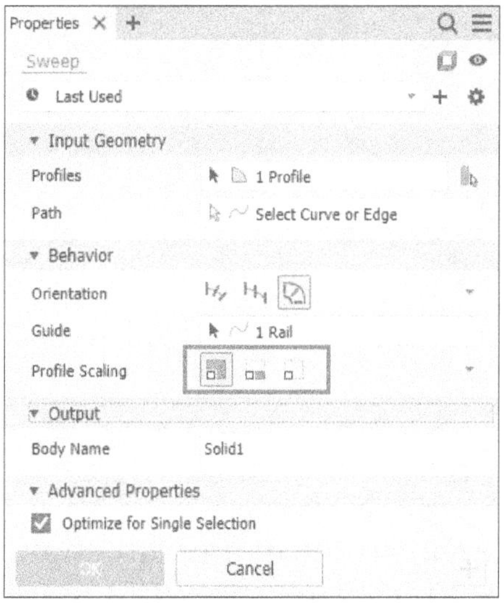

Figure-12. Profile Scaling options

- Select the **X&Y Scaling** option from the **Profile Scaling** area if you want the profile section to re-size in X and Y both directions as per the guide rail; refer to Figure-13.

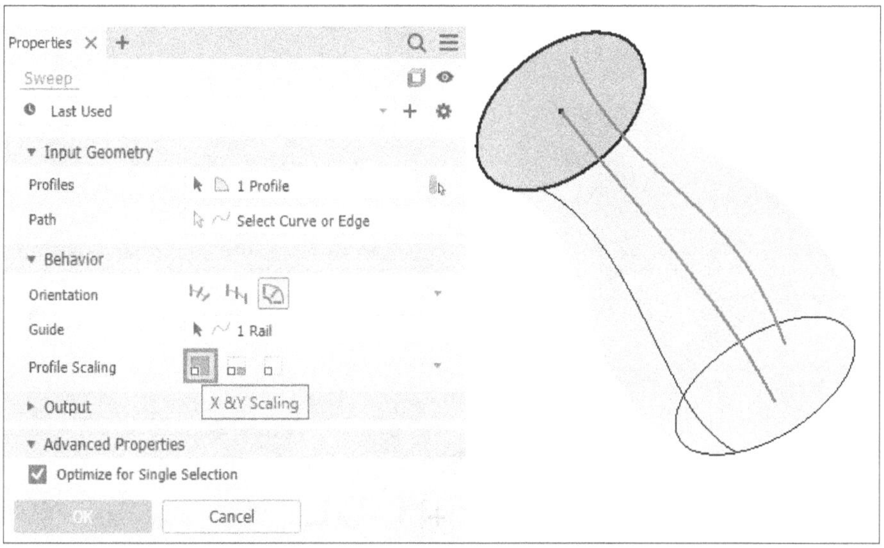

Figure-13. Sweep with XY profile scaling option

- Select the **X Scaling** option if you want the profile section to re size only in X direction as per the guide rail; refer to Figure-14.

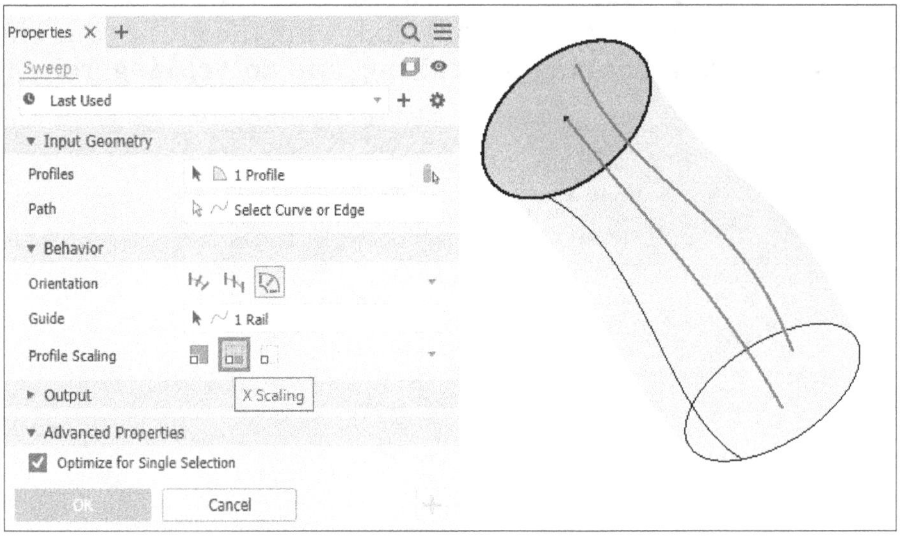

Figure-14. Sweep with X profile scaling option

- If you do not want to scale the profile in any direction then click on the **No Scaling** option from the **Profile Scaling** area; refer to Figure-15.

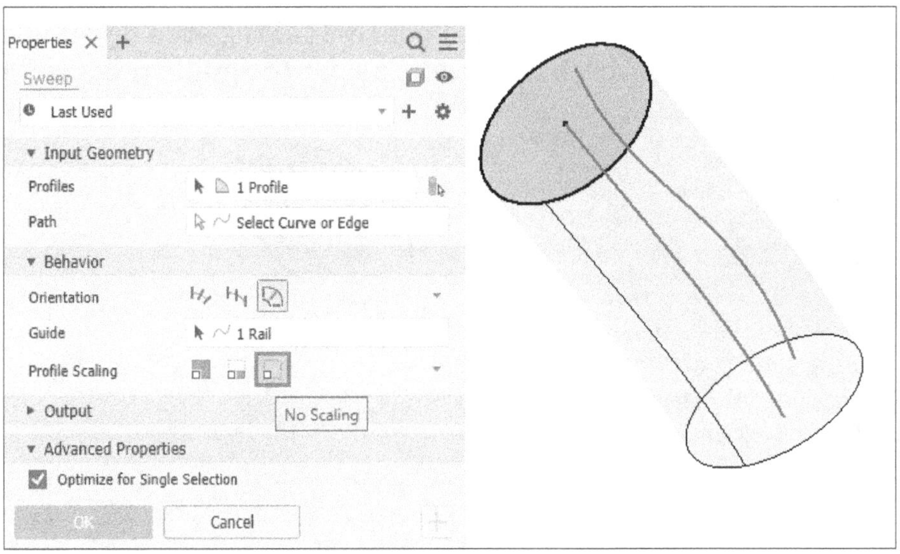

Figure-15. Sweep with No profile scaling option

LOFT TOOL

The **Loft** tool is used to create solid/surface using the transition between two or more sketches; refer to Figure-16. The procedure to use this tool is given next.

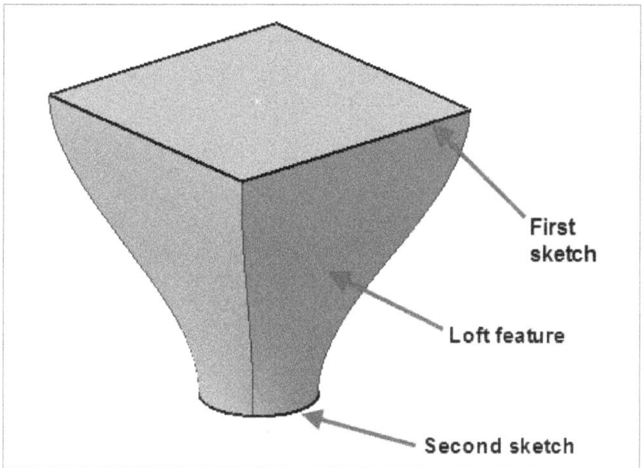

Figure-16. Example of loft feature

- Create desired shape outlines (sketches) on planes parallel to each other; refer to Figure-17.

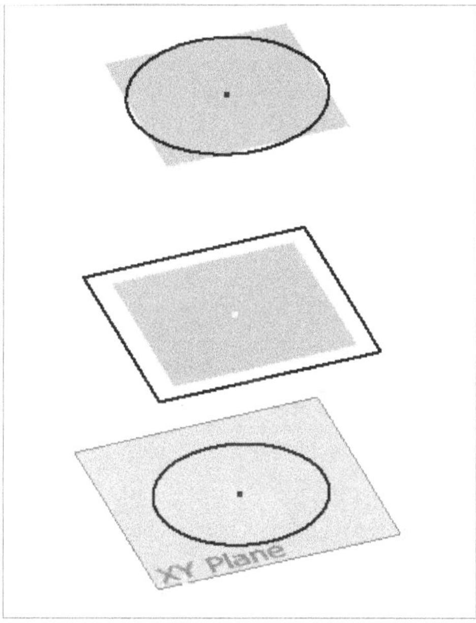

Figure-17. Sketches created on parallel planes

- Click on the **Loft** tool from **Create** panel in the **3D Model** tab of the **Ribbon**. The **Loft** dialog box will be displayed; refer to Figure-18. Also, you will be asked to select the curves.

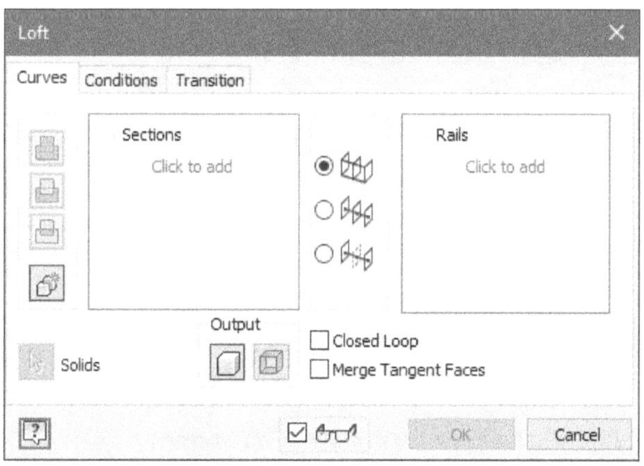

Figure-18. Loft dialog box

- One by one select the curves in a sequence by which you want the transition between curves. Preview of the loft feature will be displayed; refer to Figure-19.

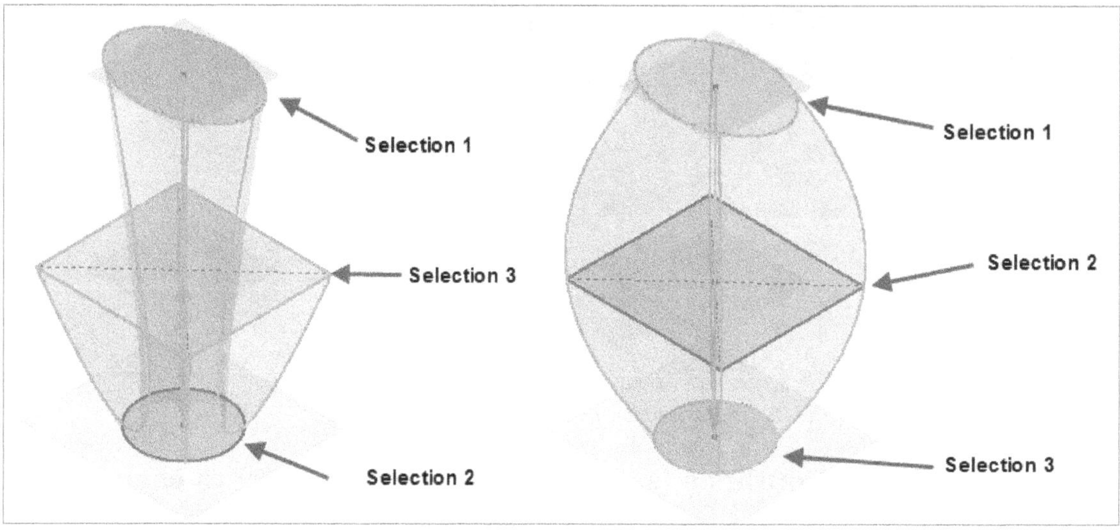

Figure-19. Preview of loft feature

- You can also select the edges of solids to create loft feature; refer to Figure-20.

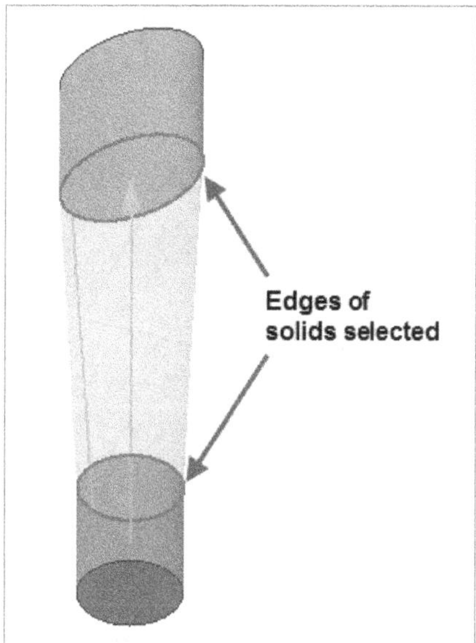

Figure-20. Creating loft using edges of solids

- You can define the transition type for loft feature in dialog box by using the **Rails**, **Center Line**, or **Area Loft** radio button; refer to Figure-21.

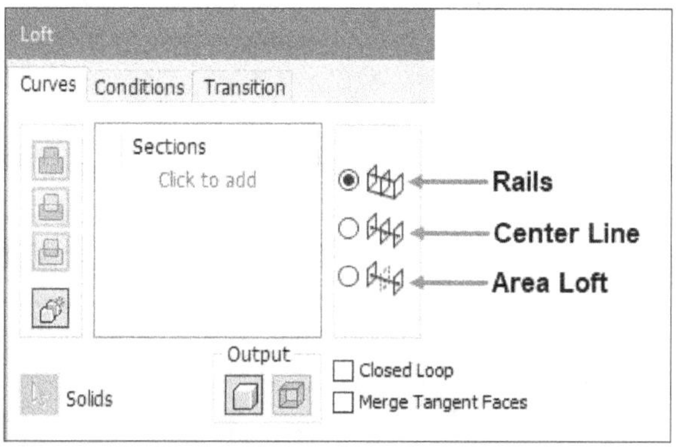

Figure-21. Options to define transition type

Loft using Rail option

- Click on the **Rail** radio button from the dialog box and select the rail for creating loft. Preview of loft following the rail curvature will be displayed; refer to Figure-22.

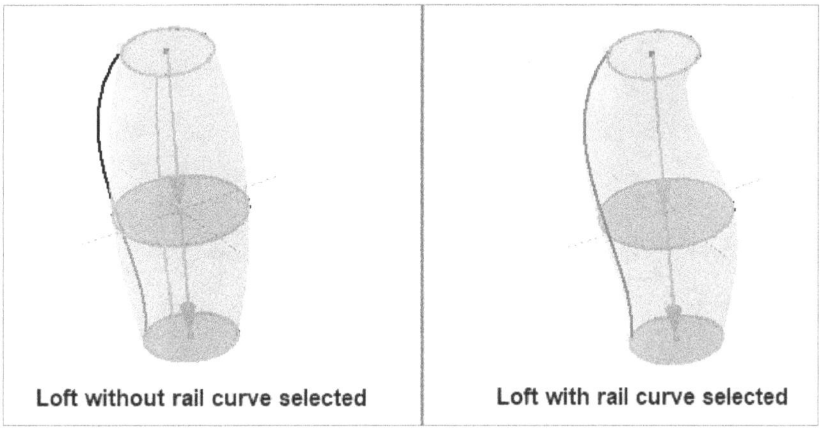

Figure-22. Preview of loft with rail curve

Note that the rail curve to be selected must intersect with all the sections (profile sketches) and that too only one time.

Loft with Center Line

Using this option, you can select a center line to refine the shape of loft as per requirement.

- Click on the **Center Line** radio button from the dialog box to activate the options related to center line in the dialog box; refer to Figure-23.

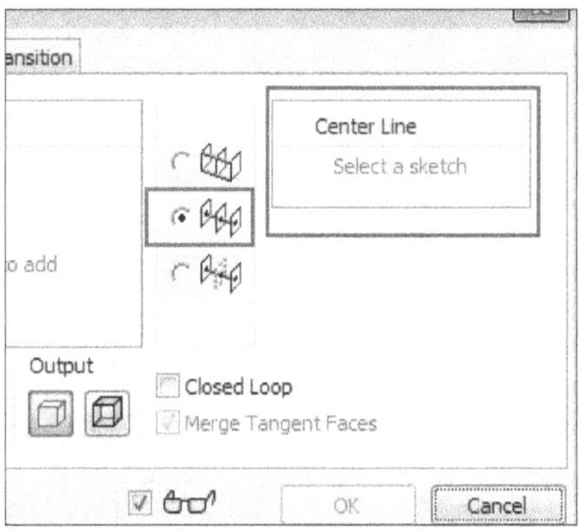

Figure-23. Center Line option in Loft dialog box

- After selecting the section sketches, click in the **Center Line** box in the dialog box and select the curve created for centerline. Preview of the loft will be displayed; refer to Figure-24.

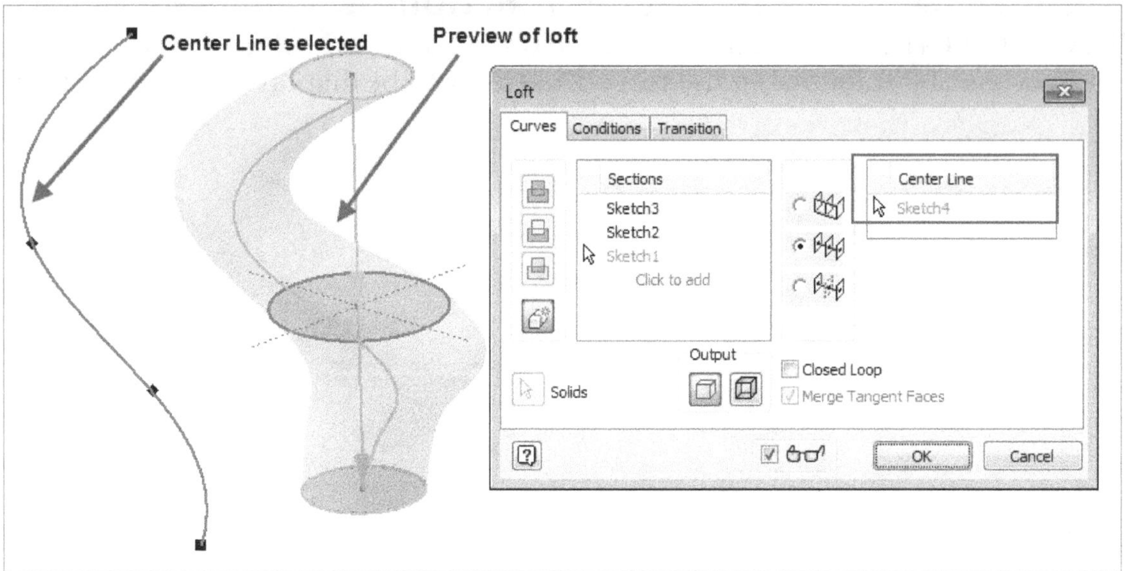

Figure-24. Preview of loft with centerline

Loft with Area Loft option

The **Area Loft** option is used to create loft feature by specifying area of the sections used for loft feature.

- Click on the **Area Loft** radio button from the dialog box. The options in the dialog box will be displayed as shown in Figure-25. Notice the area values for various positions on center line.

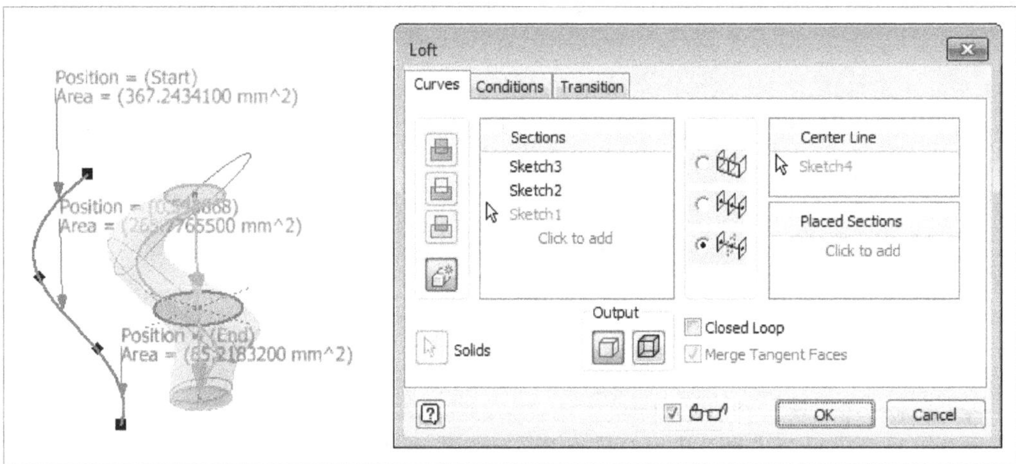

Figure-25. Loft dialog box with Area loft option

- Double-click on the area value that you want to change from the model. The **Section Dimensions** dialog box will be displayed; refer to Figure-26.

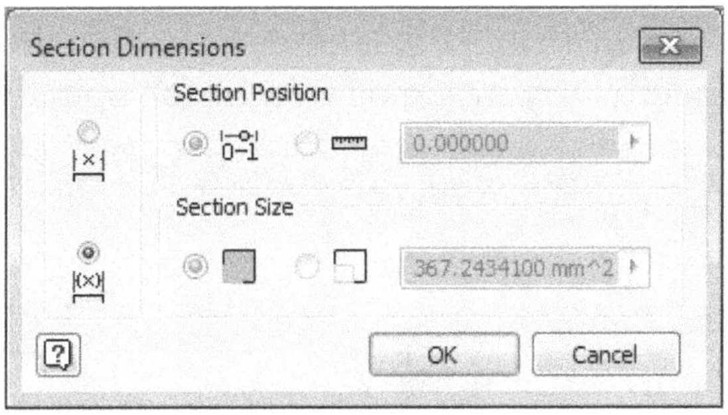

Figure-26. Section Dimensions dialog box

- Click on the **Driving Section** radio button from the dialog box. The **Section Size** area of the dialog box will become active; refer to Figure-27.

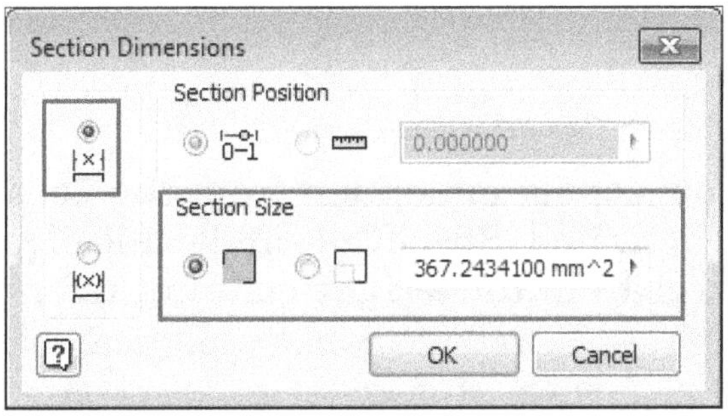

Figure-27. Driving section option of Section Dimensions dialog box

- Select desired radio button from the **Section Size** area of the dialog box and specify desired value in the edit box. If you select the **Area** radio button then you will be asked to specify the value of area of the section. If you select the **Scale Factor** radio button then you need to specify the value for the scale factor for increasing or decreasing the section area.
- Click on the **OK** button from the dialog box to change the area of the section.

Changing Conditions at the starting and end of loft

The options in the **Conditions** tab of the dialog box are used to specify the tangency conditions of the loft feature at the starting and end sections.

- Click on the **Conditions** tab in the **Loft** dialog box. The dialog box will be displayed as shown in Figure-28.

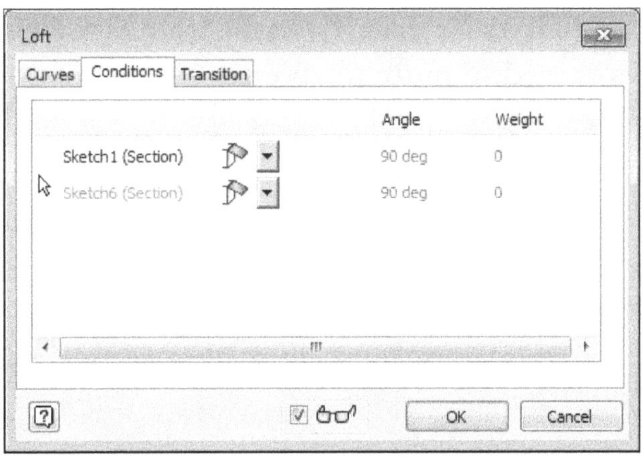

Figure-28. Loft dialog box with Conditions tab selected

- Select desired condition from the **Condition** drop-down; refer to Figure-29. By default, **Free Condition** button is selected from the drop-down and hence you will not be asked to specify any angle or weight for specifying tangency condition.

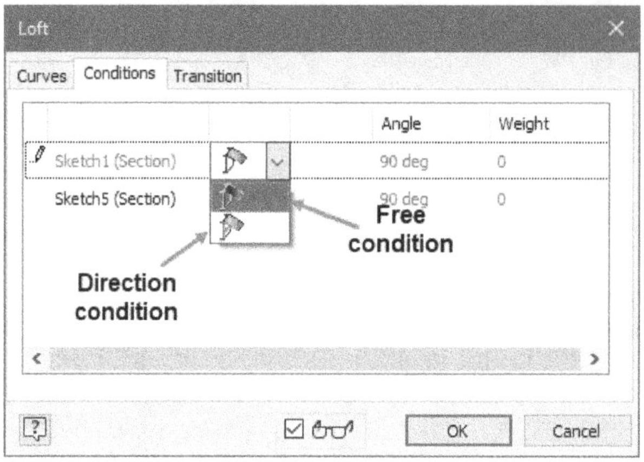

Figure-29. Conditions drop-down

- Click on the **Direction Condition** option from the **Conditions** drop-down. The related options will be activated. Specify desired value of angle in the **Angle** column and desired value of weight in the **Weight** column; refer to Figure-30.

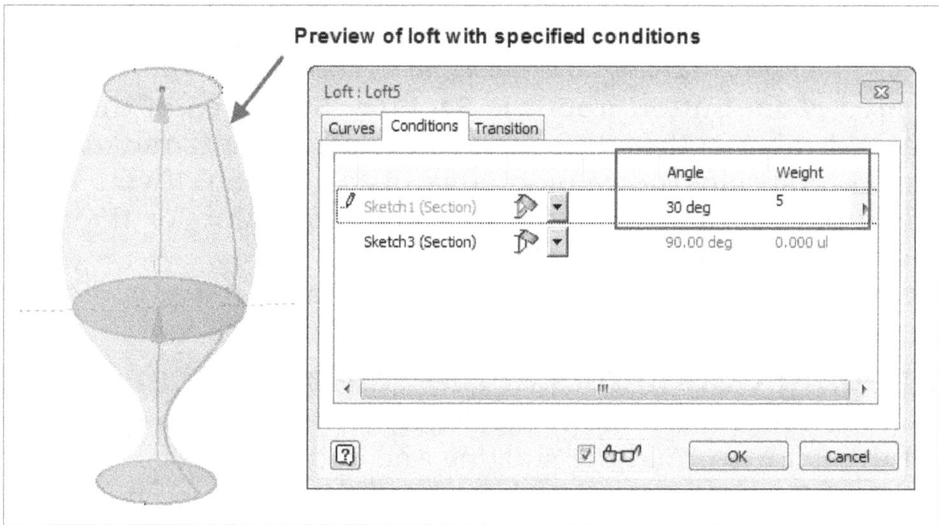

Figure-30. Preview of loft with specified end conditions

Specifying Transition Point Positions

The transition points are used to map key points of one section to the other section. The option to manage transition points is available in the **Transition** tab of the dialog box.

- Click on the **Transition** tab from the **Loft** dialog box. By default, the **Automatic Mapping** check box is selected. Hence, options to manage the transition points are not available; refer to Figure-31.

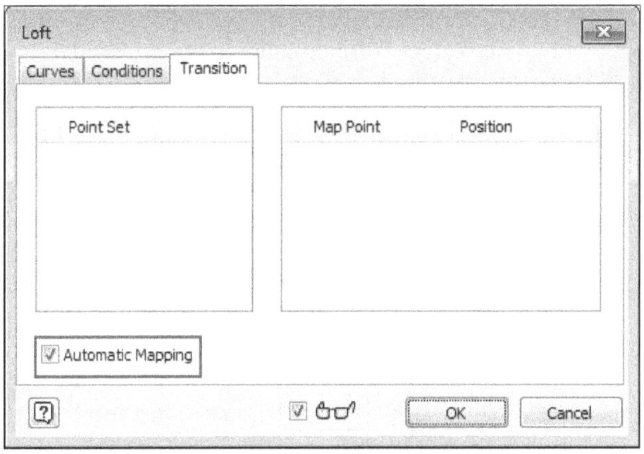

Figure-31. Transition tab of Loft dialog box

- Clear the **Automatic Mapping** check box. The options to change position of transition points will be displayed; refer to Figure-32.

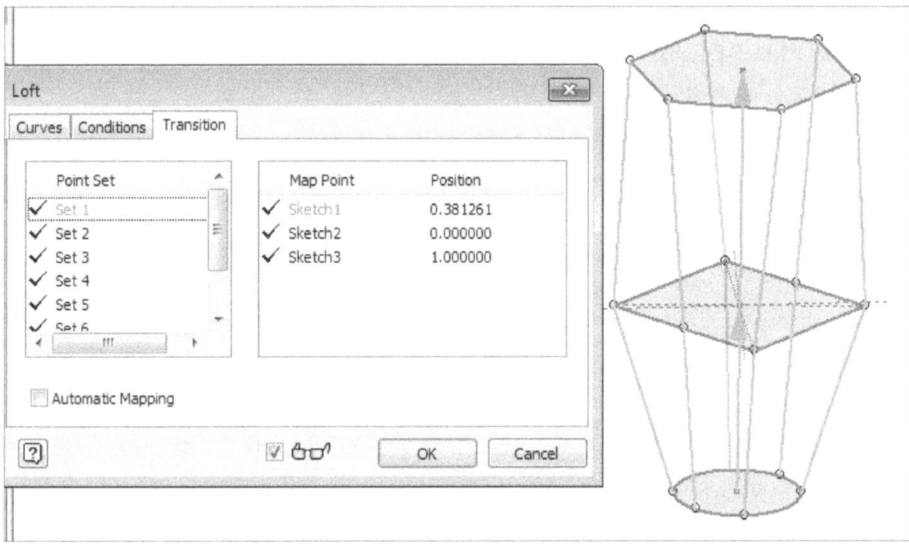

Figure-32. Options to modify position of transition points

- You can drag the key points to change the transition between the sketches.
- Click on the **OK** button from the dialog box to create the loft feature.

COIL TOOL

The **Coil** tool is used to create coil with the help of a profile and an axis. The procedure to create coil is given next.

- Create the profile for coil and an axis; refer to Figure-33.

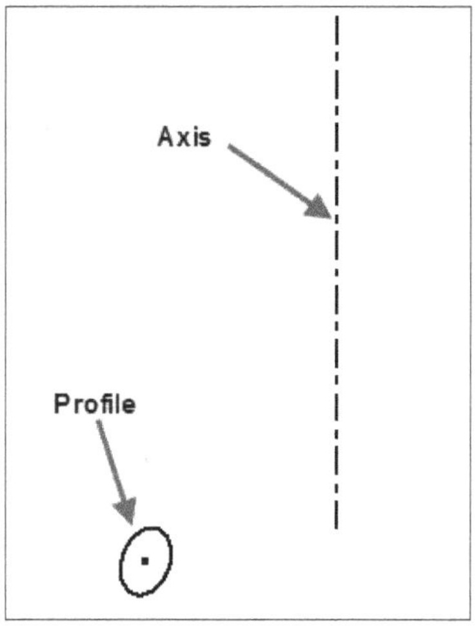

Figure-33. Profile and axis for coil

- Click on the **Coil** tool from **Create** panel in the **3D Model** tab of the **Ribbon**. The **Coil** dialog box will be displayed along with the selection of profile; refer to Figure-34. You will be asked to select the axis.

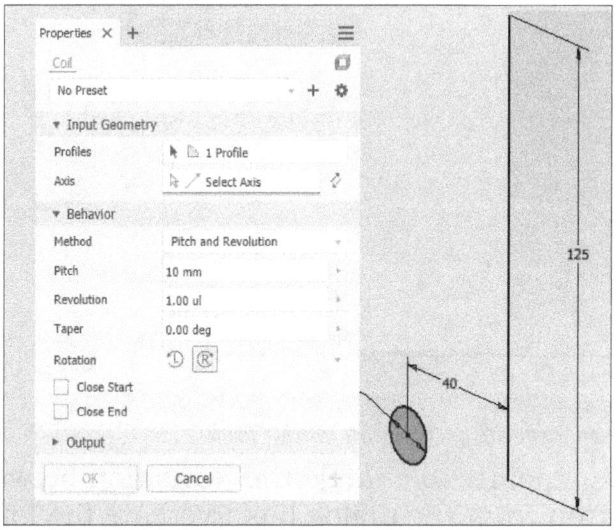

Figure-34. Coil dialog box with selection of profile

- Click on the centerline created for the coil axis. Preview of the coil will be displayed; refer to Figure-35.

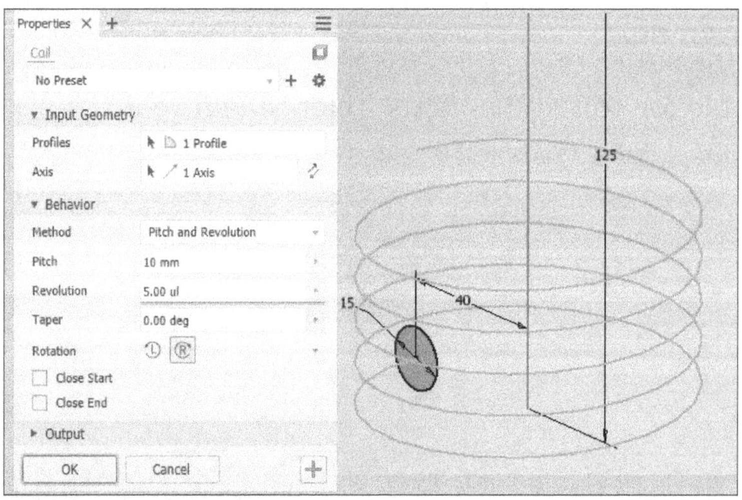

Figure-35. Preview of the coil

- Click on the flip button next to **Axis** selection button to change the direction of the coil preview between upward or downward.
- Using the buttons in the **Rotation** area of the dialog box, you can switch between left handed and right handed direction of coil creation.

Changing the coil size and Behavior

The options to change the coil size are available in the **Behavior** node of the dialog box; refer to Figure-36.

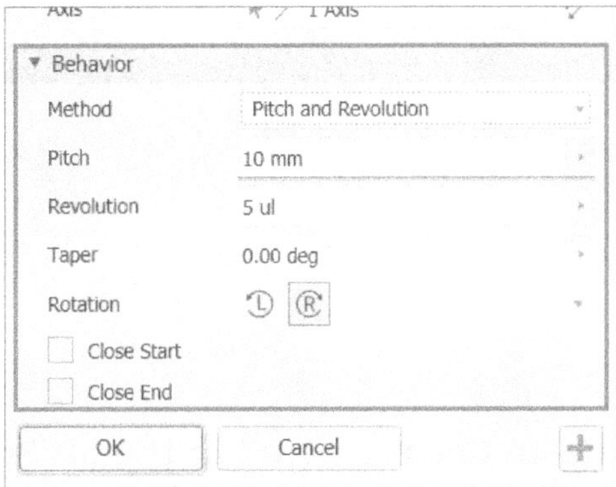

Figure-36. Coil Size tab of Coil dialog box

- There are four option in the **Method** drop-down, **Pitch and Revolution**, **Revolution and Height**, **Pitch and Height**, and **Spiral**; refer to Figure-37. Click on desired option from the drop-down. The related parameters will become active in the dialog box. The **Pitch and Revolution** option is used to specify pitch and number of revolution of the coil. The **Revolution and Height** option is used to specify total number of revolutions and total height of the coil. The **Pitch and Height** option is used to specify the pitch and total height of the coil. The **Spiral** option is used to create a spiral by specifying pitch and number of revolution.

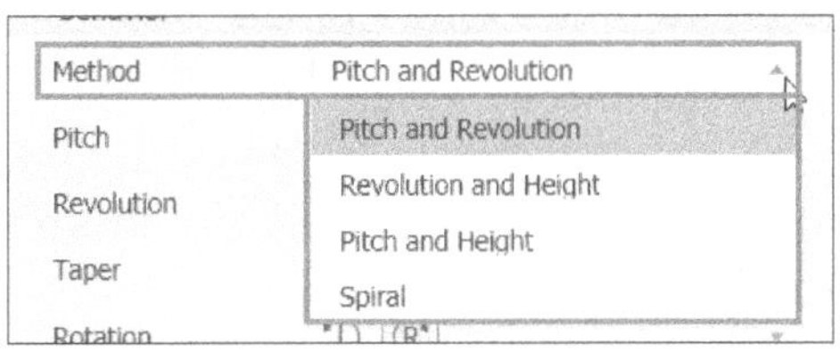

Figure-37. Method drop-down in the Coil dialog box

- Set desired parameters in the edit boxes of the **Behavior** node.
- You can also specify taper angle for the coil in the **Taper** edit box. Note that this option is not available for spiral coil.
- Select the **Close Start** check box to change direction of coil at start point. Using the **Flat Angle** and **Transition Angle** edit boxes, you can specify the starting point of the coil. Similarly, you can specify the end point of the coil.
- After setting desired parameters, click on the **OK** button from the dialog box to create the coil.

EMBOSS TOOL

The **Emboss** tool is used to emboss or engrave a profile on the selected face. Note that you need to have a sketch for embossing. The procedure to use this tool is given next.

- Create desired profile on the face on which you want it to be engraved or embossed; refer to Figure-38.

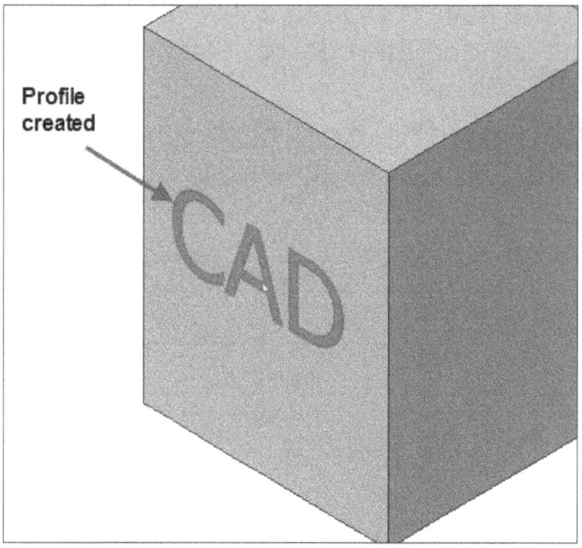

Figure-38. Profile created on face

- Click on the **Emboss** tool from **Create** panel in the **3D Model** tab of the **Ribbon**. The **Emboss** dialog box will be displayed; refer to Figure-39 and you will be asked to select the profile.

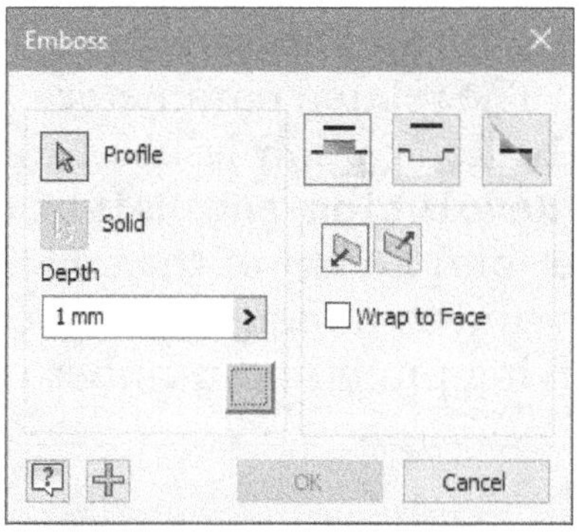

Figure-39. Emboss dialog box

- Click on the profile created earlier and click on desired button from the **Emboss** dialog box; refer to Figure-40.

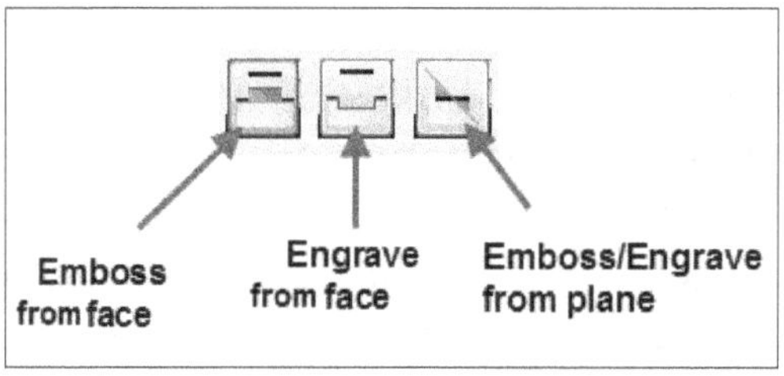

Figure-40. Buttons in Emboss dialog box

- In the **Depth** edit box, specify desired depth. You can also change the appearance of the top face of embossing/engraving by using the **Top Face Appearance** button from the dialog box; refer to Figure-41.

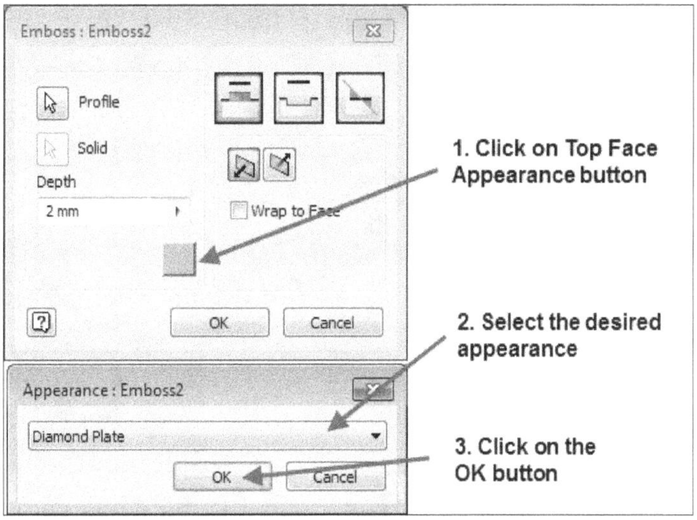

Figure-41. Changing appearance of emboss and engrave

- Click on the **OK** button from the **Emboss** dialog box to create the feature; refer to Figure-42.

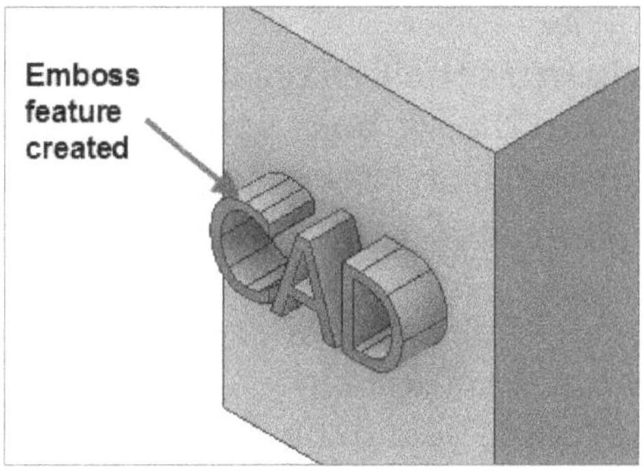

Figure-42. Emboss feature created

DERIVE TOOL

The **Derive** tool is used to create/derive part using selected Autodesk Inventor Part or Assembly model file. The procedure to use this tool is given next.

- Click on the **Derive** tool from the **Create** panel in the **3D Model** tab of the **Ribbon**. The **Open** dialog box will be displayed.
- Select desired Inventor part file or assembly file from the dialog box and click on the **Open** button from the dialog box. Preview of derived part will be displayed with the **Derived Part** dialog box; refer to Figure-43.

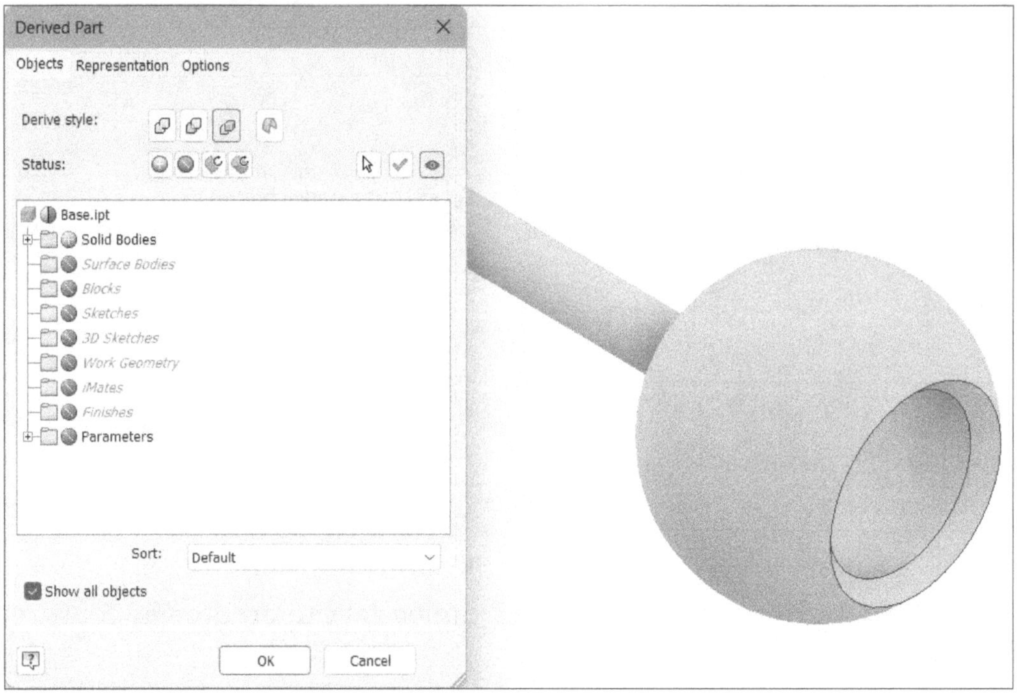

Figure-43. Derived Part dialog box

- Select desired derive style from the **Derive Style** options. There are four buttons to change derive style in the dialog box; **Single solid body merging out seams between planar faces**, **Solid body keep seams between planar faces**, **Maintain each solid as a solid body**, and **Body as Work Surface**. These buttons perform the task as per their names.
- Click on the plus sign before the component to include/exclude it from deriving.
- Similarly, you can include/exclude other properties of the part by using the plus sign. Select the **Includes bounding boxes of the selected bodies** toggle button to display an enclosure box along with selected body. Select the **Includes bounding cylinder of the selected bodies** toggle button to display enclosing cylinder around selected body in graphics area.
- Click on the **Representation** tab and select desired options from the **Model State** and **Design View** drop-downs to define design state and orientation of model, respectively.
- You can set the scale factor in the **Scale factor** edit box from **Options** tab to resize the component by proportion.
- If you want the mirror copy of derived part then select the **Mirror part** check box from **Options** tab and select desired mirror plane from the drop-down below it.
- Select the check boxes from the **Options** tab to perform related modifications and then click on the **OK** button from the dialog box to insert the part.

RIB TOOL

The **Rib** tool is used to create thin wall support in the structure. A rib can effectively increase the strength of a structure to bear load. The procedure to use this tool is given next.

- Create profile for rib feature in the model space; refer to Figure-44. Note that the profile should be connected to the edges of walls and there should be no extra portion of sketch profile hanging over the edges. In simple words, profile should connect one edge of a wall to edge of the other wall.

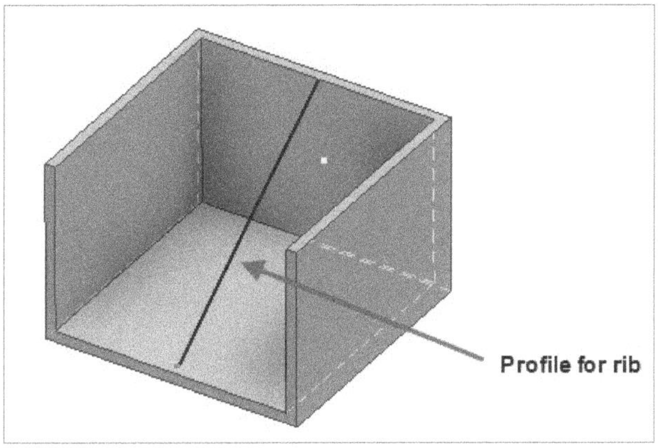

Figure-44. Profile for rib feature

- Click on the **Rib** tool from **Create** panel in the **3D Model** tab of the **Ribbon**. The **Rib** dialog box will be displayed; refer to Figure-45.

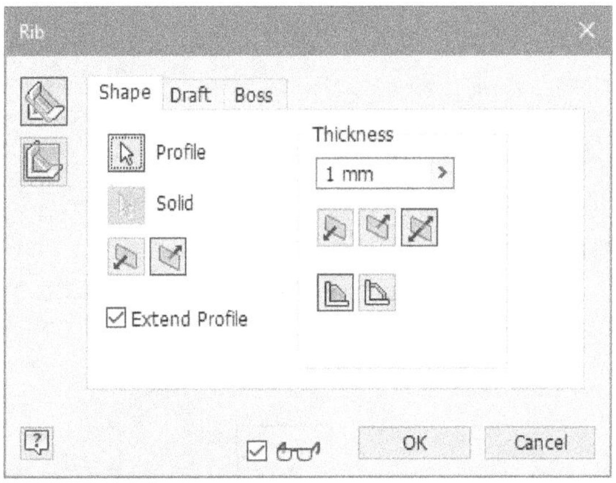

Figure-45. Rib dialog box

- Click on desired button from **Normal to Sketch Plane** and **Parallel to Sketch Plane** buttons. The **Normal to Sketch Plane** button is used to create rib feature perpendicular to the plane selected for creating profile. The **Parallel to Sketch Plane** button is used to create the rib feature parallel to the sketching plane used for creating profile.
- Select the **Direction 1** or **Direction 2** button to define the direction for creating rib feature with respect to sketching plane. Note that you will be required to switch the direction of rib feature towards the walls to create it.
- Type desired thickness in the edit box available in **Thickness** area of dialog box.
- Click on desired button from the **Thickness** area to specify the side of rib feature crcation; rcfcr to Figurc-46.

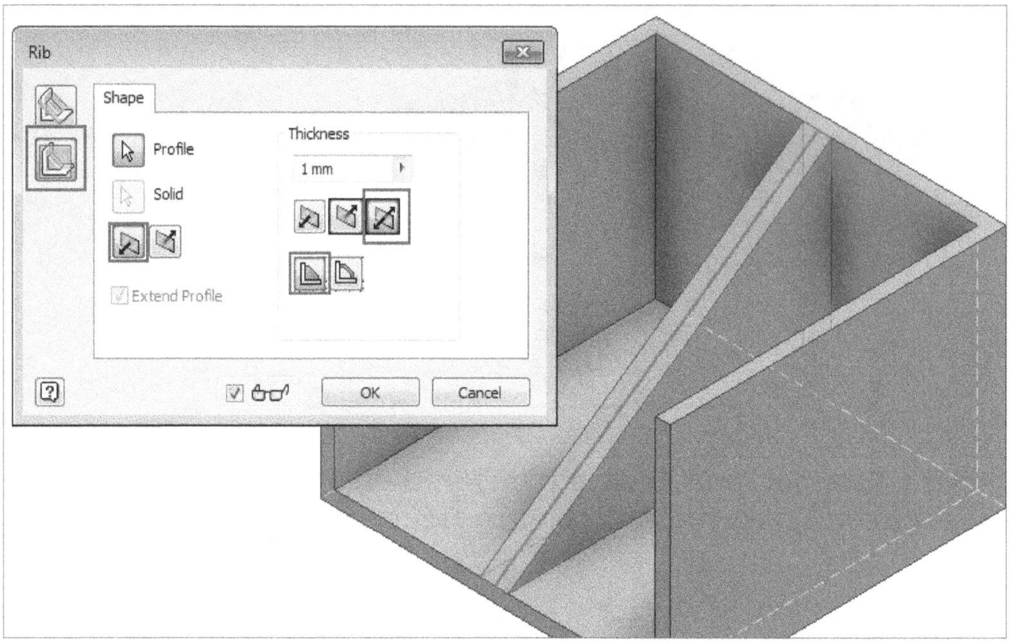

Figure-46. Preview of rib feature

- Click on desired button between **To Next** and **Finite** from the **Thickness** area to define the depth of the rib feature. The **To Next** button is selected by default and it creates the rib feature up to next face. If you select the **Finite** button then you can specify the depth of the rib in the **Extent** edit box; refer to Figure-47.

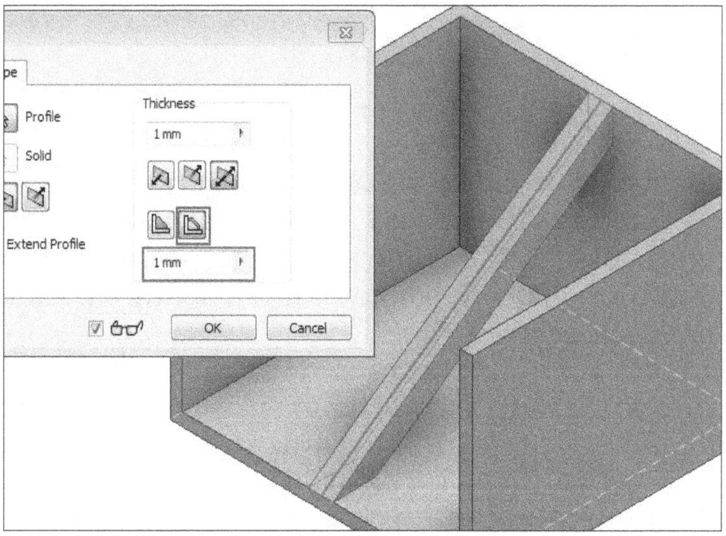

Figure-47. Specifying depth of rib feature

- If you are creating the rib feature perpendicular to the sketching plane by using the **Normal to Sketch Plane** button then **Draft** and **Boss** tabs will be available in the dialog box; refer to Figure-48.

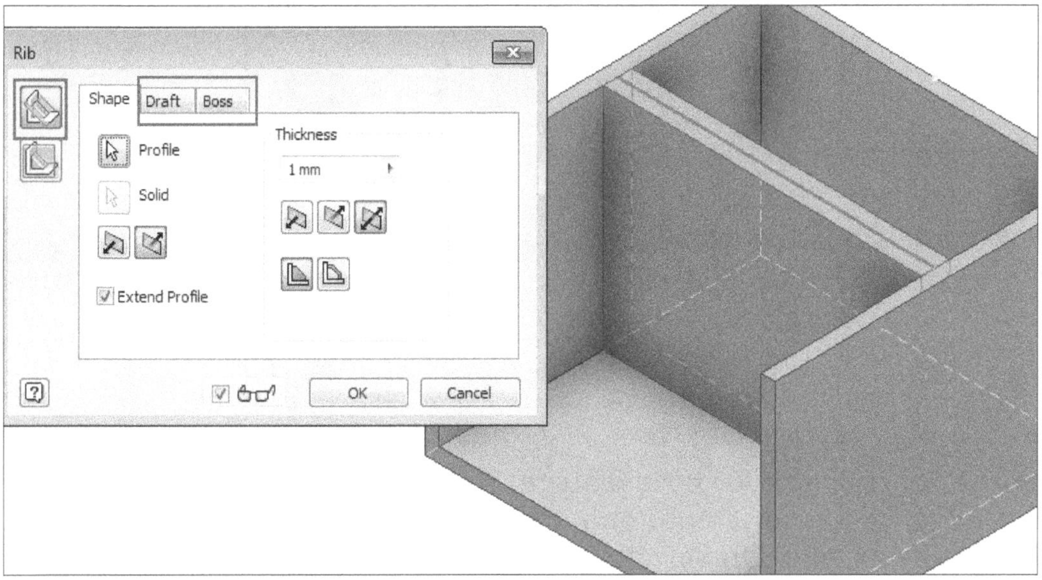

Figure-48. Normal to sketching plane rib feature

Applying Draft to Rib

- The options in the **Draft** tab are used to apply draft (taper) to the rib feature; refer to Figure-49.

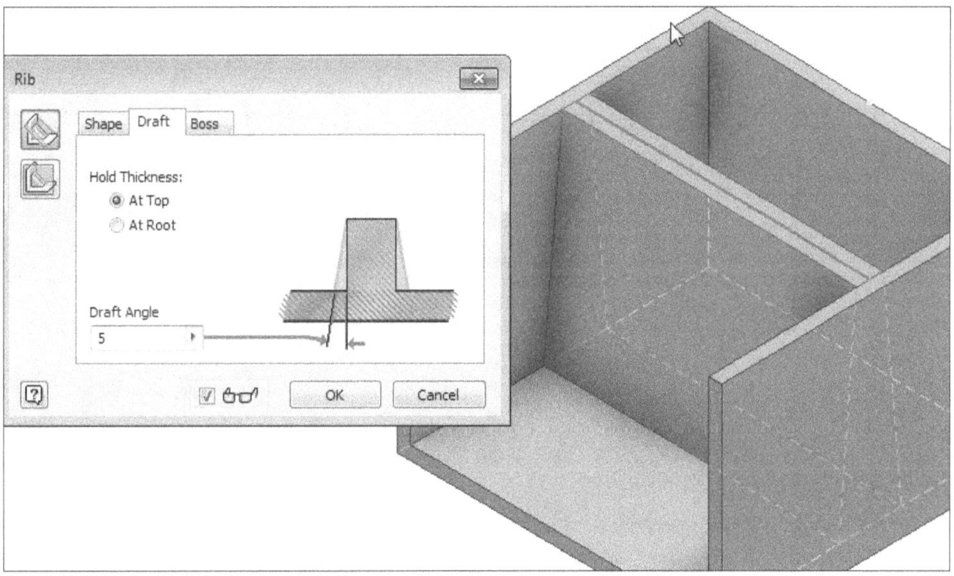

Figure-49. Applying draft to rib feature

- Specify desired draft angle value in the **Draft Angle** edit box.
- You can also define the base for applying draft by using the **At Top** and **At Root** radio buttons.

Creating Boss feature on Rib

- Click on the **Boss** tab from the **Rib** dialog box. The dialog box will be displayed as shown in Figure-50. Also, you will be asked to select center point for boss feature.

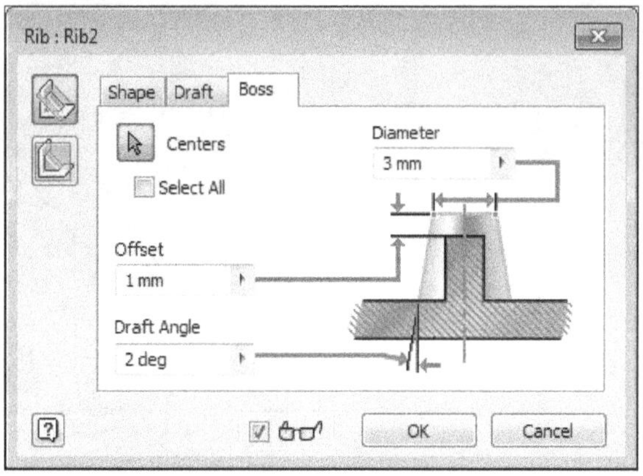

Figure-50. Boss tab of Rib dialog box

- Select the center point for boss feature. Note that the point should be coincident to the profile. You can create one or more points on the profile while creating the sketch for profile. On selecting the point, preview of the boss feature will be displayed; refer to Figure-51.

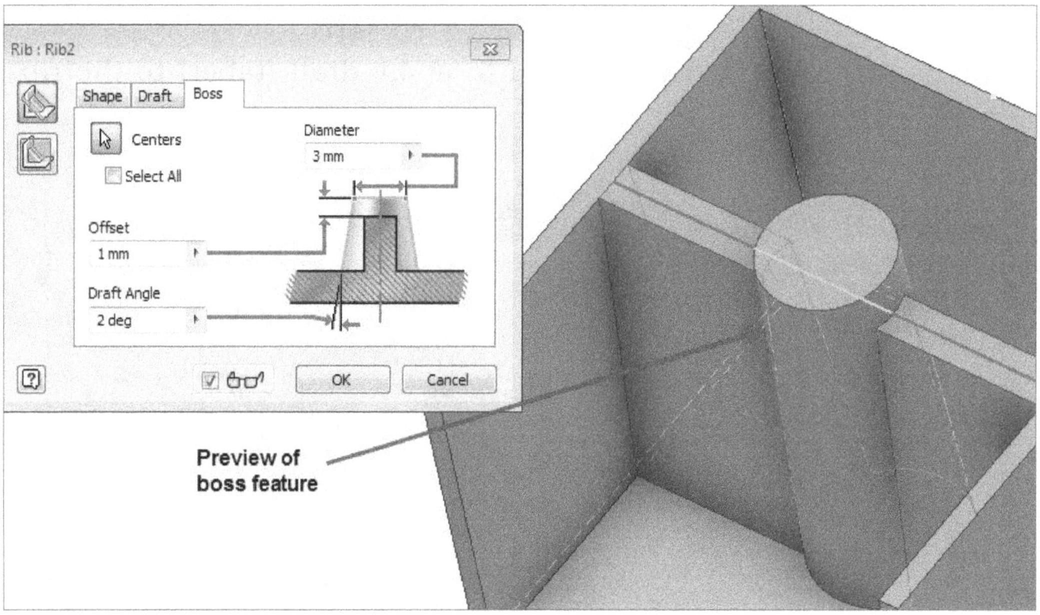

Figure-51. Preview of boss feature on rib

- Click on the **OK** button from the dialog box to create the rib feature with specified settings.

DECAL TOOL

The **Decal** tool is used to apply an image to face of the model. The procedure to use this tool is given next.

- Insert an image on sketching plane parallel to desired face (as discussed in Chapter 2); refer to Figure-52.

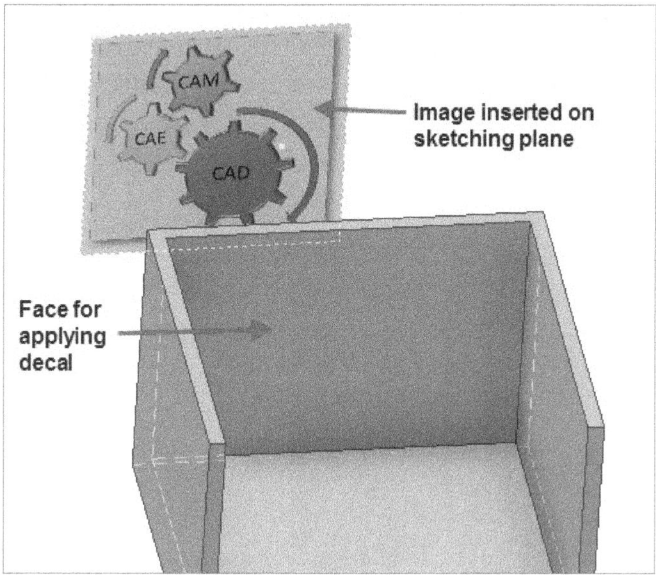

Figure-52. Image and face for decal tool

- Click on the **Decal** tool from **Create** panel in the **3D Model** tab of the **Ribbon**. The **Decal** dialog box will be displayed; refer to Figure-53. Also, you will be asked to select an image file.

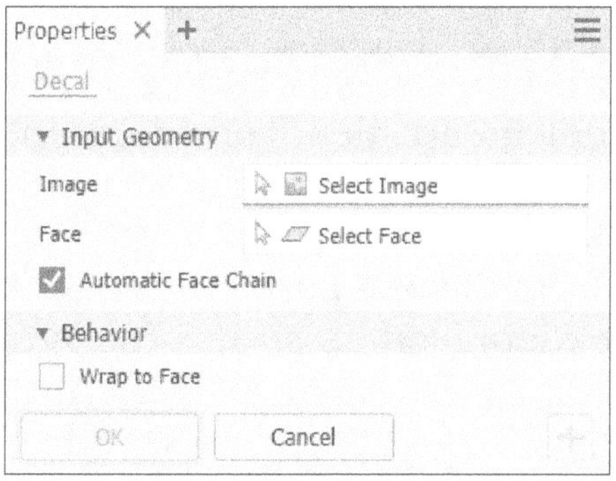

Figure-53. Decal dialog box

- Click on desired image file. You will be asked to select the face.
- Click on the face on which you want to apply decal.
- If you want to wrap the image around the selected face then select the **Wrap to Face** check box from **Behavior** node; refer to Figure-54.

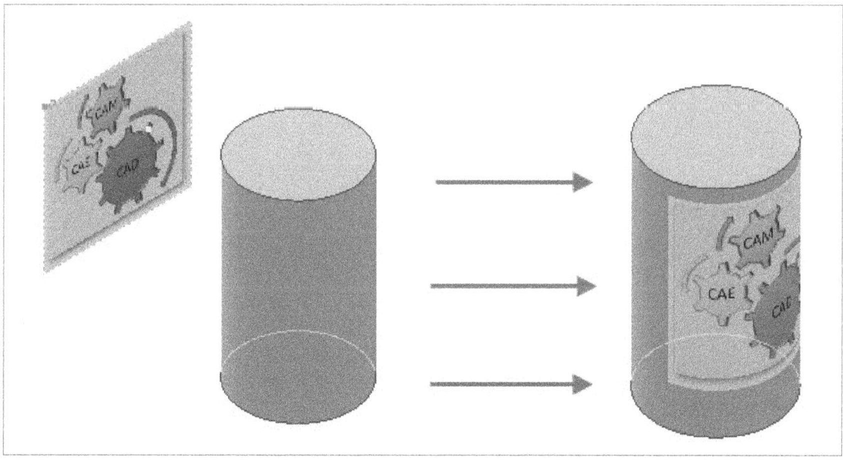

Figure-54. Preview of decal with wrap to face option selected

- If you have selected the **Automatic Face Chain** check box with **Wrap to Face** check box then you can apply decal on face smaller than the image size. The extra decal will be wrapped on the connected faces; refer to Figure-55.

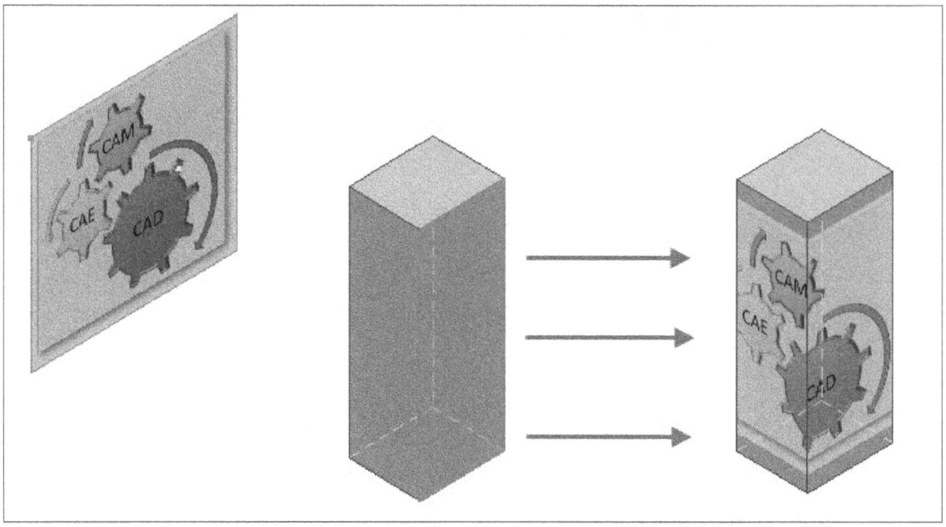

Figure-55. Applying decal on chain faces

- Click on the **OK** button from the dialog box to create the decal feature.

IMPORTING FOREIGN CAD FILES

No! Foreign file here does not mean files from different country. In CAD terms, it means CAD files of non-native format. The procedure to import files is given next.

- Click on the **Import** tool from **Create** panel in the **3D Model** tab of the **Ribbon**. The **Import** dialog box will be displayed as shown in Figure-56.

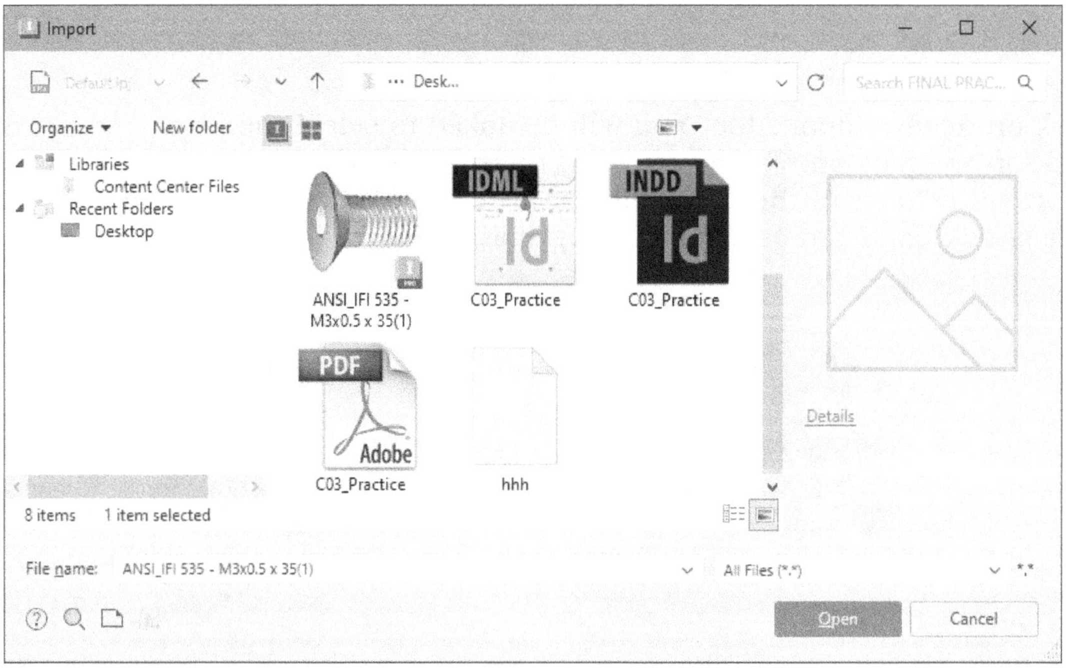

Figure-56. Import dialog box

- Click in the **Files of type** drop-down and select desired format. The files of selected format will be displayed in the file browser.

- Double-click on desired file. The **Import** dialog box with options to include various features will be displayed; refer to Figure-57.

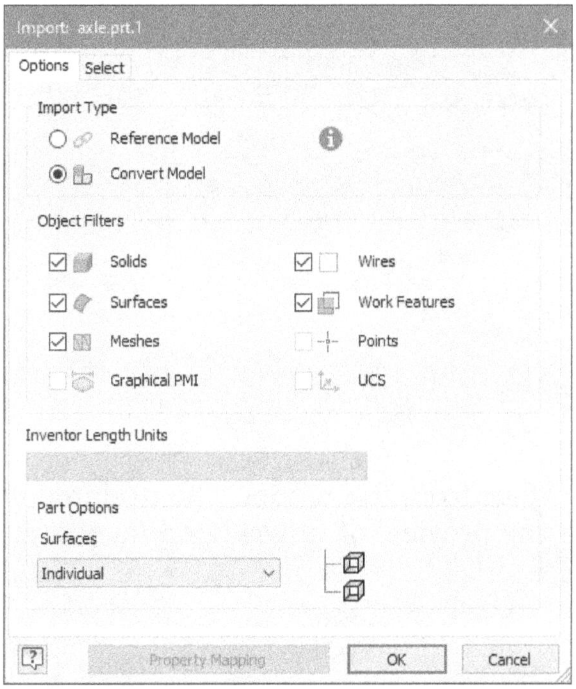

Figure-57. Import dialog box with options to include features

- There are two options in the **Import Type** area of the dialog box. Select the **Reference Model** radio button if you want the imported feature to be updated when the base model is changed in other software. Select the **Convert Model** radio button if you want to create a new model from imported file locally saved in current file.
- Select desired options from the dialog box and click on the **OK** button from the dialog box to import the model; refer to Figure-58.

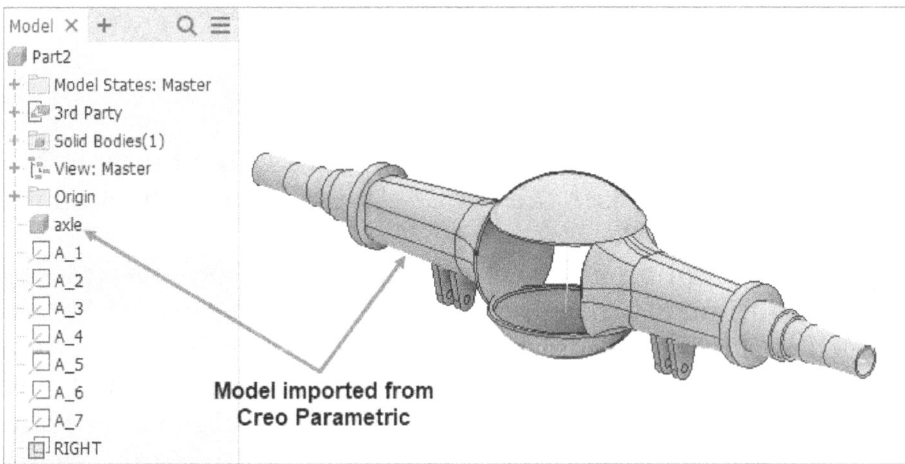

Figure-58. Model imported from Creo Parametric

Now, you can use the imported model as base solid/surface to create other features.

UNWRAP TOOL

The **Unwrap** tool is used to unwrap faces that cannot be flattened with the Unfold or sheet metal flat pattern command. The procedure to use this tool is given next.

- Click on the **Unwrap** tool from **Create** panel in the **3D Model** tab of the **Ribbon**. The **Unwrap** dialog box will be displayed; refer to Figure-59. You will be asked to select the faces.

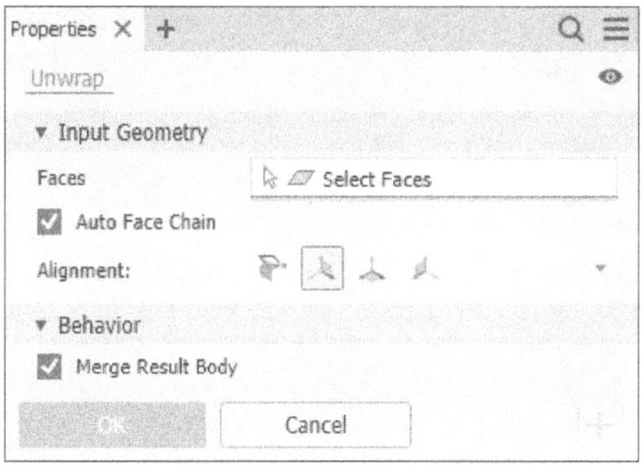

Figure-59. Unwrap dialog box

- Select the contiguous face from the model. The updated **Unwrap** dialog box will be displayed along with the preview of unwrapped faces; refer to Figure-60.

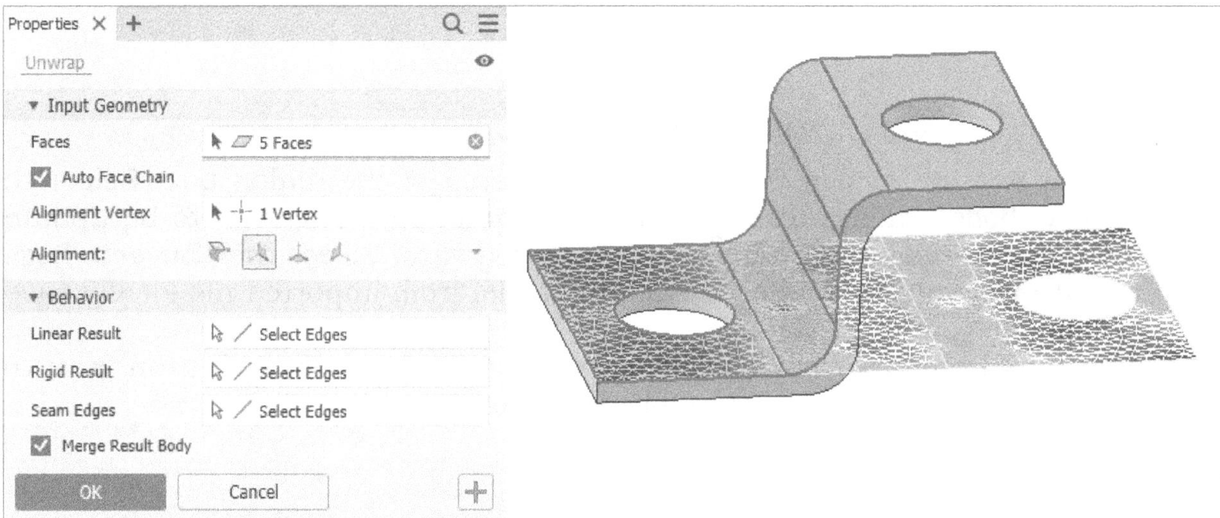

Figure-60. Preview of unwrapped faces

- Select the **Auto Face Chain** check box to select multiple faces with one pick.
- The **Alignment Vertex** area uses the vertex closest to your selection while selecting the face to unwrap.
- Select **Align to Model** option from **Alignment** area to place the unwrapped surface in the same orientation as the model. Select **Align to XY** option from area to place the unwrapped surface at the origin and in the same orientation as the **XY** plane. Select **Align to XZ** option from area to place the unwrapped surface at the origin and in the same orientation as the **XZ** plane. Select **Align to YZ** option from area to place the unwrapped surface at the origin and in the same orientation as the **YZ** plane.
- Click on the **Linear Result** area to select one or more contiguous edges to remain straight.
- Click on the **Rigid Result** area to select one or more contiguous edges to remain rigid.
- Click on the **Seam Edges** area to select edges where the model will be cut for flattening.

- Select the **Merge Result Body** check box to create the output as a single surface face.
- Click on the **OK** button from the dialog box to complete the unwrapping process.

Till this point, we have discussed the tools related to creation of features. Now, we will discuss the tools related to modifications of solids.

MODIFICATION TOOLS

The tools to modify features are available in the **Modify** panel of the **3D Model** tab in the **Ribbon**; refer to Figure-61. These tools are discussed next.

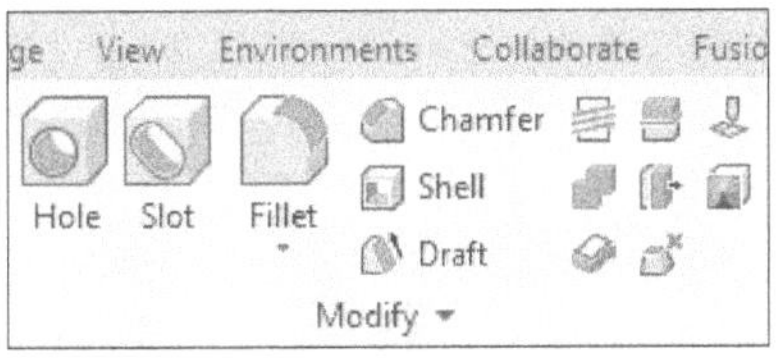

Figure-61. Modify panel

Creating Holes

The **Hole** tool in the **Modify** panel is used to create hole in the solid model. The procedure to create hole is given next.

- Click on the **Hole** tool from **Modify** panel in the **3D Model** tab of the **Ribbon**. The **Hole** dialog box will be displayed; refer to Figure-62. Also, you will be asked to specify the location of the hole.

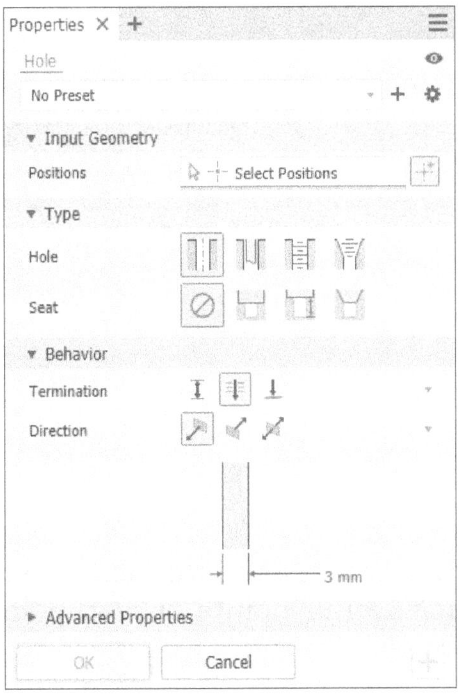

Figure-62. Hole dialog box

- Click at desired location on face of the model. Preview of the hole will be displayed; refer to Figure-63.

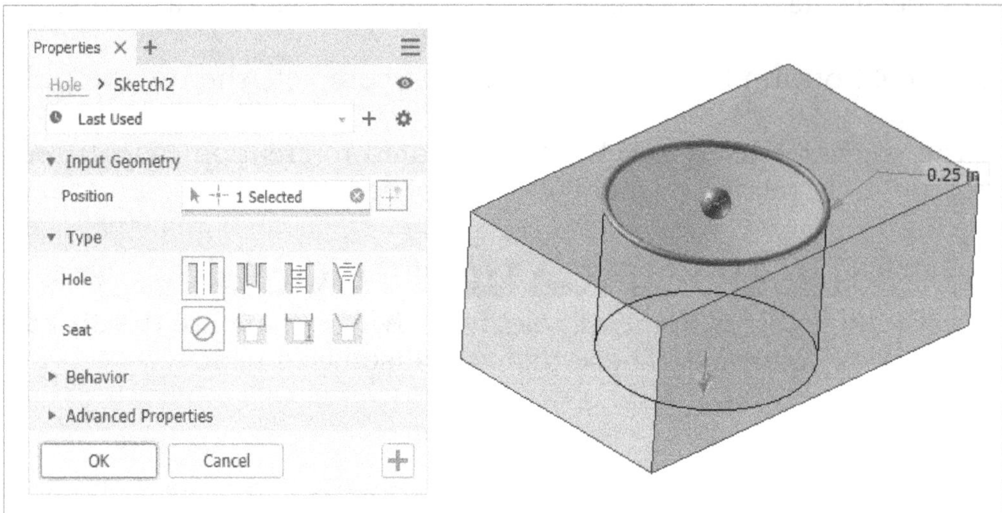

Figure-63. Preview of hole

Specifying location of hole

An existing sketch is not required for specifying the location of hole. The valid inputs for specifying hole locations include sketch point, work point, or a face.

- By default, **Allow Center Point Creation** button is **ON** in the **Position** area of the dialog box. When **Allow Center Point Creation** button is **ON**, you can add center points randomly on the part face; refer to Figure-64. Hence, you can click at any desired location on the face of model to create hole.

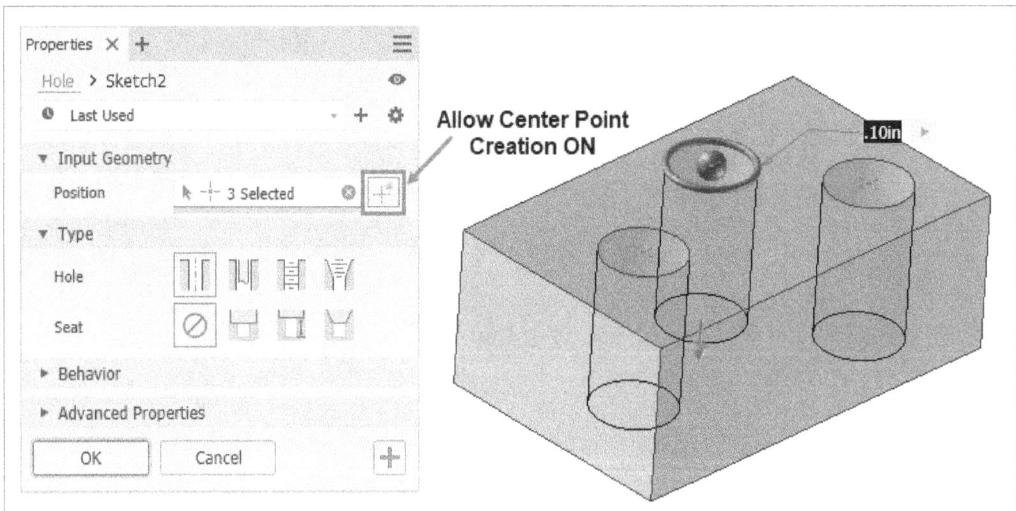

Figure-64. Preview of hole when allow center point button is ON

- When **Allow Center Point Creation** button is **OFF**, you can only select points in an existing sketch, sketch center points or workpoints to create the hole; refer to Figure-65.

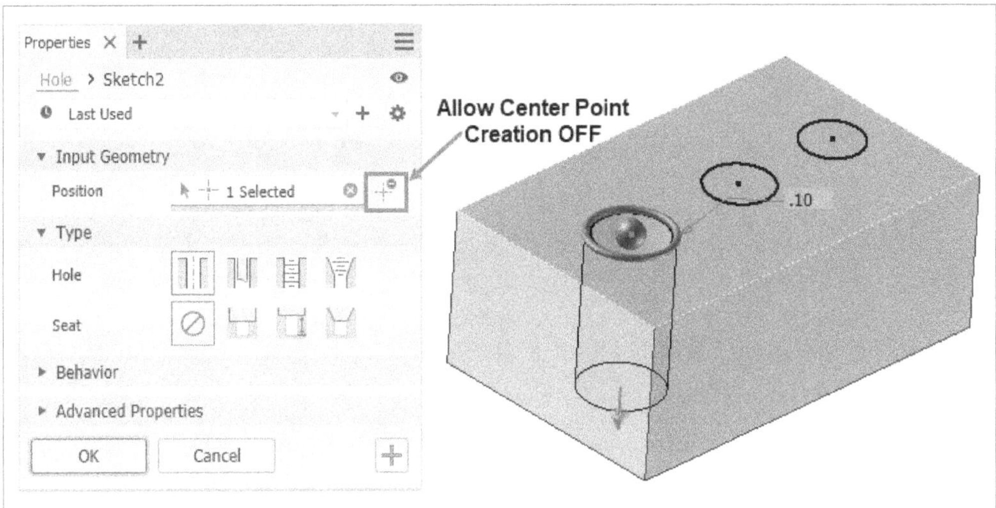

Figure-65. Preview of hole when allow center point button is OFF

- To create a hole concentric to earlier created holes, place the hole center and click the model edge or curved face the hole is to be concentric with, the preview of concentric hole will be displayed; refer to Figure-66.

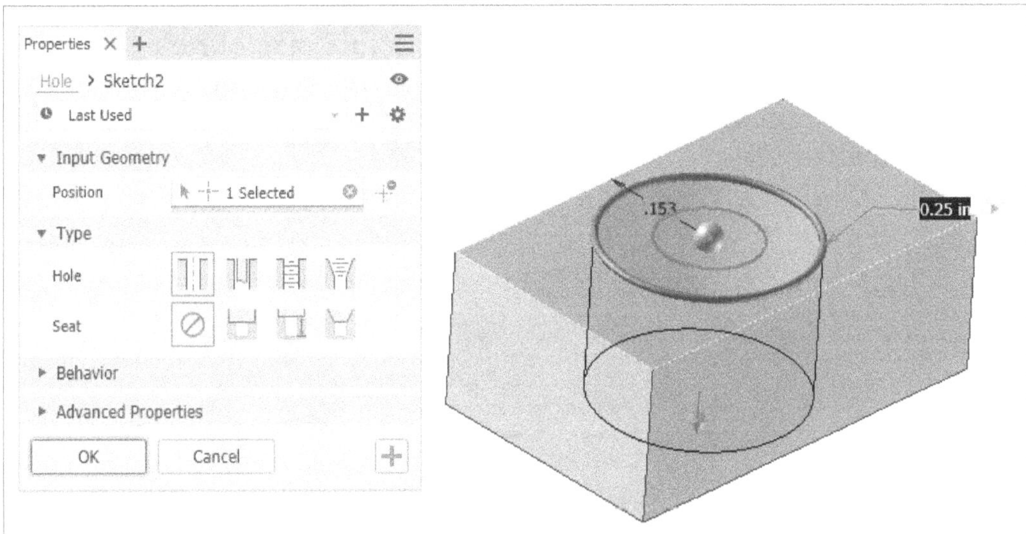

Figure-66. Preview of concentric hole

Setting Shape and Dimension of Hole

- Select desired option from **Hole** section in the **Type** area of the dialog box to define the type of hole as **Simple Hole**, **Clearance Hole**, **Tapped Hole**, and **Taper Tapped Hole**; refer to Figure-67. Options to define parameters of hole will be displayed in the **Behavior** area of the dialog box; refer to Figure-68.

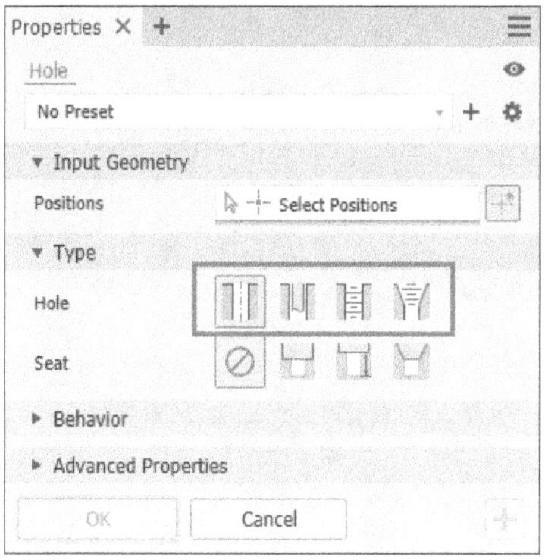

Figure-67. Options to define type of hole

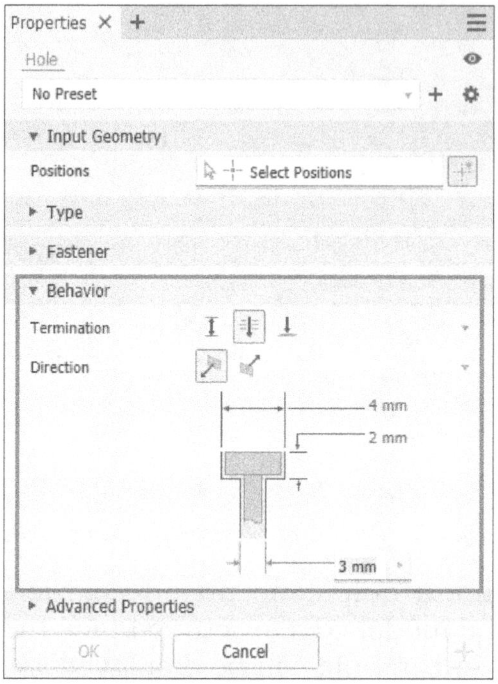

Figure-68. Options to define parameters of hole

- Type desired dimensions in the edit boxes to define size of hole.
- On selecting the **Clearance Hole** option from the type area in the dialog box, options to choose standard holes from the library will be displayed in the **Fastener** area; refer to Figure-69.

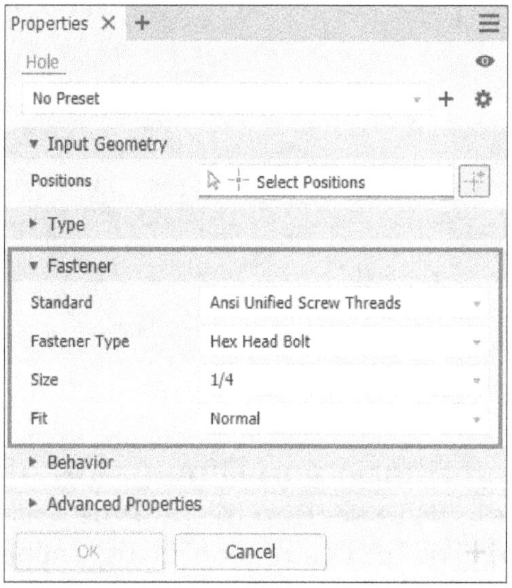

Figure-69. Fastener area

- You can also define the shape of hole by selecting the options as **None**, **Counterbore**, **Spotface**, and **Countersink** from **Seat** section in the **Type** area of the dialog box; refer to Figure-70.

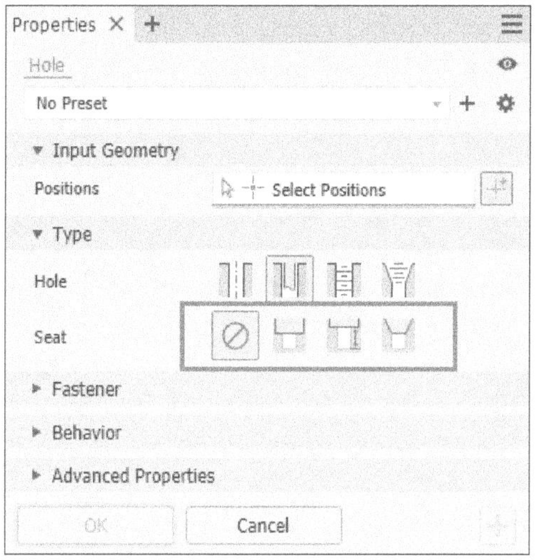

Figure-70. Options to define shape of hole

- Expand the **Advanced Properties** node and select the **iMate** check box to mark created holes for intelligent mate constraints in Assembly workspace.
- Select the Extend Start check box
- Click on the **OK** button from the dialog box to exit the **Hole** tool.

Creating Slots

The **Slot** tool is used to create a slot in the solid model. The procedure to use this tool is discussed next.

- Click on the **Slot** tool from the **Modify** panel in the **3D Model** tab of the **Ribbon**. The **Slot** dialog box will be displayed; refer to Figure-71.

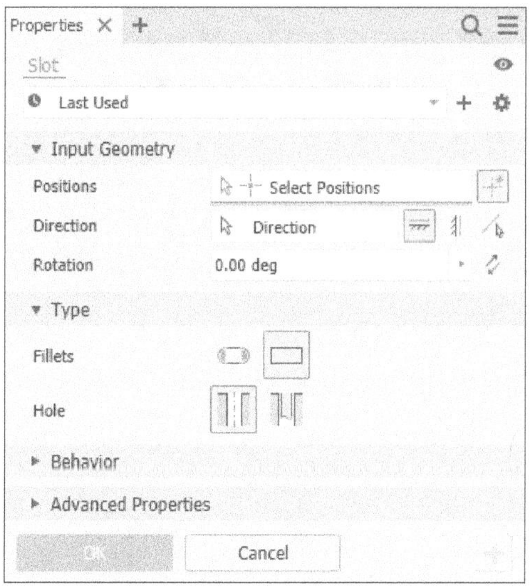

Figure-71. Slot dialog box

- Click at desired location on face of the model. Preview of the slot will be displayed; refer to Figure-72.

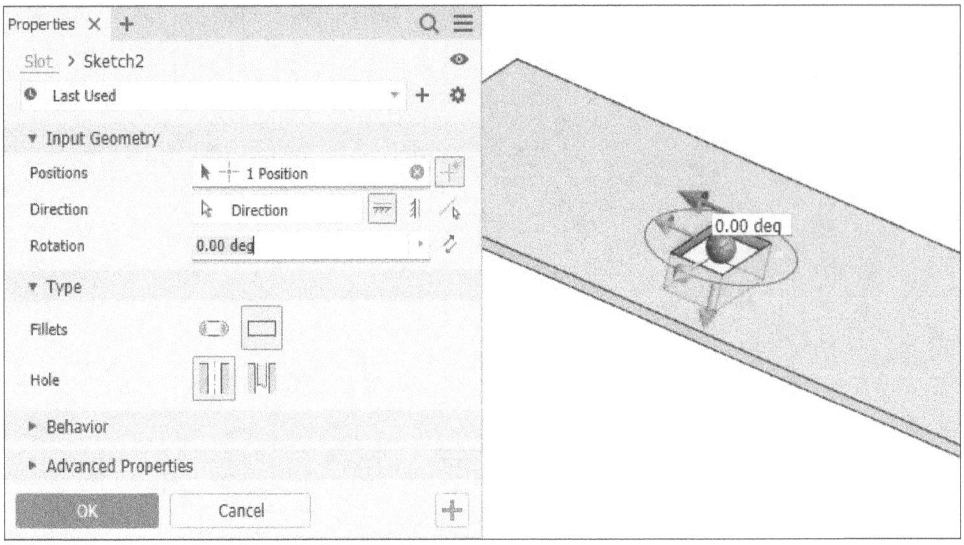

Figure-72. Preview of slot

- Select desired button from the **Direction** area to define the direction in which the slot will be created.
- Click on the button from the **Rotation** area and specify desired value to set the angular rotation of the slot.
- Click on the **Fillets** button from the **Fillets** area in the **Type** drop-down to apply round corners to the slot edges; refer to Figure-73.

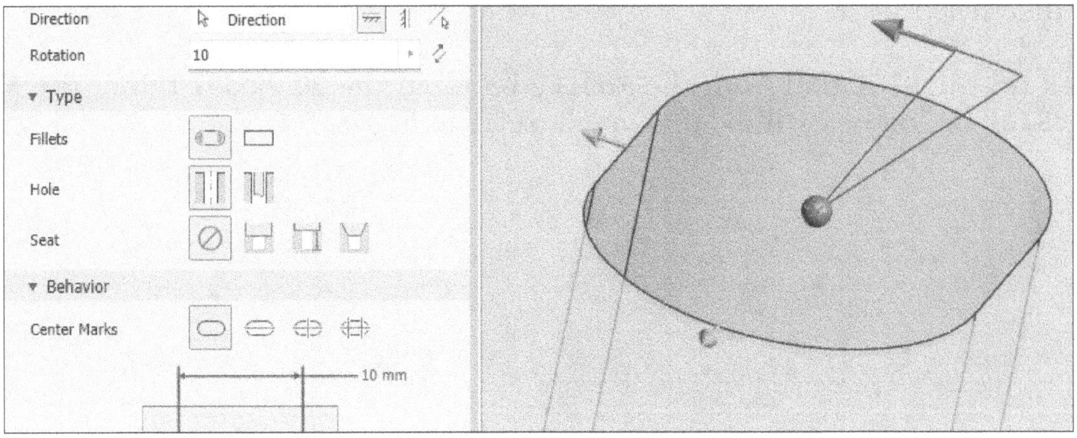

Figure-73. Preview of fillets in slot

- Select **Sharp Corners** button to create slot edges without fillets; refer to Figure-74.

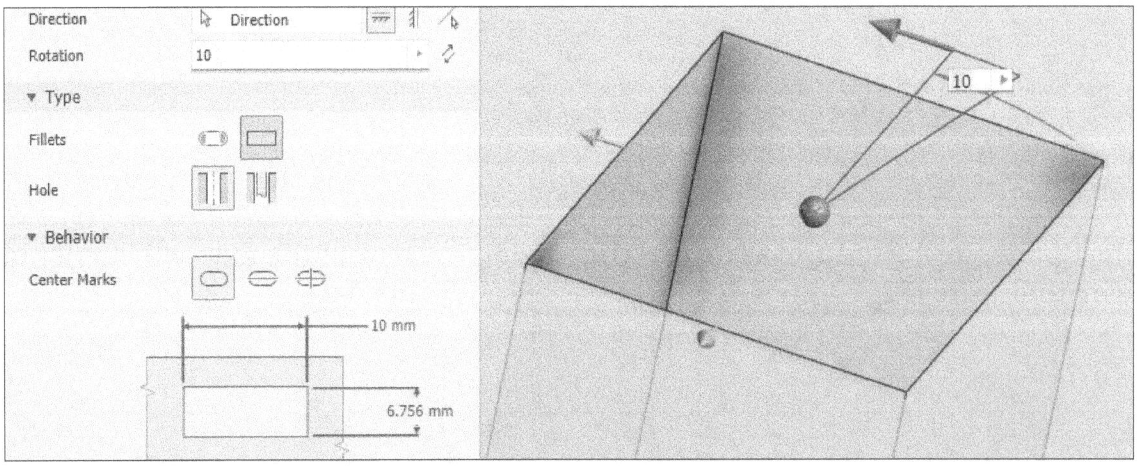

Figure-74. Preview of sharp edges in slot

- Options to define parameters of slot will be displayed in the **Behavior** area of the dialog box; refer to Figure-75.

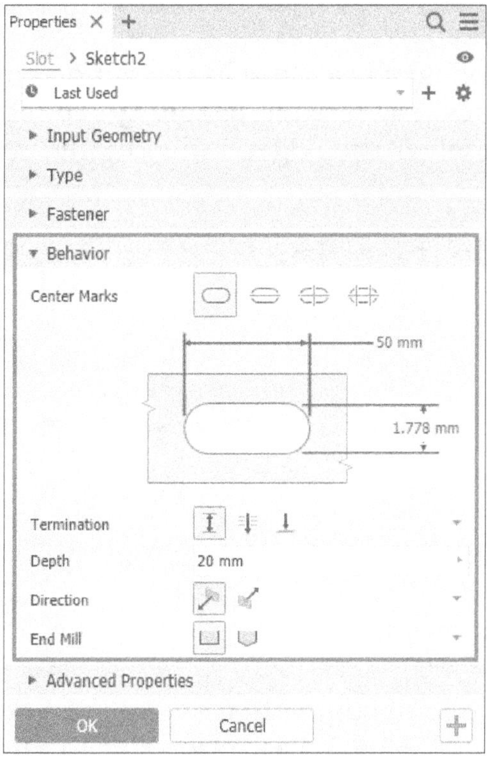

Figure-75. Options to define parameters of slot

- Select desired options from the **Center Marks** area from the **Behavior** drop-down to display center mark for the slot to assist in alignment or dimensioning.
- Type desired dimensions in the edit boxes to define size of slot.
- All the other options of the dialog box have been discussed earlier.
- Click on the **OK** button from the dialog box to exit the **Slot** tool.

Fillet Tool

The **Fillet** tool is used to apply radius at the sharp edges. The procedure to use this tool is given next.

- Click on the **Fillet** tool from the **Modify** panel in the **3D Model** tab of the **Ribbon**. The **Fillet** dialog box will be displayed; refer to Figure-76.

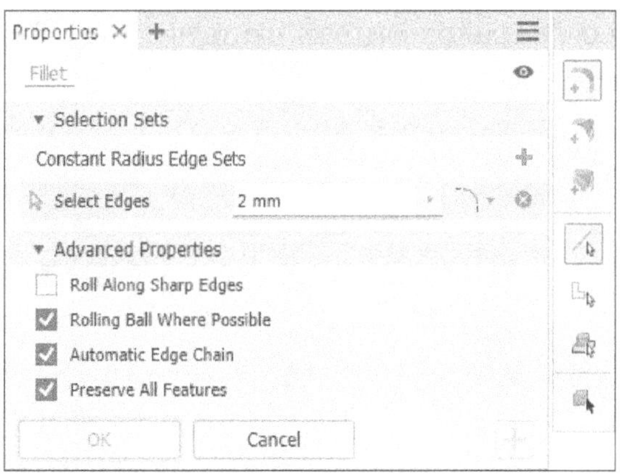

Figure-76. Fillet dialog box

Creating Constant Radius Edge Fillet

- Select the **Add constant radius edge set** button from **Tool Palette** in the dialog box, if not selected already. The options related to edge fillet will be displayed; refer to Figure-76.
- Now, there are three modes of selection in the dialog box; Edges, Edge Loops, and Features. Select the **Sets selection priority to edges** button from the **Tool Palette** if you want to select the edges individually; refer to Figure-77.

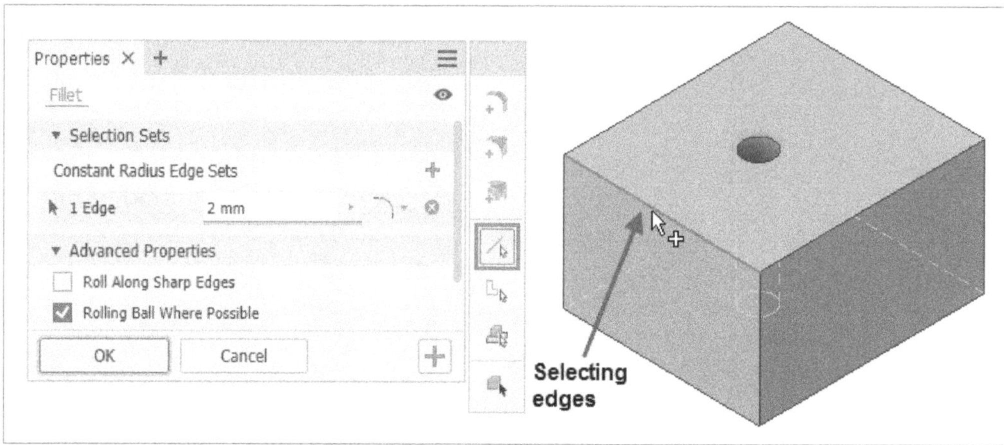

Figure-77. Selecting edges for fillet

- If you want to select a loop of edges then select the **Sets selection priority to edge loops** button from the **Tool Palette**; refer to Figure-78.

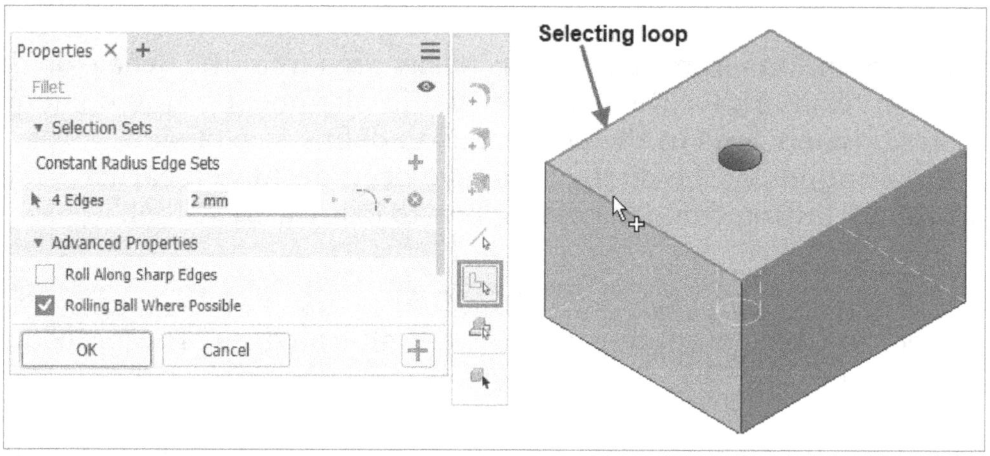

Figure-78. Selecting loop for fillet

- If you want to select the complete feature for creating fillet then select the **Sets selection priority to features** button from the **Tool Palette**; refer to Figure-79.

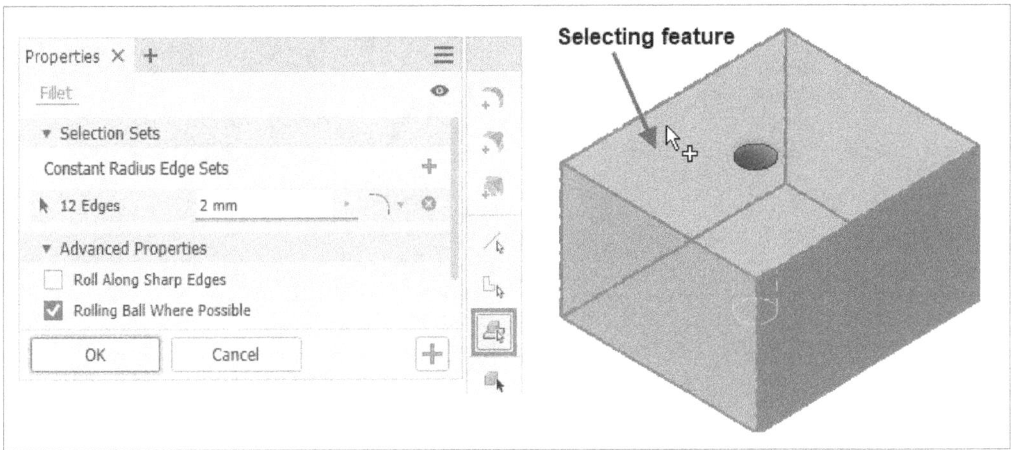

Figure-79. Selecting feature for fillet

- After making desired selection, click on the **Fillet Constant Radius** edit box. You will be asked to define the radius value; refer to Figure-80.

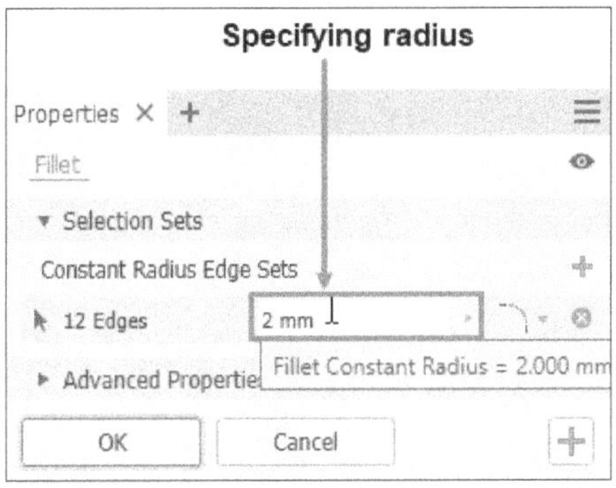

Figure-80. Specifying radius of fillet

- Specify desired radius value in the edit box.
- Select the type of fillet from the drop-down next to radius value in the dialog box. There are three options, **Tangent**, **Smooth (G2)**, and **Inverted**; refer to Figure-81.

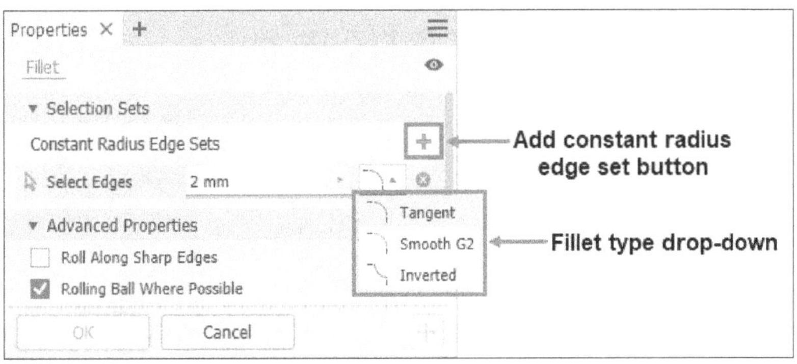

Figure-81. Fillet type drop down

- To create new set of fillet, click on the **Add constant radius edge set** button from **Constant Radius Edge Sets** area of the **Selection Sets** rollout in the dialog box. You will be asked to select a new set of edge.
- Select the new edges and specify desired radius for the new set; refer to Figure-82.

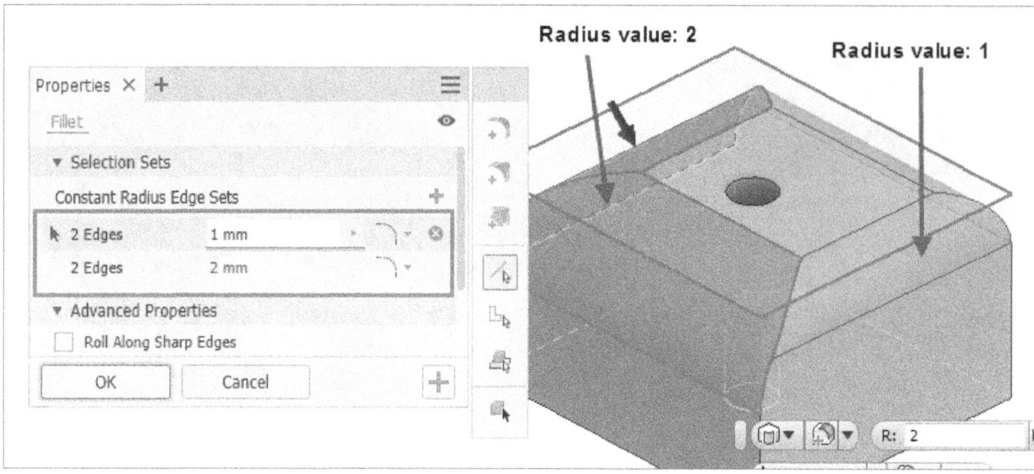

Figure-82. Applying fillet in different sets

- Click on the **Solid selection mode** button from the **Tool Palette** in the dialog box. The options related to solid selection mode will be displayed; refer to Figure-83.

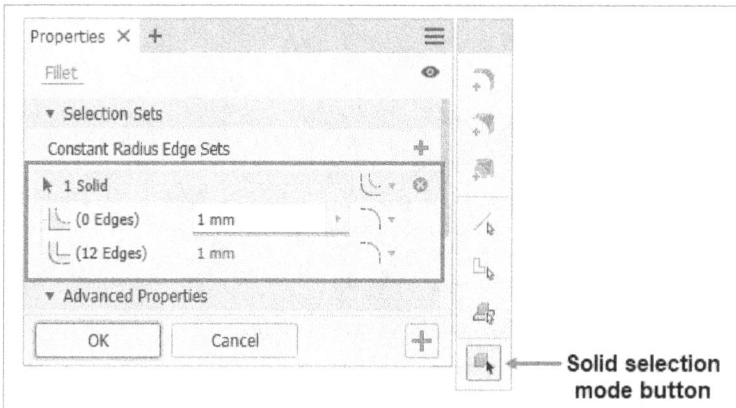

Figure-83. Solid selection mode options

- You can create fillets on all the edges of the solid by selecting the **All Rounds** option from **Solid** drop-down; refer to Figure-84.

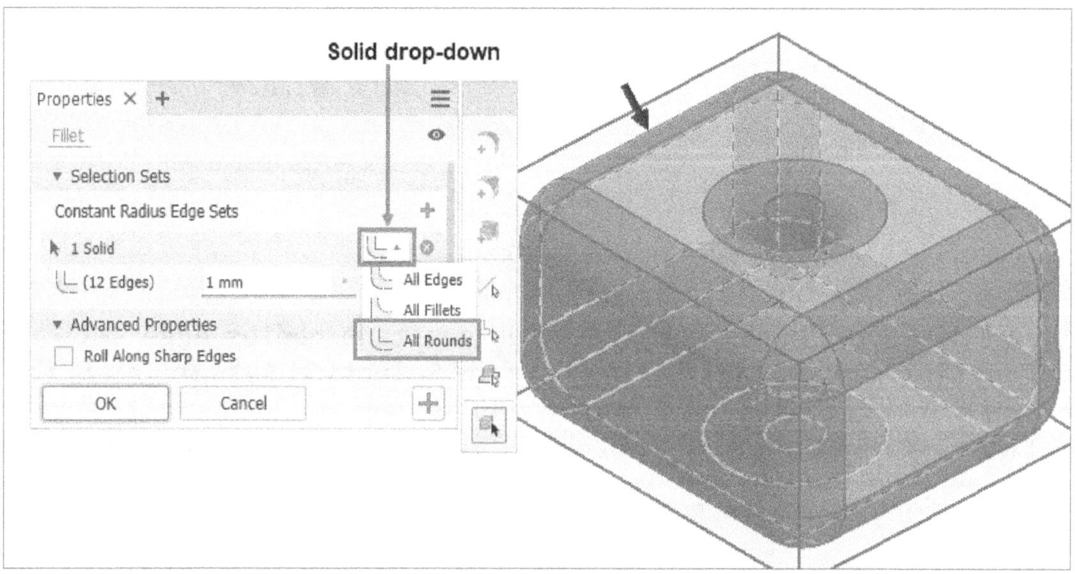

Figure-84. Creating rounds on all the edges

- After specifying the parameters, click on the **OK** button from the dialog box to complete the process.

Creating Variable Radius Edge Fillet

- Click on the **Add variable radius fillet** button from **Tool Palette** in the **Fillet** dialog box. The **Fillet** dialog box will be displayed as shown in Figure-85. Also, you will be asked to select the edges.

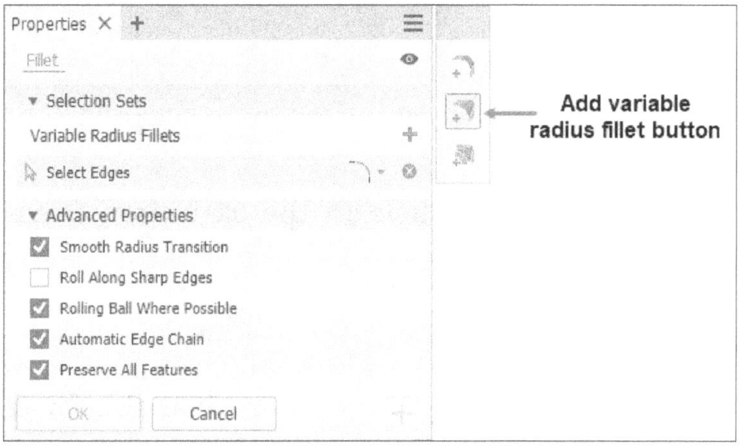

Figure-85. Fillet dialog box with variable radius fillet options

- Select desired edge from the model. You will be asked to select a point on the edge.
- Click on the edge if you want to specify radius at any intermediate point on the edge; refer to Figure-86.

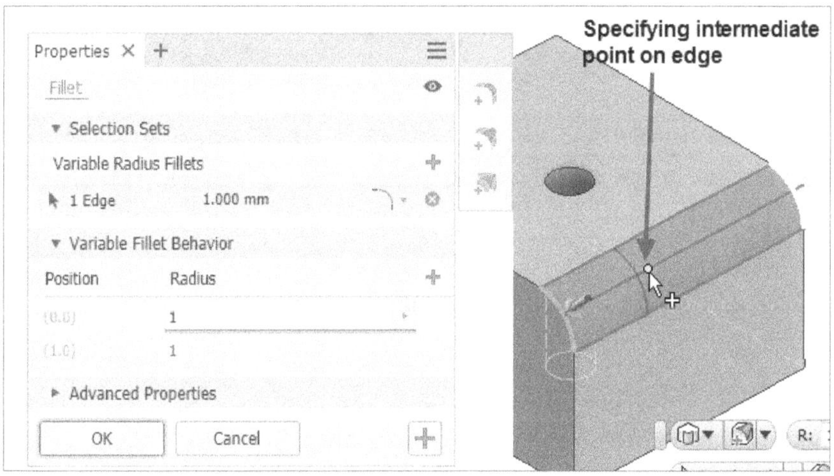

Figure-86. Specifying intermediate point on edge for variable fillet

- Click on the radius value for desired point under the **Radius** column in the **Variable Fillet Behavior** rollout of the dialog box and specify desired radius value; refer to Figure-87.

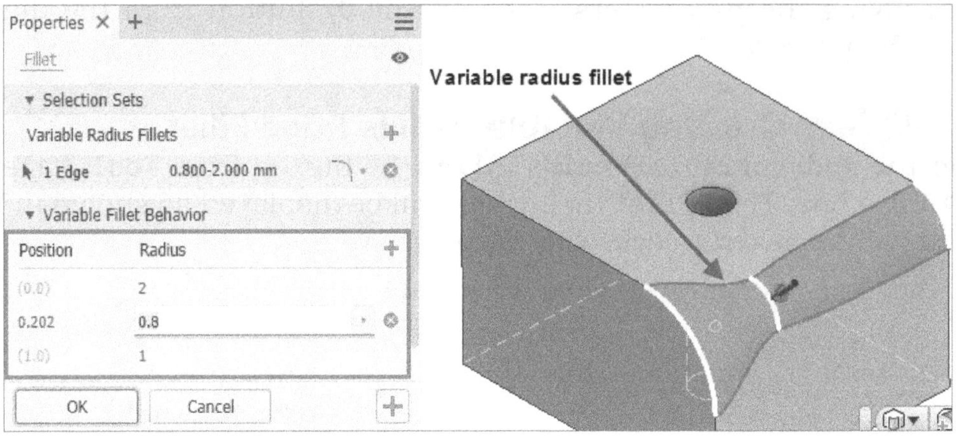

Figure-87. Variable radius fillet

- After specifying the parameters, click on the **OK** button from the dialog box to complete the process.

Specifying Setbacks

Setbacks are created at the corners where three fillets coincide at a point. You can define the shape of setbacks by using the options available by clicking on the **Add corner setback** button. The procedure is given next.

- Click on the **Add corner setback** button from **Tool Palette** in the **Fillet** dialog box. The dialog box will be displayed as shown in Figure-88. Also, you will be asked to select a vertex.

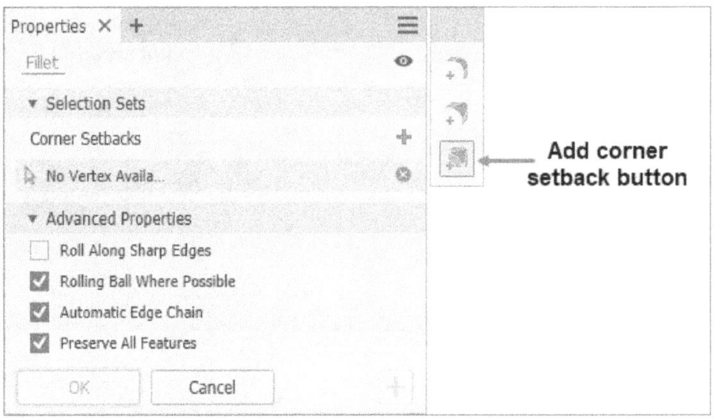

Figure-88. Setback button of Fillet dialog box

- Click at the corner point on the model for setback. The options to define parameters of setback will be displayed in the dialog box; refer to Figure-89.

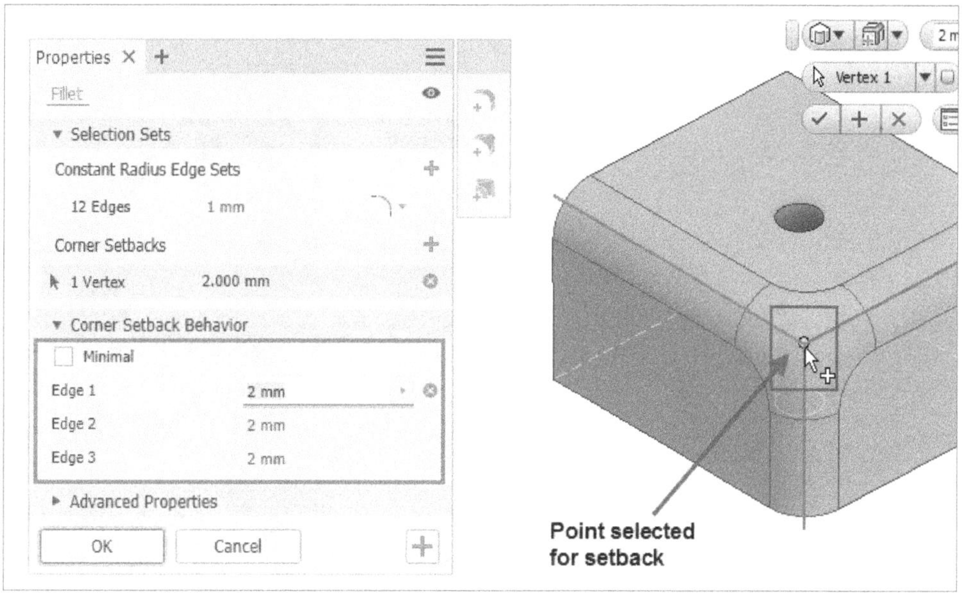

Figure-89. Setting parameters for setbacks

- Specify desired value in the **Setback Distance** edit box from **Corner Setback Behavior** rollout in the dialog box to specify parameter for setback.
- Select the **Minimal** check box from **Corner Setback Behaviour** rollout in the dialog box to set all the setbacks to minimum i.e. **0** in this case.
- After specifying the parameters, click on the **OK** button from the dialog box to complete the process.

Face Fillet Tool

You can create fillets by using faces of the model in place of selecting edges. The procedure to do so is given next.

- Click on the **Face Fillet** tool from **Fillet** drop-down in the **Modify** panel of **3D Model** tab in the **Ribbon**; refer to Figure-90. The **Face Fillet** dialog box will be displayed as shown in Figure-91. Also, you will be asked to select a face.

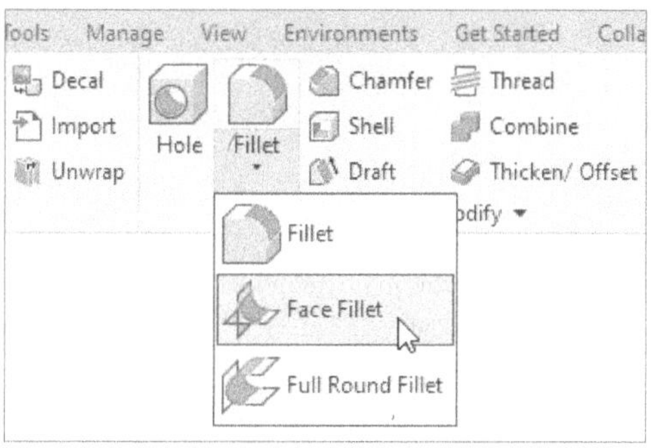

Figure-90. Face Fillet tool

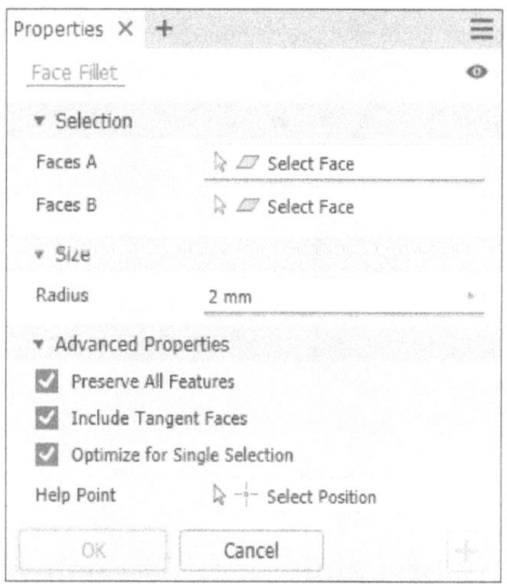

Figure-91. Face Fillet dialog box

- Click on the first face. You will be asked to select second face.
- Select the second face. Preview of the fillet will be displayed; refer to Figure-92.

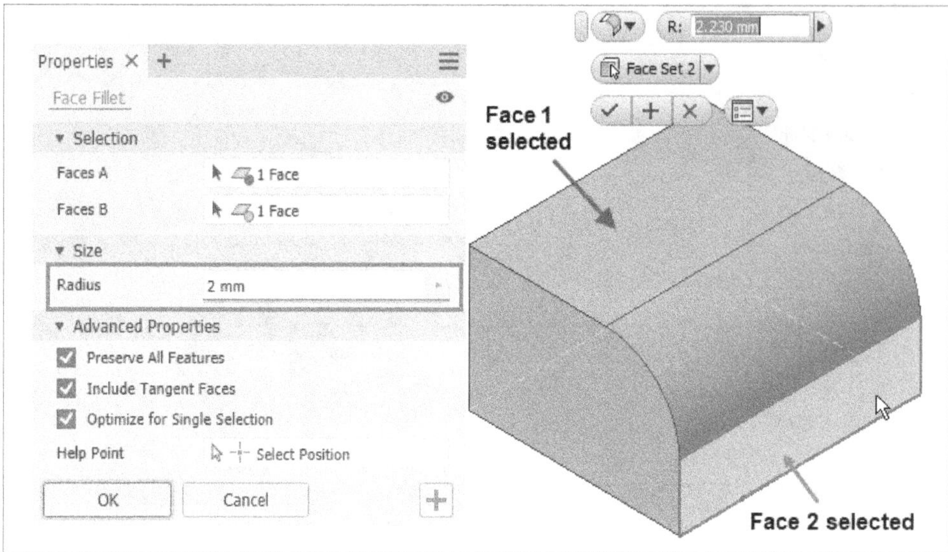

Figure-92. Preview of fillet created using faces

- Set desired radius value in the **Radius** edit box from **Size** rollout of the dialog box.
- If you select the **Include Tangent Faces** check box from **Advanced Properties** rollout then faces that are tangent to the selected faces will also be included while creating the fillet.
- After specifying the parameters, click on the **OK** button from the dialog box to complete the process.

Full Round Fillet Tool

You can create full round fillet by using the **Full Round Fillet** tool. The procedure to create full round fillet is given next.

- Click on the **Full Round Fillet** tool from **Fillet** drop-down in the **Modify** panel of **3D Model** tab in the **Ribbon**; refer to Figure-93. The options in the dialog box will be displayed as shown in Figure-94. Also, you will be asked to select first side face of the model.

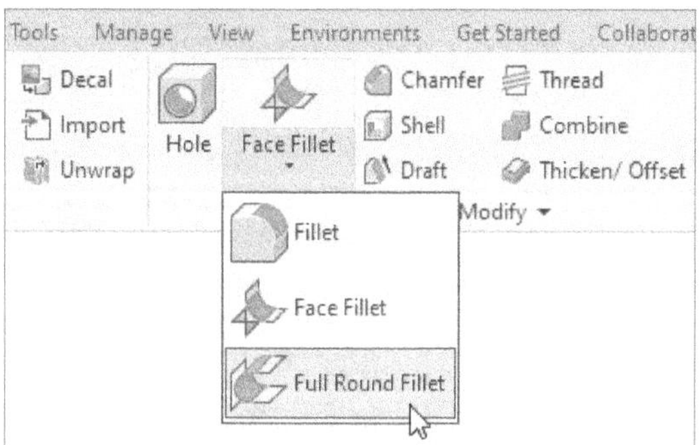

Figure-93. Full Round Fillet tool

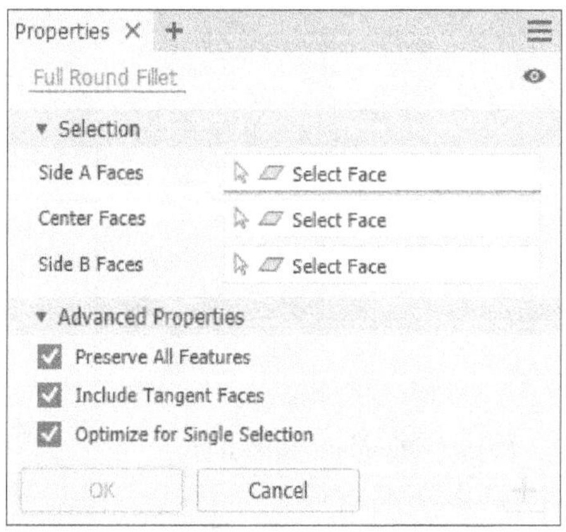

Figure-94. Full Round Fillet dialog box

- Select the first side face. You will be asked to select the center connected face.
- Select the center face. You will be asked to select the second side face.
- Select the second side face. Preview of the full round fillet will be displayed; refer to Figure-95.

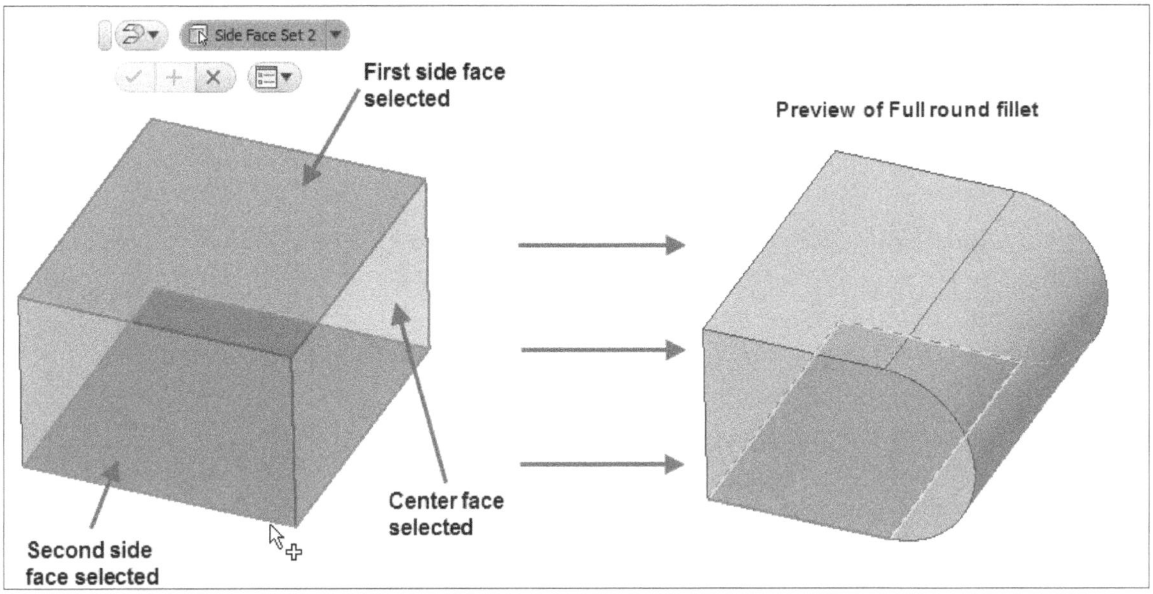

Figure-95. Faces selected for creating full round

- Click on the **OK** button from the dialog box to create the fillet/fillets.

Chamfer Tool

The **Chamfer** tool is used to chisel the sharp edges of the model. The procedure to use the **Chamfer** tool is given next.

- Click on the **Chamfer** tool from **Modify** panel in the **3D Model** tab of the **Ribbon**. The **Chamfer** dialog box will be displayed; refer to Figure-96. Also you will be asked to select the edges.

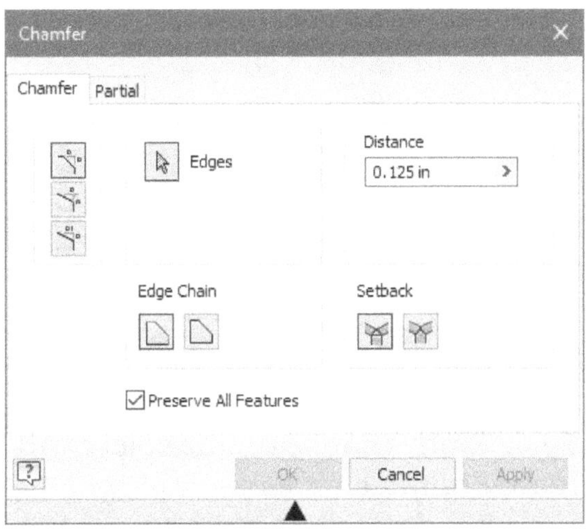

Figure-96. Chamfer dialog box

- Select the edges on which you want to apply chamfer. Preview of the chamfers will be displayed; refer to Figure-97.

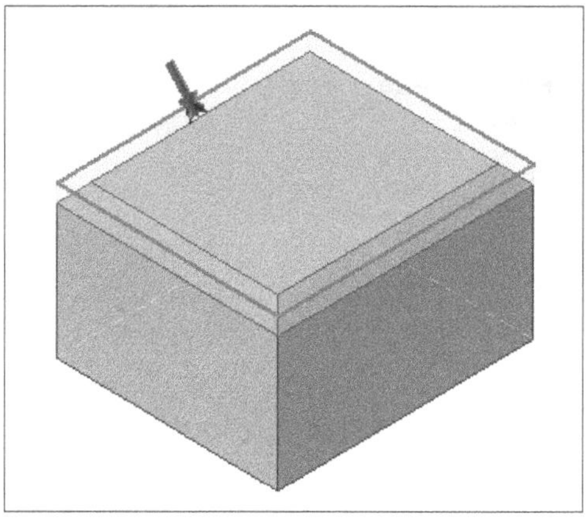

Figure-97. Preview of chamfer

Distance Chamfer

- By default, **Distance** button is selected in the dialog box so you can specify the distance value in both the direction by using the **Distance** edit box in the dialog box.

Distance and Angle Chamfer

- Select the **Distance and Angle** button from the dialog box if you want to specify distance and angle value for chamfer. The **Chamfer** dialog box will be displayed as shown in Figure-98 and you will be asked to select a face.

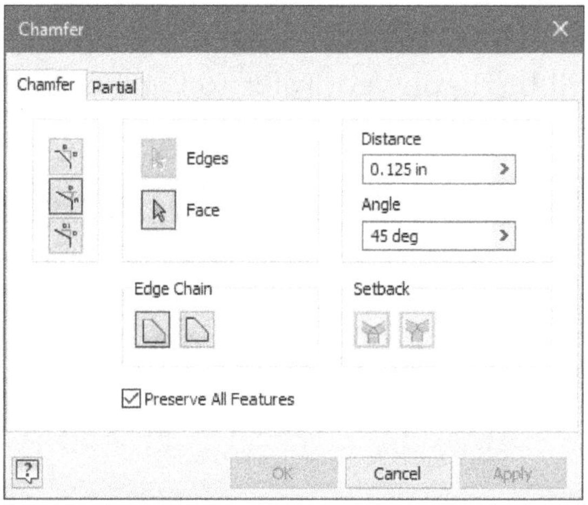

Figure-98. Chamfer dialog box with Distance and Angle button selected

- Select the face with respect to which the chamfer will be at angle. You will be asked to select the edges. Note that you can select only the boundary edges of the selected face to create chamfer.
- Select the edge(s) and specify desired parameters in the **Distance** and **Angle** edit boxes in the dialog box. Preview of the chamfer will be displayed; refer to Figure-99.

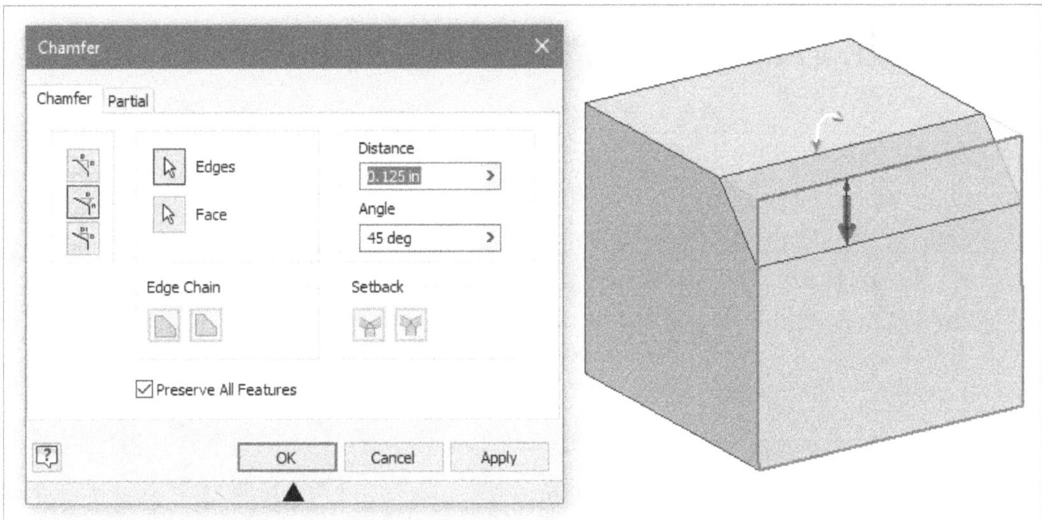

Figure-99. Preview of Distance and Angle chamfer

Two Distances Chamfer

- Select the **Two Distances** button if you want to specify different values for distances in the two directions of the chamfer. The dialog box will be displayed as shown in Figure-100. Also, you will be asked to select the edge(s).

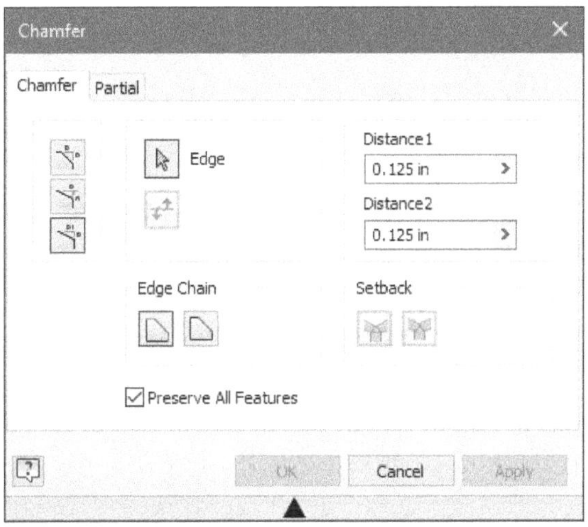

Figure-100. Chamfer dialog box with Two Distances button selected

- Select the edges on which you want to apply chamfer. Preview of the chamfer will be displayed; refer to Figure-101.

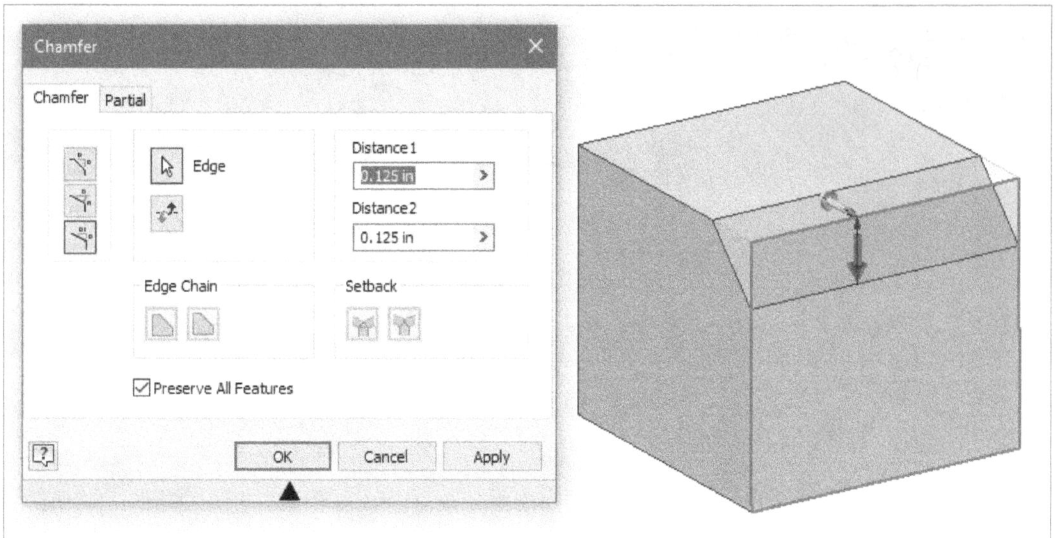

Figure-101. Chamfer created with Two Distance option

- Specify desired distance values in the edit boxes of the dialog box.
- Click on the **OK** button from the dialog box to create the chamfer.

Creating Partial Chamfers

You can create a partial chamfer by defining the location of the start and end vertices along an existing chamfer edge.

- Select the **Partial** tab from the dialog box and you will be asked to locate the end vertex.
- Click on desired chamfer edge to locate the end vertex; the preview of partial chamfer will be displayed; refer to Figure-102.

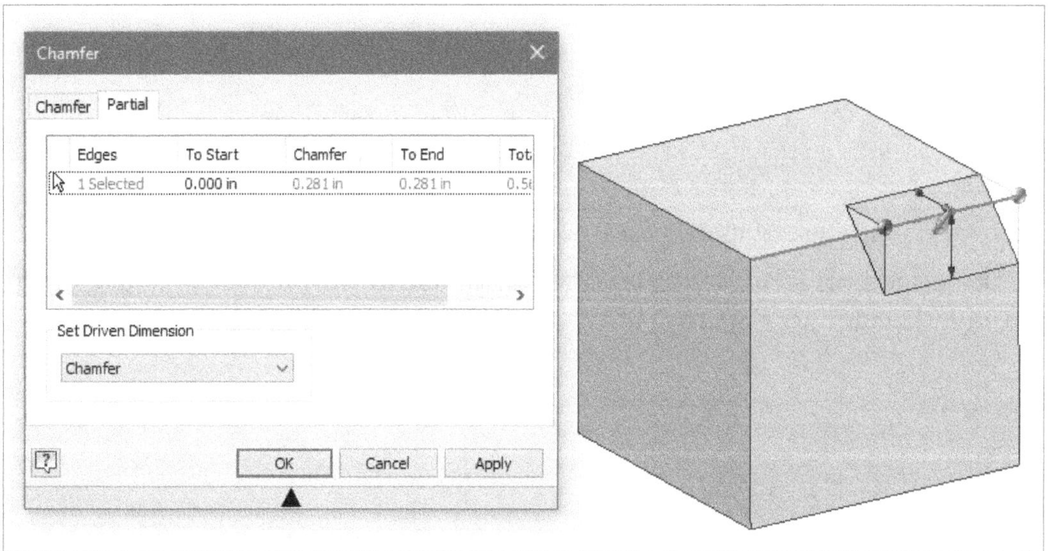

Figure-102. Preview of partial chamfer

- Specify the chamfer distance by dragging the ball or by specifying value in the edit boxes in **Partial** tab of the dialog box; refer to Figure-103.

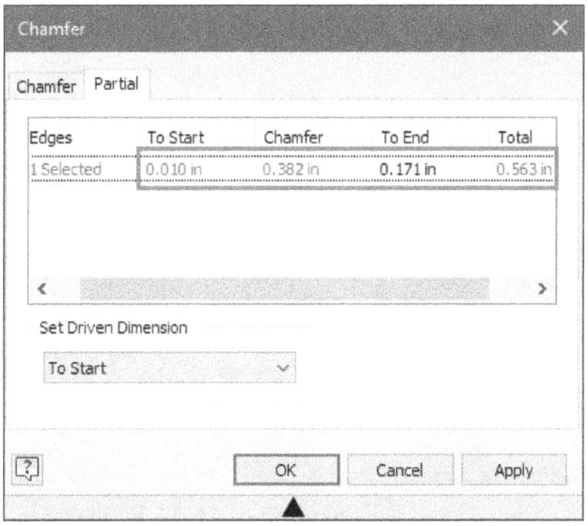

Figure-103. Edit boxes for partial chamfer

- Change the driven dimension type as desired from **Set Driven Dimension** drop-down. There are three options in this drop-down as **To Start**, **Chamfer**, and **To End**.
- Select the **To Start** option to specify the distance from start of edge to start of chamfer. The End and Chamfer length are fixed and do not change when the edge length changes.
- Select the **Chamfer** option to specify the distance as the chamfer length. The Start and End length are fixed and do not change when the edge length changes.
- Select the **To End** option to specify the distance from end of edge to end of chamfer. The Start and Chamfer length are fixed and do not change when the edge length changes.
- Click on the **OK** button from the dialog box to create the chamfer.

Shell Tool

The **Shell** tool is used to scoop out material from the solid base. The procedure to use this tool is given next.

- Click on the **Shell** tool from **Modify** panel in the **3D Model** tab of the **Ribbon**. The **Shell** dialog box will be displayed along with the preview of shell feature; refer to Figure-104. Also, you will be asked to select faces to be removed.

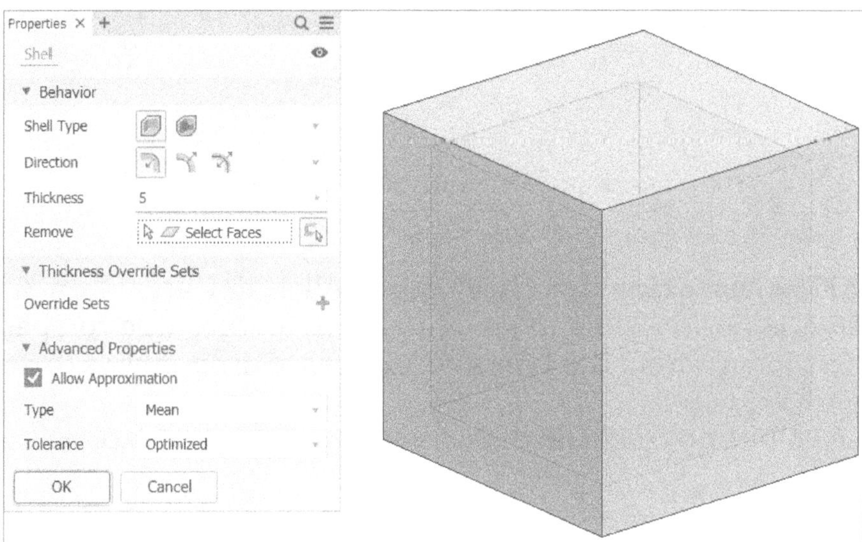

Figure-104. Shell dialog box with preview

- Click on the face(s) that you want to remove from the base model after scooping out the material; refer to Figure-105.

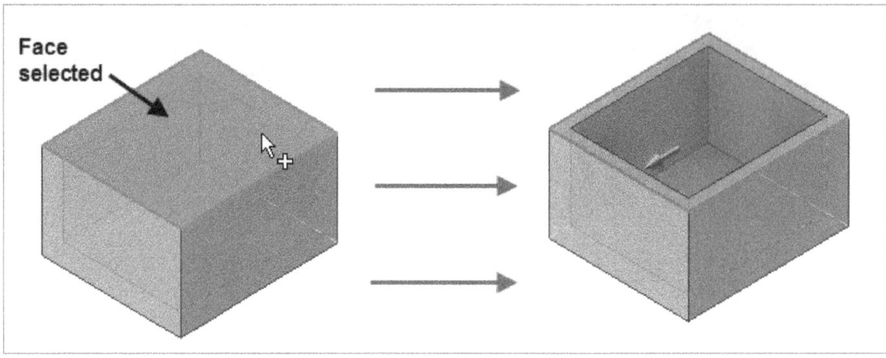

Figure-105. Face selected to remove

- Select the **Sharp Corners** button from the **Shell Type** section to generate sharp corners and select the **Rounded Corners** button from the section to generate rounded offset corners at shell boundaries.
- To specify thickness side, click on desired button from **Inside**, **Outside**, or **Center** from the dialog box.
- Type desired value in the **Thickness** edit box to define thickness of shell walls.
- Expand the **Thickness Override Sets** node and select the **Add Shell set** button to define a different thickness a selected face in the shell feature. The options to select overridden faces and define override thickness value will be displayed.
- Select desired face and type desired wall thickness value in the edit box; refer to Figure-106.

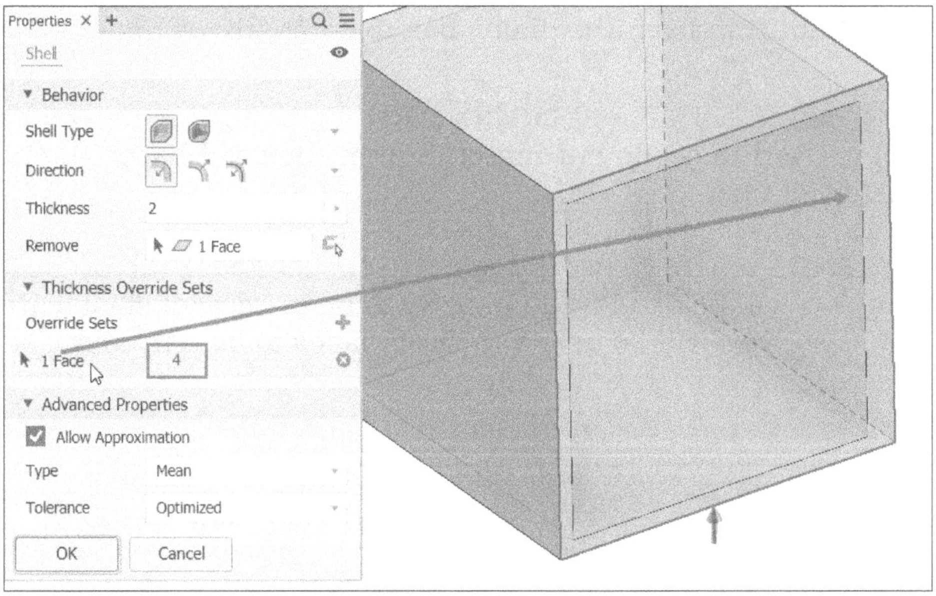

Figure-106. Shell dialog box with thickness override

- Select the **Allow Approximation** check box to allow deviation from fixed thickness value where it is not possible to generate shell feature due to space constraint. Select desired options from the **Type** and **Tolerance** drop-downs to define deviation limit.
- Click on the **OK** button from the dialog box to create the feature.

Draft Tool

The **Face Draft** tool is used to apply taper to selected face. The procedure to apply draft is given next.

- Click on the **Face Draft** tool from **Modify** panel in the **3D Model** tab of the **Ribbon**. The **Face Draft** dialog box will be displayed as shown in Figure-107. Also, you will be asked to select a reference to specify pull direction.

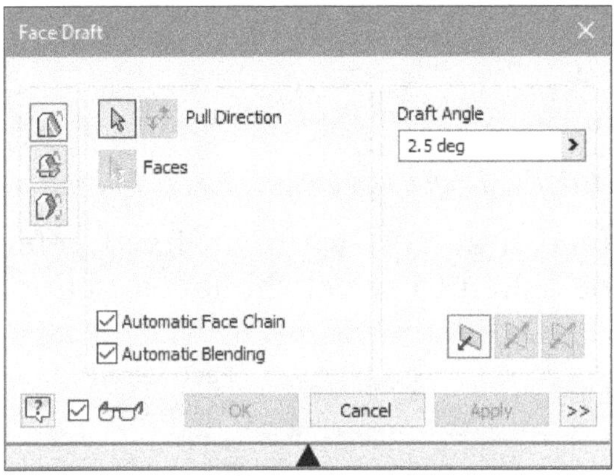

Figure-107. Face Draft dialog box

- Select an edge, plane, or face to specify direction of draft. If you select a plane or face, direction perpendicular to the selected plane or face will be selected as pull direction. If you select an edge then direction along the selected edge will be selected. On selecting the direction reference, you will be asked to select the faces for applying draft.
- Select the faces on which you want to apply draft. Preview of the draft will be displayed; refer to Figure-108.
- Enter desired angle value in the **Draft Angle** edit box.

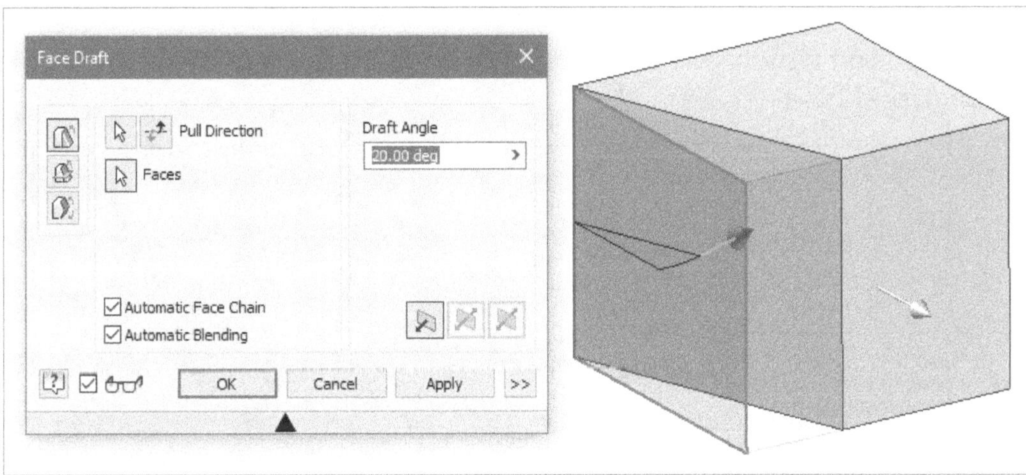

Figure-108. Preview of draft feature

Fixed Plane Draft

- Select the **Fixed Plane** button from the **Face Draft** dialog box. The dialog box will be displayed with **One Way** button selected by default as shown in Figure-109. Also, you will be asked to select a plane to be fixed as angle reference.

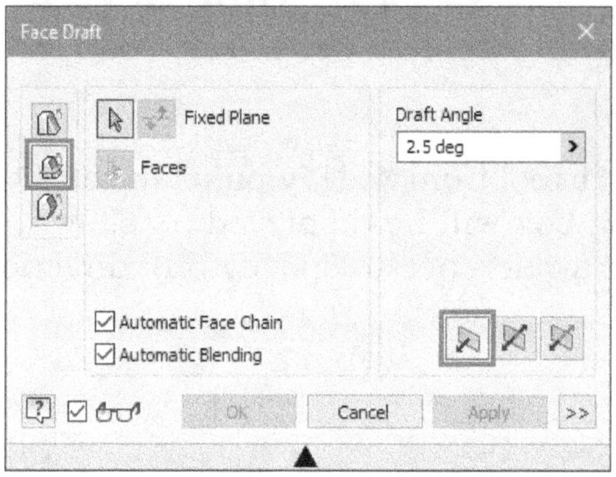

Figure-109. Face Draft dialog box with Fixed Plane button selected

- Select the plane or face that you want as fixed reference for angle; refer to Figure-110. You will be asked to select the faces to apply draft.

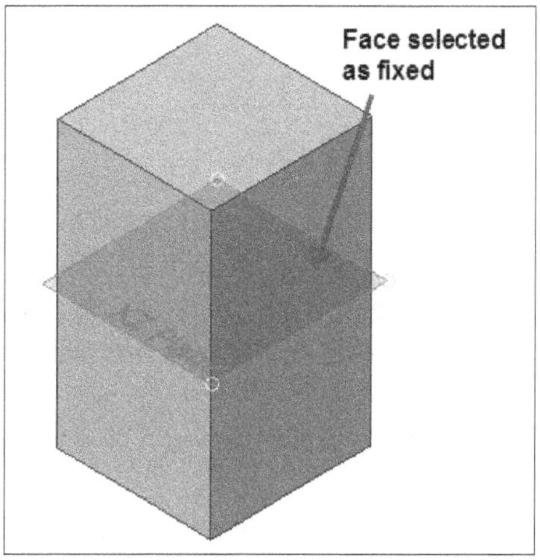

Figure-110. Face selected as fixed

- Select the faces on which you want to apply draft. Preview of draft will be displayed; refer to Figure-111.

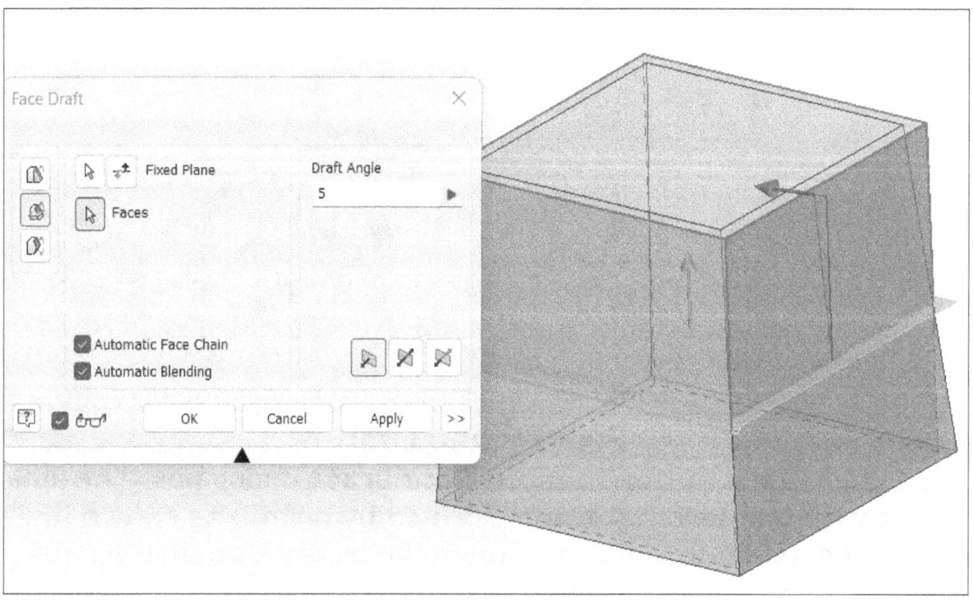

Figure-111. Preview of draft feature with Fixed Plane option

- Specify desired draft angle value in the **Draft Angle** edit box in the dialog box.
- If you want to apply symmetric draft to both sides of face divided by fixed plane then select the **Symmetric** button from the dialog box. Preview of the draft will be displayed; refer to Figure-112.

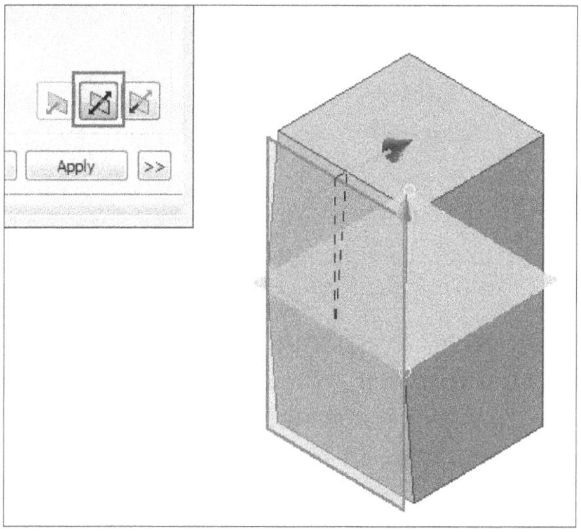

Figure-112. Preview of symmetric draft

- Specify desired angle value in the edit box.
- You can specify different values of draft for two sides of face with respect to fixed plane by using the **Asymmetric** button. Preview of the draft will be displayed with different draft angles for faces; refer to Figure-113.

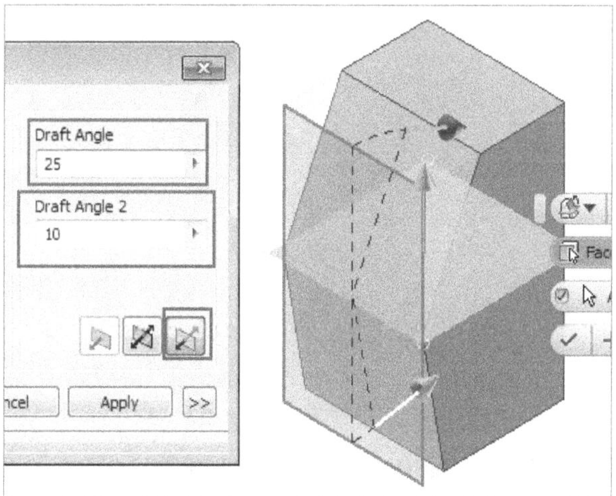

Figure-113. Preview of asymmetric draft

Draft Using Parting Line

Parting Line also works in the same way as fixed plane in draft with the only difference that now, you can also select a curve dividing the face to create different draft on either directions. The procedure to create draft with parting line is given next.

- Click on the **Parting Line** button from the **Face Draft** dialog box. The dialog box will be displayed as shown in Figure-114. Also, you will be asked to select a reference for specifying the pull direction.

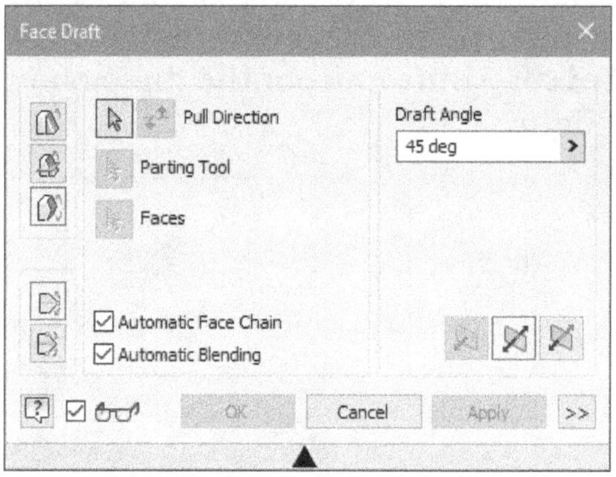

Figure-114. Face Draft dialog box with Parting Line button selected

- Select a face, plane, or edge to specify the pull direction. You will be asked to select the **Parting Tool** reference.
- Select a sketching line, plane, or surface to make it parting tool. You will be asked to select face on which the draft is to be applied.
- Select desired face. Preview of the draft feature will be displayed; refer to Figure-115.

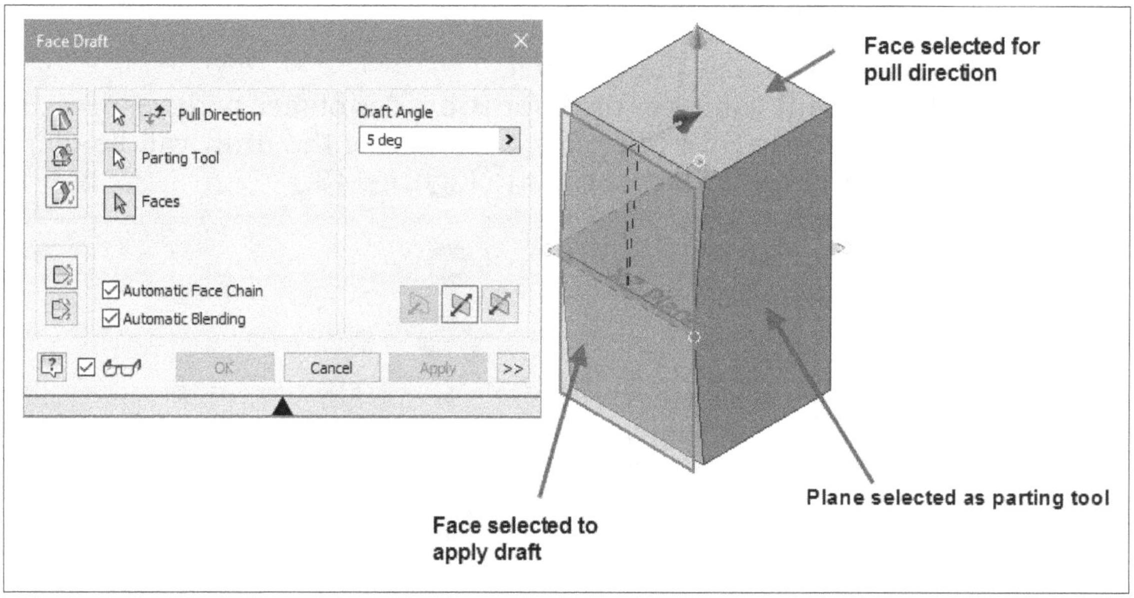

Figure-115. Preview of face draft with parting line selected

- Enter desired angle value and select the **Symmetric** or **Asymmetric** button as per your requirement.
- Click on the **OK** button to apply draft.

Thread Tool

As the name suggests, the **Thread** tool is used to create threads in selected hole or over the selected shaft. The procedure to use this tool is given next.

- Click on the **Thread** tool from **Modify** panel in the **3D Model** tab of the **Ribbon**. The **Thread** dialog box will be displayed; refer to Figure-116. Also, you will be asked to select the face on which threads are to be applied.
- Select the face on which you want to apply thread. The updated **Thread** dialog box will be displayed along with the preview of thread; refer to Figure-117.

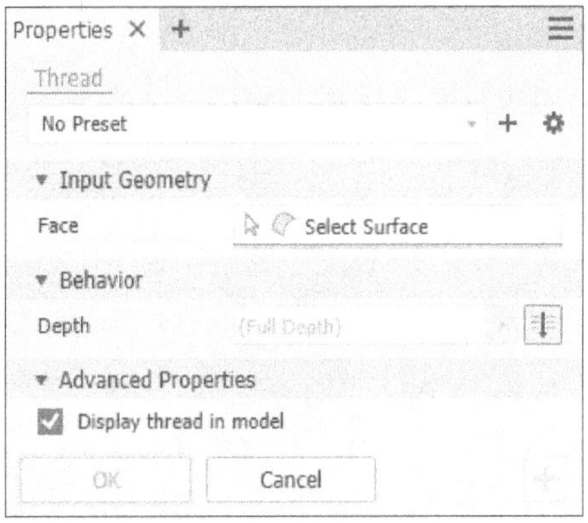

Figure-116. Thread dialog box

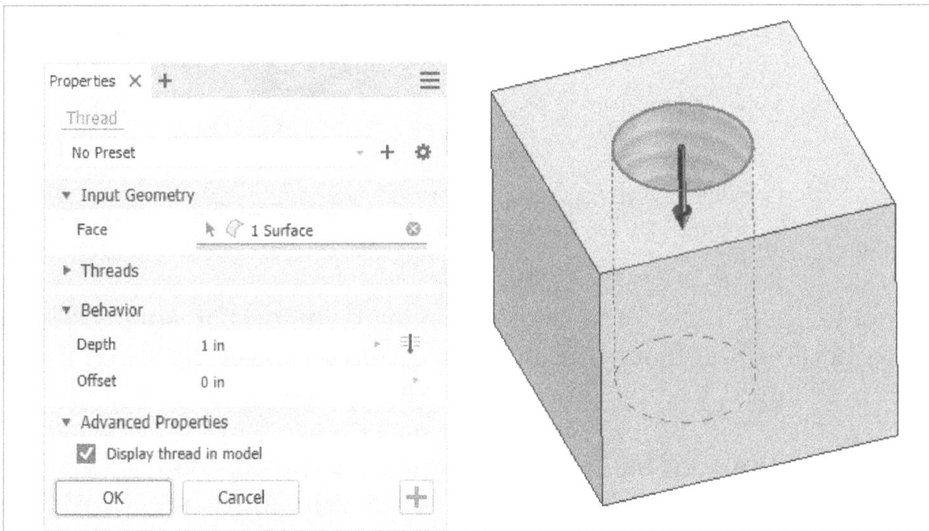

Figure-117. Preview of thread

- By default, threads are created up to full depth of hole/shaft. If you want to specify the depth of thread then specify desired values in **Depth** edit box available in **Behavior** area of the dialog box.
- Click on the **Threads** area of the dialog box to display the options related to size of thread; refer to Figure-118.

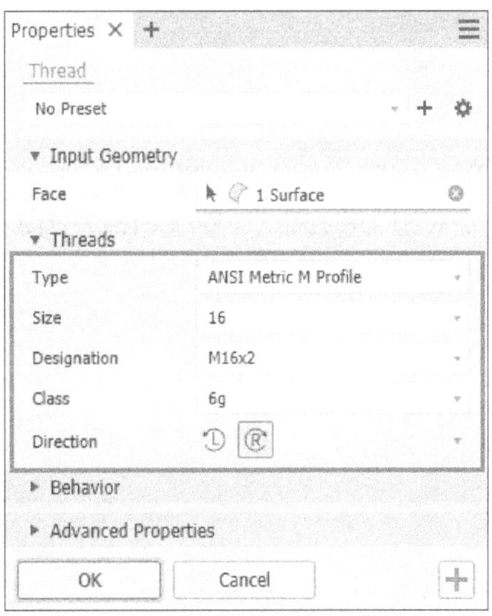

Figure-118. Threads area of the dialog box

- Select desired thread type from the **Type** drop-down and select desired size of the thread.
- Click on the **OK** button from the dialog box. The threads will be created; refer to Figure-119.

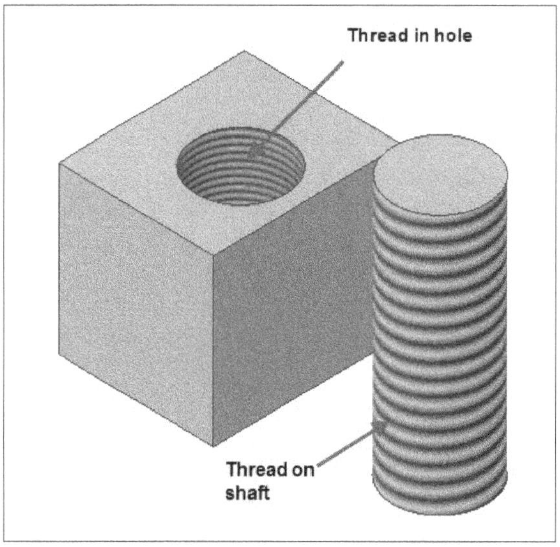

Figure-119. Threads on shaft and hole

Combine Tool

The **Combine** tool is used to perform Boolean operations on the solids. This tool is used to combine two bodies, subtract one body from another, or find out the intersecting portion between selected bodies. The procedure to use this tool is given next.

- Click on the **Combine** tool from **Modify** panel in the **3D Model** tab of the **Ribbon**. The **Combine** dialog box will be displayed; refer to Figure-120. Also, you will be asked to select the base body.

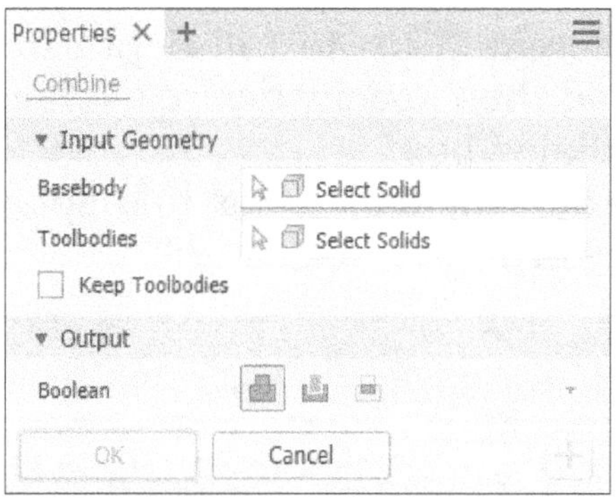

Figure-120. Combine dialog box

- Select the base body. You will be asked to select the tool body.
- Select the second solid body to perform boolean operation; refer to Figure-121.

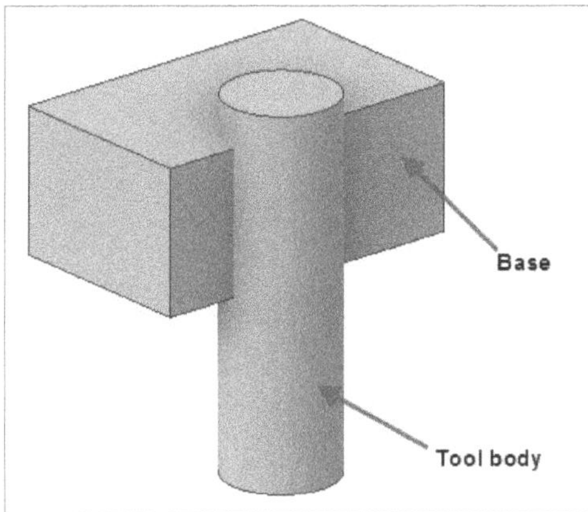

Figure-121. Base and tool body selected for combining

- If you want to join two solid bodies then click on the **Join** button from **Boolean** area in the **Output** rollout of the dialog box.
- If you want to subtract tool body from the base solid then click on the **Cut** button from **Boolean** area of the dialog box.
- If you want to find the intersecting volume of the solids then click on the **Intersect** button from **Boolean** area of the dialog box.
- Click on the **OK** button to create the feature. Note that if you want to keep the tool body even after operation then select the **Keep Toolbodies** check box in the **Input Geometry** rollout of the **Combine** dialog box.

Figure-122 shows the output of the three buttons on the model.

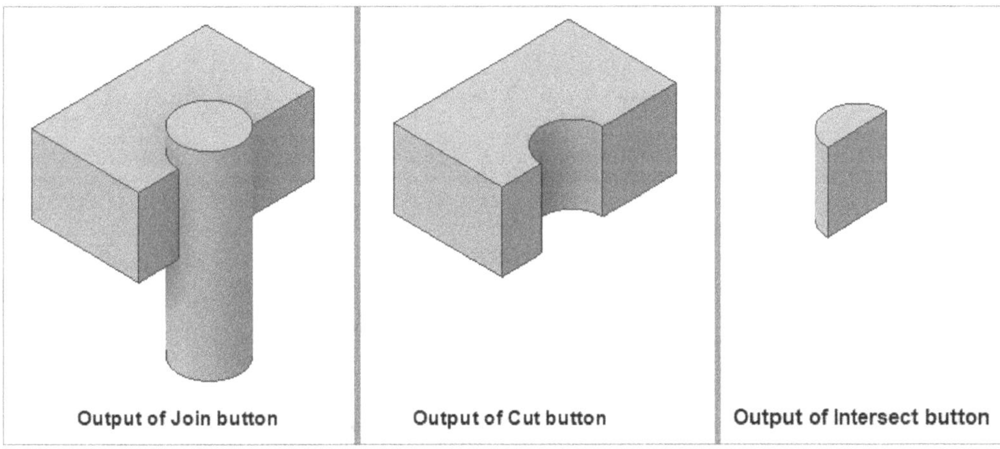

Figure-122. Output of Combining

Thicken/Offset Tool

The **Thicken/Offset** tool, as the name suggests, is used to thicken or offset the solids/ surfaces. The procedure to use this tool is given next.

- Click on the **Thicken/Offset** tool from **Modify** panel in the **3D Model** tab of **Ribbon**. The **Thicken** dialog box will be displayed; refer to Figure-123. Also, you will be asked to select the face.

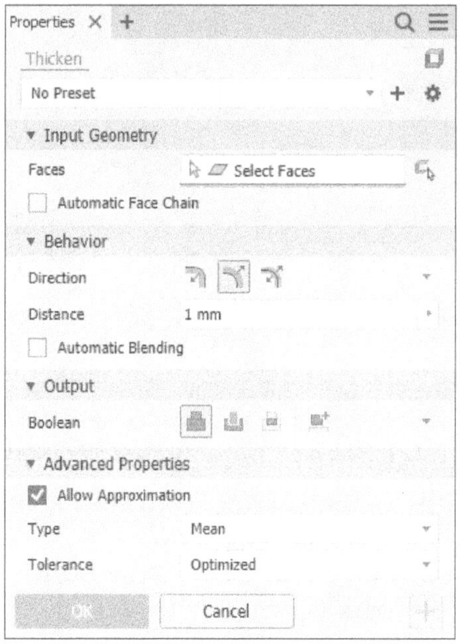

Figure-123. Thicken dialog box

- Select the face that you want to thicken or offset. Preview of the thicken/offset will be displayed; refer to Figure-124.

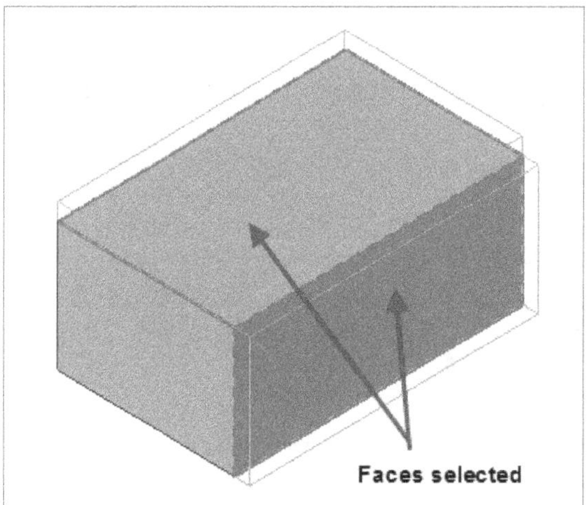

Figure-124. Faces selected for thicken or offset

- Select desired option from **Inside**, **Outside**, or **Center** option in the **Direction** area of **Behavior** rollout in the dialog box.
- Specify desired thickness or distance of the offset in the **Distance** edit box of **Behavior** rollout.
- Select **Automatic Blending** check box from **Behavior** rollout to automatically move tangential faces and also creates new blends, if required. Note that when using **Automatic Blending**, the **Output** rollout will not be available.
- Select desired option from **Boolean** area in the **Output** rollout of the dialog box. Select **Join** button to add the volume created by the Thicken feature to the solid part. Select **Cut** button to remove the volume created by the Thicken feature from the solid part. Select **Intersect** button to create a new feature from the shared volume of the Thicken feature and the solid part. Select **New Solid** button to create a new solid body.
- Click on the **Select Solids** button from the **Solids** field in the **Output** rollout of the dialog box if you want to thicken the selected face.

- Select the **Allow Approximation** check box from **Advanced Properties** rollout to allow a deviation from the specified thickness.
- Select desired option from **Type** drop-down in the **Advanced Properties** rollout of the dialog box. Select **Never too thin** option to preserve minimum distance if approximation is allowed. The deviation must fall above the specified distance. Select **Never too thick** option to preserve maximum distance if approximation is allowed. The deviation must fall below the specified distance. On selecting the **Mean** option, deviation is divided to fall both above and below the specified distance if approximation is allowed.
- Select desired option from **Tolerance** drop-down in the **Advanced Properties** rollout of the dialog box. Select **Optimized** option to compute approximation using a reasonable tolerance and minimal compute time. Select **Specified** option to compute approximation using the tolerance you specify. Valid tolerance range is from 0-100 %.
- Click on the **OK** button from the dialog box to create the feature.
- If you want to create the surface offset feature then click on the **Surface mode** button from top right corner of the **Thicken** dialog box. The **OffsetSrf** dialog box will be displayed along with the preview of surface offset feature; refer to Figure-125.

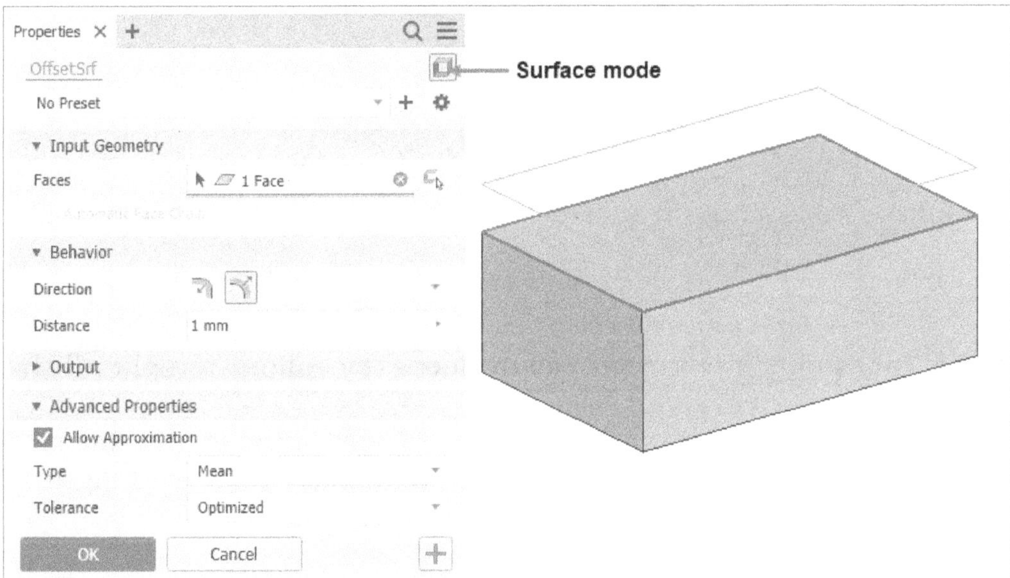

Figure-125. OffsetSrf dialog box with preview of surface offset feature

- Specify desired parameters as discussed earlier and click on **OK** button from **OffsetSrf** dialog box to create the feature.

Split Tool

The **Split** tool is used to divide the selected entity (Face or solid body) with the help of trimming reference (Sketch, Plane, or Surface). The procedure to use this tool is given next.

- Click on the **Split** tool from **Modify** panel in the **Ribbon**. The **Split** dialog box will be displayed as shown in Figure-126. Also, you will be asked to select the sketch profile, plane, or surface as split tool.

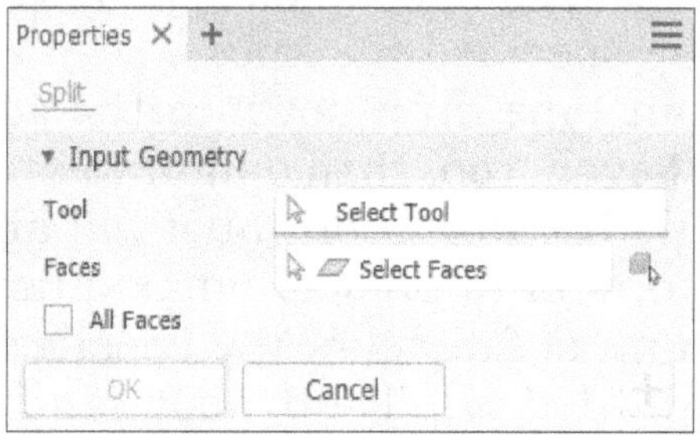

Figure-126. Split dialog box

- Select the object to be used as split tool. You will be asked to select the faces to be split up.
- Select the faces that you want to split. Preview of the splitting will be displayed; refer to Figure-127.

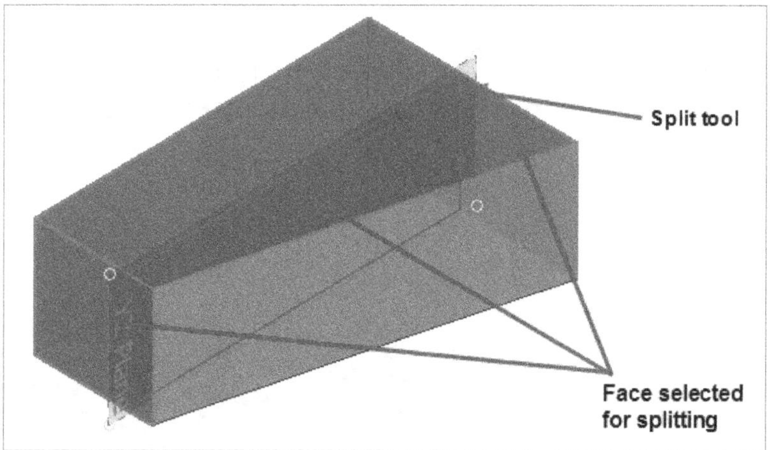

Figure-127. Selecting faces to split

- Select **All Faces** check box from **Input Geometry** rollout to split all the faces of selected body.
- Click on the **Solid selection** button from **Faces** area in the **Input Geometry** rollout. The updated **Split** dialog box will be displayed; refer to Figure-128.

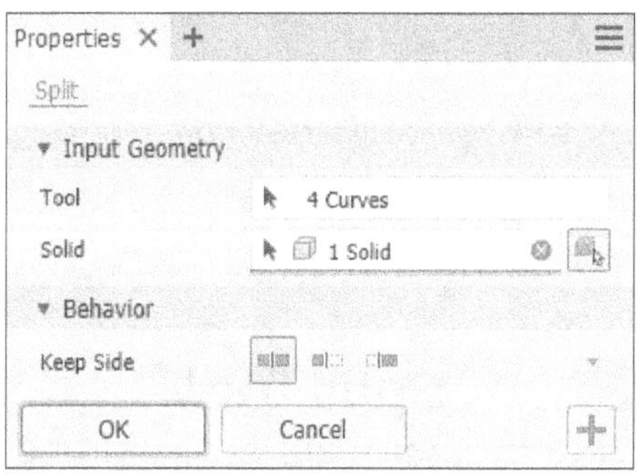

Figure-128. Updated Split dialog box

- Select desired option from **Keep Side** area in the **Behavior** rollout of the dialog box. Select **Both Sides** option to split the solid and keep both sides. Select **Default Side** option to split the body and keep the default side. Select **Flip Side** option to split the solid and keep the opposite side.
- After specifying the parameters, click on the **OK** button from the dialog box to create the feature; refer to Figure-129.

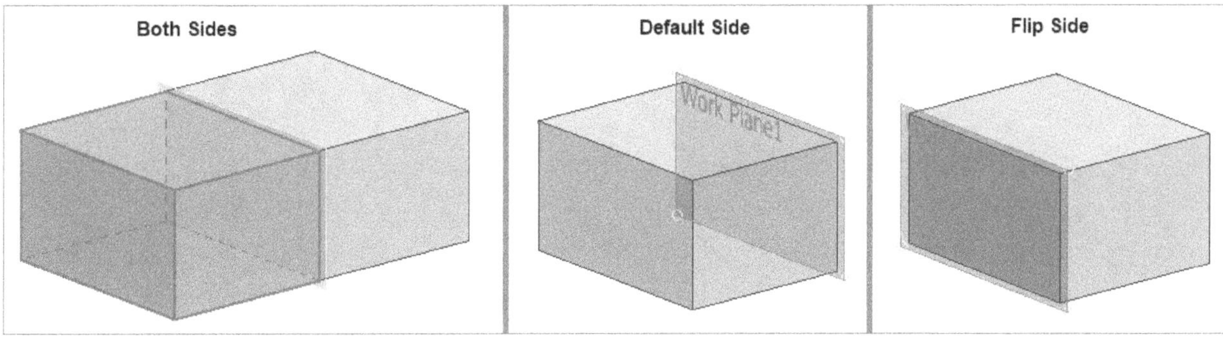

Figure-129. Splitting the body at different types

The **Direct Edit** tool is used to modify imported objects. You will learn about **Direct Edit** tool in the next chapter.

Delete Face Tool

The **Delete Face** tool is used to convert a part body into a surface body by deleting one or two faces from the solid body. The procedure to use this tool is given next.

- Click on the **Delete Face** tool from **Modify** panel in the **3D Model** tab of the **Ribbon**. The **Delete Face** dialog box will be displayed; refer to Figure-130. Also, you will be asked to select the face to be delete.

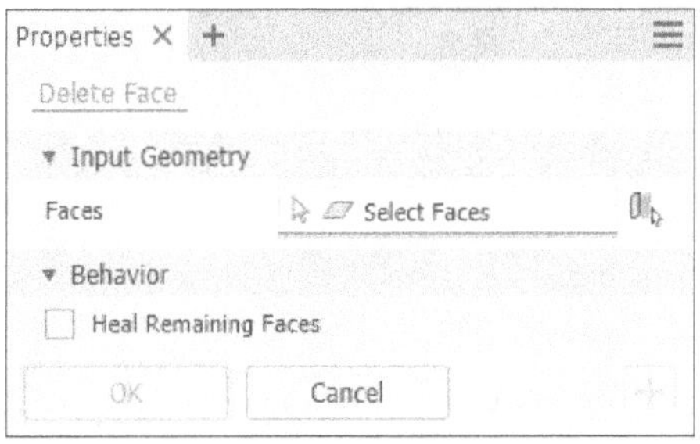

Figure-130. Delete Face dialog box

- Select desired face to be delete from the solid body.
- Select **Heal Remaining Faces** check box from **Behavior** rollout in the dialog box to heal gaps by extending adjacent faces until they intersect.
- Click on the **Lump or Void toggle** button from **Faces** area in the **Input Geometry** rollout of the dialog box and select individual faces, lumps, or voids that you want to delete.
- Click on the **OK** button from the dialog box; the selected face will be deleted; refer to Figure-131.

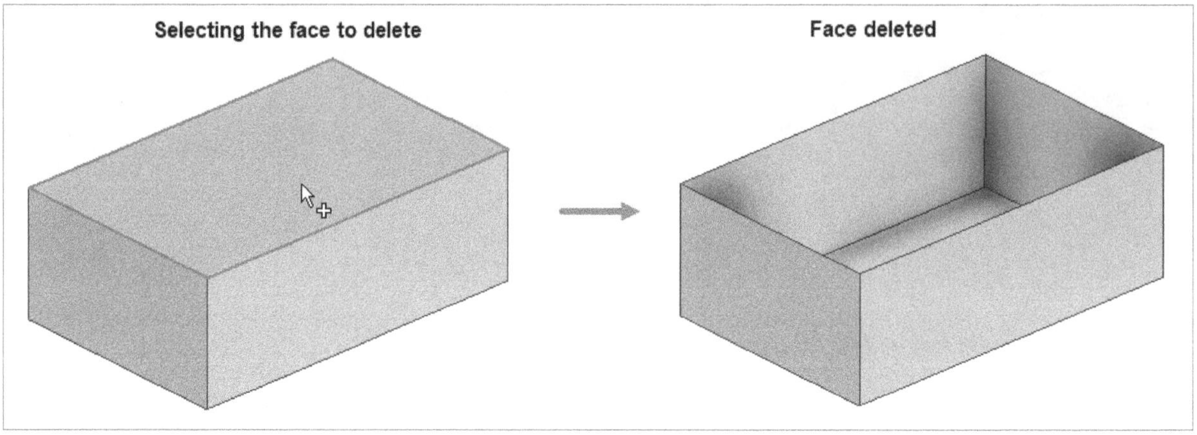

Figure-131. Selected face deleted

Mark

The **Mark** tool is used to prepare the text for machining via processes like laser marking, etching, and engraving. The procedure to use this tool is discussed next.

- Click on the **Mark** tool from **Modify** panel in the **3D Model** tab of the **Ribbon**. The **Mark** dialog box will be displayed; refer to Figure-132. You will be asked to select the object to be marked.

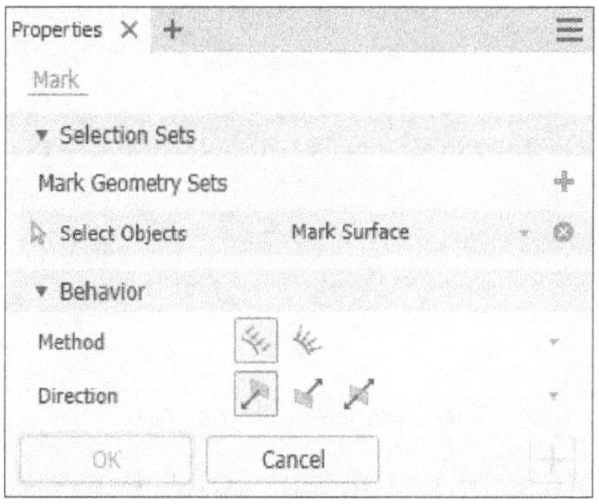

Figure-132. Mark dialog box

- Select desired geometry or text which you want to mark; refer to Figure-133.

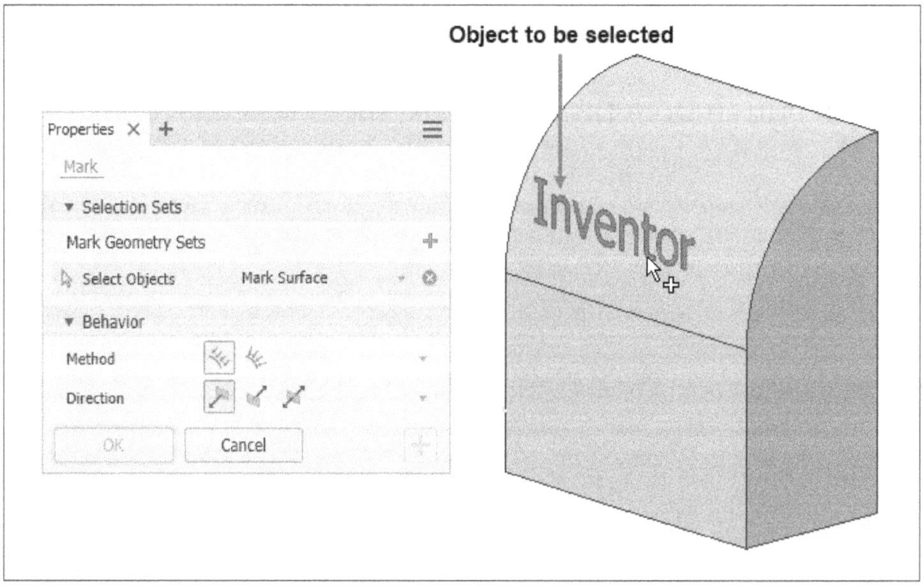

Figure-133. Selecting the object to mark

- Select desired option from the drop-down in the **Selection Sets** rollout. Select **Mark Surface** option to apply the mark to a single face and to outline the text. Select **Mark Through** option to apply the mark to multiple faces and to convert text characters to a single stroke path based on the selected font.
- Click on the plus button from **Selection Sets** rollout to add multiple mark geometry sets.
- Select desired option from the **Method** and **Direction** areas in the **Behavior** rollout of the dialog box. Select **Project** option from **Method** area and select desired direction option from **Direction** area to project the sketch geometry to a face. Select **Wrap** option from **Method** area and select desired cylindrical face for the **Face** area to wrap the sketch geometry to a cylindrical face.
- After specifying desired parameters, click on the **OK** button from the dialog box. The selected object will be marked; refer to Figure-134.

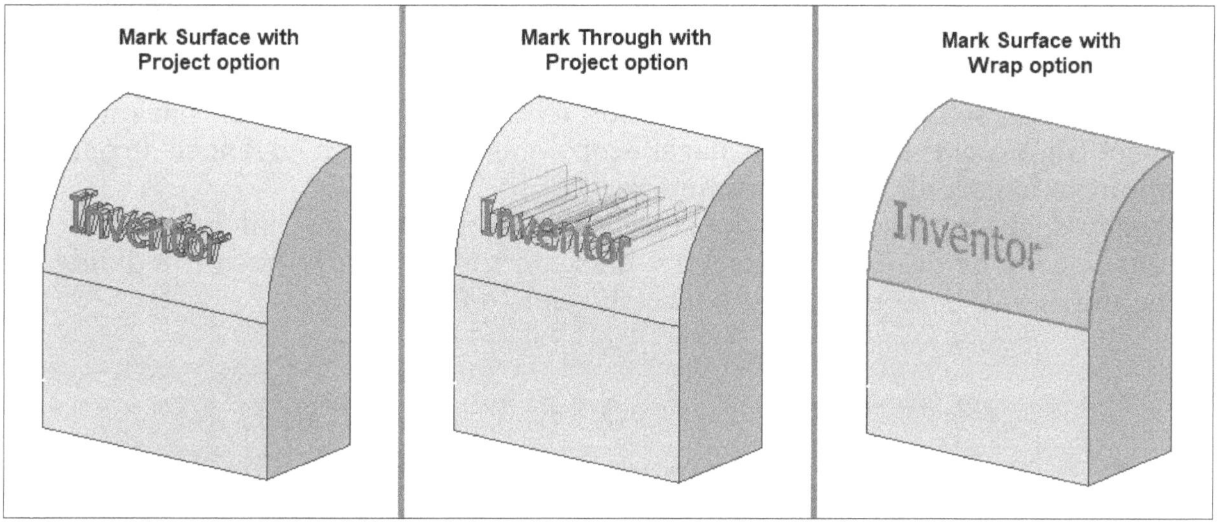

Figure-134. Object marked

Finish

The **Finish** tool is used to apply texture and material appearances to the model in graphics area. The procedure to use this tool is discussed next.

- Click on the **Finish** tool from **Modify** panel in the **3D Model** tab of the **Ribbon**. The **Finish** dialog box will be displayed; refer to Figure-135.

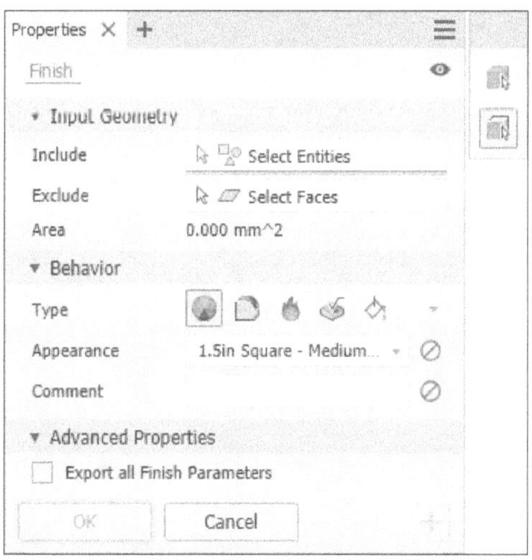

Figure-135. Finish dialog box

- Select the button to set the selection mode to find bodies first and select the button to set the selection mode to find only faces.
- Make sure the **Select Entities** selection button is active in **Include** section of **Input Geometry** rollout and then select desired faces or bodies in graphics area. Or, click on the **Select Faces** selection button in the **Exclude** section to select the faces that should be excluded from selection. Preview of appearance will be displayed in graphics area and total area of selected faces will be displayed in the **Area** section of dialog box.
- Select desired type of finish to be applied on the face(s) from **Type** section of **Behavior** rollout. Select **Apply Appearance** option to select an appearance from the Appearance library that you want to apply. Select **Apply Material Coating** option to specify the material coating to be applied to selected faces. Select **Apply Heat Treatment** option to specify the heat treatment to be applied to selected faces. Select **Apply Surface Texture** option to specify the surface texture to be applied to selected faces. Select **Apply Paint** option to specify the paint to be applied to selected faces.
- Toggle the **Disable Parameter** button to disable desired finish parameter.
- Select the **Export all Finish Parameters** check box from **Advanced Properties** rollout to export all finish parameters.
- Specify desired properties of the selected finish type in the dialog box.
- After specifying desired parameters, click on the **OK** button from the dialog box. The finish will be applied to the face(s); refer to Figure-136.

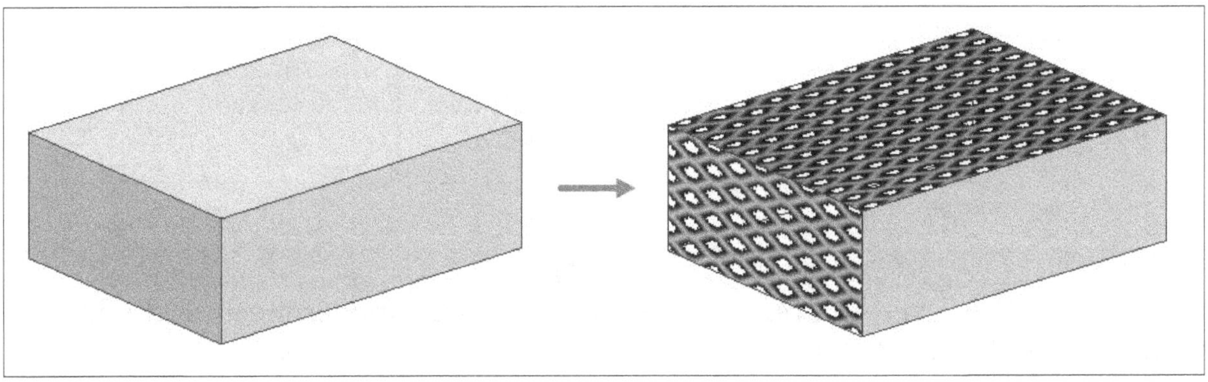

Figure-136. Finish applied to the faces

We have discussed many tools related to advanced 3D Modeling. Let's get some real-world practical on the tools.

PRACTICAL 1

In this practical, we will create a model as shown in Figure-137 using the dimensions given in Figure-138.

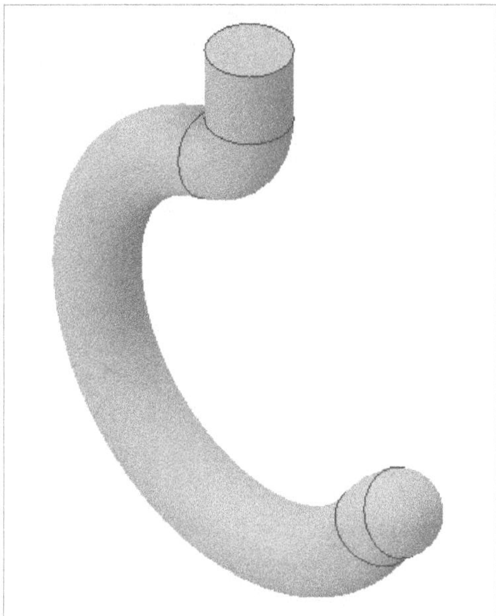

Figure-137. Model for Practical 1

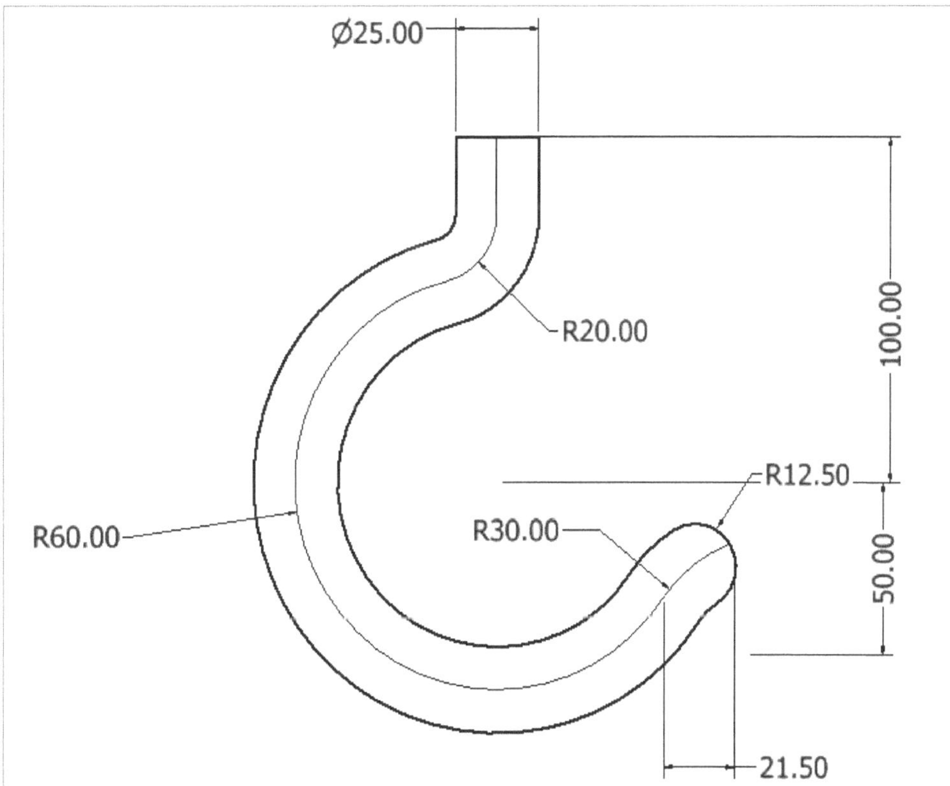

Figure-138. Practical 1 drawing view

Strategy for Creating model

1. Looking at the isometric view and orthographic views, we can find that the sketch for revolve feature should be created on the Front plane (YZ Plane).
2. Using the **Revolve** tool, we will create the solid base of the model.

3. Using the Plane tools, we will create a plane at an angle of 40 degree to the vertical wall of base feature.
4. Using the **Extrude** tool, we will create the pipe joined to the base feature.

Starting Part File

- Start Autodesk Inventor by double-clicking on the Autodesk Inventor Professional icon from the desktop. (If not started yet.)
- Click on the **New** button from the **Quick Access Toolbar**. The **Create New File** dialog box will be displayed.
- Double-click on **Standard(mm).ipt** icon from the **Metric** templates. The Part environment of Autodesk Inventor will be displayed.

Creating Sketch

- Click on the **Start 2D Sketch** button from **Sketch** panel in the **3D Model** tab of the **Ribbon**. You will be asked to select a sketching plane.
- Select the **XY** Plane (Front Plane) as sketching plane. The sketching environment will become active.
- Create the sketch as shown in Figure-139.

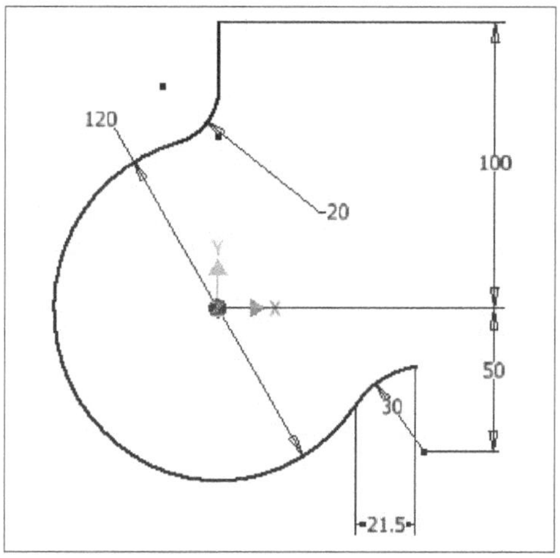

Figure-139. Sketch for practical

- Click on the **Finish Sketch** button from the **Finish** drop-down in the **Exit** panel of the **Ribbon**.
- Click on the **Plane** tool from **Plane** drop-down in the **Work Features** panel of the **3D Model** tab in the **Ribbon**. You will be asked to select the geometry for references.
- Select the top point of the sketch and then select the **XZ Plane** from the **Model Browser** bar. A plane will be created passing through the selected point and parallel to the selected **XZ** plane; refer to Figure-140.

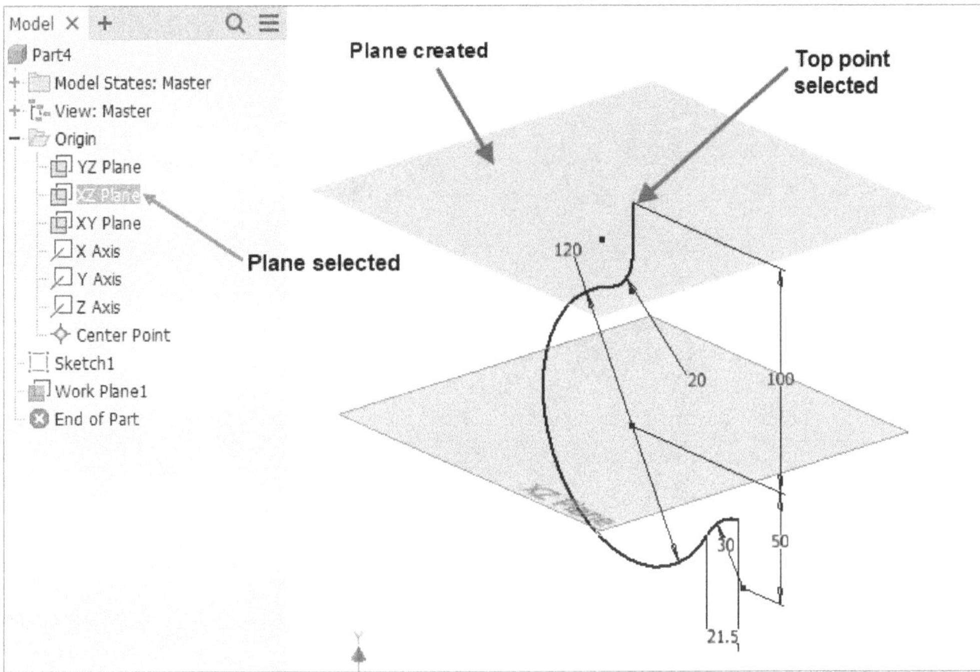

Figure-140. Plane created

- Again, click on the **Start 2D Sketch** button from **Sketch** panel in the **Ribbon**. You will be asked to select a sketching plane.
- Select the work plane recently created. The sketching environment will be displayed.
- Create the circle of diameter **25** with center at the coordinate system as shown in Figure-141.

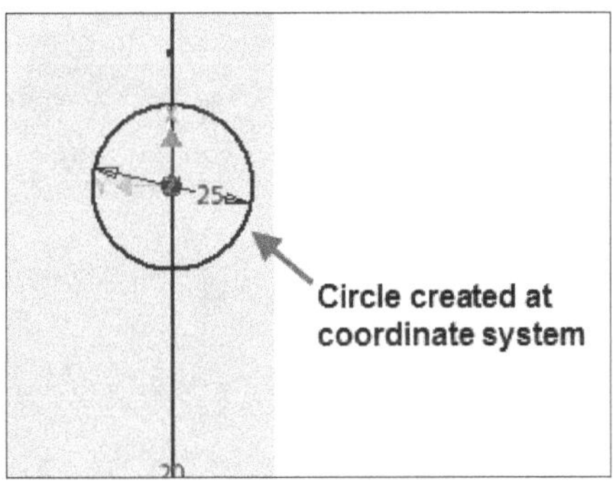

Figure-141. Circle to be created

- Click on the **Finish Sketch** button from the **Finish** drop-down to exit the sketching environment. In isometric orientation, the sketches will be displayed as shown in Figure-142.

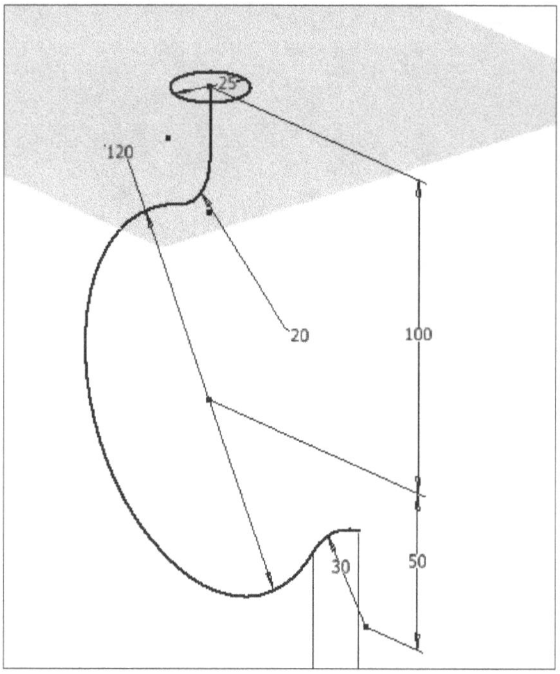

Figure-142. Sketches in isometric orientation

Creating Sweep Feature

- Click on the **Sweep** tool from **Create** panel in the **3D Model** tab of the **Ribbon**. The **Sweep** dialog box will be displayed and the profile will get selected automatically; refer to Figure-143. Also, you will be asked to select the path.

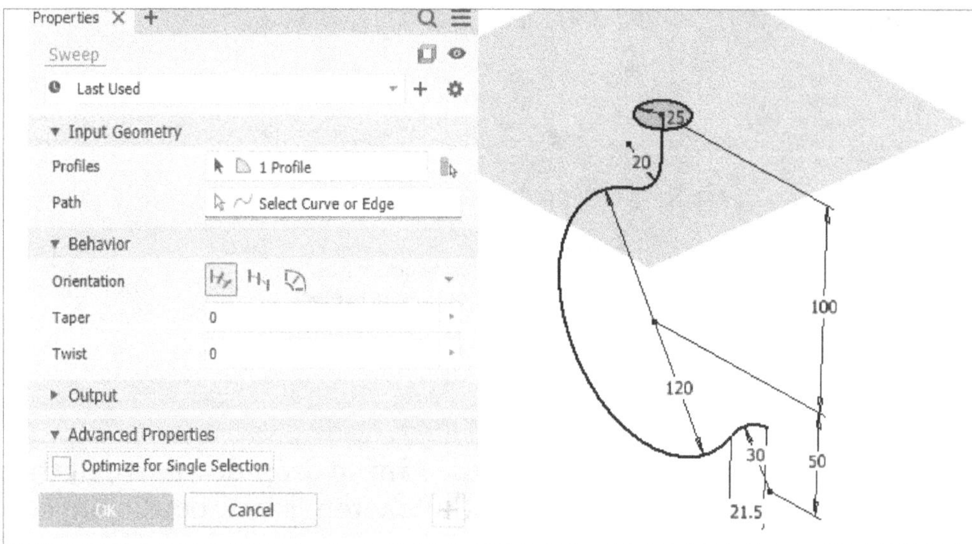

Figure-143. Sweep dialog box with profile selected

- Select the path for sweep feature. Preview of the sweep feature will be displayed; refer to Figure-144.

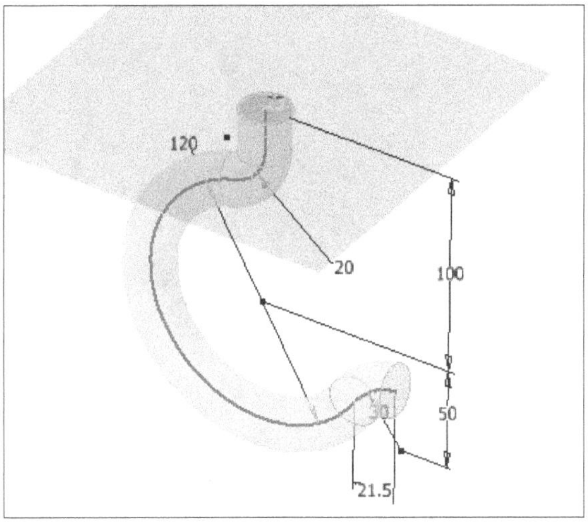

Figure-144. Preview of the sweep feature

- Click on the **OK** button from the dialog box to create the feature.

Applying Fillet

- Click on the **Fillet** tool from **Modify** panel in the **3D Model** tab of the **Ribbon**. The **Fillet** dialog box will be displayed; refer to Figure-145. Also, you will be asked to select the edge on which fillet is to be applied.

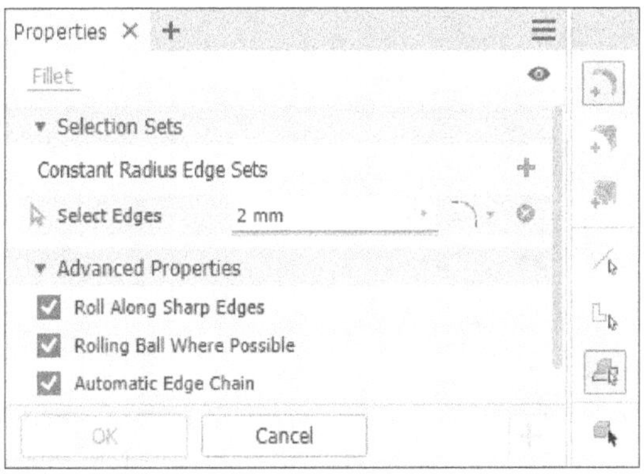

Figure-145. Fillet dialog box displayed

- Select the edge as shown in Figure-146 and specify the radius as **12.5**. Preview of the fillet will be displayed; refer to Figure-147.

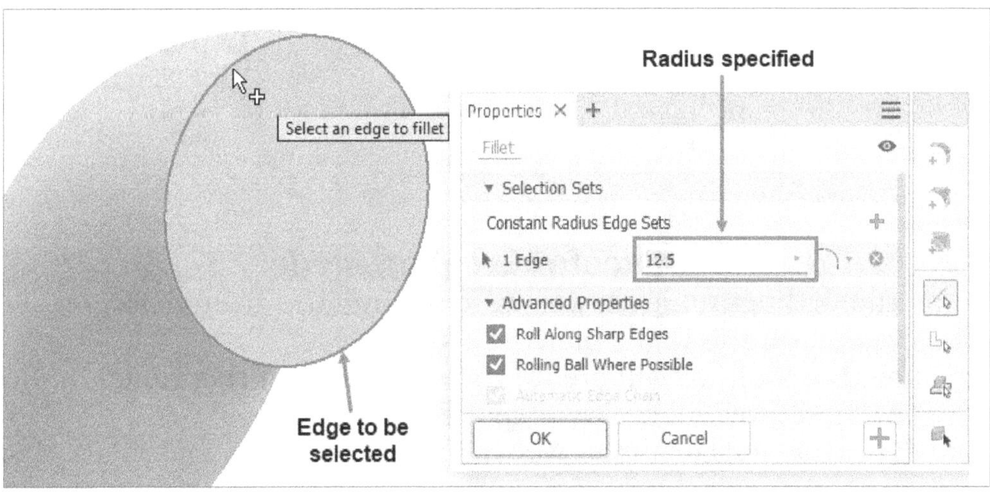

Figure-146. Edge selected for fillet

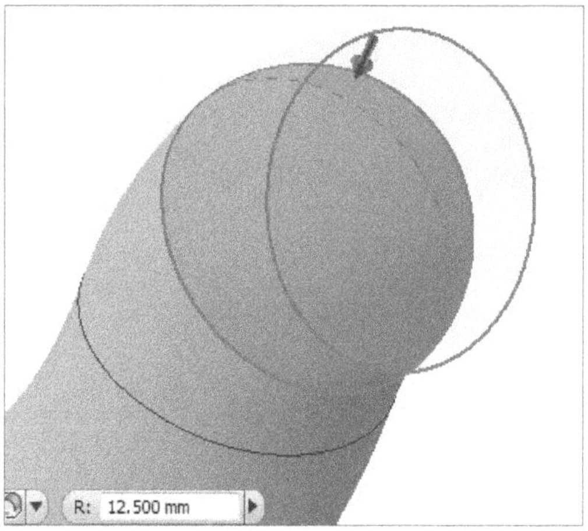

Figure-147. Preview of fillet

- Click on the **OK** button from the dialog box to create fillet.

PRACTICAL 2

Create the model using the drawings shown in Figure-148.

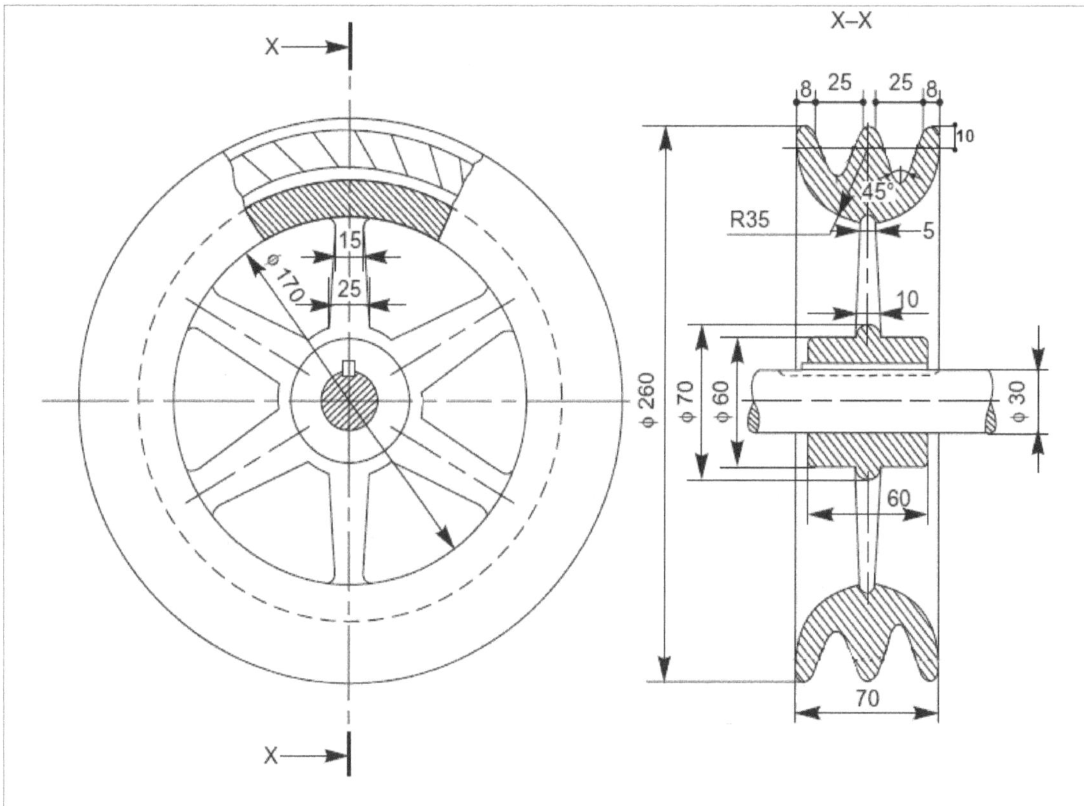

Figure-148. Rope Pulley

Strategy for Creating model

1. Looking at the orthographic views, we can find the sketch for revolve feature should be created on the Right plane (YZ Plane).
2. Using the **Revolve** tool, we will create the solid base of the model.
3. Using the **Loft** tool, we will create a spoke of the rim.
4. Using the **Circular Pattern** tool, we will create multiple instances of spokes.

Starting Part File

- Start Autodesk Inventor by double-clicking on the Autodesk Inventor Professional icon from the desktop. (If not started yet.)
- Click on the **New** button from the **Quick Access Toolbar**. The **Create New File** dialog box will be displayed.
- Double-click on **Standard(mm).ipt** icon from the **Metric** templates. The Part environment of Autodesk Inventor will be displayed.

Creating Sketch

- Click on the **Start 2D Sketch** button from **Sketch** panel in the **3D Model** tab of the **Ribbon**. You will be asked to select a sketching plane.
- Select the **YZ Plane** (Right Plane) as sketching plane. The sketching environment will become active.
- Create the sketch as shown in Figure-149.

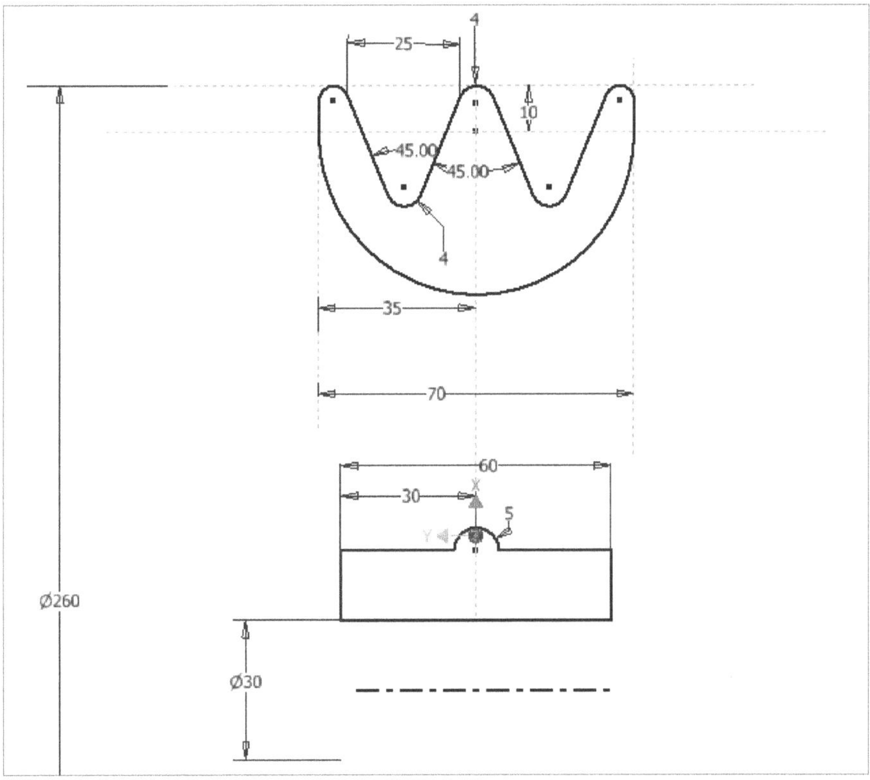

Figure-149. Sketch for practical 2

- Click on the **Finish Sketch** button from the **Finish** drop-down in the **Exit** panel of the **Ribbon**.

Creating Revolve Feature

- Click on the **Revolve** tool from **Create** panel in the **3D Model** tab of the **Ribbon**. You will be asked to select the sections to be revolved; refer to Figure-150.

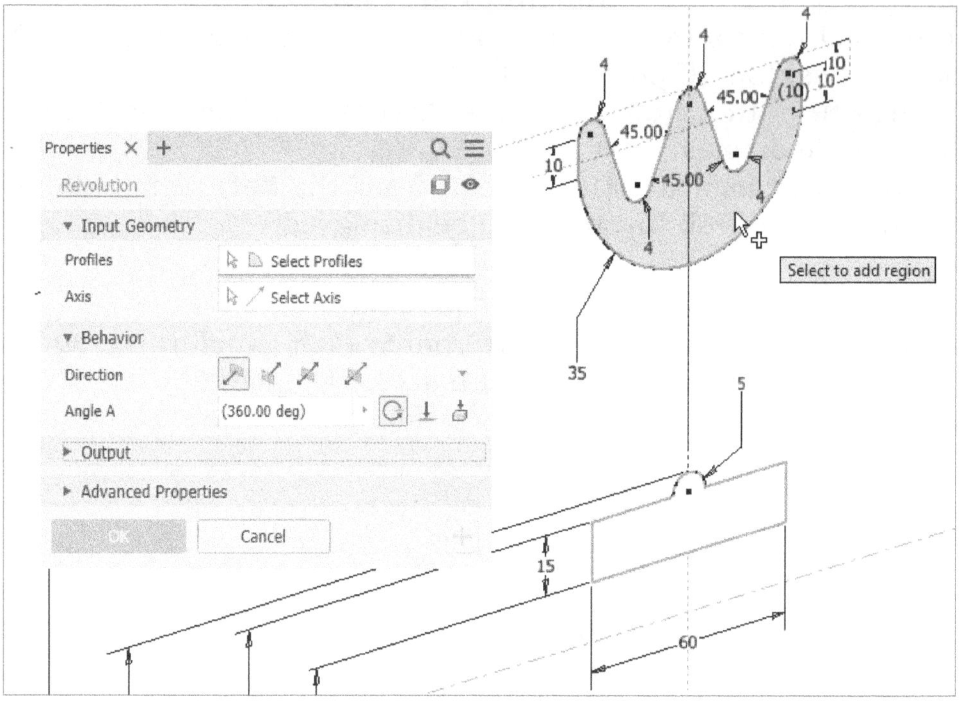

Figure-150. Selecting sections to revolve

- Select the sections as shown in Figure-151 and click on the **Select Axis** button from the **Revolve** dialog box.

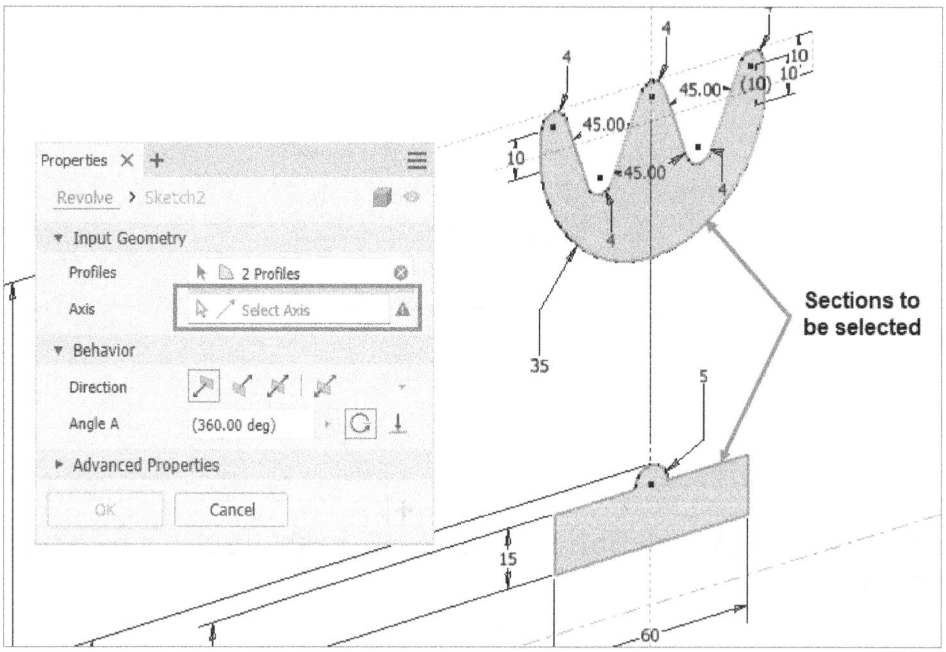

Figure-151. Sections selected

- Select the center line created in the sketch; refer to Figure-152. Preview of the revolve feature will be displayed; refer to Figure-153.

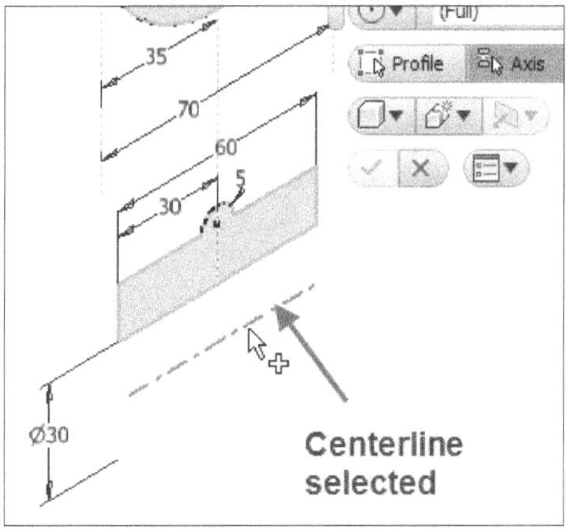

Figure-152. Centerline to select

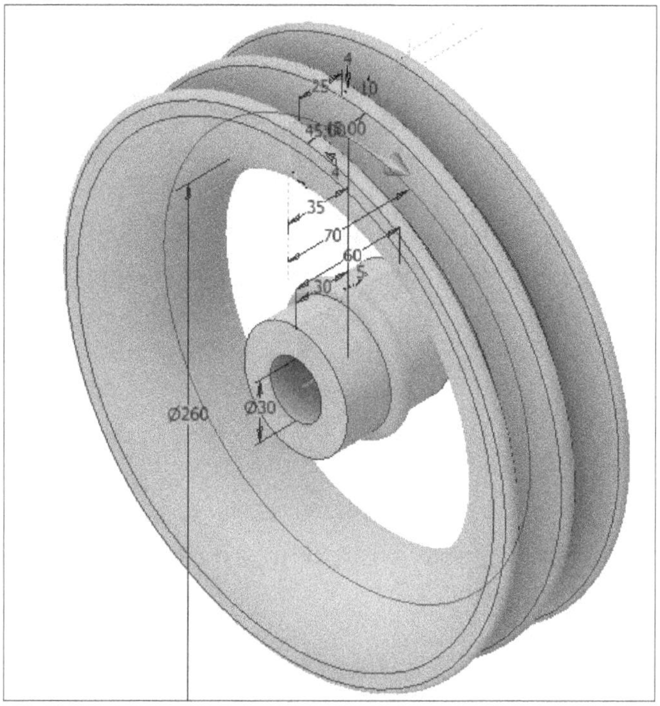
Figure-153. Preview of revolve feature

- Click on the **OK** button from the dialog box to create the feature.

Creating Planes for Sketches of Loft Feature

- Click on the **Tangent to Surface and Parallel to Plane** tool from **Plane** drop-down in the **Work Features** panel of the **Ribbon**. You will be asked to select the surface or plane.
- Select the **XZ** Plane from the **Model Browser** bar in the left of application window; refer to Figure-154. You will be asked to select the surface to be tangent.

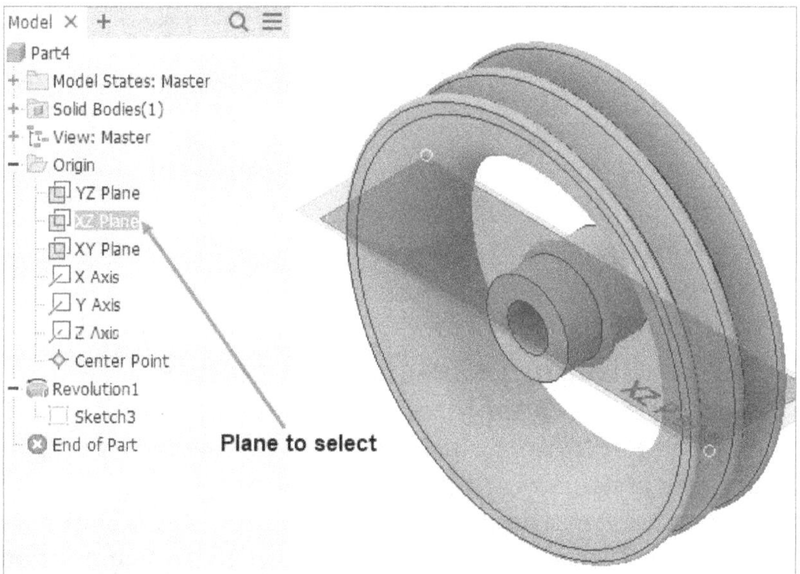

Figure-154. Selecting plane

- Select the surface as shown in Figure-155. The plane will be created.

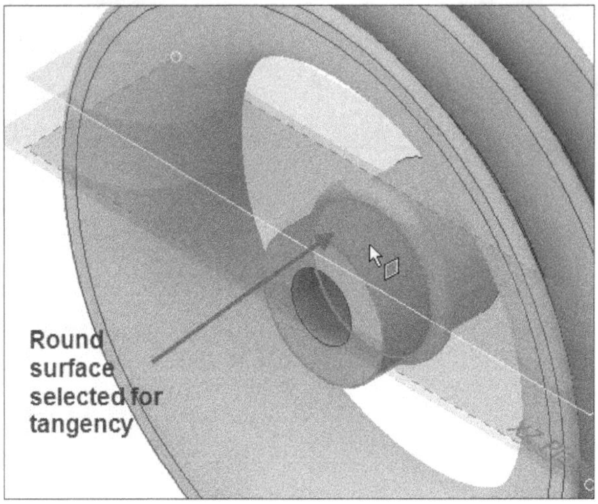

Figure-155. Surface selected for tangency

- Similarly, create a plane at an offset distance of **55** from the newly created plane; refer to Figure-156.

(If you have question like why **55** as offset distance then check the distance between these surfaces in the sketch created for revolve feature; refer to Figure-156.)

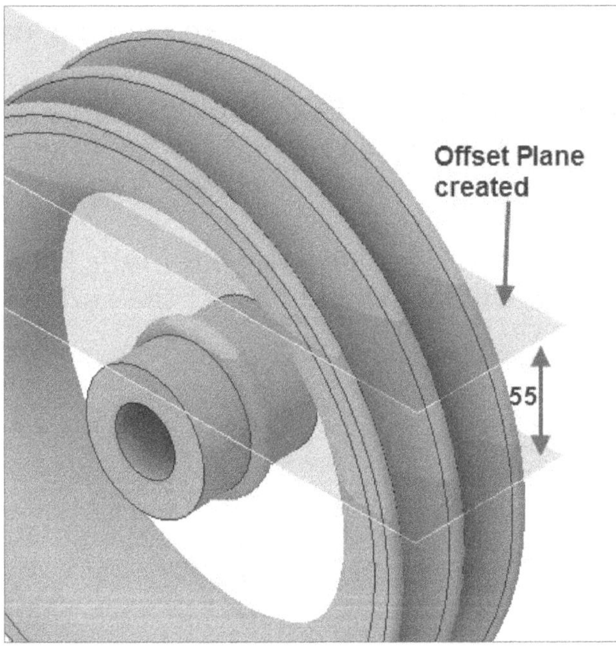

Figure-156. Offset plane created

Creating sketches on planes

- Click on the **Start 2D Sketch** tool from the **Sketch** panel in the **Ribbon**. You will be asked to select the sketching plane.
- Select the plane near centerline of revolve feature.
- Click on the **View** tab from the **Ribbon** and select the **Wireframe with Hidden Edges** option from the **Visual Style** drop-down in the **Appearance** panel of the **Ribbon**; refer to Figure-157.

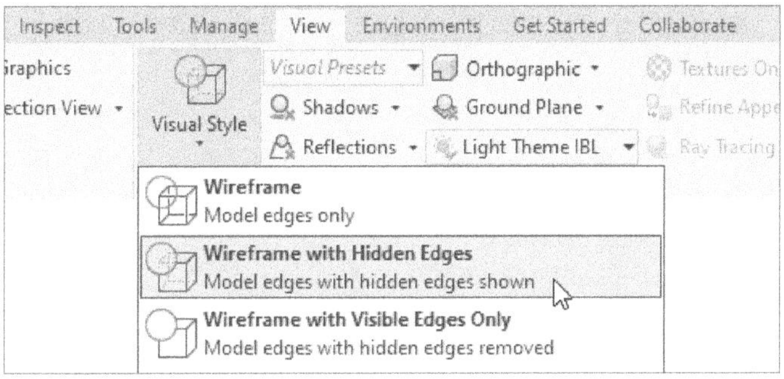

Figure-157. Visual style selected

- Create a rectangle at the center of the sketch by using the parameters as given in Figure-158.

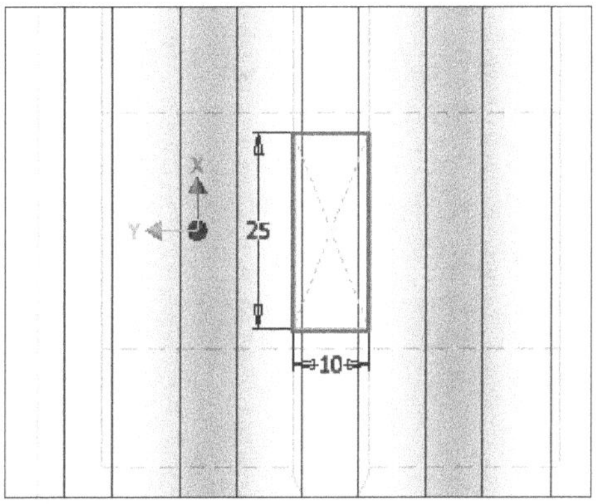

Figure-158. Rectangle created

- Click on the **Finish Sketch** button from the **Finish** drop-down in the **Exit** panel of the **Ribbon**.
- Similarly, create rectangle of size **15x5** on other plane as shown in Figure-159.

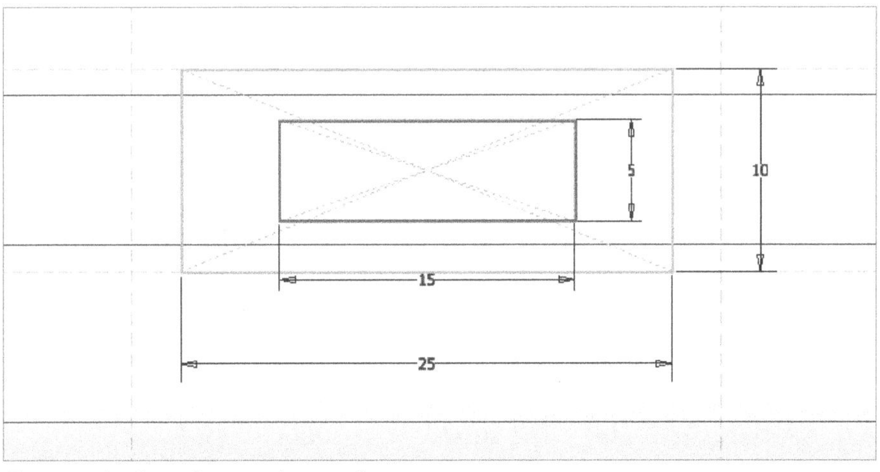

Figure-159. Second rectangle created

- Now, change the visual style to **Shaded with Edges** from the **Visual Style** drop-down in the **View** tab of **Ribbon**; refer to Figure-160.

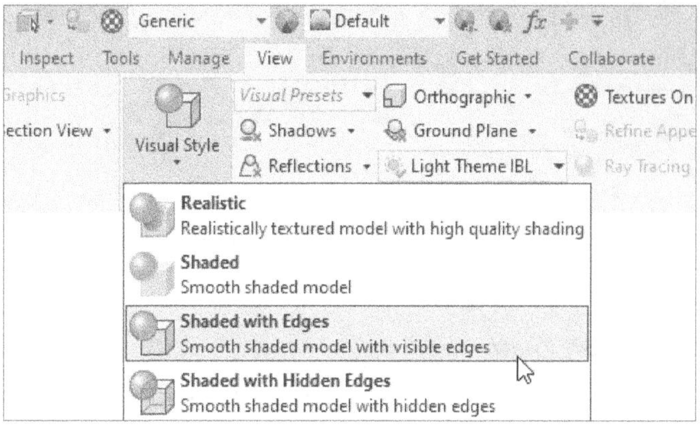

Figure-160. Selecting visual style

Creating the Loft Feature

- Click on the **Loft** tool from **Create** panel in the **3D Model** tab of the **Ribbon**. The **Loft** dialog box will be displayed and you will be asked to select the sketches.
- One by one select the two sketches created recently. Preview of the Loft feature will be displayed; refer to Figure-161.

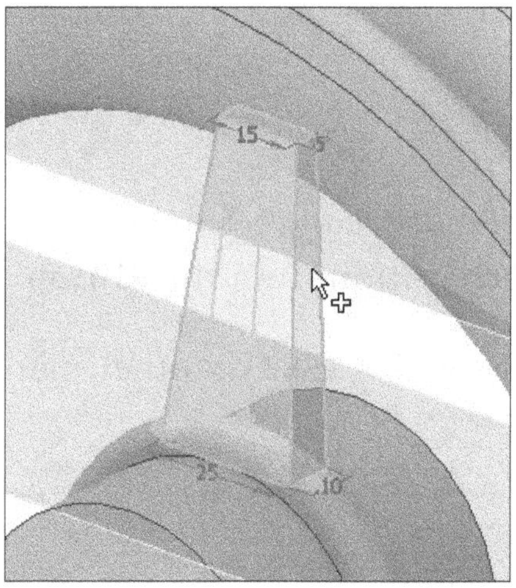

Figure-161. Preview of loft feature

- Click on the **OK** button from the dialog box to create the feature.

Creating Circular Pattern

- Click on the **Circular Pattern** tool from **Pattern** panel in the **3D Model** tab of **Ribbon**. The **Circular Pattern** dialog box will be displayed and you will be asked to select the feature to be patterned; refer to Figure-162.

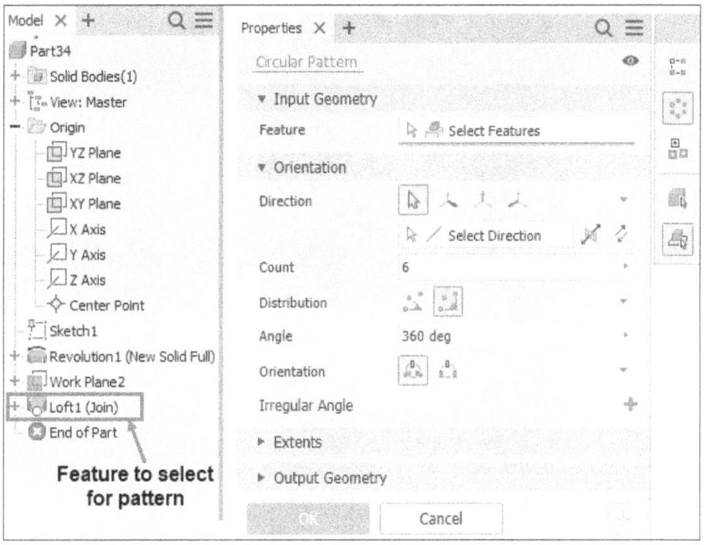

Figure-162. Circular pattern dialog box

- Select the loft feature created earlier and click on the **Rotation Axis** selection button from the dialog box; refer to Figure-163. You will be asked to select the rotation axis.

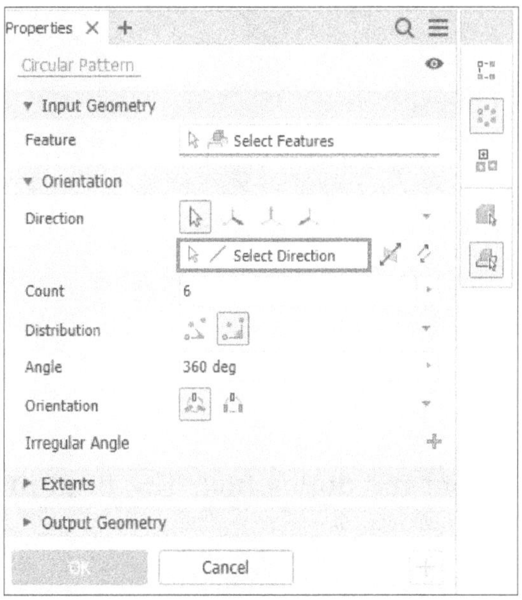

Figure-163. Rotation Axis button

- Select the circular face of the model as shown in Figure-164. Preview of the pattern will be displayed; refer to Figure-165.

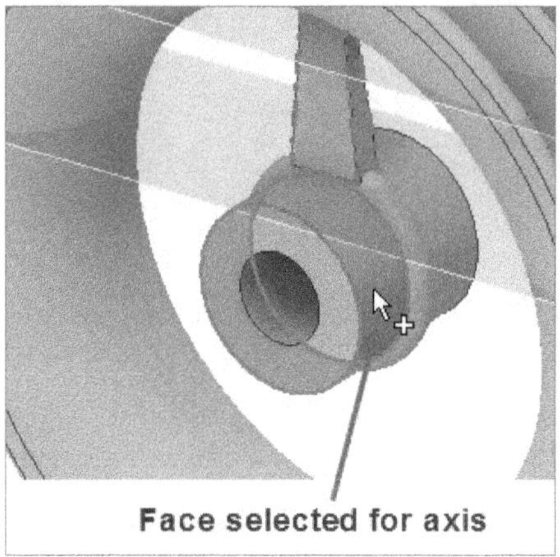

Figure-164. Selecting face for axis

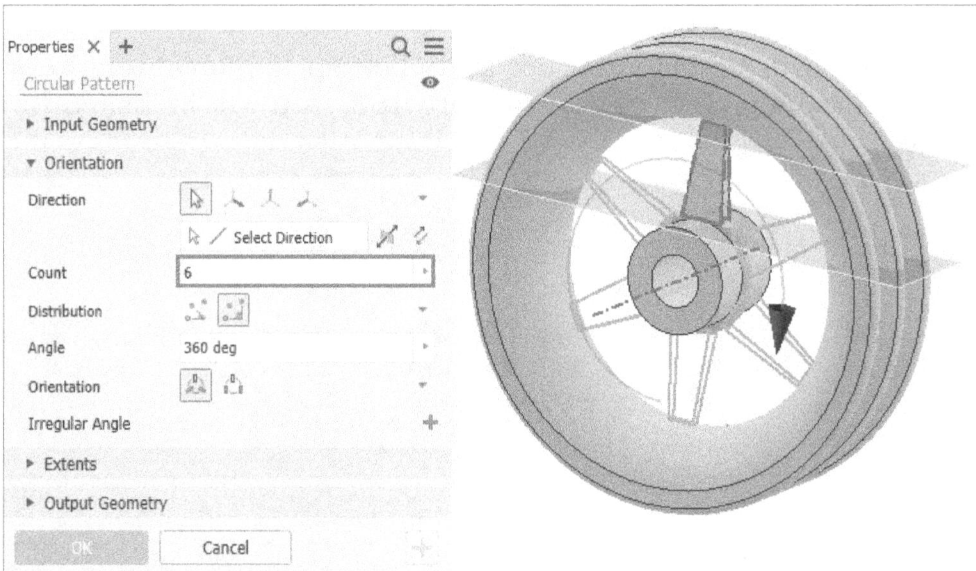

Figure-165. Preview of pattern

- Click on the **OK** button from the dialog box. The final model will be displayed.

PRACTICAL 3

Create a model as shown in Figure-166 using the dimensions given in Figure-167.

Figure-166. Model for Practical 3

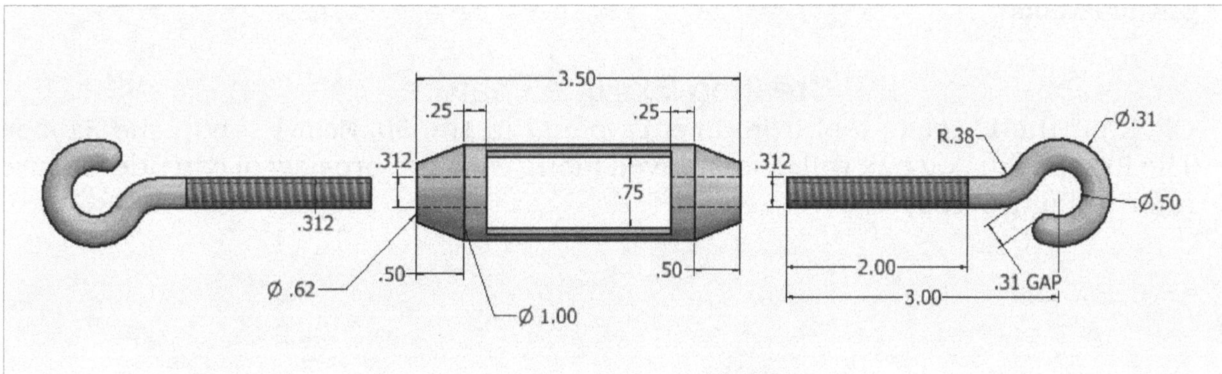

Figure-167. Practical 3 drawing view

Strategy for Creating model

1. Looking at the isometric view and orthographic views, we can find the sketch for extrude feature should be created on the Front plane (YZ Plane).
2. Using the **Extrude** and **Loft** tool, we will create the solid base of the model.
3. Using the **Plane** tools, we will create offset planes at a distance of .50mm to the vertical of loft feature created.
4. Using the **Thread** and **Sweep** tool, we will create the pulley to be joined to the base feature.

Starting Part File

- Start Autodesk Inventor by double-clicking on the Autodesk Inventor Professional icon from the desktop. (If not started yet.)
- Click on the **New** button from the **Quick Access Toolbar**. The **Create New File** dialog box will be displayed.
- Double-click on **Standard(mm).ipt** icon from the **Metric** templates. The Part environment of Autodesk Inventor will be displayed.

Creating Sketch

- Click on the **Start 2D Sketch** button from **Sketch** panel in the **3D Model** tab of the **Ribbon**. You will be asked to select a sketching plane.
- Select the **XY Plane** (Front Plane) as sketching plane. The sketching environment will become active.
- Create the sketch as shown in Figure-168.

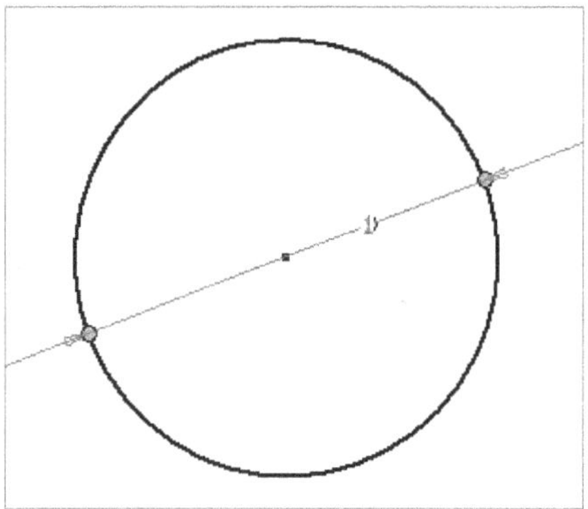

Figure-168. Sketch for Practical 3

- Click on the **Finish Sketch** button from the **Finish** drop-down in the **Exit** panel of the **Ribbon**.

Creating Extrude Feature

- Click on the **Extrude** tool from **Create** panel in the **3D Model** tab of the **Ribbon**. The **Extrude** dialog box will be displayed along with the preview of extrude feature; refer to Figure-169.

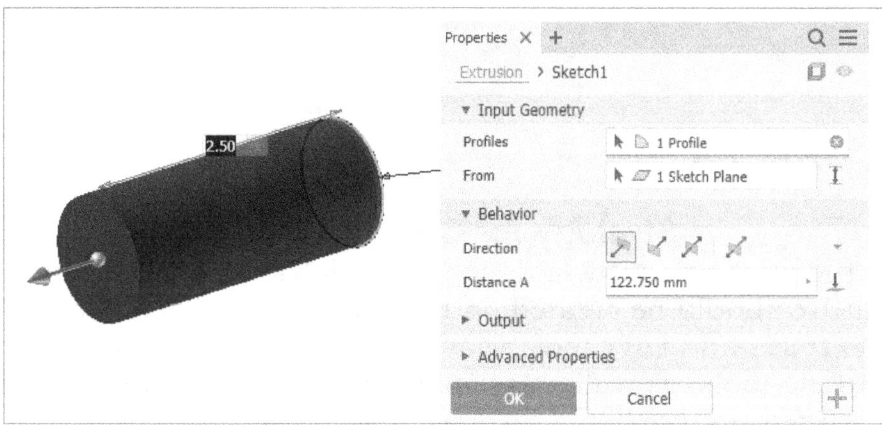

Figure-169. Preview of extrude

- Enter the extrusion value as **2.50** in the **Distace A** edit box in the dialog box.
- Click on the **OK** button from the dialog box to create the feature.

Creating planes for sketches of Loft feature

- Click on the **Offset from Plane** tool from **Plane** drop-down in the **Work Features** panel of the **Ribbon**. You will be asked to select the surface or plane.
- Select the surface as shown in Figure-170. The plane will be created.

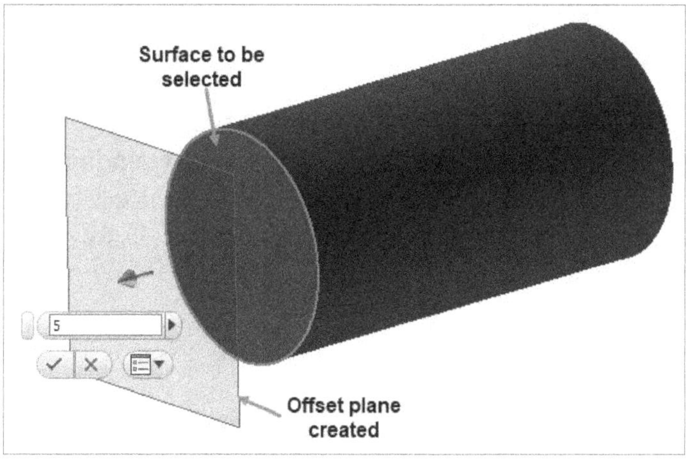

Figure-170. Offset plane creation

- Enter the Offset distance value as **.50** in the edit box displayed.
- Similarly, create another offset plane on the opposite surface of this side; refer to Figure-171.
- Click on the **OK** button to exit the tool.

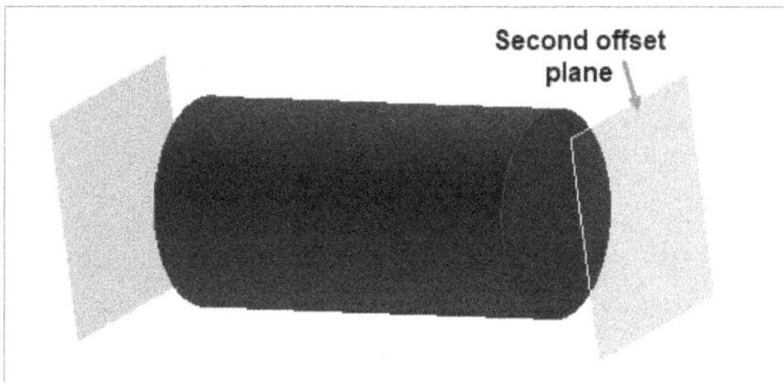

Figure-171. Second offset plane

Creating sketches on planes

- Click on the **Start 2D Sketch** tool from **Sketch** panel in the **3D Model** tab of the **Ribbon**. You will be asked to select a sketching plane.
- Select the newly created planes and create sketch on both the planes as shown in Figure-172.

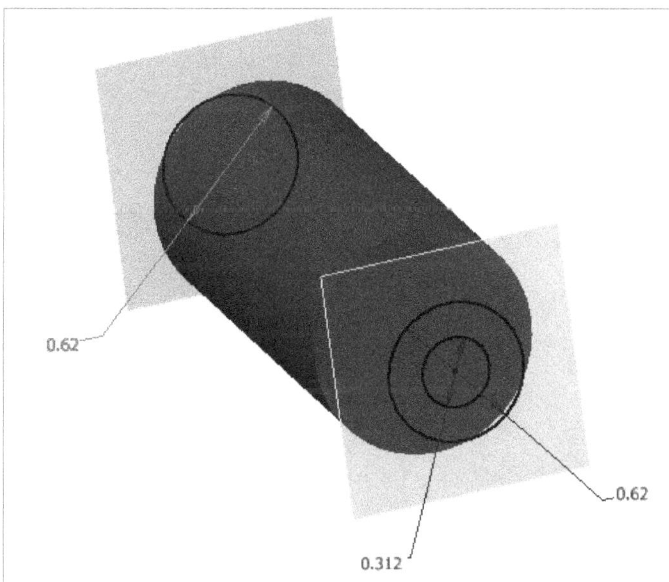

Figure-172. Sketches created for creating loft and hole

- Click on the **Finish Sketch** button from the **Finish** drop-down in the **Exit** panel of the **Ribbon**.

Creating Loft feature

- Click on the **Loft** tool from **Create** panel in the **3D Model** tab of the **Ribbon**. The **Loft** dialog box will be displayed and you will be asked to select the sketches.
- Select the newly created sketch of diameter value **0.62** and the surface on the model upto which the loft feature will be created. Preview of the loft feature will be displayed; refer to Figure-173.

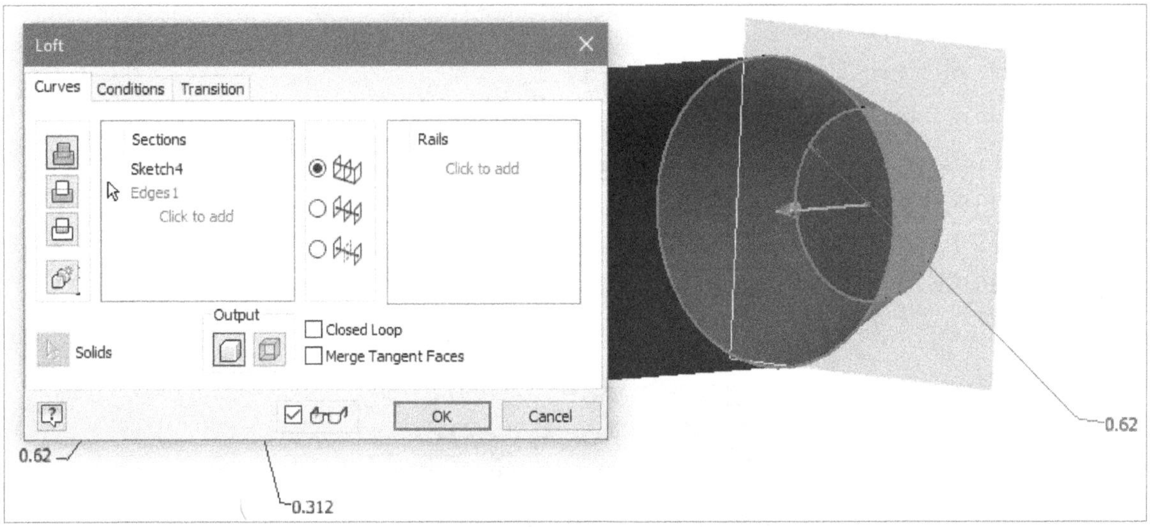

Figure-173. Preview of loft feature

- Click on the **OK** button from the dialog box to create the feature.
- Similarly, create the loft feature on the other side of the model.

Creating Extrude cut

- Click on the **Extrude** tool from **Create** panel in the **3D Model** tab of the **Ribbon**. The **Extrude** dialog box will be displayed asking you to select the profile.
- Select the sketch having diameter of **0.312** from the model and select the **Cut** option from **Boolean** drop-down in the dialog box. The preview of extrude cut will be displayed; refer to Figure-174.

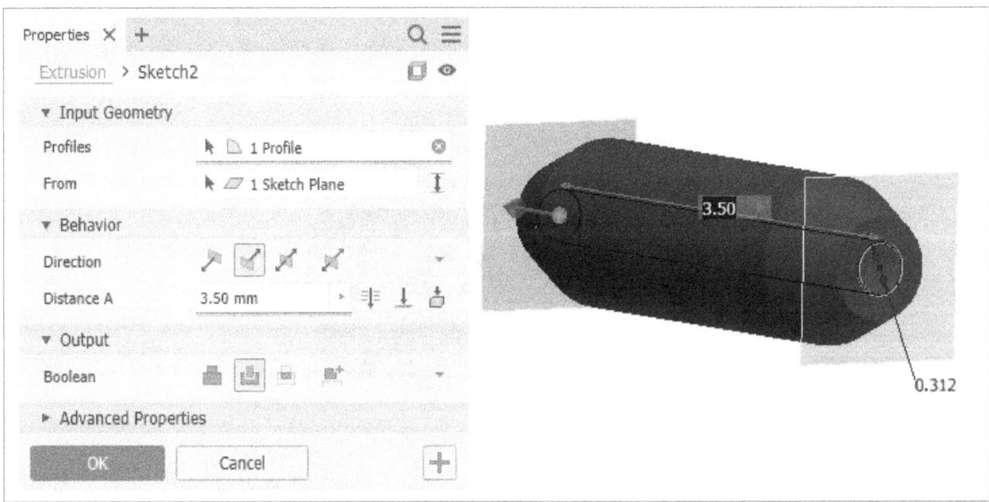

Figure-174. Preview of extrude cut

- Click on the **OK** button from the dialog box to create the feature.

Creating Offset Planes

- Click on the **Offset from Plane** tool from **Plane** drop down in the **Work Features** panel of the **Ribbon**. You will be asked to select the surface or plane.
- Select the surface from the model as shown in Figure-175. The preview of offset plane will be displayed.

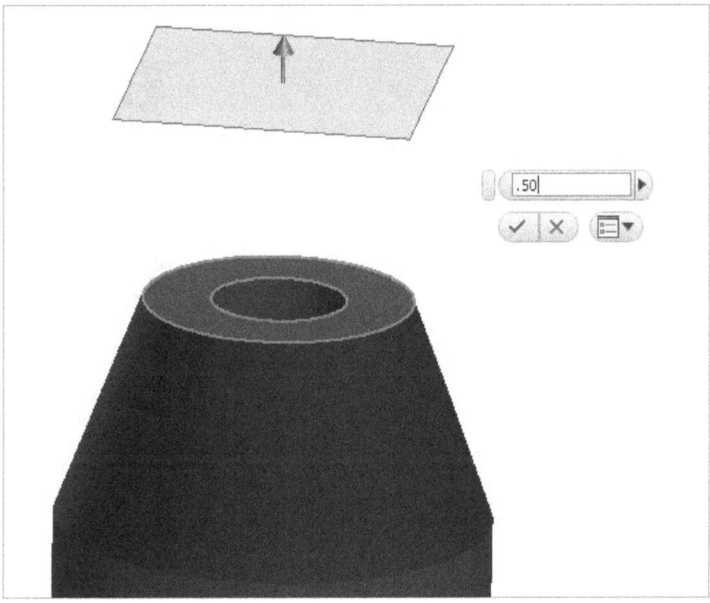

Figure-175. Offset plane created

- Enter the Offset distance value as **.50** in the edit box and click on the **OK** button to create the plane.

Creating sketch on plane

- Click on the **Start 2D Sketch** button from **Sketch** panel in the **3D Model** tab of the **Ribbon**. You will be asked to select the sketching plane.
- Select the newly created plane and create a sketch as shown in Figure-176.

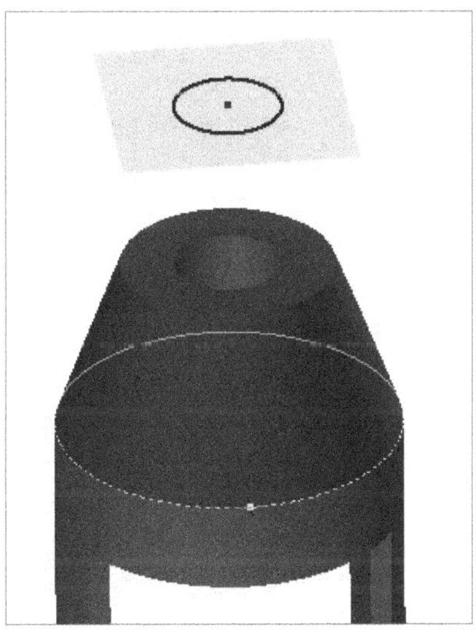

Figure-176. Sketch created on plane

- Click on the **Finish Sketch** button from the **Finish** drop-down in the **Exit** panel of the **Ribbon**.

Creating Extrude and Thread feature

- Click on the **Extrude** tool from **Create** panel in the **3D Model** tab of the **Ribbon**. The **Extrude** dialog box will be displayed along with the preview of extrusion; refer to Figure-177.

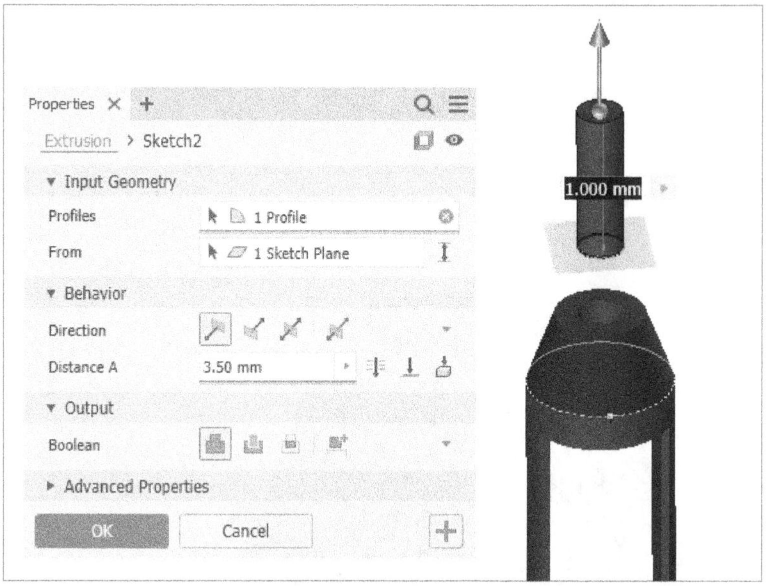

Figure-177. Preview of extrusion

- Enter the value of extrusion as **2** in the **Distance A** edit box of the dialog box.
- Click on the **OK** button from the dialog box to create the feature.
- Click on the **Thread** tool from **Modify** panel in the **3D Model** tab of the **Ribbon**. The **Thread** dialog box will be displayed and you will be asked to select the cylindrical or conical face to thread.
- Select the face to create the thread as shown in Figure-178. The preview of thread will be displayed.

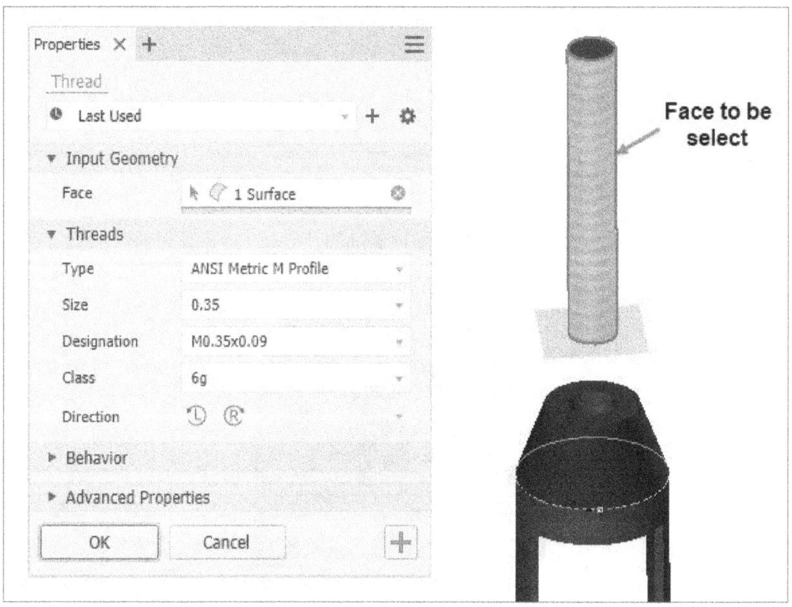

Figure-178. Preview of thread

- Click on the **OK** button from the dialog box to create the feature.

Creating sketch and plane for sweep feature

- Click on the **Start 2D Sketch** button from **Sketch** panel in the **3D Model** tab of the **Ribbon**. You will be asked to select the sketching plane.
- Click on the **XZ plane** as sketching plane. The sketching environment will become active.
- Create the sketch as shown in Figure-179.

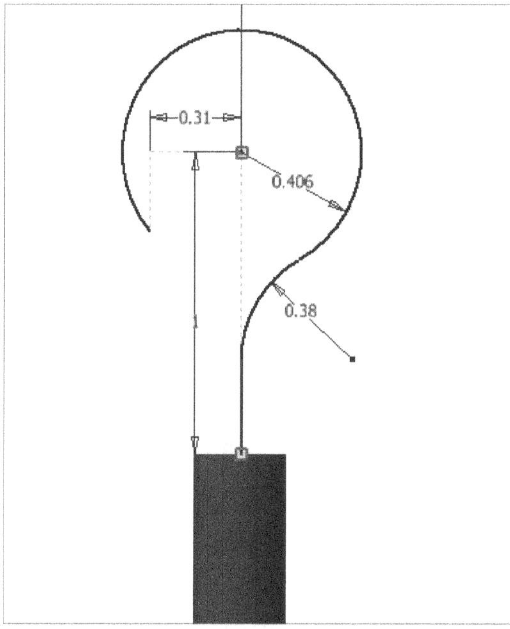

Figure-179. Creating sketch

- Click on the **Finish Sketch** button from the **Finish** drop-down in the **Exit** panel of the **Ribbon**.
- Click on the **Plane** tool from **Plane** drop-down in the **Work Features** panel from the **3D Model** tab of the **Ribbon**. You will be asked to select the geometry.
- Select the point on the newly created sketch as shown in Figure-180. The plane will be created.

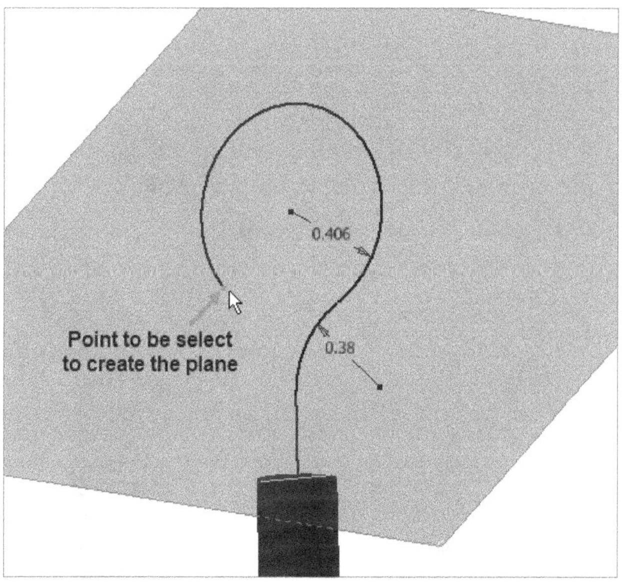

Figure-180. Plane created

- Click on the **Start 2D Sketch** button from **Sketch** panel in the **3D Model** tab of the **Ribbon**. You will be asked to select the plane.

- Select the newly created plane as sketching plane. The sketching environment will become active.
- Create the sketch as shown in Figure-181.

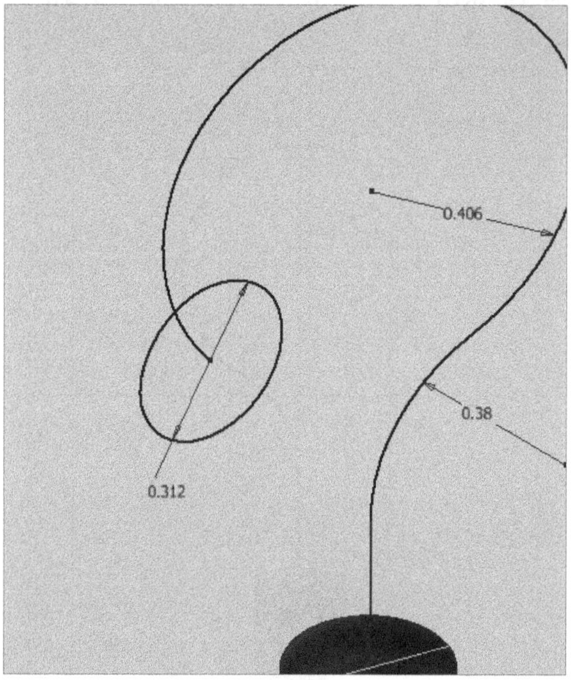

Figure-181. Sketch created

- Click on the **Finish Sketch** button from the **Finish** drop-down in the **Exit** panel of the **Ribbon**.

Creating Sweep and Fillet feature

- Click on the **Sweep** tool from **Create** panel in the **3D Model** tab of the **Ribbon**. The **Sweep** dialog box will be displayed along with the selection of profile and you will be asked to select the path for creating sweep.
- Select the curve as path for sweep as shown in Figure-182. The preview of sweep feature will be displayed.

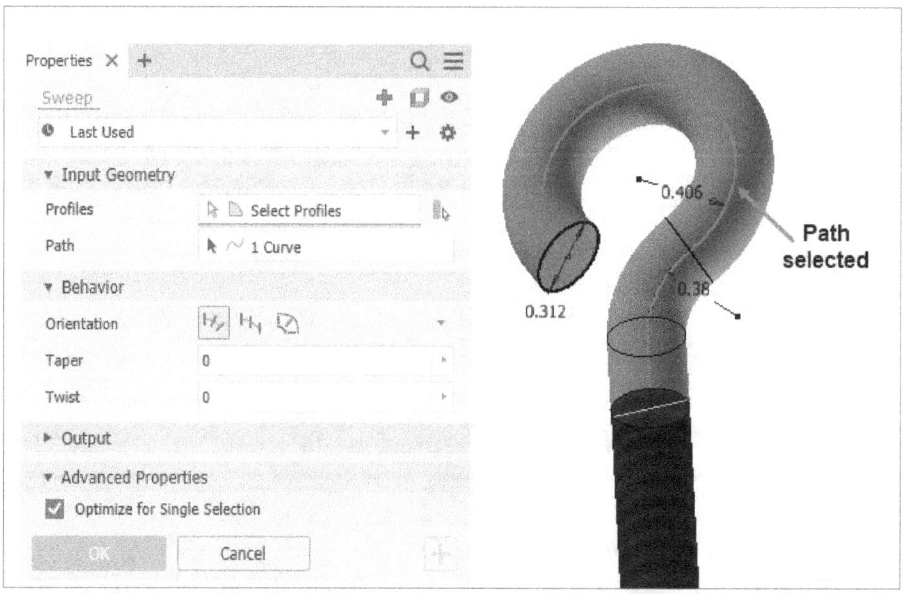

Figure-182. Sweep feature created

- Click on the **OK** button from the dialog box to create the feature.
- Click on the **Fillet** tool from **Modify** panel in the **3D Model** tab of the **Ribbon**. The **Fillet** dialog box will be displayed and you will be asked to select the edge to be fillet.
- Select the edge as shown in Figure-183. The preview of fillet will be displayed.

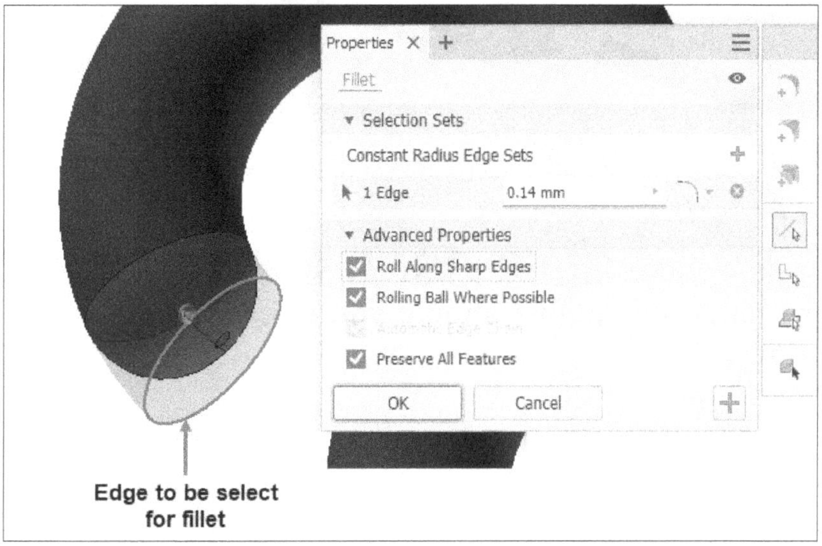

Figure-183. Preview of fillet

- Enter the radius value as **0.14** in the **Radius** edit box of the dialog box.
- Click on the **OK** button from the dialog box to create the feature.

Similarly, create the solid part as shown in Figure-184 on the opposite side of the model. The final model will be displayed; refer to Figure-185.

Figure-184. Solid part

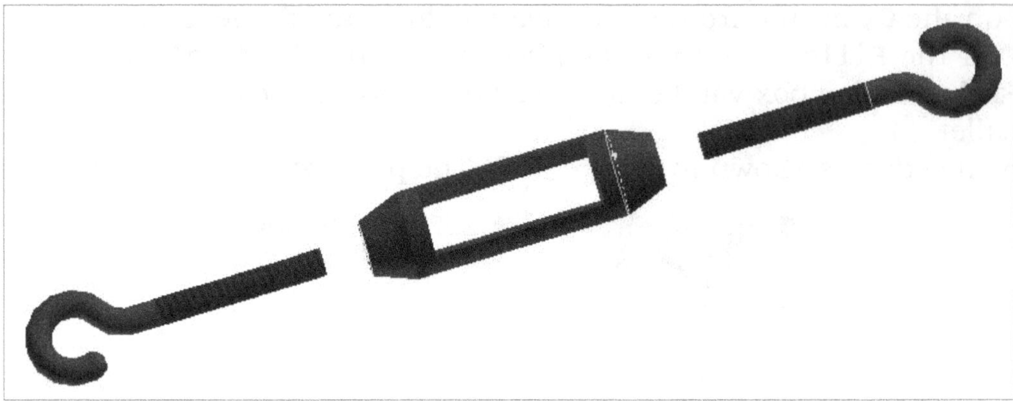

Figure-185. Final model

SELF ASSESSMENT

Q1. Which of the following options should you select to control the outer shape of the sweep feature?

a) Fixed
b) Follow Path
c) Orientation
d) Guide

Q2. In **Loft** feature, which option needs the condition that the curve to be selected for loft must be intersect with all the sections one time?

a) Rail
b) Center Line
c) Area Loft
d) None of the Above

Q3. Which of the following options can be used to create coil by specifying pitch and number of revolution?

a) Revolution and Height
b) Pitch and Height
c) Spiral
d) None of the Above

Q4. By selecting which tool, you can imprint a profile on the selected face?

a) Decal
b) Rib
c) Emboss
d) All of the above

Q5. Which of the following types of hole allow you to choose standard holes from the library?

a) Simple Hole
b) Clearance Hole
c) Tapped Hole
d) Taper Tapped Hole

Q6. Which of the following tools is used to divide the selected entity with the help of trimming reference?

a) Shell
b) Draft
c) Offset
d) Split

Q7. The **Chamfer** tool is used to chisel the sharp points of the model. (True/False)

Q8. Setbacks are created at the corners where three fillets coincide at a point. (True/False)

Q9. The Coil tool is used to create coil with the help of a profile and an axis. (True/False)

Q10. The .... tool is used to insert an image on face of the model.

Q11. The .... tool is used to apply radius at sharp edges.

Q12. The .... tool is used to flattened the faces that cannot be flattened with the Unfold or sheetmetal flat pattern command.

REVIEW QUESTIONS

Q1. What is the primary use of the Sweep tool?

A. To create holes in solid models
B. To create solid/surface features by sweeping a sketch along a path
C. To trim parts of solid models
D. To extrude shapes perpendicular to a surface

Q2. What must you create before using the Sweep tool?

A. A guide and a rail
B. A section and a loft
C. A closed loop sketch and a path
D. A 3D sketch

Q3. Which of the following orientation options is NOT available in the Sweep tool?

A. Follow Path
B. Fixed
C. Guide
D. Twist Only

Q4. When using the "Follow Path" orientation, what can you additionally specify?

A. Twist angle only
B. Taper angle only
C. Both Taper and Twist angles
D. Scale factor

Q5. Which orientation in Sweep allows profile shape/size to change along the path?

A. Follow Path
B. Guide
C. Fixed
D. Tapered

Q6. What additional sketch is required when using the "Guide" option in Sweep?

A. Center line
B. Rail
C. Guide rail
D. Axis

Q7. In the "Guide" sweep option, what does the "XY Scaling" control?

A. Scaling in X direction only
B. Scaling in both X and Y directions
C. Rotation of profile
D. Scaling in Z direction only

Q8. What is the Loft tool used for?

A. Extruding a profile
B. Sweeping a profile along a curve
C. Creating solid/surface features between two or more sketches
D. Trimming and filleting solids

Q9. What must you create before using the Loft tool?

A. A sweep profile
B. Sketches on planes parallel to each other
C. A path and a guide
D. Only one sketch

Q10. Which Loft option allows the use of a rail curve?

A. Area Loft
B. Fixed Loft
C. Center Line Loft
D. Rail Loft

Q11. What condition must a rail curve satisfy for Loft with Rail option?

A. Be perpendicular to all sketches
B. Intersect with all profile sketches once
C. Lie in a single plane
D. Have the same area as profiles

Q12. What does the Area Loft option allow you to specify?

A. Twist angle
B. Surface curvature
C. Area of sections
D. Material type

Q13. How can you change the area value in Area Loft?

A. Use the Fixed option
B. Use Section Dimensions dialog box
C. Use twist angle
D. Use taper angle

Q14. What is the function of the Conditions tab in Loft dialog box?

A. Specify material
B. Specify loft curvature
C. Specify tangency conditions at start and end
D. Specify sketch alignment

Q15. What must be unchecked to manually control transition point positions in Loft?

A. Tangency setting
B. Twist angle
C. Automatic Mapping
D. Path selection

Q16. Which tool is used to create a coil using a profile and an axis?

A. Emboss
B. Coil
C. Rib
D. Decal

Q17. In the Coil tool, which method allows you to specify pitch and number of revolutions?

A. Revolution and Height
B. Pitch and Height
C. Pitch and Revolution
D. Spiral

Q18. What is the purpose of the Emboss tool?

A. To create a coil
B. To emboss or engrave a profile on a selected face
C. To create thin wall support
D. To apply an image to a model face

Q19. Which tool is used to derive a part using a selected Autodesk Inventor Part or Assembly model file?

A. Coil
B. Emboss
C. Derive
D. Rib

Q20. What is the primary function of the Rib tool?

A. To create a coil
B. To emboss a profile
C. To create thin wall support in the structure
D. To apply an image to a model face

Q21. Which option in the Rib tool dialog box is used to create a rib feature perpendicular to the sketch plane?

A. Parallel to Sketch Plane
B. Normal to Sketch Plane
C. Direction 1
D. Direction 2

Q22. What is the purpose of the Decal tool?

A. To create a coil
B. To emboss a profile
C. To apply an image to the face of the model
D. To create thin wall support

Q23. In the Decal tool, what does selecting the "Wrap to Face" checkbox do?

A. Applies the decal only to flat surfaces
B. Wraps the image around the selected face
C. Changes the color of the decal
D. Deletes the decal

Q24. What is the function of the Import tool in Autodesk Inventor?

A. To create a coil
B. To emboss a profile
C. To import foreign CAD files
D. To apply an image to a model face

Q25. In the Import dialog box, which option allows the imported feature to be updated when the base model is changed in other software?

A. Convert Model
B. Reference Model
C. Merge Model
D. Update Model

Q26. What is the purpose of the Unwrap tool?

A. To create a coil
B. To emboss a profile
C. To unwrap faces that cannot be flattened with the Unfold command
D. To apply an image to a model face

Q27. In the Unwrap tool, what does selecting the "Auto Face Chain" checkbox do?

A. Selects multiple faces with one pick
B. Changes the color of the unwrapped surface
C. Deletes the unwrapped surface
D. Applies a decal to the unwrapped surface

Q28. Which tool is used to create a hole in the solid model?

A. Coil
B. Emboss
C. Hole
D. Rib

Q29. In the Hole tool, what does the "Allow Center Point Creation" button do when turned ON?

A. Prevents adding center points
B. Allows adding center points randomly on the part face
C. Deletes existing center points
D. Locks the center points

Q30. Which hole type allows you to choose standard holes from the library in the Hole tool?

A. Simple Hole
B. Clearance Hole
C. Tapped Hole
D. Taper Tapped Hole

Q31. What is the primary function of the Fillet tool in 3D modeling?

A. To create holes in the model
B. To apply radius at sharp edges
C. To extrude faces
D. To create threads on shafts

Q32. Which button should be selected to add a constant radius edge set in the Fillet dialog box?

A. Add variable radius fillet
B. Add constant radius edge set
C. Add corner setback
D. Add shell set

Q33. In the Fillet tool, which selection priority allows selecting a loop of edges?

A. Edges
B. Edge Loops
C. Features
D. Faces

Q34. What are the three types of fillet available in the drop-down next to the radius value?

A. Tangent, Smooth (G2), Inverted
B. Linear, Circular, Elliptical
C. Sharp, Rounded, Flat
D. None of the above

Q35. How can you create fillets on all edges of a solid?

A. By selecting each edge individually
B. By using the Edge Loops option
C. By selecting the All Rounds option from the Solid drop-down
D. By applying chamfer to all edges

Q36. What is the purpose of the Add variable radius fillet button?

A. To create fillets with a constant radius
B. To apply chamfer to edges
C. To create fillets with varying radius along an edge
D. To remove material from the model

Q37. What is a setback in the context of fillets?

A. A type of chamfer
B. A method to apply threads
C. A feature created at corners where three fillets coincide
D. A tool to combine two bodies

Q38. Which tool allows creating fillets by selecting faces instead of edges?

A. Edge Fillet
B. Face Fillet
C. Full Round Fillet
D. Chamfer

Q39. What is the function of the Full Round Fillet tool?

A. To create a fillet between two faces
B. To apply a fillet around a hole
C. To create a fillet between three faces forming a full round
D. To chamfer sharp edges

Q40. Which tool is used to chisel the sharp edges of the model?

A. Fillet
B. Chamfer
C. Shell
D. Draft

Q41. In the Chamfer tool, what does the Distance and Angle option allow?

A. Specifying two distances in different directions
B. Specifying distance and angle for chamfer
C. Applying chamfer to all edges
D. Creating variable radius fillets

Q42. How can you create a partial chamfer along an existing chamfer edge?

A. By selecting the Partial tab in the Chamfer dialog box
B. By using the Fillet tool
C. By applying a setback
D. By using the Shell tool

Q43. What is the primary function of the Shell tool?

A. To apply threads
B. To create fillets
C. To scoop out material from the solid base
D. To combine two bodies

Q44. In the Shell tool, what does the Allow Approximation option do?

A. Prevents any deviation from fixed thickness
B. Allows deviation from fixed thickness where necessary
C. Applies chamfer to edges
D. Creates threads on faces

Q45. What is the purpose of the Draft tool?

A. To create holes in the model
B. To apply taper to selected face
C. To combine two bodies
D. To apply fillets to edges

Q46. What does the Fixed Plane option in the Draft tool allow?

A. Applying draft using a fixed reference plane
B. Creating variable radius fillets
C. Applying chamfer to edges
D. Removing material from the model

Q47. How does the Parting Line option in the Draft tool differ from Fixed Plane?

A. It uses a fixed plane as reference
B. It allows selecting a curve dividing the face to create different drafts
C. It applies chamfer instead of draft
D. It combines two bodies

Q48. What is the primary function of the Thread tool?

A. To create holes in the model
B. To apply fillets to edges
C. To create threads in selected hole or over the selected shaft
D. To combine two bodies

Q49. In the Thread tool, how can you specify the depth of the thread?

A. By selecting the face
B. By entering the value in the Depth edit box
C. By choosing the thread type
D. By selecting the size of the thread

Q50. What is the function of the Combine tool?

A. To apply fillets
B. To create threads
C. To perform Boolean operations on solids
D. To apply chamfer to edges

Q51. What is the primary function of the Thicken/Offset tool?

A. To change the color of a solid
B. To modify imported models
C. To thicken or offset solids/surfaces
D. To measure distances in a sketch

Q52. Which area in the Thicken dialog box allows you to choose Inside, Outside, or Center options?

A. Output rollout
B. Behavior rollout
C. Input Geometry rollout
D. Advanced Properties rollout

Q53. What happens when the "Automatic Blending" checkbox is selected in the Behavior rollout?

A. Tangential faces are removed
B. The Output rollout becomes unavailable
C. The dialog box closes automatically
D. The face color changes

Q54. Which Boolean operation will remove the volume created by the Thicken feature from the solid part?

A. Join
B. Cut
C. Intersect
D. New Solid

Q55. What is the function of the "Allow Approximation" checkbox?

A. It prevents changes in solid
B. It creates surface offset
C. It allows deviation from specified thickness
D. It splits surfaces

Q56. What does the "Never too thick" option ensure in the Advanced Properties rollout?

A. Minimum distance is preserved
B. Deviation falls below specified distance
C. Equal distribution of deviation
D. Maximum color intensity

Q57. Which option in the Tolerance drop-down computes approximation using minimal compute time?

A. Mean
B. Optimized
C. Specified
D. Center

Q58. What tool is used to divide a face or body using a sketch, plane, or surface?

A. Thicken
B. Split
C. Finish
D. Delete Face

Q59. What does selecting the "All Faces" checkbox in the Split tool do?

A. Deletes all faces
B. Splits all faces of the selected body
C. Adds surface texture
D. Merges faces

Q60. What happens when the "Flip Side" option is selected in the Split dialog box?

A. Both sides are kept
B. The default side is kept
C. Opposite side is kept
D. Nothing changes

Q61. What is the main purpose of the Delete Face tool?

A. To color the face
B. To thicken the body
C. To convert a part body into a surface body
D. To export geometry

Q62. What does the "Heal Remaining Faces" checkbox do in the Delete Face tool?

A. Deletes the whole part
B. Extends adjacent faces to close gaps
C. Adds texture to the face
D. Selects all faces

Q63. What is the main use of the Mark tool?

A. Painting the model
B. Creating appearance finishes
C. Preparing text for processes like laser marking
D. Dividing solids

Q64. What does the "Mark Through" option do in the Mark tool?

A. Applies marks to a single face only
B. Converts text characters into a stroke path
C. Adds 3D appearance
D. Splits the geometry

Q65. In the Mark tool, what does the "Wrap" method do?

A. Projects sketch onto a flat face
B. Wraps sketch around a cylindrical face
C. Splits the part
D. Thins the surface

Q66. What is the function of the Finish tool?

A. To split parts
B. To thicken solids
C. To apply texture and material appearances
D. To delete sketches

Q67. Which finish option is used to apply heat treatment to selected faces?

A. Appearance
B. Material Coating
C. Heat Treatment
D. Surface Texture

Q68. What does the "Export all Finish Parameters" checkbox do?

A. Hides the material preview
B. Exports the entire part model
C. Exports all selected finish properties
D. Deletes finish detail

For students notes

Chapter 6

Advanced Modeling Tools and Practical

Topics Covered

The major topics covered in this chapter are:

- ***Direct Editing***
- ***Bend Tool***
- ***Practical 1 to 5***
- ***Practice***

INTRODUCTION

In this chapter, we will discuss the remaining tools in Advanced Solid Modeling. We will also practice on the tools and techniques discussed in previous chapters.

DIRECT EDIT TOOL

The **Direct Edit** tool is used to edit imported parametric features of the model by using simple drag and drop operations. The tool is available in the **Modify** panel of the **3D Model** tab in the **Ribbon**. The procedure to use this tool is given next.

- Make sure you have an imported model or solid model already created in the viewport.
- Click on the **Direct Edit** tool from **Modify** panel in the **3D Model** tab of the **Ribbon**. The **Direct Editing** toolbar will be displayed; refer to Figure-1.

Figure-1. Direct Editing toolbar

There are five options in toolbar to perform direct editing; Move, Size, Scale, Rotate, and Delete. We will discuss each of the option one by one.

Moving Faces by Direct Editing

- Click on the **Move** button from the toolbar. The toolbar will be displayed as shown in Figure-2.

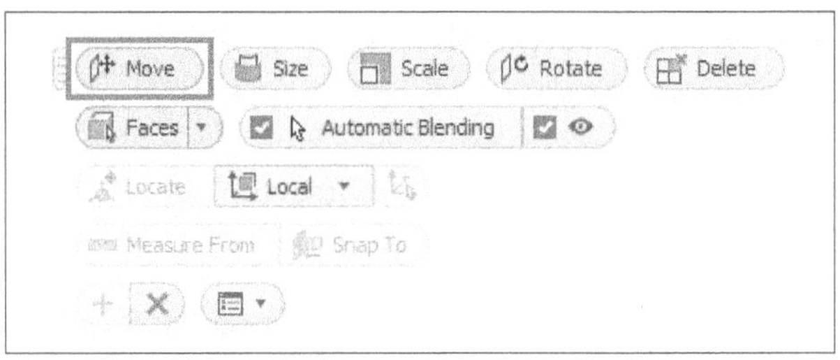

Figure-2. Move by direct editing

- Click on the face that you want to move; refer to Figure-3.
- Select the **Preview** check box to display the preview of face while modifying by direct editing.

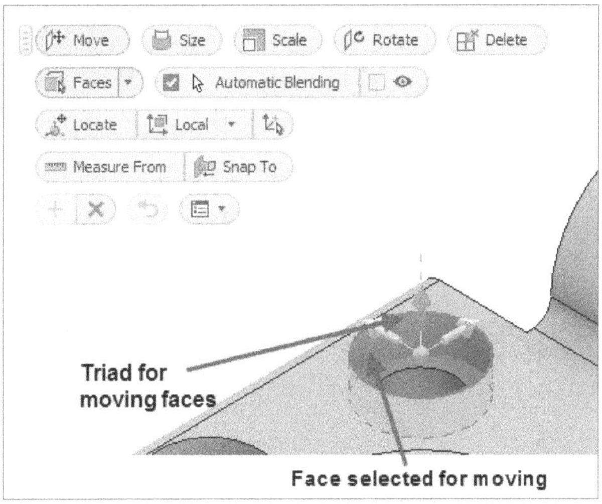

Figure-3. Selecting face for moving

- If you want to select multiple faces then you can do so by holding the **CTRL** key while selecting faces. If you want to remove a face from selection then you can do so by holding the **SHIFT** key while selecting the face.
- To change the location of triad, click on the **Locate** button from the toolbar and click at desired location to place the triad.
- By default, the triad is oriented as per the selected faces but if you want to orient the triad as per the World Coordinate system then you can do so by selecting the **World** option from the drop-down as shown in Figure-4.

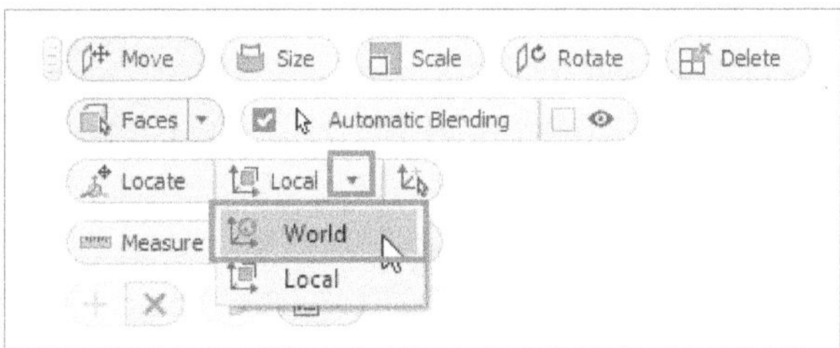

Figure-4. World orientation of triad

- Click on the arrow in desired direction and drag the arrow to move the selected face/faces; refer to Figure-5.

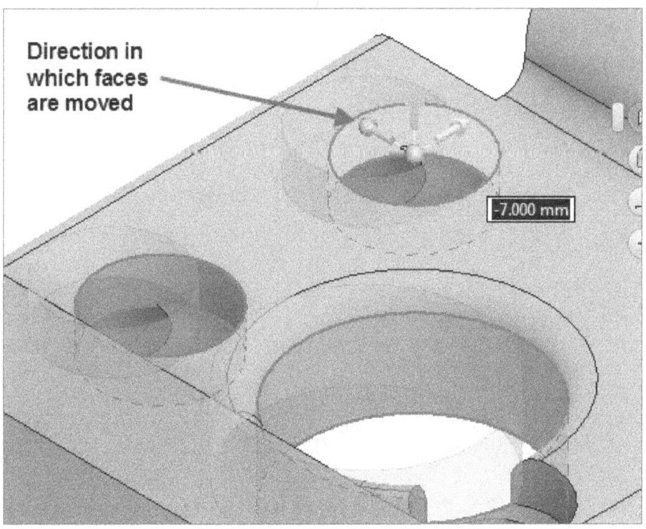

Figure-5. Direction arrow used to move faces

- You can also specify desired value of distance to be moved in the edit box displayed on dragging arrow.
- By default, the distance value is measured from the center of first selected face but you can select other entities by clicking on the **Measure From** button in the toolbar and selecting desired entity.
- You can select the target position for movement by clicking on the **Snap To** button in the toolbar and selecting the point to which you want to move the selected faces.
- Click on the **+** button from the toolbar to apply the change.

Changing Size by Direct Editing

- Click on the **Size** button from the toolbar. The toolbar will be displayed as shown in Figure-6.

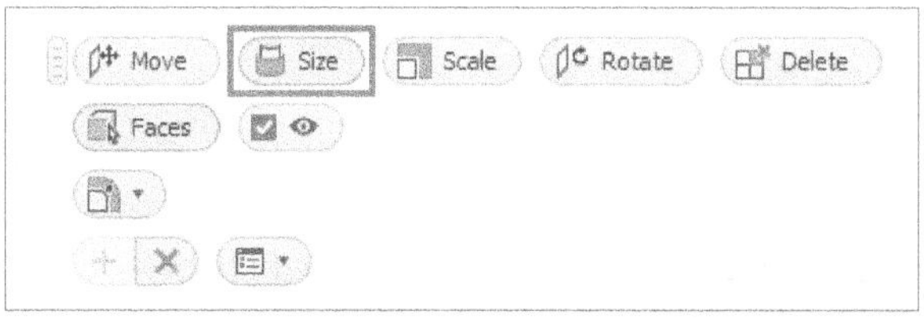

Figure-6. Size button in Direct Editing toolbar

- Select the face/faces for changing size. Triad to change the size will be displayed.
- Click on desired option from the dimension type drop-down; refer to Figure-7.

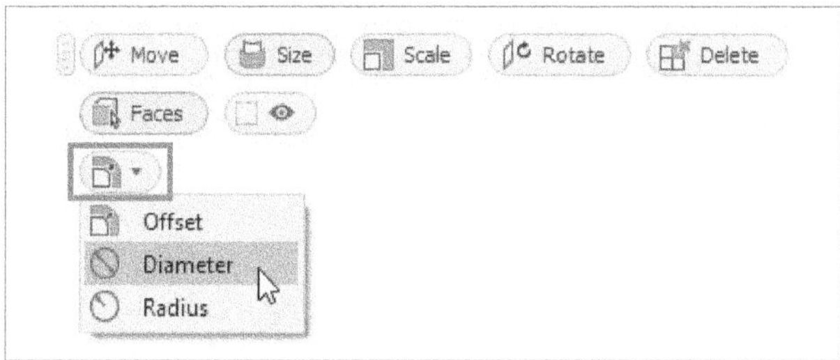

Figure-7. Options for changing size

- Specify desired value in the edit box or drag the handle in desired direction to change the value.
- Click on the **+** button to apply change.

Scaling Model by Direct Editing

- Click on the **Scale** button from the **Direct Editing** toolbar. The toolbar will be displayed as shown in Figure-8.

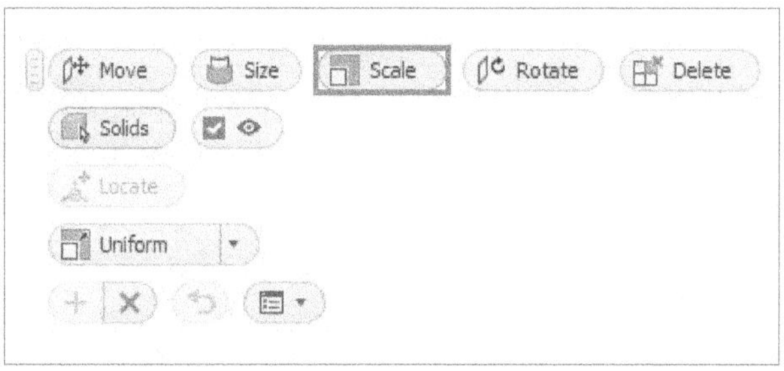

Figure-8. Scale button in Direct Editing toolbar

- Select the solid feature that you want to scale up or scale down.
- Specify desired value of scale in the edit box.

- Click on the **+** button from the toolbar to apply the changes.

Rotating Faces by Direct Editing

- Click on the **Rotate** button from the **Direct Editing** toolbar. The toolbar will be displayed as shown in Figure-9.

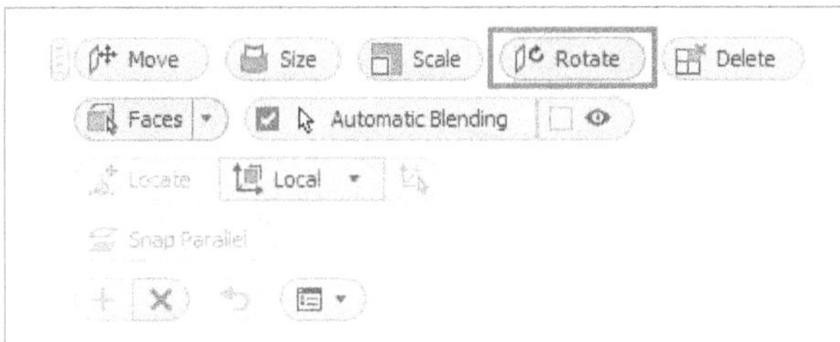

Figure-9. Rotate button in Direct Editing toolbar

- Select the face that you want to rotate. Drag handles for rotation will be displayed; refer to Figure-10.

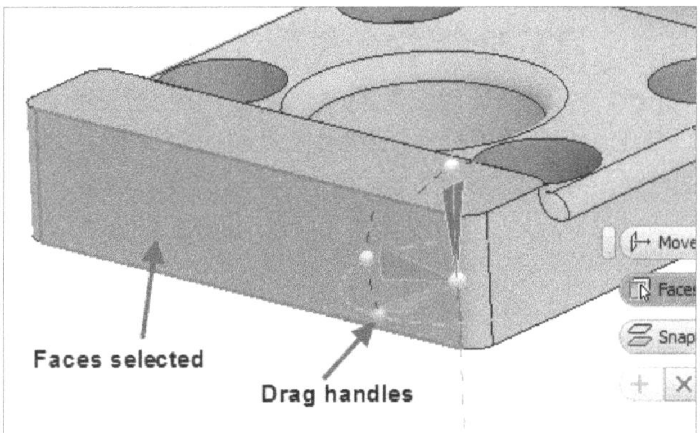

Figure-10. Drag handle for rotating face

- Click on the ball of drag handle and drag to rotate the face.
- Click on the **+** button to apply the change.

Deleting Faces by Direct Editing

- Click on the **Delete** button from the **Direct Editing** toolbar. The toolbar will be displayed as shown in Figure-11.

Figure-11. Delete button in Direct Editing toolbar

- Click on the face/faces to be deleted. Preview of the deleted faces will be displayed if feasible; refer to Figure-12.

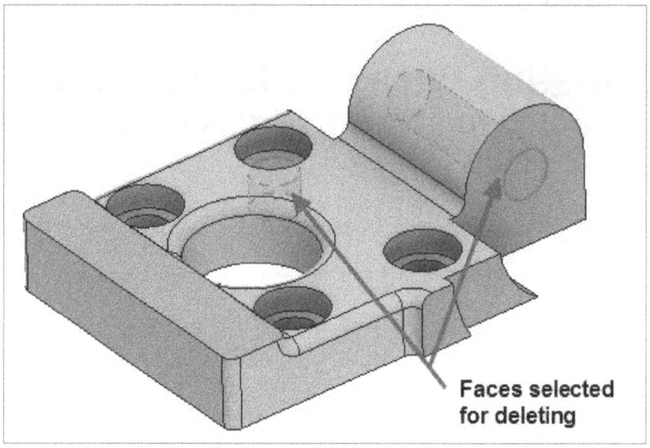

Figure-12. Faces selected for deleting

- Click on the **Apply** button to delete the faces.

BEND PART TOOL

The **Bend Part** tool is used to bend part by using sketched line. The tool is available in the expanded **Modify** panel of the **Ribbon**; refer to Figure-13. The procedure to use this tool is given next.

Figure-13. Bend Part tool

- Make sure a bend line is created by using the sketching tools.
- Click on the **Bend Part** tool from **Modify** panel in the **3D Model** tab of the **Ribbon**. The **Bend Part** dialog box will be displayed; refer to Figure-14.

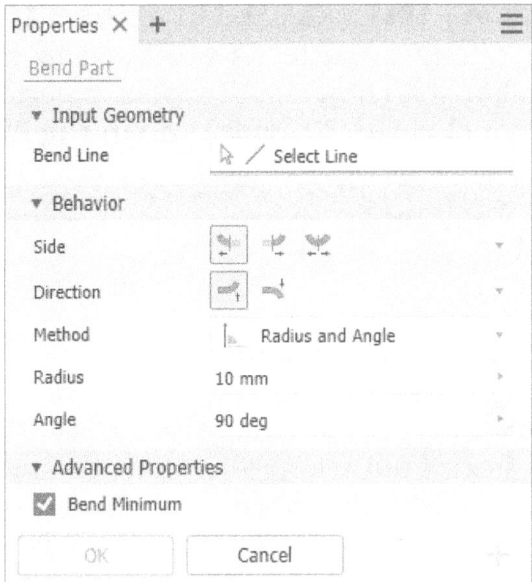

Figure-14. Bend Part dialog box

- Click on the bend line created earlier in the sketch.
- Select desired side on which part bends around the bend line from **Side** area in the **Behavior** rollout of the dialog box.
- Specify desired direction to bend the part from **Direction** area in the **Behavior** rollout.
- Select desired option from **Method** drop-down in the **Behavior** rollout. Select **Radius and Angle** option to create a feature using a radius and angle that you specify. Select **Radius and Arc Length** option to create a feature using a radius and arc length that you specify. Select **Arc Length and Angle** option to create a feature using values you specify for Arc Length and Angle.
- Specify desired radius and angle value in the **Radius** and **Angle** edit boxes, respectively.
- Select **Bend Minimum** check box from **Advanced Properties** rollout to specify which portions to bend.
- Specify desired parameters. Preview of the bend part will be displayed; refer to Figure-15.

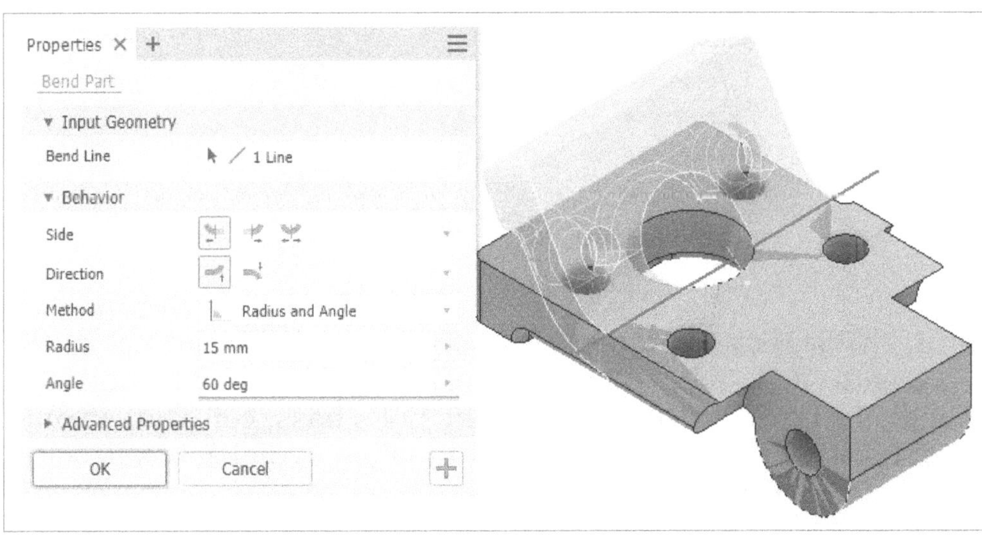

Figure-15. Preview of bended part

- Click on the **OK** button from the dialog box.

CREATING SOLID PATTERN

As discussed earlier in sketching, patterns are used to create multiple instances (copies) of selected object. For solid objects, the tools to perform pattern operation are available in the **Pattern** panel of the **3D Model** tab in the **Ribbon**; refer to Figure-16.

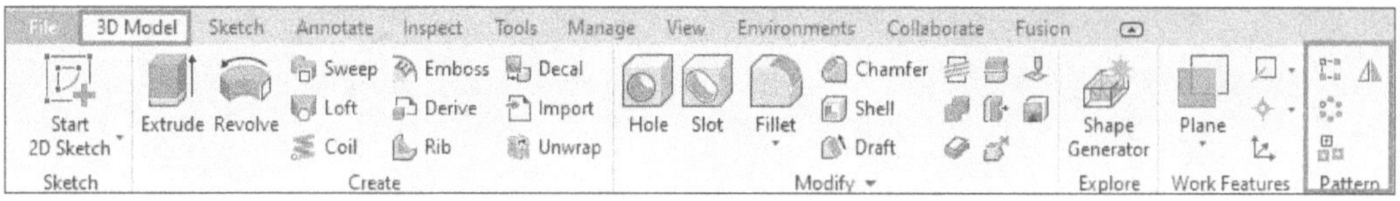

Figure-16. Pattern panel

Creating Rectangular Pattern

The Rectangular pattern is created when you want to create multiple copies of an object in two linear directions with specified distance between two consecutive instances. The procedure to create rectangular pattern is given next.

- Click on the **Rectangular Pattern** tool from **Pattern** panel in the **3D Model** tab of the **Ribbon** or press **CTRL+SHIFT+R** key from keyboard. The **Rectangular Pattern** dialog box will be displayed; refer to Figure-17.

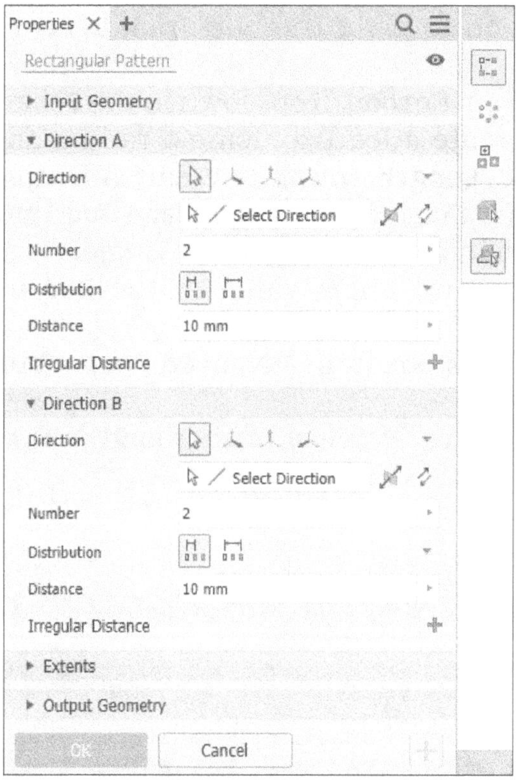

Figure-17. Rectangular Pattern dialog box

- By default, the **Select Features** selection button is active. Select the feature/ body to be patterned. Select the **Feature selection mode** button from right toolbar of dialog box to select features like hole, boss, coil, and so on. Select the **Body selection mode** button from right toolbar of dialog box to select full solid body for creating pattern.

- Select desired button from the **Direction** section to define direction of pattern. Select the **X Axis**, **Y Axis**, or **Z Axis** button to use respective axis as direction for pattern. Select the **Custom Direction** button from the **Direction** section and select desired direction reference like face, edge, and so on; refer to Figure-18.

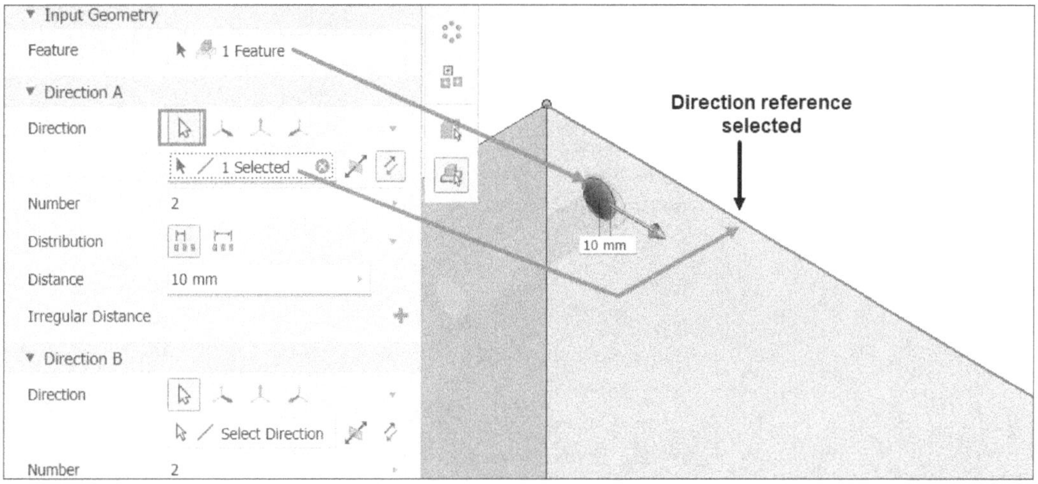

Figure-18. Selection for rectangular pattern Direction A

- Specify desired value in the **Number** edit box to define the total number of copies to be created along selected direction reference.
- Select the **Incremental** button from the **Distribution** section to define distance between two consecutive instances of object. Select the **Fitted** button from the **Distribution** section if you want to define total span within which copies of object will be fitted.
- Specify desired value in the **Distance** edit box to define distance between two consecutive instances of pattern.
- Click on the + button from **Irregular Distance** section to define a different distance of selected instance from previous instance in pattern. In simple words, you can change the default pattern distance for selected instance by using this option. Specify desired distance value for the irregular instance and then select the preview object to which you want to apply the distance; refer to Figure-19.

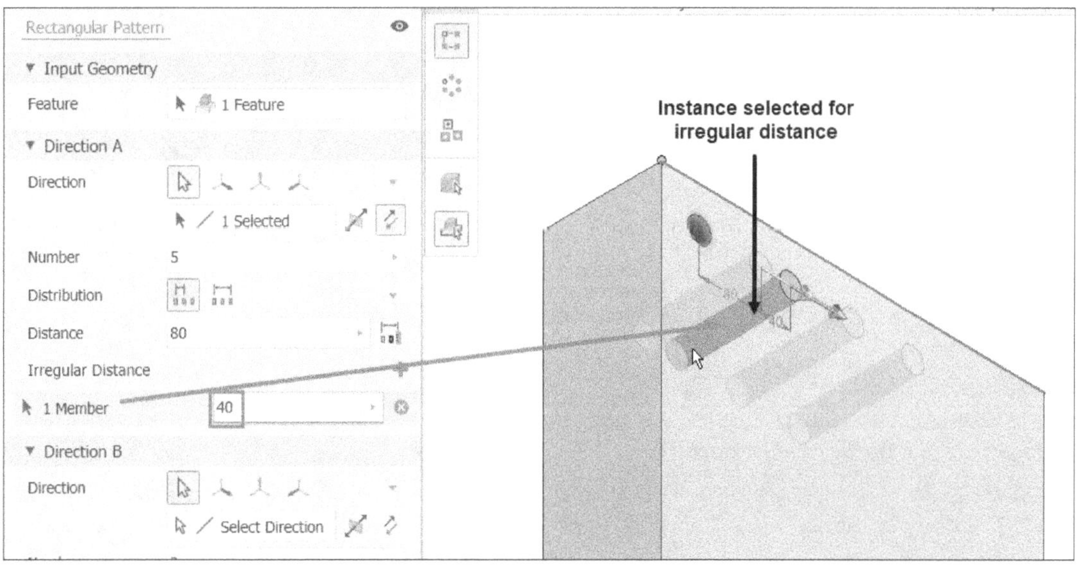

Figure-19. Preview of irregular instance

- Similarly, you can define parameters for **Direction B** of the pattern.

- Expand the **Extents** section and select desired face/sketch boundary to define the boundary within which pattern instances will be created. The options in dialog box will be displayed as shown in Figure-20.

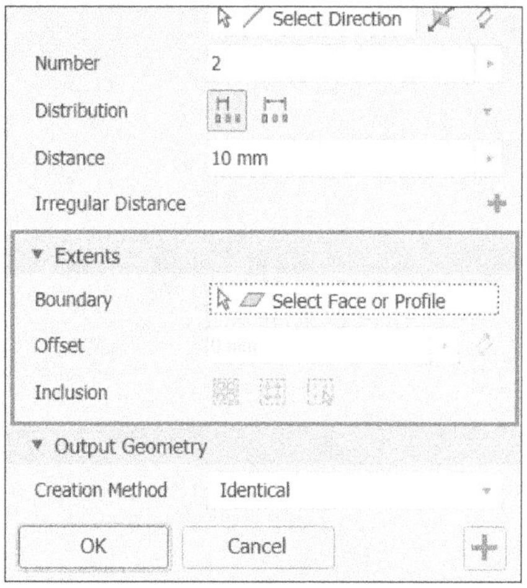

Figure-20. Extents section

- Click in the **Boundary** selection box and select desired face/sketch boundary.
- Specify desired value in the **Offset** edit box if you want to offset boundary by specified value.
- Select the button to create only the instances which fall completely inside the boundary. Select the to create instances which are even slightly touching the boundary. Select the to select a different based point for the original selected object (which was patterned). The instances whose base points fall inside the boundary will be created; refer to Figure-21.

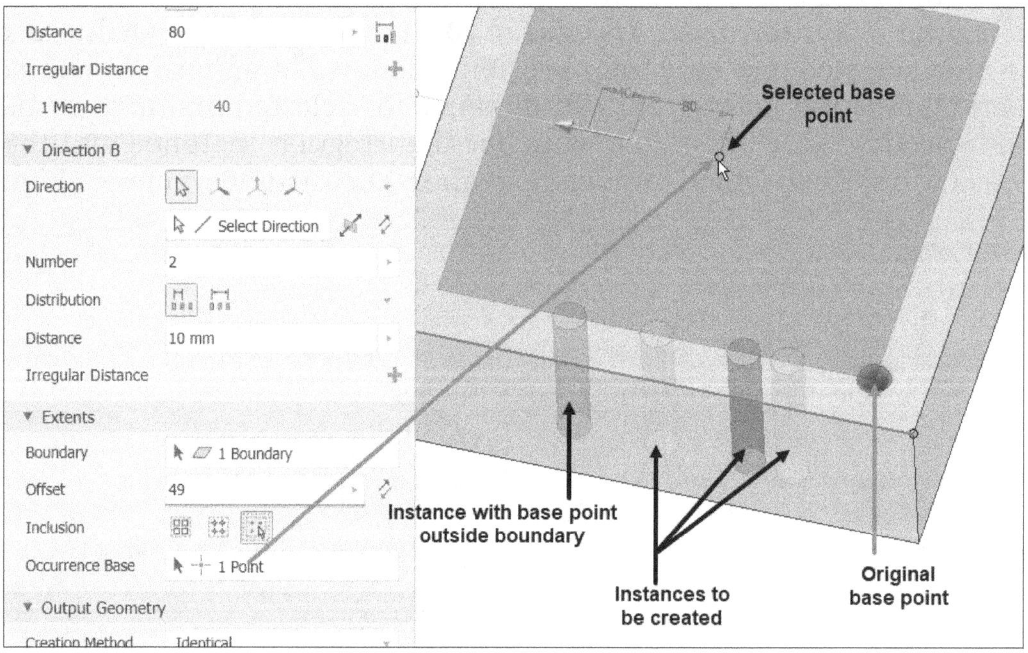

Figure-21. Using base point for extents

- Select desired method of copying from the **Create Method** drop-down in the **Output Geometry** section to define computation method for pattern. Select the **Optimized** option if there are too many instances and you are concerned about the speed of feature generation. This method may not produce correct shapes at overlapping of instances. Select the **Identical** option to create identical copies of selected object. Select the **Adjust** option if you want to allow slight deviation from the original object when creating copies depending on extent boundary, termination conditions, and other related parameters.
- After setting desired parameters, click on the **OK** button to create the pattern feature.

Creating Circular Pattern

The **Circular Pattern** tool is used to multiple copies of selected object around a common selected axis like blades in a ceiling fan. The procedure to create the circular pattern is discussed next.

- Click on the **Circular Pattern** tool from the **Pattern** panel in the **3D Model** tab of the **Ribbon**. The **Circular Pattern** dialog box will be displayed; refer to Figure-22.

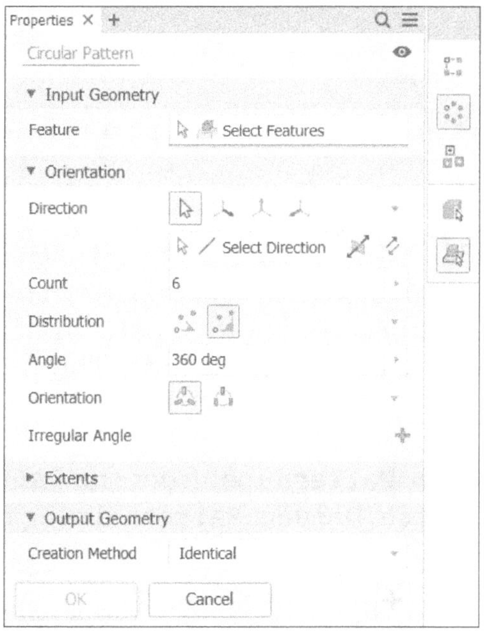

Figure-22. Circular pattern dialog box

- Select desired feature from the model to be patterned.
- Click in the **Select Direction** selection box and select desired axis to be used as center reference for pattern. Preview of the circular pattern will be displayed; refer to Figure-23.

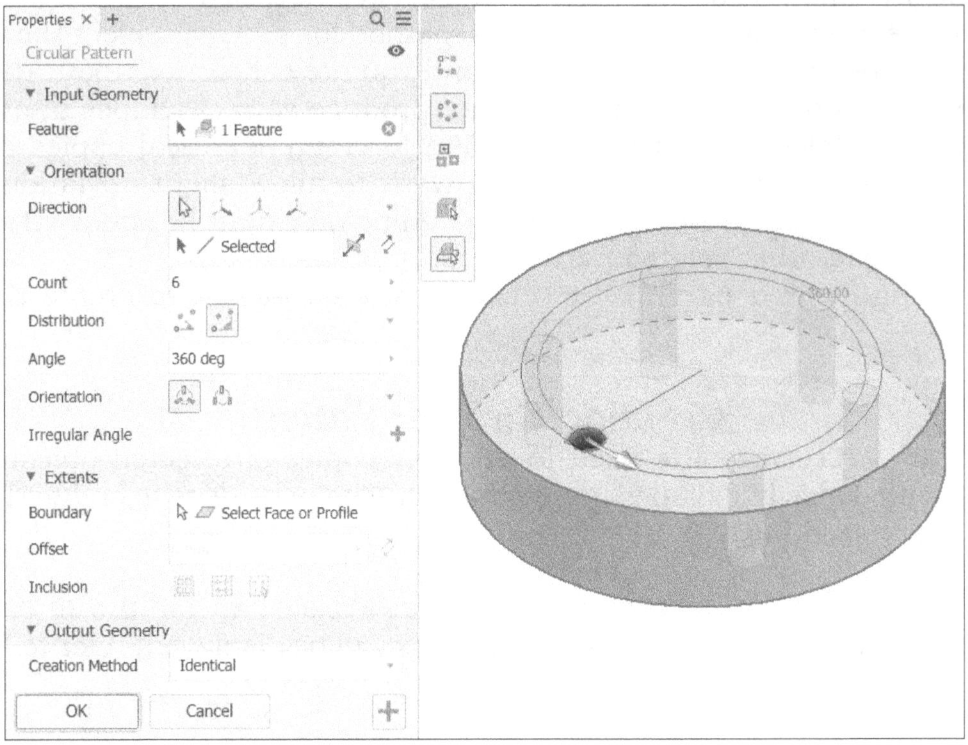

Figure-23. Preview of circular pattern

- Set the other parameters as discussed earlier and click on the **OK** button to create pattern.

Creating Sketch Driven Pattern

The **Sketch Driven Pattern** tool is used to create pattern of selected object at specified sketch points. Note that if you need to create a pattern which follows specified curve then you can use this tool to create that pattern. The procedure to use this tool is given next.

- Click on the **Sketch Driven Pattern** tool from the **Pattern** panel in the **3D Model** tab of the **Ribbon**. The **Sketch Driven Pattern** dialog box will be displayed; refer to Figure-24.

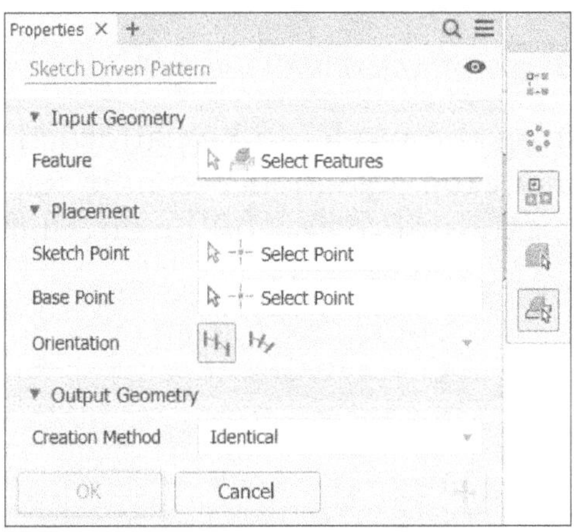

Figure-24. Sketch Driven Pattern dialog box

- Select the feature to be copied from the graphics area.

- Click in the **Sketch Point** selection box in the dialog box and select the sketch containing points at which pattern instances will be created; refer to Figure-25.

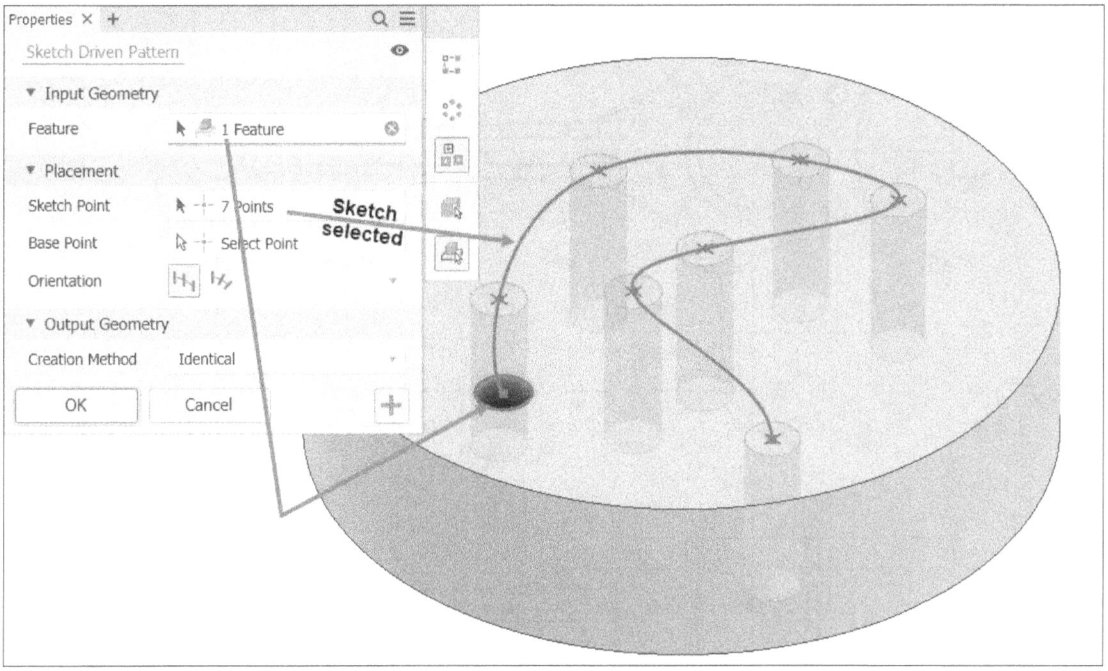

Figure-25. Preview of sketch driven pattern

- Set the other parameters as discussed earlier and click on the **OK** button from the dialog box to create the feature.

Creating Mirror

The **Mirror** tool is used to create a mirror copy of the selected entities. The procedure to use this tool have been discussed in Chapter 2.

PRACTICAL 1

Create the model as shown in Figure-26. The dimensions are given in Figure-27.

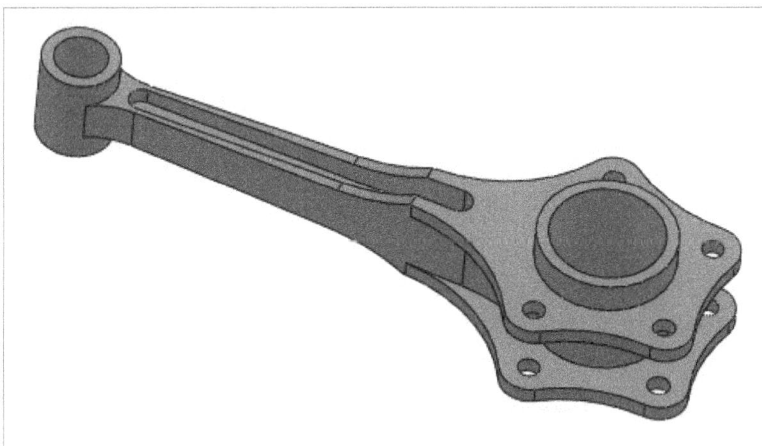

Figure-26. Practical 1

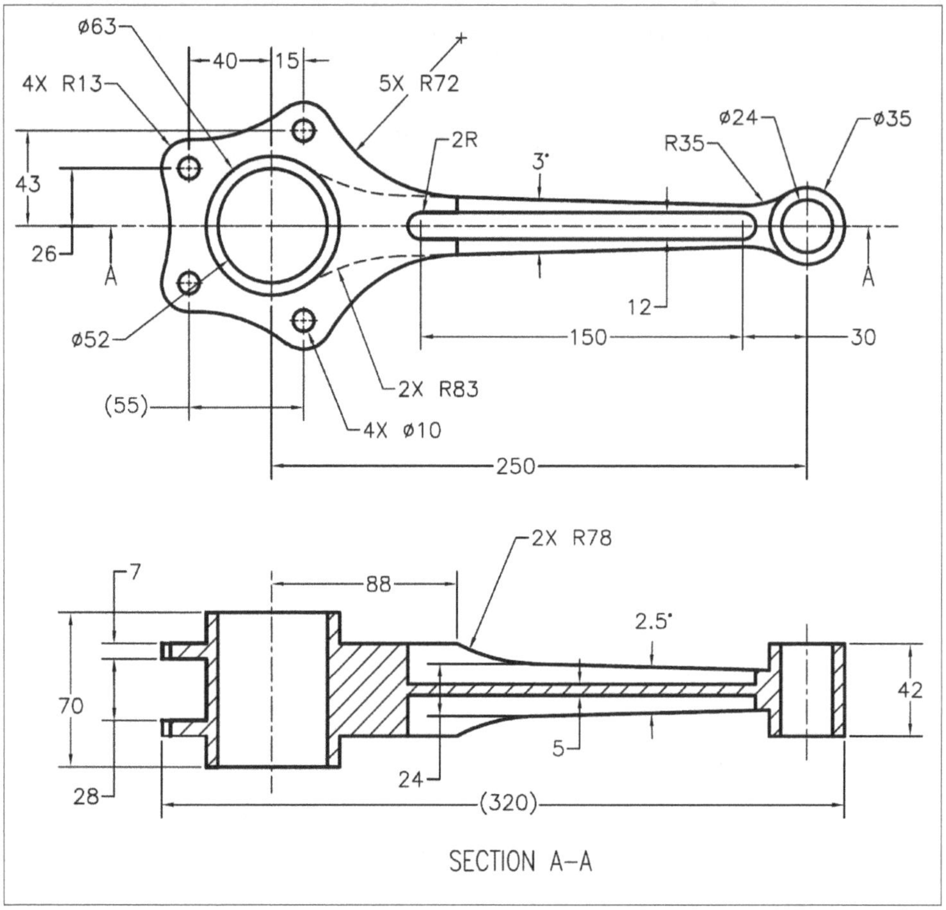

Figure-27. Practical 1 drawing

Strategy for Creating model

1. Looking at the isometric view and orthographic views, we can find that the model is created by multiple extrude features and extrude cut features.
2. First sketch (which is a ring) is to be created on the **XZ** plane (Top plane) and then it is to be extruded.
3. Create the other extrusion features and remove the extra portion from them.

Starting Part File

- Start Autodesk Inventor by double-clicking on the Autodesk Inventor Professional icon from the desktop. (If not started yet.)
- Click on the **New** button from the **Quick Access Toolbar**. The **Create New File** dialog box will be displayed.
- Double-click on **Standard(mm).ipt** icon from the **Metric** templates. The Part environment of Autodesk Inventor will be displayed.

Creating First Extrusion

- Click on the **Start 2D Sketch** button from **Sketch** panel in the **3D Model** tab of the **Ribbon**. You will be asked to select a sketching plane.
- Select the **XZ** Plane (Top Plane) as sketching plane. The sketching environment will become active.
- Create a ring of two circles as shown in Figure-28.

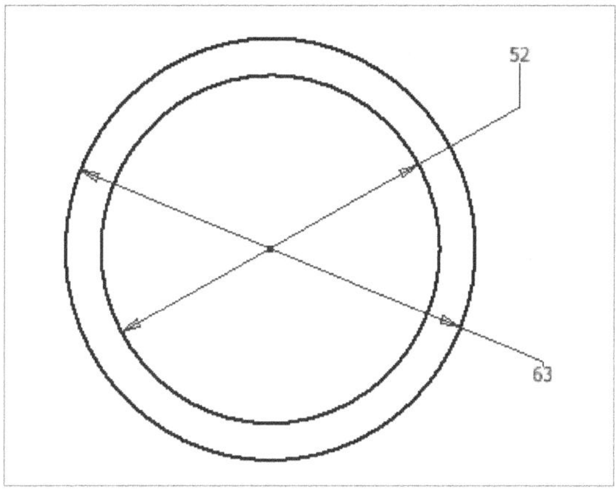

Figure-28. Circles created

- Click on the **Finish Sketch** button from the **Finish** drop-down in the **Exit** panel of the **Ribbon**.
- Click on the **Extrude** tool from **Create** panel in the **3D Model** tab of the **Ribbon**. You will be asked to select the profile for extrusion.
- Select the sketch created and extrude it to both side by **70**; refer to Figure-29.

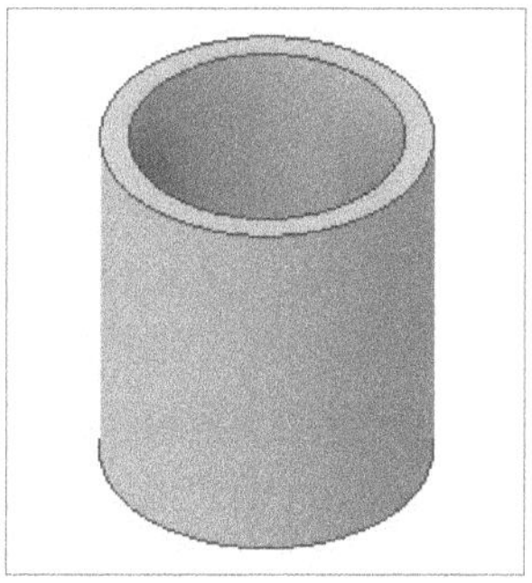

Figure-29. First Extrusion

Creating the Second Extrusion

- Click on the **Start 2D Sketch** button from **Sketch** panel in the **3D Model** tab of the **Ribbon**. You will be asked to select a sketching plane.
- Select the **XZ** Plane (Top Plane) as sketching plane.
- Create the sketch as shown in Figure-30.

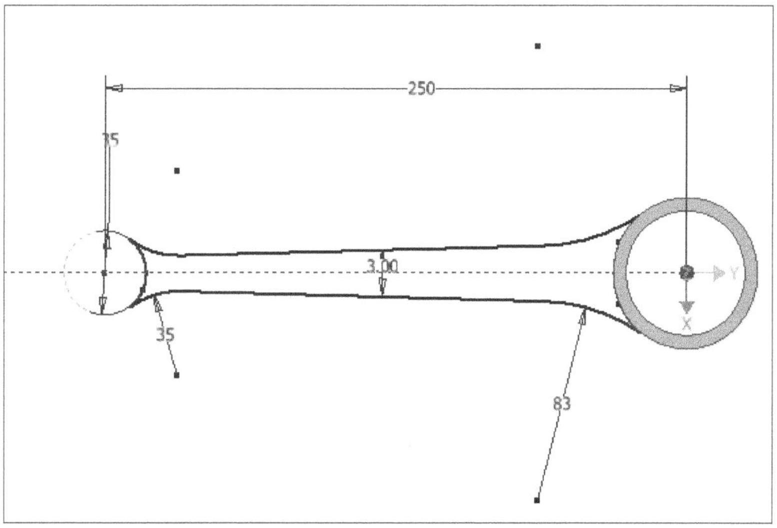

Figure-30. Sketch for second extrusion

- Click on the **Finish Sketch** button from the **Finish** drop-down in the **Exit** panel of the **Ribbon** to exit the sketching environment.
- Extrude the sketch to both side at a distance of **42**; refer to Figure-31.

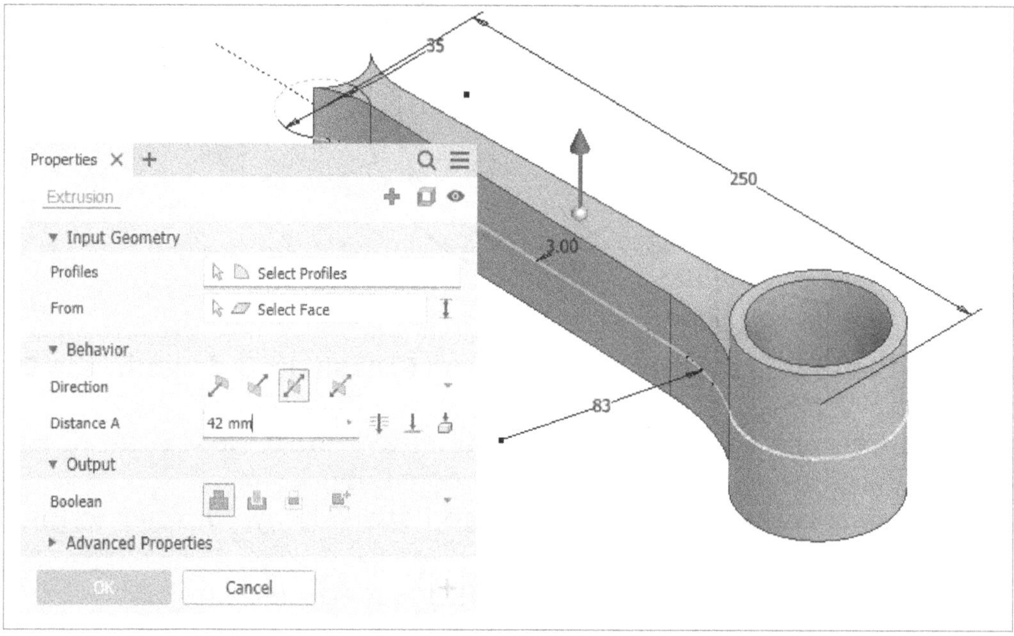

Figure-31. Second Extrusion

- Click on the **OK** button from the dialog box to create the feature.

Creating Third Extrusion Feature

- Click on the **Start 2D Sketch** button from **Sketch** panel in the **3D Model** tab of the **Ribbon**. You will be asked to select the sketching plane or face.
- Select the top face of second extrude feature. The sketch environment will display.
- Create the sketch as shown in Figure-32.

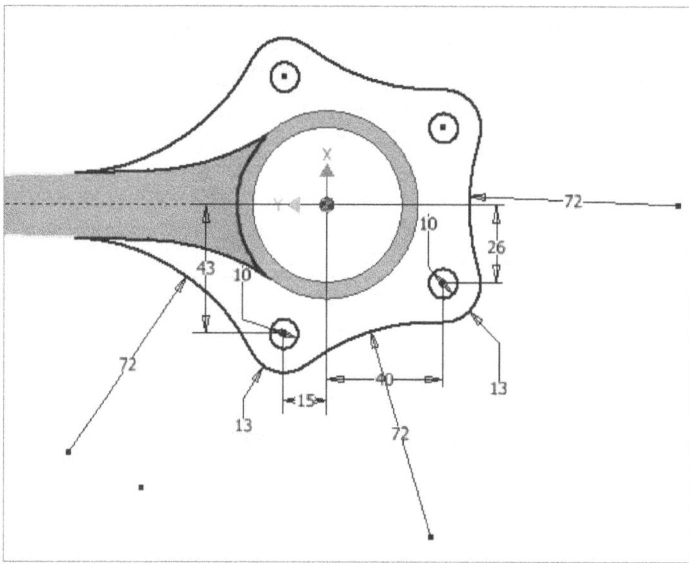

Figure-32. Sketch for third extrusion feature

- Extrude the sketch by **7** mm downward; refer to Figure-33.

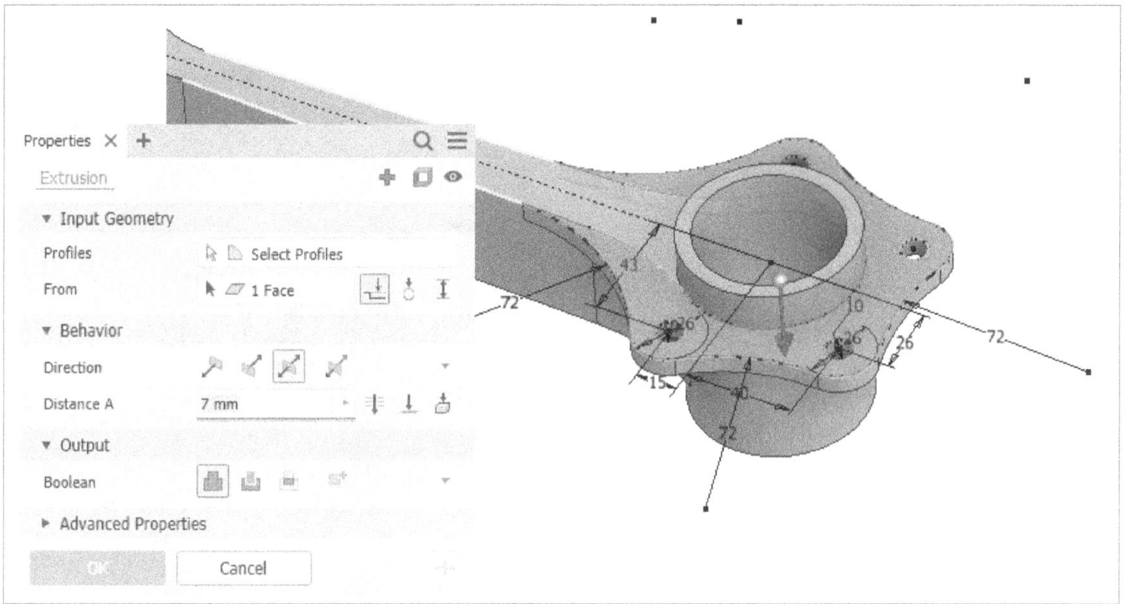

Figure-33. Extruding third feature

- Click on the **OK** button from the dialog box to create the feature.

Creating Mirror of Third Feature

- Click on the **Mirror** tool from **Pattern** panel in the **3D Model** tab of the **Ribbon**. The **Mirror** dialog box will be displayed as shown in Figure-34.

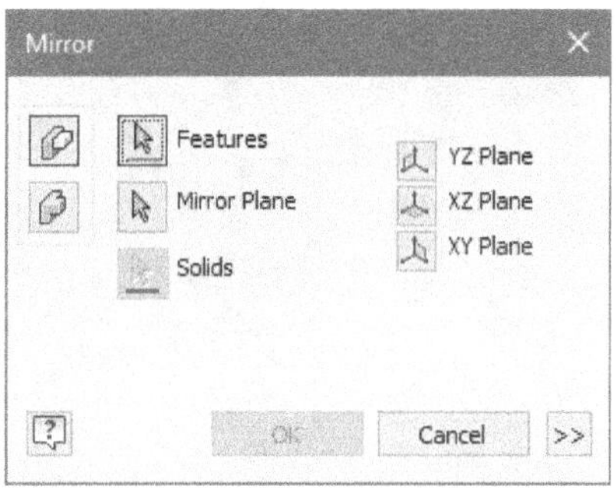

Figure-34. Mirror dialog box

- Select the third extrusion feature from the **Model Browser** bar at the left of the application window; refer to Figure-35.

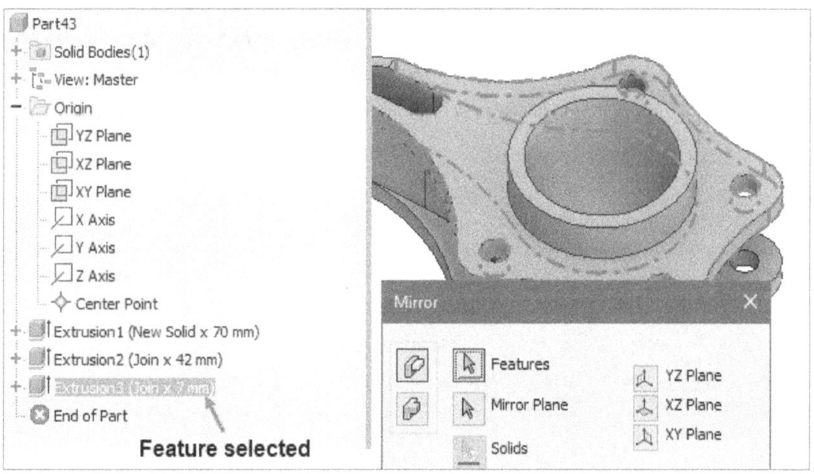

Figure-35. Selecting feature for mirroring

- Click on the **Mirror Plane** selection button from the dialog box and select the **XZ Plane** button as mirror plane from the dialog box or from the **Model Browser** bar; refer to Figure-36. Preview of the mirror feature will be displayed; refer to Figure-37.

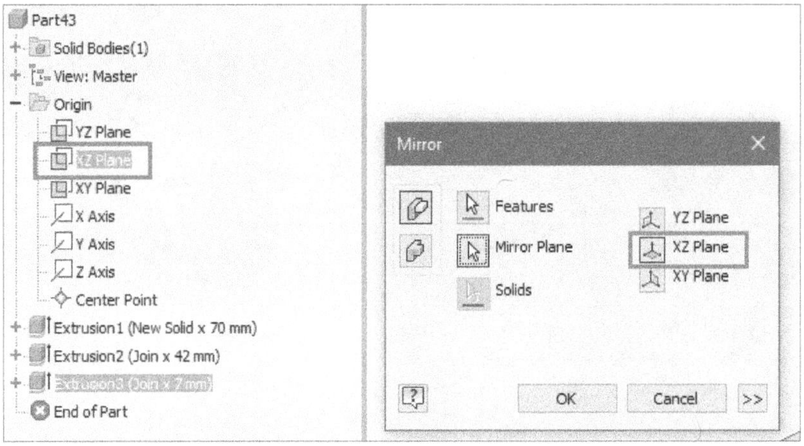

Figure-36. Plane to be selected

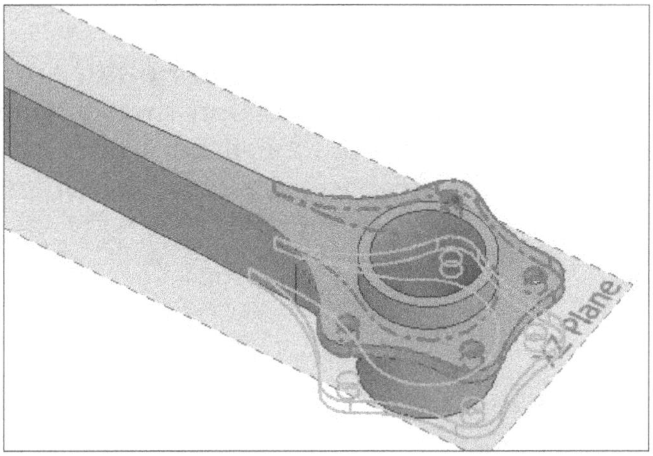

Figure-37. Preview of mirror feature

Creating First Extrude Cut Feature

- Click on the **Start 2D Sketch** button from **Sketch** panel in the **3D Model** tab of the **Ribbon**. You will be asked to select a sketching plane.
- Select the **YZ** plane as sketching plane. The sketching environment will become active.
- Create a sketch as shown in Figure-38.

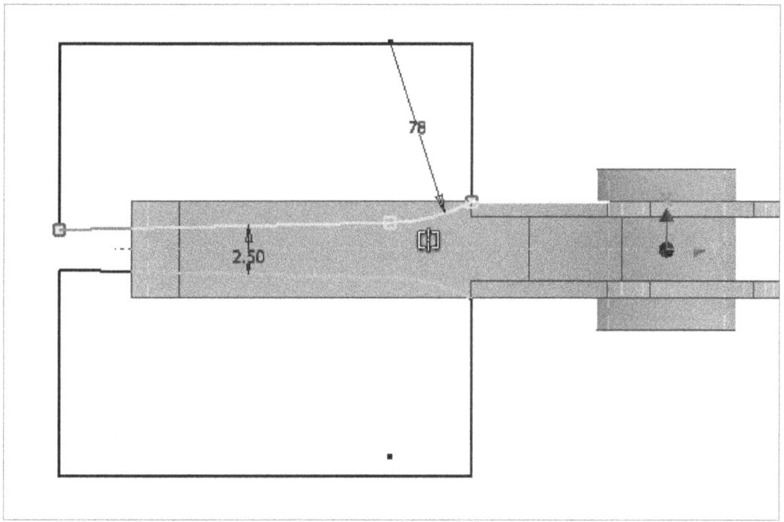

Figure-38. Sketch for extrude cut feature

- Click on the **Finish Sketch** button from the **Finish** drop-down in the **Exit** panel of the **Ribbon**.
- Click on the **Extrude** tool from **Create** panel in the **3D Model** tab of the **Ribbon**. The **Extrude** dialog box will be displayed asking you to select the profile.
- Select the newly created sketch and extrude both the sides with **Cut** option selected from **Boolean** area of the dialog box; refer to Figure-39.

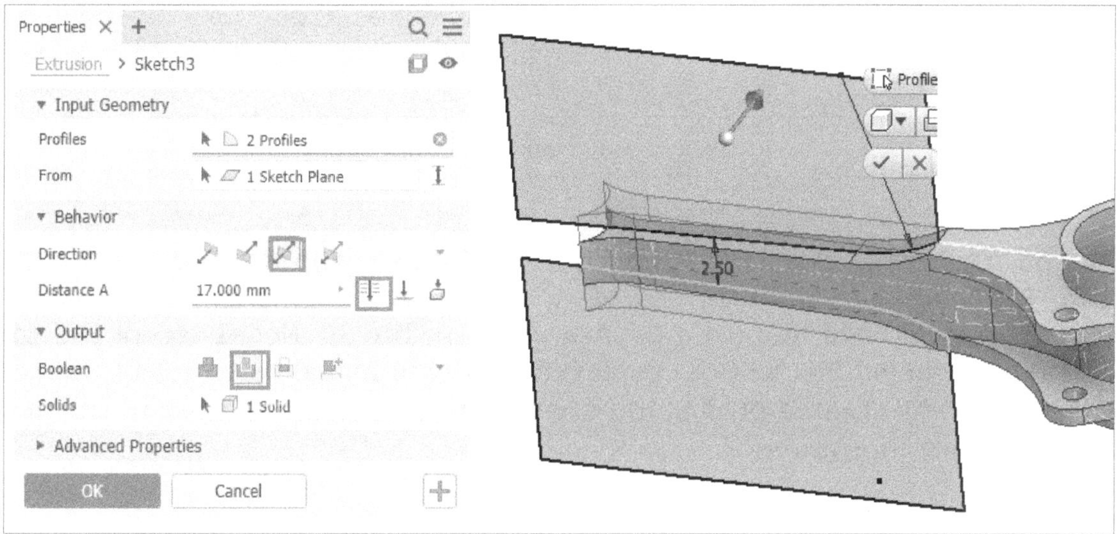

Figure-39. Creating cut feature

- Click on the **OK** button from the dialog box to create the feature.
- After creating extrude cut feature, the model will be displayed as shown in Figure-40.

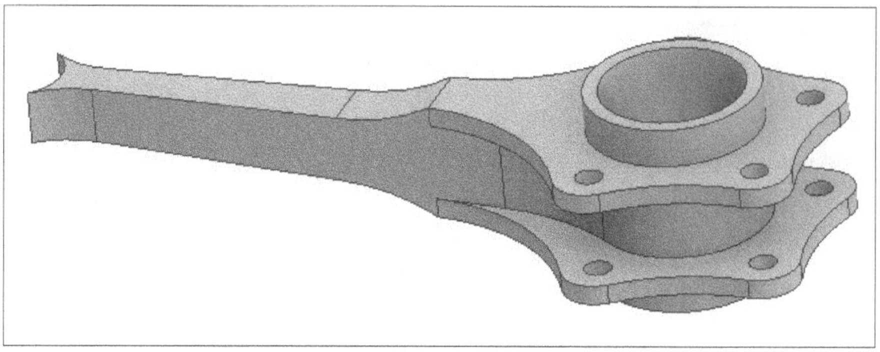

Figure-40. After creating extrude cut feature

Creating the Second and Third Extrude Cut Feature

- Click on the **Start 2D Sketch** button from **Sketch** panel in the **3D Model** tab of the **Ribbon**. You will be asked to select the sketching plane or face.
- Select the top face of the third extrusion feature created earlier as sketching face.
- Create a sketch as shown in Figure-41.

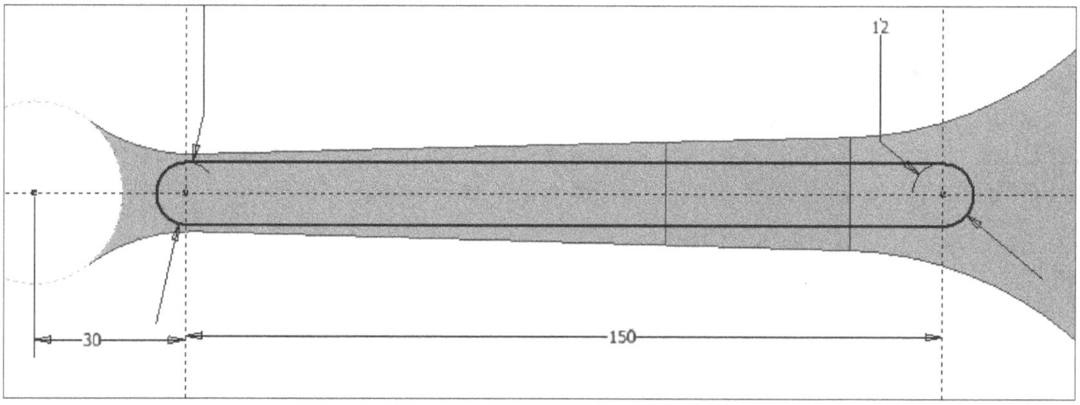

Figure-41. Sketch for second cut feature

- Click on the **Finish Sketch** button from the **Finish** drop-down in the **Exit** panel of the **Ribbon**.
- Click on the **Extrude** tool from **Create** panel in the **3D Model** tab of the **Ribbon**. The **Extrude** dialog box will be displayed. You will be asked to select the profile.
- Select the newly created profile and create an extrude cut feature to the depth of **18.5** as shown in Figure-42.

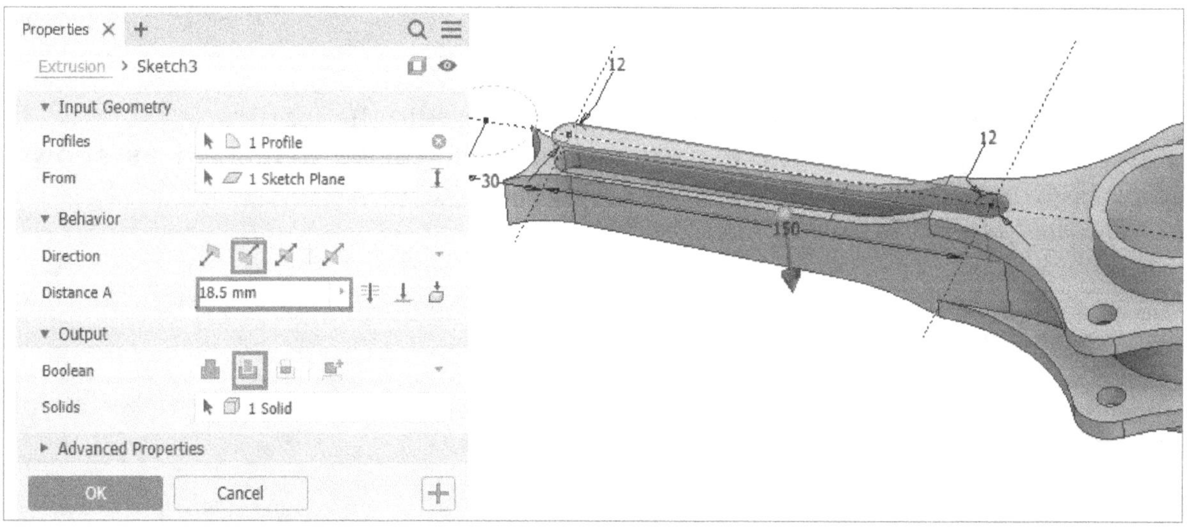

Figure-42. Second extrude cut feature

- Click on the **OK** button from the dialog box to create the feature.
- Click on the **Mirror** tool from **Pattern** panel in the **3D Model** tab of the **Ribbon**. The **Mirror** dialog box will be displayed asking you to select the feature.
- Select the newly created extrude feature to be mirrored to the other side and select the **XZ Plane** button as **Mirror Plane** from the dialog box or **Model Browser** bar. The preview of mirror feature will be displayed; refer to Figure-43.
- Click on the **OK** button from the dialog box to create the feature.

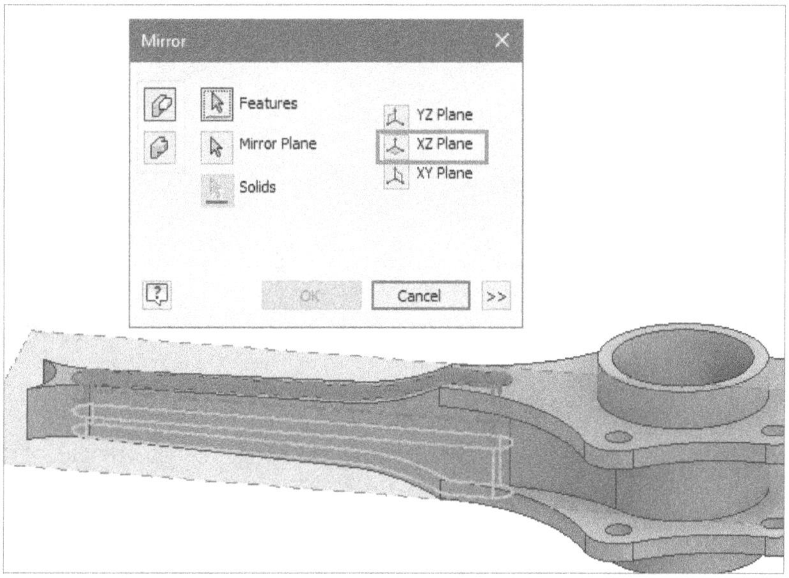

Figure-43. Mirror feature created

Creating the last extrude feature

- Click on the **Start 2D Sketch** button from **Sketch** panel in the **3D Model** tab of the **Ribbon**. You will be asked to select the sketching plane.
- Select the **XZ** plane as sketching plane and create the sketch as shown in Figure-44.

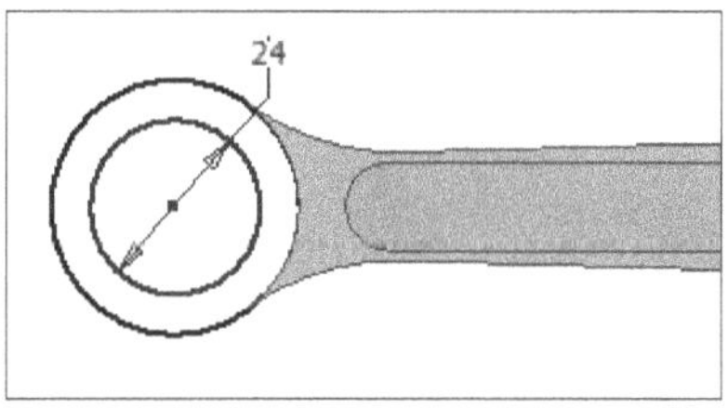

Figure-44. Sketch for last extrude feature

- Click on the **Finish Sketch** button from the **Finish** drop-down in the **Exit** panel of the **Ribbon**.
- Click on the **Extrude** tool from **Create** panel in the **3D Model** tab of the **Ribbon**. The **Extrude** dialog box will be displayed asking you to select the profile.
- Select the newly created sketch and extrude it to both the sides of distance **42** mm. The preview of extruded feature will be displayed; refer to Figure-45.

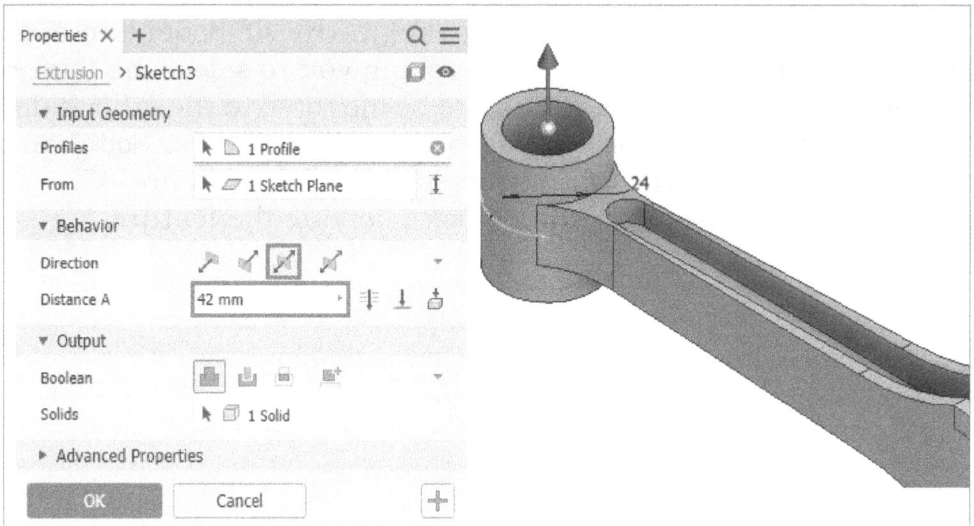

Figure-45. Extrude feature created

- Click on the **OK** button from the dialog box to create the feature.

PRACTICAL 2

In this practical, we will create a model given in Figure-46 as per the drawing given in Figure-47. The model is of a pipe with varying section and it will require the use of datum curve.

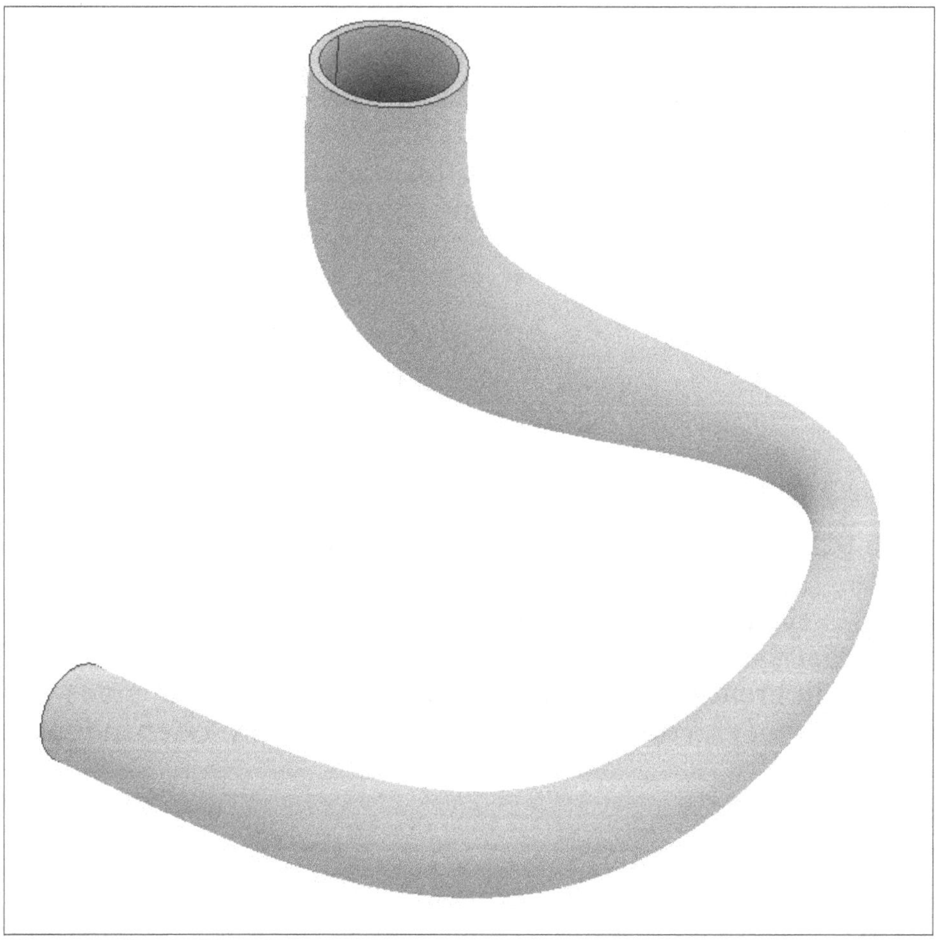

Figure-46. Practical 2 model

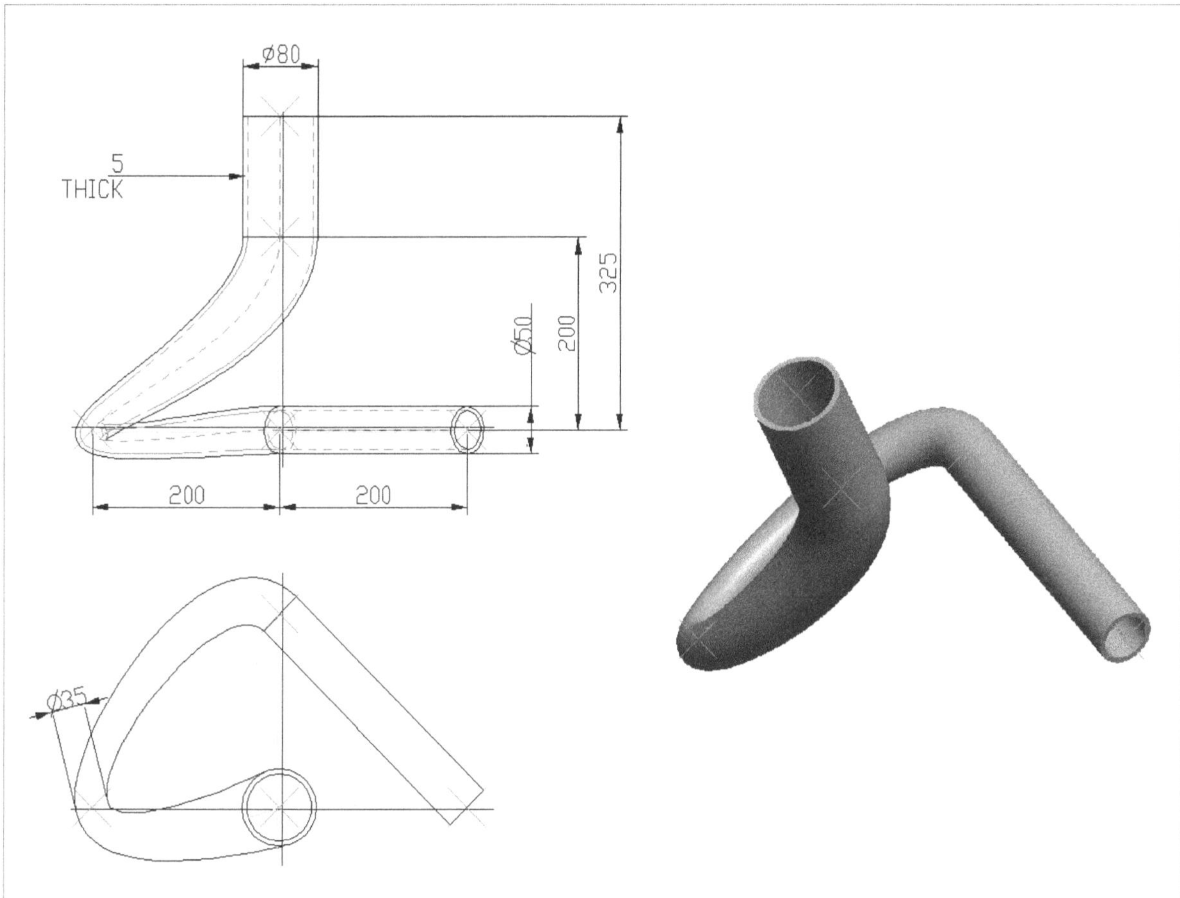

Figure-47. Practical 2

Strategy for Creating model

1. Looking at the isometric view and orthographic views, we can find that the model is created by using a spline passing through specified points.
2. First create the required points on XZ and YZ planes.
3. Create a 3D spline passing through the specified points.

Starting Part File

- Start Autodesk Inventor by double-clicking on the Autodesk Inventor Professional icon from the desktop. (If not started yet.)
- Click on the **New** button from the **Quick Access Toolbar**. The **Create New File** dialog box will be displayed.
- Double-click on **Standard(mm).ipt** icon from the **Metric** templates. The Part environment of Autodesk Inventor will be displayed.

Creating Sketch for Profile

- Click on the **Start 2D Sketch** button from the **Sketch** panel in the **3D Model** tab of the **Ribbon**. You will be asked to select a sketching plane.
- Select the **XZ** Plane (Top Plane) as sketching plane. The sketching environment will be displayed.
- Create three points on the sketching plane as shown in Figure-48.

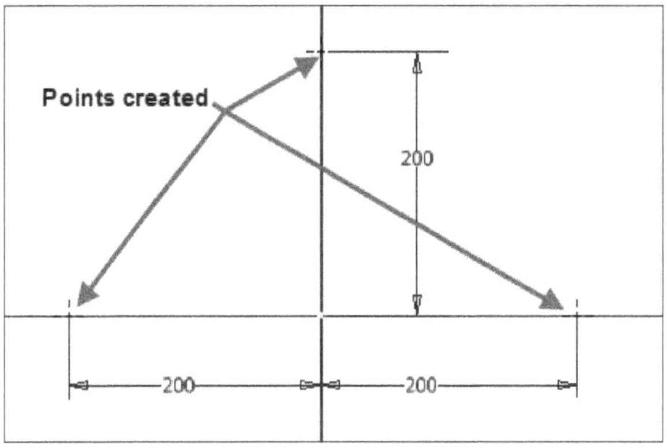

Figure-48. Points to be created

- Click on the **Finish Sketch** button from the **Finish** drop-down in the **Exit** panel of the **Ribbon**.
- Click on the **Start 2D Sketch** button again and select **YZ** Plane (Right Plane) as sketching plane. The sketching environment will be displayed.
- Draw two points as shown in Figure-49.

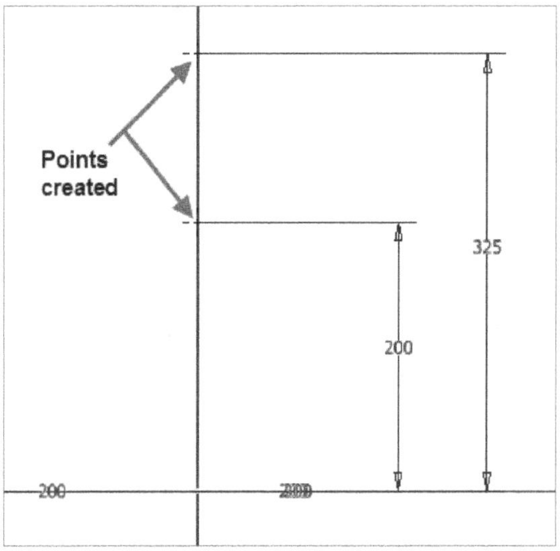

Figure-49. Points created in second sketch

- Click on the **Finish Sketch** button from the **Finish** drop-down in the **Exit** panel of the **Ribbon**.
- Click on the **Start 3D Sketch** button from **Sketch** panel in the **Sketch** tab of **Ribbon**. The tools related to 3D sketching will be displayed in the **Ribbon**.
- Click on the **Spline Interpolation** tool from the **Spline** drop-down in the **Draw** panel of **3D Sketch** tab in the **Ribbon**; refer to Figure-50. You will be asked to select starting point of spline.

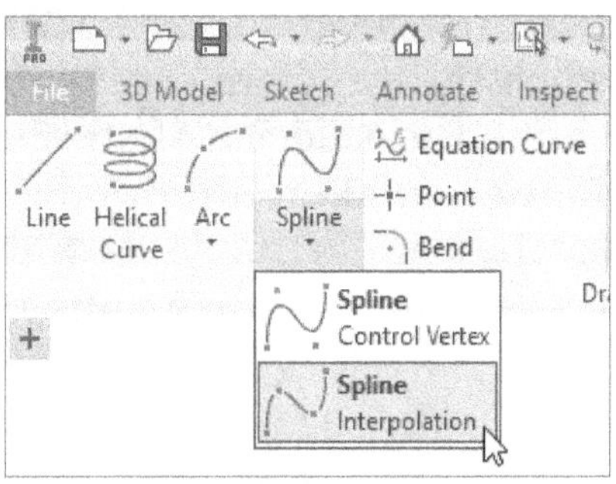

Figure-50. Spline Interpolation tool

- Create a spline passing through the earlier created points as shown in Figure-51.

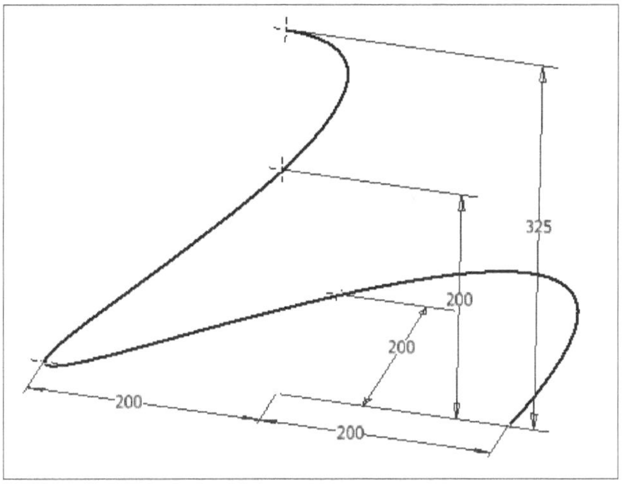

Figure-51. Spline passing through selected points

- Right-click on the spline and click on the **AutoCAD** option from the **Fit Method** cascading menu in the shortcut menu; refer to Figure-52, to change the shape of spline as per **AutoCAD** style; refer to Figure-53.

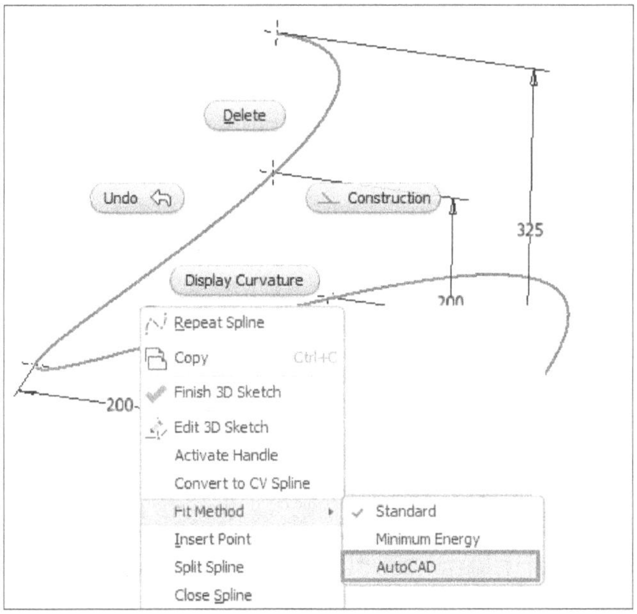

Figure-52. Changing fit method for spline

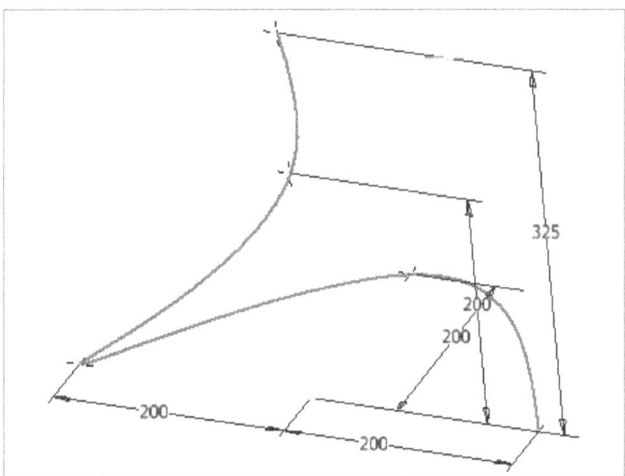

Figure-53. Spline after changing fit method

- Click on the **Finish Sketch** button from the **Finish** drop-down in the **Exit** panel of the **Ribbon**.

Creating Section Sketches

- Click on the **Plane** tool from **Plane** drop-down in the **Work Features** panel of the **Ribbon**. You will be asked to select geometry as reference for plane.
- Select the curve near the top point as shown in Figure-54.

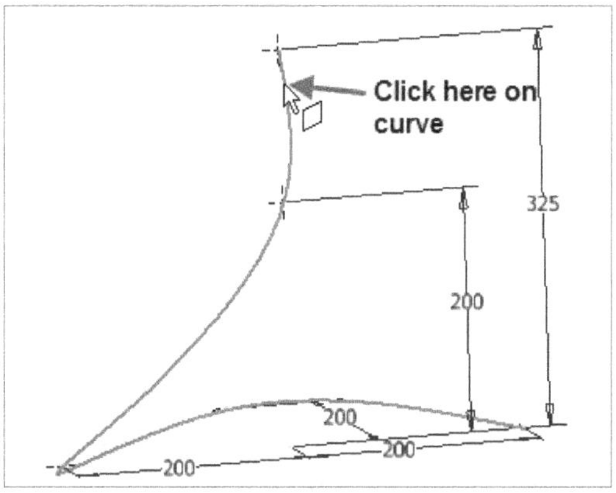

Figure-54. Selecting curve for plane creation

- Now, click on the top point to specify second reference for plane. The plane will be created as shown in Figure-55.

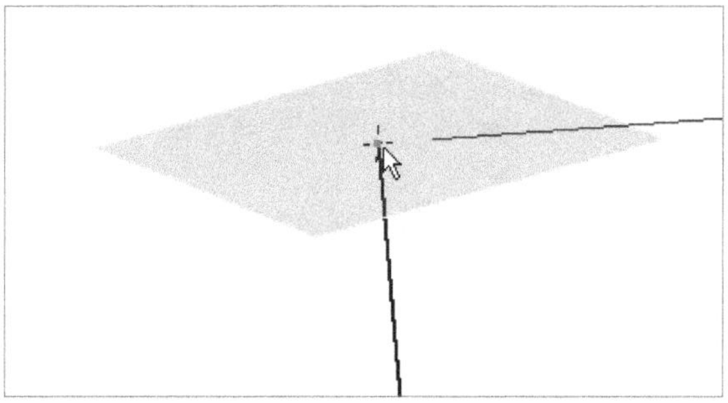

Figure-55. Plane created

- Click on the **Start 2D Sketch** button from **Sketch** panel in the **3D Model** tab of the **Ribbon**. You will be asked to select the sketching plane.
- Select the newly created plane as sketching plane. The sketching environment will be displayed.
- Create a 2D sketch as shown in Figure-56.

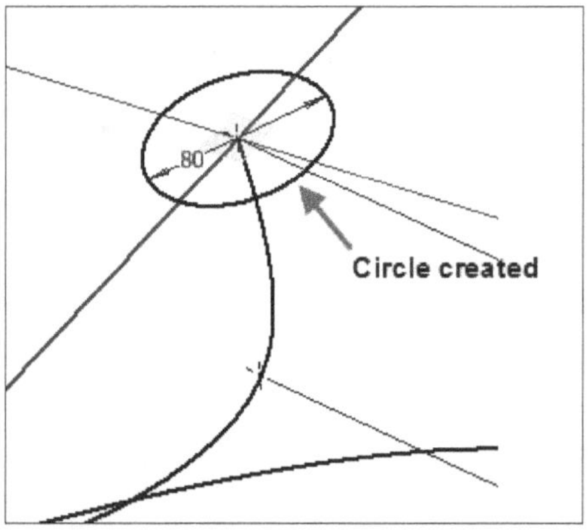

Figure-56. Circle created

- Click on the **Finish Sketch** button from the **Finish** drop-down in the **Exit** panel of the **Ribbon**.
- Similarly, create planes at other points and create sketches as shown in Figure-57.

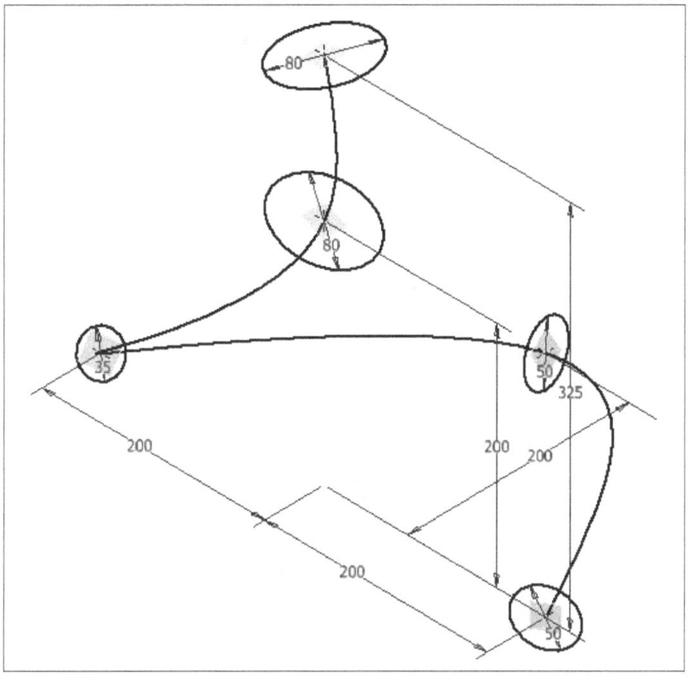

Figure-57. Sketches created on planes

Creating Loft Feature

- Click on the **Loft** tool from **Create** panel in the **3D Model** tab of the **Ribbon**. The **Loft** dialog box will be displayed as shown in Figure-58.

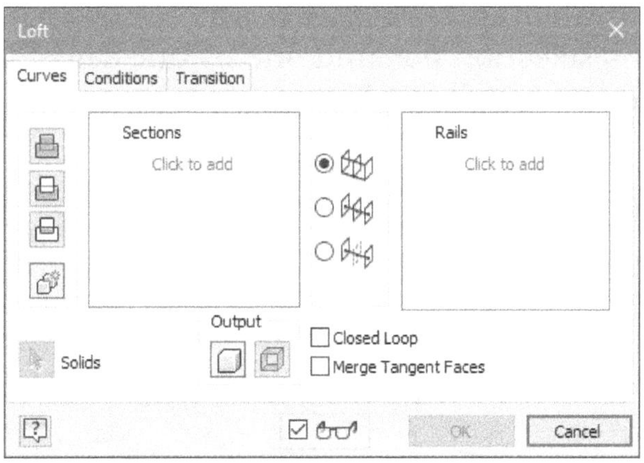

Figure-58. Loft dialog box

- Select the **Center Line** radio button from the dialog box and click in the **Center Line** selection box; refer to Figure-59.

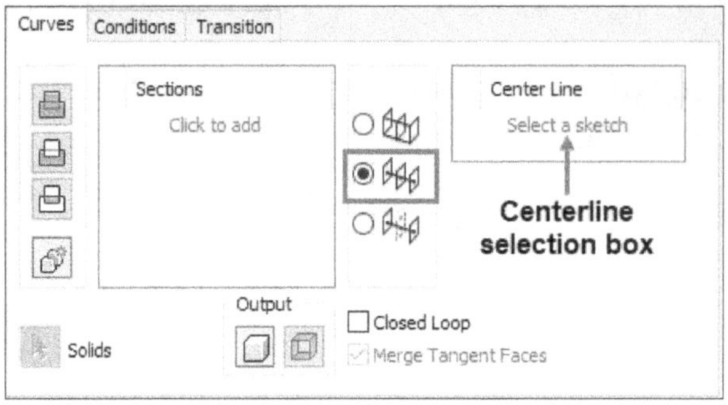

Figure-59. Centerline selection box

- Select the 3D spline created earlier; refer to Figure-60.

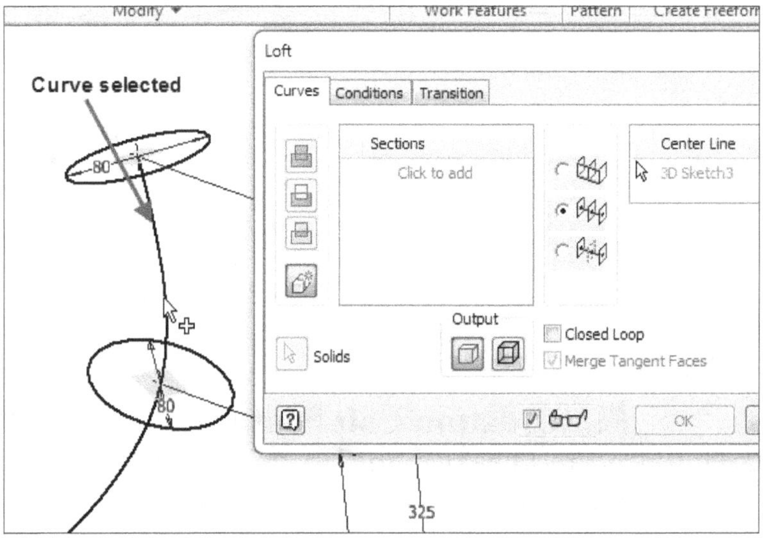

Figure-60. Curve to be selected as centerline

- Click in the **Sections** selection box and one by one select the section sketches as per the flow of loft feature; refer to Figure-61.

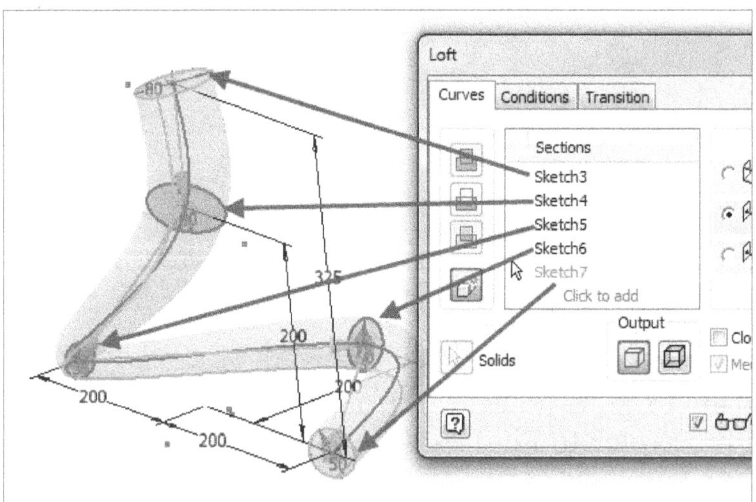

Figure-61. Sections selected

- Click on the **OK** button from the dialog box to create the feature. The loft feature will be displayed as shown in Figure-62.

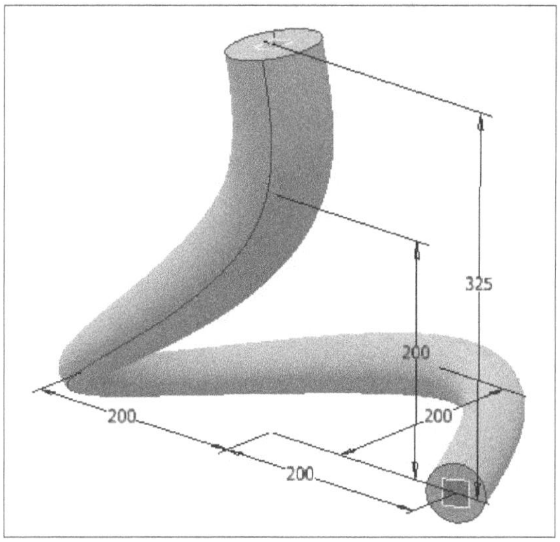

Figure-62. Loft feature created

Creating Shell feature

- Click on the **Shell** tool from **Modify** panel in the **3D Model** tab of the **Ribbon**. The **Shell** dialog box will be displayed as shown in Figure-63.

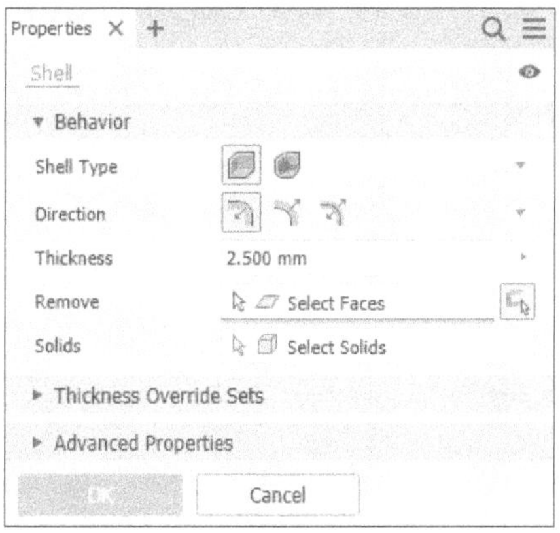

Figure-63. Shell dialog box

- Click in the **Thickness** edit box and specify the value as **5** mm.
- Select both the end faces of the loft feature to remove them; refer to Figure-64.

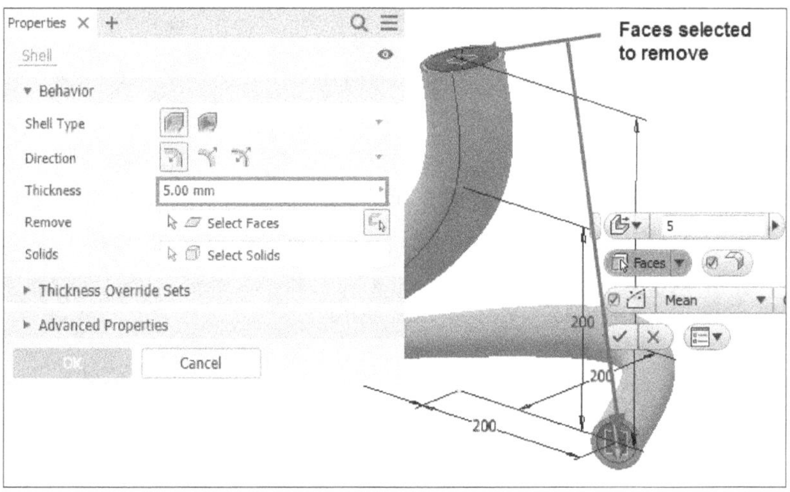

Figure-64. Faces to remove while shelling

- Click on the **OK** button from the dialog box. The feature will be created; refer to Figure-65.

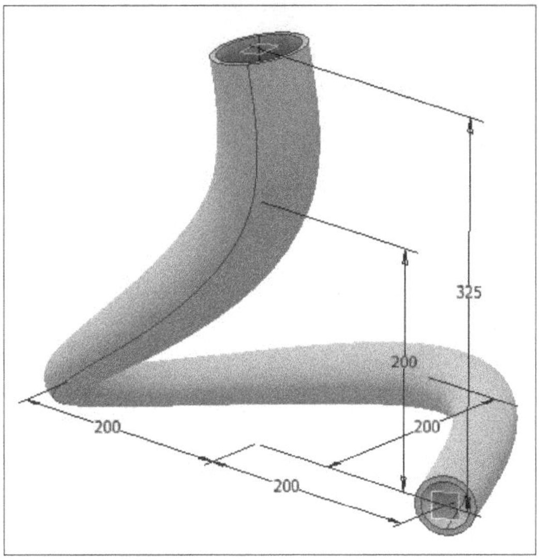

Figure-65. Model after applying shell feature

Now, select all the sketches and planes which are not required to be displayed in viewport and select the **Visibility** option from the shortcut menu displayed in the **Model Browser** bar; refer to Figure-66. The extra geometry will get hidden.

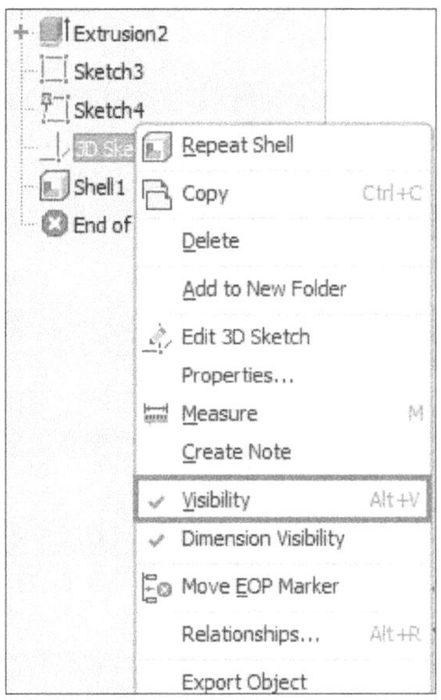

Figure-66. Visibility option

PRACTICAL 3

In this practical, you will create a model of spring as shown in Figure-67 with parameters as :

Wire Diameter : 5 mm
Pitch : 10 mm
Spring Diameter : 60 mm
Height : 150 mm

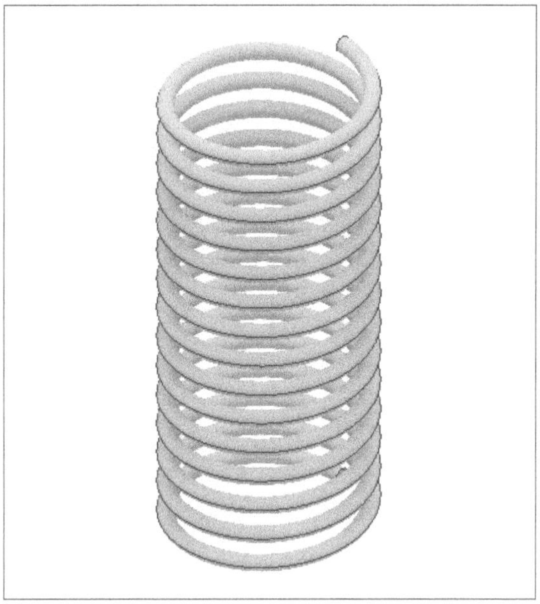

Figure-67. Model of spring

Strategy for Creating model

1. We have a direct tool to create springs in Autodesk Inventor but for using this tool, we must have a profile and an axis for the spring.
2. Create a sketch of profile with an axis.
3. Select the **Coil** tool and set the parameters of the spring.

Starting Part File

- Start Autodesk Inventor by double-clicking on the Autodesk Inventor Professional icon from the desktop. (If not started yet.)
- Click on the **New** button from the **Quick Access Toolbar**. The **Create New File** dialog box will be displayed.
- Double-click on **Standard(mm).ipt** icon from the **Metric** templates. The Part environment of Autodesk Inventor will be displayed.

Creating Sketch for Profile and axis

- Click on the **Start 2D Sketch** button from **Sketch** panel in the **3D Model** tab of the **Ribbon**. You will be asked to select a sketching plane.
- Select the **YZ** Plane (Right Plane) to create sketch.
- Create a circle and a line as shown in Figure-68.

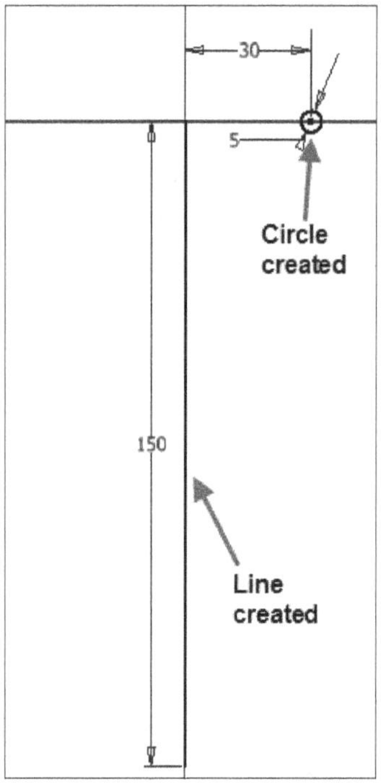

Figure-68. Sketch for spring

- Click on the **Finish Sketch** button from the **Finish** drop-down in the **Exit** panel of the **Ribbon**.
- Note that diameter of circle in this sketch represents diameter of wire and dimension of 30 represents the spring radius. Also, the line of **150** mm represents length of spring.

Creating Coil Feature

- Click on the **Coil** tool from **Create** panel in the **3D Model** tab of the **Ribbon**. The **Coil** dialog box will be displayed with profile selected automatically; refer to Figure-69. Also, you will be asked to select axis.

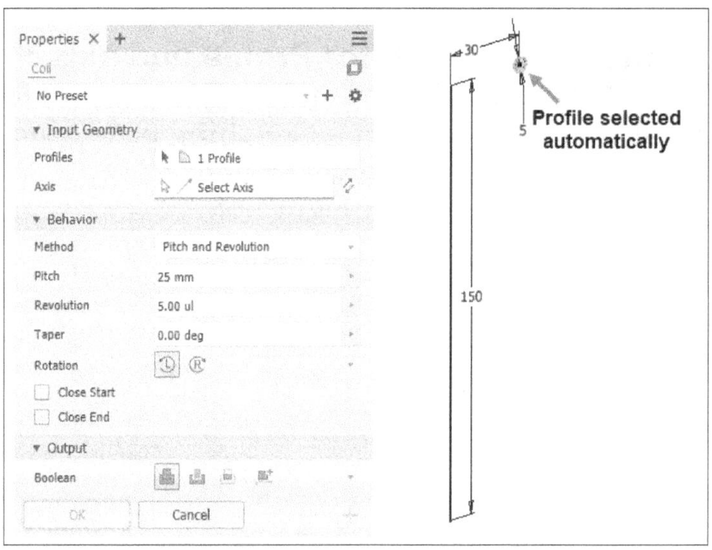

Figure-69. Coil dialog box with profile selected

- Select the line. The preview of coil will be displayed; refer to Figure-70.

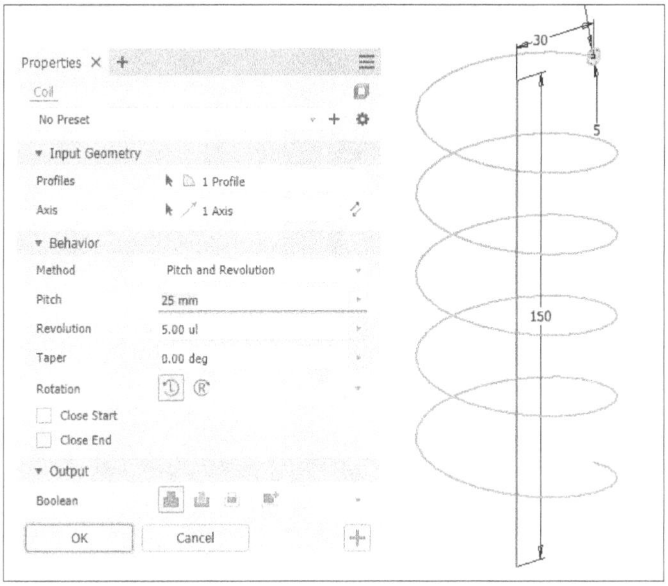

Figure-70. Preview of coil

- Click in the **Method** drop-down and select the **Pitch and Height** option from the drop-down. The **Pitch** and **Height** edit boxes will become active.
- Specify the value of pitch as **10** and height as **150** in the respective edit boxes.
- Click on the **OK** button from the dialog box. The spring will be created as shown in Figure-71.

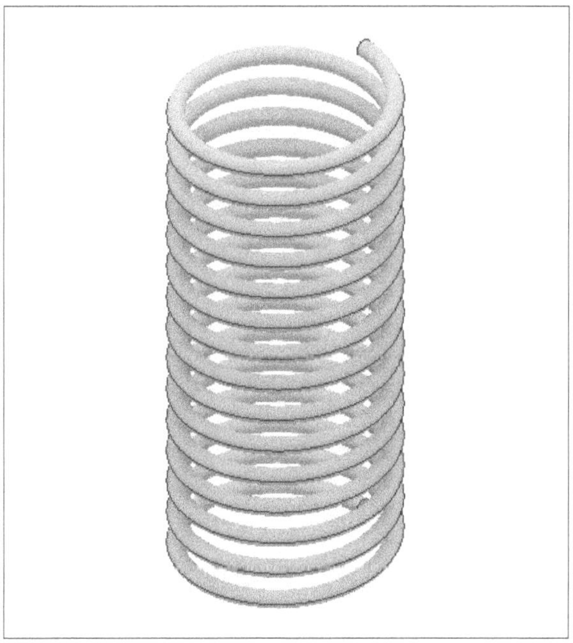

Figure-71. Model of spring

PRACTICAL 4

In this practical, you will create a model of support bracket as shown in Figure-72. Dimensions of the model are given in Figure-73.

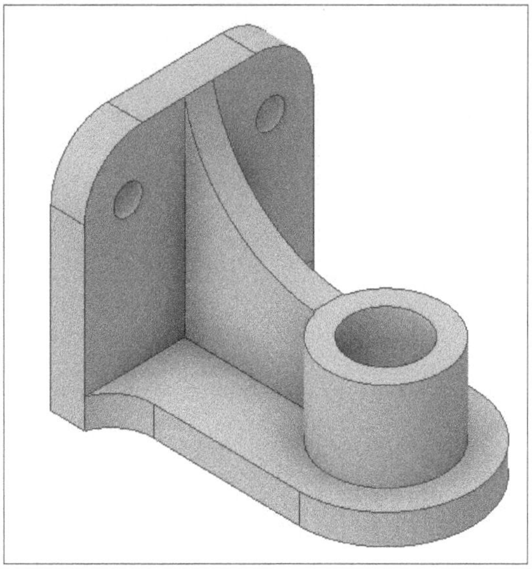

Figure-72. Model for Practical 4

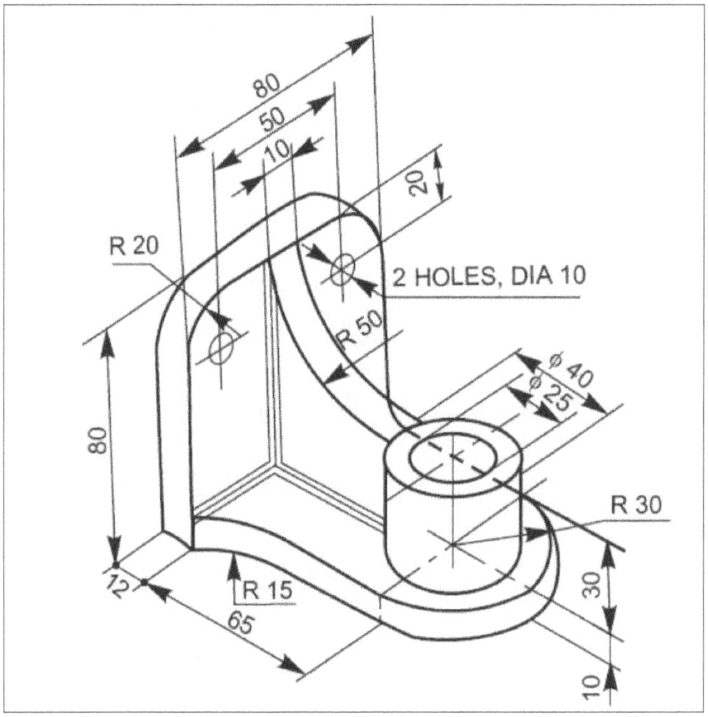

Figure-73. Dimensions for Practical 4

Strategy for Creating model

1. There are three extrude featured in the model; left side wall, bottom plate, and small tube. We will use the **Extrude** tool to create these features.
2. There is one rib feature which we will create by using the **Rib** tool.

Starting Part File

- Start Autodesk Inventor by double-clicking on the Autodesk Inventor Professional icon from the desktop. (If not started yet.)
- Click on the **New** button from the **Quick Access Toolbar**. The **Create New File** dialog box will be displayed.

- Double-click on **Standard(mm).ipt** icon from the **Metric** templates. The Part environment of Autodesk Inventor will be displayed.

Creating First Extrude Feature

- Click on the **Start 2D Sketch** button from **Sketch** panel in the **3D Model** tab of the **Ribbon**. You will be asked to select a plane.
- Select the **YZ** Plane (Right Plane) and create a sketch as shown in Figure-74.

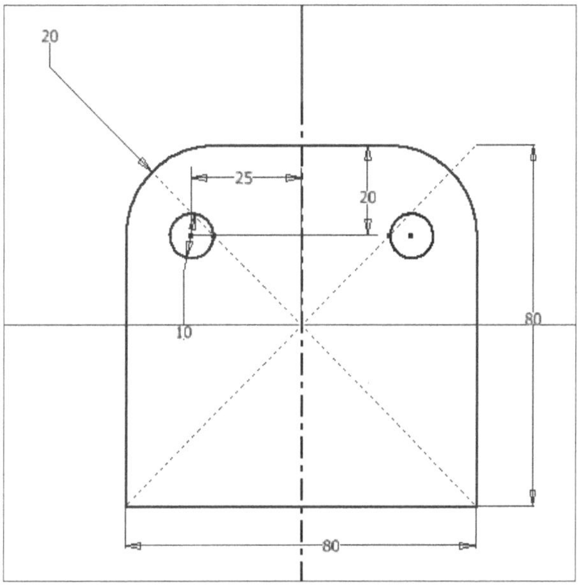

Figure-74. Sketch for base feature

- Click on the **Finish Sketch** button from the **Finish** drop-down in the **Exit** panel of the **Ribbon**.
- Click on the **Extrude** tool from **Create** panel in the **3D Model** tab of the **Ribbon**. You will be asked to select the section for extrusion.
- Select the inner loop of sketch and specify the extrusion distance as **12** in the **Distance A** edit box; refer to Figure-75. Preview of extrusion will be displayed.

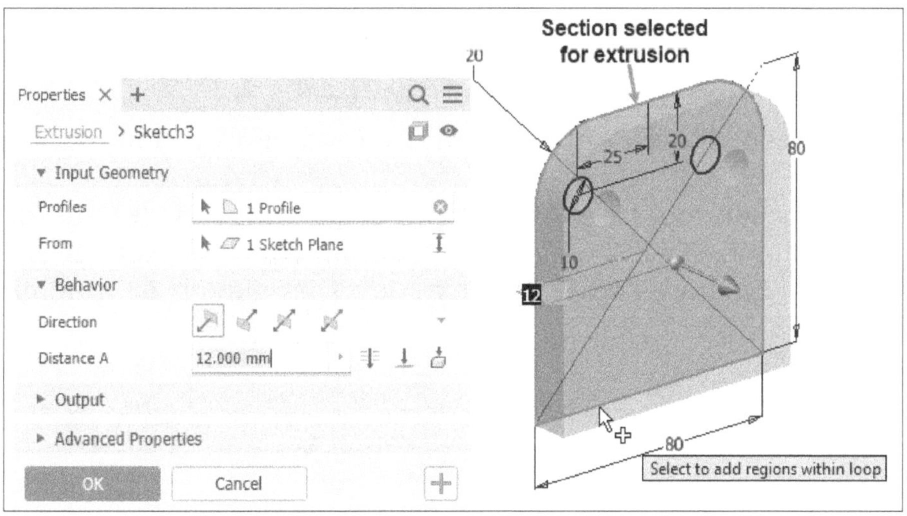

Figure-75. Section selected for extrusion

- Click on the **OK** button to create extrude feature.

Creating Second Extrude Feature

- Click on the **Start 2D Sketch** tool from **Sketch** panel in the **3D Model** tab of the **Ribbon**. You will be asked to select a sketching plane.
- Select the bottom face of extrude feature created earlier as sketching plane; refer to Figure-76.
- Create a sketch as shown in Figure-77.

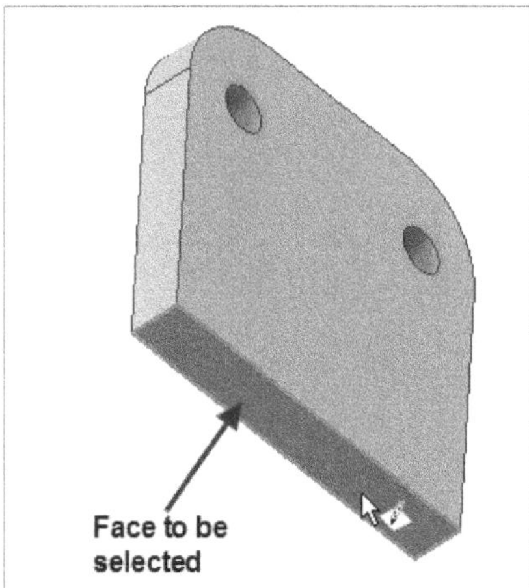

Figure-76. Face to select for sketching

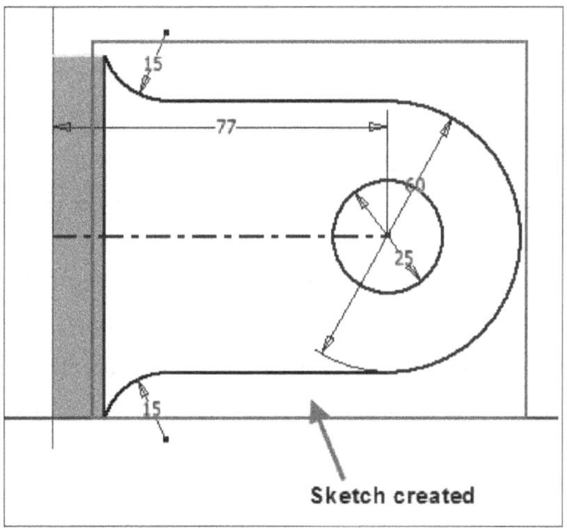

Figure-77. Sketch created for second extrusion

- Click on the **Finish Sketch** button from the **Finish** drop-down in the **Exit** panel of the **Ribbon**.
- Click on the **Extrude** tool from **Create** panel in the **3D Model** tab of the **Ribbon**. The **Extrude** dialog box will be displayed asking you to select the profile.
- Select the newly created sketch and extrude this sketch at a height of **10** mm; refer to Figure-78.

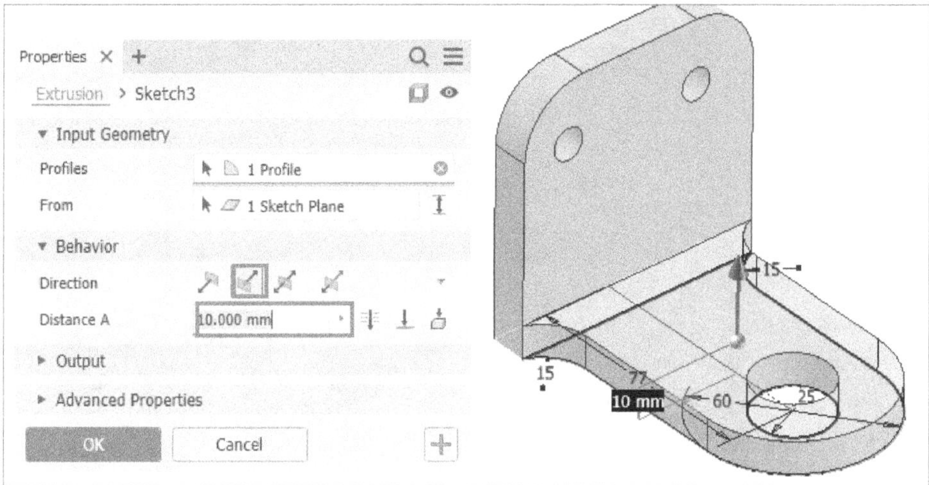

Figure-78. Extruding second sketch

- Click on the **OK** button from **Extrude** dialog box to create the feature.

Creating Third Extrusion

- Click on the **Start 2D Sketch** button from **Sketch** panel in the **3D Model** tab of the **Ribbon**. You will be asked to select the sketching plane or face.
- Select the flat face of second extrusion as sketching plane and create the sketch as shown in Figure-79.

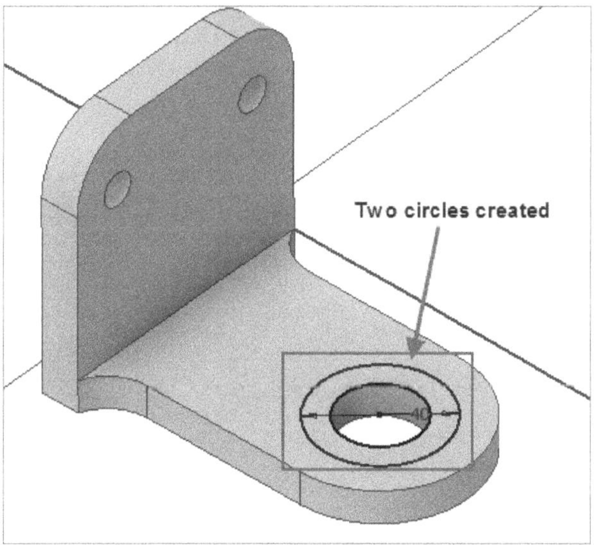

Figure-79. Sketch created on flat face

- Click on the **Finish Sketch** button from the **Finish** drop-down in the **Exit** panel of the **Ribbon**.
- Click on the **Extrude** tool from **Create** panel in the **3D Model** tab of the **Ribbon**. The **Extrude** dialog box will be displayed asking you to select the profile.
- Select the newly created sketch and extrude the sketch to the height of **30** mm; refer to Figure-80.

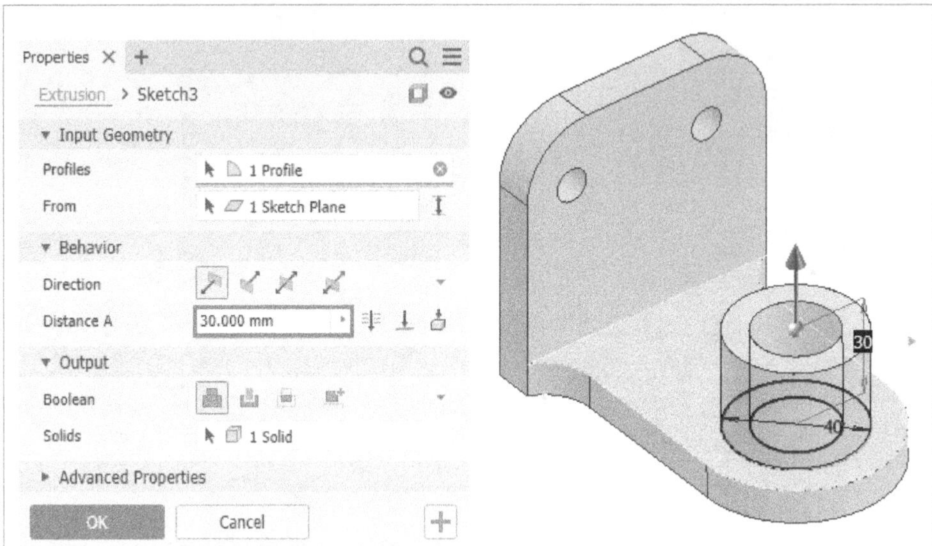

Figure-80. Third extrude feature creation

- Click on the **OK** button from the dialog box to create the feature.

Creating Rib Feature

- Click on the **Start 2D Sketch** button from **Sketch** panel in the **3D Model** tab of the **Ribbon**. You will be asked to select the sketching plane.
- Select the **XY** plane as sketching plane from the expanded **Origin** node in **Model Browser** bar. The sketching environment will become active; refer to Figure-81.

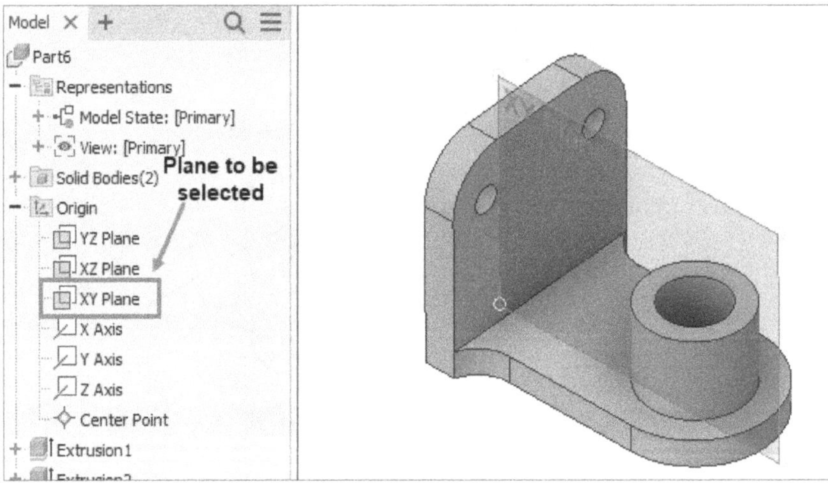

Figure-81. Selecting plane for rib feature sketch

- Create an arc of **50 mm** radius as shown in Figure-82. Note that end points of arc are coincident to faces of previous extrude features.

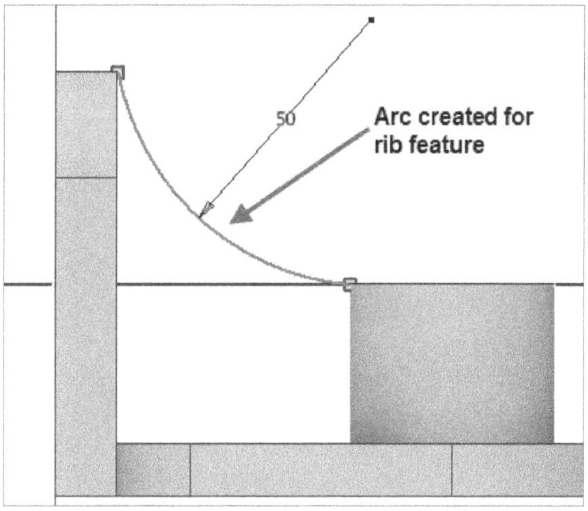

Figure-82. Sketch for rib feature

- Click on the **Finish Sketch** button from the **Finish** drop-down in the **Exit** panel of the **Ribbon**.
- Click on the **Rib** tool from **Create** panel in the **3D Model** tab of the **Ribbon**. The **Rib** dialog box will be displayed; refer to Figure-83.

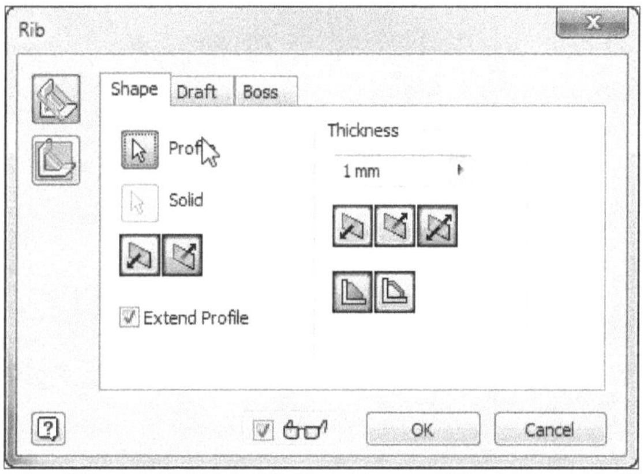

Figure-83. Rib dialog box

- Specify the thickness as **10** mm and select the **Parallel to Sketch Plane** button from the left area in the dialog box.
- Select the other buttons in the dialog box as shown in Figure-84.

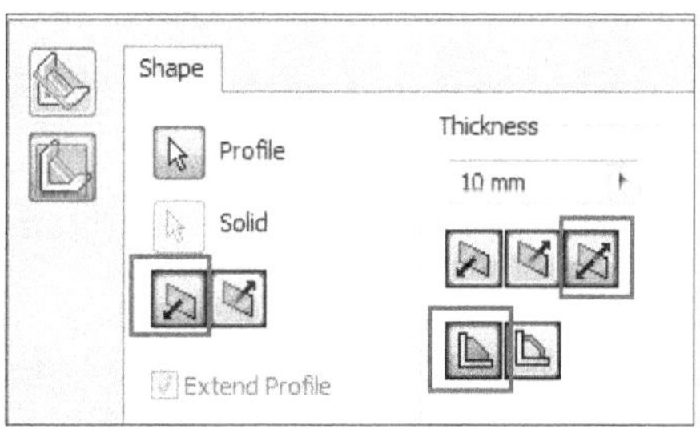

Figure-84. Buttons selected in Rib dialog box

- Click on the **OK** button from the dialog box. The rib feature will be created as shown in Figure-85.

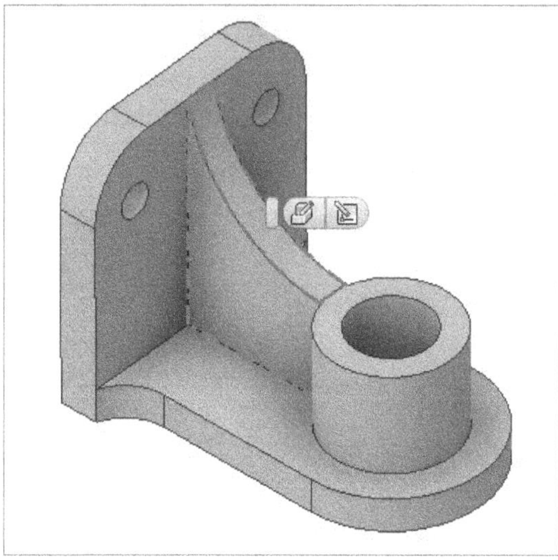

Figure-85. Rib feature created

PRACTICAL 5

In this practical, we will create a model as shown in Figure-86. Dimensions of the model are given in Figure-87.

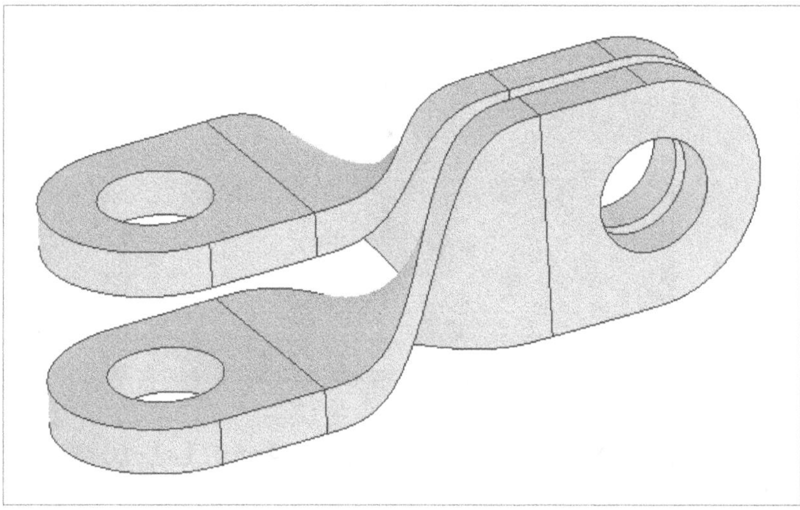

Figure-86. Model for Practical 5

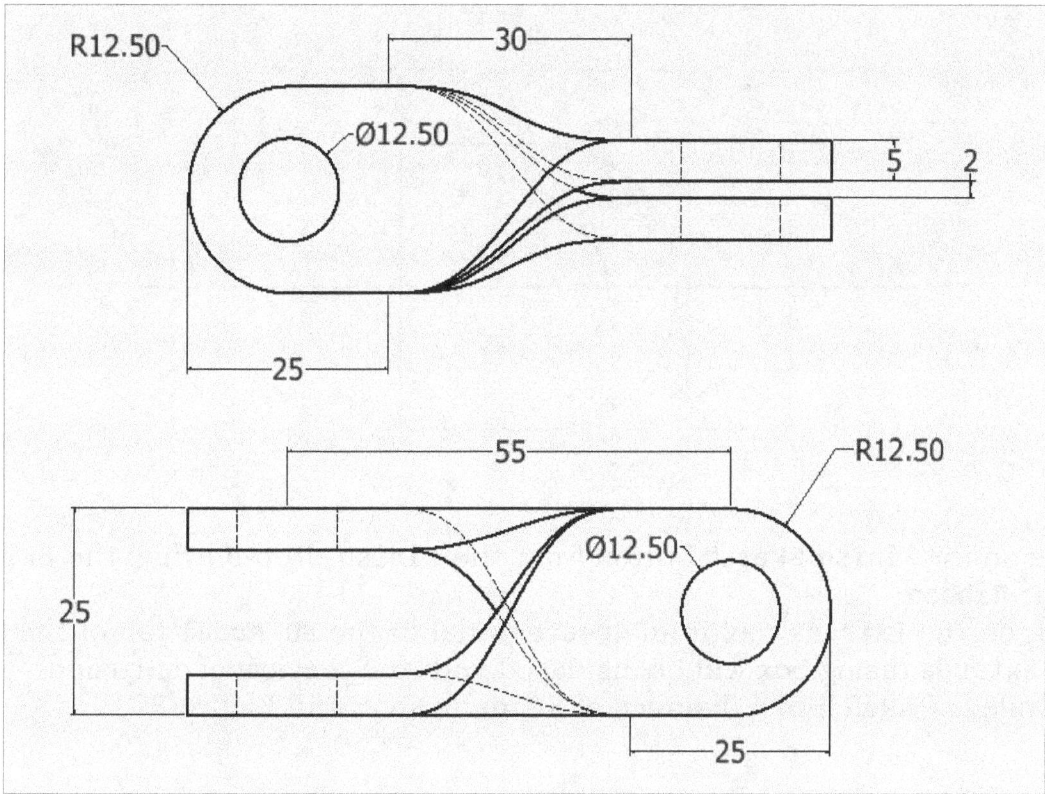

Figure-87. Dimensions for Practical 5

Strategy for Creating model

1. We need to create an extrude feature and then create rectangular pattern of that feature.
2. Similarly, we will create another extrude feature on the created offset plane and create a mirror copy of that extruded feature.
3. Using **Loft** tool, we will create loft feature between the extruded features.
4. Then, we will change the position of transition points in the **Transition** tab of the **Loft** dialog box.

Starting Part File

- Start Autodesk Inventor by double-clicking on the Autodesk Inventor Professional icon from the desktop. (If not started yet.)
- Click on the **New** button from the **Quick Access Toolbar**. The **Create New File** dialog box will be displayed.
- Double-click on **Standard(mm).ipt** icon from the **Metric** templates. The Part environment of Autodesk Inventor will be displayed.

Creating First Extrude Feature

- Click on the **Start 2D Sketch** button from **Sketch** panel in the **3D Model** tab of the **Ribbon**. You will be asked to select a sketching plane.
- Select the **XY** plane as sketching plane. The sketching environment will be displayed.
- Create a sketch as shown in Figure-88.

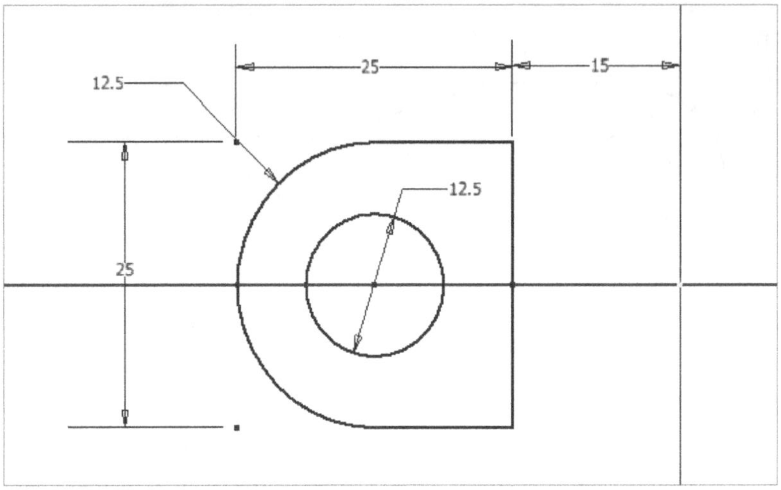

Figure-88. Creating sketch on XY plane

- Click on the **Finish Sketch** button from the **Finish** drop-down in the **Exit** panel of the **Ribbon**.
- Click on the **Extrude** tool from **Create** panel in the **3D Model** tab of the **Ribbon**. The **Extrude** dialog box will be displayed with the preview of extrusion.
- Extrude the sketch to a distance of **5** mm as shown in Figure-89.

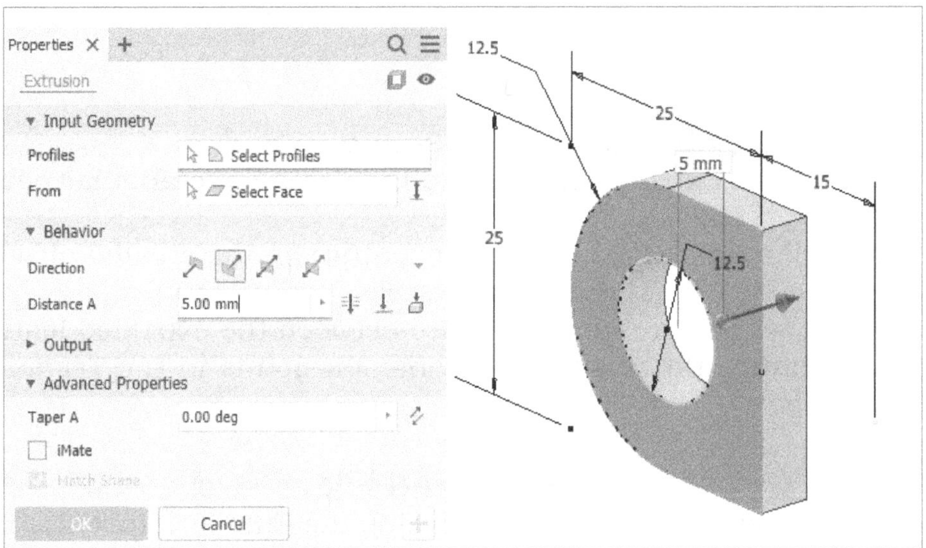

Figure-89. Extruding the sketch

- Click on the **OK** button from the **Extrude** dialog box to create the feature.

Creating pattern of the feature

- Click on the **Rectangular Pattern** tool from **Pattern** panel in the **3D Model** tab of **Ribbon**. The **Rectangular Pattern** dialog box will be displayed. You will be asked to select the feature.
- Select the recently created extrude feature to be patterned; refer to Figure-90.

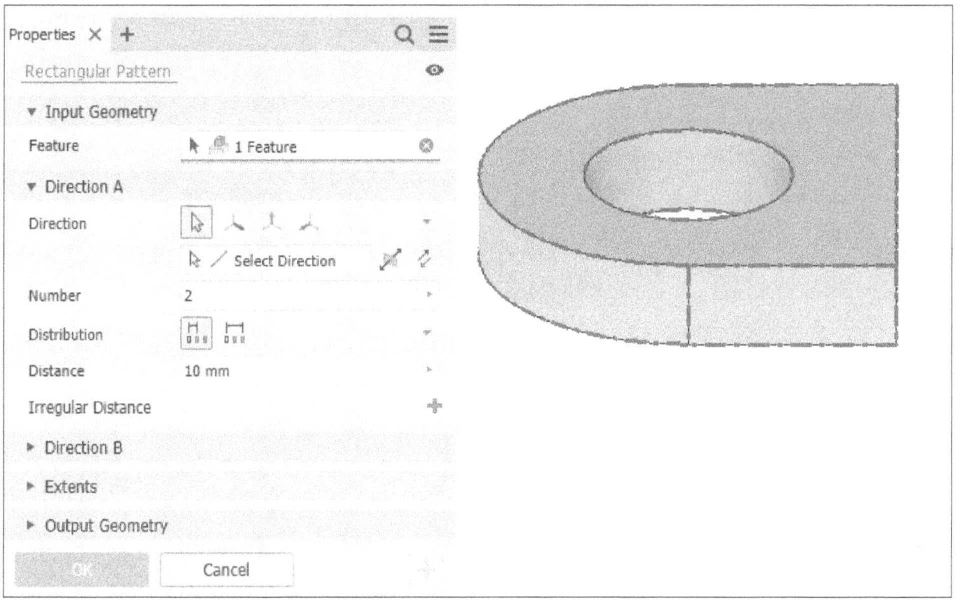

Figure-90. Selecting the feature to be patterned

- Click on the selection button of **Direction A** area of the dialog box and select the edge as shown in Figure-91.

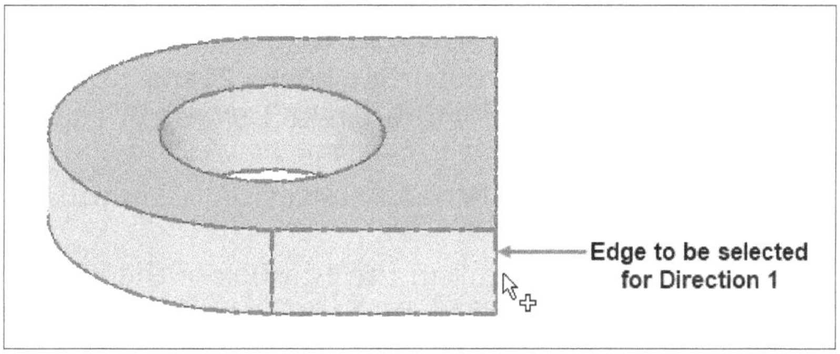

Figure-91. Edge selected for direction reference

- Specify the value of distance as **25** in the **Distance** edit box and number of instances as **2** in the **Number** edit boxes in **Direction A** area of the dialog box; refer to Figure-92.

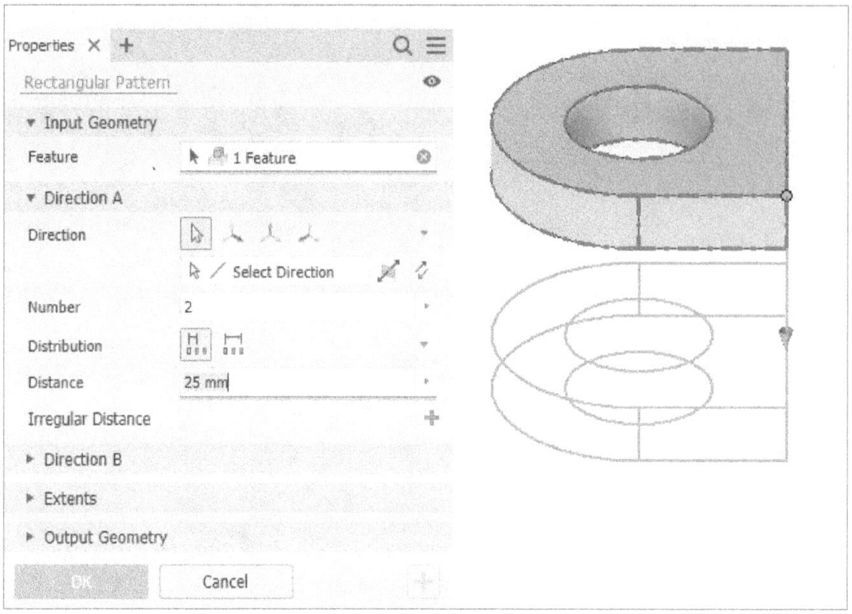

Figure-92. Specifying parameters to create the pattern

- Click on the **OK** button from the dialog box to create the feature.

Creating Second Extrude Feature

- Click on the **Offset from Plane** tool from **Work Plane** drop down in the **Work Features** panel of the **Ribbon**. You will be asked to select the plane or face as a reference to create the plane.
- Select **XZ** plane as a reference from **Model Browser** bar. You will be asked to specify the offset distance.
- Specify offset distance value as **1** mm in the edit box of the mini toolbar displayed and click on **OK** button from the mini toolbar to create the plane; refer to Figure-93.

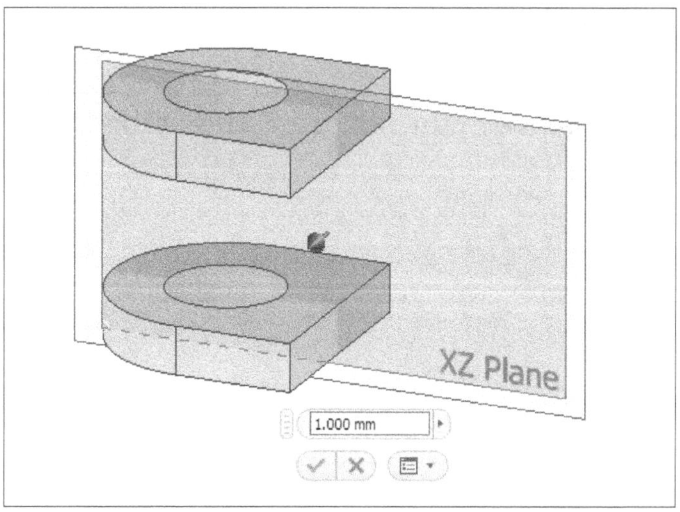

Figure-93. Specifying offset distance for plane

- Click on the **Start 2D Sketch** button from **Sketch** panel in the **3D Model** tab of the **Ribbon**. You will be asked to select a sketching plane.
- Select newly created offset plane as sketching plane. The sketching environment will be displayed.
- Create the sketch as shown in Figure-94.

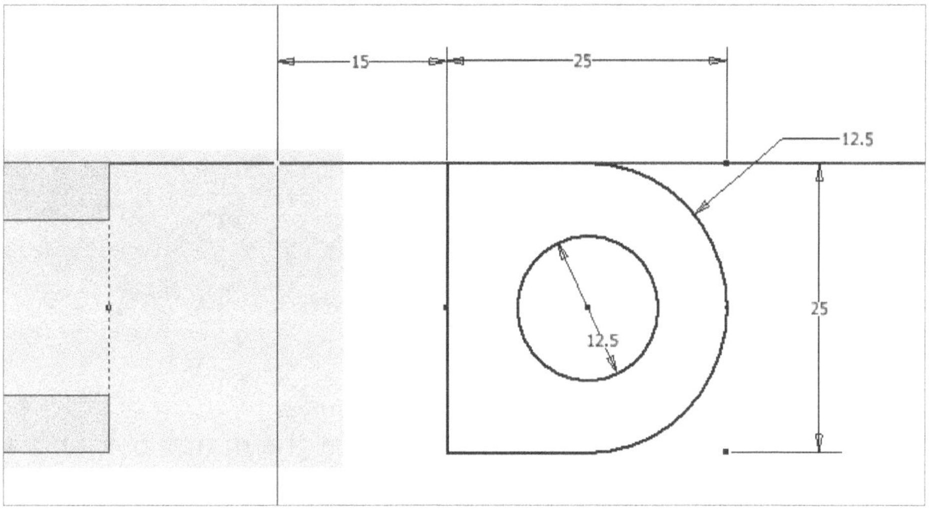

Figure-94. Creating sketch on offset plane

- Click on the **Finish Sketch** button from the **Finish** drop-down in the **Exit** panel of the **Ribbon**.
- Click on the **Extrude** tool from **Create** panel in the **3D Model** tab of the **Ribbon**. The **Extrude** dialog box will be displayed with the preview of extrusion.
- Extrude the sketch to a distance of **5** mm as shown in Figure-95.

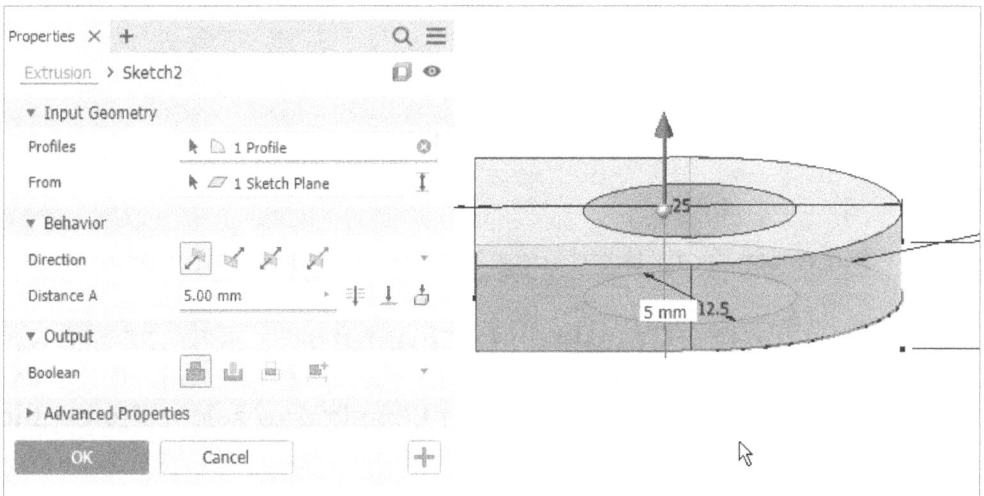

Figure-95. Extruding the second sketch

- Click on the **OK** button from the **Extrude** dialog box to create the feature.

Creating Mirror Feature

- Click on the **Mirror** tool from **Pattern** panel in the **3D Model** tab of the **Ribbon**. The **Mirror** dialog box will be displayed. You will be asked to select the feature to be mirrored.
- Select the recently created extrude feature as shown in Figure-96.

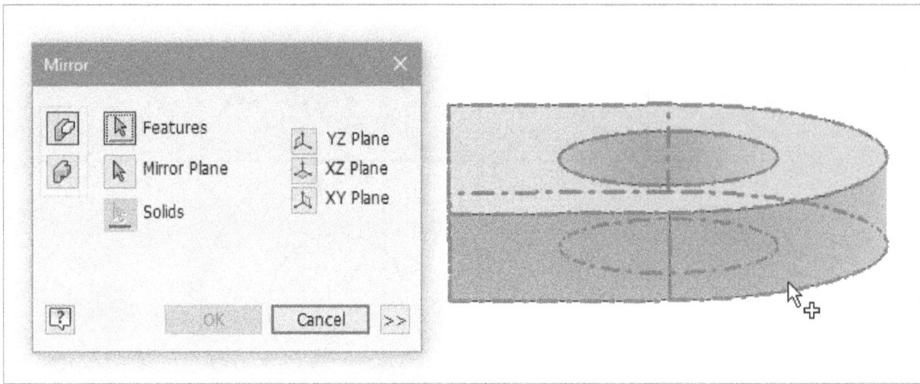

Figure-96. Selecting recently created extrude feature to be mirrored

- Click on the **Mirror Plane** selection button from the dialog box and select the **XZ Plane** button as mirror plane from the dialog box or from the **Model Browser** bar. Preview of the mirror feature will be displayed; refer to Figure-97.

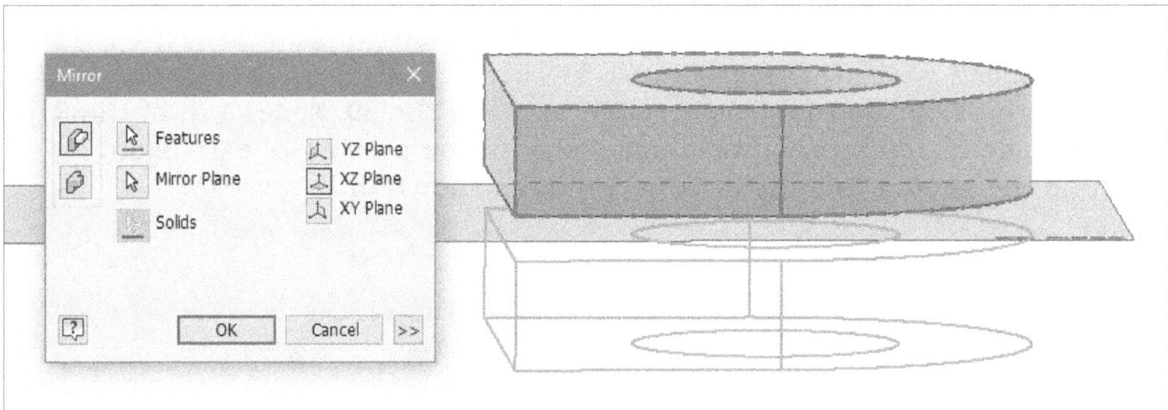

Figure-97. Selecting the mirror plane

- Click on the **OK** button from the dialog box to create the mirror feature.

Creating Loft Feature

- Click on the **Loft** tool from **Create** panel in the **3D Model** tab of the **Ribbon**. The **Loft** dialog box will be displayed. You will be asked to select the profiles to loft.
- One by one select the profiles between which you want to create the loft feature. Preview of the loft feature will be displayed; refer to Figure-98.

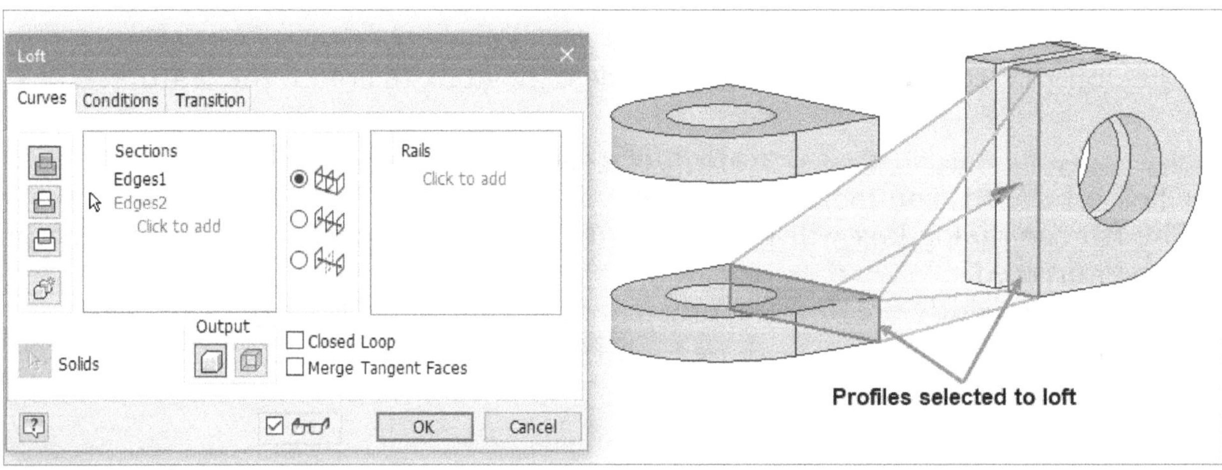

Figure-98. Preview of loft feature

- Click on the **Transition** tab of the **Loft** dialog box and clear the **Automatic Mapping** check box. The options to change position of transition points will be displayed; refer to Figure-99.

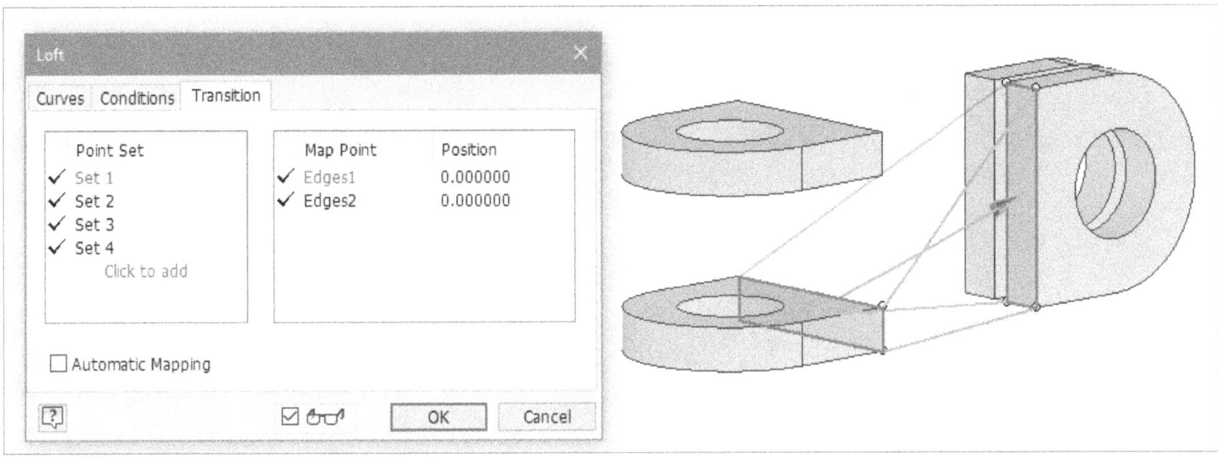

Figure-99. Options to change position of transition points

- Drag the keypoints to change the transition between the profiles as shown in Figure-100.

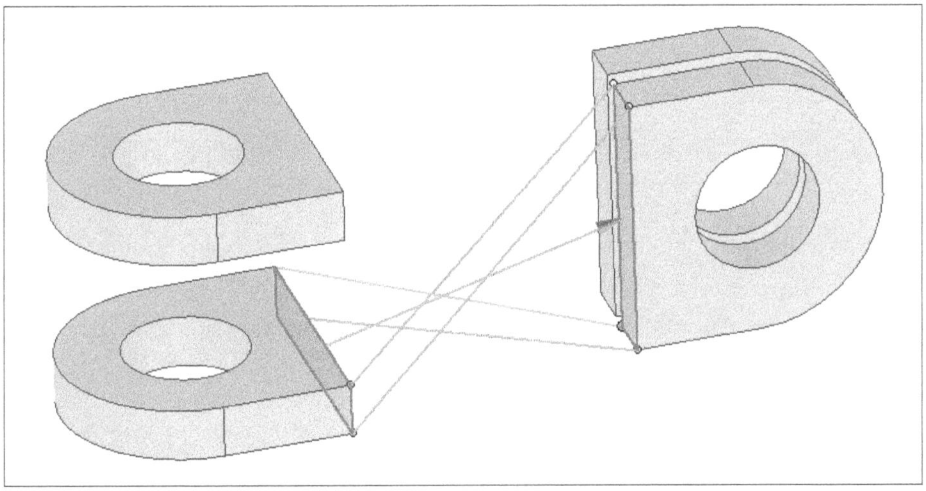

Figure-100. Changing the transition points

- Click on the **Conditions** tab of the **Loft** dialog box and select **Smooth (G2) Condition** option from **Conditions** drop-down of both the sections; refer to Figure-101.

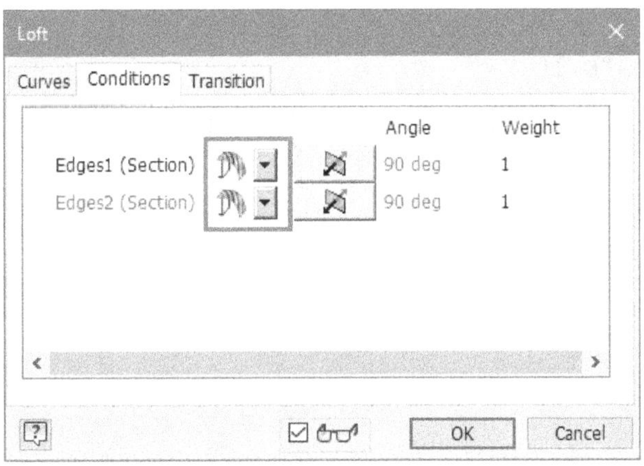

Figure-101. Specifying conditions for loft feature

- Specify the value of angle and weight for loft feature in the respective edit boxes as shown in Figure-101.
- Click on the **OK** button from the **Loft** dialog box to create the feature; refer to Figure-102.

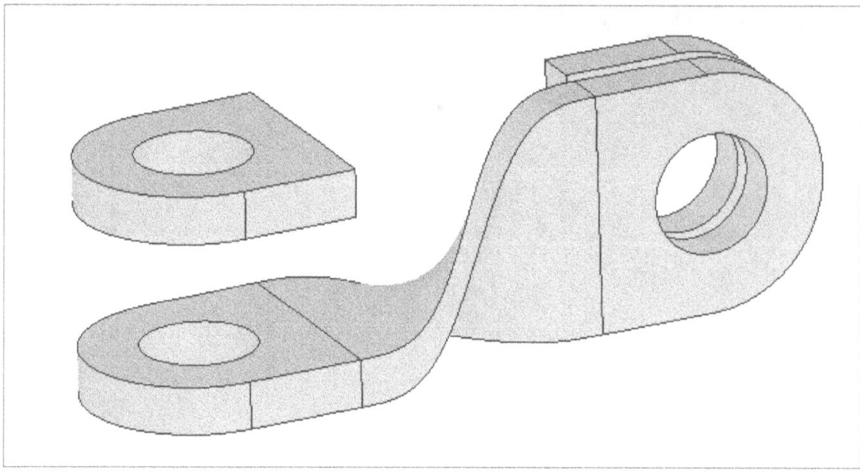

Figure-102. Creating the loft feature

- Similarly, create the second loft feature between the other profiles. The final model will be created as shown in Figure-103.

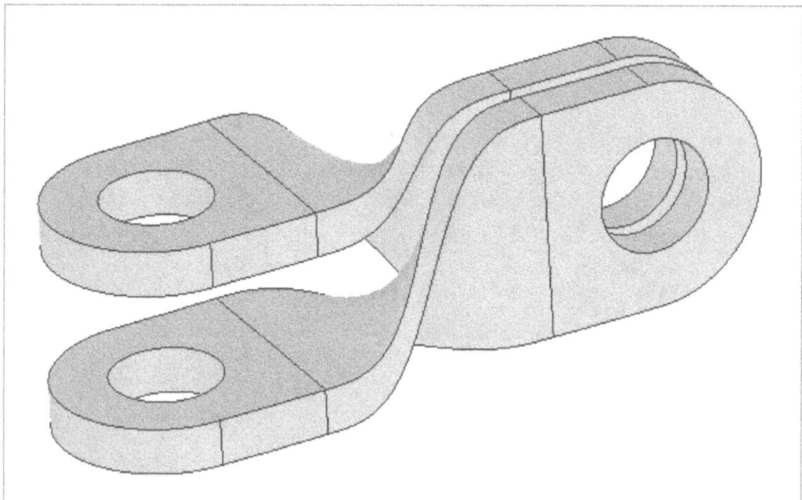

Figure-103. Final model of loft feature created

PRACTICAL 6

In this practical, we will create a model as shown in Figure-104. Dimensions of the model are given in Figure-105.

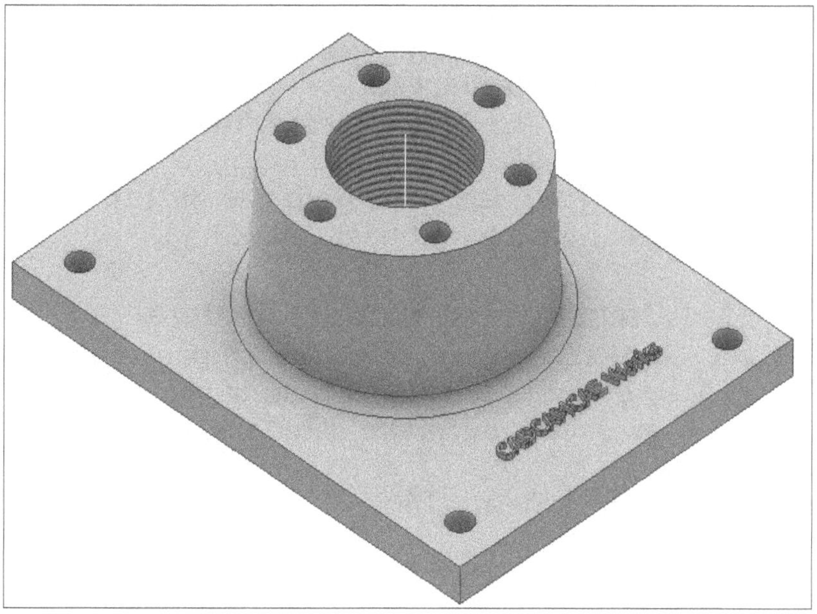

Figure-104. Practical 6 model

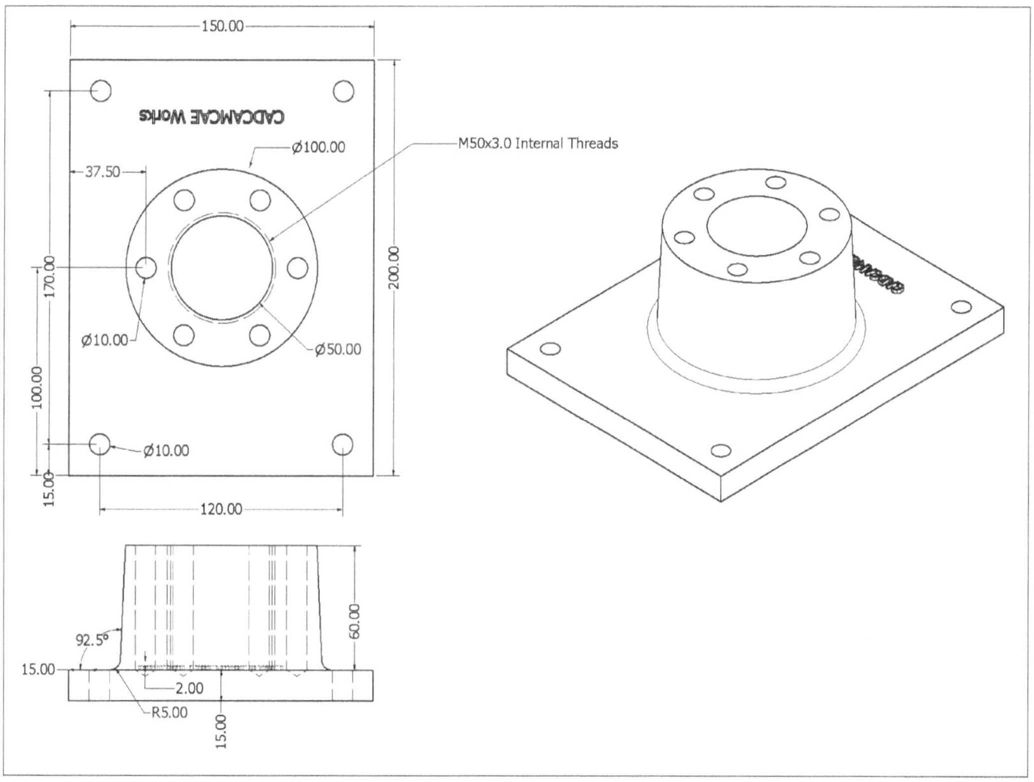

Figure-105. Practical 6 drawing

Strategy for Creating model

1. We need to create two extrude features; flat bottom plate and round tube on it.
2. We will then create one hole on tube and one hole on flat plate.
3. Using the Pattern tools, we will create multiple instances of hole.
4. We will create a sketch with the text on flat plate and then use the **Emboss** tool to emboss it on plate.

Starting Part File

- Start Autodesk Inventor by double-clicking on the Autodesk Inventor Professional icon from the desktop. (If not started yet.)
- Click on the **New** button from the **Quick Access Toolbar**. The **Create New File** dialog box will be displayed.
- Double-click on **Standard(mm).ipt** icon from the **Metric** templates. The Part environment of Autodesk Inventor will be displayed.

Creating First Extrude Feature

- Click on the **Start 2D Sketch** button from **Sketch** panel in the **3D Model** tab of the **Ribbon**. You will be asked to select a sketching plane.
- Select the **XZ** plane as sketching plane. The sketching environment will be displayed.
- Create a sketch as shown in Figure-106.

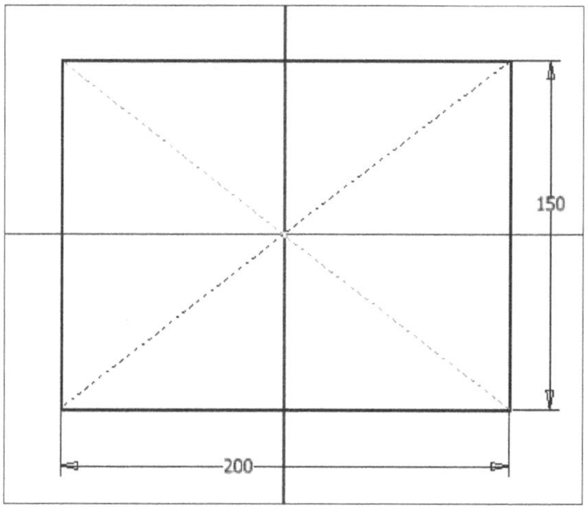

Figure-106. Sketch on XZ plane

- Click on the **Finish Sketch** button from the **Finish** drop-down in the **Exit** panel of the **Ribbon**.
- Click on the **Extrude** tool from **Create** panel in the **3D Model** tab of the **Ribbon**. The **Extrude** dialog box will be displayed with the preview of extrusion.
- Extrude the sketch to a height of **15** mm; refer to Figure-107.

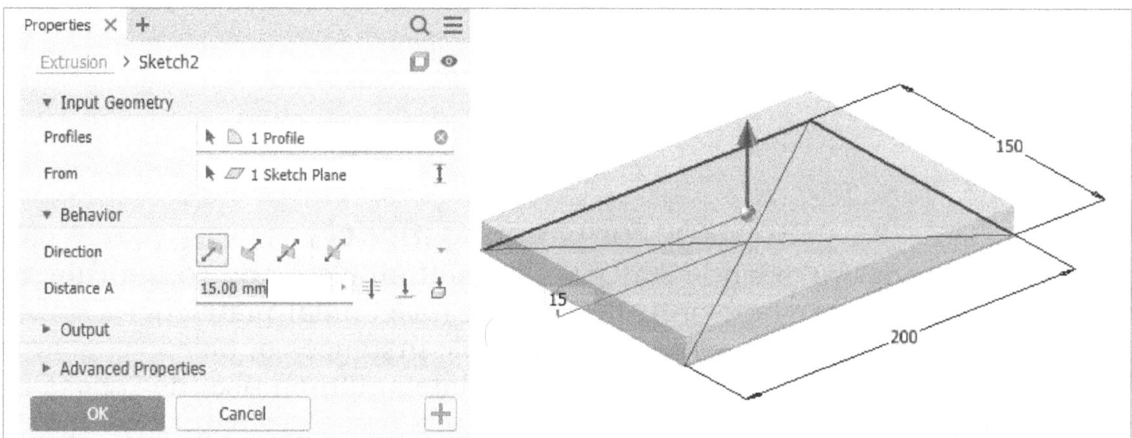

Figure-107. Extruded sketch

- Click on the **OK** button from the **Extrude** dialog box to create the feature.

Creating Second Extrude Feature

- Click on the **Start 2D Sketch** button from **Sketch** panel in the **3D Model** tab of the **Ribbon**. You will be asked to select a sketching plane.
- Select the top face of the plate as sketching plane. The sketching environment will be displayed.
- Create a sketch as shown in Figure-108.

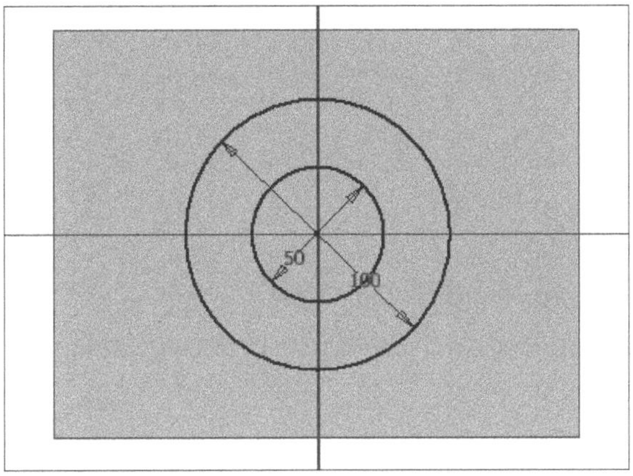

Figure-108. Sketch created on plate

- Click on the **Finish Sketch** button from the **Finish** drop-down in the **Exit** panel of the **Ribbon**.
- Click on the **Extrude** tool from **Create** panel in the **3D Model** tab of the **Ribbon**. The **Extrude** dialog box will be displayed asking you to select the profile.
- Select the newly created sketch and extrude the sketch to a height of **60** mm; refer to Figure-109.

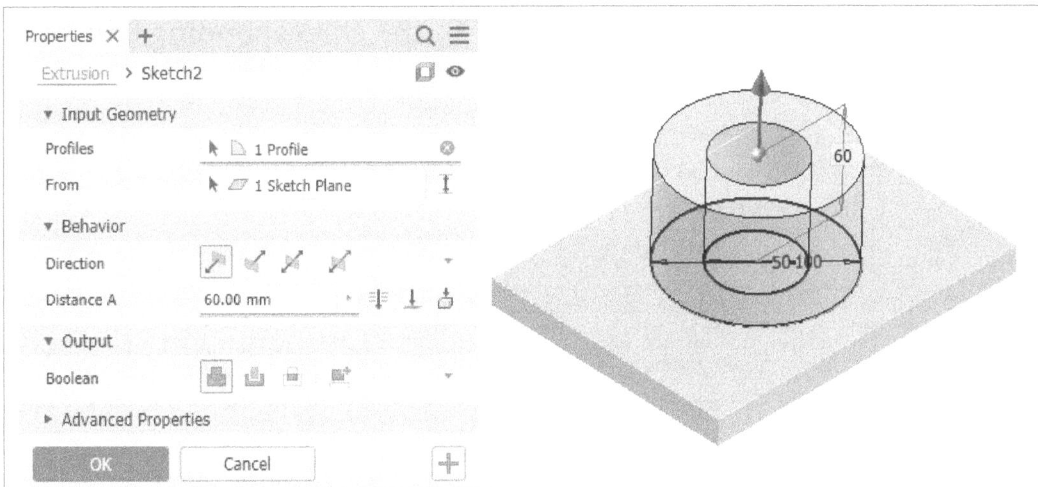

Figure-109. Extruding second feature

- Click on the **OK** button from the dialog box to create the feature.

Creating Holes

- Click on the **Hole** tool from **Modify** panel in the **3D Model** tab of the **Ribbon**. The **Hole** dialog box will be displayed; refer to Figure-110.

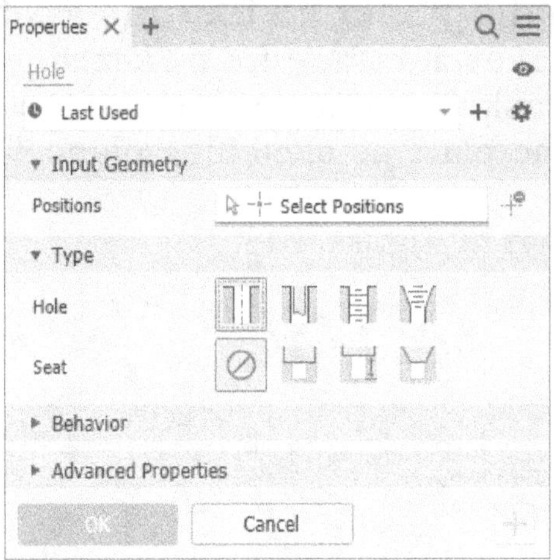

Figure-110. Hole dialog box

- Select the top face of the second extrude feature; refer to Figure-111.

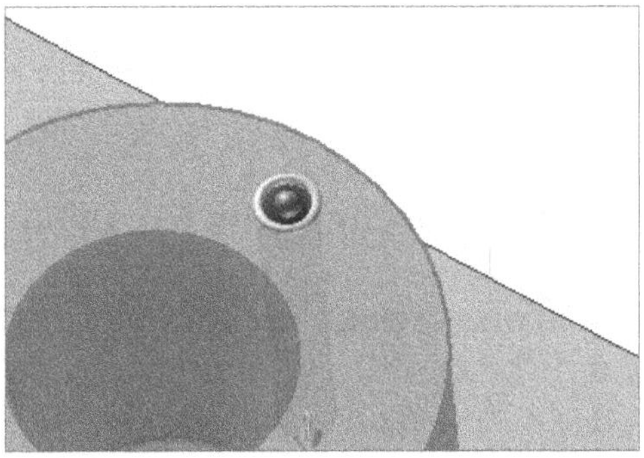

Figure-111. Position selected on the top face of extrude feature

- Specify the diameter of the hole as **10** mm in the corresponding edit box; refer to Figure-112.

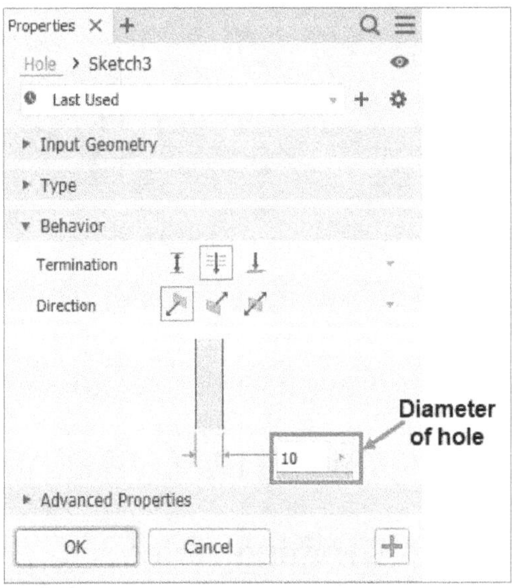

Figure-112. Edit box for specifying hole diameter

- Select the first reference linear edge to create the dimension and set the distance as **100** mm in the corresponding edit box; refer to Figure-113.

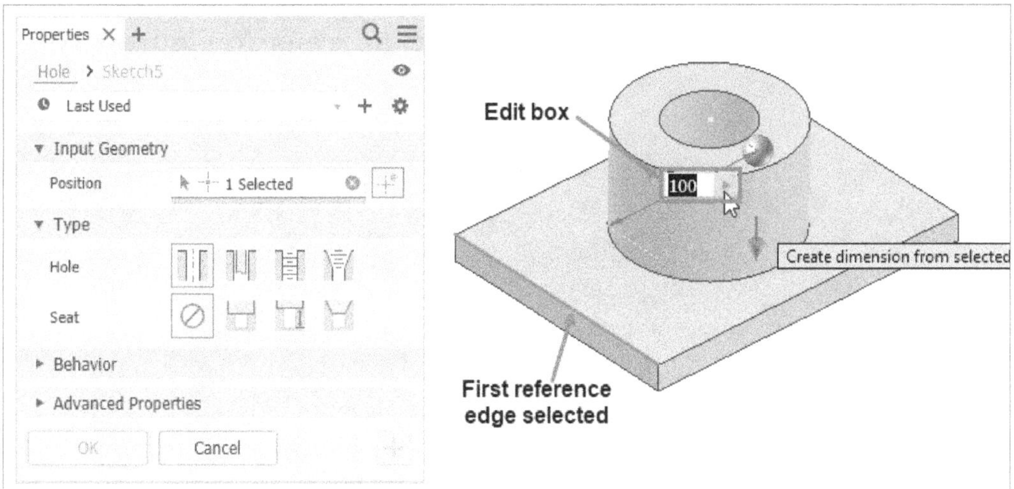

Figure-113. Selecting first reference edge

- Select the second reference linear edge to create the dimension and specify the distance as **37.5** in the corresponding edit box displayed; refer to Figure-114.

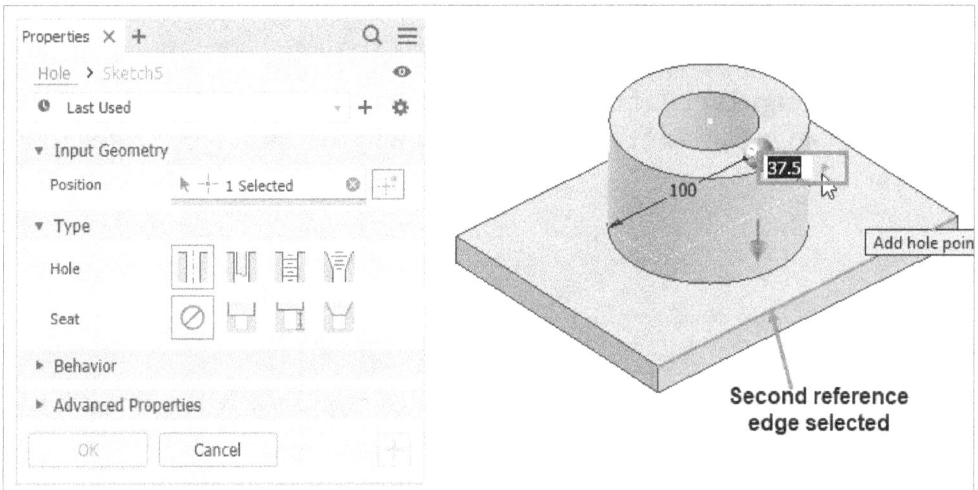

Figure-114. Selecting second reference edge

- Select the **To** button from **Behavior** drop-down in the **Termination** area of the dialog box. You will be asked to select terminating face.
- Select the top face of flat plate as terminating face; refer to Figure-115.

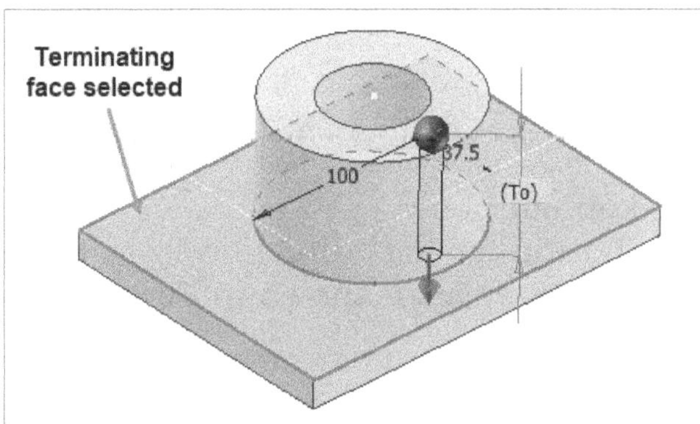

Figure-115. Terminating face selected

- Select the **Terminate feature by extending the face** button since the selected face is not intersecting with the path of hole.
- Click on the **OK** button from the dialog box to create the feature.

- Similarly, create a hole on the flat plate at a distance of **15** mm from the both edge, diameter **10** mm, and termination as through all; refer to Figure-116.

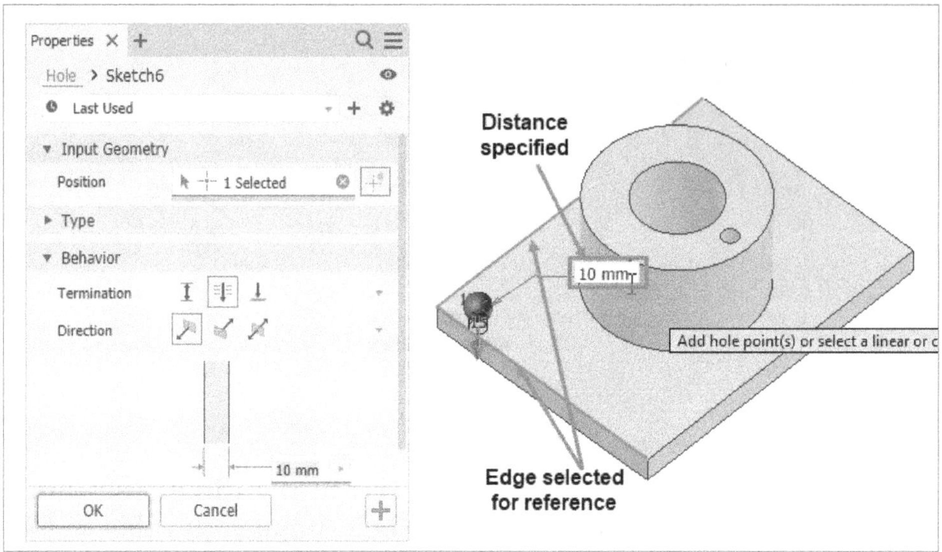

Figure-116. Creating second hole

Creating Patterns of Holes

- Click on the **Rectangular Pattern** tool from **Pattern** panel in the **3D Model** tab of **Ribbon**. The **Rectangular Pattern** dialog box will be displayed; refer to Figure-117.

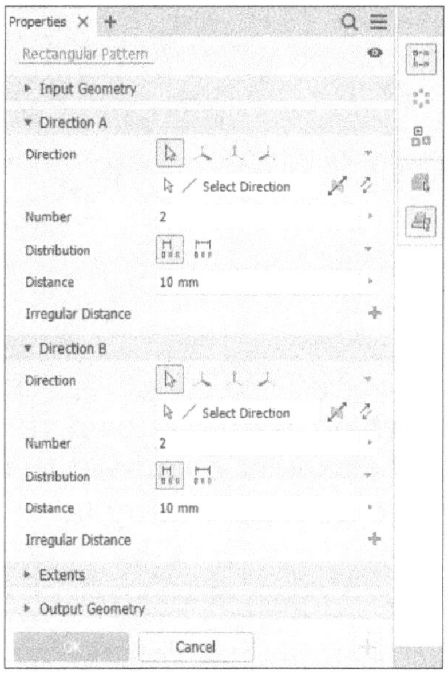

Figure-117. Rectangular Pattern dialog box

- Select the hole created on flat plate.
- Click on the selection button for first direction from the **Direction** A area of the dialog box and select the edge as shown in Figure-118.

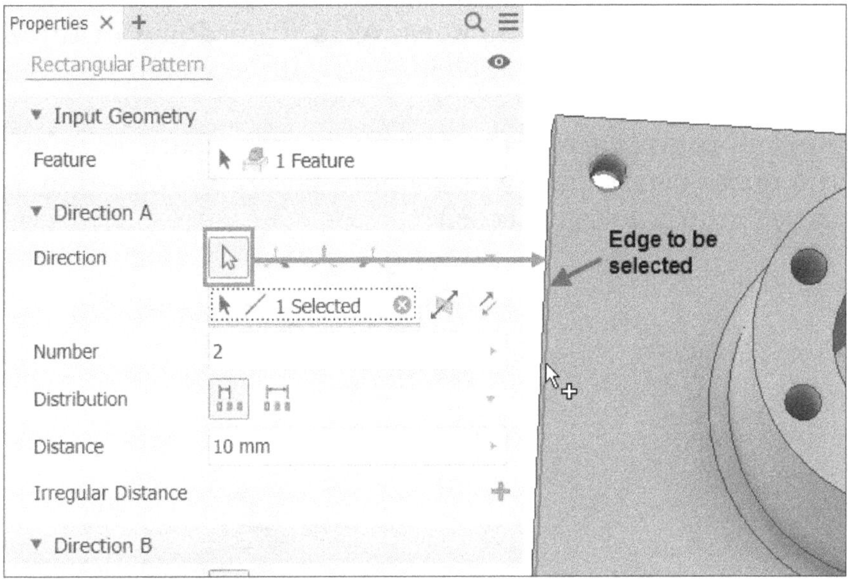

Figure-118. Edge to be selected

- Specify the value of distance as **120** and number of instances as **2** in the respective edit boxes in **Direction A** area of the dialog box; refer to Figure-119.

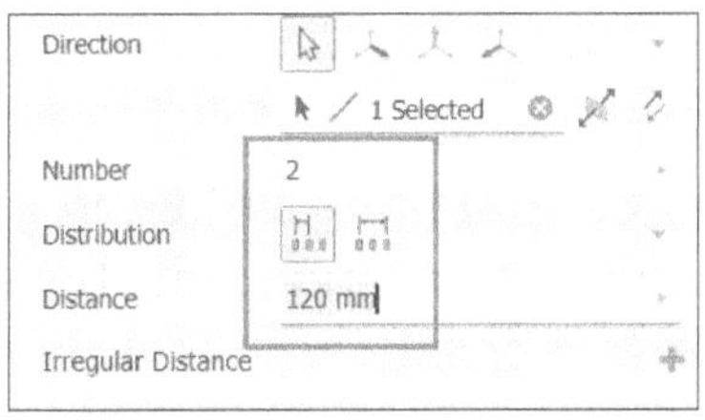

Figure-119. Parameters specified for direction 1

- Similarly, specify the distance in second direction as **170** and number of instances as **2** for Direction B area; refer to Figure-120.

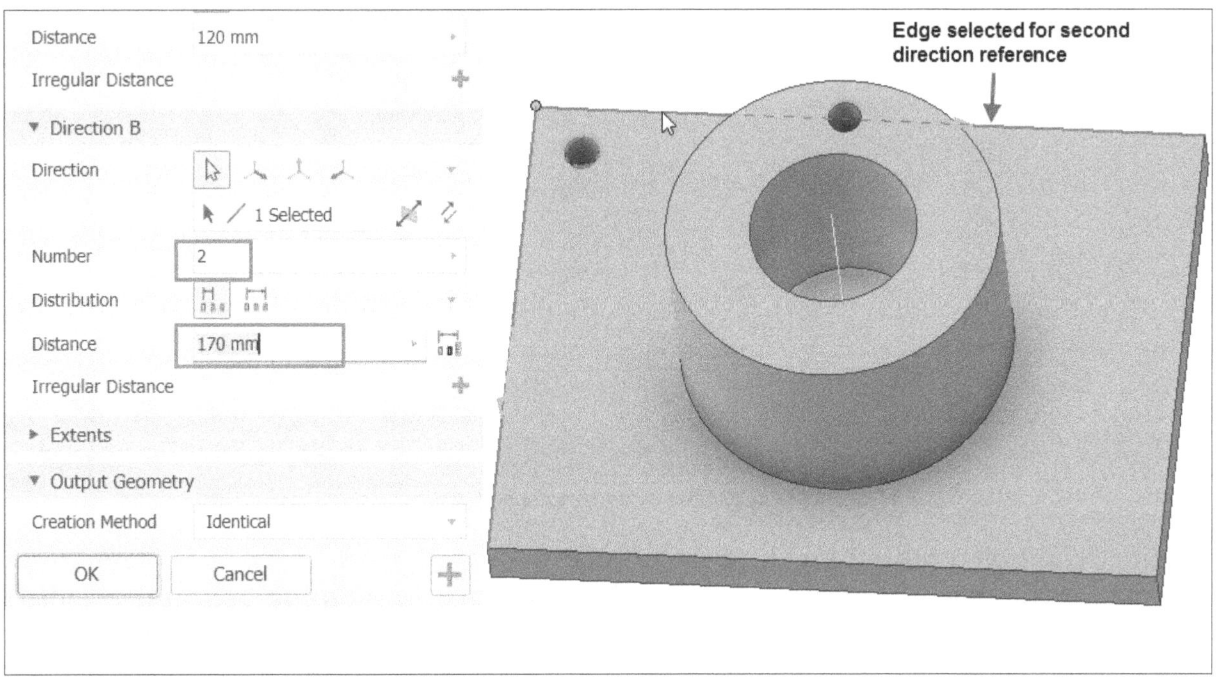

Figure-120. Parameters specified for direction 2

- Click on the **OK** button from the dialog box.
- Click on the **Axis** button from the **Work Axis** drop-down in the **Work Features** panel of the **3D Model** tab in the **Ribbon**. You will be asked to select geometry for creating axis.
- Select the internal round face of the second extrude feature; refer to Figure-121. (Note that the outer round face will become tapered after applying draft, so we are selecting the internal round face.)

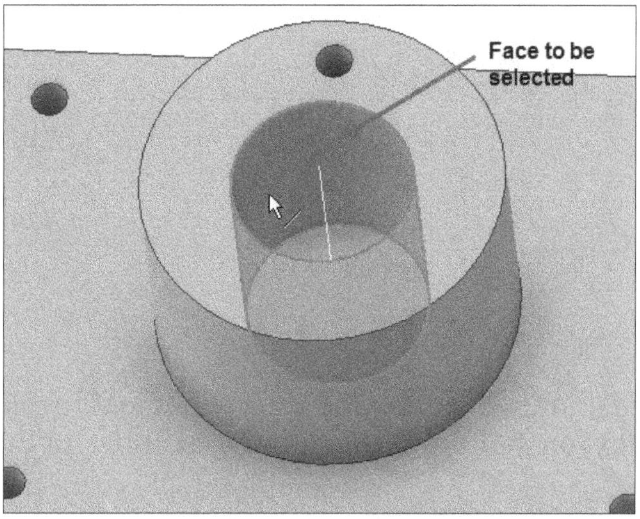

Figure-121. Selecting round face for axis

- Click on the **Circular Pattern** tool from **Pattern** panel in the **3D Model** tab of the **Ribbon**. The **Circular Pattern** dialog box will be displayed; refer to Figure-122. Also, you will be asked to select features to be patterned.

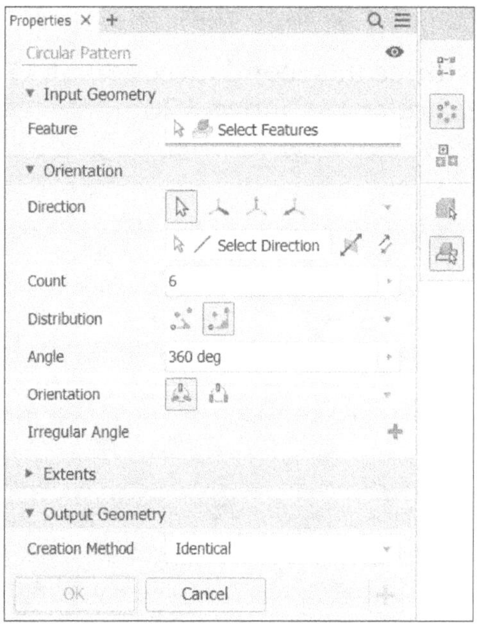

Figure-122. Circular pattern dialog box

- Select the hole created on the face of tube.
- Click on the selection button for **Rotation Axis** in the dialog box and select the axis we have created earlier; refer to Figure-123.

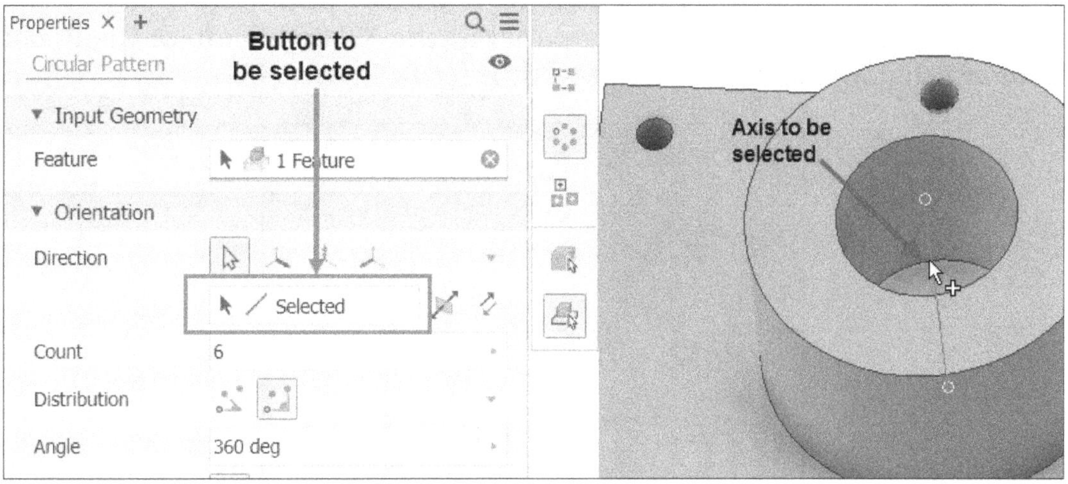

Figure-123. Axis selected for circular pattern

- Set the number of instances as **6** and Occurrence angle as **360** in the respective edit boxes in the dialog box; refer to Figure-124.

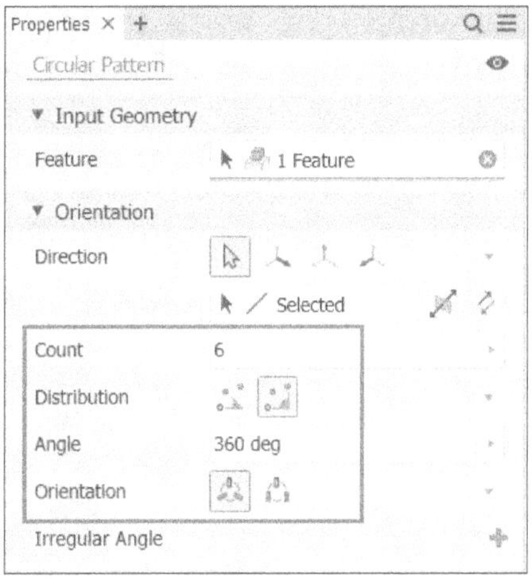

Figure-124. Parameters for circular pattern

- Click on the **OK** button from the dialog box to create the pattern; refer to Figure-125.

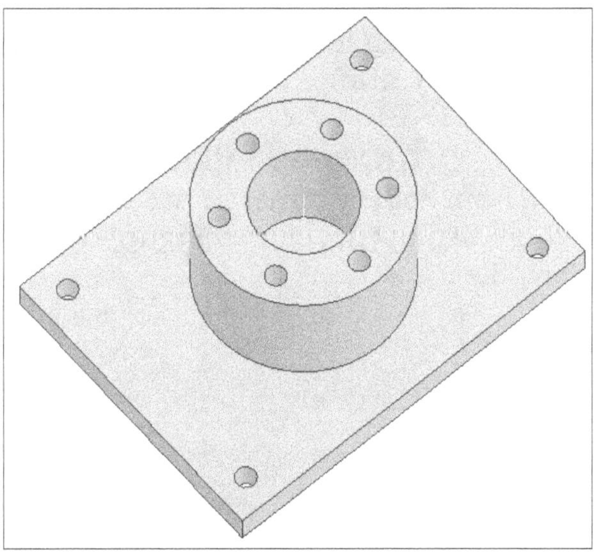

Figure-125. Model after pattern creation

Applying Draft to Round Face

- Click on the **Draft** tool from **Modify** panel in the **3D Model** tab of the **Ribbon**. The **Face Draft** dialog box will be displayed; refer to Figure-126.

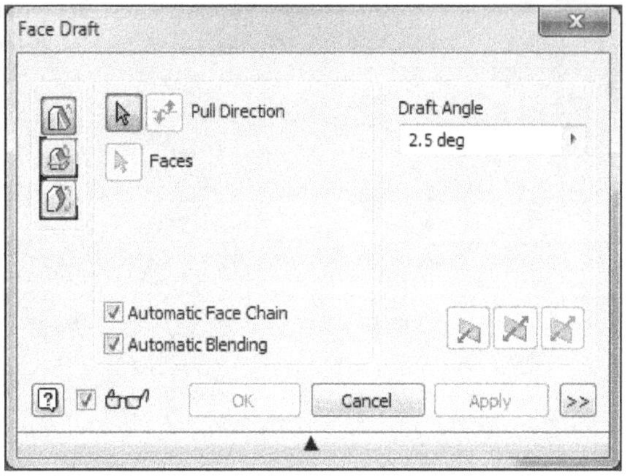

Figure-126. Face Draft dialog box

- Select the top face of the extruded tube feature as pull direction face. You will be asked to select the faces on which you want to apply draft.
- Select the round face of the tube feature; refer to Figure-127.

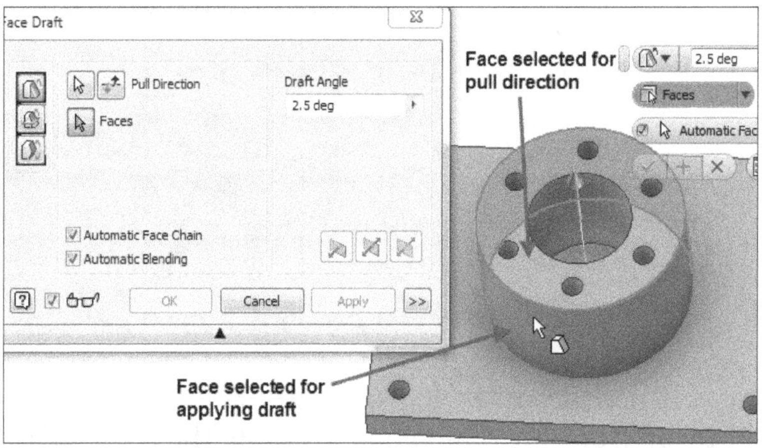

Figure-127. Faces selected for draft

- Specify the angle value as **2.5** deg in the **Draft Angle** edit box of the dialog box.
- Click on the **OK** button to apply draft.

Applying Fillet

- Click on the **Fillet** tool from **Modify** panel in the **3D Model** tab of the **Ribbon**. The **Fillet** dialog box will be displayed; refer to Figure-128. Also, you will be asked to select edges to apply fillet.

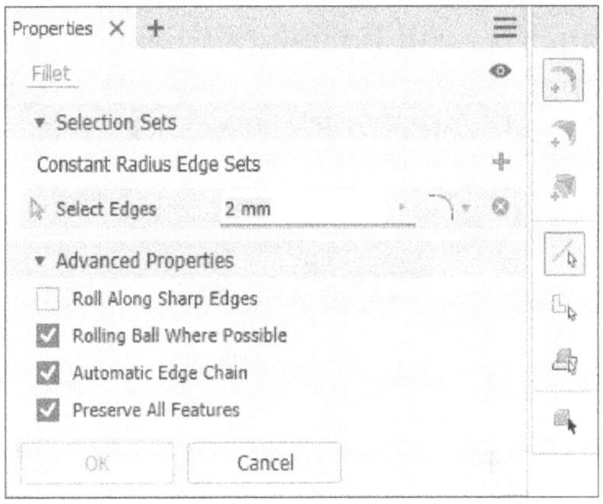

Figure-128. Fillet dialog box

- Specify the value of radius as **5** in the dialog box.
- Select the round edge of the extruded tube feature as shown in Figure-129. Preview of the fillet will be displayed.

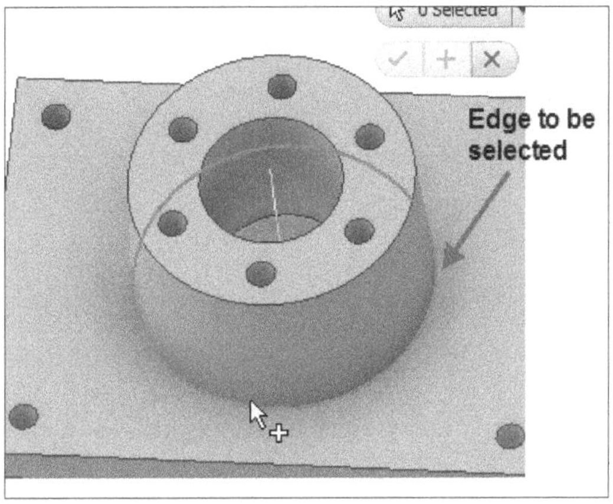

Figure-129. Edge selected for fillet

- Click on the **OK** button from the dialog box to create the feature.

Creating Emboss Feature

- Click on the **Start 2D Sketch** tool from **Sketch** panel in the **3D Model** tab of the **Ribbon**. You will be asked to select sketching plane.
- Select the top face of flat plate. The sketching environment will become active.
- Position the model as shown in Figure-130. Note that you may need to use the rotation arrows of **ViewCube** to change orientation of model; refer to Figure-131.

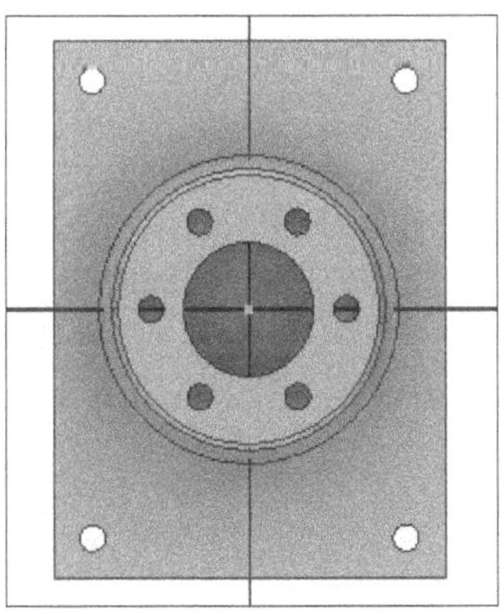

Figure-130. Model after changing orientation

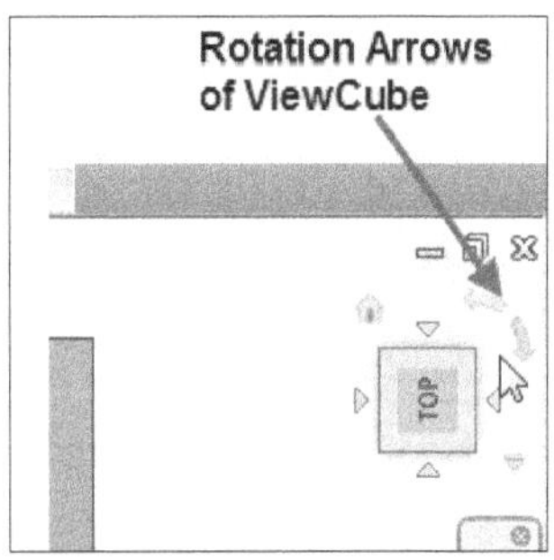

Figure-131. Rotation arrows of ViewCube

- Click on the **Text** tool from the **Geometry Text** drop-down in the **Create** panel of the **Sketch** tab in the **Ribbon**. You will be asked to specify the location of the text box.
- Click at the location approximately as shown in Figure-132. The **Format Text** dialog box will be displayed; refer to Figure-133.

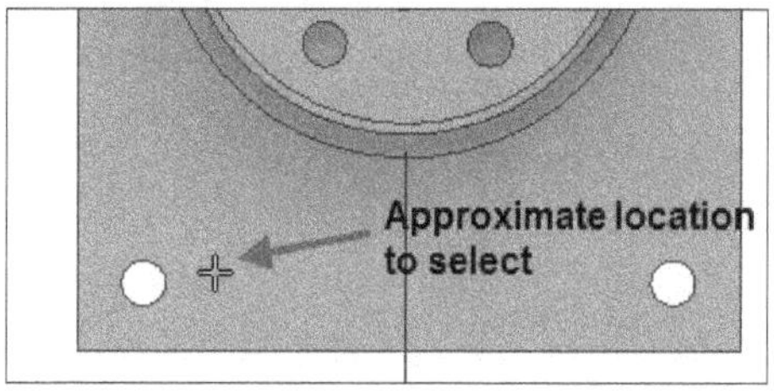

Figure-132. Approximate location to select

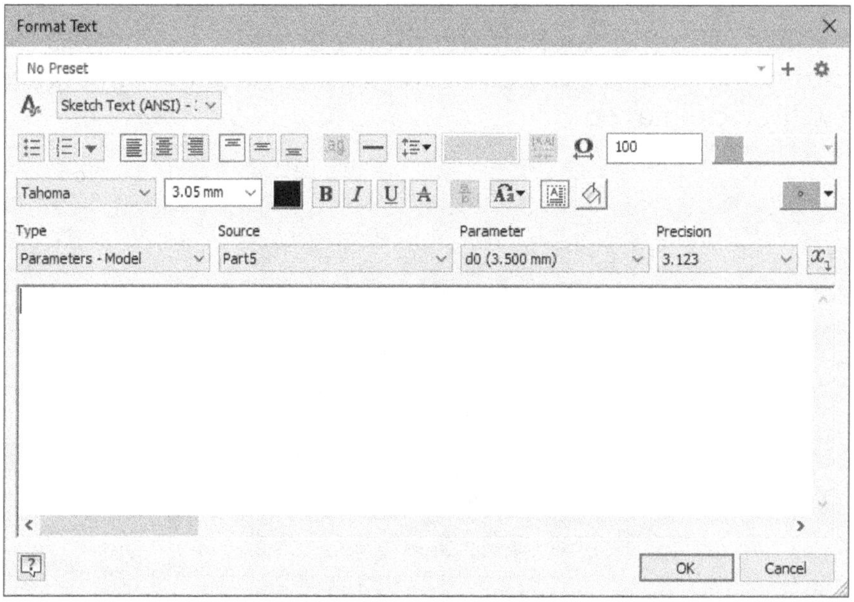

Figure-133. Format Text dialog box

- Select the font size as **6.10** from the size drop-down; refer to Figure-134.

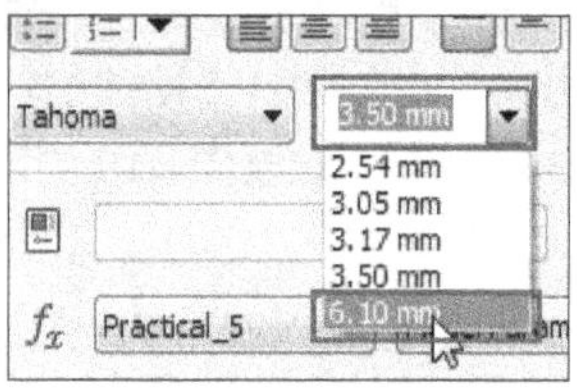

Figure-134. Font size drop-down

- Type the text as **CADCAMCAE Works** in the space provided for it.
- Click on the **OK** button from the dialog box.
- Press **ESC** from the keyboard to exit the tool.
- Click on the text created and drag it to desired position.
- Click on the **Finish Sketch** tool from **Exit** panel in the **Ribbon**.
- Click on the **Emboss** tool from **Create** panel in the **3D Model** tab of the **Ribbon**. The **Emboss** dialog box will be displayed; refer to Figure-135. Also, you will be asked to select the profile for embossing.

Figure-135. Emboss dialog box

- Click on the text created earlier. Specify the depth as **2** in the **Depth** edit box in the dialog box.
- Make sure the **Emboss from Face** button is selected and the direction of embossing is upward; refer to Figure-136.

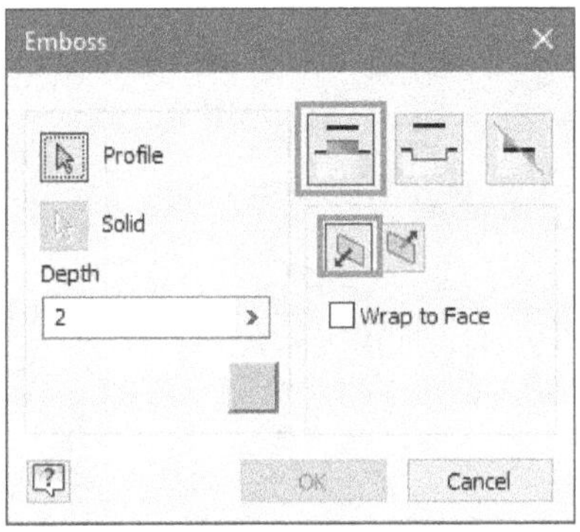

Figure-136. Option to be select for embossing

- Click on the **OK** button from the dialog box. The embossing will be created; refer to Figure-137.

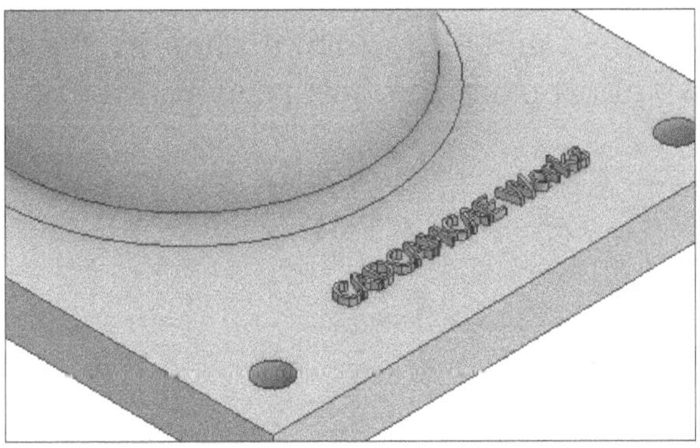

Figure-137. Embossing created

Creating Thread

- Click on the **Thread** tool from **Modify** panel in the **3D Model** tab of the **Ribbon**. The **Thread** dialog box will be displayed; refer to Figure-138.

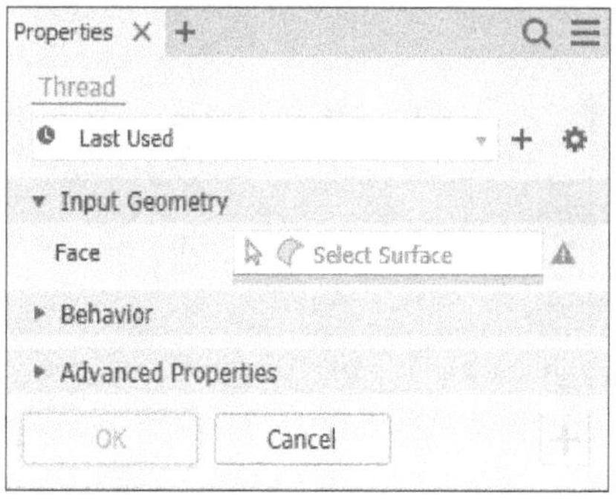

Figure-138. Thread dialog box

- Select the internal face of the extruded tube feature; refer to Figure-139. The updated **Thread** dialog box will be displayed; refer to Figure-140.

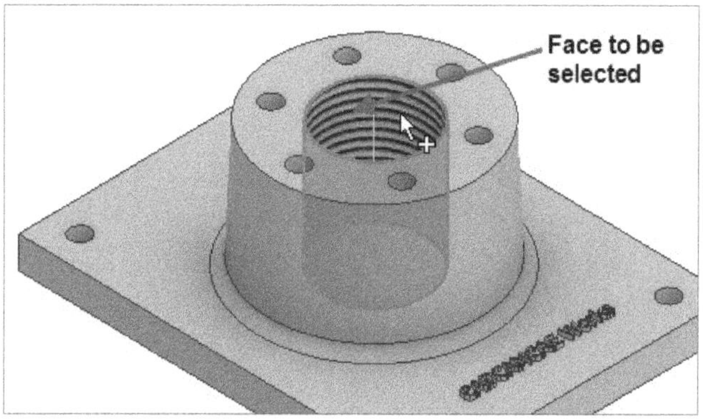

Figure-139. Face selected for thread

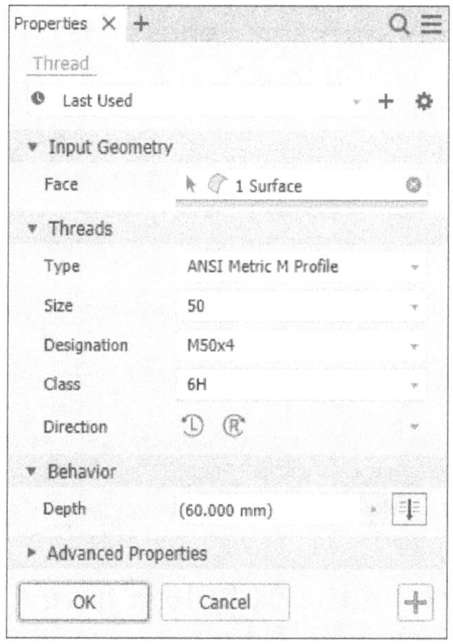

Figure-140. Updated thread dialog box

- Select the size as **50**, class as **6H**, and then click in the **Designation** drop-down and select the **M50x3** option from the list; refer to Figure-141.

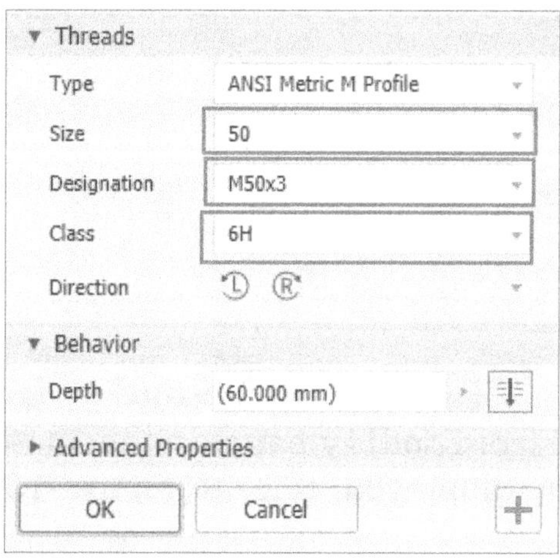

Figure-141. Parameters for thread

- Click on the **OK** button from the dialog box to create the feature; refer to Figure-142.

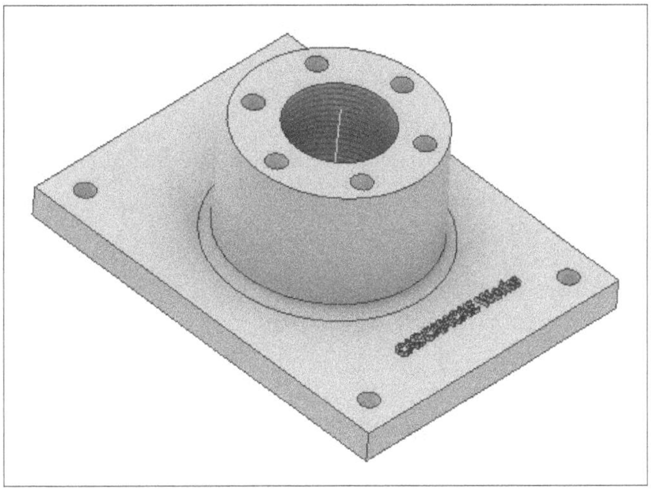

Figure-142. Thread feature created

PRACTICE 1

Create the model (isometric view) as shown in Figure-143. The dimensions of the model are given in Figure-144.

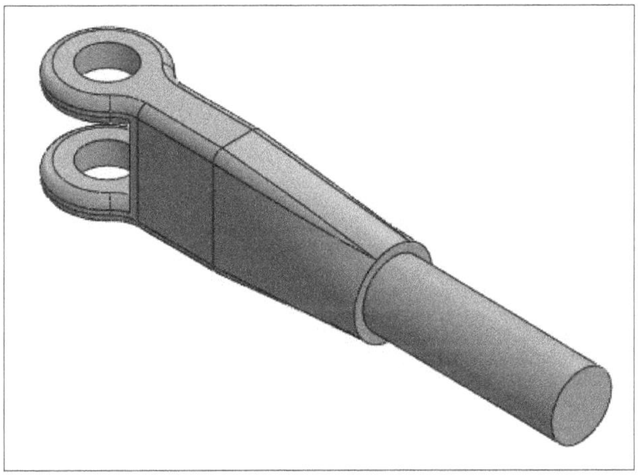

Figure-143. Model for Practice 1

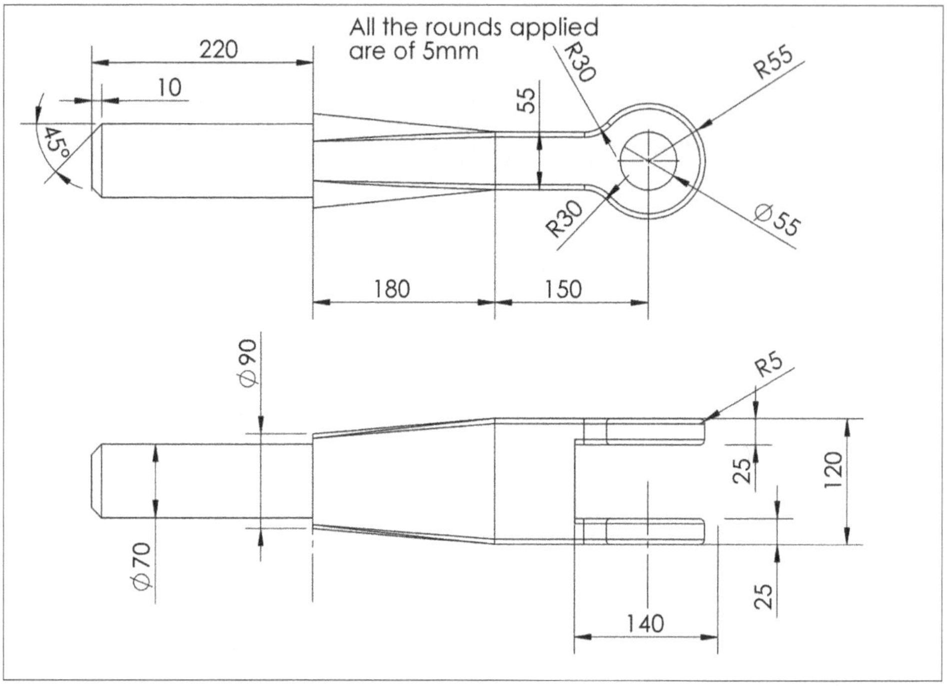

Figure-144. Practice 1 drawing views

PRACTICE 2

Create the model as shown in Figure-145. Dimensions are given in Figure-146. Assume the missing dimensions.

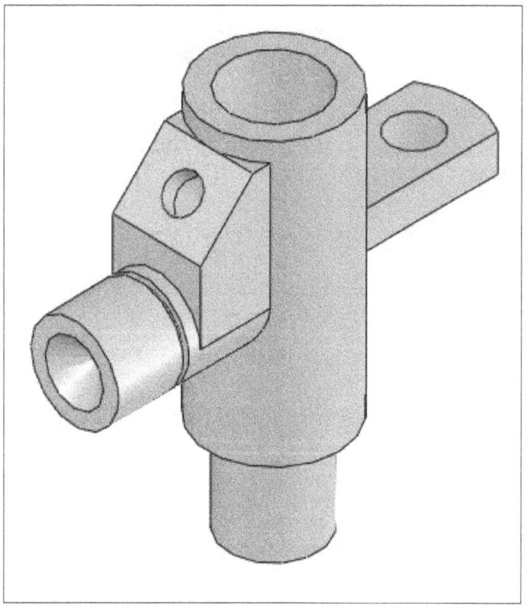

Figure-145. Practice 2 model

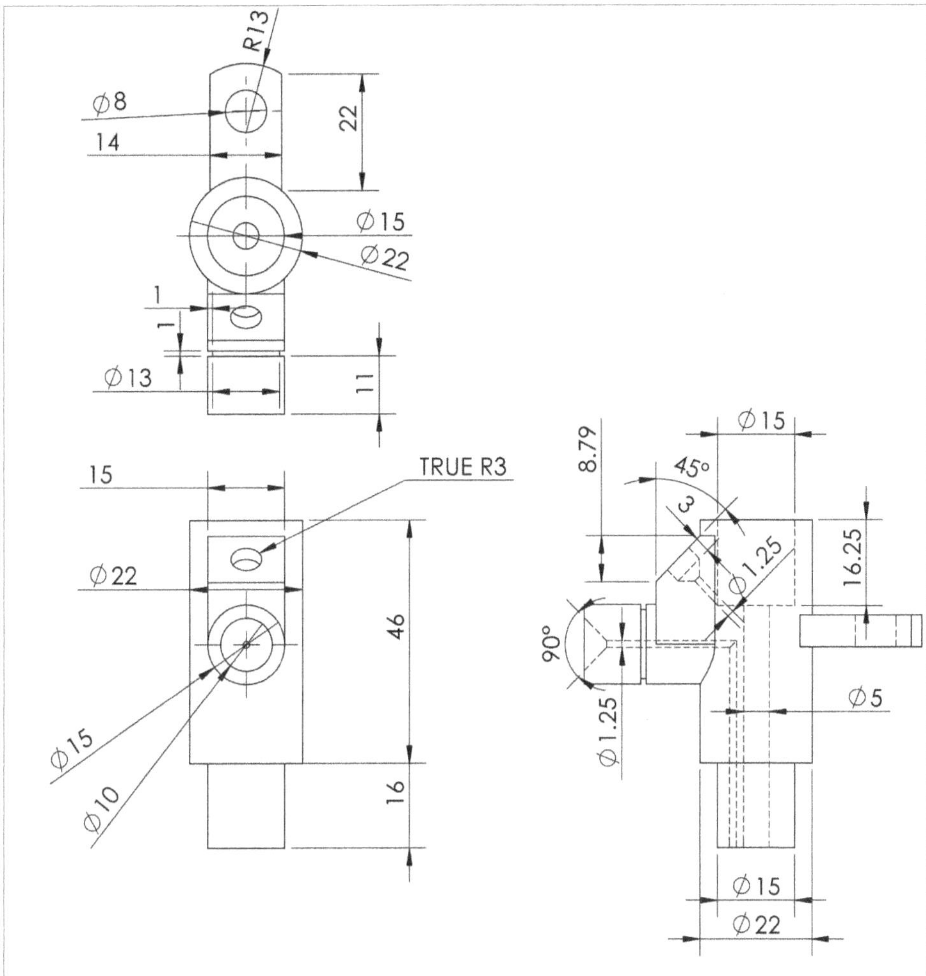

Figure-146. Practice 2

PRACTICE 3

Create the model by using the dimensions given in Figure-147.

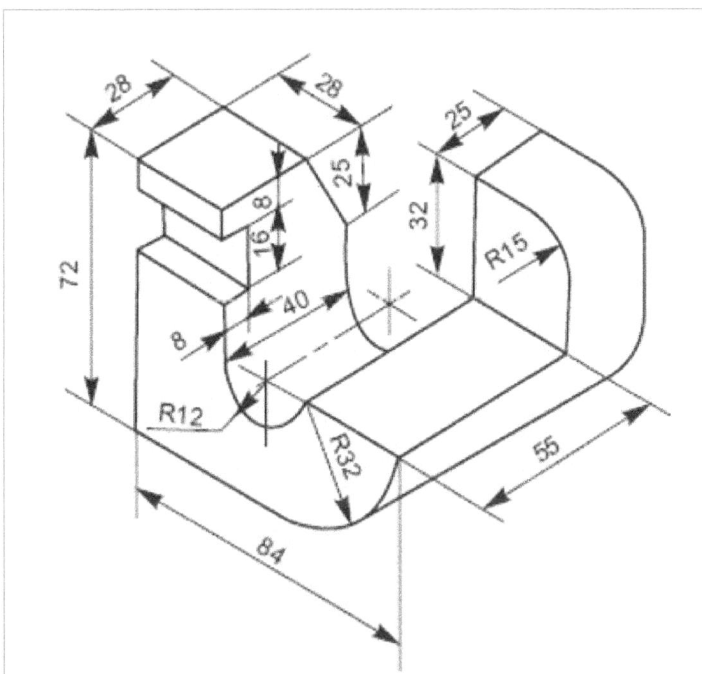

Figure-147. Practice 3

Practice 4

Create the model by using the dimensions given in Figure-148.

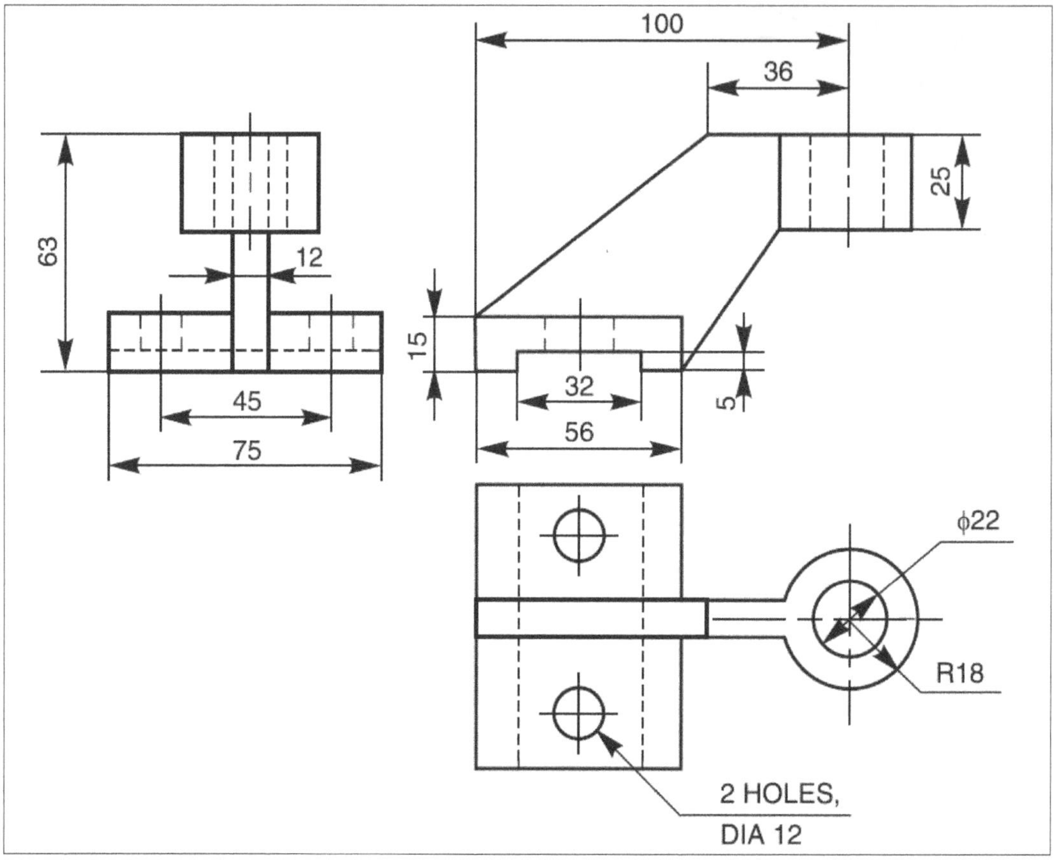

Figure-148. Practice 4

Practice 5

Create the model as shown in Figure-149 by using the dimensions given in Figure-150.

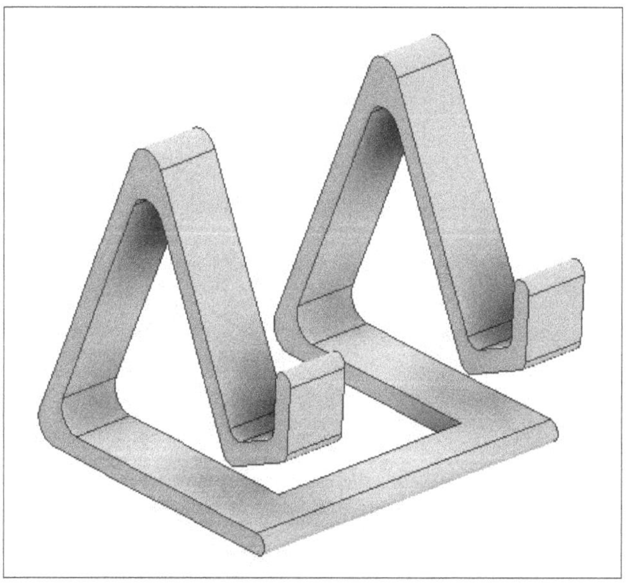

Figure-149. Practice 5

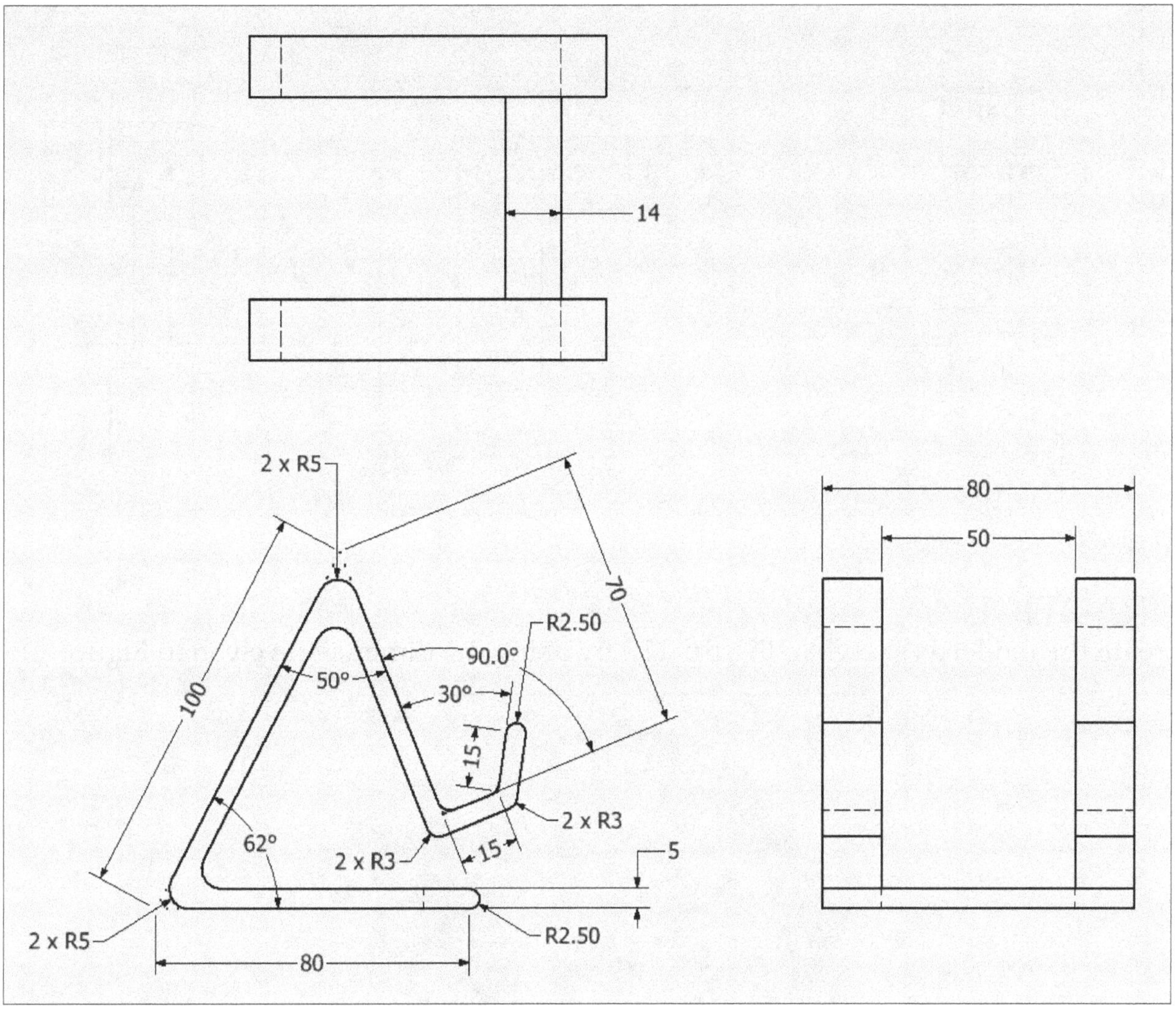

Figure-150. Practice 5 drawing

PRACTICE 6

Create the model as shown in Figure-151 by using the dimensions given in Figure-152.

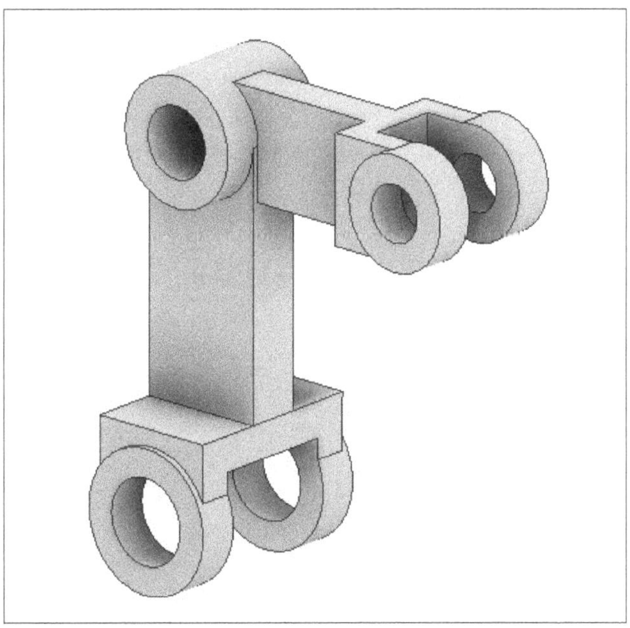

Figure-151. Practice 6

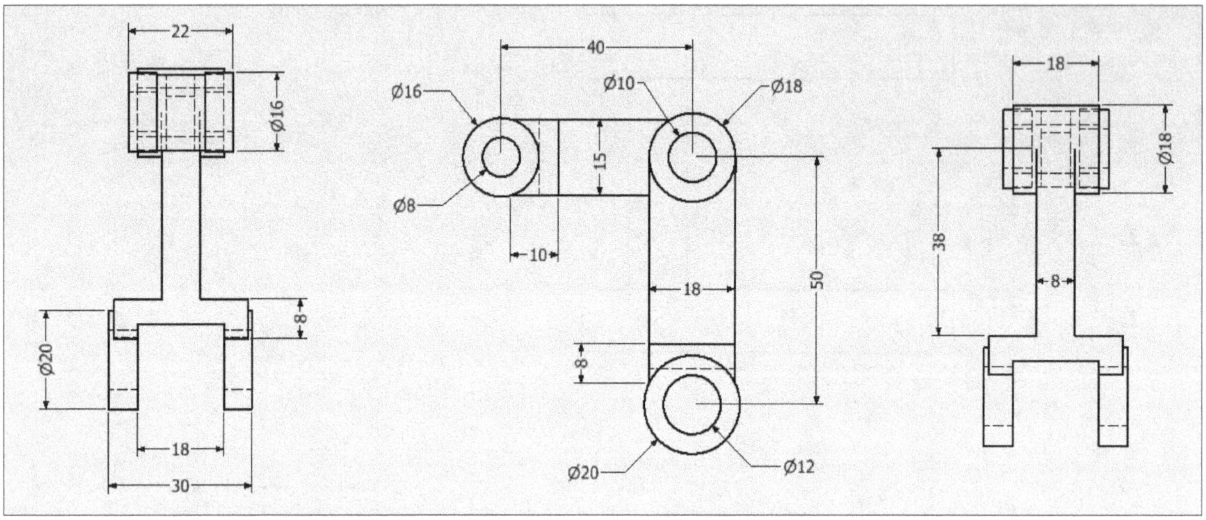

Figure-152. Practice 6 drawing

PRACTICE 7

Create the model as shown in Figure-153 by using the dimensions given in Figure-154.

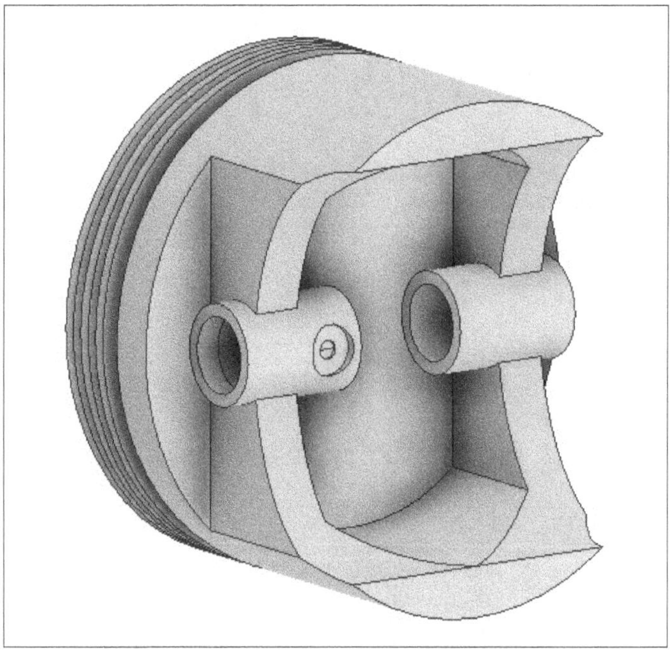

Figure-153. Practice 7

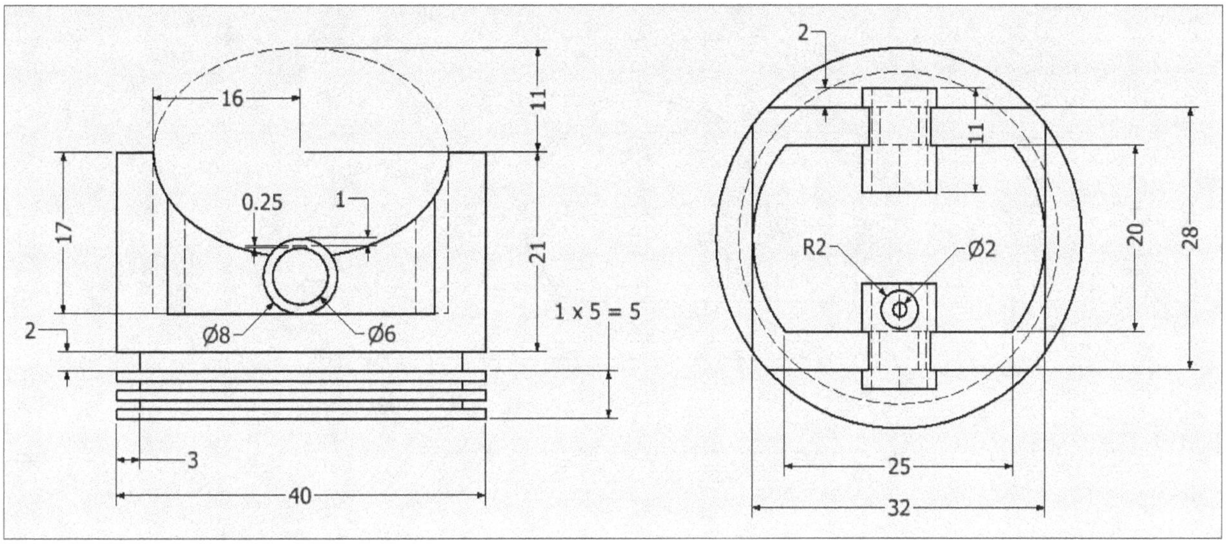

Figure-154. Practice 7 drawing

PRACTICE 8

Create the model as shown in Figure-155 by using the dimensions given in Figure-156.

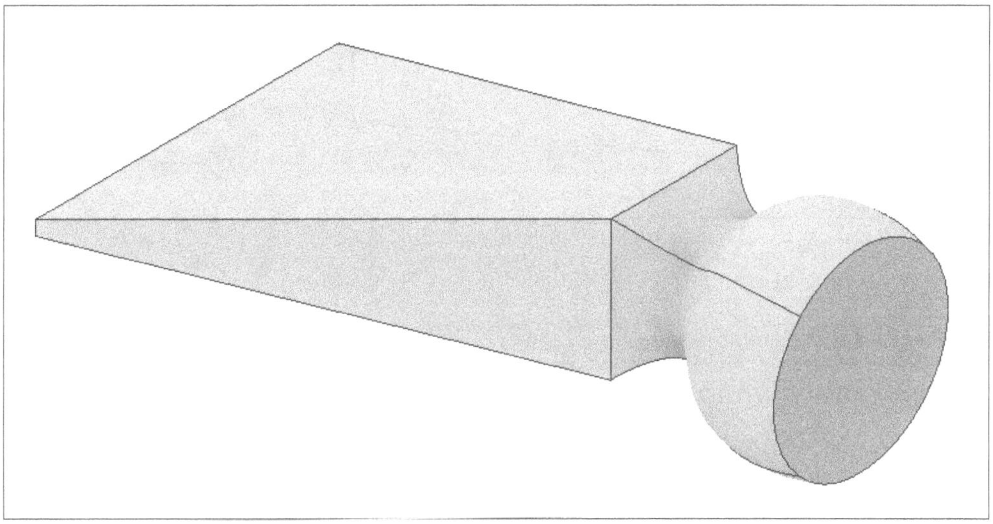

Figure-155. Practice 8

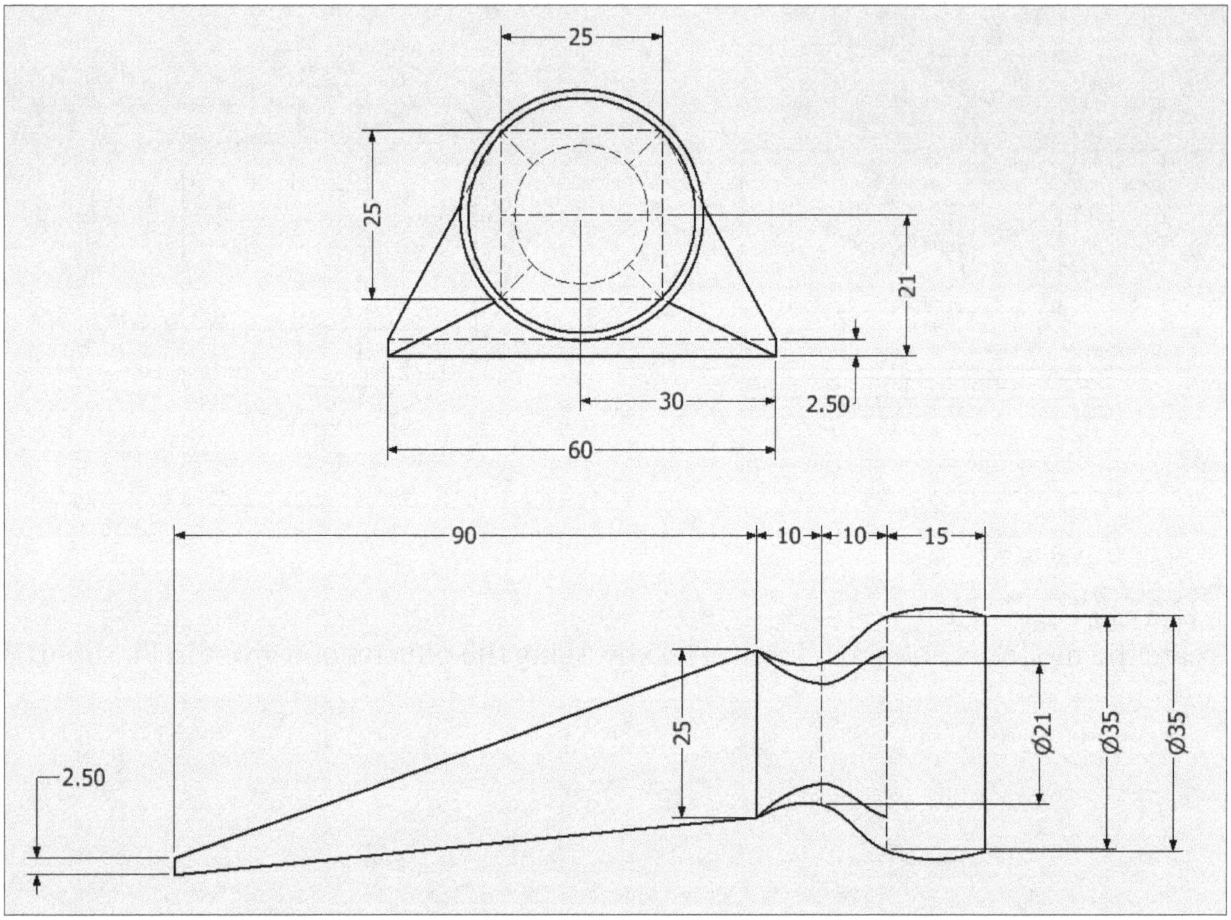

Figure-156. Practice 8 drawing

PRACTICE 9

Create the model as shown in Figure-157 by using the dimensions given in Figure-158.

Figure-157. Practice 9

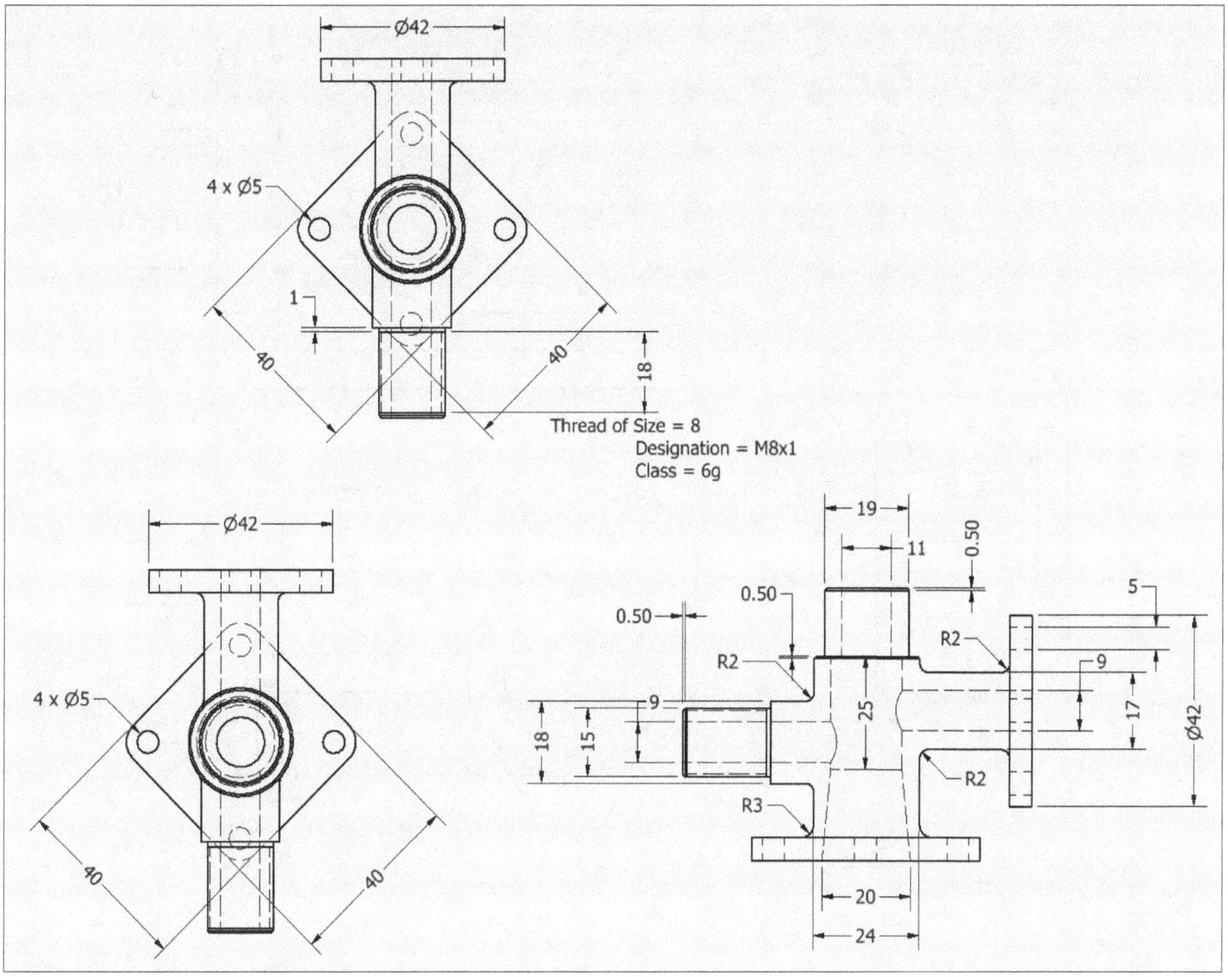

Figure-158. Practice 9 drawing

PRACTICE 10

Create the model as shown in Figure-159 by using the dimensions given in Figure-160.

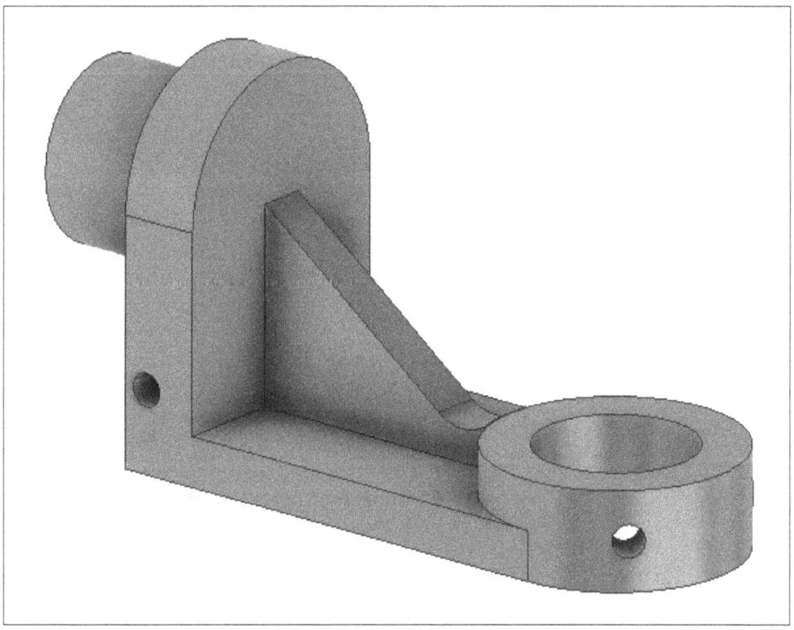

Figure-159. Practice 10

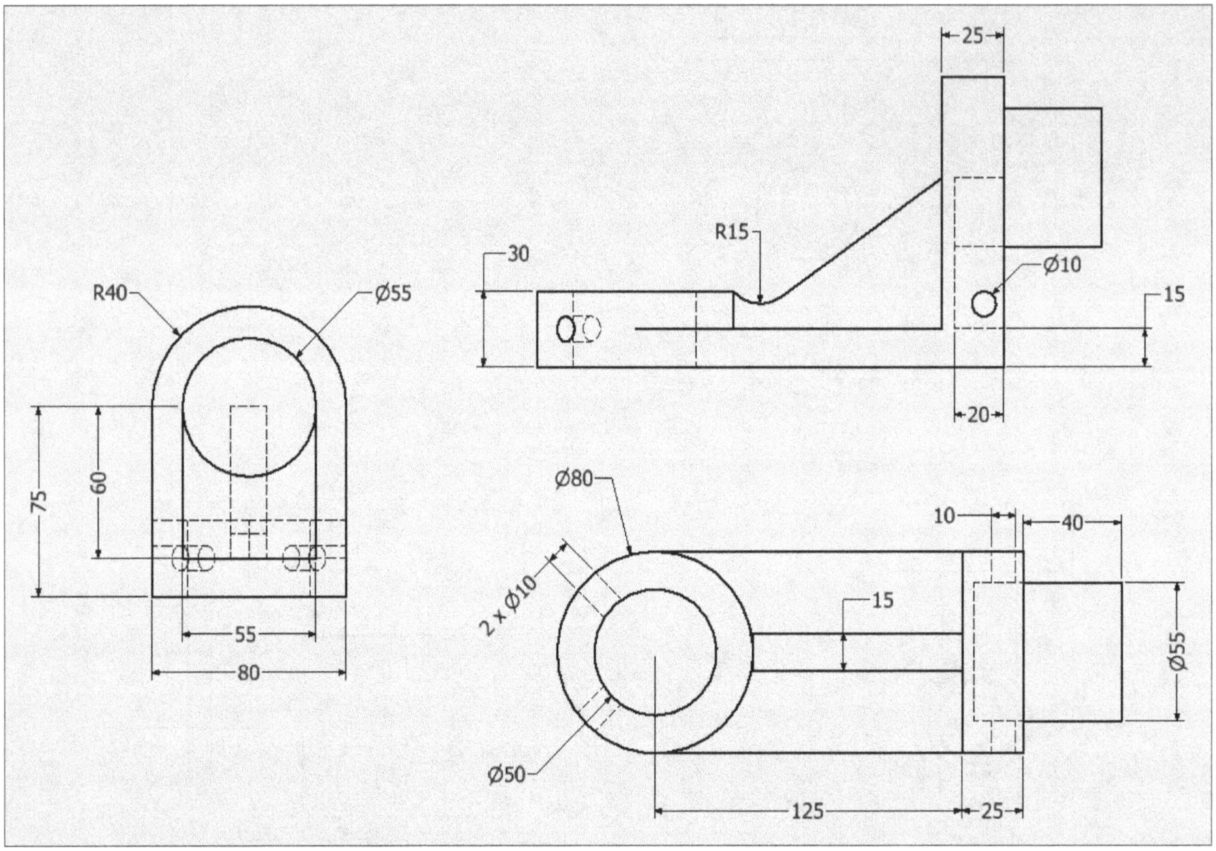

Figure-160. Practice 10 drawing

SELF ASSESSMENT

Q1. Which of the following options are available in **Direct Editing Toolbar**?

a) Move
b) Scale
c) Delete
d) All of the Above

Q2. Which button should be pressed and held while removing a face from selection?

a) Alt
b) Ctrl
c) Shift
d) Tab

Q3. The size of faces cannot be change by **Direct Editing Toolbar**. (True/False)

Q4. The **Bend Part** tool is used to bend part by using sketched line. (True/False)

Q5. The .... tool is used to edit imported parts of parametric features of the model by using simple drag and drop operations.

REVIEW QUESTIONS

Q1. What is the main function of the Direct Edit tool?
A. To create new sketches
B. To apply materials
C. To edit imported parametric features using drag and drop
D. To change the model's color

Q2. Where is the Direct Edit tool located in the Ribbon?
A. Pattern panel
B. View tab
C. Modify panel of the 3D Model tab
D. Assemble tab

Q3. Which of the following is not an option available in the Direct Edit toolbar?
A. Move
B. Size
C. Shell
D. Rotate

Q4. What must you press to select multiple faces for direct editing?
A. ALT
B. CTRL
C. SHIFT
D. ESC

Q5. What does holding the SHIFT key while selecting a face do during selection?
A. Adds face to selection
B. Zooms in on face
C. Removes face from selection
D. Opens a context menu

Q6. What does the "Locate" button do in the Direct Edit toolbar?
A. Hides the toolbar
B. Moves the model
C. Places the triad at a new location
D. Rotates the model

Q7. Which drop-down option sets the triad to World Coordinate orientation?
A. Face
B. Object
C. Local
D. World

Q8. Which tool is used to change the dimensions of a selected face in Direct Edit?
A. Scale
B. Size
C. Measure
D. Rotate

Q9. Which Direct Edit option allows increasing or decreasing the size of the whole model?
A. Size
B. Rotate
C. Scale
D. Move

Q10. What is displayed when you click on the Rotate button in Direct Edit?
A. Drag arrows
B. Triad
C. Ball handle for rotation
D. Grid

Q11. What must you click to apply changes in any Direct Edit operation?
A. Apply
B. + button
C. Done
D. Submit

Q12. What is required before using the Bend Part tool?
A. A solid object with fillet
B. A rectangular pattern
C. A bend line sketch
D. A scale value

Q13. Which area in the Bend Part dialog box is used to select the bend side?
A. Orientation
B. Direction
C. Side
D. Geometry

Q14. Which Bend Part method uses radius and angle for defining bend?
A. Radius and Arc Length
B. Radius and Angle
C. Arc Length and Angle
D. Arc Direction and Length

Q15. What panel contains the Rectangular Pattern tool?
A. Modify panel
B. Surface panel
C. Pattern panel
D. Assemble panel

Q16. What key combination opens the Rectangular Pattern tool?
A. CTRL+SHIFT+P
B. CTRL+SHIFT+R
C. ALT+R
D. CTRL+ALT+P

Q17. What does the Incremental option define in the Rectangular Pattern tool?
A. Total span of instances
B. Step size between instances
C. Axis of rotation
D. Number of instances

Q18. Which option allows adjusting spacing for a single instance in a rectangular pattern?
A. Distribution
B. Irregular Distance
C. Fitted
D. Offset

Q19. In the Extents section, what happens if you select the option that only includes fully inside instances?
A. All instances are selected
B. Only instances touching the boundary are included
C. Instances fully inside boundary are created
D. None of the above

Q20. Which method of copying provides fastest generation but might create shape errors in overlaps?
A. Optimized
B. Identical
C. Adjust
D. Manual

Q21. Which pattern tool is suitable for creating fan-blade-like features?
A. Sketch Driven Pattern
B. Rectangular Pattern
C. Circular Pattern
D. Mirror

Q22. What is required to create a circular pattern?
A. Line sketch
B. Axis reference
C. Face boundary
D. Base surface

Q23. Which tool lets you create a pattern along custom sketch points?
A. Rectangular Pattern
B. Circular Pattern
C. Mirror
D. Sketch Driven Pattern

Q24. What must be selected when using Sketch Driven Pattern tool?
A. Faces only
B. Features and sketch with points
C. Dimensions
D. Axes and planes

For Student Notes

Chapter 7

Assembly Design and Presentation

Topics Covered

The major topics covered in this chapter are:

- ***Starting Assembly Design***
- ***Placing Components in Assembly***
- ***Replacing Components***
- ***Top Down and Bottom Up Assembly approach***
- ***Creating Components in Assembly***
- ***Positioning Tools***
- ***Constraints***
- ***Joints***
- ***Contact Sets***
- ***Bill of Materials***
- ***Driving Constraints for animation/motion study***
- ***Introduction to Presentation***

INTRODUCTION

In engineer's language, assembly is the combination of two or more components and these components are constrained to each other in a specified manner called assembly constraint. In Autodesk Inventor, there is a separate environment to create assembly of parts.

STARTING ASSEMBLY ENVIRONMENT

- Start Autodesk Inventor using icon on desktop or in Start menu.
- Click on the **File Menu** button and select the **Assembly** option from **New** cascading menu; refer to Figure-1.

Or

- Click on the **Assembly** option from the **New** drop-down in **Quick Access Toolbar**; refer to Figure-2.

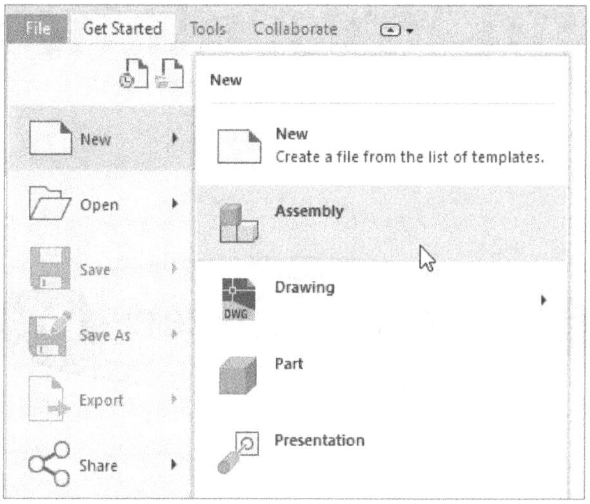

Figure-1. Assembly option

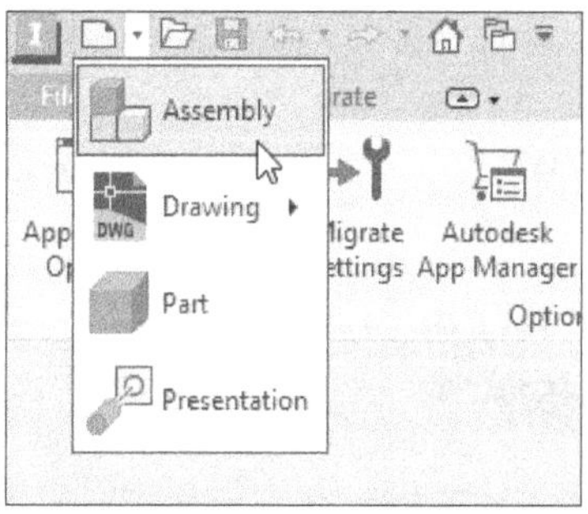

Figure-2. Assembly option in Quick Access toolbar

- The assembly environment will be displayed as shown in Figure-3.

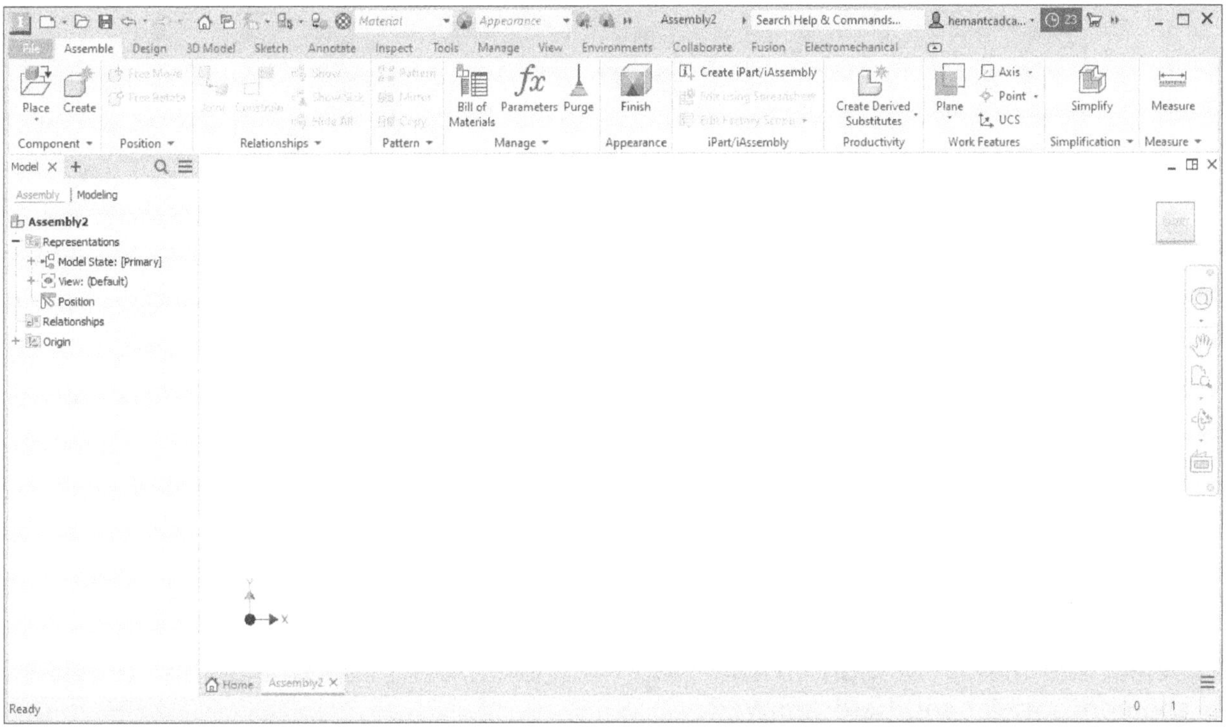

Figure-3. Assembly environment

PLACING COMPONENTS IN ASSEMBLY

There are multiple ways to insert components in an assembly in Autodesk Inventor.

- Placing Component from Local Storage
- Placing Component from Content Center
- Placing Imported CAD Files
- Placing iLogic Component
- Placing Electrical Catalog Browser

These methods of inserting components are discussed next.

Placing Component from Local Storage

Using the **Place** tool, you can insert the components in the assembly which are stored in the local drive of your computer. These components are the part files that we have created earlier. The procedure to insert components by this method is discussed next.

- Click on the **Place** tool from **Component** panel in the **Assemble** tab of the **Ribbon**. The **Place Component** dialog box will be displayed; refer to Figure-4.

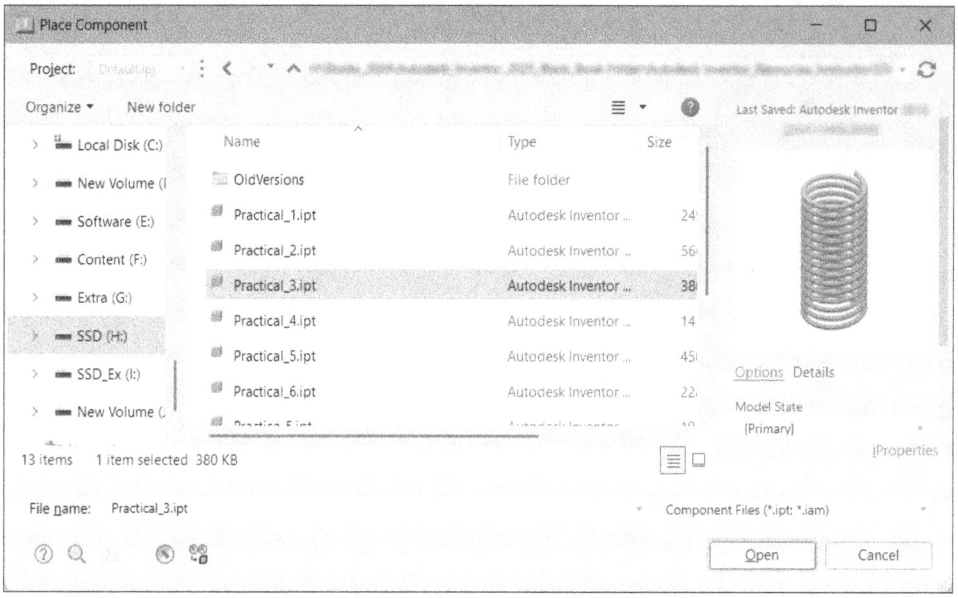

Figure-4. Place Component dialog box

- Select the file of component that you want to insert in the assembly. Preview of the component will be displayed.
- You can select desired file format from the **Files of type** drop-down if you wish to import CAD files of other software; refer to Figure-5.

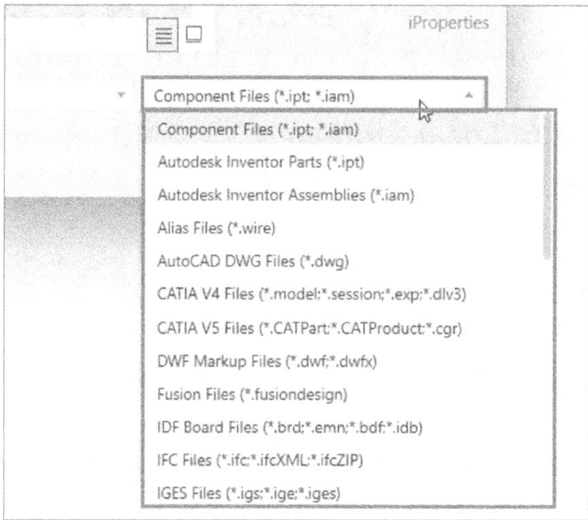

Figure-5. Files of type drop-down

- After selecting the file, click on the **Open** button from the dialog box. The component will get attached to the cursor; refer to Figure-6.

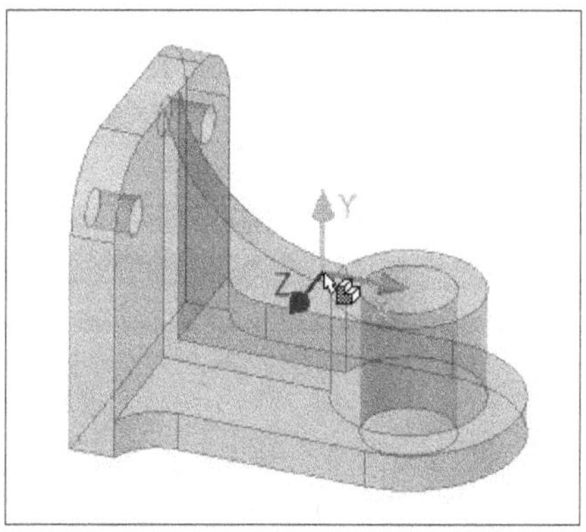

Figure-6. Component attached to cursor

- Click in the viewport to place the component.
- If you want to insert more copies of the component then click again in the viewport.
- Press **ESC** from keyboard to exit inserting more components.

Place from Content Center

- Click on the **Place from Content Center** tool from the **Place** drop-down in the **Component** panel of the **Ribbon**. The **Place from Content Center** window will be displayed; refer to Figure-7.

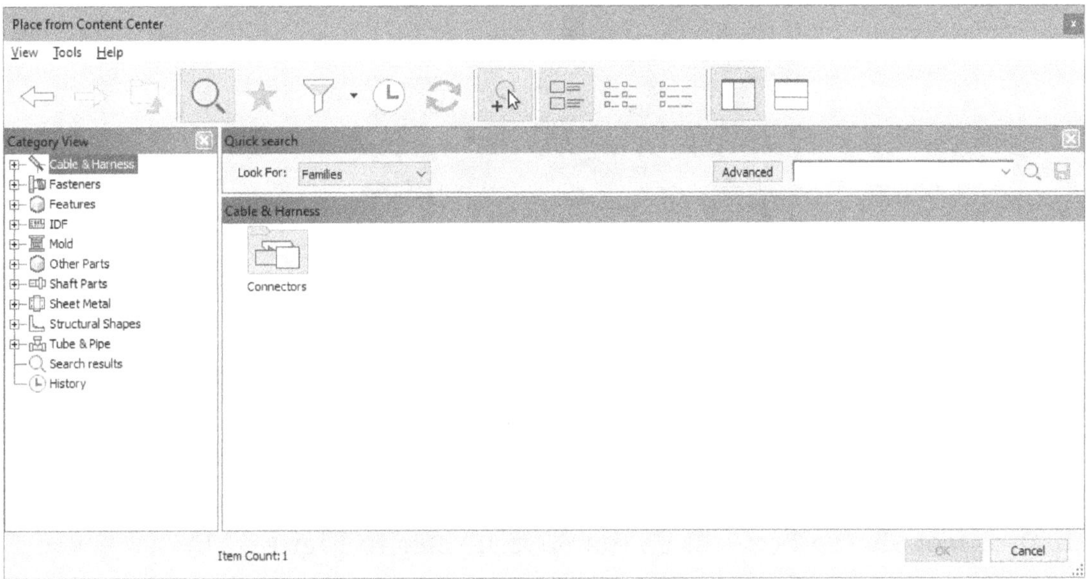

Figure-7. Place from Content Center window

- Click on desired category, components in that category will be displayed in the right; refer to Figure-8.

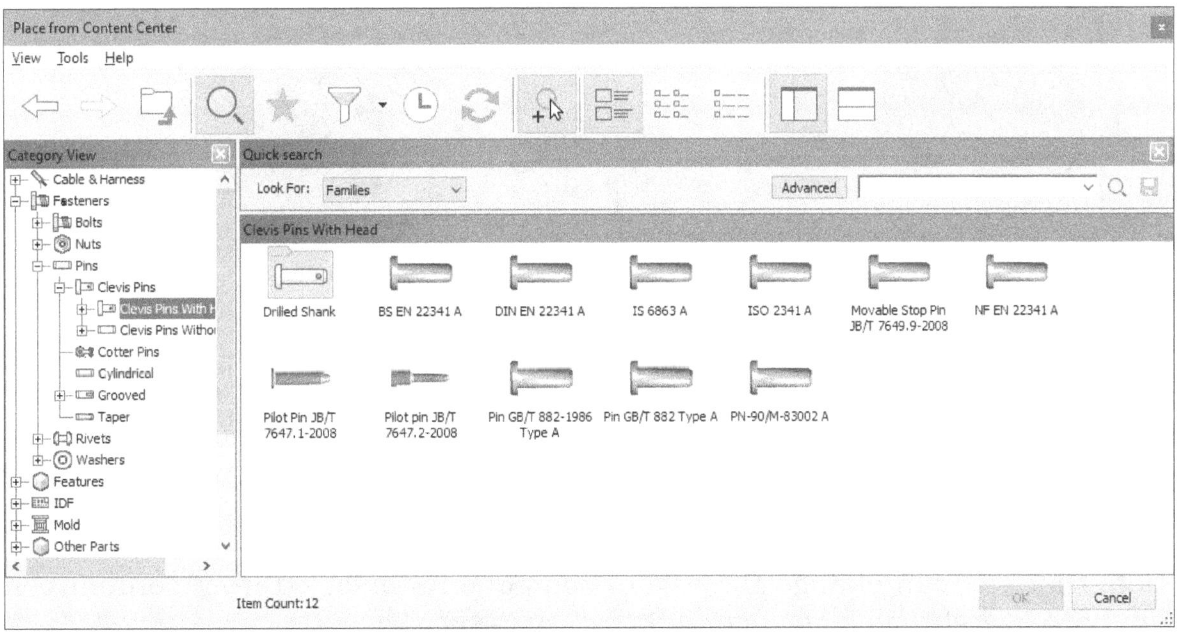

Figure-8. Categories of components

- Double-click on desired component from the right area of the window.

- Preview of the component will be displayed attached to cursor. Note that the size of pin and other similar components changes automatically based on the selected base component, once you place the component at desired location. If you hover the cursor on a hole then size of component will automatically change relative to the hole; refer to Figure-9.

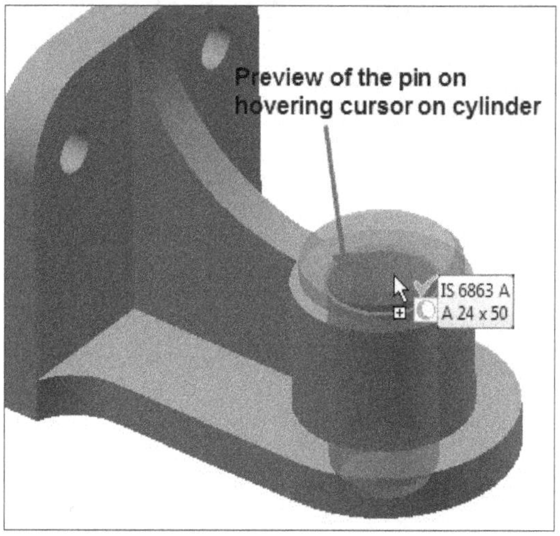

Figure-9. Preview of the pin being inserted

- If you want to place the component then click **RMB** in the modeling area and click on the **Place** button from the options displayed; refer to Figure-10. The component will be placed at its current position. But if you specify all the required references then **AutoDrop** dialog box will be displayed; refer to Figure-11.

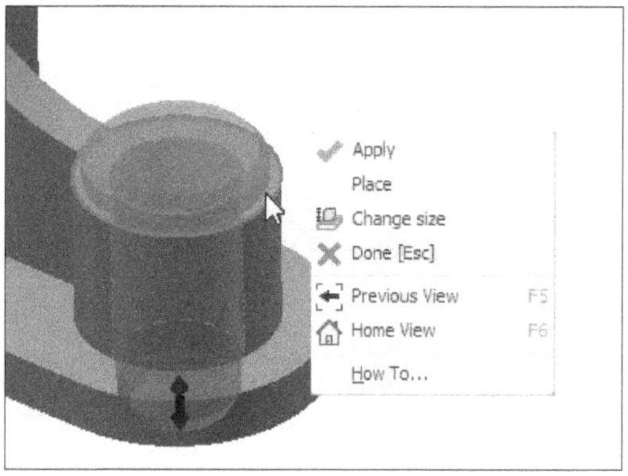

Figure-10. Options displayed on right clicking

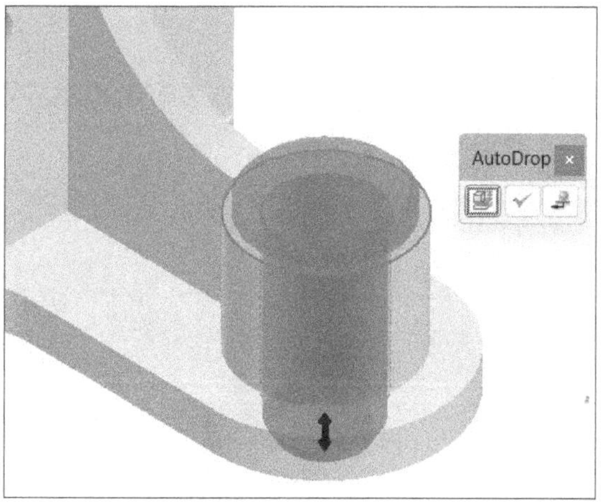

Figure-11. AutoDrop dialog box

- If you want to insert more components of same type then click on the **Apply** button in place of **Place** button.
- If you want to manually change the size of component then you can click on the **Change size** button. A dialog box with various size options will be displayed; refer to Figure-12.
- Select desired size and click on the **OK** button.
- Note that you can change the size of components inserted from content center anytime by right-click on them in **Model Browser**.

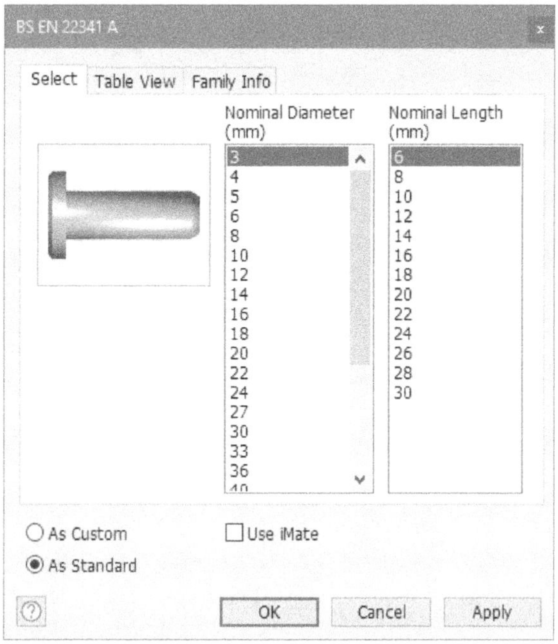

Figure-12. Size options in the dialog box

Place and Insert

The **Place and Insert** tool is used to automatically align and insert selected component in hole/hollow section in existing component of assembly. The procedure to use this tool is given next.

- Click on the **Place and Insert** tool from the **Place** drop-down in the **Component** panel of the **Ribbon**. The **Place and Insert** dialog box will be displayed; refer to Figure-13.

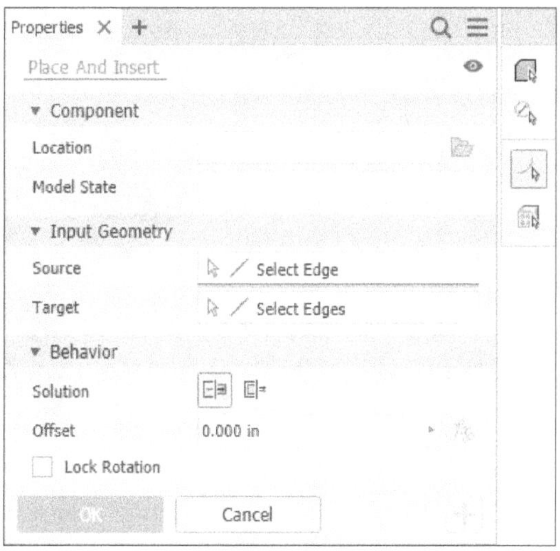

Figure-13. Place and insert dialog box

- Click on the **Browse to another component location** button to place the target body in the graphics window. The **Place Component** dialog box will be displayed as shown in Figure-14.

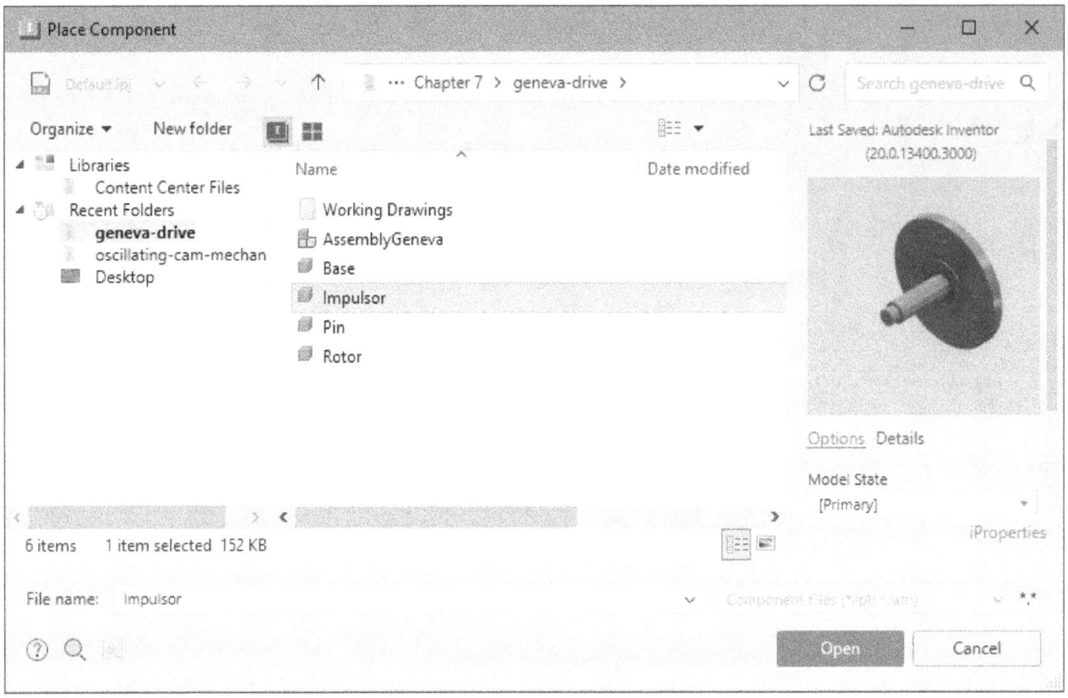

Figure-14. Place Component dialog box

- Select desired part to be inserted and click on the **Open** button from the dialog box. The part will get attach to the cursor. Click at desired location in graphics window to place the part.
- By default, the selection button of **Source** field in the dialog box will be active.
- Select desired edge of source component (component to be inserted) to be used as reference for insertion; refer to Figure-15. The selection button of **Target** field will become active.

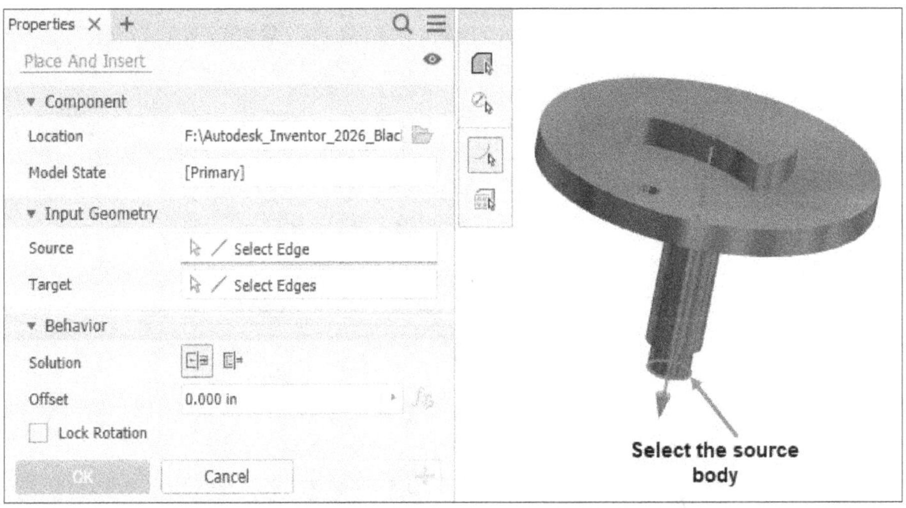

Figure-15. Selecting the geometries

- Now select desired edge of the target component in which source component edge will be inserted; refer to Figure-16. The component will be place and inserted.

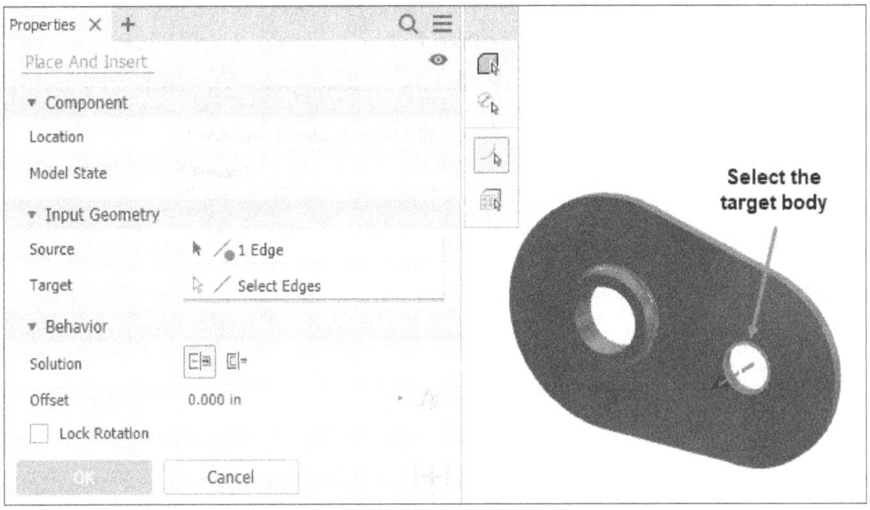

Figure-16. Selecting the target bodies

- Select desired option from the **Solution** area in the **Behavior** drop-down to define the method of placement/alignment between source and target geometry.
- Click in the **Offset** edit box and specify desired value to define the distance between source and target body during placement.
- Select **Lock Rotation** check box to restrict the rotation of the component while placing or inserting.
- After specifying desired parameters, click on the **OK** button from the dialog box. The component will be place and inserted; refer to Figure-17.

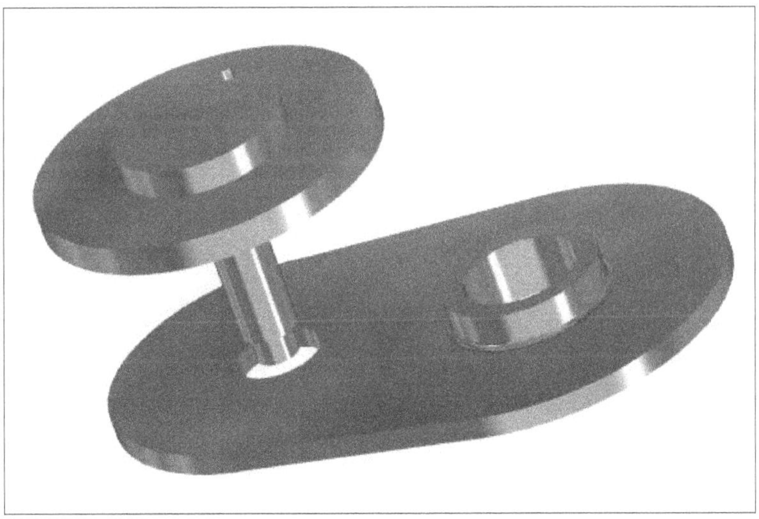

Figure-17. Place and insert displayed

Place Imported CAD files

- Click on the **Place Imported CAD Files** tool from the **Place** drop-down in the **Component** panel of the **Ribbon**. The **Place Component** dialog box will be displayed as discussed earlier.
- Note that the **All Models** option is selected in the **Files of type** drop-down in the dialog box, so you can select the model file of any CAD software.

Place iLogic Component

- Click on the **Place iLogic Component** tool from the **Place** drop-down in the **Component** panel of the **Ribbon**. The **Place iLogic Component** dialog box will be displayed; refer to Figure-18.

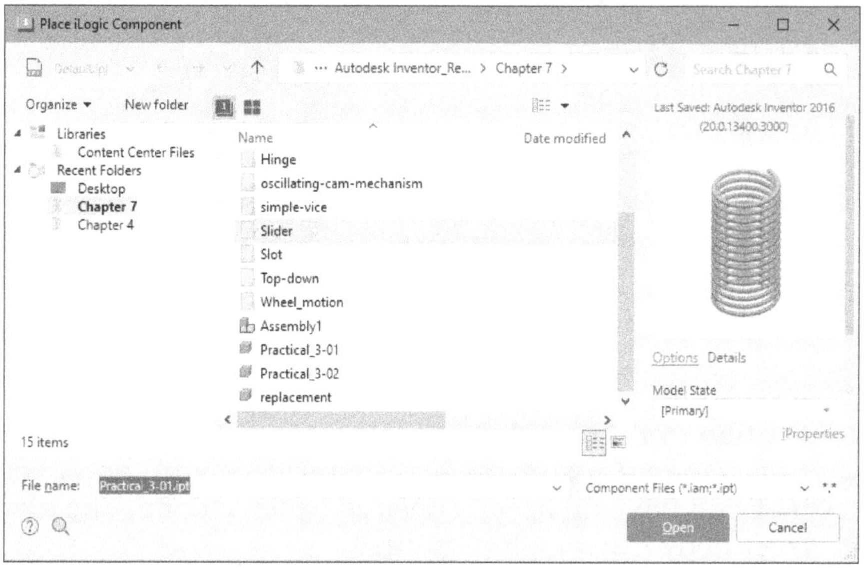

Figure-18. Place iLogic Component dialog box

- Select the file of component that you want to insert in assembly and click on the **Open** button. Selected component will be displayed with **Place iLogic Component** window; refer to Figure-19.

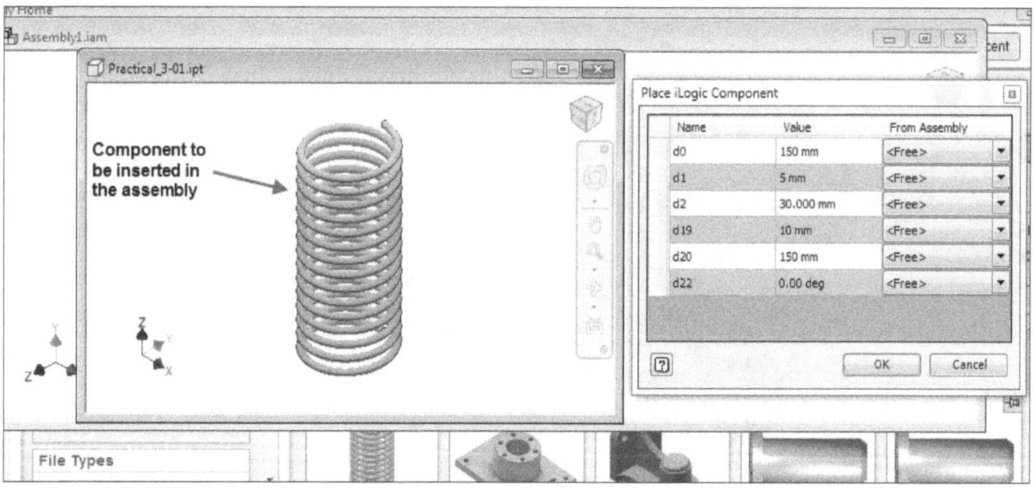

Figure-19. Place iLogic Component window

- Set desired values of dimensions in the dialog box and click on the **OK** button. The component will get attached to the cursor.
- Click in the viewport to place the component.
- Press **ESC** to exit inserting more component.

Electrical Catalog Browser

Using this option, you can insert the electrical components in Autodesk Inventor. This option is useful when you are working with electrical assemblies. The procedure to use this option is same as discussed earlier.

REPLACING COMPONENT

Sometimes, we need to replace an already existing component with a new component. You can simply delete the earlier inserted component and insert a new component but in this case, you have to specify the assembly constraints again. To solve this problem, we use **Replace** tool. The procedure is given next.

- Click on the **Replace** tool from the **Replace** drop-down in the expanded **Component** panel in the **Ribbon**; refer to Figure-20. You will be asked to select the component which you want to replace.

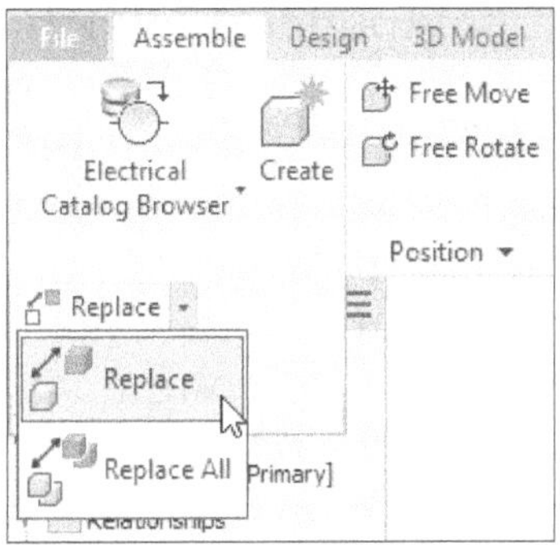

Figure-20. Replace tool

- Click on the component that you want to replace and press **ENTER** from the keyboard.
- The **Place Component** dialog box will be displayed as discussed earlier; refer to Figure-21.

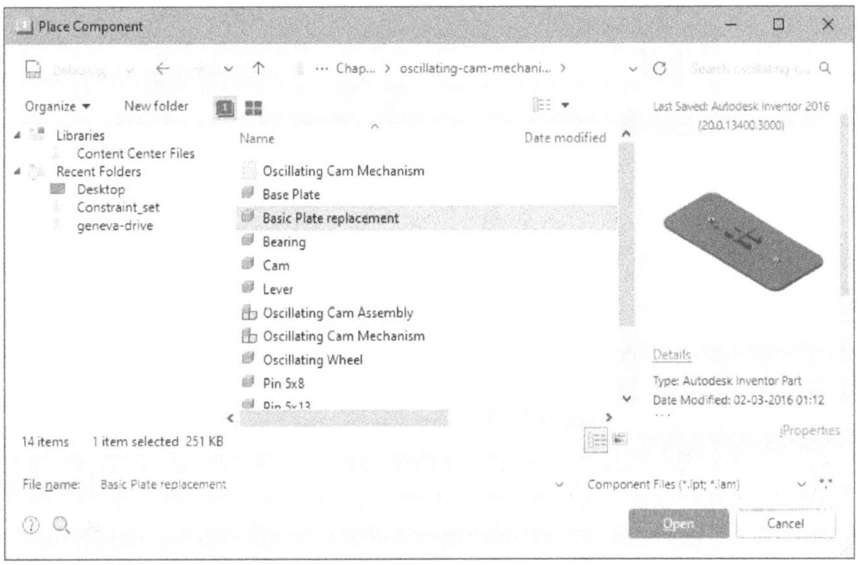

Figure-21. Place Component dialog box for replacing component

- Click on the **Open** button from the dialog box. The component will get replaced automatically if the locations of faces and other references are same.
- If you do not have the equal number of references in same orientation then an error message will be displayed.

TOP-DOWN AND BOTTOM-UP APPROACH FOR ASSEMBLY

There are two approaches in creating assembly, Top-Down approach and Bottom-Up approach. In Top-Down approach, the component are created in the assembly and constraints can be applied before creating the components. In Bottom-Up approach, the components are created in Part environment first. After creating, these components are brought in the assembly environment and are assembled by constraints.

Earlier, we have inserted the components which were already created in Part environment which means we have used the Bottom-Up approach. Now, we will create the components in assembly itself which means we will use the Top-Down approach. Now, the question arises why do we need Top-Down approach if we can easily work with Bottom-Up approach. Answer to this question lies in practical use. Sometimes, we need to design a component which fits exactly to the space left in assembly. For example, we have inserted components in an assembly as shown in Figure-22. At one stage of designing, we need a component to join the holes of discs as shown in Figure-22. In such cases, it is easy to create component in the assembly which means it is easy to use Top-Down approach in such cases.

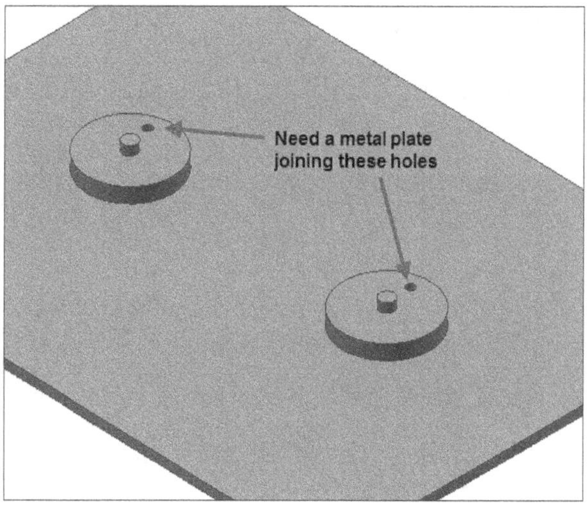

Figure-22. Example for top-down approach

CREATING COMPONENT IN ASSEMBLY

When working on some complex assemblies, you may need a new component to be created for assembly. In most of the cases, it is better to create component in the assembly itself. The procedure to create component in assembly is given next.

- Click on the **Create** tool from the **Component** panel in the **Assemble** tab of the **Ribbon**. The **Create In-Place Component** dialog box will be displayed; refer to Figure-23.

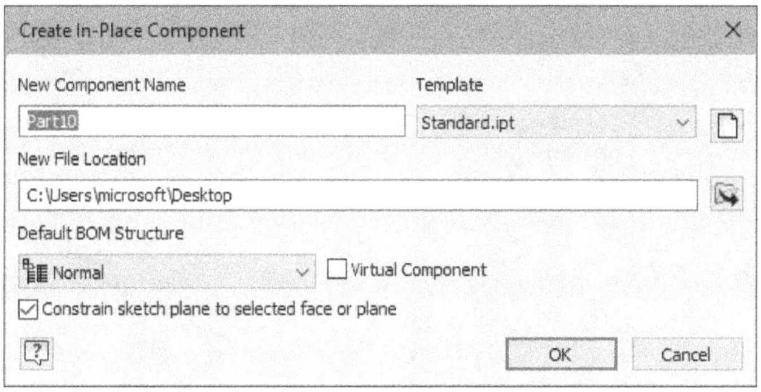

Figure-23. Create In-Place Component dialog box

- Specify desired name of the component in the **New Component Name** edit box.
- Select desired template from the **Template** drop-down. If you want to select a template from broader list then click on the **Browse Template** button. The **Open Template** dialog box will be displayed; refer to Figure-24.
- Double-click on desired template from the dialog box to select the template.
- Set desired location to save the component file in the **New File Location** edit box.
- Clear the **Constrain sketch plane to selected face or plane** check box if you do not want the sketch plane to constrained to selected plane or face.
- Click on the **OK** button from the dialog box. You will be asked to select a sketching plane/face.
- Select desired sketching plane/face; refer to Figure-25. The tools for 3D Modeling will be activated.

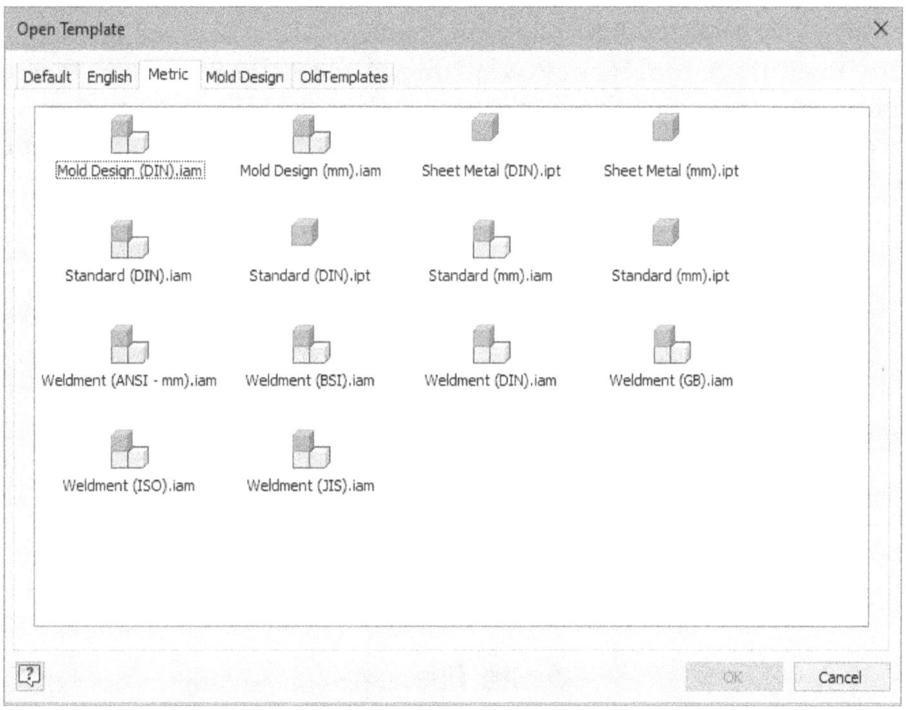

Figure-24. Open Template dialog box

- Create desired component by using 3D Modeling tools as discussed earlier; refer to Figure-26.

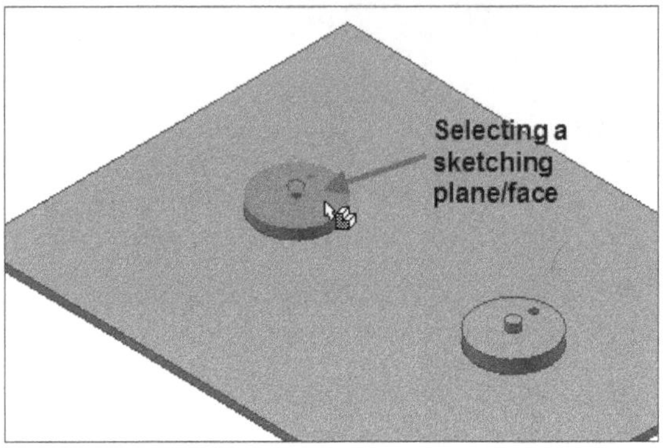

Figure-25. Selecting sketching face

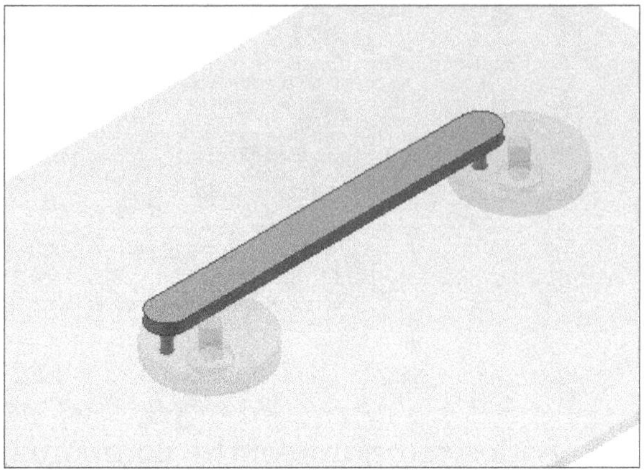

Figure-26. Part created in assembly

- Click on the **Return** tool from the **Return** panel in the **Ribbon** to return to assembly environment.

POSITIONING TOOLS

There are mainly three tools for positioning components in assembly; **Free Move**, **Free Rotate**, and **Grid Snap**. The procedures to use these tools are discussed next.

Free Move

The **Free Move** tool is used to move a component freely in 3D space of assembly environment. The procedure to use this tool is given next.

- Click on the **Free Move** tool from **Position** panel in the **Assemble** tab of the **Ribbon**. You will be asked to select the component that you want to move.
- Select the component that you want to move and drag it to desired position; refer to Figure-27.

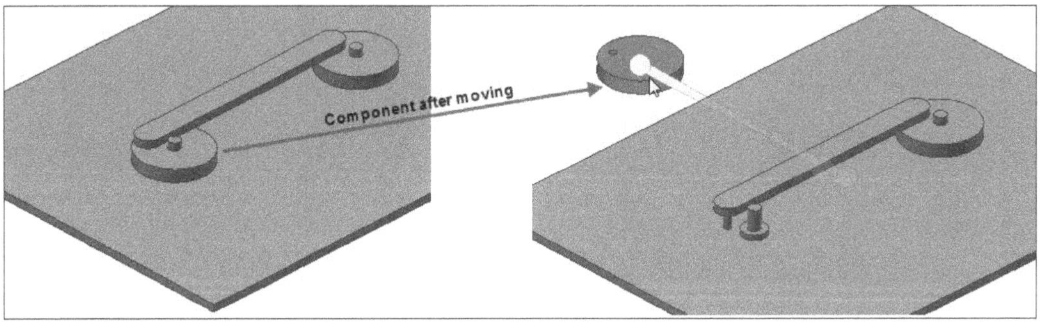

Figure-27. Freely moving component

- Note that you can move only one component at a time by using this tool.

Free Rotate

The **Free Rotate** tool works similar to **Free Move** tool but in place of moving the object is rotated freely. The procedure to use this tool is given next.

- Click on the **Free Rotate** tool from **Position** panel in the **Assemble** tab of the **Ribbon**. You will be asked to select component to be rotated.
- Select the component that you want to rotate. A window will be displayed to rotate the component; refer to Figure-28.
- Drag the component in desired direction to rotate.

- Click in the viewport to exit the tool.

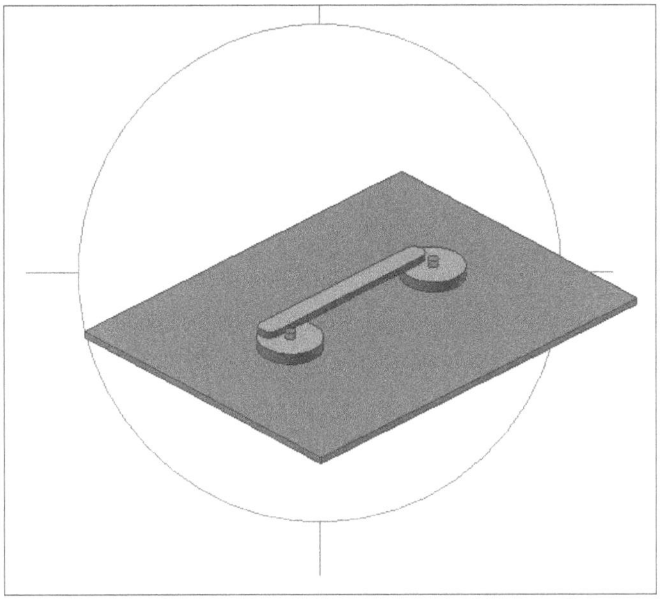

Figure-28. Free rotation orbit

Grid Snap

The **Grid Snap** tool is used to move the component in constrained environment. For example, you can make the component move in planar direction only or you can make the component move upward/downward only. The procedure to use this tool is given next.

- Click on the **Grid Snap** tool from the expanded **Position** panel in the **Assemble** tab of the **Ribbon**. You will be asked to click on a geometry of the component.
- Select desired geometry of component. Note that the selection of geometry can change the buttons displayed for movement in the toolbar; refer to Figure-29.

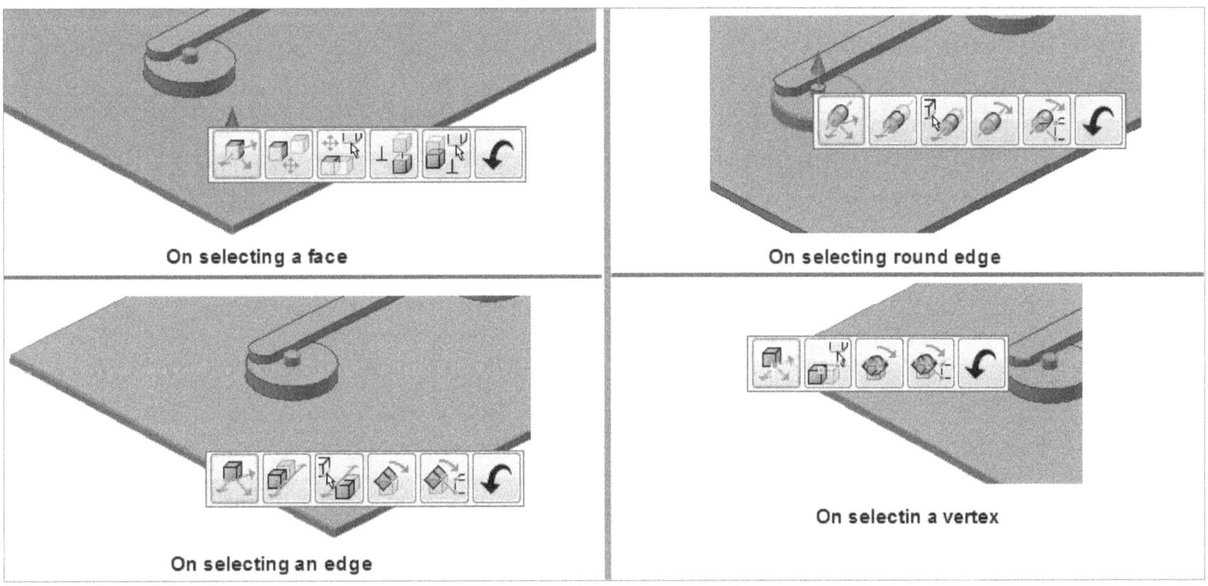

Figure-29. Buttons for movement of component

- Click on desired button to move/rotate the component.
- Move/rotate the component in the direction corresponding to the selected button.

CONSTRAINS

The Constraints are used to restrict the movement of objects. It is very important to apply constraints to the components in assembly because without them every component is free to move in any direction. Later in the book, you will perform various studies on the assembly like stress analysis, motion study, and so on. If the components are not properly constrained then results of these studies will be ambiguous. You can apply various constraints in Autodesk Inventor by using the **Constrain** tool. The procedure to apply constrain is given next.

- Click on the **Constrain** tool from the **Relationships** panel in the **Assemble** tab of the **Ribbon**. The **Place Constraint** dialog box will be displayed; refer to Figure-30.

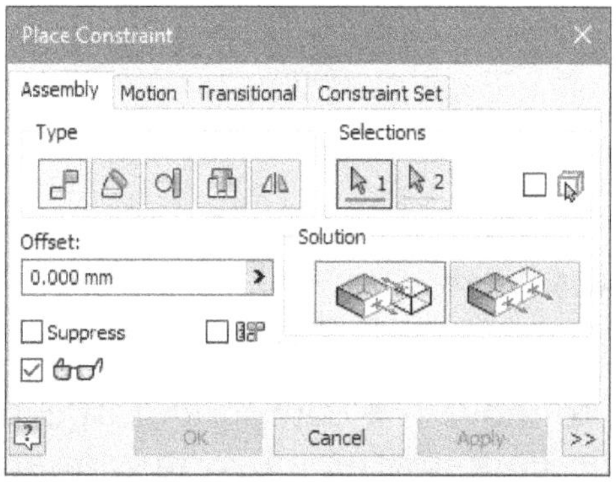

Figure-30. Place Constraint dialog box

Various constraints that can be applied in an assembly in Autodesk Inventor are discussed next.

Mate Constrain

The Mate constrain is used to make two faces or edges share the same location. This constrain can also be used to fix the distance between two faces/edges. The procedure to apply this constrain is given next.

- Click on the **Mate** button from the **Place Constraint** dialog box. You will be asked to select the first geometry.
- Click on the first geometry (Face/edge/vertex). You will be asked to select the second geometry.
- Click on the second geometry; refer to Figure-31.

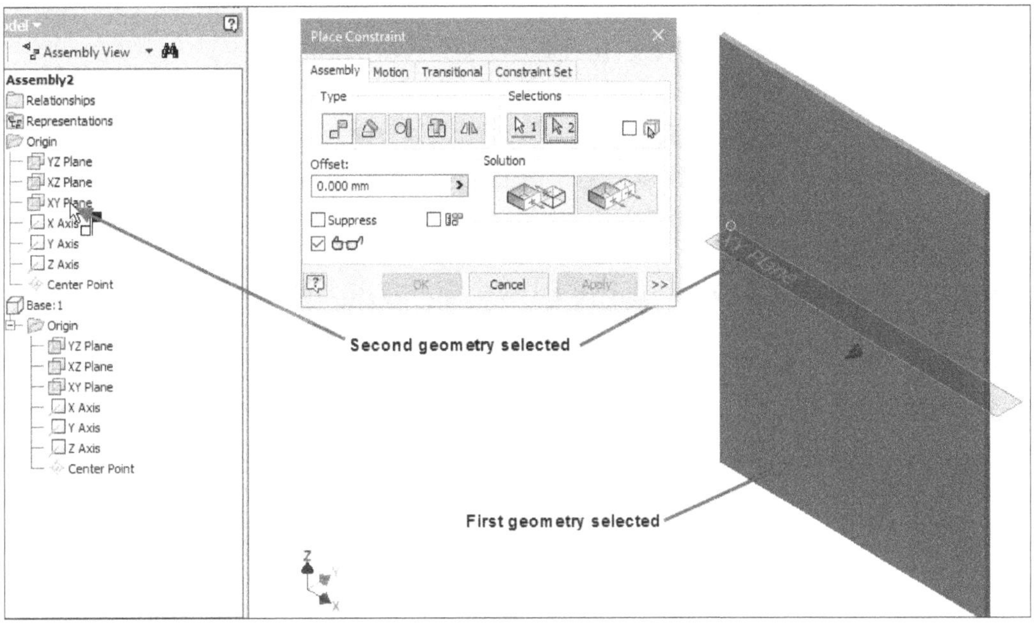

Figure-31. Selecting geometry for mate constraint

- If you want to specify an offset distance between the selected geometries then specify desired value in the **Offset** edit box.
- Select the **Suppress** check box to suppress the constraints.
- If you want to change the side of mate constraint, click on the **Flush** button  in the **Solution** area of the dialog box.
- You can also specify the limit for movement of selected geometry by using the options in expanded dialog box; refer to Figure-32. To expand the dialog box, click on the **>>** button from the dialog box.

Figure-32. Expanded Place Constraint dialog box

- Click on the **Maximum** check box and specify the maximum distance limit between the selected geometries in the edit box displayed.

- Click on the **Minimum** check box and specify the minimum distance limit between the selected geometries in the edit box displayed below.

Angle Constraint

The **Angle** constraint is used to set angle between two components. The procedure to specify angle constraint is given next.

- Click on the **Angle** button from the **Place Constraint** dialog box. The dialog box will be displayed as shown in Figure-33. Also, you will be asked to select the first geometry.

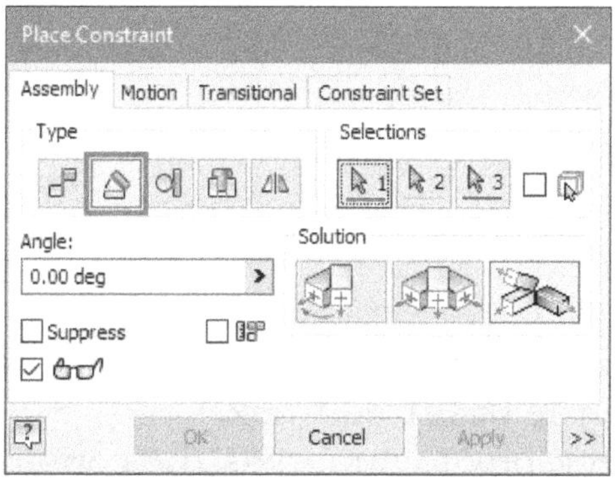

Figure-33. Place Constraint dialog box for Angle constraint

- Select the first geometry. You will be asked to select the second geometry.
- Select the second geometry. Preview of the angle constraint will be displayed; refer to Figure-34.

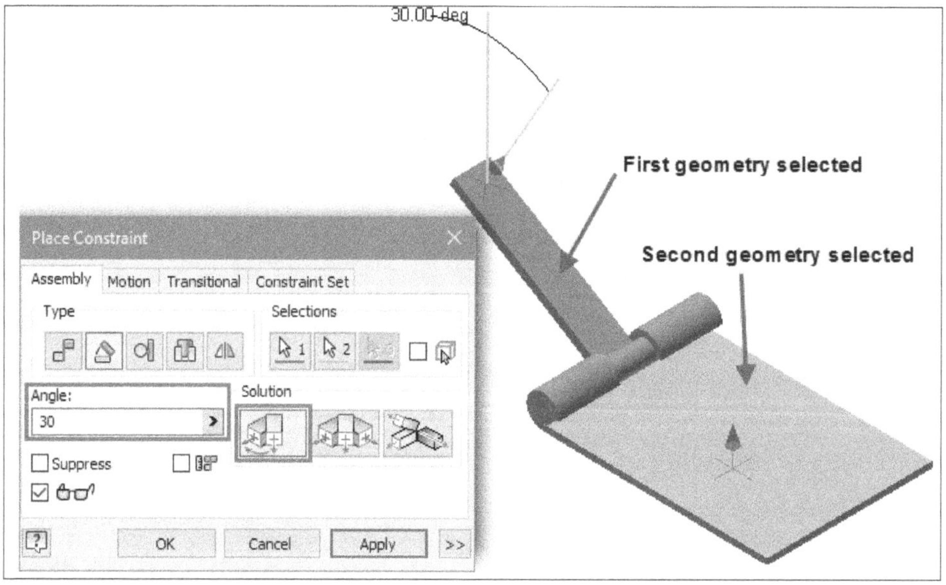

Figure-34. Preview of angle constraint

- Specify desired value in the **Angle** edit box.
- Note that there are three buttons in the **Solution** area of the dialog box; **Directed Angle**, **Undirected Angle**, and **Explicit Reference Vector**. Select the **Directed Angle** button if you want to use right-hand rule in specifying the angle. Select the **Undirected Angle** button if you want to use the left-hand rule in specifying angle between the geometries. You can select the reference vector for specifying angle direction by using the **Explicit Reference Vector** button.

- If you have selected the **Explicit Reference Vector** button then three selection buttons will be available in the **Selections** area of the dialog box; refer to Figure-35.

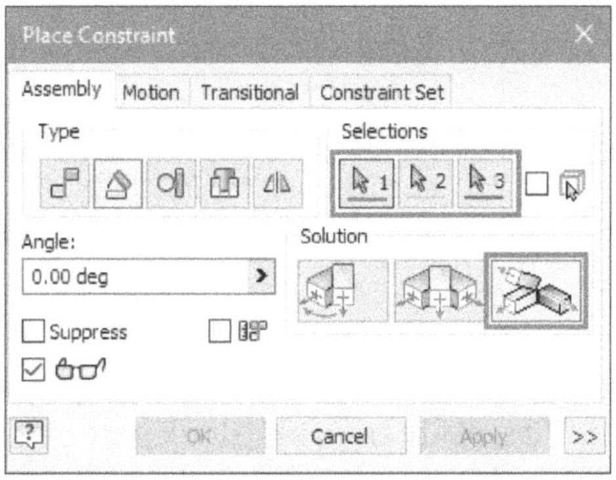

Figure-35. Explicit Reference Vector button selected

- Select the two geometries between which the angle is to be specified and then select a face/edge/axis to specify the direction for angle vector; refer to Figure-36.

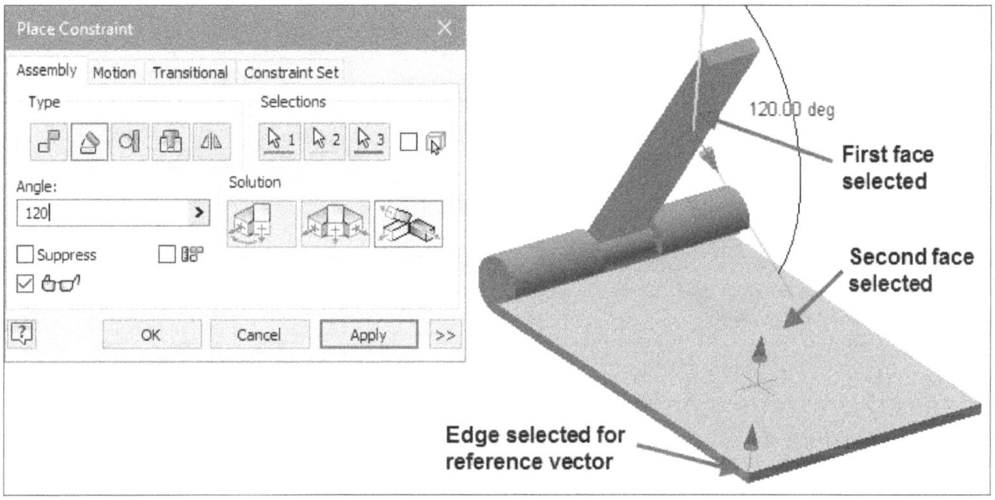

Figure-36. Preview of angle constraint with explicit vector

- Click on the **OK** button to apply the constraint.

Tangent Constraint

The **Tangent** constraint is used to make a selected geometry tangent to the other geometry. The procedure to apply this constraint is given next.

- Click on the **Tangent** button from the **Place Constraint** dialog box. The dialog box will be displayed as shown in Figure-37. Also, you will be asked to select the first geometry.

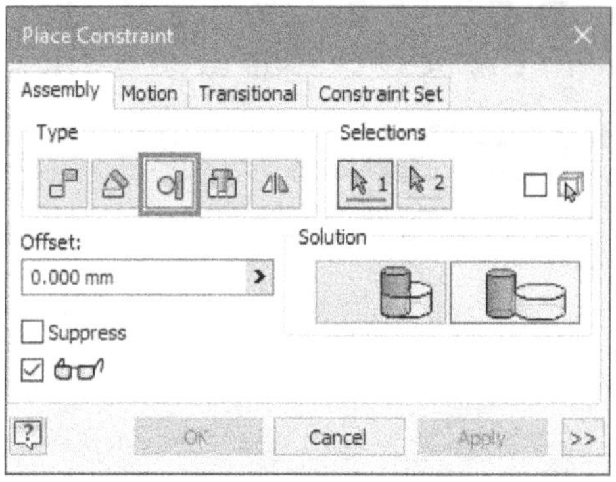

Figure-37. Place Constraint dialog box for Tangent constraint

- Select the first geometry. You will be asked to select the second geometry.
- Select the second geometry. Preview of the tangent constraint will be displayed; refer to Figure-38.

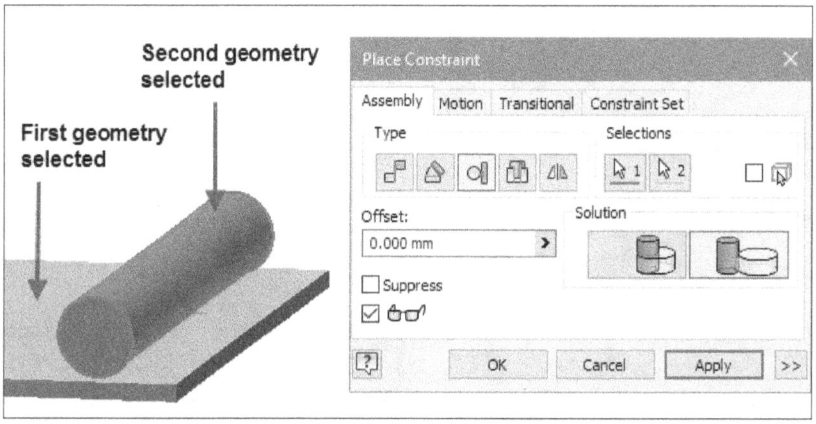

Figure-38. Preview of tangent constraint

- Select desired button from the **Solution** area of the dialog box to change the side of tangent constraint.
- If you want to specify distance between the two selected geometries then specify desired offset value in the **Offset** edit box in the dialog box.
- Click on the **OK** button from the dialog box to apply constraint.

Insert Constraint

The **Insert** constraint is used to insert pin like geometries inside hole like geometries. The procedure to use this constraint is given next.

- Click on the **Insert** button from the **Place Constraint** dialog box. The dialog box will be displayed as shown in Figure-39.

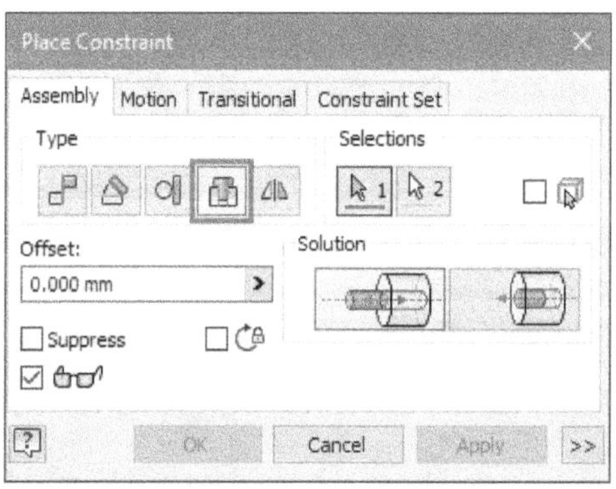

Figure-39. Place Constraint dialog box for Insert constraint

- Select the round edge of first entity. You will be asked to select the second entity.
- Select the second entity. Preview of the insert constraint will be displayed; refer to Figure-40.

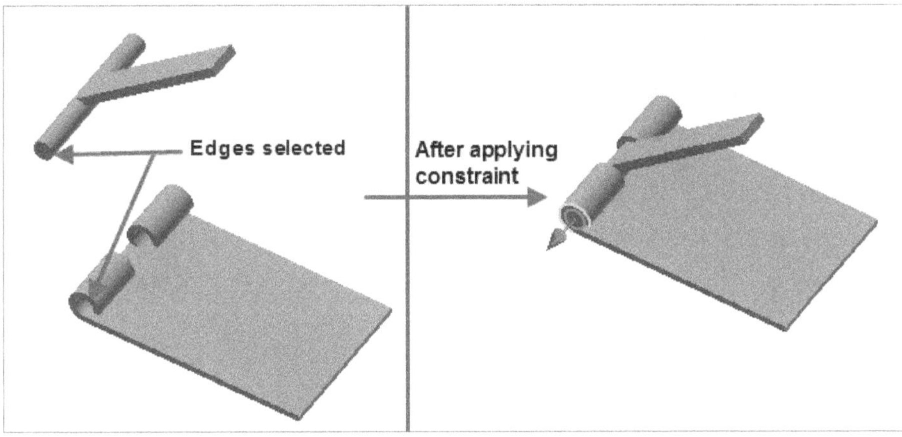

Figure-40. Preview of insert constraint

- Note that if we break down the insert constraint then it does two things, making axis of the selected geometries coincident and making selected round edges aligned in one plane.
- To change the direction of placement, select desired button from the **Solution** area of the dialog box.
- Click on the **OK** button from the dialog box to apply the constraint.

Symmetry Constraint

The **Symmetry** constraint is used to make the selected two components symmetric about the selected plane. The procedure to apply this constraint is given next.

- Click on the **Symmetry** button from the **Place Constraint** dialog box. The dialog box will be displayed as shown in Figure-41. Also, you will be asked to select a geometry.

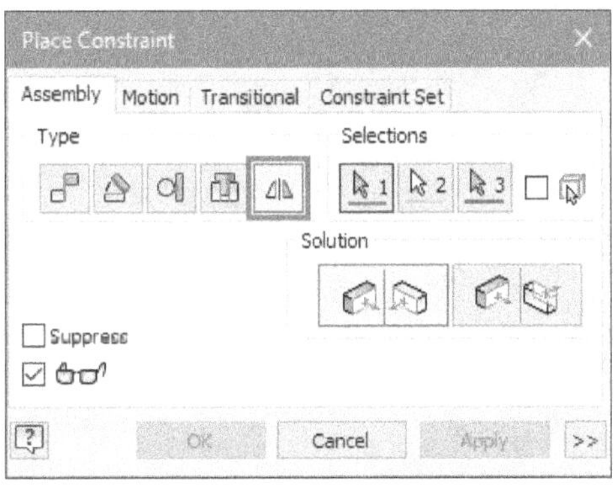

Figure-41. Place Constraint dialog box for Symmetry constraint

- Select the face/edge/axis of the first component. You will be asked to select the second geometry.
- Select the second geometry. You will be asked to select a plane for defining symmetry reference.
- Select a plane about which you want the components to be symmetric. Preview of the symmetry will be displayed; refer to Figure-42.

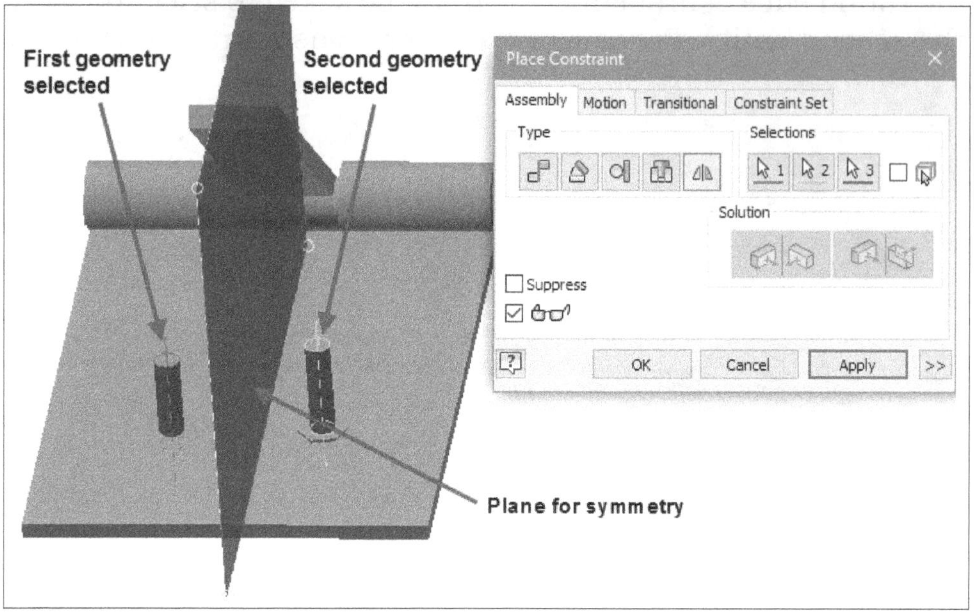

Figure-42. Preview of symmetry constraint

- Click on the **OK** button from the dialog box to apply the constraint.

Motion Constraint

There are two type of constraints for setting motion of objects in Autodesk Inventor assembly, **Rotation** and **Rotation-Translation**. Using the **Rotation** constraint, you can specify the ratio of rotation between the two objects like in gears, bearings, etc. Using the **Rotation-Translation** constraint, you can make one component translate on rotation of other component or you can make one component rotate on translation of other component. Examples can be screw jack motion, rack and pinion design, etc. The procedures to apply these constraints are discussed next.

Rotation Constraint

- Click on the **Motion** tab in the **Place Constraint** dialog box. The options in the dialog box will be displayed as shown in Figure-43.

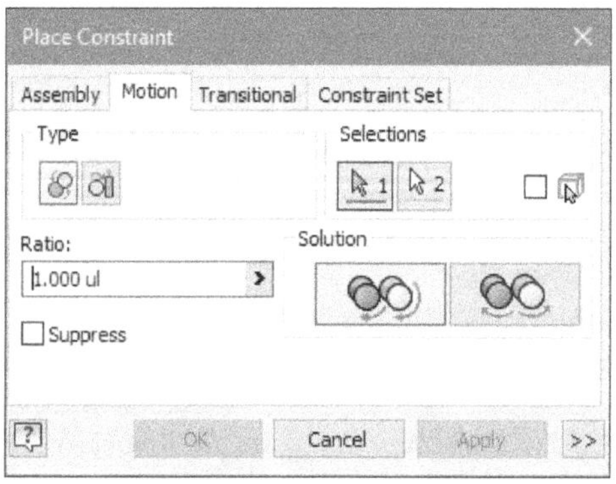

Figure-43. Place Constraint dialog box with Motion tab selected

- Click on the **Rotation** button from the **Type** area of the dialog box. You will be asked to select the first geometry.
- Select the round face of first object. You will be asked to select the second geometry.
- Select the round face of the second object.
- Specify desired ratio for rotation; refer to Figure-44.

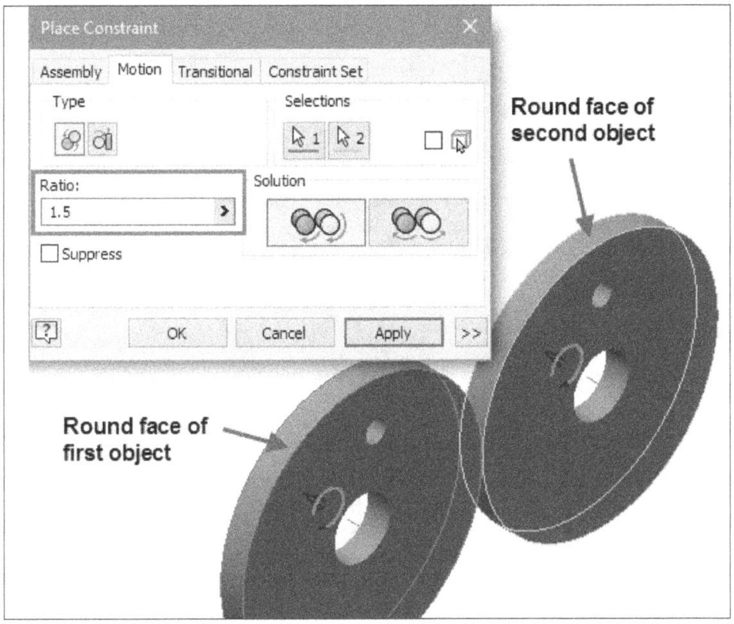

Figure-44. Options for rotation constraint

- To change the direction of rotation of the objects, click on desired button from the **Solution** area of the dialog box.
- Click on the **OK** button from the dialog box.

Rotation-Translation Constraint

- Click on the **Motion** tab in the **Place Constraint** dialog box and select the **Rotation-Translation** button. The options in the dialog box will be displayed as shown in Figure-45. Also, you will be asked to select the first geometry.

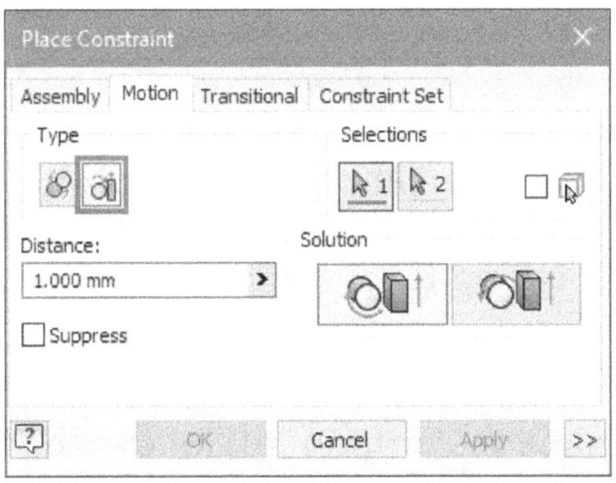

Figure-45. Place Constraint dialog box for rotation translation option

- Select the round face of the first object (disc); refer to Figure-46. You will be asked to select the second geometry.

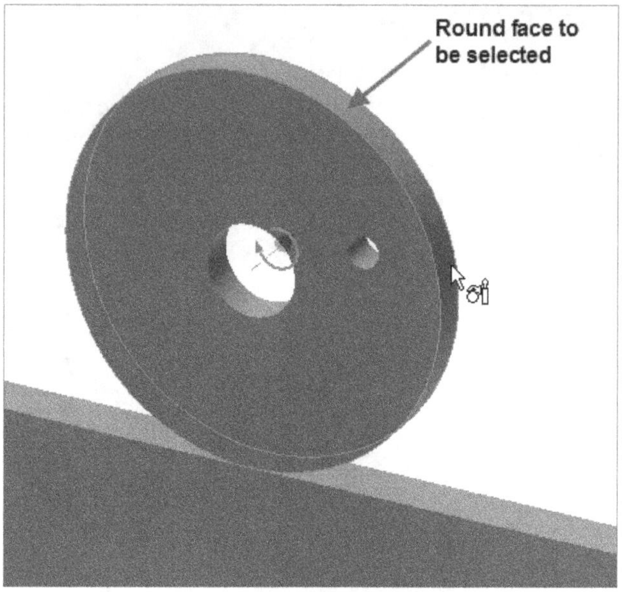

Figure-46. Round face to be selected

- Select the edge of the second object (rail) coinciding with the round face; refer to Figure-47.

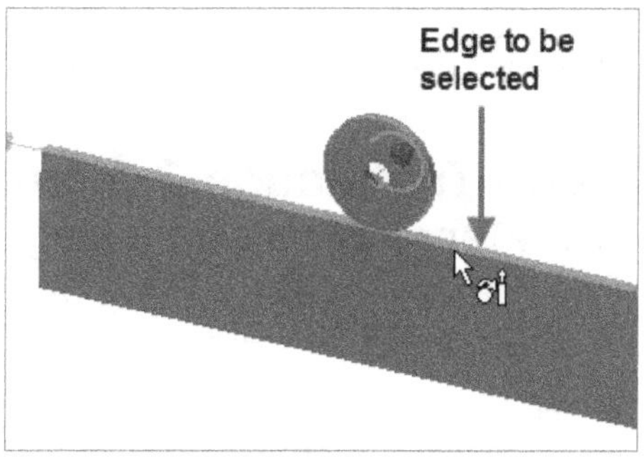

Figure-47. Edge selected for constraint

- Specify the distance moved by rail (second geometry) on one rotation of the disc object (first geometry) in the **Distance** edit box of the dialog box.
- Click on the **OK** button from the dialog box to create the constraint. Note that if you rotate the disc by dragging then the rail will move by specified distance.

Transitional Constraint

Transitional constraint makes a component follow the path of other component. You can use this constraint to make cam-follower or slot-follower mechanism. The procedure to use this constraint is given next.

- Click on the **Transitional** tab in the **Place Constraint** dialog box. The dialog box will be displayed as shown in Figure-48. Also, you will be asked to select the first geometry.

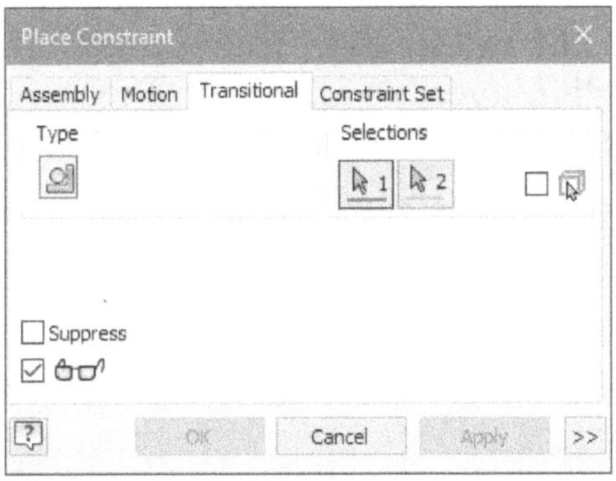

Figure-48. Place Constraint dialog box with Transitional tab selected

- Select the face of first component. You will be asked to select the second geometry.
- Select the face of slot/cam (second object). Preview of the constraint will be displayed; refer to Figure-49.

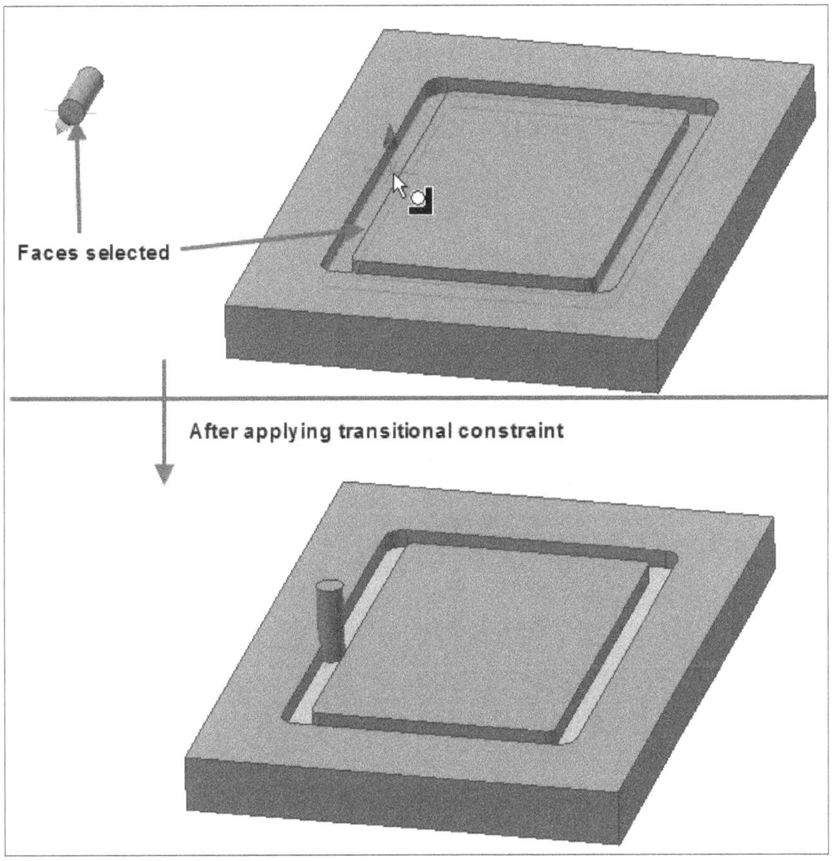

Figure-49. Preview of transitional constraint

- Click on the **OK** button from the dialog box to apply the constraint. Note that in the above example, you would have to apply the transitional constraint also on walls of the slot and follower. After applying the constraint, if you move the follower by dragging then it will move only inside the slot.

Constraint Set

The **Constraint Set** tool is used to constrain two components in such a way that coordinate systems of the two components are coincident. The procedure to apply this constraint is given next.

- Make sure that UCS are created for the components before using this constraint.
- Click on the **Constraint Set** tab in the **Place Constraint** dialog box. The options in the dialog box will be displayed as shown in Figure-50. Also, you will be asked to select the UCS of first object.

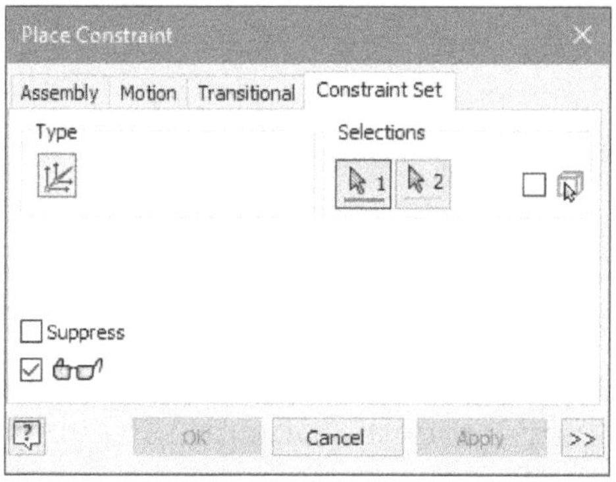

Figure-50. Place Constraint dialog box with Constraint Set tab selected

- Click on the UCS (User Coordinate System) of first component. You will be asked to select the user coordinate system of second component.
- Select the UCS of second component. The object will be placed as both UCS coincident; refer to Figure-51.

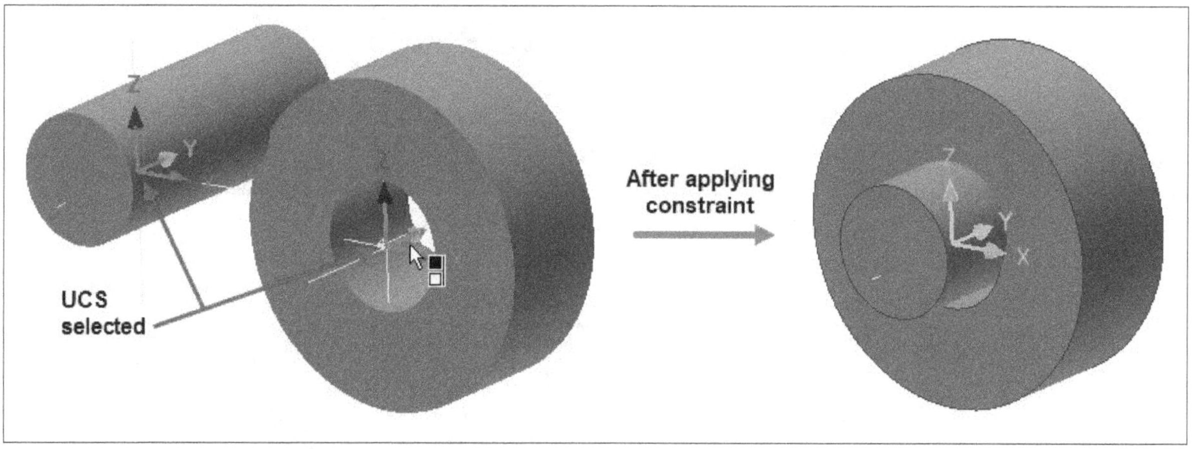

Figure-51. Preview of Constraint set

- Click on the **OK** button from the dialog box.

JOINTS

Joints are similar to constraints we have discussed earlier in terms of applying them. But, joints also provide motion along with placing the components at desired location. Various joints and procedures to apply them are discussed next.

Rigid Joint

The **Rigid joint** is used to fix a component at desired location. This type of joints are used in placing bolts, keys, pins, etc. The procedure to use this joint is given next.

- Click on the **Joint** tool from **Relationships** panel in the **Assemble** tab of the **Ribbon**. The **Place Joint** dialog box will be displayed; refer to Figure-52.

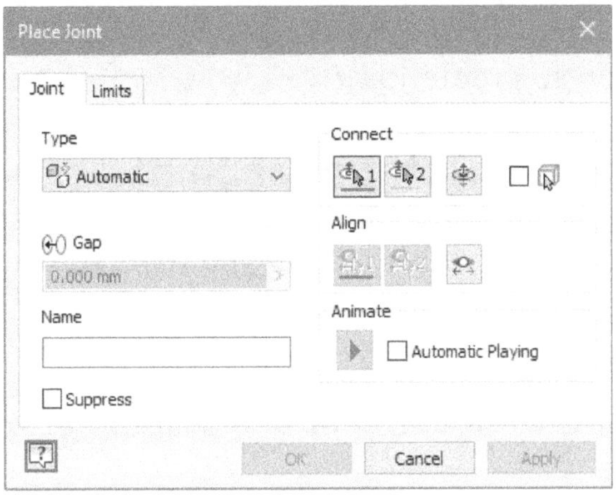

Figure-52. Place Joint dialog box

- Select the **Rigid** option from **Type** drop-down in the dialog box; refer to Figure-53. You will be asked to place origin on the first object.

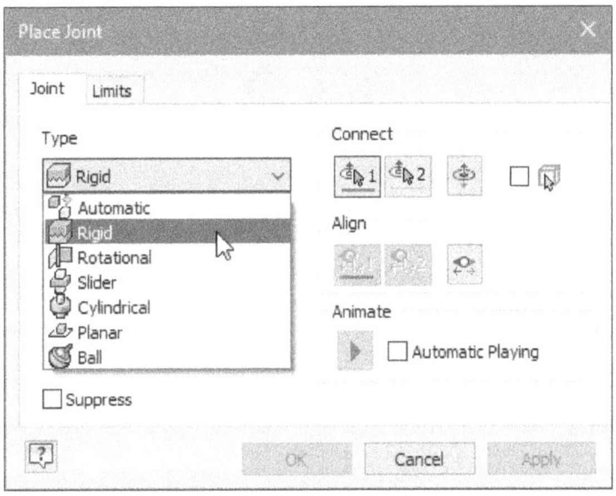

Figure-53. Rigid option in Type drop down

- Click on desired location on first object. You will be asked to place origin on the next object. Note that the location denoted by ring and point will be the origin of that component while creating joint.
- Select the location of second object; refer to Figure-54. The rigid joint will be created.

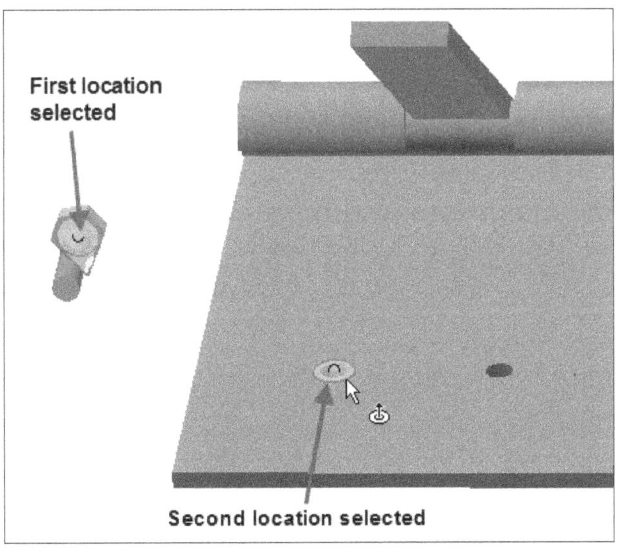

Figure-54. Selecting locations on components

- Click in the **Gap** edit box in the dialog box and specify the gap between selected faces, if required.
- Click on the **OK** button to create joint.

Rotational Joint

- Click on the **Joint** tool from **Relationships** panel in the **Assemble** tab of the **Ribbon**. The **Place Joint** dialog box will be displayed as discussed earlier.
- Select the **Rotational** option from **Type** drop-down in the dialog box; refer to Figure-55. You will be asked to place origin on the first component.

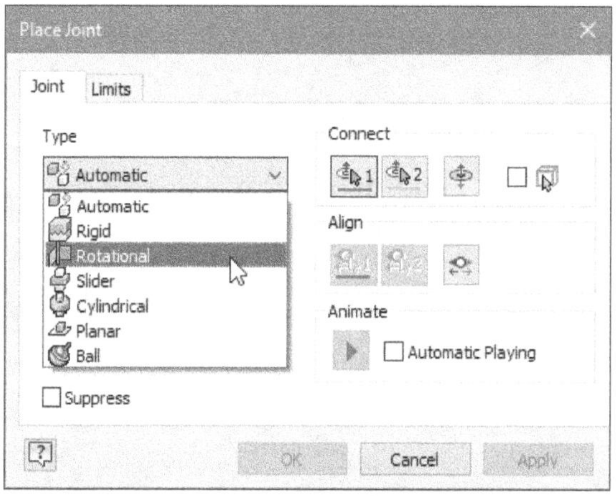

Figure-55. Rotational option in Type drop down

- Click at desired location on the first component. You will be asked to select a location on the second component.
- Click at desired location on the second component; refer to Figure-56. Preview of the rotational joint will be displayed.

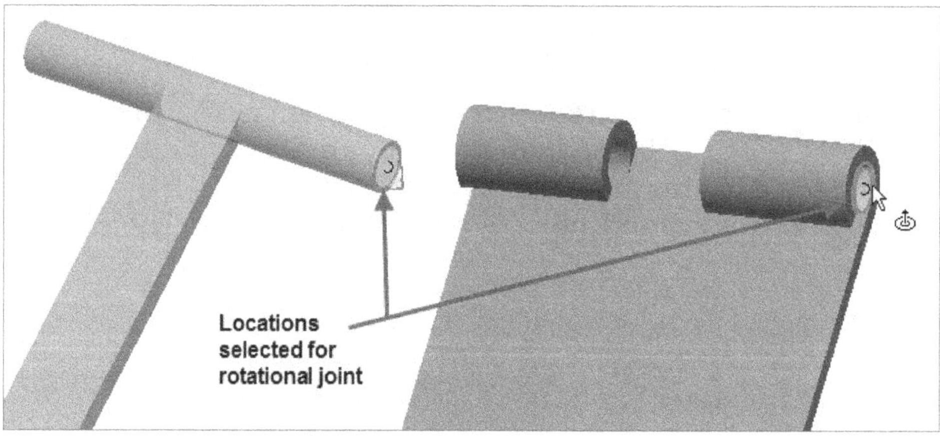

Figure-56. Locations selected for rotational joint

- If you want to set the maximum and minimum limit of rotation then click on the **Limits** tab in the dialog box. The dialog box will be displayed as shown in Figure-57.

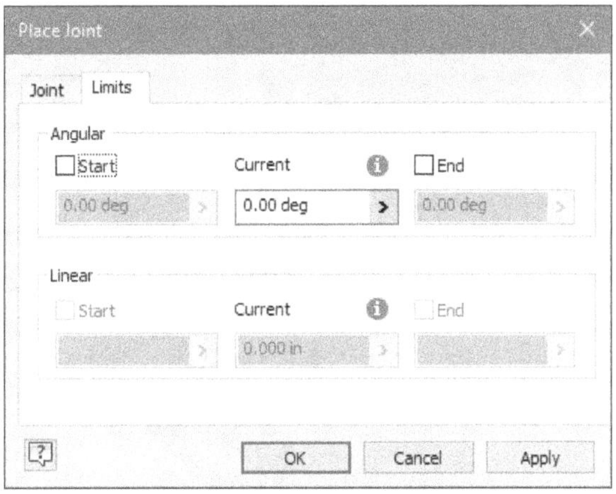

Figure-57. Limits tab in Place Joint dialog box

- Select the **Start** check box and specify the starting point of limit.
- Similarly, specify the end point of limit by using the **End** check box.
- To specify the current position of the component, click in the **Current** edit box and specify desired value of angle.
- Click on the **OK** button from the dialog box.

Slider Joint

The **Slider** joint is used to create joint when you need sliding motion of a component. For example, piston in cylinder of engine. The procedure to apply this joint is given next.

- Click on the **Joint** tool from **Relationships** panel in the **Assemble** tab of the **Ribbon**. The **Place Joint** dialog box will be displayed.
- Select the **Slider** option from **Type** drop-down in the dialog box; refer to Figure-58. You will be asked to select the first origin.

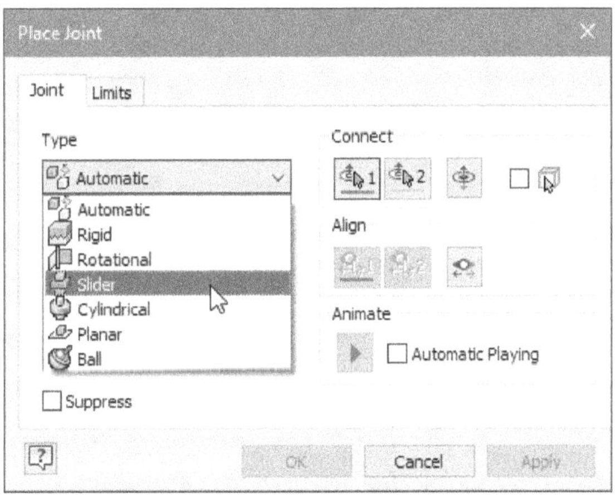

Figure-58. Slider option in Type drop down

- Select the face of first component (slider). You will be asked to select origin of the other component.
- Select the face of second component. Make sure the direction of motion is aligned properly after selection; refer to Figure-59.

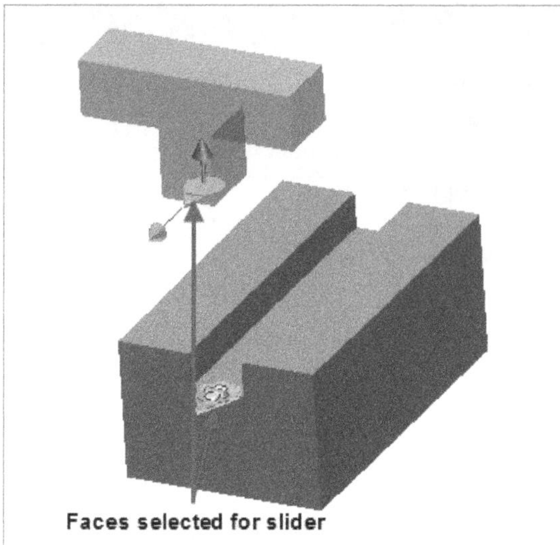

Figure-59. Faces selected for slider joint

- Set desired gap and distance limits.
- Click on the **OK** button to create the joint.

Cylindrical Joint

The **Cylindrical** joint is used to create joint when you need sliding and rotating motion of a shaft. For example, motion of a shaft in a tube. The procedure to apply this joint is given next.

- Click on the **Joint** tool from **Relationships** panel in the **Assemble** tab of the **Ribbon**. The **Place Joint** dialog box will be displayed.
- Select the **Cylindrical** option from **Type** drop-down in the dialog box; refer to Figure-60. You will be asked to select the first origin.

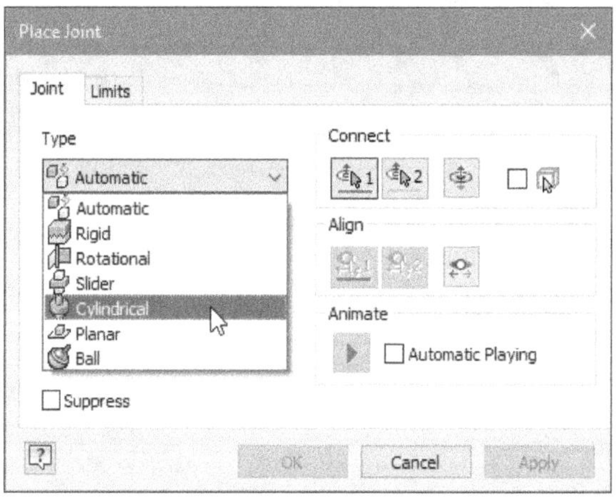

Figure-60. Cylindrical option in Type drop down

- Click on the round face of the first component. You will be asked to select origin of next component.
- Click on the round face of the second component. Preview of the joint will be displayed; refer to Figure-61.

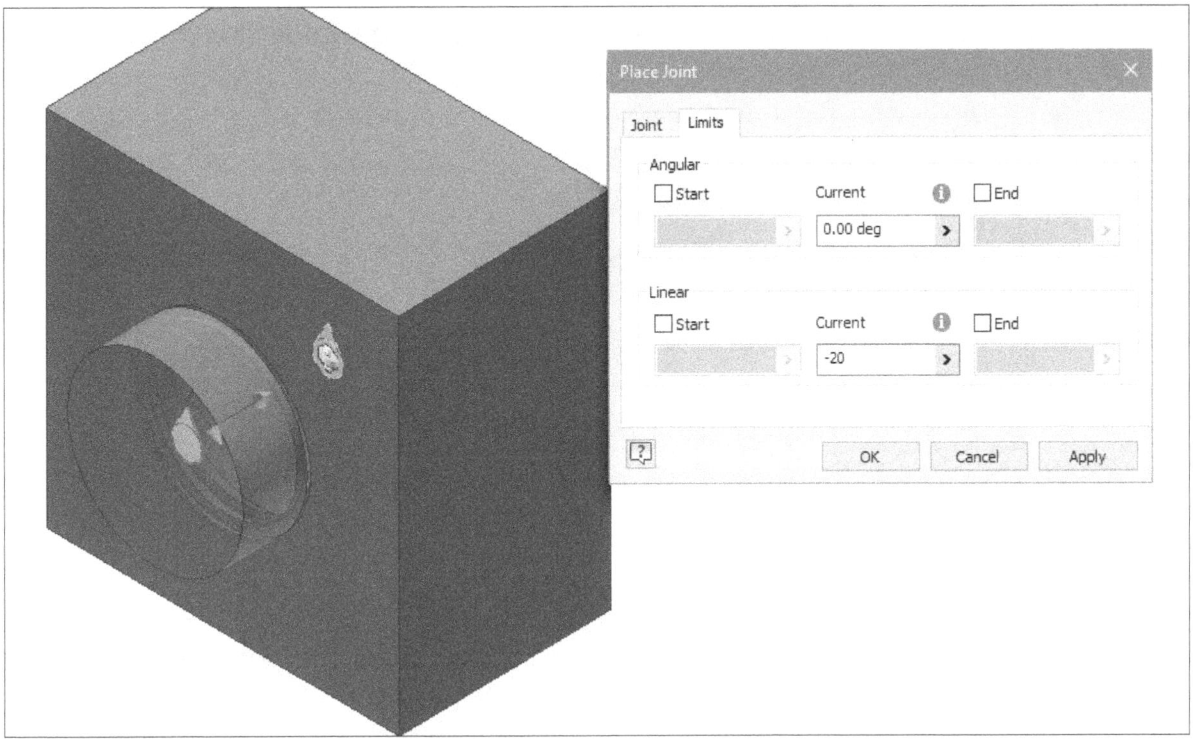

Figure-61. Preview of cylindrical joint

- Set desired limits for the component.
- Click on the **OK** button from the dialog box.

Planar Joint

The **Planar** joint is used to create joint when you need component to move in a specified plane. Note that one rotational degree of freedom will also be free of the component on applying this joint. The procedure to apply this constraint is given next.

- Click on the **Joint** tool from **Relationships** panel in the **Assemble** tab of the **Ribbon**. The **Place Joint** dialog box will be displayed.
- Select the **Planar** option from **Type** drop-down in the dialog box; refer to Figure-62. You will be asked to select the first origin.

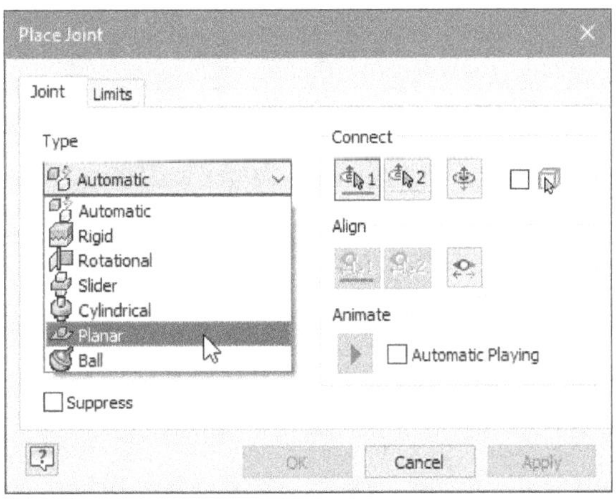

Figure-62. Planar option in Type drop down

- Click on the face of first component. You will be asked to place origin on next component.

- Click on the face of second component. Preview of the joint will be displayed.
- Set desired gap and click on the **OK** button from the dialog box to create joint; refer to Figure-63.

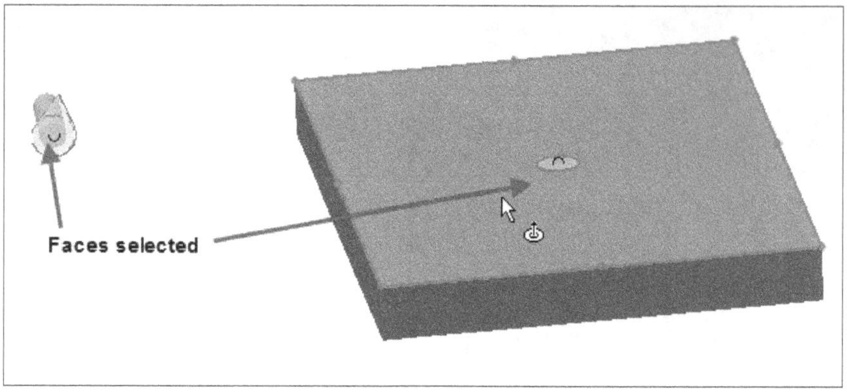

Figure-63. Faces selected for planar joint

Ball Joint

The **Ball** joint is used to create joint where you need the object free in rotational dimensions but fixed in translation. The procedure to apply this joint is given next.

- Click on the **Joint** tool from **Relationships** panel in the **Assemble** tab of the **Ribbon**. The **Place Joint** dialog box will be displayed.
- Select the **Ball** option from **Type** drop-down in the dialog box; refer to Figure-64. You will be asked to select the first origin.

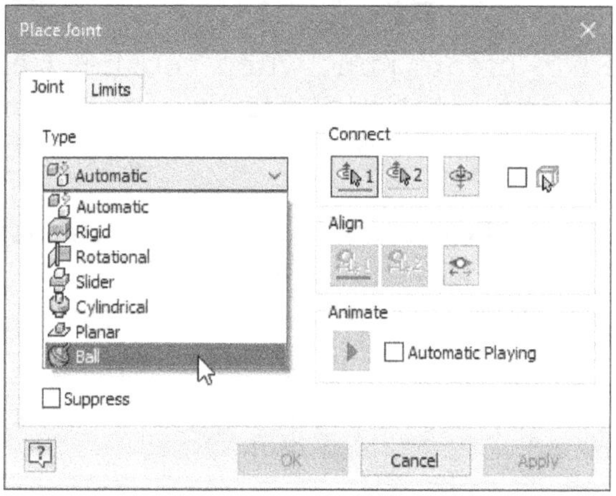

Figure-64. Ball option in Type drop down

- Select the round face of first component. You will be asked to select origin of next component.
- Select the round face of second component. The preview of ball joint will be displayed; refer to Figure-65.

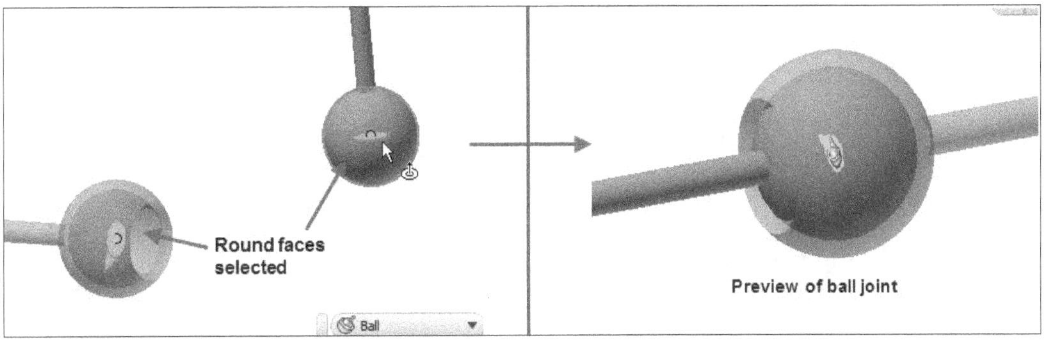

Figure-65. Creating ball joint

- Click on the **OK** button from the dialog box to create the joint.

GROUNDED CONSTRAINT

As the name suggests, the Grounded constraint is used to fix the component at its location. This constraint is generally used to fix the base component so that other components based on it does not move automatically while applying mechanism on them. The procedure to ground a component is given next.

- Right-click on the component that you want to be grounded (fixed) from the **Model Browser** bar. A shortcut menu will be displayed; refer to Figure-66.

Figure-66. Shortcut menu for component in assembly

- Click on the **Grounded** option from the shortcut menu. The component will be fixed at its current position.

CONTACT SET

The Contact set is used to make part behave in real world environment. It specifically means that parts cannot cross each other when interference occurs; refer to Figure-67. The procedure to apply contact set is given next.

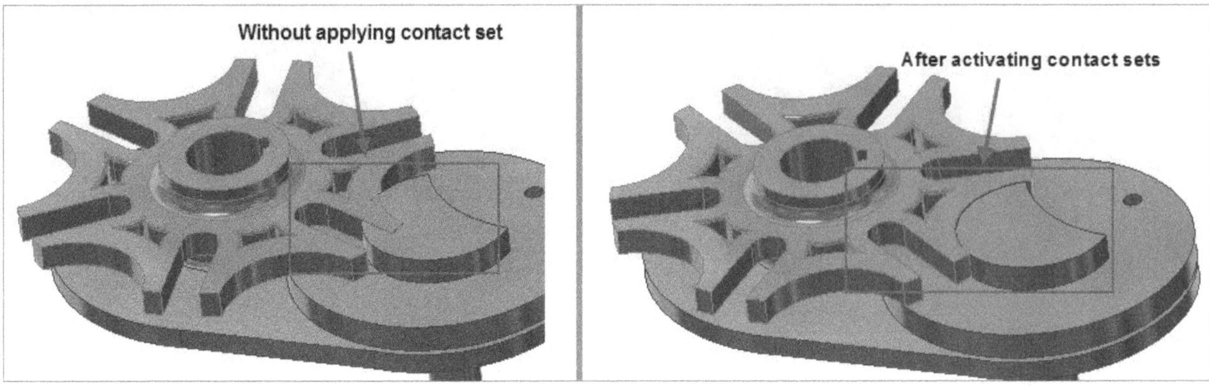

Figure-67. Interference without activating contact sets

- Right-click on the component which you want to use in contact set from the **Model Browser** bar. A shortcut menu will be displayed.
- Select the **Contact Set** option from the shortcut menu to apply contact set; refer to Figure-68. Note that the icon of component in **Model Browser** bar will change as shown in Figure-69.

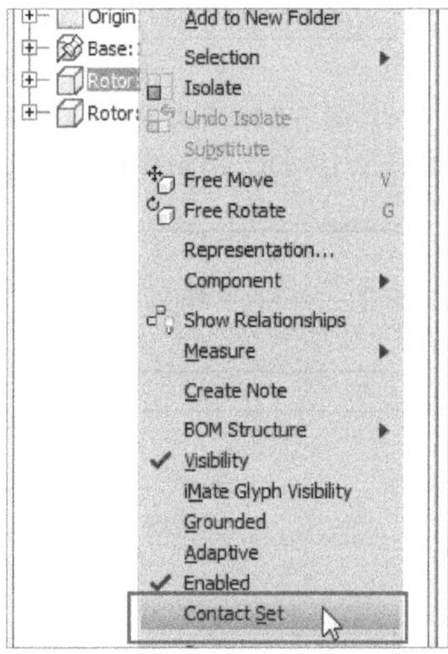

Figure-68. Contact Set option

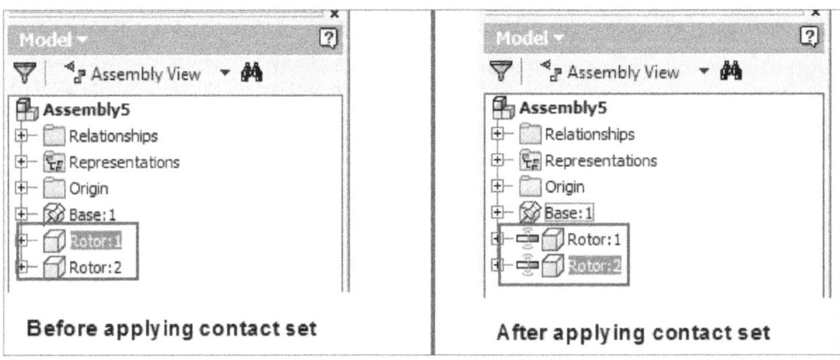

Figure-69. Applying contact set

- We have applied the contact sets but we need to activate them before making use in assembly. To do so, click on the **Inspect** tab in the **Ribbon** and select **Activate Contact Solver** button from the **Interference** panel in the **Ribbon**; refer to Figure-70. Contact sets will be activated.

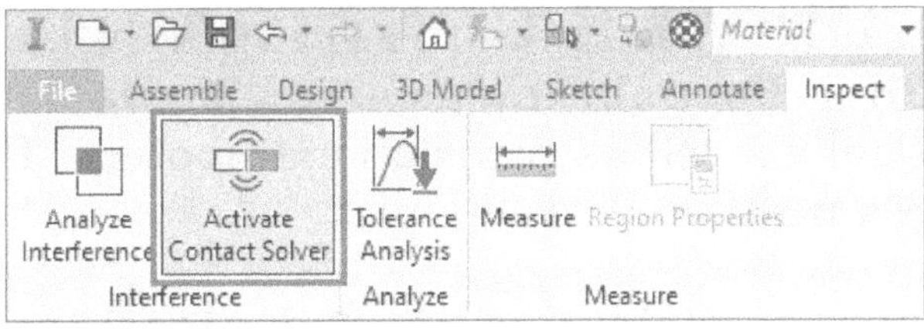

Figure-70. Activate Contact Solver button

BILL OF MATERIALS

The Bill of Materials (in short BOM) is used to form a table of components that are used in the assembly. In this table, we have name of components and their respective quantity. It becomes very important for purchasing the components from market or manage inventory of components required in making assembly. The procedure to create BOM in Autodesk Inventor is given next.

- Click on the **Bill of Materials** tool from the **Manage** panel in the **Assemble** tab of the **Ribbon**. The **Bill of Materials** dialog box will be displayed; refer to Figure-71.

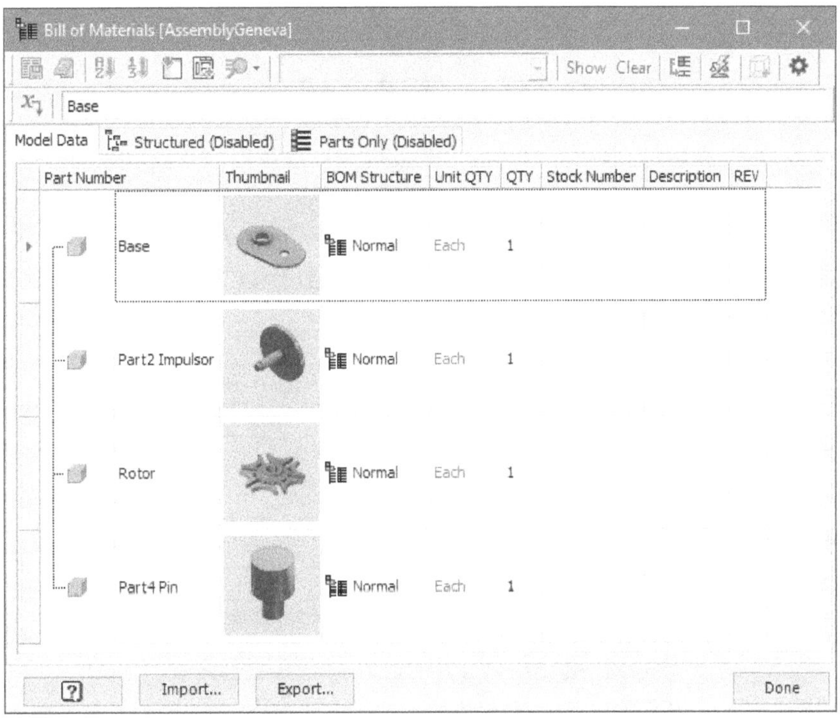

Figure-71. Bill of Materials dialog box

- Click in desired field to change the value of that item. For example, you can change the quantity from 1 to 5 in the fields under **QTY** column, you can change the name of part by clicking in the respective field, and so on.
- Enter the other details in respective fields of the dialog box.
- If you want to export the bill of material to other software in xml format then click on the **Export** button at the bottom in the dialog box. Similarly, you can import the bill of material in xml format from other software by using the **Import** button.
- Click on the **Done** button to exit the dialog box.

DRIVING CONSTRAINT

You can apply motor to a constraint by using the **Drive** option. The drive can be applied to both rotational as well as translational motion. The procedure to apply the **Drive** option is given next.

- Right-click on desired constraint from the **Relationships** category in the **Model Browser** bar. A shortcut menu will be displayed; refer to Figure-72. Note that the selected constraint should have one or more degree of freedom.

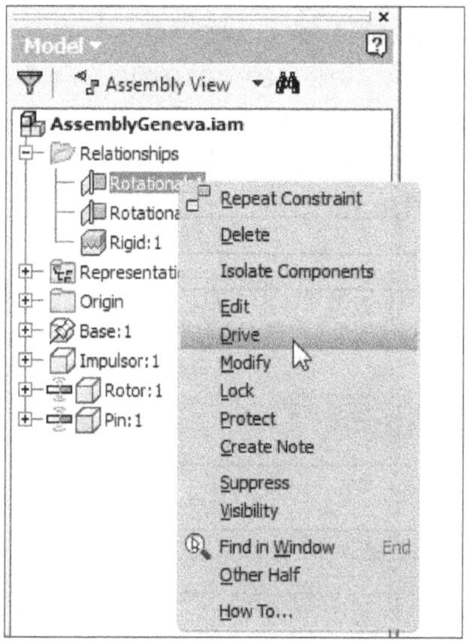

Figure-72. Shortcut menu for constraint

- Click on the **Drive** option from the shortcut menu. The **Drive** dialog box will be displayed; refer to Figure-73.

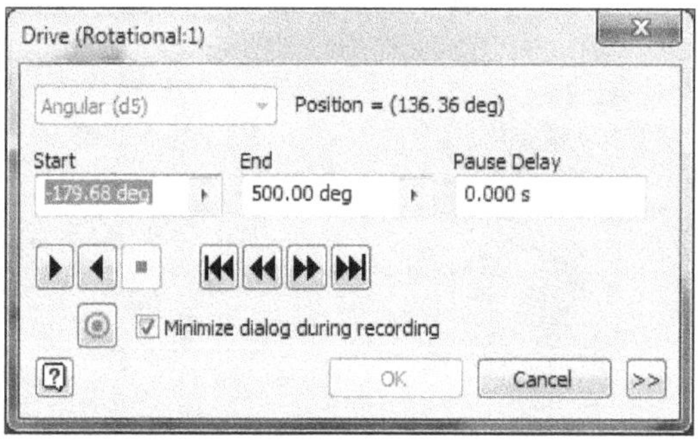

Figure-73. Drive dialog box

- Specify desired starting and end value in the respective edit boxes.
- You can specify desired amount of delay in the **Pause Delay** edit box.
- Click on the **Forward** and **Reverse** buttons from the dialog box to check the motion of assembly.
- Click on the **OK** button to apply drive.

PRACTICAL 1

Create assembly of Geneva mechanism as shown in Figure-74. The components of assembly are available in the resource kit.

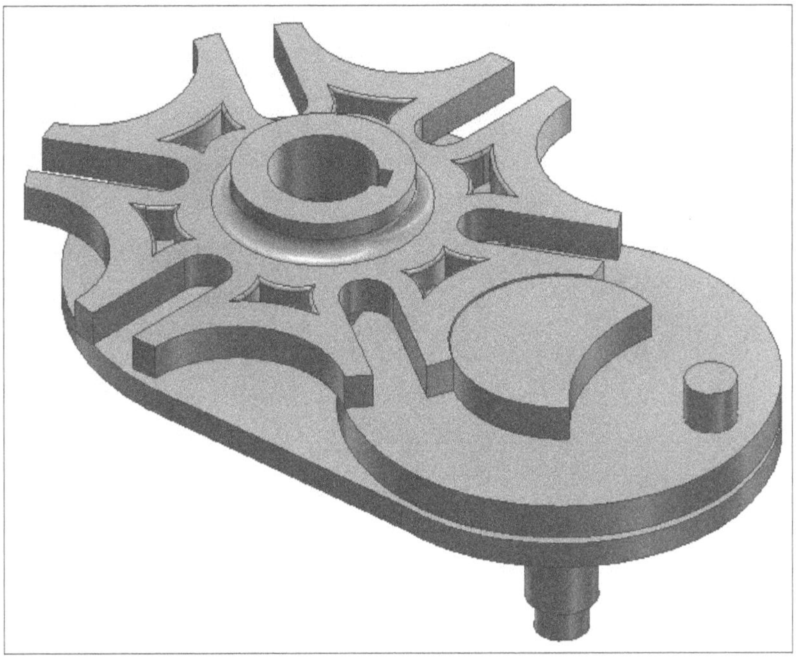

Figure-74. Geneva mechanism

Strategy for Creating model

1. Looking at the isometric view, we can find the base component which is a base plate supporting all the other components on it.
2. Insert the base plate and fix it by using Grounded option.
3. One by one insert the other components and apply constraints which provide motion also.

Starting Assembly File

- Start Autodesk Inventor by double-clicking on the Autodesk Inventor Professional icon from the desktop. (If not started yet.)
- Click on the **New** button from the **Quick Access Toolbar**. The **Create New File** dialog box will be displayed.
- Double-click on **Standard(mm).iam** icon from the Assembly category in **Metric** templates; refer to Figure-75. The Assembly environment of Autodesk Inventor will be displayed.

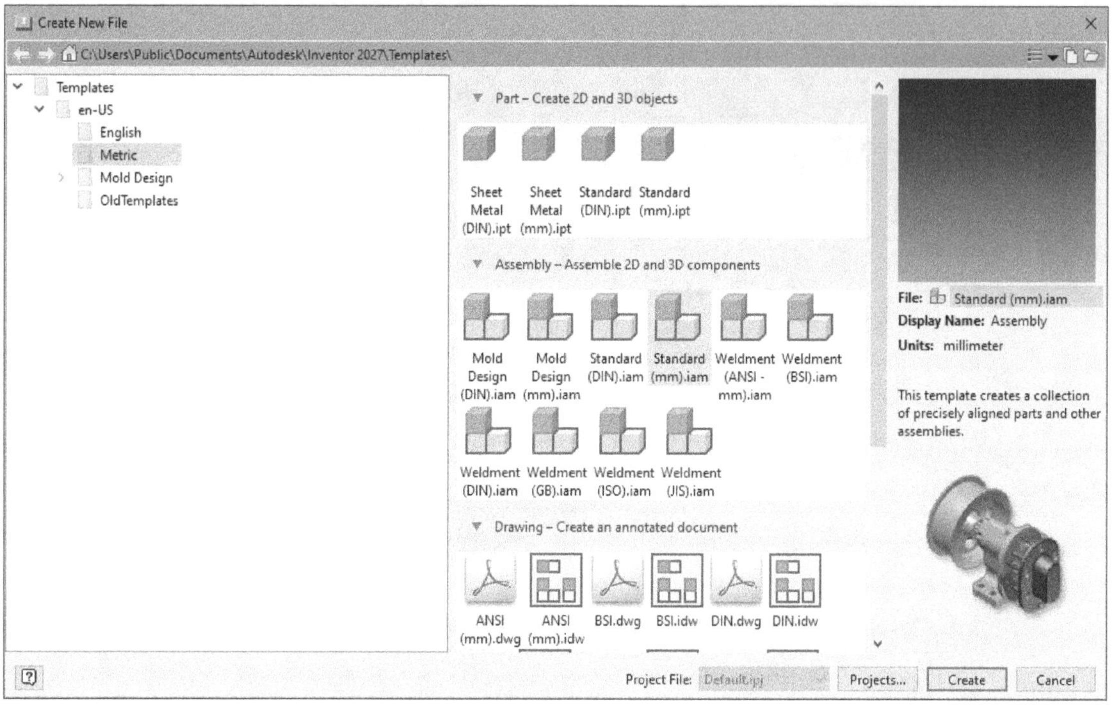

Figure-75. Assembly option in Create New File dialog box

Inserting First Component

- Click on the **Place** button from the **Component** panel in the **Assemble** tab of the **Ribbon**. The **Place Component** dialog box will be displayed.
- Select the **Base.ipt** from the dialog box and click on the **Open** button. The component will get attached to the cursor.
- Click in the viewport to place the component. A copy of the component still get attached to cursor. Press **ESC** from the keyboard to exit inserting more copies of the component.
- Right-click on the name of component from the **Model Browser** bar. A shortcut menu will be displayed; refer to Figure-76.

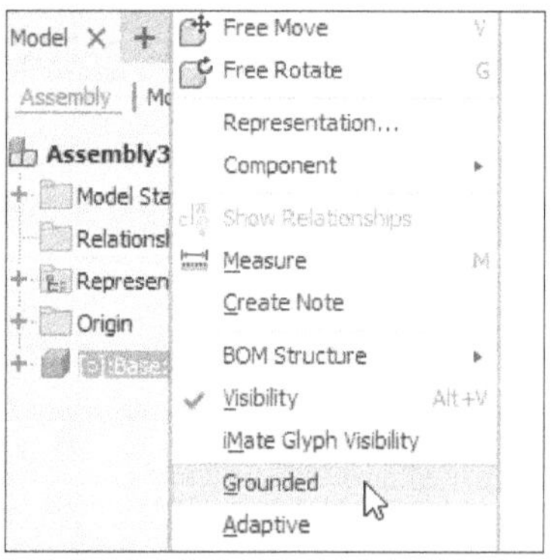

Figure-76. Shortcut menu for grounding component

- Click on the **Grounded** option from it. The component will get fixed.

Inserting Impulsor component

- Click on the **Place** tool from the **Component** panel in the **Assemble** tab of the **Ribbon**. The **Place Component** dialog box will be displayed.

- Click on the **Impulsor** component from the dialog box and click on the **Open** button. The component will get attached to the cursor.
- Click in the empty area of the viewport. The component will be placed. Press **ESC** from the keyboard to exit inserting more copies of the component.
- Click on the **Joint** tool from **Relationships** panel in the **Assemble** tab of the **Ribbon**. The **Place Joint** dialog box will be displayed; refer to Figure-77.

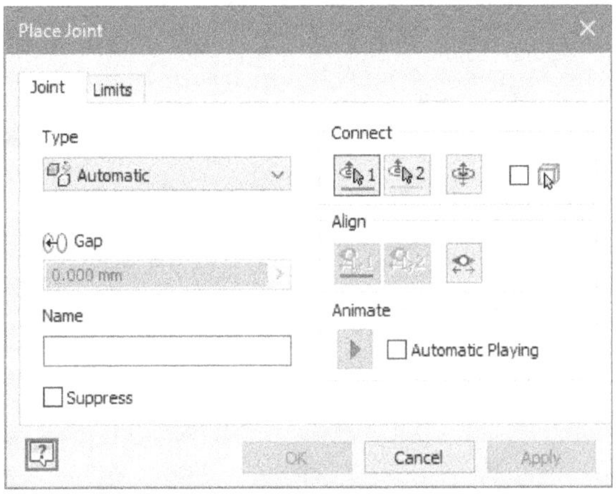

Figure-77. Place Joint dialog box

- Select the **Rotational** option from **Type** drop-down in the dialog box. You will be asked to place origin on the first component.
- Click on the face of first component; refer to Figure-78. You will be asked to place origin on the second component.
- Select the edge of second component; refer to Figure-78. The component will be placed accordingly.

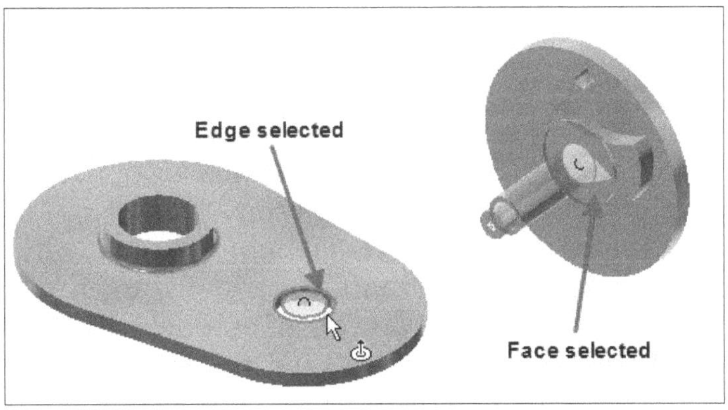

Figure-78. Entities selected for rotational joint

- Flip the side of the component if required by using the **Flip component** button from the dialog box.
- Click on the **OK** button from the dialog box to create the joint.

Inserting Rotor Component

- Click on the **Place** tool from the **Component** panel in the **Assemble** tab of the **Ribbon**. The **Place Component** dialog box will be displayed.
- Click on the **Rotor** component from the dialog box and click on the **Open** button. The component will get attached to the cursor.
- Click in the empty area of the viewport. The component will be placed. Press **ESC** from the keyboard to exit inserting more copies of the component.

- Click on the **Joint** tool from the **Relationships** panel in the **Assemble** tab of the **Ribbon**. The **Place Joint** dialog box will be displayed.
- Select the **Rotational** option from **Type** drop-down in the dialog box. You will be asked to place origin on the first component.
- Click on the edge of first component; refer to Figure-79. You will be asked to place origin on the second component.
- Select the edge of second component; refer to Figure-79. The joint will be created.

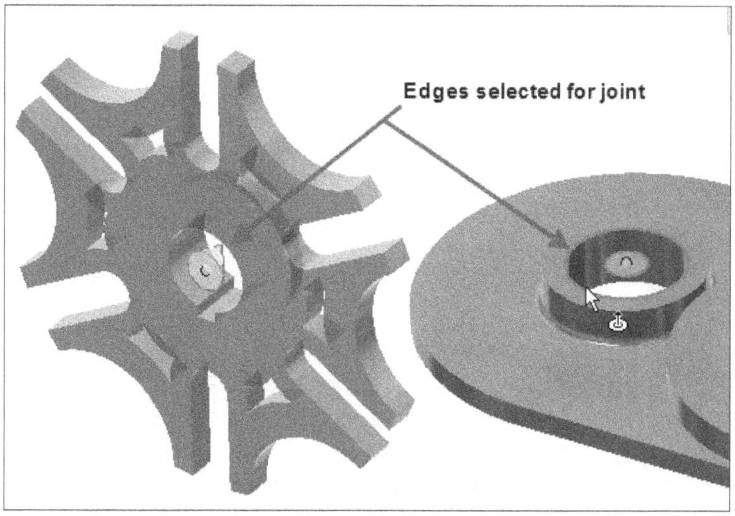

Figure-79. Edges selected for rotational joint

- Click on the **OK** button from the dialog box.
- Right-click on the **Rotor** component from the **Model Browser** bar and select the **Contact Set** option from the shortcut menu displayed.

Inserting Pin

- Click on the **Place** tool from the **Component** panel in the **Assemble** tab of the **Ribbon**. The **Place Component** dialog box will be displayed.
- Click on the **Pin** component from the dialog box and click on the **Open** button. The component will get attached to the cursor.
- Click in the empty area of the viewport. The component will be placed. Press **ESC** from the keyboard to exit inserting more copies of the component.
- Click on the **Joint** tool from the **Relationships** panel in the **Assemble** tab of the **Ribbon**. The **Place Joint** dialog box will be displayed.
- Select the **Rigid** option from **Type** drop-down in the dialog box. You will be asked to place origin on the first component.
- Click on the face of first component; refer to Figure-80. You will be asked to place origin on the next component.
- Click on the edge of second component as shown in Figure-80. The rigid joint will be created.

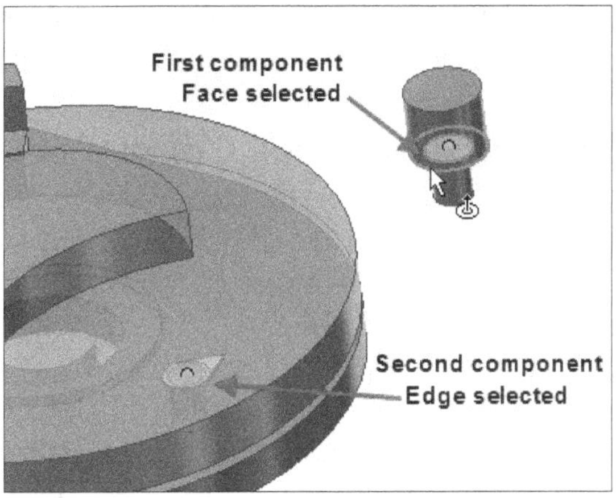

Figure-80. Entities selected for rigid joint

- Apply contact set on the **Pin** component. Procedure is same as discussed for **Rotor**.

Now, activate the contact solver by selecting the **Activate Contact Solver** button from the **Interference** panel in the **Inspect** tab of the **Ribbon**. Rotate the **Impulsor** component by dragging to check if the Geneva mechanism works as expected.

PRACTICAL 2

Create assembly of Oscillating Cam Mechanism as shown in Figure-81. The components of assembly are available in the resource kit.

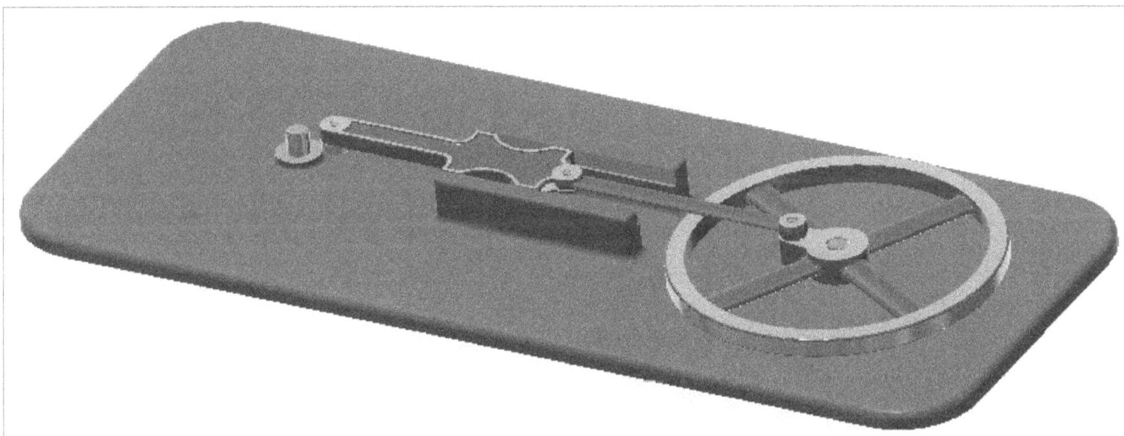

Figure-81. Partial assembly of oscillating cam mechanism

Strategy for Creating model

1. Looking at the isometric view, we can find the base component which is a base plate supporting all the other components on it.
2. Insert the base plate and fix it by using **Grounded** option.
3. One by one insert the other components and apply constraints which provide motion also.
4. Run the mechanism by dragging the wheel.

Starting Assembly File

- Start Autodesk Inventor by double-clicking on the Autodesk Inventor Professional icon from the desktop. (If not started yet.)
- Click on the **New** button from the **Quick Access Toolbar**. The **Create New File** dialog box will be displayed.

- Double-click on **Standard(mm).iam** icon from the **Assembly** category in **Metric** templates. The Assembly environment of Autodesk Inventor will be displayed.

Inserting the Base Component

- Click on the **Place** tool from the **Component** panel in the **Assemble** tab of the **Ribbon**. The **Place Component** dialog box will be displayed.
- Click on the **Base Plate** component from the dialog box and click on the **Open** button. The component will get attached to the cursor.
- Click in the empty area of the viewport. The component will be placed. Press **ESC** from the keyboard to exit inserting more copies of the component.
- Right-click on the component name in the **Model Browser** bar and select the **Grounded** option from the shortcut menu displayed. The plate will get fixed.

Inserting Oscillating Wheel Component

- Click on the **Place** tool from the **Component** panel in the **Assemble** tab of the **Ribbon**. The **Place Component** dialog box will be displayed.
- Click on the **Oscillating Wheel** component from the dialog box and click on the **Open** button. The component will get attached to the cursor.
- Click in the empty area of the viewport. The component will be placed. Press **ESC** from the keyboard to exit inserting more copies of the component.
- Click on the **Constrain** tool from **Relationships** panel in the **Assemble** tab of the **Ribbon**. The **Place Constraint** dialog box will be displayed.
- Click on the **Insert** button from the **Type** area of the dialog box and select the edges of the base component and wheel as shown in Figure-82.

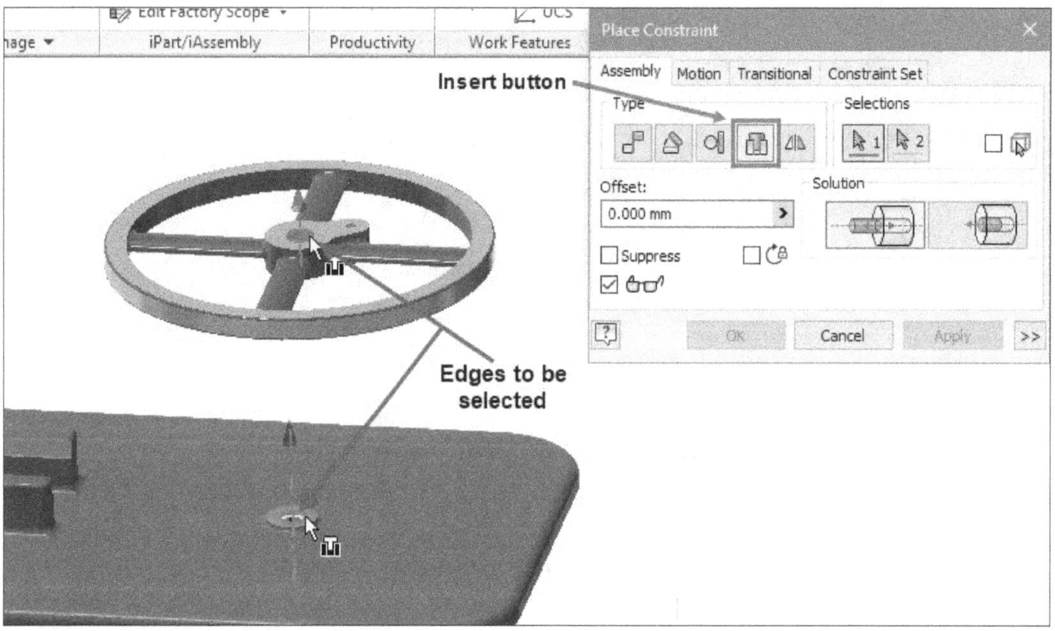

Figure-82. Inserting Oscillating wheel

- Flip the component if required and then click on the **OK** button from the dialog box.

Inserting Lever

- Click on the **Place** tool from the **Component** panel in the **Assemble** tab of the **Ribbon**. The **Place Component** dialog box will be displayed.

- Click on the **Lever** component from the dialog box and click on the **Open** button. The component will get attached to the cursor.
- Click in the empty area of the viewport. The component will be placed. Press **ESC** from the keyboard to exit inserting more copies of the component.
- Click on the **Constrain** tool from **Relationships** panel in the **Assemble** tab of the **Ribbon**. The **Place Constraint** dialog box will be displayed.
- Click on the **Insert** button from the **Type** area of the dialog box and select the edges of oscillating wheel and lever; refer to Figure-83.

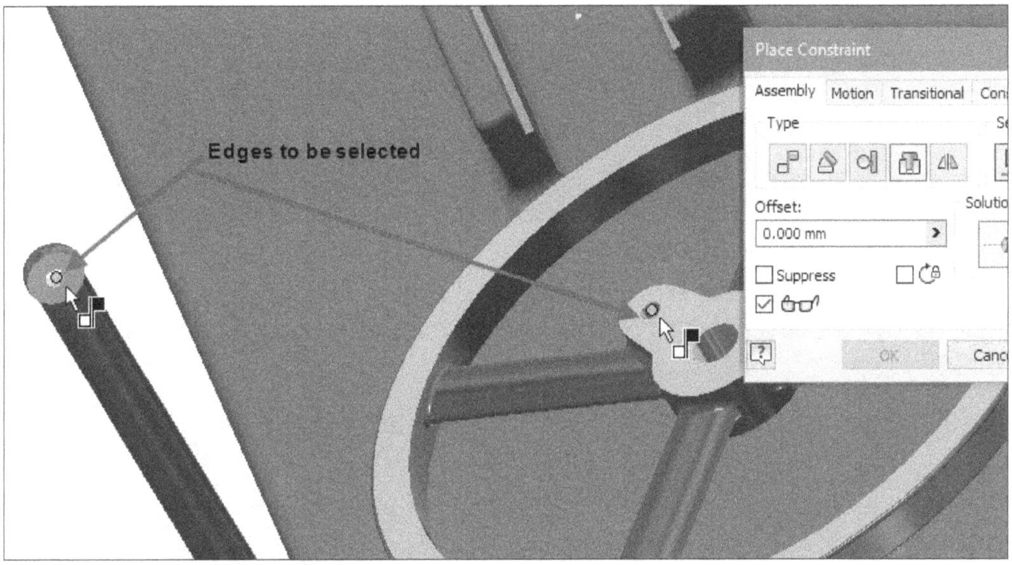

Figure-83. Edges selected for insert constraint

- Click on the **OK** button from the dialog box.

Inserting Tappet

- Click on the **Place** tool from the **Component** panel in the **Assemble** tab of the **Ribbon**. The **Place Component** dialog box will be displayed.
- Click on the **Tappet** component from the dialog box and click on the **Open** button. The component will get attached to the cursor.
- Click in the empty area of the viewport. The component will be placed. Press **ESC** from the keyboard to exit inserting more copies of the component.
- Click on the **Constrain** tool from **Relationships** panel in the **Assemble** tab of the **Ribbon**. The **Place Constraint** dialog box will be displayed.
- Click on the **Insert** button from the **Type** area of the dialog box and select the edges of oscillating wheel and lever; refer to Figure-84.

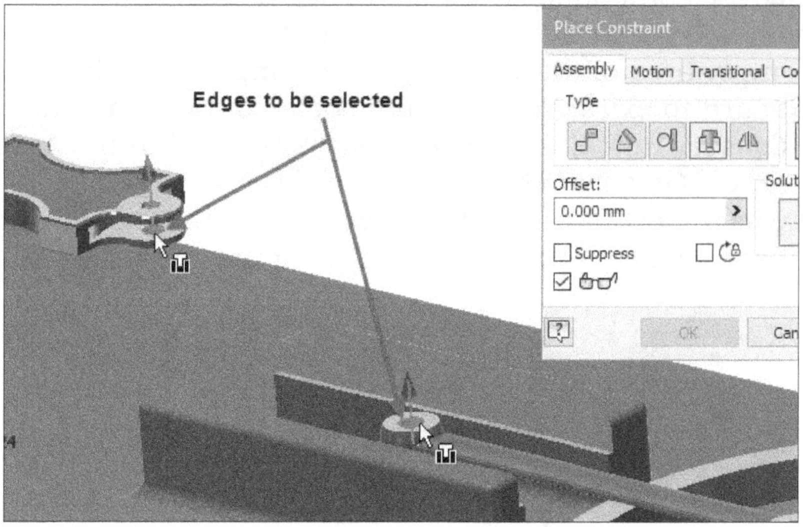

Figure-84. Connecting tappet with lever

- Click on the **Apply** button from the dialog box.
- Drag the tappet outside so that you can see the side faces of tappet; refer to Figure-85.

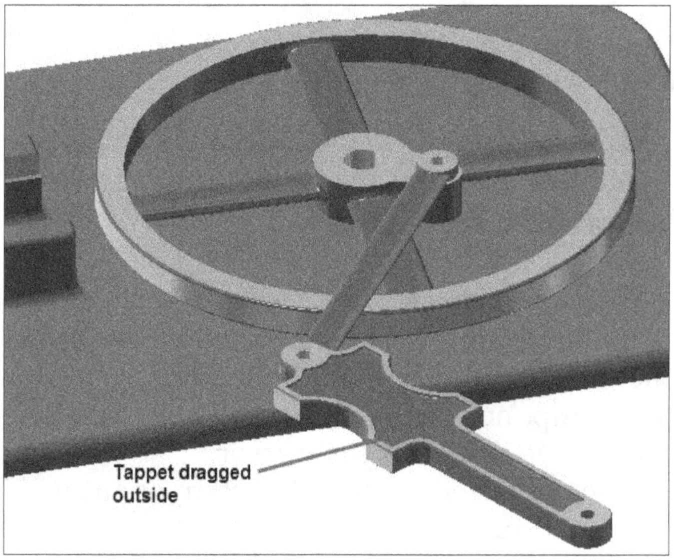

Figure-85. Tappet dragged outside

- Click on the **Mate** button from the **Type** area of the dialog box and select the side face of tappet; refer to Figure-86.

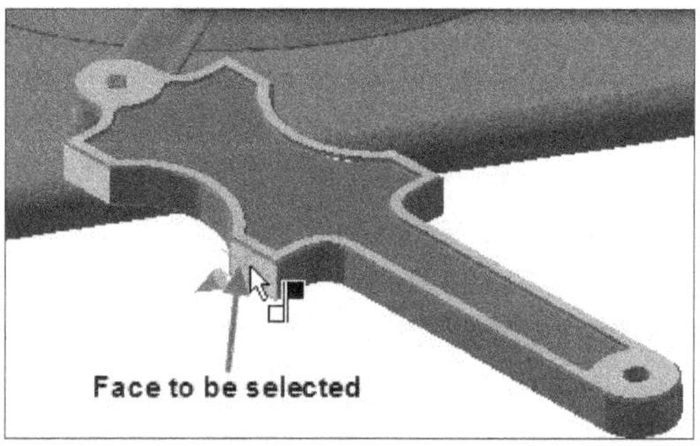

Figure-86. Face of tappet to be selected

- Select the side face of the guide in base plate; refer to Figure-87. Preview of mate constraint will be displayed.

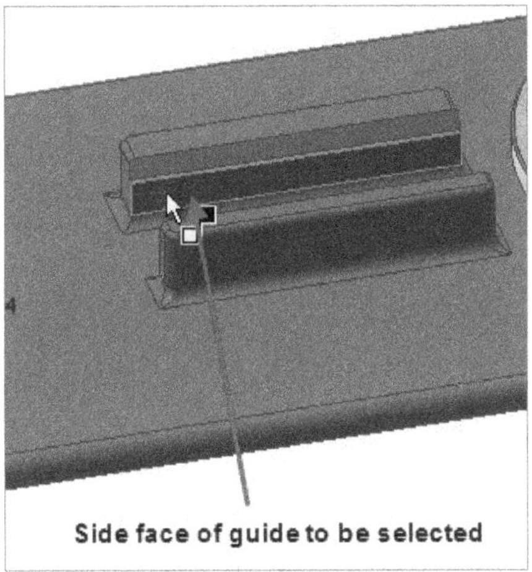

Figure-87. Side faces of guide to be selected

- Click on the **OK** button from the dialog box.

Inserting bearing

- Click on the **Place** tool from the **Component** panel in the **Assemble** tab of the **Ribbon**. The **Place Component** dialog box will be displayed.
- Click on the **Bearing** component from the dialog box and click on the **Open** button. The component will get attached to the cursor.
- Click in the empty area of the viewport. The component will be placed. Press **ESC** from the keyboard to exit inserting more copies of the component.
- Click on the **Constrain** tool from **Relationships** panel in the **Assemble** tab of the **Ribbon**. The **Place Constraint** dialog box will be displayed.
- Click on the **Insert** button from the **Type** area of the dialog box and select the edges of bearing and tappet as shown in Figure-88.

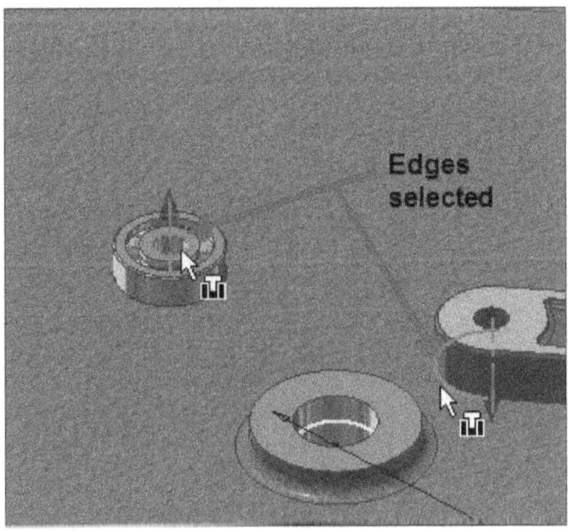

Figure-88. Inserting bearing

- Click on the **OK** button from the dialog box.

Inserting Pins

There are four different size pins to be placed at five places in the assembly. Insert these pins using the **Insert** constraint as shown in Figure-89.

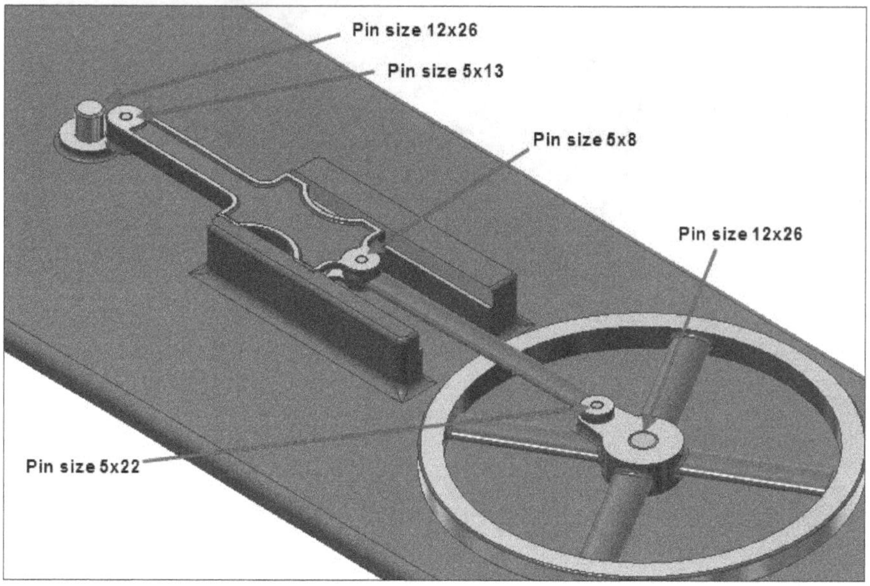

Figure-89. Pins inserted in assembly

Inserting Cam

- Click on the **Place** tool from the **Component** panel in the **Assemble** tab of the **Ribbon**. The **Place Component** dialog box will be displayed.
- Click on the **Cam** component from the dialog box and click on the **Open** button. The component will get attached to the cursor.
- Click in the empty area of the viewport. The component will be placed. Press **ESC** from the keyboard to exit inserting more copies of the component.
- Click on the **Constrain** tool from **Relationships** panel in the **Assemble** tab of the **Ribbon**. The **Place Constraint** dialog box will be displayed.
- Click on the **Insert** button from **Type** area of the dialog box and select the edges as shown in Figure-90.

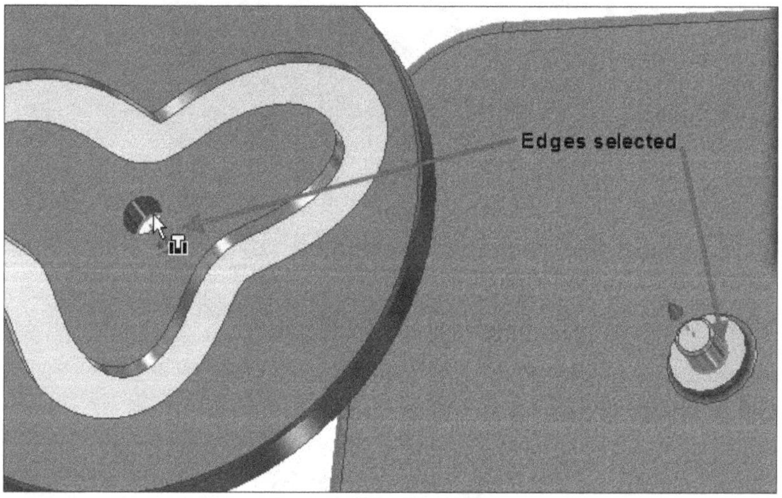

Figure-90. Edges to be selected

- Click on the **Apply** button from the dialog box.
- Click on the **Transitional** tab of the dialog box. You will be asked to select the entities to be constrained.
- Select the round face of bearing and inner face of the groove; refer to Figure-91.

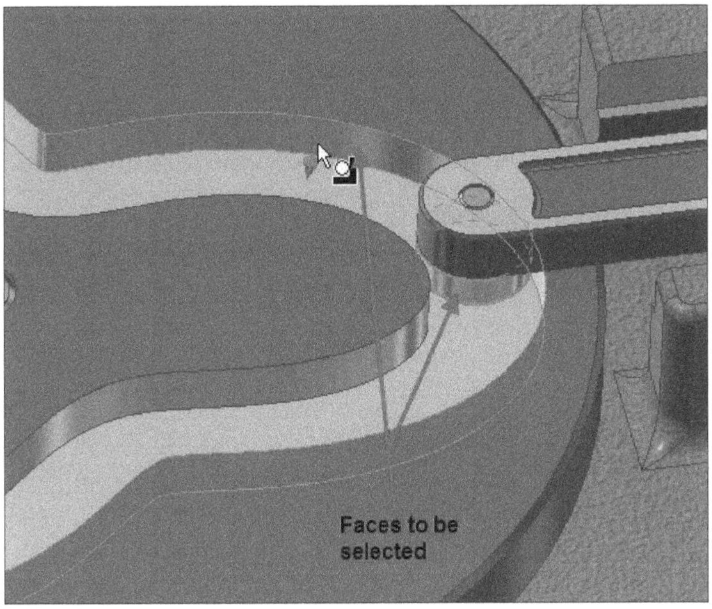

Figure-91. Faces selected for translational constraint

- Click on the **OK** button from the dialog box to apply the constraint.

PRACTICE 1

Create the working assembly of a simple vice as shown in Figure-92. The components are available in the resource kit.

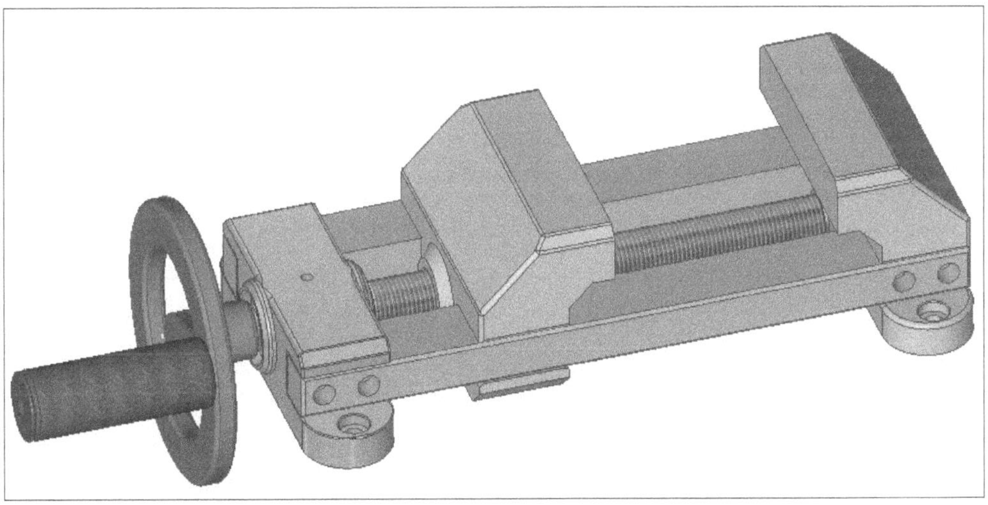

Figure-92. Simple Vice

INTRODUCTION TO PRESENTATION

The Presentation environment is used to generate snapshots and video clips of animation of the assembly. To activate this environment, click on the **Presentation** option from the **New** cascading menu of the **File** menu. The tools of Presentation environment will be displayed with **Insert** dialog box; refer to Figure-93. Select desired assembly file to be used in presentation and click on the **Open** button. Interface of presentation environment will be displayed; refer to Figure-94.

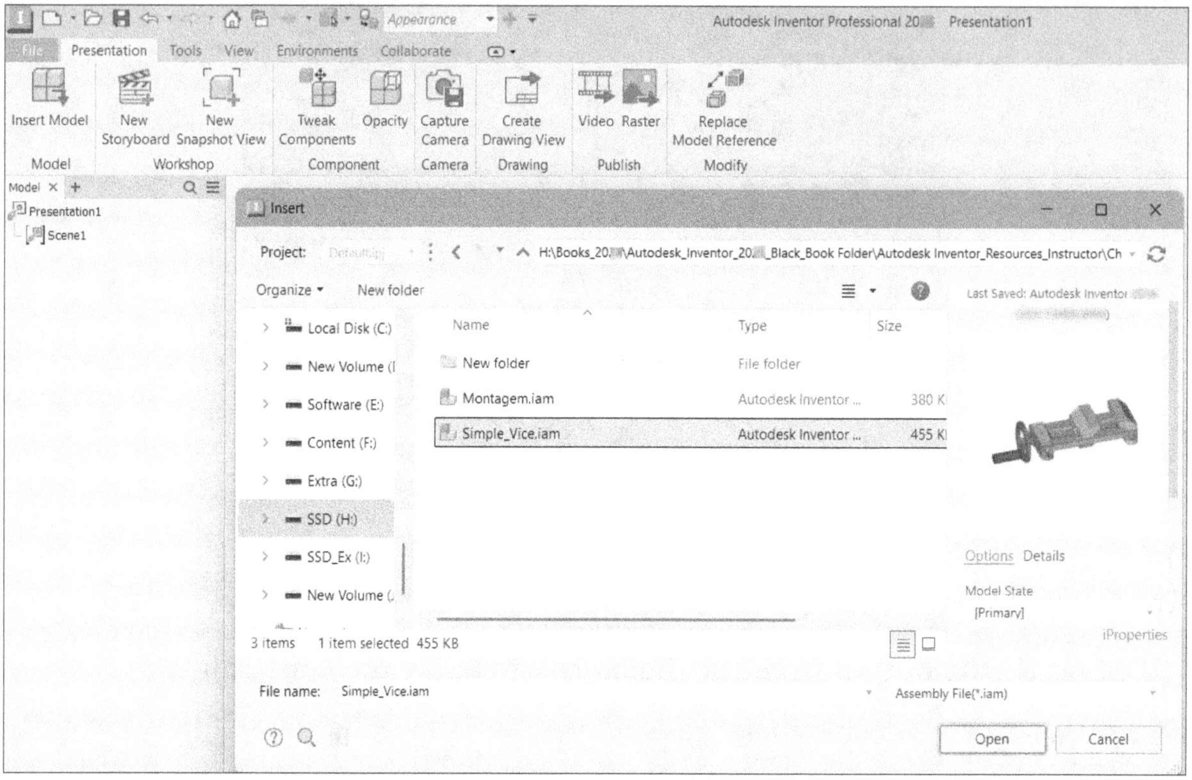

Figure-93. Presentation environment

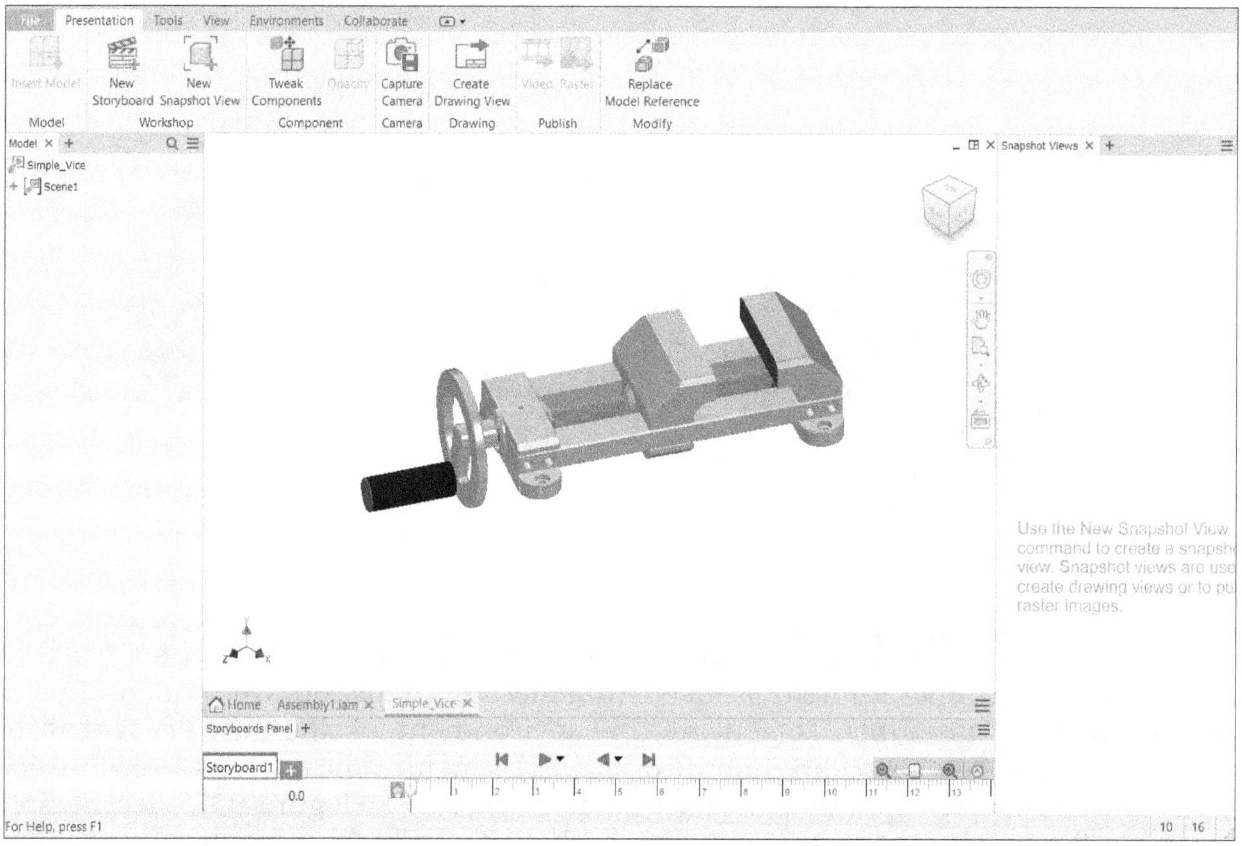

Figure-94. Presentation interface

CREATING NEW STORYBOARD

The **New Storyboard** tool is used to create a new storyboard for generating animation of assembly motion. The procedure to use this tool is given next.

- Click on the **New Storyboard** tool from the **Workshop** panel in the **Presentation** tab of the **Ribbon**. The **New Storyboard** dialog box will be displayed; refer to Figure-95.

Figure-95. New Storyboard dialog box

- Select the **Clean** option from the **Storyboard Type** drop-down to start a new storyboard using initial positions of assembly components. Select the **Start from end of previous** option from the drop-down to start a new storyboard using the positions of assembly components from previous storyboard.
- Specify desired name for the storyboard in the **Storyboard Name** edit box.
- After selecting desired option, click on the **OK** button. A new storyboard will be added in the presentation.

ADDING NEW SNAPSHOT VIEW

Snapshot is used to create drawing views and raster images. The procedure to generate a snapshot view is given next.

- Click on the **New Snapshot View** tool from the **Workshop** panel in the **Presentation** tab of the **Ribbon**. A snapshot image of current view of model will be added in the **Snapshot Views** panel of the interface; refer to Figure-96.

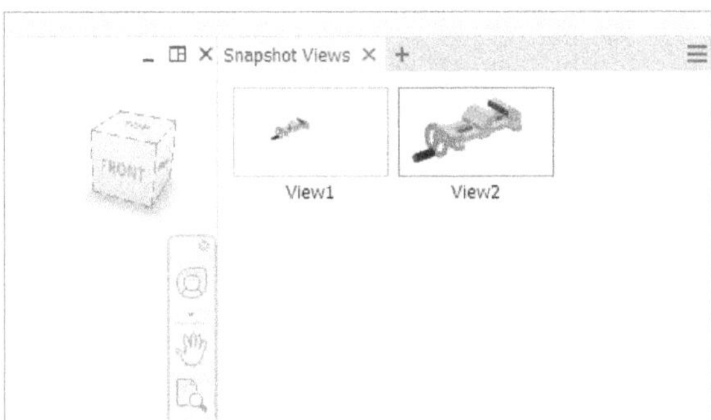

Figure-96. Snapshot images added

TWEAKING COMPONENTS

The **Tweak Components** tool is used to apply translation and rotation to the components. The procedure to use this tool is given next.

- Click on the **Tweak Components** tool from the **Component** panel in the **Presentation** tab of the **Ribbon**. The mini toolbar to move and rotate the components of assembly will be displayed; refer to Figure-97.

- Set desired value in **Duration** edit box of mini toolbar to define time in seconds within which the component will complete applied translation or rotation.
- Select desired component from the assembly and then select the **Move** or **Rotate** toggle button to define whether you want to move the component or rotate it. After selecting the toggle button, use the drag handles on the component to create motion; refer to Figure-98.

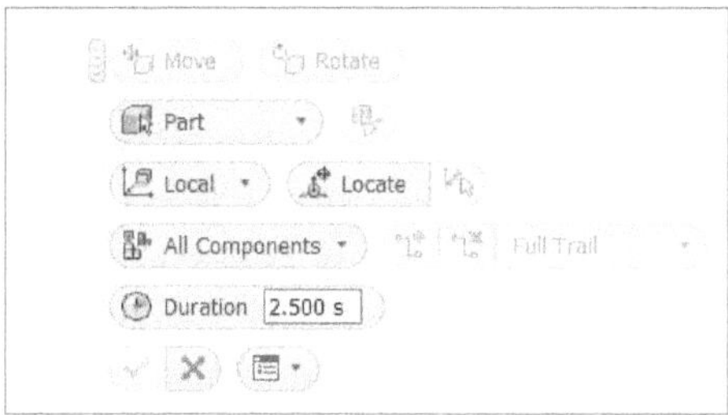

Figure-97. Mini toolbar for tweaking components

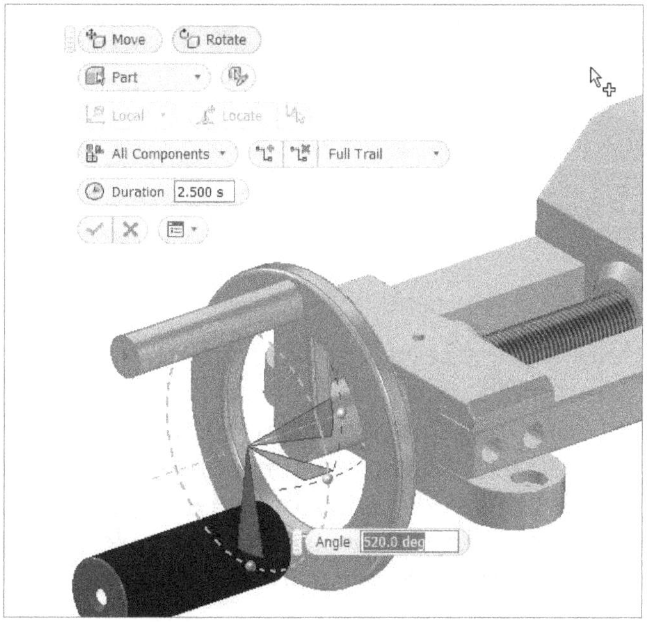

Figure-98. Rotation applied to model

- After setting desired parameters, click on the **OK** button from the mini toolbar. The tweak will be created and added in the **Model Browser**. Also, the time bar of motion will be added in the **Storyboards Panel**; refer to Figure-99.

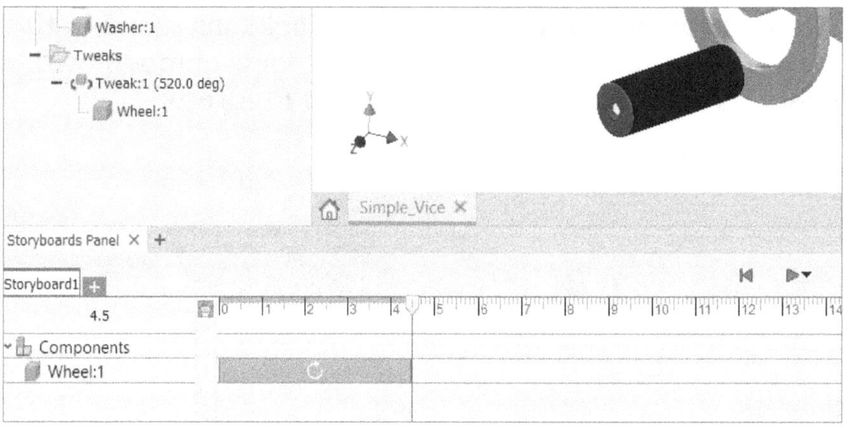

Figure-99. Tweak motion added

You can drag the motion tiles for various components in **Storyboards Panel** to desired time values. Use the standard media buttons in Storyboards Panel to check animation of motion.

SETTING OPACITY OF COMPONENTS

The **Opacity** tool is used to set transparency of selected component. The procedure to use this tool is given next.

- Select desired component from the graphics area for which you want to set opacity and click on the **Opacity** tool from the **Component** panel in the **Presentation** tab of the **Ribbon**. The **Opacity** mini toolbar will be displayed; refer to Figure-100.

Figure-100. Opacity mini toolbar

- Use the slider at the top in the mini toolbar to set transparency of selected component. After setting desired parameters, click on the **OK** button from the mini toolbar.

SETTING CAMERA POSITION

The **Capture Camera** tool is used to set position and orientation of camera for defining point of view for animation. The procedure to use this tool is given next.

- Click on the **Capture Camera** tool from the **Camera** panel in the **Presentation** tab of the **Ribbon**. The camera feature will be added in the **Storyboard Panel**; refer to Figure-101. Note that model view will reach to current status from default orientation of model in assembly file.

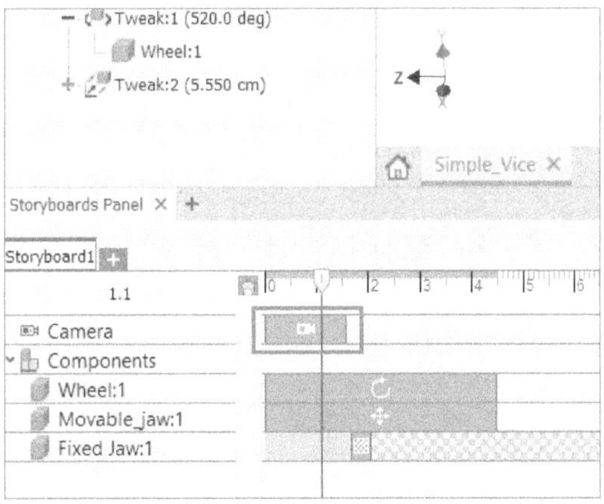

Figure-101. Camera added to storyboard

CREATING DRAWING VIEW USING SNAPSHOT

The **Create Drawing View** tool is used to generate a drawing view using selected snapshot view from the **Snapshot Views** panel in the interface. After selecting the snapshot, click on the **Create Drawing View** tool from the **Drawing** panel in the **Presentation** tab of the **Ribbon**. The drawing view will be placed in a new drawing or drawing linked with the current model.

PUBLISHING VIDEOS AND IMAGES

The **Video** tool in **Publish** panel of **Presentation** tab is used to generate video of the storyboards created in the environment. The procedure to use this tool is given next.

- Click on the **Video** tool from the **Publish** panel in the **Presentation** tab of the **Ribbon**. The **Publish to Video** dialog box will be displayed; refer to Figure-102.

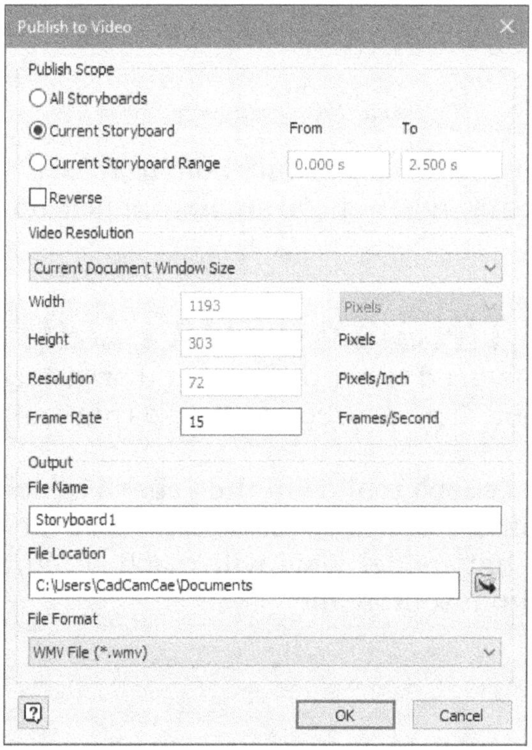

Figure-102. Publish to Video dialog box

- Specify the parameters as discussed earlier and click on the **OK** button. The **Video Compression** dialog box will be displayed; refer to Figure-103.

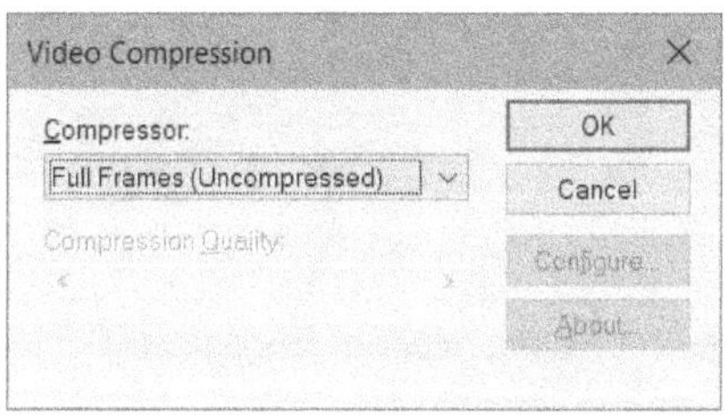

Figure-103. Video Compression dialog box

- Select desired compression option from the **Compressor** drop-down and click on the **OK** button. Video clip of animation will be generated.

Similarly, you can use the **Raster** tool from the **Publish** panel to generate image file. Use the **Replace Model Reference** tool to replace the model used in current presentation.

SELF ASSESSMENT

Q1. Which of the following ways is not used to insert components in an Assembly in Autodesk Inventor?

a) Placing Component from Local Storage
b) Placing Component from Vault
c) Placing Component from Content Center
d) Placing Exported CAM files

Q2. Which of the following tools is used to replace an existing component with a new component?

a) Electrical Catalog Browser
b) Place iLogic Component
c) Both a and b
d) None of the Above

Q3. Which of the following tools is used to move the component in constrained environment i.e. in planar direction only?

a) Grid Snap
b) Free Move
c) Free Rotate
d) None of the Above

Q4. When placing Angle constraint, which of the following options should be select to use left-hand rule in specifying angle between the geometries?

a) Directed Angle
b) Undirected Angle
c) Explicit Reference Vector
d) Both a and b

Q5. Which of the following constraints is used to make cam follower or slot follower mechanism?

a) Rotation Constraint
b) Rotation-Translation Constraint
c) Transitional Constraint
d) Mate Constraint

Q6. What is the full form of UCS?

a) Unified Combined System
b) User Combined System
c) Unified Coordinate System
d) User Coordinate System

Q7. Which of the following joints is used when you need the object free in rotational dimensions but fixed in translation?

a) Cylindrical
b) Rotational
c) Ball
d) Slider

Q8. The **Insert** Constraint is used to insert pin like geometries inside hole like geometries. (True/False)

Q9. **Driving** Constraint can only be applied to rotational motion. (True/False)

Q10. The Constraints are used to restrict the movement of objects. (True/False)

Q11. The .... is used to form a table of components that are used in the Assembly.

Q12. The .... tool is used to move a component freely in 3D space of assembly environment.

REVIEW QUESTIONS

Q1. Which menu option is used to start a new assembly in Autodesk Inventor?
A. Tools Menu
B. File Menu → Assembly
C. Insert Menu
D. Edit Menu

Q2. What tool is used to insert components from the local storage into the assembly?
A. Import
B. Insert
C. Place
D. Add

Q3. What happens when you press ESC while inserting a component?
A. Component rotates
B. Placement is confirmed
C. Insert more copies
D. Exit inserting more components

Q4. Which tool is used to insert standard components from Autodesk's library?
A. Place iLogic Component
B. Content Browser
C. Place from Content Center
D. Electrical Catalog

Q5. In Place from Content Center, which button do you use to manually select size?
A. Edit
B. Customize
C. Change size
D. Resize

Q6. How does the Content Center component adapt to holes?
A. It gets locked in position
B. It resizes automatically
C. It duplicates itself
D. It becomes transparent

Q7. Which option should you use to bring in CAD files from other software?
A. Place Imported Files
B. Import File
C. Place Imported CAD Files
D. Add from Other

Q8. What is the first step in placing an iLogic component?
A. Select geometry
B. Click on OK
C. Open dialog box and select file
D. Choose sketch plane

Q9. Which feature is specifically meant for inserting electrical components?
A. Place from Content Center
B. Electrical Catalog Browser
C. iLogic Components
D. Cable Harness Tool

Q10. Which tool is recommended when replacing an already inserted component without losing constraints?
A. Delete and Add
B. Replace
C. Swap
D. Edit

Q11. What does the Bottom-Up approach involve?
A. Creating parts within assembly
B. Importing files from other CAD
C. Designing parts first, then assembling
D. Replacing existing components

Q12. Why is Top-Down approach useful?
A. Easier modeling
B. Larger assemblies
C. Design parts that fit exactly in available space
D. Saves memory

Q13. What tool is used to create a component directly in an assembly?
A. Sketch
B. Create
C. Add Part
D. Insert

Q14. What tool is used to move components freely in 3D space?
A. Free Rotate
B. Grid Snap
C. Free Move
D. Push Pull

Q15. Which positioning tool rotates the component freely?
A. Rotate
B. Free Rotate
C. Turn
D. Spin

Q16. What does the Grid Snap tool allow you to do?
A. Rotate freely
B. Lock component
C. Move in constrained directions
D. Select multiple parts

Q17. Which tool is used to apply constraints in an assembly?
A. Position
B. Link
C. Constrain
D. Lock

Q18. Which constraint ensures two faces or edges share the same location?
A. Angle
B. Fix
C. Align
D. Mate

Q19. What feature allows setting minimum and maximum movement limits in Mate constraint?
A. Motion Limit
B. Offset Panel
C. Limit check boxes
D. Range setting

Q20. Which constraint is used to set an angle between two components?
A. Mate
B. Rotate
C. Angle
D. Direction

Q21. What is the purpose of the Explicit Reference Vector in angle constraint?
A. Rotate in 2D
B. Fix component
C. Specify angle direction
D. Flip component

Q22: What is the purpose of the Tangent constraint in Autodesk Inventor? A) To make two geometries coincident
B) To make a selected geometry tangent to another geometry
C) To specify the distance between geometries
D) To fix a geometry at a specific location

Q23: What is the first step in applying a Tangent constraint?
A) Select the second geometry
B) Specify the offset value
C) Click on the Tangent button from the Place Constraint dialog box
D) Select the face/edge/axis of the first component

Q24: What does the Insert constraint do?
A) Inserts a geometry at a specific point
B) Inserts pin-like geometries inside hole-like geometries
C) Adds a surface to a component
D) Makes geometries coincident

Q25: In the Insert constraint, what happens when it is applied?
A) The geometries are moved to align in space
B) The axis of the selected geometries becomes coincident, and their round edges align in one plane
C) It fixes the geometries in place
D) The geometries are scaled proportionally

Q26: Which type of constraint is used to make two components symmetric about a selected plane?
A) Tangent constraint
B) Symmetry constraint
C) Insert constraint
D) Rotation constraint

Q27: What is required to apply the Symmetry constraint?
A) Select the first geometry, second geometry, and plane for symmetry
B) Define the offset between the geometries
C) Select two geometries and a reference axis
D) Specify the angle of rotation

Q28: What does the Rotation constraint in Autodesk Inventor specify?
A) The distance moved by a component on rotation
B) The translation of an object based on the other
C) The ratio of rotation between two components
D) The point where a component is fixed

Q29: In the Rotation-Translation constraint, what happens when the disc object is rotated?
A) The rail moves by the specified distance
B) The rail rotates by a fixed ratio
C) The rail stays stationary
D) The rail moves linearly along a path

Q30: What is the main function of the Transitional constraint in Autodesk Inventor?
A) To make a component follow the path of another component
B) To rotate two components together
C) To set limits for rotational movement
D) To align two components in space

Q31: What does the Constraint Set tool do in Autodesk Inventor?
A) It makes two components coincide at a specified point
B) It makes the coordinate systems of two components coincident
C) It locks two components in position
D) It controls the motion of two components

Q32: What does the Rigid joint do in Autodesk Inventor?
A) It allows components to rotate relative to each other
B) It fixes a component at its desired location
C) It provides sliding motion for components
D) It restricts the translation of a component

Q33: What is the purpose of the Slider joint in Autodesk Inventor?
A) To fix a component in place
B) To allow sliding motion of a component
C) To restrict the motion of components
D) To allow rotating motion of components

Q34: How do you apply a Cylindrical joint in Autodesk Inventor?
A) Select the origin of the first and second components and allow them to rotate
B) Select a round face of the first component and the round face of the second component
C) Align the components in a plane and fix the position
D) Apply the joint to a component that needs to slide only

Q35: What does the Planar joint in Autodesk Inventor allow?
A) Allows motion of a component in a specified plane
B) Fixes the component at a specific location
C) Allows sliding and rotating motion of components
D) Makes the components symmetrical about an axis

Q36: What is the purpose of the Ball joint in Autodesk Inventor?
A) To fix a component in place
B) To allow free rotation in all directions but restrict translation
C) To allow a component to move along a specified plane
D) To allow sliding motion of a component

Q37: How do you apply the Grounded constraint in Autodesk Inventor?
A) Select the desired component and click the Grounded option from the shortcut menu
B) Apply a fixed joint to the component
C) Drag the component into position and apply a constraint
D) Use the Contact Set tool to ground the component

Q38: What is the function of the Contact Set in Autodesk Inventor?
A) To allow components to overlap in space
B) To ensure that parts do not interfere or cross each other during movement
C) To make components symmetrical about a plane
D) To align components in space

Q39: What does the Bill of Materials (BOM) help you with in Autodesk Inventor?
A) It creates a table of components used in the assembly
B) It adjusts the constraints for components
C) It adds components to the assembly
D) It provides limits for the motion of components

FOR STUDENT NOTES

Chapter 8

Drawing Creation

Topics Covered

The major topics covered in this chapter are:

- ***Elements of Engineering Drawing***
- ***Starting Drawing File and managing drawing Sheets***
- ***Views in Engineering Drawing and their placement in Autodesk Inventor***
- ***Applying annotations to drawing views***
- ***Engineering Drawing Symbols***
- ***Inserting symbols in Autodesk Inventor Drawings***
- ***GD&T and Bill of Materials***
- ***Practical and Practice on Drawing Creation***

INTRODUCTION

Drawing is a very important part of daily life of engineers in workshop. If you are manufacturing a component then there are various steps at which you will need engineering drawing of component. We need engineering drawing while,

- Programming CNC machines for machining component.
- Manufacturing dies for casting, molding, and sheetmetal work.
- Performing quality check on prepared component.
- Preparing costing and budget for manufacturing component and many other things.

In Autodesk Inventor, there is a separate environment to handle drawing. Note that the Drawing environment is well synchronized with Modeling environment and assembly environment. So, any change made in modeling environment or assembly environment is also reflected in drawing environment and vice-versa. This phenomena is called bidirectional associativity.

Before we move on to drawing creation tools in Autodesk Inventor, it is important to understand some basic concepts of engineering drawings.

ELEMENTS OF ENGINEERING DRAWING

There are various important concepts to be known to Design Engineer before he/she converts the model/assembly to drawing on paper. These concepts are discussed next.

Types of Engineering Drawings

There are mainly two types of engineering drawings for mechanical components; Part Drawing and Assembly Drawing. The part drawings are further classified as Machine Drawing and Production Drawings; refer to Figure-1.

There are various types of Assembly Drawings like Design Assembly Drawing, Installation Assembly Drawing, Catalog Drawing, and so on; refer to Figure-2.

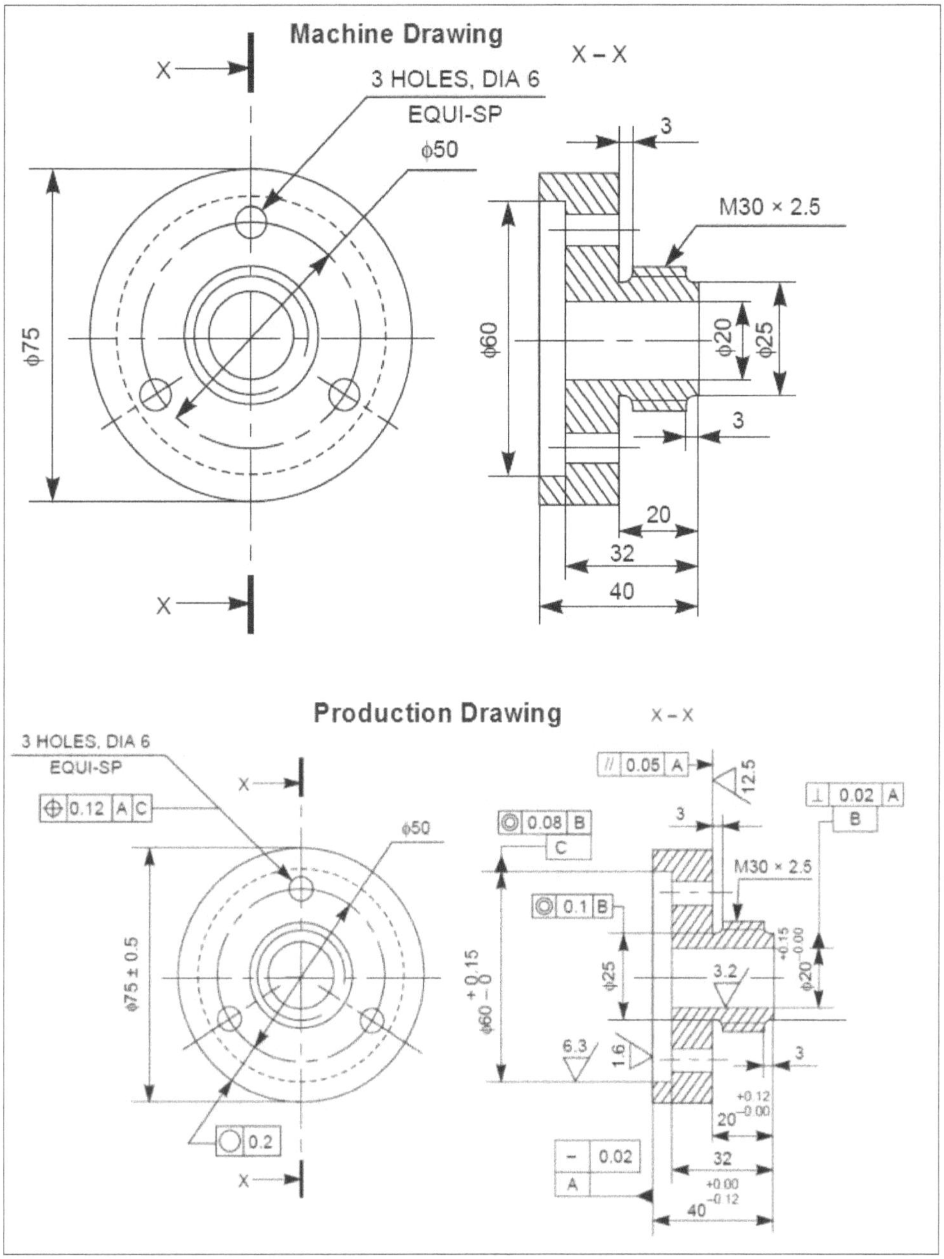

Figure-1. Classification of Part Drawings

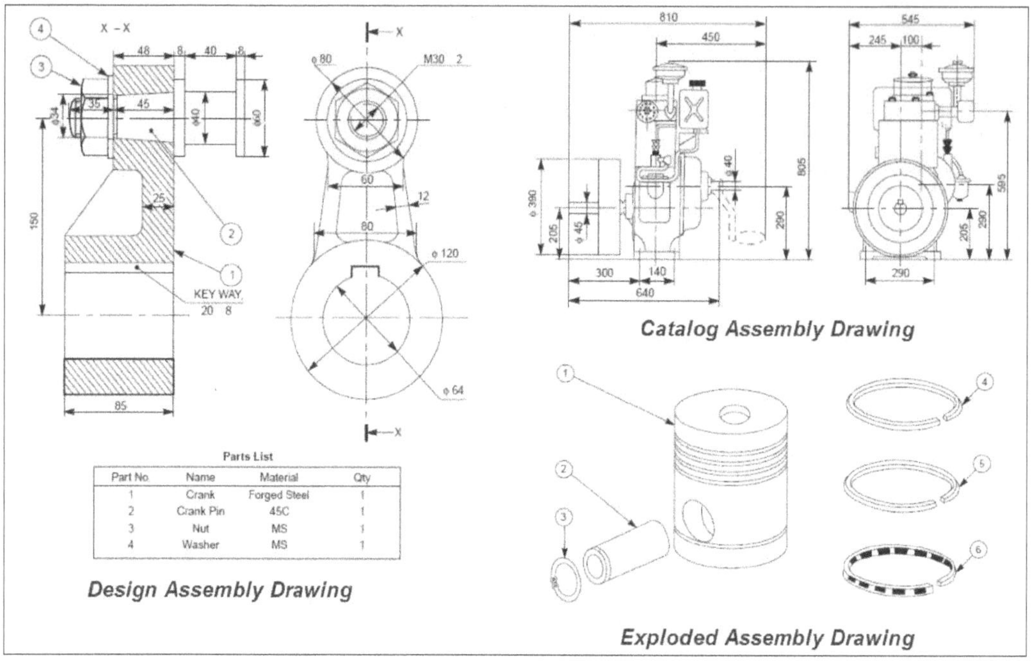

Figure-2. Types of Assembly Drawings

Standard Sheet Sizes for Engineering Drawings

The standard sheet sizes as per ISO-A used for plotting engineering drawings are:

A0	841 × 1189
A1	594 × 841
A2	420 × 594
A3	297 × 420
A4	210 × 297

Sometimes, you may need extra elongated paper size for plotting drawings. These sizes are designated as:

A3 × 3	420 × 891
A3 × 4	420 × 1188
A4 × 3	297 × 630
A4 × 4	297 × 840
A4 × 5	297 × 1050

Title Block

The title block should lie within the drawing space at the bottom right hand corner. It contains the identification information of the drawing. This must be followed for both horizontally or vertically positioned sheets; refer to Figure-3.

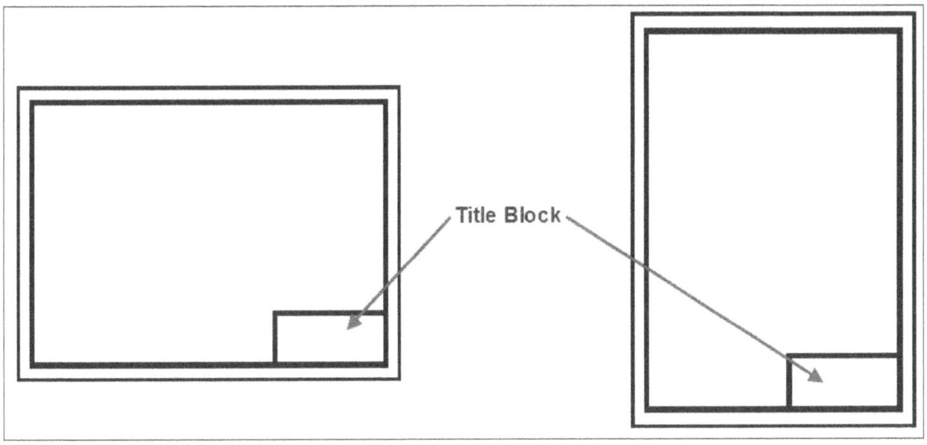

Figure-3. Title block position

The direction of viewing of the title block should correspond in general with that of the drawing. The title block can have a maximum length of **170** mm. Figure-4 shows a typical title block, providing the following information:

1. Title of the drawing
2. Sheet number
3. Scale
4. Symbol, denoting the method of projection
5. Name of the firm
6. Initials of staff drawn, checked, and approved.

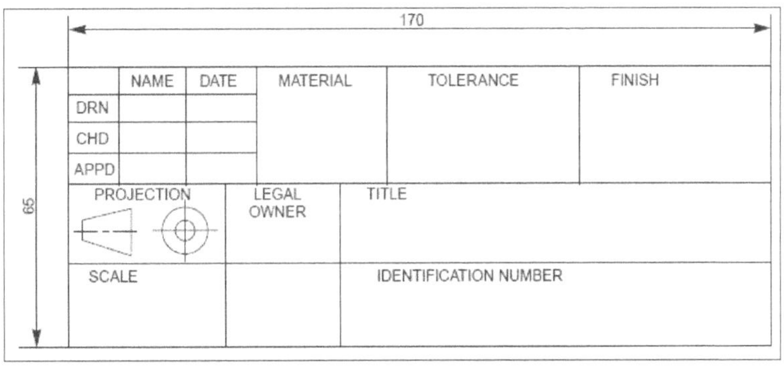

Figure-4. Typical title block

Type of Lines Used in Engineering Drawings

Lines of different types and thicknesses are used for graphical representation of objects. The types of lincs and their applications are shown in Figure-5.

These were some of the basics that you need to understand before we start using drawing creation tools in Autodesk Inventor. Note that we will keep discussing the engineering drawings concepts where ever need in this chapter.

Line	*Description*	*General Applications*
A	Continuous thick	A1 Visible outlines
B	Continuous thin (straight or curved)	B1 Imaginary lines of intersection B2 Dimension lines B3 Projection lines B4 Leader lines B5 Hatching lines B6 Outlines of revolved sections in place B7 Short centre lines
C	Continuous thin, free-hand	C1 Limits of partial or interrupted views and sections, if the limit is not a chain thin
D	Continuous thin (straight) with zigzags	D1 Line (see Fig. 2.5)
E	Dashed thick	E1 Hidden outlines
G	Chain thin	G1 Centre lines G2 Lines of symmetry G3 Trajectories
H	Chain thin, thick at ends and changes of direction	H1 Cutting planes
J	Chain thick	J1 Indication of lines or surfaces to which a special requirement applies
K	Chain thin, double-dashed	K1 Outlines of adjacent parts K2 Alternative and extreme positions of movable parts K3 Centroidal lines

Figure-5. Lines in engineering drawings

STARTING NEW DRAWING FILE

- Start Autodesk Inventor, if not started yet. Click on the **New** button from **New** cascading menu in the **File** menu of the **Ribbon**. The **Create New File** dialog box will be displayed.
- Select the **English** or **Metric** template from the **Templates** category in the dialog box and move the slider down in the dialog box; refer to Figure-6.

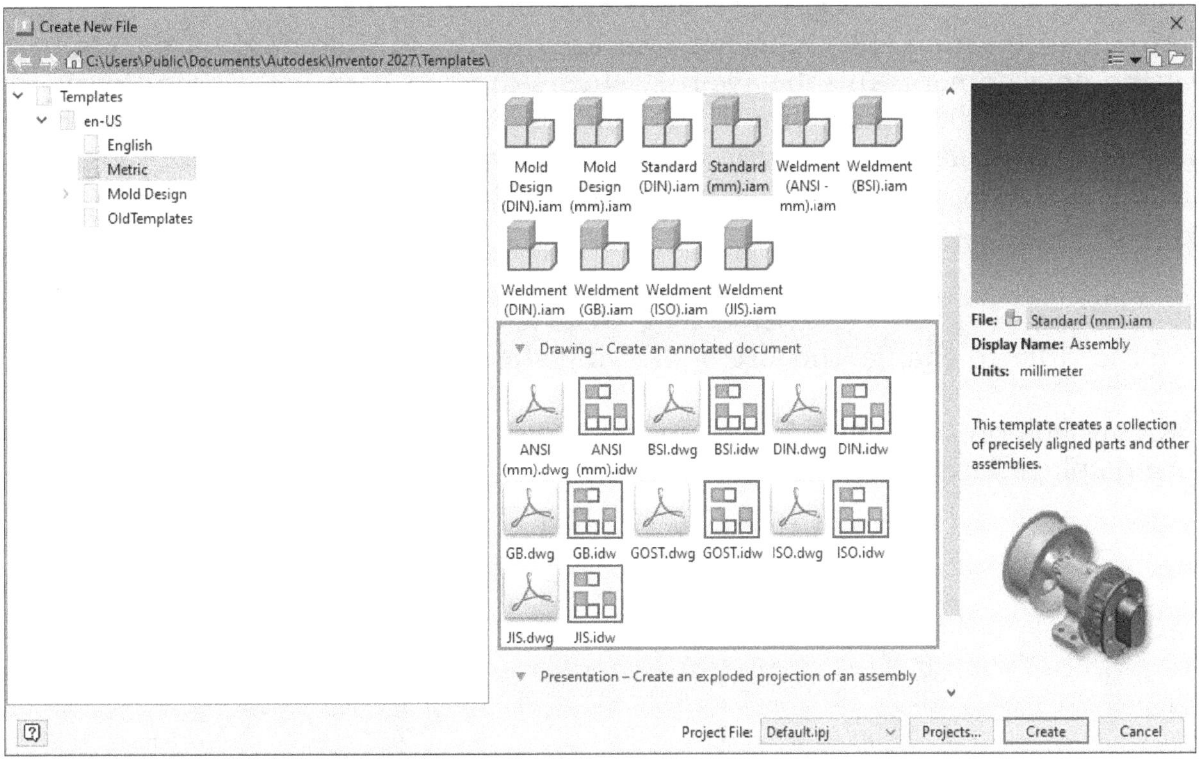

Figure-6. Create New File dialog box

- Select desired template from the **Drawing** area of the dialog box and click on the **Create** button. The drawing environment will be displayed with new file opened; refer to Figure-7 (we have selected **ANSI(mm).idw** template).

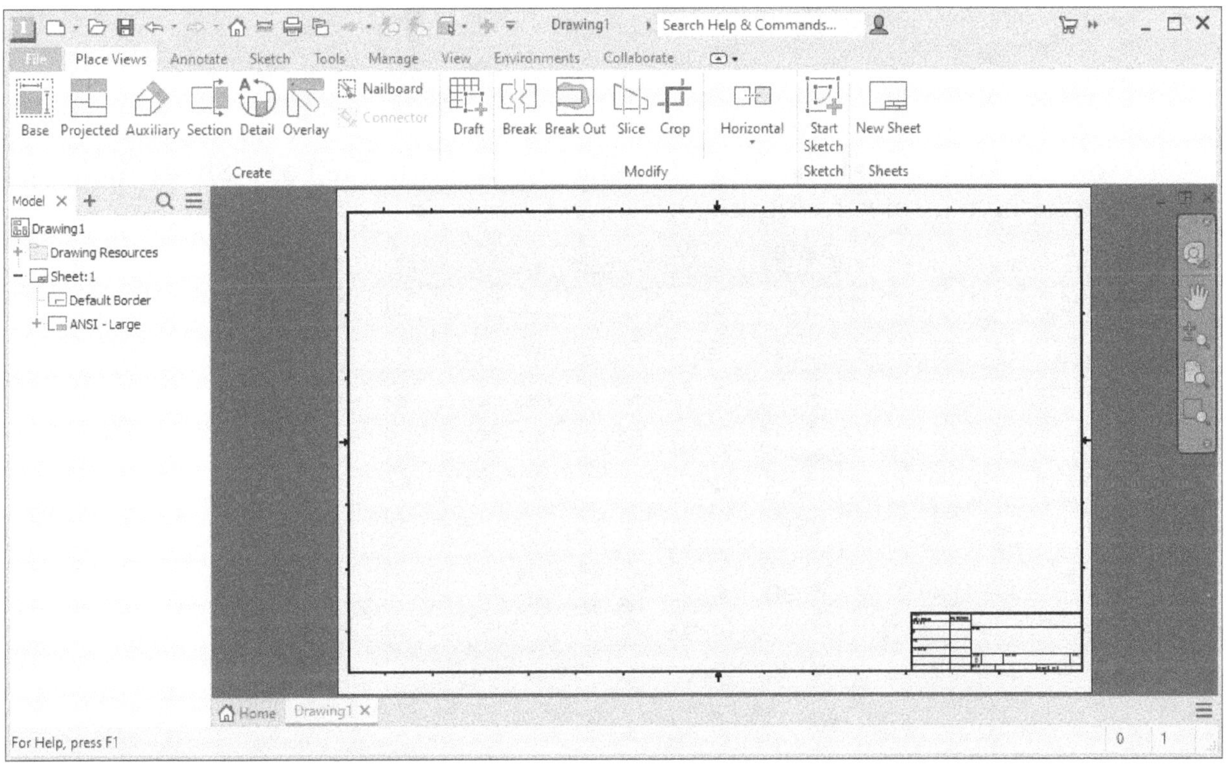

Figure-7. Drawing environment in Autodesk Inventor

SHEET MANAGEMENT

In Autodesk Inventor, all the views and annotations are created on sheets in the drawing environment. In other words, sheets are the base for drawing views and annotation just like planes are in 3D Modeling. There are few operations that we do frequently while working with sheets of drawing like changing size, positioning title block, editing borders, etc. The procedures to do some common operations are given next.

Changing Size of Sheet

The procedure to change the size of drawing sheet is given next.

- Right-click on the **Sheet:1** node in the **Model Browse Bar**. A shortcut menu will be displayed; refer to Figure-8.

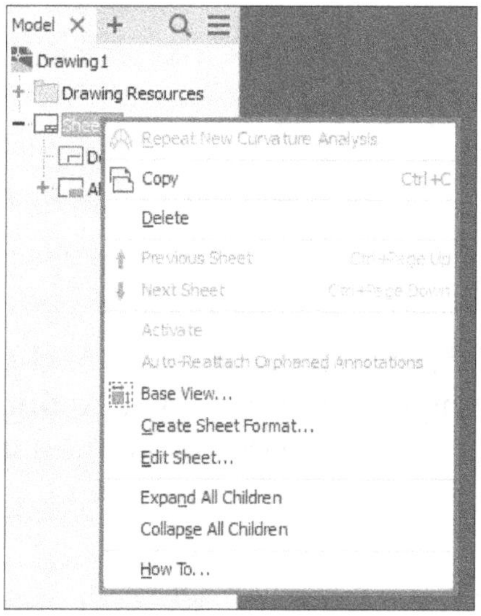

Figure-8. Right-click shortcut menu

- Click on the **Edit Sheet** tool from the shortcut menu. The **Edit Sheet** dialog box will be displayed; refer to Figure-9.

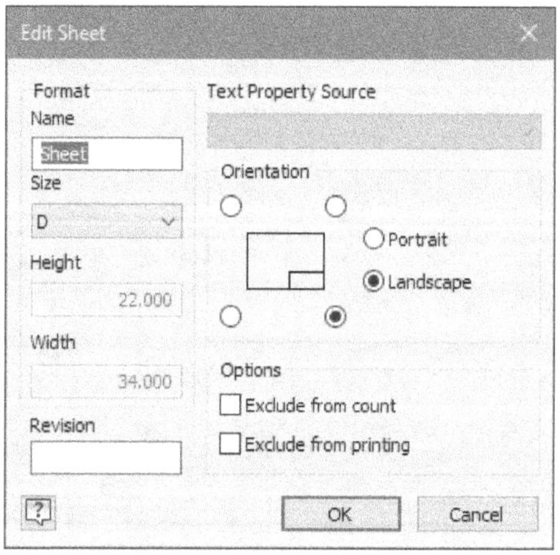

Figure-9. Edit Sheet dialog box

- Specify desired name of sheet in the **Name** edit box.
- Click in the **Size** drop-down and select desired size from the list.
- Set desired revision number in the **Revision** edit box.

- From the **Orientation** area, select radio button to define location of title block. Also, select the **Portrait** or **Landscape** radio button to define the orientation of sheet.
- If you want to exclude the current sheet from counting or printing then select the related check box from the **Options** area of the dialog box.
- Click on the **OK** button to apply the changes. The drawing sheet will be modified accordingly; refer to Figure-10.

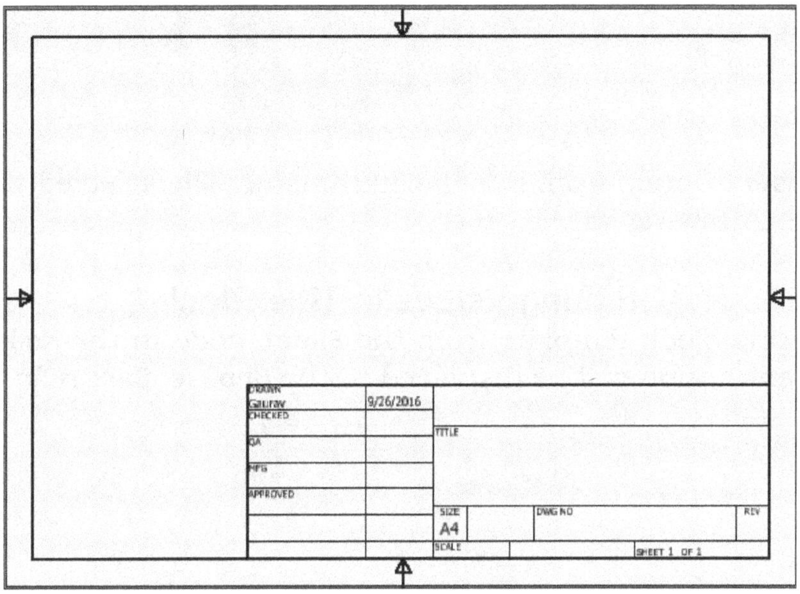

Figure-10. Drawing sheet of A4 size

Note that the size of title block has not changed as per the sheet size. We need to do this work manually.

Changing Title Block

There are two ways in which we generally modify the title block of drawing sheet; changing size of title block and changing parameters in the title block. The methods to do both the operations are discussed next.

Changing Size of Title Block

- Select the title block template from the **Sheet:1** node in the **Model Browse Bar** and press **Delete** from keyboard to delete it; refer to Figure-11.

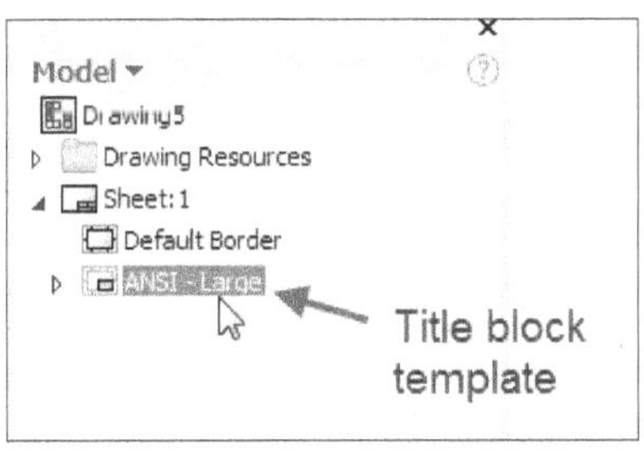

Figure-11. Title block template to delete

- Expand the **Drawing Resources** node and then **Title Blocks** node in the **Model Browse Bar**. The list of title blocks available for current sheet size will be displayed.
- Select desired size from the list and right-click to display the shortcut menu; refer to Figure-12.

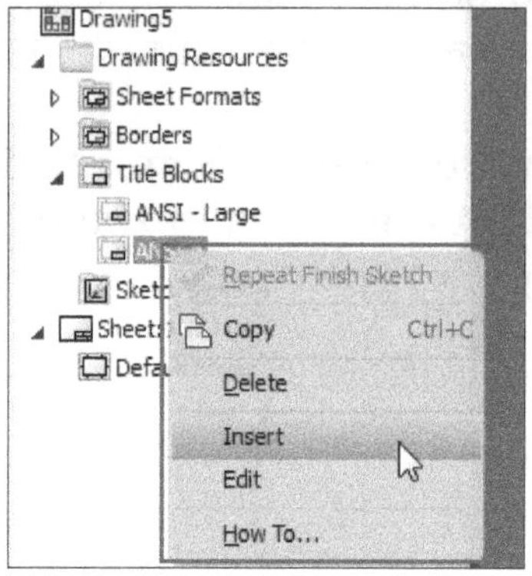

Figure-12. Shortcut menu for title block

- Select the **Insert** option from the shortcut menu. The selected title block will be inserted in the drawing sheet.

Editing Values in Title Block

- Expand the title block template from the **Sheet** node in the **Model Browse Bar**. The **Field Text** option will be displayed in the **Browse Bar**; refer to Figure-13.

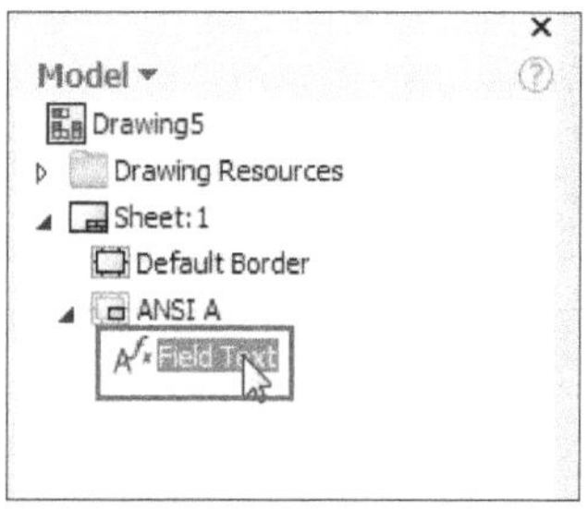

Figure-13. Field Text option

- Double-click on the option. The **Edit Property Fields** dialog box will be displayed; refer to Figure-14.

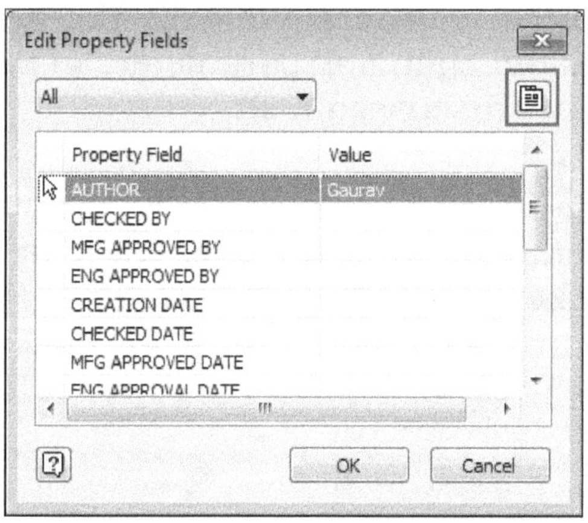

Figure-14. Edit Property Fields dialog box

- Click on the **iProperties** button at the top-right corner of the dialog box. The **Drawing iProperties** dialog box will be displayed; refer to Figure-15.
- Click on the **Summary** tab in the dialog box and specify the parameters of title block like, Title, subject, author of drawing, and so on.
- Click on the **Project** tab in the dialog box and specify the parameters like part number, description, revision number, etc.
- Similarly, specify the other parameters in the dialog box and click on the **Apply** and then **Close** button from the dialog box.

- Click on the **OK** button from the **Edit Property Fields** dialog box. The changes will be reflected in the title block.

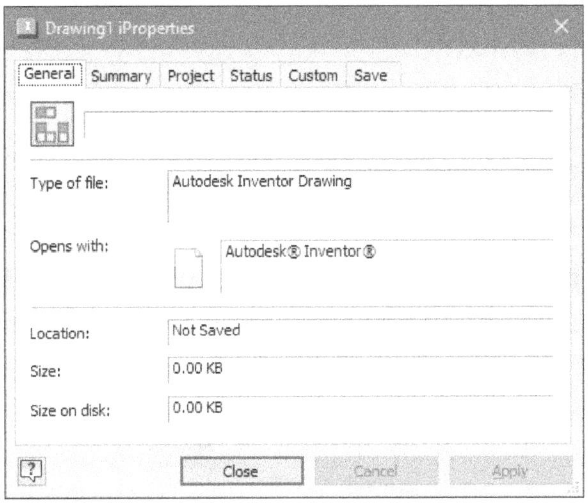

Figure-15. Drawing iProperties dialog box

Alternatively, right-click on the title block from **Sheets** node in **Model Browser Bar** and select the **Edit Definition** option from shortcut menu; refer to Figure-16. The title block will be displayed in editable mode; refer to Figure-17 Double-click on text to edit and after making changes, click **Finish** button from **Ribbon** to apply changes. You will be asked whether to save changes to title block. Click on **Yes** button from **Save Edits** dialog box displayed. The title block will be updated. Note that applied changes will modify the main definition of title block and you may not be able to change the parameters using the earlier discussed next.

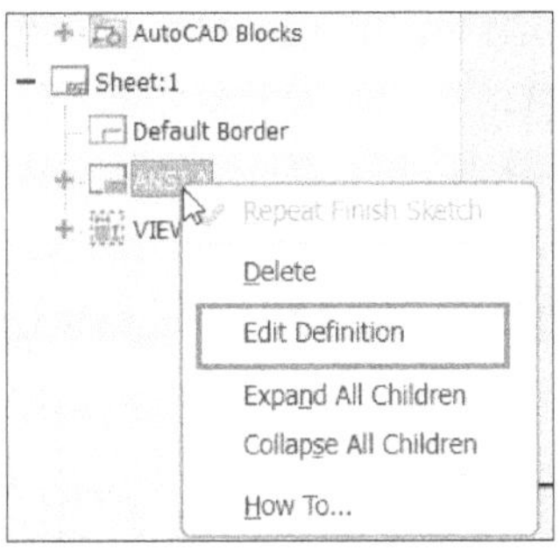

Figure-16. Edit Definition option

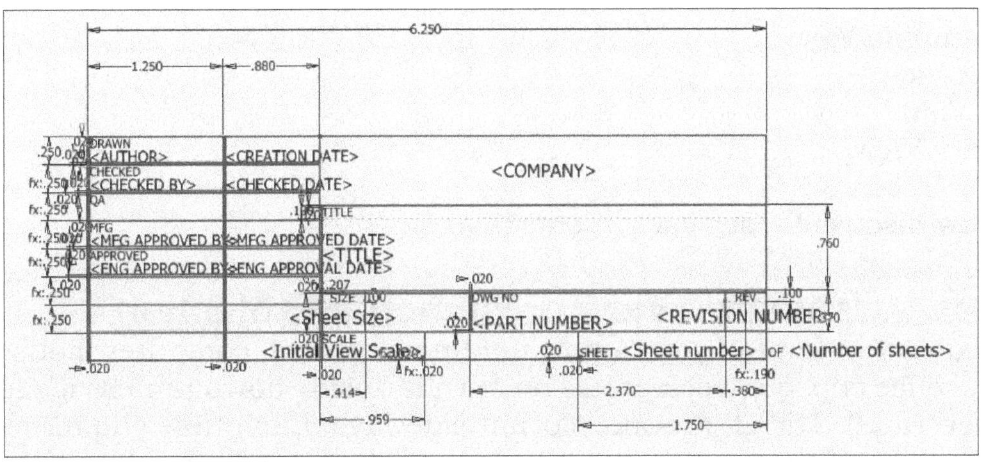

Figure-17. Title block editable mode

Inserting Sheets

Sometimes, while making drawings, you may need more sheets to insert views of the drawings like, in case of machine drawing for assembly. The procedure to insert sheets in drawing is given next.

- Click on the **New Sheet** button from the **Sheets** panel in the **Place Views** tab of the **Ribbon**. A new sheet will be added with the properties of earlier sheets.
- Keep on clicking **New Sheet** button to add as many sheets as required.

Activating and Deleting Sheet

- Right-click on the sheet in the **Model Browse Bar** that you want to activate or delete. A shortcut menu will be displayed; refer to Figure-18.

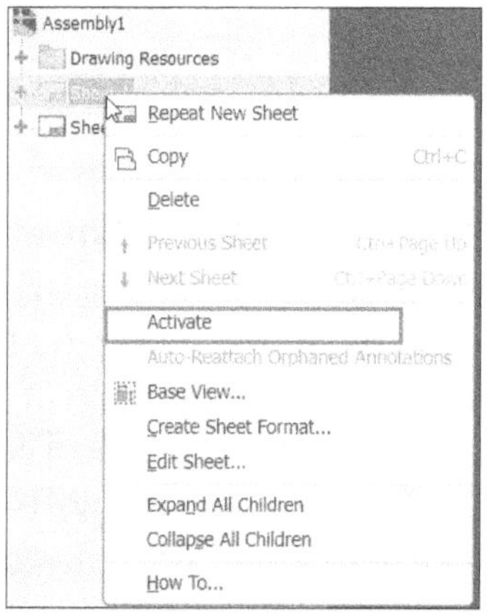

Figure-18. Shortcut menu for sheets

- Select the **Activate** button from the menu to activate the current sheet for inserting views and manipulating them.
- Select the **Delete** button from the menu to delete the current sheet.

VIEWS IN ENGINEERING DRAWING

In Engineering Drawing, 3D objects are represented on paper with the help of various views. A drawing view is projection of 3D object on paper in the direction of view. The most general drawing views used in engineering drawings are:

- Isometric View
- Orthographic View
- Section View
- Detail View
- Auxiliary View

We will now discuss these views in short.

Isometric View or Isometric Projection

Grab any object in front of you. A pencil, remote control, computer mouse, bobble-head doll, coffee cup, etc. Look at it. Now turn it upside down (unless it's full of your favorite beverage!). Turn it around. Turn it sideways. Each time you move it, you're looking at a different view of that object. You can see depth and edges. You can tell that it's not just a picture, but a real thing. Your eyes give you many clues to the objects in your world that are three-dimensional (have height, width, and depth).

A piece of paper has only two dimensions -- it is flat. If you try to draw an object on a piece of paper, you will notice that it is not easy to make the drawn object look like it has depth. One way is to use an isometric view, which is derived from the Greek words Iso means "equal" and metric means "measurement". When using an isometric view, you line up the drawing along three axes, visible or invisible guidelines that establish directions for measurement, that are separated by 120-degree angles from each other, as shown in Figure-19.

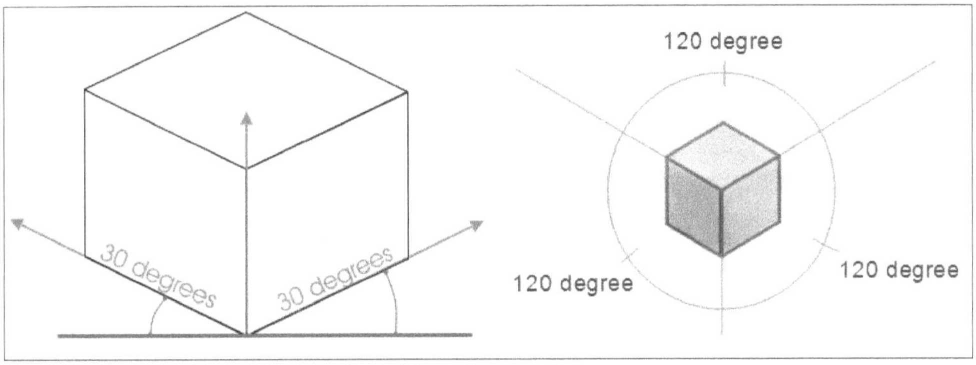

Figure-19. Isometric projection of cube

Orthographic Views or Orthographic Projection

Orthographic (ortho) views are two-dimensional drawings used to represent or describe a three-dimensional object. The ortho views represent the exact shape of an object seen from one side at a time as you are looking perpendicularly to it without showing any depth to the object.

Primarily, three ortho views (top, front, and right) adequately depict the necessary information to illustrate the object; refer to Figure-20. Sometimes, only two ortho views are needed as in a cylinder. The diameter of the cylinder and its length are the only dimension information needed to complete the drawing. A sphere only needs the diameter. It is the same from all angles and remains a perfect circle in the iso drawing.

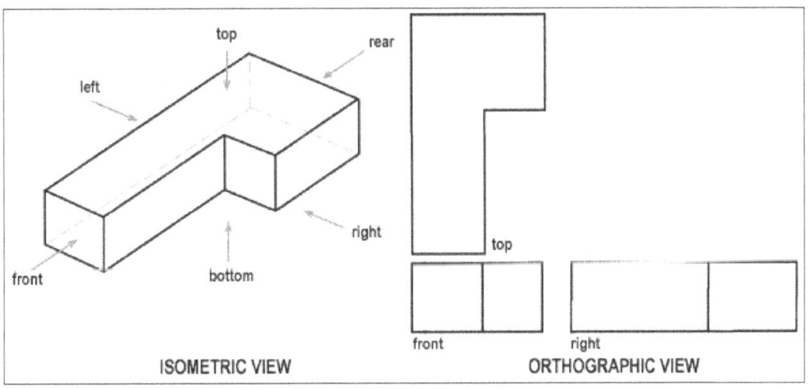

Figure-20. Isometric orthographic representation

The "six" side method is a process of making six primary ortho views that represent the entire image. This method gives you all the information to create complex object.

There are two projection methods to create orthographic views in drawings; First Angle Projection and Third Angle Projection.

First Angle Projection

In First Angle Orthographic Projection, the front, top, and side views are placed opposite to the position from where you are looking at the object. Refer to Figure-21.

In most of the countries except USA, Canada, Japan, and Australia, the First Angle projection is in use rather than Third Angle Projection. You can identify the First Angle Projection by finding symbol as shown in Figure-22.

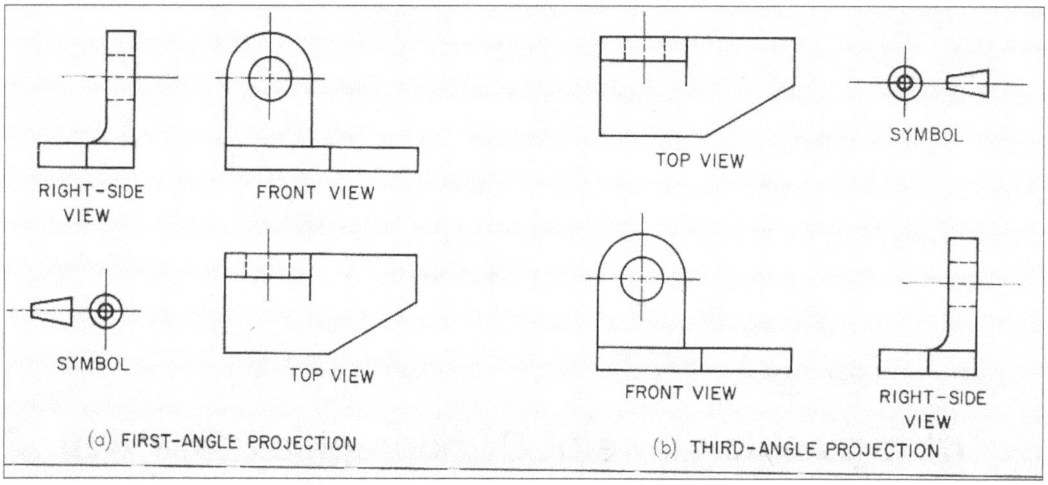

Figure-21. Example of projection

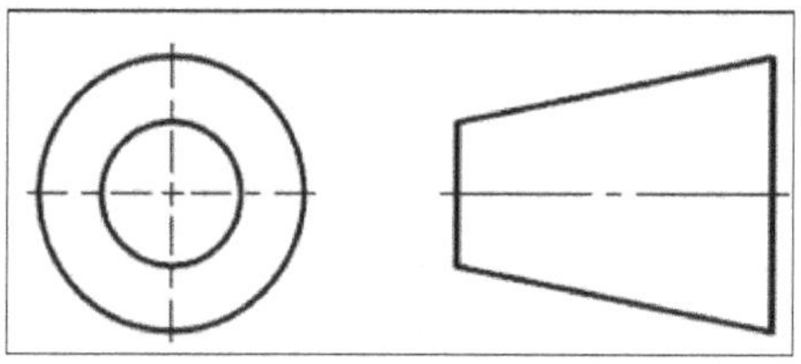

Figure-22. First Angle Projection Symbol

Third Angle Projection

In Third Angle Orthographic Projection, the top view is placed at the top of front view and right side view is placed on the right side of the front view; refer to Figure-20 and Figure-21. If you are still in confusion why have we placed the views like this in first angle and third angle projections then check Figure-23. In First Angle Projection, the object is placed in first quadrant whereas in Third Angle Projection, the object is placed in third quadrant.

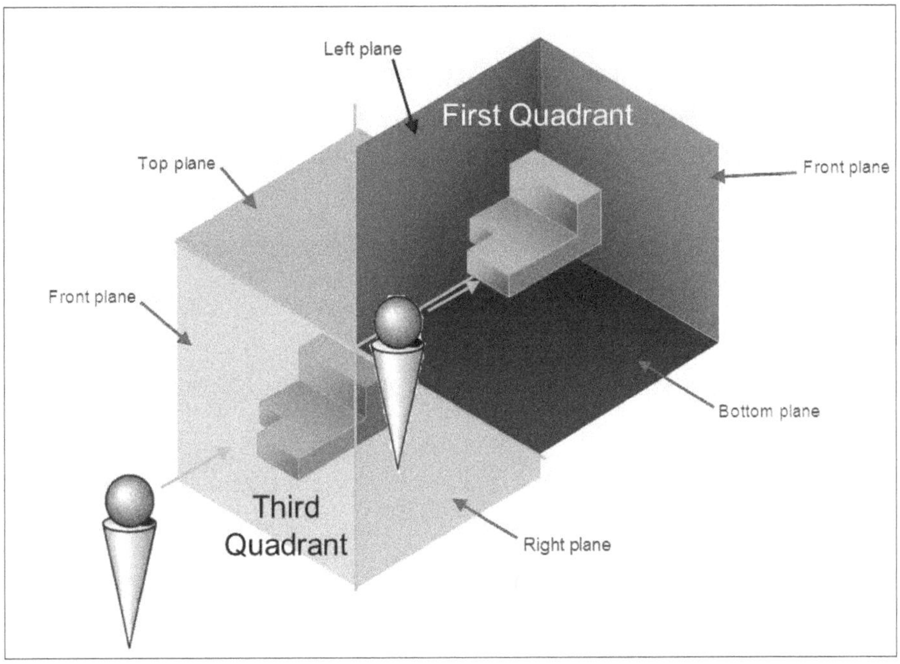

Figure-23. Placement of object in quadrants

Now, we will learn to create these projections in Autodesk Inventor drawing environment.

INSERTING BASE VIEW

In Autodesk Inventor Drawing environment, first drawing view placed is called base view and other views are generally projections. The procedure to insert base view is given next.

- Click on the **Base** tool from the **Create** panel in the **Place Views** tab in the **Ribbon**. The **Drawing View** dialog box will be displayed; refer to Figure-24.

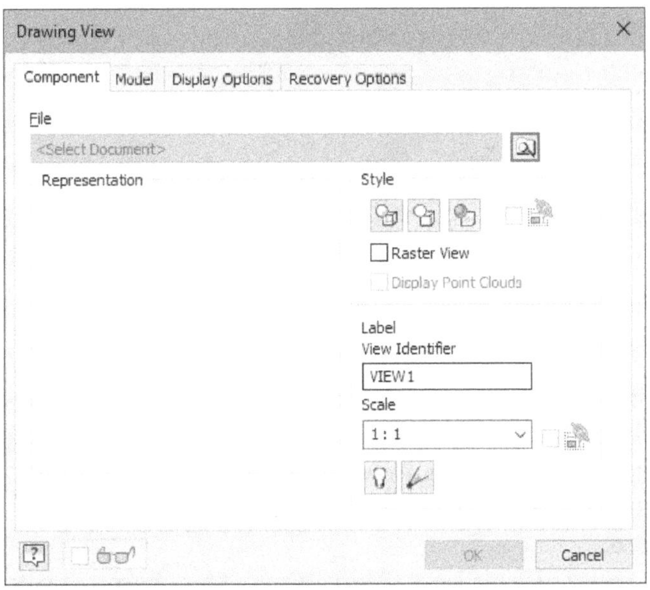

Figure-24. Drawing View dialog box

- Click on the **Open an existing file** button from the dialog box. The **Open** dialog box will be displayed.
- Select the part file or assembly file for which you want to create the drawing views and click on the **Open** button from the dialog box. The selected file will be linked in the drawing file and preview of the drawing view will be displayed on the sheet; refer to Figure-25.

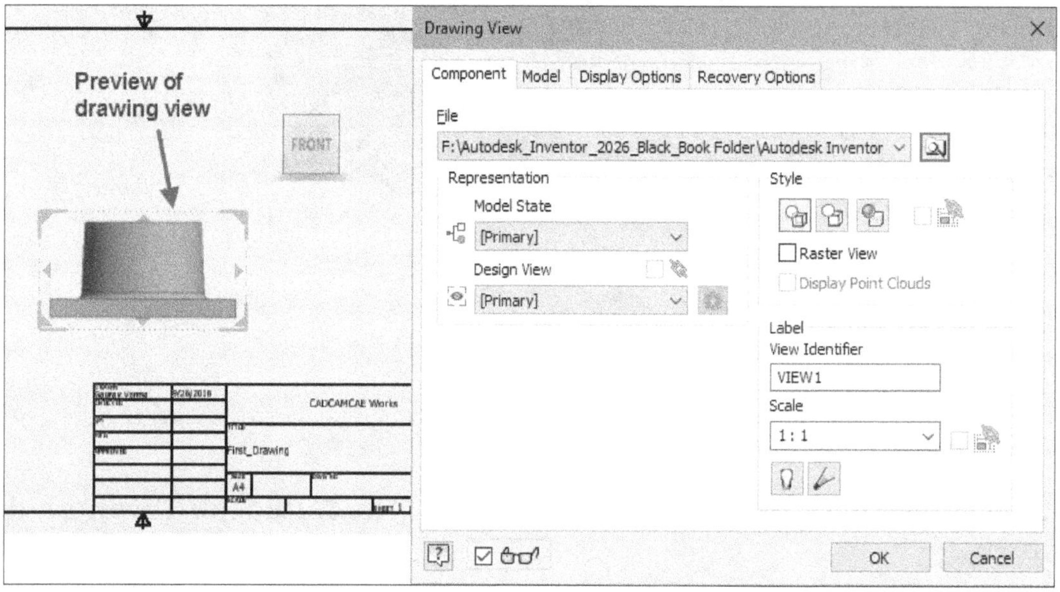

Figure-25. Preview of drawing view

- Click at desired location on the **View Cube** to orient the component to front view, top view, right view, or isometric view; refer to Figure-26.

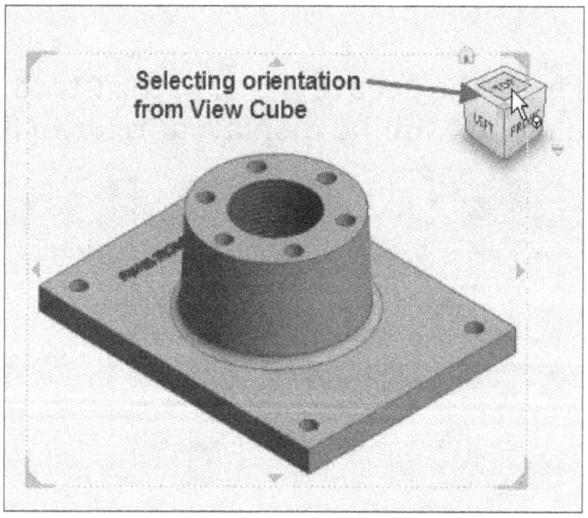

Figure-26. Changing drawing view using View Cube

- Select desired display style from the **Style** area of the dialog box. Like, you can select the **Hidden Line** button to display hidden lines in the view, you can select the **Shaded** button to display drawing view as shaded rather than wireframe or you can select the **Hidden Lines Removed** button to not display hidden lines in the drawing view.
- Select the **Raster View** check box if you want to generate pixel based views rather than accurate parametric views. Raster views are generated very fast so they are useful for large assemblies.

- Select **Display Point Clouds** check box to show point cloud data in the drawing view.
- Change the label of view and scale by using the **Label** edit box and **Scale** drop-down, respectively.
- If there are more than one model states like in case of iAssembly, iParts, or mold design assemblies then select desired model state from the drop-down in the **Model State** tab of the dialog box.
- Set desired display options from the **Display Options** tab in the dialog box.
- Click on the **OK** button to create the view.
- By default, the base view is placed at the center of sheet. Hover the cursor over the borders of view and drag it to desired location for changing placement.

Sheet Metal Drawing Options

If you are creating drawing views for a sheetmetal part then a few more options are displayed in the **Drawing View** dialog box; refer to Figure-27. These options are discussed next.

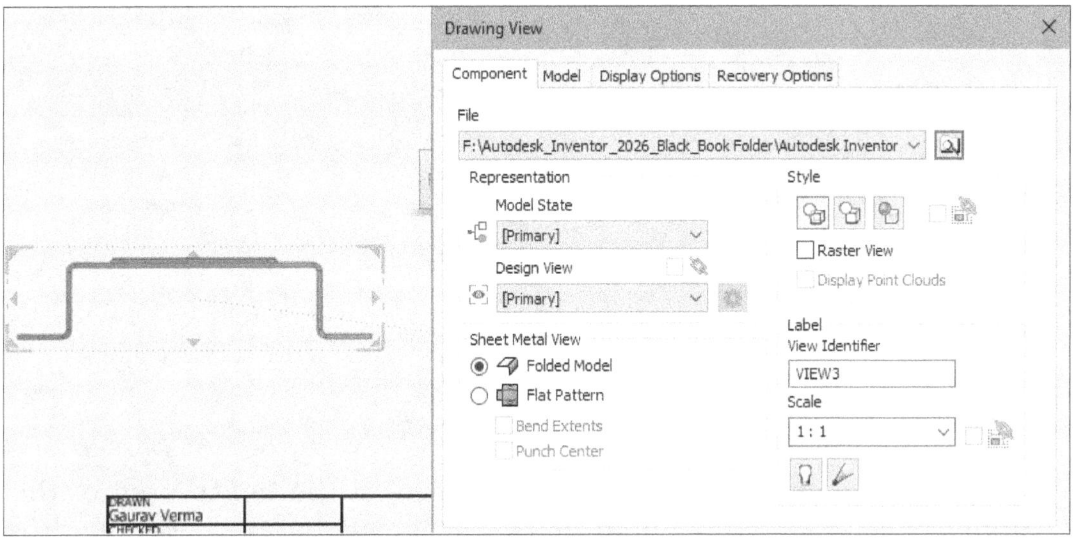

Figure-27. Sheet Metal View area in Drawing View dialog box

- By default, the **Folded Model** radio button is selected in the **Sheet Metal View** area of the dialog box. So, the model being inserted in drawing views is folded.
- Select the **Flat Pattern** radio button if you want to insert the flat pattern drawing view of the model.
- Select the **Bend Extents** check box and **Punch Center** check box if you want to display bend extends and punch center mark in the drawing view.

Similarly, you can use assembly and presentation files for view insertion. Note that exploded view of assembly are created in Presentation environment of Autodesk Inventor.

After placing the base view, next step is to insert projection views to display all details of 3D model. Before we start inserting the projection views, it is important to understand how we can change the parameters of drawing like 1st angle to 3rd angle projection, line width, drawing units, etc.

CHANGING STANDARDS AND STYLES

There are various parameters of drawing which keep on changing based on the Standards used in the company. The procedure to change the standards and styles is given next.

- Click on the **Styles Editor** tool from the **Styles and Standards** panel in the **Manage** tab of the **Ribbon**. The **Style and Standard Editor** dialog box will be displayed; refer to Figure-28.

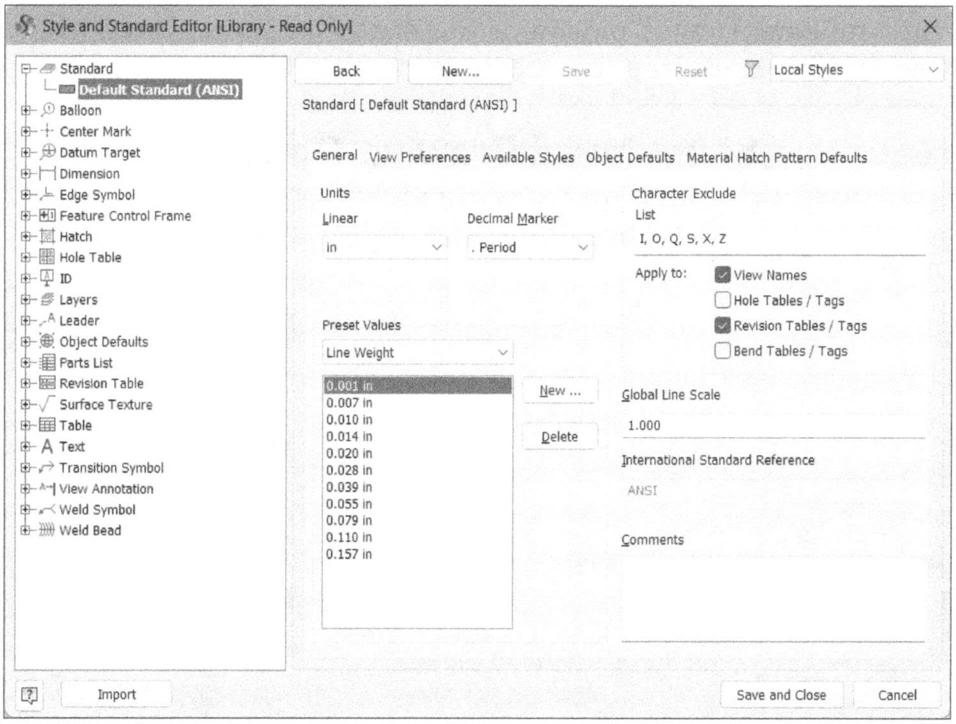

Figure-28. Style and Standard Editor dialog box

- Select desired unit from the **Linear** drop-down in the **Units** area of the dialog box. Similarly, set desired decimal marker from the **Decimal Marker** drop-down in the **Units** area.
- Set the standard line scale using the **Global Line Scale** edit box.
- After performing the changes, click on the **Save** button at the top in the dialog box.

Changing Projection Type and Other View Related Parameters

- Click on the **View Preferences** tab in the dialog box to display view related options; refer to Figure-29.

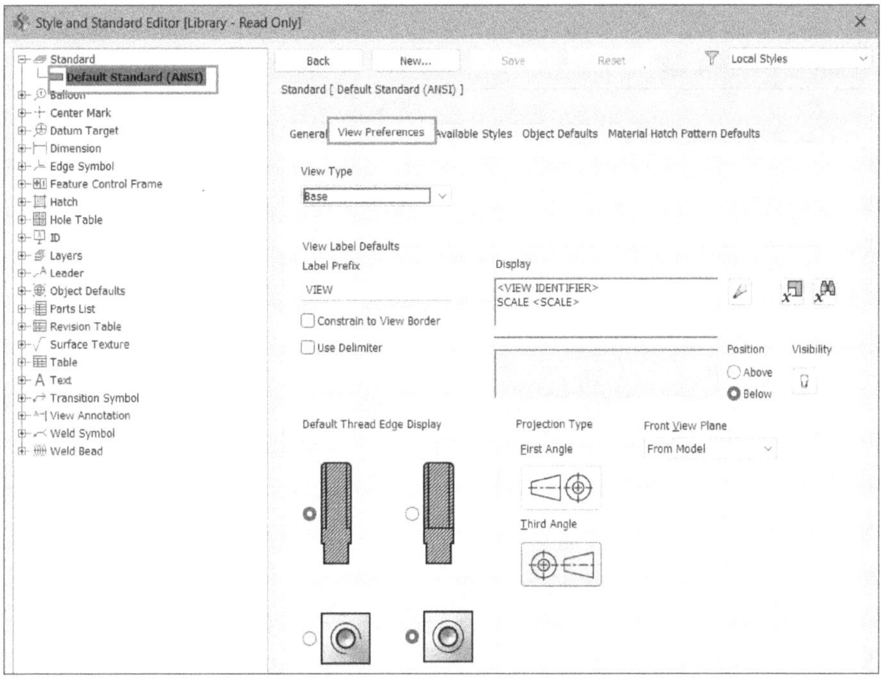

Figure-29. View Preferences tab in the Style and Standard Editor dialog box

- Select desired projection type from the **Projection Type** area of the dialog box. There are two buttons in this area; **First Angle** button to use First Angle Projection in drawing views and **Third Angle** button to use Third Angle Projection in drawing views.
- Select desired radio button in the **Default Thread Edge Display** area of the dialog box to represent threads as required in drawings.
- Similarly, you can change the default label for drawing views and toggle the visibility of labels by using the options in the **Display** area of the tab.
- After performing the changes, click on the **Save** button at the top in the dialog box.

Note that you can modify the drawing view parameters before creating the base view and projections. After creating the views, the modifications done in the dialog box will not be reflected in the drawing.

Modifying Layers of Drawing Objects

- Expand the **Layers** node in the left area of the dialog box. The list of various layers will be displayed; refer to Figure-30.

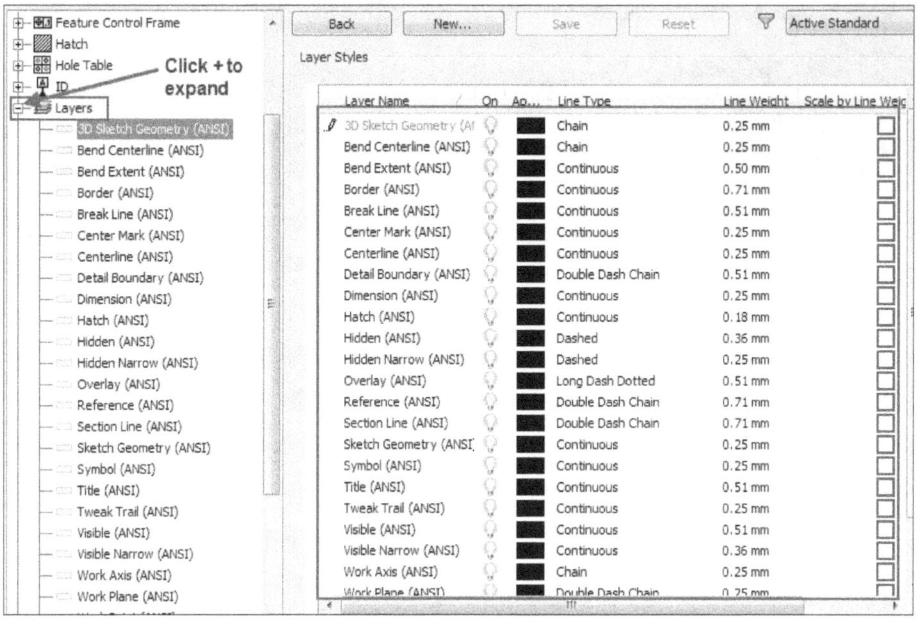

Figure-30. Expanded list of layers

- Select the layer of object and click on the value of the layer to modify it in the table. The option to change it will be displayed. Like, if you want to change the list type for **Bend Centerline (ANSI)** then click on the **Chain** option for it in the table. The selected value will change to a drop-down; refer to Figure-31.

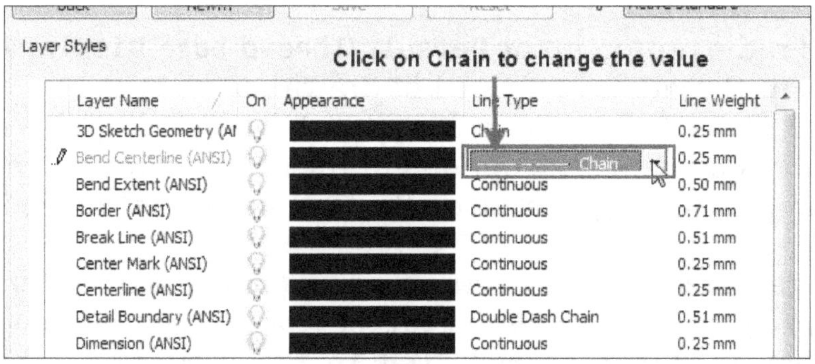

Figure-31. Changing parameters for layer

- Click again on the value to expand the drop-down and select desired value. Similarly, you can change the other values in the table.
- After performing the changes, click on the **Save** button at the top in the dialog box.

There are various other parameters which will be used later in this chapter. You will learn to modify them later in this chapter. For now, click on the **Save and Close** button from the dialog box to exit.

CREATING PROJECTED VIEWS

Projected views are used to present the model on paper from different sides and angles. The procedure to create the projected views is given next.

- Click on the **Projected** button from the **Create** panel in the **Place Views** tab of the **Ribbon**. You will be asked to select a view for projection.

- Select the base view earlier created. The projected view will get attached to cursor and gets modified as you move the cursor around the base view; refer to Figure-32.

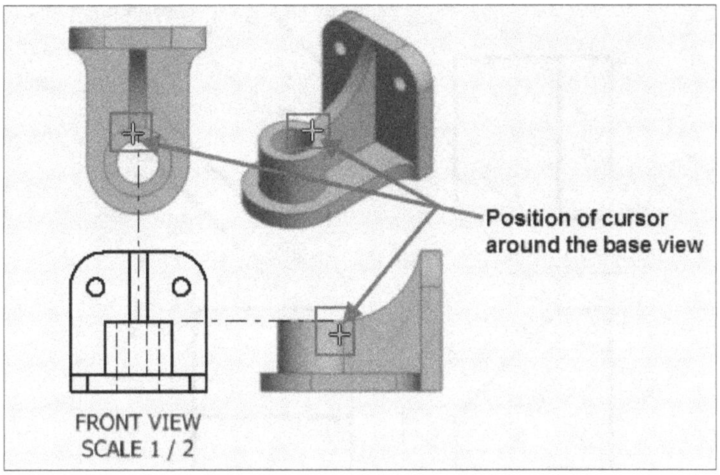

Figure-32. Preview of Projected view

- Click in desired location to place the projection view. Note that the projection view is automatically created based on the Projection Type selected in the **Style and Standard Editor** dialog box.
- You can click at other locations to place more projected views of the model.
- After placing desired number of views, right-click in the drawing area and select the **Create** button from the interactive shortcut menu displayed. The projections views will be created; refer to Figure-33.

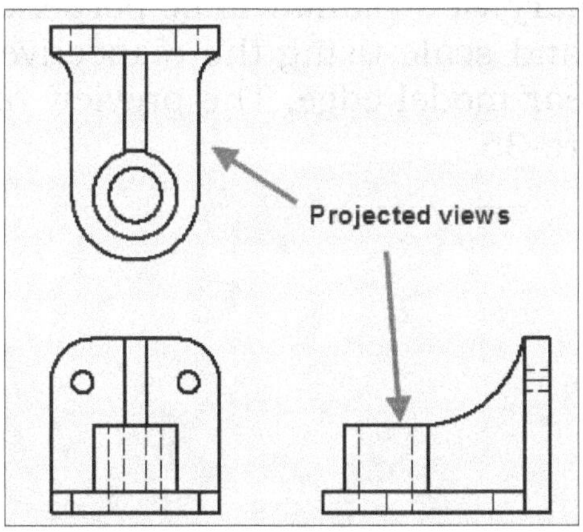

Figure-33. Projected views created

Note that the properties of base view are automatically applied to the projected views. Like, if base view is not shaded then projected views will also be not shaded by default.

CREATING AUXILIARY VIEW

Auxiliary view is an orthographic view taken in such a manner that the lines of sight are not parallel to the principal projection planes (frontal, horizontal, or profile). There are an infinite number of possible auxiliary views of any given object. When creating engineering drawings, it is often necessary to show features in a view where they appear true size so that they can be dimensioned. The object is normally positioned such that the major surfaces and features are either parallel or perpendicular to the principal planes; refer to Figure-34.

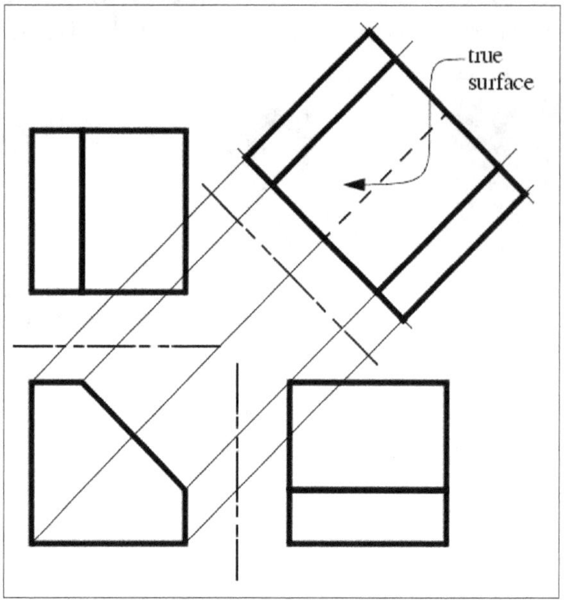

Figure-34. Auxiliary view example

The procedure to create auxiliary view is discussed next.

- Click on the **Auxiliary** tool from the **Create** panel in the **Place Views** tab of the **Ribbon**. You will be asked to select a view.
- Select the view using which you want to create the auxiliary view. The **Auxiliary View** dialog box will be displayed and you will be asked to select the linear model edge to which the auxiliary view plane will be perpendicular.
- Set the view identifier and scale using the respective options in the dialog box and then select the linear model edge. The preview of the auxiliary view will be displayed; refer to Figure-35.

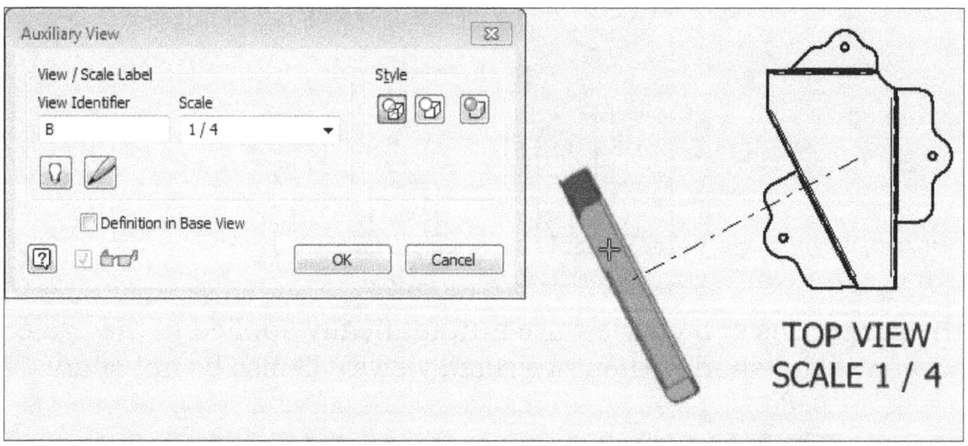

Figure-35. Preview of auxiliary view

- Click in the drawing area to place the view; refer to Figure-36.

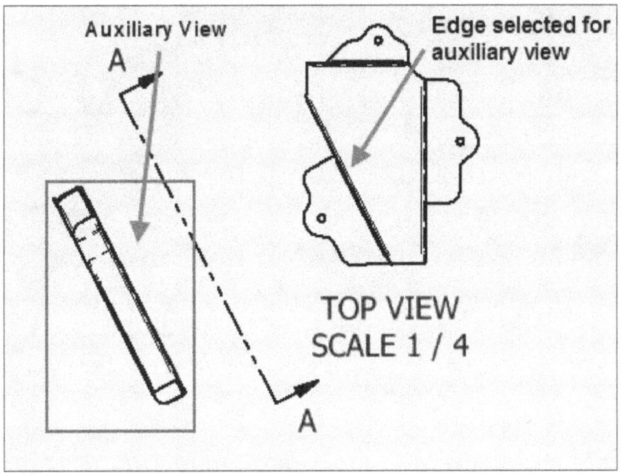

Figure-36. Auxiliary view created

CREATING SECTION VIEW

The **Section View** tool in Autodesk Inventor Drawing Environment is used to create section of the solid model to display inner details. The procedure to use this tool is given next.

- Click on the **Section view** tool from the **Create** panel in the **Place Views** tab of the **Ribbon**. You will be asked to select a base view whose section is to be created.
- Select a view from the drawing area. You will be asked to specify end points of the section line.
- Click to specify the first end point (or say starting point). You will be asked to specify next point of the line segment.
- Click on desired locations to create the section line; refer to Figure-37. Note that the section line is multiline entity.

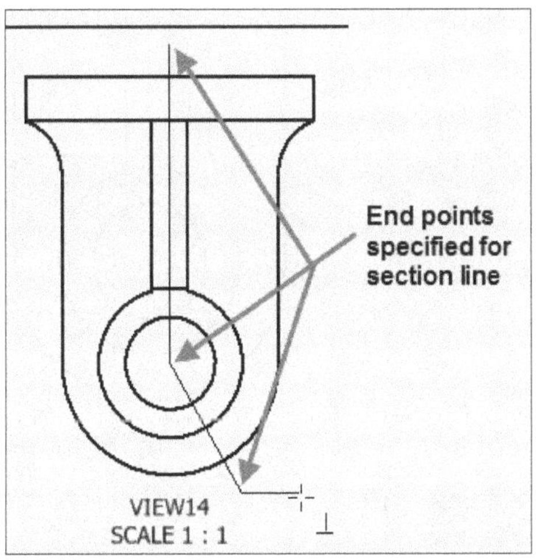

Figure-37. End points of section-line

- Right-click in the drawing area and click on **Continue** button from the shortcut menu. Preview of the section view will be displayed along with **Section View** dialog box; refer to Figure-38.

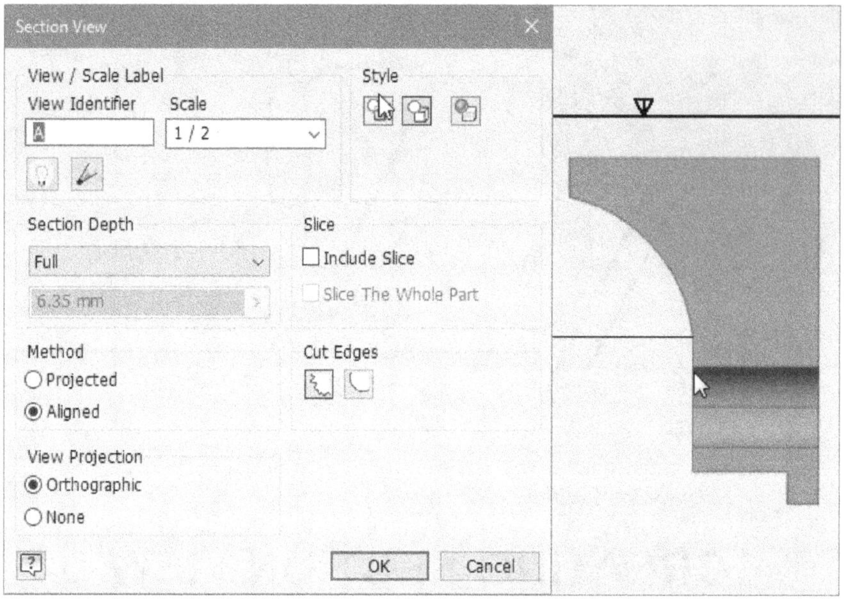

Figure-38. Preview of section view with Section View dialog box

- Specify the alphabet for view identifier in the **View Identifier** edit box.
- Select desired scale from the **Scale** drop-down in the dialog box.
- If you want to create section up to specified depth then select the **Distance** option from the drop-down in the **Section Depth** area and specify the distance value in the edit box below drop-down. Preview of the section will be displayed; refer to Figure-39.

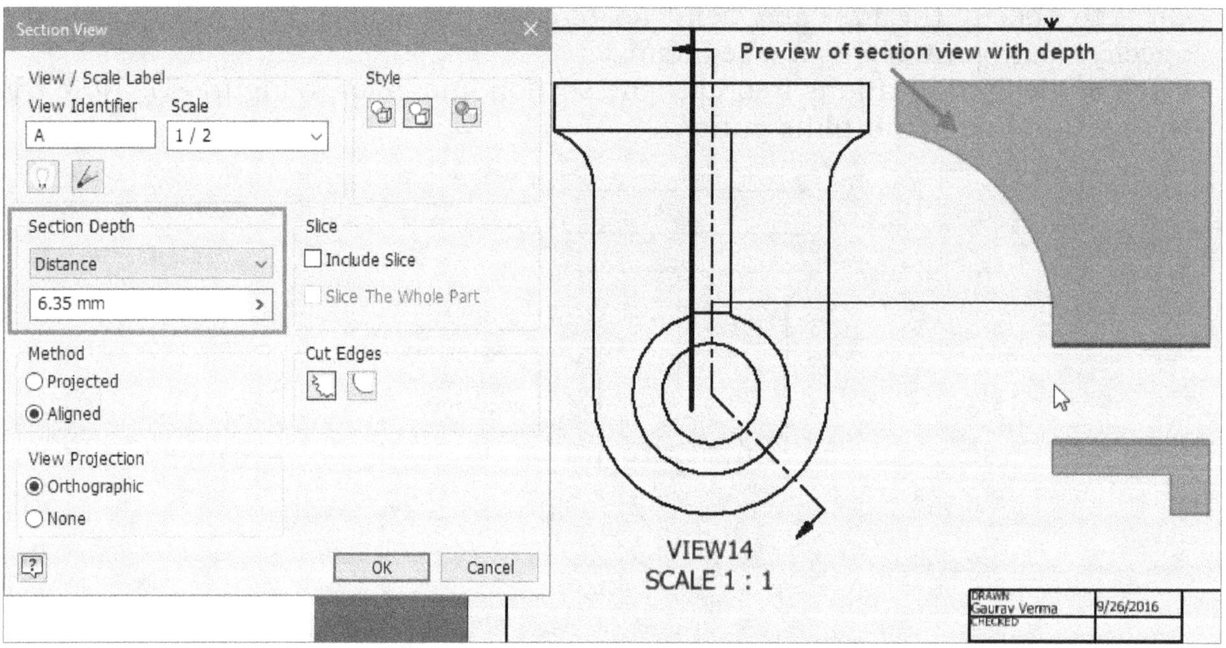

Figure-39. Preview of section view with depth

- Select desired option from the **Slice** area to include slices created for the part in modeling environment. Drawing view shown in Figure-40 is a section view with **Slice The Whole Part** check box selected.
- Select the **Aligned** radio button to create section view aligned to the base view. Select the **Projected** radio button to make the section view projection of section lines; refer to Figure-41.

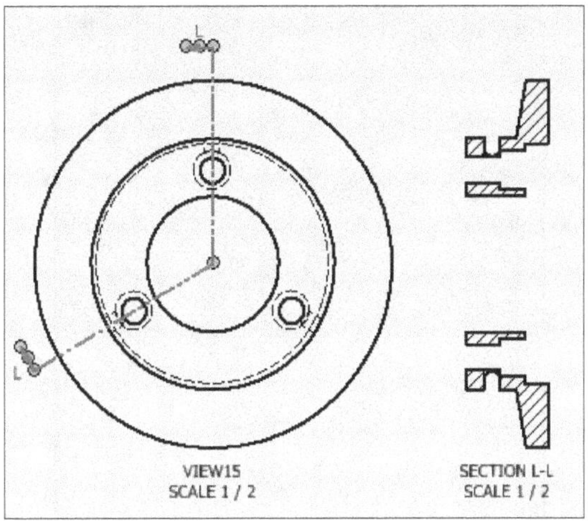

Figure-40. Section view with slice the whole part check box selected

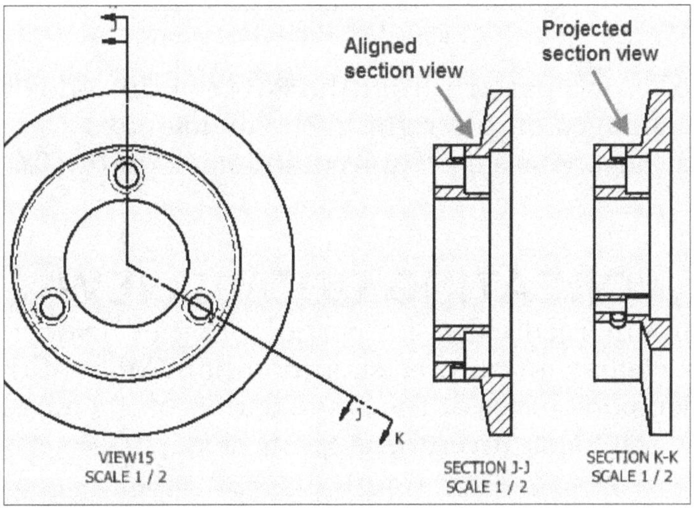

Figure-41. Section views created

- Click in the drawing area to place the view.

Modifying Hatching in Section View

Sometimes, you need to change the hatch pattern in section view to represent different type of materials. The procedure to change hatching is given next.

- Double-click on the hatching in section view. The **Edit Hatch Pattern** dialog box will be displayed; refer to Figure-42.

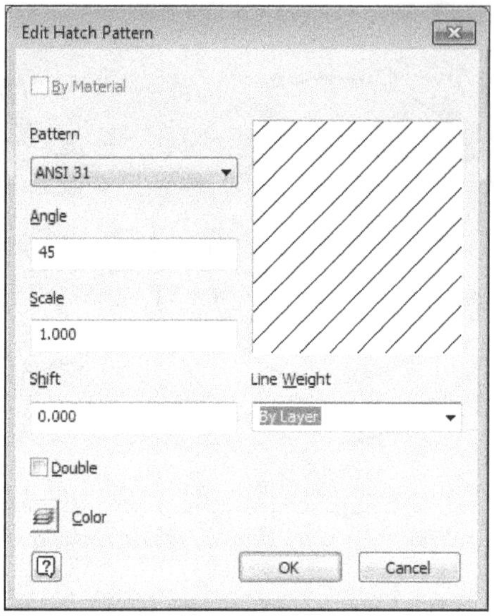

Figure-42. Edit Hatch Pattern dialog box

- Select the type of hatch pattern from the **Pattern** drop-down in the dialog box. Preview will be displayed on the right in the dialog box.
- Specify the other parameters as required and click on the **OK** button to apply the changes.

CREATING DETAIL VIEW

The detail view is an enlarged view of a portion of other drawing view. Detail views are used to provide clearer, more precise annotation. Most of the time detail views are provided to dimension curves at the small corner of the model. The procedure to create detail view in Autodesk Inventor is given next.

- Click on the **Detail View** tool from the **Create** panel in the **Place Views** tab of the **Ribbon**. You will be asked to select the view for which detail view is to be generated.
- Click on the view for creating detail view fence. The **Detail View** dialog box will be displayed and you will be asked to specify the center point of the detail view fence.
- Select the **Circular** or **Rectangular** button from the dialog box to set the shape of detail view fence.
- Click on the location for which detail view is to be generated. You will be asked to specify end point of the fence; refer to Figure-43.

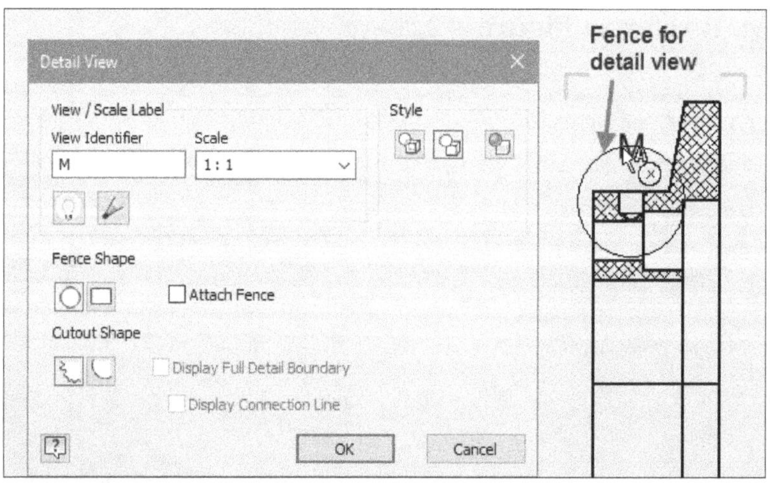

Figure-43. Detail View dialog box with detail view fence

- Click to specify the span of detail view fence. The detail view get attached to the cursor.
- Select the **Attach Fence** check box to select fence center point where the detail view will be fixed.
- Specify desired parameters in the **Detail View** dialog box and click to place the detail view; refer to Figure-44.

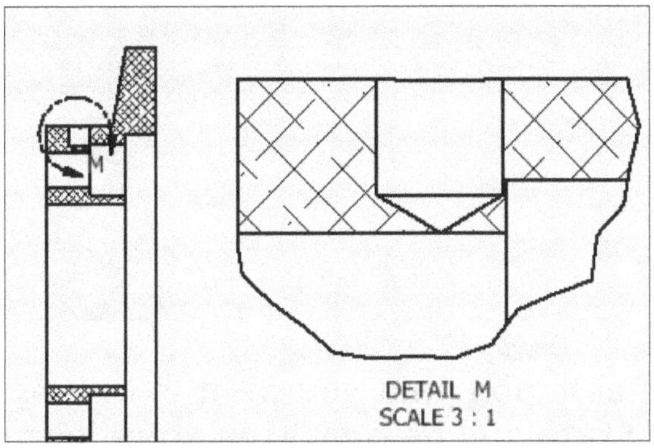

Figure-44. Detail view created

CREATING OVERLAY VIEW

The Overlay view, also called multi-positional view, is used to represent various positions of components of assembly in single view; refer to Figure-45. The procedure to create overlay view is given next.

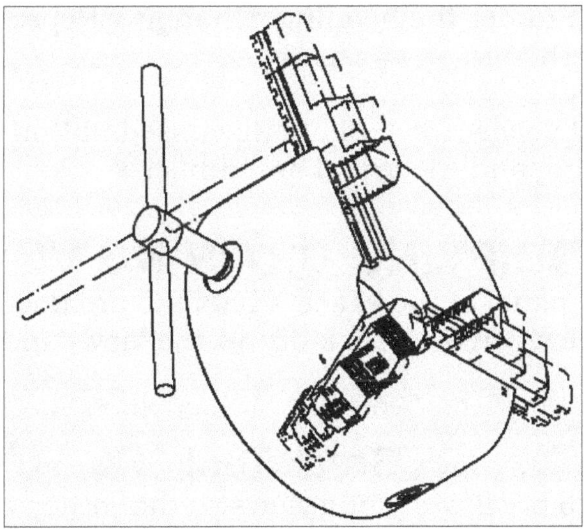

Figure-45. Overlay view example

- Click on the **Overlay** button from the **Create** panel in the **Place Views** tab of the **Ribbon**. You will be asked to select the drawing view for which overlay views are to be created.
- Select the drawing view. The **Overlay View** dialog box will be displayed; refer to Figure-46.

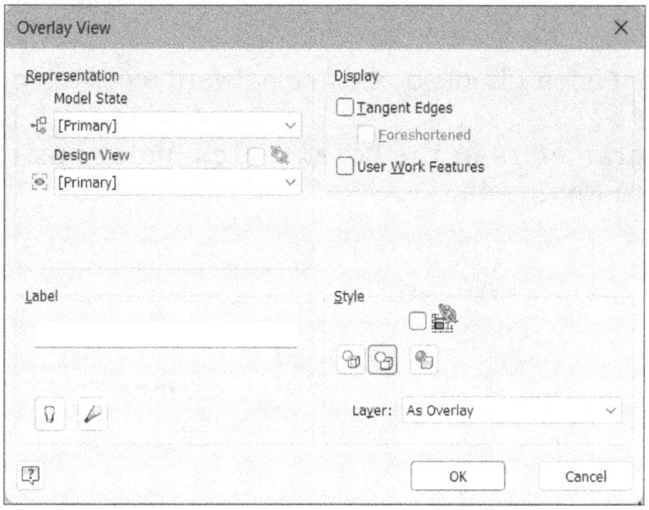

Figure-46. Overlay View dialog box

- Select the position of assembly that you want to overlay on the current drawing view from the **Model State** and **Design View** drop-downs in the **Representation** area of the dialog box.
- Set the other parameters in the dialog box as required and click on the **OK** button. The overlay feature will be created.

Note that the assembly used for overlay drawing view must have more than one positional views. You have learned about creating positional representations in Chapter 12 of this book under the heading "Changing Representation of Mold". You can apply the same method to any assembly.

The **Nailboard** tool and **Connector** tool are discussed in 2nd part of the book where we have discussed Piping and Electrical assemblies.

MODIFYING DRAWING VIEW

The tools in the **Modify** panel of the **Place Views** tab are used to modify the drawing views like break long view, create break out in the view, and so on. These tools are discussed next.

Break Tool

The **Break** tool is used to break very long views so that other views can accommodate in smaller sheet; refer to Figure-47. The procedure to use this tool is given next.

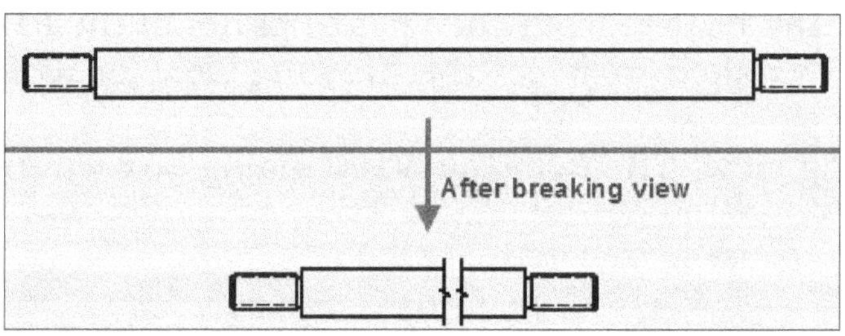

Figure-47. Example of breaking view

- Click on the **Break** tool from the **Modify** panel in the **Place Views** tab of the **Ribbon**. You will be asked to select a view.

- Select the view on which you want to apply break. The **Break** dialog box will be displayed and you will be asked to specify the start point of break section; refer to Figure-48.

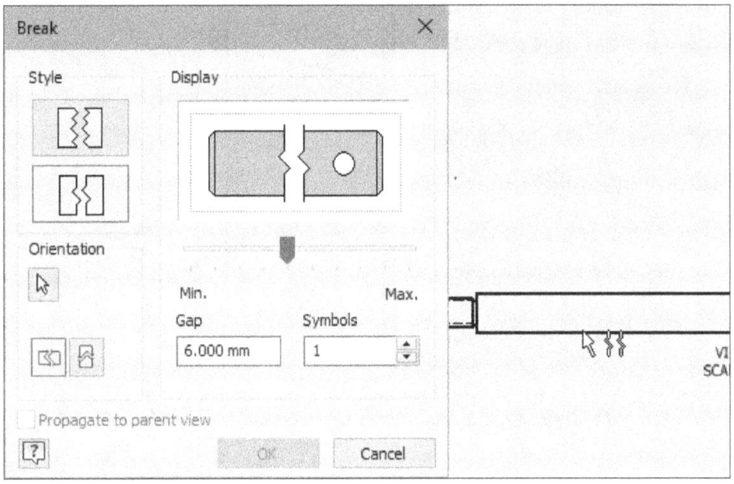

Figure-48. Break dialog box

- Select the style and orientation of the break feature from the **Style** and **Orientation** area of the dialog box.
- Set the gap of break symbol and number of symbols using the **Gap** and **Symbols** edit boxes, respectively.
- Click on the drawing view to specify starting and then end point; refer to Figure-49. The break feature will be applied to the view.

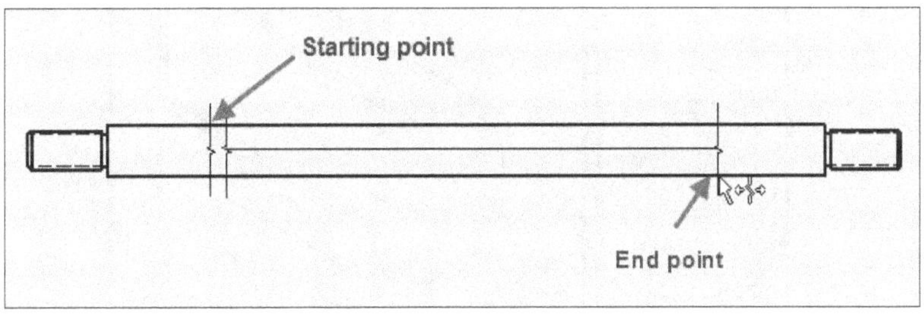

Figure-49. Specifying starting and end point for break

Creating Break Out View

The break out views are used to display inner details of smaller sections of the component. The procedure to create break out view is given next.

- Click on the **Start Sketch** tool from the **Sketch** panel in the **Place Views** tab of the **Ribbon**. You will be asked to select the view to create sketch section for break out view.
- Select the drawing view. Tools of the sketching environment will be activated.
- Create a closed section at desired location on the drawing view and click on the **Finish Sketch** button from the **Exit** panel in the **Ribbon**.
- Now, click on the **Break Out** tool from the **Modify** panel in the **Place Views** tab of the **Ribbon**. You will be asked to select the view with sketch created earlier.
- Select the drawing view. The sketch section will get selected automatically and you will be asked to specify a point for depth reference. Also, the **Break Out** dialog box will be displayed; refer to Figure-50.

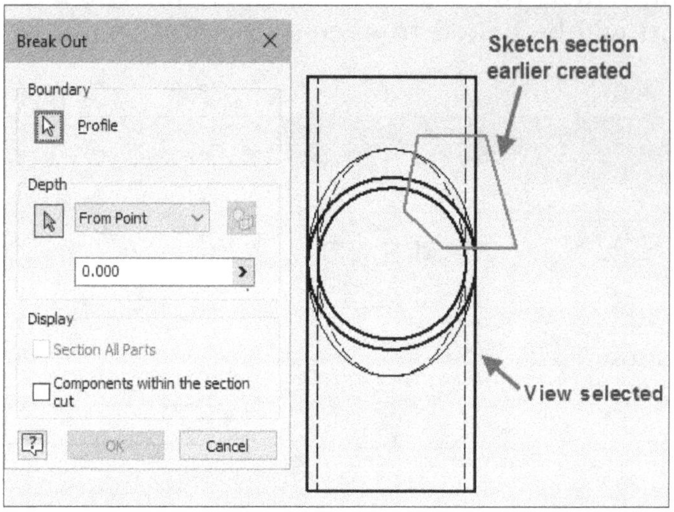

Figure-50. Break Out dialog box with drawing view selected

- Click at desired location inside the sketch created to specify the reference for depth.
- Specify desired value of depth of break out section and click on the **OK** button. The break out view will be created. You can create a projected view of the break out view to give better view of the inside of component; refer to Figure-51.

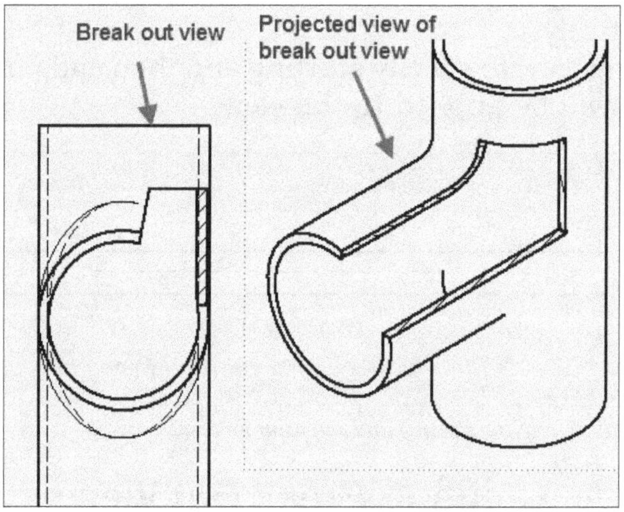

Figure-51. Break out view with its projected view

Creating Slice of Drawing View

The **Slice** tool is used to create 2D slices of the selected drawing view in its projected representation. The procedure to use this tool is given next.

- Click on the **Start Sketch** tool from the **Sketch** panel in the **Place Views** tab of the **Ribbon**. You will be asked to select the view to create sketch section for break out view.
- Select the drawing view. Tools of the sketching environment will be activated.
- Create an open loop sketch at desired location on the drawing view and click on the **Finish Sketch** button from the **Exit** panel in the **Ribbon**; refer to Figure-52.

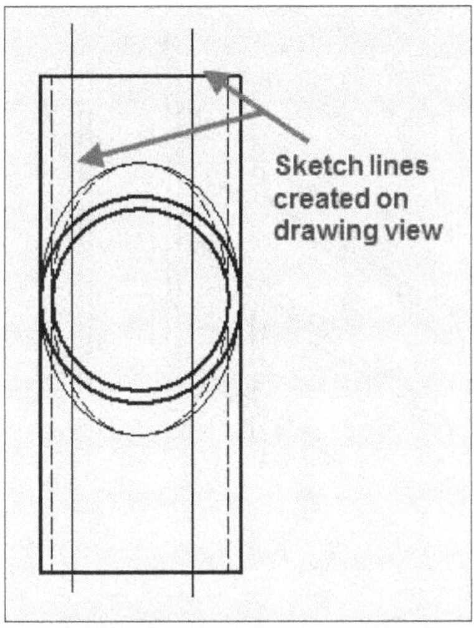

Figure-52. Sketch created for slice

- Click on the **Projected** tool from the **Create** panel in the **Place Views** tab of the **Ribbon** and create a projected view of base view; refer to Figure-53.

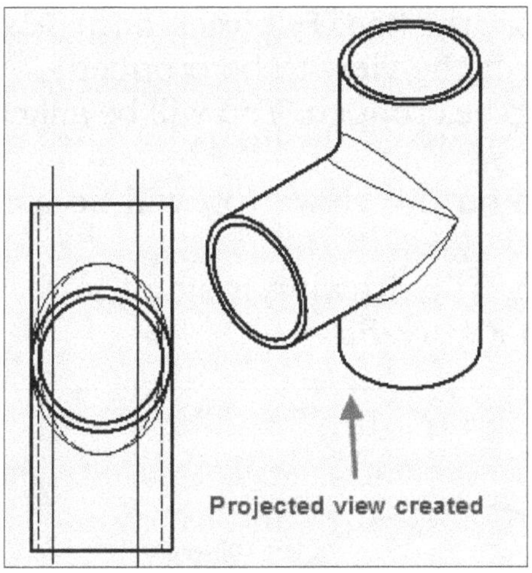

Figure-53. Projected view created

- Click on the **Slice** tool from the **Modify** panel in the **Place Views** tab of the **Ribbon**. You will be asked to select the view to be sliced.
- Select the projected view. The **Slice** dialog box will be displayed and you will be asked to select the sketch for slicing.
- Select the sketch earlier created for slicing. The **OK** button in **Slice** dialog box will become active.
- Select the **Slice All Parts** check box to slice the complete part in view and click on the **OK** button from the **Slice** dialog box displayed. The sliced view will be displayed; refer to Figure-54.

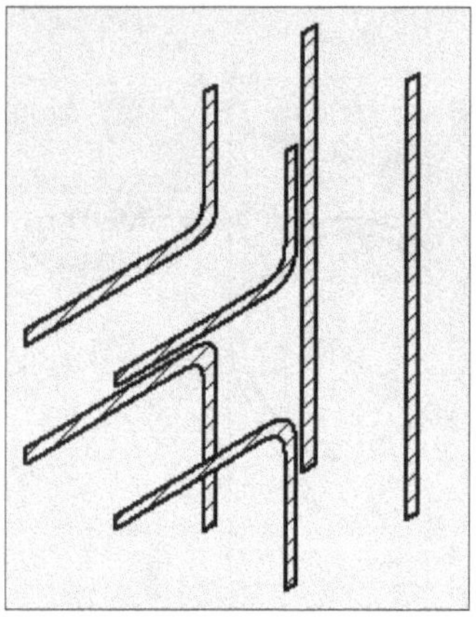

Figure-54. Sliced view

Cropping View

The **Crop** tool is used to crop the drawing view so that only small portion of the drawing can be displayed. The procedure to use this tool is given next.

- Click on the **Crop** tool from the **Modify** panel in the **Place Views** tab of the **Ribbon**. You will be asked to select the view to be cropped.
- Select the drawing view to be cropped. You will be asked to select the first rectangle corner.
- Click at desired location on the view. You will be asked to select second corner of the crop rectangle.
- Click at desired location. The drawing inside the rectangle will remain and rest will be removed; refer to Figure-55.

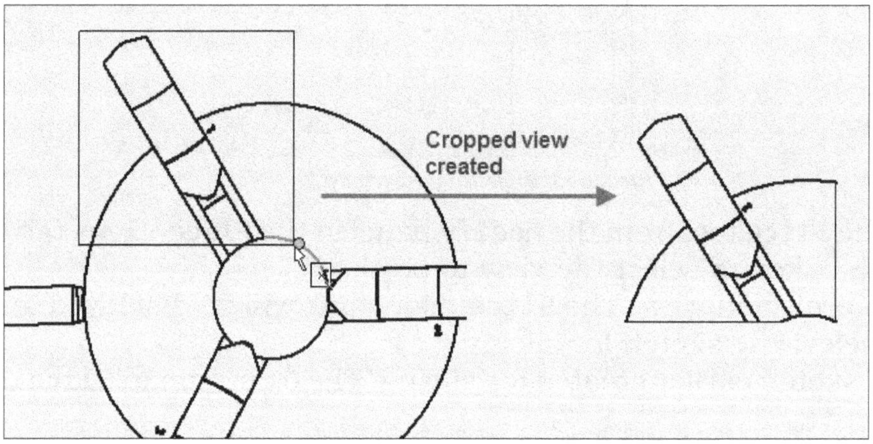

Figure-55. Cropped view created

The alignment tools available in the **Break Alignment** drop-down of the **Modify** panel are used to break or modify the alignment between base view and other child views; refer to Figure-56. I hope you can work on them by yourself. If you get any doubt, please E-mail at **cadcamcaeworks@gmail.com**

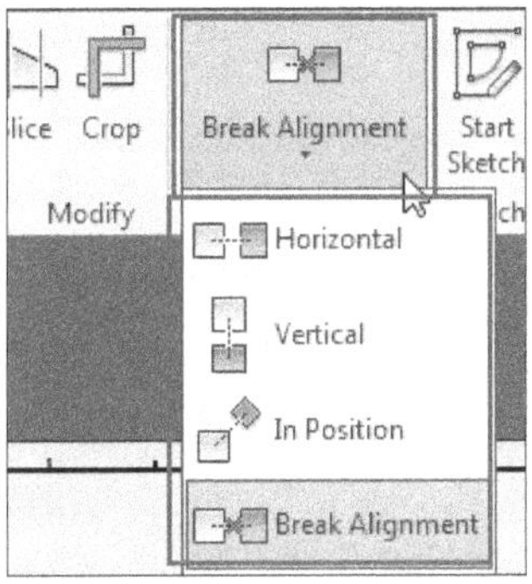

Figure-56. Alignment drop-down

Placing the views in drawing is less half of the drawing work done. The actual use of drawing is to express the real size and shape of the object. To express the size and shape of object, we use different type of annotations in drawing. Now, we will discuss different type of annotations and their related tools in Autodesk Inventor.

ANNOTATION TOOLS

As discussed earlier, the annotations are used to express the real size and shape of object to be manufactured. In Engineering field, annotations are group of different type of dimensions and symbols permitted by national and international standards of drafting. Each type of dimension and symbol has unique and clear meaning in drawing. The tools to apply annotations to drawing views are available in the **Annotate** tab in the **Ribbon**; refer to Figure-57.

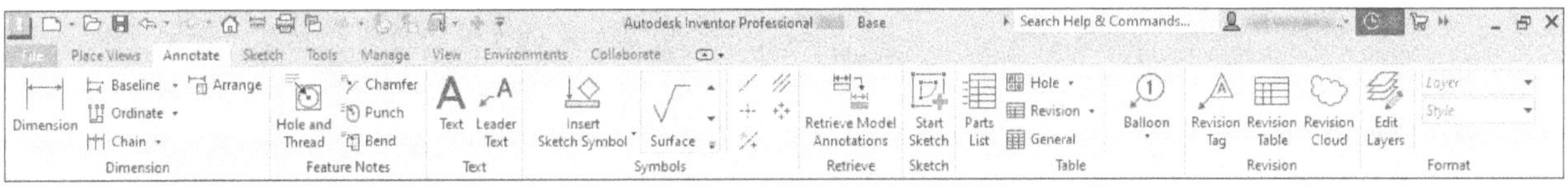

Figure-57. Annotate tab in Ribbon

The tools in the tab are discussed next.

Retrieve Model Annotations Tool

Retrieve The **Retrieve Model Annotations** tool is used to retrieve all the dimensions applied to the model in the 3D modeling environment. If you have not applied any dimension to the model then you will retrieve nothing by using this tool. Note that while working in Industry, you will apply this tool after placing the views to get all the modeling dimension. The procedure to use this tool is given next.

- Click on the **Retrieve Model Annotations** tool from the **Retrieve** panel in the **Annotate** tab of the **Ribbon**. The **Retrieve Model Annotation** dialog box will be displayed; refer to Figure-58. Also, you will be asked to select the view whose dimensions are to be retrieved.

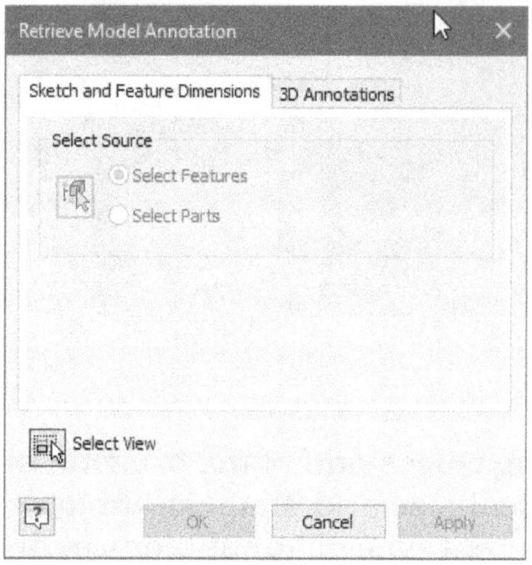

Figure-58. Retrieve Model Annotation dialog box

- Select the drawing view from the drawing area, the preview of dimensions will be displayed; refer to Figure-59. You will be asked to select the features of the model or the dimensions to retrieve.

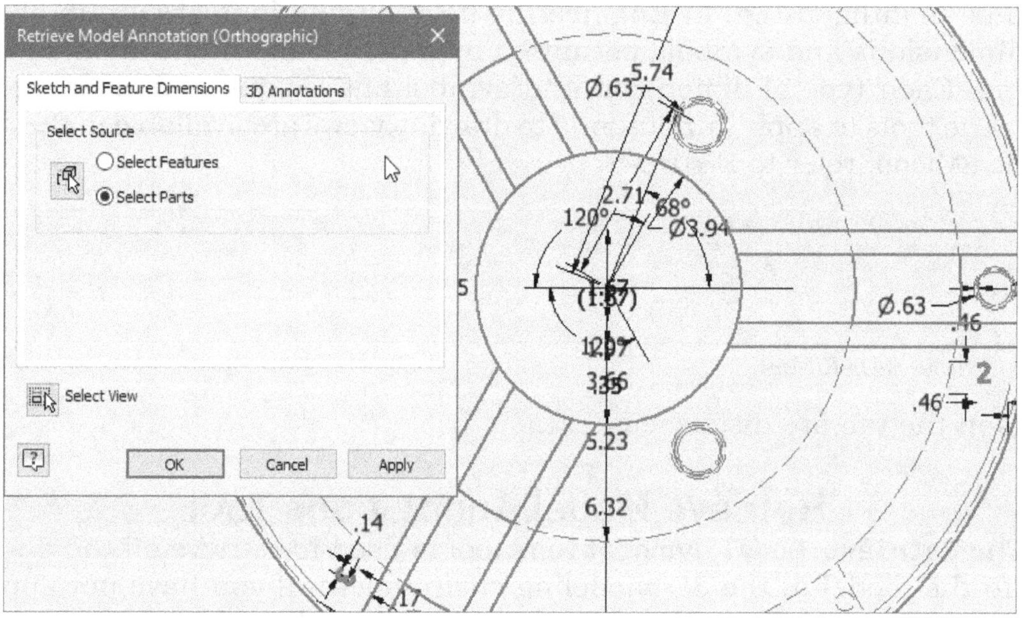

Figure-59. Preview of dimensions retrieved

- Select desired features or the dimensions. If you want to select the parts then select the **Select Parts** radio button from the **Select Source** area in the **Sketch and Feature Dimensions** tab of the dialog box. Note that you can make window selections to select multiple dimensions at one time to retrieve.
- Click on the **OK** button from the dialog box.

Dimension Tool

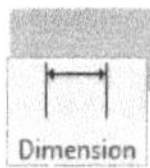

The **Dimension** tool is used to apply dimension to the selected entity in the drawing view. The procedure to use this tool is given next.

- Click on the **Dimension** tool from the **Dimension** panel in the **Annotate** tab of the **Ribbon**. You will be asked to select the geometry to be dimensioned.

- Select the entity/entities to be dimensioned. The dimension will get attached to cursor; refer to Figure-60. Note that the pattern of selecting entities for dimensioning is same as discussed in 3D Modeling environment.

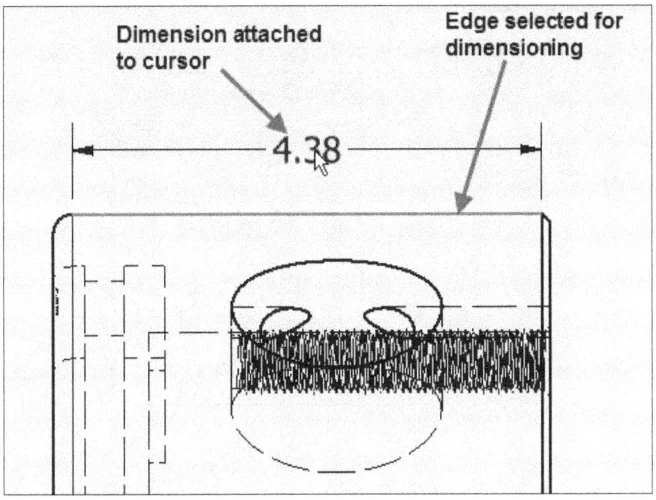

Figure-60. Dimensioning entities

- Click in the drawing area to place the dimension. The **Edit dimension** dialog box will be displayed; refer to Figure-61.

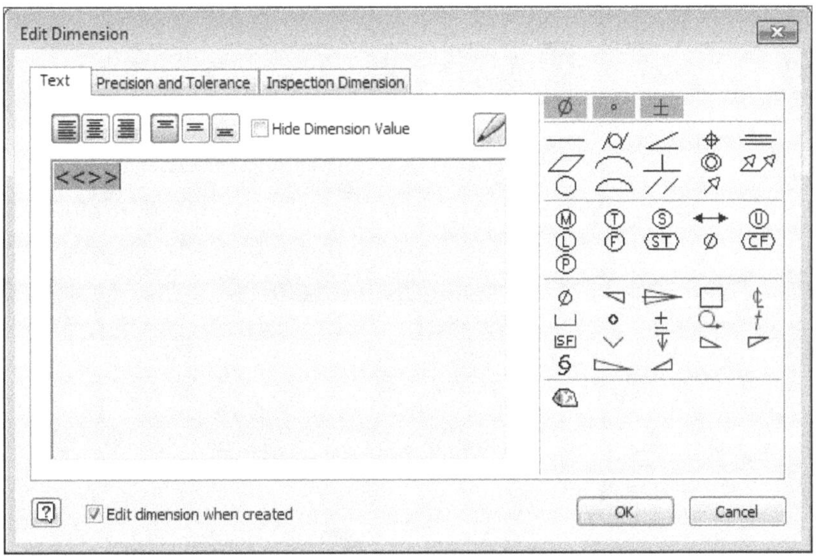

Figure-61. Edit Dimension dialog box

- Specify desired parameters in the dialog box and click on the **OK** button to create the dimension.

The options in the **Edit Dimension** dialog box are discussed next.

Text Options

The options to edit text of dimension are available in the **Text** tab of the dialog box. The major options in this tab are discussed next.

- Type desired text in the text box to add text to the dimension.
- Set the alignment of the text using justification buttons above the text box in the dialog box. 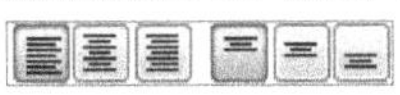

- Select the **Hide Dimension Value** check box to hide the dimension value and display only user defined text.
- You can insert the symbols in the dimension text by using the panel in the right of dialog box; refer to Figure-62.

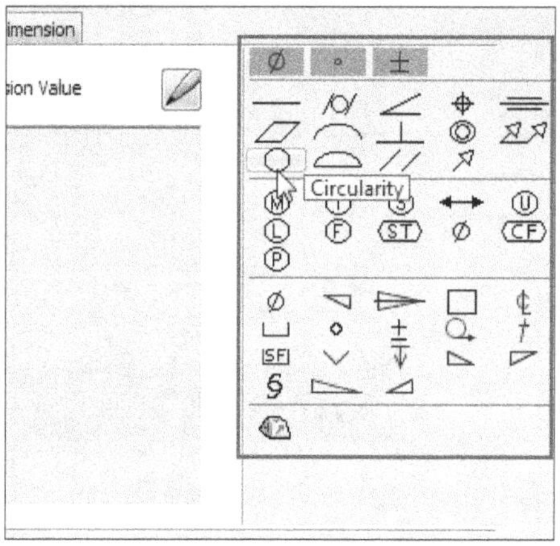

Figure-62. Panel for inserting symbols in the dimension

- If you want to change the formatting of text like changing font, boldface, font size, etc. then click on the **Launch Text Editor** button from the dialog box. The **Format Text** dialog box will be displayed; refer to Figure-63.

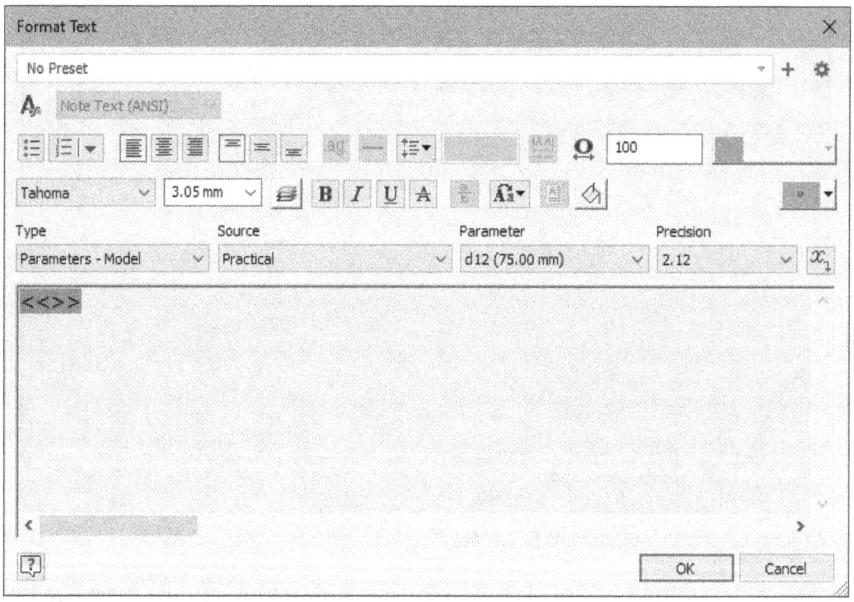

Figure-63. Format Text dialog box

- Using the options in the dialog box, change the formatting of text and then click on the **OK** button.

Precision and Tolerance Options

The options in the **Precision and Tolerance** tab are used to specify the dimensioning tolerance and limits of the component. Select desired tolerance method from the **Tolerance Method** area of the dialog box and set the precision of tolerance from the **Precision** area of the dialog box; refer to Figure-64. Set the value of tolerances in the edit boxes below **Tolerance Method** selection list in the dialog box.

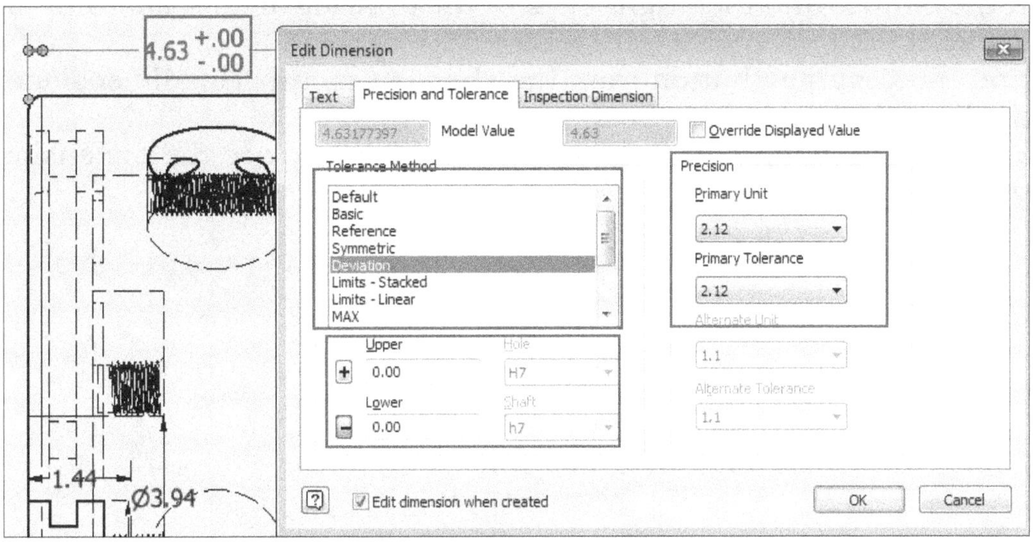

Figure-64. Precision and Tolerance tab in the dialog box

Inspection Dimension Options

The options in the **Inspection Dimension** tab are used to set the inspection criteria for the current dimension. Select the **Inspection Dimension** check box and specify desired values for inspection rate of current dimension; refer to Figure-65.

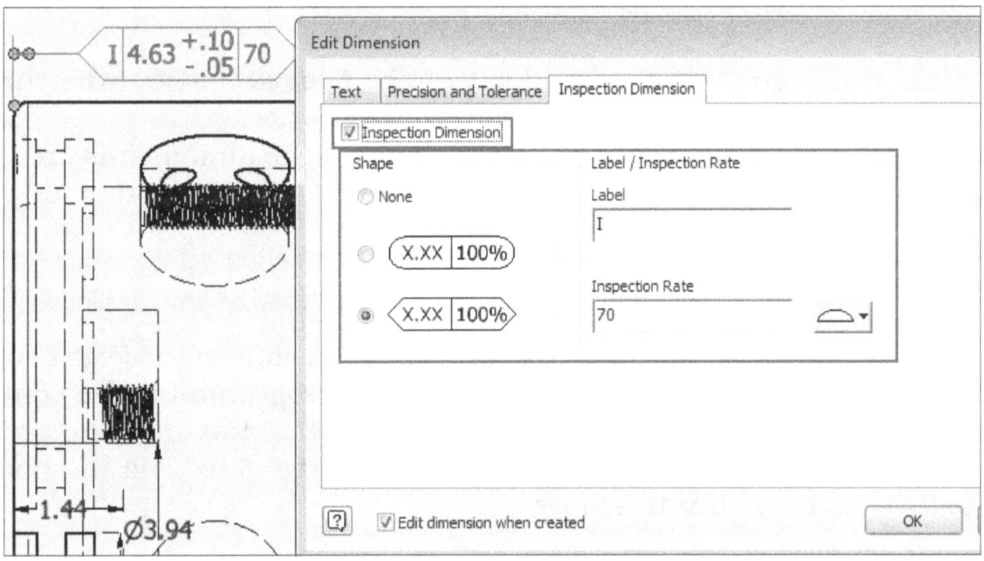

Figure-65. Inspection Dimension options

Click on the **OK** button from the dialog box after specifying desired parameters.

Baseline Dimensioning

There are two tools to create baseline dimensions, **Baseline** and **Baseline Set**. The method of using both the tools is same as discussed next.

- Click on the **Baseline** or **Baseline Set** tool from the **Baseline Dimension** drop-down in the **Dimension** panel of the **Annotate** tab in the **Ribbon**. You will be asked to select the entity on model which you want to be base for all other dimensions.
- Select an edge or curve from the drawing view. You will be asked to select geometry to be dimensioned.

- Select the entities and then right-click in the drawing area. A shortcut menu will be displayed.
- Click on the **Continue** button from the shortcut menu. The dimensions will get attached to the cursor.
- Move the cursor along X or Y direction and click to place the dimensions; refer to Figure-66.

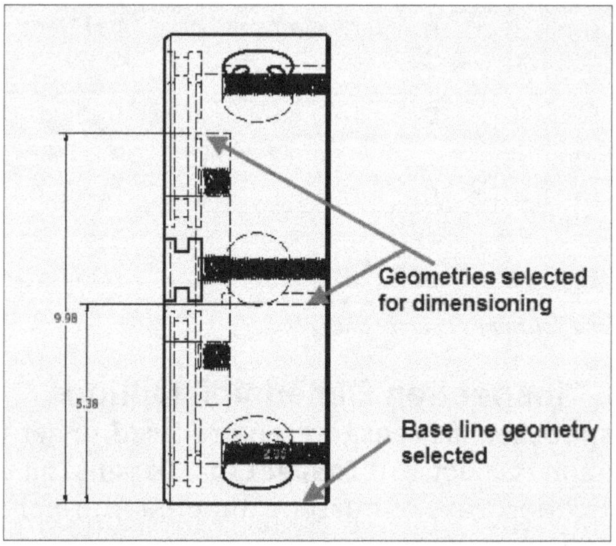

Figure-66. Baseline dimensioning

- Right-click in the drawing area and select the **Create** option from the shortcut menu.
- Note that if you use the **Baseline Set** tool then all the dimensions created will be part of a group. If you select one dimension of the baseline set then all dimension will get selected.

Ordinate Dimensioning

The Ordinate dimensioning is used to display the dimensions in the form of coordinate. This type of dimensioning is useful in manual CAM programming the component or when there are lots of dimension in small section of the drawing. The are two tools to create ordinate dimensions; **Ordinate** and **Ordinate Set**. The method of using both the tools is same as discussed next.

- Click on the **Ordinate** or **Ordinate Set** tool from the **Ordinate Dimension** drop-down in the **Dimension** panel of the **Annotate** tab in **Ribbon**. You will be asked to select the drawing view to be dimensioned.
- Select the drawing view. You will be asked to specify the origin location.
- Click at desired location in the drawing view to specify **0** level of ordinate dimension. You will be asked to select the geometries to be dimensioned.
- Select the entities in the drawing view and right-click in the drawing area. A shortcut menu will be displayed.
- Select the **Continue** button from the shortcut menu. You will be asked to specify location for placing dimensions.
- Click at desired location in the drawing area to place the dimension; refer to Figure-67.

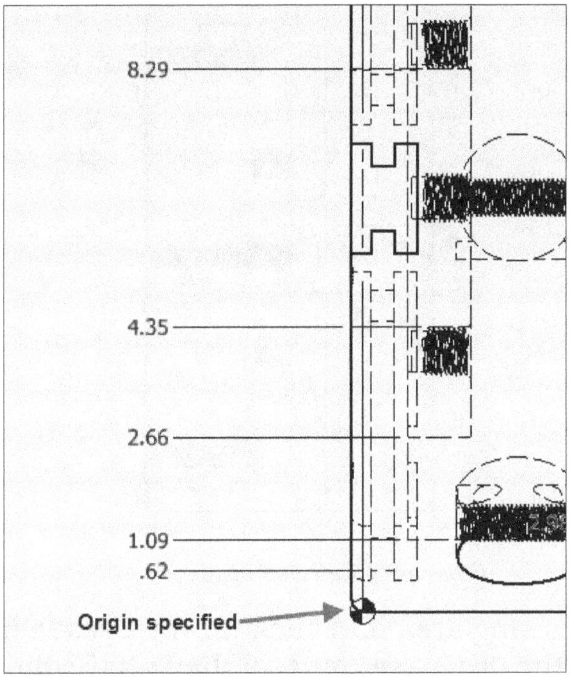

Figure-67. Ordinate dimension

- Right-click in the drawing area and select the **OK** button from the shortcut menu displayed.
- Note that if you use the **Ordinate Set** tool then all the dimensions created will be part of a group. If you select one dimension of the ordinate set then all dimensions will get selected.

Chain Dimensioning

The chain dimensioning is used to create dimensions linked one after the other. There are two tools to create chain dimensions; **Chain** and **Chain Set**. The method of using both the tools is same as discussed next.

- Click on the **Chain** or **Chain Set** tool from the **Chain Dimension** drop-down in the **Dimension** panel of the **Annotate** tab in the **Ribbon**. You will be asked to select entity for base of chain dimensioning.
- Select the geometry from the drawing view. You will be asked to select geometries to be dimensioned.
- Select the entities and right-click in the drawing area. A shortcut menu will be displayed.
- Click on the **Continue** button from the menu. The dimensions will get attached to cursor.
- Click in the drawing area to place the dimensions; refer to Figure-68.

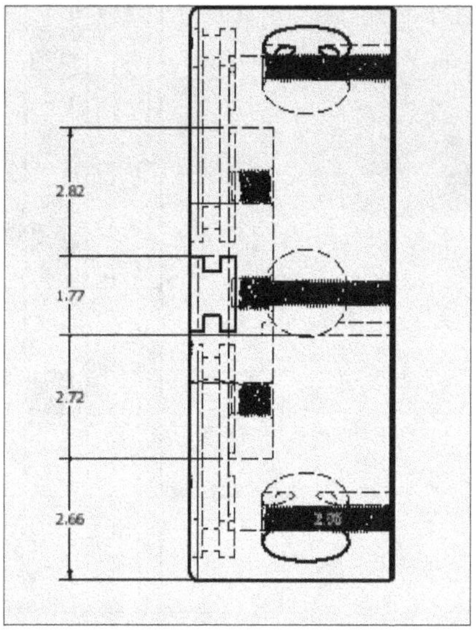

Figure-68. Chain dimensioning

- Right-click in the drawing area and click on the **Create** button.
- Note that if you use the **Ordinate Set** tool then all the dimensions created will be part of a group. If you select one dimension of the ordinate set then all dimension will get selected.

Hole and Thread Tool

The **Hole and Thread** tool is used to annotate holes and threads. The procedure to use this tool is given next.

- Click on the **Hole and Thread** tool from the **Feature Notes** panel in the **Annotate** tab of the **Ribbon**. You will be asked to select hole or thread edges in the drawing view.
- Select the edge of the hole/thread. The annotation will get attached to cursor.
- Click at desired location in the drawing to place the annotation; refer to Figure-69.

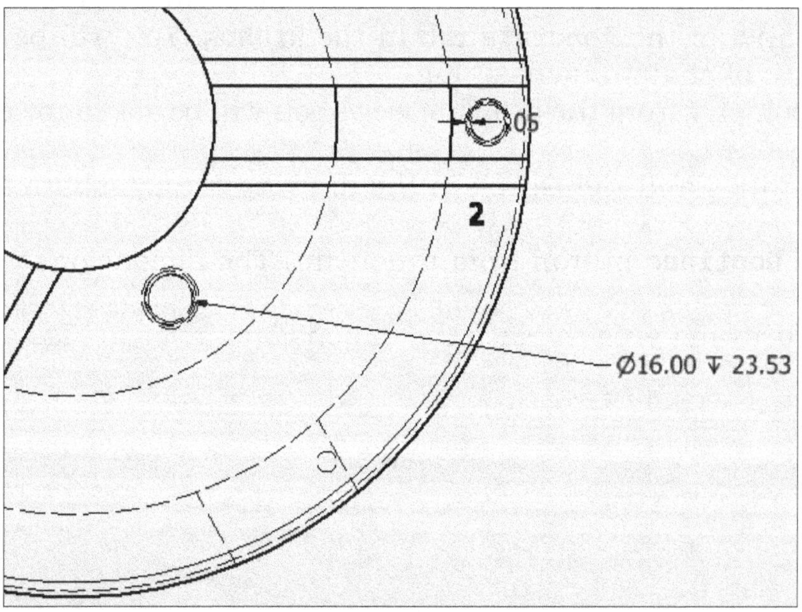

Figure-69. Hole annotation

- You will be asked to select hole or thread edge. Click on the edge and repeat the procedure till you have required annotations.
- Right-click in the drawing area and click on the **OK** button to exit the tool.

Chamfer Tool

The **Chamfer** tool is used to annotate chamfer in the drawing view. The procedure to use this tool is given next.

- Click on the **Chamfer** tool from the **Feature Notes** panel in the **Annotate** tab of the **Ribbon**. You will be asked to select the chamfer edge.
- Click on the chamfered edge. You will be asked to select the reference edge. The chamfer annotation will get attached to the cursor; refer to Figure-70.

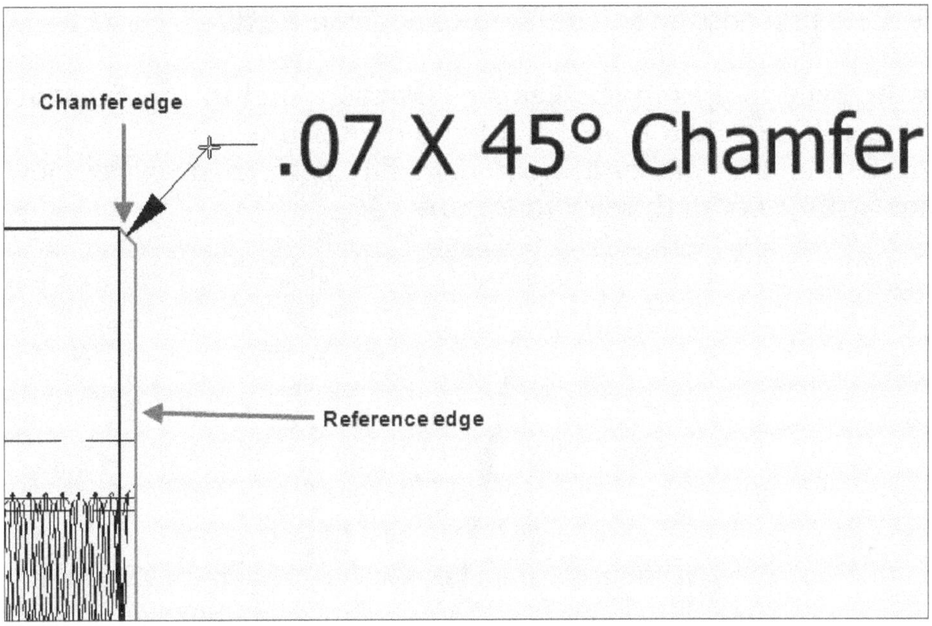

Figure-70. Chamfer dimension

- Click in the drawing area to place the dimension.
- Right-click in the drawing area and click on the **OK** button to exit the tool.

Punch Tool

The **Punch** tool is used to annotate punch mark of the sheetmetal flat pattern drawing views. The procedure to use this tool is given next.

- Click on the **Punch** tool from the **Feature Notes** panel in the **Annotate** tab of the **Ribbon**. You will be asked to select the punch geometry or punch center mark.
- Select the geometry of center mark of punch from the drawing view. The annotation will get attached to the cursor.
- Click in the drawing area to place the annotation. The annotation will be created; refer to Figure-71. You will be asked to select next punch mark or geometry for annotation.
- Select the entity if you want to annotate more punch marks otherwise press **ESC** from keyboard to exit the tool.

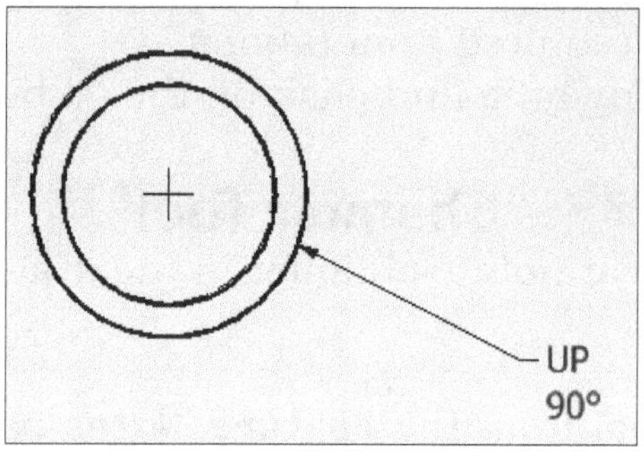

Figure-71. Punch mark annotation

Bend Tool

The **Bend** tool in the **Feature Notes** panel is used to create annotations for sheet metal bends. The procedure to use this tool is given next.

- Click on the **Bend** tool from the **Feature Notes** panel in the **Annotate** tab of the **Ribbon**. You will be asked to select a bend center line.
- Select the center line of bend created in flat pattern drawing view. The bend annotation will be created; refer to Figure-72.

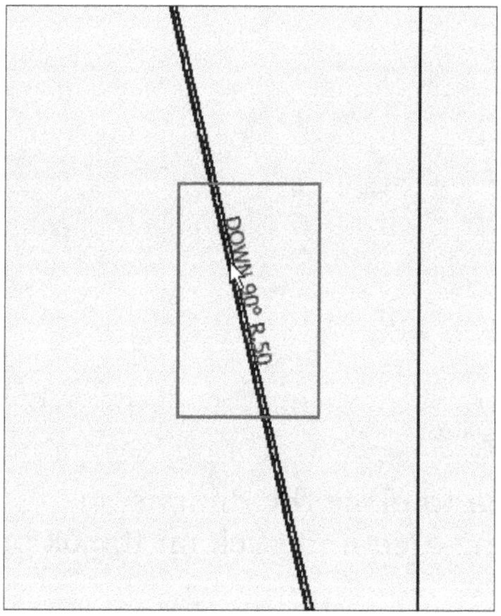

Figure-72. Bend annotation created

- Select the other bend lines to annotate them or press **ESC** to exit the tool.

Text Tool

The **Text** tool is used to write desired text in the drawing like, notes for manufacturer or machinist. The procedure to use this tool is given next.

- Click on the **Text** tool from the **Text** panel in the **Annotate** tab of the **Ribbon**. You will be asked to specify the location of the text.
- Click at desired location to place the text. The **Format Text** dialog box will be displayed as discussed earlier.
- Write desired text in the text box and set the formatting as required.
- Click on the **OK** button from the dialog box to create the text.
- Press **ESC** to exit the tool.

Leader Text

The **Leader Text** tool is used to create text with leader attached to it. The procedure to use this tool is given next.

- Click on the **Leader Text** tool from the **Text** panel in the **Annotate** tab of the **Ribbon**. You will be asked to click on a location.
- Click at desired location to specify the starting point of the leader.
- Click at desired locations to specify the other points of the leader and then right-click. A shortcut menu will be displayed.
- Select the **Continue** button from the shortcut menu. The **Format Text** dialog box will be displayed as discussed earlier.
- Set desired text and click on the **OK** button. The leader text will be created; refer to Figure-73.
- Press **ESC** from keyboard to exit the tool.

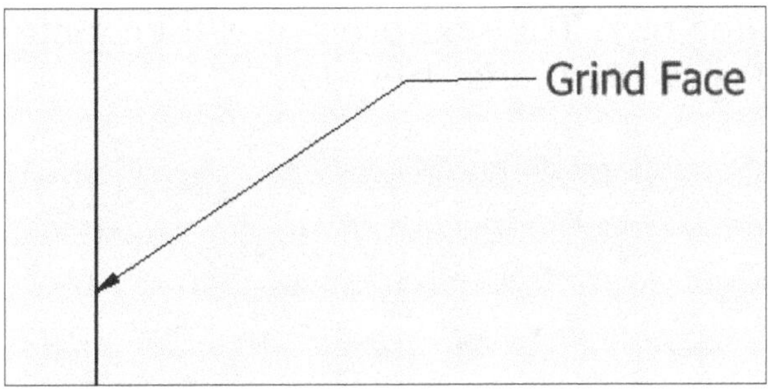

Figure-73. Leader text created

INSERTING SYMBOLS

The tools to insert drawing symbols in the drawing view are available in the **Symbols** panel of the **Annotate** tab in the **Ribbon**; refer to Figure-74. The tools in this panel are discussed next.

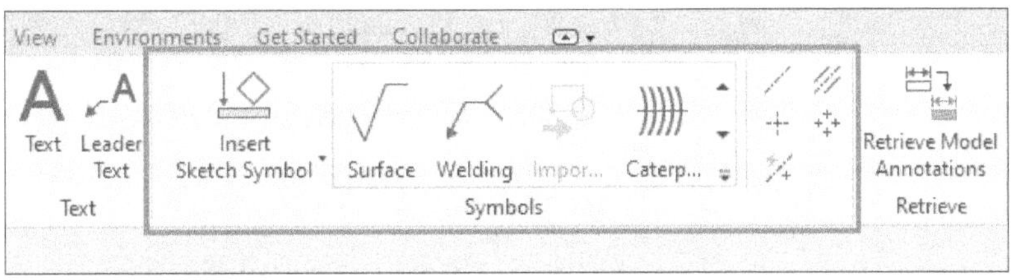

Figure-74. Symbols panel

Insert Sketch Symbol

The **Insert Sketch Symbol** tool is used to insert the symbols saved in local directory of drawing file. Before using this tool, you must have sketched symbols created by using the **Define New Symbol** tool in the **Symbols** panel. The procedure to create and insert symbols is discussed next.

Creating Symbol

- Click on the **Define New Symbol** tool from the **Insert Symbols** drop-down in the **Symbols** panel of the **Annotate** tab in the **Ribbon**; refer to Figure-75. The sketching environment will be displayed and you will be asked to create sketch of the symbol.

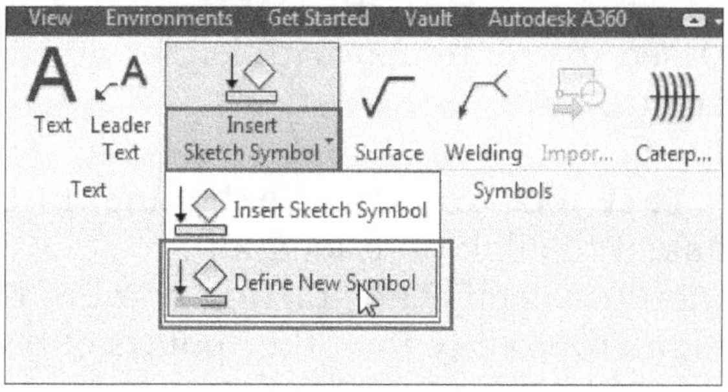

Figure-75. Define New Symbol tool

- If you want to be prompted for specifying text after placing the symbol then click on the **Text** tool from the **Create** panel in the **Sketch** contextual tab. Specify the location of text near the symbol by clicking. The **Format Text** dialog box will be displayed. Select the **Prompted Entry** option from the **Type** drop-down in the dialog box; refer to Figure-76. Set the other parameters and click on the **OK** button from the **Format Text** dialog box. The text prompt will be connected with the symbol; refer to Figure-77. Press **ESC** to exit the tool.

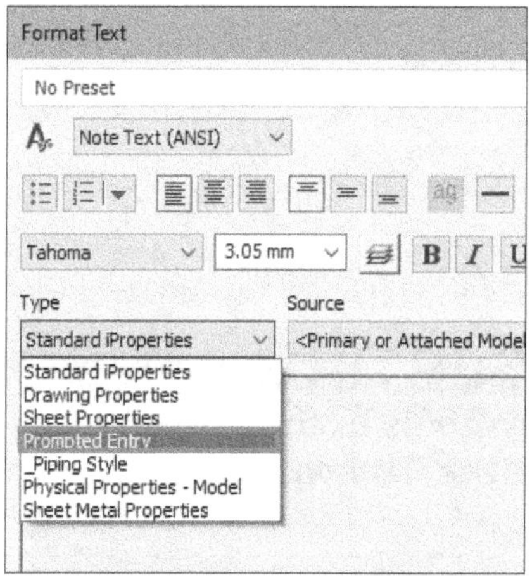

Figure-76. Prompted Entry option

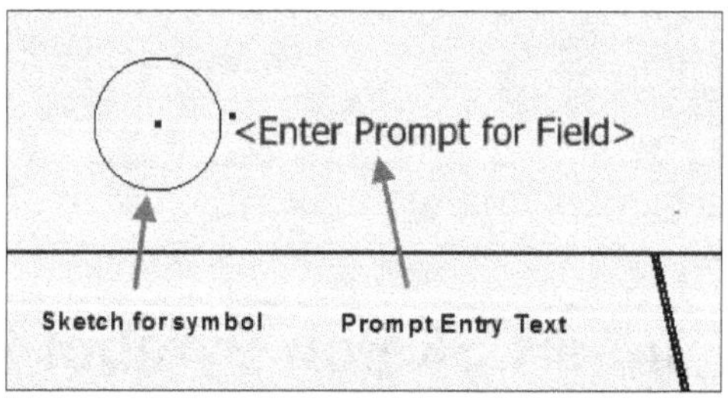

Figure-77. Sketch symbol created

- Click on the **Finish Sketch** button from the **Ribbon**. The **Sketched Symbol** dialog box will be displayed; refer to Figure-78.

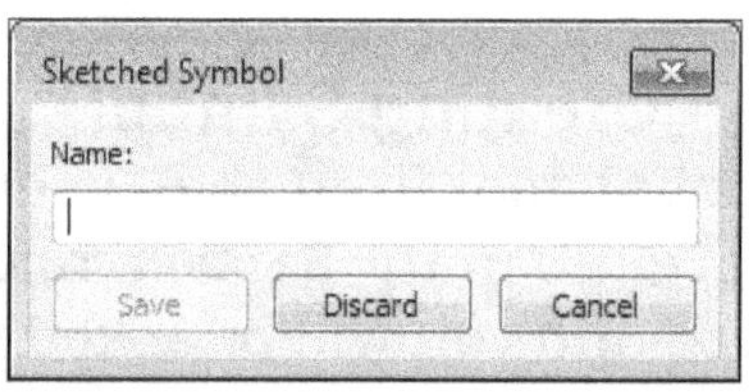

Figure-78. Sketched Symbol dialog box

- Specify the name of symbol in the **Name** edit box of dialog box and click on the **Save** button. The symbol will be added in the **Sketch Symbols** category of **Model Browse Bar**; refer to Figure-79.

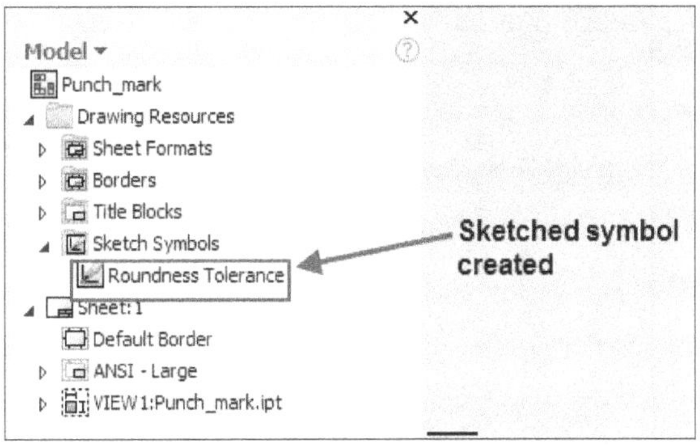

Figure-79. Symbol added in Model Browse Bar

Inserting Sketch Symbol

- Click on the **Insert Sketch Symbol** tool from the **Insert Symbol** drop-down in the **Symbols** panel of the **Annotate** tab in the **Ribbon**. The **Sketch Symbols** dialog box will be displayed; refer to Figure-80.

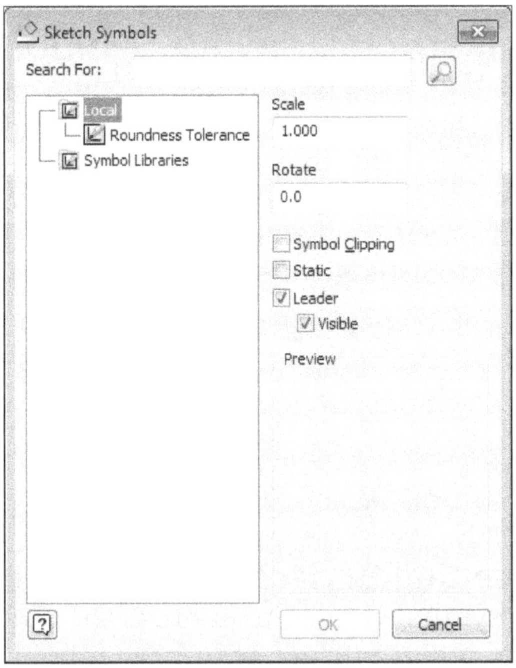

Figure-80. Sketch Symbols dialog box

- Select the symbol from the left area of the dialog box. Preview of the symbol will be displayed.
- Set the parameters like scale, rotation, symbol clipping, etc. in the dialog box and then click on the **OK** button. The symbol will get attached to the cursor and if you have selected the **Leader** check box in the dialog box then you will be asked to specify location of the leader start point.
- Click in the drawing area to specify starting position of symbol leader. You will be asked to specify next point of leader.
- Specify the next point(s) and right-click in the drawing area. A shortcut menu will be displayed.

- Click on the **Continue** button from the shortcut menu. If you have used the **Prompted Entry** option for symbol then **Prompted Texts** dialog box will be displayed; refer to Figure-81.

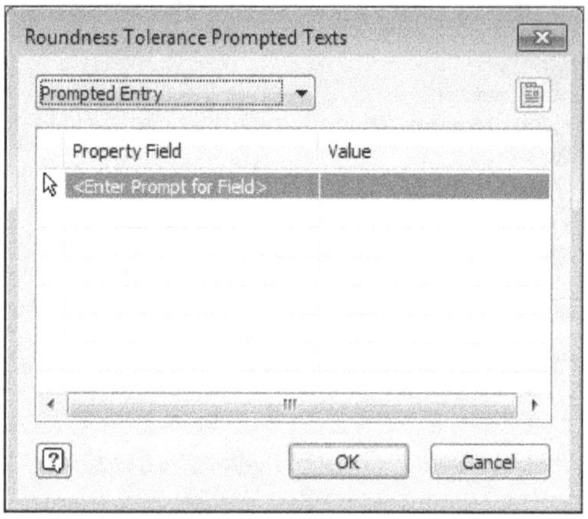

Figure-81. Prompted Texts dialog box

- Click in the **Value** field and specify desired text for symbol.
- Click on the **OK** button from the dialog box. The symbol will be created. Press **ESC** from keyboard to exit the tool.

Inserting Drawing Symbols

There are various symbols that we generally use in engineering drawings like surface finish symbol, Geometric Dimensioning and Tolerance (GD&T) symbols, welding symbols, datum symbols, and so on. In Autodesk Inventor, you do not need to create each and every symbol by using sketch as there are ready to use symbols available in the tool box of **Symbols** panel in the **Annotate** tab of **Ribbon**; refer to Figure-82. The procedure to insert symbols is given next.

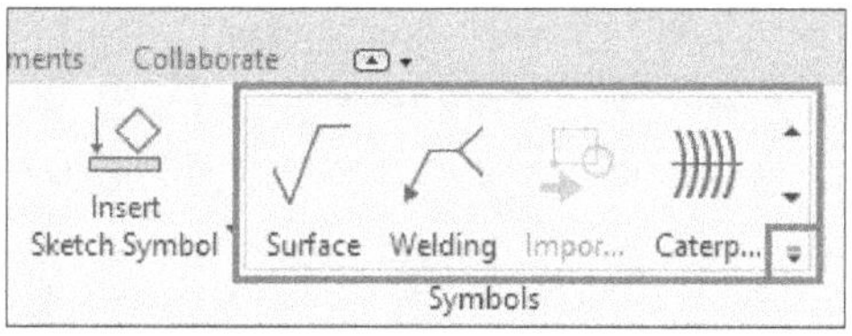

Figure-82. Toolbox in Symbols panel

Inserting Surface Texture Symbol

The Surface Texture symbol is used to express the material condition of surface of metal. The procedure to insert surface texture symbol is given next.

- Click on the **Surface** button in the toolbox of **Symbols** panel in the **Annotate** tab of **Ribbon**. The symbol will get attached to cursor.
- Click at desired location to place the symbol. If you want to create leader with symbol then move the cursor to desired location and click to specify the leader point. Once you have specified desired leader points, right-click and select the **Continue** button from the shortcut menu. If you do not want leader to be created with symbol then right-click after placing the symbol and select the **Continue** button from the shortcut menu. On doing so, the **Surface Texture** dialog box will be displayed; refer to Figure-83.

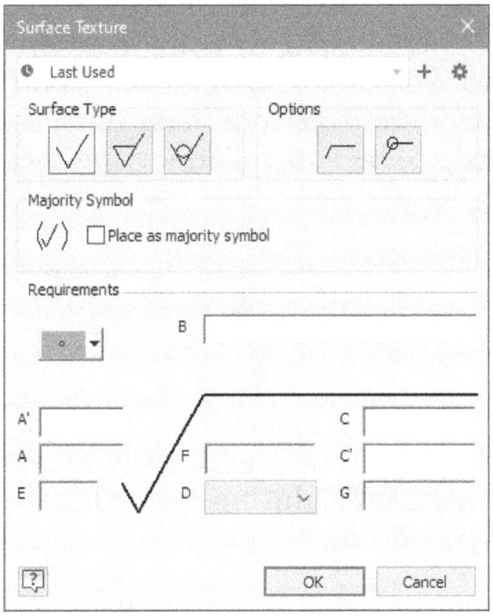

Figure-83. Surface Texture dialog box

- Select desired symbol type from **Surface Type** area of the dialog box.
- Specify the other parameters for the symbol and click on the **OK** button.
- Press **ESC** to exit the tool.

In the same way, you can use the other symbols in the toolbox.

Engineering Drawing Symbols

In this topic, you will learn about the common engineering symbols and their meanings in manufacturing.

Surface Texture Symbols or Surface Roughness Symbols

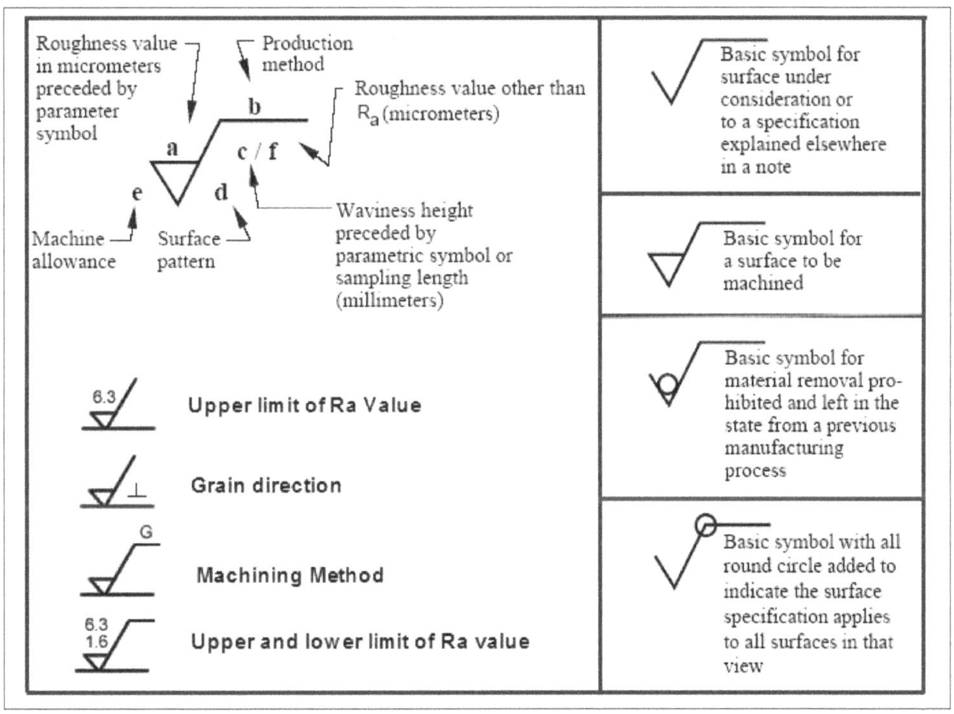

Datum Identifier

A datum is theoretical exact plane, axis, or point location that GD&T or dimensional tolerances are referenced to. You can think of them as an anchor for the entire part; where the other features are referenced from. A datum feature is usually an important functional feature that needs to be controlled during measurement as well.

All GD&T symbols except for the form tolerances (straightness, flatness, circularity, and cylindricity) can use datums to help specify what geometrical control is needed on the part. When it comes to GD&T, datum symbols are your starting points where all other features are referenced from.

Placement of Datum identifier is given in Figure-84.

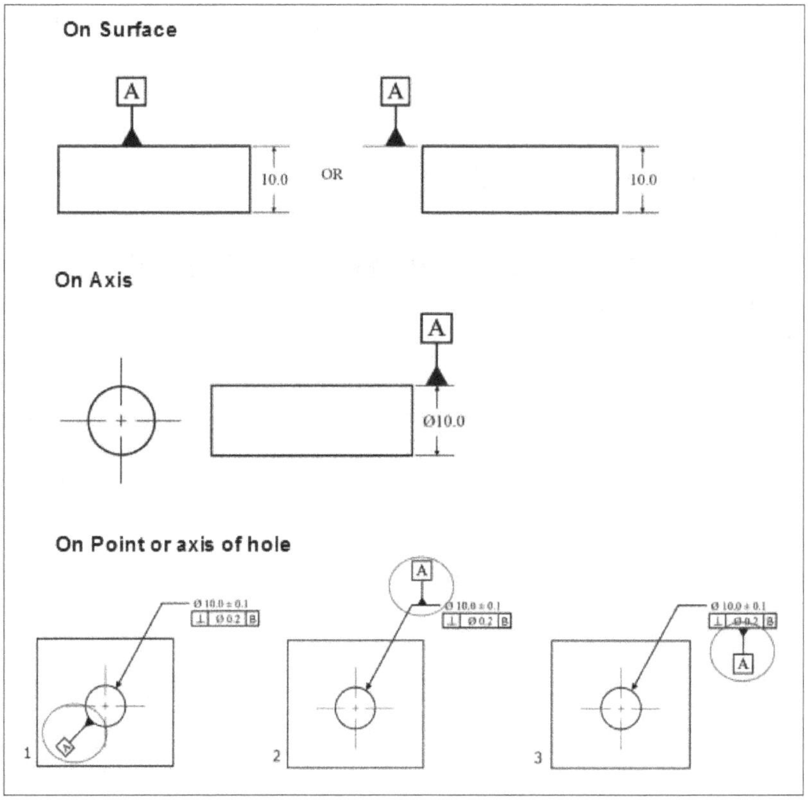

Figure-84. Placement of Datum Identifier

Datum Target Symbols

Some manufacturing processes, such as casting, forging, welding, and heat treating, are likely to produce uneven or irregular surfaces. Datum targets may be used to immobilize parts with such uneven or irregular surfaces. Datum targets may also be used to support irregular-shaped parts that are not easily mounted in a datum reference frame. Datum targets are used only when necessary because, once they are specified, costly manufacturing and inspection tooling is required to process them. The datum target is to be the place of contact (supports of the workpiece) for the manufacturing and inspection equipment.
Note that the upper half of datum target symbol is used only for circular targets and lower half gives Datum identifier with target number; refer to Figure-85. In datum target symbol, A1, A2, A3 are datum target areas and B1, B2 are datum target points and C1 is datum target line.

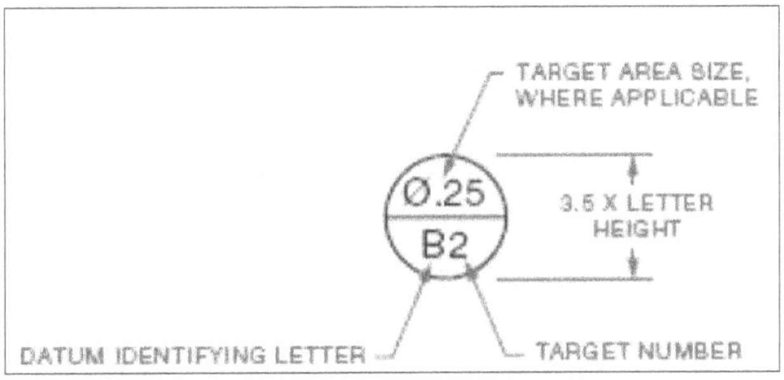

Figure-85. Datum target symbol

In Autodesk Inventor, we have five different tools to insert symbols for datum targets on different geometrical entities.

Feature Control Frame

The feature control frame is also known as GD&T box in laymen's language. The method to insert Feature Control Frame in drawing is same as discussed for Surface Finish symbol. In GD&T, a feature control frame is required to describe the conditions and tolerances of a geometric control on a part's feature. The feature control frame consists of four pieces of information:

1. GD&T symbol or control symbol
2. Tolerance zone type and dimensions
3. Tolerance zone modifiers: features of size, projections...
4. Datum references (if required by the GD&T symbol)

This information provides everything you need to determine what geometrical tolerance needs to be on the part and how to measure or determine if the part is in specification; refer to Figure-86. The common elements of feature control frame are discussed next.

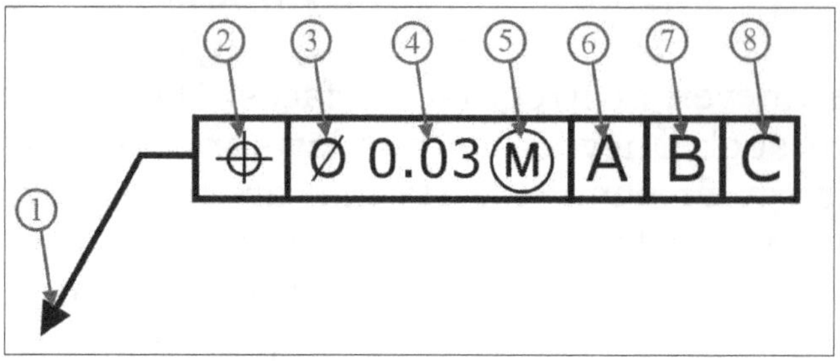

Figure-86. Feature control frame

1. **Leader Arrow** – This arrow points to the feature that the geometric control is placed on. If the arrow points to a surface then the surface is controlled by the GD&T. If it points to a diametric dimension then the axis is controlled by GD&T. The arrow is optional but helps clarify the feature being controlled.
2. **Geometric Symbol** – This is where your geometric control is specified.
3. **Diameter Symbol (if required)** – If the geometric control is a diametrical tolerance then the diameter symbol (Ø) will be in front of the tolerance value.
4. **Tolerance Value** – If the tolerance is a diameter, you will see the Ø symbol next to the dimension signifying a diametric tolerance zone. The tolerance of the GD&T is in same unit of measure that the drawing is written in.
5. **Feature of Size or Tolerance Modifiers (if required)** – This is where you call out max material condition or a projected tolerance in the feature control frame.
6. **Primary Datum (if required)** – If a datum is required, this is the main datum used for the GD&T control. The letter corresponds to a feature somewhere on the part which will be marked with the same letter. This is the datum that must be constrained first when measuring the part. Note: The order of the datum is important for measurement of the part. The primary datum is usually held in three places to fix 3 degrees of freedom.
7. **Secondary Datum (if required)** – If a secondary datum is required, it will be to the right of the primary datum. This letter corresponds to a feature somewhere on the part which will be marked with the same letter. During measurement, this is the datum fixated after the primary datum.
8. **Tertiary Datum (if required)** – If a third datum is required, it will be to the right of the secondary datum. This letter corresponds to a feature somewhere on the part which will be marked with the same letter. During measurement, this is the datum fixated last.

Reading Feature Control Frame

The feature control frame forms a kind of sentence when you read it. Below is how you would read the frame in order to describe the feature.

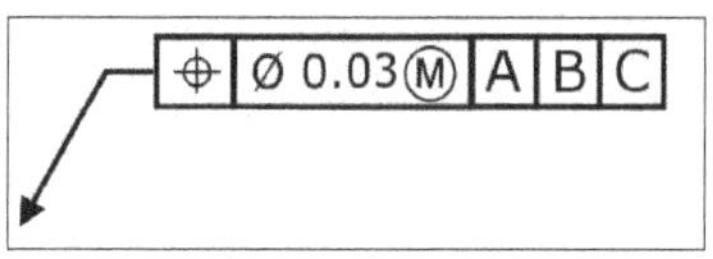

gives meaning of

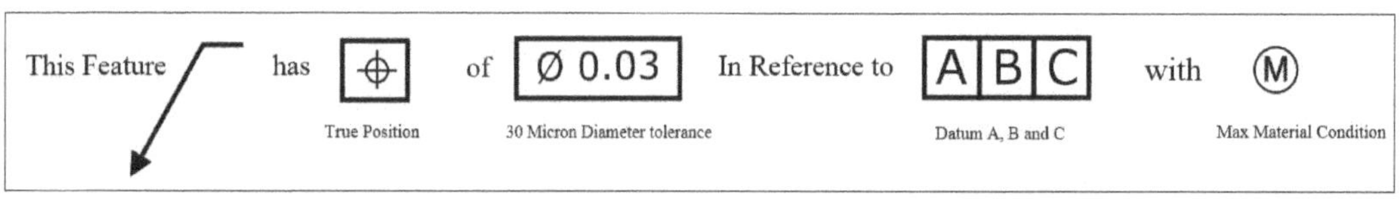

Meaning of various geometric symbols are given in Figure-87.

SYMBOL	CHARACTERISTICS	CATEGORY
⏤	Straightness	Form
▱	Flatness	
○	Circulatity	
⌭	Cylindricity	
⌒	Profile of a Line	Profile
⌓	Profile of Surface	
∠	Angularity	Orientation
⊥	Perpendicularity	
//	Parallelism	
⌖	Position	Location
◎	Concentricity	
⌯	Symmetry	
↗	Circular Runout	Runout
⌰	Total Runout	

Figure-87. Geometric Symbols

Figure-88 and Figure-89 shows the use of geometric tolerances in real-world.

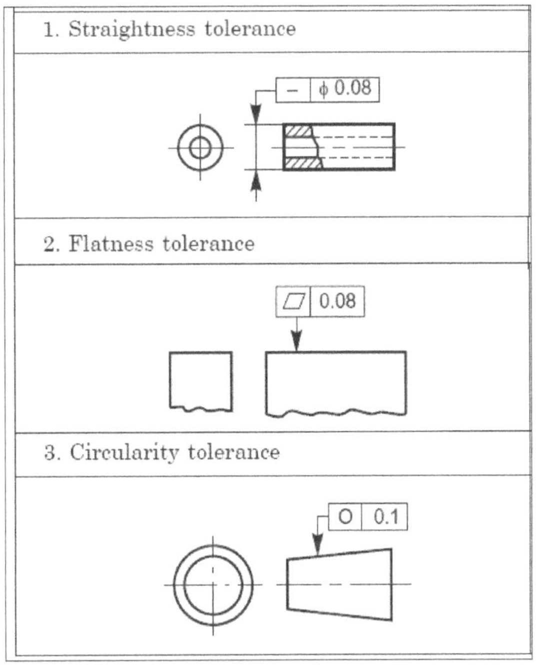

Figure-88. Use of geometric tolerance 1

Note that in applying most of the Geometrical tolerances, you need to define a datum plane like in Perpendicularity, Parallelism, and so on.

There are a few dimensioning symbols also used in geometric dimensioning and tolerances, which are given in Figure-90.

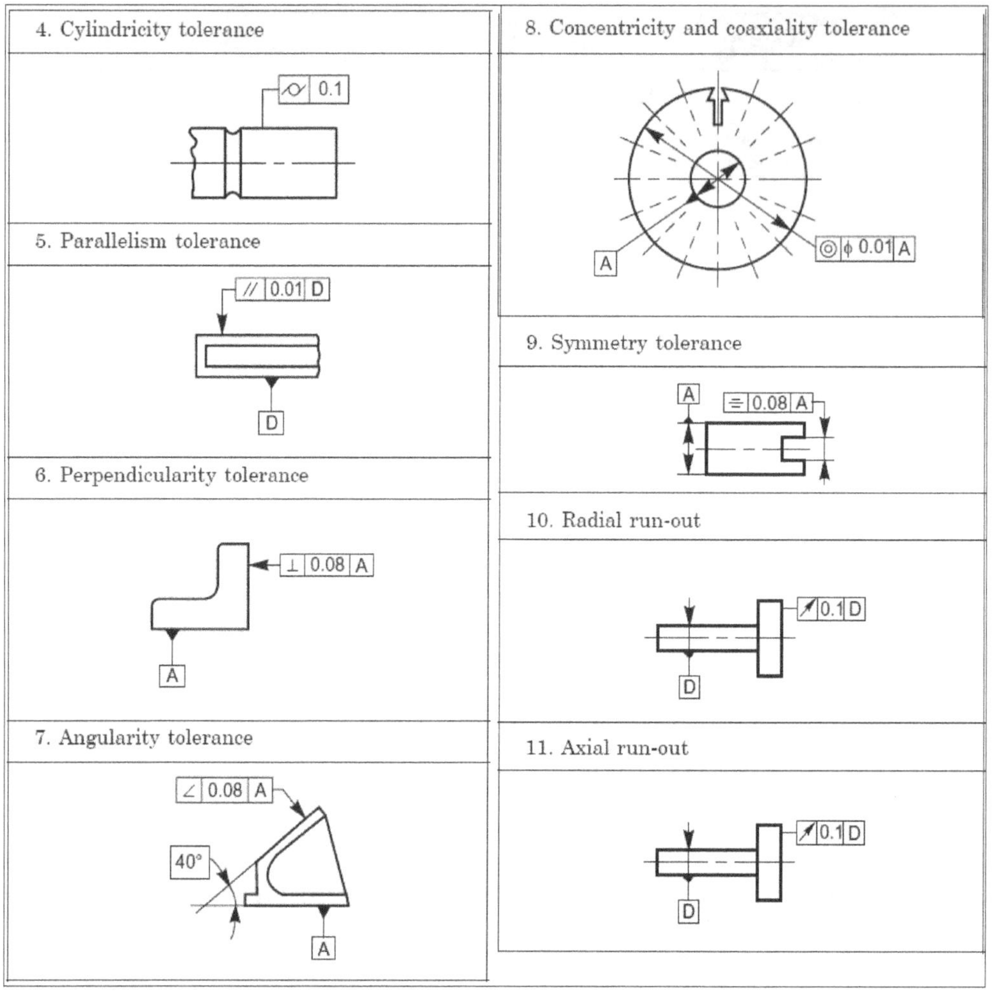

Figure-89. Use of geometric tolerance 2

Symbol	Meaning	Symbol	Meaning
Ⓛ	LMC – Least Material Condition	◀⊕	Dimension Origin
Ⓜ	MMC – Maximum Material Condition	⌴	Counterbore
Ⓣ	Tangent Plane	⌵	Countersink
Ⓟ	Projected Tolerance Zone	↧	Depth
Ⓕ	Free State	⌀↗	All Around
Ø	Diameter	↔	Between
R	Radius	✕	Target Point
SR	Spherical Radius	⌲	Conical Taper
SØ	Spherical Diameter	⌳	Slope
CR	Controlled Radius	□	Square
(ST)	Statistical Tolerance		
[77]	Basic Dimension		
(77)	Reference Dimension		
5X	Places		

Figure-90. Dimensioning symbols

INSERTING BILL OF MATERIALS (BOM)

Bill of Materials is used to display the parts of assembly in a tabulated form in the engineering drawing. There may be other informations like material of parts, number of parts, and so on. Note that we generally insert BOM in a drawing where exploded view of assembly is present so that we can also assign balloons to the parts in BOM. The procedure to insert Bill of Materials is given next.

- Click on the **Parts List** tool from the **Table** panel in the **Annotate** tab of the **Ribbon**. The **Parts List** dialog box will be displayed; refer to Figure-91. Also, you will be asked to select the view for BOM is being generated.

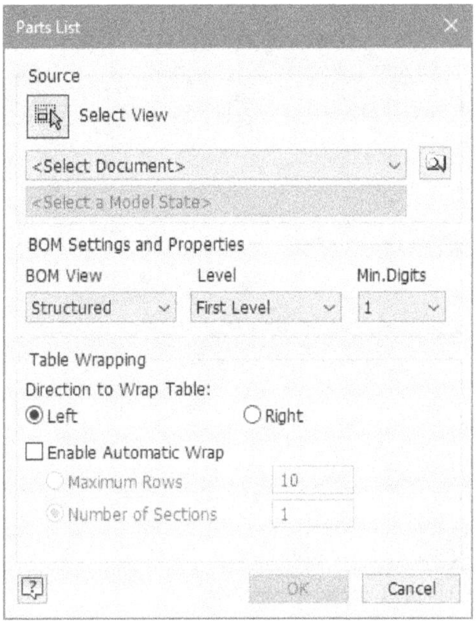

Figure-91. Parts List dialog box

- Select the drawing view from drawing area. The **OK** button will become active in the dialog box.
- Set the parameters in dialog box as required and then click on the **OK** button. The Bill of Material will get attached to cursor.
- Click at desired location in drawing to place the BOM; refer to Figure-92.

PARTS LIST			
ITEM	QTY	PART NUMBER	DESCRIPTION
1	1	Base	
2	1	Slider	
3	1	Slider Shaft	
4	1	Head Shaft	
5	1	Shaft handle	
6	2	Shaft Handle Head	
7	2	Block	
8	1	Shaft Housing	
9	1	Stopper	

Figure-92. Bill of Materials

Editing Bill of Materials

- Double-click on the Bill of Materials created. The **Parts List** dialog box will be displayed as shown in Figure-93.

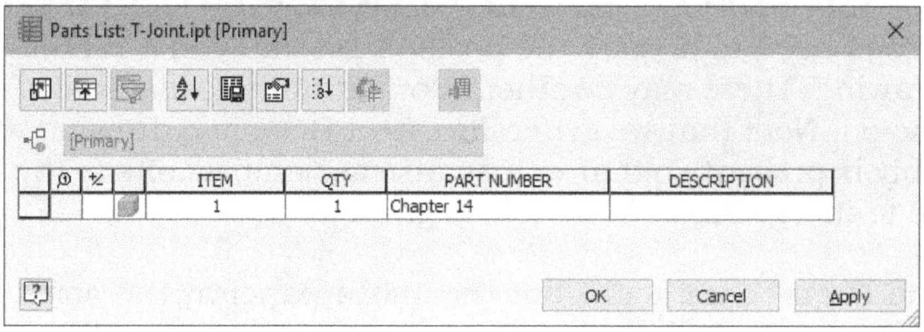

Figure-93. Parts List dialog box

- Click on the **Column Chooser** button from the dialog box. The **Parts List Column Chooser** dialog box will be displayed; refer to Figure-94.

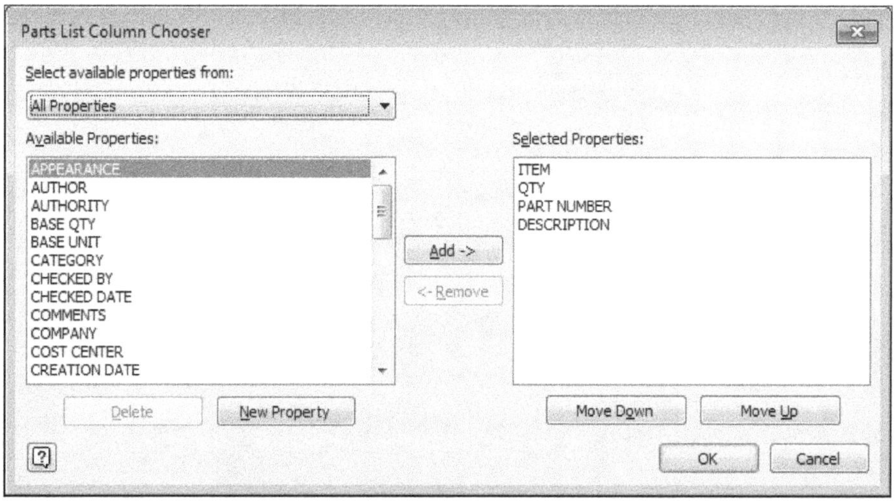

Figure-94. Part List Column Chooser dialog box

- Select the options in the **Available Properties** list box and click on the **Add** button to add column in BOM. To remove a column from BOM, select the option from **Selected Properties** list box and click on the **Remove** button from the dialog box.
- Click on the **OK** button to apply the changes.
- Set the other options in the **Parts List** dialog box as required and then click on the **OK** button.

Creating Balloons

Balloons are used to identify parts in the assembly as per the Bill Of Materials. The procedure to assign balloons to the parts is given next.

- Click on the **Balloon** tool from the **Table** panel in the **Annotate** tab of the **Ribbon**; refer to Figure-95. You will be asked to select a component.

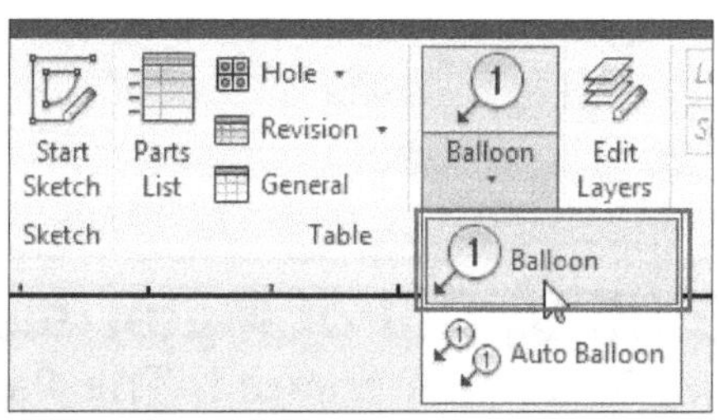

Figure-95. Balloon tool

- Select the component from the assembly. The balloon gets attached to the cursor; refer to Figure-96.

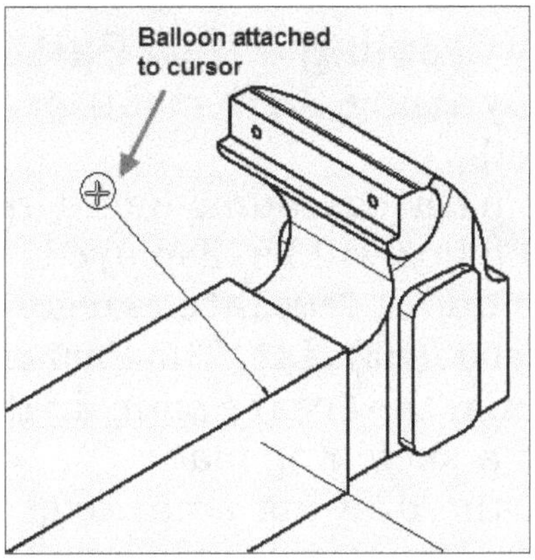

Figure-96. Balloon attached to cursor

- Click to specify the placement location and right-click in the drawing area. A shortcut menu will be displayed.
- Select the **Continue** button from the shortcut menu. The balloon will be placed and you will be asked to select the next part.
- Repeat the procedure for other parts and **Esc** button from keyboard to exit the tool.

You can also use the **Auto Balloon** tool to place balloons automatically.

Note that you can edit the style and standards of balloons, text size, feature control frame, datum identifiers, etc. by using the Styles Editor tool in the Styles and Standards panel of the Manage tab in the Ribbon as discussed earlier.

PRACTICAL

In this practical, you will first create the model of part as per the production drawing given in Figure-97 and then you will create the same production drawing of part using the model.

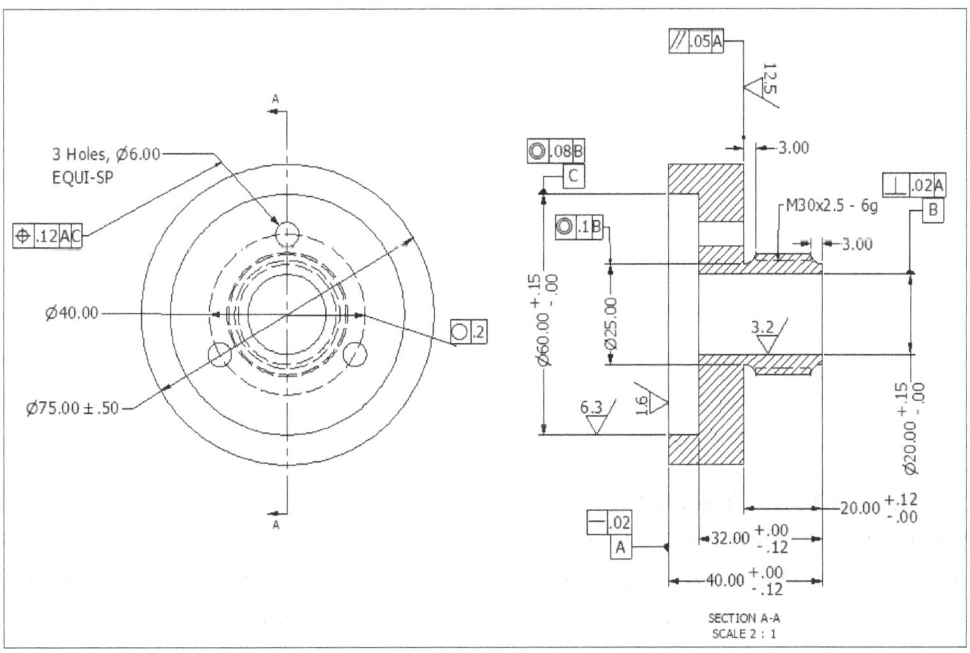

Figure-97. Production drawing for practical 1

If you see the model carefully then you will find that it is single part and can be created in Autodesk Inventor by Part Modeling. The steps to create the part are given next.

Creating a New Part

- Start Autodesk Inventor by using Start menu or icon on the desktop of your computer (If not started yet).
- Click on the **New** button from **New** cascading menu in the **File** menu of the **Ribbon**. The **Create New File** dialog box will be displayed.
- Click on the **Metric** folder under **Template** category in the left of the dialog box and double click on **Standard (mm).ipt**. The Part environment will be displayed.
- Click on the **Revolve** tool from the **Create** panel in the **3D Model** tab of the **Ribbon**. You will be asked to select a sketching plane.
- Select the **YZ Plane** from the drawing area; refer to Figure-98. The Sketching environment will be activated.

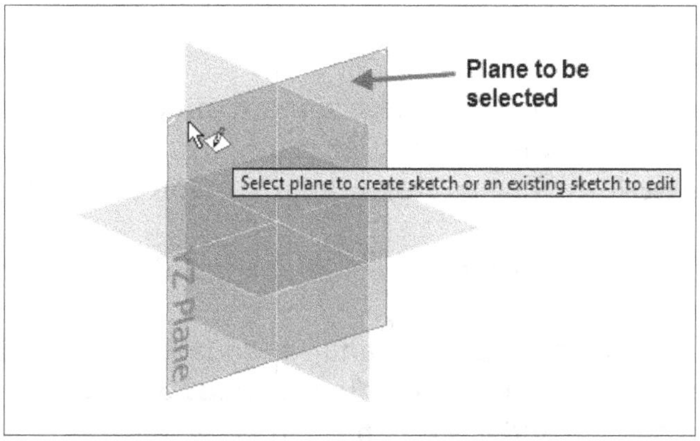

Figure-98. Selecting plane for sketch

- Create the sketch as shown in Figure-99 based on drawing.

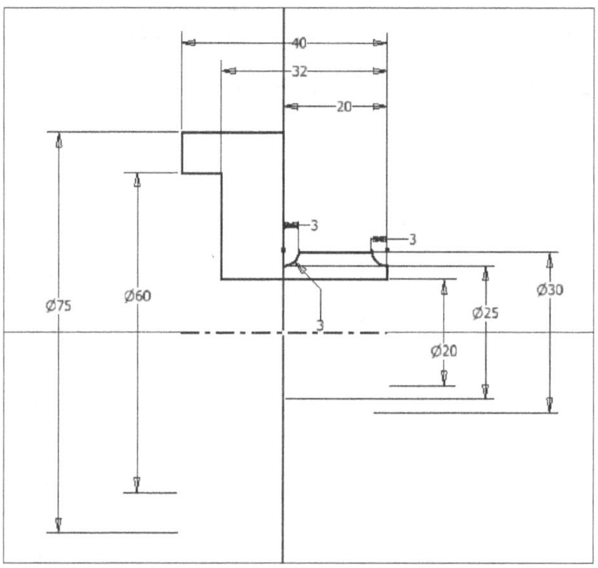

Figure-99. Creating sketch for revolve feature

- Click on the **Finish Sketch** button from the **Finish** drop-down in the **Exit** panel of the **Ribbon**. The sketch will be displayed.
- Click on the **Revolve** button from the **Sketch** contextual tab. The **Revolve** dialog box will be displayed and you will be asked to select the sketch to be revolve.

- Select the newly created sketch and axis to create the feature. Preview of the feature will be displayed; refer to Figure-100.

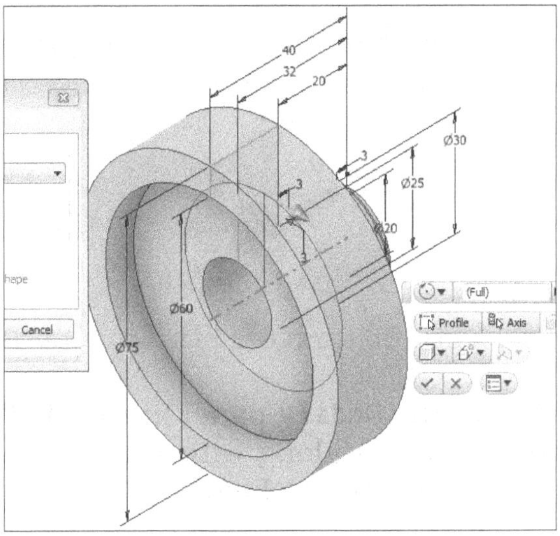

Figure-100. Preview of revolve feature

- Make sure the revolve feature is created as full round. Click on the **OK** button from the dialog box to create revolve feature.
- Click on the **Start 2D Sketch** tool from the **Sketch** panel in the **Ribbon**. You will be asked to select a plane/face.
- Click on the inner flat face of the revolve feature; refer to Figure-101. The sketching environment will be activated.

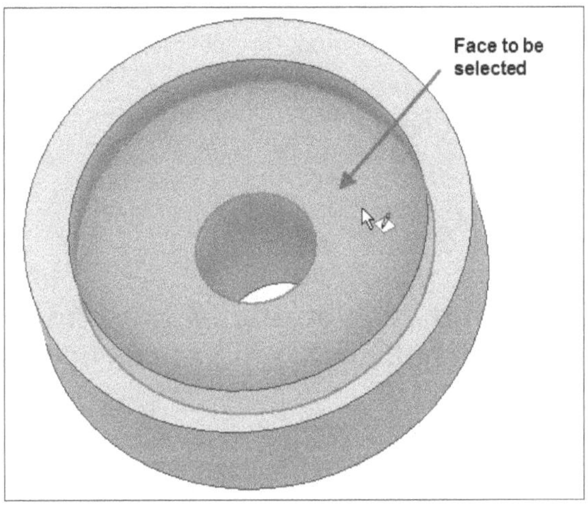

Figure-101. Face selected for creating sketch

- Click on the **Point** tool from the **Create** panel in the **Sketch** contextual tab of **Ribbon**. You will be asked to specify location of point.
- Move the cursor on Y axis in the sketch and specify coordinates as **0** along X and **20** along Y axis as shown in Figure-102. Press **ENTER** to create the point.

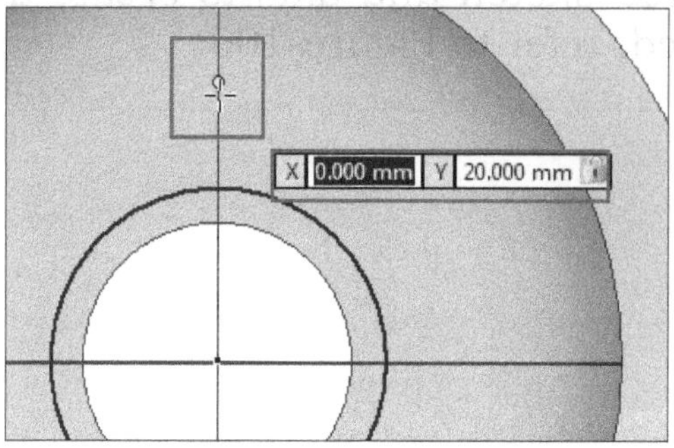

Figure-102. Specifying coordinates of point

- Click on the **Finish Sketch** button from the **Finish** drop-down to exit the Sketching environment.
- Click on the **Hole** tool from the **Modify** panel in the **3D Model** tab of **Ribbon**. The **Hole** dialog box will be displayed along with the preview of hole located at the sketched point created earlier; refer to Figure-103.

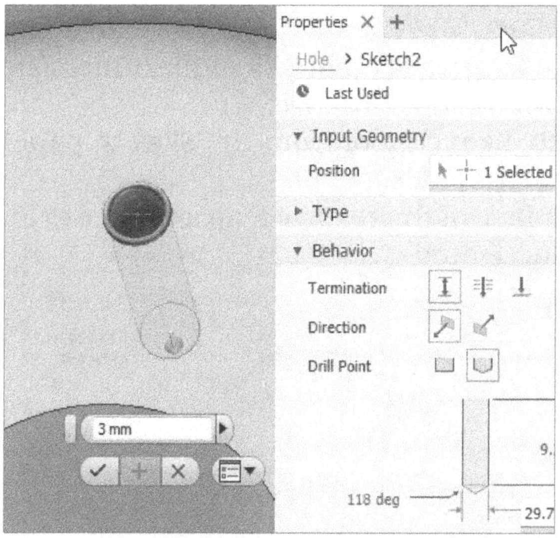

Figure-103. Preview of hole

- Set the hole size as **6** mm and click on the **OK** button from dialog box.
- Create the circular pattern of hole with 3 instances in 360 degree revolution; refer to Figure-104.

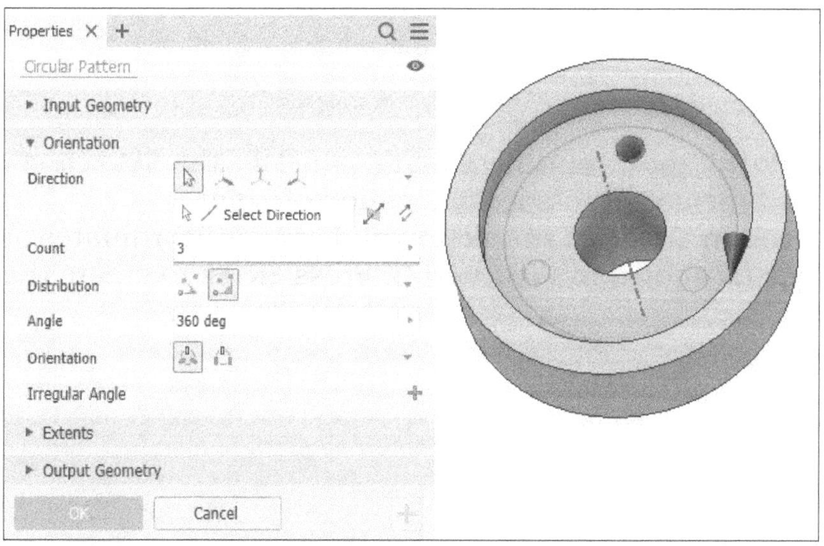

Figure-104. Preview of circular pattern

- Click on the **Thread** tool from the **Modify** panel in the **3D Model** tab of the **Ribbon**. The **Thread** dialog box will be displayed.
- Select the face of hub as shown in Figure-105. Preview of thread will be displayed.

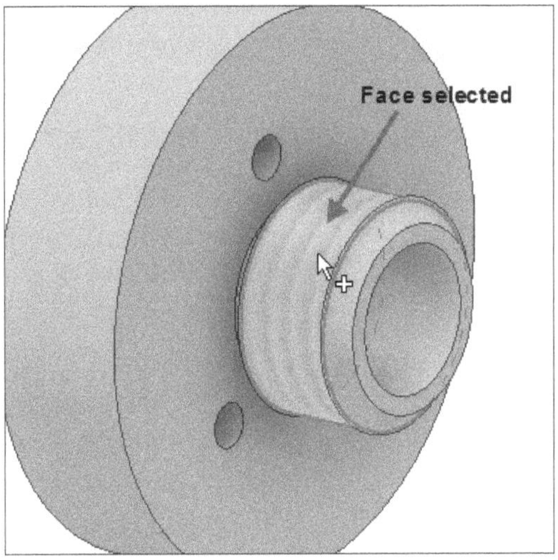

Figure-105. Face selected for Thread tool

- Click on the **Designation** drop-down from **Threads** area of the dialog box and select **M30x2.5** thread; refer to Figure-106.
- Click on the **OK** button from the dialog box.

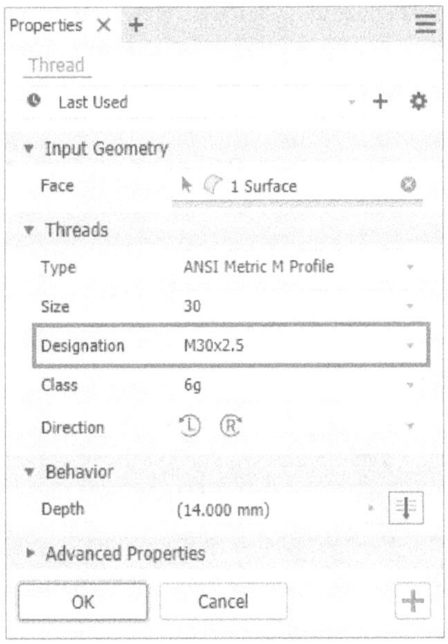

Figure-106. Thread selected in Thread dialog box

Starting A New Drawing

- Click on the **New** button from the **Quick Access Toolbar**. The **Create New File** dialog box will be displayed.
- Double-click on **ANSI(mm).idw** template in the dialog box (because we want the annotations in mm). The drawing environment will be displayed.

Placing Views

- Click on the **Base** tool from the **Create** panel in the **Place Views** tab of the **Ribbon**. The **Drawing View** dialog box will be displayed with preview of base view.

- Set the parameters as required and place the view at the left in the drawing area; refer to Figure-107.

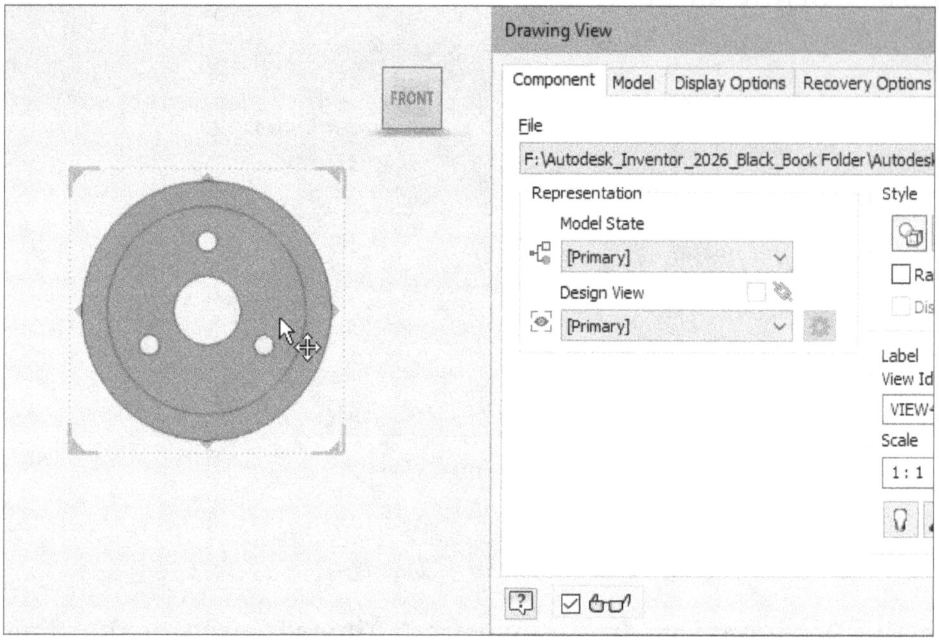

Figure-107. Placing drawing view

- Click on the **OK** button from the dialog box.
- Click on the **Section** tool from the **Create** panel in the **Place Views** tab of the **Ribbon**. You will be asked to select the view for sectioning.
- Select the view you have placed earlier. You will be asked to specify end points of the section line.
- Click at the points shown in Figure-108 and right-click. A shortcut menu will be displayed.

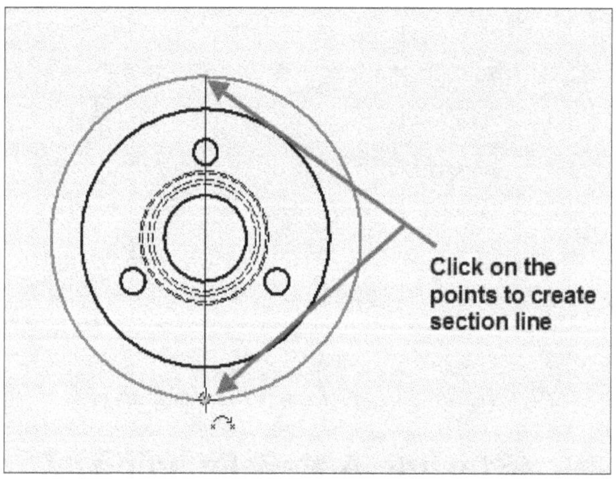

Figure-108. Points selected for section line

- Click on the **Continue** button from the shortcut menu. The preview of section will get attached to cursor.
- Click in the drawing at adequate distance from base view to place the section view.

Applying Annotations

- Click on the **Retrieve Model Annotations** tool from the **Retrieve** panel in the **Annotate** tab of the **Ribbon**. The **Retrieve Model Annotation** dialog box will be displayed. Also, you will be asked to select the view for retrieving dimensions.

- Select the section view created in drawing. The preview of dimensions will be displayed; refer to Figure-109. You will be asked to select the features or the dimensions to be retrieve.

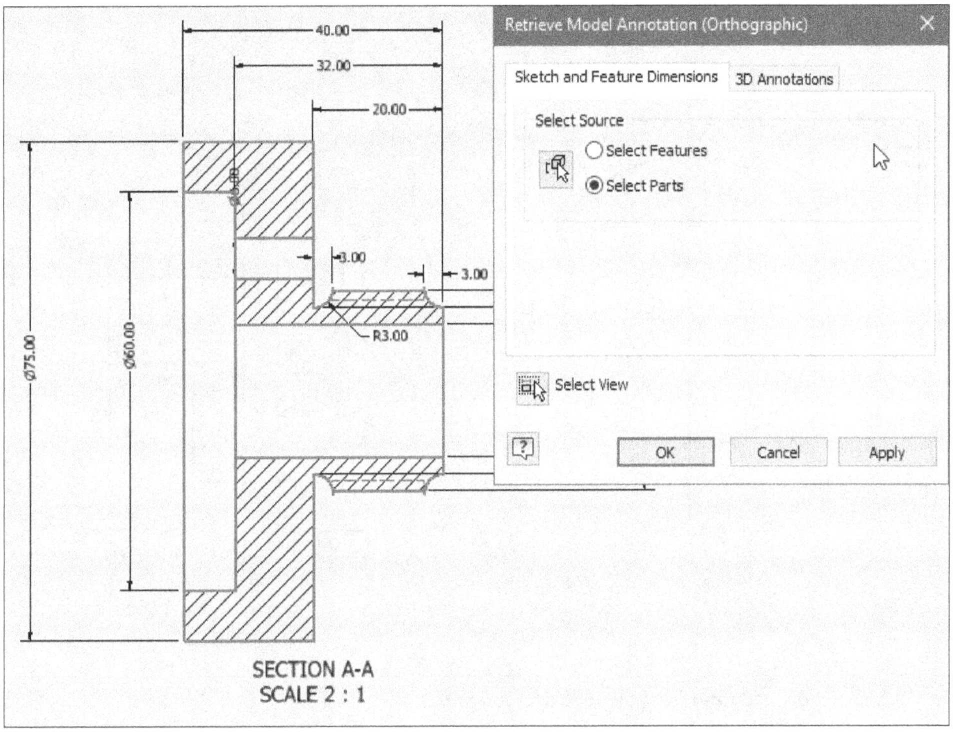

Figure-109. Preview of dimensions

- Select all the dimensions except diameter **6** dimension of hole.
- Click on the **Apply** button to apply dimensions to the view. You will be asked to select the next view for dimensioning.
- Select base view and repeat the procedure to create the dimension in base view.
- Click on the **OK** button to apply dimensions.
- Create the pitch circle for holes in the base view using sketching tools in **Sketch** tab of **Ribbon**; refer to Figure-110.

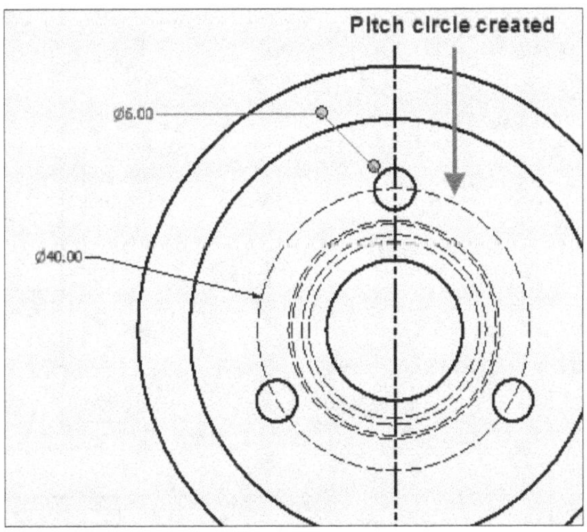

Figure-110. Pitch circle for holes

- Apply the symbols for Datum Identifier, Surface Finish, and Feature Control Frame; refer to Figure-111. Also, double-click on the dimensions and set tolerances as shown in the figure.

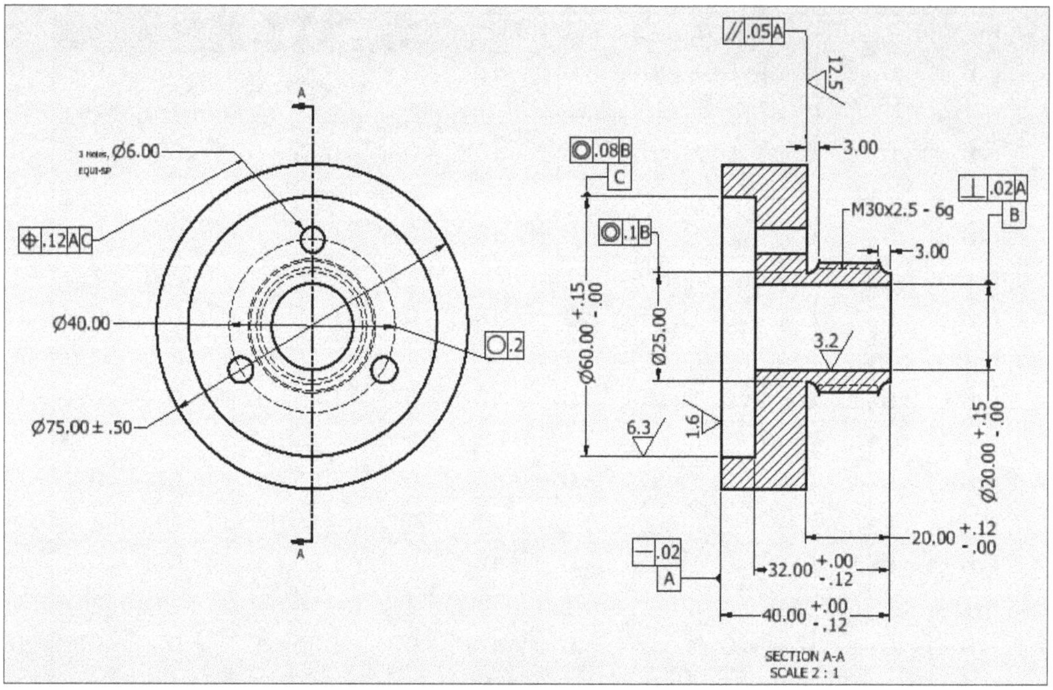

Figure-111. Drawing after applying symbols and tolerances

- Save the drawing using **CTRL+S** at desired location. Yes! It is common sense in Computer works.

Printing Drawing

- Right-click on the sheet from the **Model Browse Bar** and select the **Edit Sheet** from the shortcut menu. The **Edit Sheet** dialog box will be displayed.
- Select the size of sheet which is suitable to accommodate drawing views and annotations; refer to Figure-112.

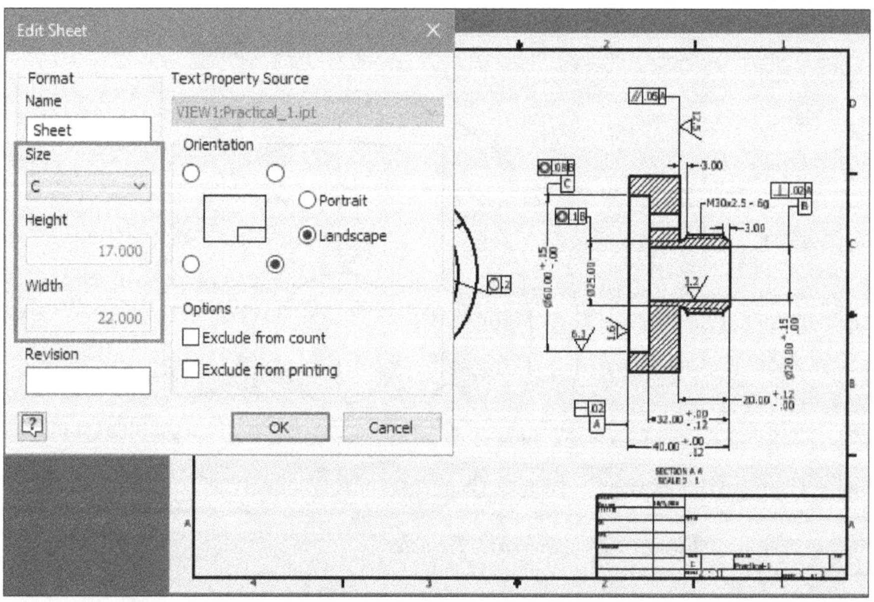

Figure-112. Changing size of sheet

- Press **CTRL+P** from keyboard. The **Print Drawing** dialog box will be displayed; refer to Figure-113.

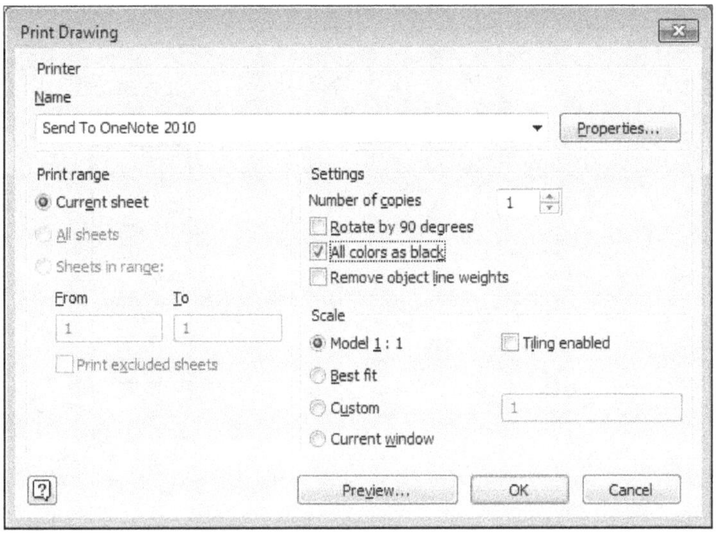

Figure-113. Print Drawing dialog box

- Select the printer from **Name** drop-down in the **Printer** area of the dialog box.
- Set the other parameters as required and then click on the **Preview** button. If you find the preview satisfactory then click on the **Print** button from the **Preview** window and then click on the **OK** button from the dialog box displayed. If you are not satisfied by preview then click on the **Close** button from preview window and make the changes; refer to Figure-114.

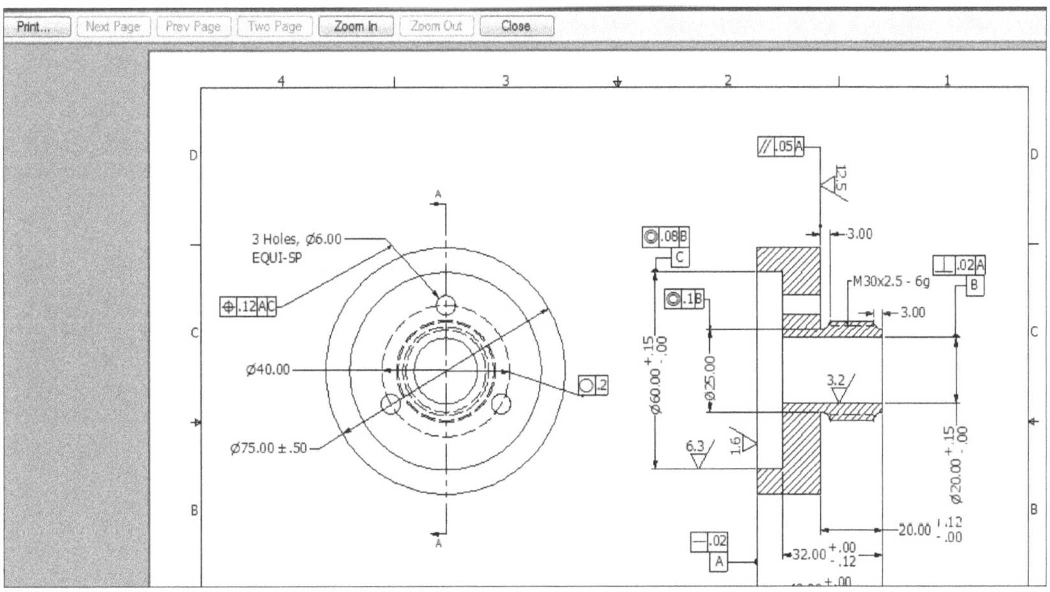

Figure-114. Partial preview of the drawing

PRACTICE 1

Create the model and drawing given in Figure-115.

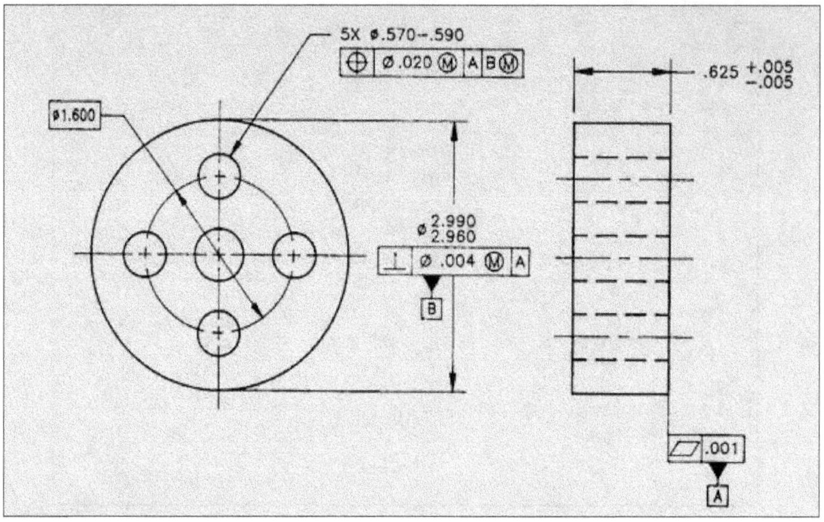

Figure-115. Practice 1

PRACTICE 2

Create the model and drawing given in Figure-116.

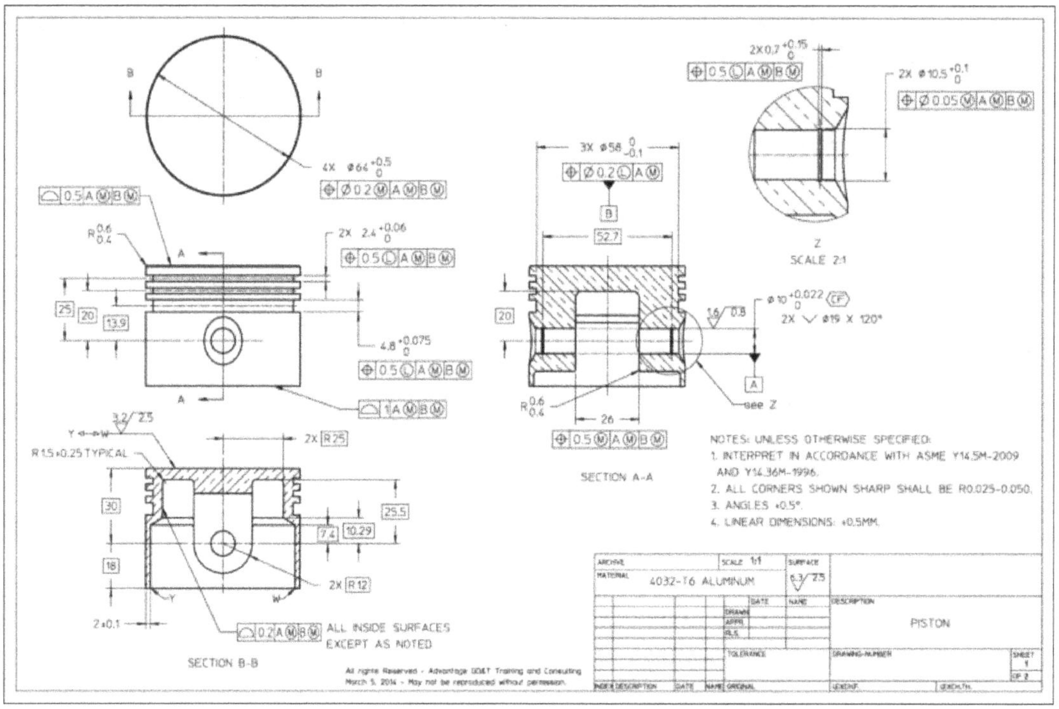

Figure-116. Practice 2

Note that the drawings given in this book are for practice purpose only.

SELF ASSESSMENT

Q1. Which of the following statements is correct about the phenomena of bidirectional associativity?

a) Any change made in modeling environment is also reflected in drawing environment.
b) Any change made in assembly environment is also reflected in drawing environment.
c) Any change made in drawing environment is not reflected in assembly environment.
d) Both a and b

Q2. What is the standard sheet size of A4 as per ISO-A used for plotting engineering drawings?

a) 594 x 841
b) 420 x 594
c) 297 x 420
d) 210 x 297

Q3. Which of the following information is not provided by the title block?

a) Title of the drawing
b) Roll Number
c) Symbol denoting the method of projection
d) Name of the firm

Q4. From which of the following views, the 3D objects are not represented on paper in engineering drawings?

a) Detail view
b) Orthographic view
c) Summary view
d) Both a and c

Q5. Which of the following tools is used to create the view to display the inner details of the solid model?

a) Projected View
b) Auxilliary View
c) Section View
d) Detail View

Q6. Which of the following tools is used to get all the modeling dimensions after placing the views?

a) Retrieve Model Annotations
b) Dimension
c) Chain Set
d) Ordinate Set

Q7. Which of the following dimension tool is used in manual CAM programming of a component?

a) Chain Set
b) Ordinate Set
c) Punch
d) Precision and Tolerance

Q8. Which of the following statements is correct about Datum Target Symbols in Engineering Drawings?

a) A1, A2, A3 are datum target areas and B1, B2 are datum target lines and C1 is datum target point.

b) A1, A2, A3 are datum target areas and B1, B2 are datum target points and C1 is datum target line.

c) A1, A2, A3 are datum target points and B1, B2 are datum target areas and C1 is datum target line.

d) None of the Above

Q9. Which of the following geometrical tolerances represent the cylindricity tolerance?

a)

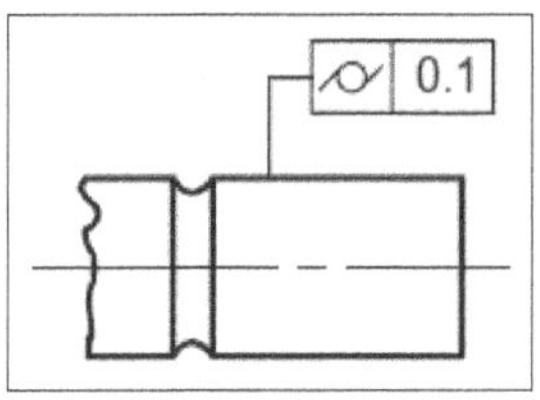

b)

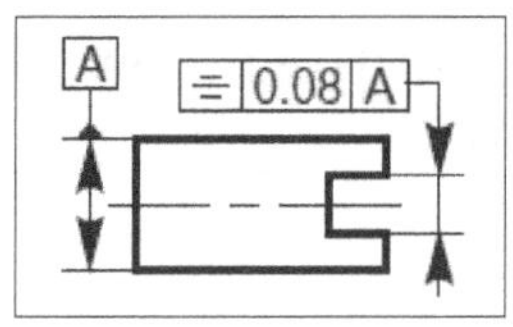

c)

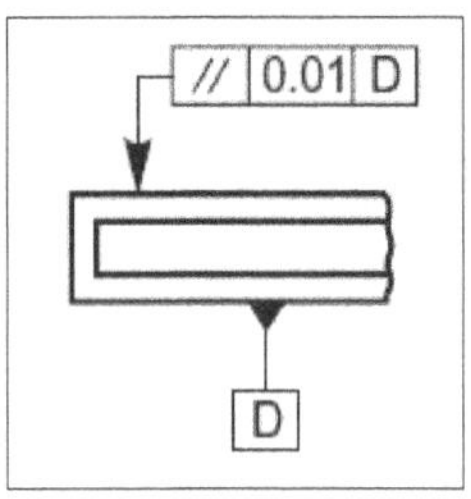

d)

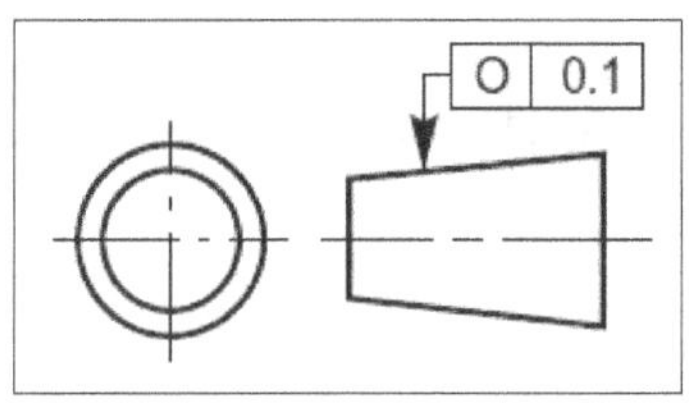

Q10. Bill of Materials is used to display the parts of assembly in a tabulated form in engineering drawing. (True/False)

Q11. In the Drawing View dialog box, select the .... check box if you want to generate pixel based views rather than accurate parametric views.

Q12. The .... also called multi-positional view, is used to represent various positions of components of assembly in single view.

REVIEW QUESTIONS

Q1. What is the term for the mutual update between modeling, assembly, and drawing environments in Autodesk Inventor?
A. Dual editing
B. Bidirectional associativity
C. Multi environment linking
D. Associative drafting

Q2. Which of the following is not mentioned as a reason for needing engineering drawings during manufacturing?
A. Operating CNC machines
B. Estimating budget
C. Conducting interviews
D. Performing quality checks

Q3. What are the two main types of engineering drawings for mechanical components?
A. Sketch and Blueprint
B. Part Drawing and Assembly Drawing
C. Section Drawing and Wireframe
D. Model Drawing and Rendering Drawing

Q4. What does the title block in an engineering drawing typically include?
A. Revision history and CAD commands
B. Drawing title, scale, projection symbol, and more
C. Wireframe view and coordinate system
D. Material list and texture details

Q5. Which of the following is an elongated paper size used in plotting drawings?
A. A1
B. A3 × 3
C. A4
D. A2

Q6. In Autodesk Inventor, where can you change the orientation of the drawing sheet?
A. Edit Title Block dialog
B. Drawing View dialog
C. Edit Sheet dialog
D. Properties menu

Q7. What is the first step to insert a base view in Autodesk Inventor Drawing environment?
A. Select the shaded view
B. Activate the desired sheet
C. Click on the Base tool in the Ribbon
D. Create a new assembly

Q8. Which drawing view gives a 3D appearance on a 2D paper?
A. Orthographic View
B. Detail View
C. Section View
D. Isometric View

Q9. In Third Angle Projection, where is the right side view placed in relation to the front view?
A. On the left
B. On the top
C. On the right
D. Below

Q10. How can you insert a new sheet in Autodesk Inventor?
A. From File > Insert Sheet
B. Click the New Sheet button in Place Views tab
C. Click Edit Sheet and select Add
D. Right-click title block and choose Add Sheet

Q11. What option must be selected to insert the flat pattern drawing view of a sheet metal model in Autodesk Inventor?
A. Folded Model
B. Flat Pattern
C. Bend Extents
D. Punch Center

Q12. Which checkbox enables display of the punch center mark in sheet metal drawing views?
A. Flat Pattern
B. Folded Model
C. Punch Center
D. Center Mark

Q13. Where are exploded views of assemblies created in Autodesk Inventor?
A. Drawing environment
B. Sketch environment
C. Presentation environment
D. Assembly environment

Q14. Which tool is used to change the projection type and view-related options in Inventor?
A. View Preferences
B. Styles Editor
C. Edit Sheet
D. Display Manager

Q15. What is used to adjust the decimal marker and unit system in Inventor's drawings?
A. View Preferences tab
B. Layers tab
C. Units area of Style and Standard Editor
D. Sheet Properties

Q16. Which tool is used to create projection views after placing the base view?
A. Base View
B. Section View
C. Projected
D. Slice

Q17. What type of drawing view allows you to represent features in true size for dimensioning purposes?
A. Isometric view
B. Auxiliary view
C. Detail view
D. Overlay view

Q18. What tool is used to create a section view of a component in Autodesk Inventor?
A. Break Out
B. Slice
C. Section View
D. Overlay

Q19. How do you change the hatch pattern in a section view?
A. Use the Hatch Style tool
B. Right-click the view and select Hatch Settings
C. Double-click on the hatching
D. Use the Modify panel

Q20. What type of view enlarges a portion of another drawing view for more precise annotation?
A. Detail View
B. Auxiliary View
C. Section View
D. Break Out View

Q21. What is the function of the Overlay view tool?
A. Enlarges specific part of model
B. Represents multiple positions of components in a single view
C. Creates a flat pattern
D. Displays internal sections of component

Q22. Which tool is used to break very long views in a drawing to fit them in a smaller sheet?
A. Slice
B. Break
C. Crop
D. Overlay

Q23. Before using the Break Out tool, which step must be performed?
A. Place a detail view
B. Create an auxiliary view
C. Create a closed sketch section
D. Insert base view

Q24. What sketch is required to use the Slice tool on a projected view?
A. Closed loop sketch
B. Open loop sketch
C. Rectangular sketch
D. Circular sketch

Q25. What happens when you use the Crop tool in a drawing view?
A. Crops model geometry permanently
B. Crops the selected portion of drawing view to display only the selected area
C. Slices the model for flat pattern
D. Adds break line to the component

Q26. What is the use of the Retrieve Model Annotations tool?
A. Import 2D sketches
B. Add annotations manually
C. Retrieve dimensions from 3D model
D. Export drawing to PDF

Q27. What is required for the Retrieve Model Annotations tool to work properly?
A. The model must be exploded
B. Dimensions must be applied in the modeling environment
C. Drawing sheet must be active
D. Base view must be hidden

Q28. What panel contains the Dimension tool in Autodesk Inventor?
A. View tab
B. Annotate tab
C. Place Views tab
D. Tools tab

Q29. Which dialog box is used to add text to a dimension in Autodesk Inventor?
A. Format Text dialog box
B. Style and Standard Editor
C. Edit Hatch Pattern
D. Properties dialog box

Q30. What does the Inspection Dimension tab allow you to define?
A. Units and projections
B. Hatch pattern style
C. Dimension text and format
D. Inspection criteria for the dimension

Q31. What is the main function of the Baseline Dimensioning tools?
A. Annotate chamfers
B. Create holes and threads
C. Create dimensions from a common base point
D. Insert datum symbols

Q32. What happens if you use the Baseline Set tool instead of the Baseline tool?
A. You can only create one dimension at a time
B. Dimensions created are grouped together
C. Only circular dimensions can be created
D. It disables the dimensioning

Q33. Ordinate dimensioning is particularly useful for:
A. Creating surface finish symbols
B. Manual CAM programming
C. Defining threads
D. Adding chamfer annotations

Q34. What is the first step when using the Ordinate or Ordinate Set tool?
A. Select dimension entities
B. Select geometry origin
C. Select the drawing view
D. Press ESC to begin

Q35. In Chain Dimensioning, the dimensions are:
A. Random
B. Unrelated
C. Linked one after the other
D. Grouped by diameter

Q36. When using the Hole and Thread tool, the user is prompted to:
A. Sketch the hole manually
B. Click the origin
C. Select thread/hole edges
D. Enter text annotation

Q37. Which tool is used to annotate chamfers?
A. Hole tool
B. Chamfer tool
C. Punch tool
D. Surface symbol tool

Q38. What does the Punch tool annotate in sheet metal drawings?
A. Holes
B. Threads
C. Punch marks
D. Datum lines

Q39. What is selected first when using the Bend tool?
A. Hole edge
B. Leader start point
C. Bend center line
D. Datum target

Q40. What does the Text tool allow you to add to a drawing?
A. Balloons
B. Symbols
C. Custom text or notes
D. Thread features

Q41. The Leader Text tool includes which of the following features?
A. Annotating only circles
B. Writing text without leaders
C. Text with attached leader lines
D. Only usable in 3D views

Q42. What must be created before using the Insert Sketch Symbol tool?
A. Datum identifier
B. Surface symbol
C. Sketched symbol
D. Leader text

Q43. What option must be selected for adding custom text prompts to a sketch symbol?
A. Leader
B. Prompted Entry
C. Continue
D. Annotate Text

Q44. What is the function of the Surface Texture symbol?
A. Indicates coordinate system
B. Shows tolerance
C. Shows material surface condition
D. Identifies part numbers

Q45. Datum identifiers serve what purpose in GD&T?
A. Add finishing textures
B. Create threads
C. Act as reference points
D. Generate BOM automatically

Q46. What are Datum Targets used for?
A. Defining thread depths
B. Measuring surface texture
C. Supporting irregular parts
D. Creating bend features

Q47. A feature control frame provides information on:
A. Dimensions and materials
B. Chamfer size only
C. Tolerances and geometric controls
D. Texture and threads

Q48. In a Feature Control Frame, the primary datum is:
A. Least important
B. Used only for circular parts
C. Fixed first during measurement
D. Always optional

Q49. The GD&T symbol for flatness would be placed in:
A. Datum target
B. BOM table
C. Feature control frame
D. Surface finish panel

Q50. The tool used to insert a BOM is found under which panel?
A. Symbols
B. Feature Notes
C. Table
D. Dimensions

Q51. What must be selected to activate the OK button when inserting a BOM?
A. Datum reference
B. Drawing view
C. Parts list icon
D. Table border

Q52. What does the Column Chooser allow you to do in the Parts List dialog box?
A. Place bend lines
B. Add or remove BOM columns
C. Insert symbols
D. Change units

Q53. The Balloon tool is used to:
A. Indicate surface finish
B. Annotate welds
C. Label parts in assembly
D. Mark datum planes

Q54. What does Auto Balloon do?
A. Removes all balloons
B. Adds balloons to all parts automatically
C. Only works in exploded views
D. Prompts user for datum

Q55. Which figure would you refer to for Feature Control Frame details?
A. Figure-78
B. Figure-66
C. Figure-86
D. Figure-91

Q56. To specify a text prompt in a sketched symbol, you use which dialog box?
A. Format Text
B. Parts List
C. Surface Finish
D. Insert Symbol

Q57. How do you exit most annotation tools?
A. Click Save
B. Click Create
C. Press ESC
D. Close Ribbon

Q58. What does the upper half of a datum target symbol represent?
A. Tolerance zone
B. Leader text
C. Circular target
D. Feature control

Q59. What does the Leader arrow in a Feature Control Frame indicate?
A. Drawing scale
B. Part orientation
C. The controlled feature
D. Text style

Q60. What is the significance of the primary, secondary, and tertiary datums?
A. Describe surface types
B. Indicate different drawing views
C. Define order of constraint during measurement
D. Only used in text annotations

Chapter 9

Application Management

Topics Covered

The major topics covered in this chapter are:

- ***Introduction***
- ***Managing Materials***
- ***Appearance***
- ***Application Options***
- ***Document Settings***
- ***Manage Tab***
- ***Styles Editor***
- ***Deriving and Importing Objects***
- ***Attaching Point Cloud Data***
- ***iParts, iMates, and iFeatures***
- ***Adding Rules***

INTRODUCTION

In previous chapters, you have learned about the tools used to create various objects and you have also performed various analyses to check the model for production. In this chapter, you will learn about the tools used for managing application level settings. You will also learn to customize various aspects of the software. These tools are available in **Tools**, **Manage**, and **View** tab of the **Ribbon**.

MANAGING MATERIALS

The **Material** tool in **Tools** tab is used to create and manage various materials applied to the models for representing physical properties of the object. The procedure to use this tool is given next.

- Click on the **Material** tool from the **Material and Appearance** panel in the **Tools** tab of the **Ribbon**. The **Material Browser** will be displayed; refer to Figure-1.

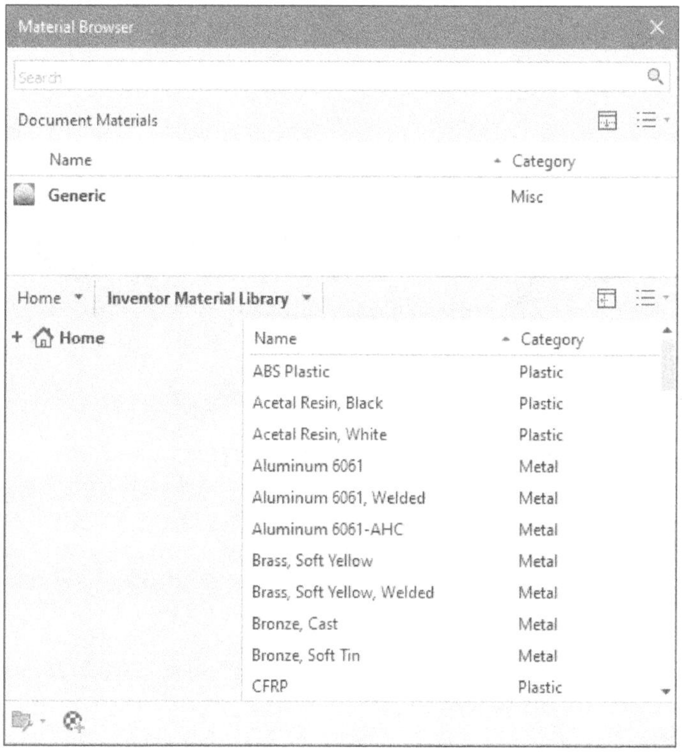

Figure-1. Material Browser

- To apply a material to current part model, select the desired material from the list of materials in the **Material Browser**. By default, the **Inventor Material Library** is selected in the **Browser**. If you want to use another library installed in your system then click on the down button next to **Home** tile and select desired library option; refer to Figure-2.

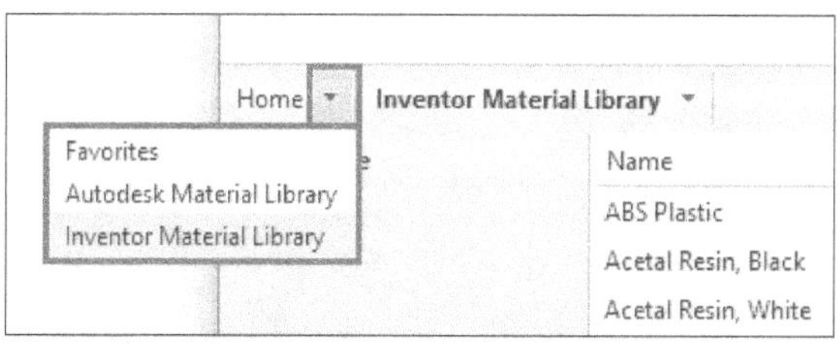

Figure-2. Material library drop-down

- You can filter the list of materials by selecting desired category from the drop-down displayed on clicking down button next to Inventor Material Library tile; refer to Figure-3. For example if you want to use metals in model then select the **Metal** option from the drop-down.

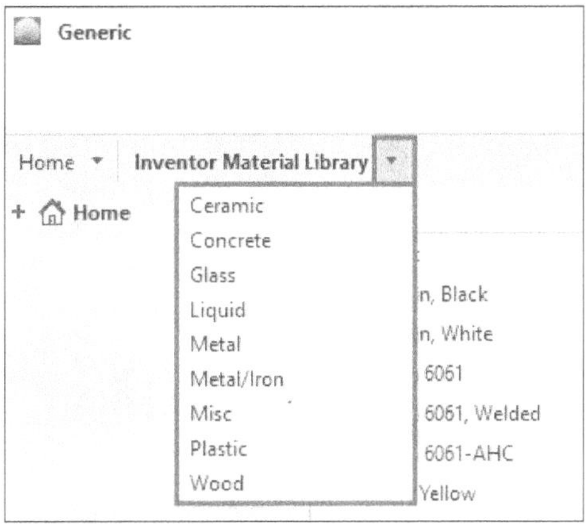

Figure-3. Category drop-down

- If you want to change the style of displaying material in the **Browser** then click on the **View Type** button from the dialog. A drop-down will be displayed with options to modify view style; refer to Figure-4.

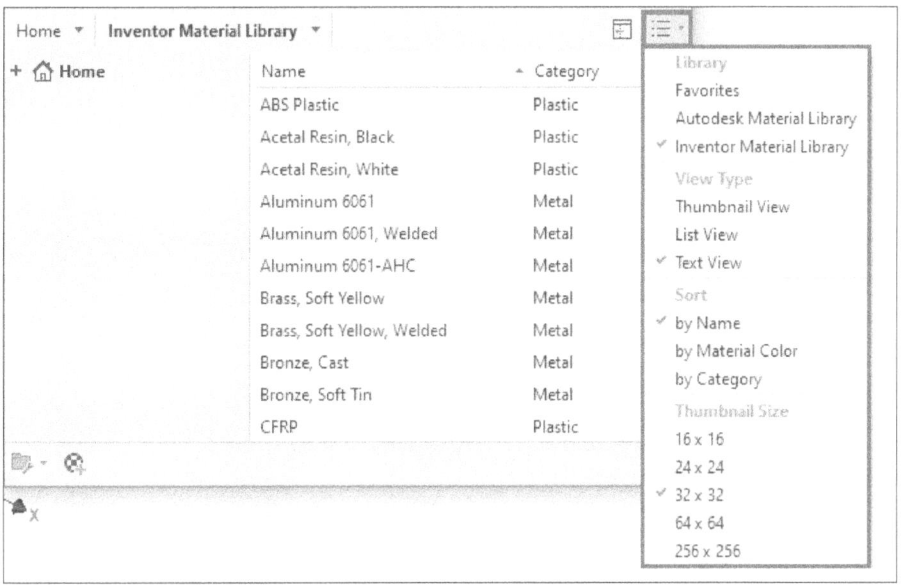

Figure-4. View Type drop-down

- Set desired options in the drop-down. The materials will be displayed accordingly in the **Browser**; refer to Figure-5.

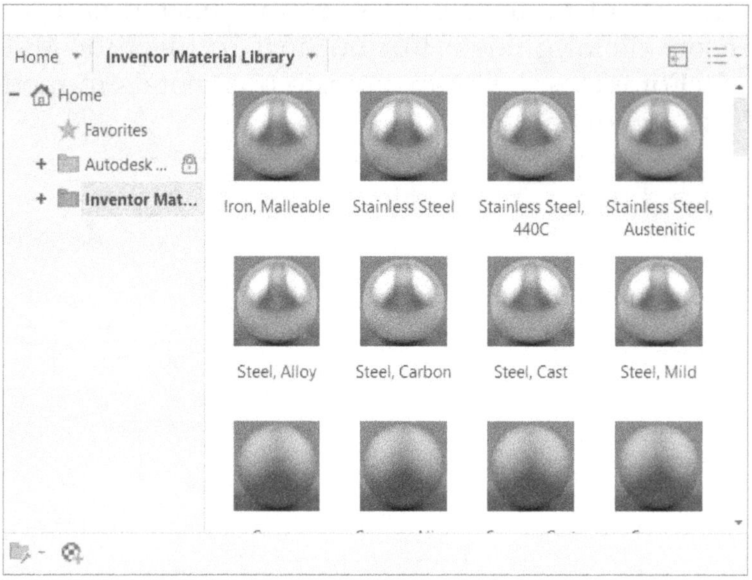

Figure-5. Material displayed in Thumbnail view

- To add materials in the current document, hover the cursor on desired material and click on the **Adds material to document** button; refer to Figure-6. You can add multiple materials to the document for checking different variations of the model.

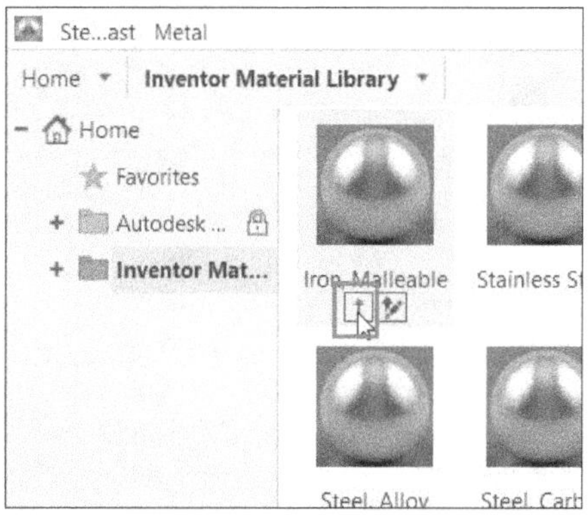

Figure-6. Adds material to document button

Editing Materials

- If you want to edit the properties of material before adding to document then click on the **Adds material to document and displays in editor** button after hovering cursor on desired material in the **Material Browser**; refer to Figure-7. The **Material Editor** dialog box will be displayed; refer to Figure-8.

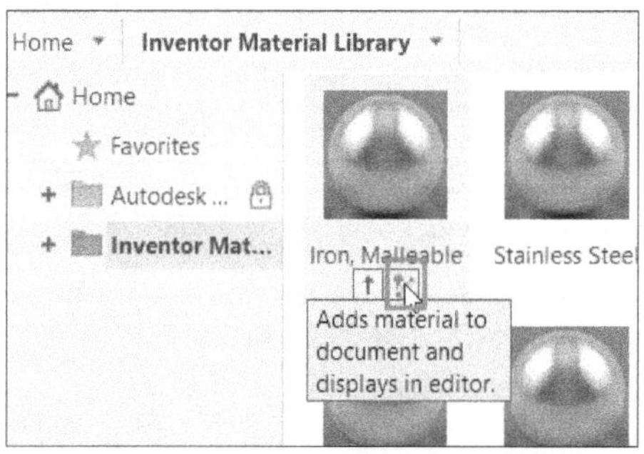

Figure-7. Adds material to document and displays in editor button

Figure-8. Material Editor dialog box

- The options in various tabs of this dialog box change based on material type. Specify the parameters and click on the **OK** button to modify material and apply to the document. Various parameters related to material are discussed in next topic.

General Parameters of Materials

There are three categories in which properties of materials are defined: Identity, Appearance, and Physical. These categories are available as tabs in the **Material Editor** dialog box when you edit a material or create a new material; refer to Figure-8. The parameters specified in these tabs are discussed next.

Identity Parameters (common for all type of materials)

The parameters of **Identity** tab are used to define description and type of material, manufacturer of material, cost of material and other related data. These parameters are discussed next.

- Specify desired text in the **Description** edit box to add user-define description of material which can be used to identify general use of the material.
- Select desired option from the **Type** drop-down to define type of the material. Note that the type selected here will define the category in which material will be placed in Material Library.
- Specify desired text in the **Comments** edit box to define comments about the material meant to warn or notify the user of material. Like, material is fragile, material is explosive, and so on.
- Specify desired identification keywords in the **Keywords** edit box separated by comma (,) to enable fast filtering of material in the browser based on specified keywords.

- The options in **Product Information** section of this tab are used when generating reports for production or performing cost calculations. Specify desired text in the **Manufacturer** edit box to define the name of vendor from whom your organization purchases the material.
- Specify desired value in the **Model** edit box to define model number of material if provided by your manufacturer.
- Specify desired value in the **Cost** edit box to define cost of material. Note that value specified in this edit box is in the form of text which is not used for any mathematical formula.
- Specify desired value in the **URL** edit box to define website link for the material. If you have Revit installed in your system then you will also find options for **Revit Annotation Information** category. Specify the parameters as discussed earlier.

Any modification in appearance of material does not affect the results of analysis but they can make huge difference when generating rendered images of model. Some important parameters of all five categories of material appearances are discussed next.

Appearance Tab (For metal type materials)

If you are defining parameters of appearance for a metal type material then options in the **Material Editor** will be displayed as shown in Figure-9.

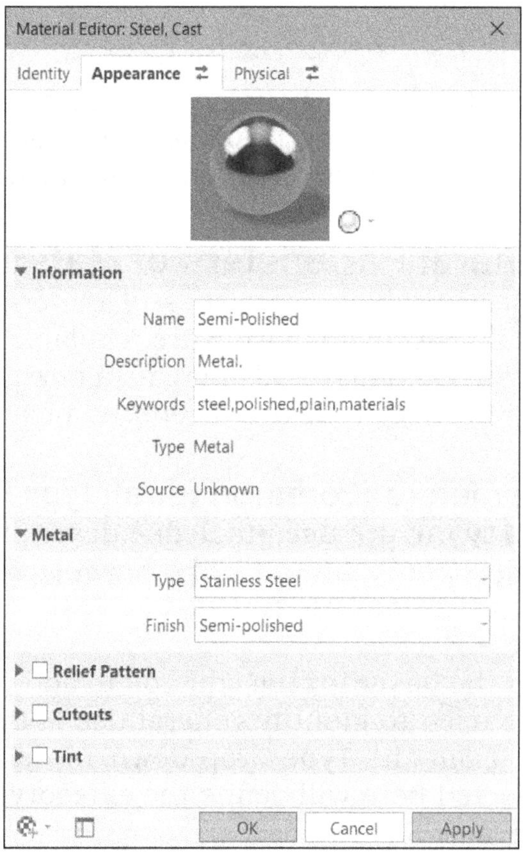

Figure-9. Appearance tab for metal type

- The options in the **Information** section of dialog box are used to define general information about the appearance of material so that user can easily identify the type of material. In this section, you need to specify name, description, and keywords for the material.

- The options in the **Metal** section are used to define color and roughness of surface of material. Click in the field for **Type** option and select desired metallic color. Using the options in **Finish** field, you can define the roughness of surface of material for reflectivity.
- Select the **Relief Pattern** check box to add bumps in the texture of material. Bumps create an illusion of irregularities generally found on surfaces of real objects; refer to Figure-10. Select desired pattern for relief in the **Type** drop-down. Set desired value in **Amount** field to define depth of the bump. Using the **Scale** field, you can define the size of bump. Note that a larger value in **Scale** field means finer pattern. The appearance of material will be modified accordingly.

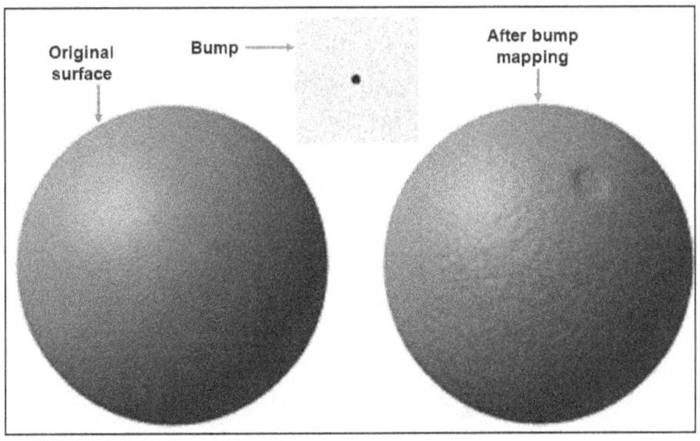

Figure-10. Bump mapping

- Select the **Cutout** check box to make net like texture of material where some portion of material will be transparent and some portion will be opaque; refer to Figure-11. After selecting check box, set desired cutout pattern in the **Type** drop-down and specify related parameters as discussed earlier.

Figure-11. Cutout texture

- Select the **Tint** check box to add shade of selected color to the material surface.

Appearance Tab (Generic)

If you are defining parameters of appearance for generic type material then options in **Material Editor** will be displayed as shown in Figure-12. Most of the options in this tab are same as discussed for metals. The other options of this tab are discussed next.

- Expand the **Generic** node to modify basic appearance of material. Click in the **Color** field and specify desired color for the model. If you want to use image as appearance texture then click in the **Image** field. The **Texture Editor** window will be displayed; refer to Figure-13. Click in the **Source** field of window and select desired image file. Set the other parameters as desired in the window and close it using button on top-right corner.

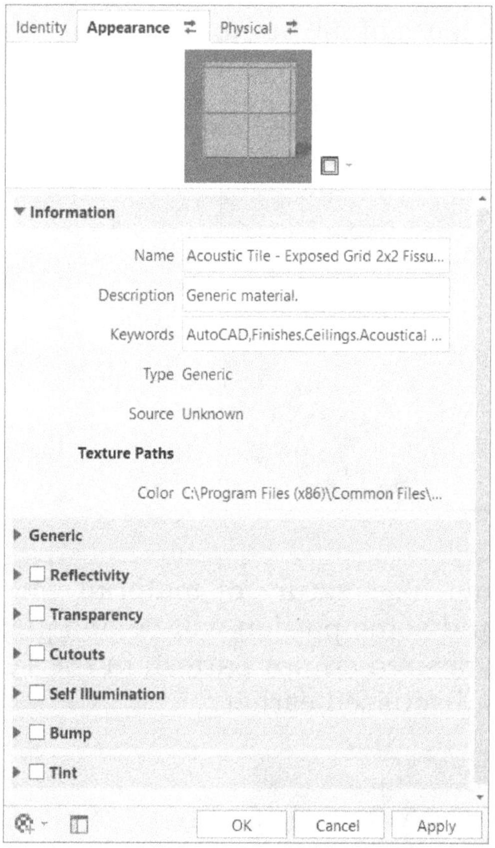

Figure-12. Appearance tab for generic type

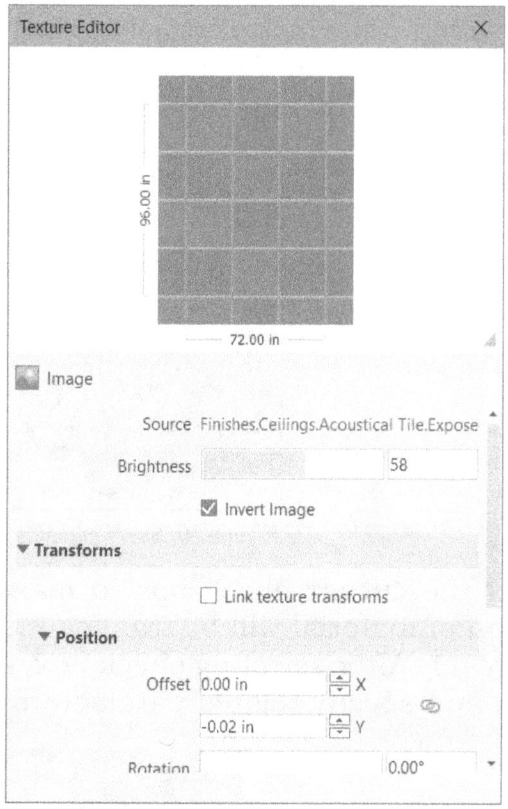

Figure-13. Texture Editor window

- Set desired value in the **Image Fade** field to transparency of image. Similarly, set desired value in the **Glossiness** field to define smoothness of material surface to provide it shine. Select desired option from the **Highlights** drop-down to define whether material surface is metallic or non-metallic.
- Select the **Reflectivity** check box to define how much light will be reflected from the surface of material. Specify desired values in **Direct** and **Oblique** fields to define amount of light that will be reflected when material face is directly in line with light source and when material face is at an angle to the light source, respectively.
- Select the **Transparency** check box to define parameters for free transmission of light through the material. After selecting check box, specify desired value of amount of light which will be freely transmitted though the material using **Amount** slider. Specify desired amount of light to be absorbed by the material surface to give self glow effect in the **Translucency** field. Select desired option from the **Refraction** drop-down to define the medium through which light passes before and after striking the surface of material. The value in edit box next to the drop-down will change based on selected medium. You can specify desired value from 0 to 5 in the edit box to define refraction index of medium.

- Select the **Self Illumination** check box to apply self illumination of material under light. After selecting check box, set desired value using the **Luminance** drop-down to define brightness of light emitting from material in candelas per meter square unit. Set desired value in **Filter Color** selection box to define color of self illuminance. Using the options in **Color Temperature** drop-down, you can define the warmth or coolness of the self illuminance light.

Physical Tab

The options in **Physical** tab are used to define properties that affect the physical data of material used by various simulations (analyses). Parameters like thermal conductivity, yield strength, young's modulus are some example of physical properties. On selecting this tab in **Material Editor** dialog box, the options will be displayed as shown in Figure-14. The options in **Information** section are same as discussed earlier. The other options are discussed next.

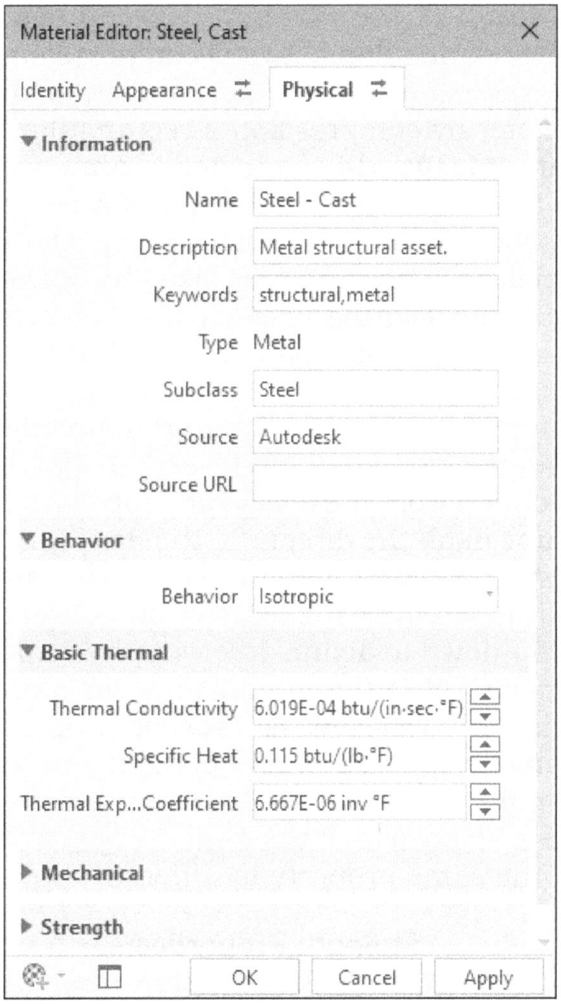

Figure-14. Physical tab for materials

Basic Thermal Properties

- The options in **Basic Thermal** section are used to define how much heat can be transferred through the material and related parameters. Specify desired value in **Thermal Conductivity** edit box to define the amount of heat in W that can be transferred through the unit length of material at unit temperature. Specify desired value in **Specific Heat** edit box to define the amount of heat energy required by unit mass of material to raise its temperature by 1 unit. Specify desired value in the **Thermal Expansion Coefficient** edit box to define the amount of length increase in material due to unit increase in temperature.

Mechanical Properties

- The options in **Mechanical** section are used to define parameters like Young's modulus, Poisson's ratio, and so on. Specify desired value in **Young's Modulus** edit box to define the amount of stress required for per unit strain in the material. This parameter is also called **Modulus of elasticity** and defines relationship between stress and strain of the material. Specify desired value in **Poisson's Ratio** edit box to define relationship between compression applied on one direction of material causing expansion in other perpendicular direction. You can check the role of this parameter by compression a rectangular piece of sponge. Specify desired value in **Shear Modulus** edit box to define amount of shear stress required for unit shear strain to occur in material. Shear forces cause objects to tilt while their base is fixed. Specify desired value in **Density** edit box to define mass of per unit volume of material. This parameter is used to determine mass of the model. Specify desired value in the **Damping Coefficient** edit box to define a ratio by which oscillations in the material are dissipated. Note that if there is no damping in a spring placed in vacuum then it will keep on oscillating forever once stretched and released. The damping coefficient of material directly affects results of Modal analysis and other frequency related analyses.
- Select the **Isotropic** option from the **Behavior** drop-down to define that properties of the material are same in all the direction. It means you can apply 100 N load in any direction (X, Y, or Z) of material and it will cause same stress in the material because Young's Modulus is same in all directions. Select the **Orthotropic** option from the **Behavior** drop-down to define different physical properties in X, Y, and Z directions for the material. Note that a non-uniform effect of load occurs in these type of materials. Select the **Transverse Isotropic** option from the drop-down if your material has same properties in one plane (transverse plane) and different in direction perpendicular to the plane. Based on selected material behavior, you may get two or three edit boxes for the same property in the dialog box. These edit boxes represent the same property in different directions.

Strength Properties

- The options in **Strength** section are used to define strength parameters of material up to which the material will be useful for mechanical applications. Specify desired value in the **Yield Strength** edit box to define the amount of stress at which permanent deformation will occur in material. Specify desired value in the **Tensile Strength** edit box to define amount of stress required to break off the material. Tensile strength is also called ultimate tensile strength and ultimate strength of material. Select the **Thermally Treated** check box to mark material as thermally treated for drawing representation. Generally, thermal treatment is performed on the material to harden its surface or make the material ductile/brittle.

- After specify desired parameters, click on the **OK** button to apply modifications to material.

Creating a New Material

The **Creates a new material in the document** button is available at the bottom in the **Material Browser**. This button is used to create a new material depending on the user requirements. The procedure to use this button is given next.

- Click on the **Creates a new material in the document** button from the bottom in the **Material Browser**. The **Material Editor** dialog box will be displayed as discussed earlier.
- Specify desired parameters in the dialog box and click on the **OK** button. The material will be created and added in the list of document materials.

Similarly, you can use the options in the **Material library** drop-down to create and manage material libraries; refer to Figure-15. After performing desired operations, close the **Material Browser**.

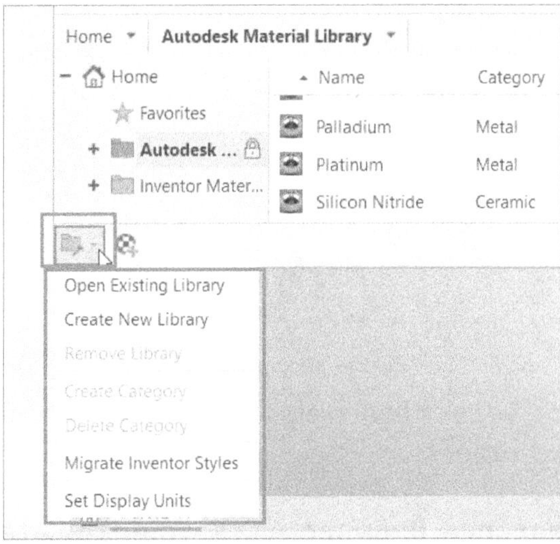

Figure-15. Material library drop-down

APPEARANCE

Appearance represents the way in which material will be displayed when rendering is performed. Applying appearance is similar to applying material without physical properties. You can also use appearance to enhance look of material in graphics area. The **Appearance** tool in **Tools** tab is used to create and manage appearances in Autodesk Inventor. The procedure to use this tool is given next.

- Click on the **Appearance** tool from the **Material and Appearance** panel in the **Tools** tab of the **Ribbon**. The **Appearance Browser** will be displayed; refer to Figure-16.

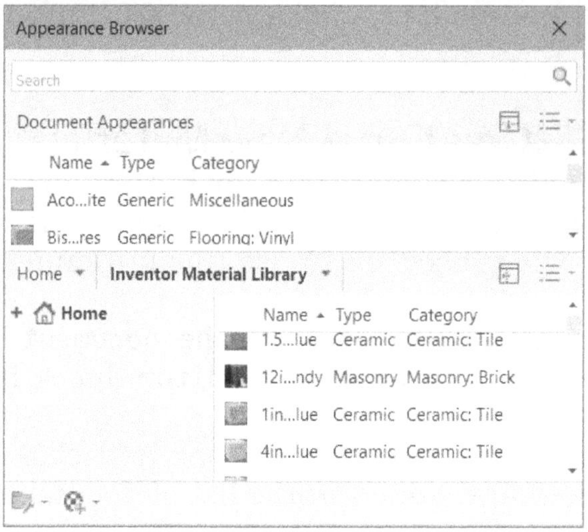

Figure-16. Appearance Browser

- To apply appearance to the model, select desired object from the graphics area and right-click on the appearance to be applied. A shortcut menu will be displayed; refer to Figure-17.

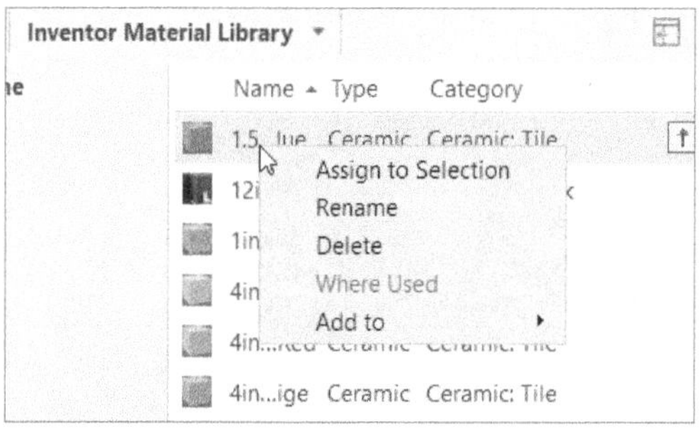

Figure-17. Shortcut menu for appearance

- Select the **Assign to Selection** option from the shortcut menu to apply the appearance to selected objects.

Other options of the **Appearance Browser** are similar to **Material Browser** discussed earlier.

Clearing Appearances

The **Clear** tool in **Tools** tab is used to remove any appearances applied to selected objects. The procedure to use this tool is given next.

- Click on the **Clear** tool from the **Material and Appearance** panel in the **Tools** tab of the **Ribbon**. A mini toolbar will be displayed for managing appearances; refer to Figure-18.

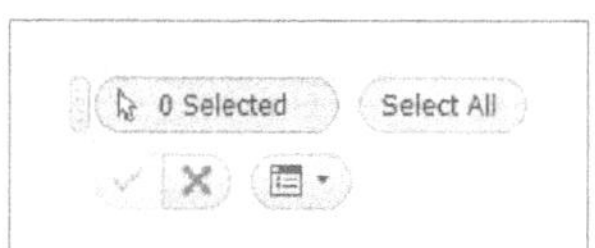

Figure-18. Appearance mini toolbar

- Select desired faces from the model to remove their appearances. If you want to remove appearances from all the faces in the model then click on the **Select All** button.
- Click on the **OK** button from the mini toolbar to remove the appearances.

Adjusting Appearance

The **Adjust** tool in **Tools** tab is used to scale and modify appearance applied to a face. The procedure to use this tool is given next.

- Click on the **Adjust** tool from the **Material and Appearance** panel in the **Tools** tab of the **Ribbon**. The **Adjust Appearance** mini toolbar will be displayed; refer to Figure-19.

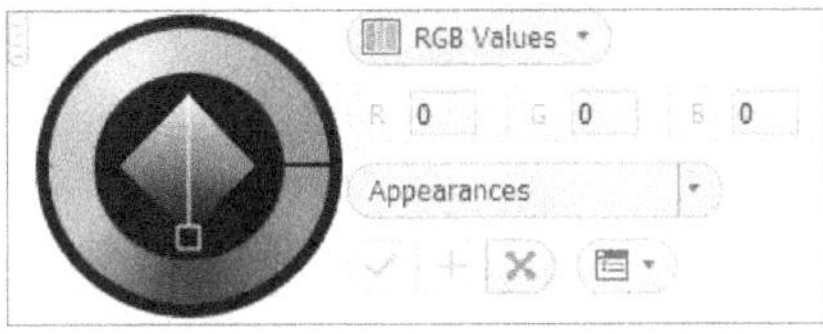

Figure-19. Adjust appearance mini toolbar

- Select the face whose appearance is to be changed. Scale and rotate handles will be displayed on selected face and options in the mini toolbar will be modified according to selected face; refer to Figure-20.

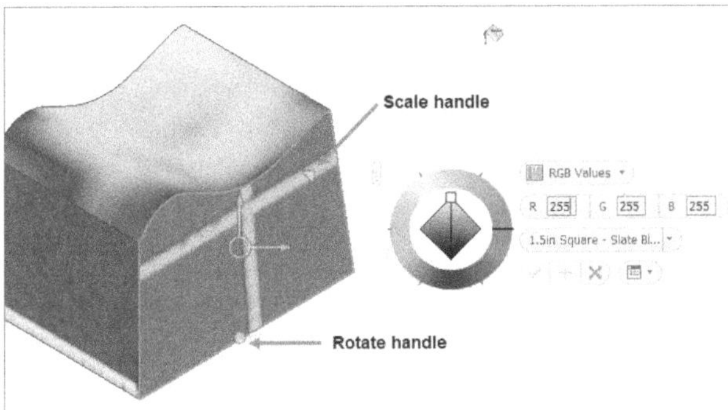

Figure-20. Handles for adjusting appearances

- Drag the handles to scale and rotate appearances. Click on the faces other than earlier selected one to copy the appearance to them.
- Set the other parameters in mini toolbar as discussed earlier and click on the **OK** button to apply adjustments.

The **Finish** tool has been discussed earlier in Chapter 5.

APPLICATION OPTIONS

The **Application Options** tool is used to modify common application parameters like interface colors, template file locations, save reminders, display quality, and so on. The procedure to use this tool is given next.

- Click on the **Application Options** tool from the **Options** panel in the **Tools** tab of the **Ribbon**. The **Application Options** dialog box will be displayed; refer to Figure-21.

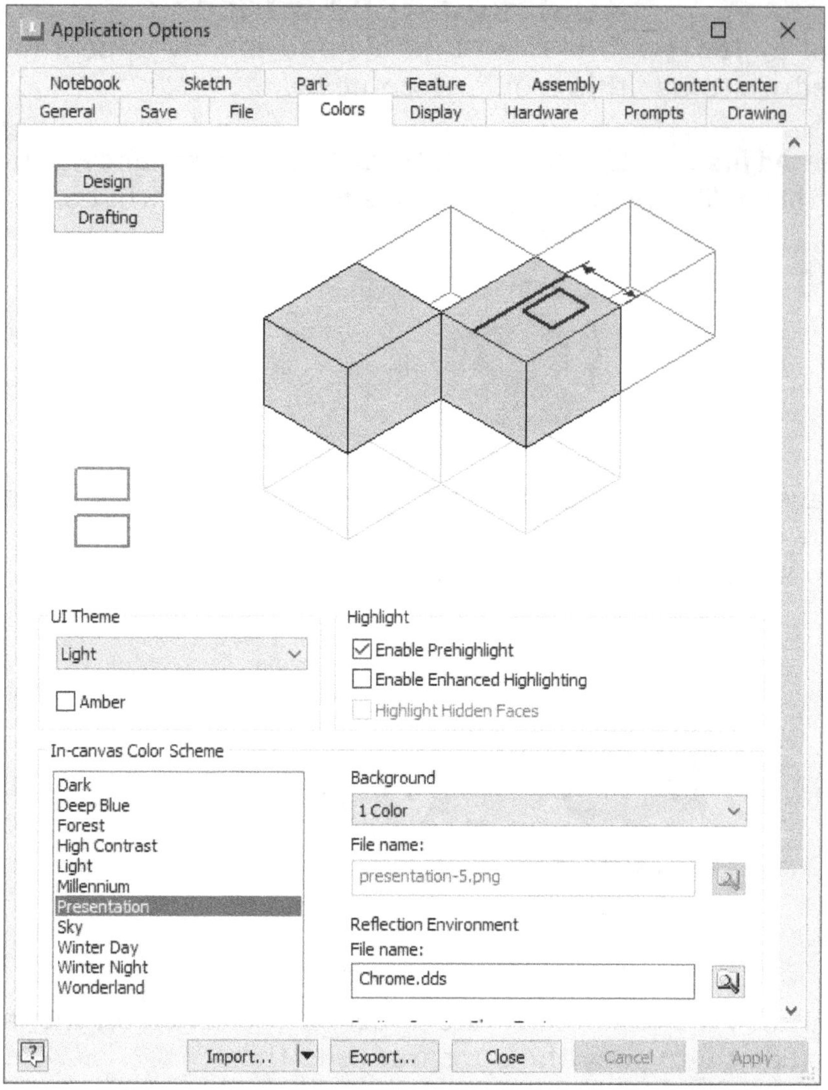

Figure-21. Application Options dialog box

There are enough options in this dialog box that a new chapter can be dedicated to this dialog box. Here, we will given an overview of various tabs in the dialog box and discuss some commonly used options.

General Tab Options

Click on the **General** tab from the dialog box to modify general application parameters; refer to Figure-22. The options in this tab are discussed next.

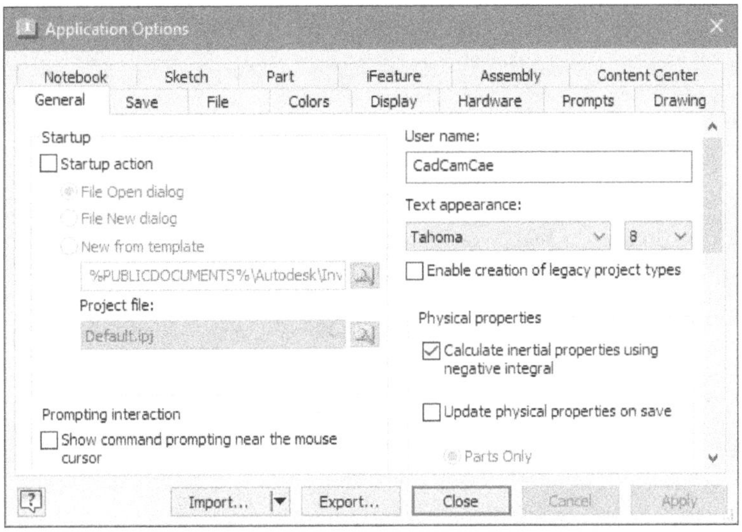

Figure-22. General tab

- Click in the **User name** edit box and specify desired name of software user which is you. Note that this name will also display in model properties and drawing title block.
- Set desired options in the **Text appearance** drop-downs to define text font and text size for text displayed in various dialog boxes of application.
- Select the **Startup action** check box to set action to be performed as soon as software starts. After selecting check box, select the **File Open dialog** radio button to display dialog box for opening an existing file. Select the **File New dialog** radio button to display dialog box for starting a new model. Select the **New from template** radio button to use specified template file and start a new model file.
- Select the **Show command prompting near the mouse cursor** check box to display command prompt near cursor when a tool is active; refer to Figure-23.

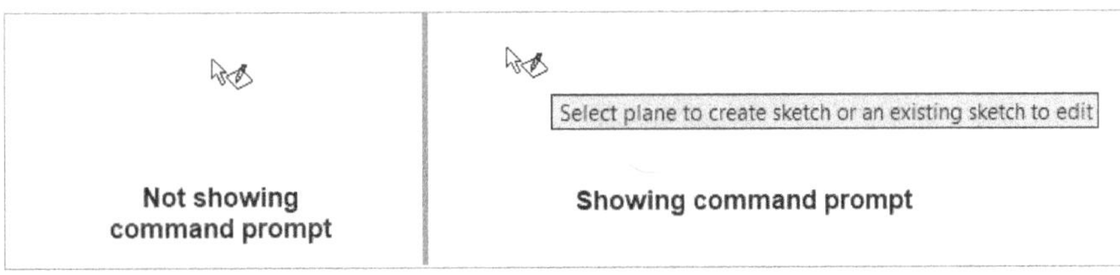

Figure-23. Command prompt near cursor

- Select the **Show Tooltips** check box to display tips about a tool/option when you hover cursor on it. You can set the delay in seconds in edit box below the check box to define the time before tool tip is displayed when you hover cursor on the tool/option.
- If there is an expanded tooltip available for the option then select the **Show second-level Tooltips** check box and specify the delay time as discussed earlier.
- If you want to install local copy of help file then click on the **Download Local Help** link button at the bottom in the dialog box. The download link will open in your default web browser.

Save Tab Options

The options in **Save** tab of **Application Options** dialog box are used to manage parameters related to how software saves the files; refer to Figure-24.

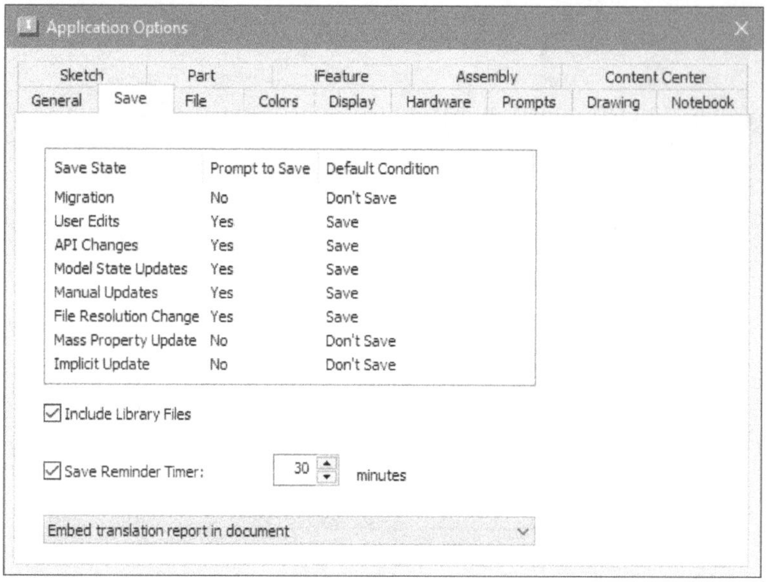

Figure-24. Save tab

- Select the **Include Library Files** check box if you want to save the files used from inventor library with the model file when saving any assembly.
- Select the **Save Reminder Timer** check box and specify desired time duration in edit box next to it so that system prompts you to save any unsaved work after specified time has elapsed.
- If you have performed translation in the model for various texts and annotations then select desired option from the **Translation report** drop-down at the bottom in the dialog box to define how report is saved with the document.

File Tab Options

Select the **File** tab from the dialog box to define options related to file templates and how software opens a file by default; refer to Figure-25.

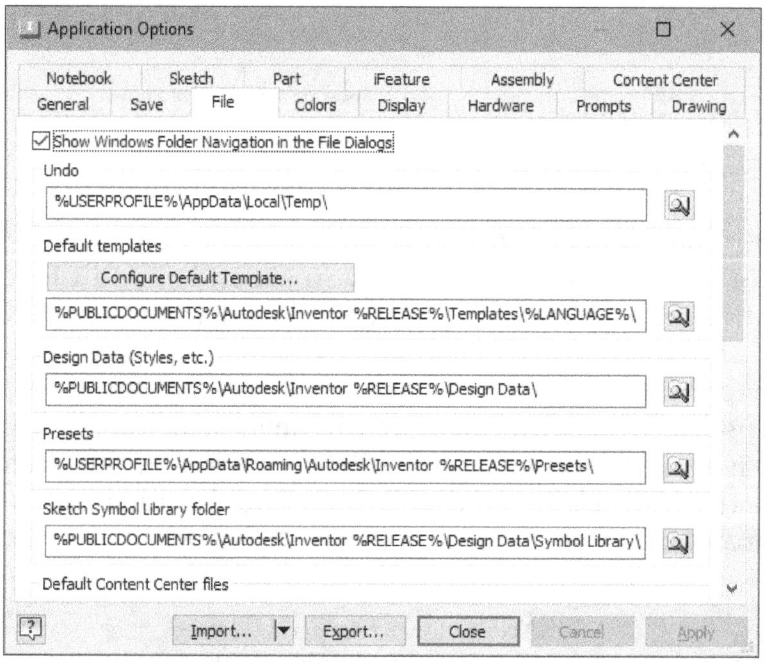

Figure-25. File tab options

- Click on the **Configure Default Template** button from the dialog box to define settings for default templates. The **Configure Default Template** dialog box will be displayed; refer to Figure-26. Select desired radio buttons for default unit and drawing standard to be used in the document. After selecting desired radio buttons, click on the **OK** button from the dialog box. You will be asked whether to overwrite standard template based on specified modifications. Click on the **Overwrite** button to apply changes.

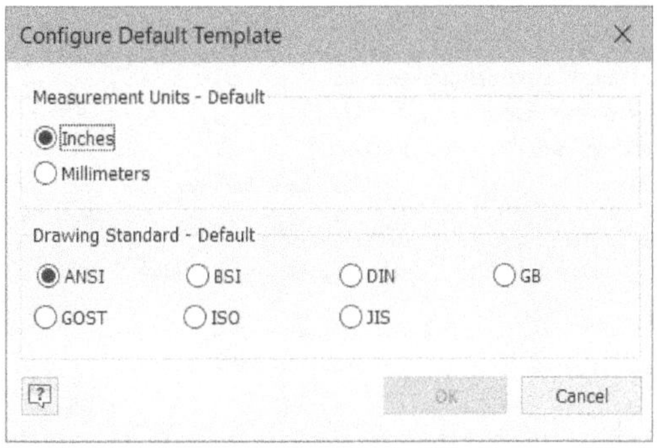

Figure-26. Configure Default Template dialog box

- Click on the **File Open** button from the **Options** area in the dialog box to define the model state and view in which model files will be opened by default by the software.
- Set desired paths for various data files in the fields of this tab.

Colors Tab Options

Using the options in the **Colors** tab of the dialog box, you can set color for background and various objects in the interface as well as drawing area. Select desired option from the **In-canvas Color Scheme** list box in this tab to change the colors using predefined themes.

Display Tab Options

The options in **Display** tab of the dialog box are used to set quality of object display in the drawing area.

- Select desired option from the **Display quality** drop-down to define how smooth the objects will be displayed in the graphics area.
- Using the **Scroll Wheel Sensitivity** slider, you can set the sensitivity of mouse wheel to slower or faster.
- Using the drop-downs in **Middle Mouse Button** area of the dialog box, you can change the functions of various MMB key combinations.

Hardware Tab Options

The options in the **Hardware** tab are used to modify graphic settings for the software. Select the **Quality** radio button to display visualizations in high quality. Select the **Performance** radio button to perform modeling with high performance against the quality of visualizations. Select the **Conservative** radio button to get maximum performance in modeling at the cost of quality of display. If your graphics card is not recognized and you want to use software for visualization performance then select the **Software graphics** check box.

Drawing Tab Options

The options in the **Drawing** tab are used to define settings related to drawing environment; refer to Figure-27.

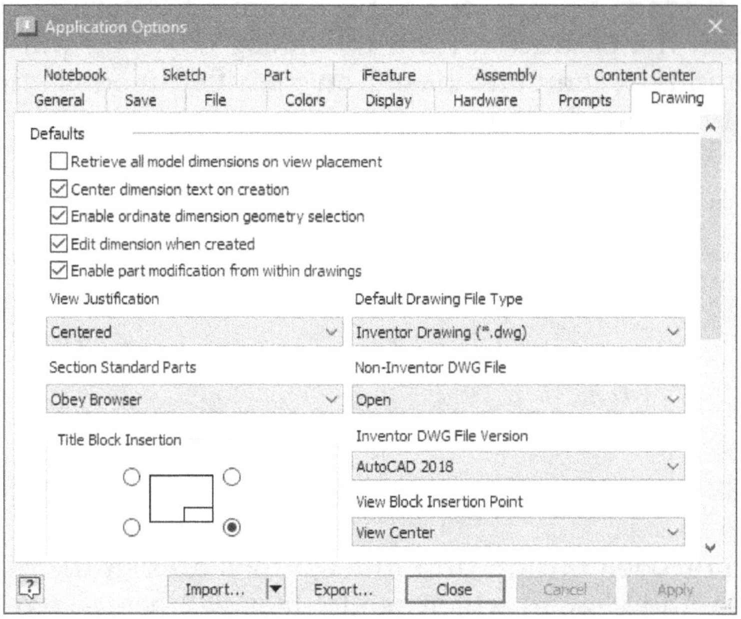

Figure-27. Drawing tab

- Select the **Retrieve all model dimensions on view placement** check box to automatically place model dimensions in the drawing when you place a new view in the drawing.
- Set the other parameters like title block location, default drawing file format, dimension type preferences, and so on in the tab.

Sketch Tab Options

The options in the **Sketch** tab are used to set default settings for sketching environment of Autodesk Inventor; refer to Figure-28.

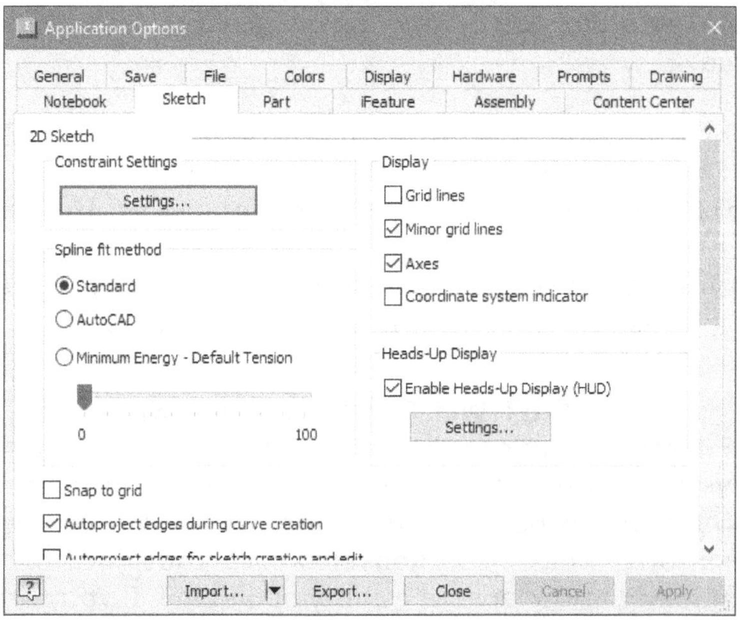

Figure-28. Sketch tab options

- Select desired check boxes from the **Display** area of the dialog box to display various interface elements like grid lines, axes, coordinate system indicator, and so on.

Similarly, you can specify other parameters in the dialog box to define application options. After setting desired parameters, click on the **OK** button from the dialog box.

DOCUMENT SETTINGS

The **Document Settings** tool is used to define default parameters for current open document. The procedure to use this tool is given next.

- Click on the **Document Settings** tool from the **Options** panel in the **Tools** tab of the **Ribbon**. The **Document Settings** dialog box will be displayed; refer to Figure-29.

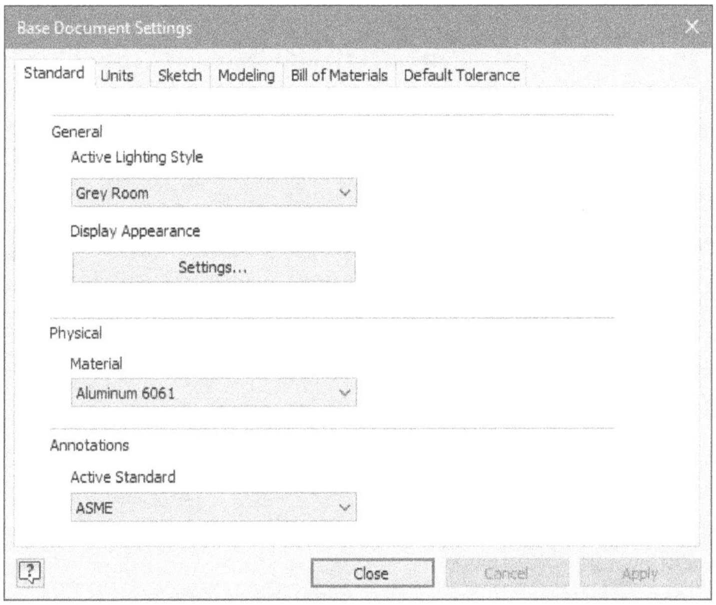

Figure-29. Document Settings dialog box

- Select desired option from the **Active Lighting Style** drop-down to define light setup for rendering model.
- Select desired option from the **Material** drop-down to define physical material used for the model.
- Select desired option from the **Active Standard** drop-down to define units to be used for annotations.
- Select the **Units** tab and set desired parameters in the dialog box to define unit system to be used for various parameters of the model.
- Select the **Default Tolerance** tab from the dialog box and select check boxes to assign tolerance values. After selecting the check box, click in the **Linear** and **Angular** tables to set default tolerance values.
- After setting desired parameters, click on the **OK** button from the dialog box.

MANAGE TAB

The tools and options in the **Manage** tab of **Ribbon** are used to manage styles, parameters, and content related to model; refer to Figure-30.

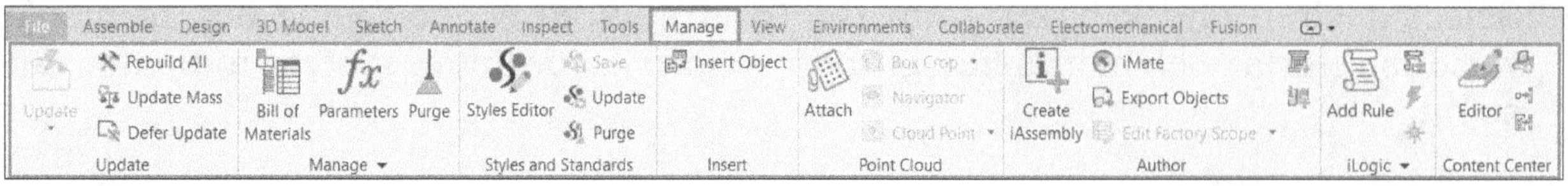

Figure-30. Manage tab

Update Options

The options in the **Update** panel are used to update the changes in the model. Select desired option from the **Update** drop-down to update changes in the assembly, drawing, and modeling environment when you have changed properties of the model but they are not yet reflected in the graphics area. Click on the **Rebuild All** tool from the panel to reflect the changes made in parameters of the model. Click on the **Update Mass** tool from the **Update** panel to update mass of the model based on changes specified in density and other physical properties of the model.

Parameters

The **Parameters** tool is used to create and manage different type of parameters in the model like user parameter and model parameter. The procedure to use this tool is given next.

- Click on the **Parameters** tool from the **Manage** panel in the **Manage** tab of the **Ribbon**. The **Parameters** dialog box will be displayed showing all the model dimensions as parameters; refer to Figure-31.

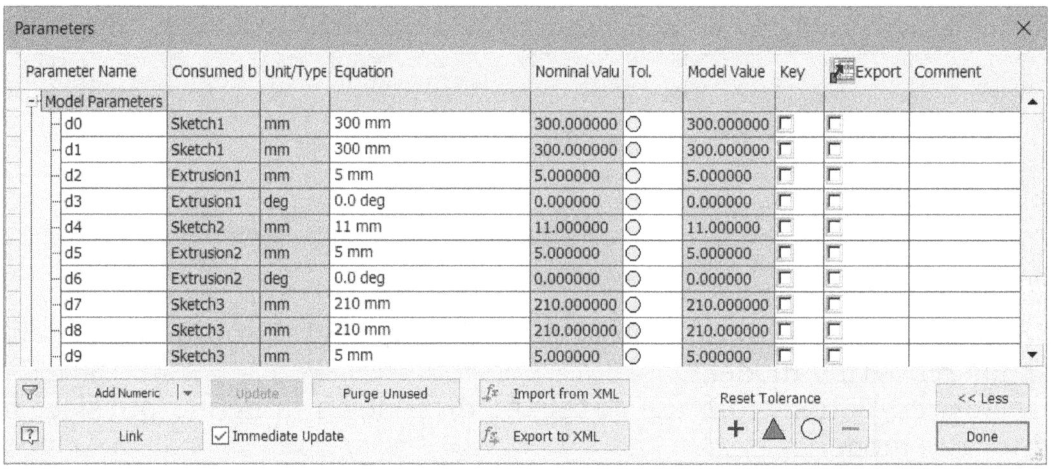

Figure-31. Parameters dialog box

- You can modify the values of all the dimensions by using the fields in the **Equation** column. You can also specify formula for dimension by using the Equation field; refer to Figure-32.

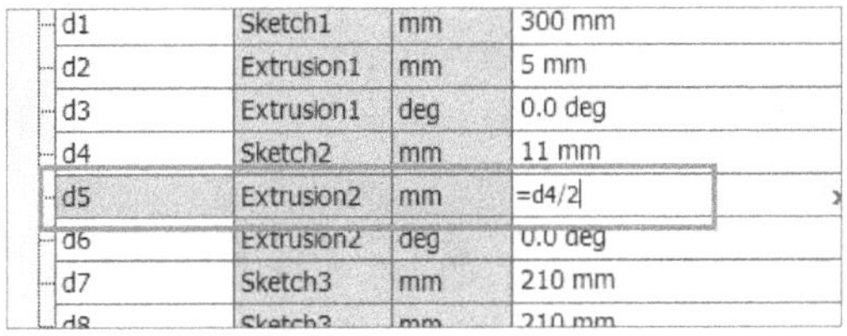

Figure-32. Creating formula using parameter

- If you want to add a new parameter then select desired type of parameter from the **New Parameter** drop-down; refer to Figure-33. Respective parameter will be added in the table under **User Parameters** category.

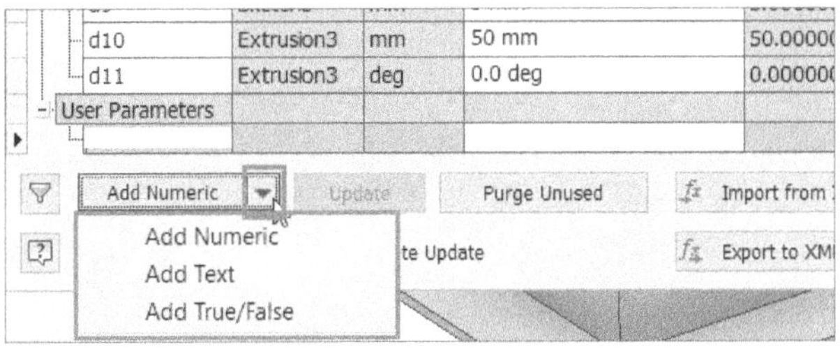

Figure-33. New Parameters drop-down

- Specify desired name for the parameter and define related values in various fields of the dialog box.
- After setting desired parameters, click on the **Done** button. Click on the **Rebuild All** tool from the **Update** panel to update model after changing parameters.

PURGE

The **Purge** tool is used to delete the unused sketches and work features from the active document. The procedure to use this tool is discussed next.

- Click on the **Purge** tool from **Manage** panel in the **Manage** tab of the **Ribbon**. The **Purge Unused** dialog box will be displayed; refer to Figure-34.

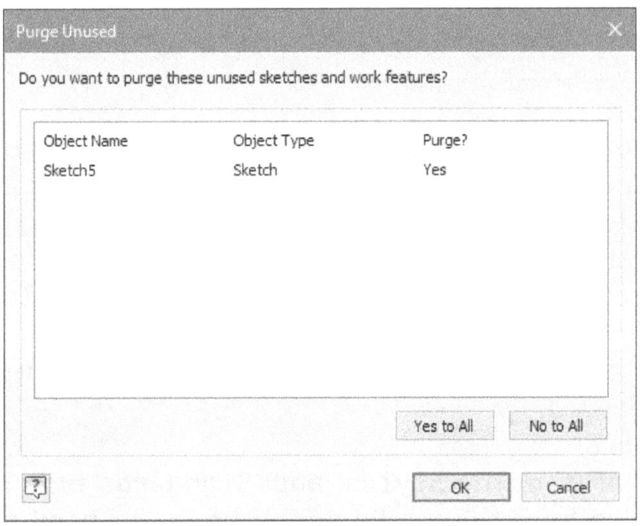

Figure-34. Purge Unused dialog box

- By default, the **Yes** button is selected in the **Purge?** section.
- Click on the **Yes** button from **Purge?** section in the list box to replace with **No** button.

- Click on the **Yes to All** button to purge all the unused sketches or click on the **No to All** button to not to purge any unused sketch.
- After specifying desired parameters, click on the **OK** button from the dialog box.

STYLES EDITOR

The **Styles Editor** tool is used to styles for text and lighting. The procedure to use this tool is given next.

- Click on the **Styles Editor** tool from the **Styles and Standards** panel in the **Manage** tab of the **Ribbon**. The **Styles and Standard Editor** dialog box will be displayed; refer to Figure-35.

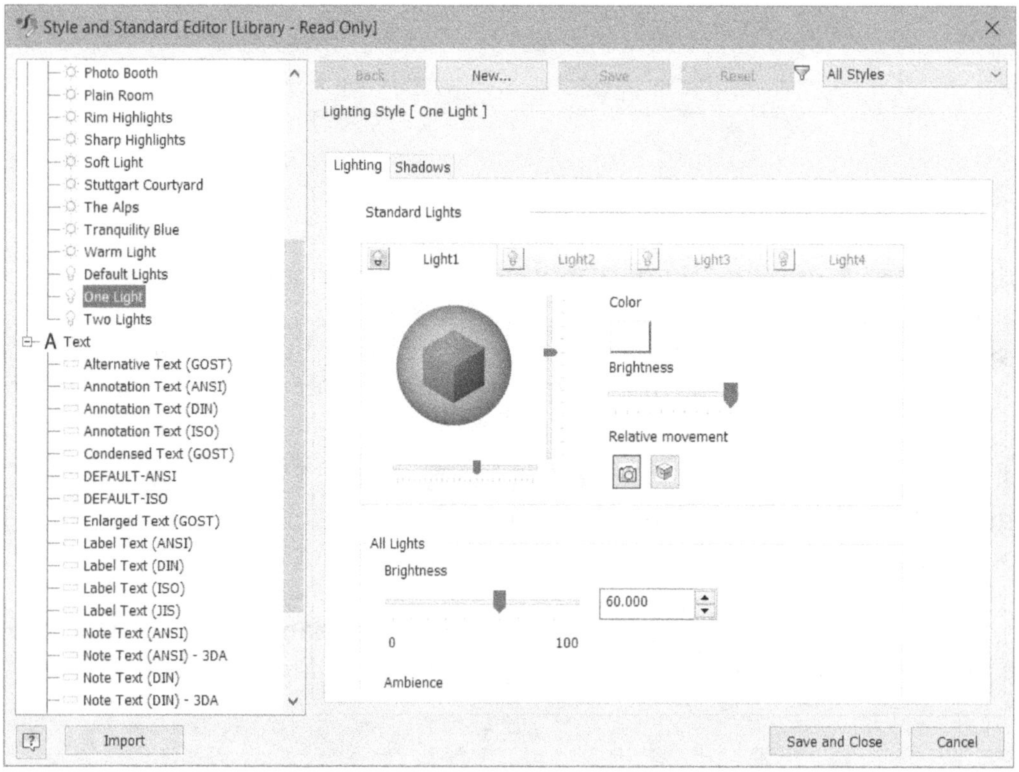

Figure-35. Style and Standard Editor dialog box

- Select desired option from the left area in the dialog box and define the parameters. For example, if you have selected a light then you can define color, brightness, ambience, and location of light.
- The options to modify text style have been discussed earlier.
- After setting desired parameters, click on the **Save and Close** button.

Click on the **Update** tool from the **Styles and Standards** panel to update modified styles in the graphics area.

Click on the **Purge** tool from the **Styles and Standards** panel of **Manage** tab in the **Ribbon** to remove styles from the model which have not been used.

DERIVING COMPONENTS

The **Derive** tool is used to create parts using another part or assembly model as base feature. This tool is useful in creating a multi-body part model. The procedure to use this tool is given next.

- Click on the **Derive** tool (in Part Design environment) from the **Insert** panel in the **Manage** tab of the **Ribbon**. The **Open** dialog box will be displayed and you will be asked to open an existing Autodesk Inventor model file.
- Select desired model file from the dialog box and click on the **Open** button. The **Derived Part** dialog box will be displayed; refer to Figure-36.
- The options in this dialog box have been discussed earlier. Specify the options as discussed earlier and click on the **OK** button.

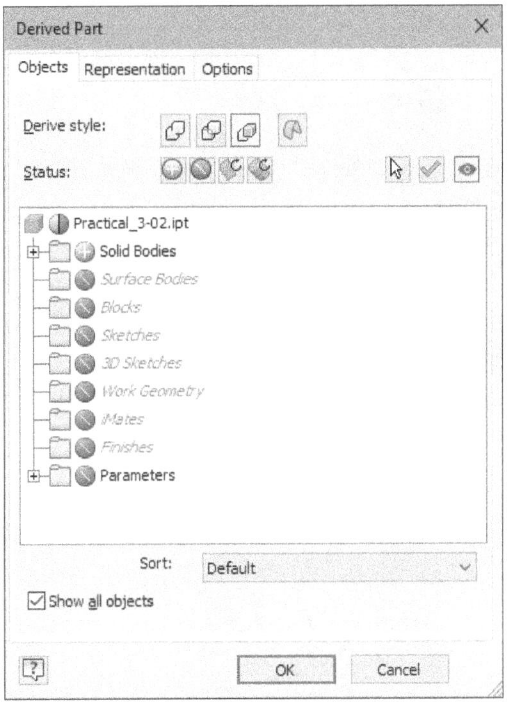

Figure-36. Derived Part dialog box

PLACING FEATURES FROM CONTENT CENTER

The **Feature** tool is used to place objects from content center. The procedure to use this tool is given next.

- Click on the **Feature** tool from the **Insert** panel in the **Manage** tab of the **Ribbon**. The **Place feature from Content Center** dialog box will be displayed; refer to Figure-37.

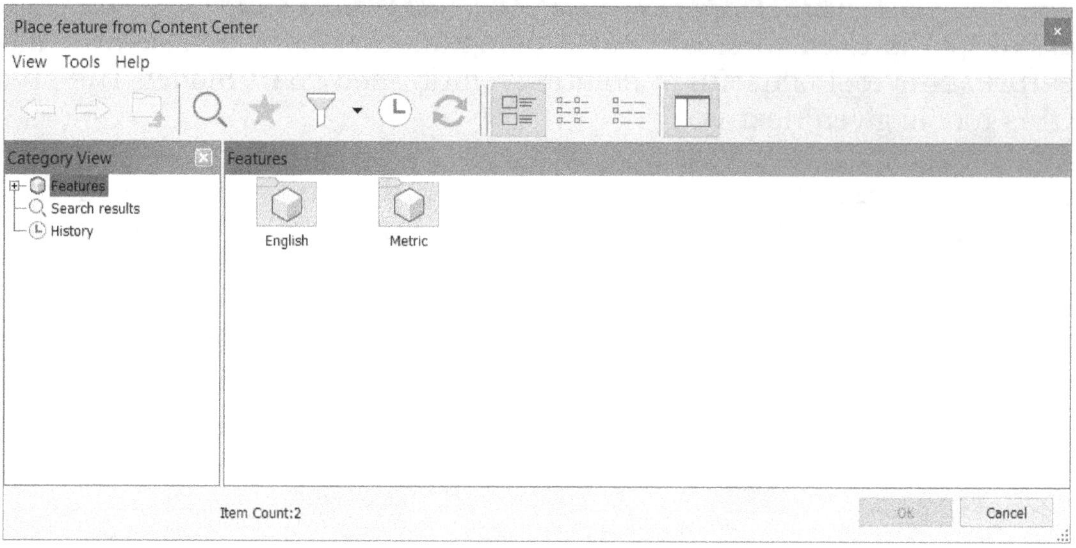

Figure-37. Place feature from Content Center dialog box

- Double-click on the **English** folder to use parts with imperial dimension units or double-click on the **Metric** folder to use parts with metric dimension units. Various categories of parts will be displayed in the dialog box.
- Double-click on the folder of desired category. Related features will be displayed in the dialog box. Note that most of the features will have two options; create a solid protrusion or create a cut using the feature.
- Double-click on desired feature from the dialog box. Related dialog box will be displayed; refer to Figure-38.

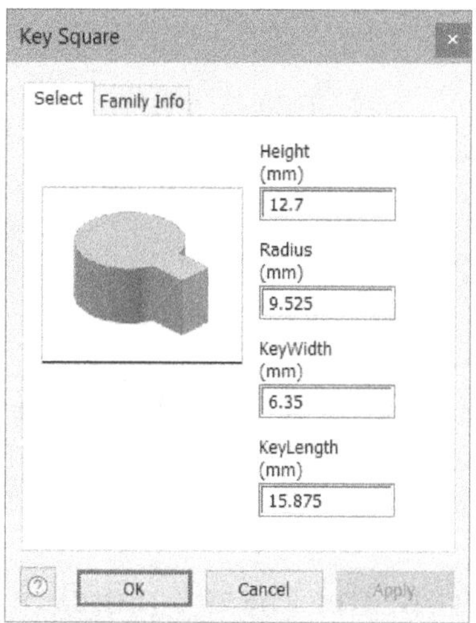

Figure-38. Key Square dialog box

- Set desired parameters in the dialog box and click on the **OK** button. You will be asked to select a face or plane on which the feature will be created.
- Select desired face or plane to be used as base reference for the feature. Preview of the feature will be displayed; refer to Figure-39. Note that when you hover cursor on key points of the model, arrow handles are displayed.
- Drag these arrow handles to modify shape of the model.

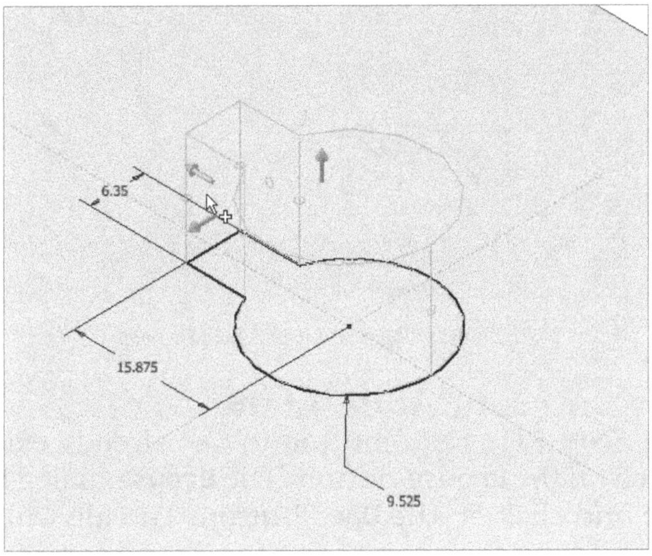

Figure-39. Preview of content center feature

- After setting desired parameters, right-click in the drawing area and select the **Done** option from shortcut menu. The feature will be created.

INSERTING SYSTEM SUPPORTED OBJECTS

The **Insert Object** tool is used to insert objects supported by software installed in your system. For example, if you have Microsoft Excel installed in your system then you can insert excel sheets in the model. The procedure to use this tool is given next.

- Click on the **Insert Object** tool from the **Insert** panel in the **Manage** tab of the **Ribbon**. The **Insert Object** dialog box will be displayed; refer to Figure-40.

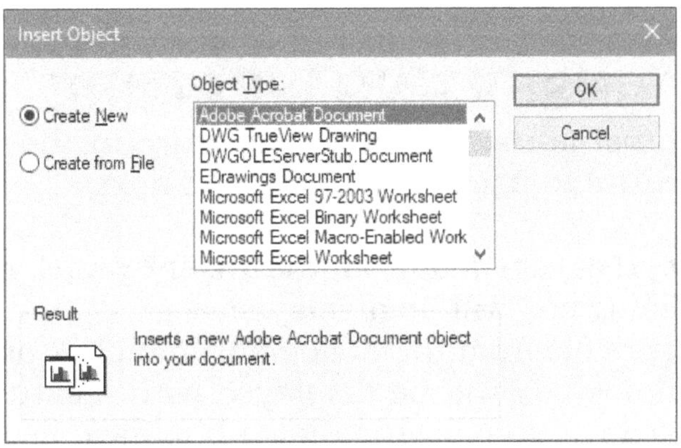

Figure-40. Insert Object dialog box

Creating New File

- Select the **Create New** radio button to create a new object by using the software option available in the **Object Type** area of the dialog box. After selecting radio button, click on the **OK** button. Respective software will open.
- Create the file, save it, and exit the software. Created file will be added in the **3rd Party** node of **Model Browser**; refer to Figure-41. You can edit the object anytime by double-clicking on it.

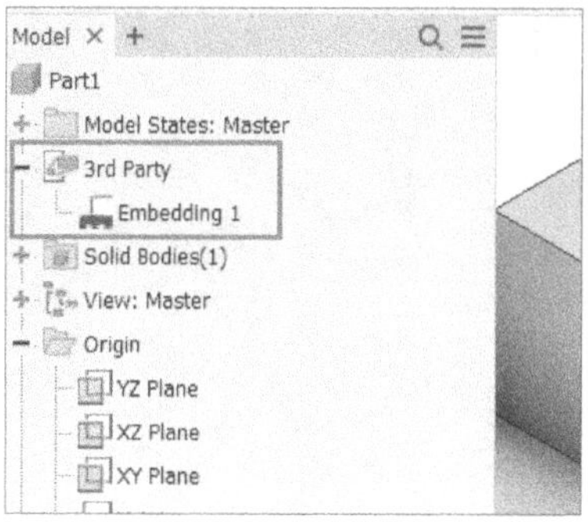

Figure-41. Object added in Model Browser

Using File

- Select the **Create from File** radio button to use already existing object from the local drive and click on the **Browse** button. The **Browse** dialog box will be displayed.
- Select desired file and click on the **Open** button. The file will be added in the edit box.
- Select the **Link** check box to use the file as link in place of saving local copy of the file in project.
- After setting desired parameters, click on the **OK** button from the dialog box. The file will be added in the **Model Browser**.

IMPORTING A CAD FILE MODEL

The **Import** tool is used to import model from a CAD file. The procedure to use this tool is given next.

- Click on the **Import** tool from the **Insert** panel in the **Manage** tab of **Ribbon**. The **Import** dialog box will be displayed. The options of this dialog box have been discussed earlier.

INSERTING iFEATURE

The **Insert iFeature** tool is used to insert iFeature in the part using a plane or planar face. The procedure to use this tool is given next.

- Click on the **Insert iFeature** tool from the **Insert** panel in the **Manage** tab of the **Ribbon**. The **Open** dialog box will be displayed.
- Select desired iFeature file from the dialog box and click on the **Open** button. The **Insert iFeature** dialog box will be displayed with iFeature attached to cursor; refer to Figure-42. The options in the dialog box have been discussed earlier in Chapter 1.

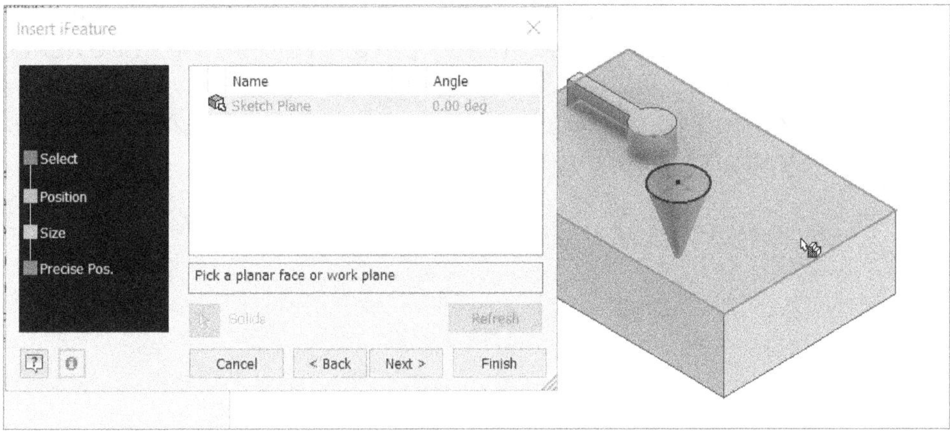

Figure-42. Insert iFeature dialog box and feature attached to cursor

INSERTING FEATURES FROM iFEATURE CATALOG

The options in the **Place iFeature from the iFeature Catalog** drop-down in the **Insert** panel of **Manage** tab in the **Ribbon** are used to insert iFeatures from the catalog of iFeatures. Select desired option from the drop-down and rest of the procedure is same as discussed for Insert iFeature tool. Note that iFeatures saved in C:\Users\Public\Documents\Autodesk\Inventor 2027\Catalog folder (default) will be displayed automatically in the drop-down.

ATTACHING POINT CLOUD

The **Attach** tool is used to insert point cloud data in the model. Note that when you use 3D Scanner to generate rough model of scanned object, you are generating point cloud data. The procedure to use this tool is given next.

- Click on the **Attach** tool from the **Point Cloud** panel in the **Manage** tab of the **Ribbon**. The **Select Point Cloud File** dialog box will be displayed; refer to Figure-43.

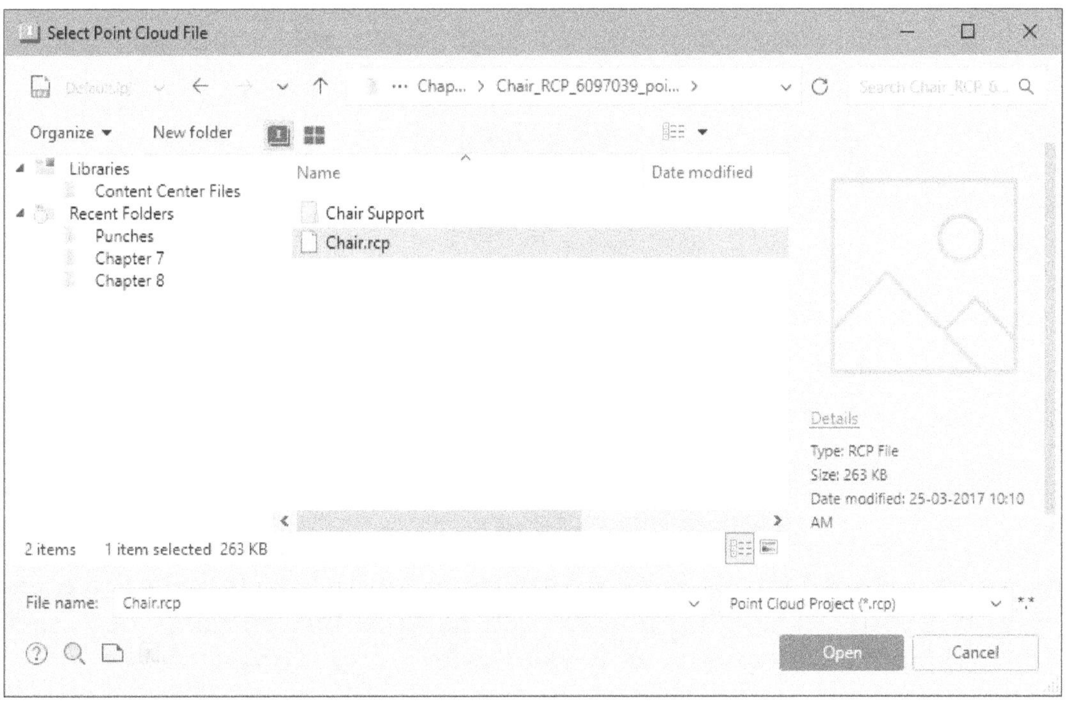

Figure-43. Select Point Cloud File dialog box

- Select desired point cloud data file from the dialog box and click on the **Open** button. The point cloud will be attached to cursor and you will be asked to specify the location to place it.
- Click at desired location to place the data model. The **Attach Point Cloud** dialog box will be displayed; refer to Figure-44.

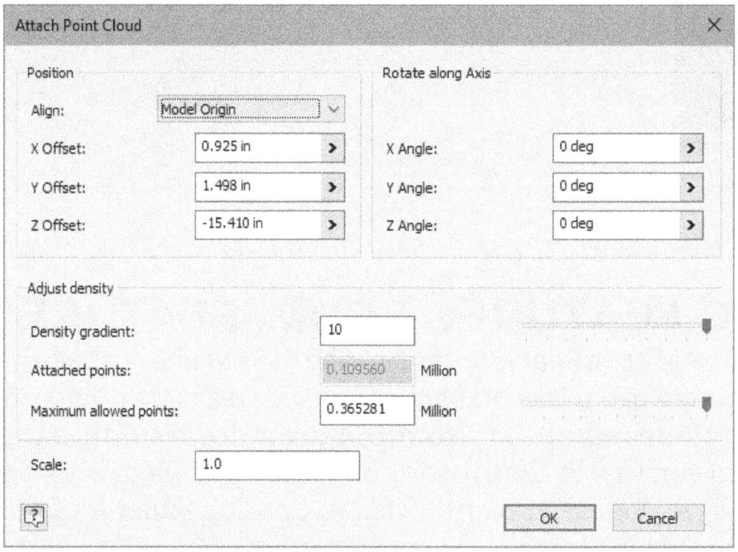

Figure-44. Attach Point Cloud dialog box

- Select **Model Origin** option from the **Align** drop-down from the **Position** area to align the point cloud coordinate system with the model origin coordinates.
- Select **UCS1** or **UCS2** option from the drop-down to align the point cloud with the selected UCS coordinates.
- Specify desired parameters in the dialog box like scale value, density, location, and so on.
- Click on the **OK** button to complete the process. The model will be displayed in graphics area; refer to Figure-45.

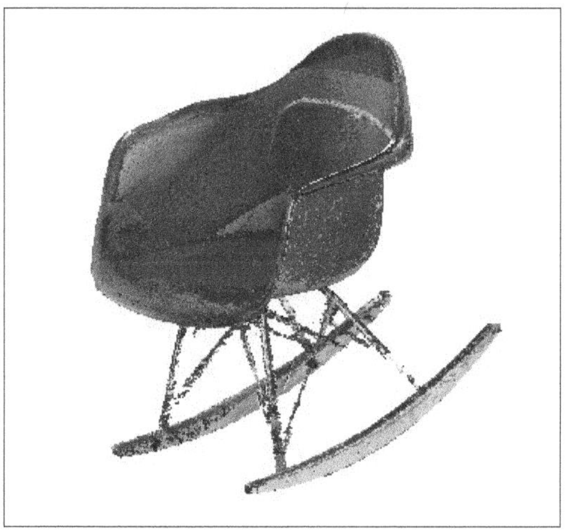

Figure-45. Point cloud model

You can use the other tools in Point Cloud panel to further modify the point cloud data. Note that you can use the point cloud as base for creating your features as points in the point cloud can be easily references for creating features.

MAKING PART USING SELECTED OBJECTS

The **Make Part** tool is used to create a new part model using selected objects as reference. This tool is useful when you have multi-body model file and you want to create individual parts using the bodies so that you can create a functional assembly model. The procedure to use this tool is given next.

- Click on the **Make Part** tool from the **Layout** panel in the **Manage** tab of the **Ribbon**. The **Make Part** dialog box will be displayed with list of all the features in the model; refer to Figure-46.

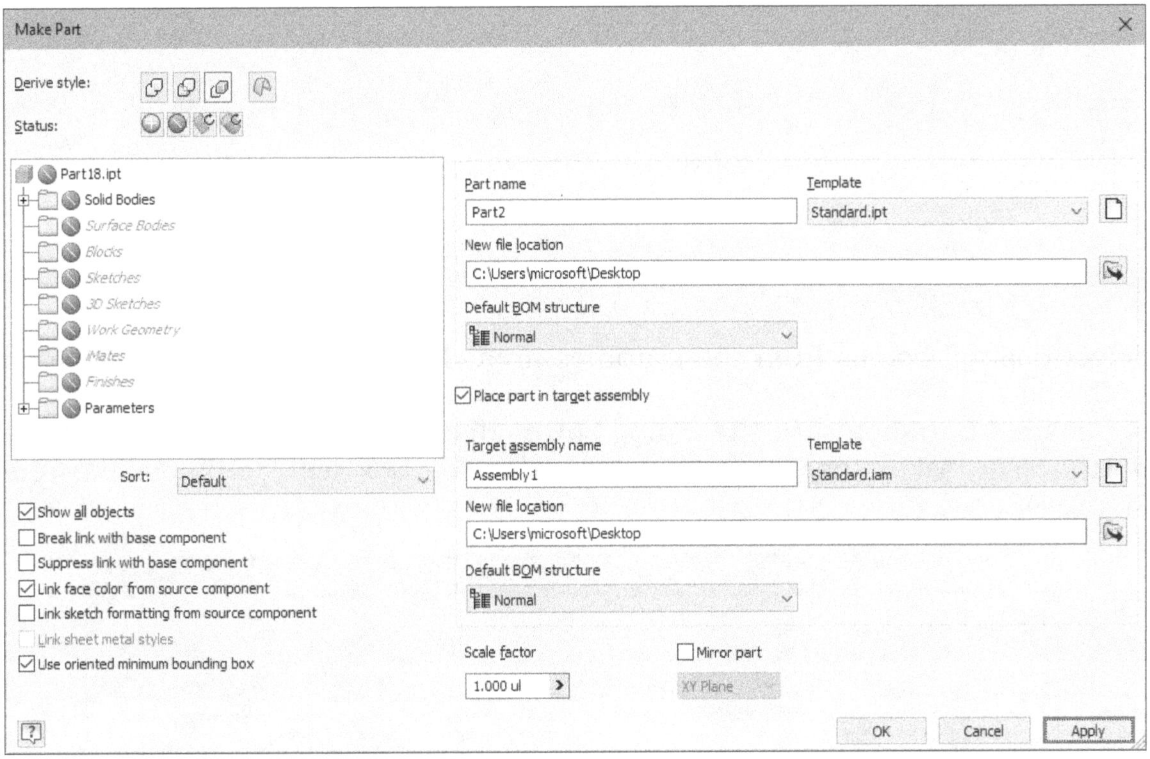

Figure-46. Make Part dialog box

- Double-click on desired bodies, sketches, and features that you want to include in your new part from the list box. Make sure a button is displayed against selected feature which means selected feature is derived in the part.
- Click in the **Part name** edit box and specify name of the part file to be created.
- Select desired template from the **Template** drop-down to define basic parameters of model file.
- Click in the **New file location** edit box to define save location for the file.
- You can select the Bill of Materials structure for the model by using options in the **Default BOM structure** drop-down.
- Clear the **Place part in target assembly** check box if you do not want to place the newly created part in an assembly.
- Similarly, set the other parameters and click on the **OK** button. The part file will be created and displayed in the application.

MAKING COMPONENTS

The **Make Components** tool is used to generate components from selected bodies and place them in an assembly file as per their current placements. The procedure to do so is given next.

- Open a multi body part file or create one and then click on the **Make Components** tool from the **Layout** panel in the **Manage** tab of the **Ribbon**. The **Make Components : Selection** dialog box will be displayed; refer to Figure-47.

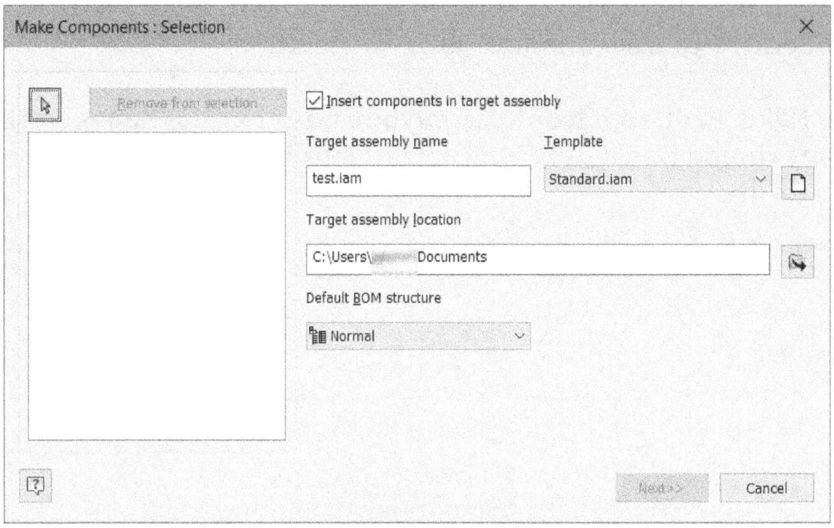

Figure-47. Make Components : Selection dialog box

- Select desired bodies from the graphics area. The selected bodies will be added in the list.
- Set desired parameters in the dialog box as discussed next and click on the **Next** button. The **Make Components : Bodies** dialog box will be displayed; refer to Figure-48.

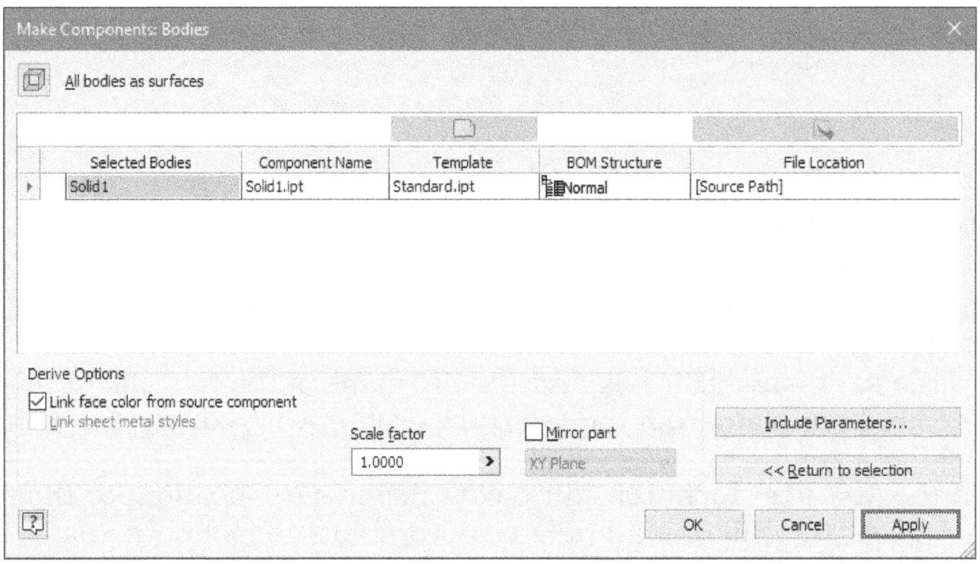

Figure-48. Make Components Bodies dialog box

- You can still modify the parameters as desired by clicking the fields of table. Set the other parameters as discussed earlier and click on the **Apply** button. The assembly file will be created using the bodies as components. Click on the **Cancel** button to exit the dialog box and select the assembly file tile from the bottom bar.

CREATING IPART

The **Create iPart** tool is used to create a table driven part model in which shape/ size of model can be changed by specifying parameters in the table. The procedure to use this tool is given next.

- Click on the **Create iPart** tool from the **Author** panel in the **Manage** tab of the **Ribbon**. The **iPart Author** dialog box will be displayed; refer to Figure-49.

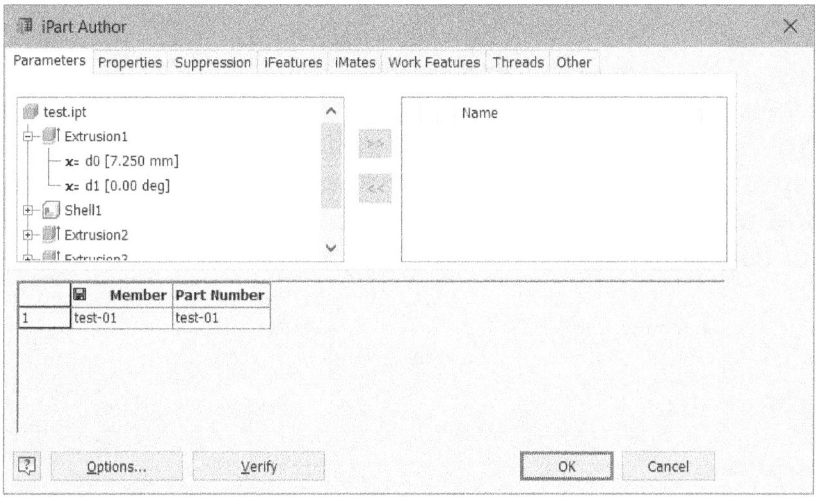

Figure-49. iPart Author dialog box

- Select desired parameter to be added in the iPart from left list box in the dialog box and click on the **>>** button. Selected parameter will be added in the table for customizing part; refer to Figure-50.

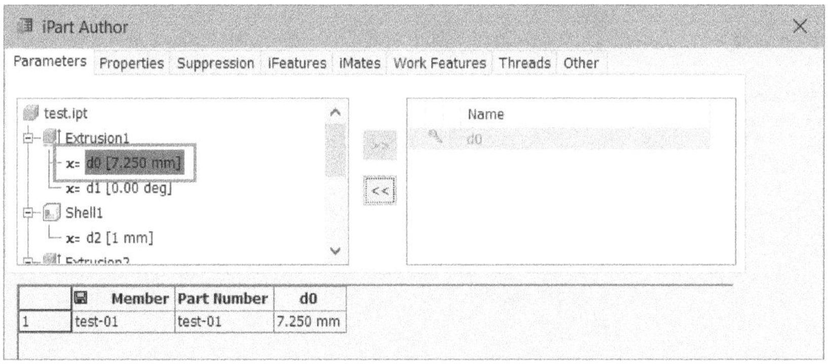

Figure-50. Parameter added for customization

- If you want to remove a parameter from customization list then select the parameter from right list box and click on thc **<<** button.
- Click on the **Properties** tab to add parameters from properties of the model. The procedure to add property parameter is same as discussed earlier.
- Click on the **Suppression** tab and select the features to be set as suppressed and unsuppressed in variations of the part.
- Similarly, add other parameters of various tabs in the dialog box to vary the instances of the iPart.
- Right-click in any field of the first row and select the **Insert Row** option from the shortcut menu displayed; refer to Figure-51. A new row will be added in the table.

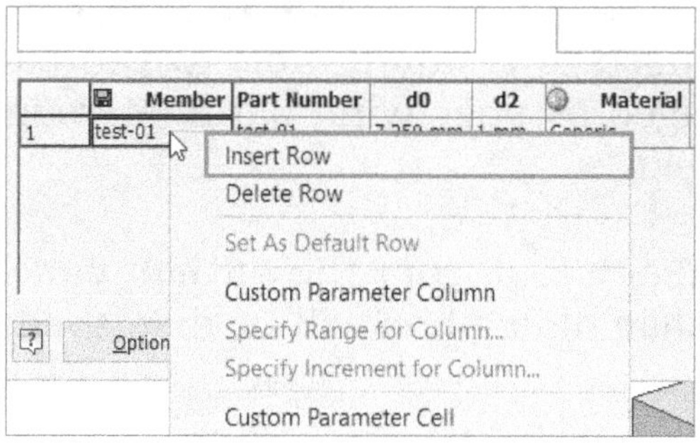

Figure-51. Insert Row option

- Change the parameters as desired for the new configuration of iPart; refer to Figure-52. Note that we have typed the values of materials and compute in the table. After specifying desired parameters, click on the **OK** button. The iPart will be created and table for managing configurations of iPart will be displayed in the **Table** node of **Model Browser**; refer to Figure-53.

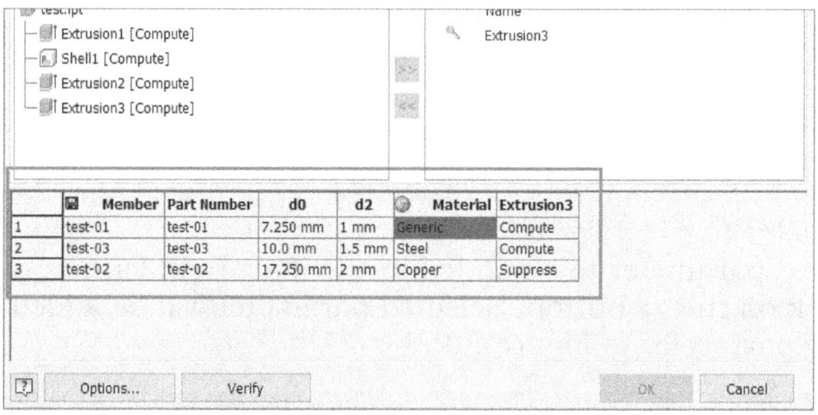

Figure-52. Changing parameters in table

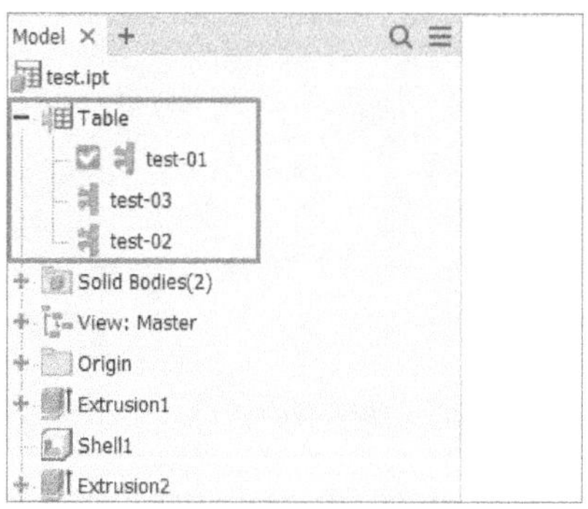

Figure-53. Table of iPart

- Double-click on desired configuration from the **Table** node to activate it in graphics area.
- You can modify the parameters in the dialog box as discussed earlier if needed. Click on the **OK** button from the dialog box to activate the configuration.

DEFINING IMATE

The **iMates** are used to assign default assembly constraints to the part when inserted in an assembly. For example, you can assign Insert constraint to a cylindrical face of part so that when this part is inserted in assembly, it will ask for mating cylindrical face by default. The procedure to define iMate is given next.

- Click on the **iMate** tool from the **Author** panel in the **Manage** tab of the **Ribbon**. The **Create iMate** dialog box will be displayed; refer to Figure-54.

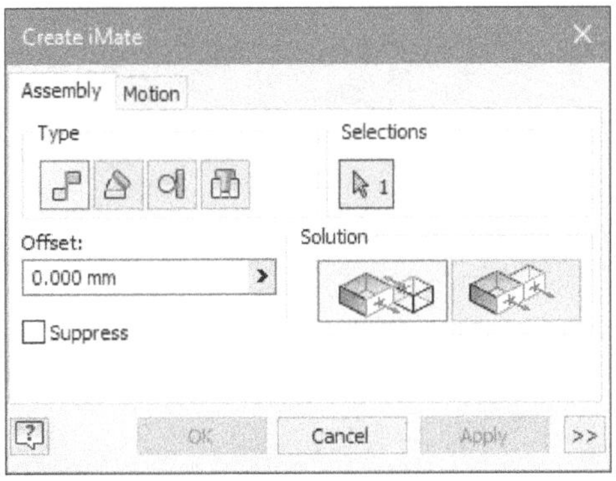

Figure-54. Create iMate dialog box

- Select desired constraint type and set related parameters as discussed earlier in chapter related to Assembly.
- Select desired mate reference (face/edge/axis/point) from the model in graphics area and click on the **OK** button. The iMate will be applied to part.

EXTRACTING IFEATURES

The **Extract iFeature** tool is used to extract features from current model and save them as iFeatures for later use. The procedure to use this tool is given next.

- Click on the **Extract iFeature** tool from the **Author** panel in the **Manage** tab of the **Ribbon**. The **Extract iFeature** dialog box will be displayed; refer to Figure-55.

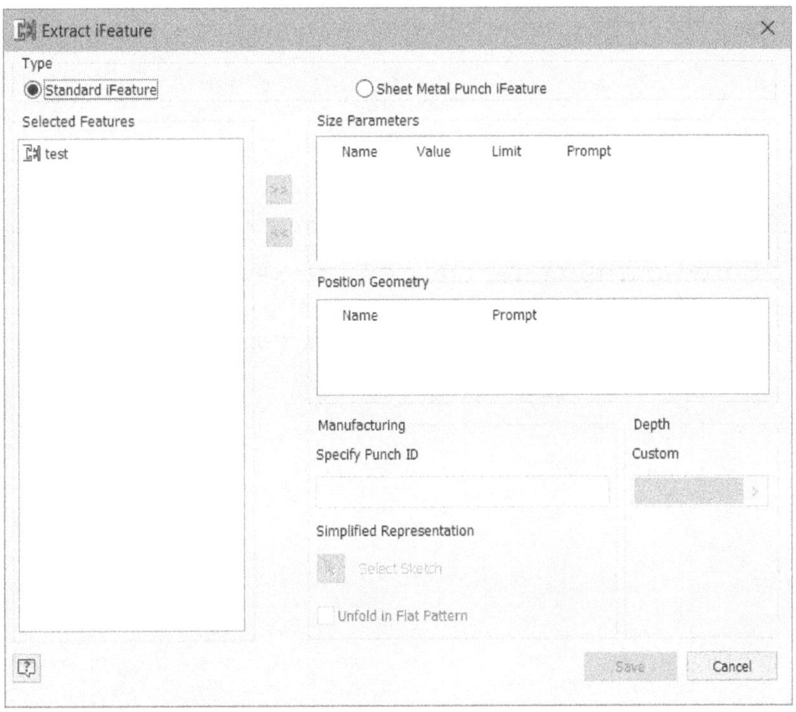

Figure-55. Extract iFeature dialog box

- Select desired feature from the model in graphics area to be used as iFeature. Selected features will be displayed in the **Selected Features** area of the dialog box; refer to Figure-56.

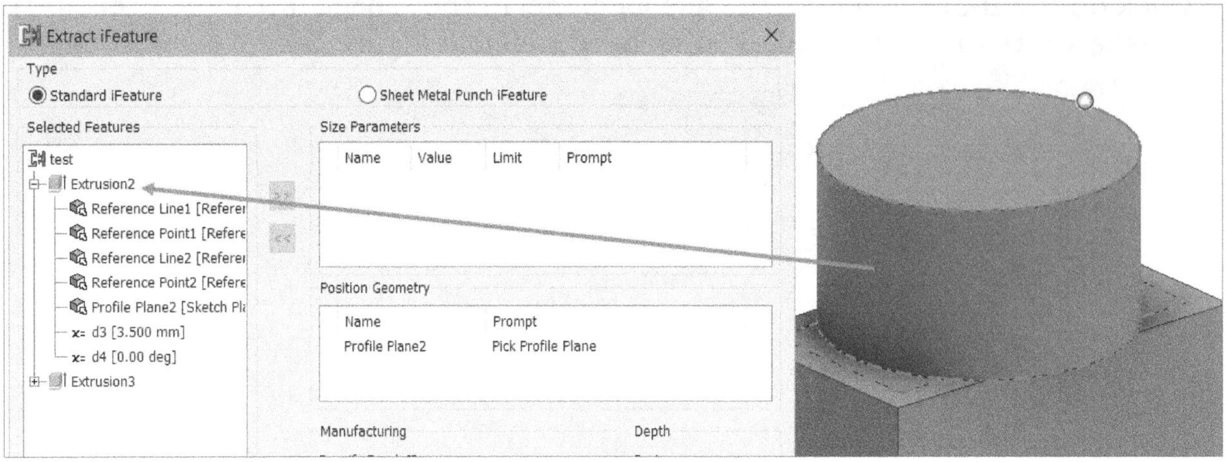

Figure-56. Selected features

- Select desired parameter to be used for size variation from the **Selected Features** area and click on the **>>** button. The parameter will be added in Size Parameters table.
- Similarly, you can add references from the model to be used as positioning geometry; refer to Figure-57.

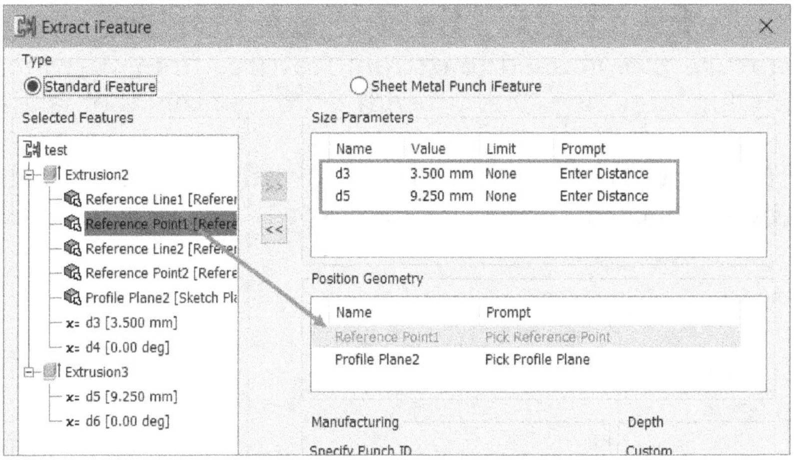

Figure-57. Adding size parameters and position geometry

- After setting desired parameters, click on the **Save** button from the dialog box to save the iFeature. The **Save As** dialog box will be displayed; refer to Figure-58.

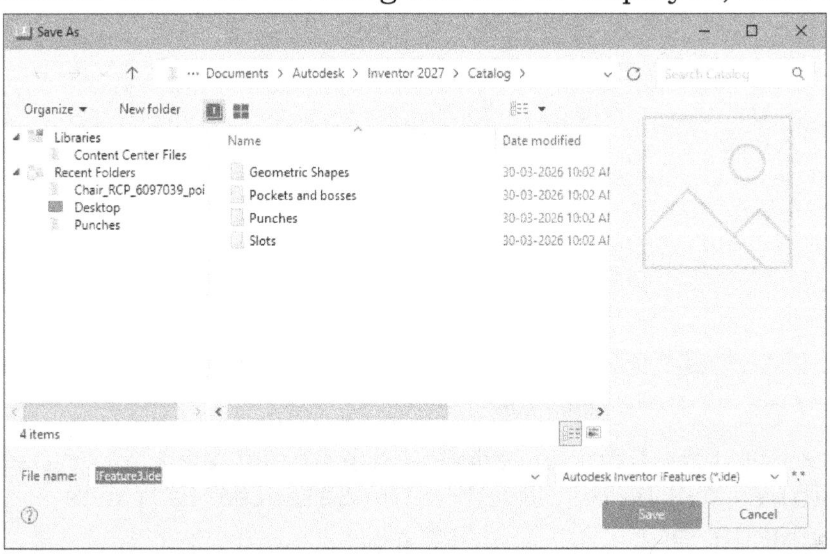

Figure-58. Save As dialog box

- Specify desired name and location of the file, and click on the **Save** button to save iFeature file.

Similarly, you can use the tools in **Component** drop-down of **Author** panel to create iFeature like components related to specific categories.

ADDING RULES TO MODEL

Rules are used to define logic and equations in the model to automate some designing tasks. The procedure to create rules is given next.

- Click on the **Add Rule** tool from the **iLogic** panel in the **Manage** tab of the **Ribbon**. The **Rule Name** dialog box will be displayed; refer to Figure-59.

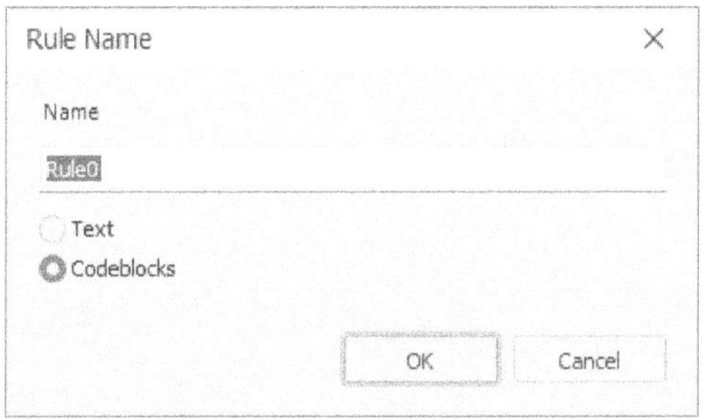

Figure-59. Rule Name dialog box

- Specify desired name for the rule in the **Name** edit box.

Using Text based Rules

- Select **Text** radio button to apply the normal text content and click on the **OK** button from the dialog box. The **Edit Rule** dialog box will be displayed; refer to Figure-60.

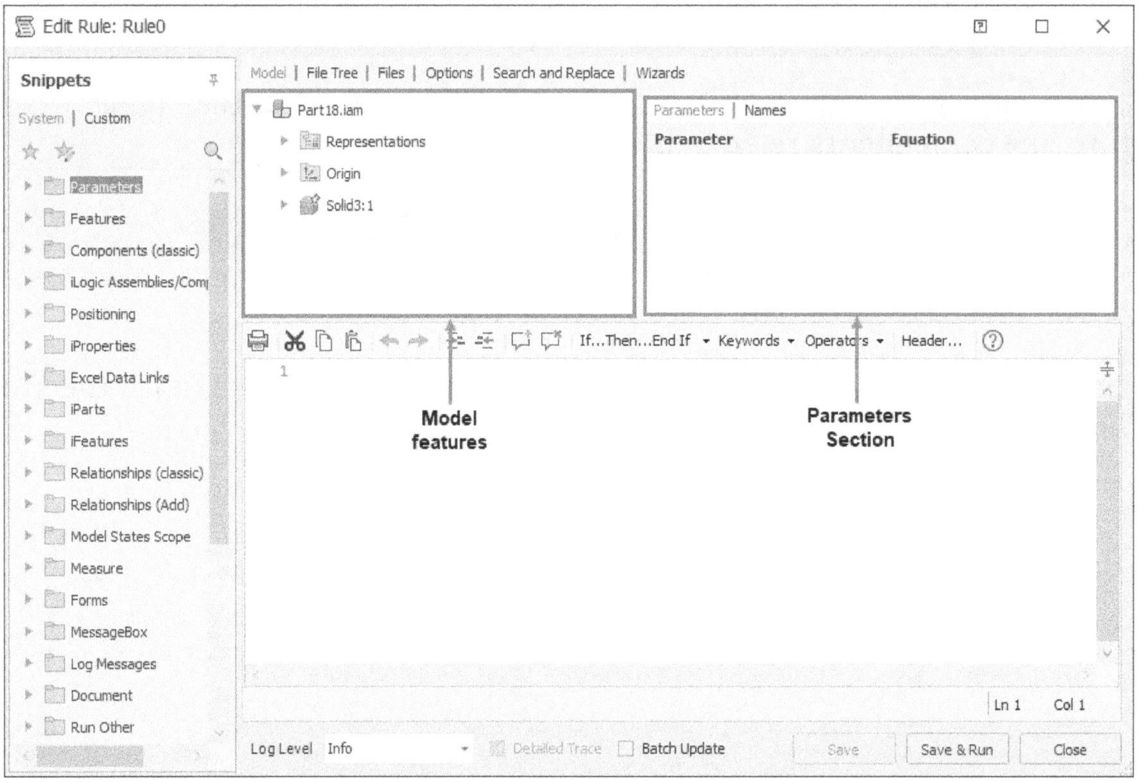

Figure-60. Edit Rule dialog box

- Select desired feature from the **Model** tab to display related parameters in the **Parameters** section of the dialog box.
- Double-click on desired parameter from the **Parameters** section to use it in equation.
- You can create desired arithmetic and logical equations in the equations area of the dialog box; refer to Figure-61.

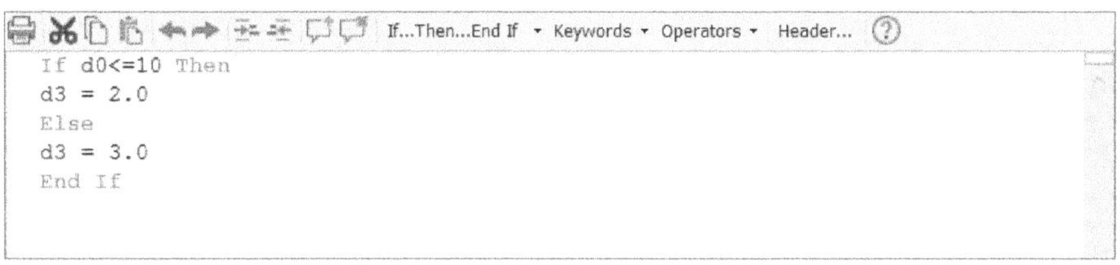

Figure-61. Sample equation

- Click on the **Save & Run** button from the dialog box after typing the equation. If there is an error then a message box will be displayed otherwise, model will be modified based on specified rule.

Using Codeblocks Rule

- Select **Codeblocks** radio button to apply only the code section in the model and click on the **OK** button from the dialog box. The **Codeblocks** dialog box will be displayed; refer to Figure-62.

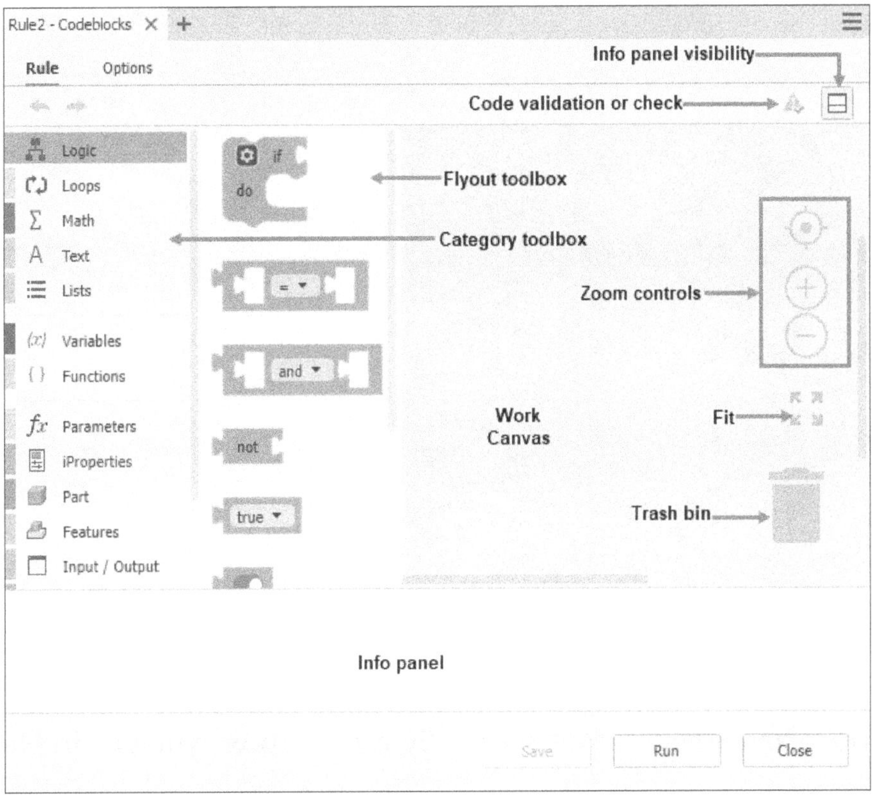

Figure-62. Codeblocks dialog box

- Select **Logic** category to apply decision making condition such as if else in the program.
- Select **Loops** category to repeat a set of instruction multiple times based on a condition.
- Select **Math** category to perform mathematical calculation like addition, subtraction, multiple, and division.
- Select **Text** category to used a handle and manipulate string or text data.
- Select **Lists** category to manage a collection of multiple values in the sequence.

Now we will explain the formation of code blocks using an example where one side of rectangular block is double of other side; refer to Figure-63.

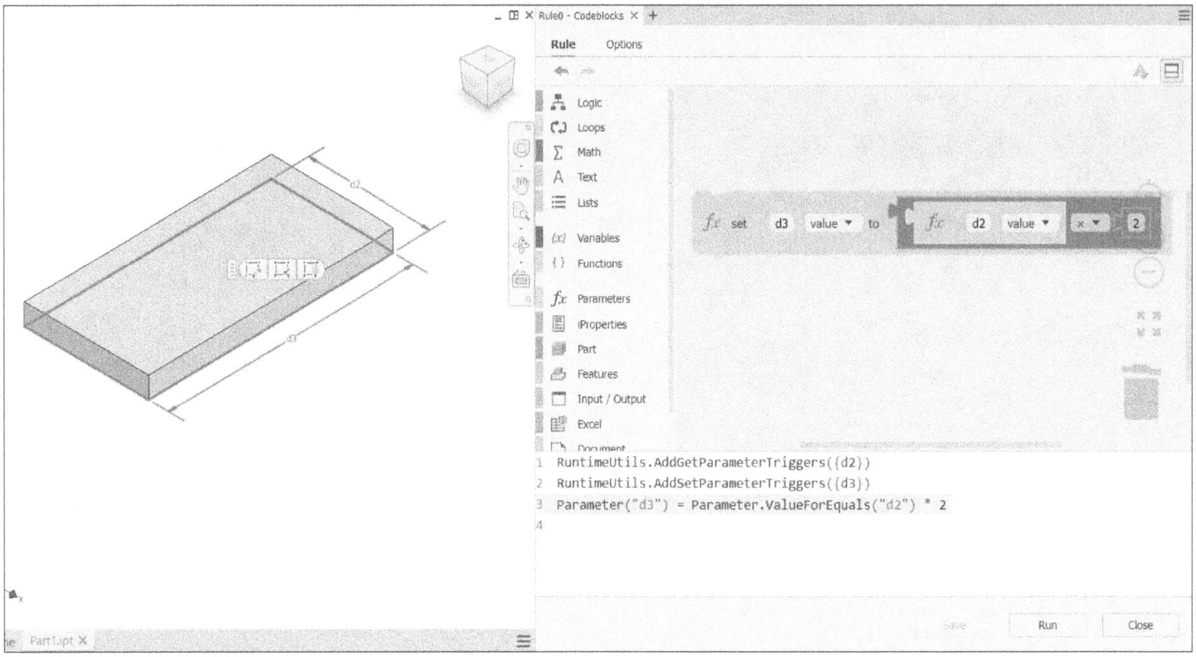

Figure-63. Codeblock example

- Click on the **Parameters** category, a flyout toolbox will be displayed; refer to Figure-64.

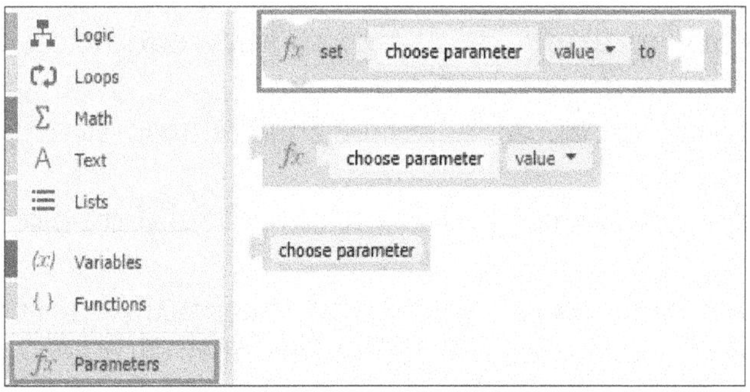

Figure-64. Parameters category toolbox

- Click on the code block as shown in Figure-64. The codeblock will be placed in the work canvas.
- Click on the **Math** category and select the code block as shown in Figure-65. The code block will be placed in work canvas.

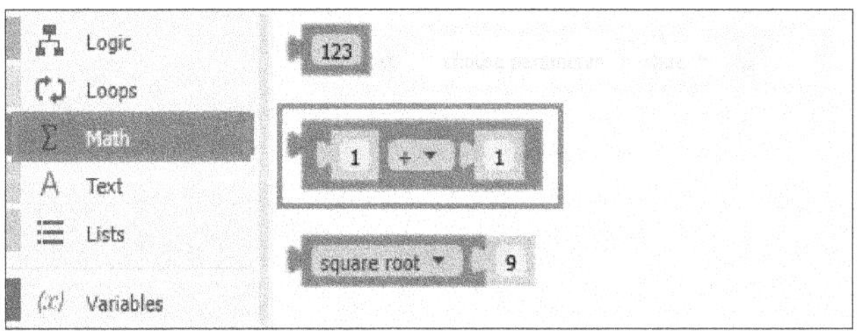

Figure-65. Math category toolbox

- Drag and place the codeblock of **Math** category inside code block of the **Parameters** category; refer to Figure-66.

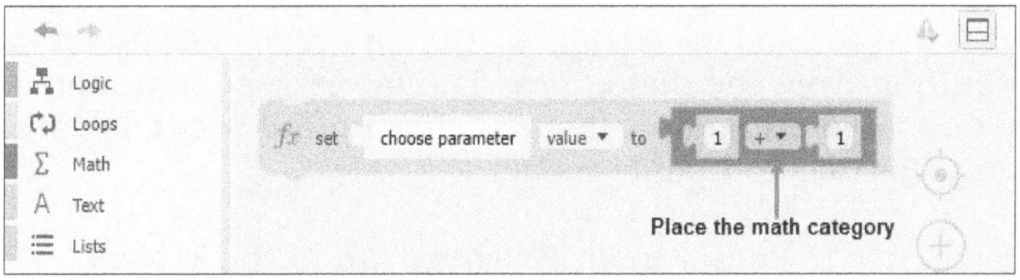

Figure-66. Placing the math category

- Again click on the **Parameters** category and select the code block as shown in Figure-67. The code block will be placed in work canvas.

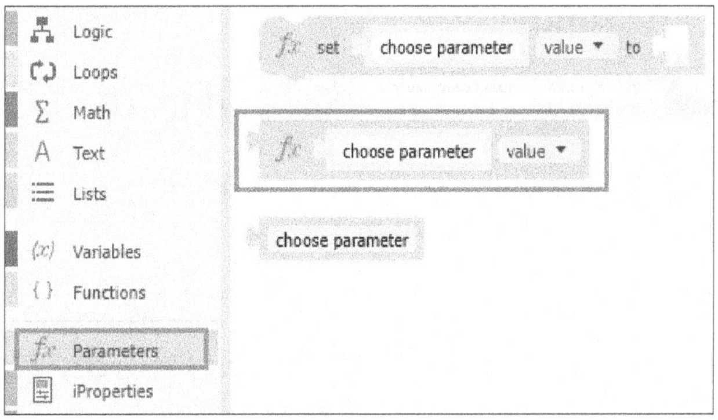

Figure-67. Parameters category toolbox

- Drag and place this newly added code block inside the code block of **Math** category; refer to Figure-68.

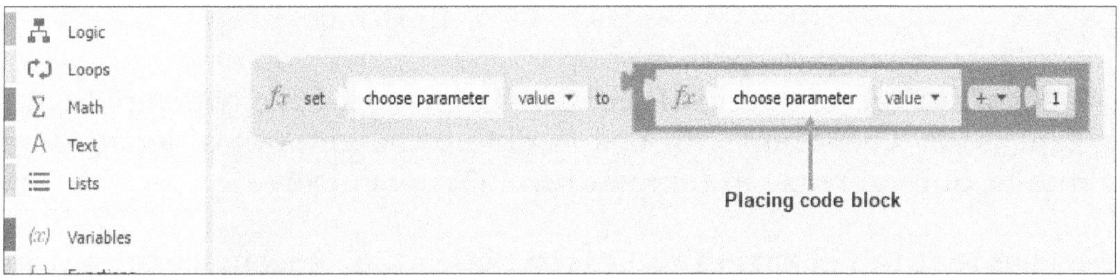

Figure-68. Placing codeblock

- Click on the **choose parameter** button from the **Parameters** flyout, a list of options will be displayed; refer to Figure-69.

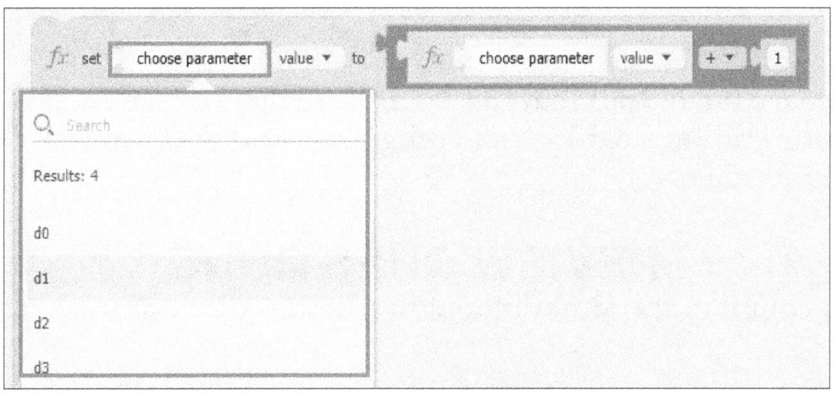

Figure-69. Displaying the flyout

- Select the **d3** option from the options displayed then click on the **choose parameters** button from the **Math** category and select the **d2** option from the options displayed.

- Change mathematical operator to “x” for multiplication and multiplier value to 2 in the input box at the end in codeblock. After specifying desired parameters, click on the **Run** button from the dialog box. The model will be updated. If the model does not get updated automatically then click on the **Local Update** tool from the **Quick Access Toolbar** to update model.

Similarly, you can use the other tools of **Manage** tab in the **Ribbon**.

SELF ASSESSMENT

Q1. Define iMate with an example.

Q2. What is the difference between Make Part and iPart?

Q3. In the **Material Editor** dialog box, which of the following fields is used to define roughness of surface of material for reflectivity?

a) Finish
b) Amount
c) Scale
d) Source

Q4. In the **Material Editor** dialog box, which of the following check boxes should be selected to add shade of selected color to the material surface?

a) Reflectivity
b) Self Illumination
c) Tint
d) Bump

Q5. In the **Physical** tab of **Material Editor** dialog box, specify desired value in the **Thermal Expansion Coefficient** edit box to define the amount of length increase in material due to unit increase in temperature. (True/False)

Q6. In the **Physical** tab of **Material Editor** dialog box, specify desired value in the **Damping Coefficient** edit box to define a ratio by which oscillations in the material are dissipated. (True/False)

Q7. The .... tool in **Tools** tab is used to scale and modify appearance applied to a face.

Q8. In the **Hardware** tab of **Application Options** dialog box, select the .... check box if your graphics card is not recognized and you want to use software for visualization performance.

REVIEW QUESTIONS

Q1. Which tab contains the Material tool in Autodesk Inventor?
A. Home
B. Manage
C. Tools
D. View

Q2. What is the function of the Material Browser?
A. To edit geometry of a model
B. To create and manage material appearances only
C. To create and manage materials applied to models
D. To manage layers in sketches

Q3. Which option is used to filter materials by category in the Material Browser?
A. Library Switcher
B. View Type
C. Category drop-down
D. Material Editor

Q4. What must be done to edit a material before adding it to a document?
A. Click "Add to library"
B. Use "Adjust Appearance" tool
C. Click "Adds material to document and displays in editor"
D. Use "Clear" tool

Q5. What does the Identity tab of the Material Editor define?
A. Thermal properties
B. Surface finish
C. Description and type of material
D. Transparency

Q6. Which field is used to define the cost of a material?
A. Comments
B. Cost
C. Type
D. URL

Q7. In the Appearance tab for metal materials, what does the Relief Pattern option do?
A. Changes surface color
B. Adds bumps to simulate texture
C. Makes material reflective
D. Enhances glossiness

Q8. What does the Cutout option in material appearance settings do?
A. Applies shading
B. Creates a translucent effect
C. Creates a net-like texture with transparent sections
D. Adds a logo to the material

Q9. Which parameter in the generic appearance tab defines how smooth a surface is?
A. Glossiness
B. Tint
C. Scale
D. Relief Pattern

Q10. What does the Reflectivity setting define in material appearance?
A. The light absorbed
B. The light emitted
C. The amount of light reflected
D. The weight of material

Q11. What property is defined using the Thermal Conductivity field in the Physical tab?
A. Rate of cooling
B. Material thickness
C. Heat transfer capability
D. Temperature resistance

Q12. What does Young's Modulus measure?
A. Material weight
B. Rate of thermal expansion
C. Stress per unit strain
D. Energy absorption

Q13. What does selecting the Orthotropic behavior option signify?
A. Uniform properties in all directions
B. Properties vary in X, Y, and Z directions
C. Properties vary only on the surface
D. Same properties in one direction only

Q14. What strength property defines the stress at which permanent deformation begins?
A. Shear Modulus
B. Yield Strength
C. Density
D. Damping Coefficient

Q15. Which tool is used to remove appearances from a model?
A. Adjust
B. Clear
C. Material Editor
D. Application Options

Q16. Which tool lets you scale and rotate appearance on a face?
A. Clear
B. Appearance Browser
C. Adjust
D. Edit

Q17. What does the Application Options dialog box help configure?
A. Appearance only
B. Materials only
C. General application settings
D. Drawing formats only

Q18. What is the function of the Save Reminder Timer?
A. Automatically closes unsaved files
B. Reminds user to save work at intervals
C. Saves files in backup folder
D. Disables auto-save

Q19. What can be changed in the File tab of Application Options?
A. Background color
B. Drawing environment
C. Default templates and file paths
D. Interface layout

Q20. What does selecting "Software graphics" in the Hardware tab do?
A. Disables graphics card
B. Uses software rendering for visualization
C. Enables 3D view
D. Improves material rendering only

Q21. What is the purpose of the Configure Default Template button under the File tab options?
A. To open files from specific locations
B. To set units and drawing standards for default templates
C. To save templates to cloud storage
D. To configure the interface theme

Q22. What action is prompted after clicking the OK button in the Configure Default Template dialog box?
A. Restarting the software
B. Saving template to library
C. Overwriting the standard template
D. Updating the drawing tab

Q23. What does the File Open button in the File tab options allow you to configure?
A. Display resolution
B. Default file type
C. Model state and view for opening files
D. Grid size in drawing area

Q24. In the Colors tab, what can be changed using the In-canvas Color Scheme list box?
A. Sketch behavior
B. Object lighting
C. Colors using predefined themes
D. Export file formats

Q25. What does the Scroll Wheel Sensitivity slider in the Display tab adjust?
A. Zoom level
B. Display contrast
C. Mouse wheel sensitivity
D. Background color

Q26. Which radio button in the Hardware tab should be selected for maximum modeling performance at the cost of visual quality?
A. Quality
B. Conservative
C. Performance
D. Software graphics

Q27. What happens when you select the Retrieve all model dimensions on view placement checkbox in the Drawing tab?
A. Dimensions are manually entered
B. All model dimensions are automatically placed in the drawing
C. Dimensions are removed
D. View is locked

Q28. What tool is used to define default parameters for the currently open document?
A. Document Control
B. Document Settings
C. Template Manager
D. Display Settings

Q29. What tab in the Document Settings dialog box allows setting the unit system for various parameters?
A. Lighting
B. Tolerance
C. Units
D. Display

Q30. What is the purpose of the Rebuild All tool in the Update panel?
A. Save all files
B. Delete unused sketches
C. Reflect parameter changes in the model
D. Lock model dimensions

Q31. How do you create a new user parameter using the Parameters tool?
A. Click Add Field
B. Use the + symbol
C. Select from the New Parameter drop-down
D. Click Update

Q32. What does the Purge tool do?
A. Save the model
B. Export unused styles
C. Delete unused sketches and work features
D. Clean the system cache

Q33. What does the Styles Editor allow you to modify?
A. Viewports
B. Hardware settings
C. Lighting and text styles
D. Export settings

Q34. Which dialog box is displayed when using the Derive tool to create parts from existing models?
A. Derive Features
B. Derived Part
C. Component Creator
D. Feature Base

Q35. In the Place Feature from Content Center dialog, how are imperial parts accessed?
A. Select the ISO folder
B. Double-click the Metric folder
C. Double-click the English folder
D. Use the Settings menu

Q36. What does the Insert Object tool allow you to do?
A. Open AutoCAD drawings
B. Add point clouds
C. Insert system-supported objects like Excel files
D. Define new document templates

Q37. What must you do to create a new part from selected bodies using the Make Part tool?
A. Click Export
B. Select from the BOM panel
C. Name the part and define save location
D. Choose Update All

Q38. What is created when using the Make Components tool from selected bodies?
A. Sheet views
B. Sub-assemblies
C. Complete drawing sheets
D. Individual parts

Q39. What is the function of the iPart tool?
A. Insert animated objects
B. Create configuration-driven part models
C. Insert Excel tables
D. Measure distances

Q40. What does an iMate do in an assembly?
A. Adds lights
B. Defines automatic constraints
C. Imports 3D scans
D. Sets colors

Q41. Which tool is used to save existing features as iFeatures for later reuse?
A. Insert Feature
B. Extract iFeature
C. Save As Template
D. Convert to Component

Q42. What is the primary use of the Add Rule tool in the iLogic panel?
A. Insert text notes
B. Control lighting settings
C. Define logic and automate design
D. Generate assemblies

FOR STUDENT NOTES

Index

Symbols

A

B

C

D

Ethics of an Engineer

- Engineers shall hold paramount the safety, health and welfare of the public and shall strive to comply with the principles of sustainable development in the performance of their professional duties.
- Engineers shall perform services only in areas of their competence.
- Engineers shall issue public statements only in an objective and truthful manner.
- Engineers shall act in professional manners for each employer or client as faithful agents or trustees, and shall avoid conflicts of interest.
- Engineers shall build their professional reputation on the merit of their services and shall not compete unfairly with others.
- Engineers shall act in such a manner as to uphold and enhance the honor, integrity, and dignity of the engineering profession and shall act with zero-tolerance for bribery, fraud, and corruption.
- Engineers shall continue their professional development throughout their careers, and shall provide opportunities for the professional development of those engineers under their supervision.

www.ingramcontent.com/pod-product-compliance
Lightning Source LLC
LaVergne TN
LVHW082011200926
848481LV00010B/2838
9781774592144